State Profiles

State Profiles

The Population and Economy of Each U.S. State

Fifth Edition
2013

Edited by Shana Hertz Hattis

Bernan Press

Bernan Press
Lanham, Maryland

Published in the United States of America
by Bernan Press, a wholly owned subsidiary of
The Rowman & Littlefield Publishing Group, Inc.
4501 Forbes Boulevard, Suite 200
Lanham, Maryland 20706

Bernan Press
800-865-3457
www.bernan.com

ISBN 13: 978-1-59888-640-5
E-ISBN: 978-1-59888-641-2

∞™ The paper used in this publication meets the minimum requirements of American National Standard for Information Sciences—Permanence of Paper for Printed Library Materials, ANSI/NISO Z39.48-1992.
Manufactured in the United States of America.

CONTENTS

LIST OF TABLES

The following tables are included for each state and the District of Columbia

PREFACE

Bernan Press is pleased to present the fifth edition of *State Profiles*, a publication that provides a state-by-state view of the United States. Topics covered include population composition by age, sex, race, and ethnicity; marital status; migration, origin, and language; households and housing; income and poverty; health insurance; employment; educational indicators; voting; crime; and other important aspects of the economy.

The publication's primary focus is on the 50 states and the District of Columbia, each of which possesses considerable differences in economic structure and demographics and has experienced various changes over time. Changes at the national level, including the diminished importance of agriculture and manufacturing and the growing influence of global trade, have resulted in today's information-based, service-providing economy. While national trends have laid the broad framework for change, each state has been affected differently. Cyclical fluctuations have also affected states in various ways during the nationwide recessions and the subsequent recovery periods. Recessions and recoveries spread unevenly among regions and states. Migration patterns have also reflected these changes, as states have inexperienced different influxes of workers from within the country and new residents from abroad.

Beyond the market forces, economic circumstances have been influenced by local and national government policies and expenditures on items such as education, health care, energy production and conservation, national defense, and homeland security.

The information provided in *State Profiles* aims to illuminate these trends. As such, the analysis and statistics are of interest not only to researchers and policy analysts but also to businesses seeking a broad basis for investments and expansion or relocation plans. The volume also profiles recent voting patterns, which will be of interest to political scientists.

DATA SELECTION

This edition of *State Profiles* generally continues the broad selection of information from previous editions. Most, but not all, of the data items have been updated through 2010, 2011, and even 2012, as demographic estimates from the U.S. Census Bureau became available. Agriculture data are not included in this edition, as the most recent data available is from the 2007 Census of Agriculture.

As in the past, space constraints have influenced the amount of data presented for each state. The most meaningful and relevant data have thus been selected, analyzed, and highlighted. This edition expands upon the available information to include more detailed data on the demographics of each state, especially in regard to diversity of spoken languages and the foreign-born population. For most of the subjects addressed in this edition, further data are generally available from the source government agencies. Locations of sources information are listed in notes and definitions at the end of the volume.

Although the editor has taken care to present accurate data, all statistical data are subject to a degree of error, resulting from sampling variability, erroneous reporting, and other causes. Many of the data are subject to subsequent revision.

The data in this book meet the publication standards of the federal agencies from which they were obtained. The responsibilities of the editor and publisher of this volume are limited to reasonable care in the reproduction and presentation of the data from the established sources.

Shana Hertz Hattis, editor of this edition of *State Profiles*, has worked as an editor and writer for Bernan since 2005. In addition to her federally oriented publications, her work has spanned the fields of hospitality, business, and popular culture. She studied journalism and education at Northwestern University.

USING THIS BOOK: ORGANIZATION AND CONTENTS

STATE PROFILES 2013 PROVIDES:

- Rankings of states for key demographic and economic indicators
- A chapter for each state, complete with tables and figures that summarize and illustrate common demographic and economic characteristics
- Notes and definitions to assist with interpreting the information contained in this volume

THE U.S. OVERVIEW. This short introduction to the demographics of the United States provides commentary on overall trends within the country.

THE STATE RANKINGS. The ranking tables that follow the national overview give state rankings by more than 25 characteristics, including population, demographic and age composition, income, per capita gross domestic product, homeownership, poverty, health indicators, education, and federal aid. These rankings provide the user with a quick analysis of the performance of each state in relation to the other states.

THE STATE CHAPTERS. The state chapters are the focus of this book. Each chapter follows a standard format and contains text highlighting the key features shown in the tables and figures. Some of these tables and figures contain references to the U.S. averages for the same characteristics.

Each of the state chapters is organized as follows:

Population: This table provides data on the state's total population and average annual population growth in comparison with the national average. It also shows the major population groups by sex, age, race, and ethnicity.

Marital status: The table shows the marital status for all men and women age 15 years and over.

Income, migration, and language. This table provides statistics on residence one year ago, year of entry, place of origin, language spoken at home, and the native-born and foreign-born populations.

Households: Data on household types, size, units (whether owner- or renter-occupied), median gross rent, and median value of owner-occupied housing are included.

Income and poverty: Median household and family income and poverty rates by sex and age are contained in this table.

Health insurance coverage: This table provides information on health insurance, by type and coverage.

Employment: This section presents various tables that illustrate each state's particular economic configuration. Employment status by detailed demographic group, labor force, participation rates, employment, unemployment, average wages and salaries by industry, and employment by family type.

Education: This section provides the user with details on educational attainment, elementary and secondary school enrollment, student/teacher ratios, per student expenditures, and higher education enrollments.

Voter participation: Information is given on voter registration and voter participation in the 2012 presidential election, categorized by sex and race and ethnicity.

Crime: This table include the number and rates of violent and property crime.

Government finance: This section provides data on revenues and expenditures by source. In addition, state government tax information is included.

NOTES AND DEFINITIONS. Each chapter relies on the same standard set of federal data sources. Since the basic data sources are common to all chapters, the main body of the volume contains few footnotes. Basic data and corresponding definitions and sources are identified in the notes and definition section at the end of the volume. It provides brief descriptions, methodologies, data availability, information on calculations made by the editors, and references to additional sources of information.

United States

Introduction

During the early 2000s, the United States experienced several economic fluctuations that greatly impacted the strength, size, and performance of its economy. The recession that began in March 2001 was concluded in a few months; however, the longer-lasting recession that began in December 2007 has had a more serious impact on the country. This edition of *State Profiles: The Population and Economy of Each U.S. State* creates a snapshot of the people and economy in each state and the District of Columbia. Each chapter (one per state/district) includes information on topics such as population, health, marital status, crime, government finance, housing, education, language, and citizen participation in the 2012 election.

Summary

The U.S. population grew 1.7 percent between 2010 and 2012. The District of Columbia experienced the largest population growth in the nation at 5.1 percent. The 11 states with the largest population growth included North Dakota (4.0 percent), Texas (3.6 percent), Utah (3.3 percent), Colorado (3.1 percent), Alaska (3.0 percent), Florida (2.7 percent), Washington (2.6 percent), Arizona (2.5 percent), Georgia (2.4 percent), Hawaii (2.4 percent), and South Dakota (2.4 percent). States that grew in population by 0.5 percent or less included Connecticut, Pennsylvania, Illinois, New Hampshire, Maine, Ohio, and West Virginia. Michigan and Vermont experienced near-zero growth, while the population of Rhode Island fell by 0.2 percent.

Vermont and Maine had the highest percentage of White alone residents in 2012, at 95.4 and 95.3 percent, followed by New Hampshire at 94.4 percent. Hawaii had the lowest number of White alone residents, at 26.1 percent. The District of Columbia had the highest percentage of Black alone residents in 2012, at 50.1 percent, followed by Mississippi at 37.4 percent. At 0.6 percent, Montana had the lowest percentage of Black alone residents. Hispanic and Latino residents may be of any race, and New Mexico (47.0 percent) and Maine (1.4 percent) had the highest and lowest resident percentages, respectively.

In 2011, the median household income in the United States was $50,502. Maryland had the highest median household income at $70,004, followed by Alaska ($67,285), New Jersey ($67,458), Connecticut ($65,753), and the District of Columbia ($63,124). The states with the lowest median household incomes were Mississippi ($36,919), West Virginia ($28,482), Arkansas ($38,758), Kentucky ($41,141), and Alabama ($41,415). Some correlation to the percentage of residents with a bachelor's degree or more can be inferred, as Maryland, the District of Columbia, and Connecticut rank in the top 5 states in this category, with New Jersey ranking 6th and Alaska 24th. Mississippi, West Virginia, Arkansas, and Kentucky rank within the bottom 5 states in this category, with Alabama ranking 46th. The unemployment rate for the United States was 8.1 percent in 2012, with Nevada (11.1 percent) having the highest percentage of unemployed residents and North Dakota (3.1 percent) having the lowest percentage of unemployed residents.

In the United States in 2011, 15.9 percent of the population lived below the poverty level. Mississippi, which had the lowest median household income, also had the highest poverty rate, with 22.6 percent of its residents below the poverty level. New Hampshire had the lowest poverty rate, at 8.8 percent, and was the only state with a poverty rate below 10 percent. Mississippi had the highest rate of persons under 18 years of age below the poverty level (31.8 percent), followed by New Mexico (30.7 percent), the District of Columbia (30.3 percent), Louisiana (28.8 percent), and Arkansas (28.1 percent). The states with the fewest residents under 18 years of age below the poverty level included New Hampshire (12.0 percent), Maryland (13.5 percent), Alaska (14.5 percent), North Dakota (14.6 percent), and New Jersey (14.7 percent). Connecticut and Vermont also had rates below 15 percent.

UNITED STATES RANKINGS

Population, 2012

Rank	State	Population
	United States	313,914,040
1	California	38,041,430
2	Texas	26,059,203
3	New York	19,570,261
4	Florida	19,317,568
5	Illinois	12,875,255
6	Pennsylvania	12,763,536
7	Ohio	11,544,225
8	Georgia	9,919,945
9	Michigan	9,883,360
10	North Carolina	9,752,073
11	New Jersey	8,864,590
12	Virginia	8,185,867
13	Washington	6,897,012
14	Massachusetts	6,646,144
15	Arizona	6,553,255
16	Indiana	6,537,334
17	Tennessee	6,456,243
18	Missouri	6,021,988
19	Maryland	5,884,563
20	Wisconsin	5,726,398
21	Minnesota	5,379,139
22	Colorado	5,187,582
23	Alabama	4,822,023
24	South Carolina	4,723,723
25	Louisiana	4,601,893
26	Oregon	3,899,353
27	Oklahoma	3,814,820
28	Connecticut	3,590,347
29	Iowa	3,074,186
30	Mississippi	2,984,926
31	Arkansas	2,949,131
32	Kansas	2,885,905
33	Kentucky	2,885,905
34	Utah	2,855,287
35	Nevada	2,758,931
36	New Mexico	2,085,538
37	Nebraska	1,855,525
38	West Virginia	1,855,413
39	Idaho	1,595,728
40	Hawaii	1,392,313
41	Maine	1,329,192
42	New Hampshire	1,320,718
43	Rhode Island	1,050,292
44	Montana	1,005,141
45	Delaware	917,092
46	South Dakota	833,354
47	Alaska	731,449
48	North Dakota	699,628
49	District of Columbia	632,323
50	Vermont	626,011
51	Wyoming	576,412

Population, Percent Change, 2010–2012

Rank	State	Percent
	United States	1.7
1	District of Columbia	5.1
2	North Dakota	4.0
3	Texas	3.6
4	Utah	3.3
5	Colorado	3.1
6	Alaska	3.0
7	Florida	2.7
8	Washington	2.6
9	Arizona	2.5
10	Georgia	2.4
10	Hawaii	2.4
10	South Dakota	2.4
13	North Carolina	2.3
13	Virginia	2.3
13	Wyoming	2.3
16	Nevada	2.2
17	California	2.1
17	Delaware	2.1
17	South Carolina	2.1
20	Maryland	1.9
21	Idaho	1.8
21	Oregon	1.8
23	Oklahoma	1.7
23	Tennessee	1.7
25	Montana	1.6
25	Nebraska	1.6
27	Louisiana	1.5
27	Massachusetts	1.5
29	Minnesota	1.4
30	New Mexico	1.3
31	Arkansas	1.1
31	Kansas	1.1
33	New York	1.0
34	Alabama	0.9
34	Iowa	0.9
34	Kentucky	0.9
37	Indiana	0.8
37	New Jersey	0.8
39	Wisconsin	0.7
40	Mississippi	0.6
40	Missouri	0.6
42	Connecticut	0.5
42	Pennsylvania	0.5
44	Illinois	0.3
44	New Hampshire	0.3
46	Maine	0.1
46	Ohio	0.1
46	West Virginia	0.1
49	Michigan	Z
49	Vermont	Z
51	Rhode Island	-0.2

Z = Value greater than zero but less than half of the unit shown.

Population Under 18 Years Old, 2012

Rank	State	Percent
	United States	23.5
1	Utah	31.1
2	Texas	26.8
3	Idaho	26.7
4	Alaska	25.6
5	Georgia	25.1
5	Kansas	25.1
7	Mississippi	25.0
7	Nebraska	25.0
9	Arizona	24.7
9	New Mexico	24.7
11	Oklahoma	24.6
12	South Dakota	24.5
13	California	24.3
13	Indiana	24.3
13	Louisiana	24.3
16	Arkansas	24.1
16	Nevada	24.1
18	Illinois	23.8
19	Colorado	23.7
19	Minnesota	23.7
21	Iowa	23.5
21	Wyoming	23.5
23	North Carolina	23.4
24	Alabama	23.3
24	Missouri	23.3
26	Kentucky	23.2
27	Ohio	23.1
27	Tennessee	23.1
29	Washington	23.0
29	Wisconsin	23.0
31	Michigan	22.9
31	New Jersey	22.9
31	South Carolina	22.9
34	Maryland	22.8
35	Virginia	22.7
36	Delaware	22.4
37	Connecticut	22.1
37	Montana	22.1
37	North Dakota	22.1
37	Oregon	22.1
41	Hawaii	21.8
41	New York	21.8
43	Pennsylvania	21.5
44	Massachusetts	21.1
45	New Hampshire	20.8
46	Florida	20.7
46	West Virginia	20.7
48	Rhode Island	20.6
49	Maine	20.0
50	Vermont	19.8
51	District of Columbia	17.3

Population 65 Years and Over, 2012

Rank	State	Percent
	United States	13.7
1	Florida	18.2
2	Maine	17.0
3	West Virginia	16.8
4	Pennsylvania	16.0
5	Montana	15.7
5	Vermont	15.7
7	Delaware	15.3
7	Iowa	15.3
9	Hawaii	15.1
9	Rhode Island	15.1
11	Arkansas	15.0
12	Oregon	14.9
13	Arizona	14.8
13	Connecticut	14.8
13	Ohio	14.8
16	Missouri	14.7
16	New Hampshire	14.7
16	South Carolina	14.7
16	South Dakota	14.7
20	Michigan	14.6
21	Alabama	14.5
22	Massachusetts	14.4
22	North Dakota	14.4
22	Wisconsin	14.4
25	Tennessee	14.2
26	New Jersey	14.1
26	New Mexico	14.1
26	New York	14.1
29	Kentucky	14.0
29	Oklahoma	14.0
31	Nebraska	13.9
32	North Carolina	13.8
33	Kansas	13.7
34	Indiana	13.6
34	Minnesota	13.6
36	Mississippi	13.5
37	Idaho	13.3
38	Illinois	13.2
38	Washington	13.2
40	Nevada	13.1
40	Wyoming	13.1
42	Maryland	13.0
42	Virginia	13.0
44	Louisiana	12.9
45	California	12.1
46	Colorado	11.8
47	Georgia	11.5
48	District of Columbia	11.4
49	Texas	10.9
50	Utah	9.5
51	Alaska	8.5

Percent White Alone, 2012

Rank	State	Percent
	United States	77.9
1	Vermont	95.4
2	Maine	95.3
3	New Hampshire	94.4
4	Idaho	93.8
5	Wyoming	93.1
6	Iowa	92.8
7	Utah	91.8
8	North Dakota	90.1
9	Nebraska	89.9
10	Montana	89.7
11	Kentucky	88.6
12	Oregon	88.3
13	Wisconsin	88.2
14	Colorado	88.1
15	Kansas	87.2
16	Indiana	86.6
17	Minnesota	86.5
18	South Dakota	86.2
19	Rhode Island	85.9
20	Arizona	84.3
21	Missouri	83.9
22	Massachusetts	83.7
23	Pennsylvania	83.5
24	Ohio	83.4
24	West Virginia	83.4
26	New Mexico	83.2
27	Connecticut	82.0
28	Washington	81.6
29	Texas	80.6
30	Michigan	80.1
31	Arkansas	80.0
32	Tennessee	79.3
33	Florida	78.3
34	Illinois	77.9
35	Nevada	77.1
36	Oklahoma	75.5
37	New Jersey	73.8
38	California	73.7
39	North Carolina	71.9
40	Delaware	71.4
41	New York	71.2
42	Virginia	71.1
43	Alabama	70.0
44	South Carolina	68.4
45	Alaska	67.5
46	Louisiana	63.7
47	Georgia	62.8
48	Maryland	60.8
49	Mississippi	59.9
50	District of Columbia	42.9
51	Hawaii	26.1

Percent Black or African American Alone, 2012

Rank	State	Percent
	United States	13.1
1	District of Columbia	50.1
2	Mississippi	37.4
3	Louisiana	32.4
4	Georgia	31.2
5	Maryland	30.0
6	South Carolina	28.0
7	Alabama	26.5
8	Delaware	22.0
8	North Carolina	22.0
10	Virginia	19.7
11	New York	17.5
12	Tennessee	17.0
13	Florida	16.6
14	Arkansas	15.6
15	Illinois	14.8
16	New Jersey	14.7
17	Michigan	14.3
18	Ohio	12.5
18	West Virginia	12.5
20	Texas	12.3
21	Missouri	11.7
22	Pennsylvania	11.4
23	Connecticut	11.2
24	Indiana	9.4
25	Nevada	8.9
26	Kentucky	8.1
27	Massachusetts	7.9
28	Oklahoma	7.6
29	Rhode Island	7.3
30	California	6.6
31	Wisconsin	6.5
32	Kansas	6.2
33	Minnesota	5.5
34	Nebraska	4.8
35	Arizona	4.5
36	Colorado	4.3
37	Washington	3.9
38	Alaska	3.7
39	Iowa	3.2
40	New Mexico	2.4
41	Hawaii	2.1
42	Oregon	2.0
43	South Dakota	1.7
44	North Dakota	1.5
44	Wyoming	1.5
46	New Hampshire	1.4
47	Maine	1.3
47	Utah	1.3
49	Vermont	1.1
50	Idaho	0.8
51	Montana	0.6

Percent American Indian and Alaska Native Alone, 2012

Rank	State	Percent
	United States	1.2
1	Alaska	14.8
2	New Mexico	10.2
3	Oklahoma	9.0
4	South Dakota	8.9
5	Montana	6.5
6	North Dakota	5.5
7	Arizona	5.3
8	Wyoming	2.6
9	Oregon	1.8
9	Washington	1.8
11	California	1.7
11	Idaho	1.7
13	Colorado	1.6
13	Nevada	1.6
15	North Carolina	1.5
15	Utah	1.5
17	Minnesota	1.3
17	Nebraska	1.3
19	Kansas	1.2
20	Wisconsin	1.1
21	New York	1.0
21	Texas	1.0
23	Arkansas	0.9
23	Rhode Island	0.9
25	Alabama	0.7
25	Delaware	0.7
25	Louisiana	0.7
25	Maine	0.7
25	Michigan	0.7
30	District of Columbia	0.6
30	Illinois	0.6
30	Mississippi	0.6
30	New Jersey	0.6
34	Connecticut	0.5
34	Florida	0.5
34	Georgia	0.5
34	Iowa	0.5
34	Maryland	0.5
34	Massachusetts	0.5
34	Missouri	0.5
34	South Carolina	0.5
34	Virginia	0.5
43	Hawaii	0.4
43	Indiana	0.4
43	Tennessee	0.4
43	Vermont	0.4
47	Kentucky	0.3
47	New Hampshire	0.3
47	Ohio	0.3
47	Pennsylvania	0.3
47	West Virginia	0.3

Percent Asian Alone, 2012

Rank	State	Percent
	United States	5.1
1	Hawaii	38.3
2	California	13.9
3	New Jersey	9.0
4	New York	8.0
5	Nevada	7.9
6	Washington	7.7
7	Maryland	6.0
7	Virginia	6.0
9	Massachusetts	5.8
10	Alaska	5.7
11	Illinois	5.0
12	Minnesota	4.4
13	Connecticut	4.2
13	Texas	4.2
15	Oregon	4.0
16	District of Columbia	3.8
17	Delaware	3.5
17	Georgia	3.5
19	Rhode Island	3.2
20	Arizona	3.1
21	Colorado	3.0
21	Pennsylvania	3.0
23	Florida	2.7
24	Kansas	2.6
24	Michigan	2.6
26	North Carolina	2.5
26	Wisconsin	2.5
28	New Hampshire	2.4
29	Utah	2.2
30	Iowa	2.0
30	Nebraska	2.0
32	Oklahoma	1.9
33	Indiana	1.8
33	Missouri	1.8
33	Ohio	1.8
33	West Virginia	1.8
37	Louisiana	1.7
38	New Mexico	1.6
38	Tennessee	1.6
40	Arkansas	1.4
40	Idaho	1.4
40	South Carolina	1.4
40	Vermont	1.4
44	Kentucky	1.3
45	Alabama	1.2
46	Maine	1.1
46	North Dakota	1.1
46	South Dakota	1.1
49	Mississippi	0.9
49	Wyoming	0.9
51	Montana	0.7

Percent Native Hawaiian and Other Pacific Islander Alone, 2012

Rank	State	Percent
	United States	0.2
1	Hawaii	10.1
2	Alaska	1.2
3	Utah	1.0
4	Nevada	0.7
4	Washington	0.7
6	California	0.5
7	Oregon	0.4
8	Arizona	0.3
8	Arkansas	0.3
10	Colorado	0.2
10	District of Columbia	0.2
10	Idaho	0.2
10	New Mexico	0.2
10	Oklahoma	0.2
10	Rhode Island	0.2
16	Alabama	0.1
16	Connecticut	0.1
16	Delaware	0.1
16	Florida	0.1
16	Georgia	0.1
16	Illinois	0.1
16	Indiana	0.1
16	Iowa	0.1
16	Kansas	0.1
16	Kentucky	0.1
16	Louisiana	0.1
16	Maryland	0.1
16	Massachusetts	0.1
16	Minnesota	0.1
16	Mississippi	0.1
16	Missouri	0.1
16	Montana	0.1
16	Nebraska	0.1
16	New Jersey	0.1
16	New York	0.1
16	North Carolina	0.1
16	North Dakota	0.1
16	Pennsylvania	0.1
16	South Carolina	0.1
16	South Dakota	0.1
16	Tennessee	0.1
16	Texas	0.1
16	Virginia	0.1
16	Wyoming	0.1
45	Maine	Z
45	Michigan	Z
45	New Hampshire	Z
45	Ohio	Z
45	Vermont	Z
45	West Virginia	Z
45	Wisconsin	Z

Z = Value greater than zero but less than half of the unit shown.

Percent Two or More Races, 2012

Rank	State	Percent
	United States	2.4
1	Hawaii	23.0
2	Alaska	7.1
3	Oklahoma	5.8
4	Washington	4.3
5	Nevada	3.8
6	California	3.6
7	Oregon	3.5
8	Colorado	2.8
9	Kansas	2.7
10	Virginia	2.6
11	Arizona	2.5
11	District of Columbia	2.5
11	Maryland	2.5
11	Montana	2.5
11	Rhode Island	2.5
16	Delaware	2.4
16	New Mexico	2.4
18	Utah	2.3
19	Idaho	2.2
19	Michigan	2.2
19	Minnesota	2.2
19	New York	2.2
23	Connecticut	2.1
23	South Dakota	2.1
25	Massachusetts	2.0
25	Missouri	2.0
25	North Carolina	2.0
25	Ohio	2.0
25	West Virginia	2.0
30	Florida	1.9
30	Nebraska	1.9
30	New Jersey	1.9
33	Arkansas	1.8
33	Georgia	1.8
33	Indiana	1.8
33	North Dakota	1.8
33	Wyoming	1.8
38	Illinois	1.7
38	Pennsylvania	1.7
38	Texas	1.7
38	Vermont	1.7
38	Wisconsin	1.7
43	Iowa	1.6
43	Kentucky	1.6
43	South Carolina	1.6
43	Tennessee	1.6
47	Alabama	1.5
47	Maine	1.5
47	New Hampshire	1.5
50	Louisiana	1.4
51	Mississippi	1.1

Percent Hispanic or Latino,[1] 2012

Rank	State	Percent
	United States	16.9
1	New Mexico	47.0
2	California	38.2
2	Texas	38.2
4	Arizona	30.2
5	Nevada	27.3
6	Florida	23.2
7	Colorado	21.0
8	New Jersey	18.5
9	New York	18.2
10	Illinois	16.3
11	Connecticut	14.2
12	Utah	13.3
13	Rhode Island	13.2
14	Oregon	12.2
15	Washington	11.7
16	Idaho	11.6
17	Kansas	11.0
18	Massachusetts	10.1
19	District of Columbia	9.9
20	Nebraska	9.7
21	Hawaii	9.5
21	Wyoming	9.5
23	Oklahoma	9.3
24	Georgia	9.2
25	Maryland	8.7
25	North Carolina	8.7
27	Delaware	8.6
28	Virginia	8.4
29	Arkansas	6.8
30	Indiana	6.3
31	Wisconsin	6.2
32	Alaska	6.1
32	Pennsylvania	6.1
34	Iowa	5.3
34	South Carolina	5.3
36	Minnesota	4.9
37	Tennessee	4.8
38	Michigan	4.6
39	Louisiana	4.5
40	Alabama	4.1
41	Missouri	3.7
42	Ohio	3.3
42	West Virginia	3.3
44	Kentucky	3.2
45	Montana	3.1
45	South Dakota	3.1
47	New Hampshire	3.0
48	Mississippi	2.9
49	North Dakota	2.5
50	Vermont	1.6
51	Maine	1.4

[1] May be of any race.

Percent White Alone, Not Hispanic or Latino, 2012

Rank	State	Percent
	United States	63.0
1	Maine	94.1
2	Vermont	94.0
3	New Hampshire	91.9
4	North Dakota	88.1
5	Iowa	88.0
6	Montana	87.2
7	Kentucky	85.9
8	Wyoming	84.6
9	South Dakota	83.8
10	Idaho	83.5
11	Wisconsin	82.8
12	Minnesota	82.4
13	Nebraska	81.4
14	Indiana	81.0
15	Ohio	80.7
15	West Virginia	80.7
17	Missouri	80.6
18	Utah	79.9
19	Pennsylvania	78.8
20	Oregon	77.8
21	Kansas	77.5
22	Michigan	76.2
23	Rhode Island	75.9
24	Massachusetts	75.8
25	Tennessee	75.1
26	Arkansas	73.9
27	Washington	71.6
28	Connecticut	70.3
29	Colorado	69.6
30	Oklahoma	67.9
31	Alabama	66.6
32	North Carolina	64.7
33	Delaware	64.6
34	Virginia	64.1
35	South Carolina	64.0
36	Alaska	63.1
37	Illinois	63.0
38	Louisiana	59.9
39	New Jersey	58.2
40	Mississippi	57.6
40	New York	57.6
42	Arizona	57.1
43	Florida	57.0
44	Georgia	55.1
45	Maryland	53.9
46	Nevada	52.9
47	Texas	44.5
48	New Mexico	39.8
49	California	39.4
50	District of Columbia	35.5
51	Hawaii	22.8

Infant Mortality Rate, 2008		
Rank	State	Rate per 1,000 live births (infants under 1 year old)
	United States	6.6
1	District of Columbia	11.2
2	Mississippi	10.0
3	Alabama	9.5
4	Louisiana	9.0
5	Delaware	8.4
6	South Dakota	8.3
7	North Carolina	8.2
7	Tennessee	8.2
9	South Carolina	8.1
10	Maryland	8.0
10	Georgia	8.0
12	Ohio	7.7
12	Virginia	7.7
14	Michigan	7.4
14	Pennsylvania	7.4
14	Wyoming	7.4
14	Arkansas	7.4
18	Kansas	7.3
18	West Virginia	7.3
18	Florida	7.3
21	Illinois	7.2
21	Montana	7.2
21	Oklahoma	7.2
24	Missouri	7.1
25	Kentucky	6.9
26	Indiana	6.8
27	Wisconsin	6.4
27	Arizona	6.4
29	Colorado	6.2
29	Texas	6.2
31	Alaska	6.0
32	Connecticut	5.9
32	Minnesota	5.9
32	Rhode Island	5.9
35	North Dakota	5.8
36	Idaho	5.7
36	Iowa	5.7
36	Hawaii	5.7
39	New Mexico	5.6
40	Nebraska	5.5
40	New Jersey	5.5
40	New York	5.5
43	Maine	5.4
43	Nevada	5.4
45	California	5.1
45	Oregon	5.1
47	Massachusetts	5.0
48	Washington	4.9
49	Utah	4.7
50	Vermont	4.6
51	New Hampshire	3.9

Birth Rate, 2011		
Rank	State	Rate per 1,000 population
	United States	12.7
1	Utah	18.2
2	Alaska	15.8
3	District of Columbia	15.1
4	Texas	14.7
5	South Dakota	14.4
6	Idaho	14.1
7	Nebraska	14.0
8	North Dakota	13.9
9	Hawaii	13.8
9	Kansas	13.8
9	Oklahoma	13.8
12	Georgia	13.5
12	Louisiana	13.5
14	Mississippi	13.4
15	California	13.3
16	Arizona	13.2
16	Arkansas	13.2
18	New Mexico	13.1
19	Nevada	13.0
19	Wyoming	13.0
21	Indiana	12.8
21	Minnesota	12.8
23	Colorado	12.7
23	Kentucky	12.7
23	Missouri	12.7
23	Virginia	12.7
23	Washington	12.7
28	Illinois	12.5
28	Iowa	12.5
28	Maryland	12.5
28	North Carolina	12.5
32	Alabama	12.4
32	Delaware	12.4
32	New York	12.4
32	Tennessee	12.4
36	South Carolina	12.3
37	Montana	12.1
38	New Jersey	12.0
39	Ohio	11.9
39	Wisconsin	11.9
41	Oregon	11.7
42	Michigan	11.5
43	Florida	11.2
43	Pennsylvania	11.2
43	West Virginia	11.2
46	Massachusetts	11.1
47	Connecticut	10.4
47	Rhode Island	10.4
49	New Hampshire	9.7
49	Vermont	9.7
51	Maine	9.6

Voting Population, 2012		
Rank	State	Percent voted, total population
	United States	56.5
1	Mississippi	73.3
2	Wisconsin	71.9
3	Minnesota	70.5
4	District of Columbia	67.7
5	Maine	67.2
6	New Hampshire	66.9
7	Iowa	66.7
8	Colorado	65.4
8	Massachusetts	65.4
10	Louisiana	64.7
11	Michigan	64.5
11	Montana	64.5
13	North Carolina	63.7
14	Oregon	63.3
15	Missouri	62.3
16	Delaware	62.2
16	North Dakota	62.2
16	South Carolina	62.2
19	Vermont	62.1
20	Virginia	62.0
21	Ohio	61.7
22	Washington	60.7
23	Idaho	60.2
24	South Dakota	60.1
25	Alabama	59.9
26	Pennsylvania	59.1
26	Rhode Island	59.1
28	Kansas	58.9
29	Maryland	58.7
30	Nebraska	58.2
31	Georgia	58.1
32	Wyoming	57.8
33	Indiana	57.7
34	Kentucky	57.6
35	Connecticut	57.5
36	New Mexico	56.5
37	Illinois	56.2
38	Alaska	56.0
39	New Jersey	54.5
40	Florida	53.9
41	Tennessee	53.7
42	Utah	53.3
43	Nevada	51.4
44	Arkansas	51.1
45	Oklahoma	51.0
46	New York	50.9
47	Arizona	49.6
48	California	47.5
48	West Virginia	47.5
50	Hawaii	47.4
51	Texas	46.4

Percent of Persons 25 Years and Over with a Bachelor's Degree or More, 2007–2011

Rank	State	Percent
	United States	28.2
1	District of Columbia	50.5
2	Massachusetts	38.7
3	Colorado	36.3
4	Maryland	36.1
5	Connecticut	35.7
6	New Jersey	35.0
7	Virginia	34.4
8	Vermont	33.8
9	New Hampshire	33.1
10	New York	32.5
11	Minnesota	31.8
12	Washington	31.4
13	Illinois	30.7
14	Rhode Island	30.6
15	California	30.2
16	Kansas	29.7
17	Utah	29.6
18	Hawaii	29.5
19	Oregon	29.0
20	Montana	28.2
21	Delaware	28.0
22	Nebraska	27.8
23	Georgia	27.5
24	Alaska	27.2
25	Maine	27.1
26	Pennsylvania	26.7
27	North Carolina	26.5
27	North Dakota	26.5
29	Arizona	26.4
30	Texas	26.1
31	Florida	26.0
31	Wisconsin	26.0
33	South Dakota	25.8
34	Missouri	25.4
34	New Mexico	25.4
36	Michigan	25.3
37	Iowa	24.9
38	Idaho	24.6
39	Ohio	24.5
40	South Carolina	24.2
40	Wyoming	24.2
42	Oklahoma	23.0
42	Tennessee	23.0
44	Indiana	22.7
45	Nevada	22.2
46	Alabama	22.0
47	Louisiana	21.1
48	Kentucky	20.6
49	Mississippi	19.7
50	Arkansas	19.6
51	West Virginia	17.6

Violent Crime, 2011

Rank	State	Rate per 100,000 population
	United States	386.3
1	District of Columbia[1]	1,202.1
2	Tennessee	608.2
3	Alaska	606.5
4	South Carolina	571.9
5	New Mexico	567.5
6	Nevada	562.1
7	Delaware	559.5
8	Louisiana	555.3
9	Florida	515.3
10	Maryland	494.1
11	Arkansas	480.9
12	Oklahoma	454.8
13	Missouri	447.4
14	Michigan	445.3
15	Illinois	429.3
16	Massachusetts	428.4
17	Alabama	420.1
18	California	411.1
19	Texas	408.5
20	Arizona	405.9
21	New York	398.1
22	Georgia	373.2
23	Pennsylvania	355.0
24	Kansas	353.9
25	North Carolina	349.8
26	Indiana	331.8
27	Colorado	320.2
28	West Virginia	315.9
29	New Jersey	308.4
30	Ohio	307.4
31	Washington	294.6
32	Hawaii	287.2
33	Connecticut	272.8
34	Mississippi	269.8
35	Montana	267.5
36	Iowa	255.6
37	South Dakota	254.1
38	Nebraska	253.2
39	Oregon	247.6
40	Rhode Island	247.5
41	North Dakota	247.0
42	Kentucky	238.2
43	Wisconsin	236.9
44	Minnesota[2]	221.2
45	Wyoming	219.3
46	Idaho	200.9
47	Virginia	196.7
48	Utah	195.0
49	New Hampshire	188.0
50	Vermont	135.2
51	Maine	123.2

[1] Includes offenses reported by the Zoological Police and the Metro Transit Police.
[2] The data collection methodology for the offense of forcible rape used by the Minnesota state Uniform Crime Reporting (UCR) Program (with the exception of Minneapolis and St. Paul, Minnesota) does not comply with national UCR Program guidelines. Consequently, its figures for forcible rape and violent crime (of which forcible rape is a part) are not published in this table.

Property Crime, 2011

Rank	State	Rate per 100,000 population
	United States	2,908.7
1	District of Columbia	4,795.5
2	South Carolina	3,905.2
3	Arkansas	3,754.1
4	Louisiana	3,688.5
5	Georgia	3,626.5
6	Alabama	3,606.1
7	Tennessee	3,595.9
8	Washington	3,574.6
9	Arizona	3,554.5
10	New Mexico	3,531.5
11	North Carolina	3,526.8
12	Florida	3,522.0
13	Texas	3,472.3
14	Delaware	3,410.6
15	Oklahoma	3,356.2
16	Ohio	3,354.7
17	Hawaii	3,337.8
18	Missouri	3,308.8
19	Indiana	3,161.8
20	Oregon	3,114.6
21	Kansas	3,080.1
22	Mississippi	3,025.5
23	Utah	2,973.1
24	Maryland	2,860.2
25	Nebraska	2,752.9
26	Kentucky	2,708.8
27	Illinois	2,688.8
28	Rhode Island	2,676.8
29	Alaska	2,632.8
30	Michigan	2,612.1
31	Colorado	2,606.3
32	California	2,583.8
33	Nevada	2,560.5
34	Minnesota	2,549.4
35	Maine	2,545.5
36	Wisconsin	2,432.7
37	Iowa	2,330.3
38	Montana	2,319.7
39	Vermont	2,309.0
40	New Hampshire	2,283.9
41	West Virginia	2,273.9
42	Wyoming	2,266.4
43	Massachusetts	2,258.7
44	Virginia	2,249.6
45	Pennsylvania	2,222.3
46	Connecticut	2,167.4
47	New Jersey	2,150.7
48	Idaho	2,068.6
49	North Dakota	1,936.7
50	New York	1,912.4
51	South Dakota	1,817.7

Federal Aid to State and Local Governments Per Capita, 2010

Rank	State	Thousands of dollars
	United States	630,170
1	California	66,565
2	New York	61,341
3	Texas	43,732
4	Florida	27,731
5	Pennsylvania	26,291
6	Illinois	23,194
7	Ohio	23,072
8	Michigan	19,646
9	New Jersey	16,309
10	Georgia	15,879
11	North Carolina	15,522
12	Massachusetts	15,121
13	Louisiana	13,437
14	Arizona	13,370
15	Missouri	12,717
16	Tennessee	12,514
17	Washington	11,945
18	Minnesota	10,872
19	Maryland	10,832
20	Wisconsin	10,710
21	Virginia	10,647
22	Indiana	10,400
23	District of Columbia	9,942
24	Kentucky	9,756
25	Mississippi	8,611
26	Alabama	8,609
27	South Carolina	8,296
28	Oklahoma	8,022
29	Oregon	7,849
30	Connecticut	7,673
31	Colorado	7,651
32	New Mexico	6,811
33	Arkansas	6,418
34	Iowa	5,871
35	Kansas	4,980
36	West Virginia	4,830
37	Utah	4,212
38	Nevada	3,610
39	Maine	3,581
40	Alaska	3,326
41	Delaware	3,325
42	Nebraska	3,122
43	Idaho	3,057
44	Rhode Island	2,944
45	Montana	2,810
46	Hawaii	2,520
47	Wyoming	2,356
48	New Hampshire	2,355
49	North Dakota	2,169
50	South Dakota	2,145
51	Vermont	2,044

Unemployment Rate, 2012

Rank	State	Unemployment rate
	United States	8.1
1	Nevada	11.1
2	California	10.5
3	Rhode Island	10.4
4	New Jersey	9.5
4	North Carolina	9.5
6	Mississippi	9.2
7	Michigan	9.1
7	South Carolina	9.1
9	Georgia	9.0
10	District of Columbia	8.9
10	Illinois	8.9
12	Oregon	8.7
13	Florida	8.6
14	New York	8.5
15	Connecticut	8.4
15	Indiana	8.4
17	Arizona	8.3
18	Kentucky	8.2
18	Washington	8.2
20	Colorado	8.0
20	Tennessee	8.0
22	Pennsylvania	7.9
23	Alabama	7.3
23	Arkansas	7.3
23	Maine	7.3
23	West Virginia	7.3
27	Ohio	7.2
28	Delaware	7.1
28	Idaho	7.1
30	Alaska	7.0
31	Missouri	6.9
31	New Mexico	6.9
31	Wisconsin	6.9
34	Maryland	6.8
34	Texas	6.8
36	Massachusetts	6.7
37	Louisiana	6.4
38	Montana	6.0
39	Virginia	5.9
40	Hawaii	5.8
41	Kansas	5.7
41	Utah	5.7
43	Minnesota	5.6
44	New Hampshire	5.5
45	Wyoming	5.4
46	Iowa	5.2
46	Oklahoma	5.2
48	Vermont	5.0
49	South Dakota	4.4
50	Nebraska	3.9
51	North Dakota	3.1

Private Nonfarm Employment, Percent Change, 2010–2011

Rank	State	Percent
	United States	1.3
1	North Dakota	3.8
2	Nebraska	3.7
3	District of Columbia	3.1
4	Michigan	2.8
5	Texas	2.3
6	Arizona	2.1
7	Pennsylvania	2.0
8	Ohio	1.8
8	Rhode Island	1.8
10	Indiana	1.7
10	Kentucky	1.7
12	Arkansas	1.6
12	Florida	1.6
12	Oklahoma	1.6
12	Tennessee	1.6
12	Wyoming	1.6
17	Minnesota	1.5
17	North Carolina	1.5
19	Hawaii	1.4
19	Maryland	1.4
19	New York	1.4
19	West Virginia	1.4
19	Wisconsin	1.4
24	California	1.3
25	Illinois	1.2
25	South Carolina	1.2
25	Washington	1.2
28	Louisiana	1.1
28	Massachusetts	1.1
30	Virginia	1.0
31	Colorado	0.9
32	Iowa	0.8
32	Utah	0.8
34	Mississippi	0.6
35	Connecticut	0.4
35	Georgia	0.4
37	Alabama	0.3
37	Missouri	0.3
37	New Jersey	0.3
40	Delaware	0.2
41	Alaska	0.1
42	Vermont	0.0
43	Nevada	-0.2
44	Maine	-0.3
45	New Mexico	-0.4
46	Montana	-0.7
46	Oregon	-0.7
46	South Dakota	-0.7
49	Idaho	-1.1
50	Kansas	-1.2
51	New Hampshire	-1.5

Per Capita Money Income in the Past 12 Months, 2007–2011 (2011 Dollars)

Rank	State	Dollars
	United States	27,915
1	District of Columbia	43,993
2	Connecticut	37,627
3	Maryland	35,751
4	New Jersey	35,678
5	Massachusetts	35,051
6	Virginia	33,040
7	New Hampshire	32,357
8	Alaska	31,944
9	New York	31,796
10	Colorado	30,816
11	Washington	30,481
12	Minnesota	30,310
13	Rhode Island	29,685
14	Delaware	29,659
15	California	29,634
16	Illinois	29,376
17	Hawaii	29,203
18	Wyoming	28,952
19	Vermont	28,376
20	Pennsylvania	27,824
21	Nevada	27,625
22	North Dakota	27,305
23	Wisconsin	27,192
24	Florida	26,733
25	Oregon	26,561
26	Kansas	26,545
27	Maine	26,195
28	Nebraska	26,113
29	Iowa	26,110
30	Arizona	25,784
31	Ohio	25,618
32	Texas	25,548
33	Michigan	25,482
34	Georgia	25,383
35	Missouri	25,371
36	North Carolina	25,256
37	South Dakota	24,925
38	Montana	24,640
39	Indiana	24,497
40	Tennessee	24,197
41	South Carolina	23,854
42	Louisiana	23,853
43	Oklahoma	23,770
44	Utah	23,650
45	New Mexico	23,537
46	Alabama	23,483
47	Kentucky	23,033
48	Idaho	22,788
49	West Virginia	22,010
50	Arkansas	21,833
51	Mississippi	20,521

Gross Domestic Product in Chained (2005) Dollars, 2011

Rank	State	Dollars (billions)
	United States	13,108
1	California	1,692
2	Texas	1,156
3	New York	1,025
4	Florida	656
5	Illinois	583
6	Pennsylvania	503
7	New Jersey	432
8	Ohio	426
9	North Carolina	383
10	Virginia	381
11	Georgia	366
12	Massachusetts	346
13	Michigan	341
14	Washington	314
15	Maryland	268
16	Indiana	247
17	Minnesota	244
18	Colorado	235
19	Tennessee	233
20	Arizona	225
21	Wisconsin	222
22	Missouri	217
23	Connecticut	197
24	Louisiana	196
25	Oregon	180
26	Alabama	155
27	South Carolina	147
28	Kentucky	145
29	Oklahoma	135
30	Iowa	127
31	Kansas	117
32	Utah	108
33	Arkansas	93
34	District of Columbia	91
35	Mississippi	84
36	Nebraska	82
37	New Mexico	71
38	Hawaii	61
38	Nevada	61
40	Delaware	56
40	New Hampshire	56
42	West Virginia	55
43	Idaho	51
44	Maine	46
45	Alaska	44
46	Rhode Island	43
47	South Dakota	36
48	North Dakota	34
49	Montana	33
50	Wyoming	31
51	Vermont	24

Gross Domestic Product in Chained (2005) Dollars, Percent Change, 2010–2011

Rank	State	Percent
	United States	1.6
1	North Dakota	7.8
2	South Dakota	4.4
3	Texas	3.6
4	Michigan	3.5
4	Oregon	3.5
6	Kansas	3.2
7	Ohio	2.9
8	Utah	2.8
9	Montana	2.4
9	Tennessee	2.4
11	South Carolina	2.3
12	Indiana	2.2
12	Iowa	2.2
12	New Hampshire	2.2
15	Georgia	2.1
15	Hawaii	2.1
15	Illinois	2.1
18	Kentucky	2.0
18	Washington	2.0
20	Nebraska	1.9
20	Oklahoma	1.9
20	Pennsylvania	1.9
20	West Virginia	1.9
24	Nevada	1.8
25	Alaska	1.7
25	Arizona	1.7
25	Colorado	1.7
25	Massachusetts	1.7
29	District of Columbia	1.6
29	Maryland	1.6
29	Minnesota	1.6
32	Vermont	1.3
32	Wisconsin	1.3
34	California	1.2
34	New York	1.2
36	Virginia	1.1
37	Alabama	1.0
38	Delaware	0.9
38	Florida	0.9
40	Arkansas	0.7
41	North Carolina	0.5
42	Maine	0.4
43	Missouri	0.3
44	New Jersey	0.2
45	Idaho	0.0
45	Rhode Island	0.0
47	Connecticut	-0.1
48	New Mexico	-0.4
49	Mississippi	-1.1
50	Wyoming	-2.4
51	Louisiana	-2.6

Median Household Income, 2011

Rank	State	Dollars
	United States	50,502
1	Maryland	70,004
2	Alaska	67,825
3	New Jersey	67,458
4	Connecticut	65,753
5	District of Columbia	63,124
6	Massachusetts	62,859
7	New Hampshire	62,647
8	Virginia	61,882
9	Hawaii	61,821
10	Delaware	58,814
11	California	57,287
12	Minnesota	56,954
13	Washington	56,835
14	Wyoming	56,322
15	Utah	55,869
16	Colorado	55,387
17	New York	55,246
18	Rhode Island	53,636
19	Illinois	53,234
20	Vermont	52,776
21	North Dakota	51,704
22	Wisconsin	50,395
23	Nebraska	50,296
24	Pennsylvania	50,228
25	Iowa	49,427
26	Texas	49,392
27	Kansas	48,964
28	Nevada	48,927
29	South Dakota	48,321
30	Oregon	46,816
31	Arizona	46,709
32	Indiana	46,438
33	Maine	46,033
34	Georgia	46,007
35	Michigan	45,981
36	Ohio	45,749
37	Missouri	45,247
38	Florida	44,299
39	Montana	44,222
40	North Carolina	43,916
41	Idaho	43,341
42	Oklahoma	43,225
43	South Carolina	42,637
44	New Mexico	41,963
45	Louisiana	41,734
46	Tennessee	41,693
47	Alabama	41,415
48	Kentucky	41,141
49	Arkansas	38,758
50	West Virginia	38,482
51	Mississippi	36,919

Median Family Income, 2011

Rank	State	Dollars
	United States	69,821
1	Maryland	83,823
2	Connecticut	83,106
3	New Jersey	82,255
4	Massachusetts	80,425
5	New Hampshire	76,609
6	Alaska	75,786
7	District of Columbia	75,603
8	Virginia	74,500
9	Hawaii	74,234
10	Minnesota	71,321
11	Delaware	69,663
12	Rhode Island	69,604
13	Colorado	69,110
14	Wyoming	68,629
15	Washington	68,628
16	North Dakota	66,924
17	New York	66,852
18	Vermont	66,190
19	Illinois	65,579
20	California	65,476
21	Wisconsin	63,732
22	Nebraska	63,491
23	Pennsylvania	63,283
24	Iowa	62,821
25	Utah	62,809
26	South Dakota	62,059
27	Kansas	61,947
28	Ohio	58,565
29	Maine	58,375
30	Oregon	58,356
31	Michigan	58,068
32	Texas	58,016
33	Indiana	57,148
34	Missouri	56,616
35	Nevada	56,544
36	Montana	56,217
37	Arizona	55,328
38	Georgia	55,001
39	North Carolina	54,082
40	Florida	53,958
41	Oklahoma	53,742
42	Louisiana	53,601
43	Idaho	52,814
44	Tennessee	52,273
45	South Carolina	52,240
46	Alabama	51,991
47	Kentucky	51,917
48	New Mexico	51,744
49	West Virginia	49,693
50	Arkansas	48,713
51	Mississippi	46,304

Persons Below Poverty Level, 2011

Rank	State	Percent
	United States	15.9
1	Mississippi	22.6
2	New Mexico	21.5
3	Louisiana	20.4
4	Arkansas	19.5
5	Georgia	19.1
5	Kentucky	19.1
7	Alabama	19.0
7	Arizona	19.0
9	South Carolina	18.9
10	District of Columbia	18.7
11	West Virginia	18.6
12	Texas	18.5
13	Tennessee	18.3
14	North Carolina	17.9
15	Michigan	17.5
15	Oregon	17.5
17	Oklahoma	17.2
18	Florida	17.0
19	California	16.6
20	Idaho	16.5
21	Ohio	16.4
22	Indiana	16.0
22	New York	16.0
24	Nevada	15.9
25	Missouri	15.8
26	Illinois	15.0
27	Montana	14.8
28	Rhode Island	14.7
29	Maine	14.1
30	South Dakota	13.9
30	Washington	13.9
32	Kansas	13.8
32	Pennsylvania	13.8
34	Colorado	13.5
34	Utah	13.5
36	Nebraska	13.1
36	Wisconsin	13.1
38	Iowa	12.8
39	North Dakota	12.2
40	Hawaii	12.0
41	Delaware	11.9
41	Minnesota	11.9
43	Massachusetts	11.6
44	Vermont	11.5
44	Virginia	11.5
46	Wyoming	11.3
47	Connecticut	10.9
48	Alaska	10.5
49	New Jersey	10.4
50	Maryland	10.1
51	New Hampshire	8.8

Persons Under 18 Years Old Below Poverty Level, 2011

Rank	State	Percent
	United States	15.9
1	Mississippi	31.8
2	New Mexico	30.7
3	District of Columbia	30.3
4	Louisiana	28.8
5	Arkansas	28.1
6	South Carolina	27.8
7	Alabama	27.6
8	Kentucky	27.4
9	Arizona	27.2
10	Texas	26.6
11	Georgia	26.3
11	Tennessee	26.3
13	West Virginia	25.8
14	North Carolina	25.6
15	Florida	24.9
16	Michigan	24.8
17	Ohio	24.2
18	Oregon	23.6
19	Oklahoma	23.4
20	Indiana	23.0
21	California	22.8
22	New York	22.6
23	Missouri	22.1
23	Nevada	22.1
25	Rhode Island	21.9
26	Illinois	21.6
27	Idaho	20.4
28	Montana	19.7
29	Pennsylvania	19.6
30	Kansas	18.8
30	Maine	18.8
32	Washington	18.3
33	South Dakota	18.2
33	Wisconsin	18.2
35	Nebraska	18.1
36	Colorado	17.9
37	Delaware	17.5
38	Iowa	17.3
39	Hawaii	17.0
40	Utah	15.9
41	Wyoming	15.6
42	Minnesota	15.4
43	Virginia	15.3
44	Massachusetts	15.2
45	Connecticut	14.9
45	Vermont	14.9
47	New Jersey	14.7
48	North Dakota	14.6
49	Alaska	14.5
50	Maryland	13.5
51	New Hampshire	12.0

Energy Consumption Per Capita, 2011

Rank	State	Million Btu
	United States	312
1	Wyoming	975
2	Louisiana	886
3	Alaska	881
4	North Dakota	768
5	Iowa	494
6	Texas	476
7	Nebraska	473
8	South Dakota	464
9	Indiana	440
10	Kentucky	438
11	Oklahoma	421
12	Kansas	405
13	Alabama	402
14	Montana	398
15	Mississippi	391
16	West Virginia	390
17	Arkansas	380
18	Minnesota	349
19	South Carolina	345
20	Tennessee	344
21	Idaho	332
21	Ohio	332
23	New Mexico	331
24	Missouri	313
25	Wisconsin	313
26	Maine	311
27	Illinois	309
28	Georgia	306
29	Washington	305
30	Delaware	299
31	Virginia	295
32	Pennsylvania	292
33	District of Columbia	291
34	Colorado	289
35	Michigan	284
36	Utah	283
37	New Jersey	276
38	North Carolina	267
39	Oregon	262
40	Maryland	244
41	Vermont	238
42	Nevada	233
43	New Hampshire	222
44	Arizona	221
44	Florida	221
46	Massachusetts	211
47	California	209
48	Hawaii	208
49	Connecticut	207
50	New York	185
51	Rhode Island	175

Homeownership Rate, 2011

Rank	State	Percent
	United States	66.1
1	West Virginia	78.7
2	Mississippi	74.8
3	Vermont	74.6
4	Delaware	74.2
4	South Carolina	74.2
6	Michigan	74.1
6	New Hampshire	74.1
8	Maine	73.9
9	Alabama	72.9
10	Idaho	72.4
11	Indiana	72.1
12	Utah	71.4
13	Minnesota	71.3
14	Iowa	71.2
15	Missouri	71.1
15	Pennsylvania	71.1
15	Wyoming	71.1
18	Connecticut	70.6
19	Louisiana	70.1
20	Maryland	69.7
21	Oklahoma	69.4
22	South Dakota	69.3
22	Tennessee	69.3
24	Kentucky	69.1
24	New Mexico	69.1
26	Florida	69.0
27	Nebraska	68.9
27	Ohio	68.9
29	Wisconsin	68.5
30	Illinois	68.4
30	Montana	68.4
32	North Carolina	68.3
32	North Dakota	68.3
34	Virginia	67.9
35	Arkansas	67.6
36	New Jersey	66.4
36	Oregon	66.4
38	Georgia	66.2
39	Arizona	66.0
40	Colorado	65.9
41	Kansas	65.4
42	Massachusetts	65.3
43	Alaska	64.4
44	Texas	64.3
45	Washington	64.2
46	Rhode Island	63.4
47	Nevada	56.2
48	Hawaii	55.4
49	California	55.3
50	New York	53.6
51	District of Columbia	44.8

One-Unit Detached or Attached Housing Units, Percent of Total Occupied Units, 2011

Rank	State	Percent
	United States	68.9
1	Kansas	78.6
2	Iowa	78.5
3	Indiana	77.9
4	Nebraska	77.7
5	Michigan	77.3
6	Idaho	76.6
6	Oklahoma	76.6
8	Pennsylvania	76.4
9	Delaware	76.3
10	Utah	75.8
11	Missouri	75.7
12	Minnesota	75.1
12	Ohio	75.1
14	Virginia	74.5
15	West Virginia	74.0
16	Maryland	73.9
17	Tennessee	73.1
18	Montana	73.0
18	South Dakota	73.0
20	Mississippi	72.7
21	Arkansas	72.6
21	Wyoming	72.6
23	Alabama	72.5
24	Georgia	71.7
24	Wisconsin	71.7
26	Kentucky	71.2
27	Colorado	71.1
28	North Carolina	70.6
29	Arizona	70.5
30	Vermont	69.8
31	Texas	69.7
32	Louisiana	69.6
33	Alaska	69.1
34	Maine	68.7
35	Oregon	68.6
36	New Hampshire	68.4
37	New Mexico	68.0
38	South Carolina	67.9
39	North Dakota	67.7
40	Washington	67.6
41	Connecticut	66.5
42	Illinois	66.4
43	Nevada	66.0
44	California	65.6
44	Hawaii	65.6
46	Florida	65.2
47	New Jersey	64.4
48	Rhode Island	59.3
49	Massachusetts	57.1
50	New York	47.3
51	District of Columbia	39.2

Mobile Homes, Percent of Total Housing Units, 2011

Rank	State	Percent
	United States	6.5
1	New Mexico	17.2
2	South Carolina	16.9
3	Mississippi	15.3
4	West Virginia	15.0
5	Alabama	13.9
6	Louisiana	13.8
7	North Carolina	13.7
7	Wyoming	13.7
9	Arkansas	13.3
10	Kentucky	12.7
11	Montana	10.9
12	Arizona	10.4
13	Tennessee	10.1
14	Oklahoma	9.8
15	Georgia	9.4
16	Maine	9.3
17	Florida	9.1
18	Delaware	8.9
19	Idaho	8.5
19	South Dakota	8.5
21	Oregon	8.0
22	North Dakota	7.9
23	Texas	7.6
24	Vermont	6.9
24	Washington	6.9
26	Missouri	6.3
27	Nevada	6.2
28	New Hampshire	5.7
29	Michigan	5.6
30	Virginia	5.5
31	Alaska	5.4
32	Indiana	5.1
33	Kansas	4.9
34	Pennsylvania	4.2
35	Colorado	4.0
35	Ohio	4.0
37	Iowa	3.9
38	California	3.8
38	Utah	3.8
38	Wisconsin	3.8
41	Nebraska	3.7
42	Minnesota	3.6
43	Illinois	2.6
44	New York	2.5
45	Maryland	1.7
46	New Jersey	1.0
46	Rhode Island	1.0
48	Connecticut	0.9
48	Massachusetts	0.9
50	Hawaii	0.2
51	District of Columbia	0.0

Traffic Fatalities Per 100 Million Vehicle Miles, 2011

Rank	State	Rate
	United States	1.10
1	Montana	1.79
2	West Virginia	1.78
3	South Carolina	1.70
4	Arkansas	1.67
5	Mississippi	1.62
5	North Dakota	1.62
7	Alaska	1.57
8	Kentucky	1.50
9	Oklahoma	1.47
10	Wyoming	1.46
11	Louisiana	1.45
12	Alabama	1.38
12	Arizona	1.38
12	New Mexico	1.38
15	Tennessee	1.34
16	Pennsylvania	1.30
17	Kansas	1.29
18	Texas	1.27
19	Florida	1.25
20	South Dakota	1.23
21	North Carolina	1.18
22	Iowa	1.15
23	Missouri	1.14
24	Georgia	1.13
25	Delaware	1.10
26	Wisconsin	1.07
27	Idaho	1.05
28	Nevada	1.02
29	Hawaii	0.99
29	Oregon	0.99
31	Indiana	0.98
32	Colorado	0.96
33	Maine	0.95
33	Nebraska	0.95
35	Michigan	0.94
35	Virginia	0.94
37	New York	0.92
37	Utah	0.92
39	Ohio	0.91
40	Illinois	0.89
41	California	0.87
42	Maryland	0.86
42	New Jersey	0.86
44	Rhode Island	0.84
45	Washington	0.80
46	Vermont	0.77
47	District of Columbia	0.76
48	Connecticut	0.71
48	New Hampshire	0.71
50	Minnesota	0.65
51	Massachusetts	0.62

ALABAMA

Facts and Figures

Location: Southeastern United States; bordered on the N by Tennessee, on the E by Georgia, on the S by Florida and the Gulf of Mexico, and on the W by Mississippi

Area: 52,419 sq. mi. (135,765 sq. km.); rank—30th

Population: 4,822,023 (2012 est.); rank—23rd

Principal Cities: capital—Montgomery; largest—Birmingham

Statehood: December 14, 1819; 22nd state

U.S. Congress: 2 senators, 7 representatives

State Motto: *Audemus jura nostra defendere* ("We dare defend our rights")

State Song: "Alabama"

State Nicknames: The Yellowhammer State; The Heart of Dixie; The Cotton State

Abbreviations: AL; Ala.

State Symbols: flower—camellia; tree—Southern longleaf pine; bird—yellowhammer

At a Glance

- With an increase in population of 5.9 percent, Alabama ranked 25th among the states in growth from 2000 to 2009.
- An estimated 37,300 marriages took place in Alabama in 2009, compared to 20,200 divorces.
- The 2008 homeownership rate in Alabama was 73.0 percent, giving it a ranking of 15th among the states.
- Alabama's violent crime rate in 2011 was 420.1 per 100,000 population, compared to 386.3 for the entire nation.
- In the 2012 election, 61.9 percent of Alabama's eligible voters voted, compared to 61.8 percent of eligible voters nationwide.
- In 2007, Alabama exported $616 million worth of agricultural products, less than 1 percent of the U.S. total.

Table AL-1. Population by Age, Sex, Race, and Hispanic Origin

(Number, percent, except where noted.)

Sex, age, race, and Hispanic origin	2000	2010	2012	Average annual percent change, 2010–2012
Total Population	4,447,100	4,779,736	4,822,023	0.3
Percent of total U.S. population	1.6	1.5	1.5	X
Sex				
Male	2,146,504	2,320,188	2,338,671	0.3
Female	2,300,596	2,459,548	2,483,342	0.3
Age				
Under 5 years	295,992	304,957	305,267	-
5 to 19 years	960,177	971,355	951,199	-0.7
20 to 64 years	2,611,133	2,845,632	2,866,177	0.2
65 years and over	579,798	657,792	699,380	2.0
Median age (years)	35.8	37.9	38.2	0.3
Race and Hispanic Origin				
One race				
White	3,162,808	3,362,877	3,373,844	0.1
Black	1,155,930	1,259,224	1,279,805	0.5
American Indian and Alaska Native	22,430	32,903	33,579	0.7
Asian	31,346	55,240	59,602	2.4
Native Hawaiian or Other Pacific Islander	1,409	5,208	5,270	0.4
Two or more races	44,179	64,284	69,923	2.7
Hispanic (of any race)	75,830	192,498	203,558	1.8

X = Not applicable.
- = Zero or rounds to zero.

Population by Selected Race and Hispanic Origin, 2012

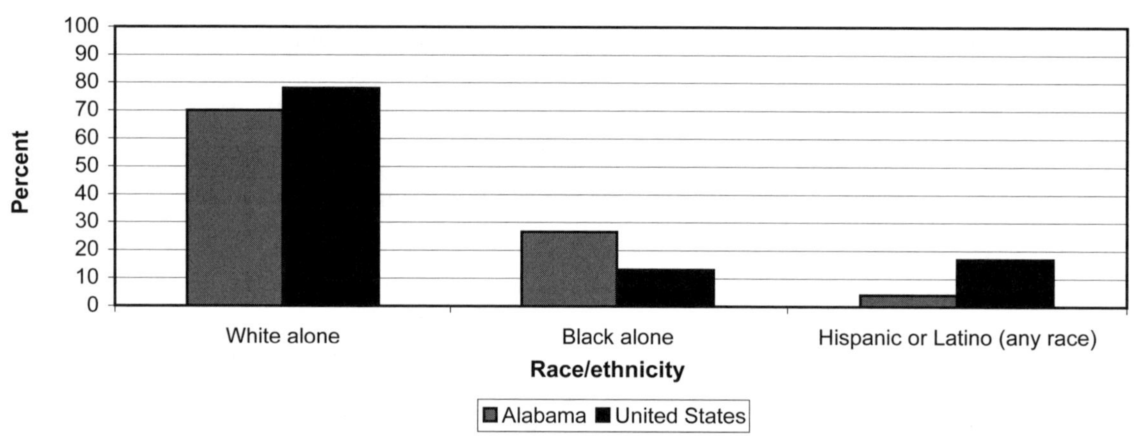

Table AL-2. Marital Status

(Number, percent distribution.)

Sex, age, race, and Hispanic origin	2000	2010	2011
Males, 15 Years and Over	1,666,798	1,844,661	1,854,464
Never married	26.7	32.5	32.1
Now married, except separated	59.0	50.6	51.5
Separated	1.8	2.5	2.2
Widowed	2.8	3.0	2.9
Divorced	9.8	11.4	11.3
Females, 15 Years and Over	1,847,401	2,004,450	2,020,294
Never married	21.4	26.1	26.2
Now married, except separated	52.5	45.9	46.4
Separated	2.5	3.1	3.1
Widowed	12.4	11.2	10.9
Divorced	11.2	13.6	13.3

Table AL-3. Households and Housing Characteristics

(Number, percent, dollars.)

Item	2000	2010	2011	Average annual percent change, 2000–2011
Total Households	1,737,080	1,815,152	1,844,546	0.5
Family households	1,215,968	1,227,884	1,251,795	0.2
Married-couple family	906,916	868,946	889,810	-0.2
Other family	309,052	358,938	361,985	1.4
Male householder, no wife present	62,586	79,308	79,578	2.3
Female householder, no husband present	246,466	279,630	282,407	1.2
Nonfamily households	521,112	587,268	592,751	1.1
Householder living alone	453,898	511,708	520,241	1.2
Householder not living alone	67,214	75,560	72,510	0.7
Housing Characteristics				
Total housing units	1,963,711	2,174,428	2,182,199	0.9
Occupied housing units	1,737,080	1,815,152	1,844,546	0.5
Owner occupied	1,258,705	1,272,846	1,289,217	0.2
Renter occupied	478,375	542,306	555,329	1.3
Average size	2.49	2.57	2.54	0.2
Financial Characteristics				
Median gross rent of renter-occupied housing	447	667	687	4.5
Median monthly owner costs for housing units with a mortgage	816	1,130	1,134	3.2
Median value of owner-occupied housing units	85,100	123,900	122,700	3.7

Table AL-4. Migration, Origin, and Language

(Number, percent.)

Characteristic	State			U.S.		
	2010	2011	Percent change	2010	2011	Percent change
Residence 1 Year Ago						
Population 1 year and over	4,729,509	4,745,278	0.3	305,628,607	307,900,319	0.7
Same house	84.3	84.8	0.6	84.6	84.8	0.2
Different house in the U.S.	15.4	14.9	-3.2	14.8	14.6	-1.4
Same county	9.6	9.3	-3.1	9.4	9.2	-2.1
Different county	5.8	5.6	-3.4	5.4	5.4	-
Same state	3.5	3.1	-11.4	3.2	3.1	-3.1
Different state	2.3	2.5	8.7	2.2	2.3	4.5
Abroad	0.3	0.3	-	0.6	0.6	-
Place of Birth						
Native born	4,616,702	4,640,067	0.5	269,393,835	271,214,059	0.7
Male	48.4	48.3	-0.2	49.2	49.2	-
Female	51.6	51.7	0.2	50.8	50.8	-
Foreign born	168,596	162,673	-3.5	39,955,854	40,377,860	1.1
Male	52.1	52.0	-0.2	49.1	48.9	-0.4
Female	47.9	48.0	0.2	50.9	51.1	0.4
Foreign born; naturalized U.S. citizen	48,099	57,576	19.7	17,476,082	18,140,192	3.8
Male	43.8	46.5	6.2	45.8	45.8	-
Female	56.2	53.5	-4.8	54.2	54.2	-
Foreign born; not a U.S. citizen	120,497	105,097	-12.8	22,479,772	22,237,668	-1.1
Male	55.4	55.0	-0.7	51.6	51.5	-0.2
Female	44.6	45.0	0.9	48.4	48.5	0.2
Entered 2000 or later	56.5	49.7	-12.0	34.7	35.7	2.9
Entered 1990 to 1999	22.0	22.8	3.6	27.2	26.7	-1.8
Entered before 1990	21.4	27.5	28.5	38.1	37.6	-1.3
World Region of Birth, Foreign						
Foreign-born population, excluding population born at sea	168,596	162,673	-3.5	39,955,673	40,377,757	1.1
Europe	9.9	11.8	19.2	12.1	12.1	-
Asia	26.3	26.7	1.5	28.2	28.6	1.4
Africa	3.3	4.7	42.4	4	4.1	2.5
Oceania	0.4	0.3	-25.0	0.5	0.5	-
Latin America	58.0	54.9	-5.3	53.1	52.6	-0.9
North America	2.0	1.5	-25.0	2	2.0	-
Language Spoken at Home and Ability to Speak English						
Population 5 years and over	4,477,229	4,504,275	0.6	289,215,746	291,524,091	0.8
English only	94.8	94.8	-	79.4	79.2	-0.3
Language other than English	5.2	5.2	-	20.6	20.8	1.0
Speaks English less than "very well"	2.4	2.3	-4.2	8.7	8.7	-

- = Zero or rounds to zero.

Table AL-5. Median Income and Poverty Status, 2011

(Number, percent, except as noted.)

Characteristic	State		U.S.	
	Number	Percent	Number	Percent
Median Income				
Households (dollars)	41,415	X	50,502	X
Families (dollars)	51,991	X	61,455	X
Below Poverty Level (All People)	892,483	19.0	48,452,035	15.9
Sex				
Male	386,574	17.2	21,825,281	14.7
Female	505,909	20.8	26,626,754	17.2
Age				
Under 18 years	306,973	27.6	16,386,500	22.5
Related children under 18 years	303,606	27.4	16,087,074	22.2
18 to 64 years	518,036	17.7	28,335,079	14.8
65 years and over	67,474	10.3	3,730,456	9.3

X = Not applicable.

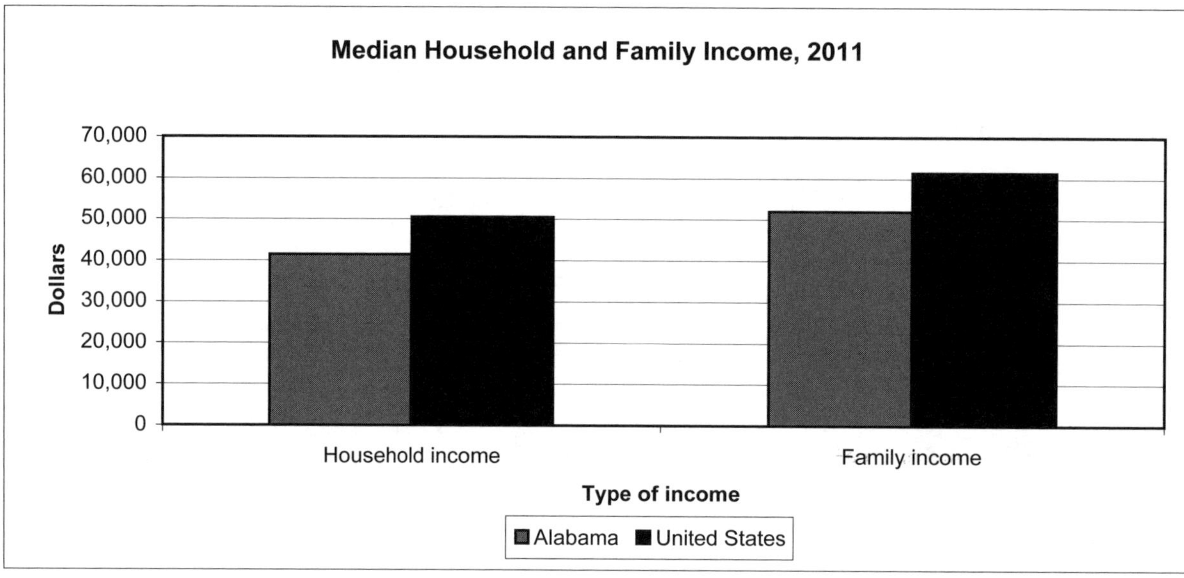

Table AL-6. Health Insurance Coverage Status for the Civilian Noninstitutionalized Population and Children Under 18 Years of Age

(Numbers in thousands, percent.)

Item	2004	2005	2006	2007	2008	2009	2010	2011
Civilian Noninstitutionalized Population	4,512	4,524	4,532	4,570	4,574	4,616	4,703	4,720
Covered by Private or Public Insurance								
Number	3,950	3,867	3,843	4,021	4,023	3,979	4,016	4,046
Percent	87.5	85.5	84.8	88.0	88.0	86.2	85.4	85.7
Not Covered								
Number	562	657	689	549	551	637	687	674
Percent	19.7	14.5	15.2	12.0	12.0	13.8	14.6	14.3
Percent in the U.S. not covered	14.9	15.3	15.8	15.3	15.1	15.1	15.5	15.1
Children Under 18 Years of Age	1,096	1,083	1,114	1,083	1,120	1,124	1,134	1,122
Covered by Private or Public Insurance								
Number	1,027	1,034	1,032	1,041	1,030	1,057	1,067	1,063
Percent	93.7	95.5	92.6	92.7	92.0	94.1	94.1	94.7
Not Covered								
Number	69	49	82	82	90	67	67	59
Percent	6.3	4.5	7.4	7.3	8.0	5.9	5.9	5.3
Percent in the U.S. not covered	10.5	10.9	11.7	11.0	9.7	8.6	8.0	7.5

Table AL-7. Employment Status by Demographic Group, Preliminary 2012

(Numbers in thousands, percent.)

Characteristic	Civilian noninstitutional population	Civilian labor force		Employed		Unemployed	
		Number	Percent of population	Number	Percent of population	Number	Percent of population
Total	3,752	2,178	58.1	2,003	53.4	175	8.0
Sex							
Male	1,776	1,151	64.8	1,056	59.5	95	8.2
Female	1,977	1,028	52.0	947	47.9	81	7.9
Race, Sex, and Hispanic Origin							
White	2,704	1,598	59.1	1,498	55.4	101	6.3
Male	1,308	896	68.5	839	64.1	57	6.4
Female	1,397	702	50.3	659	47.2	43	6.2
Black or African American	942	515	54.6	448	47.6	67	12.9
Male	415	223	53.7	191	46.0	32	14.2
Female	526	292	55.4	257	48.8	35	11.9
Hispanic	97	70	71.8	60	62.0	10	13.8
Male	49	41	84.0	37	75.2	4	10.4
Female	48	29	59.5	23	48.5	5	18.5
Age							
16 to 19 years	280	80	28.6	66	23.7	14	17.1
20 to 24 years	303	203	66.9	170	56.2	32	16.0
25 to 34 years	610	476	78.1	423	69.4	53	11.1
35 to 44 years	602	463	76.9	435	72.3	28	6.1
45 to 54 years	654	492	75.4	465	71.2	27	5.5
55 to 64 years	639	367	57.4	353	55.2	14	3.8
65 years and over	665	97	14.6	90	13.5	7	7.1

NOTE: Data in Table 7 are from the Current Population Survey (CPS) and do not match the estimates in Table 8. See notes and definitions for further information.

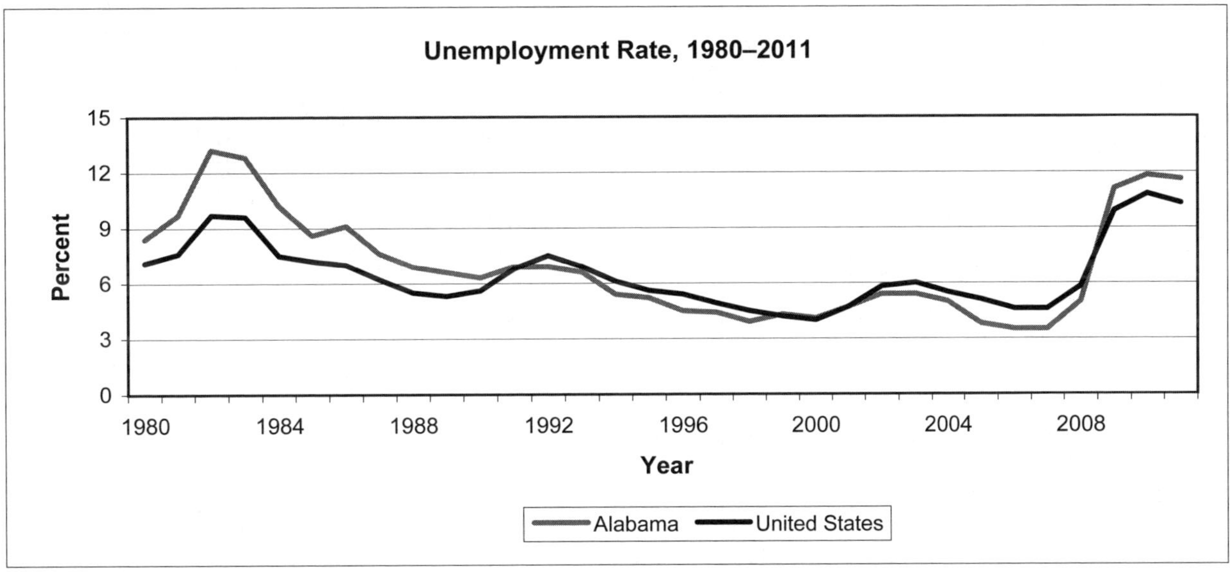

Table AL-8. Employment Status of the Civilian Noninstitutional Population Age 16 Years and Over

(Number, percent.)

Year	Civilian labor force	Civilian participation rate	Employed	Unemployed	Unemployment rate
2005	2,124,149	61.1	2,042,925	81,224	3.8
2006	2,166,071	61.5	2,090,387	75,684	3.5
2007	2,175,716	61.1	2,099,615	76,101	3.5
2008	2,162,479	60.2	2,053,502	108,977	5.0
2009	2,257,446	60.9	1,986,034	247,536	11.1
2010	2,244,208	59.3	1,978,825	265,383	11.8
2011	2,240,441	58.8	1,981,095	259,376	11.6

Table AL-9. Employment and Average Wages by Industry

(Estimates before 2007 are based on the 2002 *North American Industry Classification System* [NAICS]. Estimates from 2007 onward are based on the 2007 NAICS.)

Industry	2005	2006	2007	2008	2009	2010	2011
				Number of jobs			
Wage and Salary Employment by Industry	2,041,001	2,078,844	2,101,829	2,082,617	1,978,414	1,960,904	1,962,049
Farm Wage and Salary Employment	8,327	9,025	7,648	7,750	9,482	7,957	8,074
Nonfarm Wage and Salary Employment	2,032,674	2,069,819	2,094,181	2,074,867	1,968,932	1,952,947	1,953,975
Private wage and salary employment	1,632,480	1,664,991	1,683,982	1,664,029	1,557,480	1,539,991	1,545,888
Forestry, fishing, and related activities	9,486	9,178	9,055	8,708	8,503	8,727	8,857
Mining	8,026	8,331	8,178	8,267	7,723	7,771	8,289
Utilities	12,667	12,947	13,350	13,971	13,865	14,093	14,262
Construction	109,904	114,243	116,957	112,693	95,983	91,361	85,262
Manufacturing	299,230	303,097	296,645	282,951	246,592	236,733	237,815
Durable goods manufacturing	178,308	187,425	186,669	178,501	152,566	146,428	148,023
Nondurable goods manufacturing	120,922	115,672	109,976	104,450	94,026	90,305	89,792
Wholesale trade	79,802	81,854	82,557	81,737	75,203	72,336	72,563
Retail trade	238,626	238,662	244,471	240,716	228,378	226,793	228,106
Transportation and warehousing	55,900	58,167	58,854	58,524	53,443	53,269	54,180
Information	30,935	30,221	28,042	27,380	25,325	24,016	23,098
Finance and insurance	73,503	73,767	73,486	73,664	71,718	70,355	71,988
Real estate and rental and leasing	25,389	25,551	26,393	25,659	24,041	22,753	21,878
Professional, scientific, and technical services	91,660	95,730	98,192	100,795	97,910	95,809	95,059
Management of companies and enterprises	12,317	13,335	14,705	14,439	15,190	15,496	15,982
Administrative and waste services	105,319	107,221	110,544	108,209	94,485	100,596	104,600
Educational services	24,386	25,864	25,698	25,905	27,042	28,053	28,817
Health care and social assistance	181,761	188,134	193,279	196,005	195,152	197,749	199,466
Arts, entertainment, and recreation	16,832	17,237	17,777	17,787	18,082	16,616	16,278
Accommodation and food services	149,687	154,435	158,106	158,467	153,918	153,104	155,098
Other services, except public administration	107,050	107,017	107,693	108,152	104,927	104,361	104,290
Government and government enterprises	400,194	404,828	410,199	410,838	411,452	412,956	408,087
				Dollars			
Average Wages and Salaries by Industry	34,001	35,517	36,846	38,085	38,701	39,607	40,461
Average Farm Wages and Salaries	19,717	19,603	25,831	23,102	18,923	22,692	20,050
Average Nonfarm Wages and Salaries	34,060	35,587	36,886	38,141	38,796	39,676	40,546
Average private wages and salaries	33,611	35,131	36,253	37,345	37,841	38,802	39,653
Forestry, fishing, and related activities	27,421	28,343	29,335	30,634	29,997	32,117	32,801
Mining	58,979	58,506	61,865	67,255	68,446	74,346	77,705
Utilities	80,620	80,493	83,860	81,835	80,520	78,785	85,859
Construction	34,946	36,917	39,197	40,970	41,761	43,398	43,496
Manufacturing	40,530	42,313	43,679	45,149	45,770	48,313	49,094
Durable goods manufacturing	43,185	44,927	45,898	47,563	48,039	51,079	51,728
Nondurable goods manufacturing	36,614	38,076	39,912	41,026	42,088	43,827	44,752
Wholesale trade	47,627	49,958	51,799	53,580	53,268	54,900	56,108
Retail trade	22,537	23,324	23,719	23,821	24,139	24,523	24,734
Transportation and warehousing	37,630	38,507	39,691	40,641	40,471	41,919	43,059
Information	45,968	47,158	47,982	48,804	47,929	48,328	50,897
Finance and insurance	52,079	57,229	58,404	58,570	58,364	58,243	62,143
Real estate and rental and leasing	30,200	31,751	33,138	33,444	32,982	35,275	36,598
Professional, scientific, and technical services	53,663	56,308	58,573	62,245	65,076	65,906	68,022
Management of companies and enterprises	65,341	67,212	70,037	70,406	69,189	74,595	78,602
Administrative and waste services	22,035	22,723	23,394	24,258	25,148	26,251	26,113
Educational services	22,461	22,680	23,811	23,660	24,069	24,045	24,536
Health care and social assistance	36,310	37,676	38,614	39,966	41,221	41,615	42,230
Arts, entertainment, and recreation	17,750	19,290	19,900	19,310	18,934	18,935	18,915
Accommodation and food services	12,923	13,292	14,125	14,346	14,700	15,353	15,715
Other services, except public administration	22,629	23,590	24,740	25,935	26,389	27,569	28,092
Government and government enterprises	35,890	37,460	39,484	41,366	42,412	42,937	43,929

Table AL-10. Employment Characteristics by Family Type

(Number, percent.)

Family type and labor force status	2009 Total	2009 Families with own children under 18 years	2010 Total	2010 Families with own children under 18 years	2011 Total	2011 Families with own children under 18 years
All families	1,246,056	532,733	1,227,884	511,392	1,251,795	519,269
Family type and labor force status						
Married-couple families	884,533	338,979	868,946	320,947	889,810	331,712
Both husband and wife in labor force	49.6	65.2	49.6	66.4	48.4	65.2
Husband in labor force, wife not in labor force	23.4	27.9	22.6	26.7	22.9	27.9
Wife in labor force, husband not in labor force	8.2	4.5	7.9	4.2	8.8	4.3
Both husband and wife not in labor force	18.9	2.3	19.9	2.7	19.9	2.6
Other families	361,523	193,754	358,938	190,445	361,985	187,557
Female householder, no husband present	78.7	82.1	77.9	80.9	78.0	81.4
In labor force	52.5	67.2	49.4	62.2	51.2	64.7
Not in labor force	26.2	14.9	28.5	18.7	26.8	16.7
Male householder, no wife present	21.3	17.9	22.1	19.1	22.0	18.6
In labor force	15.9	16.1	15.9	16.9	15.6	15.7
Not in labor force	5.4	1.7	6.1	2.2	6.4	2.9

Table AL-11. School Enrollment and Educational Attainment, 2011

(Number, percent.)

Item	State	U.S.
Enrollment		
Total population 3 years and over, enrolled in school	1,241,786	83,131,910
Enrolled in nursery school or preschool (percent)	5.3	6.0
Enrolled in kindergarten (percent)	5.4	5.1
Enrolled in elementary school, grades 1-8 (percent)	41.4	39.5
Enrolled in high school, grades 9-12 (percent)	20.9	20.7
Enrolled in college or graduate school (percent)	27.1	28.7
Attainment		
Total population 25 years and over	3,193,078	206,471,670
Less than ninth grade (percent)	5.6	6.0
9th to 12th grade, no diploma (percent)	11.7	8.1
High school graduate, including equivalency (percent)	30.9	28.4
Some college, no degree (percent)	22.2	21.2
Associate's degree (percent)	7.4	7.8
Bachelor's degree (percent)	13.9	17.9
Graduate or professional degree (percent)	8.4	10.6
High school graduate or higher (percent)	82.7	85.9
Bachelor's degree or higher (percent)	22.3	28.5

Table AL-12. Educational Indicators

(Number, percent; data derived from National Center of Education Statistics.)

Item	State	U.S.
Public Schools, 2009–2010 (except where noted)		
Number of school districts	133	13,629
Number of schools	1,600	99,834
Number of students (in thousands)	749	49,373
Student-teacher ratio	15.8	15.4
Expenditures per student (dollars)	10,210	10,591
Averaged freshman graduation rate, 2008–2009	69.9	75.5[1]
Dropout rate, 2008–2009	1.5	4.1
Students eligible for free or reduced-price lunch (percent)	55.1	48.0
English language learners, 2010–2011 (percent)	2.4	9.8[1]
Students with IEP (percent)	11.1	13.1
Private Schools, 2009–2010 (except where noted)		
Number of schools	578	33,366
Number of students (in thousands)	78	4,700
High school graduates, 2008–2009	5,277	308,813
Student-teacher ratio	8.9	10.7

Table AL-13. Reported Voting and Registration of the Voting-Age Population, November 2012

(Numbers in thousands, percent.)

Item	Total population	Total citizen population	Registered			Voted		
			Total registered	Percent registered (total population)	Percent registered (total citizen population)	Total voted	Percent voted (total population)	Percent voted (total citizen population)
U.S. Total	235,248	215,081	153,157	65.1	71.2	132,948	56.5	61.8
State Total	3,594	3,479	2,556	71.1	73.5	2,154	59.9	61.9
Sex	1,703	1,649	1,201	70.5	72.9	1,009	59.2	61.2
Male	1,891	1,831	1,354	71.6	74.0	1,145	60.6	62.6
Female								
Race								
White alone	2,580	2,502	1,878	72.8	75.1	1,530	59.3	61.2
White, non-Hispanic alone	2,473	2,467	1,866	75.5	75.6	1,530	61.9	62.0
Black alone	891	888	610	68.5	68.7	560	62.8	63.1
Asian alone	59	25	17	B	B	17	B	B
Hispanic (of any race)	107	35	12	11.5	35.1	-	B	B
Age								
18 to 24 years	439	428	212	48.3	49.6	155	35.3	36.2
25 to 44 years	1,191	1,116	770	64.6	69.0	601	50.5	53.8
45 to 64 years	1,297	1,275	1,051	81.0	82.4	939	72.4	73.7
65 to 74 years	381	378	293	77.0	77.6	260	68.3	68.8
75 years and over	286	282	230	80.4	81.4	199	69.5	70.4

- = Zero or rounds to zero.
B = Base is less than 75,000 and therefore too small to show the derived measure.

Table AL-14. Crime

(Number, rate per 100,000. Data are derived from the FBI Uniform Crime Reports.)

Item	State			U.S.		
	2010	2011	Percent change	2010	2011	Percent change
TOTAL POPULATION	4,785,401	4,802,740	0.4	309,330,219	311,591,917	0.7
VIOLENT CRIME						
Number	18,363	20,174	9.9	1,251,248	1,203,564	-3.8
Rate	383.7	420.1	9.5	404.5	386.3	-4.5
Murder and Nonnegligent Manslaughter						
Number	275	301	9.5	14,722	14,612	-0.7
Rate	5.7	6.3	10.5	4.8	4.7	-2.1
Forcible Rape						
Number	1,355	1,371	1.2	85,593	83,425	-2.5
Rate	28.3	28.5	0.7	27.7	26.8	-3.2
Robbery						
Number	4,864	4,910	0.9	369,089	354,396	-4.0
Rate	101.6	102.2	0.6	119.3	113.7	-4.7
Aggravated Assault						
Number	11,869	13,592	14.5	781,844	751,131	-3.9
Rate	248.0	283.0	14.1	252.8	241.1	-4.6
PROPERTY CRIME						
Number	168,828	173,190	2.6	9,112,625	9,063,173	-0.5
Rate	3,528.0	3,606.1	2.2	2,945.9	2,908.7	-1.3
Burglary						
Number	42,484	51,117	20.3	2,168,459	2,188,005	0.9
Rate	887.8	1,064.3	19.9	701.0	702.2	0.2
Larceny-Theft						
Number	115,564	111,411	-3.6	6,204,601	6,159,795	-0.7
Rate	2,414.9	2,319.7	-3.9	2,005.8	1,976.9	-1.4
Motor Vehicle Theft						
Number	10,780	10,662	-1.1	739,565	715,373	-3.3
Rate	225.3	222.0	-1.5	239.1	229.6	-4.0

Table AL-15. State Government Finances, 2011

(Dollar amounts in thousands, percent distribution.)

Item	Dollars	Percent distribution
Total Revenue	26,305,162	100.0
General revenue	23,276,781	88.5
Intergovernmental revenue	8,881,520	33.8
Taxes	8,635,527	32.8
General sales	2,174,639	8.3
Selective sales	2,400,488	9.1
License taxes	496,117	1.9
Individual income tax	2,795,906	10.6
Corporate income tax	301,178	1.1
Other taxes	467,199	1.8
Current charges	4,452,308	16.9
Miscellaneous general revenue	1,307,426	5.0
Utility revenue	0	0.0
Liquor stores revenue	266,951	1.0
Insurance trust revenue [1]	2,761,430	10.5
Total Expenditure	28,061,237	100.0
Intergovernmental expenditure	6,800,787	24.2
Direct expenditure	21,260,450	75.8
Current operation	14,898,156	53.1
Capital outlay	1,920,251	6.8
Insurance benefits and repayments	3,526,164	12.6
Assistance and subsidies	565,447	2.0
Interest on debt	350,432	1.2
Exhibit: Salaries and wages	4,665,923	16.6
Total Expenditure	28,061,237	100.0
General expenditure	24,290,468	86.6
Intergovernmental expenditure	6,800,787	24.2
Direct expenditure	17,489,681	62.3
General expenditure, by function:		
Education	10,938,129	39.0
Public welfare	5,961,891	21.2
Hospitals	1,948,230	6.9
Health	609,367	2.2
Highways	1,616,245	5.8
Police protection	183,957	0.7
Correction	563,058	2.0
Natural resources	270,950	1.0
Parks and recreation	36,497	0.1
Governmental administration	579,928	2.1
Interest on general debt	350,432	1.2
Other and unallocable	1,231,784	4.4
Utility expenditure	0	0.0
Liquor stores expenditure	244,605	0.9
Insurance trust expenditure	3,526,164	12.6
Debt at End of Fiscal Year	9,067,280	X
Cash and Security Holdings	34,335,207	X

X = Not applicable.

[1] Within insurance trust revenue, net earnings of state retirement systems is a calculated statistic (the item code in the data file is X08), and thus can be positive or negative. Net earnings is the sum of earnings on investments plus gains on investments minus losses on investments.

Table AL-16. State Government Tax Collections, 2012

(Dollars in thousands, percent.)

Item	Dollars	Percent distribution
Total Taxes	9,052,880	100.0
Property taxes	325,116	3.6
Sales and gross receipts	4,626,357	51.1
General sales and gross receipts	2,274,658	25.1
Selective sales and gross receipts	2,351,699	26.0
Alcoholic beverages	173,251	1.9
Amusements	53	
Insurance premiums	278,242	3.1
Motor fuels	541,499	6.0
Pari-mutuels	1,841	-
Public utilities	736,533	8.1
Tobacco products	126,151	1.4
Other selective sales	494,129	5.5
Licenses	517,676	5.7
Alcoholic beverages	4,229	-
Amusements	0	0.0
Corporations in general	130,843	1.4
Hunting and fishing	20,688	0.2
Motor vehicle	201,875	2.2
Motor vehicle operators	21,679	0.2
Public utilities	14,367	0.2
Occupation and business, NEC	123,994	1.4
Other licenses	1	-
Income taxes	3,430,690	37.9
Individual income	3,017,437	33.3
Corporation net income	413,253	4.6
Other taxes	153,041	1.7
Death and gift	303	-
Documentary and stock transfer	36,271	0.4
Severance	116,467	1.3
Taxes, NEC	0	0.0

- = Rounds to zero.

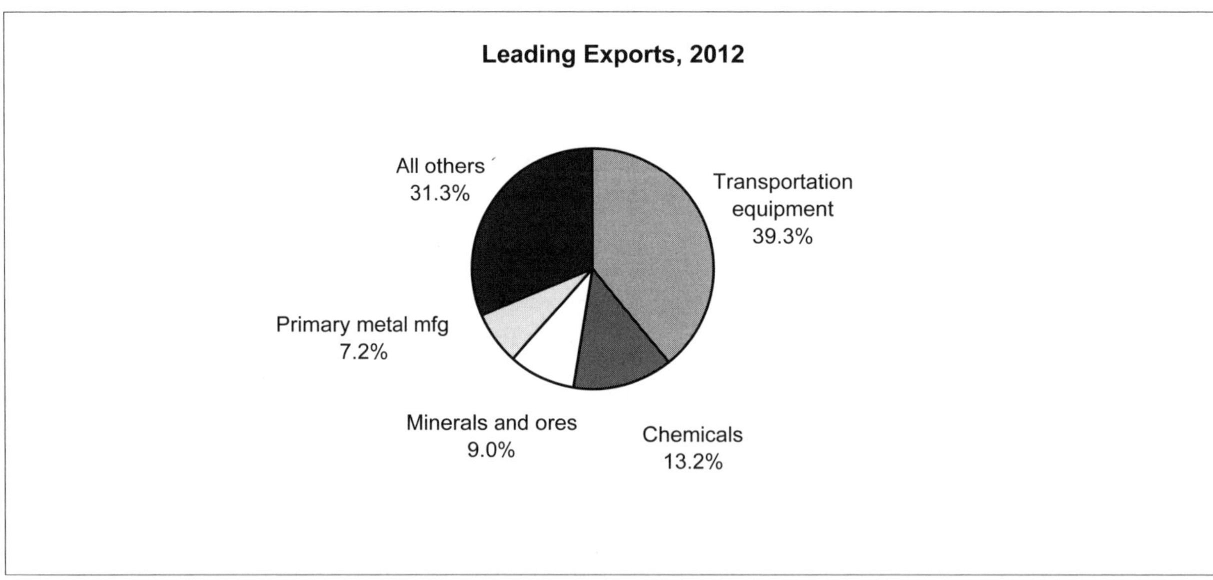

ALASKA

Facts and Figures

Location: Northwestern North America; bordered on the N by the Arctic Ocean, on the E by Canada, on the S by the Pacific Ocean and the Gulf of Alaska, and on the W by the Bering Sea

Area: 663,267 sq. mi. (1,717,854 sq. sq. km.); rank—1st

Population: 731,449 (2012 est.); rank—47th

Principal Cities: capital—Juneau; largest—Anchorage

Statehood: January 3, 1959; 49th state

U.S. Congress: 2 senators, 1 representative

State Motto: North to the Future

State Song: "Alaska's Flag"

State Nicknames: The Last Frontier; The Land of the Midnight Sun

Abbreviations: AK

State Symbols: flower—forget-me-not; tree—Sitka spruce; bird—willow ptarmigan

At a Glance

- With an increase in population of 11.5 percent, Alaska ranked 41st among the states in growth from 2000 to 2009.
- Approximately 5,500 marriages took place in Alaska in 2009, compared to 3,300 divorces.
- Alaska's violent crime rate in 2011 was 606.5 per 100,000 population, compared to 386.3 for the entire nation.
- In the 2012 election, 58.4 percent of Alaska's eligible voters voted, compared to 61.8 percent of eligible voters nationwide.
- In 2007, Alaska exported $4 million worth of agricultural products, less than 1 percent of the U.S. total.

Table AK-1. Population by Age, Sex, Race, and Hispanic Origin

(Number, percent, except where noted.)

Sex, age, race, and Hispanic origin	2000	2010	2012[1]	Average annual percent change, 2010–2012
Total Population	626,932	710,231	731,449	1.0
Percent of total U.S. population	0.2	0.2	0.2	X
Sex				
Male	324,112	369,628	381,238	1.0
Female	302,820	240,603	350,211	10.4
Age				
Under 5 years	47,591	53,996	54,791	0.5
5 to 19 years	160,526	153,844	151,866	-0.4
20 to 64 years	383,116	447,453	462,295	1.1
65 years and over	35,699	54,938	62,497	4.0
Median age (years)	32.4	33.8	33.7	-0.1
Race and Hispanic Origin				
One race				
White	434,534	483,873	493,430	0.6
Black	21,787	24,441	27,373	3.6
American Indian and Alaska Native	98,043	106,268	108,249	0.6
Asian	25,116	38,882	41,986	2.5
Native Hawaiian or Other Pacific Islander	3,309	7,622	8,558	3.6
Two or more races	34,146	49,105	51,853	1.8
Hispanic (of any race)	25,852	44,490	50,422	3.9

X = Not applicable.
[1]Population figures for 2012 are July 1 estimates. The 2010 estimates are taken from the 2010 Census.

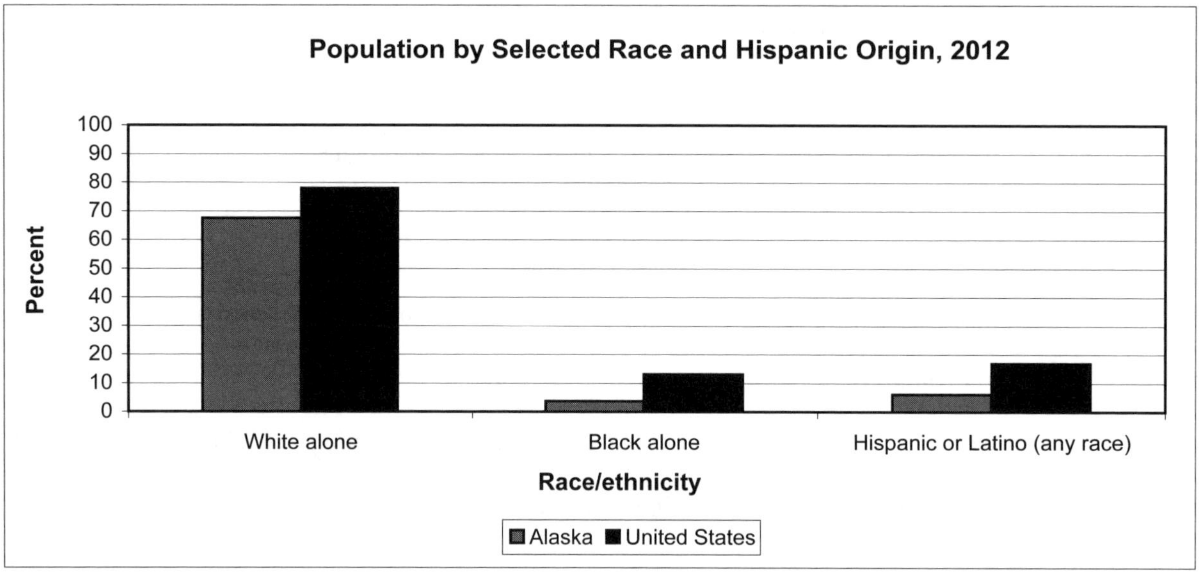

Table AK-2. Marital Status

(Number, percent distribution.)

Sex, age, race, and Hispanic origin	2000	2010	2011
Males, 15 Years and Over	243,024	290,598	292,160
Never married	32.5	35.5	36.0
Now married, except separated	53.6	49.7	48.8
Separated	1.7	1.7	2.0
Widowed	1.4	1.8	1.8
Divorced	10.8	11.4	11.4
Females, 15 Years and Over	225,837	267,563	273,002
Never married	24.1	27.3	28.4
Now married, except separated	55.6	50.2	50.2
Separated	2.3	2.6	2.1
Widowed	5.6	6.1	5.8
Divorced	12.5	13.7	13.5

Table AK-3. Households and Housing Characteristics

(Number, percent, dollars.)

Item	2000	2010	2011	Average annual percent change, 2000–2011
Total Households	221,600	254,610	257,330	1.3
Family households	152,337	170,859	173,279	1.1
Married-couple family	116,318	127,969	127,277	0.8
Other family	36,019	42,890	46,002	2.3
Male householder, no wife present	12,082	14,211	15,744	2.5
Female householder, no husband present	23,937	28,679	30,258	2.2
Nonfamily households	69,263	83,751	84,051	1.8
Householder living alone	52,060	63,698	64,846	2.0
Householder not living alone	17,203	20,053	19,205	1.0
Housing Characteristics				
Total housing units	260,978	307,065	311,182	1.6
Occupied housing units	221,600	254,610	257,330	1.3
Owner occupied	138,509	162,785	162,312	1.4
Renter occupied	83,091	91,825	95,018	1.2
Average size	2.74	2.70	2.71	-0.1
Financial Characteristics				
Median gross rent of renter-occupied housing	720	981	1,049	3.8
Median monthly owner costs for housing units with a mortgage	1,315	1,772	1,794	3.0
Median value of owner-occupied housing units	144,200	241,400	238,300	5.4

Table AK-4. Migration, Origin, and Language

(Number, percent.)

Characteristic	State			U.S.		
	2010	2011	Percent change	2010	2011	Percent change
Residence 1 Year Ago						
Population 1 year and over	702,974	711,962	1.3	305,628,607	307,900,319	0.7
Same house	80.4	80.3	-0.1	84.6	84.8	0.2
Different house in the U.S.	18.8	19.0	1.1	14.8	14.6	-1.4
Same county	10.9	11.4	4.6	9.4	9.2	-2.1
Different county	8.0	7.7	-3.8	5.4	5.4	-
Same state	2.8	2.7	-3.6	3.2	3.1	-3.1
Different state	5.2	4.9	-5.8	2.2	2.3	4.5
Abroad	0.8	0.7	-12.5	0.6	0.6	-
Place of Birth						
Native born	664,666	671,115	1.0	269,393,835	271,214,059	0.7
Male	52.3	52.1	-0.4	49.2	49.2	-
Female	47.7	47.9	0.4	50.8	50.8	-
Foreign born	49,319	51,603	4.6	39,955,854	40,377,860	1.1
Male	50.4	45.5	-9.7	49.1	48.9	-0.4
Female	49.6	54.5	9.9	50.9	51.1	0.4
Foreign born; naturalized U.S. citizen	24,102	26,602	10.4	17,476,082	18,140,192	3.8
Male	48.0	42.1	-12.3	45.8	45.8	-
Female	52.0	57.9	11.3	54.2	54.2	-
Foreign born; not a U.S. citizen	25,217	25,001	-0.9	22,479,772	22,237,668	-1.1
Male	52.6	49.2	-6.5	51.6	51.5	-0.2
Female	47.4	50.8	7.2	48.4	48.5	0.2
Entered 2000 or later	35.1	38.3	9.1	34.7	35.7	2.9
Entered 1990 to 1999	29.7	25.9	-12.8	27.2	26.7	-1.8
Entered before 1990	35.2	35.9	2.0	38.1	37.6	-1.3
World Region of Birth, Foreign						
Foreign-born population, excluding population born at sea	49,307	51,603	4.7	39,955,673	40,377,757	1.1
Europe	17.0	21.1	24.1	12.1	12.1	-
Asia	52.3	52.0	-0.6	28.2	28.6	1.4
Africa	5.0	3.2	-36.0	4	4.1	2.5
Oceania	1.8	2.8	55.6	0.5	0.5	-
Latin America	19.2	16.1	-16.1	53.1	52.6	-0.9
North America	4.6	4.8	4.3	2	2.0	-
Language Spoken at Home and Ability to Speak English						
Population 5 years and over	660,403	668,687	1.3	289,215,746	291,524,091	0.8
English only	83.5	83.4	-0.1	79.4	79.2	-0.3
Language other than English	16.5	16.6	0.6	20.6	20.8	1.0
Speaks English less than "very well"	5.7	5.1	-10.5	8.7	8.7	-

- = Zero or rounds to zero.

Table AK-5. Median Income and Poverty Status, 2011

(Number, percent, except as noted.)

Characteristic	State		U.S.	
	Number	Percent	Number	Percent
Median Income				
Households (dollars)	67,825	X	50,502	X
Families (dollars)	75,786	X	61,455	X
Below Poverty Level (All People)	73,905	10.5	48,452,035	15.9
Sex				
Male	33,986	9.4	21,825,281	14.7
Female	39,919	11.5	26,626,754	17.2
Age				
Under 18 years	26,941	14.5	16,386,500	22.5
Related children under 18 years	26,387	14.3	16,087,074	22.2
18 to 64 years	43,402	9.3	28,335,079	14.8
65 years and over	3,562	6.3	3,730,456	9.3

X = Not applicable.

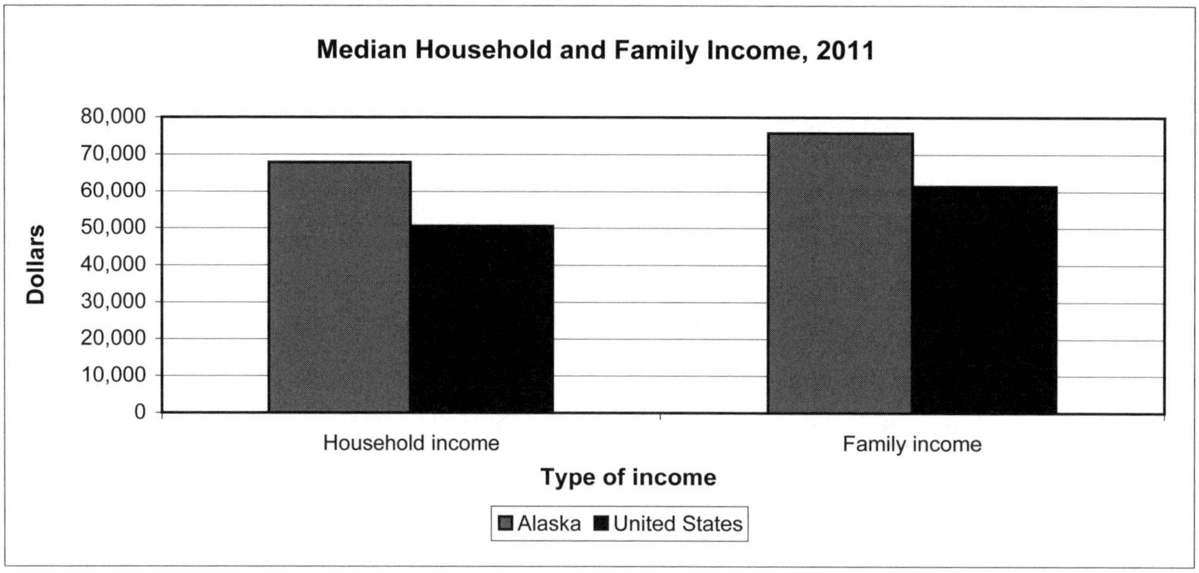

Table AK-6. Health Insurance Coverage Status for the Civilian Noninstitutionalized Population and Children Under 18 Years of Age

(Numbers in thousands, percent.)

Item	2004	2005	2006	2007	2008	2009	2010	2011
Civilian Noninstitutionalized Population	649	659	659	675	659	678	689	699
Covered by Private or Public Insurance								
Number	542	545	550	552	635	535	552	559
Percent	83.5	82.8	83.5	81.8	96.4	78.9	80.1	79.9
Not Covered								
Number	107	113	109	123	24	143	137	141
Percent	16.5	17.2	16.5	18.2	3.6	21.1	19.9	20.1
Percent in the U.S. not covered	14.9	15.3	15.8	15.3	15.1	15.1	15.5	15.1
Children Under 18 Years of Age	185	187	181	185	180	183	188	188
Covered by Private or Public Insurance								
Number	167	171	163	164	156	158	165	166
Percent	90.3	91.6	89.7	88.6	86.7	86.4	87.8	88.2
Not Covered								
Number	18	16	19	21	24	25	23	22
Percent	9.7	8.4	10.3	11.4	13.3	13.6	12.2	11.8
Percent in the U.S. not covered	10.5	10.9	11.7	11.0	9.7	8.6	8.0	7.5

Table AK-7. Employment Status by Demographic Group, Preliminary 2012

(Numbers in thousands, percent.)

Characteristic	Civilian noninstitutional population	Civilian labor force		Employed		Unemployed	
		Number	Percent of population	Number	Percent of population	Number	Percent of population
Total	536	365	68.2	338	63.1	27	7.4
Sex							
Male	272	197	72.6	180	66.3	17	8.6
Female	264	168	63.6	158	59.8	10	6.1
Race, Sex, and Hispanic Origin							
White	397	270	68.0	253	63.8	16	6.1
Male	206	149	72.6	139	67.4	11	7.2
Female	191	120	63.0	115	59.9	6	4.8
Black or African American	18	13	70.3	12	63.3	1	10.2
Male	NA	NA	NA	NA	NA	NA	NA
Female	NA	NA	NA	NA	NA	NA	NA
Hispanic	27	20	72.3	19	68.7	1	5.0
Male	NA	NA	NA	NA	NA	NA	NA
Female	NA	NA	NA	NA	NA	NA	NA
Age							
16 to 19 years	43	16	37.8	13	29.9	3	20.6
20 to 24 years	48	36	74.7	32	65.5	4	12.3
25 to 34 years	100	82	81.8	76	75.9	6	7.2
35 to 44 years	87	71	82.1	67	77.1	4	6.0
45 to 54 years	96	81	83.7	75	77.9	6	7.0
55 to 64 years	96	64	67.0	61	63.9	3	4.7
65 years and over	64	14	22.2	14	21.4	1	3.7

NOTE: Data in Table 7 are from the Current Population Survey (CPS) and do not match the estimates in Table 8. See notes and definitions for further information.
NA = Not available.

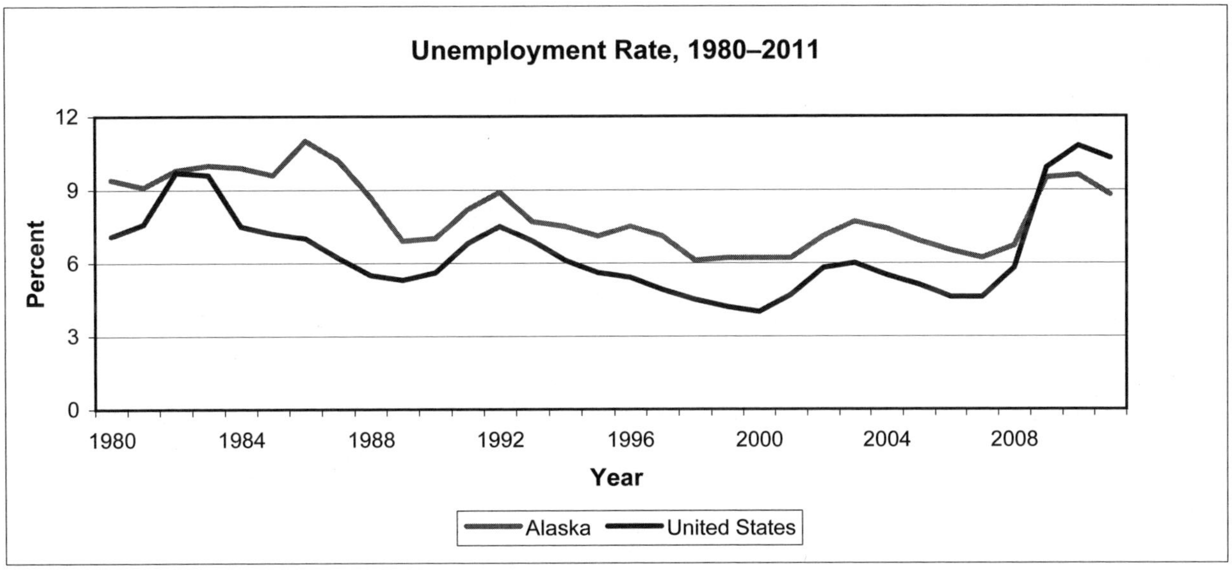

Table AK-8. Employment Status of the Civilian Noninstitutional Population Age 16 Years and Over

(Number, percent.)

Year	Civilian labor force	Civilian participation rate	Employed	Unemployed	Unemployment rate
2005	344,379	71.6	320,644	23,735	6.9
2006	349,733	71.3	326,852	22,881	6.5
2007	351,701	20.8	330,065	21,636	6.2
2008	357,136	71.2	333,376	23,760	6.7
2009	368,338	61.3	33,464	34,874	9.5
2010	373,703	68.3	337,683	36,020	9.6
2011	377,710	68.1	344,343	33,367	8.8

Table AK-9. Employment and Average Wages by Industry

(Estimates before 2007 are based on the 2002 *North American Industry Classification System* [NAICS]. Estimates from 2007 onward are based on the 2007 NAICS.)

Industry	2005	2006	2007	2008	2009	2010	2011
	Number of jobs						
Wage and Salary Employment by Industry	335,796	343,297	347,537	351,532	351,192	353,467	359,669
Farm Wage and Salary Employment	206	208	195	179	175	187	210
Nonfarm Wage and Salary Employment	335,590	343,089	347,342	351,353	351,017	353,280	359,459
Private wage and salary employment	234,263	238,777	242,285	245,649	243,126	245,102	250,423
Forestry, fishing, and related activities	741	615	529	485	508	677	941
Mining	10,408	12,192	13,716	15,206	14,877	15,040	15,591
Utilities	1,844	1,840	1,843	1,895	1,982	2,142	2,107
Construction	19,209	18,738	18,196	17,945	17,050	16,812	16,673
Manufacturing	12,566	13,274	13,206	13,015	12,879	12,771	13,708
Durable goods manufacturing	1,964	1,964	2,119	2,186	2,042	1,891	1,865
Nondurable goods manufacturing	10,602	11,310	11,087	10,829	10,837	10,880	11,843
Wholesale trade	6,469	6,624	6,663	6,596	6,376	6,333	6,360
Retail trade	36,260	36,286	36,566	36,724	36,150	36,033	36,275
Transportation and warehousing	19,435	19,880	20,018	20,264	19,575	19,141	19,416
Information	6,921	6,967	6,934	7,000	6,607	6,458	6,316
Finance and insurance	8,897	9,005	9,112	9,145	8,955	9,085	9,047
Real estate and rental and leasing	5,146	5,113	4,988	4,801	4,899	5,073	5,013
Professional, scientific, and technical services	11,822	12,203	12,678	13,379	13,825	14,055	14,641
Management of companies and enterprises	1,136	1,216	1,187	1,206	1,247	1,156	1,240
Administrative and waste services	11,195	11,251	11,596	11,979	11,571	11,474	11,636
Educational services	2,923	3,015	3,054	3,048	3,023	3,128	3,236
Health care and social assistance	35,049	35,957	36,352	37,103	38,701	40,627	42,054
Arts, entertainment, and recreation	4,295	4,300	4,487	4,638	4,573	4,463	4,860
Accommodation and food services	26,973	27,437	27,978	27,979	26,908	27,379	28,039
Other services, except public administration	12,974	12,864	13,182	13,241	13,420	13,255	13,270
Government and government enterprises	101,327	104,312	105,057	105,704	107,891	108,178	109,036
	Dollars						
Average Wages and Salaries by Industry	41,387	43,013	45,208	47,088	48,401	49,543	50,806
Average Farm Wages and Salaries	25,451	25,168	26,528	28,430	28,320	28,487	29,324
Average Nonfarm Wages and Salaries	41,397	43,024	45,218	47,098	48,411	49,554	50,819
Average private wages and salaries	39,718	41,394	43,929	46,001	47,125	48,041	49,206
Forestry, fishing, and related activities	44,849	42,649	43,611	45,831	44,037	47,266	51,692
Mining	95,333	99,085	104,512	110,499	114,364	116,055	118,956
Utilities	63,406	63,557	66,598	70,620	74,032	73,526	78,613
Construction	56,347	58,773	63,032	66,902	69,498	71,000	70,793
Manufacturing	36,864	36,478	38,452	38,163	37,869	39,476	39,535
Durable goods manufacturing	42,112	43,998	45,862	47,471	49,774	49,620	49,568
Nondurable goods manufacturing	35,891	35,172	37,035	36,285	35,625	37,713	37,955
Wholesale trade	46,156	47,140	49,307	51,329	52,283	52,303	53,477
Retail trade	26,655	27,276	27,953	28,441	28,536	28,997	29,478
Transportation and warehousing	49,104	49,813	53,810	55,641	58,086	59,113	60,778
Information	49,828	51,045	52,803	55,511	56,738	56,105	59,742
Finance and insurance	50,042	53,111	55,339	56,815	57,805	59,910	61,358
Real estate and rental and leasing	30,889	31,757	33,020	35,354	37,045	38,255	38,912
Professional, scientific, and technical services	52,720	55,013	59,519	63,161	64,443	65,970	68,859
Management of companies and enterprises	66,894	74,617	76,695	77,402	77,772	81,629	79,747
Administrative and waste services	34,045	35,938	38,168	39,836	41,766	42,586	42,389
Educational services	27,647	28,102	28,261	28,340	28,229	28,092	27,795
Health care and social assistance	36,960	38,096	39,920	41,597	43,000	43,588	45,279
Arts, entertainment, and recreation	18,689	19,915	20,914	19,874	19,137	20,478	21,405
Accommodation and food services	20,155	20,760	22,318	22,199	21,907	22,619	23,430
Other services, except public administration	28,334	29,741	30,522	31,682	32,817	34,283	34,569
Government and government enterprises	45,277	46,755	48,192	49,647	51,309	52,980	54,522

Table AK-10. Employment Characteristics by Family Type

(Number, percent.)

Family type and labor force status	2009		2010		2011	
	Total	Families with own children under 18 years	Total	Families with own children under 18 years	Total	Families with own children under 18 years
All families	159,940	79,973	170,859	88,925	173,279	86,512
Family type and labor force status						
Married-couple families	119,143	55,160	127,969	61,175	127,277	56,973
Both husband and wife in labor force	59.4	63.8	58.0	63.5	58.4	64.0
Husband in labor force, wife not in labor force	23.0	30.3	25.2	30.2	21.9	29.4
Wife in labor force, husband not in labor force	7.7	3.6	8.2	5.2	8.7	4.5
Both husband and wife not in labor force	9.9	2.2	8.7	1.0	11.0	2.1
Other families	40,797	24,813	42,890	27,750	46,002	29,539
Female householder, no husband present	66.2	71.3	66.9	69.2	65.8	65.0
In labor force	50.2	58.4	48.6	53.2	50.9	54.0
Not in labor force	16.0	12.9	18.3	16.0	14.9	11.1
Male householder, no wife present	33.8	28.7	33.1	30.8	34.2	35.0
In labor force	27.5	26.0	26.4	27.3	26.5	28.3
Not in labor force	6.3	2.7	6.7	3.5	7.7	6.6

Table AK-11. School Enrollment and Educational Attainment, 2011

(Number, percent.)

Item	State	U.S.
Enrollment		
Total population 3 years and over, enrolled in school	196,240	83,131,910
Enrolled in nursery school or preschool (percent)	4.7	6.0
Enrolled in kindergarten (percent)	5.2	5.1
Enrolled in elementary school, grades 1-8 (percent)	42.3	39.5
Enrolled in high school, grades 9-12 (percent)	21.8	20.7
Enrolled in college or graduate school (percent)	26.0	28.7
Attainment		
Total population 25 years and over	456,862	206,471,670
Less than ninth grade (percent)	3.1	6.0
9th to 12th grade, no diploma (percent)	5.2	8.1
High school graduate, including equivalency (percent)	28.1	28.4
Some college, no degree (percent)	29.9	21.2
Associate's degree (percent)	7.4	7.8
Bachelor's degree (percent)	16.9	17.9
Graduate or professional degree (percent)	9.5	10.6
High school graduate or higher (percent)	91.8	85.9
Bachelor's degree or higher (percent)	26.4	28.5

Table AK-12. Educational Indicators

(Number, percent; data derived from National Center of Education Statistics.)

Item	State	U.S.
Public Schools, 2009–2010 (except where noted)		
Number of school districts	53	13,629
Number of schools	506	99,834
Number of students (in thousands)	132	49,373
Student-teacher ratio	16.3	15.4
Expenditures per student (dollars)	17,951	10,591
Averaged freshman graduation rate, 2008–2009	72.6	75.5[1]
Dropout rate, 2008–2009	7.0	4.1
Students eligible for free or reduced-price lunch (percent)	42.2	48.0
English language learners, 2010–2011 (percent)	11.3	9.8[1]
Students with IEP (percent)	13.6	13.1
Private Schools, 2009–2010 (except where noted)		
Number of schools	123[2]	33,366
Number of students (in thousands)	4	4,700
High school graduates, 2008–2009	189	308,813
Student-teacher ratio	8.4	10.7

[1]U.S. total includes estimates for nonreporting states.
[2]Interpret data with caution. The coefficient of variation for this estimate is larger than 25 percent.

Table AK-13. Reported Voting and Registration of the Voting-Age Population, November 2012

(Numbers in thousands, percent.)

Item	Total population	Total citizen population	Registered			Voted		
			Total registered	Percent registered (total population)	Percent registered (total citizen population)	Total voted	Percent voted (total population)	Percent voted (total citizen population)
U.S. Total	235,248	215,081	153,157	65.1	71.2	132,948	56.5	61.8
State Total	516	495	361	69.9	72.8	289	56.0	58.4
Sex								
Male	261	254	181	69.3	71.3	140	53.6	55.1
Female	255	241	180	70.5	74.4	149	58.6	61.8
Race								
White alone	373	365	283	75.7	77.4	232	62.1	63.4
White, non-Hispanic alone	355	352	273	76.8	77.5	225	63.3	63.9
Black alone	21	20	10	B	B	6	B	B
Asian alone	30	21	13	B	B	10	B	B
Hispanic (of any race)	23	18	10	B	B	7	B	B
Age								
18 to 24 years	63	61	31	B	B	20	B	B
25 to 44 years	195	183	130	66.8	71.0	97	49.6	52.8
45 to 64 years	186	182	144	77.6	79.3	122	65.7	67.1
65 to 74 years	46	45	35	B	77.1	32	B	70.5
75 years and over	26	24	20	B	B	19	B	B

B = Base is less than 75,000 and therefore too small to show the derived measure.

Table AK-14. Crime

(Number, rate per 100,000. Data are derived from the FBI Uniform Crime Reports.)

Item	State			U.S.		
	2010	2011	Percent change	2010	2011	Percent change
TOTAL POPULATION	714,146	722,718	1.2	309,330,219	311,591,917	0.7
VIOLENT CRIME						
Number	4,537	4,383	-3.4	1,251,248	1,203,564	-3.8
Rate	635.3	606.5	-4.5	404.5	386.3	-4.5
Murder and Nonnegligent Manslaughter						
Number	31	29	-6.5	14,722	14,612	-0.7
Rate	4.3	4.0	-7.0	4.8	4.7	-2.1
Forcible Rape						
Number	533	420	-21.2	85,593	83,425	-2.5
Rate	74.6	58.1	-22.1	27.7	26.8	-3.2
Robbery						
Number	594	576	-3.0	369,089	354,396	-4.0
Rate	83.2	79.7	-4.2	119.3	113.7	-4.7
Aggravated Assault						
Number	3,379	3,358	-0.6	781,844	751,131	-3.9
Rate	473.2	464.6	-1.8	252.8	241.1	-4.6
PROPERTY CRIME						
Number	20,259	19,028	-6.1	9,112,625	9,063,173	-0.5
Rate	2,836.8	2,632.8	-7.2	2,945.9	2,908.7	-1.3
Burglary						
Number	3,105	2,826	-9.0	2,168,459	2,188,005	0.9
Rate	434.8	391.0	-10.1	701.0	702.2	0.2
Larceny-Theft						
Number	15,535	14,859	-4.4	6,204,601	6,159,795	-0.7
Rate	2,175.3	2,056.0	-5.5	2,005.8	1,976.9	-1.4
Motor Vehicle Theft						
Number	1,619	1,343	-17.0	739,565	715,373	-3.3
Rate	226.7	185.8	-18.0	239.1	229.6	-4.0

Table AK-15. State Government Finances, 2011

(Dollar amounts in thousands, percent distribution.)

Item	Dollars	Percent distribution
Total Revenue	14,920,900	100.0
General revenue	12,665,675	84.9
Intergovernmental revenue	3,040,677	20.4
Taxes	5,537,679	37.1
General sales	0	0.0
Selective sales	256,014	1.7
License taxes	137,889	0.9
Individual income tax	0	0.0
Corporate income tax	720,733	4.8
Other taxes	4,423,043	29.6
Current charges	586,262	3.9
Miscellaneous general revenue	3,501,057	23.5
Utility revenue	17,613	0.1
Liquor stores revenue	0	0.0
Insurance trust revenue [1]	2,237,612	15.0
Total Expenditure	11,320,127	100.0
Intergovernmental expenditure	1,723,023	15.2
Direct expenditure	9,597,104	84.8
Current operation	6,661,701	58.8
Capital outlay	1,218,201	10.8
Insurance benefits and repayments	1,244,060	11.0
Assistance and subsidies	183,766	1.6
Interest on debt	289,376	2.6
Exhibit: Salaries and wages	1,774,592	15.7
Total Expenditure	11,320,127	100.0
General expenditure	9,956,134	88.0
Intergovernmental expenditure	1,723,023	15.2
Direct expenditure	8,233,111	72.7
General expenditure, by function:		
Education	2,475,486	21.9
Public welfare	1,917,737	16.9
Hospitals	66,227	0.6
Health	362,760	3.2
Highways	1,412,087	12.5
Police protection	118,154	1.0
Correction	283,764	2.5
Natural resources	391,462	3.5
Parks and recreation	21,012	0.2
Governmental administration	585,703	5.2
Interest on general debt	283,836	2.5
Other and unallocable	2,037,906	18.0
Utility expenditure	119,933	1.1
Liquor stores expenditure	0	0.0
Insurance trust expenditure	1,244,060	11.0
Debt at End of Fiscal Year	6,417,682	X
Cash and Security Holdings	69,279,035	X

X = Not applicable.

[1] Within insurance trust revenue, net earnings of state retirement systems is a calculated statistic (the item code in the data file is X08), and thus can be positive or negative. Net earnings is the sum of earnings on investments plus gains on investments minus losses on investments. The change made in 2002 for asset valuation from book to market value in accordance with Statement 34 of the Governmental Accounting Standards Board is reflected in the calculated statistics.

Table AK-16. State Government Tax Collections, 2012

(Dollars in thousands, percent.)

Item	Dollars	Percent distribution
Total Taxes	7,049,398	100.0
Property taxes	215,407	3.1
Sales and gross receipts	248,432	3.5
General sales and gross receipts	0	0.0
Selective sales and gross receipts	248,432	3.5
Alcoholic beverages	40,230	0.6
Amusements	7,712	0.1
Insurance premiums	61,684	0.9
Motor fuels	40,980	0.6
Pari-mutuels	0	0.0
Public utilities	4,114	0.1
Tobacco products	67,382	1.0
Other selective sales	26,330	0.4
Licenses	135,055	1.9
Alcoholic beverages	1,864	0.0
Amusements	1	-
Corporations in general	0	0.0
Hunting and fishing	27,316	0.4
Motor vehicle	58,196	0.8
Motor vehicle operators	0	0.0
Public utilities	604	0.0
Occupation and business, NEC	38,936	0.6
Other licenses	8,138	0.1
Income taxes	663,144	9.4
Individual income	0	0.0
Corporation net income	663,144	9.4
Other taxes	5,787,360	82.1
Death and gift	0	0.0
Documentary and stock transfer	0	0.0
Severance	5,787,360	82.1
Taxes, NEC	0	0.0

- = Rounds to zero.

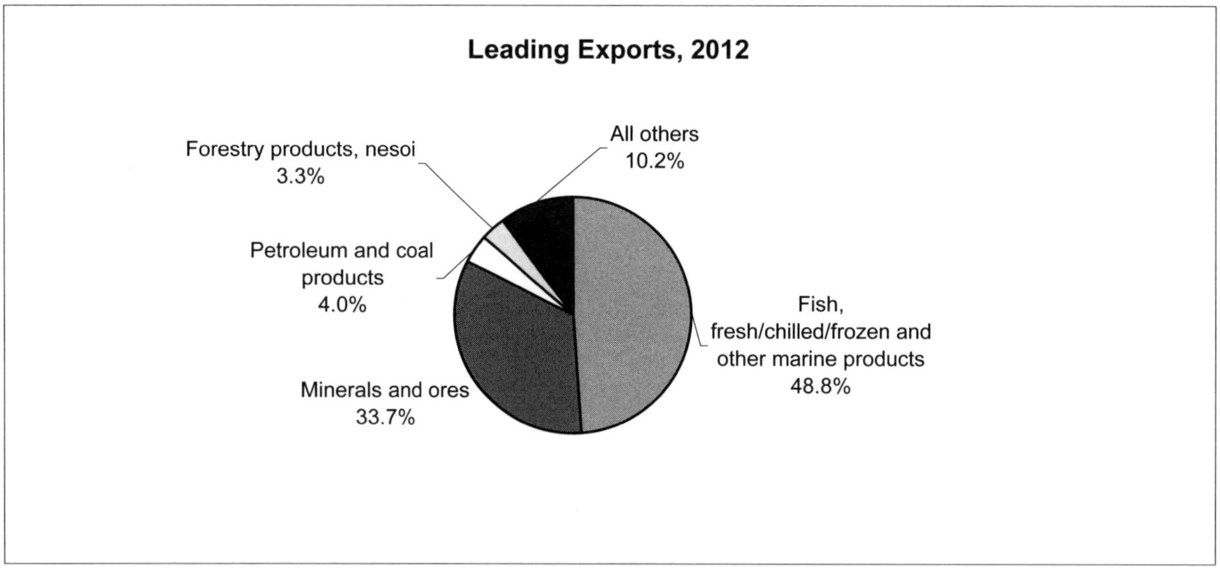

ARIZONA

Facts and Figures

Location: Southwestern United States; bordered on the North by Utah, on the East by New Mexico, on the South by Mexico, and on the West by Nevada and California; Arizona is one of the Four Corner states—at its NE corner it touches Colorado, New Mexico, and Utah

Area: 113,998 sq, mi. (295,254 sq. km.); rank—6th

Population: 6,553,255 (2012 est.); rank—15th

Principal Cities: capital—Phoenix; largest—Phoenix

Statehood: February 14, 1912; 48th state

U.S. Congress: 2 senators, 9 representatives

State Motto: *Ditat Deus* ("God enriches")

State Song: "Arizona"

State Nickname: The Grand Canyon State

Abbreviations: AZ; Ariz.

State Symbols: flower—saguaro cactus blossom; tree—paloverde; bird—cactus wren

At a Glance

- With an increase in population of 28.6 percent, Arizona ranked 5th among the states in growth from 2000 to 2009.
- In 2009, approximately 35,300 marriages and 23,100 divorces took place in Arizona.
- Arizona's median household income in 2011 was $46,709, and 15.9 percent of its population lived below the poverty level.
- In 2011, 17.2 percent of Arizonans did not have health insurance, compared to 15.1 percent of the total U.S. population.
- Approximately 55.9 percent of Arizonans voted in the 2012 election, compared with 61.8 of the total U.S. population.
- In 2007, Arizona exported $506 million worth of agricultural products, less than 1 percent of the U.S. total.

Table AZ-1. Population by Age, Sex, Race, and Hispanic Origin

(Number, percent, except where noted.)

Sex, age, race, and Hispanic origin	2000	2010	2012[1]	Average annual percent change, 2010–2012
Total Population	5,130,632	6,392,017	6,553,255	0.8
Percent of total U.S. population	1.8	2.1	2.1	X
Sex				
Male	2,561,057	3,175,823	3,258,483	0.8
Female	2,569,575	3,216,814	3,294,772	0.8
Age				
Under 5 years	382,386	455,715	439,633	-1.2
5 to 19 years	1,135,802	1,363,926	1,359,779	-0.1
20 to 64 years	2,944,605	3,690,545	3,782,310	0.8
65 years and over	667,839	881,831	971,533	3.1
Median age (years)	34.2	35.9	36.5	0.5
Race and Hispanic Origin				
One race				
White	3,873,611	5,418,483	5,522,144	0.6
Black	158,873	280,905	297,985	1.9
American Indian and Alaska Native	255,879	335,278	345,622	1.0
Asian	92,236	188,456	204,840	2.7
Native Hawaiian or Other Pacific Islander	6,733	16,112	16,922	1.6
Two or more races	146,526	152,783	165,742	2.6
Hispanic (of any race)	1,295,617	1,943,466	2,028,540	1.4

X = Not applicable.
[1]Population figures for 2012 are July 1 estimates. The 2010 estimates are taken from the 2010 Census.

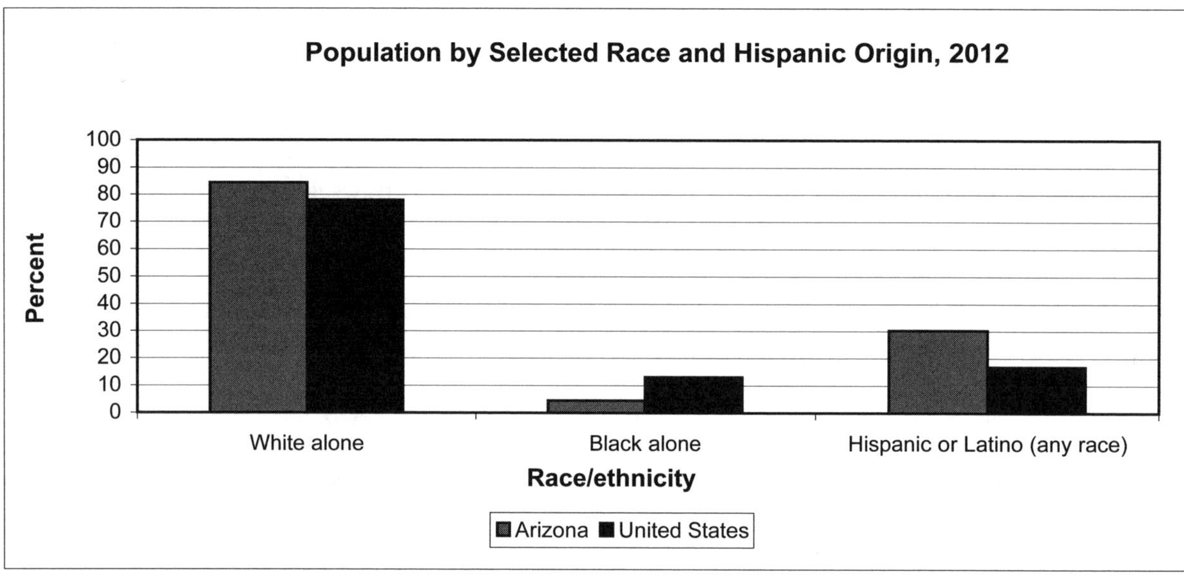

Table AZ-2. Marital Status

(Number, percent distribution.)

Sex, age, race, and Hispanic origin	2000	2010	2011
Males, 15 Years and Over	1,966,032	2,492,590	2,534,739
Never married	29.6	35.3	35.8
Now married, except separated	56.4	50.1	49.0
Separated	1.6	1.4	1.7
Widowed	2.6	2.5	2.7
Divorced	9.8	10.7	10.8
Females, 15 Years and Over	2,013,304	2,559,409	2,594,670
Never married	22.5	28.0	28.5
Now married, except separated	53.6	48.0	46.4
Separated	2.1	2.2	2.2
Widowed	9.4	8.3	8.4
Divorced	12.3	13.5	14.4

Table AZ-3. Households and Housing Characteristics

(Number, percent, dollars.)

Item	2000	2010	2011	Average annual percent change, 2000–2011
Total Households	1,901,327	2,334,050	2,356,055	2.0
Family households	1,287,367	1,548,428	1,543,923	1.7
Married-couple family	986,303	1,134,229	1,110,350	1.0
Other family	310,064	414,199	433,573	3.3
Male householder, no wife present	90,283	123,772	127,496	3.4
Female householder, no husband present	210,781	290,427	306,077	3.8
Nonfamily households	613,960	785,622	812,132	2.7
Householder living alone	472,006	621,291	650,612	3.2
Householder not living alone	141,954	164,331	161,520	1.1
Housing Characteristics				
Total housing units	2,189,189	2,846,738	2,864,360	2.6
Occupied housing units	1,901,327	2,334,050	2,356,055	2.0
Owner occupied	1,293,556	1,522,938	1,501,528	1.3
Renter occupied	607,771	811,112	854,527	3.4
Average size	2.64	2.69	2.69	0.2
Financial Characteristics				
Median gross rent of renter-occupied housing	619	844	850	3.1
Median monthly owner costs for housing units with a mortgage	1,039	1,442	1,365	2.6
Median value of owner-occupied housing units	121,300	168,800	153,800	2.2

Table AZ-4. Migration, Origin, and Language

(Number, percent.)

Characteristic	State			U.S.		
	2010	2011	Percent change	2010	2011	Percent change
Residence 1 Year Ago						
Population 1 year and over	6,332,786	6,402,301	1.1	305,628,607	307,900,319	0.7
Same house	80.0	79.8	-0.3	84.6	84.8	0.2
Different house in the U.S.	19.3	19.5	1.0	14.8	14.6	-1.4
Same county	13.9	14.1	1.4	9.4	9.2	-2.1
Different county	5.5	5.5	-	5.4	5.4	-
Same state	1.9	2.0	5.3	3.2	3.1	-3.1
Different state	3.5	3.5	-	2.2	2.3	4.5
Abroad	0.6	0.7	16.7	0.6	0.6	-
Place of Birth						
Native born	5,557,074	5,610,838	1.0	269,393,835	271,214,059	0.7
Male	50.0	49.9	-0.2	49.2	49.2	-
Female	50.0	50.1	0.2	50.8	50.8	-
Foreign born	856,663	871,667	1.8	39,955,854	40,377,860	1.1
Male	48.3	48.9	1.2	49.1	48.9	-0.4
Female	51.7	51.1	-1.2	50.9	51.1	0.4
Foreign born; naturalized U.S. citizen	310,835	327,453	5.3	17,476,082	18,140,192	3.8
Male	45.4	45.9	1.1	45.8	45.8	-
Female	54.6	54.1	-0.9	54.2	54.2	-
Foreign born; not a U.S. citizen	545,828	544,214	-0.3	22,479,772	22,237,668	-1.1
Male	50.0	50.7	1.4	51.6	51.5	-0.2
Female	50.0	49.3	-1.4	48.4	48.5	0.2
Entered 2000 or later	31.7	33.0	4.1	34.7	35.7	2.9
Entered 1990 to 1999	28.7	27.3	-4.9	27.2	26.7	-1.8
Entered before 1990	39.6	39.6	-	38.1	37.6	-1.3
World Region of Birth, Foreign						
Foreign-born population, excluding population born at sea	856,663	871,667	1.8	39,955,673	40,377,757	1.1
Europe	9.2	10.1	9.8	12.1	12.1	-
Asia	17.0	17.8	4.7	28.2	28.6	1.4
Africa	2.8	2.4	-14.3	4	4.1	2.5
Oceania	0.3	0.4	33.3	0.5	0.5	-
Latin America	66.8	65.3	-2.2	53.1	52.6	-0.9
North America	3.8	4.0	5.3	2	2.0	-
Language Spoken at Home and Ability to Speak English						
Population 5 years and over	5,957,961	6,034,541	1.3	289,215,746	291,524,091	0.8
English only	73.3	73.0	-0.4	79.4	79.2	-0.3
Language other than English	26.7	27.0	1.1	20.6	20.8	1.0
Speaks English less than "very well"	9.9	9.3	-6.1	8.7	8.7	-

- = Zero or rounds to zero.

Table AZ-5. Median Income and Poverty Status, 2011

(Number, percent, except as noted.)

Characteristic	State Number	State Percent	U.S. Number	U.S. Percent
Median Income				
Households (dollars)	46,709	X	50,502	X
Families (dollars)	55,328	X	61,455	X
Below Poverty Level (All People)	1,203,501	19.0	48,452,035	15.9
Sex				
Male	571,297	18.3	21,825,281	14.7
Female	632,204	19.7	26,626,754	17.2
Age				
Under 18 years	434,950	27.2	16,386,500	22.5
Related children under 18 years	428,162	26.9	16,087,074	22.2
18 to 64 years	690,692	18.0	28,335,079	14.8
65 years and over	77,859	8.5	3,730,456	9.3

X = Not applicable.

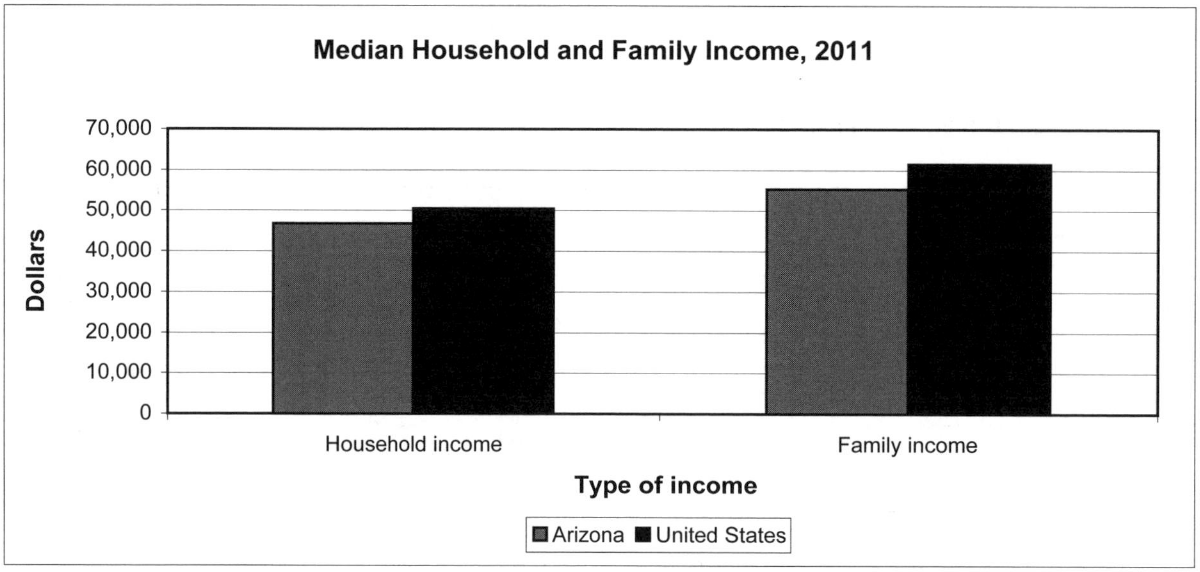

Table AZ-6. Health Insurance Coverage Status for the Civilian Noninstitutionalized Population and Children Under 18 Years of Age

(Numbers in thousands, percent.)

Item	2004	2005	2006	2007	2008	2009	2010	2011
Civilian Noninstitutionalized Population	5,768	6,047	6,269	6,368	6,403	6,502	6,310	6,378
Covered by Private or Public Insurance								
Number	4,807	4,864	4,958	5,204	5,207	5,375	5,245	5,283
Percent	83.3	80.4	79.1	81.7	81.3	82.7	83.1	82.8
Not Covered								
Number	961	1,183	1,311	1,164	1,196	1,127	1,065	1,095
Percent	16.7	19.6	20.9	18.3	18.7	17.3	16.9	17.2
Percent in the U.S. not covered	14.9	15.3	15.8	15.3	15.1	15.1	15.5	15.1
Children Under 18 Years of Age	1,567	1,627	1,662	1,697	1,706	1,730	1,630	1,622
Covered by Private or Public Insurance								
Number	1,350	1,359	1,379	1,463	1,430	1,522	1,422	1,622
Percent	86.2	83.6	83.0	86.2	83.8	88.0	87.2	87.1
Not Covered								
Number	217	267	283	234	276	208	208	208
Percent	13.8	16.4	17.0	13.8	16.2	12.0	12.8	12.9
Percent in the U.S. not covered	10.5	10.9	11.7	11.0	9.7	8.6	8.0	7.5

Table AZ-7. Employment Status by Demographic Group, Preliminary 2012

(Numbers in thousands, percent.)

Characteristic	Civilian noninstitutional population	Civilian labor force		Employed		Unemployed	
		Number	Percent of population	Number	Percent of population	Number	Percent of population
Total	4,987	3,011	60.4	2,764	55.4	248	8.2
Sex							
Male	2,428	1,629	67.1	1,495	61.6	134	8.2
Female	2,558	1,382	54.0	1,268	49.6	114	8.2
Race, Sex, and Hispanic Origin							
White	4,323	2,612	60.4	2,401	55.5	211	8.1
Male	2,118	1,419	67.0	1,301	61.5	117	8.3
Female	2,206	1,193	54.1	1,100	49.9	94	7.9
Black or African American	229	139	60.6	126	55.1	13	9.2
Male	113	71	63.1	65	57.8	6	8.3
Female	117	68	58.3	61	52.3	7	10.2
Hispanic	1,451	895	61.7	800	55.1	95	10.6
Male	724	515	71.1	464	64.1	51	9.9
Female	727	380	52.2	336	46.2	44	11.5
Age							
16 to 19 years	341	121	35.6	86	25.3	35	28.9
20 to 24 years	440	321	72.9	278	63.2	43	13.3
25 to 34 years	830	637	76.8	586	70.6	51	8.0
35 to 44 years	843	668	79.3	629	74.6	39	5.9
45 to 54 years	823	638	77.6	595	72.3	43	6.8
55 to 64 years	817	493	60.3	469	57.3	24	4.8
65 years and over	892	133	14.9	121	13.5	12	9.2

NOTE: Data in Table 7 are from the Current Population Survey (CPS) and do not match the estimates in Table 8. See notes and definitions for further information.

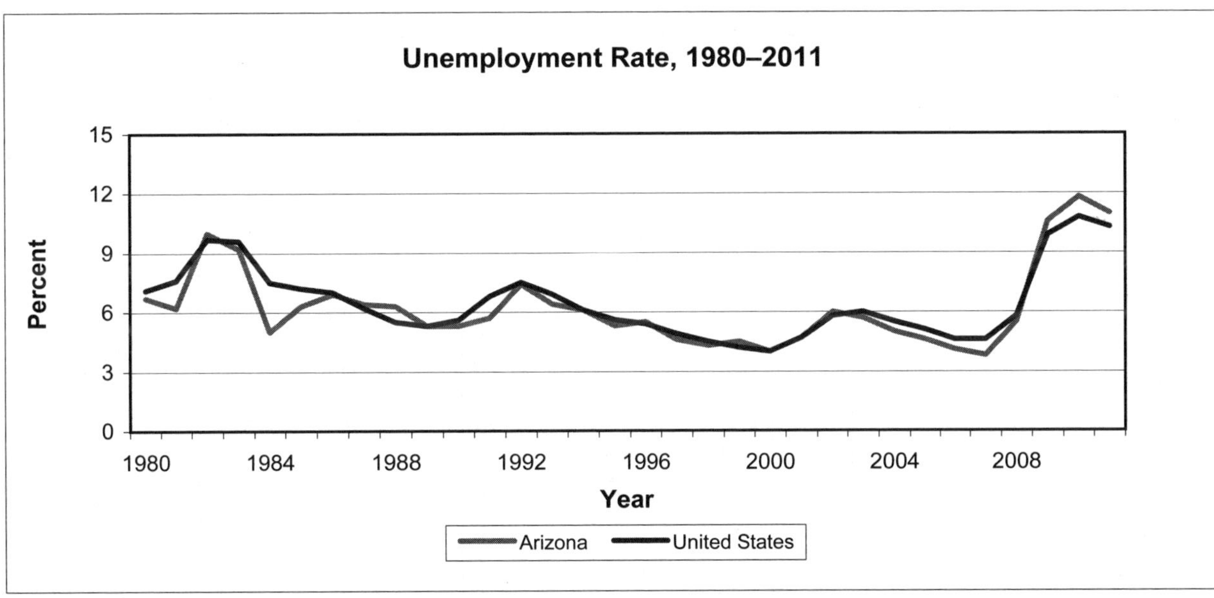

Table AZ-8. Employment Status of the Civilian Noninstitutional Population Age 16 Years and Over

(Number, percent.)

Year	Civilian labor force	Civilian participation rate	Employed	Unemployed	Unemployment rate
2005	2,866,720	64.3	2,733,551	133,169	4.6
2006	2,971,211	64.2	2,849,057	122,154	4.1
2007	3,036,011	63.8	2,920,242	115,769	3.8
2008	3,132,667	64.2	2,960,199	172,468	5.5
2009	3,128,500	62.0	2,795,318	333,182	10.6
2010	3,011,568	60.7	2,655,557	356,011	11.8
2011	3,025,208	60.0	2,687,991	337,217	11.0

Table AZ-9. Employment and Average Wages by Industry

(Estimates before 2007 are based on the 2002 *North American Industry Classification System* [NAICS]. Estimates from 2007 onward are based on the 2007 NAICS.)

Industry	2005	2006	2007	2008	2009	2010	2011
	Number of jobs						
Wage and Salary Employment by Industry	2,613,915	2,743,333	2,779,312	2,713,899	2,524,521	2,483,674	2,510,358
Farm Wage and Salary Employment	13,815	13,423	13,272	11,632	12,134	11,583	11,342
Nonfarm Wage and Salary Employment	2,600,100	2,729,910	2,766,040	2,702,267	2,512,387	2,472,091	2,499,016
Private wage and salary employment	2,167,936	2,292,524	2,316,269	2,243,239	2,059,730	2,024,116	2,058,758
Forestry, fishing, and related activities	14,142	14,465	14,204	13,180	11,880	12,431	12,954
Mining	8,502	9,829	11,483	12,976	10,559	10,285	10,925
Utilities	11,818	12,402	12,745	12,738	12,435	12,079	11,975
Construction	228,399	249,620	233,245	193,649	134,757	116,705	117,015
Manufacturing	180,400	185,215	180,972	172,214	151,959	146,695	148,251
Durable goods manufacturing	145,421	149,583	146,899	139,141	121,379	116,492	117,601
Nondurable goods manufacturing	34,979	35,632	34,073	33,073	30,580	30,203	30,650
Wholesale trade	101,236	106,879	111,475	110,611	102,513	98,769	98,543
Retail trade	312,604	328,153	337,173	326,188	302,597	297,827	299,718
Transportation and warehousing	70,960	75,405	75,978	74,922	70,120	67,604	70,860
Information	45,034	44,549	42,056	40,878	38,185	36,733	36,683
Finance and insurance	127,854	134,064	134,236	127,573	123,284	121,948	125,932
Real estate and rental and leasing	50,734	53,476	54,989	53,938	49,042	47,092	46,332
Professional, scientific, and technical services	120,381	132,002	135,762	135,400	125,170	123,415	125,862
Management of companies and enterprises	23,343	25,299	26,938	27,646	26,577	25,422	25,216
Administrative and waste services	229,387	243,836	244,960	229,569	199,382	197,672	200,946
Educational services	38,202	40,955	41,829	45,006	47,281	51,291	53,767
Health care and social assistance	238,845	253,157	265,727	279,644	285,598	296,275	304,151
Arts, entertainment, and recreation	32,153	33,983	36,021	36,226	33,492	33,467	33,781
Accommodation and food services	226,635	237,180	240,783	236,949	225,280	223,334	228,368
Other services, except public administration	107,307	112,055	115,693	113,932	109,619	105,072	107,479
Government and government enterprises	432,164	437,386	449,771	459,028	452,657	447,975	440,258
	Dollars						
Average Wages and Salaries by Industry	38,743	40,699	42,367	43,309	43,580	44,145	45,396
Average Farm Wages and Salaries	28,813	29,014	32,451	35,735	38,035	34,616	36,679
Average Nonfarm Wages and Salaries	38,796	40,757	42,415	43,341	43,607	44,190	45,435
Average private wages and salaries	38,543	40,471	42,144	42,994	43,149	43,948	45,258
Forestry, fishing, and related activities	17,911	19,109	20,385	20,414	22,363	22,730	23,549
Mining	57,589	60,019	63,423	70,644	68,479	71,447	78,827
Utilities	73,946	76,831	83,264	87,512	91,045	92,192	95,114
Construction	38,609	41,448	43,123	45,101	44,867	45,018	45,931
Manufacturing	54,809	57,893	59,605	62,020	63,447	66,902	70,052
Durable goods manufacturing	58,967	62,408	64,079	67,051	69,137	73,482	77,173
Nondurable goods manufacturing	37,520	38,939	40,317	40,856	40,862	41,523	42,728
Wholesale trade	56,674	59,007	62,610	62,201	62,405	64,391	66,939
Retail trade	28,227	29,249	29,382	28,964	28,679	29,366	30,909
Transportation and warehousing	43,146	44,497	46,682	46,428	46,747	48,814	49,744
Information	49,207	52,497	54,718	55,738	57,476	57,915	59,814
Finance and insurance	58,740	60,716	61,382	60,329	58,925	61,003	63,500
Real estate and rental and leasing	40,642	43,906	43,007	43,606	42,085	42,624	44,623
Professional, scientific, and technical services	57,125	59,773	63,522	65,255	66,152	67,406	69,857
Management of companies and enterprises	65,410	67,918	77,033	76,555	75,094	74,940	77,325
Administrative and waste services	28,482	29,793	31,383	32,804	33,206	33,325	33,607
Educational services	33,313	33,503	35,475	37,183	39,065	39,625	40,119
Health care and social assistance	41,502	43,742	45,763	47,546	48,233	48,018	48,532
Arts, entertainment, and recreation	31,753	35,319	35,182	34,719	36,293	37,062	37,101
Accommodation and food services	17,777	18,338	20,334	19,778	19,475	20,005	20,467
Other services, except public administration	24,733	26,224	27,307	28,105	27,993	28,541	29,086
Government and government enterprises	40,061	42,254	43,810	45,037	45,691	45,281	46,265

Table AZ-10. Employment Characteristics by Family Type

(Number, percent.)

Family type and labor force status	2009		2010		2011	
	Total	Families with own children under 18 years	Total	Families with own children under 18 years	Total	Families with own children under 18 years
All families	1,514,235	686,216	1,548,428	680,624	1,543,923	674,157
Family type and labor force status						
Married-couple families	1,125,825	459,511	1,134,229	441,343	1,110,350	428,287
Both husband and wife in labor force	47.8	60.9	46.8	61.2	46.9	59.8
Husband in labor force, wife not in labor force	24.1	33.9	23.5	32.6	23.0	34.1
Wife in labor force, husband not in labor force	6.7	3.3	7.8	4.1	7.5	4.1
Both husband and wife not in labor force	21.3	1.9	21.9	2.2	22.6	2.1
Other families	388,410	226,705	414,199	239,281	433,573	245,870
Female householder, no husband present	69.9	71.8	70.1	72.7	70.6	71.7
In labor force	51.0	58.6	50.0	59.0	51.0	58.9
Not in labor force	18.9	13.2	20.1	13.6	19.6	12.9
Male householder, no wife present	30.1	28.2	29.9	27.3	29.4	28.3
In labor force	24.7	25.3	24.4	25.1	23.2	25.1
Not in labor force	5.4	2.9	5.5	2.2	6.2	3.2

Table AZ-11. School Enrollment and Educational Attainment, 2011

(Number, percent.)

Item	State	U.S.
Enrollment		
Total population 3 years and over, enrolled in school	1,751,916	83,131,910
Enrolled in nursery school or preschool (percent)	4.7	6.0
Enrolled in kindergarten (percent)	4.8	5.1
Enrolled in elementary school, grades 1-8 (percent)	41.6	39.5
Enrolled in high school, grades 9-12 (percent)	20.7	20.7
Enrolled in college or graduate school (percent)	28.2	28.7
Attainment		
Total population 25 years and over	4,211,223	206,471,670
Less than ninth grade (percent)	6.2	6.0
9th to 12th grade, no diploma (percent)	8.1	8.1
High school graduate, including equivalency (percent)	24.6	28.4
Some college, no degree (percent)	26.2	21.2
Associate's degree (percent)	8.3	7.8
Bachelor's degree (percent)	17.1	17.9
Graduate or professional degree (percent)	9.5	10.6
High school graduate or higher (percent)	85.7	85.9
Bachelor's degree or higher (percent)	26.6	28.5

Table AZ-12. Educational Indicators

(Number, percent; data derived from National Center of Education Statistics.)

Item	State	U.S.
Public Schools, 2009–2010 (except where noted)		
Number of school districts	224	13,629
Number of schools	2,248	99,834
Number of students (in thousands)	1,078	49,373
Student-teacher ratio	20.7	15.4
Expenditures per student (dollars)	9,391	10,591
Averaged freshman graduation rate, 2008–2009	72.5	75.5[1]
Dropout rate, 2008–2009	8.3	4.1
Students eligible for free or reduced-price lunch (percent)	45.3	48.0
English language learners, 2010–2011 (percent)	7.5	9.8[1]
Students with IEP (percent)	11.7	13.1
Private Schools, 2009–2010 (except where noted)		
Number of schools	360	33,366
Number of students (in thousands)	45	4,700
High school graduates, 2008–2009	2,755	308,813
Student-teacher ratio	11.4	10.7

[1] U.S. total includes estimates for nonreporting states.

Table AZ-13. Reported Voting and Registration of the Voting-Age Population, November 2012

(Numbers in thousands, percent.)

Item	Total population	Total citizen population	Registered			Voted		
			Total registered	Percent registered (total population)	Percent registered (total citizen population)	Total voted	Percent voted (total population)	Percent voted (total citizen population)
U.S. Total	235,248	215,081	153,157	65.1	71.2	132,948	56.5	61.8
State Total	4,863	4,314	2,812	57.8	65.2	2,412	49.6	55.9
Sex								
Male	2,361	2,110	1,398	59.2	66.2	1,193	50.5	56.6
Female	2,501	2,204	1,414	56.5	64.2	1,219	48.7	55.3
Race								
White alone	4,130	3,660	2,445	59.2	66.8	2,123	51.4	58.0
White, non-Hispanic alone	2,854	2,784	1,963	68.8	70.5	1,737	60.8	62.4
Black alone	211	207	122	57.5	58.6	95	45.1	46.0
Asian alone	227	160	51	22.5	32.0	43	19.0	27.1
Hispanic (of any race)	1,396	989	516	37.0	52.2	400	28.7	40.4
Age								
18 to 24 years	586	545	301	51.4	55.3	234	40.0	43.0
25 to 44 years	1,729	1,422	837	48.4	58.8	671	38.8	47.2
45 to 64 years	1,656	1,502	1,015	61.3	67.6	901	54.4	60.0
65 to 74 years	504	474	368	73.0	77.6	351	69.5	73.9
75 years and over	388	371	291	75.1	78.5	255	65.8	68.8

Table AZ-14. Crime

(Number, rate per 100,000. Data are derived from the FBI Uniform Crime Reports.)

Item	State			U.S.		
	2010	2011	Percent change	2010	2011	Percent change
TOTAL POPULATION	6,413,158	6,482,505	1.1	309,330,219	311,591,917	0.7
VIOLENT CRIME						
Number	26,528	26,311	-0.8	1,251,248	1,203,564	-3.8
Rate	413.6	405.9	-1.9	404.5	386.3	-4.5
Murder and Nonnegligent Manslaughter						
Number	408	405	-0.7	14,722	14,612	-0.7
Rate	6.4	6.2	-3.1	4.8	4.7	-2.1
Forcible Rape						
Number	2,191	2,264	3.3	85,593	83,425	-2.5
Rate	34.2	34.9	2.0	27.7	26.8	-3.2
Robbery						
Number	6,953	7,127	2.5	369,089	354,396	-4.0
Rate	108.4	109.9	1.4	119.3	113.7	-4.7
Aggravated Assault						
Number	16,976	16,515	-2.7	781,844	751,131	-3.9
Rate	264.7	254.8	-3.7	252.8	241.1	-4.6
PROPERTY CRIME						
Number	226,802	230,422	1.6	9,112,625	9,063,173	-0.5
Rate	3,536.5	3,554.5	0.5	2,945.9	2,908.7	-1.3
Burglary						
Number	50,932	54,929	7.8	2,168,459	2,188,005	0.9
Rate	794.2	847.3	6.7	701.0	702.2	0.2
Larceny-Theft						
Number	154,137	155,664	1.0	6,204,601	6,159,795	-0.7
Rate	2,403.4	2,401.3	-0.1	2,005.8	1,976.9	-1.4
Motor Vehicle Theft						
Number	21,733	19,829	-8.8	739,565	715,373	-3.3
Rate	338.9	305.9	-9.7	239.1	229.6	-4.0

Table AZ-15. State Government Finances, 2011

(Dollar amounts in thousands, percent distribution.)

Item	Dollars	Percent distribution
Total Revenue	36,611,494	100.0
General revenue	27,048,737	73.9
Intergovernmental revenue	12,360,358	33.8
Taxes	10,848,179	29.6
General sales	4,462,557	12.2
Selective sales	1,743,812	4.8
License taxes	418,938	1.1
Individual income tax	2,863,658	7.8
Corporate income tax	560,236	1.5
Other taxes	798,978	2.2
Current charges	2,277,144	6.2
Miscellaneous general revenue	1,563,056	4.3
Utility revenue	29,511	0.1
Liquor stores revenue	0	0.0
Insurance trust revenue [1]	9,533,246	26.0
Total Expenditure	32,875,412	100.0
Intergovernmental expenditure	8,668,387	26.4
Direct expenditure	24,207,025	73.6
Current operation	16,547,532	50.3
Capital outlay	1,648,490	5.0
Insurance benefits and repayments	4,720,412	14.4
Assistance and subsidies	627,999	1.9
Interest on debt	662,592	2.0
Exhibit: Salaries and wages	3,169,426	9.6
Total Expenditure	32,875,412	100.0
General expenditure	28,123,095	85.5
Intergovernmental expenditure	8,668,387	26.4
Direct expenditure	19,454,708	59.2
General expenditure, by function:		
Education	9,121,942	27.7
Public welfare	9,511,299	28.9
Hospitals	52,314	0.2
Health	1,822,334	5.5
Highways	2,038,165	6.2
Police protection	240,169	0.7
Correction	906,213	2.8
Natural resources	256,522	0.8
Parks and recreation	97,087	0.3
Governmental administration	655,362	2.0
Interest on general debt	660,422	2.0
Other and unallocable	2,761,266	8.4
Utility expenditure	31,905	0.1
Liquor stores expenditure	0	0.0
Insurance trust expenditure	4,720,412	14.4
Debt at End of Fiscal Year	14,163,076	X
Cash and Security Holdings	47,487,739	X

X = Not applicable.

[1] Within insurance trust revenue, net earnings of state retirement systems is a calculated statistic (the item code in the data file is X08), and thus can be positive or negative. Net earnings is the sum of earnings on investments plus gains on investments minus losses on investments. The change made in 2002 for asset valuation from book to market value in accordance with Statement 34 of the Governmental Accounting Standards Board is reflected in the calculated statistics.

Table AZ-16. State Government Tax Collections, 2012

(Dollars in thousands, percent.)

Item	Dollars	Percent distribution
Total Taxes	12,973,265	100.0
Property taxes	754,428	5.8
Sales and gross receipts	8,066,124	62.2
General sales and gross receipts	6,210,756	47.9
Selective sales and gross receipts	1,855,368	14.3
Alcoholic beverages	68,379	0.5
Amusements	521	-
Insurance premiums	426,497	3.3
Motor fuels	896,983	6.9
Pari-mutuels	254	-
Public utilities	21,339	0.2
Tobacco products	319,467	2.5
Other selective sales	121,928	0.9
Licenses	370,222	2.9
Alcoholic beverages	4,918	-
Amusements	0	0.0
Corporations in general	10,518	0.1
Hunting and fishing	29,258	0.2
Motor vehicle	146,214	1.1
Motor vehicle operators	29,898	0.2
Public utilities	16,299	0.1
Occupation and business, NEC	128,759	1.0
Other licenses	4,358	-
Income taxes	3,741,713	28.8
Individual income	3,093,904	23.8
Corporation net income	647,809	5.0
Other taxes	40,778	0.3
Death and gift	200	-
Documentary and stock transfer	0	0.0
Severance	40,578	0.3
Taxes, NEC	0	0.0

- = Rounds to zero.

Leading Exports, 2012

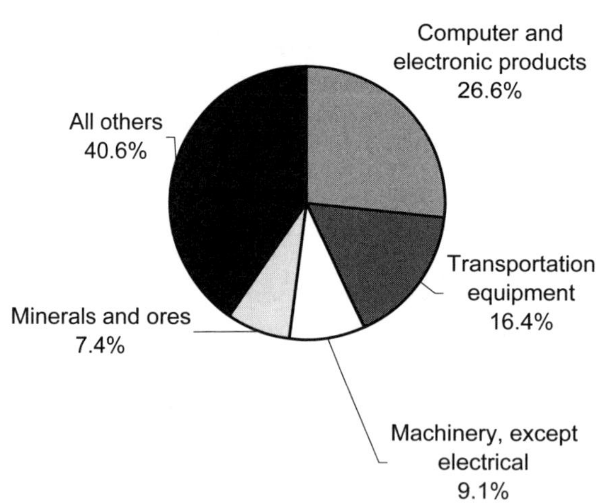

ARKANSAS

Facts and Figures

Location: South central United States; bordered on the N by Missouri, on the E by Tennessee and Mississippi, on the S by Louisiana, and on the W by Oklahoma and Texas

Area: 53,179 sq. mi. (137,733 sq. km.); rank—29th

Population: 2,949,131 (2012 est.); rank—32nd

Principal Cities: capital—Little Rock; largest—Little Rock

Statehood: June 15, 1836; 25th state

U.S. Congress: 2 senators, 4 representatives

State Motto: *Regnat populus* ("The people rule")

State Song: "Arkansas"

State Nicknames: The Natural State; The Land of Opportunity

Abbreviations: AR; Ark.

State Symbols: flower—apple blossom; tree—pine; bird—mockingbird

At a Glance

- With an increase in population of 8.1 percent, Arkansas ranked 29th among the states in growth from 2000 to 2009.
- An estimated 31,600 marriages took place in Arkansas in 2009, compared to 16,300 divorces.
- Arkansas's median household income in 2011 was $38,758, and 19.5 percent of its population lived below the poverty level.
- In 2011, 17.1 percent of Arkansans did not have health insurance, compared to 15.1 percent of the total U.S. population.
- Arkansas's violent crime rate in 2011 was 480.9 per 100,000 population, compared to 386.3 for the entire nation.
- In 2007, Arkansas exported $2.1 billion worth of agricultural products, about 2.6 percent of the U.S. total.

Table AR-1. Population by Age, Sex, Race, and Hispanic Origin

(Number, percent, except where noted.)

Sex, age, race, and Hispanic origin	2000	2010	2012[1]	Average annual percent change, 2010–2012
Total Population	2,673,400	2,915,918	2,949,131	0.4
Percent of total U.S. population	0.9	0.9	0.9	X
Sex				
Male	1,304,693	1,431,637	1,448,490	0.4
Female	1,368,707	1,484,281	1,500,641	0.4
Age				
Under 5 years	181,585	197,689	194,019	-0.6
5 to 19 years	578,924	598,241	594,674	-0.2
20 to 64 years	1,538,872	1,700,007	1,717,848	0.3
65 years and over	374,019	419,981	442,590	1.7
Median age (years)	36.0	37.4	37.6	0.2
Race and Hispanic Origin				
One race				
White	2,138,598	2,342,403	2,359,569	0.2
Black	418,950	454,021	459,739	0.4
American Indian and Alaska Native	17,808	26,134	27,647	1.8
Asian	20,220	37,537	41,338	3.1
Native Hawaiian or Other Pacific Islander	1,668	6,685	7,495	3.6
Two or more races	35,744	49,138	53,343	2.6
Hispanic (of any race)	86,866	191,535	205,720	2.3

X = Not applicable.
[1]Population figures for 2012 are July 1 estimates. The 2010 estimates are taken from the 2010 Census.

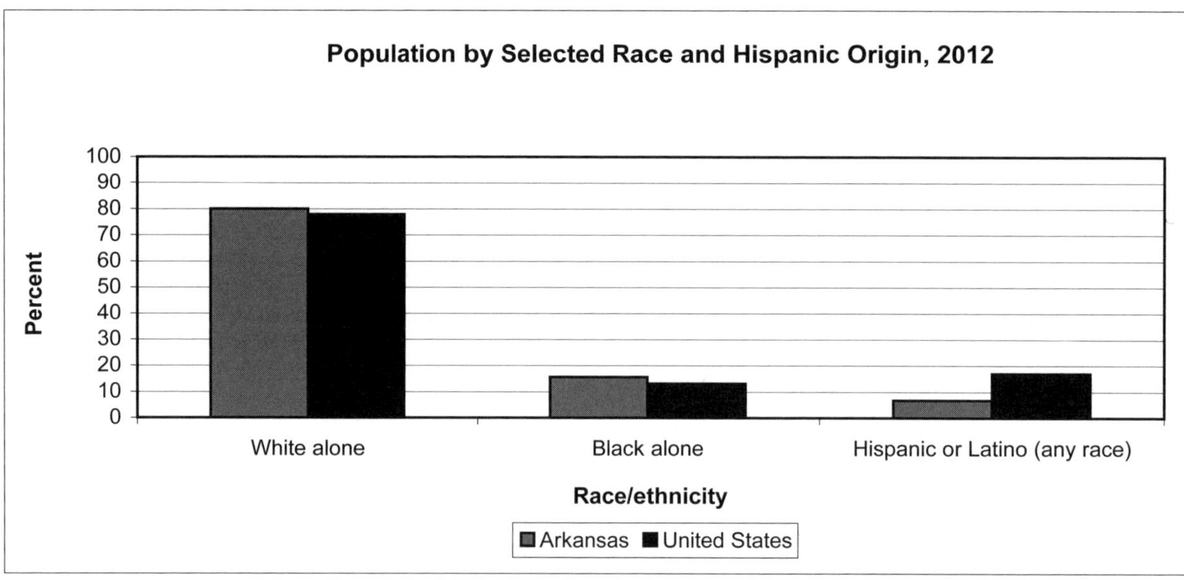

Table AR-2. Marital Status

(Number, percent distribution.)

Sex, age, race, and Hispanic origin	2000	2010	2011
Males, 15 Years and Over	1,015,594	1,128,804	1,141,046
Never married	24.2	29.5	29.5
Now married, except separated	61.0	53.3	53.2
Separated	1.6	2.2	2.1
Widowed	2.7	3.1	2.7
Divorced	10.4	12.0	12.6
Females, 15 Years and Over	1,096,069	1,200,974	1,201,330
Never married	18.4	23.5	22.9
Now married, except separated	55.7	48.8	49.5
Separated	2.2	2.9	2.8
Widowed	12.2	11.2	10.7
Divorced	11.6	13.6	14.1

Table AR-3. Households and Housing Characteristics

(Number, percent, dollars.)

Item	2000	2010	2011	Average annual percent change, 2000–2011
Total Households	1,042,696	1,114,902	1,127,621	0.7
Family households	732,261	761,361	757,205	0.3
Married-couple family	566,401	554,946	556,108	-0.2
Other family	165,860	206,415	201,097	1.8
Male householder, no wife present	39,299	51,620	48,001	1.8
Female householder, no husband present	126,561	154,795	153,096	1.7
Nonfamily households	310,435	353,541	370,416	1.6
Householder living alone	266,585	302,127	316,351	1.6
Householder not living alone	43,850	51,414	54,065	1.9
Housing Characteristics				
Total housing units	1,173,043	1,317,818	1,324,471	1.1
Occupied housing units	1,042,696	1,114,902	1,127,621	0.7
Owner occupied	723,535	751,568	750,984	0.3
Renter occupied	319,161	363,334	376,637	1.5
Average size	2.49	2.55	2.54	0.2
Financial Characteristics				
Median gross rent of renter-occupied housing	453	638	639	3.4
Median monthly owner costs for housing units with a mortgage	737	987	988	2.8
Median value of owner-occupied housing units	72,800	106,300	106,300	3.8

Table AR-4. Migration, Origin, and Language

(Number, percent.)

Characteristic	State			U.S.		
	2010	2011	Percent change	2010	2011	Percent change
Residence 1 Year Ago						
Population 1 year and over	2,888,304	2,906,632	0.6	305,628,607	307,900,319	0.7
Same house	82.7	83.3	0.7	84.6	84.8	0.2
Different house in the U.S.	17.0	16.4	-3.5	14.8	14.6	-1.4
Same county	10.1	10.5	4.0	9.4	9.2	-2.1
Different county	6.9	5.8	-15.9	5.4	5.4	-
Same state	4.2	3.4	-19.0	3.2	3.1	-3.1
Different state	2.7	2.4	-11.1	2.2	2.3	4.5
Abroad	0.3	0.3	-	0.6	0.6	-
Place of Birth						
Native born	2,789,939	2,809,170	0.7	269,393,835	271,214,059	0.7
Male	48.9	49.1	0.4	49.2	49.2	-
Female	51.1	50.9	-0.4	50.8	50.8	-
Foreign born	131,667	128,809	-2.2	39,955,854	40,377,860	1.1
Male	50.7	52.5	3.6	49.1	48.9	-0.4
Female	49.3	47.5	-3.7	50.9	51.1	0.4
Foreign born; naturalized U.S. citizen	36,435	36,376	-0.2	17,476,082	18,140,192	3.8
Male	46.1	44.4	-3.7	45.8	45.8	-
Female	53.9	55.6	3.2	54.2	54.2	-
Foreign born; not a U.S. citizen	95,232	92,433	-2.9	22,479,772	22,237,668	-1.1
Male	52.5	55.8	6.3	51.6	51.5	-0.2
Female	47.5	44.2	-6.9	48.4	48.5	0.2
Entered 2000 or later	47.5	45.8	-3.6	34.7	35.7	2.9
Entered 1990 to 1999	27.3	26.3	-3.7	27.2	26.7	-1.8
Entered before 1990	25.2	27.9	10.7	38.1	37.6	-1.3
World Region of Birth, Foreign						
Foreign-born population, excluding population born at sea	131,667	128,809	-2.2	39,955,673	40,377,757	1.1
Europe	7.4	7.3	-1.4	12.1	12.1	-
Asia	19.4	21.2	9.3	28.2	28.6	1.4
Africa	1.0	2.2	120.0	4	4.1	2.5
Oceania	3.2	3.4	6.2	0.5	0.5	-
Latin America	66.5	64.4	-3.2	53.1	52.6	-0.9
North America	2.6	1.7	-34.6	2	2.0	-
Language Spoken at Home and Ability to Speak English						
Population 5 years and over	2,727,155	2,740,313	0.5	289,215,746	291,524,091	0.8
English only	93.1	92.5	-0.6	79.4	79.2	-0.3
Language other than English	6.9	7.5	8.7	20.6	20.8	1.0
Speaks English less than "very well"	3.2	3.4	6.2	8.7	8.7	-

- = Zero or rounds to zero.

Table AR-5. Median Income and Poverty Status, 2011

(Number, percent, except as noted.)

Characteristic	State Number	State Percent	U.S. Number	U.S. Percent
Median Income				
Households (dollars)	38,758	X	50,502	X
Families (dollars)	48,713	X	61,455	X
Below Poverty Level (All People)	555,876	19.5	48,452,035	15.9
Sex				
Male	248,549	17.8	21,825,281	14.7
Female	307,327	21.1	26,626,754	17.2
Age				
Under 18 years	196,538	28.1	16,386,500	22.5
Related children under 18 years	193,010	27.7	16,087,074	22.2
18 to 64 years	316,187	18.1	28,335,079	14.8
65 years and over	43,151	10.5	3,730,456	9.3

X = Not applicable.

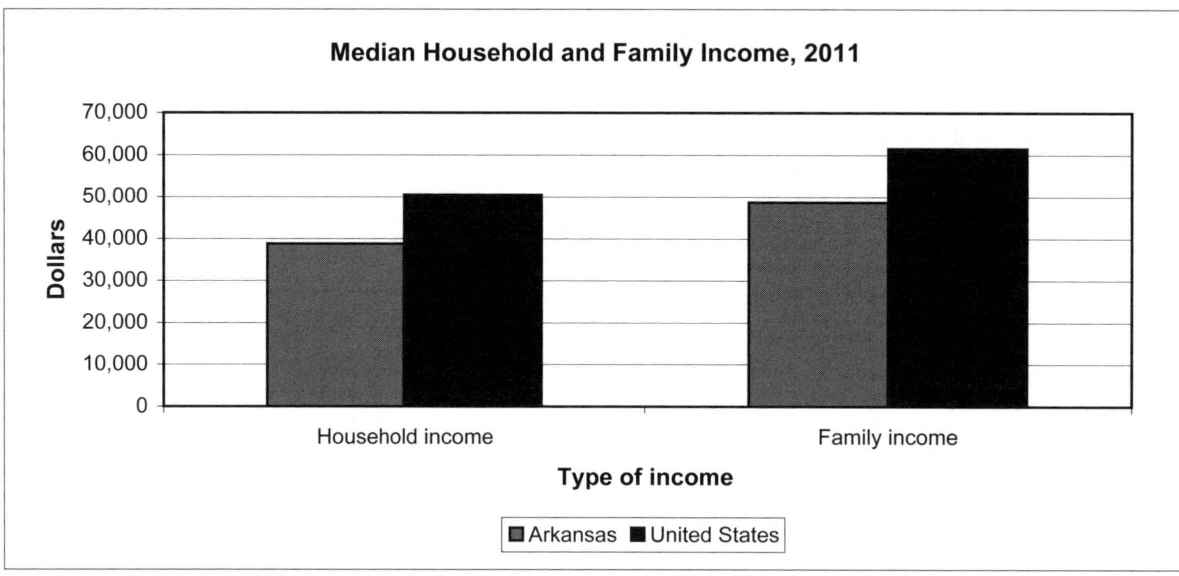

Table AR-6. Health Insurance Coverage Status for the Civilian Noninstitutionalized Population and Children Under 18 Years of Age

(Numbers in thousands, percent.)

Item	2004	2005	2006	2007	2008	2009	2010	2011
Civilian Noninstitutionalized Population	2,731	2,760	2,758	2,805	2,802	2,833	2,868	2,885
Covered by Private or Public Insurance								
Number	2,290	2,277	2,237	2,354	2,296	2,351	2,367	2,393
Percent	83.8	82.5	81.1	83.9	81.9	83.0	82.5	82.9
Not Covered								
Number	441	482	521	451	506	483	501	492
Percent	16.2	17.5	18.9	16.1	18.1	17.0	17.5	17.1
Percent in the U.S. not covered	14.9	15.3	15.8	15.3	15.1	15.1	15.5	15.1
Children Under 18 Years of Age	692	673	699	720	701	707	709	709
Covered by Private or Public Insurance								
Number	649	600	634	679	640	663	663	669
Percent	93.8	89.3	90.7	93.8	91.3	93.8	93.4	94.4
Not Covered								
Number	43	72	65	44	61	44	46	40
Percent	6.2	10.7	9.3	6.2	8.7	6.2	6.6	5.6
Percent in the U.S. not covered	10.5	10.9	11.7	11.0	9.7	8.6	8.0	7.5

Table AR-7. Employment Status by Demographic Group, Preliminary 2012

(Numbers in thousands, percent.)

Characteristic	Civilian noninstitutional population	Civilian labor force		Employed		Unemployed	
		Number	Percent of population	Number	Percent of population	Number	Percent of population
Total	2,271	1,354	59.6	1,252	55.1	102	7.6
Sex							
Male	1,095	718	65.6	663	60.6	54	7.6
Female	1,176	636	54.1	588	50.0	48	7.6
Race, Sex, and Hispanic Origin							
White	1,853	1,091	58.9	1,026	55.4	65	6.0
Male	905	592	65.4	556	61.4	36	6.1
Female	948	499	52.7	470	49.6	29	5.9
Black or African American	327	201	61.5	169	51.7	32	15.9
Male	147	91	62.2	76	51.5	16	17.3
Female	181	110	61.0	94	52.0	16	14.8
Hispanic	114	80	70.6	76	66.7	4	5.5
Male	62	51	81.5	48	77.0	3	5.5
Female	52	30	57.6	28	54.4	2	5.6
Age							
16 to 19 years	137	51	36.8	37	27.2	13	26.2
20 to 24 years	197	147	74.5	125	63.5	22	14.8
25 to 34 years	399	321	80.5	298	74.5	24	7.4
35 to 44 years	355	282	79.2	263	73.9	19	6.7
45 to 54 years	408	310	76.1	294	72.2	16	5.1
55 to 64 years	352	181	51.6	176	49.9	6	3.3
65 years and over	422	62	14.6	59	14.0	3	4.2

NOTE: Data in Table 7 are from the Current Population Survey (CPS) and do not match the estimates in Table 8. See notes and definitions for further information.

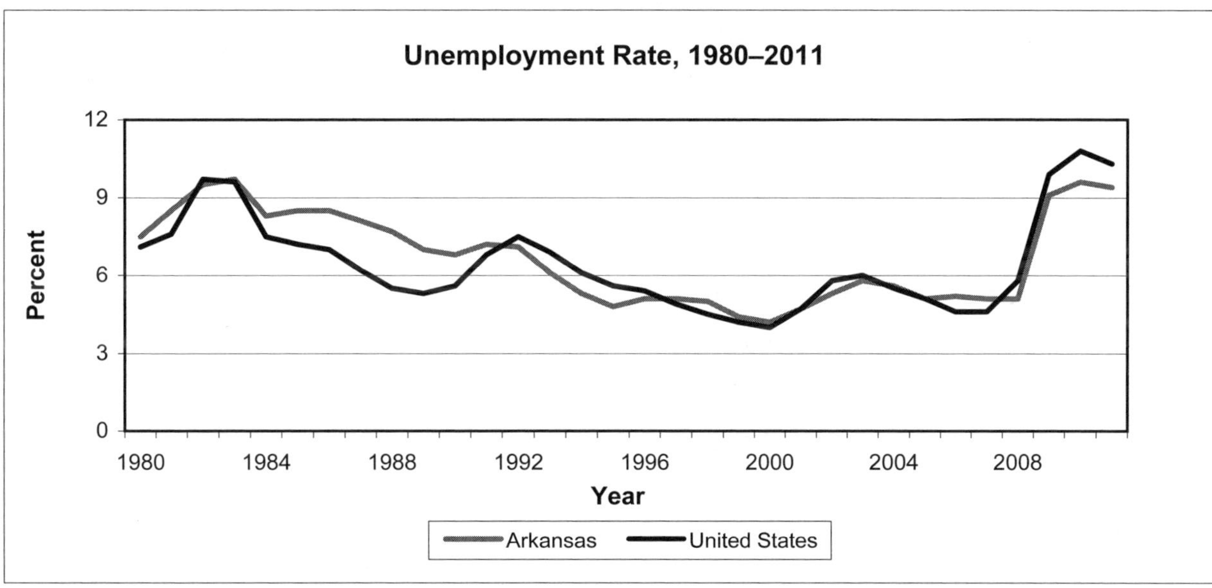

Table AR-8. Employment Status of the Civilian Noninstitutional Population Age 16 Years and Over

(Number, percent.)

Year	Civilian labor force	Civilian participation rate	Employed	Unemployed	Unemployment rate
2005	1,335,550	63.3	1,267,655	67,895	5.1
2006	1,354,156	63.4	1,284,177	69,979	5.2
2007	1,361,176	63.0	1,291,981	69,195	5.1
2008	1,370,259	62.9	1,300,542	69,717	5.1
2009	1,371,228	60.7	1,245,923	125,305	9.1
2010	1,377,434	60.1	1,245,328	132,106	9.6
2011	1,363,235	59.2	1,235,755	127,480	9.4

Table AR-9. Employment and Average Wages by Industry

(Estimates before 2007 are based on the 2002 *North American Industry Classification System* [NAICS]. Estimates from 2007 onward are based on the 2007 NAICS.)

Industry	2005	2006	2007	2008	2009	2010	2011
				Number of jobs			
Wage and Salary Employment by Industry	1,234,501	1,259,810	1,262,522	1,263,298	1,227,077	1,226,354	1,229,913
Farm Wage and Salary Employment	10,934	12,236	10,700	12,453	12,493	13,208	11,972
Nonfarm Wage and Salary Employment	1,223,567	1,247,574	1,251,822	1,250,845	1,214,584	1,213,146	1,217,941
Private wage and salary employment	1,000,702	1,019,019	1,022,030	1,018,122	978,490	976,519	983,731
Forestry, fishing, and related activities	8,790	8,499	8,245	8,061	7,774	8,163	8,244
Mining	4,107	4,902	6,806	8,322	8,432	8,574	9,014
Utilities	6,609	6,829	6,956	6,971	7,028	7,315	7,170
Construction	56,781	59,102	58,651	58,642	54,361	51,129	49,824
Manufacturing	201,253	199,086	189,188	181,870	162,703	159,290	158,294
Durable goods manufacturing	106,904	106,600	100,214	94,796	80,067	77,864	78,484
Nondurable goods manufacturing	94,349	92,486	88,974	87,074	82,636	81,426	79,810
Wholesale trade	47,922	48,262	48,761	49,087	47,341	46,792	46,968
Retail trade	133,260	134,721	135,881	135,130	131,360	131,391	133,167
Transportation and warehousing	60,405	61,724	61,848	59,287	53,350	52,891	54,211
Information	20,078	19,945	19,617	18,518	17,437	16,545	16,077
Finance and insurance	37,141	38,282	38,551	37,616	36,472	36,135	36,797
Real estate and rental and leasing	14,094	14,661	14,849	14,754	14,334	14,074	13,719
Professional, scientific, and technical services	36,218	37,800	39,216	39,391	38,313	39,141	39,756
Management of companies and enterprises	23,580	24,102	24,998	26,130	26,357	25,904	26,048
Administrative and waste services	52,841	53,419	54,593	53,823	50,018	53,783	56,173
Educational services	12,814	13,552	13,857	14,170	14,454	14,841	15,224
Health care and social assistance	135,118	140,143	144,051	149,162	153,207	156,158	157,082
Arts, entertainment, and recreation	9,468	9,556	9,933	10,026	9,954	9,881	9,875
Accommodation and food services	85,691	89,004	90,756	91,945	90,991	90,288	91,548
Other services, except public administration	54,532	55,430	55,273	55,217	54,604	54,224	54,540
Government and government enterprises	222,865	228,555	229,792	232,723	236,094	236,627	234,210
				Dollars			
Average Wages and Salaries by Industry	31,701	32,900	34,611	35,321	36,032	36,686	37,787
Average Farm Wages and Salaries	21,792	19,506	23,814	22,276	18,839	19,023	19,145
Average Nonfarm Wages and Salaries	31,790	33,031	34,703	35,451	36,209	36,878	37,970
Average private wages and salaries	31,496	32,802	34,586	35,251	35,914	36,667	37,771
Forestry, fishing, and related activities	25,531	27,104	28,078	29,126	29,499	30,403	31,440
Mining	46,591	53,043	55,172	61,034	62,564	64,277	67,647
Utilities	64,743	64,361	67,942	72,220	72,644	71,533	74,513
Construction	33,150	34,547	36,691	39,321	40,284	40,169	40,709
Manufacturing	35,296	36,467	37,903	38,563	38,731	40,788	42,050
Durable goods manufacturing	36,213	37,615	39,237	40,064	40,397	42,621	44,068
Nondurable goods manufacturing	34,256	35,144	36,402	36,928	37,116	39,036	40,066
Wholesale trade	46,577	49,844	52,052	54,190	54,294	56,314	57,927
Retail trade	20,832	21,739	22,350	23,004	23,340	23,904	24,286
Transportation and warehousing	38,111	39,106	39,669	40,824	40,433	41,564	44,092
Information	41,875	44,631	77,610	50,957	65,601	48,243	50,025
Finance and insurance	44,373	46,449	48,536	50,838	51,213	52,920	55,027
Real estate and rental and leasing	26,737	28,119	29,162	30,007	30,480	31,376	32,788
Professional, scientific, and technical services	45,465	47,080	49,095	50,492	51,509	53,072	56,330
Management of companies and enterprises	68,646	73,541	73,220	77,734	81,263	90,405	91,222
Administrative and waste services	20,460	21,439	22,460	24,195	25,240	25,843	26,898
Educational services	21,323	22,106	23,091	24,105	25,937	26,232	26,894
Health care and social assistance	33,136	33,994	34,778	35,599	36,104	36,284	37,279
Arts, entertainment, and recreation	16,636	18,702	19,573	19,771	19,644	19,311	20,360
Accommodation and food services	12,417	12,904	13,800	13,826	14,097	14,688	15,144
Other services, except public administration	21,899	23,053	24,093	25,237	25,244	26,277	26,864
Government and government enterprises	33,109	34,051	35,223	36,323	37,431	37,749	38,808

Table AR-10. Employment Characteristics by Family Type

(Number, percent.)

Family type and labor force status	2009 Total	2009 Families with own children under 18 years	2010 Total	2010 Families with own children under 18 years	2011 Total	2011 Families with own children under 18 years
All families	768,492	336,779	761,361	318,766	757,205	320,053
Family type and labor force status						
Married-couple families	566,397	217,509	554,946	202,668	556,108	205,856
Both husband and wife in labor force	50.4	68.0	50.1	66.6	47.7	64.2
Husband in labor force, wife not in labor force	21.6	25.6	20.4	26.0	21.8	27.7
Wife in labor force, husband not in labor force	8.5	4.3	8.9	4.8	9.3	4.9
Both husband and wife not in labor force	19.6	2.2	20.6	2.6	21.2	3.1
Other families	202,095	119,270	206,415	116,098	201,097	114,197
Female householder, no husband present	75.5	81.1	75.0	78.5	76.1	78.5
In labor force	52.2	64.2	52.9	63.7	52.4	63.8
Not in labor force	23.3	16.9	22.1	14.7	23.8	14.7
Male householder, no wife present	24.5	18.9	25.0	21.5	23.9	21.5
In labor force	17.8	16.3	17.9	18.6	17.3	18.8
Not in labor force	6.7	2.6	7.1	2.9	6.6	2.7

Table AR-11. School Enrollment and Educational Attainment, 2011

(Number, percent.)

Item	State	U.S.
Enrollment		
Total population 3 years and over, enrolled in school	752,121	83,131,910
Enrolled in nursery school or preschool (percent)	6.9	6.0
Enrolled in kindergarten (percent)	4.9	5.1
Enrolled in elementary school, grades 1-8 (percent)	42.1	39.5
Enrolled in high school, grades 9-12 (percent)	20.5	20.7
Enrolled in college or graduate school (percent)	25.6	28.7
Attainment		
Total population 25 years and over	1,943,427	206,471,670
Less than ninth grade (percent)	6.2	6.0
9th to 12th grade, no diploma (percent)	10	8.1
High school graduate, including equivalency (percent)	35.7	28.4
Some college, no degree (percent)	22	21.2
Associate's degree (percent)	5.8	7.8
Bachelor's degree (percent)	13.1	17.9
Graduate or professional degree (percent)	7.2	10.6
High school graduate or higher (percent)	83.8	85.9
Bachelor's degree or higher (percent)	20.3	28.5

Table AR-12. Educational Indicators

(Number, percent; data derived from National Center of Education Statistics.)

Item	State	U.S.
Public Schools, 2009–2010 (except where noted)		
Number of school districts	244	13,629
Number of schools	1,120	99,834
Number of students (in thousands)	481	49,373
Student-teacher ratio	12.9	15.4
Expenditures per student (dollars)	10,978	10,591
Averaged freshman graduation rate, 2008–2009	74.0	75.5[1]
Dropout rate, 2008–2009	4.1	4.1
Students eligible for free or reduced-price lunch (percent)	60.4	48.0
English language learners, 2010–2011 (percent)	6.6	9.8[1]
Students with IEP (percent)	13.5	13.1
Private Schools, 2009–2010 (except where noted)		
Number of schools	224	33,366
Number of students (in thousands)	24	4,700
High school graduates, 2008–2009	1,330	308,813
Student-teacher ratio	10.0	10.7

[1] U.S. total includes estimates for nonreporting states.

Table AR-13. Reported Voting and Registration of the Voting-Age Population, November 2012

(Numbers in thousands, percent.)

Item	Total population	Total citizen population	Registered			Voted		
			Total registered	Percent registered (total population)	Percent registered (total citizen population)	Total voted	Percent voted (total population)	Percent voted (total citizen population)
U.S. Total	235,248	215,081	153,157	65.1	71.2	132,948	56.5	61.8
State Total	2,198	2,109	1,376	62.6	65.3	1,124	51.1	53.3
Sex								
Male	1,044	1,006	637	61.0	63.4	531	50.9	52.8
Female	1,154	1,103	739	64.1	67.0	593	51.4	53.7
Race								
White alone	1,788	1,726	1,148	64.2	66.5	941	52.7	54.5
White, non-Hispanic alone	1,681	1,676	1,138	67.7	67.9	933	55.5	55.7
Black alone	313	313	192	61.3	61.3	155	49.4	49.4
Asian alone	33	21	9	B	B	9	B	B
Hispanic (of any race)	143	73	16	11.3	B	14	9.5	B
Age								
18 to 24 years	288	281	126	43.8	44.8	70	24.3	24.8
25 to 44 years	719	676	428	59.6	63.3	345	48.0	51.0
45 to 64 years	742	704	498	67.1	70.8	442	59.6	62.8
65 to 74 years	301	299	212	70.6	71.0	185	61.7	62.0
75 years and over	149	149	111	75.0	75.0	81	54.7	54.7

B = Base is less than 75,000 and therefore too small to show the derived measure.

Table AR-14. Crime

(Number, rate per 100,000. Data are derived from the FBI Uniform Crime Reports.)

Item	State			U.S.		
	2010	2011	Percent change	2010	2011	Percent change
TOTAL POPULATION	2,921,588	2,937,979	0.6	309,330,219	311,591,917	0.7
VIOLENT CRIME						
Number	14,711	14,129	-4.0	1,251,248	1,203,564	-3.8
Rate	503.5	480.9	-4.5	404.5	386.3	-4.5
Murder and Nonnegligent Manslaughter						
Number	134	162	20.9	14,722	14,612	-0.7
Rate	4.6	5.5	19.6	4.8	4.7	-2.1
Forcible Rape						
Number	1,321	1,213	-8.2	85,593	83,425	-2.5
Rate	45.2	41.3	-8.6	27.7	26.8	-3.2
Robbery						
Number	2,369	2,428	2.5	369,089	354,396	-4.0
Rate	81.1	82.6	1.8	119.3	113.7	-4.7
Aggravated Assault						
Number	10,887	10,326	-5.2	781,844	751,131	-3.9
Rate	372.6	351.5	-5.7	252.8	241.1	-4.6
PROPERTY CRIME						
Number	103,820	110,295	6.2	9,112,625	9,063,173	-0.5
Rate	3,553.5	3,754.1	5.6	2,945.9	2,908.7	-1.3
Burglary						
Number	32,463	34,471	6.2	2,168,459	2,188,005	0.9
Rate	1,111.1	1,173.3	5.6	701.0	702.2	0.2
Larceny-Theft						
Number	65,796	70,012	6.4	6,204,601	6,159,795	-0.7
Rate	2,252.1	2,383.0	5.8	2,005.8	1,976.9	-1.4
Motor Vehicle Theft						
Number	5,561	5,812	4.5	739,565	715,373	-3.3
Rate	190.3	197.8	3.9	239.1	229.6	-4.0

Table AR-15. State Government Finances, 2011

(Dollar amounts in thousands, percent distribution.)

Item	Dollars	Percent distribution
Total Revenue	22,807,859	100.0
General revenue	17,453,870	76.5
Intergovernmental revenue	6,313,263	27.7
Taxes	7,975,526	35.0
General sales	2,736,946	12.0
Selective sales	1,140,036	5.0
License taxes	361,548	1.6
Individual income tax	2,270,383	10.0
Corporate income tax	376,874	1.7
Other taxes	1,089,739	4.8
Current charges	2,319,881	10.2
Miscellaneous general revenue	845,200	3.7
Utility revenue	0	0.0
Liquor stores revenue	0	0.0
Insurance trust revenue [1]	5,353,989	23.5
Total Expenditure	18,861,507	100.0
Intergovernmental expenditure	5,151,981	27.3
Direct expenditure	13,709,526	72.7
Current operation	10,101,909	53.6
Capital outlay	898,800	4.8
Insurance benefits and repayments	2,001,596	10.6
Assistance and subsidies	555,837	2.9
Interest on debt	151,384	0.8
Exhibit: Salaries and wages	2,903,305	15.4
Total Expenditure	18,861,507	100.0
General expenditure	16,859,911	89.4
Intergovernmental expenditure	5,151,981	27.3
Direct expenditure	11,707,930	62.1
General expenditure, by function:		
Education	7,508,042	39.8
Public welfare	4,493,896	23.8
Hospitals	856,818	4.5
Health	278,329	1.5
Highways	1,081,300	5.7
Police protection	97,386	0.5
Correction	411,436	2.2
Natural resources	339,085	1.8
Parks and recreation	59,730	0.3
Governmental administration	576,327	3.1
Interest on general debt	151,384	0.8
Other and unallocable	1,006,178	5.3
Utility expenditure	0	0.0
Liquor stores expenditure	0	0.0
Insurance trust expenditure	2,001,596	10.6
Debt at End of Fiscal Year	3,748,749	X
Cash and Security Holdings	26,065,733	X

X = Not applicable.

[1] Within insurance trust revenue, net earnings of state retirement systems is a calculated statistic (the item code in the data file is X08), and thus can be positive or negative. Net earnings is the sum of earnings on investments plus gains on investments minus losses on investments. The change made in 2002 for asset valuation from book to market value in accordance with Statement 34 of the Governmental Accounting Standards Board is reflected in the calculated statistics.

Table AR-16. State Government Tax Collections, 2012

(Dollars in thousands, percent.)

Item	Dollars	Percent distribution
Total Taxes	8,287,744	100.0
Property taxes	1,008,707	12.2
Sales and gross receipts	3,982,832	48.1
General sales and gross receipts	2,809,416	33.9
Selective sales and gross receipts	1,173,416	14.2
Alcoholic beverages	48,803	0.6
Amusements	27,640	0.3
Insurance premiums	156,828	1.9
Motor fuels	467,055	5.6
Pari-mutuels	3,526	-
Public utilities	0	0.0
Tobacco products	246,976	3.0
Other selective sales	222,588	2.7
Licenses	359,012	4.3
Alcoholic beverages	4,170	0.1
Amusements	450	-
Corporations in general	24,690	0.3
Hunting and fishing	21,696	0.3
Motor vehicle	154,095	1.9
Motor vehicle operators	17,604	0.2
Public utilities	10,015	0.1
Occupation and business, NEC	125,492	1.5
Other licenses	800	-
Income taxes	2,805,985	33.9
Individual income	2,401,902	29.0
Corporation net income	404,083	4.9
Other taxes	131,208	1.6
Death and gift	0	0.0
Documentary and stock transfer	25,750	0.3
Severance	82,770	1.0
Taxes, NEC	22,688	0.3

- = Rounds to zero.

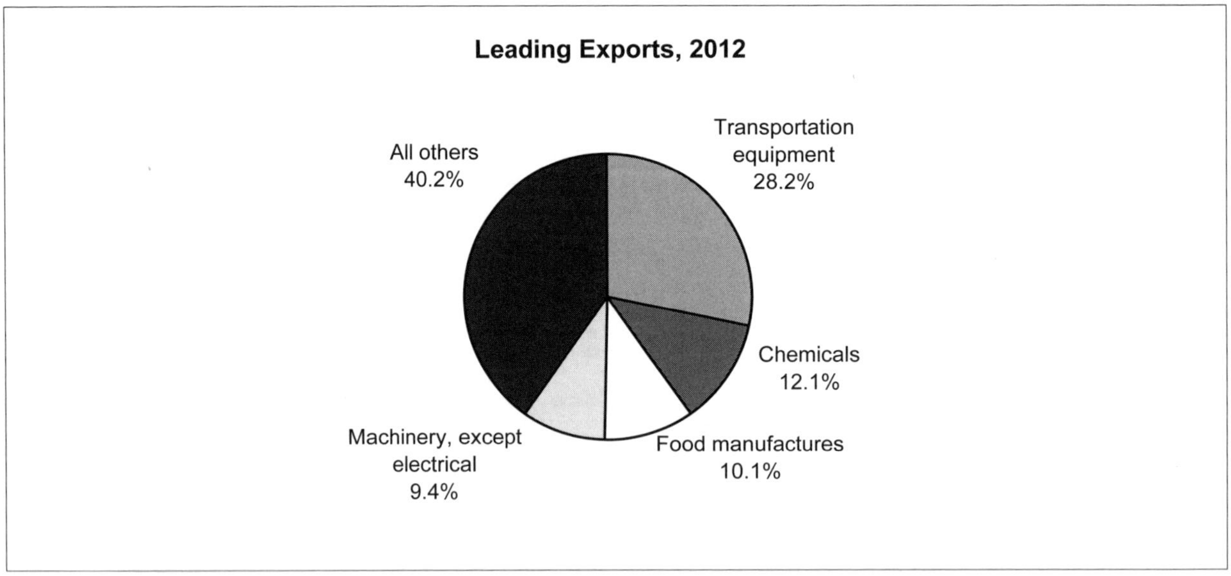

CALIFORNIA

Facts and Figures

Location: Western United States; bordered on the N by Oregon, on the E by Nevada and Arizona, on the S by Mexico, and on the W by the Pacific Ocean

Area: 163,696 sq. mi. (423,970 sq. km.); rank—3rd

Population: 38,041,430 (2012 est.); rank—1st

Principal Cities: capital—Sacramento; largest—Los Angeles

Statehood: September 9, 1850; 31st state

U.S. Congress: 2 senators, 53 representatives

State Motto: *Eureka* ("I have found it")

State Song: "I Love You, California"

State Nickname: The Golden State

Abbreviations: CA; Calif.

State Symbols: flower—California poppy; tree—redwood; bird—California valley quail

At a Glance

- With an increase in population of 9.1 percent, California ranked 2nd among the states in growth from 2000 to 2009.
- An estimated 213,900 marriages took place in California in 2009; California does not report its number of divorces.
- California's median household income in 2011 was $57,287, and 16.6 percent of the population lived below the poverty level.
- California's violent crime rate in 2011 was 411.1 per 100,000 population, compared to 386.3 for the entire nation.
- In the 2012 election, 57.5 percent of California's eligible voters voted, compared to 61.8 percent of the total U.S. population.
- In 2007, California exported $1.3 billion worth of agricultural products, 14 percent of the U.S. total.

Table CA-1. Population by Age, Sex, Race, and Hispanic Origin

(Number, percent, except where noted.)

Sex, age, race, and Hispanic origin	2000	2010	2012	Average annual percent change, 2010–2012
Total Population	33,871,648	37,253,956	38,041,430	0.7
Percent of total U.S. population	12.0	12.1	12.1	X
Sex				
Male	16,874,892	18,517,830	18,918,564	0.7
Female	16,996,756	18,736,126	19,122,866	0.7
Age				
Under 5 years	2,486,981	2,531,333	2,541,497	0.1
5 to 19 years	7,747,590	7,920,709	7,797,982	-0.5
20 to 64 years	20,041,419	22,555,400	23,101,866	0.8
65 years and over	3,595,658	4,246,514	4,600,085	2.6
Median age (years)	33.3	35.2	35.5	0.3
Race and Hispanic Origin				
One race				
White	20,170,059	27,636,403	28,033,826	0.5
Black	2,263,882	2,486,549	2,515,716	0.4
American Indian and Alaska Native	333,346	622,107	639,740	0.9
Asian	3,697,513	5,038,123	5,294,255	1.6
Native Hawaiian or Other Pacific Islander	116,961	181,431	187,855	1.1
Two or more races	1,607,646	1,289,343	1,370,038	2.0
Hispanic (of any race)	10,966,556	14,440,187	14,994,375	1.2

X = Not applicable.

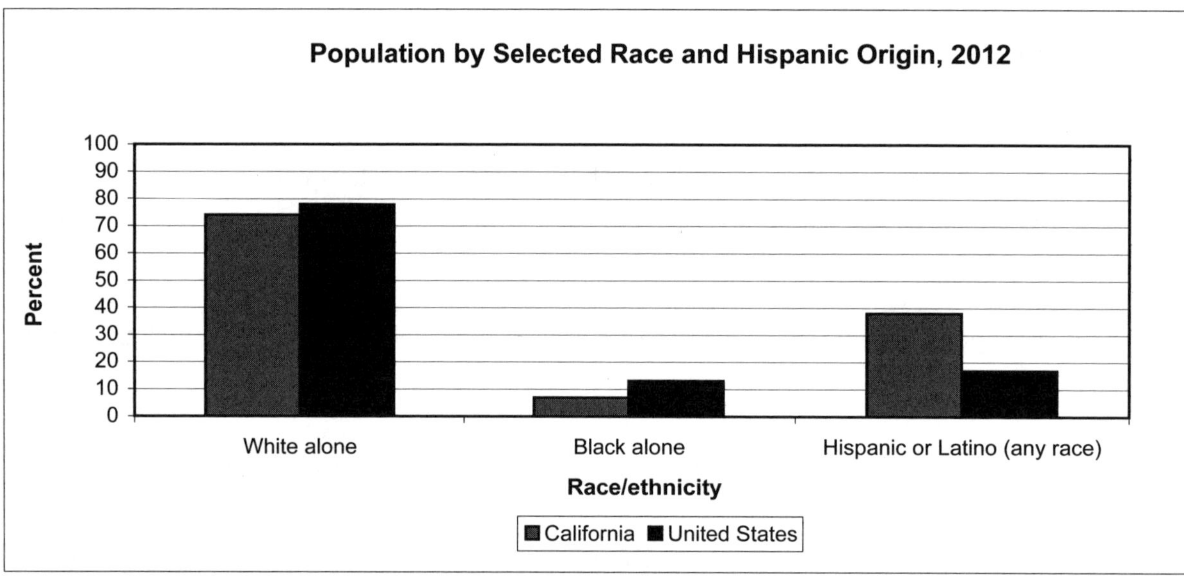

Table CA-2. Marital Status

(Number, percent distribution.)

Sex, age, race, and Hispanic origin	2000	2010	2011
Males, 15 Years and Over	12,844,669	14,662,335	14,850,044
Never married	33.8	39.8	40.1
Now married, except separated	54.1	48.2	47.6
Separated	2.0	1.9	1.9
Widowed	2.2	2.1	2.1
Divorced	7.9	8.0	8.2
Females, 15 Years and Over	13,231,494	15,043,190	15,212,346
Never married	26.5	32.3	32.6
Now married, except separated	50.7	45.7	45.3
Separated	2.9	2.7	2.8
Widowed	8.9	8.1	8.1
Divorced	11.0	11.2	11.2

Table CA-3. Households and Housing Characteristics

(Number, percent, dollars.)

Item	2000	2010	2011	Average annual percent change, 2000–2011
Total Households	11,502,870	12,406,475	12,468,743	0.7
Family households	7,920,049	8,507,856	8,518,518	0.6
Married-couple family	5,877,084	6,082,566	6,059,185	0.3
Other family	2,042,965	2,425,290	2,459,333	1.7
Male householder, no wife present	594,455	736,626	748,432	2.2
Female householder, no husband present	1,448,510	1,688,664	1,710,901	1.5
Nonfamily households	3,582,821	3,898,619	3,950,225	0.9
Householder living alone	2,708,308	3,001,307	3,050,172	1.1
Householder not living alone	874,513	897,312	900,053	0.2
Housing Characteristics				
Total housing units	12,214,549	13,682,976	13,721,187	1.0
Occupied housing units	11,502,870	12,406,475	12,468,743	0.7
Owner occupied	6,546,334	6,903,175	6,843,369	0.4
Renter occupied	4,956,536	5,503,300	5,625,374	1.1
Average size	2.87	2.94	2.96	0.3
Financial Characteristics				
Median gross rent of renter-occupied housing	747	1,163	1,174	4.8
Median monthly owner costs for housing units with a mortgage	1,478	2,242	2,182	4.0
Median value of owner-occupied housing units	211,500	370,900	355,600	5.7

Table CA-4. Migration, Origin, and Language

(Number, percent.)

Characteristic	State			U.S.		
	2010	2011	Percent change	2010	2011	Percent change
Residence 1 Year Ago						
Population 1 year and over	36,907,897	37,222,678	0.9	305,628,607	307,900,319	0.7
Same house	83.4	83.9	0.6	84.6	84.8	0.2
Different house in the U.S.	15.9	15.4	-3.1	14.8	14.6	-1.4
Same county	11.7	11.3	-3.4	9.4	9.2	-2.1
Different county	4.2	4.1	-2.4	5.4	5.4	-
Same state	3.0	2.9	-3.3	3.2	3.1	-3.1
Different state	1.2	1.3	8.3	2.2	2.3	4.5
Abroad	0.7	0.7	-	0.6	0.6	-
Place of Birth						
Native born	27,198,934	27,496,855	1.1	269,393,835	271,214,059	0.7
Male	50.1	50.2	0.2	49.2	49.2	-
Female	49.9	49.8	-0.2	50.8	50.8	-
Foreign born	10,150,429	10,195,057	0.4	39,955,854	40,377,860	1.1
Male	48.8	48.6	-0.4	49.1	48.9	-0.4
Female	51.2	51.4	0.4	50.9	51.1	0.4
Foreign born; naturalized U.S. citizen	4,633,509	4,771,515	3.0	17,476,082	18,140,192	3.8
Male	45.9	46.0	0.2	45.8	45.8	-
Female	54.1	54.0	-0.2	54.2	54.2	-
Foreign born; not a U.S. citizen	5,516,920	5,423,542	-1.7	22,479,772	22,237,668	-1.1
Male	51.2	50.9	-0.6	51.6	51.5	-0.2
Female	48.8	49.1	0.6	48.4	48.5	0.2
Entered 2000 or later	27.8	28.5	2.5	34.7	35.7	2.9
Entered 1990 to 1999	26.5	25.9	-2.3	27.2	26.7	-1.8
Entered before 1990	45.7	45.6	-0.2	38.1	37.6	-1.3
World Region of Birth, Foreign						
Foreign-born population, excluding population born at sea	10,150,369	10,195,057	0.4	39,955,673	40,377,757	1.1
Europe	6.6	6.5	-1.5	12.1	12.1	-
Asia	35.9	36.6	1.9	28.2	28.6	1.4
Africa	1.6	1.6	0.0	4	4.1	2.5
Oceania	0.7	0.8	14.3	0.5	0.5	-
Latin America	54.0	53.4	-1.1	53.1	52.6	-0.9
North America	1.3	1.2	-7.7	2	2.0	-
Language Spoken at Home and Ability to Speak English						
Population 5 years and over	34,820,465	35,158,257	1.0	289,215,746	291,524,091	0.8
English only	56.3	56.2	-0.2	79.4	79.2	-0.3
Language other than English	43.7	43.8	0.2	20.6	20.8	1.0
Speaks English less than "very well"	19.8	19.4	-2.0	8.7	8.7	-

- = Zero or rounds to zero.

Table CA-5. Median Income and Poverty Status, 2011

(Number, percent, except as noted.)

Characteristic	State		U.S.	
	Number	Percent	Number	Percent
Median Income				
Households (dollars)	57,287	X	50,502	X
Families (dollars)	65,476	X	61,455	X
Below Poverty Level (All People)	6,118,803	16.6	48,452,035	15.9
Sex				
Male	2,818,467	15.4	21,825,281	14.7
Female	3,300,336	17.7	26,626,754	17.2
Age				
Under 18 years	2,084,522	22.8	16,386,500	22.5
Related children under 18 years	2,044,902	22.5	16,087,074	22.2
18 to 64 years	3,601,969	15.3	28,335,079	14.8
65 years and over	432,312	10.0	3,730,456	9.3

X = Not applicable.

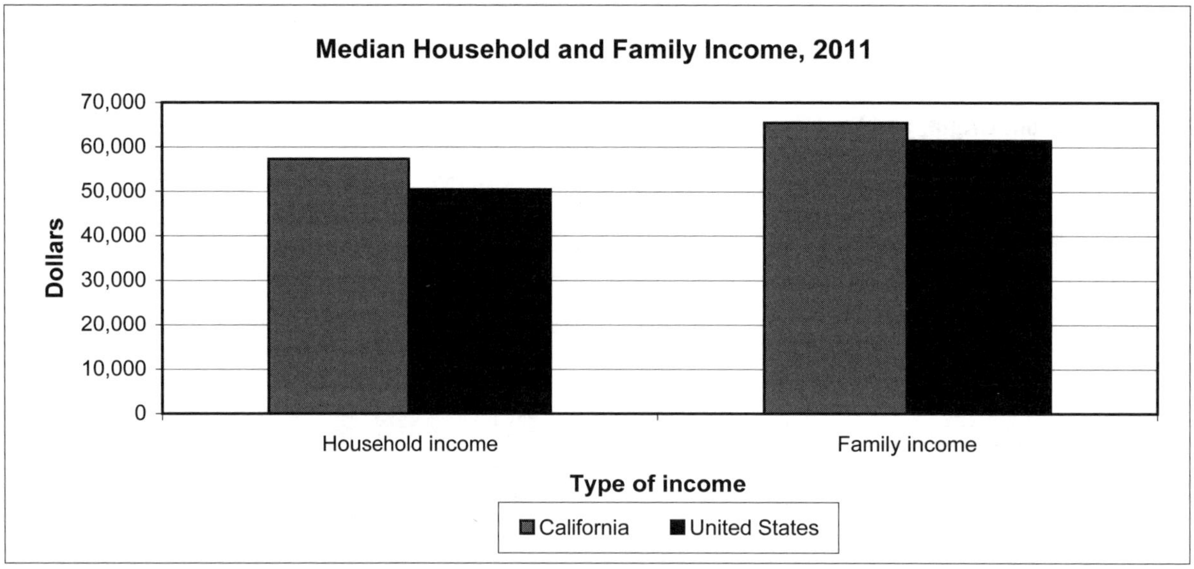

Table CA-6. Health Insurance Coverage Status for the Civilian Noninstitutionalized Population and Children Under 18 Years of Age

(Numbers in thousands, percent.)

Item	2004	2005	2006	2007	2008	2009	2010	2011
Civilian Noninstitutionalized Population	35,854	35,940	36,208	36,295	36,161	36,377	36,816	37,162
Covered by Private or Public Insurance								
Number	29,413	29,182	29,417	29,682	29,730	29,818	29,990	30,436
Percent	82.0	81.2	81.2	81.8	82.2	82.0	81.5	81.9
Not Covered								
Number	6,441	6,757	6,791	6,613	6,431	6,559	6,835	6,726
Percent	18.0	18.8	18.8	18.2	17.8	18.0	18.5	18.1
Percent in the U.S. not covered	14.9	15.3	15.8	15.3	15.1	15.1	15.5	15.1
Children Under 18 Years of Age	9,590	9,738	9,571	9,423	9,348	9,423	9,289	9,252
Covered by Private or Public Insurance								
Number	8,462	8,429	8,346	8,410	8,337	8,532	8,456	8,507
Percent	88.2	86.6	87.2	89.3	89.2	90.5	91.0	92.0
Not Covered								
Number	1,128	1,309	1,225	1,013	1,011	891	833	745
Percent	11.8	13.4	12.8	10.7	10.8	9.5	9.0	8.0
Percent in the U.S. not covered	10.5	10.9	11.7	11.0	9.7	8.6	8.0	7.5

Table CA-7. Employment Status by Demographic Group, Preliminary 2012

(Numbers in thousands, percent.)

Characteristic	Civilian noninstitutional population	Civilian labor force		Employed		Unemployed	
		Number	Percent of population	Number	Percent of population	Number	Percent of population
Total	29,297	18,454	63.0	16,529	56.4	1,925	10.4
Sex							
Male	14,316	10,110	70.6	9,056	63.3	1,054	10.4
Female	14,980	8,344	55.7	7,473	49.9	871	10.4
Race, Sex, and Hispanic Origin							
White	21,903	13,888	63.4	12,484	57.0	1,404	10.1
Male	10,860	7,788	71.7	7,005	64.5	783	10.1
Female	11,043	6,100	55.2	5,479	49.6	621	10.2
Black or African American	1,858	1,057	56.9	875	47.1	183	17.3
Male	873	512	58.7	421	48.2	91	17.8
Female	985	545	55.3	454	46.0	92	16.8
Hispanic	10,338	6,796	65.7	5,936	57.4	861	12.7
Male	5,202	3,978	76.5	3,498	67.2	480	12.1
Female	5,136	2,818	54.9	2,438	47.5	380	13.5
Age							
16 to 19 years	2,219	593	26.7	388	17.5	205	34.6
20 to 24 years	2,937	1,957	66.6	1,646	56.0	311	15.9
25 to 34 years	5,300	4,224	79.7	3,795	71.6	429	10.1
35 to 44 years	4,933	4,001	81.1	3,663	74.3	338	8.5
45 to 54 years	5,163	4,080	79.0	3,743	72.5	337	8.3
55 to 64 years	4,271	2,754	64.5	2,527	59.2	227	8.2
65 years and over	4,474	844	18.9	765	17.1	78	9.3

NOTE: Data in Table 7 are from the Current Population Survey (CPS) and do not match the estimates in Table 8. See notes and definitions for further information.

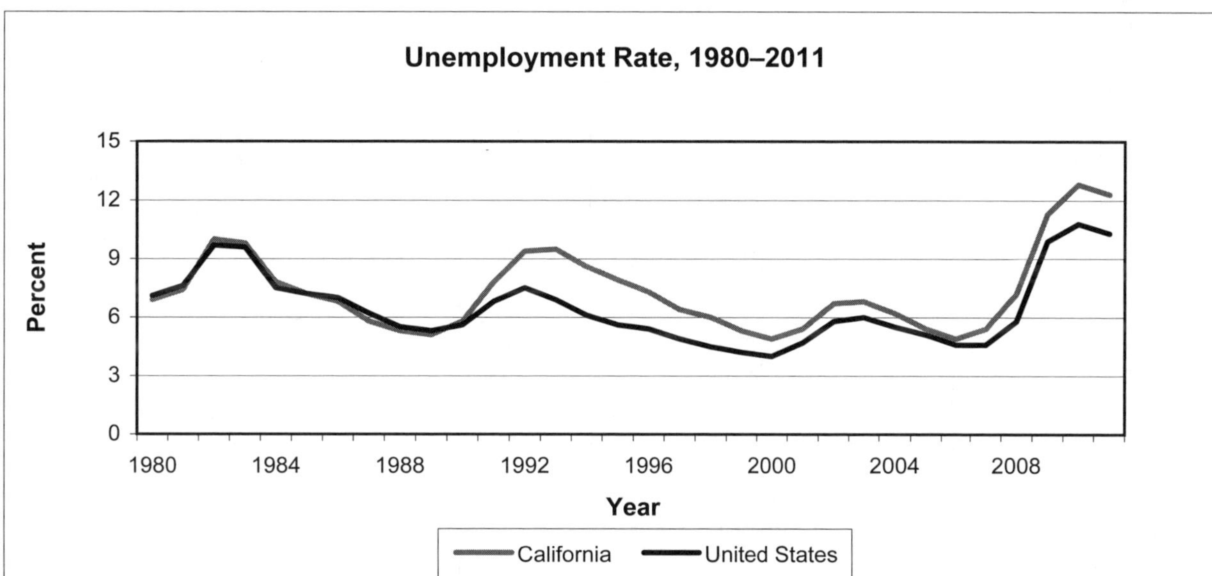

Table CA-8. Employment Status of the Civilian Noninstitutional Population Age 16 Years and Over

(Number, percent.)

Year	Civilian labor force	Civilian participation rate	Employed	Unemployed	Unemployment rate
2005	17,629,159	65.5	16,671,914	957,245	5.4
2006	17,821,106	65.4	16,948,374	872,732	4.9
2007	18,077,963	65.6	17,108,702	969,261	5.4
2008	18,391,144	65.9	17,059,574	1,333,270	7.2
2009	18,541,318	64.8	16,454,578	2,086,740	11.3
2010	18,625,515	63.9	16,243,172	2,382,343	12.8
2011	18,737,749	63.5	16,426,694	2,311,055	12.3

Table CA-9. Employment and Average Wages by Industry

(Estimates before 2007 are based on the 2002 *North American Industry Classification System* [NAICS]. Estimates from 2007 onward are based on the 2007 NAICS.)

Industry	2005	2006	2007	2008	2009	2010	2011
				Number of jobs			
Wage and Salary Employment by Industry	15,900,117	16,151,887	16,289,089	16,110,889	15,233,396	15,047,583	15,204,435
Farm Wage and Salary Employment	178,410	158,978	167,671	156,022	161,058	169,614	160,906
Nonfarm Wage and Salary Employment	15,721,707	15,992,909	16,121,418	15,954,867	15,072,338	14,877,969	15,043,529
Private wage and salary employment	13,071,716	13,320,945	13,405,324	13,198,099	12,342,534	12,195,802	12,422,179
Forestry, fishing, and related activities	178,255	180,151	186,995	191,649	181,927	192,710	201,708
Mining	22,096	23,893	24,940	26,281	23,952	24,427	26,341
Utilities	56,039	56,455	58,048	58,774	60,033	57,126	58,304
Construction	940,868	967,867	925,124	818,256	650,724	585,150	590,831
Manufacturing	1,506,024	1,499,742	1,460,834	1,422,847	1,284,607	1,241,475	1,246,809
Durable goods manufacturing	963,312	956,912	925,445	898,963	800,113	770,103	777,998
Nondurable goods manufacturing	542,712	542,830	535,389	523,884	484,494	471,372	468,811
Wholesale trade	680,007	705,757	724,378	714,862	655,084	650,177	663,909
Retail trade	1,679,446	1,703,109	1,713,694	1,666,081	1,546,001	1,538,490	1,559,965
Transportation and warehousing	436,745	441,692	452,924	453,409	420,712	414,620	420,114
Information	474,847	473,372	475,159	464,230	435,783	427,352	429,627
Finance and insurance	658,841	663,772	636,275	591,900	558,634	536,180	544,545
Real estate and rental and leasing	294,639	299,623	291,708	286,684	267,267	261,542	258,009
Professional, scientific, and technical services	977,636	1,036,357	1,078,632	1,107,746	1,040,459	1,037,800	1,074,788
Management of companies and enterprises	223,904	212,876	208,041	206,764	198,742	192,985	199,149
Administrative and waste services	973,072	1,002,354	1,004,860	959,603	854,098	868,144	890,638
Educational services	300,832	308,082	312,605	326,221	335,608	338,629	349,487
Health care and social assistance	1,327,422	1,357,083	1,402,382	1,443,788	1,470,049	1,502,221	1,527,790
Arts, entertainment, and recreation	243,856	247,435	255,496	258,853	249,738	250,178	255,015
Accommodation and food services	1,245,339	1,286,407	1,320,487	1,329,333	1,270,556	1,272,004	1,301,337
Other services, except public administration	851,848	854,918	872,742	870,818	838,560	804,592	823,813
Government and government enterprises	2,649,991	2,671,964	2,716,094	2,756,768	2,729,804	2,682,167	2,621,350
				Dollars			
Average Wages and Salaries by Industry	46,762	49,089	51,411	52,474	52,641	54,355	56,097
Average Farm Wages and Salaries	27,775	31,366	26,134	32,196	33,633	31,788	29,768
Average Nonfarm Wages and Salaries	46,978	49,265	51,674	52,672	52,844	54,613	56,379
Average private wages and salaries	46,794	49,096	51,441	52,262	52,307	54,298	56,170
Forestry, fishing, and related activities	19,370	20,393	21,658	22,278	22,579	23,173	24,053
Mining	89,309	97,892	107,441	118,023	114,505	130,923	129,702
Utilities	87,425	94,046	95,311	96,972	100,935	103,261	108,002
Construction	46,188	48,877	52,267	55,127	55,846	55,814	57,238
Manufacturing	60,779	64,254	67,413	67,279	69,765	74,165	76,527
Durable goods manufacturing	67,941	73,071	76,717	75,953	77,579	85,553	88,777
Nondurable goods manufacturing	48,065	48,710	51,330	52,396	56,860	55,560	56,199
Wholesale trade	57,605	60,622	63,563	64,144	63,855	65,842	68,418
Retail trade	30,151	30,816	31,821	31,597	31,114	31,923	32,639
Transportation and warehousing	43,533	45,705	46,976	47,251	47,191	48,557	49,951
Information	85,395	88,960	92,317	92,922	92,646	101,563	107,712
Finance and insurance	85,513	88,731	93,779	93,323	89,206	93,938	97,258
Real estate and rental and leasing	45,803	49,177	50,812	50,237	48,526	49,852	52,639
Professional, scientific, and technical services	74,397	78,515	83,278	86,900	87,010	91,051	94,848
Management of companies and enterprises	79,609	86,244	93,262	92,037	90,436	97,434	103,817
Administrative and waste services	31,312	32,955	35,207	36,602	36,916	38,007	39,229
Educational services	33,172	35,026	36,592	37,941	39,081	41,151	42,187
Health care and social assistance	44,510	46,860	48,858	50,943	52,548	53,445	54,684
Arts, entertainment, and recreation	47,591	50,791	52,174	52,827	52,078	53,203	55,439
Accommodation and food services	19,072	19,722	21,333	21,205	20,815	21,455	22,154
Other services, except public administration	25,486	26,588	27,747	28,655	28,515	29,752	30,353
Government and government enterprises	47,883	50,107	52,826	54,632	55,274	56,041	57,366

Table CA-10. Employment Characteristics by Family Type

(Number, percent.)

Family type and labor force status	2009 Total	2009 Families with own children under 18 years	2010 Total	2010 Families with own children under 18 years	2011 Total	2011 Families with own children under 18 years
All families	8,366,253	4,079,715	8,507,856	4,103,443	8,518,518	4,064,364
Family type and labor force status						
Married-couple families	6,041,210	2,875,001	6,082,566	2,858,983	6,059,185	2,793,349
Both husband and wife in labor force	53.5	62.7	52.7	61.7	52.2	61.5
Husband in labor force, wife not in labor force	25.1	31.9	25.4	32.5	25.3	32.7
Wife in labor force, husband not in labor force	6.9	3.5	7.1	3.9	7.3	3.7
Both husband and wife not in labor force	14.5	1.9	14.8	1.9	15.3	2.0
Other families	2,325,043	1,204,714	2,425,290	1,244,460	2,459,333	1,271,015
Female householder, no husband present	68.5	71.7	69.6	72.9	69.6	72.2
In labor force	49.1	57.6	49.1	57.7	49.4	58.2
Not in labor force	19.4	14.1	20.5	15.2	20.2	14.0
Male householder, no wife present	31.5	28.3	30.4	27.1	30.4	27.8
In labor force	26.3	26.1	24.8	24.6	24.9	25.6
Not in labor force	5.1	2.2	5.6	2.5	5.6	2.2

Table CA-11. School Enrollment and Educational Attainment, 2011

(Number, percent.)

Item	State	U.S.
Enrollment		
Total population 3 years and over, enrolled in school	10,584,220	83,131,910
Enrolled in nursery school or preschool (percent)	5.6	6.0
Enrolled in kindergarten (percent)	4.8	5.1
Enrolled in elementary school, grades 1-8 (percent)	38.4	39.5
Enrolled in high school, grades 9-12 (percent)	21.3	20.7
Enrolled in college or graduate school (percent)	29.9	28.7
Attainment		
Total population 25 years and over	24,443,872	206,471,670
Less than ninth grade (percent)	10.3	6.0
9th to 12th grade, no diploma (percent)	8.6	8.1
High school graduate, including equivalency (percent)	21.1	28.4
Some college, no degree (percent)	22.1	21.2
Associate's degree (percent)	7.7	7.8
Bachelor's degree (percent)	19.2	17.9
Graduate or professional degree (percent)	11.1	10.6
High school graduate or higher (percent)	81.1	85.9
Bachelor's degree or higher (percent)	30.3	28.5

Table CA-12. Educational Indicators

(Number, percent; data derived from National Center of Education Statistics.)

Item	State	U.S.
Public Schools, 2009–2010 (except where noted)		
Number of school districts	958	13,629
Number of schools	10,068	99,834
Number of students (in thousands)	6,263	49,373
Student-teacher ratio	20.0	15.4
Expenditures per student (dollars)	10,933	10,591
Averaged freshman graduation rate, 2008–2009	71.0	75.5[1]
Dropout rate, 2008–2009	5.0	4.1
Students eligible for free or reduced-price lunch (percent)	54.1	48.0
English language learners, 2010–2011 (percent)	28.9[2]	9.8[1]
Students with IEP (percent)	10.8	13.1
Private Schools, 2009–2010 (except where noted)		
Number of schools	3,644	33,366
Number of students (in thousands)	540	4,700
High school graduates, 2008–2009	35,256	308,813
Student-teacher ratio	11.8	10.7

[1] U.S. total includes estimates for nonreporting states.
[2] Imputation for survey nonresponse. State-level imputations were based on the percentages reported by the state for other years applied to the enrollment for the given year

Table CA-13. Reported Voting and Registration of the Voting-Age Population, November 2012

(Numbers in thousands, percent.)

Item	Total population	Total citizen population	Registered			Voted		
			Total registered	Percent registered (total population)	Percent registered (total citizen population)	Total voted	Percent voted (total population)	Percent voted (total citizen population)
U.S. Total	235,248	215,081	153,157	65.1	71.2	132,948	56.5	61.8
State Total	28,357	23,419	15,356	54.2	65.6	13,462	47.5	57.5
Sex								
Male	13,887	11,374	7,245	52.2	63.7	6,326	45.6	55.6
Female	14,470	12,044	8,111	56.1	67.3	7,137	49.3	59.3
Race								
White alone	21,330	17,692	11,785	55.2	66.6	10,391	48.7	58.7
White, non-Hispanic alone	12,317	11,866	8,544	69.4	72.0	7,628	61.9	64.3
Black alone	1,810	1,740	1,192	65.8	68.5	1,063	58.7	61.1
Asian alone	3,915	2,839	1,645	42.0	57.9	1,380	35.2	48.6
Hispanic (of any race)	9,935	6,510	3,684	37.1	56.6	3,157	31.8	48.5
Age								
18 to 24 years	3,962	3,479	1,787	45.1	51.4	1,447	36.5	41.6
25 to 44 years	10,386	7,828	5,026	48.4	64.2	4,188	40.3	53.5
45 to 64 years	9,356	7,827	5,459	58.3	69.7	4,926	52.6	62.9
65 to 74 years	2,591	2,358	1,696	65.5	71.9	1,612	62.2	68.3
75 years and over	2,062	1,926	1,388	67.3	72.1	1,290	62.6	67.0

Table CA-14. Crime

(Number, rate per 100,000. Data are derived from the FBI Uniform Crime Reports.)

Item	State			U.S.		
	2010	2011	Percent change	2010	2011	Percent change
TOTAL POPULATION	37,338,198	37,691,912	0.9	309,330,219	311,591,917	0.7
VIOLENT CRIME						
Number	164,133	154,944	-5.6	1,251,248	1,203,564	-3.8
Rate	439.6	411.1	-6.5	404.5	386.3	-4.5
Murder and Nonnegligent Manslaughter						
Number	1,809	1,792	-0.9	14,722	14,612	-0.7
Rate	4.8	4.8	0.0	4.8	4.7	-2.1
Forcible Rape						
Number	8,331	7,663	-8.0	85,593	83,425	-2.5
Rate	22.3	20.3	-9.0	27.7	26.8	-3.2
Robbery						
Number	58,116	54,292	-6.6	369,089	354,396	-4.0
Rate	155.6	144.0	-7.5	119.3	113.7	-4.7
Aggravated Assault						
Number	95,877	91,197	-4.9	781,844	751,131	-3.9
Rate	256.8	242.0	-5.8	252.8	241.1	-4.6
PROPERTY CRIME						
Number	981,939	973,901	-0.8	9,112,625	9,063,173	-0.5
Rate	2,629.9	2,583.8	-1.8	2,945.9	2,908.7	-1.3
Burglary						
Number	228,857	230,090	0.5	2,168,459	2,188,005	0.9
Rate	612.9	610.4	-0.4	701.0	702.2	0.2
Larceny-Theft						
Number	600,558	596,963	-0.6	6,204,601	6,159,795	-0.7
Rate	1,608.4	1,583.8	-1.5	2,005.8	1,976.9	-1.4
Motor Vehicle Theft						
Number	152,524	146,848	-3.7	739,565	715,373	-3.3
Rate	408.5	389.6	-4.6	239.1	229.6	-4.0

Table CA-15. State Government Finances, 2011

(Dollar amounts in thousands, percent distribution.)

Item	Dollars	Percent distribution
Total Revenue	334,233,317	100.0
General revenue	211,358,143	63.2
Intergovernmental revenue	68,430,680	20.5
Taxes	116,695,284	34.9
General sales	30,996,372	9.3
Selective sales	14,151,285	4.2
License taxes	8,186,412	2.4
Individual income tax	50,508,441	15.1
Corporate income tax	9,613,594	2.9
Other taxes	3,239,180	1.0
Current charges	16,701,739	5.0
Miscellaneous general revenue	9,530,440	2.9
Utility revenue	2,496,154	0.7
Liquor stores revenue	0	0.0
Insurance trust revenue [1]	120,379,020	36.0
Total Expenditure	280,212,581	100.0
Intergovernmental expenditure	91,501,553	32.7
Direct expenditure	188,711,028	67.3
Current operation	117,525,130	41.9
Capital outlay	7,881,389	2.8
Insurance benefits and repayments	52,116,136	18.6
Assistance and subsidies	3,537,207	1.3
Interest on debt	7,651,166	2.7
Exhibit: Salaries and wages	31,679,660	11.3
Total Expenditure	280,212,581	100.0
General expenditure	224,992,157	80.3
Intergovernmental expenditure	91,501,553	32.7
Direct expenditure	133,490,604	47.6
General expenditure, by function:		
Education	74,992,505	26.8
Public welfare	77,464,948	27.6
Hospitals	11,297,876	4.0
Health	7,352,206	2.6
Highways	10,623,812	3.8
Police protection	1,646,807	0.6
Correction	6,589,627	2.4
Natural resources	3,843,151	1.4
Parks and recreation	538,898	0.2
Governmental administration	8,496,967	3.0
Interest on general debt	7,302,166	2.6
Other and unallocable	14,843,194	5.3
Utility expenditure	3,104,288	1.1
Liquor stores expenditure	0	0.0
Insurance trust expenditure	52,116,136	18.6
Debt at End of Fiscal Year	149,670,954	X
Cash and Security Holdings	535,101,067	X

X = Not applicable.

[1] Within insurance trust revenue, net earnings of state retirement systems is a calculated statistic (the item code in the data file is X08), and thus can be positive or negative. Net earnings is the sum of earnings on investments plus gains on investments minus losses on investments. The change made in 2002 for asset valuation from book to market value in accordance with Statement 34 of the Governmental Accounting Standards Board is reflected in the calculated statistics.

Table CA-16. State Government Tax Collections, 2012

(Dollars in thousands, percent.)

Item	Dollars	Percent distribution
Total Taxes	112,372,263	100.0
Property taxes	2,079,878	1.9
Sales and gross receipts	38,623,797	34.4
General sales and gross receipts	28,536,238	25.4
Selective sales and gross receipts	10,087,559	9.0
Alcoholic beverages	346,000	0.3
Amusements	0	0.0
Insurance premiums	2,416,073	2.2
Motor fuels	5,544,530	4.9
Pari-mutuels	15,838	-
Public utilities	766,361	0.7
Tobacco products	895,677	0.8
Other selective sales	103,080	0.1
Licenses	8,658,041	7.7
Alcoholic beverages	53,169	-
Amusements	15,850	-
Corporations in general	53,003	-
Hunting and fishing	98,840	0.1
Motor vehicle	3,529,137	3.1
Motor vehicle operators	306,882	0.3
Public utilities	289,461	0.3
Occupation and business, NEC	4,293,352	3.8
Other licenses	18,347	-
Income taxes	62,973,435	56.0
Individual income	55,024,435	49.0
Corporation net income	7,949,000	7.1
Other taxes	37,112	-
Death and gift	0	0.0
Documentary and stock transfer	0	0.0
Severance	37,112	-
Taxes, NEC	0	0.0

- = Rounds to zero.

Leading Exports, 2012

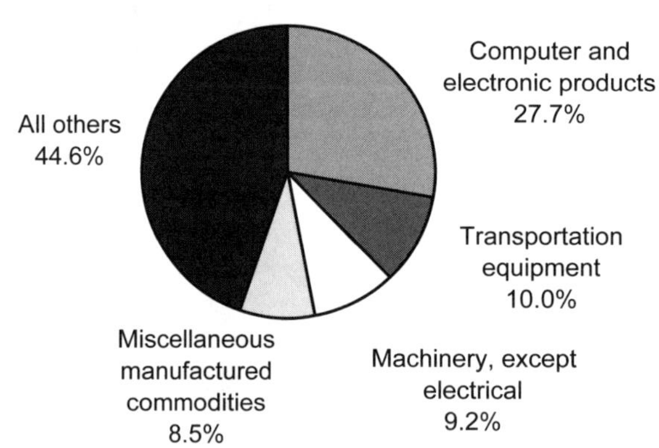

COLORADO

Facts and Figures

Location: Western United States; bordered on the N by Wyoming and Nebraska, on the E by Nebraska and Kansas, on the S by Oklahoma and New Mexico, and on the W by Utah; Colorado is one of the Four Corner states—at its SW corner it touches Arizona, New Mexico, and Utah

Area: 104,094 sq. mi. (269,601 sq. km.); rank—8th

Population: 5,187,582 (2012 est.); rank—22nd

Principal Cities: capital—Denver; largest—Denver

Statehood: August 1, 1876; 38th state

U.S. Congress: 2 senators, 7 representatives

State Motto: *Nil sine numine* ("Nothing without providence")

State Songs: "Where the Columbines Grow"; "Rocky Mountain High"

State Nicknames: The Centennial State; Colorful Colorado

Abbreviations: CO; Colo.

State Symbols: flower—Rocky Mountain columbine; tree—Colorado blue spruce; bird—lark bunting

At a Glance

- With an increase in population of 16.8 percent, Colorado ranked 9th among the states in growth from 2000 to 2009.
- An estimated 37,400 marriages took place in Colorado in 2009, compared to 21,200 divorces.
- In 2011, 15.1 percent of Coloradans did not have health insurance, the same percentage as that for the total U.S. population.
- In the 2012 election, 70.4 percent of Colorado's eligible voters voted, compared to 61.8 percent of eligible voters nationwide.
- In 2007, Colorado exported $1.1 billion worth of agricultural products, 1.4 percent of the U.S. total.

Table CO-1. Population by Age, Sex, Race, and Hispanic Origin

(Number, percent, except where noted.)

Sex, age, race, and Hispanic origin	2000	2010	2012[1]	Average annual percent change, 2010–2012
Total Population	4,301,261	5,029,196	5,187,582	1.0
Percent of total U.S. population	1.5	1.6	1.7	X
Sex				
Male	2,165,983	2,520,662	2,603,705	1.1
Female	2,135,278	2,508,534	2,583,877	1.0
Age				
Under 5 years	297,505	343,960	337,568	-0.6
5 to 19 years	927,163	1,020,732	1,035,207	0.5
20 to 64 years	2,660,520	3,114,879	3,201,566	0.9
65 years and over	416,073	549,625	613,241	3.5
Median age (years)	34.3	36.1	36.3	0.2
Race and Hispanic Origin				
One race				
White	3,560,005	4,450,623	4,572,022	0.9
Black	165,063	214,919	225,390	1.5
American Indian and Alaska Native	44,241	78,144	81,688	1.4
Asian	95,213	144,819	155,031	2.2
Native Hawaiian or Other Pacific Islander	4,621	8,420	9,231	2.9
Two or more races	122,187	132,271	144,220	2.8
Hispanic (of any race)	735,601	1,078,225	1,131,582	1.6

X = Not applicable.
[1] Population figures for 2012 are July 1 estimates. The 2010 estimates are taken from the 2010 Census.

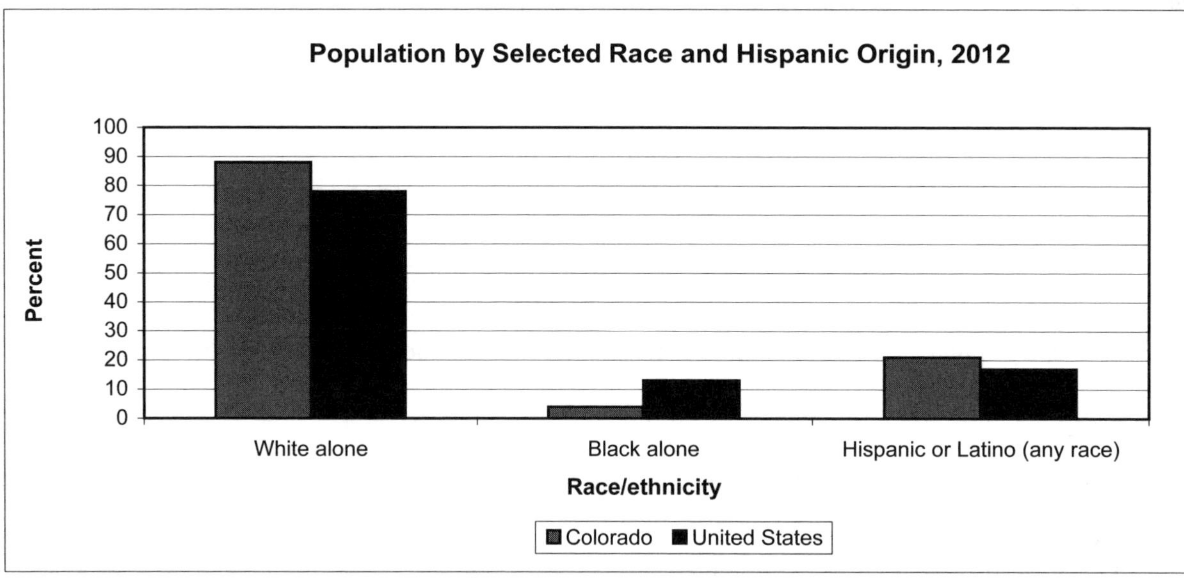

Table CO-2. Marital Status

(Number, percent distribution.)

Sex, age, race, and Hispanic origin	2000	2010	2011
Males, 15 Years and Over	1,694,635	2,004,303	2,040,728
Never married	30.5	34.4	34.5
Now married, except separated	56.6	51.7	52.0
Separated	1.4	1.6	1.5
Widowed	1.9	2.0	2.2
Divorced	9.6	10.3	9.9
Females, 15 Years and Over	1,690,734	2,017,425	2,046,428
Never married	23.4	26.9	27.3
Now married, except separated	54.7	50.8	49.8
Separated	1.8	2.0	1.9
Widowed	7.6	7.0	7.1
Divorced	12.5	13.3	13.9

Table CO-3. Households and Housing Characteristics

(Number, percent, dollars.)

Item	2000	2010	2011	Average annual percent change, 2000–2011
Total Households	1,658,238	1,960,585	1,975,388	1.6
Family households	1,084,461	1,258,885	1,256,471	1.3
Married-couple family	858,671	959,624	970,556	1.1
Other family	225,790	299,261	285,915	2.2
Male householder, no wife present	66,811	90,518	87,794	2.6
Female householder, no husband present	158,979	208,743	198,121	2.1
Nonfamily households	573,777	701,700	718,917	2.1
Householder living alone	435,778	555,080	568,963	2.5
Householder not living alone	137,999	146,620	149,954	0.7
Housing Characteristics				
Total housing units	1,808,037	2,214,262	2,224,661	1.9
Occupied housing units	1,658,238	1,960,585	1,975,388	1.6
Owner occupied	1,116,173	1,292,792	1,271,804	1.2
Renter occupied	542,101	667,793	703,584	2.5
Average size	2.53	2.52	2.53	-
Financial Characteristics				
Median gross rent of renter-occupied housing	671	863	900	2.8
Median monthly owner costs for housing units with a mortgage	1,197	1,590	1,560	2.5
Median value of owner-occupied housing units	166,600	236,600	233,700	3.4

Table CO-4. Migration, Origin, and Language

(Number, percent.)

Characteristic	State			U.S.		
	2010	2011	Percent change	2010	2011	Percent change
Residence 1 Year Ago						
Population 1 year and over	4,988,190	5,048,443	1.2	305,628,607	307,900,319	0.7
Same house	81.0	80.2	-1.0	84.6	84.8	0.2
Different house in the U.S.	18.3	19.1	4.4	14.8	14.6	-1.4
Same county	9.8	9.9	1.0	9.4	9.2	-2.1
Different county	8.5	9.2	8.2	5.4	5.4	-
Same state	4.7	5.2	10.6	3.2	3.1	-3.1
Different state	3.7	4.0	8.1	2.2	2.3	4.5
Abroad	0.7	0.7	-	0.6	0.6	-
Place of Birth						
Native born	4,551,966	4,622,036	1.5	269,393,835	271,214,059	0.7
Male	50.1	50.2	0.2	49.2	49.2	-
Female	49.9	49.8	-0.2	50.8	50.8	-
Foreign born	497,105	494,760	-0.5	39,955,854	40,377,860	1.1
Male	50.0	50.0	-	49.1	48.9	-0.4
Female	50.0	50.0	-	50.9	51.1	0.4
Foreign born; naturalized U.S. citizen	177,346	177,752	0.2	17,476,082	18,140,192	3.8
Male	46.0	45.4	-1.3	45.8	45.8	-
Female	54.0	54.6	1.1	54.2	54.2	-
Foreign born; not a U.S. citizen	319,759	317,008	-0.9	22,479,772	22,237,668	-1.1
Male	52.3	52.6	0.6	51.6	51.5	-0.2
Female	47.7	47.4	-0.6	48.4	48.5	0.2
Entered 2000 or later	40.1	40.1	0.0	34.7	35.7	2.9
Entered 1990 to 1999	29.4	29.8	1.4	27.2	26.7	-1.8
Entered before 1990	30.4	30.0	-1.3	38.1	37.6	-1.3
World Region of Birth, Foreign						
Foreign-born population, excluding population born at sea	497,105	494,760	-0.5	39,955,673	40,377,757	1.1
Europe	13.8	13.7	-0.7	12.1	12.1	-
Asia	21.3	21.6	1.4	28.2	28.6	1.4
Africa	5.1	5.8	13.7	4	4.1	2.5
Oceania	0.7	0.7	-	0.5	0.5	-
Latin America	55.3	55.9	1.1	53.1	52.6	-0.9
North America	3.7	2.2	-40.5	2	2.0	-
Language Spoken at Home and Ability to Speak English						
Population 5 years and over	4,706,794	4,775,755	1.5	289,215,746	291,524,091	0.8
English only	82.9	83.3	0.5	79.4	79.2	-0.3
Language other than English	17.1	16.7	-2.3	20.6	20.8	1.0
Speaks English less than "very well"	7.0	6.4	-8.6	8.7	8.7	-

- = Zero or rounds to zero.

Table CO-5. Median Income and Poverty Status, 2011

(Number, percent, except as noted.)

Characteristic	State		U.S.	
	Number	Percent	Number	Percent
Median Income				
Households (dollars)	55,387	X	50,502	X
Families (dollars)	69,110	X	61,455	X
Below Poverty Level (All People)	674,195	13.5	48,452,035	15.9
Sex				
Male	318,670	12.8	21,825,281	14.7
Female	355,525	14.2	26,626,754	17.2
Age				
Under 18 years	217,049	17.9	16,386,500	22.5
Related children under 18 years	211,228	17.5	16,087,074	22.2
18 to 64 years	413,569	12.8	28,335,079	14.8
65 years and over	43,577	7.8	3,730,456	9.3

X = Not applicable.

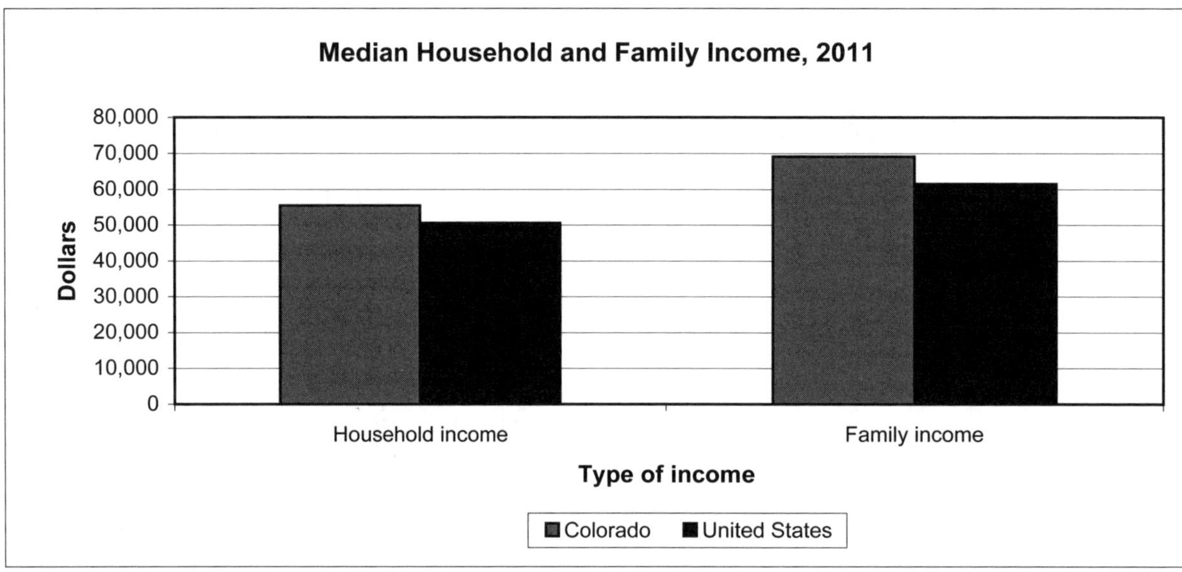

Table CO-6. Health Insurance Coverage Status for the Civilian Noninstitutionalized Population and Children Under 18 Years of Age

(Numbers in thousands, percent.)

Item	2004	2005	2006	2007	2008	2009	2010	2011
Civilian Noninstitutionalized Population	4,524	4,641	4,803	4,877	4,853	4,930	4,957	5,025
Covered by Private or Public Insurance								
Number	3,806	3,869	3,977	4,077	4,020	4,152	4,168	4,265
Percent	84.1	83.4	82.8	83.6	82.8	84.2	84.1	84.9
Not Covered								
Number	719	772	826	801	833	778	789	760
Percent	15.9	16.6	17.2	16.4	17.2	15.8	15.9	15.1
Percent in the U.S. not covered	14.9	15.3	15.8	15.3	15.1	15.1	15.5	15.1
Children Under 18 Years of Age	1,169	1,187	1,209	1,208	1,204	1,225	1,226	1,227
Covered by Private or Public Insurance								
Number	998	1,024	1,033	1,051	1,031	1,101	1,102	1,111
Percent	85.4	86.3	85.4	87.0	85.6	89.8	89.9	90.6
Not Covered								
Number	170	163	176	157	173	124	124	116
Percent	14.6	13.7	14.6	13.0	14.4	10.2	10.1	9.4
Percent in the U.S. not covered	10.5	10.9	11.7	11.0	9.7	8.6	8.0	7.5

Table CO-7. Employment Status by Demographic Group, Preliminary 2012

(Numbers in thousands, percent.)

Characteristic	Civilian noninstitutional population	Civilian labor force		Employed		Unemployed	
		Number	Percent of population	Number	Percent of population	Number	Percent of population
Total	3,975	2,725	68.6	2,505	63.0	220	8.1
Sex							
Male	1,959	1,474	75.2	1,353	69.1	121	8.2
Female	2,017	1,251	62.0	1,152	57.1	99	7.9
Race, Sex, and Hispanic Origin							
White	3,589	2,459	68.5	2,263	63.0	197	8.0
Male	1,774	1,332	75.1	1,222	68.9	109	8.2
Female	1,815	1,127	62.1	1,040	57.3	87	7.7
Black or African American	153	105	68.9	96	62.7	10	9.0
Male	76	58	76.4	54	70.6	4	7.6
Female	77	47	61.5	42	54.9	5	10.8
Hispanic	715	485	67.8	424	59.3	61	12.6
Male	370	277	74.9	244	65.9	33	12.0
Female	345	208	60.3	180	52.2	28	13.3
Age							
16 to 19 years	264	104	39.3	76	29.0	27	26.2
20 to 24 years	359	265	73.7	231	64.2	34	12.9
25 to 34 years	713	601	84.2	559	78.3	42	7.0
35 to 44 years	703	607	86.4	569	80.9	38	6.3
45 to 54 years	721	609	84.4	569	78.9	40	6.5
55 to 64 years	596	414	69.5	386	64.8	28	6.8
65 years and over	619	126	20.4	116	18.8	10	7.9

NOTE: Data in Table 7 are from the Current Population Survey (CPS) and do not match the estimates in Table 8. See notes and definitions for further information.

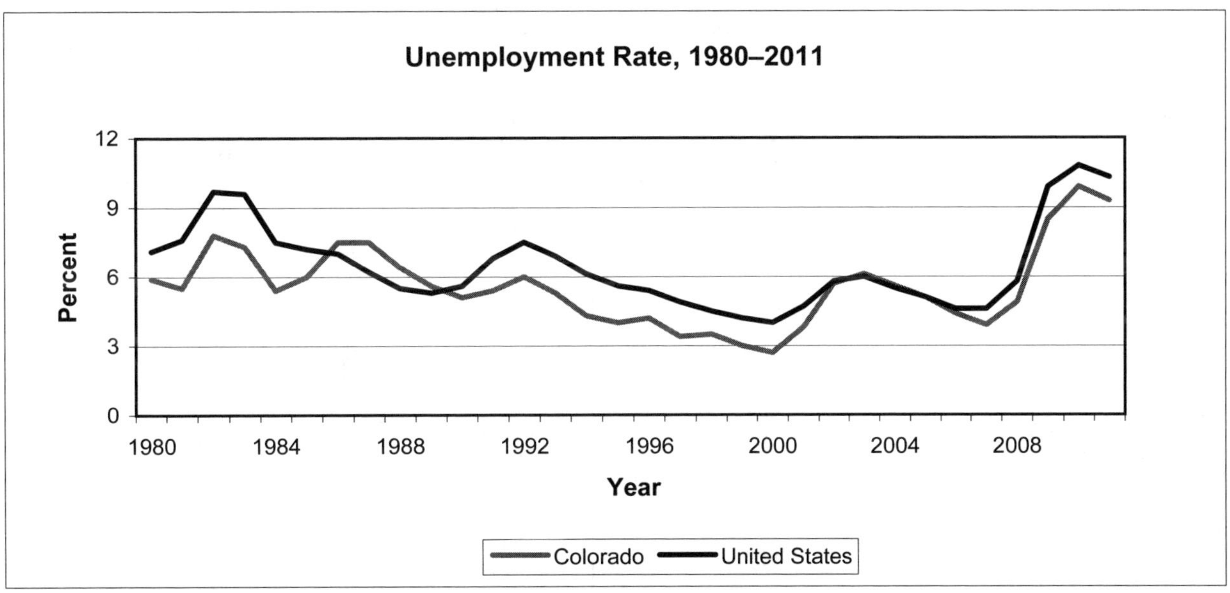

Table CO-8. Employment Status of the Civilian Noninstitutional Population Age 16 Years and Over

(Number, percent.)

Year	Civilian labor force	Civilian participation rate	Employed	Unemployed	Unemployment rate
2005	2,580,752	72.6	2,448,150	132,602	5.1
2006	2,642,744	72.8	2,526,986	115,758	4.4
2007	2,686,427	72.6	2,582,486	103,941	3.9
2008	2,730,447	72.3	2,596,309	134,138	4.9
2009	2,710,648	69.0	2,480,113	230,535	8.5
2010	2,714,224	68.6	2,446,674	267,550	9.9
2011	2,747,663	68.3	2,492,419	255,244	9.3

Table CO-9. Employment and Average Wages by Industry

(Estimates before 2007 are based on the 2002 *North American Industry Classification System* [NAICS]. Estimates from 2007 onward are based on the 2007 NAICS.)

Industry	2005	2006	2007	2008	2009	2010	2011
	Number of jobs						
Wage and Salary Employment by Industry	2,349,288	2,402,553	2,451,987	2,478,747	2,373,917	2,355,555	2,393,084
Farm Wage and Salary Employment	14,128	13,968	11,903	12,505	12,051	12,775	11,691
Nonfarm Wage and Salary Employment	2,335,160	2,388,585	2,440,084	2,466,242	2,361,866	2,342,780	2,381,393
Private wage and salary employment	1,922,425	1,971,771	2,016,672	2,028,998	1,914,438	1,888,408	1,926,691
Forestry, fishing, and related activities	4,642	4,775	4,727	4,967	5,035	5,304	5,598
Mining	16,874	20,594	24,918	28,423	23,956	24,096	27,633
Utilities	7,949	8,109	7,958	8,142	8,313	8,181	8,140
Construction	166,292	174,000	174,101	168,329	137,237	120,670	118,361
Manufacturing	150,882	149,870	146,827	144,043	129,909	125,705	129,345
Durable goods manufacturing	101,067	100,911	98,670	95,828	84,535	81,247	84,053
Nondurable goods manufacturing	49,815	48,959	48,157	48,215	45,374	44,458	45,292
Wholesale trade	94,141	97,023	100,175	100,941	94,114	91,575	92,873
Retail trade	248,949	251,636	257,093	256,017	242,207	240,644	243,733
Transportation and warehousing	65,450	66,063	68,054	67,863	63,291	61,351	62,042
Information	77,439	76,076	76,943	77,101	74,824	71,864	72,033
Finance and insurance	109,540	111,926	110,499	107,554	103,408	101,846	102,542
Real estate and rental and leasing	48,263	49,070	49,231	48,596	44,742	43,415	42,920
Professional, scientific, and technical services	157,788	164,765	173,024	178,999	172,348	170,403	174,799
Management of companies and enterprises	25,034	27,155	28,600	29,026	28,556	28,823	29,921
Administrative and waste services	136,545	143,183	150,667	148,263	133,816	135,539	139,134
Educational services	35,632	36,924	37,154	39,631	39,930	40,984	42,344
Health care and social assistance	201,017	206,748	215,012	224,710	230,712	237,152	244,151
Arts, entertainment, and recreation	44,347	44,503	45,387	46,337	45,357	45,435	46,757
Accommodation and food services	216,687	223,525	228,146	229,772	220,157	220,787	228,234
Other services, except public administration	114,954	115,826	118,156	120,284	116,526	114,634	116,131
Government and government enterprises	412,735	416,814	423,412	437,244	447,428	454,372	454,702
	Dollars						
Average Wages and Salaries by Industry	42,099	44,050	46,070	47,201	47,427	48,477	49,788
Average Farm Wages and Salaries	29,428	28,879	37,147	34,126	39,317	32,222	36,532
Average Nonfarm Wages and Salaries	42,175	44,139	46,113	47,267	47,469	48,566	49,853
Average private wages and salaries	42,370	44,506	46,608	47,647	47,684	48,872	50,279
Forestry, fishing, and related activities	19,389	19,963	21,913	22,560	23,827	24,186	25,041
Mining	83,582	84,452	87,626	97,885	91,239	100,062	106,045
Utilities	73,934	94,788	80,115	82,256	82,187	87,106	91,672
Construction	42,146	43,823	46,201	48,488	48,650	48,775	49,866
Manufacturing	55,096	56,417	57,597	59,136	59,687	61,692	63,392
Durable goods manufacturing	59,486	61,104	62,688	63,279	64,868	67,783	69,996
Nondurable goods manufacturing	46,189	46,756	47,166	50,903	50,033	50,561	51,137
Wholesale trade	59,296	62,968	67,347	68,909	66,832	69,618	73,015
Retail trade	26,264	26,805	27,515	27,695	27,633	27,840	28,170
Transportation and warehousing	41,717	44,801	44,804	45,394	45,346	46,404	47,767
Information	69,924	77,627	78,618	78,235	79,114	83,528	85,778
Finance and insurance	63,868	66,952	70,679	72,428	70,751	73,396	76,280
Real estate and rental and leasing	39,596	42,013	44,200	42,676	41,997	43,100	45,260
Professional, scientific, and technical services	68,342	72,081	76,618	78,227	78,876	81,054	82,808
Management of companies and enterprises	101,948	106,094	116,961	112,467	119,266	127,683	133,814
Administrative and waste services	30,850	31,638	32,989	34,214	34,764	35,342	36,183
Educational services	28,759	30,109	31,819	32,160	32,943	34,003	34,312
Health care and social assistance	39,773	41,085	42,756	44,061	45,218	45,370	46,052
Arts, entertainment, and recreation	30,428	34,280	35,861	34,056	33,864	33,778	34,527
Accommodation and food services	17,210	17,756	19,546	19,501	19,261	19,882	20,598
Other services, except public administration	28,048	29,429	30,718	31,887	31,959	32,860	33,368
Government and government enterprises	41,269	42,404	43,756	45,504	46,549	47,295	48,050

Table CO-10. Employment Characteristics by Family Type

(Number, percent.)

Family type and labor force status	2009		2010		2011	
	Total	Families with own children under 18 years	Total	Families with own children under 18 years	Total	Families with own children under 18 years
All families	1,233,139	576,089	1,258,885	587,254	1,256,471	587,062
Family type and labor force status						
Married-couple families	969,768	420,576	959,624	411,308	970,556	420,122
Both husband and wife in labor force	57.5	65.1	57.5	66.5	56.7	66.0
Husband in labor force, wife not in labor force	22.5	29.6	22.1	28.9	22.5	29.2
Wife in labor force, husband not in labor force	6.4	3.8	6.4	3.1	6.8	3.4
Both husband and wife not in labor force	13.6	1.5	14.0	1.5	14.0	1.4
Other families	263,371	155,513	299,261	175,946	285,915	166,940
Female householder, no husband present	71.1	75.3	69.8	72.1	69.3	69.6
In labor force	55.4	63.5	53.5	60.8	52.5	58.6
Not in labor force	15.7	11.7	16.2	11.2	16.8	11.0
Male householder, no wife present	28.9	24.7	30.2	27.9	30.7	30.4
In labor force	24.5	23.2	26.4	25.9	26.1	27.9
Not in labor force	4.4	1.5	3.9	2.0	4.6	2.4

Table CO-11. School Enrollment and Educational Attainment, 2011

(Number, percent.)

Item	State	U.S.
Enrollment		
Total population 3 years and over, enrolled in school	1,377,803	83,131,910
Enrolled in nursery school or preschool (percent)	6.5	6.0
Enrolled in kindergarten (percent)	4.9	5.1
Enrolled in elementary school, grades 1-8 (percent)	39.6	39.5
Enrolled in high school, grades 9-12 (percent)	19.8	20.7
Enrolled in college or graduate school (percent)	29.2	28.7
Attainment		
Total population 25 years and over	3,387,310	206,471,670
Less than ninth grade (percent)	4.0	6.0
9th to 12th grade, no diploma (percent)	5.8	8.1
High school graduate, including equivalency (percent)	22.4	28.4
Some college, no degree (percent)	22.8	21.2
Associate's degree (percent)	8.3	7.8
Bachelor's degree (percent)	23.3	17.9
Graduate or professional degree (percent)	13.4	10.6
High school graduate or higher (percent)	90.2	85.9
Bachelor's degree or higher (percent)	36.7	28.5

Table CO-12. Educational Indicators

(Number, percent; data derived from National Center of Education Statistics.)

Item	State	U.S.
Public Schools, 2009–2010 (except where noted)		
Number of school districts	178	13,629
Number of schools	1,793	99,834
Number of students (in thousands)	832	49,373
Student-teacher ratio	17.0	15.4
Expenditures per student (dollars)	10,778	10,591
Averaged freshman graduation rate, 2008–2009	77.6	75.51
Dropout rate, 2008–2009	6.1	4.1
Students eligible for free or reduced-price lunch (percent)	39.9	48.0
English language learners, 2010–2011 (percent)	11.8	9.8[1]
Students with IEP (percent)	10.1	13.1
Private Schools, 2009–2010 (except where noted)		
Number of schools	488	33,366
Number of students (in thousands)	49	4,700
High school graduates, 2008–2009	2,838	308,813
Student-teacher ratio	10.1	10.7

[1] U.S. total includes estimates for nonreporting states.

Table CO-13. Reported Voting and Registration of the Voting-Age Population, November 2012

(Numbers in thousands, percent.)

Item	Total population	Total citizen population	Registered: Total registered	Registered: Percent registered (total population)	Registered: Percent registered (total citizen population)	Voted: Total voted	Voted: Percent voted (total population)	Voted: Percent voted (total citizen population)
U.S. Total	235,248	215,081	153,157	65.1	71.2	132,948	56.5	61.8
State Total	3,817	3,544	2,635	69.0	74.4	2,495	65.4	70.4
Sex								
Male	1,882	1,725	1,251	66.5	72.5	1,179	62.7	68.4
Female	1,935	1,818	1,384	71.5	76.1	1,316	68.0	72.4
Race								
White alone	3,474	3,253	2,471	71.1	76.0	2,345	67.5	72.1
White, non-Hispanic alone	2,852	2,800	2,205	77.3	78.7	2,105	73.8	75.2
Black alone	140	125	75	53.6	60.1	69	49.6	55.6
Asian alone	119	98	39	32.9	40.0	31	26.0	31.6
Hispanic (of any race)	681	497	284	41.7	57.2	259	38.0	52.1
Age								
18 to 24 years	493	461	278	56.5	60.3	259	52.5	56.1
25 to 44 years	1,377	1,218	895	65.0	73.5	816	59.2	66.9
45 to 64 years	1,354	1,287	1,025	75.7	79.7	989	73.0	76.9
65 to 74 years	344	330	262	76.4	79.4	258	75.0	78.0
75 years and over	250	247	174	69.7	70.6	174	69.7	70.6

Table CO-14. Crime

(Number, rate per 100,000. Data are derived from the FBI Uniform Crime Reports.)

Item	State: 2010	State: 2011	State: Percent change	U.S.: 2010	U.S.: 2011	U.S.: Percent change
TOTAL POPULATION	5,047,692	5,116,796	1.4	309,330,219	311,591,917	0.7
VIOLENT CRIME						
Number	16,339	16,383	0.3	1,251,248	1,203,564	-3.8
Rate	323.7	320.2	-1.1	404.5	386.3	-4.5
Murder and Nonnegligent Manslaughter						
Number	129	149	15.5	14,722	14,612	-0.7
Rate	2.6	2.9	11.5	4.8	4.7	-2.1
Forcible Rape						
Number	2,230	2,278	2.2	85,593	83,425	-2.5
Rate	44.2	44.5	0.7	27.7	26.8	-3.2
Robbery						
Number	3,164	3,306	4.5	369,089	354,396	-4.0
Rate	62.7	64.6	3.0	119.3	113.7	-4.7
Aggravated Assault						
Number	10,816	10,650	-1.5	781,844	751,131	-3.9
Rate	214.3	208.1	-2.9	252.8	241.1	-4.6
PROPERTY CRIME						
Number	135,001	133,361	-1.2	9,112,625	9,063,173	-0.5
Rate	2,674.5	2,606.3	-2.6	2,945.9	2,908.7	-1.3
Burglary						
Number	26,196	25,768	-1.6	2,168,459	2,188,005	0.9
Rate	519.0	503.6	-3.0	701.0	702.2	0.2
Larceny-Theft						
Number	97,534	96,546	-1.0	6,204,601	6,159,795	-0.7
Rate	1,932.2	1,886.8	-2.3	2,005.8	1,976.9	-1.4
Motor Vehicle Theft						
Number	11,271	11,047	-2.0	739,565	715,373	-3.3
Rate	223.3	215.9	-3.3	239.1	229.6	-4.0

Table CO-15. State Government Finances, 2011

(Dollar amounts in thousands, percent distribution.)

Item	Dollars	Percent distribution
Total Revenue	30,248,080	100.0
General revenue	21,864,224	72.3
Intergovernmental revenue	7,007,888	23.2
Taxes	9,467,684	31.3
General sales	2,173,882	7.2
Selective sales	1,623,488	5.4
License taxes	599,455	2.0
Individual income tax	4,540,586	15.0
Corporate income tax	383,513	1.3
Other taxes	146,760	0.5
Current charges	3,333,064	11.0
Miscellaneous general revenue	2,055,588	6.8
Utility revenue	0	0.0
Liquor stores revenue	0	0.0
Insurance trust revenue [1]	8,383,856	27.7
Total Expenditure	29,169,425	100.0
Intergovernmental expenditure	7,090,961	24.3
Direct expenditure	22,078,464	75.7
Current operation	13,061,655	44.8
Capital outlay	1,698,430	5.8
Insurance benefits and repayments	6,108,159	20.9
Assistance and subsidies	313,645	1.1
Interest on debt	896,575	3.1
Exhibit: Salaries and wages	3,986,076	13.7
Total Expenditure	29,169,425	100.0
General expenditure	23,030,329	79.0
Intergovernmental expenditure	7,090,961	24.3
Direct expenditure	15,939,368	54.6
General expenditure, by function:		
Education	9,250,143	31.7
Public welfare	5,663,074	19.4
Hospitals	660,019	2.3
Health	1,232,255	4.2
Highways	1,436,154	4.9
Police protection	137,732	0.5
Correction	1,023,871	3.5
Natural resources	336,507	1.2
Parks and recreation	127,871	0.4
Governmental administration	926,146	3.2
Interest on general debt	872,349	3.0
Other and unallocable	1,364,208	4.7
Utility expenditure	30,937	0.1
Liquor stores expenditure	0	0.0
Insurance trust expenditure	6,108,159	20.9
Debt at End of Fiscal Year	16,335,260	X
Cash and Security Holdings	62,786,242	X

X = Not applicable.
[1] Within insurance trust revenue, net earnings of state retirement systems is a calculated statistic (the item code in the data file is X08), and thus can be positive or negative. Net earnings is the sum of earnings on investments plus gains on investments minus losses on investments. The change made in 2002 for asset valuation from book to market value in accordance with Statement 34 of the Governmental Accounting Standards Board is reflected in the calculated statistics.

Table CO-16. State Government Tax Collections, 2012

(Dollars in thousands, percent.)

Item	Dollars	Percent distribution
Total Taxes	10,250,628	100.0
Property taxes	0	0.0
Sales and gross receipts	4,090,645	39.9
General sales and gross receipts	2,302,333	22.5
Selective sales and gross receipts	1,788,312	17.4
Alcoholic beverages	38,817	0.4
Amusements	93,223	0.9
Insurance premiums	197,914	1.9
Motor fuels	630,573	6.2
Pari-mutuels	595	-
Public utilities	11,974	0.1
Tobacco products	203,399	2.0
Other selective sales	611,817	6.0
Licenses	616,752	6.0
Alcoholic beverages	6,221	0.1
Amusements	837	-
Corporations in general	15,690	0.2
Hunting and fishing	67,629	0.7
Motor vehicle	455,744	4.4
Motor vehicle operators	30,986	0.3
Public utilities	0	0.0
Occupation and business, NEC	38,705	0.4
Other licenses	940	-
Income taxes	5,367,851	52.4
Individual income	4,875,627	47.6
Corporation net income	492,224	4.8
Other taxes	175,380	1.7
Death and gift	290	-
Documentary and stock transfer	0	0.0
Severance	175,090	1.7
Taxes, NEC	0	0.0

- = Rounds to zero.

Leading Exports, 2012

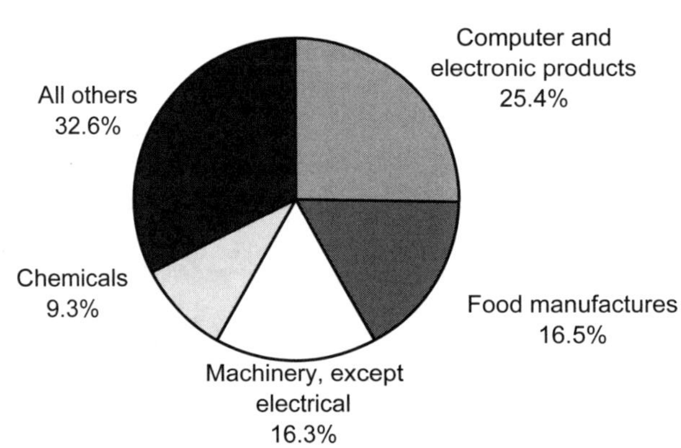

CONNECTICUT

Facts and Figures

Location: Northeastern United States; bordered on the N by Massachusetts, on the E by Rhode Island, on the S by Long Island Sound, and on the W by New York

Area: 5,543 sq. mi. (14,357); rank—48th

Population: 3,590,347 (2012 est.); rank—29th

Principal Cities: capital—Hartford; largest—Bridgeport

Statehood: January 9, 1788; 5th state

U.S. Congress: 2 senators, 5 representatives

State Motto: *Qui transtulit sustinet* ("He who transplanted still sustains")

State Song: "Yankee Doodle"

State Nicknames: The Constitution State; The Nutmeg State

Abbreviations: CT; Conn.

State Symbols: flower—mountain laurel; tree—white oak; bird—American robin

At a Glance

- With an increase in population of 3.3 percent, Connecticut ranked 33rd among the states in growth from 2000 to 2009.
- An estimated 19,800 marriages took place in Connecticut in 2009, compared to 10,900 divorces.
- Connecticut's median household income in 2011 was $65,673, and 10.9 percent of its population was below the poverty level.
- In 2012, 8.4 percent of Connecticuters were unemployed.
- Connecticut's violent crime rate in 2011 was 272.8 per 100,000 population, compared to 386.3 for the entire nation.
- In 2007, Connecticut exported $116 million worth of agricultural products, less than 1 percent of the U.S. total.

Table CT-1. Population by Age, Sex, Race, and Hispanic Origin

(Number, percent, except where noted.)

Sex, age, race, and Hispanic origin	2000	2010	2012[1]	Average annual percent change, 2010–2012
Total Population	3,405,565	3,574,097	3,590,347	0.2
Percent of total U.S. population	1.2	1.2	1.1	X
Sex				
Male	1,649,319	1,739,614	1,749,916	0.2
Female	1,756,246	1,834,483	1,840,431	0.1
Age				
Under 5 years	233,344	202,106	193,456	-1.5
5 to 19 years	702,358	713,670	708,224	-0.3
20 to 64 years	2,009,680	2,151,762	2,155,955	0.1
65 years and over	470,183	506,559	532,712	1.6
Median age (years)	37.4	40.0	40.5	0.4
Race and Hispanic Origin				
One race				
White	2,780,355	2,950,820	2,942,355	-0.1
Black	309,843	392,131	401,496	0.8
American Indian and Alaska Native	9,639	16,734	17,688	1.8
Asian	82,313	140,516	155,031	3.1
Native Hawaiian or Other Pacific Islander	1,366	3,491	3,541	0.5
Two or more races	74,848	70,405	74,658	1.9
Hispanic (of any race)	320,323	498,638	531,832	2.1

X = Not applicable.
[1] Population figures for 2012 are July 1 estimates. The 2010 estimates are taken from the 2010 Census.

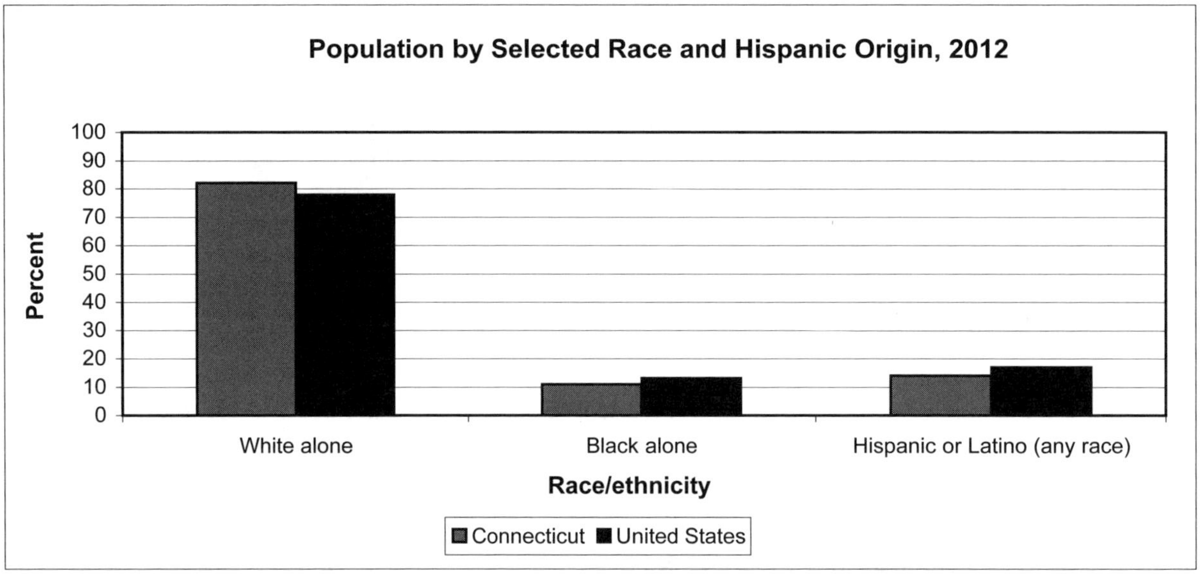

Table CT-2. Marital Status

(Number, percent distribution.)

Sex, age, race, and Hispanic origin	2000	2010	2011
Males, 15 Years and Over	1,284,881	1,399,329	1,408,200
Never married	30.0	36.3	36.4
Now married, except separated	58.0	50.6	50.8
Separated	1.3	1.1	1.2
Widowed	2.7	2.7	2.7
Divorced	7.9	9.3	8.9
Females, 15 Years and Over	1,411,369	1,512,492	1,517,622
Never married	24.5	29.9	30.1
Now married, except separated	52.3	46.5	46.2
Separated	1.8	1.8	2.0
Widowed	10.8	9.3	9.4
Divorced	10.5	12.5	12.3

Table CT-3. Households and Housing Characteristics

(Number, percent, dollars.)

Item	2000	2010	2011	Average annual percent change, 2000–2011
Total Households	1,301,670	1,358,809	1,351,643	0.3
Family households	881,170	890,770	893,101	0.1
Married-couple family	676,467	656,629	660,299	-0.2
Other family	204,703	234,141	232,802	1.1
Male householder, no wife present	47,292	58,325	53,467	1.1
Female householder, no husband present	157,411	175,816	179,335	1.2
Nonfamily households	420,500	468,039	458,542	0.8
Householder living alone	334,224	384,382	384,135	1.2
Householder not living alone	76,276	83,657	74,407	-0.2
Housing Characteristics				
Total housing units	1,385,975	1,488,215	1,494,042	0.6
Occupied housing units	1,301,670	1,358,809	1,351,643	0.3
Owner occupied	869,729	923,617	911,059	0.4
Renter occupied	431,941	435,192	440,584	0.2
Average size	2.53	2.55	2.56	0.1
Financial Characteristics				
Median gross rent of renter-occupied housing	681	992	1,021	4.2
Median monthly owner costs for housing units with a mortgage	1,426	2,068	2,052	3.7
Median value of owner-occupied housing units	166,900	288,800	278,700	5.6

Table CT-4. Migration, Origin, and Language

(Number, percent.)

Characteristic	State			U.S.		
	2010	2011	Percent change	2010	2011	Percent change
Residence 1 Year Ago						
Population 1 year and over	3,541,146	3,548,667	0.2	305,628,607	307,900,319	0.7
Same house	87.6	88.5	1.0	84.6	84.8	0.2
Different house in the U.S.	11.9	10.9	-8.4	14.8	14.6	-1.4
Same county	7.7	7.0	-9.1	9.4	9.2	-2.1
Different county	4.2	3.9	-7.1	5.4	5.4	-
Same state	2.0	1.9	-5.0	3.2	3.1	-3.1
Different state	2.2	2.0	-9.1	2.2	2.3	4.5
Abroad	0.6	0.6	-	0.6	0.6	-
Place of Birth						
Native born	3,089,953	3,102,386	0.4	269,393,835	271,214,059	0.7
Male	48.6	48.8	0.4	49.2	49.2	-
Female	51.4	51.2	-0.4	50.8	50.8	-
Foreign born	487,120	478,323	-1.8	39,955,854	40,377,860	1.1
Male	48.5	48.2	-0.6	49.1	48.9	-0.4
Female	51.5	51.8	0.6	50.9	51.1	0.4
Foreign born; naturalized U.S. citizen	228,059	236,346	3.6	17,476,082	18,140,192	3.8
Male	45.6	44.6	-2.2	45.8	45.8	-
Female	54.4	55.4	1.8	54.2	54.2	-
Foreign born; not a U.S. citizen	259,061	241,977	-6.6	22,479,772	22,237,668	-1.1
Male	51.1	51.8	1.4	51.6	51.5	-0.2
Female	48.9	48.2	-1.4	48.4	48.5	0.2
Entered 2000 or later	37.4	37.0	-1.1	34.7	35.7	2.9
Entered 1990 to 1999	25.7	26.0	1.2	27.2	26.7	-1.8
Entered before 1990	36.9	37.1	0.5	38.1	37.6	-1.3
World Region of Birth, Foreign						
Foreign-born population, excluding population born at sea	487,120	478,323	-1.8	39,955,673	40,377,757	1.1
Europe	28.5	27.6	-3.2	12.1	12.1	-
Asia	22.0	23.3	5.9	28.2	28.6	1.4
Africa	3.6	4.4	22.2	4	4.1	2.5
Oceania	0.3	0.2	-33.3	0.5	0.5	-
Latin America	42.1	41.0	-2.6	53.1	52.6	-0.9
North America	3.4	3.5	2.9	2	2.0	-
Language Spoken at Home and Ability to Speak English						
Population 5 years and over	3,375,388	3,384,503	0.3	289,215,746	291,524,091	0.8
English only	78.7	78.6	-0.1	79.4	79.2	-0.3
Language other than English	21.3	21.4	0.5	20.6	20.8	1.0
Speaks English less than "very well"	8.7	8.2	-5.7	8.7	8.7	-

- = Zero or rounds to zero.

Table CT-5. Median Income and Poverty Status, 2011

(Number, percent, except as noted.)

Characteristic	State		U.S.	
	Number	Percent	Number	Percent
Median Income				
Households (dollars)	65,753	X	50,502	X
Families (dollars)	83,106	X	61,455	X
Below Poverty Level (All People)	377,856	10.9	48,452,035	15.9
Sex				
Male	166,124	9.8	21,825,281	14.7
Female	211,732	11.9	26,626,754	17.2
Age				
Under 18 years	118,809	14.9	16,386,500	22.5
Related children under 18 years	116,925	14.8	16,087,074	22.2
18 to 64 years	225,295	10.3	28,335,079	14.8
65 years and over	33,752	6.8	3,730,456	9.3

X = Not applicable.

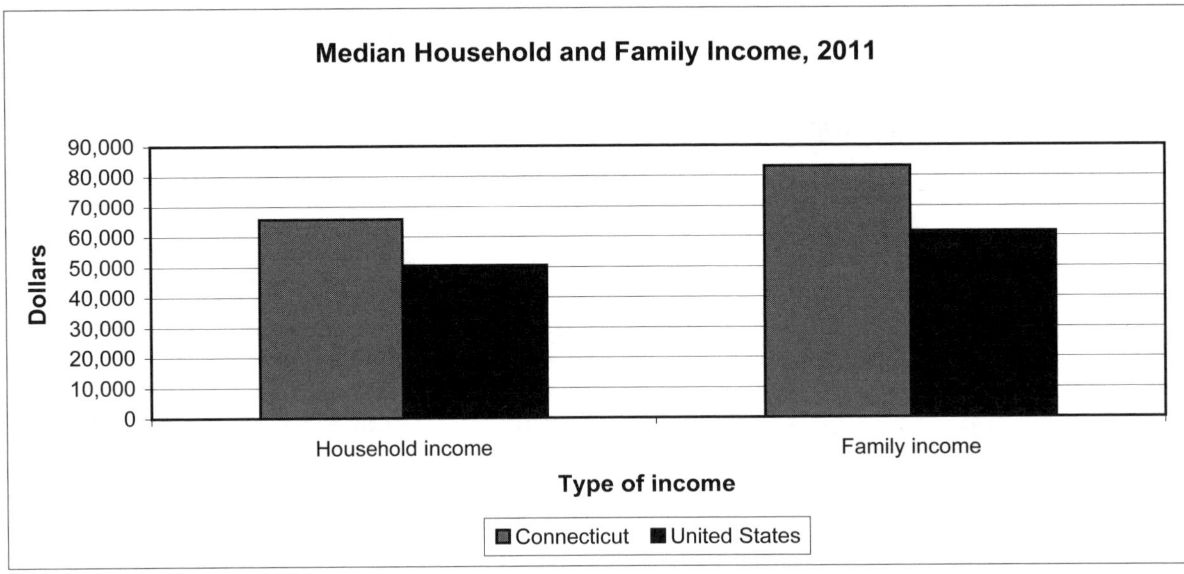

Table CT-6. Health Insurance Coverage Status for the Civilian Noninstitutionalized Population and Children Under 18 Years of Age

(Numbers in thousands, percent.)

Item	2004	2005	2006	2007	2008	2009	2010	2011
Civilian Noninstitutionalized Population	3,492	3,487	3,462	3,476	3,441	3,457	3,520	3,523
Covered by Private or Public Insurance								
Number	3,112	3,106	3,137	3,150	3,130	3,152	3,200	3,214
Percent	89.1	89.1	90.6	90.6	91.0	91.2	90.9	91.2
Not Covered								
Number	381	381	325	326	311	305	320	309
Percent	10.9	10.9	9.4	9.4	9.0	8.8	9.1	8.8
Percent in the U.S. not covered	14.9	15.3	15.8	15.3	15.1	15.1	15.5	15.1
Children Under 18 Years of Age	840	832	820	819	810	807	815	803
Covered by Private or Public Insurance								
Number	780	768	771	776	770	777	791	780
Percent	92.9	92.3	94.0	94.8	95.1	96.2	97.0	97.1
Not Covered								
Number	60	64	49	43	40	30	24	23
Percent	7.1	7.7	6.0	5.2	4.9	3.8	3.0	2.9
Percent in the U.S. not covered	10.5	10.9	11.7	11.0	9.7	8.6	8.0	7.5

Table CT-7. Employment Status by Demographic Group, Preliminary 2012

(Numbers in thousands, percent.)

Characteristic	Civilian noninstitutional population	Civilian labor force		Employed		Unemployed	
		Number	Percent of population	Number	Percent of population	Number	Percent of population
Total	2,841	1,881	66.2	1,722	60.6	159	8.4
Sex							
Male	1,363	983	72.1	893	65.6	89	9.1
Female	1,478	898	60.7	828	56.0	69	7.7
Race, Sex, and Hispanic Origin							
White	2,351	1,545	65.7	1,425	60.6	120	7.8
Male	1,134	812	71.6	746	65.8	66	8.1
Female	1,217	733	60.2	679	55.8	54	7.3
Black or African American	293	196	67.1	167	57.1	29	14.9
Male	133	95	71.6	77	58.0	18	19.1
Female	160	101	63.4	90	56.5	11	11.0
Hispanic	318	210	66.1	177	55.7	33	15.7
Male	154	109	71.0	90	58.8	19	17.1
Female	164	101	61.5	87	52.8	14	14.2
Age							
16 to 19 years	222	74	33.6	56	25.0	19	25.4
20 to 24 years	232	174	74.9	151	64.9	23	13.4
25 to 34 years	398	336	84.5	305	76.8	30	9.1
35 to 44 years	450	378	84.1	353	78.6	25	6.5
45 to 54 years	582	491	84.3	457	78.5	34	6.9
55 to 64 years	451	320	71.0	301	66.7	19	6.0
65 years and over	507	107	21.1	99	19.5	8	7.6

NOTE: Data in Table 7 are from the Current Population Survey (CPS) and do not match the estimates in Table 8. See notes and definitions for further information.

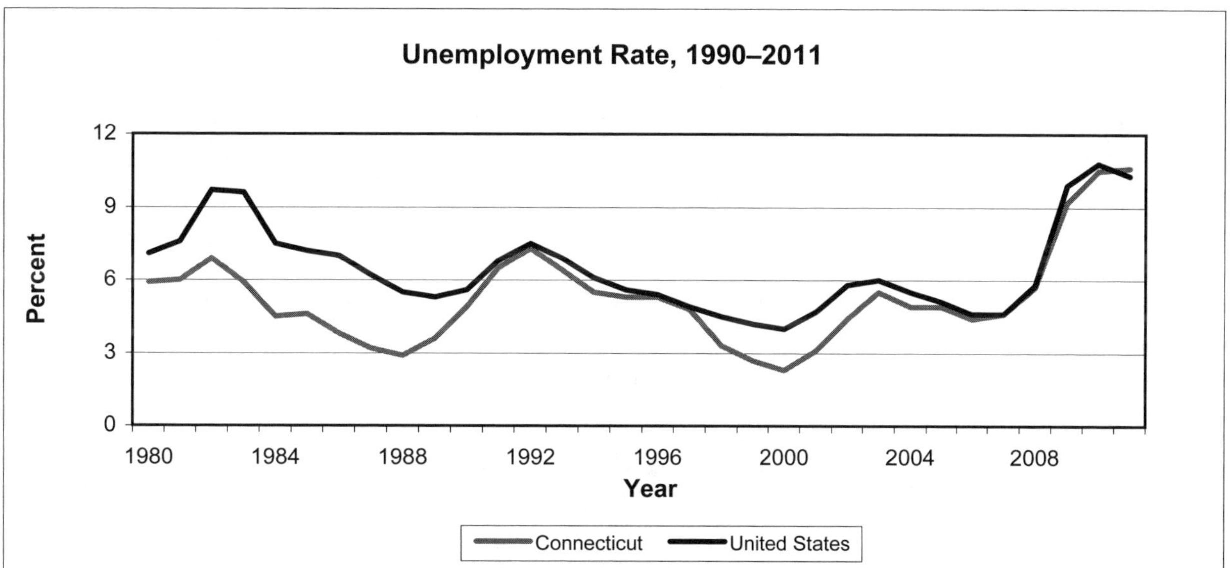

Table CT-8. Employment Status of the Civilian Noninstitutional Population Age 16 Years and Over

(Number, percent.)

Year	Civilian labor force	Civilian participation rate	Employed	Unemployed	Unemployment rate
2005	1,808,762	67.4	1,720,346	88,416	4.9
2006	1,829,024	67.7	1,748,368	80,656	4.4
2007	1,850,345	68.2	1,765,835	84,510	4.6
2008	1,876,125	68.8	1,769,223	106,902	5.7
2009	1,917,746	68.3	1,740,760	176,986	9.2
2010	1,939,959	67.8	1,736,446	203,513	10.5
2011	1,949,486	67.8	1,742,494	206,992	10.6

Table CT-9. Employment and Average Wages by Industry

(Estimates before 2007 are based on the 2002 *North American Industry Classification System* [NAICS]. Estimates from 2007 onward are based on the 2007 NAICS.)

Industry	2005	2006	2007	2008	2009	2010	2011
	Number of jobs						
Wage and Salary Employment by Industry	1,733,450	1,750,386	1,766,024	1,768,627	1,697,796	1,678,439	1,695,049
Farm Wage and Salary Employment	4,910	4,433	4,227	4,612	4,449	4,460	4,730
Nonfarm Wage and Salary Employment	1,728,540	1,745,953	1,761,797	1,764,015	1,693,347	1,673,979	1,690,319
Private wage and salary employment	1,461,417	1,478,387	1,493,426	1,491,508	1,424,167	1,407,694	1,428,832
Forestry, fishing, and related activities	775	822	811	815	800	830	906
Mining	705	740	715	737	629	571	542
Utilities	8,574	6,675	6,657	6,759	6,644	6,310	6,173
Construction	68,518	69,684	71,158	67,888	57,044	52,304	54,272
Manufacturing	195,455	193,956	191,381	187,230	171,479	165,835	166,442
Durable goods manufacturing	145,776	145,419	144,475	143,485	132,078	127,377	128,576
Nondurable goods manufacturing	49,679	48,537	46,906	43,745	39,401	38,458	37,866
Wholesale trade	66,999	68,225	68,612	69,891	65,526	63,209	63,914
Retail trade	194,868	193,987	194,127	191,035	181,585	181,490	183,247
Transportation and warehousing	42,853	43,272	43,539	43,337	40,829	40,274	41,375
Information	38,163	37,809	38,105	37,521	34,261	31,827	31,446
Finance and insurance	123,952	125,914	125,734	125,204	120,584	118,635	118,257
Real estate and rental and leasing	21,387	21,715	21,707	21,279	19,820	19,780	19,485
Professional, scientific, and technical services	89,761	92,841	93,691	93,970	88,629	87,408	89,298
Management of companies and enterprises	25,019	26,248	26,638	28,516	27,779	27,826	28,622
Administrative and waste services	87,133	88,916	90,627	87,546	77,461	78,853	81,765
Educational services	55,923	57,162	59,117	61,087	63,159	64,153	66,405
Health care and social assistance	224,984	229,860	236,470	243,264	248,409	251,509	255,468
Arts, entertainment, and recreation	24,585	24,121	24,155	24,211	23,964	23,873	24,538
Accommodation and food services	106,599	109,898	112,762	114,430	111,349	111,542	114,648
Other services, except public administration	85,164	86,542	87,420	86,788	84,216	81,465	82,029
Government and government enterprises	267,123	267,566	268,371	272,507	269,180	266,285	261,487
	Dollars						
Average Wages and Salaries by Industry	51,801	54,012	57,139	57,517	56,809	58,501	60,138
Average Farm Wages and Salaries	21,839	27,678	32,758	28,805	28,367	26,728	22,547
Average Nonfarm Wages and Salaries	51,886	54,079	57,198	57,592	56,884	58,585	60,243
Average private wages and salaries	53,007	55,326	58,490	58,670	57,627	59,713	61,357
Forestry, fishing, and related activities	20,227	20,799	21,705	22,004	23,028	22,981	23,056
Mining	57,562	61,165	61,070	64,171	64,526	67,965	68,950
Utilities	87,740	97,072	105,485	109,587	106,692	103,576	111,584
Construction	51,425	52,916	55,934	57,966	57,799	58,614	58,336
Manufacturing	63,036	65,726	69,254	70,484	70,207	73,403	76,894
Durable goods manufacturing	61,787	64,448	67,776	69,674	69,702	73,005	76,332
Nondurable goods manufacturing	66,700	69,552	73,806	73,142	71,900	74,724	78,801
Wholesale trade	72,750	77,599	80,003	79,758	79,147	81,467	83,383
Retail trade	28,807	29,554	30,207	30,356	30,636	30,909	31,211
Transportation and warehousing	41,191	43,115	47,411	47,040	46,145	46,410	47,499
Information	63,365	65,699	69,484	70,196	71,374	77,158	78,945
Finance and insurance	127,438	134,446	145,391	141,147	130,078	143,395	152,330
Real estate and rental and leasing	46,861	49,686	53,543	52,902	51,556	54,133	58,140
Professional, scientific, and technical services	75,788	77,931	83,165	85,411	85,225	88,164	89,592
Management of companies and enterprises	130,148	137,143	157,905	136,632	135,450	135,150	139,171
Administrative and waste services	32,290	33,791	36,770	38,188	38,583	40,063	40,837
Educational services	38,680	40,553	42,330	44,406	45,609	46,391	47,415
Health care and social assistance	41,474	42,756	44,072	45,815	46,433	46,972	47,523
Arts, entertainment, and recreation	28,197	31,168	31,101	29,742	29,230	29,054	29,259
Accommodation and food services	18,513	19,017	20,226	19,788	19,804	20,491	20,779
Other services, except public administration	27,130	28,142	29,273	30,166	30,344	31,253	31,708
Government and government enterprises	45,750	47,193	50,003	51,688	52,951	52,625	54,157

Table CT-10. Employment Characteristics by Family Type

(Number, percent.)

Family type and labor force status	2009		2010		2011	
	Total	Families with own children under 18 years	Total	Families with own children under 18 years	Total	Families with own children under 18 years
All families	890,530	414,959	890,770	407,963	893,101	402,424
Family type and labor force status						
Married-couple families	667,948	292,752	656,629	280,390	660,299	275,446
Both husband and wife in labor force	60.7	72.1	60.0	71.9	59.5	71.6
Husband in labor force, wife not in labor force	19.7	24.8	19.3	24.5	19.9	24.7
Wife in labor force, husband not in labor force	6.4	2.2	6.6	2.9	7.0	3.0
Both husband and wife not in labor force	13.2	0.9	14.2	0.7	13.6	0.8
Other families	222,582	122,207	234,141	127,573	232,802	126,978
Female householder, no husband present	75.1	79.9	75.1	80.1	77.0	80.7
In labor force	57.7	69.4	56.1	67.8	58.5	69.0
Not in labor force	17.4	10.5	19.0	12.3	18.5	11.7
Male householder, no wife present	24.9	20.1	24.9	19.9	23.0	19.3
In labor force	20.2	18.6	20.2	18.4	18.6	17.6
Not in labor force	4.7	1.4	4.7	1.5	4.4	1.8

Table CT-11. School Enrollment and Educational Attainment, 2011

(Number, percent.)

Item	State	U.S.
Enrollment		
Total population 3 years and over, enrolled in school	943,212	83,131,910
Enrolled in nursery school or preschool (percent)	6.4	6.0
Enrolled in kindergarten (percent)	4.6	5.1
Enrolled in elementary school, grades 1-8 (percent)	39.2	39.5
Enrolled in high school, grades 9-12 (percent)	22.2	20.7
Enrolled in college or graduate school (percent)	27.7	28.7
Attainment		
Total population 25 years and over	2,444,403	206,471,670
Less than ninth grade (percent)	4.4	6.0
9th to 12th grade, no diploma (percent)	6.5	8.1
High school graduate, including equivalency (percent)	27.7	28.4
Some college, no degree (percent)	17.9	21.2
Associate's degree (percent)	7.3	7.8
Bachelor's degree (percent)	20.5	17.9
Graduate or professional degree (percent)	15.7	10.6
High school graduate or higher (percent)	89.1	85.9
Bachelor's degree or higher (percent)	36.2	28.5

Table CT-12. Educational Indicators

(Number, percent; data derived from National Center of Education Statistics.)

Item	State	U.S.
Public Schools, 2009–2010 (except where noted)		
Number of school districts	169	13,629
Number of schools	1,165	99,834
Number of students (in thousands)	564	49,373
Student-teacher ratio	12.9	15.4
Expenditures per student (dollars)	17,611	10,591
Averaged freshman graduation rate, 2008–2009	75.4	75.5[1]
Dropout rate, 2008–2009	3.1	4.1
Students eligible for free or reduced-price lunch (percent)	34.1	48.0
English language learners, 2010–2011 (percent)	5.6	9.8[1]
Students with IEP (percent)	12.2	13.1
Private Schools, 2009–2010 (except where noted)		
Number of schools	405	33,366
Number of students (in thousands)	64	4,700
High school graduates, 2008–2009	6,233	308,813
Student-teacher ratio	8.7	10.7

[1] U.S. total includes estimates for nonreporting states.

Table CT-13. Reported Voting and Registration of the Voting-Age Population, November 2012

(Numbers in thousands, percent.)

Item	Total population	Total citizen population	Registered			Voted		
			Total registered	Percent registered (total population)	Percent registered (total citizen population)	Total voted	Percent voted (total population)	Percent voted (total citizen population)
U.S. Total	235,248	215,081	153,157	65.1	71.2	132,948	56.5	61.8
State Total	2,726	2,499	1,760	64.6	70.4	1,568	57.5	62.7
Sex								
Male	1,297	1,188	811	62.6	68.3	712	54.9	59.9
Female	1,429	1,311	949	66.4	72.4	856	59.9	65.3
Race								
White alone	2,238	2,115	1,520	67.9	71.8	1,352	60.4	63.9
White, non-Hispanic alone	2,004	1,931	1,420	70.9	73.5	1,271	63.4	65.8
Black alone	279	256	164	58.7	64.0	159	57.1	62.2
Asian alone	147	80	37	25.1	46.1	23	15.8	29.0
Hispanic (of any race)	292	220	127	43.5	57.7	103	35.4	47.0
Age								
18 to 24 years	333	308	145	43.6	47.1	123	36.9	39.8
25 to 44 years	843	713	464	55.1	65.2	400	47.4	56.1
45 to 64 years	1,047	993	768	73.3	77.4	695	66.3	70.0
65 to 74 years	276	264	212	76.6	80.2	206	74.5	78.0
75 years and over	226	222	172	75.8	77.3	145	64.0	65.3

Table CT-14. Crime

(Number, rate per 100,000. Data are derived from the FBI Uniform Crime Reports.)

Item	State			U.S.		
	2010	2011	Percent change	2010	2011	Percent change
TOTAL POPULATION	3,575,498	3,580,709	0.1	309,330,219	311,591,917	0.7
VIOLENT CRIME						
Number	10,083	9,767	-3.1	1,251,248	1,203,564	-3.8
Rate	282.0	272.8	-3.3	404.5	386.3	-4.5
Murder and Nonnegligent Manslaughter						
Number	133	128	-3.8	14,722	14,612	-0.7
Rate	3.7	3.6	-2.7	4.8	4.7	-2.1
Forcible Rape						
Number	595	686	15.3	85,593	83,425	-2.5
Rate	16.6	19.2	15.7	27.7	26.8	-3.2
Robbery						
Number	3,553	3,677	3.5	369,089	354,396	-4.0
Rate	99.4	102.7	3.3	119.3	113.7	-4.7
Aggravated Assault						
Number	5,802	5,276	-9.1	781,844	751,131	-3.9
Rate	162.3	147.3	-9.2	252.8	241.1	-4.6
PROPERTY CRIME						
Number	78,259	77,609	-0.8	9,112,625	9,063,173	-0.5
Rate	2,188.8	2,167.4	-1.0	2,945.9	2,908.7	-1.3
Burglary						
Number	15,145	15,679	3.5	2,168,459	2,188,005	0.9
Rate	423.6	437.9	3.4	701.0	702.2	0.2
Larceny-Theft						
Number	56,413	55,218	-2.1	6,204,601	6,159,795	-0.7
Rate	1,577.8	1,542.1	-2.3	2,005.8	1,976.9	-1.4
Motor Vehicle Theft						
Number	6,701	6,712	0.2	739,565	715,373	-3.3
Rate	187.4	187.4	0.0	239.1	229.6	-4.0

Table CT-15. State Government Finances, 2011

(Dollar amounts in thousands, percent distribution.)

Item	Dollars	Percent distribution
Total Revenue	28,927,902	100.0
General revenue	23,508,277	81.3
Intergovernmental revenue	6,561,366	22.7
Taxes	13,432,252	46.4
General sales	3,252,123	11.2
Selective sales	2,270,657	7.8
License taxes	446,755	1.5
Individual income tax	6,469,246	22.4
Corporate income tax	672,816	2.3
Other taxes	320,655	1.1
Current charges	2,096,873	7.2
Miscellaneous general revenue	1,417,786	4.9
Utility revenue	31,060	0.1
Liquor stores revenue	0	0.0
Insurance trust revenue [1]	5,388,565	18.6
Total Expenditure	28,094,106	100.0
Intergovernmental expenditure	4,485,808	16.0
Direct expenditure	23,608,298	84.0
Current operation	14,822,195	52.8
Capital outlay	1,522,409	5.4
Insurance benefits and repayments	5,228,718	18.6
Assistance and subsidies	551,181	2.0
Interest on debt	1,483,795	5.3
Exhibit: Salaries and wages	4,314,655	15.4
Total Expenditure	28,094,106	100.0
General expenditure	22,249,079	79.2
Intergovernmental expenditure	4,485,808	16.0
Direct expenditure	17,763,271	63.2
General expenditure, by function:		
Education	6,747,698	24.0
Public welfare	6,362,163	22.6
Hospitals	1,475,928	5.3
Health	932,699	3.3
Highways	1,013,420	3.6
Police protection	201,969	0.7
Correction	698,030	2.5
Natural resources	143,541	0.5
Parks and recreation	35,864	0.1
Governmental administration	1,177,686	4.2
Interest on general debt	1,483,795	5.3
Other and unallocable	1,976,286	7.0
Utility expenditure	616,309	2.2
Liquor stores expenditure	0	0.0
Insurance trust expenditure	5,228,718	18.6
Debt at End of Fiscal Year	30,523,708	X
Cash and Security Holdings	42,652,669	X

X = Not applicable.

[1] Within insurance trust revenue, net earnings of state retirement systems is a calculated statistic (the item code in the data file is X08), and thus can be positive or negative. Net earnings is the sum of earnings on investments plus gains on investments minus losses on investments. The change made in 2002 for asset valuation from book to market value in accordance with Statement 34 of the Governmental Accounting Standards Board is reflected in the calculated statistics.

Table CT-16. State Government Tax Collections, 2012

(Dollars in thousands, percent.)

Item	Dollars	Percent distribution
Total Taxes	15,419,556	100.0
Property taxes	0	0.0
Sales and gross receipts	6,677,074	43.3
General sales and gross receipts	3,758,881	24.4
Selective sales and gross receipts	2,918,193	18.9
Alcoholic beverages	60,595	0.4
Amusements	379,333	2.5
Insurance premiums	205,587	1.3
Motor fuels	487,104	3.2
Pari-mutuels	6,876	-
Public utilities	251,168	1.6
Tobacco products	418,231	2.7
Other selective sales	1,109,299	7.2
Licenses	441,341	2.9
Alcoholic beverages	8,378	0.1
Amusements	213	-
Corporations in general	27,947	0.2
Hunting and fishing	4,714	-
Motor vehicle	209,109	1.4
Motor vehicle operators	43,522	0.3
Public utilities	676	-
Occupation and business, NEC	143,726	0.9
Other licenses	3,056	-
Income taxes	7,996,509	51.9
Individual income	7,371,189	47.8
Corporation net income	625,320	4.1
Other taxes	304,632	2.0
Death and gift	174,554	1.1
Documentary and stock transfer	130,014	0.8
Severance	64	-
Taxes, NEC	0	0.0

- = Rounds to zero.

Leading Exports, 2012

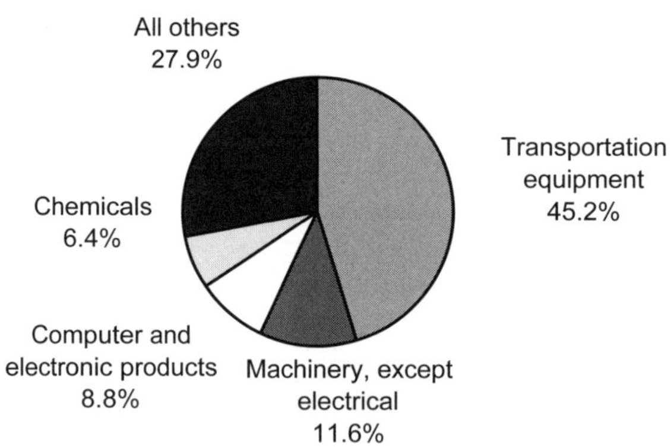

DELAWARE

Facts and Figures

Location: Northeastern United States; bordered on the N by Pennsylvania, on the E by New Jersey, and on the S and W by Maryland

Area: 2,489 sq. mi. (6,447 sq. km.); rank—49th

Population: 917,092 (2012 est.); rank—45th

Principal Cities: capital—Dover; largest—Wilmington

Statehood: December 7, 1787; 1st state

U.S. Congress: 2 senators, 1 representative

State Motto: Liberty and Independence

State Song: "Our Delaware"

State Nickname: The First State

Abbreviations: DE; Del.

State Symbols: flower—peach blossom; tree—American holly; bird—blue hen chicken

At a Glance

- An estimated 5,100 marriages took place in Delaware in 2008, compared to 3,400 divorces.
- In 2011, 9.4 percent of Delawareans did not have health insurance, compared to 15.1 percent of the total U.S. population.
- Delaware's violent crime rate in 2011 was 559.5 per 100,000 population, compared to 386.3 for the entire nation.
- In the 2012 election, 67.3 percent of Delaware's eligible voters voted, compared to 61.8 percent of eligible voters nationwide.
- In 2007, Delaware exported $160 million worth of agricultural products, less than 1 percent of the U.S. total.

Table DE-1. Population by Age, Sex, Race, and Hispanic Origin

(Number, percent, except where noted.)

Sex, age, race, and Hispanic origin	2000	2010	2012[1]	Average annual percent change, 2010–2012
Total Population	783,600	897,934	917,092	0.7
Percent of total U.S. population	0.3	0.3	0.3	X
Sex				
Male	380,541	434,939	444,358	0.7
Female	403,059	462,995	472,734	0.7
Age				
Under 5 years	51,531	55,886	56,279	0.2
5 to 19 years	166,719	177,917	178,718	0.1
20 to 64 years	463,624	648,387	665,275	0.8
65 years and over	101,726	15,744	16,820	2.1
Median age (years)	36.0	38.8	39.2	0.3
Race and Hispanic Origin				
One race				
White	584,773	645,770	654,352	0.4
Black	150,666	196,281	202,090	1.0
American Indian and Alaska Native	2,731	5,929	6,161	1.3
Asian	16,259	29,342	32,141	2.9
Native Hawaiian or Other Pacific Islander	283	690	766	3.3
Two or more races	13,033	19,922	21,528	2.5
Hispanic (of any race)	37,277	76,137	82,059	2.4

X = Not applicable.
[1] Population figures for 2012 are July 1 estimates. The 2010 estimates are taken from the 2010 Census.

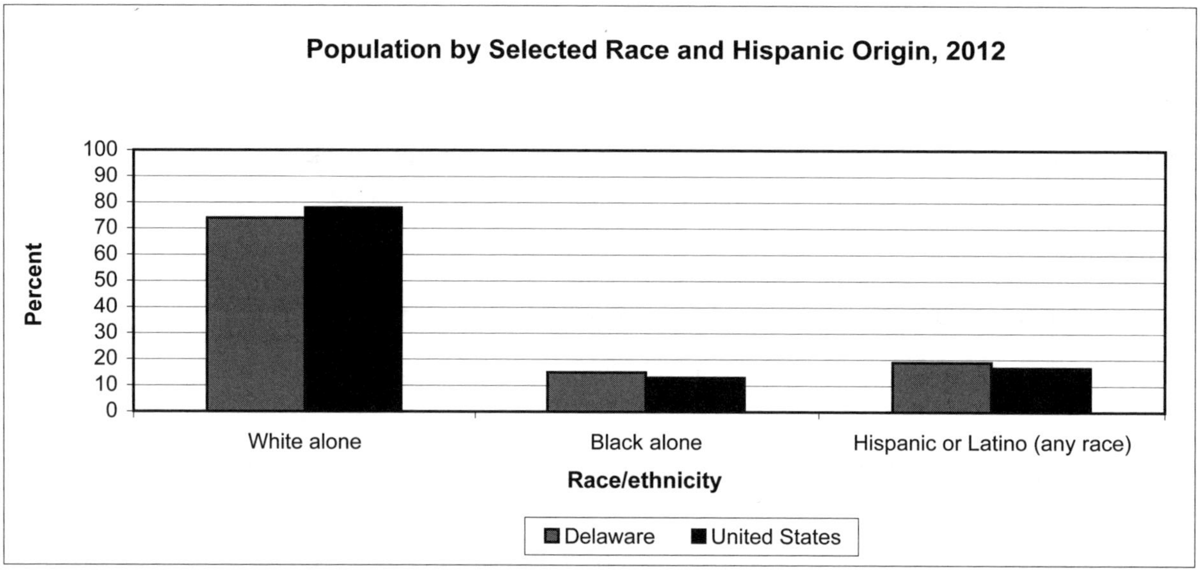

Table DE-2. Marital Status

(Number, percent distribution.)

Sex, age, race, and Hispanic origin	2000	2010	2011
Males, 15 Years and Over	296,619	350,025	353,526
Never married	29.4	35.3	36.4
Now married, except separated	57.4	50.4	49.3
Separated	1.8	1.9	1.7
Widowed	2.8	2.9	3.2
Divorced	8.7	9.4	9.5
Females, 15 Years and Over	324,042	380,618	384,321
Never married	25.3	30.8	30.6
Now married, except separated	50.9	45.3	45.1
Separated	2.2	2.0	2.1
Widowed	10.7	9.8	9.2
Divorced	10.9	12.1	10.0

Table DE-3. Households and Housing Characteristics

(Number, percent, dollars.)

Item	2000	2010	2011	Average annual percent change, 2000–2011
Total Households	298,736	328,765	333,192	1.0
Family households	204,590	221,233	227,101	0.9
Married-couple family	153,136	161,575	161,755	0.5
Other family	51,454	59,658	65,346	2.2
Male householder, no wife present	12,468	14,124	18,685	4.2
Female householder, no husband present	38,986	45,534	46,661	1.6
Nonfamily households	94,146	107,532	106,091	1.1
Householder living alone	74,639	86,990	84,187	1.1
Householder not living alone	19,507	20,542	21,904	1.0
Housing Characteristics				
Total housing units	343,072	406,489	409,779	1.6
Occupied housing units	298,736	328,765	333,192	1.0
Owner occupied	216,038	239,884	238,560	0.9
Renter occupied	86,698	88,881	94,632	0.8
Average size	2.54	2.66	2.65	0.4
Financial Characteristics				
Median gross rent of renter-occupied housing	639	952	960	4.2
Median monthly owner costs for housing units with a mortgage	1,101	1,569	1,567	3.5
Median value of owner-occupied housing units	130,400	243,600	236,900	6.8

Table DE-4. Migration, Origin, and Language

(Number, percent.)

Characteristic	State			U.S.		
	2010	2011	Percent change	2010	2011	Percent change
Residence 1 Year Ago						
Population 1 year and over	889,812	897,187	0.8	305,628,607	307,900,319	0.7
Same house	85.9	86.4	0.6	84.6	84.8	0.2
Different house in the U.S.	13.6	13.0	-4.4	14.8	14.6	-1.4
Same county	9.3	8.3	-10.8	9.4	9.2	-2.1
Different county	4.3	4.7	9.3	5.4	5.4	-
Same state	0.8	1.0	25.0	3.2	3.1	-3.1
Different state	3.5	3.8	8.6	2.2	2.3	4.5
Abroad	0.5	0.5	-	0.6	0.6	-
Place of Birth						
Native born	827,901	830,773	0.3	269,393,835	271,214,059	0.7
Male	48.6	48.4	-0.4	49.2	49.2	-
Female	51.4	51.6	0.4	50.8	50.8	-
Foreign born	71,868	76,362	6.3	39,955,854	40,377,860	1.1
Male	47.3	49.9	5.5	49.1	48.9	-0.4
Female	52.7	50.1	-4.9	50.9	51.1	0.4
Foreign born; naturalized U.S. citizen	33,473	32,547	-2.8	17,476,082	18,140,192	3.8
Male	44.6	46.4	4.0	45.8	45.8	-
Female	55.4	53.6	-3.2	54.2	54.2	-
Foreign born; not a U.S. citizen	38,395	43,815	14.1	22,479,772	22,237,668	-1.1
Male	49.6	52.5	5.8	51.6	51.5	-0.2
Female	50.4	47.5	-5.8	48.4	48.5	0.2
Entered 2000 or later	43.0	46.3	7.7	34.7	35.7	2.9
Entered 1990 to 1999	27.1	24.8	-8.5	27.2	26.7	-1.8
Entered before 1990	29.9	28.9	-3.3	38.1	37.6	-1.3
World Region of Birth, Foreign						
Foreign-born population, excluding population born at sea	71,868	76,362	6.3	39,955,673	40,377,757	1.1
Europe	12.8	15.2	18.8	12.1	12.1	-
Asia	30.9	30.0	-2.9	28.2	28.6	1.4
Africa	7.8	11.4	46.2	4	4.1	2.5
Oceania	0.1	0.1	-	0.5	0.5	-
Latin America	47.2	41.1	-12.9	53.1	52.6	-0.9
North America	1.1	2.2	100.0	2	2.0	-
Language Spoken at Home and Ability to Speak English						
Population 5 years and over	843,674	851,887	1.0	289,215,746	291,524,091	0.8
English only	88.0	86.4	-1.8	79.4	79.2	-0.3
Language other than English	12.0	13.6	13.3	20.6	20.8	1.0
Speaks English less than "very well"	4.6	4.7	2.2	8.7	8.7	-

- = Zero or rounds to zero.

Table DE-5. Median Income and Poverty Status, 2011

(Number, percent, except as noted.)

Characteristic	State		U.S.	
	Number	Percent	Number	Percent
Median Income				
Households (dollars)	58,814	X	50,502	X
Families (dollars)	69,663	X	61,455	X
Below Poverty Level (All People)	104,831	11.9	48,452,035	15.9
Sex				
Male	43,229	10.2	21,825,281	14.7
Female	61,602	13.5	26,626,754	17.2
Age				
Under 18 years	35,216	17.5	16,386,500	22.5
Related children under 18 years	33,697	16.8	16,087,074	22.2
18 to 64 years	62,179	11.3	28,335,079	14.8
65 years and over	7,436	5.7	3,730,456	9.3

X = Not applicable.

Median Household and Family Income, 2011

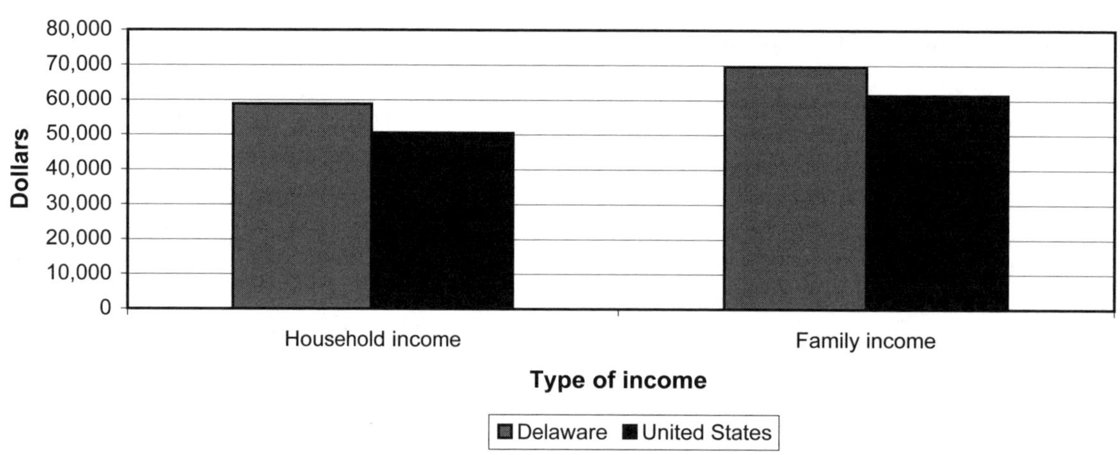

Table DE-6. Health Insurance Coverage Status for the Civilian Noninstitutionalized Population and Children Under 18 Years of Age

(Numbers in thousands, percent.)

Item	2004	2005	2006	2007	2008	2009	2010	2011
Civilian Noninstitutionalized Population	826	844	862	863	856	869	885	892
Covered by Private or Public Insurance								
Number	717	742	757	766	768	780	799	808
Percent	86.7	87.8	87.9	88.8	89.7	89.8	90.3	90.6
Not Covered								
Number	110	103	105	96	88	89	86	84
Percent	13.3	12.2	12.1	11.2	10.3	10.2	9.7	9.4
Percent in the U.S. not covered	14.9	15.3	15.8	15.3	15.1	15.1	15.5	15.1
Children Under 18 Years of Age	195	197	206	209	206	207	206	204
Covered by Private or Public Insurance								
Number	172	173	182	194	190	196	195	110
Percent	88.5	88.1	88.3	92.5	92.2	94.5	94.7	95.4
Not Covered								
Number	22	23	24	10	10	11	11	94
Percent	11.5	11.9	11.7	7.5	7.8	5.5	5.3	4.6
Percent in the U.S. not covered	10.5	10.9	11.7	11.0	9.7	8.6	8.0	7.5

Table DE-7. Employment Status by Demographic Group, Preliminary 2012

(Numbers in thousands, percent.)

Characteristic	Civilian noninstitutional population	Civilian labor force		Employed		Unemployed	
		Number	Percent of population	Number	Percent of population	Number	Percent of population
Total	718	446	62.2	414	57.7	32	7.2
Sex							
Male	340	226	66.5	208	61.3	18	7.8
Female	378	220	58.3	206	54.5	15	6.6
Race, Sex, and Hispanic Origin							
White	534	329	61.6	308	57.8	20	6.2
Male	256	169	66.1	157	61.4	12	7.0
Female	277	160	57.5	151	54.5	9	5.3
Black or African American	148	93	63.3	83	56.4	10	10.8
Male	66	43	65.5	38	58.3	5	11.1
Female	82	50	61.4	45	54.9	5	10.5
Hispanic	59	40	67.5	36	61.5	4	8.9
Male	29	25	84.2	23	78.3	2	7.0
Female	30	15	50.9	13	44.7	2	12.1
Age							
16 to 19 years	49	16	33.4	13	25.5	4	23.8
20 to 24 years	60	42	70.9	37	62.5	5	12.0
25 to 34 years	111	91	81.6	83	74.9	7	8.3
35 to 44 years	114	95	83.2	90	78.6	5	5.5
45 to 54 years	126	102	80.6	97	76.5	5	5.0
55 to 64 years	120	77	64.0	73	60.7	4	5.1
65 years and over	137	24	17.3	22	16.1	2	6.5

NOTE: Data in Table 7 are from the Current Population Survey (CPS) and do not match the estimates in Table 8. See notes and definitions for further information.

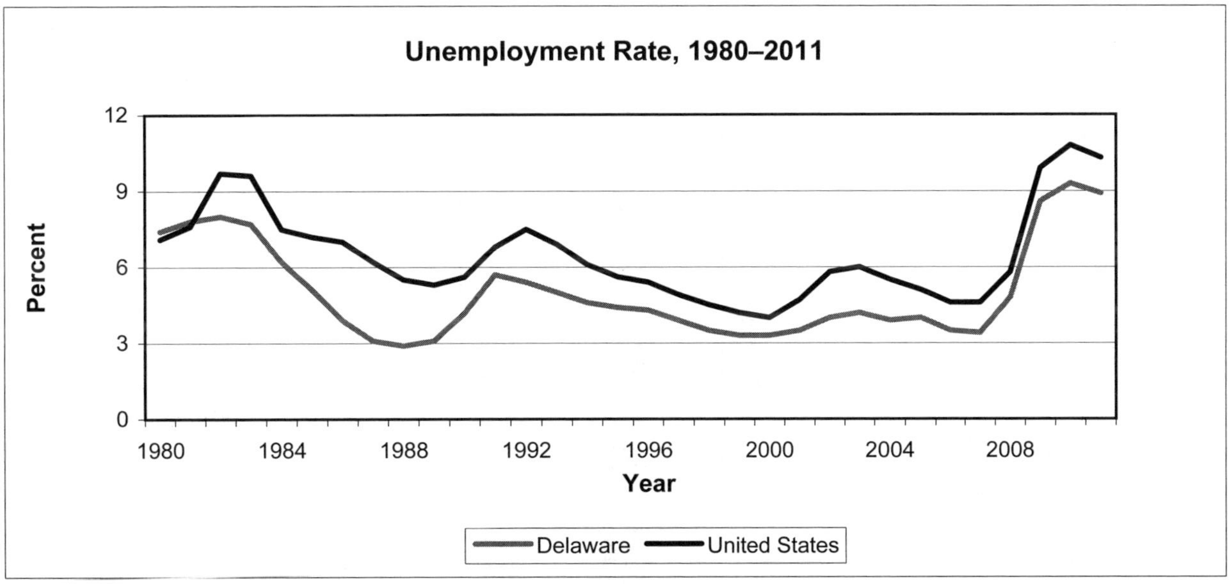

Table DE-8. Employment Status of the Civilian Noninstitutional Population Age 16 Years and Over

(Number, percent.)

Year	Civilian labor force	Civilian participation rate	Employed	Unemployed	Unemployment rate
2005	432,701	67.1	415,491	17,210	4.0
2006	438,617	66.9	423,267	15,350	3.5
2007	440,912	66.2	425,707	15,205	3.4
2008	442,902	65.5	421,838	21,064	4.8
2009	457,002	65.1	417,673	39,329	8.6
2010	453,206	63.2	411,120	42,086	9.3
2011	461,640	63.5	420,365	41,275	8.9

Table DE-9. Employment and Average Wages by Industry

(Estimates before 2007 are based on the 2002 *North American Industry Classification System* [NAICS]. Estimates from 2007 onward are based on the 2007 NAICS.)

Industry	2005	2006	2007	2008	2009	2010	2011
	Number of jobs						
Wage and Salary Employment by Industry	446,298	450,887	452,042	451,791	430,104	428,089	432,161
Farm Wage and Salary Employment	1,247	1,284	1,200	1,069	1,036	1,161	1,126
Nonfarm Wage and Salary Employment	445,051	449,603	450,842	450,722	429,068	426,928	431,035
Private wage and salary employment	376,773	380,019	380,353	379,042	357,441	354,081	358,212
Forestry, fishing, and related activities	334	323	318	D	D	D	D
Mining	D	16	L	D	D	D	D
Utilities	2,177	2,176	2,127	2,204	2,129	2,090	1,961
Construction	D	30,380	27,837	25,636	20,959	20,265	20,318
Manufacturing	33,264	33,330	33,394	31,813	27,987	26,181	25,698
Durable goods manufacturing	13,718	14,110	13,937	12,968	10,211	9,737	9,691
Nondurable goods manufacturing	19,546	19,220	19,457	18,845	17,776	16,444	16,007
Wholesale trade	15,023	15,227	14,873	14,667	13,355	12,599	12,592
Retail trade	54,225	54,367	55,073	53,635	50,475	50,723	51,364
Transportation and warehousing	10,809	11,281	11,478	11,196	10,215	10,092	10,261
Information	6,694	6,720	6,941	7,072	6,502	5,985	5,661
Finance and insurance	41,226	39,868	39,207	39,591	38,507	37,764	37,845
Real estate and rental and leasing	6,772	6,688	6,843	6,708	6,164	5,894	5,732
Professional, scientific, and technical services	25,351	25,163	25,624	26,132	24,563	24,166	26,292
Management of companies and enterprises	12,459	12,019	11,403	10,745	9,933	9,409	8,048
Administrative and waste services	23,365	24,103	24,685	23,737	21,527	21,440	22,068
Educational services	6,594	6,984	7,006	6,981	6,865	6,974	7,179
Health care and social assistance	47,573	48,887	50,899	55,114	56,354	57,290	58,699
Arts, entertainment, and recreation	9,021	8,873	8,489	8,439	8,223	8,817	9,224
Accommodation and food services	32,151	32,550	32,966	33,497	33,233	34,064	34,748
Other services, except public administration	20,730	21,064	21,181	21,532	20,085	19,925	19,978
Government and government enterprises	68,278	69,584	70,489	71,680	71,627	72,847	72,823
	Dollars						
Average Wages and Salaries by Industry	43,832	45,485	46,570	46,831	47,075	47,961	49,661
Average Farm Wages and Salaries	21,834	24,452	29,762	32,054	31,419	26,482	24,429
Average Nonfarm Wages and Salaries	43,893	45,545	46,614	46,866	47,113	48,020	49,727
Average private wages and salaries	44,262	46,001	46,972	47,097	47,132	48,446	50,316
Forestry, fishing, and related activities	19,278	20,858	21,786	D	D	D	D
Mining	D	37,125	L	D	D	D	D
Utilities	80,767	83,770	83,612	88,640	94,420	94,430	96,294
Construction	D	45,971	47,432	49,628	48,641	49,049	52,483
Manufacturing	52,166	54,044	59,626	56,464	57,897	56,995	56,148
Durable goods manufacturing	58,890	62,775	72,649	64,317	69,954	65,811	67,990
Nondurable goods manufacturing	47,447	47,635	50,297	51,059	50,971	51,776	48,979
Wholesale trade	63,559	72,018	70,604	69,948	72,291	76,872	82,623
Retail trade	24,396	25,040	25,474	25,504	25,714	25,809	26,002
Transportation and warehousing	38,073	38,299	39,053	40,885	43,197	43,126	44,551
Information	52,167	53,765	54,653	55,013	55,492	56,439	57,380
Finance and insurance	81,889	84,143	80,783	76,765	74,028	79,068	84,043
Real estate and rental and leasing	37,188	38,404	39,771	40,138	39,671	40,745	41,443
Professional, scientific, and technical services	71,914	73,218	76,696	79,826	80,985	85,311	89,362
Management of companies and enterprises	67,403	77,445	80,450	90,221	88,304	105,373	127,272
Administrative and waste services	27,798	29,529	30,326	31,245	31,075	32,443	32,770
Educational services	30,500	31,824	32,808	34,012	35,465	35,617	36,172
Health care and social assistance	42,403	43,606	45,541	45,687	46,857	47,294	48,700
Arts, entertainment, and recreation	23,256	25,756	28,368	26,862	27,626	28,568	30,865
Accommodation and food services	16,941	17,810	19,056	18,840	18,364	18,853	18,637
Other services, except public administration	26,309	27,708	28,389	28,818	28,893	29,255	29,443
Government and government enterprises	41,858	43,056	45,541	45,687	47,015	45,948	46,827

D = Not shown to avoid disclosure of confidential information, but the estimates for this item are included in the total.
L = Less than 10 jobs, but the estimates for this item are included in the total.

Table DE-10. Employment Characteristics by Family Type

(Number, percent.)

Family type and labor force status	2009		2010		2011	
	Total	Families with own children under 18 years	Total	Families with own children under 18 years	Total	Families with own children under 18 years
All families	220,655	95,181	221,233	96,460	227,101	94,229
Family type and labor force status						
Married-couple families	159,862	61,412	161,575	62,148	161,755	59,348
Both husband and wife in labor force	54.4	71.4	54.8	72.7	53.5	70.1
Husband in labor force, wife not in labor force	19.8	24.2	17.9	20.4	19.4	24.7
Wife in labor force, husband not in labor force	8.2	3.4	9.1	4.4	7.8	3.5
Both husband and wife not in labor force	17.6	1.0	18.3	2.6	19.3	1.8
Other families	60,793	33,769	59,658	34,312	65,346	34,881
Female householder, no husband present	74.9	78.9	76.3	78.3	71.4	71.6
In labor force	59.5	71.1	55.6	66.2	54.1	62.8
Not in labor force	15.4	7.8	20.8	12.1	17.3	8.8
Male householder, no wife present	25.1	21.1	23.7	21.7	28.6	28.4
In labor force	19.9	20.0	18.8	20.9	24.1	27.8
Not in labor force	5.2	1.2	4.9	0.8	4.5	0.6

Table DE-11. School Enrollment and Educational Attainment, 2011

(Number, percent.)

Item	State	U.S.
Enrollment		
Total population 3 years and over, enrolled in school	237,520	83,131,910
Enrolled in nursery school or preschool (percent)	6.2	6.0
Enrolled in kindergarten (percent)	5.7	5.1
Enrolled in elementary school, grades 1-8 (percent)	38.3	39.5
Enrolled in high school, grades 9-12 (percent)	19.9	20.7
Enrolled in college or graduate school (percent)	30.0	28.7
Attainment		
Total population 25 years and over	611,120	206,471,670
Less than ninth grade (percent)	4.7	6.0
9th to 12th grade, no diploma (percent)	8.3	8.1
High school graduate, including equivalency (percent)	31.6	28.4
Some college, no degree (percent)	19.6	21.2
Associate's degree (percent)	7.0	7.8
Bachelor's degree (percent)	17.1	17.9
Graduate or professional degree (percent)	11.7	10.6
High school graduate or higher (percent)	87	85.9
Bachelor's degree or higher (percent)	28.8	28.5

Table DE-12. Educational Indicators

(Number, percent; data derived from National Center of Education Statistics.)

Item	State	U.S.
Public Schools, 2009–2010 (except where noted)		
Number of school districts	19	13,629
Number of schools	217	99,834
Number of students (in thousands)	127	49,373
Student-teacher ratio	14.7	15.4
Expenditures per student (dollars)	14,329	10,591
Averaged freshman graduation rate, 2008–2009	73.7	75.5[1]
Dropout rate, 2008–2009	5.1	4.1
Students eligible for free or reduced-price lunch (percent)	48.9	48.0
English language learners, 2010–2011 (percent)	5.6	9.8[1]
Students with IEP (percent)	15.3	13.1
Private Schools, 2009–2010 (except where noted)		
Number of schools	135	33,366
Number of students (in thousands)	23	4,700
High school graduates, 2008–2009	1,847	308,813
Student-teacher ratio	11.0	10.7

[1] U.S. total includes estimates for nonreporting states.

Table DE-13. Reported Voting and Registration of the Voting-Age Population, November 2012

(Numbers in thousands, percent.)

Item	Total population	Total citizen population	Registered: Total registered	Registered: Percent registered (total population)	Registered: Percent registered (total citizen population)	Voted: Total voted	Voted: Percent voted (total population)	Voted: Percent voted (total citizen population)
U.S. Total	235,248	215,081	153,157	65.1	71.2	132,948	56.5	61.8
State Total	693	641	470	67.8	73.3	431	62.2	67.3
Sex								
Male	329	302	218	66.1	72.1	196	59.6	65.0
Female	363	339	252	69.3	74.4	235	64.6	69.3
Race								
White alone	521	488	365	70.1	74.7	336	64.5	68.8
White, non-Hispanic alone	474	468	355	74.9	75.9	328	69.0	69.9
Black alone	142	134	91	64.0	67.5	86	60.5	63.7
Asian alone	26	15	12	B	B	8	B	B
Hispanic (of any race)	56	24	11	B	B	10	B	B
Age								
18 to 24 years	82	77	38	46.1	49.4	33	40.5	43.4
25 to 44 years	225	187	131	58.2	70.1	117	51.8	62.3
45 to 64 years	240	232	182	75.9	78.6	168	69.9	72.3
65 to 74 years	83	82	66	80.0	80.4	63	76.7	77.1
75 years and over	63	63	52	B	B	50	B	B

B = Base is less than 75,000 and therefore too small to show the derived measure.

Table DE-14. Crime

(Number, rate per 100,000. Data are derived from the FBI Uniform Crime Reports.)

Item	State: 2010	State: 2011	State: Percent change	U.S.: 2010	U.S.: 2011	U.S.: Percent change
TOTAL POPULATION	899,792	907,135	0.8	309,330,219	311,591,917	0.7
VIOLENT CRIME						
Number	5,608	5,075	-9.5	1,251,248	1,203,564	-3.8
Rate	623.3	559.5	-10.2	404.5	386.3	-4.5
Murder and Nonnegligent Manslaughter						
Number	51	41	-19.6	14,722	14,612	-0.7
Rate	5.7	4.5	-21.1	4.8	4.7	-2.1
Forcible Rape						
Number	326	289	-11.3	85,593	83,425	-2.5
Rate	36.2	31.9	-11.9	27.7	26.8	-3.2
Robbery						
Number	1,839	1,538	-16.4	369,089	354,396	-4.0
Rate	204.4	169.5	-17.1	119.3	113.7	-4.7
Aggravated Assault						
Number	3,392	3,207	-5.5	781,844	751,131	-3.9
Rate	377.0	353.5	-6.2	252.8	241.1	-4.6
PROPERTY CRIME						
Number	31,078	30,939	-0.4	9,112,625	9,063,173	-0.5
Rate	3,453.9	3,410.6	-1.3	2,945.9	2,908.7	-1.3
Burglary						
Number	7,550	7,531	-0.3	2,168,459	2,188,005	0.9
Rate	839.1	830.2	-1.1	701.0	702.2	0.2
Larceny-Theft						
Number	21,593	21,878	1.3	6,204,601	6,159,795	-0.7
Rate	2,399.8	2,411.8	0.5	2,005.8	1,976.9	-1.4
Motor Vehicle Theft						
Number	1,935	1,530	-20.9	739,565	715,373	-3.3
Rate	215.0	168.7	-21.5	239.1	229.6	-4.0

Table DE-15. State Government Finances, 2011

(Dollar amounts in thousands, percent distribution.)

Item	Dollars	Percent distribution
Total Revenue	9,105,971	100.0
General revenue	7,309,677	80.3
Intergovernmental revenue	1,890,925	20.8
Taxes	3,017,837	33.1
General sales	0	0.0
Selective sales	493,195	5.4
License taxes	1,172,354	12.9
Individual income tax	962,321	10.6
Corporate income tax	322,537	3.5
Other taxes	67,430	0.7
Current charges	1,134,111	12.5
Miscellaneous general revenue	1,266,804	13.9
Utility revenue	16,142	0.2
Liquor stores revenue	0	0.0
Insurance trust revenue [1]	1,780,152	19.5
Total Expenditure	7,936,467	100.0
Intergovernmental expenditure	1,293,106	16.3
Direct expenditure	6,643,361	83.7
Current operation	4,731,765	59.6
Capital outlay	666,590	8.4
Insurance benefits and repayments	752,501	9.5
Assistance and subsidies	225,552	2.8
Interest on debt	266,953	3.4
Exhibit: Salaries and wages	2,286,930	28.8
Total Expenditure	7,936,467	100.0
General expenditure	7,057,717	88.9
Intergovernmental expenditure	1,293,106	16.3
Direct expenditure	5,764,611	72.6
General expenditure, by function:		
Education	2,543,765	32.1
Public welfare	1,762,406	22.2
Hospitals	51,908	0.7
Health	395,092	5.0
Highways	460,695	5.8
Police protection	114,070	1.4
Correction	266,666	3.4
Natural resources	99,770	1.3
Parks and recreation	37,934	0.5
Governmental administration	439,594	5.5
Interest on general debt	266,953	3.4
Other and unallocable	618,864	7.8
Utility expenditure	126,249	1.6
Liquor stores expenditure	0	0.0
Insurance trust expenditure	752,501	9.5
Debt at End of Fiscal Year	5,807,957	X
Cash and Security Holdings	14,799,103	X

X = Not applicable.
[1] Within insurance trust revenue, net earnings of state retirement systems is a calculated statistic (the item code in the data file is X08), and thus can be positive or negative. Net earnings is the sum of earnings on investments plus gains on investments minus losses on investments. The change made in 2002 for asset valuation from book to market value in accordance with Statement 34 of the Governmental Accounting Standards Board is reflected in the calculated statistics.

Table DE-16. State Government Tax Collections, 2012

(Dollars in thousands, percent.)

Item	Dollars	Percent distribution
Total Taxes	3,360,235	100.0
Property taxes	0	0.0
Sales and gross receipts	491,044	14.6
General sales and gross receipts	0	0.0
Selective sales and gross receipts	491,044	14.6
Alcoholic beverages	17,654	0.5
Amusements	0	0.0
Insurance premiums	91,763	2.7
Motor fuels	112,908	3.4
Pari-mutuels	96	-
Public utilities	59,694	1.8
Tobacco products	120,850	3.6
Other selective sales	88,079	2.6
Licenses	1,230,286	36.6
Alcoholic beverages	1,465	-
Amusements	324	-
Corporations in general	625,394	18.6
Hunting and fishing	2,736	0.1
Motor vehicle	49,601	1.5
Motor vehicle operators	5,470	0.2
Public utilities	0	0.0
Occupation and business, NEC	374,732	11.2
Other licenses	170,564	5.1
Income taxes	1,573,967	46.8
Individual income	1,311,589	39.0
Corporation net income	262,378	7.8
Other taxes	64,938	1.9
Death and gift	12,017	0.4
Documentary and stock transfer	51,598	1.5
Severance	0	0.0
Taxes, NEC	1,323	-

- = Rounds to zero.

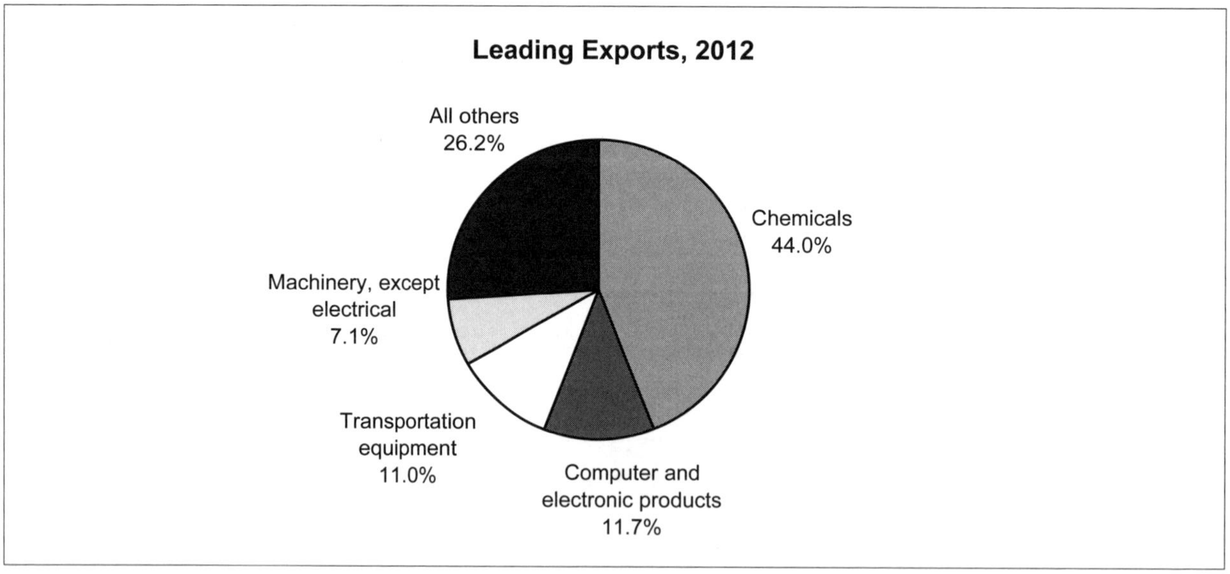

DISTRICT OF COLUMBIA

Facts and Figures

Location: South Atlantic United States; bordered on the SE, NE, and NW by Maryland and on the SW by Virginia

Area: 61.4 sq. mi. (2000 est.)

Population: 632,323 (2012 est.); rank—49th

Official Motto: Justitia omnibus ("Justice for All")

U.S. Congress: 1 delegate

Abbreviation: D.C.

Symbols: flower—American beauty rose; tree—scarlet oak; bird—wood thrush

At a Glance

- From 2000 to 2009, the population of the District of Columbia increased by 4.8 percent.
- In 2009, there were approximately 1,900 marriages and 1,300 divorces in the District of Columbia.
- The violent crime rate in the District of Columbia was 1,202.1 per 100,000 population, compared to 386.3 for the U.S. as a whole.
- Approximately 75.9 percent of District of Columbia residents voted in the 2012 election, while 61.9 percent of U.S. residents voted.
- Median gross rent was $1,216 in 2012.
- In 2011, 18.7 percent of people were in poverty. The poverty rate was higher for women (19.8 percent) than for men (17.4 percent).

Table DC-1. Population by Age, Sex, Race, and Hispanic Origin

(Number, percent, except where noted.)

Sex, age, race, and Hispanic origin	2000	2010	2012[1]	Average annual percent change, 2010–2012
Total Population	572,059	601,723	632,323	1.6
Percent of total U.S. population	0.2	0.2	0.2	X
Sex				
Male	269,366	284,222	299,041	1.7
Female	302,693	317,501	333,282	1.6
Age				
Under 5 years	32,536	32,613	38,876	5.4
5 to 19 years	103,270	91,107	93,333	0.8
20 to 64 years	366,355	409,194	428,225	1.5
65 years and over	69,898	68,809	71,889	1.4
Median age (years)	34.8	33.8	33.6	-0.2
Race and Hispanic Origin				
One race				
White	176,101	251,265	271,323	2.5
Black	343,312	310,379	316,482	0.6
American Indian and Alaska Native	1,713	3,264	3,488	2.1
Asian	15,189	21,705	24,034	3.2
Native Hawaiian or Other Pacific Islander	348	770	1,131	10.6
Two or more races	13,446	14,340	15,865	3.2
Hispanic (of any race)	44,953	57,833	66,135	4.2

X = Not applicable.
[1] Population figures for 2012 are July 1 estimates. The 2010 estimates are taken from the 2010 Census.

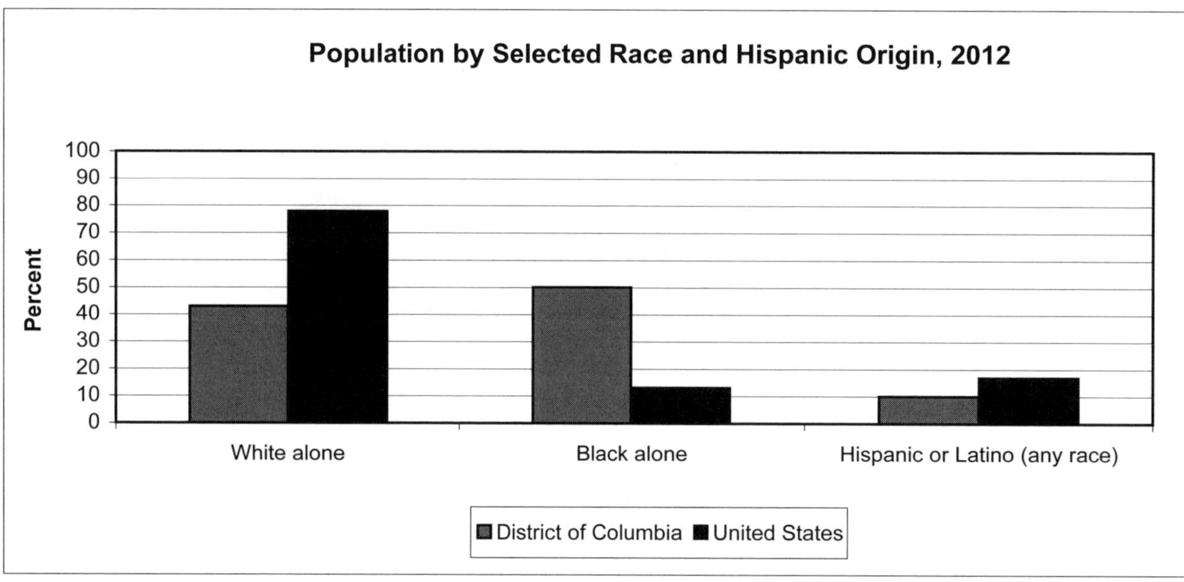

Table DC-2. Marital Status

(Number, percent distribution.)

Sex, age, race, and Hispanic origin	2000	2010	2011
Males, 15 Years and Over	219,706	243,152	247,251
Never married	51.2	58.9	59.3
Now married, except separated	32.8	28.2	27.1
Separated	3.9	2.4	2.2
Widowed	3.4	2.1	2.4
Divorced	8.7	8.4	8.9
Females, 15 Years and Over	254,711	277,203	281,817
Never married	46.0	55.8	56.9
Now married, except separated	27.5	22.8	23.1
Separated	4.4	3.1	2.5
Widowed	11.6	7.5	7.8
Divorced	10.6	10.8	9.7

Table DC-3. Households and Housing Characteristics

(Number, percent, dollars.)

Item	2000	2010	2011	Average annual percent change, 2000–2011
Total Households	248,338	252,388	268,670	0.7
Family households	114,166	101,519	114,045	-
Married-couple family	56,631	57,275	57,247	0.1
Other family	57,535	44,244	56,798	-0.1
Male householder, no wife present	10,503	8,740	11,128	0.5
Female householder, no husband present	47,032	35,504	45,670	-0.2
Nonfamily households	134,172	150,869	154,625	1.3
Householder living alone	108,744	121,036	121,522	1.0
Householder not living alone	25,428	29,833	33,103	2.5
Housing Characteristics				
Total housing units	274,845	296,836	298,908	0.7
Occupied housing units	248,338	252,388	268,670	0.7
Owner occupied	101,214	107,193	110,625	0.8
Renter occupied	147,124	145,195	158,045	0.6
Average size	2.16	2.24	2.15	-
Financial Characteristics				
Median gross rent of renter-occupied housing	618	1,198	1,216	8.1
Median monthly owner costs for housing units with a mortgage	1,291	2,297	2,224	6.0
Median value of owner-occupied housing units	157,200	426,900	422,400	14.1

- = Zero or rounds to zero.

Table DC-4. Migration, Origin, and Language

(Number, percent.)

Characteristic	State			U.S.		
	2010	2011	Percent change	2010	2011	Percent change
Residence 1 Year Ago						
Population 1 year and over	596,747	611,608	2.5	305,628,607	307,900,319	0.7
Same house	79.5	80.1	0.8	84.6	84.8	0.2
Different house in the U.S.	19.3	18.7	-3.1	14.8	14.6	-1.4
Same county	10.7	10.9	1.9	9.4	9.2	-2.1
Different county	8.6	7.9	-8.1	5.4	5.4	-
Same state	0.0	0.0	-	3.2	3.1	-3.1
Different state	8.6	7.9	-8.1	2.2	2.3	4.5
Abroad	1.2	1.2	-	0.6	0.6	-
Place of Birth						
Native born	522,719	534,397	2.2	269,393,835	271,214,059	0.7
Male	46.6	47.1	1.1	49.2	49.2	-
Female	53.4	52.9	-0.9	50.8	50.8	-
Foreign born	81,734	83,599	2.3	39,955,854	40,377,860	1.1
Male	51.4	48.7	-5.3	49.1	48.9	-0.4
Female	48.6	51.3	5.6	50.9	51.1	0.4
Foreign born; naturalized U.S. citizen	32,412	31,573	-2.6	17,476,082	18,140,192	3.8
Male	49.2	45.7	-7.1	45.8	45.8	-
Female	50.8	54.3	6.9	54.2	54.2	-
Foreign born; not a U.S. citizen	49,322	52,026	5.5	22,479,772	22,237,668	-1.1
Male	52.9	50.5	-4.5	51.6	51.5	-0.2
Female	47.1	49.5	5.1	48.4	48.5	0.2
Entered 2000 or later	45.1	46.3	2.7	34.7	35.7	2.9
Entered 1990 to 1999	21.6	21.7	0.5	27.2	26.7	-1.8
Entered before 1990	33.3	32.0	-3.9	38.1	37.6	-1.3
World Region of Birth, Foreign						
Foreign-born population, excluding population born at sea	81,734	83,599	2.3	39,955,673	40,377,757	1.1
Europe	17.5	20.3	16.0	12.1	12.1	-
Asia	18.6	18.8	1.1	28.2	28.6	1.4
Africa	16.1	14.2	-11.8	4	4.1	2.5
Oceania	1.9	0.4	-78.9	0.5	0.5	-
Latin America	44.1	44.9	1.8	53.1	52.6	-0.9
North America	1.8	1.5	-16.7	2	2.0	-
Language Spoken at Home and Ability to Speak English						
Population 5 years and over	571,592	581,764	1.8	289,215,746	291,524,091	0.8
English only	85.5	85.0	-0.6	79.4	79.2	-0.3
Language other than English	14.5	15.0	3.4	20.6	20.8	1.0
Speaks English less than "very well"	4.2	4.1	-2.4	8.7	8.7	-

- = Zero or rounds to zero.

Table DC-5. Median Income and Poverty Status, 2011

(Number, percent, except as noted.)

Characteristic	State		U.S.	
	Number	Percent	Number	Percent
Median Income				
Households (dollars)	63,124	X	50,502	X
Families (dollars)	75,603	X	61,455	X
Below Poverty Level (All People)	109,363	18.7	48,452,035	15.9
Sex				
Male	48,227	17.4	21,825,281	14.7
Female	61,136	19.8	26,626,754	17.2
Age				
Under 18 years	31,769	30.3	16,386,500	22.5
Related children under 18 years	31,598	30.2	16,087,074	22.2
18 to 64 years	69,155	16.8	28,335,079	14.8
65 years and over	8,439	12.5	3,730,456	9.3

X = Not applicable.

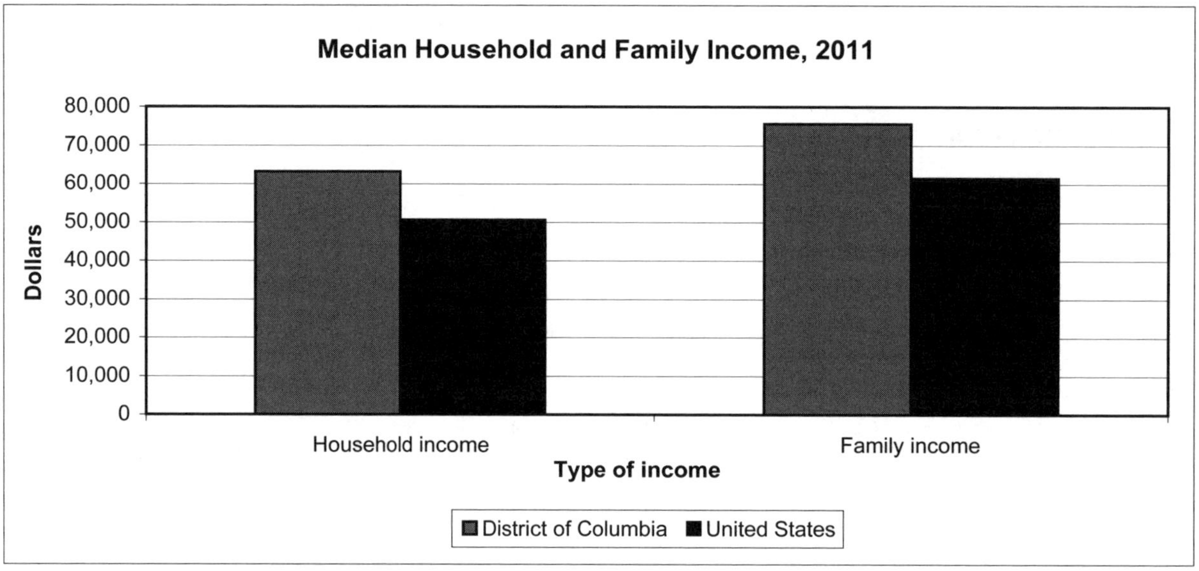

Table DC-6. Health Insurance Coverage Status for the Civilian Noninstitutionalized Population and Children Under 18 Years of Age

(Numbers in thousands, percent.)

Item	2004	2005	2006	2007	2008	2009	2010	2011
Civilian Noninstitutionalized Population	547	540	569	582	580	589	594	608
Covered by Private or Public Insurance								
Number	479	468	503	526	534	548	549	566
Percent	87.7	86.8	88.5	90.5	92.1	93.0	92.4	93.1
Not Covered								
Number	67	71	66	55	46	41	45	42
Percent	12.3	13.2	11.6	9.5	7.9	7.0	7.6	6.9
Percent in the U.S. not covered	14.9	15.3	15.8	15.3	15.1	15.1	15.5	15.1
Children Under 18 Years of Age	113	112	115	112	111	114	101	105
Covered by Private or Public Insurance								
Number	105	105	105	105	106	111	99	101
Percent	92.6	93.7	91.3	93.8	95.5	97.2	97.7	96.1
Not Covered								
Number	8	7	10	7	5	3	2	4
Percent	7.4	6.3	8.7	6.2	4.5	2.8	2.3	3.9
Percent in the U.S. not covered	10.5	10.9	11.7	11.0	9.7	8.6	8.0	7.5

Table DC-7. Employment Status by Demographic Group, Preliminary 2012

(Numbers in thousands, percent.)

Characteristic	Civilian noninstitutional population	Civilian labor force		Employed		Unemployed	
		Number	Percent of population	Number	Percent of population	Number	Percent of population
Total	523	363	69.3	330	63.1	33	9.0
Sex							
Male	242	179	74.0	164	67.6	15	8.6
Female	281	183	65.3	166	59.2	17	9.3
Race, Sex, and Hispanic Origin							
White	239	196	81.9	189	79.1	7	3.5
Male	119	102	85.6	99	82.7	3	3.3
Female	120	94	78.3	90	75.5	3	3.6
Black or African American	252	144	57.2	120	47.4	25	17.0
Male	110	68	62.0	57	51.7	11	16.7
Female	142	76	53.4	63	44.1	13	17.4
Hispanic	53	40	76.4	37	70.4	3	7.8
Male	28	23	82.9	21	76.2	2	8.2
Female	25	17	69.2	16	64.3	1	7.2
Age							
16 to 19 years	22	4	19.9	3	13.0	2	34.0
20 to 24 years	60	44	72.9	38	62.9	6	13.7
25 to 34 years	145	124	85.6	114	79.1	9	7.6
35 to 44 years	85	75	87.8	70	81.7	5	7.0
45 to 54 years	72	57	80.0	51	71.5	6	10.6
55 to 64 years	62	41	66.2	37	60.5	4	8.7
65 years and over	78	18	22.8	17	21.8	1	4.3

NOTE: Data in Table 7 are from the Current Population Survey (CPS) and do not match the estimates in Table 8. See notes and definitions for further information.

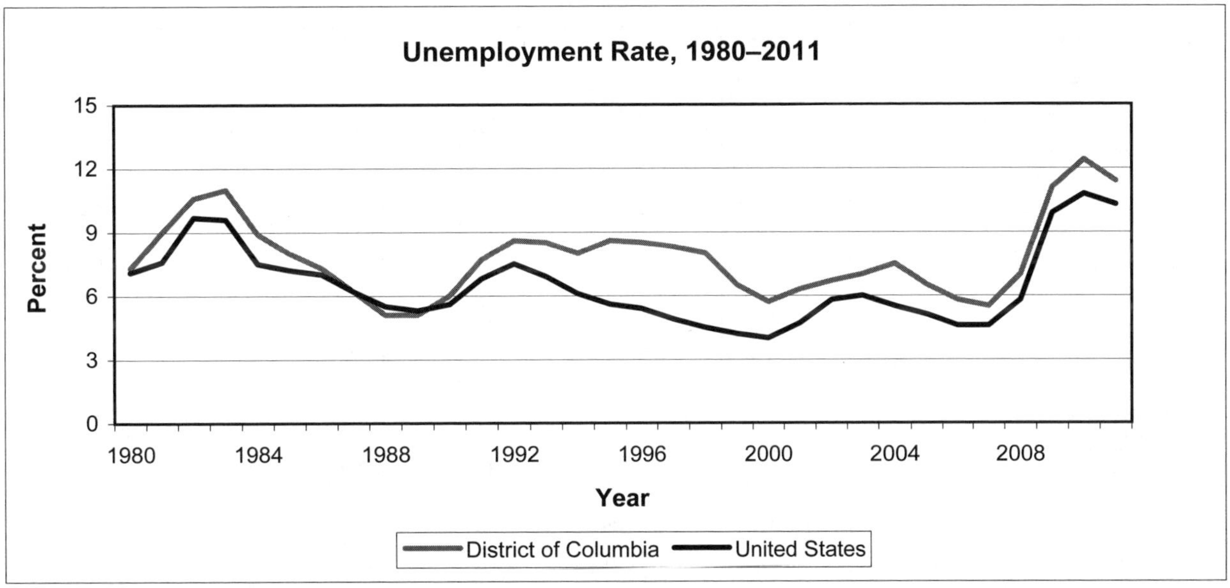

Table DC-8. Employment Status of the Civilian Noninstitutional Population Age 16 Years and Over

(Number, percent.)

Year	Civilian labor force	Civilian participation rate	Employed	Unemployed	Unemployment rate
2005	318,472	67.9	297,710	20,762	7.5
2006	321,442	67.8	302,893	18,549	5.8
2007	327,218	68.5	309,116	18,102	5.5
2008	332,703	69.0	309,528	23,175	7.0
2009	330,607	66.3	293,927	36,680	11.1
2010	341,495	66.3	299,127	42,368	12.4
2011	350,483	67.0	310,607	39,876	11.4

Table DC-9. Employment and Average Wages by Industry

(Estimates before 2007 are based on the 2002 *North American Industry Classification System* [NAICS]. Estimates from 2007 onward are based on the 2007 NAICS.)

Industry	2005	2006	2007	2008	2009	2010	2011
	Number of jobs						
Wage and Salary Employment by Industry	715,764	723,167	729,092	733,517	733,350	744,878	757,818
Farm Wage and Salary Employment	0	0	0	0	0	0	0
Nonfarm Wage and Salary Employment	715,764	723,167	729,092	733,517	733,350	744,878	757,818
Private wage and salary employment	462,232	469,642	478,923	481,877	474,925	476,224	489,895
Forestry, fishing, and related activities	0	0	0	0	0	0	0
Mining	D	0	0	0	0	0	0
Utilities	2,600	2,461	2,398	2,346	2,459	1,833	1,830
Construction	D	13,305	13,306	13,598	12,281	11,251	12,828
Manufacturing	2,139	1,783	1,708	1,623	1,431	1,280	1,043
Durable goods manufacturing	710	624	566	579	528	476	424
Nondurable goods manufacturing	1,429	1,159	1,142	1,044	903	804	619
Wholesale trade	4,704	4,813	5,012	4,852	4,673	4,819	4,651
Retail trade	18,116	18,531	18,693	18,906	18,309	18,993	18,983
Transportation and warehousing	5,027	4,554	4,202	4,132	4,102	4,165	4,080
Information	22,956	22,755	22,413	20,900	19,379	18,759	18,690
Finance and insurance	16,752	16,756	16,689	15,746	14,746	15,029	14,956
Real estate and rental and leasing	10,278	10,424	10,562	10,481	10,563	10,456	10,641
Professional, scientific, and technical services	100,089	102,746	103,754	105,097	102,924	102,220	104,222
Management of companies and enterprises	1,452	1,383	1,366	1,422	1,294	2,020	2,018
Administrative and waste services	43,956	44,431	45,373	44,695	42,286	42,712	45,578
Educational services	45,452	48,207	49,313	48,206	49,770	49,090	50,908
Health care and social assistance	52,511	52,677	55,840	56,702	58,017	59,950	61,752
Arts, entertainment, and recreation	6,382	6,150	6,343	7,296	7,338	7,207	7,164
Accommodation and food services	48,725	49,584	50,033	51,596	51,897	53,781	56,053
Other services, except public administration	67,740	69,082	71,918	74,279	73,456	72,659	74,498
Government and government enterprises	253,532	253,525	250,169	251,640	258,425	268,654	267,923
	Dollars						
Average Wages and Salaries by Industry	65,619	68,636	72,022	74,759	75,910	78,560	79,851
Average Farm Wages and Salaries	0	0	0	0	0	0	0
Average Nonfarm Wages and Salaries	65,619	68,636	72,022	74,759	75,910	78,560	79,851
Average private wages and salaries	60,835	64,373	67,954	70,075	69,872	72,019	73,536
Forestry, fishing, and related activities	0	0	0	0	0	0	0
Mining	D	0	0	0	0	0	0
Utilities							
Construction	D	52,234	54,148	55,750	56,397	61,048	63,382
Manufacturing	75,668	78,477	76,138	77,417	80,783	84,192	104,606
Durable goods manufacturing	100,414	95,095	80,072	79,097	78,275	78,029	83,026
Nondurable goods manufacturing	63,373	69,530	74,187	76,486	82,250	87,841	119,388
Wholesale trade	81,059	84,075	89,460	95,595	97,341	100,782	107,748
Retail trade	28,519	29,179	29,318	29,003	29,420	30,688	31,739
Transportation and warehousing	50,816	54,147	58,770	67,129	65,654	66,085	69,395
Information	89,765	91,724	97,249	103,994	102,813	103,198	106,842
Finance and insurance	110,463	124,703	138,096	133,784	120,567	128,361	137,434
Real estate and rental and leasing	60,589	69,072	71,384	69,104	64,471	70,628	74,778
Professional, scientific, and technical services	95,701	102,104	108,801	113,138	113,173	117,448	120,221
Management of companies and enterprises	167,169	208,094	277,063	237,873	273,999	218,147	201,919
Administrative and waste services	35,157	37,766	40,409	42,388	42,808	43,764	45,846
Educational services	38,600	38,627	39,687	43,550	44,413	45,190	45,369
Health care and social assistance	48,513	51,310	52,686	54,254	55,691	56,786	57,529
Arts, entertainment, and recreation	51,431	57,931	55,746	60,157	61,914	63,999	55,361
Accommodation and food services	28,641	29,371	32,025	30,918	30,575	31,751	32,479
Other services, except public administration	59,604	61,795	64,572	67,754	69,914	72,831	75,100
Government and government enterprises	74,342	76,534	79,811	83,727	87,005	90,156	91,399

D = Not shown to avoid disclosure of confidential information, but the estimates for this item are included in the total.

Table DC-10. Employment Characteristics by Family Type

(Number, percent.)

Family type and labor force status	2009		2010		2011	
	Total	Families with own children under 18 years	Total	Families with own children under 18 years	Total	Families with own children under 18 years
All families	109,030	44,124	101,519	42,063	114,045	46,540
Family type and labor force status						
Married-couple families	56,695	18,402	57,275	20,732	57,247	19,337
Both husband and wife in labor force	60.9	68.6	60.8	73.8	64.2	77.3
Husband in labor force, wife not in labor force	19.2	26.4	19.7	21.8	15.2	17.0
Wife in labor force, husband not in labor force	7.8	4.3	8.7	4.5	7.7	4.0
Both husband and wife not in labor force	12.0	0.7	10.7	0.0	12.9	1.7
Other families	52,335	25,722	44,244	21,331	56,798	27,203
Female householder, no husband present	83.2	84.3	80.2	83.2	80.4	82.4
In labor force	55.3	67.3	51.6	64.7	52.2	64.9
Not in labor force	27.9	17.0	28.6	18.5	28.2	17.5
Male householder, no wife present	16.8	15.7	19.8	16.8	19.6	17.6
In labor force	12.3	12.8	13.6	15.3	15.0	15.6
Not in labor force	4.5	2.9	6.1	1.5	4.6	2.0

Table DC-11. School Enrollment and Educational Attainment, 2011

(Number, percent.)

Item	State	U.S.
Enrollment		
Total population 3 years and over, enrolled in school	160,469	83,131,910
Enrolled in nursery school or preschool (percent)	6.8	6.0
Enrolled in kindergarten (percent)	5.1	5.1
Enrolled in elementary school, grades 1-8 (percent)	25.5	39.5
Enrolled in high school, grades 9-12 (percent)	15.3	20.7
Enrolled in college or graduate school (percent)	47.3	28.7
Attainment		
Total population 25 years and over	428,261	206,471,670
Less than ninth grade (percent)	5.1	6.0
9th to 12th grade, no diploma (percent)	7.7	8.1
High school graduate, including equivalency (percent)	17.7	28.4
Some college, no degree (percent)	14.2	21.2
Associate's degree (percent)	2.8	7.8
Bachelor's degree (percent)	23.3	17.9
Graduate or professional degree (percent)	29.2	10.6
High school graduate or higher (percent)	87.2	85.9
Bachelor's degree or higher (percent)	52.5	28.5

Table DC-12. Educational Indicators

(Number, percent; data derived from National Center of Education Statistics.)

Item	State	U.S.
Public Schools, 2009–2010 (except where noted)		
Number of school districts	1	13,629
Number of schools	233	99,834
Number of students (in thousands)	69	49,373
Student-teacher ratio	10.9	15.4
Expenditures per student (dollars)	24,358	10,591
Averaged freshman graduation rate, 2008–2009	62.4	75.5[1]
Dropout rate, 2008–2009	7.0	4.1
Students eligible for free or reduced-price lunch (percent)	73.1	48.0
English language learners, 2010–2011 (percent)	8.4	9.8[1]
Students with IEP (percent)	16.4	13.1
Private Schools, 2009–2010 (except where noted)		
Number of schools	86	33,366
Number of students (in thousands)	16	4,700
High school graduates, 2008–2009	1,339	308,813
Student-teacher ratio	8.4	10.7

[1] U.S. total includes estimates for nonreporting states.

Table DC-13. Reported Voting and Registration of the Voting-Age Population, November 2012

(Numbers in thousands, percent.)

Item	Total population	Total citizen population	Registered			Voted		
			Total registered	Percent registered (total population)	Percent registered (total citizen population)	Total voted	Percent voted (total population)	Percent voted (total citizen population)
U.S. Total	235,248	215,081	153,157	65.1	71.2	132,948	56.5	61.8
State Total	517	461	385	74.4	83.4	350	67.7	75.9
Sex								
Male	240	212	173	71.8	81.4	154	64.2	72.7
Female	277	249	212	76.6	85.0	196	70.8	78.6
Race								
White alone	246	212	180	73.2	85.1	161	65.3	75.9
White, non-Hispanic alone	208	197	171	82.0	86.4	151	72.8	76.7
Black alone	244	231	191	78.0	82.6	177	72.6	76.8
Asian alone	20	13	10	B	B	9	B	B
Hispanic (of any race)	48	19	14	B	B	13	B	B
Age								
18 to 24 years	71	61	43	B	B	38	B	B
25 to 44 years	233	200	173	74.2	86.3	156	67.2	78.1
45 to 64 years	140	129	109	77.7	84.4	99	70.9	77.0
65 to 74 years	40	38	34	B	B	33	B	B
75 years and over	34	33	26	B	B	24	B	B

B = Base is less than 75,000 and therefore too small to show the derived measure.

Table DC-14. Crime

(Number, rate per 100,000. Data are derived from the FBI Uniform Crime Reports.)

Item	State			U.S.		
	2010	2011	Percent change	2010	2011	Percent change
TOTAL POPULATION	604,912	617,996	2.2	309,330,219	311,591,917	0.7
VIOLENT CRIME						
Number	8,026	7,429	-7.4	1,251,248	1,203,564	-3.8
Rate	1,326.8	1,202.1	-9.4	404.5	386.3	-4.5
Murder and Nonnegligent Manslaughter						
Number	132	108	-18.2	14,722	14,612	-0.7
Rate	21.8	17.5	-19.7	4.8	4.7	-2.1
Forcible Rape						
Number	187	173	-7.5	85,593	83,425	-2.5
Rate	30.9	28.0	-9.4	27.7	26.8	-3.2
Robbery						
Number	4,325	4,093	-5.4	369,089	354,396	-4.0
Rate	715.0	662.3	-7.4	119.3	113.7	-4.7
Aggravated Assault						
Number	3,382	3,055	-9.7	781,844	751,131	-3.9
Rate	559.1	494.3	-11.6	252.8	241.1	-4.6
PROPERTY CRIME						
Number	28,802	29,636	2.9	9,112,625	9,063,173	-0.5
Rate	4,761.4	4,795.5	0.7	2,945.9	2,908.7	-1.3
Burglary						
Number	4,233	3,850	-9.0	2,168,459	2,188,005	0.9
Rate	699.8	623.0	-11.0	701.0	702.2	0.2
Larceny-Theft						
Number	19,514	21,330	9.3	6,204,601	6,159,795	-0.7
Rate	3,225.9	3,451.5	7.0	2,005.8	1,976.9	-1.4
Motor Vehicle Theft						
Number	5,055	4,456	-11.8	739,565	715,373	-3.3
Rate	835.7	721.0	-13.7	239.1	229.6	-4.0

Table DC-15. State Government Finances, 2011

(Dollar amounts in thousands, percent distribution.)

Item	Dollars	Percent distribution
Total Revenue	11,643,413	100.0
General revenue	10,330,632	88.7
Intergovernmental revenue	3,926,319	33.7
Taxes	5,029,797	43.2
General sales	860,466	7.4
Selective sales	499,645	4.3
License taxes	22,985	0.2
Individual income tax	1,107,139	9.5
Corporate income tax	328,563	2.8
Other taxes	351,873	3.0
Current charges	506,619	4.4
Miscellaneous general revenue	867,897	7.5
Utility revenue	884,337	7.6
Liquor stores revenue	0	0.0
Insurance trust revenue [1]	428,444	3.7
Total Expenditure	13,682,043	100.0
Intergovernmental expenditure	0	0.0
Direct expenditure	10,223,841	74.7
Current operation	2,194,859	16.0
Capital outlay	1,671,719	12.2
Insurance benefits and repayments	671,632	4.9
Assistance and subsidies	149,190	1.1
Interest on debt	442,521	3.2
Exhibit: Salaries and wages	3,299,510	24.1
Total Expenditure	13,682,043	100.0
General expenditure	13,682,043	100.0
Intergovernmental expenditure	0	0.0
Direct expenditure	10,780,681	78.8
General expenditure, by function:		
Education	2,379,998	17.4
Public welfare	2,679,348	19.6
Hospitals	150,780	1.1
Health	468,943	3.4
Highways	562,532	4.1
Police protection	568,915	4.2
Correction	257,885	1.9
Natural resources	40,884	0.3
Parks and recreation	232,750	1.7
Governmental administration	619,388	4.5
Interest on general debt	422,941	3.1
Other and unallocable	734,713	5.4
Utility expenditure	2,229,730	16.3
Liquor stores expenditure	0	0.0
Insurance trust expenditure	671,632	4.9
Debt at End of Fiscal Year	10,330,553	X
Cash and Security Holdings	10,188,144	X

X = Not applicable.
[1] Within insurance trust revenue, net earnings of state retirement systems is a calculated statistic (the item code in the data file is X08), and thus can be positive or negative. Net earnings is the sum of earnings on investments plus gains on investments minus losses on investments. The change made in 2002 for asset valuation from book to market value in accordance with Statement 34 of the Governmental Accounting Standards Board is reflected in the calculated statistics.

Table DC-16. State Government Tax Collections, 2012

(Dollars in thousands, percent.)

Item	Dollars	Percent distribution
Total Taxes	5,029,797	100.0
Property taxes	1,859,126	37.0
Sales and gross receipts	1,360,111	27.0
General sales and gross receipts	860,466	17.1
Selective sales and gross receipts	499,645	9.9
Alcoholic beverages	5,855	0.1
Amusements	NA	X
Insurance premiums	NA	X
Motor fuels	22,323	0.4
Pari-mutuels	NA	X
Public utilities	209,949	4.2
Tobacco products	33,394	0.7
Other selective sales	228,124	4.5
Licenses		
Alcoholic beverages	NA	X
Amusements	NA	X
Corporations in general	NA	X
Hunting and fishing	NA	X
Motor vehicle	22,985	
Motor vehicle operators	NA	X
Public utilities	NA	X
Occupation and business, NEC	NA	X
Other licenses	NA	X
Income taxes		
Individual income	1,107,139	22.0
Corporation net income	328,563	6.5
Other taxes		
Death and gift	NA	X
Documentary and stock transfer	NA	X
Severance	NA	X
Taxes, NEC	1,810,560	36.0

Leading Exports, 2012

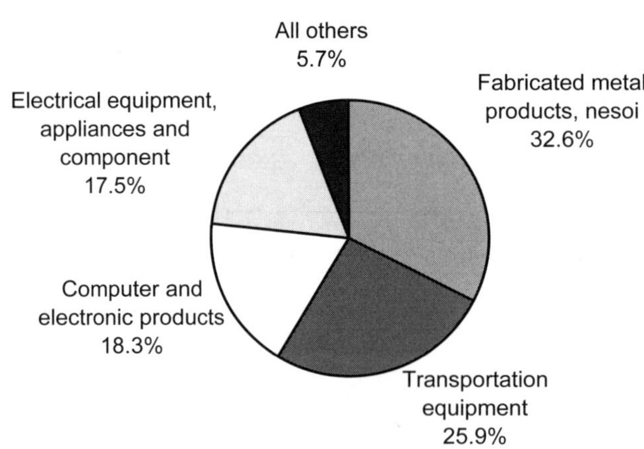

FLORIDA

Facts and Figures

Location: Southeastern United States; bordered on the N by Georgia and Alabama, on the E by the Atlantic Ocean, on the S by the Straits of Florida, and on the W by Alabama and the Gulf of Mexico

Area: 65,755 sq. mi. (170,304 sq. km.); rank—22nd

Population: 19,317,568 (2012 est.); rank—4th

Principal Cities: capital—Tallahassee; largest—Jacksonville

Statehood: March 3, 1845; 27th state

U.S. Congress: 2 senators, 27 representatives

State Motto: In God We Trust

State Song: "The Swanee River (Old Folks at Home)"

State Nickname: The Sunshine State

Abbreviations: FL; Fla.

State Symbols: flower—orange blossom; tree—Sabal palm (cabbage palm); bird—mockingbird

At a Glance

- With an increase in population of 16.0 percent, Florida ranked 3rd among the states in growth from 2000 to 2009.
- An estimated 141,200 marriages took place in Florida in 2009, compared to 79,900 divorces.
- Florida's violent crime rate in 2011 was 515.3 per 100,000 population, compared to 386.3 for the entire nation.
- In the 2012 election, 60.8 percent of Florida's eligible voters voted, compared to 61.8 percent of eligible voters nationwide.
- In 2007, Florida exported $1.9 billion worth of agricultural products, 2.3 percent of the U.S. total.

Table FL-1. Population by Age, Sex, Race, and Hispanic Origin

(Number, percent, except where noted.)

Sex, age, race, and Hispanic origin	2000	2010	2012[1]	Average annual percent change, 2010–2012
Total Population	15,982,378	18,801,310	19,317,568	0.9
Percent of total U.S. population	5.7	6.1	6.1	X
Sex				
Male	7,797,715	9,189,355	9,447,827	0.9
Female	8,184,663	9,611,955	9,859,741	0.8
Age				
Under 5 years	945,823	1,073,506	1,071,463	-0.1
5 to 19 years	3,102,809	3,439,484	3,405,696	-0.3
20 to 64 years	9,126,149	11,034,718	11,330,721	0.9
65 years and over	2,807,597	3,259,602	3,509,715	2.4
Median age (years)	38.7	40.7	39.7	-0.8
Race and Hispanic Origin				
One race				
White	12,465,029	14,808,867	15,120,082	0.7
Black	2,335,505	3,078,067	3,206,350	1.3
American Indian and Alaska Native	53,541	89,119	95,218	2.1
Asian	266,256	474,199	511,960	2.5
Native Hawaiian or Other Pacific Islander	8,625	18,790	20,454	2.7
Two or more races	376,315	332,268	363,504	2.9
Hispanic (of any race)	2,682,715	4,301,853	4,570,972	2.0

X = Not applicable.
[1] Population figures for 2012 are July 1 estimates. The 2010 estimates are taken from the 2010 Census.

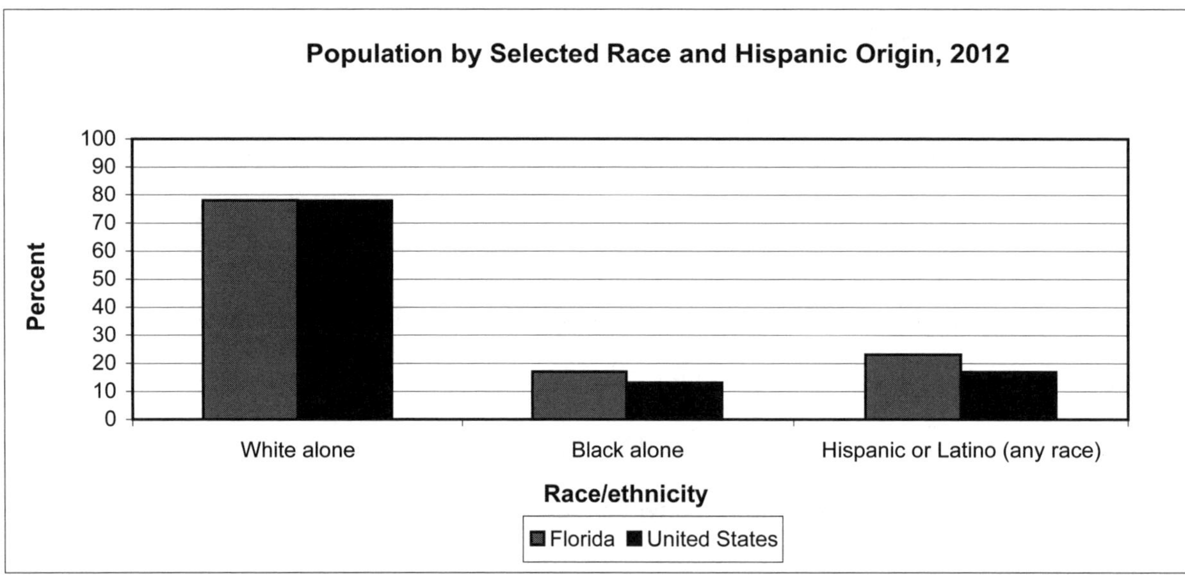

Table FL-2. Marital Status

(Number, percent distribution.)

Sex, age, race, and Hispanic origin	2000	2010	2011
Males, 15 Years and Over	6,232,987	7,534,535	7,641,196
Never married	27.3	33.9	35.0
Now married, except separated	56.9	49.3	48.0
Separated	2.1	2.2	2.3
Widowed	3.2	3.2	3.2
Divorced	10.5	11.5	11.4
Females, 15 Years and Over	6,714,003	8,021,290	8,129,069
Never married	20.5	26.6	27.4
Now married, except separated	51.9	45.1	44.5
Separated	2.7	3.0	2.9
Widowed	12.3	10.8	10.9
Divorced	12.7	14.5	14.3

Table FL-3. Households and Housing Characteristics

(Number, percent, dollars.)

Item	2000	2010	2011	Average annual percent change, 2000–2011
Total Households	6,337,929	7,035,068	7,106,283	1.0
Family households	4,210,760	4,556,930	4,559,858	0.7
Married-couple family	3,192,266	3,307,884	3,293,055	0.3
Other family	1,018,494	1,249,046	1,266,803	2.0
Male householder, no wife present	259,924	313,305	324,085	2.1
Female householder, no husband present	759,000	935,741	942,718	2.0
Nonfamily households	2,127,169	2,478,138	2,546,425	1.6
Householder living alone	1,687,303	2,013,028	2,078,284	1.9
Householder not living alone	439,886	465,110	468,141	0.5
Housing Characteristics				
Total housing units	7,302,947	8,994,091	9,027,271	2.0
Occupied housing units	6,337,929	7,035,068	7,106,283	1.0
Owner occupied	4,441,799	4,794,130	4,741,169	0.6
Renter occupied	1,896,130	2,240,938	2,365,114	2.1
Average size	2.46	2.62	2.62	0.5
Financial Characteristics				
Median gross rent of renter-occupied housing	641	947	949	4.0
Median monthly owner costs for housing units with a mortgage	1,004	1,505	1,470	3.9
Median value of owner-occupied housing units	105,500	164,200	151,000	3.6

Table FL-4. Migration, Origin, and Language

(Number, percent.)

Characteristic	State			U.S.		
	2010	2011	Percent change	2010	2011	Percent change
Residence 1 Year Ago						
Population 1 year and over	18,647,600	18,863,948	1.2	305,628,607	307,900,319	0.7
Same house	83.4	83.5	0.1	84.6	84.8	0.2
Different house in the U.S.	15.8	15.7	-0.6	14.8	14.6	-1.4
Same county	10.3	10.0	-2.9	9.4	9.2	-2.1
Different county	5.5	5.6	1.8	5.4	5.4	-
Same state	2.9	3.0	3.4	3.2	3.1	-3.1
Different state	2.6	2.6	-	2.2	2.3	4.5
Abroad	0.8	0.9	-	0.6	0.6	-
Place of Birth						
Native born	15,185,283	15,354,915	1.1	269,393,835	271,214,059	0.7
Male	49.2	49.4	0.4	49.2	49.2	-
Female	50.8	50.6	-0.4	50.8	50.8	-
Foreign born	3,658,043	3,702,627	1.2	39,955,854	40,377,860	1.1
Male	47.5	47.0	-1.1	49.1	48.9	-0.4
Female	52.5	53.0	1.0	50.9	51.1	0.4
Foreign born; naturalized U.S. citizen	1,773,148	1,840,016	3.8	17,476,082	18,140,192	3.8
Male	44.2	43.3	-2.0	45.8	45.8	-
Female	55.8	56.7	1.6	54.2	54.2	-
Foreign born; not a U.S. citizen	1,884,895	1,862,611	-1.2	22,479,772	22,237,668	-1.1
Male	50.5	50.8	0.6	51.6	51.5	-0.2
Female	49.5	49.2	-0.6	48.4	48.5	0.2
Entered 2000 or later	35.3	36.1	2.3	34.7	35.7	2.9
Entered 1990 to 1999	24.2	24.1	-0.4	27.2	26.7	-1.8
Entered before 1990	40.5	39.9	-1.5	38.1	37.6	-1.3
World Region of Birth, Foreign						
Foreign-born population, excluding population born at sea	3,658,043	3,702,627	1.2	39,955,673	40,377,757	1.1
Europe	10.6	10.4	-1.9	12.1	12.1	-
Asia	9.7	10.0	3.1	28.2	28.6	1.4
Africa	1.6	1.6	-	4	4.1	2.5
Oceania	0.1	0.2	100.0	0.5	0.5	-
Latin America	75.2	75.0	-0.3	53.1	52.6	-0.9
North America	2.7	2.9	7.4	2	2.0	-
Language Spoken at Home and Ability to Speak English						
Population 5 years and over	17,775,340	17,983,218	1.2	289,215,746	291,524,091	0.8
English only	72.6	72.4	-0.3	79.4	79.2	-0.3
Language other than English	27.4	27.6	0.7	20.6	20.8	1.0
Speaks English less than "very well"	11.9	11.9	-	8.7	8.7	-

- = Zero or rounds to zero.

Table FL-5. Median Income and Poverty Status, 2011

(Number, percent, except as noted.)

Characteristic	State		U.S.	
	Number	Percent	Number	Percent
Median Income				
Households (dollars)	44,299	X	50,502	X
Families (dollars)	53,958	X	61,455	X
Below Poverty Level (All People)	3,173,456	17.0	48,452,035	15.9
Sex				
Male	1,452,721	16.0	21,825,281	14.7
Female	1,720,735	17.9	26,626,754	17.2
Age				
Under 18 years	980,002	24.9	16,386,500	22.5
Related children under 18 years	965,366	24.6	16,087,074	22.2
18 to 64 years	1,864,891	16.3	28,335,079	14.8
65 years and over	328,563	10.0	3,730,456	9.3

X = Not applicable.

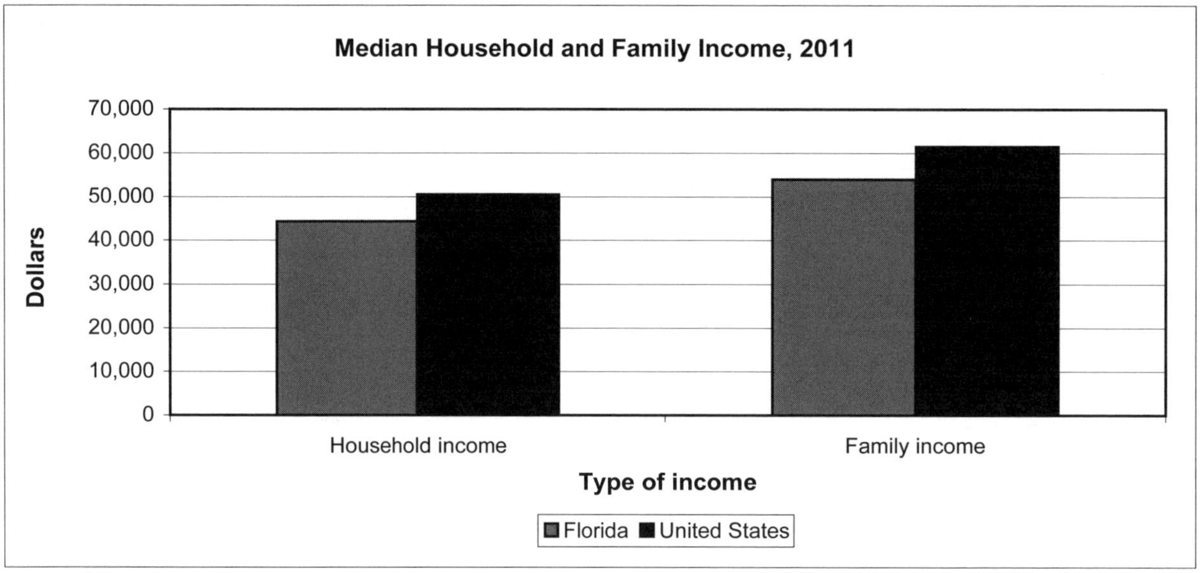

Table FL-6. Health Insurance Coverage Status for the Civilian Noninstitutionalized Population and Children Under 18 Years of Age

(Numbers in thousands, percent.)

Item	2004	2005	2006	2007	2008	2009	2010	2011
Civilian Noninstitutionalized Population	17,468	17,886	18,062	18,074	17,996	18,193	18,534	18,752
Covered by Private or Public Insurance								
Number	14,086	14,270	14,233	14,426	14,247	14,397	14,593	14,841
Percent	80.6	79.8	78.8	79.8	79.2	79.1	78.7	79.1
Not Covered								
Number	3,382	3,616	3,828	3,648	3,749	3,795	3,941	3,911
Percent	19.4	20.2	21.2	20.2	20.8	20.9	21.3	20.9
Percent in the U.S. not covered	14.9	15.3	15.8	15.3	15.1	15.1	15.5	15.1
Children Under 18 Years of Age	4,060	4,038	4,076	4,084	3,996	4,051	3,990	3,987
Covered by Private or Public Insurance								
Number	3,477	3,307	3,305	3,298	3,295	3,450	3,483	3,512
Percent	85.6	81.9	81.1	80.8	82.5	85.2	87.3	88.1
Not Covered								
Number	583	731	771	785	701	601	507	475
Percent	14.4	18.1	18.9	19.2	17.5	14.8	12.7	11.9
Percent in the U.S. not covered	10.5	10.9	11.7	11.0	9.7	8.6	8.0	7.5

Table FL-7. Employment Status by Demographic Group, Preliminary 2012

(Numbers in thousands, percent.)

Characteristic	Civilian noninstitutional population	Civilian labor force		Employed		Unemployed	
		Number	Percent of population	Number	Percent of population	Number	Percent of population
Total	15,431	9,358	60.6	8,572	55.5	786	8.4
Sex							
Male	7,391	4,898	66.3	4,460	60.3	438	8.9
Female	8,040	4,460	55.5	4,111	51.1	348	7.8
Race, Sex, and Hispanic Origin							
White	12,452	7,507	60.3	6,951	55.8	556	7.4
Male	6,008	3,991	66.4	3,677	61.2	313	7.8
Female	6,443	3,516	54.6	3,274	50.8	242	6.9
Black or African American	2,330	1,430	61.4	1,233	52.9	197	13.8
Male	1,065	680	63.8	575	54.0	104	15.3
Female	1,264	751	59.4	658	52.0	93	12.4
Hispanic	3,363	2,211	65.8	2,002	59.5	209	9.4
Male	1,623	1,185	73.0	1,074	66.2	111	9.4
Female	1,740	1,026	59.0	928	53.4	98	9.5
Age							
16 to 19 years	893	242	27.1	185	20.8	57	23.5
20 to 24 years	1,173	820	70.0	703	59.9	117	14.3
25 to 34 years	2,347	1,892	80.6	1,730	73.7	162	8.5
35 to 44 years	2,429	2,008	82.7	1,871	77.0	138	6.9
45 to 54 years	2,791	2,224	79.7	2,065	74.0	159	7.1
55 to 64 years	2,506	1,644	65.6	1,532	61.1	113	6.8
65 years and over	1,459	281	19.3	257	17.6	24	8.7

NOTE: Data in Table 7 are from the Current Population Survey (CPS) and do not match the estimates in Table 8. See notes and definitions for further information.

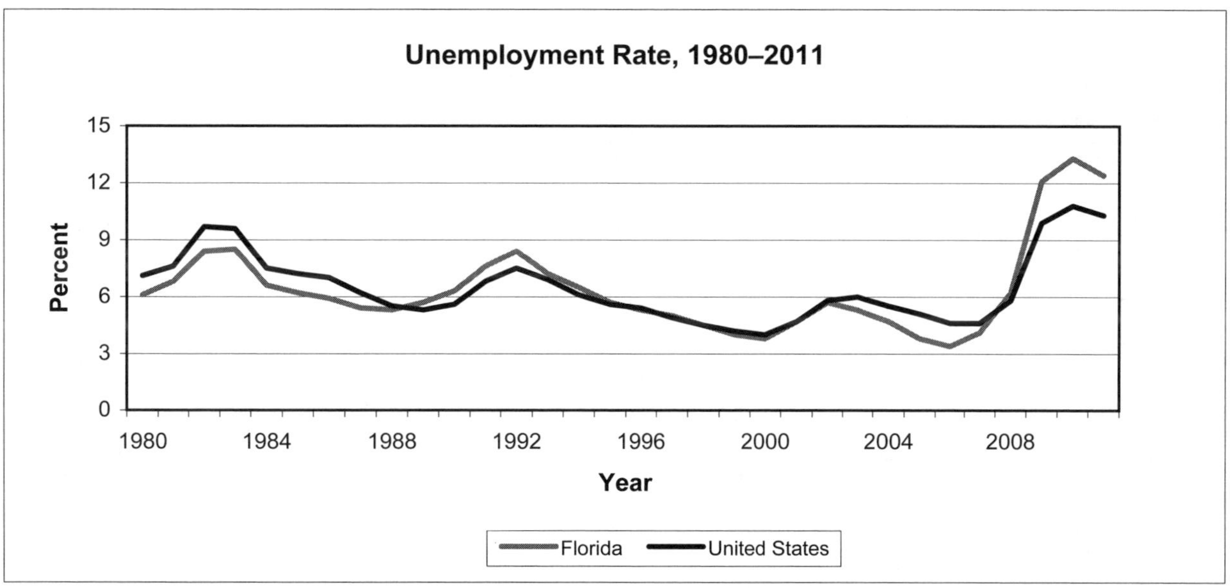

Table FL-8. Employment Status of the Civilian Noninstitutional Population Age 16 Years and Over

(Number, percent.)

Year	Civilian labor force	Civilian participation rate	Employed	Unemployed	Unemployment rate
2005	8,630,977	62.3	8,300,224	330,753	3.8
2006	8,889,263	62.9	8,587,732	301,531	3.4
2007	9,088,439	63.5	8,716,798	371,641	4.1
2008	9,231,462	63.9	8,659,856	571,606	6.2
2009	9,093,655	60.9	7,995,087	1,098,568	12.1
2010	9,203,585	60.0	7,974,945	1,228,640	13.3
2011	9,249,754	59.5	8,101,898	1,147,856	12.4

Table FL-9. Employment and Average Wages by Industry

(Estimates before 2007 are based on the 2002 *North American Industry Classification System* [NAICS]. Estimates from 2007 onward are based on the 2007 NAICS.)

Industry	2005	2006	2007	2008	2009	2010	2011
	Number of jobs						
Wage and Salary Employment by Industry	8,177,529	8,398,140	8,401,090	8,125,945	7,630,376	7,563,323	7,649,469
Farm Wage and Salary Employment	44,978	46,993	46,988	45,006	40,631	43,823	43,610
Nonfarm Wage and Salary Employment	8,132,551	8,351,147	8,354,102	8,080,939	7,589,745	7,519,500	7,605,859
Private wage and salary employment	6,954,962	7,155,768	7,139,936	6,861,100	6,385,235	6,317,449	6,425,016
Forestry, fishing, and related activities	46,206	47,129	46,639	46,733	45,698	47,225	48,809
Mining	5,349	4,644	4,779	4,491	3,716	3,621	3,867
Utilities	24,268	24,711	23,966	23,899	23,635	22,536	22,449
Construction	626,768	686,701	628,439	533,034	411,498	363,731	352,460
Manufacturing	403,709	411,086	396,293	371,848	324,409	307,997	311,760
Durable goods manufacturing	272,686	281,059	267,971	250,147	214,229	202,824	205,712
Nondurable goods manufacturing	131,023	130,027	128,322	121,701	110,180	105,173	106,048
Wholesale trade	343,623	353,805	362,217	349,063	321,204	310,983	310,640
Retail trade	1,002,039	1,030,157	1,032,619	1,002,198	938,837	943,845	970,895
Transportation and warehousing	221,639	226,690	227,058	224,977	209,413	206,261	213,907
Information	169,704	168,512	162,786	156,989	143,058	136,033	134,453
Finance and insurance	364,913	379,172	376,700	360,662	334,599	331,483	340,393
Real estate and rental and leasing	178,479	188,613	182,644	177,961	161,689	158,406	157,696
Professional, scientific, and technical services	441,654	464,406	467,854	465,317	440,476	441,971	452,113
Management of companies and enterprises	72,532	74,313	79,498	82,146	79,963	78,138	81,001
Administrative and waste services	766,859	728,679	714,819	603,182	541,284	540,834	534,702
Educational services	118,452	122,786	128,587	135,985	139,499	146,429	151,325
Health care and social assistance	826,354	864,528	892,867	915,482	922,747	936,552	954,874
Arts, entertainment, and recreation	177,407	181,242	188,356	188,382	186,789	186,468	194,114
Accommodation and food services	731,808	754,189	770,630	770,528	735,030	745,657	773,615
Other services, except public administration	433,199	444,405	453,185	448,223	421,691	409,279	415,943
Government and government enterprises	1,177,589	1,195,379	1,214,166	1,219,839	1,204,510	1,202,051	1,180,843
	Dollars						
Average Wages and Salaries by Industry	37,951	39,663	41,029	41,818	42,146	42,871	43,660
Average Farm Wages and Salaries	23,557	26,759	24,790	28,713	30,381	28,183	25,536
Average Nonfarm Wages and Salaries	38,030	39,736	41,120	41,891	42,209	42,956	43,764
Average private wages and salaries	37,364	39,104	40,435	41,051	41,209	42,029	42,933
Forestry, fishing, and related activities	20,043	20,861	21,436	21,531	21,449	22,205	23,045
Mining	50,305	54,620	58,004	57,534	56,325	59,818	61,206
Utilities	69,602	67,390	70,306	76,318	80,133	80,142	84,153
Construction	38,816	40,909	42,272	42,914	42,484	42,173	42,044
Manufacturing	44,982	47,205	48,964	50,491	52,102	53,838	54,449
Durable goods manufacturing	46,772	49,375	51,278	52,660	54,854	56,778	57,454
Nondurable goods manufacturing	41,257	42,514	44,131	46,034	46,751	48,168	48,621
Wholesale trade	54,205	57,359	58,885	60,133	60,012	62,426	64,969
Retail trade	26,951	27,742	27,681	27,581	27,740	28,095	28,326
Transportation and warehousing	40,777	42,413	44,062	45,062	45,607	47,072	48,077
Information	54,637	56,645	58,681	60,097	60,896	63,321	66,495
Finance and insurance	61,495	64,003	66,790	66,651	65,488	68,184	70,986
Real estate and rental and leasing	39,842	40,751	40,986	39,866	39,360	40,310	41,834
Professional, scientific, and technical services	56,787	59,926	62,488	64,195	64,394	65,418	66,954
Management of companies and enterprises	83,510	86,370	92,335	86,320	85,668	91,656	95,799
Administrative and waste services	28,521	29,755	30,890	32,267	33,037	33,431	34,123
Educational services	31,033	32,680	34,432	35,264	35,821	36,176	37,532
Health care and social assistance	40,186	41,593	43,031	44,290	45,327	45,926	46,711
Arts, entertainment, and recreation	33,323	35,911	37,288	37,133	36,096	36,864	37,366
Accommodation and food services	19,372	20,036	21,457	20,810	20,434	21,174	21,844
Other services, except public administration	25,440	26,803	27,782	28,520	28,746	29,697	29,872
Government and government enterprises	41,964	43,517	45,151	46,613	47,508	47,829	48,285

Table FL-10. Employment Characteristics by Family Type

(Number, percent.)

Family type and labor force status	2009		2010		2011	
	Total	Families with own children under 18 years	Total	Families with own children under 18 years	Total	Families with own children under 18 years
All families	4,542,466	1,830,555	4,556,930	1,790,226	4,559,858	1,788,705
Family type and labor force status						
Married-couple families	3,335,399	1,183,620	3,307,884	1,141,058	3,293,055	1,126,757
Both husband and wife in labor force	49.2	67.2	48.1	67.6	47.0	66.8
Husband in labor force, wife not in labor force	20.1	27.1	20.1	26.2	20.1	26.5
Wife in labor force, husband not in labor force	7.4	4.0	8.1	4.4	8.3	4.7
Both husband and wife not in labor force	23.3	1.7	23.7	1.8	24.6	2.1
Other families	1,207,067	646,935	1,249,046	649,168	1,266,803	661,948
Female householder, no husband present	74.3	77.2	74.9	78.4	74.4	77.0
In labor force	54.5	65.4	54.5	66.2	54.6	65.3
Not in labor force	19.9	11.7	20.4	12.2	19.8	11.7
Male householder, no wife present	25.7	22.8	25.1	21.6	25.6	23.0
In labor force	20.7	20.7	19.4	19.5	19.9	20.4
Not in labor force	4.9	2.1	5.7	2.1	5.7	2.6

Table FL-11. School Enrollment and Educational Attainment, 2011

(Number, percent.)

Item	State	U.S.
Enrollment		
Total population 3 years and over, enrolled in school	4,682,575	83,131,910
Enrolled in nursery school or preschool (percent)	6.4	6.0
Enrolled in kindergarten (percent)	4.7	5.1
Enrolled in elementary school, grades 1-8 (percent)	38.4	39.5
Enrolled in high school, grades 9-12 (percent)	20.3	20.7
Enrolled in college or graduate school (percent)	30.3	28.7
Attainment		
Total population 25 years and over	13,267,581	206,471,670
Less than ninth grade (percent)	5.6	6.0
9th to 12th grade, no diploma (percent)	8.4	8.1
High school graduate, including equivalency (percent)	30.4	28.4
Some college, no degree (percent)	20.8	21.2
Associate's degree (percent)	8.9	7.8
Bachelor's degree (percent)	16.5	17.9
Graduate or professional degree (percent)	9.3	10.6
High school graduate or higher (percent)	85.9	85.9
Bachelor's degree or higher (percent)	25.8	28.5

Table FL-12. Educational Indicators

(Number, percent; data derived from National Center of Education Statistics.)

Item	State	U.S.
Public Schools, 2009–2010 (except where noted)		
Number of school districts	67	13,629
Number of schools	4,043	99,834
Number of students (in thousands)	2,635	49,373
Student-teacher ratio	14.3	15.4
Expenditures per student (dollars)	10,491	10,591
Averaged freshman graduation rate, 2008–2009	68.9	75.5[1]
Dropout rate, 2008–2009	2.6	4.1
Students eligible for free or reduced-price lunch (percent)	56.0	48.0
English language learners, 2010–2011 (percent)	8.7	9.8[1]
Students with IEP (percent)	14.3	13.1
Private Schools, 2009–2010 (except where noted)		
Number of schools	1,962	33,366
Number of students (in thousands)	288	4,700
High school graduates, 2008–2009	18,255	308,813
Student-teacher ratio	10.8	10.7

[1] U.S. total includes estimates for nonreporting states.

Table FL-13. Reported Voting and Registration of the Voting-Age Population, November 2012

(Numbers in thousands, percent.)

Item	Total population	Total citizen population	Registered			Voted		
			Total registered	Percent registered (total population)	Percent registered (total citizen population)	Total voted	Percent voted (total population)	Percent voted (total citizen population)
U.S. Total	235,248	215,081	153,157	65.1	71.2	132,948	56.5	61.8
State Total	15,034	13,326	9,102	60.5	68.3	8,107	53.9	60.8
Sex								
Male	7,179	6,346	4,234	59.0	66.7	3,727	51.9	58.7
Female	7,855	6,980	4,869	62.0	69.8	4,379	55.8	62.7
Race								
White alone	12,054	10,834	7,515	62.3	69.4	6,712	55.7	62.0
White, non-Hispanic alone	9,024	8,771	6,039	66.9	68.9	5,430	60.2	61.9
Black alone	2,244	1,919	1,262	56.3	65.8	1,104	49.2	57.6
Asian alone	496	360	174	35.1	48.4	155	31.2	43.0
Hispanic (of any race)	3,349	2,250	1,622	48.4	72.1	1,399	41.8	62.2
Age								
18 to 24 years	1,669	1,467	751	45.0	51.2	614	36.8	41.9
25 to 44 years	4,715	3,863	2,493	52.9	64.5	2,164	45.9	56.0
45 to 64 years	5,345	4,814	3,474	65.0	72.2	3,107	58.1	64.5
65 to 74 years	1,881	1,802	1,344	71.5	74.6	1,259	66.9	69.9
75 years and over	1,423	1,381	1,040	73.1	75.3	963	67.6	69.7

Table FL-14. Crime

(Number, rate per 100,000. Data are derived from the FBI Uniform Crime Reports.)

Item	State			U.S.		
	2010	2011	Percent change	2010	2011	Percent change
TOTAL POPULATION	18,838,613	19,057,542	1.2	309,330,219	311,591,917	0.7
VIOLENT CRIME						
Number	101,969	98,199	-3.7	1,251,248	1,203,564	-3.8
Rate	541.3	515.3	-4.8	404.5	386.3	-4.5
Murder and Nonnegligent Manslaughter						
Number	987	984	-0.3	14,722	14,612	-0.7
Rate	5.2	5.2	-1.4	4.8	4.7	-2.1
Forcible Rape						
Number	5,373	5,274	-1.8	85,593	83,425	-2.5
Rate	28.5	27.7	-2.8	27.7	26.8	-3.2
Robbery						
Number	26,086	25,622	-1.8	369,089	354,396	-4.0
Rate	138.5	134.4	-3.0	119.3	113.7	-4.7
Aggravated Assault						
Number	69,523	66,319	-4.6	781,844	751,131	-3.9
Rate	369.0	348.0	-5.7	252.8	241.1	-4.6
PROPERTY CRIME						
Number	669,035	671,200	0.3	9,112,625	9,063,173	-0.5
Rate	3,551.4	3,522.0	-0.8	2,945.9	2,908.7	-1.3
Burglary						
Number	169,119	170,171	0.6	2,168,459	2,188,005	0.9
Rate	897.7	892.9	-0.5	701.0	702.2	0.2
Larceny-Theft						
Number	458,454	461,408	0.6	6,204,601	6,159,795	-0.7
Rate	2,433.6	2,421.1	-0.5	2,005.8	1,976.9	-1.4
Motor Vehicle Theft						
Number	41,462	39,621	-4.4	739,565	715,373	-3.3
Rate	220.1	207.9	-5.5	239.1	229.6	-4.0

Table FL-15. State Government Finances, 2011

(Dollar amounts in thousands, percent distribution.)

Item	Dollars	Percent distribution
Total Revenue	106,165,531	100.0
General revenue	75,290,282	70.9
Intergovernmental revenue	27,804,346	26.2
Taxes	32,557,946	30.7
General sales	19,353,000	18.2
Selective sales	7,803,056	7.3
License taxes	2,132,280	2.0
Individual income tax	0	0.0
Corporate income tax	1,869,870	1.8
Other taxes	1,399,740	1.3
Current charges	9,034,401	8.5
Miscellaneous general revenue	5,893,589	5.6
Utility revenue	20,342	0.0
Liquor stores revenue	0	0.0
Insurance trust revenue [1]	30,854,907	29.1
Total Expenditure	84,633,065	100.0
Intergovernmental expenditure	19,725,217	23.3
Direct expenditure	64,907,848	76.7
Current operation	43,852,094	51.8
Capital outlay	5,059,074	6.0
Insurance benefits and repayments	12,509,675	14.8
Assistance and subsidies	2,055,395	2.4
Interest on debt	1,431,610	1.7
Exhibit: Salaries and wages	9,093,287	10.7
Total Expenditure	84,633,065	100.0
General expenditure	71,984,886	85.1
Intergovernmental expenditure	19,725,217	23.3
Direct expenditure	52,259,669	61.7
General expenditure, by function:		
Education	24,882,722	29.4
Public welfare	22,302,600	26.4
Hospitals	948,858	1.1
Health	3,749,538	4.4
Highways	5,449,166	6.4
Police protection	439,294	0.5
Correction	2,465,017	2.9
Natural resources	1,133,964	1.3
Parks and recreation	116,607	0.1
Governmental administration	2,757,756	3.3
Interest on general debt	1,431,610	1.7
Other and unallocable	6,307,754	7.5
Utility expenditure	138,504	0.2
Liquor stores expenditure	0	0.0
Insurance trust expenditure	12,509,675	14.8
Debt at End of Fiscal Year	43,471,755	X
Cash and Security Holdings	191,713,677	X

X = Not applicable.

[1] Within insurance trust revenue, net earnings of state retirement systems is a calculated statistic (the item code in the data file is X08), and thus can be positive or negative. Net earnings is the sum of earnings on investments plus gains on investments minus losses on investments. The change made in 2002 for asset valuation from book to market value in accordance with Statement 34 of the Governmental Accounting Standards Board is reflected in the calculated statistics.

Table FL-16. State Government Tax Collections, 2012

(Dollars in thousands, percent.)

Item	Dollars	Percent distribution
Total Taxes	32,997,012	100.0
Property taxes	140	-
Sales and gross receipts	27,267,196	82.6
General sales and gross receipts	19,403,788	58.8
Selective sales and gross receipts	7,863,408	23.8
Alcoholic beverages	527,016	1.6
Amusements	157,108	0.5
Insurance premiums	704,760	2.1
Motor fuels	2,273,685	6.9
Pari-mutuels	9,360	-
Public utilities	3,162,560	9.6
Tobacco products	381,485	1.2
Other selective sales	647,434	2.0
Licenses	2,205,376	6.7
Alcoholic beverages	8,268	-
Amusements	12,000	-
Corporations in general	275,849	0.8
Hunting and fishing	15,379	-
Motor vehicle	1,305,028	4.0
Motor vehicle operators	350,141	1.1
Public utilities	27,321	0.1
Occupation and business, NEC	203,720	0.6
Other licenses	7,670	-
Income taxes	2,003,490	6.1
Individual income	0	0.0
Corporation net income	2,003,490	6.1
Other taxes	1,520,810	4.6
Death and gift	360	-
Documentary and stock transfer	1,470,590	4.5
Severance	49,860	0.2
Taxes, NEC	0	0.0

- = Rounds to zero.

Leading Exports, 2012

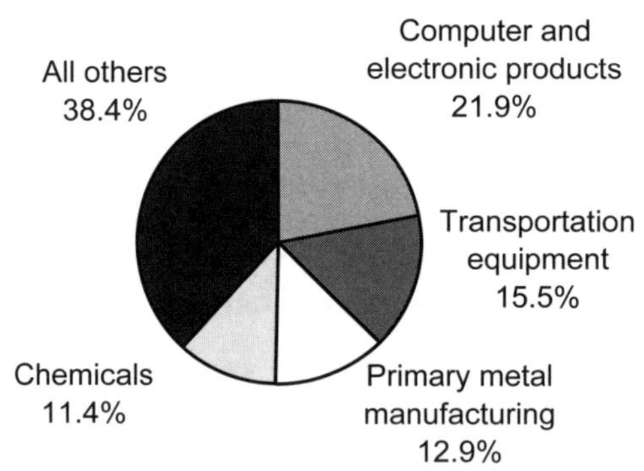

GEORGIA

Facts and Figures

Location: Southeastern United States; bordered on the N by Tennessee and North Carolina, on the E by South Carolina and the Atlantic Ocean, on the S by Florida, and on the W by Florida and Alabama

Area: 59,425 sq. mi. (153,909 sq. km.); rank—24th

Population: 9,919,945 (2012 est.); rank—8th

Principal Cities: capital—Atlanta; largest—Atlanta

Statehood: January 2, 1788; 4th state

U.S. Congress: 2 senators, 14 representatives

State Motto: Wisdom, Justice, and Moderation

State Song: "Georgia on My Mind"

State Nicknames: The Empire State of the South; The Peach State

Abbreviations: GA; Ga.

State Symbols: flower—Cherokee rose; tree—live oak; bird—brown thrasher

At a Glance

- With an increase in population of 20.1 percent, Georgia ranked 4th among the states in growth from 2000 to 2009.
- An estimated 63,600 marriages took place in Georgia in 2009; Georgia does not report its number of divorces.
- Georgia's median household income in 2011 was $46,007, and 19.1 percent of the population lived below the poverty level.
- In 2011, 19.6 percent of Georgians did not have health insurance, compared to 15.1 percent of the total U.S. population.
- In 2007, Georgia exported $1.5 billion worth of agricultural products, 1.8 percent of the U.S. total.

Table GA-1. Population by Age, Sex, Race, and Hispanic Origin

(Number, percent, except where noted.)

Sex, age, race, and Hispanic origin	2000	2010	2012[1]	Average annual percent change, 2010–2012
Total Population	8,186,453	9,687,653	9,919,945	0.8
Percent of total U.S. population	2.9	3.1	3.2	X
Sex				
Male	4,027,113	4,729,171	4,851,024	0.8
Female	4,159,340	4,958,482	5,068,921	0.7
Age				
Under 5 years	595,150	686,785	675,032	-0.6
5 to 19 years	1,819,620	2,094,844	2,103,201	0.1
20 to 64 years	4,986,408	5,873,989	6,002,013	0.7
65 years and over	785,275	1,032,035	1,139,699	3.1
Median age (years)	33.4	35.3	35.7	0.4
Race and Hispanic Origin				
One race				
White	5,327,281	6,144,931	6,231,978	0.5
Black	2,349,542	2,993,927	3,091,904	1.1
American Indian and Alaska Native	21,737	48,599	50,539	1.3
Asian	173,170	323,459	351,734	2.7
Native Hawaiian or Other Pacific Islander	4,246	10,454	11,061	1.8
Two or more races	114,188	166,283	182,729	3.0
Hispanic (of any race)	435,227	911,863	941,431	1.0

X = Not applicable.
[1] Population figures for 2012 are July 1 estimates. The 2010 estimates are taken from the 2010 Census.

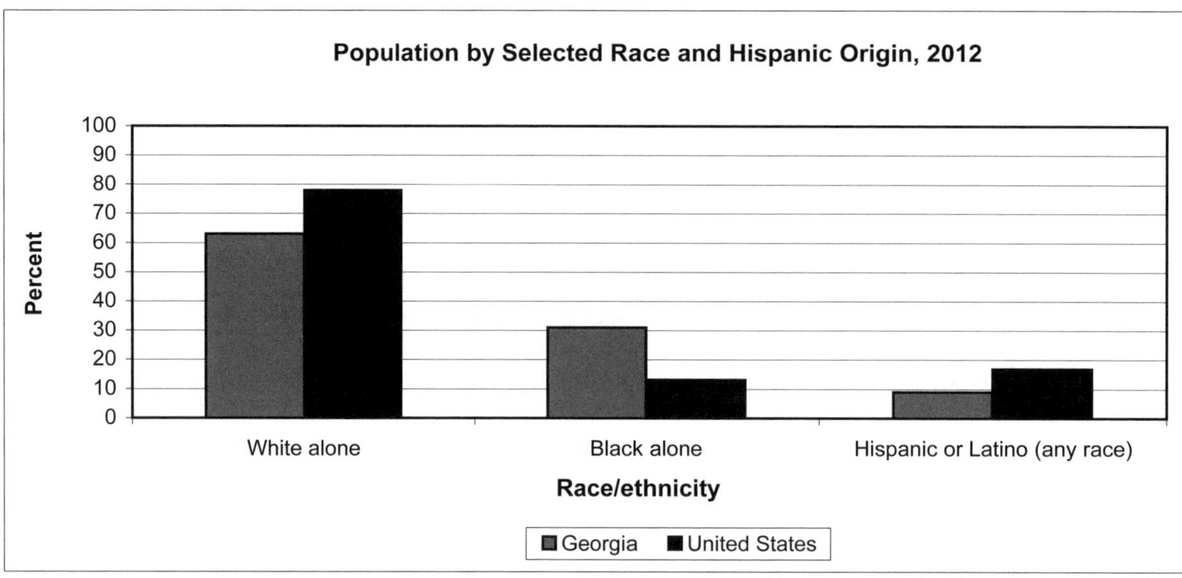

Table GA-2. Marital Status

(Number, percent distribution.)

Sex, age, race, and Hispanic origin	2000	2010	2011
Males, 15 Years and Over	3,092,736	3,683,258	3,739,449
Never married	30.4	35.4	36.0
Now married, except separated	56.5	50.5	49.6
Separated	2.0	2.1	2.2
Widowed	2.1	2.2	2.3
Divorced	9.0	9.9	9.9
Females, 15 Years and Over	3,273,889	3,954,542	3,996,814
Never married	24.4	29.7	30.5
Now married, except separated	51.5	46.1	44.9
Separated	2.7	2.9	3.2
Widowed	9.8	8.6	8.7
Divorced	11.6	12.7	12.8

Table GA-3. Households and Housing Characteristics

(Number, percent, dollars.)

Item	2000	2010	2011	Average annual percent change, 2000–2011
Total Households	3,006,369	3,482,420	3,494,542	1.4
Family households	2,111,647	2,385,969	2,376,008	1.0
Married-couple family	1,548,800	1,688,896	1,667,698	0.6
Other family	562,847	697,073	708,310	2.2
Male householder, no wife present	127,437	161,001	164,952	2.5
Female householder, no husband present	435,410	536,072	543,358	2.1
Nonfamily households	894,722	1,096,451	1,118,534	2.1
Householder living alone	710,523	921,005	929,969	2.6
Householder not living alone	184,199	175,446	188,565	0.2
Housing Characteristics				
Total housing units	3,281,737	4,091,482	4,103,118	2.1
Occupied housing units	3,006,369	3,482,420	3,494,542	1.4
Owner occupied	2,029,154	2,304,165	2,256,703	0.9
Renter occupied	977,215	1,178,255	1,237,839	2.2
Average size	2.65	2.72	2.74	0.3
Financial Characteristics				
Median gross rent of renter-occupied housing	613	819	833	3.0
Median monthly owner costs for housing units with a mortgage	1,039	1,390	1,371	2.7
Median value of owner-occupied housing units	111,200	156,200	147,100	2.7

Table GA-4. Migration, Origin, and Language

(Number, percent.)

Characteristic	State			U.S.		
	2010	2011	Percent change	2010	2011	Percent change
Residence 1 Year Ago						
Population 1 year and over	9,587,237	9,699,859	1.2	305,628,607	307,900,319	0.7
Same house	83.6	83.5	-0.1	84.6	84.8	0.2
Different house in the U.S.	15.9	16.1	1.3	14.8	14.6	-1.4
Same county	8.7	8.4	-3.4	9.4	9.2	-2.1
Different county	7.3	7.7	5.5	5.4	5.4	-
Same state	4.7	4.9	4.3	3.2	3.1	-3.1
Different state	2.6	2.8	7.7	2.2	2.3	4.5
Abroad	0.5	0.5	-	0.6	0.6	-
Place of Birth						
Native born	8,769,628	8,872,289	1.2	269,393,835	271,214,059	0.7
Male	48.5	48.7	0.4	49.2	49.2	-
Female	51.5	51.3	-0.4	50.8	50.8	-
Foreign born	942,959	942,921	-	39,955,854	40,377,860	1.1
Male	52.1	51.6	-1.0	49.1	48.9	-0.4
Female	47.9	48.4	1.0	50.9	51.1	0.4
Foreign born; naturalized U.S. citizen	329,875	373,068	13.1	17,476,082	18,140,192	3.8
Male	47.7	47.5	-0.4	45.8	45.8	-
Female	52.3	52.5	0.4	54.2	54.2	-
Foreign born; not a U.S. citizen	613,084	569,853	-7.1	22,479,772	22,237,668	-1.1
Male	54.5	54.4	-0.2	51.6	51.5	-0.2
Female	45.5	45.6	0.2	48.4	48.5	0.2
Entered 2000 or later	43.3	43.3	-	34.7	35.7	2.9
Entered 1990 to 1999	31.7	30.9	-2.5	27.2	26.7	-1.8
Entered before 1990	24.9	25.8	3.6	38.1	37.6	-1.3
World Region of Birth, Foreign						
Foreign-born population, excluding population born at sea	942,959	942,921	-	39,955,673	40,377,757	1.1
Europe	9.4	8.9	-5.3	12.1	12.1	-
Asia	26.1	26.8	2.7	28.2	28.6	1.4
Africa	7.9	8.5	-	4	4.1	2.5
Oceania	0.2	0.3	50.0	0.5	0.5	-
Latin America	54.7	54.0	-1.3	53.1	52.6	-0.9
North America	1.7	1.6	-5.9	2	2.0	-
Language Spoken at Home and Ability to Speak English						
Population 5 years and over	9,030,273	9,141,183	1.2	289,215,746	291,524,091	0.8
English only	86.9	86.7	-0.2	79.4	79.2	-0.3
Language other than English	13.1	13.3	1.5	20.6	20.8	1.0
Speaks English less than "very well"	5.8	5.7	-1.7	8.7	8.7	-

- = Zero or rounds to zero.

Table GA-5. Median Income and Poverty Status, 2011

(Number, percent, except as noted.)

Characteristic	State		U.S.	
	Number	Percent	Number	Percent
Median Income				
Households (dollars)	46,007	X	50,502	X
Families (dollars)	55,001	X	61,455	X
Below Poverty Level (All People)	1,827,743	19.1	48,452,035	15.9
Sex				
Male	824,886	17.8	21,825,281	14.7
Female	1,002,857	20.4	26,626,754	17.2
Age				
Under 18 years	646,824	26.3	16,386,500	22.5
Related children under 18 years	639,080	26.1	16,087,074	22.2
18 to 64 years	1,066,876	17.6	28,335,079	14.8
65 years and over	114,043	10.9	3,730,456	9.3

X = Not applicable.

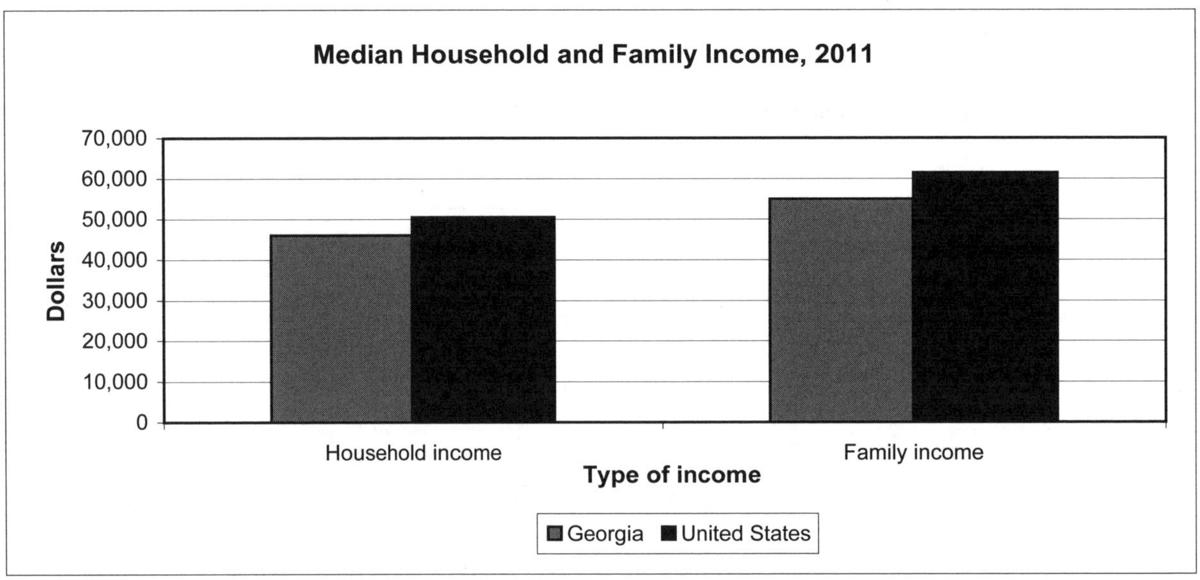

Table GA-6. Health Insurance Coverage Status for the Civilian Noninstitutionalized Population and Children Under 18 Years of Age

(Numbers in thousands, percent.)

Item	2004	2005	2006	2007	2008	2009	2010	2011
Civilian Noninstitutionalized Population	8,706	9,045	9,347	9,493	9,473	9,594	9,520	9,620
Covered by Private or Public Insurance								
Number	7,237	7,391	7,688	7,831	7,694	7,758	7,644	7,737
Percent	83.1	81.7	82.3	82.5	81.2	80.9	80.3	80.4
Not Covered								
Number	1,469	1,654	1,659	1,662	1,779	1,836	1,876	1,883
Percent	16.9	18.3	17.7	17.5	18.8	19.1	19.7	19.6
Percent in the U.S. not covered	14.9	15.3	15.8	15.3	15.1	15.1	15.5	15.1
Children Under 18 Years of Age	2,340	2,371	2,455	2,517	2,536	2,576	2,492	2,485
Covered by Private or Public Insurance								
Number	2,073	2,110	2,141	2,228	2,245	2,295	2,248	2,248
Percent	88.6	89.0	87.2	88.5	88.5	89.1	90.2	90.5
Not Covered								
Number	267	260	314	289	291	281	244	237
Percent	11.4	11.0	12.8	11.5	11.5	10.9	9.8	9.5
Percent in the U.S. not covered	10.5	10.9	11.7	11.0	9.7	8.6	8.0	7.5

Table GA-7. Employment Status by Demographic Group, Preliminary 2012

(Numbers in thousands, percent.)

Characteristic	Civilian noninstitutional population	Civilian labor force		Employed		Unemployed	
		Number	Percent of population	Number	Percent of population	Number	Percent of population
Total	7,456	4,803	64.4	4,365	58.5	438	9.1
Sex							
Male	3,537	2,520	71.2	2,307	65.2	212	8.4
Female	3,919	2,283	58.3	2,057	52.5	226	9.9
Race, Sex, and Hispanic Origin							
White	4,794	3,080	64.2	2,853	59.5	227	7.4
Male	2,343	1,707	72.9	1,593	68.0	114	6.7
Female	2,451	1,373	56.0	1,260	51.4	113	8.2
Black or African American	2,230	1,428	64.0	1,237	55.5	191	13.4
Male	989	657	66.4	567	57.3	90	13.7
Female	1,241	771	62.1	670	54.0	101	13.1
Hispanic	510	376	73.7	338	66.3	38	10.1
Male	268	232	86.7	214	79.9	18	7.8
Female	242	143	59.4	124	51.1	20	13.9
Age							
16 to 19 years	565	162	28.7	114	20.2	48	29.6
20 to 24 years	690	469	68.1	387	56.1	82	17.5
25 to 34 years	1,301	1,060	81.5	955	73.5	104	9.8
35 to 44 years	1,317	1,095	83.1	1,012	76.8	83	7.6
45 to 54 years	1,497	1,192	79.6	1,118	74.7	73	6.2
55 to 64 years	1,081	654	60.5	613	56.7	40	6.2
65 years and over	1,005	171	17.1	164	16.4	7.0	4.1

NOTE: Data in Table 7 are from the Current Population Survey (CPS) and do not match the estimates in Table 8. See notes and definitions for further information.

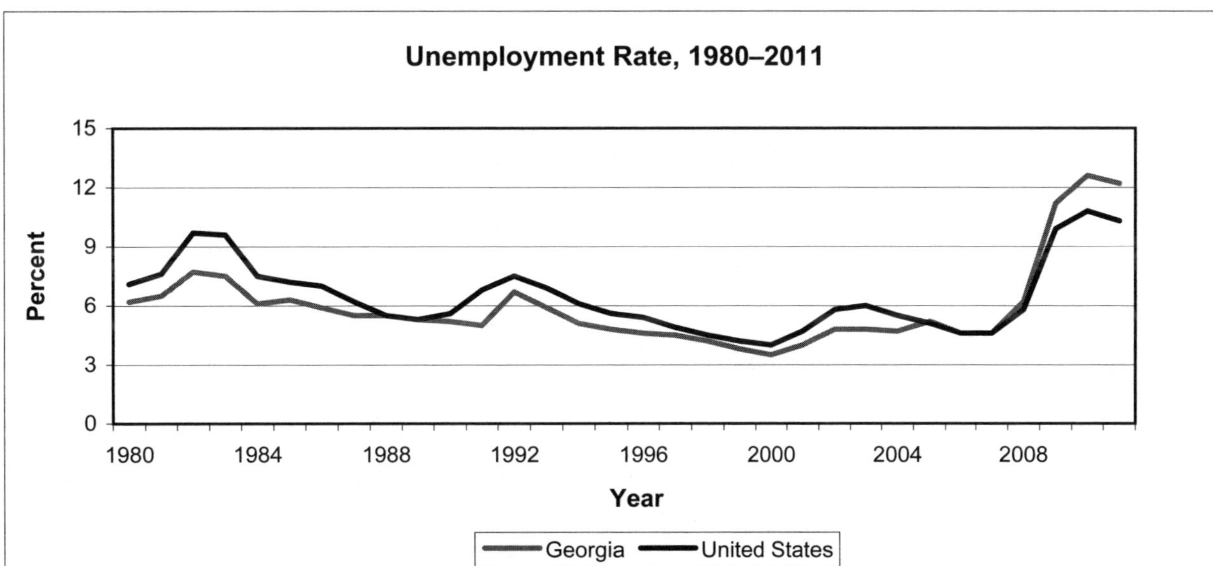

Table GA-8. Employment Status of the Civilian Noninstitutional Population Age 16 Years and Over

(Number, percent.)

Year	Civilian labor force	Civilian participation rate	Employed	Unemployed	Unemployment rate
2005	4,613,585	68.3	4,373,348	240,237	5.2
2006	4,727,059	68.3	4,507,769	219,290	4.6
2007	4,798,003	67.8	4,578,828	219,175	4.6
2008	4,847,650	67.3	4,545,675	301,975	6.2
2009	4,847,607	64.4	4,304,791	542,816	11.2
2010	2,765,482	63.6	4,165,453	600,029	12.6
2011	4,774,331	62.8	4,193,776	580,555	12.2

Table GA-9. Employment and Average Wages by Industry

(Estimates before 2007 are based on the 2002 *North American Industry Classification System* [NAICS]. Estimates from 2007 onward are based on the 2007 NAICS.)

Industry	2005	2006	2007	2008	2009	2010	2011
				Number of jobs			
Wage and Salary Employment by Industry	4,213,329	4,305,608	4,364,184	4,326,738	4,092,799	4,050,847	4,089,152
Farm Wage and Salary Employment	19,872	15,676	15,603	17,301	16,401	13,804	14,578
Nonfarm Wage and Salary Employment	4,193,457	4,289,932	4,348,581	4,309,437	4,076,398	4,037,043	4,074,574
Private wage and salary employment	3,437,889	3,519,082	3,560,787	3,500,784	3,275,382	3,240,704	3,292,162
Forestry, fishing, and related activities	14,533	14,931	14,244	14,169	13,756	14,477	14,895
Mining	6,943	7,045	6,984	5,943	5,013	4,942	4,792
Utilities	19,937	20,196	20,681	20,625	20,437	19,738	20,011
Construction	217,860	227,879	230,627	213,709	174,419	157,079	154,046
Manufacturing	450,906	449,714	434,068	411,541	359,528	346,160	351,084
Durable goods manufacturing	208,464	209,374	202,291	190,194	161,496	155,681	161,698
Nondurable goods manufacturing	242,442	240,340	231,777	221,347	198,032	190,479	189,386
Wholesale trade	214,268	218,674	222,616	219,879	201,601	198,258	199,538
Retail trade	466,262	478,076	486,556	472,635	444,911	441,958	448,738
Transportation and warehousing	163,730	167,264	171,967	173,231	162,834	162,081	165,995
Information	114,031	113,911	112,649	110,244	101,744	97,935	98,631
Finance and insurance	164,718	169,160	169,227	164,341	160,226	156,825	159,145
Real estate and rental and leasing	64,399	66,639	66,779	64,997	59,978	58,451	58,078
Professional, scientific, and technical services	206,932	217,635	223,809	231,527	221,601	221,109	227,474
Management of companies and enterprises	53,490	53,163	52,860	54,251	52,583	52,879	54,026
Administrative and waste services	284,731	290,140	291,922	278,869	247,546	259,493	269,090
Educational services	69,491	71,392	73,722	75,806	77,301	79,567	81,954
Health care and social assistance	355,603	367,453	379,788	387,896	394,137	402,734	408,783
Arts, entertainment, and recreation	39,236	40,667	42,533	42,415	41,471	39,828	41,138
Accommodation and food services	337,395	349,169	359,069	357,622	342,524	339,751	345,699
Other services, except public administration	193,424	195,974	200,686	201,084	193,772	187,439	189,045
Government and government enterprises	755,568	770,850	787,794	808,653	801,016	796,339	782,412
				Dollars			
Average Wages and Salaries by Industry	39,777	41,198	42,916	43,568	43,873	44,924	46,170
Average Farm Wages and Salaries	18,653	19,950	25,789	23,731	18,790	23,004	20,178
Average Nonfarm Wages and Salaries	39,877	41,276	42,977	43,648	43,974	44,999	46,263
Average private wages and salaries	40,219	41,635	43,440	43,988	44,160	45,335	46,678
Forestry, fishing, and related activities	26,770	28,185	29,599	29,761	30,078	31,128	31,585
Mining	54,332	55,381	58,728	54,253	53,581	55,430	57,491
Utilities	74,405	75,397	75,808	78,570	81,539	76,775	84,511
Construction	40,589	42,461	44,224	45,449	45,940	46,524	47,134
Manufacturing	43,502	45,506	46,817	47,931	48,957	51,805	53,702
Durable goods manufacturing	45,730	48,652	49,012	50,599	52,057	54,755	56,989
Nondurable goods manufacturing	41,586	42,765	44,900	45,639	46,429	49,394	50,895
Wholesale trade	59,915	62,874	65,045	65,646	65,394	67,527	69,803
Retail trade	25,460	26,236	26,552	26,557	26,631	27,112	27,388
Transportation and warehousing	44,853	44,405	50,000	49,645	48,753	51,081	52,918
Information	66,877	70,071	75,337	74,449	73,878	76,733	79,875
Finance and insurance	64,714	68,243	71,496	72,191	70,080	72,883	76,669
Real estate and rental and leasing	43,073	47,055	48,352	46,902	45,213	45,955	48,695
Professional, scientific, and technical services	62,700	65,404	68,997	70,645	70,734	72,372	74,401
Management of companies and enterprises	92,019	84,496	91,384	83,871	85,454	89,287	94,652
Administrative and waste services	29,603	30,683	32,317	33,546	34,251	34,517	35,021
Educational services	32,300	36,084	37,625	39,002	39,754	40,262	41,022
Health care and social assistance	39,606	40,518	42,023	43,174	44,342	44,681	45,588
Arts, entertainment, and recreation	31,478	32,460	33,829	33,577	33,892	35,321	35,834
Accommodation and food services	16,462	17,046	17,937	17,731	17,778	18,519	19,027
Other services, except public administration	25,880	27,028	28,039	28,617	28,691	29,763	30,144
Government and government enterprises	38,322	39,637	40,887	42,174	43,213	43,633	44,514

Table GA-10. Employment Characteristics by Family Type

(Number, percent.)

Family type and labor force status	2009 Total	2009 Families with own children under 18 years	2010 Total	2010 Families with own children under 18 years	2011 Total	2011 Families with own children under 18 years
All families	2,370,143	1,125,508	2,385,969	1,109,259	2,376,008	1,103,003
Family type and labor force status						
Married-couple families	1,676,830	734,870	1,688,896	727,342	1,667,698	718,977
Both husband and wife in labor force	55.1	66.3	53.7	65.3	52.3	64.3
Husband in labor force, wife not in labor force	23.4	29.0	23.4	29.1	24.2	30.0
Wife in labor force, husband not in labor force	7.0	3.2	7.8	3.9	8.0	4.1
Both husband and wife not in labor force	14.5	1.5	15.1	1.8	15.5	1.6
Other families	693,313	390,638	697,073	381,917	708,310	384,026
Female householder, no husband present	77.1	80.4	76.9	80.5	76.7	80.4
In labor force	56.5	67.8	56.4	68.3	54.3	65.8
Not in labor force	20.6	12.6	20.5	12.2	22.4	14.6
Male householder, no wife present	22.9	19.6	23.1	19.5	23.3	19.6
In labor force	18.5	18.1	18.4	18.1	18.4	17.4
Not in labor force	4.4	1.4	4.7	1.4	4.9	2.2

Table GA-11. School Enrollment and Educational Attainment, 2011

(Number, percent.)

Item	State	U.S.
Enrollment		
Total population 3 years and over, enrolled in school	2,782,980	83,131,910
Enrolled in nursery school or preschool (percent)	6.4	6.0
Enrolled in kindergarten (percent)	5.5	5.1
Enrolled in elementary school, grades 1-8 (percent)	40.4	39.5
Enrolled in high school, grades 9-12 (percent)	20.1	20.7
Enrolled in college or graduate school (percent)	27.6	28.7
Attainment		
Total population 25 years and over	6,308,961	206,471,670
Less than ninth grade (percent)	5.8	6.0
9th to 12th grade, no diploma (percent)	9.8	8.1
High school graduate, including equivalency (percent)	29.3	28.4
Some college, no degree (percent)	20.8	21.2
Associate's degree (percent)	6.7	7.8
Bachelor's degree (percent)	17.7	17.9
Graduate or professional degree (percent)	9.8	10.6
High school graduate or higher (percent)	84.3	85.9
Bachelor's degree or higher (percent)	27.6	28.5

Table GA-12. Educational Indicators

(Number, percent; data derived from National Center of Education Statistics.)

Item	State	U.S.
Public Schools, 2009–2010 (except where noted)		
Number of school districts	180	13,629
Number of schools	2,461	99,834
Number of students (in thousands)	1,668	49,373
Student-teacher ratio	14.4	15.4
Expenditures per student (dollars)	10,704	10,591
Averaged freshman graduation rate, 2008–2009	67.8	75.5[1]
Dropout rate, 2008–2009	4.2	4.1
Students eligible for free or reduced-price lunch (percent)	57.4	48.0
English language learners, 2010–2011 (percent)	4.9	9.8[1]
Students with IEP (percent)	10.6	13.1
Private Schools, 2009–2010 (except where noted)		
Number of schools	823	33,366
Number of students (in thousands)	130	4,700
High school graduates, 2008–2009	8,322	308,813
Student-teacher ratio	9.8	10.7

[1] U.S. total includes estimates for nonreporting states.

Table GA-13. Reported Voting and Registration of the Voting-Age Population, November 2012

(Numbers in thousands, percent.)

Item	Total population	Total citizen population	Registered			Voted		
			Total registered	Percent registered (total population)	Percent registered (total citizen population)	Total voted	Percent voted (total population)	Percent voted (total citizen population)
U.S. Total	235,248	215,081	153,157	65.1	71.2	132,948	56.5	61.8
State Total	7,179	6,738	4,767	66.4	70.7	4,168	58.1	61.9
Sex								
Male	3,424	3,206	2,178	63.6	67.9	1,899	55.5	59.2
Female	3,755	3,532	2,589	68.9	73.3	2,269	60.4	64.2
Race								
White alone	4,659	4,388	3,121	67.0	71.1	2,683	57.6	61.1
White, non-Hispanic alone	4,227	4,176	3,006	71.1	72.0	2,590	61.3	62.0
Black alone	2,151	2,063	1,491	69.3	72.3	1,340	62.3	65.0
Asian alone	274	198	86	31.4	43.6	83	30.2	41.9
Hispanic (of any race)	489	238	140	28.7	59.0	114	23.3	47.8
Age								
18 to 24 years	920	867	469	51.0	54.1	349	37.9	40.2
25 to 44 years	2,649	2,376	1,673	63.1	70.4	1,426	53.8	60.0
45 to 64 years	2,658	2,547	1,886	70.9	74.0	1,741	65.5	68.4
65 to 74 years	615	615	492	79.9	79.9	446	72.5	72.5
75 years and over	336	333	248	73.6	74.3	206	61.2	61.8

Table GA-14. Crime

(Number, rate per 100,000. Data are derived from the FBI Uniform Crime Reports.)

Item	State			U.S.		
	2010	2011	Percent change	2010	2011	Percent change
TOTAL POPULATION	9,712,157	9,815,210	1.1	309,330,219	311,591,917	0.7
VIOLENT CRIME						
Number	39,068	36,634	-6.2	1,251,248	1,203,564	-3.8
Rate	402.3	373.6	-7.1	404.5	386.3	-4.5
Murder and Nonnegligent Manslaughter						
Number	555	554	-0.2	14,722	14,612	-0.7
Rate	5.7	5.6	-1.8	4.8	4.7	-2.1
Forcible Rape						
Number	2,107	2,053	-2.6	85,593	83,425	-2.5
Rate	21.7	20.8	-4.1	27.7	26.8	-3.2
Robbery						
Number	12,372	12,148	-1.8	369,089	354,396	-4.0
Rate	127.4	123.8	-2.8	119.3	113.7	-4.7
Aggravated Assault						
Number	24,034	21,879	-9.0	781,844	751,131	-3.9
Rate	247.5	222.9	-9.9	252.8	241.1	-4.6
PROPERTY CRIME						
Number	353,449	355,952	0.7	9,112,625	9,063,173	-0.5
Rate	3,639.2	3,626.5	-0.3	2,945.9	2,908.7	-1.3
Burglary						
Number	96,947	95,657	-1.3	2,168,459	2,188,005	0.9
Rate	998.2	974.6	-2.4	701.0	702.2	0.2
Larceny-Theft						
Number	226,161	230,820	2.1	6,204,601	6,159,795	-0.7
Rate	2,328.6	2,351.7	1.0	2,005.8	1,976.9	-1.4
Motor Vehicle Theft						
Number	30,341	29,475	-2.9	739,565	715,373	-3.3
Rate	312.4	300.3	-3.9	239.1	229.6	-4.0

Table GA-15. State Government Finances, 2011

(Dollar amounts in thousands, percent distribution.)

Item	Dollars	Percent distribution
Total Revenue	52,294,783	100.0
General revenue	37,167,825	71.1
Intergovernmental revenue	15,266,487	29.2
Taxes	16,003,250	30.6
General sales	5,080,777	9.7
Selective sales	2,027,885	3.9
License taxes	477,056	0.9
Individual income tax	7,658,782	14.6
Corporate income tax	670,410	1.3
Other taxes	88,340	0.2
Current charges	3,922,860	7.5
Miscellaneous general revenue	1,975,228	3.8
Utility revenue	9,824	0.0
Liquor stores revenue	0	0.0
Insurance trust revenue [1]	15,117,134	28.9
Total Expenditure	44,750,297	100.0
Intergovernmental expenditure	10,600,099	23.7
Direct expenditure	34,150,198	76.3
Current operation	22,210,411	49.6
Capital outlay	2,639,401	5.9
Insurance benefits and repayments	7,296,018	16.3
Assistance and subsidies	1,316,050	2.9
Interest on debt	688,318	1.5
Exhibit: Salaries and wages	5,588,929	12.5
Total Expenditure	44,750,297	100.0
General expenditure	37,410,466	83.6
Intergovernmental expenditure	10,600,099	23.7
Direct expenditure	26,810,367	59.9
General expenditure, by function:		
Education	17,429,181	38.9
Public welfare	10,366,884	23.2
Hospitals	838,523	1.9
Health	1,159,244	2.6
Highways	1,640,847	3.7
Police protection	298,050	0.7
Correction	1,462,044	3.3
Natural resources	559,431	1.3
Parks and recreation	195,353	0.4
Governmental administration	810,105	1.8
Interest on general debt	688,318	1.5
Other and unallocable	1,962,486	4.4
Utility expenditure	43,813	0.1
Liquor stores expenditure	0	0.0
Insurance trust expenditure	7,296,018	16.3
Debt at End of Fiscal Year	13,402,568	X
Cash and Security Holdings	77,103,782	X

X = Not applicable.

[1] Within insurance trust revenue, net earnings of state retirement systems is a calculated statistic (the item code in the data file is X08), and thus can be positive or negative. Net earnings is the sum of earnings on investments plus gains on investments minus losses on investments. The change made in 2002 for asset valuation from book to market value in accordance with Statement 34 of the Governmental Accounting Standards Board is reflected in the calculated statistics.

Table GA-16. State Government Tax Collections, 2012

(Dollars in thousands, percent.)

Item	Dollars	Percent distribution
Total Taxes	16,576,903	100.0
Property taxes	68,951	0.4
Sales and gross receipts	7,253,554	43.8
General sales and gross receipts	5,303,524	32.0
Selective sales and gross receipts	1,950,030	11.8
Alcoholic beverages	175,051	1.1
Amusements	0	0.0
Insurance premiums	309,193	1.9
Motor fuels	880,987	5.3
Pari-mutuels	0	0.0
Public utilities	0	0.0
Tobacco products	227,146	1.4
Other selective sales	357,653	2.2
Licenses	505,618	3.1
Alcoholic beverages	2,357	-
Amusements	785	-
Corporations in general	44,089	0.3
Hunting and fishing	23,840	0.1
Motor vehicle	308,342	1.9
Motor vehicle operators	46,986	0.3
Public utilities	0	0.0
Occupation and business, NEC	73,556	0.4
Other licenses	5,663	-
Income taxes	8,733,047	52.7
Individual income	8,142,371	49.1
Corporation net income	590,676	3.6
Other taxes	15,733	0.1
Death and gift	28	-
Documentary and stock transfer	15,705	0.1
Severance	0	0.0
Taxes, NEC	0	0.0

- = Rounds to zero.

Leading Exports, 2012

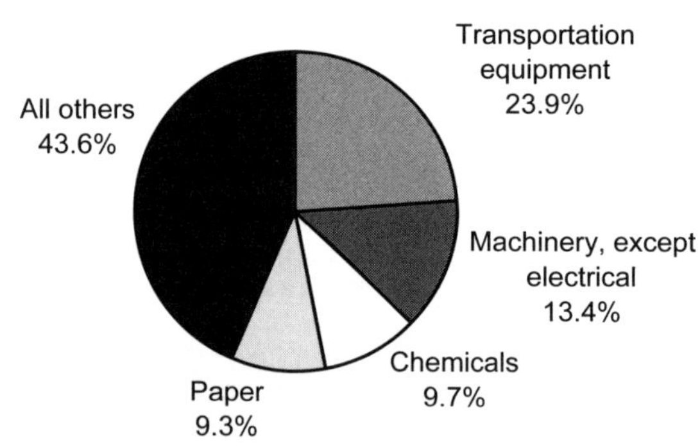

HAWAII

Facts and Figures

Location: North Pacific Ocean

Area: 10,931 sq. mi. (28,311 sq. km.); rank—43rd

Population: 1,392,313 (2012 est.); rank—40th

Principal Cities: capital—Honolulu; largest—Honolulu

Statehood: August 21, 1959; 50th state

U.S. Congress: 2 senators, 2 representatives

State Motto: *Ua mau ke ea o ka'ina i ka pono* ("The life of the land is perpetuated in righteousness")

State Song: "Hawai'i Pono' (Hawaii's Own)"

State Nickname: The Aloha State

Abbreviations: HI

State Symbols: flower—native yellow hibiscus; tree—kukui (candlenut tree); bird—nene (Hawaiian goose)

At a Glance

- With an increase in population of 6.9 percent, Hawaii ranked 38th among the states in growth from 2000 to 2008.
- An estimated 22,200 marriages took place in Hawaii in 2009; Hawaii does not report divorces.
- In 2011, 7.1 percent of Hawaiians did not have health insurance, compared to 15.1 percent of the total U.S. population.
- Hawaii's violent crime rate in 2011 was 287.2 per 100,000 population, compared to 386.3 for the entire nation.
- In the 2012 election, 51.6 percent of Hawaii's eligible voters voted, compared to 61.8 percent of eligible voters nationwide.
- In 2007, Hawaii exported $88 million worth of agricultural products, less than 1 percent of the U.S. total.

Table HI-1. Population by Age, Sex, Race, and Hispanic Origin

(Number, percent, except where noted.)

Sex, age, race, and Hispanic origin	2000	2010	2012[1]	Average annual percent change, 2010–2012
Total Population	1,211,537	1,360,301	1,392,313	0.8
Percent of total U.S. population	0.4	0.4	0.4	X
Sex				
Male	563,891	681,243	701,965	1.0
Female	544,338	679,058	690,348	0.5
Age				
Under 5 years	78,163	87,407	89,147	0.7
5 to 19 years	249,088	250,894	246,942	-0.5
20 to 64 years	723,685	826,868	845,423	0.7
65 years and over	160,601	195,138	210,801	2.5
Median age (years)	36.2	38.6	38.3	-0.3
Race and Hispanic Origin				
One race				
White	294,102	349,051	363,544	1.3
Black	22,003	22,473	29,905	8.3
American Indian and Alaska Native	3,535	4,960	5,507	3.3
Asian	503,868	531,633	532,599	0.1
Native Hawaiian or Other Pacific Islander	113,539	138,292	140,112	0.4
Two or more races	259,343	313,892	320,646	0.7
Hispanic (of any race)	87,699	202,324	217,537	2.3

X = Not applicable.
[1] Population figures for 2012 are July 1 estimates. The 2010 estimates are taken from the 2010 Census.

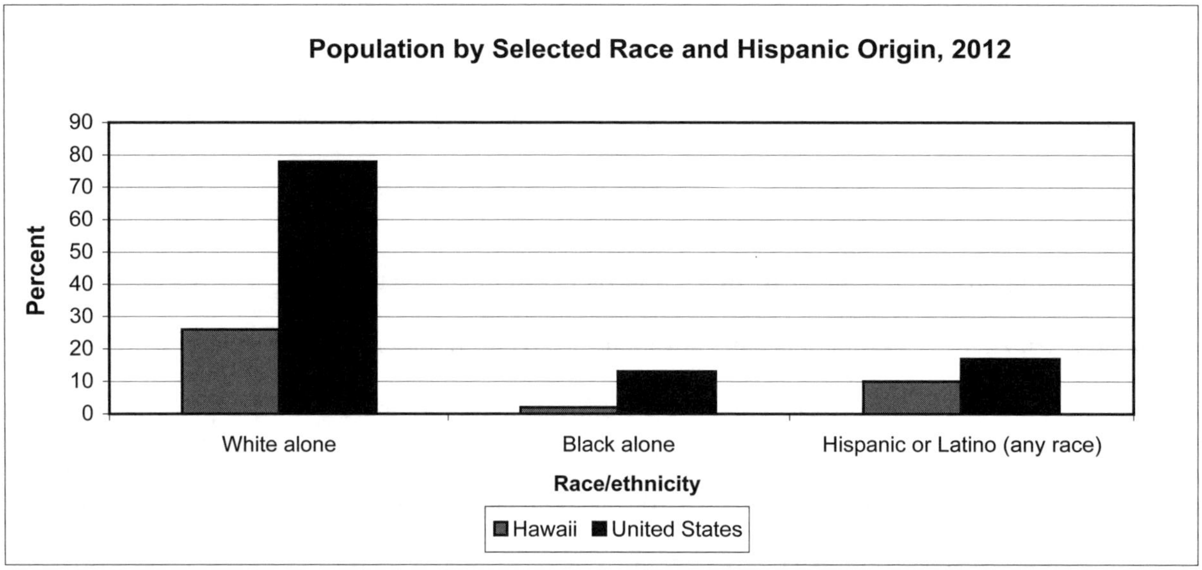

Table HI-2. Marital Status

(Number, percent distribution.)

Sex, age, race, and Hispanic origin	2000	2010	2011
Males, 15 Years and Over	481,768	554,154	558,393
Never married	34.6	37.8	36.7
Now married, except separated	53.7	49.1	51.3
Separated	1.4	1.2	1.3
Widowed	2.2	2.7	2.4
Divorced	8.1	9.2	8.3
Females, 15 Years and Over	484,107	556,915	562,960
Never married	25.9	28.7	28.3
Now married, except separated	52.5	48.5	49.7
Separated	1.7	1.8	1.5
Widowed	9.8	10.1	10.0
Divorced	10.0	11.0	10.4

Table HI-3. Households and Housing Characteristics

(Number, percent, dollars.)

Item	2000	2010	2011	Average annual percent change, 2000–2011
Total Households	403,240	445,812	448,563	0.9
Family households	287,068	303,075	311,789	0.7
Married-couple family	216,077	224,402	229,641	0.5
Other family	70,991	78,673	82,148	1.3
Male householder, no wife present	21,068	24,247	25,768	1.9
Female householder, no husband present	49,923	54,426	56,380	1.1
Nonfamily households	116,172	142,737	136,774	1.5
Householder living alone	88,153	108,872	108,071	1.9
Householder not living alone	28,019	33,865	28,703	0.2
Housing Characteristics				
Total housing units	460,542	519,992	522,314	1.1
Occupied housing units	403,240	445,812	448,563	0.9
Owner occupied	227,888	258,533	254,700	1.0
Renter occupied	175,352	187,279	193,863	0.9
Average size	2.92	2.96	2.97	0.1
Financial Characteristics				
Median gross rent of renter-occupied housing	779	1,291	1,308	5.7
Median monthly owner costs for housing units with a mortgage	1,636	2,240	2,221	3.0
Median value of owner-occupied housing units	272,700	525,400	487,400	6.6

Table HI-4. Migration, Origin, and Language

(Number, percent.)

Characteristic	State			U.S.		
	2010	2011	Percent change	2010	2011	Percent change
Residence 1 Year Ago						
Population 1 year and over	1,346,274	1,357,806	0.9	305,628,607	307,900,319	0.7
Same house	84.7	85.5	0.9	84.6	84.8	0.2
Different house in the U.S.	14.0	13.3	-5.0	14.8	14.6	-1.4
Same county	9.2	8.5	-7.6	9.4	9.2	-2.1
Different county	4.8	4.8	0.0	5.4	5.4	-
Same state	0.8	0.6	-25.0	3.2	3.1	-3.1
Different state	4.0	4.2	5.0	2.2	2.3	4.5
Abroad	1.3	1.2	-7.7	0.6	0.6	-
Place of Birth						
Native born	1,115,408	1,128,719	1.2	269,393,835	271,214,059	0.7
Male	51.7	51.6	-0.2	49.2	49.2	-
Female	48.3	48.4	0.2	50.8	50.8	-
Foreign born	248,213	246,091	-0.9	39,955,854	40,377,860	1.1
Male	43.2	43.0	-0.5	49.1	48.9	-0.4
Female	56.8	57.0	0.4	50.9	51.1	0.4
Foreign born; naturalized U.S. citizen	141,320	137,458	-2.7	17,476,082	18,140,192	3.8
Male	44.5	43.2	-2.9	45.8	45.8	-
Female	55.5	56.8	2.3	54.2	54.2	-
Foreign born; not a U.S. citizen	106,893	108,633	1.6	22,479,772	22,237,668	-1.1
Male	41.5	42.8	3.1	51.6	51.5	-0.2
Female	58.5	57.2	-2.2	48.4	48.5	0.2
Entered 2000 or later	31.4	33.3	6.1	34.7	35.7	2.9
Entered 1990 to 1999	21.0	22.2	5.7	27.2	26.7	-1.8
Entered before 1990	47.5	44.4	-6.5	38.1	37.6	-1.3
World Region of Birth, Foreign						
Foreign-born population, excluding population born at sea	248,213	246,091	-0.9	39,955,673	40,377,757	1.1
Europe	5.1	5.0	-2.0	12.1	12.1	-
Asia	76.8	78.6	2.3	28.2	28.6	1.4
Africa	0.7	0.3	-57.1	4	4.1	2.5
Oceania	10.5	10.4	-1.0	0.5	0.5	-
Latin America	5.1	4.4	-13.7	53.1	52.6	-0.9
North America	1.8	1.3	-27.8	2	2.0	-
Language Spoken at Home and Ability to Speak English						
Population 5 years and over	1,276,928	1,286,790	0.8	289,215,746	291,524,091	0.8
English only	74.1	74.8	0.9	79.4	79.2	-0.3
Language other than English	25.9	25.2	-2.7	20.6	20.8	1.0
Speaks English less than "very well"	11.8	12.0	1.7	8.7	8.7	-

- = Zero or rounds to zero.

Table HI-5. Median Income and Poverty Status, 2011

(Number, percent, except as noted.)

Characteristic	State		U.S.	
	Number	Percent	Number	Percent
Median Income				
Households (dollars)	61,821	X	50,502	X
Families (dollars)	74,234	X	61,455	X
Below Poverty Level (All People)	161,290	12.0	48,452,035	15.9
Sex				
Male	73,612	11.1	21,825,281	14.7
Female	87,678	13.0	26,626,754	17.2
Age				
Under 18 years	50,834	17.0	16,386,500	22.5
Related children under 18 years	49,781	16.7	16,087,074	22.2
18 to 64 years	94,102	11.2	28,335,079	14.8
65 years and over	16,354	8.2	3,730,456	9.3

X = Not applicable.

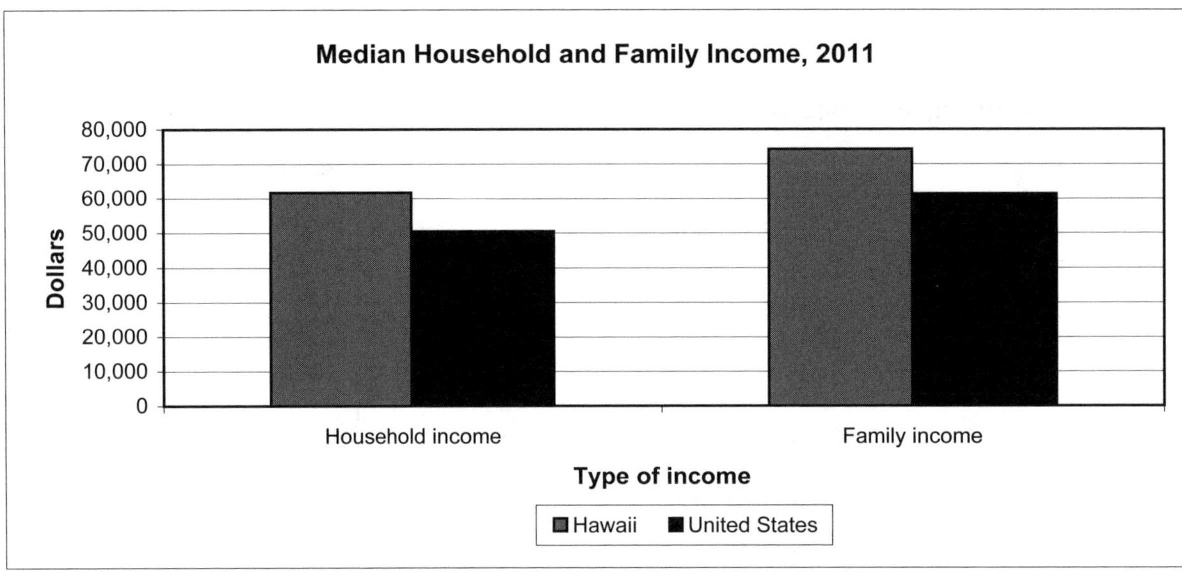

Table HI-6. Health Insurance Coverage Status for the Civilian Noninstitutionalized Population and Children Under 18 Years of Age

(Numbers in thousands, percent.)

Item	2004	2005	2006	2007	2008	2009	2010	2011
Civilian Noninstitutionalized Population	1,249	1,279	1,255	1,267	1,237	1,232	1,316	1,326
Covered by Private or Public Insurance								
Number	1,145	1,169	1,144	1,172	1,154	1,146	1,212	1,232
Percent	91.7	91.4	91.2	92.5	93.3	93.0	92.1	92.9
Not Covered								
Number	104	110	110	96	83	86	104	94
Percent	8.3	8.6	8.8	7.5	6.7	7.0	7.9	7.1
Percent in the U.S. not covered	14.9	15.3	15.8	15.3	15.1	15.1	15.5	15.1
Children Under 18 Years of Age	286	306	298	291	284	288	304	304
Covered by Private or Public Insurance								
Number	275	290	279	277	274	281	293	293
Percent	96.1	94.7	93.7	47.5	96.5	97.5	96.3	96.4
Not Covered								
Number	11	16	19	14	10	7	11	11
Percent	3.9	5.3	6.3	4.8	3.5	2.5	3.7	3.6
Percent in the U.S. not covered	10.5	10.9	11.7	11.0	9.7	8.6	8.0	7.5

Table HI-7. Employment Status by Demographic Group, Preliminary 2012

(Numbers in thousands, percent.)

Characteristic	Civilian noninstitutional population	Civilian labor force		Employed		Unemployed	
		Number	Percent of population	Number	Percent of population	Number	Percent of population
Total	1,060	642	60.5	603	56.9	39	6.0
Sex							
Male	515	340	66.2	319	62.0	21	6.3
Female	545	301	55.2	284	52.1	17	5.7
Race, Sex, and Hispanic Origin							
White	241	150	62.3	142	58.9	8	5.5
Male	123	83	67.7	78	63.8	5	5.9
Female	117	67	56.7	63	53.8	3	5.0
Black or African American	18	10	52.8	8	43.0	2	18.8
Male	95	59	62.3	51	53.8	8	13.6
Female	46	30	65.7	26	56.6	4	13.8
Hispanic	50	29	59.1	25	51.0	4	13.5
Male							
Female							
	76	19	25.1	13	17.6	6	29.7
Age	96	68	71.0	62	64.7	6	8.9
16 to 19 years	167	133	79.8	125	74.8	8	6.3
20 to 24 years	155	125	81.0	120	77.7	5	4.0
25 to 34 years	78	58	74.7	56	72.0	2	3.7
35 to 44 years	91	68	74.5	66	72.2	2	3.0
45 to 54 years	92	58	63.1	56	60.6	2	4.0
55 to 64 years	113	15	13.5	14	12.6	1	7.0
65 years and over	1,005	171	17.1	164	16.4	7.0	4.1

NOTE: Data in Table 7 are from the Current Population Survey (CPS) and do not match the estimates in Table 8. See notes and definitions for further information.

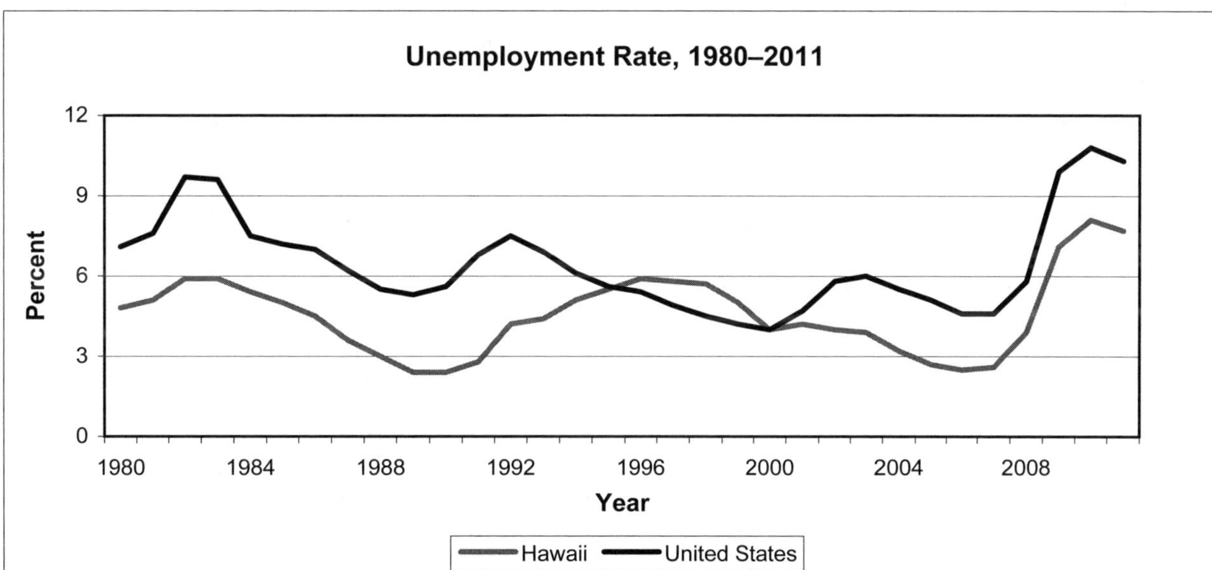

Table HI-8. Employment Status of the Civilian Noninstitutional Population Age 16 Years and Over

(Number, percent.)

Year	Civilian labor force	Civilian participation rate	Employed	Unemployed	Unemployment rate
2005	630,624	65.7	613,372	17,252	2.7
2006	642,891	66.2	627,058	15,833	2.5
2007	645,947	65.8	628,902	17,045	2.6
2008	654,261	66.0	628,429	25,832	3.9
2009	654,223	63.0	607,551	46,672	7.1
2010	694,445	63.5	638,191	56,254	8.1
2011	681,799	61.9	629,523	52,276	7.7

Table HI-9. Employment and Average Wages by Industry

(Estimates before 2007 are based on the 2002 *North American Industry Classification System* [NAICS]. Estimates from 2007 onward are based on the 2007 NAICS.)

Industry	2005	2006	2007	2008	2009	2010	2011
	Number of jobs						
Wage and Salary Employment by Industry	675,401	691,920	700,378	695,721	668,418	665,430	674,452
Farm Wage and Salary Employment	6,791	6,791	6,331	5,822	5,699	6,087	6,808
Nonfarm Wage and Salary Employment	668,610	685,129	694,047	689,899	662,719	659,343	667,644
Private wage and salary employment	496,166	510,267	517,707	509,528	481,507	477,378	484,522
Forestry, fishing, and related activities	1,326	1,360	1,199	1,193	1,151	1,171	1,285
Mining	288	286	305	330	340	338	332
Utilities	2,873	2,935	3,020	3,086	3,193	3,215	3,329
Construction	35,884	38,588	40,264	39,066	32,516	29,925	29,882
Manufacturing	15,610	15,540	15,303	14,906	13,716	12,954	13,179
Durable goods manufacturing	4,506	4,513	4,625	4,607	4,154	3,793	3,881
Nondurable goods manufacturing	11,104	11,027	10,678	10,299	9,562	9,161	9,298
Wholesale trade	17,830	18,138	18,574	18,937	17,992	17,849	17,596
Retail trade	70,576	71,360	71,331	70,876	67,641	67,119	68,182
Transportation and warehousing	28,631	30,470	30,429	26,686	23,862	23,478	23,997
Information	10,856	10,757	10,721	10,083	9,095	9,931	8,510
Finance and insurance	17,054	17,519	17,386	17,206	16,725	16,154	16,016
Real estate and rental and leasing	13,286	13,553	13,519	13,126	11,864	11,888	11,775
Professional, scientific, and technical services	23,732	24,612	24,959	25,447	25,039	24,553	24,675
Management of companies and enterprises	7,348	7,525	7,620	7,442	7,001	6,649	6,926
Administrative and waste services	40,129	43,142	44,552	43,516	40,458	41,345	44,446
Educational services	14,272	14,255	14,939	15,664	15,778	15,790	16,072
Health care and social assistance	57,410	58,575	60,025	60,819	61,416	62,098	62,401
Arts, entertainment, and recreation	12,012	11,828	12,240	11,767	10,877	10,548	10,836
Accommodation and food services	96,000	97,625	98,788	96,394	90,989	90,918	93,410
Other services, except public administration	31,049	32,199	32,533	32,984	31,854	31,455	31,673
Government and government enterprises	172,444	174,862	176,340	180,371	181,212	181,965	183,122
	Dollars						
Average Wages and Salaries by Industry	37,375	38,929	40,893	42,012	42,708	43,202	44,085
Average Farm Wages and Salaries	25,402	25,189	26,512	28,365	28,219	28,395	29,353
Average Nonfarm Wages and Salaries	37,497	39,065	41,024	42,127	42,833	43,338	44,236
Average private wages and salaries	35,200	36,590	38,389	39,090	39,306	39,925	40,572
Forestry, fishing, and related activities	22,503	22,424	21,793	22,105	21,284	21,976	22,674
Mining	86,764	86,357	81,807	81,870	77,894	73,485	77,443
Utilities	72,310	75,140	75,765	78,450	80,427	83,879	88,489
Construction	53,840	55,850	59,313	62,052	62,750	62,573	63,604
Manufacturing	33,673	35,561	37,680	38,773	38,818	39,245	40,354
Durable goods manufacturing	40,714	43,410	45,647	47,183	47,850	48,272	50,996
Nondurable goods manufacturing	30,816	32,348	34,229	35,012	34,894	35,508	35,912
Wholesale trade	43,227	44,963	47,290	47,975	48,169	48,175	49,747
Retail trade	25,046	25,997	26,798	27,064	27,419	28,193	28,183
Transportation and warehousing	36,513	36,317	38,829	41,197	41,024	42,112	43,535
Information	47,910	53,049	53,494	54,887	55,815	55,593	57,663
Finance and insurance	55,215	56,310	56,595	56,764	56,897	58,145	60,284
Real estate and rental and leasing	39,072	40,339	41,570	40,717	40,386	41,368	42,542
Professional, scientific, and technical services	55,070	57,442	60,197	61,791	62,342	63,054	63,420
Management of companies and enterprises	71,651	69,862	71,907	71,675	71,200	76,806	79,812
Administrative and waste services	25,724	26,618	28,111	29,299	30,283	30,312	29,710
Educational services	28,489	30,340	30,494	31,430	32,337	33,386	34,416
Health care and social assistance	38,885	40,253	41,360	43,364	45,348	45,549	46,630
Arts, entertainment, and recreation	24,701	27,173	28,638	29,078	29,151	28,107	27,292
Accommodation and food services	26,497	27,606	30,276	28,777	27,819	29,329	30,557
Other services, except public administration	26,891	28,313	29,391	30,402	30,727	31,896	32,405
Government and government enterprises	44,105	46,287	48,760	50,707	52,204	52,294	53,929

Table HI-10. Employment Characteristics by Family Type

(Number, percent.)

Family type and labor force status	2009 Total	2009 Families with own children under 18 years	2010 Total	2010 Families with own children under 18 years	2011 Total	2011 Families with own children under 18 years
All families	310,366	130,295	303,075	119,941	311,789	125,077
Family type and labor force status						
Married-couple families	228,864	93,016	224,402	88,908	229,641	89,648
Both husband and wife in labor force	56.3	70.9	53.8	69.5	53.0	67.2
Husband in labor force, wife not in labor force	19.7	23.6	19.4	25.2	20.0	26.1
Wife in labor force, husband not in labor force	7.4	3.7	9.3	3.9	8.5	4.0
Both husband and wife not in labor force	16.7	1.9	17.5	1.4	18.5	2.8
Other families	81,502	37,279	78,673	31,033	82,148	35,429
Female householder, no husband present	68.3	67.7	69.2	73.1	68.6	70.0
In labor force	45.4	57.3	45.7	61.5	41.5	54.9
Not in labor force	22.8	10.4	23.5	11.6	27.1	15.1
Male householder, no wife present	31.7	32.3	30.8	26.9	31.4	30.0
In labor force	26.1	30.9	22.9	24.3	23.8	27.8
Not in labor force	5.6	1.3	7.9	2.6	7.6	2.1

Table HI-11. School Enrollment and Educational Attainment, 2011

(Number, percent.)

Item	State	U.S.
Enrollment		
Total population 3 years and over, enrolled in school	336,724	83,131,910
Enrolled in nursery school or preschool (percent)	5.7	6.0
Enrolled in kindergarten (percent)	4.8	5.1
Enrolled in elementary school, grades 1-8 (percent)	38.7	39.5
Enrolled in high school, grades 9-12 (percent)	20.8	20.7
Enrolled in college or graduate school (percent)	29.9	28.7
Attainment		
Total population 25 years and over	939,512	206,471,670
Less than ninth grade (percent)	4.4	6.0
9th to 12th grade, no diploma (percent)	5.0	8.1
High school graduate, including equivalency (percent)	28.5	28.4
Some college, no degree (percent)	23	21.2
Associate's degree (percent)	10.0	7.8
Bachelor's degree (percent)	19.2	17.9
Graduate or professional degree (percent)	9.9	10.6
High school graduate or higher (percent)	90.6	85.9
Bachelor's degree or higher (percent)	29.1	28.5

Table HI-12. Educational Indicators

(Number, percent; data derived from National Center of Education Statistics.)

Item	State	U.S.
Public Schools, 2009–2010 (except where noted)		
Number of school districts	1	13,629
Number of schools	289	99,834
Number of students (in thousands)	180	49,373
Student-teacher ratio	15.8	15.4
Expenditures per student (dollars)	12,896	10,591
Averaged freshman graduation rate, 2008–2009	75.3	75.5[1]
Dropout rate, 2008–2009	4.9	4.1
Students eligible for free or reduced-price lunch (percent)	46.8	48.0
English language learners, 2010–2011 (percent)	10.6	9.8[1]
Students with IEP (percent)	11.1	13.1
Private Schools, 2009–2010 (except where noted)		
Number of schools	135	33,366
Number of students (in thousands)	34	4,700
High school graduates, 2008–2009	2,659	308,813
Student-teacher ratio	11.0	10.7

[1] U.S. total includes estimates for nonreporting states.

Table HI-13. Reported Voting and Registration of the Voting-Age Population, November 2012

(Numbers in thousands, percent.)

Item	Total population	Total citizen population	Registered			Voted		
			Total registered	Percent registered (total population)	Percent registered (total citizen population)	Total voted	Percent voted (total population)	Percent voted (total citizen population)
U.S. Total	235,248	215,081	153,157	65.1	71.2	132,948	56.5	61.8
State Total	1,013	930	547	54.1	58.9	480	47.4	51.6
Sex								
Male	493	463	256	51.9	55.3	225	45.7	48.7
Female	520	467	292	56.1	62.4	255	49.1	54.6
Race								
White alone	238	228	170	71.3	74.4	153	64.2	66.9
White, non-Hispanic alone	212	210	160	75.4	76.0	143	67.6	68.2
Black alone	18	18	12	B	B	12	B	B
Asian alone	459	403	227	49.5	56.3	201	43.7	49.7
Hispanic (of any race)	81	73	33	41.0	B	25	31.4	B
Age								
18 to 24 years	107	91	33	30.6	36.0	24	22.1	26.0
25 to 44 years	338	307	148	43.9	48.3	124	36.6	40.3
45 to 64 years	343	317	217	63.2	68.4	196	57.0	61.8
65 to 74 years	124	119	79	63.8	66.5	73	59.1	61.6
75 years and over	100	96	70	70.1	73.4	63	63.4	66.3

B = Base is less than 75,000 and therefore too small to show the derived measure.

Table HI-14. Crime

(Number, rate per 100,000. Data are derived from the FBI Uniform Crime Reports.)

Item	State			U.S.		
	2010	2011	Percent change	2010	2011	Percent change
TOTAL POPULATION	1,363,359	1,274,810	-6.5	309,330,219	311,591,917	0.7
VIOLENT CRIME						
Number	3,603	3,949	9.6	1,251,248	1,203,564	-3.8
Rate	264.3	287.2	8.7	404.5	386.3	-4.5
Murder and Nonnegligent Manslaughter						
Number	25	17	-32.0	14,722	14,612	-0.7
Rate	1.8	1.2	-33.3	4.8	4.7	-2.1
Forcible Rape						
Number	377	434	15.1	85,593	83,425	-2.5
Rate	27.7	31.6	14.1	27.7	26.8	-3.2
Robbery						
Number	1,065	1,042	-2.2	369,089	354,396	-4.0
Rate	78.1	75.8	-2.9	119.3	113.7	-4.7
Aggravated Assault						
Number	2,136	2,456	15.0	781,844	751,131	-3.9
Rate	156.7	178.6	14.0	252.8	241.1	-4.6
PROPERTY CRIME						
Number	45,667	45,889	0.5	9,112,625	9,063,173	-0.5
Rate	3,349.6	3,337.8	-0.4	2,945.9	2,908.7	-1.3
Burglary						
Number	8,706	10,008	15.0	2,168,459	2,188,005	0.9
Rate	638.6	728.0	14.0	701.0	702.2	0.2
Larceny-Theft						
Number	31,681	31,697	0.1	6,204,601	6,159,795	-0.7
Rate	2,323.7	2,305.6	-0.8	2,005.8	1,976.9	-1.4
Motor Vehicle Theft						
Number	5,280	4,184	-20.8	739,565	715,373	-3.3
Rate	387.3	304.3	-21.4	239.1	229.6	-4.0

Table HI-15. State Government Finances, 2011

(Dollar amounts in thousands, percent distribution.)

Item	Dollars	Percent distribution
Total Revenue	12,931,811	100.0
General revenue	10,203,676	78.9
Intergovernmental revenue	2,918,445	22.6
Taxes	4,857,729	37.6
General sales	2,495,807	19.3
Selective sales	839,755	6.5
License taxes	151,525	1.2
Individual income tax	1,247,291	9.6
Corporate income tax	67,859	0.5
Other taxes	55,492	0.4
Current charges	1,599,757	12.4
Miscellaneous general revenue	827,745	6.4
Utility revenue	0	0.0
Liquor stores revenue	0	0.0
Insurance trust revenue [1]	2,728,135	21.1
Total Expenditure	11,475,771	100.0
Intergovernmental expenditure	207,988	1.8
Direct expenditure	11,267,783	98.2
Current operation	8,411,885	73.3
Capital outlay	862,111	7.5
Insurance benefits and repayments	1,507,373	13.1
Assistance and subsidies	125,206	1.1
Interest on debt	361,208	3.1
Exhibit: Salaries and wages	2,146,707	18.7
Total Expenditure	11,475,771	100.0
General expenditure	9,963,247	86.8
Intergovernmental expenditure	207,988	1.8
Direct expenditure	9,755,259	85.0
General expenditure, by function:		
Education	3,345,134	29.1
Public welfare	2,086,752	18.2
Hospitals	666,713	5.8
Health	620,003	5.4
Highways	357,387	3.1
Police protection	31,656	0.3
Correction	191,030	1.7
Natural resources	97,119	0.8
Parks and recreation	110,006	1.0
Governmental administration	417,053	3.6
Interest on general debt	361,208	3.1
Other and unallocable	1,679,186	14.6
Utility expenditure	5,151	0.0
Liquor stores expenditure	0	0.0
Insurance trust expenditure	1,507,373	13.1
Debt at End of Fiscal Year	7,912,833	X
Cash and Security Holdings	15,603,693	X

X = Not applicable.
[1] Within insurance trust revenue, net earnings of state retirement systems is a calculated statistic (the item code in the data file is X08), and thus can be positive or negative. Net earnings is the sum of earnings on investments plus gains on investments minus losses on investments. The change made in 2002 for asset valuation from book to market value in accordance with Statement 34 of the Governmental Accounting Standards Board is reflected in the calculated statistics.

Table HI-16. State Government Tax Collections, 2012

(Dollars in thousands, percent.)

Item	Dollars	Percent distribution
Total Taxes	5,516,146	100.0
Property taxes	0	0.0
Sales and gross receipts	3,581,652	64.9
General sales and gross receipts	2,697,951	48.9
Selective sales and gross receipts	883,701	16.0
Alcoholic beverages	48,854	0.9
Amusements	0	0.0
Insurance premiums	122,401	2.2
Motor fuels	93,349	1.7
Pari-mutuels	0	0.0
Public utilities	150,528	2.7
Tobacco products	121,971	2.2
Other selective sales	346,598	6.3
Licenses	258,795	4.7
Alcoholic beverages	0	0.0
Amusements	0	0.0
Corporations in general	1,539	-
Hunting and fishing	465	0.0
Motor vehicle	206,164	3.7
Motor vehicle operators	487	-
Public utilities	17,810	0.3
Occupation and business, NEC	31,168	0.6
Other licenses	1,162	-
Income taxes	1,621,002	29.4
Individual income	1,540,746	27.9
Corporation net income	80,256	1.5
Other taxes	54,697	1.0
Death and gift	14,125	0.3
Documentary and stock transfer	40,572	0.7
Severance	0	0.0
Taxes, NEC	0	0.0

- = Rounds to zero.

Leading Exports, 2012

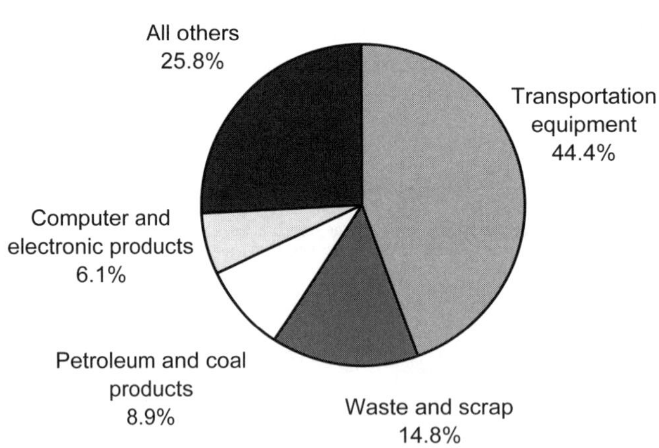

IDAHO

Facts and Figures

Location: Northwestern United States; bordered on the N by Canada, on the E by Montana and Wyoming, on the S by Nevada and Utah, and on the W by Washington and Oregon

Area: 83,570 sq. mi. (216,446 sq. km.); rank—14th

Population: 1,595,728 (2012 est.); rank—39th

Principal Cities: capital—Boise; largest—Boise

Statehood: July 3, 1890; 43rd state

U.S. Congress: 2 senators, 2 representatives

State Motto: *Esto perpetua* ("Let it be perpetual")

State Song: "Here We Have Idaho"

State Nickname: The Gem State

Abbreviations: ID

State Symbols: flower—syringa (mock orange); tree—Western white pine; bird—mountain bluebird

At a Glance

- With an increase in population of 19.5 percent, Idaho ranked 26th among the states in growth from 2000 to 2009.
- An estimated 13,900 marriages took place in Idaho in 2009, compared to 7,700 divorces.
- Idaho's violent crime rate in 2011 was 200.9 per 100,000 population, compared to 386.3 for the entire nation.
- In the 2012 election, 63.9 percent of Idaho's eligible voters voted, compared to 61.8 percent of eligible voters nationwide.
- In 2007, Idaho exported $1.2 billion worth of agricultural products, about 1.4 percent of the U.S. total.

Table ID-1. Population by Age, Sex, Race, and Hispanic Origin

(Number, percent, except where noted.)

Sex, age, race, and Hispanic origin	2000	2010	2012[1]	Average annual percent change, 2010–2012
Total Population	1,293,953	1,567,582	1,595,728	0.6
Percent of total U.S. population	0.5	0.5	0.5	X
Sex				
Male	648,660	785,324	798,612	0.6
Female	645,293	782,258	797,116	0.6
Age				
Under 5 years	97,643	121,772	115,972	-1.7
5 to 19 years	316,222	353,509	355,212	0.2
20 to 64 years	734,172	897,633	911,966	0.5
65 years and over	145,916	194,668	212,578	2.8
Median age (years)	33.2	34.6	35.2	0.6
Race and Hispanic Origin				
One race				
White	1,177,304	1,476,097	1,497,404	0.5
Black	5,456	10,950	12,037	3.0
American Indian and Alaska Native	17,645	25,782	26,684	1.1
Asian	11,889	20,034	21,899	2.8
Native Hawaiian or Other Pacific Islander	1,308	2,786	2,916	1.5
Two or more races	25,609	31,933	34,788	2.7
Hispanic (of any race)	101,690	182,424	192,262	1.7

X = Not applicable.
[1] Population figures for 2012 are July 1 estimates. The 2010 estimates are taken from the 2010 Census.

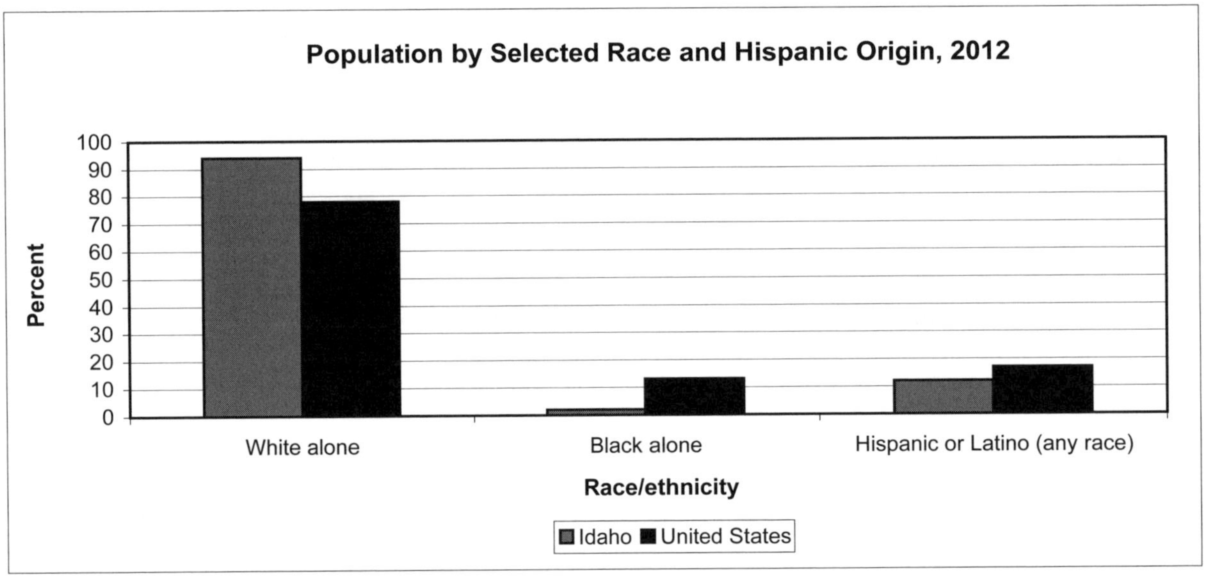

Table ID-2. Marital Status

(Number, percent distribution.)

Sex, age, race, and Hispanic origin	2000	2010	2011
Males, 15 Years and Over	493,045	602,308	609,408
Never married	26.1	28.3	28.9
Now married, except separated	61.0	57.0	56.6
Separated	1.0	1.4	1.1
Widowed	2.1	2.4	1.8
Divorced	9.9	10.9	11.7
Females, 15 Years and Over	498,579	608,900	615,004
Never married	19.6	22.4	23.0
Now married, except separated	59.0	55.3	54.5
Separated	1.3	1.6	1.4
Widowed	8.6	7.6	7.9
Divorced	11.4	13.1	13.2

Table ID-3. Households and Housing Characteristics

(Number, percent, dollars.)

Item	2000	2010	2011	Average annual percent change, 2000–2011
Total Households	469,645	576,709	580,193	2.0
Family households	333,588	401,806	398,682	1.6
Married-couple family	276,511	322,129	319,270	1.3
Other family	59,077	79,677	79,412	2.9
Male householder, no wife present	18,228	23,583	25,194	3.2
Female householder, no husband present	40,849	56,094	54,218	2.7
Nonfamily households	134,057	174,903	181,511	2.9
Householder living alone	105,175	139,909	144,079	3.1
Householder not living alone	28,882	34,994	37,432	2.5
Housing Characteristics				
Total housing units	527,824	668,634	674,394	2.3
Occupied housing units	469,645	576,709	580,193	2.0
Owner occupied	339,960	401,532	398,816	1.4
Renter occupied	129,685	175,177	181,377	3.3
Average size	2.69	2.67	2.68	-
Financial Characteristics				
Median gross rent of renter-occupied housing	515	683	689	2.8
Median monthly owner costs for housing units with a mortgage	887	1,187	1,212	3.1
Median value of owner-occupied housing units	106,300	165,100	158,800	4.1

- = Zero or rounds to zero.

Table ID-4. Migration, Origin, and Language

(Number, percent.)

Characteristic	State			U.S.		
	2010	2011	Percent change	2010	2011	Percent change
Residence 1 Year Ago						
Population 1 year and over	1,550,967	1,559,637	0.6	305,628,607	307,900,319	0.7
Same house	82.5	82.4	-0.1	84.6	84.8	0.2
Different house in the U.S.	17.1	17.2	0.6	14.8	14.6	-1.4
Same county	10.1	10.0	-1.0	9.4	9.2	-2.1
Different county	7.0	7.2	2.9	5.4	5.4	-
Same state	3.4	3.3	-2.9	3.2	3.1	-3.1
Different state	3.6	3.9	8.3	2.2	2.3	4.5
Abroad	0.4	0.4	-	0.6	0.6	-
Place of Birth						
Native born	1,484,352	1,489,599	0.4	269,393,835	271,214,059	0.7
Male	50.2	50.2	-	49.2	49.2	-
Female	49.8	49.8	-	50.8	50.8	-
Foreign born	87,098	95,386	9.5	39,955,854	40,377,860	1.1
Male	49.3	49.1	-0.4	49.1	48.9	-0.4
Female	50.7	50.9	0.4	50.9	51.1	0.4
Foreign born; naturalized U.S. citizen	29,550	31,019	5.0	17,476,082	18,140,192	3.8
Male	46.1	41.2	-10.6	45.8	45.8	-
Female	53.9	58.8	9.1	54.2	54.2	-
Foreign born; not a U.S. citizen	57,548	64,367	11.8	22,479,772	22,237,668	-1.1
Male	51.0	52.9	3.7	51.6	51.5	-0.2
Female	49.0	47.1	-3.9	48.4	48.5	0.2
Entered 2000 or later	35.8	37.9	5.9	34.7	35.7	2.9
Entered 1990 to 1999	28.6	25.5	-10.8	27.2	26.7	-1.8
Entered before 1990	35.7	36.6	2.5	38.1	37.6	-1.3
World Region of Birth, Foreign						
Foreign-born population, excluding population born at sea	87,098	95,386	9.5	39,955,673	40,377,757	1.1
Europe	16.4	13.9	-15.2	12.1	12.1	-
Asia	11.8	19.5	65.3	28.2	28.6	1.4
Africa	3.1	1.4	-54.8	4	4.1	2.5
Oceania	1.9	0.3	-84.2	0.5	0.5	-
Latin America	62.4	58.6	-6.1	53.1	52.6	-0.9
North America	4.3	6.1	41.9	2	2.0	-
Language Spoken at Home and Ability to Speak English						
Population 5 years and over	1,450,742	1,466,499	1.1	289,215,746	291,524,091	0.8
English only	89.5	89.6	0.1	79.4	79.2	-0.3
Language other than English	10.5	10.4	-1.0	20.6	20.8	1.0
Speaks English less than "very well"	3.7	3.9	5.4	8.7	8.7	-

- = Zero or rounds to zero.

Table ID-5. Median Income and Poverty Status, 2011

(Number, percent, except as noted.)

Characteristic	State		U.S.	
	Number	Percent	Number	Percent
Median Income				
Households (dollars)	43,341	X	50,502	X
Families (dollars)	52,814	X	61,455	X
Below Poverty Level (All People)	255,027	16.5	48,452,035	15.9
Sex				
Male	118,472	15.3	21,825,281	14.7
Female	136,555	17.6	26,626,754	17.2
Age				
Under 18 years	85,173	20.4	16,386,500	22.5
Related children under 18 years	82,521	19.9	16,087,074	22.2
18 to 64 years	156,303	16.8	28,335,079	14.8
65 years and over	13,551	6.8	3,730,456	9.3

X = Not applicable.

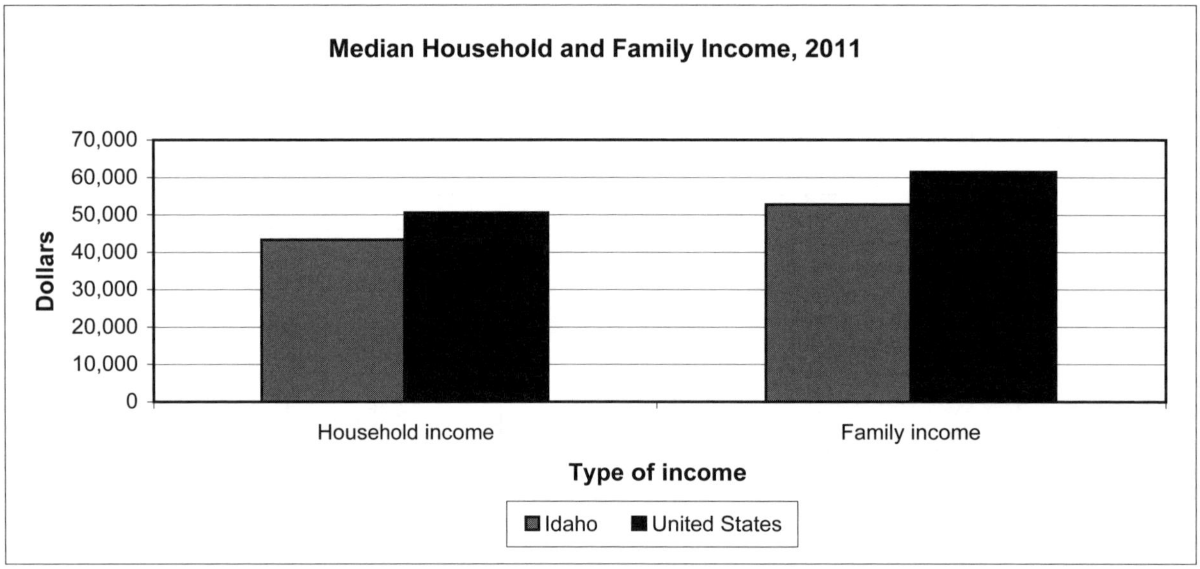

Table ID-6. Health Insurance Coverage Status for the Civilian Noninstitutionalized Population and Children Under 18 Years of Age

(Numbers in thousands, percent.)

Item	2004	2005	2006	2007	2008	2009	2010	2011
Civilian Noninstitutionalized Population	1,375	1,442	1,475	1,501	1,499	1,521	1,552	1,566
Covered by Private or Public Insurance								
Number	1,175	1,229	1,248	1,292	1,232	1,256	1,276	1,307
Percent	85.5	85.2	84.6	86.1	82.2	82.6	82.3	83.5
Not Covered								
Number	200	213	227	209	267	264	275	259
Percent	14.5	14.8	15.4	13.9	17.8	17.4	17.7	16.5
Percent in the U.S. not covered	14.9	15.3	15.8	15.3	15.1	15.1	15.5	15.1
Children Under 18 Years of Age	384	394	420	415	413	418	428	427
Covered by Private or Public Insurance								
Number	352	349	350	369	357	371	383	388
Percent	91.5	88.6	87.0	89.0	86.4	88.8	89.5	90.9
Not Covered								
Number	33	45	52	46	56	47	45	39
Percent	8.5	11.4	13.0	11.0	13.6	11.2	10.5	9.1
Percent in the U.S. not covered	10.5	10.9	11.7	11.0	9.7	8.6	8.0	7.5

Table ID-7. Employment Status by Demographic Group, Preliminary 2012

(Numbers in thousands, percent.)

Characteristic	Civilian noninstitutional population	Civilian labor force		Employed		Unemployed	
		Number	Percent of population	Number	Percent of population	Number	Percent of population
Total	1,194	772	64.6	717	60.1	55	7.1
Sex							
Male	588	430	73.0	402	68.2	28	6.5
Female	606	342	56.5	316	52.1	27	7.8
Race, Sex, and Hispanic Origin							
White	1,144	741	64.7	689	60.2	52	7.0
Male	564	413	73.2	386	68.4	27	6.5
Female	581	328	56.5	303	52.2	25	7.7
Black or African American	NA	NA	NA	NA	NA	NA	NA
Male	NA	NA	NA	NA	NA	NA	NA
Female	NA	NA	NA	NA	NA	NA	NA
Hispanic	136	98	72.3	91	67.2	7	7.1
Male	77	65	84.0	62	80.0	3	4.7
Female	59	33	56.9	29	50.3	4	11.7
Age							
16 to 19 years	97	42	43.0	32	33.3	9	22.5
20 to 24 years	87	66	76.7	57	66.0	9	14.0
25 to 34 years	209	167	80.0	155	74.2	12	7.2
35 to 44 years	203	169	83.3	161	79.1	9	5.1
45 to 54 years	203	170	84.1	164	80.8	7	3.9
55 to 64 years	180	122	68.1	115	63.9	8	6.1
65 years and over	216	35	16.1	34	15.6	1	3.4

NOTE: Data in Table 7 are from the Current Population Survey (CPS) and do not match the estimates in Table 8. See notes and definitions for further information.

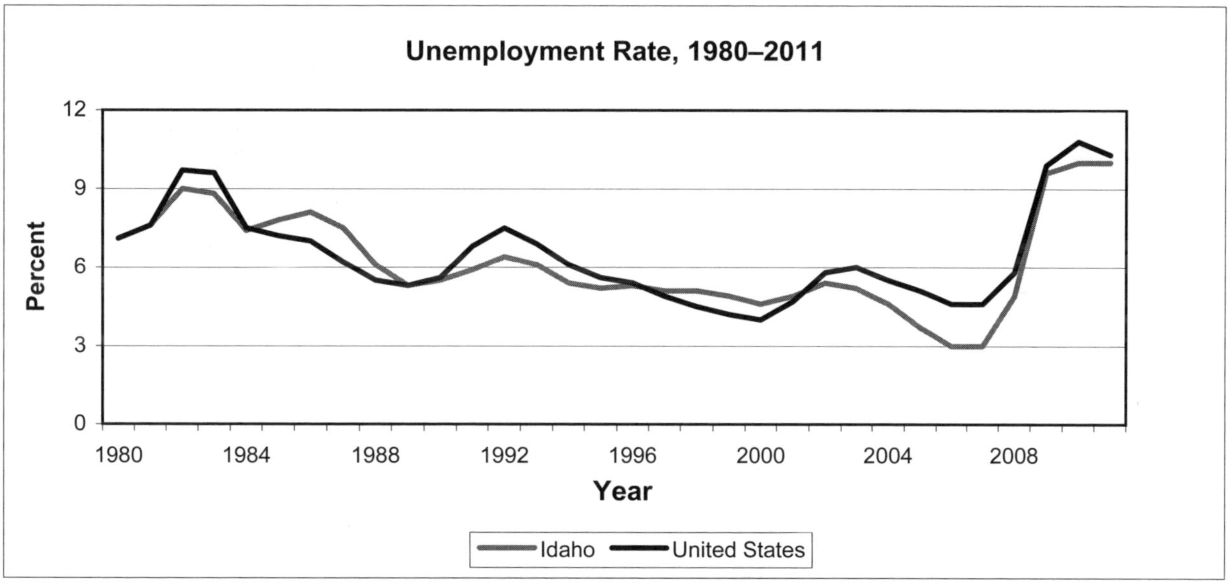

Table ID-8. Employment Status of the Civilian Noninstitutional Population Age 16 Years and Over

(Number, percent.)

Year	Civilian labor force	Civilian participation rate	Employed	Unemployed	Unemployment rate
2005	720,673	68.4	693,851	26,822	3.7
2006	735,859	68.0	713,520	22,339	3.0
2007	748,709	67.5	726,091	22,618	3.0
2008	754,879	66.7	718,097	36,782	4.9
2009	758,533	64.6	685,475	73,058	9.6
2010	757,590	63.8	681,907	75,683	10.0
2011	760,733	63.4	684,916	75,817	10.0

Table ID-9. Employment and Average Wages by Industry

(Estimates before 2007 are based on the 2002 *North American Industry Classification System* [NAICS]. Estimates from 2007 onward are based on the 2007 NAICS.)

Industry	2005	2006	2007	2008	2009	2010	2011
	Number of jobs						
Wage and Salary Employment by Industry	656,257	684,570	701,608	694,229	653,408	646,725	649,999
Farm Wage and Salary Employment	15,134	15,278	14,490	15,287	14,323	14,700	16,442
Nonfarm Wage and Salary Employment	641,123	669,292	687,118	678,942	639,085	632,025	633,557
Private wage and salary employment	516,114	543,693	560,150	550,215	510,255	503,538	507,403
Forestry, fishing, and related activities	8,014	7,801	7,630	7,502	7,128	7,316	7,485
Mining	2,167	2,383	2,655	2,780	2,167	2,273	2,568
Utilities	1,948	2,018	2,069	2,161	2,098	2,729	2,798
Construction	46,905	54,096	54,383	47,063	36,067	32,693	31,140
Manufacturing	63,031	66,046	66,436	63,059	55,052	53,383	54,598
Durable goods manufacturing	40,653	42,822	42,473	38,378	31,182	29,954	31,309
Nondurable goods manufacturing	22,378	23,224	23,963	24,681	23,870	23,429	23,289
Wholesale trade	26,794	27,059	28,238	27,922	26,315	25,950	26,413
Retail trade	77,685	81,461	84,629	83,774	77,551	76,232	76,151
Transportation and warehousing	18,022	18,646	19,340	19,358	18,402	18,377	18,504
Information	10,334	10,614	10,920	11,075	10,077	9,702	9,424
Finance and insurance	20,269	21,847	22,248	21,997	21,063	20,980	21,343
Real estate and rental and leasing	8,289	8,962	9,081	8,615	7,515	7,168	6,924
Professional, scientific, and technical services	31,338	33,429	34,598	34,494	33,003	32,795	32,794
Management of companies and enterprises	7,684	7,707	7,846	7,250	6,719	5,863	5,874
Administrative and waste services	39,666	41,316	41,401	40,620	36,959	36,571	37,024
Educational services	8,686	9,105	9,677	9,890	10,043	10,295	10,585
Health care and social assistance	61,331	63,911	67,347	70,562	73,380	76,111	77,474
Arts, entertainment, and recreation	7,832	8,482	9,131	9,038	8,704	8,621	8,663
Accommodation and food services	50,012	51,902	54,675	54,748	50,606	50,047	51,144
Other services, except public administration	26,107	26,908	27,846	28,307	27,406	26,432	26,497
Government and government enterprises	125,009	125,599	126,968	128,727	128,830	128,487	126,154
	Dollars						
Average Wages and Salaries by Industry	31,532	33,278	34,391	34,651	35,066	35,781	36,452
Average Farm Wages and Salaries	31,900	32,165	39,021	35,696	42,301	35,808	33,216
Average Nonfarm Wages and Salaries	31,523	33,303	34,293	34,628	34,904	35,781	36,536
Average private wages and salaries	31,384	33,300	34,331	34,467	34,647	35,729	36,595
Forestry, fishing, and related activities	25,042	26,427	27,313	27,349	26,300	27,268	28,854
Mining	46,546	51,399	56,599	59,909	57,883	67,925	69,470
Utilities	55,161	57,779	59,417	62,911	65,184	73,834	75,159
Construction	32,668	34,135	37,952	38,167	37,942	39,040	39,436
Manufacturing	43,843	46,397	47,408	48,028	48,132	50,941	51,881
Durable goods manufacturing	48,922	51,939	53,096	54,184	54,423	58,795	58,355
Nondurable goods manufacturing	34,615	36,177	37,327	38,455	39,913	40,900	43,177
Wholesale trade	40,393	43,311	45,542	45,887	45,910	47,440	48,927
Retail trade	24,773	26,089	25,652	25,270	25,330	25,847	26,308
Transportation and warehousing	34,445	35,590	36,201	37,119	37,036	37,745	39,150
Information	37,806	39,423	39,759	41,268	41,888	42,599	44,478
Finance and insurance	44,469	46,679	47,936	47,440	47,444	48,734	49,575
Real estate and rental and leasing	27,242	28,870	29,602	28,616	28,478	28,465	28,854
Professional, scientific, and technical services	47,330	49,623	50,967	52,533	54,833	56,536	58,158
Management of companies and enterprises	69,061	87,621	83,910	77,648	78,219	81,421	87,177
Administrative and waste services	22,678	23,945	25,026	25,777	26,126	26,740	27,217
Educational services	23,514	23,554	23,988	24,594	25,495	26,243	26,993
Health care and social assistance	31,261	32,827	34,300	35,224	35,982	36,401	37,454
Arts, entertainment, and recreation	17,720	19,863	20,960	19,585	18,399	19,522	18,973
Accommodation and food services	12,937	13,687	14,484	14,306	14,482	15,110	15,442
Other services, except public administration	20,177	21,422	22,461	23,208	23,040	23,855	24,065
Government and government enterprises	32,096	33,315	34,127	35,315	35,921	35,983	36,296

Table ID-10. Employment Characteristics by Family Type

(Number, percent.)

Family type and labor force status	2009		2010		2011	
	Total	Families with own children under 18 years	Total	Families with own children under 18 years	Total	Families with own children under 18 years
All families	397,214	191,250	401,806	187,262	398,682	180,257
Family type and labor force status						
Married-couple families	321,795	142,303	322,129	136,620	319,270	132,413
Both husband and wife in labor force	53.1	63.4	52.8	63.5	50.8	60.3
Husband in labor force, wife not in labor force	23.8	32.0	23.0	31.3	23.4	34.1
Wife in labor force, husband not in labor force	6.8	2.6	6.8	3.6	7.2	3.9
Both husband and wife not in labor force	16.3	2.0	17.4	1.7	18.6	1.8
Other families	75,419	48,947	79,677	50,642	79,412	47,844
Female householder, no husband present	68.6	70.7	70.4	73.5	68.3	70.2
In labor force	50.7	59.8	52.9	62.9	48.4	56.1
Not in labor force	18.0	10.8	17.5	10.6	19.9	14.2
Male householder, no wife present	31.4	29.3	29.6	26.5	31.7	29.8
In labor force	26.5	27.7	22.5	23.4	25.2	26.8
Not in labor force	4.9	1.6	7.1	3.1	6.5	3.0

Table ID-11. School Enrollment and Educational Attainment, 2011

(Number, percent.)

Item	State	U.S.
Enrollment		
Total population 3 years and over, enrolled in school	452,340	83,131,910
Enrolled in nursery school or preschool (percent)	5.3	6.0
Enrolled in kindergarten (percent)	5.2	5.1
Enrolled in elementary school, grades 1-8 (percent)	41.9	39.5
Enrolled in high school, grades 9-12 (percent)	21.0	20.7
Enrolled in college or graduate school (percent)	26.7	28.7
Attainment		
Total population 25 years and over	998,460	206,471,670
Less than ninth grade (percent)	4.5	6.0
9th to 12th grade, no diploma (percent)	6.9	8.1
High school graduate, including equivalency (percent)	27.5	28.4
Some college, no degree (percent)	26.9	21.2
Associate's degree (percent)	8.9	7.8
Bachelor's degree (percent)	17.5	17.9
Graduate or professional degree (percent)	7.8	10.6
High school graduate or higher (percent)	88.6	85.9
Bachelor's degree or higher (percent)	25.2	28.5

Table ID-12. Educational Indicators

(Number, percent; data derived from National Center of Education Statistics.)

Item	State	U.S.
Public Schools, 2009–2010 (except where noted)		
Number of school districts	116	13,629
Number of schools	752	99,834
Number of students (in thousands)	276	49,373
Student-teacher ratio	18.2	15.4
Expenditures per student (dollars)	8,234	10,591
Averaged freshman graduation rate, 2008–2009	80.6	75.5[1]
Dropout rate, 2008–2009	1.6	4.1
Students eligible for free or reduced-price lunch (percent)	44.7	48.0
English language learners, 2010–2011 (percent)	5.8	9.8[1]
Students with IEP (percent)	10.1	13.1
Private Schools, 2009–2010 (except where noted)		
Number of schools	197[2]	33,366
Number of students (in thousands)	14[2]	4,700
High school graduates, 2008–2009	11	308,813
Student-teacher ratio	10.62	10.7

[1] U.S. total includes estimates for nonreporting states.
[2] Interpret data with caution. The coefficient of variation for this estimate is larger than 25 percent.

Table ID-13. Reported Voting and Registration of the Voting-Age Population, November 2012

(Numbers in thousands, percent.)

Item	Total population	Total citizen population	Registered			Voted		
			Total registered	Percent registered (total population)	Percent registered (total citizen population)	Total voted	Percent voted (total population)	Percent voted (total citizen population)
U.S. Total	235,248	215,081	153,157	65.1	71.2	132,948	56.5	61.8
State Total	1,129	1,064	745	65.9	70.0	679	60.2	63.9
Sex								
Male	553	519	354	64.1	68.3	323	58.4	62.2
Female	577	545	390	67.7	71.6	357	61.8	65.4
Race								
White alone	1,077	1,021	726	67.4	71.1	661	61.4	64.8
White, non-Hispanic alone	960	956	691	72.0	72.3	634	66.1	66.4
Black alone	7	7	-	B	B	-	B	B
Asian alone	15	6	2	B	B	2	B	B
Hispanic (of any race)	119	68	35	29.6	B	27	22.5	B
Age								
18 to 24 years	130	121	51	39.0	41.8	39	29.8	31.9
25 to 44 years	397	359	256	64.4	71.1	231	58.1	64.2
45 to 64 years	401	382	274	68.3	71.7	250	62.3	65.4
65 to 74 years	112	112	90	80.7	80.7	86	77.1	77.1
75 years and over	89	89	74	82.6	82.6	74	82.6	82.6

- = Zero or rounds to zero.
B = Base is less than 75,000 and therefore too small to show the derived measure.

Table ID-14. Crime

(Number, rate per 100,000. Data are derived from the FBI Uniform Crime Reports.)

Item	State			U.S.		
	2010	2011	Percent change	2010	2011	Percent change
TOTAL POPULATION	1,571,102	1,584,985	0.9	309,330,219	311,591,917	0.7
VIOLENT CRIME						
Number	3,464	3,184	-8.1	1,251,248	1,203,564	-3.8
Rate	220.5	200.9	-8.9	404.5	386.3	-4.5
Murder and Nonnegligent Manslaughter						
Number	22	36	63.6	14,722	14,612	-0.7
Rate	1.4	2.3	64.3	4.8	4.7	-2.1
Forcible Rape						
Number	533	435	-18.4	85,593	83,425	-2.5
Rate	33.9	27.4	-19.2	27.7	26.8	-3.2
Robbery						
Number	213	184	-13.6	369,089	354,396	-4.0
Rate	13.6	11.6	-14.7	119.3	113.7	-4.7
Aggravated Assault						
Number	2,696	2,529	-6.2	781,844	751,131	-3.9
Rate	171.6	159.6	-7.0	252.8	241.1	-4.6
PROPERTY CRIME						
Number	31,436	32,787	4.3	9,112,625	9,063,173	-0.5
Rate	2,000.9	2,068.6	3.4	2,945.9	2,908.7	-1.3
Burglary						
Number	6,513	6,920	6.2	2,168,459	2,188,005	0.9
Rate	414.5	436.6	5.3	701.0	702.2	0.2
Larceny-Theft						
Number	23,594	24,534	4.0	6,204,601	6,159,795	-0.7
Rate	1,501.7	1,547.9	3.1	2,005.8	1,976.9	-1.4
Motor Vehicle Theft						
Number	1,329	1,333	0.3	739,565	715,373	-3.3
Rate	84.6	84.1	-0.6	239.1	229.6	-4.0

Table ID-15. State Government Finances, 2011

(Dollar amounts in thousands, percent distribution.)

Item	Dollars	Percent distribution
Total Revenue	10,776,454	100.0
General revenue	7,344,101	68.1
Intergovernmental revenue	2,804,663	26.0
Taxes	3,261,722	30.3
General sales	1,187,070	11.0
Selective sales	425,655	3.9
License taxes	297,648	2.8
Individual income tax	1,169,247	10.9
Corporate income tax	170,214	1.6
Other taxes	11,888	0.1
Current charges	801,841	7.4
Miscellaneous general revenue	475,875	4.4
Utility revenue	0	0.0
Liquor stores revenue	121,520	1.1
Insurance trust revenue [1]	3,310,833	30.7
Total Expenditure	8,733,485	100.0
Intergovernmental expenditure	2,036,312	23.2
Direct expenditure	6,697,173	76.3
Current operation	4,430,640	50.5
Capital outlay	691,443	7.9
Insurance benefits and repayments	1,235,285	14.1
Assistance and subsidies	163,543	1.9
Interest on debt	176,262	2.0
Exhibit: Salaries and wages	1,035,307	11.8
Total Expenditure	8,733,485	99.5
General expenditure	7,404,749	84.4
Intergovernmental expenditure	2,036,312	23.2
Direct expenditure	5,368,437	61.2
General expenditure, by function:		
Education	2,700,603	30.8
Public welfare	2,174,866	24.8
Hospitals	44,305	0.5
Health	159,152	1.8
Highways	836,014	9.5
Police protection	52,386	0.6
Correction	219,042	2.5
Natural resources	194,745	2.2
Parks and recreation	35,329	0.4
Governmental administration	272,690	3.1
Interest on general debt	176,262	2.0
Other and unallocable	539,355	6.1
Utility expenditure	0	0.0
Liquor stores expenditure	93,451	1.1
Insurance trust expenditure	1,235,285	14.1
Debt at End of Fiscal Year	3,928,080	X
Cash and Security Holdings	18,352,520	X

X = Not applicable.

[1] Within insurance trust revenue, net earnings of state retirement systems is a calculated statistic (the item code in the data file is X08), and thus can be positive or negative. Net earnings is the sum of earnings on investments plus gains on investments minus losses on investments. The change made in 2002 for asset valuation from book to market value in accordance with Statement 34 of the Governmental Accounting Standards Board is reflected in the calculated statistics.

Table ID-16. State Government Tax Collections, 2012

(Dollars in thousands, percent.)

Item	Dollars	Percent distribution
Total Taxes	3,374,304	100.0
Property taxes	0	0.0
Sales and gross receipts	1,664,615	49.5
General sales and gross receipts	1,224,656	36.4
Selective sales and gross receipts	439,959	13.1
Alcoholic beverages	8,099	0.2
Amusements	0	0.0
Insurance premiums	69,722	2.1
Motor fuels	236,769	7.0
Pari-mutuels	1,269	-
Public utilities	2,983	0.1
Tobacco products	48,461	1.4
Other selective sales	72,656	2.2
Licenses	299,443	8.9
Alcoholic beverages	1,399	-
Amusements	321	-
Corporations in general	1,963	0.1
Hunting and fishing	33,590	1.0
Motor vehicle	127,813	3.8
Motor vehicle operators	11,463	0.3
Public utilities	49,085	1.5
Occupation and business, NEC	69,894	2.1
Other licenses	3,915	0.1
Income taxes	1,401,924	41.7
Individual income	1,213,335	36.1
Corporation net income	188,589	5.6
Other taxes	8,322	0.2
Death and gift	13	-
Documentary and stock transfer	0	0.0
Severance	8,309	0.2
Taxes, NEC	0	0.0

- = Rounds to zero.

Leading Exports, 2012

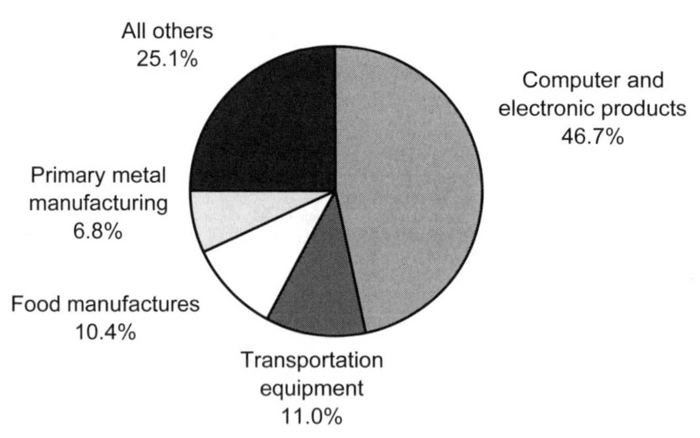

ILLINOIS

Facts and Figures

Location: North central United States; bordered on the N by Wisconsin, on the E by Lake Michigan and Indiana, on the S by Kentucky, and on the W by Iowa and Missouri

Area: 57,914 sq. mi. (149,998 sq. km.); rank—25th

Population: 12,875,255 (2012 est.); rank—5th

Principal Cities: capital—Springfield; largest—Chicago

Statehood: December 3, 1818; 21st state

U.S. Congress: 2 senators, 18 representatives

State Motto: State Sovereignty, National Union

State Song: "Illinois"

State Nicknames: The Prairie State; The Land of Lincoln

Abbreviations: IL; Ill.

State Symbols: flower—native violet; tree—white oak; bird—cardinal

At a Glance

- An estimated 72,700 marriages took place in Illinois in 2009, compared to 32,700 divorces.
- In 2011, 13.1 percent of Illinoisans did not have health insurance, compared to 15.1 percent of the total U.S. population.
- In the 2012 election, 61.5 percent of Illinois's eligible voters voted, compared to 61.8 percent of eligible voters nationwide.
- In 2007, Illinois exported $4.8 billion worth of agricultural products, 5.8 percent of the U.S. total.

Table IL-1. Population by Age, Sex, Race, and Hispanic Origin

(Number, percent, except where noted.)

Sex, age, race, and Hispanic origin	2000	2010	2012[1]	Average annual percent change, 2010–2012
Total Population	12,419,293	12,830,632	12,875,255	0.1
Percent of total U.S. population	4.4	4.2	4.1	X
Sex				
Male	6,080,336	6,292,276	6,319,455	0.1
Female	6,338,957	6,538,356	6,555,800	0.1
Age				
Under 5 years	876,549	859,405	848,914	-0.4
5 to 19 years	2,728,957	2,660,945	2,607,044	-0.7
20 to 64 years	7,313,762	7,701,069	7,724,860	0.1
65 years and over	1,500,025	1,609,213	1,694,437	1.7
Median age (years)	34.7	36.6	37.0	0.4
Race and Hispanic Origin				
One race				
White	9,125,471	10,030,587	10,028,832	-
Black	1,878,875	1,903,458	1,900,578	-0.1
American Indian and Alaska Native	31,006	73,486	75,948	1.1
Asian	423,603	604,399	638,108	1.8
Native Hawaiian or Other Pacific Islander	4,610	7,436	7,877	1.9
Two or more races	235,016	210,906	232,912	3.1
Hispanic (of any race)	1,530,262	2,073,054	2,149,798	1.2

X = Not applicable.
- = Zero or rounds to zero.
[1] Population figures for 2012 are July 1 estimates. The 2010 estimates are taken from the 2010 Census.

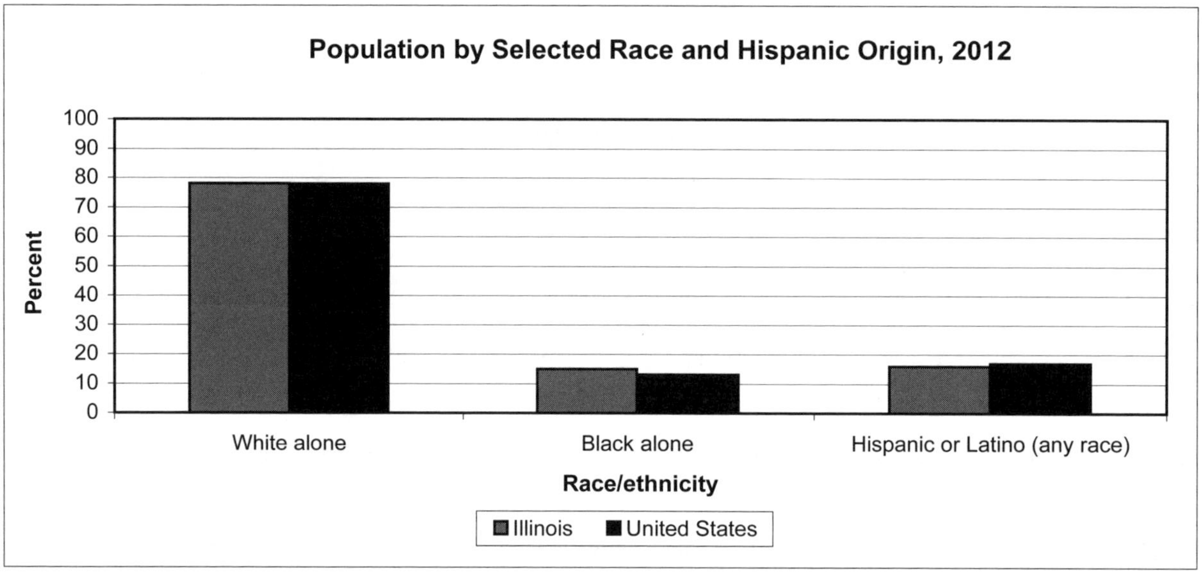

Table IL-2. Marital Status

(Number, percent distribution.)

Sex, age, race, and Hispanic origin	2000	2010	2011
Males, 15 Years and Over	4,685,982	4,977,964	5,009,508
Never married	31.9	37.2	37.5
Now married, except separated	56.1	50.0	49.6
Separated	1.6	1.4	1.5
Widowed	2.5	2.6	2.5
Divorced	7.9	8.8	8.9
Females, 15 Years and Over	5,021,855	5,289,803	5,307,191
Never married	26.1	31.1	31.9
Now married, except separated	51.3	46.3	45.7
Separated	2.0	2.1	2.0
Widowed	10.7	9.5	9.4
Divorced	9.9	11.0	11.0

Table IL-3. Households and Housing Characteristics

(Number, percent, dollars.)

Item	2000	2010	2011	Average annual percent change, 2000–2011
Total Households	4,591,779	4,752,857	4,737,208	0.3
Family households	3,105,513	3,133,813	3,098,864	-
Married-couple family	2,353,892	2,301,009	2,269,243	-0.3
Other family	751,621	832,804	829,621	0.9
Male householder, no wife present	187,903	220,197	212,106	1.1
Female householder, no husband present	563,718	612,607	617,515	0.8
Nonfamily households	1,486,266	1,619,044	1,638,344	0.9
Householder living alone	1,229,807	1,340,394	1,372,272	1.0
Householder not living alone	256,459	278,650	266,072	0.3
Housing Characteristics				
Total housing units	4,885,615	5,297,077	5,296,209	0.7
Occupied housing units	4,591,779	4,752,857	4,737,208	0.3
Owner occupied	3,088,884	3,219,338	3,190,282	0.3
Renter occupied	1,502,895	1,533,519	1,546,926	0.2
Average size	2.63	2.64	2.65	0.1
Financial Characteristics				
Median gross rent of renter-occupied housing	605	848	859	3.5
Median monthly owner costs for housing units with a mortgage	1,198	1,655	1,646	3.1
Median value of owner-occupied housing units	130,800	191,800	178,500	3.0

- = Zero or rounds to zero.

Table IL-4. Migration, Origin, and Language

(Number, percent.)

Characteristic	State 2010	State 2011	State Percent change	U.S. 2010	U.S. 2011	U.S. Percent change
Residence 1 Year Ago						
Population 1 year and over	12,680,126	12,718,402	0.3	305,628,607	307,900,319	0.7
Same house	86.8	87.1	0.3	84.6	84.8	0.2
Different house in the U.S.	12.7	12.3	-3.1	14.8	14.6	-1.4
Same county	8.6	8.2	-4.7	9.4	9.2	-2.1
Different county	4.1	4.1	0.0	5.4	5.4	-
Same state	2.5	2.4	-4.0	3.2	3.1	-3.1
Different state	1.6	1.7	6.2	2.2	2.3	4.5
Abroad	0.5	0.6	20.0	0.6	0.6	-
Place of Birth						
Native born	11,083,307	11,070,444	-0.1	269,393,835	271,214,059	0.7
Male	48.8	48.8	-	49.2	49.2	-
Female	51.2	51.2	-	50.8	50.8	-
Foreign born	1,759,859	1,798,815	2.2	39,955,854	40,377,860	1.1
Male	50.1	50.1	-	49.1	48.9	-0.4
Female	49.9	49.9	-	50.9	51.1	0.4
Foreign born; naturalized U.S. citizen	768,664	837,193	8.9	17,476,082	18,140,192	3.8
Male	47.5	47.7	0.4	45.8	45.8	-
Female	52.5	52.3	-0.4	54.2	54.2	-
Foreign born; not a U.S. citizen	991,195	961,622	-3.0	22,479,772	22,237,668	-1.1
Male	52.1	52.3	0.4	51.6	51.5	-0.2
Female	47.9	47.7	-0.4	48.4	48.5	0.2
Entered 2000 or later	32.5	33.7	3.7	34.7	35.7	2.9
Entered 1990 to 1999	30.5	30.4	-0.3	27.2	26.7	-1.8
Entered before 1990	37.0	36.0	-2.7	38.1	37.6	-1.3
World Region of Birth, Foreign						
Foreign-born population, excluding population born at sea	1,759,859	1,798,815	2.2	39,955,673	40,377,757	1.1
Europe	22.1	20.8	-5.9	12.1	12.1	-
Asia	26.5	27.4	3.4	28.2	28.6	1.4
Africa	2.5	3.0	20.0	4	4.1	2.5
Oceania	0.2	0.2	0.0	0.5	0.5	-
Latin America	47.9	47.6	-0.6	53.1	52.6	-0.9
North America	0.9	0.9	-	2	2.0	-
Language Spoken at Home and Ability to Speak English						
Population 5 years and over	12,010,235	12,042,289	0.3	289,215,746	291,524,091	0.8
English only	78.0	77.3	-0.9	79.4	79.2	-0.3
Language other than English	22.0	22.7	3.2	20.6	20.8	1.0
Speaks English less than "very well"	9.6	9.7	1.0	8.7	8.7	-

- = Zero or rounds to zero.

Table IL-5. Median Income and Poverty Status, 2011

(Number, percent, except as noted.)

Characteristic	State		U.S.	
	Number	Percent	Number	Percent
Median Income				
Households (dollars)	53,234	X	50,502	X
Families (dollars)	65,579	X	61,455	X
Below Poverty Level (All People)	1,879,965	15.0	48,452,035	15.9
Sex				
Male	846,939	13.8	21,825,281	14.7
Female	1,033,026	16.1	26,626,754	17.2
Age				
Under 18 years	658,340	21.6	16,386,500	22.5
Related children under 18 years	648,592	21.3	16,087,074	22.2
18 to 64 years	1,091,542	13.8	28,335,079	14.8
65 years and over	130,083	8.2	3,730,456	9.3

X = Not applicable.

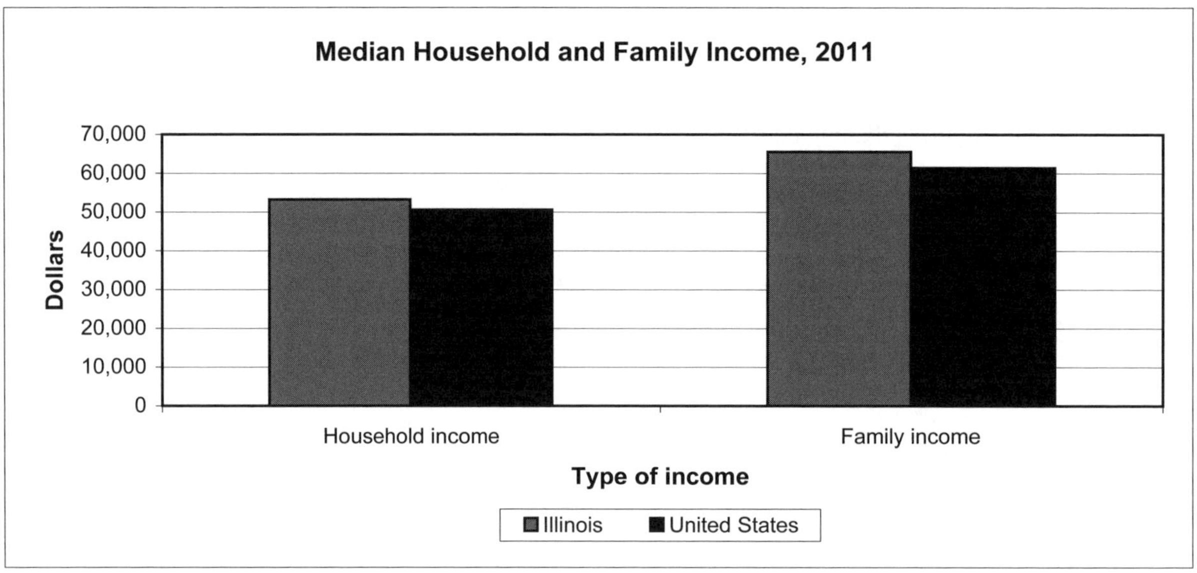

Table IL-6. Health Insurance Coverage Status for the Civilian Noninstitutionalized Population and Children Under 18 Years of Age

(Numbers in thousands, percent.)

Item	2004	2005	2006	2007	2008	2009	2010	2011
Civilian Noninstitutionalized Population	12,592	12,608	12,644	12,688	12,709	12,720	12,673	12,689
Covered by Private or Public Insurance								
Number	10,952	10,878	10,867	10,988	11,086	11,025	10,928	11,029
Percent	87.0	86.3	86.0	86.6	87.2	86.7	86.2	86.9
Not Covered								
Number	1,640	1,730	1,776	1,700	1,623	1,694	1,746	1,659
Percent	13.0	13.7	14.0	13.4	12.8	13.3	13.8	13.1
Percent in the U.S. not covered	14.9	15.3	15.8	15.3	15.1	15.1	15.5	15.1
Children Under 18 Years of Age	3,242	3,276	3,188	3,180	3,176	3,168	3,122	3,092
Covered by Private or Public Insurance								
Number	2,900	2,947	2,886	2,970	2,997	3,026	2,982	2,979
Percent	89.4	89.9	90.5	93.4	94.4	95.5	95.5	96.3
Not Covered								
Number	342	329	302	210	179	142	140	113
Percent	10.6	10.1	9.5	6.6	5.6	4.5	4.5	3.7
Percent in the U.S. not covered	10.5	10.9	11.7	11.0	9.7	8.6	8.0	7.5

Table IL-7. Employment Status by Demographic Group, Preliminary 2012

(Numbers in thousands, percent.)

Characteristic	Civilian noninstitutional population	Civilian labor force		Employed		Unemployed	
		Number	Percent of population	Number	Percent of population	Number	Percent of population
Total	10,007	6,616	66.1	6,039	60.3	577	8.7
Sex							
Male	4,828	3,492	72.3	3,177	65.8	315	9.0
Female	5,179	3,124	60.3	2,862	55.3	262	8.4
Race, Sex, and Hispanic Origin							
White	7,936	5,328	67.1	4,915	61.9	413	7.7
Male	3,890	2,881	74.1	2,646	68.0	235	8.2
Female	4,046	2,447	60.5	2,269	56.1	178	7.3
Black or African American	1,404	841	59.9	706	50.3	135	16.0
Male	621	370	59.6	304	48.9	67	18.1
Female	783	471	60.1	403	51.4	68	14.4
Hispanic	1,286	894	69.5	803	62.4	91	10.2
Male	662	530	80.0	477	72.1	53	9.9
Female	624	364	58.3	326	52.2	38	10.5
Age							
16 to 19 years	695	264	38.0	193	27.7	72	27.1
20 to 24 years	906	650	71.8	553	61.1	97	15.0
25 to 34 years	1,796	1,507	83.9	1,388	77.3	119	7.9
35 to 44 years	1,606	1,332	83.0	1,244	77.5	88	6.6
45 to 54 years	1,839	1,509	82.0	1,388	75.5	121	8.0
55 to 64 years	1,533	1,025	66.9	960	62.6	65	6.4
65 years and over	1,632	328	20.1	313	19.2	15	4.6

NOTE: Data in Table 7 are from the Current Population Survey (CPS) and do not match the estimates in Table 8. See notes and definitions for further information.

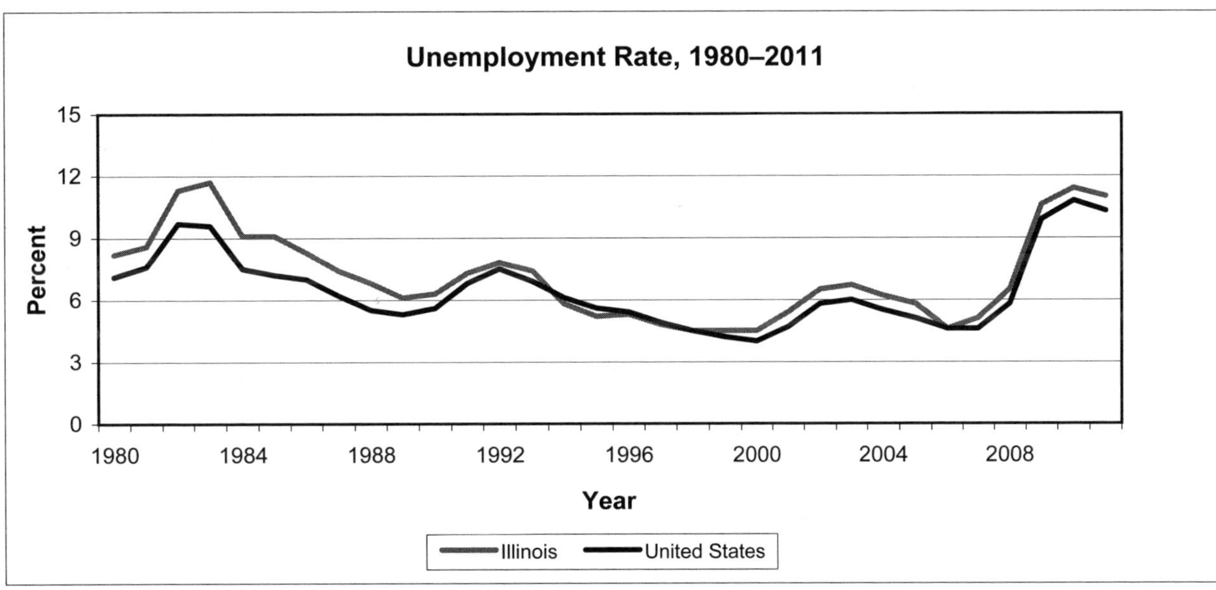

Table IL-8. Employment Status of the Civilian Noninstitutional Population Age 16 Years and Over

(Number, percent.)

Year	Civilian labor force	Civilian participation rate	Employed	Unemployed	Unemployment rate
2005	6,443,119	66.6	6,061,314	371,805	5.8
2006	6,557,959	67.4	6,255,169	302,790	4.6
2007	6,689,636	68.2	6,348,650	340,986	5.1
2008	6,697,335	67.8	6,263,651	433,684	6.5
2009	6,744,354	66.8	6,029,349	715,005	10.6
2010	6,674,563	66.2	5,911,495	763,068	11.4
2011	6,661,181	65.7	5,926,849	734,332	11.0

Table IL-9. Employment and Average Wages by Industry

(Estimates before 2007 are based on the 2002 *North American Industry Classification System* [NAICS]. Estimates from 2007 onward are based on the 2007 NAICS.)

Industry	2005	2006	2007	2008	2009	2010	2011
	Number of jobs						
Wage and Salary Employment by Industry	6,053,479	6,134,058	6,181,343	6,153,026	5,869,095	5,821,234	5,882,915
Farm Wage and Salary Employment	17,271	18,006	17,831	16,207	15,271	18,237	17,069
Nonfarm Wage and Salary Employment	6,036,208	6,116,052	6,163,512	6,136,819	5,853,824	5,802,997	5,865,846
Private wage and salary employment	5,142,967	5,221,135	5,266,000	5,228,543	4,939,399	4,896,135	4,976,577
Forestry, fishing, and related activities	4,335	4,135	4,342	4,362	4,261	3,820	4,068
Mining	9,690	10,147	9,976	9,672	9,303	9,052	9,507
Utilities	23,415	23,111	23,063	23,520	23,716	23,189	23,528
Construction	279,195	286,908	281,896	269,100	229,839	208,243	206,472
Manufacturing	690,597	685,106	676,962	659,693	579,317	561,722	574,540
Durable goods manufacturing	419,327	421,154	416,173	403,843	340,047	329,461	343,356
Nondurable goods manufacturing	271,270	263,952	260,789	255,850	239,270	232,261	231,184
Wholesale trade	303,625	309,324	313,563	312,742	295,062	288,749	291,888
Retail trade	635,115	637,817	645,575	637,807	606,122	598,108	605,006
Transportation and warehousing	237,614	240,963	244,776	244,327	230,887	231,795	238,612
Information	118,960	117,225	117,018	115,305	106,957	101,883	100,183
Finance and insurance	319,900	323,577	320,786	313,174	298,307	293,720	291,833
Real estate and rental and leasing	86,681	87,566	86,906	83,548	77,976	75,984	74,436
Professional, scientific, and technical services	350,577	365,268	369,993	374,287	353,699	351,122	360,573
Management of companies and enterprises	92,480	95,873	96,939	97,693	95,264	96,365	98,340
Administrative and waste services	393,327	404,082	412,987	398,574	348,271	366,269	383,498
Educational services	131,926	139,884	142,874	148,711	155,293	160,381	165,620
Health care and social assistance	635,587	648,939	663,991	678,901	690,647	700,048	711,121
Arts, entertainment, and recreation	81,799	81,310	81,905	81,602	78,617	77,391	78,617
Accommodation and food services	437,346	448,250	457,989	458,044	445,269	444,352	450,849
Other services, except public administration	310,798	311,650	314,459	317,481	310,592	303,942	307,886
Government and government enterprises	893,241	894,917	897,512	908,276	914,425	906,862	889,269
	Dollars						
Average Wages and Salaries by Industry	44,154	46,147	48,330	49,415	49,012	50,271	51,711
Average Farm Wages and Salaries	25,750	22,666	28,313	32,632	31,157	24,440	34,006
Average Nonfarm Wages and Salaries	44,206	46,216	48,388	49,459	49,059	50,353	51,762
Average private wages and salaries	44,485	46,641	48,954	49,988	49,335	50,673	52,169
Forestry, fishing, and related activities	23,134	24,842	26,622	29,039	30,025	28,236	28,973
Mining	56,359	57,848	61,144	61,714	61,591	68,078	66,616
Utilities	90,762	94,835	98,659	102,320	98,866	98,417	104,422
Construction	52,892	55,862	57,679	61,204	60,378	59,921	60,768
Manufacturing	51,488	53,852	56,337	57,654	57,560	61,015	63,001
Durable goods manufacturing	52,300	54,794	57,153	58,749	58,578	61,613	64,517
Nondurable goods manufacturing	50,234	52,350	55,036	55,925	56,113	60,167	60,748
Wholesale trade	60,312	63,436	67,124	67,928	66,951	69,366	73,149
Retail trade	25,479	26,287	27,248	26,771	26,537	27,260	27,824
Transportation and warehousing	44,646	47,359	47,597	48,425	47,509	48,979	50,597
Information	60,209	62,510	66,952	68,607	67,216	68,704	72,819
Finance and insurance	77,554	83,233	91,732	94,533	89,628	91,361	97,120
Real estate and rental and leasing	47,601	52,769	54,018	51,702	49,771	51,723	53,603
Professional, scientific, and technical services	72,951	75,901	79,005	81,811	81,516	84,215	86,166
Management of companies and enterprises	101,060	103,460	112,118	108,889	107,457	114,816	117,501
Administrative and waste services	28,863	29,971	32,280	33,970	33,908	34,811	35,004
Educational services	34,408	35,952	37,772	39,346	40,063	40,989	42,103
Health care and social assistance	39,027	40,496	41,960	43,195	44,120	44,654	45,209
Arts, entertainment, and recreation	30,419	32,585	34,608	33,922	33,922	34,953	35,783
Accommodation and food services	17,004	17,766	19,066	18,906	18,807	19,510	20,189
Other services, except public administration	28,778	30,032	31,462	32,578	32,808	33,887	34,749
Government and government enterprises	42,601	43,736	45,064	46,412	47,565	48,623	49,487

Table IL-10. Employment Characteristics by Family Type

(Number, percent.)

Family type and labor force status	2009		2010		2011	
	Total	Families with own children under 18 years	Total	Families with own children under 18 years	Total	Families with own children under 18 years
All families	3,120,138	1,449,612	3,133,813	1,435,817	3,098,864	1,405,017
Family type and labor force status						
Married-couple families	2,310,026	1,010,710	2,301,009	994,964	2,269,243	966,588
Both husband and wife in labor force	57.3	68.6	56.5	68.4	55.7	66.5
Husband in labor force, wife not in labor force	21.3	27.2	21.7	27.4	21.7	28.8
Wife in labor force, husband not in labor force	6.8	2.9	7.0	3.1	7.3	3.2
Both husband and wife not in labor force	14.6	1.4	14.8	1.1	15.3	1.5
Other families	810,112	438,902	832,804	440,853	829,621	438,429
Female householder, no husband present	73.5	76.5	73.6	76.8	74.4	77.2
In labor force	54.1	64.4	53.5	64.2	54.2	65.1
Not in labor force	19.4	12.1	20.1	12.6	20.3	12.1
Male householder, no wife present	26.5	23.5	26.4	23.2	25.6	22.8
In labor force	21.3	21.8	20.8	20.9	20.8	21.1
Not in labor force	5.2	1.7	5.6	2.4	4.8	1.7

Table IL-11. School Enrollment and Educational Attainment, 2011

(Number, percent.)

Item	State	U.S.
Enrollment		
Total population 3 years and over, enrolled in school	3,516,919	83,131,910
Enrolled in nursery school or preschool (percent)	6.8	6.0
Enrolled in kindergarten (percent)	4.8	5.1
Enrolled in elementary school, grades 1-8 (percent)	39.2	39.5
Enrolled in high school, grades 9-12 (percent)	21.1	20.7
Enrolled in college or graduate school (percent)	28.0	28.7
Attainment		
Total population 25 years and over	8,521,694	206,471,670
Less than ninth grade (percent)	5.6	6.0
9th to 12th grade, no diploma (percent)	7.2	8.1
High school graduate, including equivalency (percent)	27.6	28.4
Some college, no degree (percent)	21.3	21.2
Associate's degree (percent)	7.3	7.8
Bachelor's degree (percent)	19.3	17.9
Graduate or professional degree (percent)	11.7	10.6
High school graduate or higher (percent)	87.2	85.9
Bachelor's degree or higher (percent)	31.0	28.5

Table IL-12. Educational Indicators

(Number, percent; data derived from National Center of Education Statistics.)

Item	State	U.S.
Public Schools, 2009–2010 (except where noted)		
Number of school districts	869	13,629
Number of schools	4,405	99,834
Number of students (in thousands)	2,104	49,373
Student-teacher ratio	15.2	15.4
Expenditures per student (dollars)	13,403	10,591
Averaged freshman graduation rate, 2008–2009	77.7	75.5[1]
Dropout rate, 2008–2009	NA	4.1
Students eligible for free or reduced-price lunch (percent)	46.6	48.0
English language learners, 2010–2011 (percent)	8.4	9.8 1
Students with IEP (percent)	14.9	13.1
Private Schools, 2009–2010 (except where noted)		
Number of schools	1,733	33,366
Number of students (in thousands)	243	4,700
High school graduates, 2008–2009	15,107	308,813
Student-teacher ratio	12.0	10.7

NA = Not available.
[1] U.S. total includes estimates for nonreporting states.

Table IL-13. Reported Voting and Registration of the Voting-Age Population, November 2012

(Numbers in thousands, percent.)

Item	Total population	Total citizen population	Registered			Voted		
			Total registered	Percent registered (total population)	Percent registered (total citizen population)	Total voted	Percent voted (total population)	Percent voted (total citizen population)
U.S. Total	235,248	215,081	153,157	65.1	71.2	132,948	56.5	61.8
State Total	9,651	8,831	6,425	66.6	72.7	5,428	56.2	61.5
Sex								
Male	4,638	4,244	3,010	64.9	70.9	2,517	54.3	59.3
Female	5,013	4,588	3,415	68.1	74.4	2,911	58.1	63.5
Race								
White alone	7,673	7,115	5,150	67.1	72.4	4,275	55.7	60.1
White, non-Hispanic alone	6,553	6,408	4,762	72.7	74.3	3,986	60.8	62.2
Black alone	1,322	1,278	987	74.7	77.2	918	69.5	71.8
Asian alone	557	356	228	40.9	64.0	198	35.5	55.4
Hispanic (of any race)	1,200	770	415	34.6	53.9	295	24.6	38.3
Age								
18 to 24 years	1,228	1,122	608	49.5	54.2	396	32.2	35.3
25 to 44 years	3,396	2,961	2,086	61.4	70.5	1,719	50.6	58.0
45 to 64 years	3,407	3,182	2,471	72.5	77.7	2,206	64.7	69.3
65 to 74 years	946	920	763	80.7	82.9	688	72.7	74.7
75 years and over	674	646	495	73.5	76.7	420	62.4	65.1

Table IL-14. Crime

(Number, rate per 100,000. Data are derived from the FBI Uniform Crime Reports.)

Item	State			U.S.		
	2010	2011	Percent change	2010	2011	Percent change
TOTAL POPULATION	12,841,980	12,869,257	0.2	309,330,219	311,591,917	0.7
VIOLENT CRIME						
Number	57,132	55,247	-3.3	1,251,248	1,203,564	-3.8
Rate	444.9	429.3	-3.5	404.5	386.3	-4.5
Murder and Nonnegligent Manslaughter						
Number	704	721	2.4	14,722	14,612	-0.7
Rate	5.5	5.6	1.8	4.8	4.7	-2.1
Forcible Rape						
Number	3,066	3,708	20.9	85,593	83,425	-2.5
Rate	23.9	28.8	20.5	27.7	26.8	-3.2
Robbery						
Number	20,386	20,254	-0.6	369,089	354,396	-4.0
Rate	158.7	157.4	-0.8	119.3	113.7	-4.7
Aggravated Assault						
Number	32,976	30,564	-7.3	781,844	751,131	-3.9
Rate	256.8	237.5	-7.5	252.8	241.1	-4.6
PROPERTY CRIME						
Number	349,064	346,025	-0.9	9,112,625	9,063,173	-0.5
Rate	2,718.1	2,688.8	-1.1	2,945.9	2,908.7	-1.3
Burglary						
Number	77,472	77,746	0.4	2,168,459	2,188,005	0.9
Rate	603.3	604.1	0.1	701.0	702.2	0.2
Larceny-Theft						
Number	242,681	239,510	-1.3	6,204,601	6,159,795	-0.7
Rate	1,889.7	1,861.1	-1.5	2,005.8	1,976.9	-1.4
Motor Vehicle Theft						
Number	28,911	28,769	-0.5	739,565	715,373	-3.3
Rate	225.1	223.5	-0.7	239.1	229.6	-4.0

Table IL-15. State Government Finances, 2011

(Dollar amounts in thousands, percent distribution.)

Item	Dollars	Percent distribution
Total Revenue	79,512,457	100.0
General revenue	58,202,342	73.2
Intergovernmental revenue	19,586,991	24.6
Taxes	29,433,475	37.0
General sales	7,420,829	9.3
Selective sales	6,192,798	7.8
License taxes	2,525,341	3.2
Individual income tax	11,225,000	14.1
Corporate income tax	1,851,000	2.3
Other taxes	218,507	0.3
Current charges	4,731,611	6.0
Miscellaneous general revenue	4,450,265	5.6
Utility revenue	0	0.0
Liquor stores revenue	0	0.0
Insurance trust revenue [1]	21,310,115	26.8
Total Expenditure	74,655,351	100.0
Intergovernmental expenditure	15,711,058	21.0
Direct expenditure	58,944,293	78.9
Current operation	35,433,844	47.5
Capital outlay	3,867,268	5.2
Insurance benefits and repayments	15,150,850	20.3
Assistance and subsidies	1,235,360	1.7
Interest on debt	3,256,971	4.4
Exhibit: Salaries and wages	8,785,932	11.8
Total Expenditure	74,655,351	100.0
General expenditure	59,504,501	79.7
Intergovernmental expenditure	15,711,058	21.0
Direct expenditure	43,793,443	58.7
General expenditure, by function:		
Education	17,130,559	22.9
Public welfare	19,508,223	26.1
Hospitals	1,183,689	1.6
Health	2,233,917	3.0
Highways	5,110,368	6.8
Police protection	440,245	0.6
Correction	1,514,033	2.0
Natural resources	253,236	0.3
Parks and recreation	179,401	0.2
Governmental administration	1,313,020	1.8
Interest on general debt	3,256,971	4.4
Other and unallocable	7,380,839	9.9
Utility expenditure	0	0.0
Liquor stores expenditure	0	0.0
Insurance trust expenditure	15,150,850	20.3
Debt at End of Fiscal Year	64,801,423	X
Cash and Security Holdings	123,283,282	X

X = Not applicable.
[1] Within insurance trust revenue, net earnings of state retirement systems is a calculated statistic (the item code in the data file is X08), and thus can be positive or negative. Net earnings is the sum of earnings on investments plus gains on investments minus losses on investments. The change made in 2002 for asset valuation from book to market value in accordance with Statement 34 of the Governmental Accounting Standards Board is reflected in the calculated statistics.

Table IL-16. State Government Tax Collections, 2012

(Dollars in thousands, percent.)

Item	Dollars	Percent distribution
Total Taxes	36,437,803	100.0
Property taxes	65,106	0.2
Sales and gross receipts	14,295,688	39.2
General sales and gross receipts	8,034,466	22.0
Selective sales and gross receipts	6,261,222	17.2
Alcoholic beverages	279,270	0.8
Amusements	546,819	1.5
Insurance premiums	369,117	1.0
Motor fuels	1,290,266	3.5
Pari-mutuels	7,212	-
Public utilities	1,750,459	4.8
Tobacco products	606,422	1.7
Other selective sales	1,411,657	3.9
Licenses	2,602,296	7.1
Alcoholic beverages	11,845	-
Amusements	74,255	0.2
Corporations in general	321,319	0.9
Hunting and fishing	41,177	0.1
Motor vehicle	1,620,595	4.4
Motor vehicle operators	104,581	0.3
Public utilities	17,936	-
Occupation and business, NEC	390,975	1.1
Other licenses	19,613	0.1
Income taxes	19,186,890	52.7
Individual income	15,692,351	43.1
Corporation net income	3,494,539	9.6
Other taxes	287,823	0.8
Death and gift	234,864	0.6
Documentary and stock transfer	52,959	0.1
Severance	0	0.0
Taxes, NEC	0	0.0

- = Rounds to zero.

Leading Exports, 2012

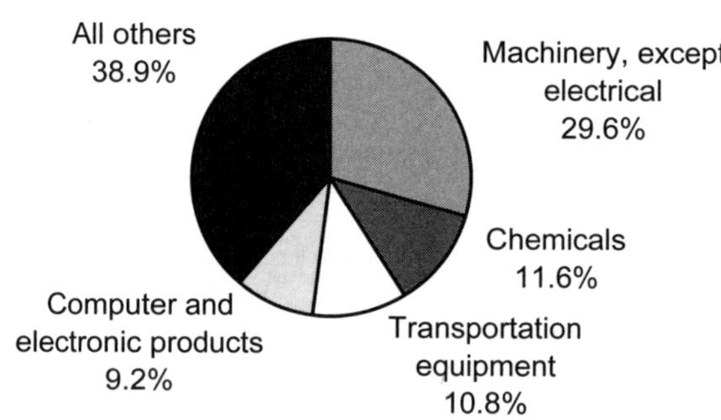

INDIANA

Facts and Figures

Location: East north central United States; bordered on the N by Michigan and Lake Michigan, on the E by Ohio, on the S by Kentucky, and on the W by Illinois

Area: 36,418 sq. mi. (94,321 sq. km.); rank—38th

Population: 6,537,334 (2012 est.); rank—16th

Principal Cities: capital—Indianapolis; largest—Indianapolis

Statehood: December 11, 1816; 19th state

U.S. Congress: 2 senators, 9 representatives

State Motto: The Crossroads of America

State Song: "On the Banks of the Wabash, Far Away"

State Nickname: The Hoosier State

Abbreviations: IN; Ind.

State Symbols: flower—peony; tree—tulip tree; bird—cardinal

At a Glance

- With an increase in population of 5.6 percent, Indiana ranked 20th among the states in growth from 2000 to 2009.
- An estimated 52,900 marriages took place in Indiana in 2009; Indiana does not report its number of divorces.
- Indiana's violent crime rate in 2011 was 331.8 per 100,000 population, compared to 386.3 for the entire nation.
- In the 2012 election, 59.3 percent of Indiana's eligible voters voted, compared to 61.8 percent of eligible voters nationwide.
- In 2007, Indiana exported $2.4 billion worth of agricultural products, about 2.9 percent of the U.S. total.

Table IN-1. Population by Age, Sex, Race, and Hispanic Origin

(Number, percent, except where noted.)

Sex, age, race, and Hispanic origin	2000	2010	2012[1]	Average annual percent change, 2010–2012
Total Population	6,080,485	6,483,802	6,537,344	0.3
Percent of total U.S. population	2.2	2.1	2.1	X
Sex				
Male	2,982,474	3,189,737	3,218,190	0.3
Female	3,098,011	3,294,065	3,319,144	0.3
Age				
Under 5 years	423,215	434,075	425,503	-0.7
5 to 19 years	1,340,171	1,372,507	1,353,186	-0.5
20 to 64 years	3,564,268	3,836,112	3,869,507	0.3
65 years and over	752,831	841,108	889,148	1.8
Median age (years)	35.2	37.0	37.2	0.2
Race and Hispanic Origin				
One race				
White	5,320,022	5,638,833	5,659,668	0.1
Black	510,034	603,797	616,199	0.7
American Indian and Alaska Native	15,815	24,487	25,494	1.3
Asian	59,126	105,535	116,029	3.0
Native Hawaiian or Other Pacific Islander	2,005	3,532	3,769	2.1
Two or more races	75,672	107,618	166,175	11.7
Hispanic (of any race)	214,536	403,234	427,525	1.9

X = Not applicable.
[1] Population figures for 2012 are July 1 estimates. The 2010 estimates are taken from the 2010 Census.

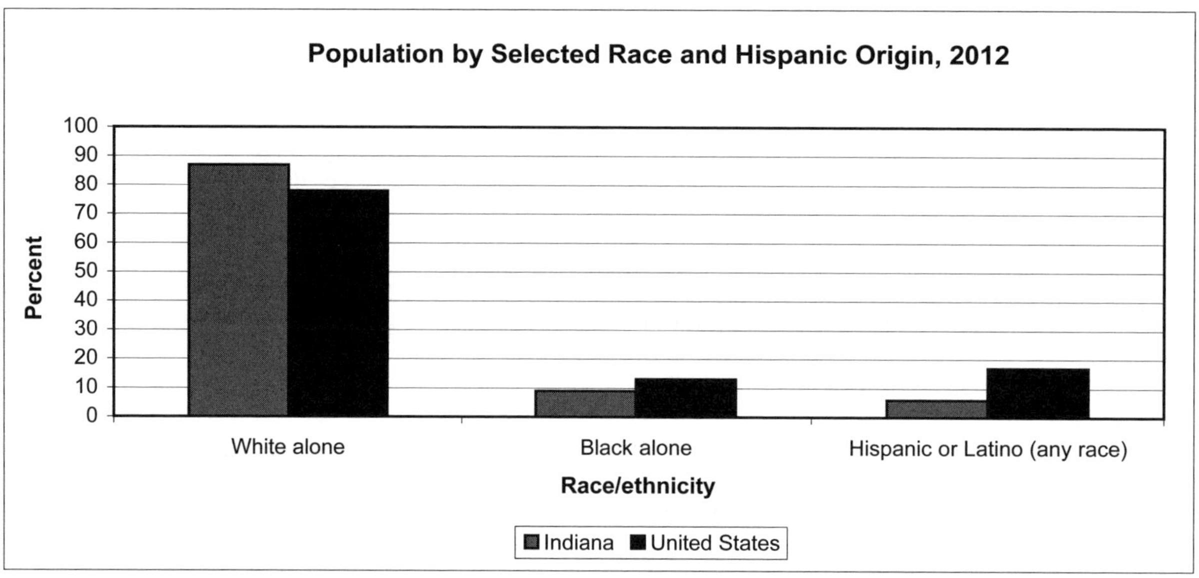

Table IN-2. Marital Status

(Number, percent distribution.)

Sex, age, race, and Hispanic origin	2000	2010	2011
Males, 15 Years and Over	2,308,917	2,513,953	2,532,594
Never married	27.9	32.6	33.5
Now married, except separated	58.5	52.3	51.4
Separated	1.3	1.1	1.3
Widowed	2.4	2.5	2.4
Divorced	10.0	11.4	11.5
Females, 15 Years and Over	2,462,123	2,644,068	2,661,753
Never married	22.0	26.7	27.5
Now married, except separated	54.3	49.1	47.7
Separated	1.5	1.8	1.9
Widowed	10.6	9.2	9.5
Divorced	11.6	13.2	13.5

Table IN-3. Households and Housing Characteristics

(Number, percent, dollars.)

Item	2000	2010	2011	Average annual percent change, 2000–2011
Total Households	2,336,306	2,470,905	2,467,111	0.5
Family households	1,602,501	1,656,386	1,641,389	0.2
Married-couple family	1,251,458	1,236,518	1,217,034	-0.2
Other family	351,043	419,868	424,355	1.7
Male householder, no wife present	91,671	110,663	110,790	1.7
Female householder, no husband present	259,372	309,205	313,565	1.7
Nonfamily households	733,805	814,519	825,722	1.0
Householder living alone	605,428	678,460	687,171	1.1
Householder not living alone	128,377	136,059	138,551	0.7
Housing Characteristics				
Total housing units	2,532,319	2,797,172	2,800,799	0.9
Occupied housing units	2,336,306	2,470,905	2,467,111	0.5
Owner occupied	1,669,192	1,736,751	1,720,062	0.3
Renter occupied	667,144	734,154	747,049	1.0
Average size	2.53	2.55	2.57	0.1
Financial Characteristics				
Median gross rent of renter-occupied housing	521	683	707	3.0
Median monthly owner costs for housing units with a mortgage	869	1,090	1,091	2.1
Median value of owner-occupied housing units	94,300	123,300	122,400	2.5

Table IN-4. Migration, Origin, and Language

(Number, percent.)

Characteristic	State			U.S.		
	2010	2011	Percent change	2010	2011	Percent change
Residence 1 Year Ago						
Population 1 year and over	6,414,862	6,437,155	0.3	305,628,607	307,900,319	0.7
Same house	84.7	85.1	0.5	84.6	84.8	0.2
Different house in the U.S.	15.0	14.6	-2.7	14.8	14.6	-1.4
Same county	9.4	9.1	-3.2	9.4	9.2	-2.1
Different county	5.5	5.5	-	5.4	5.4	-
Same state	3.5	3.5	-	3.2	3.1	-3.1
Different state	2.0	2.0	-	2.2	2.3	4.5
Abroad	0.4	0.3	-25.0	0.6	0.6	-
Place of Birth						
Native born	6,189,832	6,209,728	0.3	269,393,835	271,214,059	0.7
Male	49.2	49.1	-0.2	49.2	49.2	-
Female	50.8	50.9	0.2	50.8	50.8	-
Foreign born	300,789	307,194	2.1	39,955,854	40,377,860	1.1
Male	50.9	50.8	-0.2	49.1	48.9	-0.4
Female	49.1	49.2	0.2	50.9	51.1	0.4
Foreign born; naturalized U.S. citizen	109,717	107,751	-1.8	17,476,082	18,140,192	3.8
Male	44.8	46.1	2.9	45.8	45.8	-
Female	55.2	53.9	-2.4	54.2	54.2	-
Foreign born; not a U.S. citizen	191,072	199,443	4.4	22,479,772	22,237,668	-1.1
Male	54.5	53.3	-2.2	51.6	51.5	-0.2
Female	45.5	46.7	2.6	48.4	48.5	0.2
Entered 2000 or later	48.0	49.3	2.7	34.7	35.7	2.9
Entered 1990 to 1999	25.3	25.3	-	27.2	26.7	-1.8
Entered before 1990	26.7	25.5	-4.5	38.1	37.6	-1.3
World Region of Birth, Foreign						
Foreign-born population, excluding population born at sea	300,789	307,194	2.1	39,955,673	40,377,757	1.1
Europe	14.1	14.4	2.1	12.1	12.1	-
Asia	29.4	29.4	0.0	28.2	28.6	1.4
Africa	6.3	5.2	-17.5	4	4.1	2.5
Oceania	0.4	0.4	-	0.5	0.5	-
Latin America	47.6	48.1	1.1	53.1	52.6	-0.9
North America	2.2	2.5	13.6	2	2.0	-
Language Spoken at Home and Ability to Speak English						
Population 5 years and over	6,057,306	6,088,598	0.5	289,215,746	291,524,091	0.8
English only	92.0	91.8	-0.2	79.4	79.2	-0.3
Language other than English	8.0	8.2	2.5	20.6	20.8	1.0
Speaks English less than "very well"	3.2	3.3	3.1	8.7	8.7	-

- = Zero or rounds to zero.

Table IN-5. Median Income and Poverty Status, 2011

(Number, percent, except as noted.)

Characteristic	State		U.S.	
	Number	Percent	Number	Percent
Median Income				
Households (dollars)	46,438	X	50,502	X
Families (dollars)	57,148	X	61,455	X
Below Poverty Level (All People)	1,011,017	16.0	48,452,035	15.9
Sex				
Male	447,464	14.4	21,825,281	14.7
Female	563,553	17.5	26,626,754	17.2
Age				
Under 18 years	360,859	23.0	16,386,500	22.5
Related children under 18 years	350,272	22.5	16,087,074	22.2
18 to 64 years	591,483	15.0	28,335,079	14.8
65 years and over	58,675	7.2	3,730,456	9.3

X = Not applicable.

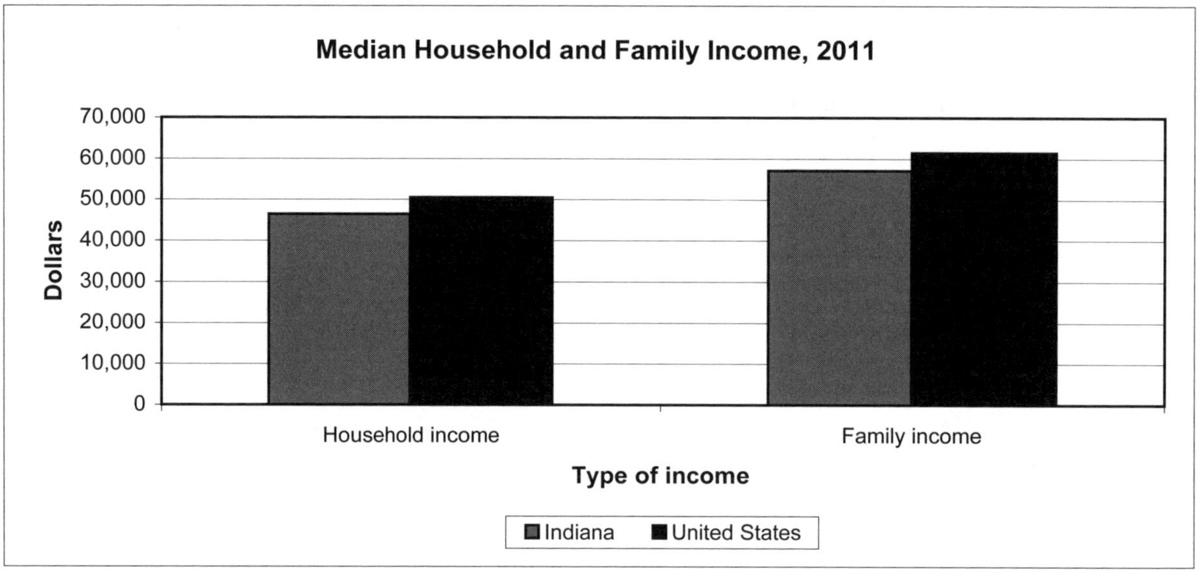

Table IN-6. Health Insurance Coverage Status for the Civilian Noninstitutionalized Population and Children Under 18 Years of Age

(Numbers in thousands, percent.)

Item	2004	2005	2006	2007	2008	2009	2010	2011
Civilian Noninstitutionalized Population	6,136	6,141	6,337	6,263	6,271	6,316	6,391	6,418
Covered by Private or Public Insurance								
Number	5,289	5,308	5,590	5,546	5,400	5,415	5,444	5,487
Percent	86.2	86.4	88.2	88.6	86.1	85.7	85.2	85.5
Not Covered								
Number	847	832	748	717	871	901	948	931
Percent	13.8	13.6	11.8	11.4	13.9	14.3	14.8	14.5
Percent in the U.S. not covered	14.9	15.3	15.8	15.3	15.1	15.1	15.5	15.1
Children Under 18 Years of Age	1,605	1,614	1,582	1,593	1,580	1,583	1,602	1,594
Covered by Private or Public Insurance								
Number	1,469	1,457	1,459	1,511	1,420	1,443	1,459	1,465
Percent	91.5	90.2	92.2	94.8	89.9	91.2	91.1	91.9
Not Covered								
Number	137	158	123	83	160	140	143	129
Percent	8.5	9.8	7.8	5.2	10.1	8.8	8.9	8.1
Percent in the U.S. not covered	10.5	10.9	11.7	11.0	9.7	8.6	8.0	7.5

Table IN-7. Employment Status by Demographic Group, Preliminary 2012

(Numbers in thousands, percent.)

Characteristic	Civilian noninstitutional population	Civilian labor force		Employed		Unemployed	
		Number	Percent of population	Number	Percent of population	Number	Percent of population
Total	5,043	3,159	62.6	2,898	57.5	261	8.3
Sex							
Male	2,443	1,677	68.7	1,542	63.1	136	8.1
Female	2,600	1,481	57.0	1,356	52.2	125	8.5
Race, Sex, and Hispanic Origin							
White	4,520	2,834	62.7	2,627	58.1	207	7.3
Male	2,216	1,530	69.0	1,415	63.9	115	7.5
Female	2,304	1,304	56.6	1,211	52.6	93	7.1
Black or African American	398	252	63.4	202	50.8	50	19.8
Male	168	107	63.8	88	52.4	19	17.8
Female	230	145	63.1	114	49.6	31	21.3
Hispanic	223	150	67.5	136	61.1	14	9.4
Male	120	95	78.8	87	72.6	8	7.9
Female	103	56	54.1	49	47.6	7	12.1
Age							
16 to 19 years	390	140	35.9	110	28.1	31	21.9
20 to 24 years	439	332	75.7	293	66.7	40	12.0
25 to 34 years	814	669	82.3	606	74.5	63	9.4
35 to 44 years	822	683	83.0	628	76.3	55	8.1
45 to 54 years	868	702	80.9	663	76.4	39	5.6
55 to 64 years	787	478	60.7	452	57.4	26	5.5
65 years and over	923	154	16.7	147	15.9	7	4.8

NOTE: Data in Table 7 are from the Current Population Survey (CPS) and do not match the estimates in Table 8. See notes and definitions for further information.

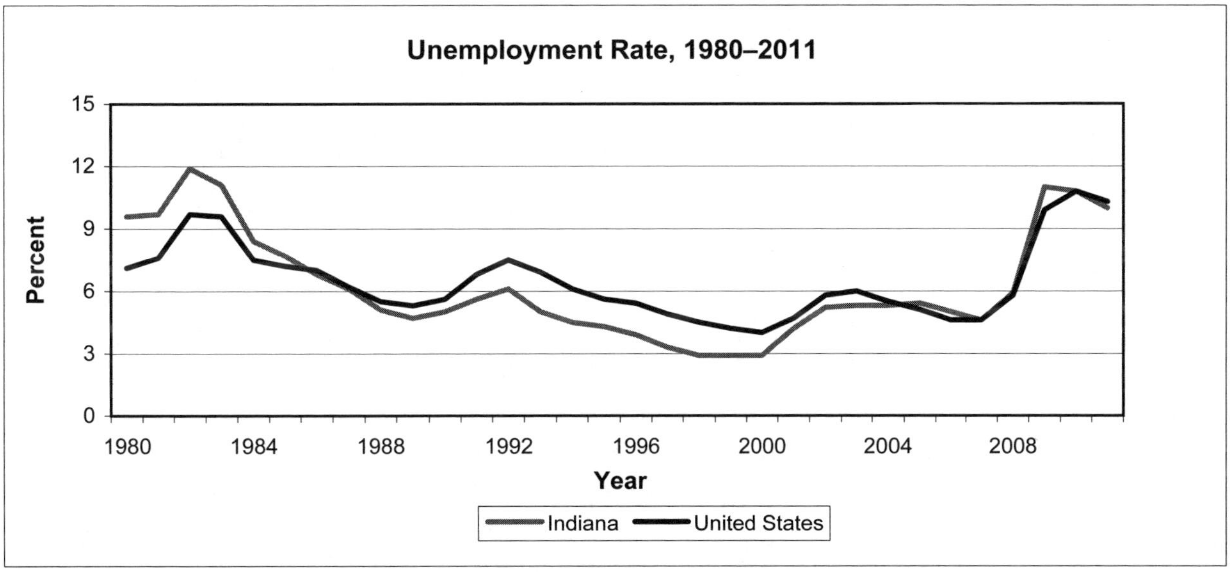

Table IN-8. Employment Status of the Civilian Noninstitutional Population Age 16 Years and Over

(Number, percent.)

Year	Civilian labor force	Civilian participation rate	Employed	Unemployed	Unemployment rate
2005	3,200,103	67.3	3,028,470	171,633	5.4
2006	3,235,132	67.5	3,074,927	160,205	5.0
2007	3,221,054	66.6	3,074,079	146,975	4.8
2008	3,230,367	66.3	3,039,795	190,572	5.9
2009	3,296,045	65.8	2,934,902	361,143	11.0
2010	3,250,476	64.1	2,898,761	351,715	10.8
2011	3,260,792	63.9	2,934,500	326,292	10.0

Table IN-9. Employment and Average Wages by Industry

(Estimates before 2007 are based on the 2002 *North American Industry Classification System* [NAICS]. Estimates from 2007 onward are based on the 2007 NAICS.)

Industry	2005	2006	2007	2008	2009	2010	2011
				Number of jobs			
Wage and Salary Employment by Industry	3,033,785	3,059,032	3,075,446	3,042,659	2,877,302	2,886,635	2,930,409
Farm Wage and Salary Employment	11,466	13,193	12,146	9,368	10,488	13,576	10,314
Nonfarm Wage and Salary Employment	3,022,319	3,045,839	3,063,300	3,033,291	2,866,814	2,873,059	2,920,095
Private wage and salary employment	2,581,400	2,601,895	2,612,334	2,572,832	2,405,042	2,415,138	2,470,191
Forestry, fishing, and related activities	3,233	3,314	3,378	3,152	2,985	3,158	3,183
Mining	6,456	6,596	6,663	6,455	6,296	6,268	6,580
Utilities	14,709	14,797	14,748	14,996	15,291	14,952	14,729
Construction	154,113	156,417	157,062	150,313	126,089	121,231	126,627
Manufacturing	571,139	565,677	550,333	521,405	442,761	448,527	464,552
Durable goods manufacturing	419,078	414,487	401,509	377,451	309,284	314,026	330,610
Nondurable goods manufacturing	152,061	151,190	148,824	143,954	133,477	134,501	133,942
Wholesale trade	122,533	124,251	126,612	126,047	116,318	114,851	115,978
Retail trade	335,895	334,488	332,963	326,542	312,887	309,475	312,756
Transportation and warehousing	114,229	117,750	119,658	118,012	110,784	111,987	115,179
Information	40,403	39,972	40,345	39,759	37,772	35,811	34,274
Finance and insurance	102,812	103,446	103,035	101,823	98,256	97,609	98,073
Real estate and rental and leasing	37,712	37,790	37,006	35,920	34,329	33,286	33,249
Professional, scientific, and technical services	92,373	95,218	98,308	100,029	97,236	97,668	99,962
Management of companies and enterprises	26,441	26,735	28,535	29,218	27,518	26,995	28,043
Administrative and waste services	158,654	161,106	163,566	157,324	139,298	153,626	164,333
Educational services	55,516	57,421	59,673	61,830	61,146	62,728	64,520
Health care and social assistance	316,091	323,722	332,863	341,927	349,939	355,805	360,872
Arts, entertainment, and recreation	44,588	43,761	43,803	44,269	43,782	42,417	41,966
Accommodation and food services	236,185	240,512	243,587	243,915	236,425	234,685	239,687
Other services, except public administration	148,318	148,922	150,196	149,896	145,930	144,059	145,628
Government and government enterprises	440,919	443,944	450,966	460,459	461,772	457,921	449,904
				Dollars			
Average Wages and Salaries by Industry	35,853	37,037	38,066	38,950	38,869	39,885	40,970
Average Farm Wages and Salaries	25,677	21,521	27,880	33,586	32,706	25,400	33,141
Average Nonfarm Wages and Salaries	35,891	37,104	38,106	38,966	38,891	39,954	40,998
Average private wages and salaries	36,157	37,464	38,531	39,396	39,153	40,335	41,461
Forestry, fishing, and related activities	20,209	21,322	22,473	21,266	21,845	22,565	23,165
Mining	52,467	56,115	58,324	59,481	59,059	62,666	65,326
Utilities	66,338	69,321	70,756	75,360	76,469	79,645	82,447
Construction	41,357	42,667	45,347	47,883	47,845	50,401	52,444
Manufacturing	49,332	51,247	52,408	53,793	54,025	56,098	57,108
Durable goods manufacturing	49,804	51,485	52,754	53,426	53,484	55,455	56,727
Nondurable goods manufacturing	48,032	50,595	51,476	54,757	55,279	57,600	58,047
Wholesale trade	48,546	50,971	52,748	53,909	53,345	55,051	57,000
Retail trade	22,555	23,054	23,450	23,642	23,809	24,497	24,866
Transportation and warehousing	38,325	39,483	40,830	41,521	41,056	41,857	43,020
Information	44,605	45,966	47,724	49,087	49,371	50,488	52,277
Finance and insurance	51,060	53,401	54,536	54,888	54,304	56,496	59,275
Real estate and rental and leasing	30,743	32,467	33,552	34,066	34,024	35,267	36,779
Professional, scientific, and technical services	48,236	49,862	52,685	55,068	54,734	56,197	58,657
Management of companies and enterprises	74,050	76,072	75,849	75,634	74,953	79,612	84,796
Administrative and waste services	24,180	25,295	25,910	27,130	27,832	28,019	28,591
Educational services	25,118	26,614	26,998	27,890	29,731	30,030	30,984
Health care and social assistance	36,535	37,640	38,672	39,857	40,532	40,982	41,982
Arts, entertainment, and recreation	29,924	32,538	34,528	32,893	31,624	32,922	32,971
Accommodation and food services	13,350	13,776	14,464	14,374	14,553	15,157	15,576
Other services, except public administration	24,352	25,250	26,137	27,037	27,043	28,031	28,512
Government and government enterprises	34,337	34,990	35,644	36,564	37,526	37,946	38,455

Table IN-10. Employment Characteristics by Family Type

(Number, percent.)

Family type and labor force status	2009 Total	2009 Families with own children under 18 years	2010 Total	2010 Families with own children under 18 years	2011 Total	2011 Families with own children under 18 years
All families	1,657,555	751,748	1,656,386	738,436	1,641,389	725,540
Family type and labor force status						
Married-couple families	1,251,350	510,674	1,236,518	489,020	1,217,034	474,838
Both husband and wife in labor force	56.1	69.1	54.9	68.8	54.5	68.9
Husband in labor force, wife not in labor force	20.6	25.5	20.9	25.7	20.7	26.1
Wife in labor force, husband not in labor force	7.3	3.8	7.7	3.6	8.0	3.5
Both husband and wife not in labor force	15.9	1.7	16.6	1.9	16.8	1.5
Other families	406,205	241,074	419,868	249,416	424,355	250,702
Female householder, no husband present	73.9	75.4	73.6	75.6	73.9	76.7
In labor force	54.7	62.7	53.6	62.6	53.7	63.1
Not in labor force	19.2	12.7	20.1	13.0	20.2	13.6
Male householder, no wife present	26.1	24.6	26.4	24.4	26.1	23.3
In labor force	20.9	22.2	20.9	21.9	20.8	21.2
Not in labor force	5.2	2.4	5.5	2.5	5.3	2.1

Table IN-11. School Enrollment and Educational Attainment, 2011

(Number, percent.)

Item	State	U.S.
Enrollment		
Total population 3 years and over, enrolled in school	1,761,848	83,131,910
Enrolled in nursery school or preschool (percent)	6.1	6.0
Enrolled in kindergarten (percent)	5.0	5.1
Enrolled in elementary school, grades 1-8 (percent)	40.7	39.5
Enrolled in high school, grades 9-12 (percent)	20.5	20.7
Enrolled in college or graduate school (percent)	27.7	28.7
Attainment		
Total population 25 years and over	4,255,459	206,471,670
Less than ninth grade (percent)	4.2	6.0
9th to 12th grade, no diploma (percent)	8.6	8.1
High school graduate, including equivalency (percent)	35.5	28.4
Some college, no degree (percent)	20.9	21.2
Associate's degree (percent)	7.9	7.8
Bachelor's degree (percent)	14.8	17.9
Graduate or professional degree (percent)	8.2	10.6
High school graduate or higher (percent)	87.3	85.9
Bachelor's degree or higher (percent)	23.0	28.5

Table IN-12. Educational Indicators

(Number, percent; data derived from National Center of Education Statistics.)

Item	State	U.S.
Public Schools, 2009–2010 (except where noted)		
Number of school districts	294	13,629
Number of schools	1,961	99,834
Number of students (in thousands)	1,047	49,373
Student-teacher ratio	16.8	15.4
Expenditures per student (dollars)	10,845	10,591
Averaged freshman graduation rate, 2008–2009	75.2	75.5[1]
Dropout rate, 2008–2009	1.7	4.1
Students eligible for free or reduced-price lunch (percent)	46.7	48.0
English language learners, 2010–2011 (percent)	4.7	9.8[1]
Students with IEP (percent)	16.4	13.1
Private Schools, 2009–2010 (except where noted)		
Number of schools	910	33,366
Number of students (in thousands)	104	4,700
High school graduates, 2008–2009	5,232	308,813
Student-teacher ratio	12.4	10.7

[1] U.S. total includes estimates for nonreporting states.

Table IN-13. Reported Voting and Registration of the Voting-Age Population, November 2012

(Numbers in thousands, percent.)

Item	Total population	Total citizen population	Registered			Voted		
			Total registered	Percent registered (total population)	Percent registered (total citizen population)	Total voted	Percent voted (total population)	Percent voted (total citizen population)
U.S. Total	235,248	215,081	153,157	65.1	71.2	132,948	56.5	61.8
State Total	4,852	4,724	3,270	67.4	69.2	2,801	57.7	59.3
Sex								
Male	2,326	2,247	1,542	66.3	68.7	1,331	57.2	59.2
Female	2,526	2,478	1,727	68.4	69.7	1,470	58.2	59.3
Race								
White alone	4,349	4,255	2,926	67.3	68.8	2,509	57.7	59.0
White, non-Hispanic alone	4,179	4,151	2,861	68.4	68.9	2,460	58.9	59.3
Black alone	385	385	309	80.3	80.3	263	68.4	68.4
Asian alone	75	41	19	B	B	14	B	B
Hispanic (of any race)	184	118	71	38.5	59.7	49	26.5	41.1
Age								
18 to 24 years	570	558	269	47.2	48.2	203	35.7	36.4
25 to 44 years	1,688	1,602	1,012	59.9	63.2	776	45.9	48.4
45 to 64 years	1,754	1,733	1,329	75.8	76.7	1,212	69.1	70.0
65 to 74 years	478	473	377	79.0	79.9	360	75.3	76.2
75 years and over	362	359	283	78.1	78.7	250	69.1	69.6

B = Base is less than 75,000 and therefore too small to show the derived measure.

Table IN-14. Crime

(Number, rate per 100,000. Data are derived from the FBI Uniform Crime Reports.)

Item	State			U.S.		
	2010	2011	Percent change	2010	2011	Percent change
TOTAL POPULATION	6,490,622	6,516,922	0.4	309,330,219	311,591,917	0.7
VIOLENT CRIME						
Number	20,983	21,626	3.1	1,251,248	1,203,564	-3.8
Rate	323.3	331.8	2.6	404.5	386.3	-4.5
Murder and Nonnegligent Manslaughter						
Number	268	312	16.4	14,722	14,612	-0.7
Rate	4.1	4.8	17.1	4.8	4.7	-2.1
Forcible Rape						
Number	1,760	1,757	-0.2	85,593	83,425	-2.5
Rate	27.1	27.0	-0.4	27.7	26.8	-3.2
Robbery						
Number	6,559	6,978	6.4	369,089	354,396	-4.0
Rate	101.1	107.1	5.9	119.3	113.7	-4.7
Aggravated Assault						
Number	12,396	12,579	1.5	781,844	751,131	-3.9
Rate	191.0	193.0	1.0	252.8	241.1	-4.6
PROPERTY CRIME						
Number	199,274	206,055	3.4	9,112,625	9,063,173	-0.5
Rate	3,070.2	3,161.8	3.0	2,945.9	2,908.7	-1.3
Burglary						
Number	48,570	50,551	4.1	2,168,459	2,188,005	0.9
Rate	748.3	775.7	3.7	701.0	702.2	0.2
Larceny-Theft						
Number	137,204	140,668	2.5	6,204,601	6,159,795	-0.7
Rate	2,113.9	2,158.8	2.1	2,005.8	1,976.9	-1.4
Motor Vehicle Theft						
Number	13,500	14,816	9.7	739,565	715,373	-3.3
Rate	208.0	227.3	9.3	239.1	229.6	-4.0

Table IN-15. State Government Finances, 2011

(Dollar amounts in thousands, percent distribution.)

Item	Dollars	Percent distribution
Total Revenue	38,894,976	100.0
General revenue	31,449,911	80.9
Intergovernmental revenue	10,858,319	27.9
Taxes	14,909,416	38.3
General sales	6,269,721	16.1
Selective sales	2,562,091	6.6
License taxes	625,782	1.6
Individual income tax	4,583,977	11.8
Corporate income tax	717,207	1.8
Other taxes	150,638	0.4
Current charges	3,709,260	9.5
Miscellaneous general revenue	1,972,916	5.1
Utility revenue	0	0.0
Liquor stores revenue	0	0.0
Insurance trust revenue [1]	7,445,065	19.1
Total Expenditure	35,261,522	100.0
Intergovernmental expenditure	9,265,386	26.3
Direct expenditure	25,996,136	73.7
Current operation	17,396,095	49.3
Capital outlay	2,268,396	6.4
Insurance benefits and repayments	4,359,127	12.4
Assistance and subsidies	973,086	2.8
Interest on debt	999,432	2.8
Exhibit: Salaries and wages	3,940,904	11.2
Total Expenditure	35,261,522	100.0
General expenditure	30,902,395	87.6
Intergovernmental expenditure	9,265,386	26.3
Direct expenditure	21,637,009	61.4
General expenditure, by function:		
Education	14,055,154	39.9
Public welfare	8,396,983	23.8
Hospitals	177,353	0.5
Health	565,707	1.6
Highways	2,680,023	7.6
Police protection	226,750	0.6
Correction	661,358	1.9
Natural resources	303,525	0.9
Parks and recreation	73,011	0.2
Governmental administration	551,909	1.6
Interest on general debt	999,432	2.8
Other and unallocable	2,211,190	6.3
Utility expenditure	0	0.0
Liquor stores expenditure	0	0.0
Insurance trust expenditure	4,359,127	12.4
Debt at End of Fiscal Year	22,144,251	X
Cash and Security Holdings	56,822,466	X

X = Not applicable.

[1] Within insurance trust revenue, net earnings of state retirement systems is a calculated statistic (the item code in the data file is X08), and thus can be positive or negative. Net earnings is the sum of earnings on investments plus gains on investments minus losses on investments. The change made in 2002 for asset valuation from book to market value in accordance with Statement 34 of the Governmental Accounting Standards Board is reflected in the calculated statistics.

Table IN-16. State Government Tax Collections, 2012

(Dollars in thousands, percent.)

Item	Dollars	Percent distribution
Total Taxes	15,704,680	100.0
Property taxes	173	-
Sales and gross receipts	9,172,715	58.4
General sales and gross receipts	6,621,954	42.2
Selective sales and gross receipts	2,550,761	16.2
Alcoholic beverages	44,155	0.3
Amusements	822,881	5.2
Insurance premiums	203,123	1.3
Motor fuels	783,897	5.0
Pari-mutuels	3,845	-
Public utilities	216,458	1.4
Tobacco products	465,200	3.0
Other selective sales	11,202	0.1
Licenses	629,260	4.0
Alcoholic beverages	11,598	0.1
Amusements	5,890	-
Corporations in general	12,055	0.1
Hunting and fishing	17,875	0.1
Motor vehicle	320,480	2.0
Motor vehicle operators	221,323	1.4
Public utilities	0	0.0
Occupation and business, NEC	32,419	0.2
Other licenses	7,620	-
Income taxes	5,724,366	36.5
Individual income	4,765,566	30.3
Corporation net income	958,800	6.1
Other taxes	178,166	1.1
Death and gift	175,954	1.1
Documentary and stock transfer	0	0.0
Severance	2,212	-
Taxes, NEC	0	0.0

- = Rounds to zero.

Leading Exports, 2012

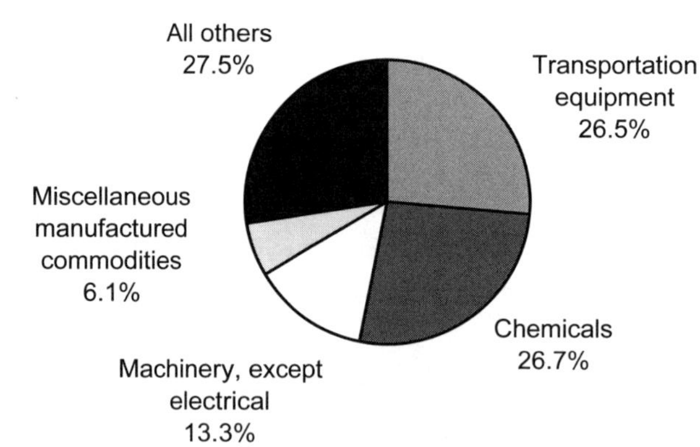

IOWA

Facts and Figures

Location: North central United States; bordered on the N by Minnesota, on the E by Wisconsin and Illinois, on the S by Missouri, and on the W by Nebraska and South Dakota

Area: 56,272 sq. mi. (145,743 sq. km.); rank—26th

Population: 3,074,186 (2012 est.); rank—30th

Principal Cities: capital—Des Moines; largest—Des Moines

Statehood: December 28, 1846; 29th state

U.S. Congress: 2 senators, 4 representatives

State Motto: Our Liberties We Prize and Our Rights We Will Maintain

State Song: "The Song of Iowa"

State Nickname: The Hawkeye State

Abbreviations: IA; Ia.

State Symbols: flower—wild prairie rose; tree—oak; bird—Eastern goldfinch

At a Glance

- With an increase in population of 2.8 percent, Iowa ranked 39th among the states in growth from 2000 to 2009.
- An estimated 21,200 marriages took place in Iowa in 2009, compared to 7,300 divorces.
- Iowa's median household income in 2011 was $49,427, and 12.8 percent of the population lived below the poverty level.
- In 2011, 8.9 percent of Iowans did not have health insurance, compared to 15.1 percent of the total U.S. population.
- In the 2012 election, 69.4 percent of Iowa's eligible voters voted, compared to 61.8 percent of eligible voters nationwide.
- In 2007, Iowa exported $5.2 billion worth of agricultural products, about 6.4 percent of the U.S. total.

Table IA-1. Population by Age, Sex, Race, and Hispanic Origin

(Number, percent, except where noted.)

Sex, age, race, and Hispanic origin	2000	2010	2012[1]	Average annual percent change, 2010–2012
Total Population	2,926,324	3,046,355	3,074,186	0.3
Percent of total U.S. population	1.0	1.0	1.0	X
Sex				
Male	1,435,515	1,508,319	1,524,488	0.4
Female	1,490,809	1,538,036	1,549,698	0.3
Age				
Under 5 years	188,413	202,123	196,366	-1.0
5 to 19 years	639,570	618,387	618,351	-
20 to 64 years	1,662,128	1,772,957	1,789,164	0.3
65 years and over	436,213	452,888	470,305	1.2
Median age (years)	36.6	38.1	38.1	-
Race and Hispanic Origin				
One race				
White	2,748,640	2,839,615	2,851,533	0.1
Black	61,853	91,695	97,080	1.8
American Indian and Alaska Native	8,989	13,563	14,179	1.4
Asian	36,635	54,232	60,004	3.2
Native Hawaiian or Other Pacific Islander	1,009	2,419	2,634	2.7
Two or more races	31,778	44,831	48,756	2.7
Hispanic (of any race)	82,473	156,932	167,077	2.0

X = Not applicable.
- = Zero or rounds to zero.
[1] Population figures for 2012 are July 1 estimates. The 2010 estimates are taken from the 2010 Census.

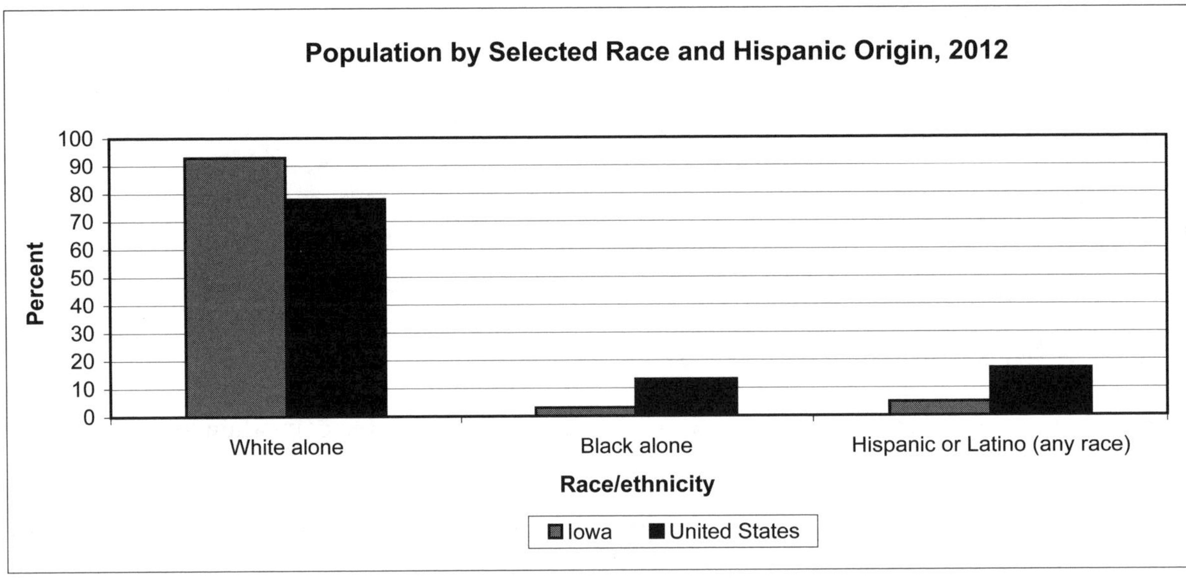

Table IA-2. Marital Status

(Number, percent distribution.)

Sex, age, race, and Hispanic origin	2000	2010	2011
Males, 15 Years and Over	1,126,566	1,199,509	1,206,487
Never married	28.2	31.3	32.2
Now married, except separated	59.8	55.2	53.9
Separated	0.9	1.1	1.1
Widowed	2.5	2.6	2.6
Divorced	8.5	9.7	10.2
Females, 15 Years and Over	1,198,297	1,250,612	1,255,187
Never married	21.8	24.7	25.4
Now married, except separated	55.8	52.4	51.5
Separated	1.1	1.5	1.5
Widowed	11.6	10.2	10.2
Divorced	9.6	11.2	11.4

Table IA-3. Households and Housing Characteristics

(Number, percent, dollars.)

Item	2000	2010	2011	Average annual percent change, 2000–2011
Total Households	1,149,276	1,223,439	1,216,765	0.5
Family households	769,684	793,768	784,895	0.2
Married-couple family	633,254	633,602	625,231	-0.1
Other family	136,430	160,166	159,664	1.4
Male householder, no wife present	38,160	46,829	47,231	2.0
Female householder, no husband present	98,270	113,337	112,433	1.2
Nonfamily households	379,592	429,671	431,870	1.1
Householder living alone	313,083	349,736	358,391	1.2
Householder not living alone	66,509	79,935	73,479	0.9
Housing Characteristics				
Total housing units	1,232,511	1,337,563	1,340,588	0.7
Occupied housing units	1,149,276	1,223,439	1,216,765	0.5
Owner occupied	831,419	885,284	880,368	0.5
Renter occupied	317,857	338,155	336,397	0.5
Average size	2.46	2.41	2.44	-0.1
Financial Characteristics				
Median gross rent of renter-occupied housing	470	629	643	3.1
Median monthly owner costs for housing units with a mortgage	829	1,140	1,144	3.2
Median value of owner-occupied housing units	82,500	123,400	123,400	4.1

Table IA-4. Migration, Origin, and Language

(Number, percent.)

Characteristic	State			U.S.		
	2010	2011	Percent change	2010	2011	Percent change
Residence 1 Year Ago						
Population 1 year and over	3,013,053	3,027,718	0.5	305,628,607	307,900,319	0.7
Same house	84.7	85.0	0.4	84.6	84.8	0.2
Different house in the U.S.	14.9	14.6	-2.0	14.8	14.6	-1.4
Same county	8.9	8.3	-6.7	9.4	9.2	-2.1
Different county	5.9	6.2	5.1	5.4	5.4	-
Same state	3.5	3.9	11.4	3.2	3.1	-3.1
Different state	2.4	2.3	-4.2	2.2	2.3	4.5
Abroad	0.4	0.4	-	0.6	0.6	-
Place of Birth						
Native born	2,910,406	2,928,762	0.6	269,393,835	271,214,059	0.7
Male	49.3	49.3	-	49.2	49.2	-
Female	50.7	50.7	-	50.8	50.8	-
Foreign born	139,477	133,547	-4.3	39,955,854	40,377,860	1.1
Male	50.9	51.1	0.4	49.1	48.9	-0.4
Female	49.1	48.9	-0.4	50.9	51.1	0.4
Foreign born; naturalized U.S. citizen	51,709	50,232	-2.9	17,476,082	18,140,192	3.8
Male	49.3	48.5	-1.6	45.8	45.8	-
Female	50.7	51.5	1.6	54.2	54.2	-
Foreign born; not a U.S. citizen	87,768	83,315	-5.1	22,479,772	22,237,668	-1.1
Male	51.8	52.7	1.7	51.6	51.5	-0.2
Female	48.2	47.3	-1.9	48.4	48.5	0.2
Entered 2000 or later	46.1	48.5	5.2	34.7	35.7	2.9
Entered 1990 to 1999	30.8	26.7	-13.3	27.2	26.7	-1.8
Entered before 1990	23.0	24.8	7.8	38.1	37.6	-1.3
World Region of Birth, Foreign						
Foreign-born population, excluding population born at sea	139,477	133,547	-4.3	39,955,673	40,377,757	1.1
Europe	15.8	15.7	-0.6	12.1	12.1	-
Asia	29.7	33.6	13.1	28.2	28.6	1.4
Africa	7.7	7.1	-7.8	4	4.1	2.5
Oceania	0.4	1.1	175.0	0.5	0.5	-
Latin America	42.7	39.9	-6.6	53.1	52.6	-0.9
North America	3.6	2.5	-30.6	2	2.0	-
Language Spoken at Home and Ability to Speak English						
Population 5 years and over	2,850,218	2,864,107	0.5	289,215,746	291,524,091	0.8
English only	92.6	92.7	0.1	79.4	79.2	-0.3
Language other than English	7.4	7.3	-1.4	20.6	20.8	1.0
Speaks English less than "very well"	3.0	3.0	-	8.7	8.7	-

- = Zero or rounds to zero.

Table IA-5. Median Income and Poverty Status, 2011

(Number, percent, except as noted.)

Characteristic	State		U.S.	
	Number	Percent	Number	Percent
Median Income				
Households (dollars)	49,427	X	50,502	X
Families (dollars)	62,821	X	61,455	X
Below Poverty Level (All People)	378,864	12.8	48,452,035	15.9
Sex				
Male	169,662	11.6	21,825,281	14.7
Female	209,202	13.9	26,626,754	17.2
Age				
Under 18 years	122,828	17.3	16,386,500	22.5
Related children under 18 years	119,907	17.0	16,087,074	22.2
18 to 64 years	226,259	12.4	28,335,079	14.8
65 years and over	29,777	6.9	3,730,456	9.3

X = Not applicable.

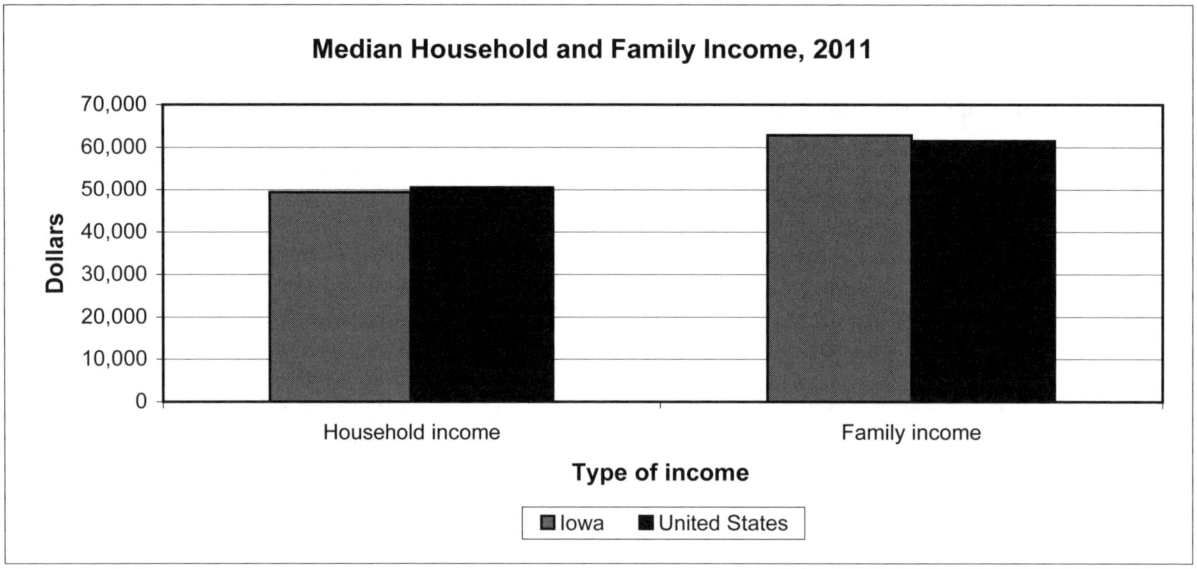

Table IA-6. Health Insurance Coverage Status for the Civilian Noninstitutionalized Population and Children Under 18 Years of Age

(Numbers in thousands, percent.)

Item	2004	2005	2006	2007	2008	2009	2010	2011
Civilian Noninstitutionalized Population	2,906	2,909	2,919	2,970	2,951	2,957	3,005	3,017
Covered by Private or Public Insurance								
Number	2,604	2,639	2,612	2,695	2,683	2,702	2,725	2,748
Percent	90.8	91.7	89.5	90.7	90.9	91.4	90.7	91.1
Not Covered								
Number	266	241	307	275	268	255	280	269
Percent	9.2	8.3	10.5	9.3	9.1	8.6	9.3	8.9
Percent in the U.S. not covered	14.9	15.3	15.8	15.3	15.1	15.1	15.5	15.1
Children Under 18 Years of Age	683	683	708	709	708	707	722	722
Covered by Private or Public Insurance								
Number	642	649	664	675	668	675	693	690
Percent	94.1	95.0	93.7	95.2	94.4	95.4	96.0	95.6
Not Covered								
Number	40	34	44	34	40	32	29	32
Percent	5.9	5.0	6.3	4.8	5.6	4.6	4.0	4.4
Percent in the U.S. not covered	10.5	10.9	11.7	11.0	9.7	8.6	8.0	7.5

Table IA-7. Employment Status by Demographic Group, Preliminary 2012

(Numbers in thousands, percent.)

Characteristic	Civilian noninstitutional population	Civilian labor force		Employed		Unemployed	
		Number	Percent of population	Number	Percent of population	Number	Percent of population
Total	2,397	1,650	68.8	1,565	65.3	85	5.1
Sex							
Male	1,177	863	73.3	815	69.3	48	5.5
Female	1,221	787	64.5	750	61.4	37	4.7
Race, Sex, and Hispanic Origin							
White	2,237	1,539	68.8	1,464	65.4	75	4.8
Male	1,102	805	73.1	762	69.2	43	5.3
Female	1,136	734	64.6	702	61.8	32	4.3
Black or African American	61	43	69.4	36	58.5	7	15.8
Male	27	20	75.8	17	63.5	3	16.3
Female	35	23	64.6	19	54.8	3	15.2
Hispanic	118	85	71.9	77	65.3	8	9.1
Male	63	51	80.8	47	74.0	4	8.4
Female	55	34	61.7	31	55.4	4	10.2
Age							
16 to 19 years	160	78	48.9	65	40.7	13	16.8
20 to 24 years	218	173	79.4	159	72.7	15	8.4
25 to 34 years	374	322	86.1	305	81.6	17	5.3
35 to 44 years	378	333	88.3	319	84.4	15	4.4
45 to 54 years	424	367	86.5	354	83.4	13	3.6
55 to 64 years	411	294	71.5	285	69.4	9	3.0
65 years and over	432	82	19.0	79	18.2	3	4.2

NOTE: Data in Table 7 are from the Current Population Survey (CPS) and do not match the estimates in Table 8. See notes and definitions for further information.

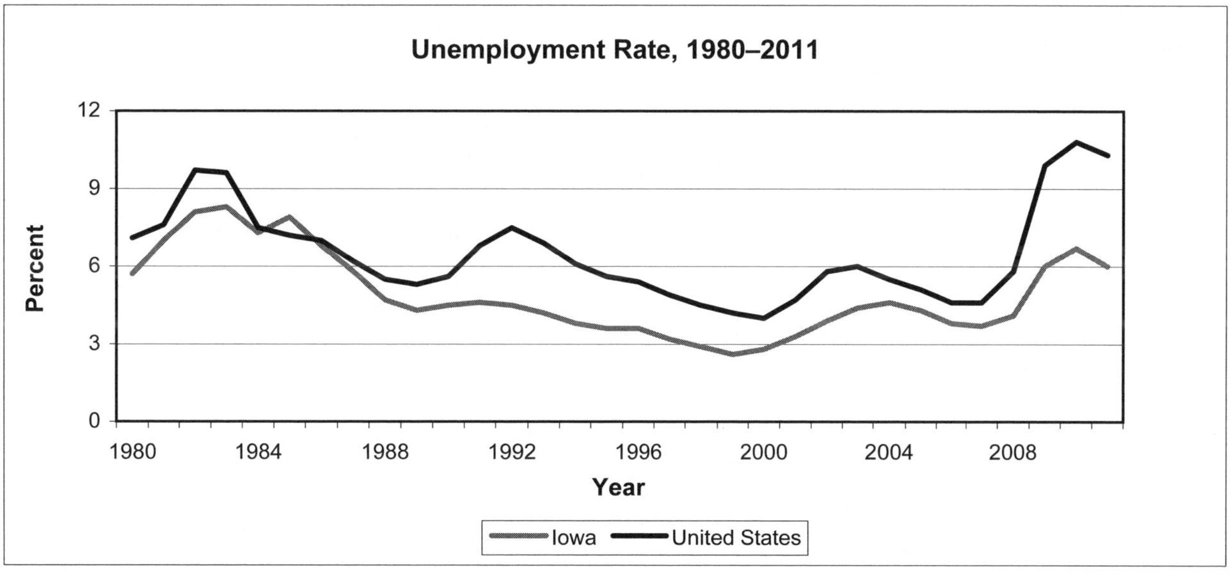

Table IA-8. Employment Status of the Civilian Noninstitutional Population Age 16 Years and Over

(Number, percent.)

Year	Civilian labor force	Civilian participation rate	Employed	Unemployed	Unemployment rate
2005	1,630,003	71.6	1,559,555	70,448	4.3
2006	1,656,855	72.3	1,594,628	62,227	3.8
2007	1,664,431	72.1	1,602,147	62,284	3.7
2008	1,675,981	72.1	1,606,976	69,005	4.1
2009	1,650,987	69.3	1,552,500	98,487	6.0
2010	1,651,501	68.6	1,540,038	111,463	6.7
2011	1,637,404	67.6	1,538,756	96,648	6.0

Table IA-9. Employment and Average Wages by Industry

(Estimates before 2007 are based on the 2002 *North American Industry Classification System* [NAICS]. Estimates from 2007 onward are based on the 2007 NAICS.)

Industry	2005	2006	2007	2008	2009	2010	2011
				Number of jobs			
Wage and Salary Employment by Industry	1,547,335	1,570,960	1,582,832	1,590,045	1,546,421	1,541,196	1,556,200
Farm Wage and Salary Employment	17,579	15,986	15,557	18,140	16,360	18,966	18,011
Nonfarm Wage and Salary Employment	1,529,756	1,554,974	1,567,275	1,571,905	1,530,061	1,522,230	1,538,189
Private wage and salary employment	1,269,819	1,293,172	1,303,854	1,305,760	1,260,011	1,253,690	1,270,493
Forestry, fishing, and related activities	5,113	5,287	5,425	5,606	5,754	6,550	6,776
Mining	2,084	2,149	2,120	2,148	2,181	2,132	2,175
Utilities	6,938	6,895	6,997	7,103	7,007	6,785	6,605
Construction	74,212	77,102	75,445	75,946	67,998	64,513	65,729
Manufacturing	229,658	232,003	230,103	227,885	203,661	201,315	206,393
Durable goods manufacturing	140,822	143,308	142,141	139,276	117,787	116,664	122,271
Nondurable goods manufacturing	88,836	88,695	87,962	88,609	85,874	84,651	84,122
Wholesale trade	67,522	67,725	68,514	69,641	67,350	66,581	67,390
Retail trade	182,083	182,428	181,595	180,283	177,577	175,618	176,933
Transportation and warehousing	53,883	55,871	56,994	57,393	55,432	55,371	56,908
Information	33,318	33,037	32,451	31,944	30,269	28,786	28,192
Finance and insurance	85,844	89,224	91,640	92,084	91,221	92,004	92,320
Real estate and rental and leasing	15,173	15,011	14,332	14,278	14,489	14,089	13,531
Professional, scientific, and technical services	39,208	41,056	43,442	43,946	42,881	43,288	43,841
Management of companies and enterprises	11,751	12,582	13,020	12,934	13,152	13,208	14,902
Administrative and waste services	63,342	64,849	67,805	67,482	62,500	66,552	68,103
Educational services	35,238	36,251	35,823	36,887	37,938	38,091	38,752
Health care and social assistance	163,763	167,264	169,980	173,569	177,162	179,031	180,609
Arts, entertainment, and recreation	19,935	20,838	21,199	20,988	20,764	19,931	20,701
Accommodation and food services	111,938	114,692	117,553	115,983	113,441	111,486	112,472
Other services, except public administration	68,816	68,908	69,416	69,660	69,234	68,359	68,161
Government and government enterprises	259,937	261,802	263,421	266,145	270,050	268,540	267,696
				Dollars			
Average Wages and Salaries by Industry	32,362	33,589	35,210	36,259	36,413	37,323	38,386
Average Farm Wages and Salaries	22,879	23,509	40,135	30,211	33,470	29,462	30,892
Average Nonfarm Wages and Salaries	32,471	33,692	35,162	36,328	36,445	37,421	38,473
Average private wages and salaries	32,381	33,630	35,070	36,106	36,023	37,179	38,333
Forestry, fishing, and related activities	20,579	21,096	22,850	24,169	24,953	25,161	26,320
Mining	42,616	42,153	43,865	44,226	42,644	43,546	45,485
Utilities	67,328	67,770	74,234	75,231	75,802	76,433	80,037
Construction	38,182	40,635	42,158	44,009	43,507	43,749	45,122
Manufacturing	43,073	44,340	45,996	47,181	47,287	49,765	51,117
Durable goods manufacturing	45,287	46,874	48,515	49,249	49,696	52,516	54,519
Nondurable goods manufacturing	39,562	40,246	41,926	43,930	43,982	45,972	46,171
Wholesale trade	43,440	45,120	47,325	49,557	49,730	51,514	53,943
Retail trade	20,477	20,855	21,399	22,018	22,307	22,646	23,212
Transportation and warehousing	37,229	38,225	39,861	39,718	39,061	40,388	41,255
Information	39,633	41,966	42,387	43,267	43,600	45,192	46,745
Finance and insurance	50,425	53,699	55,943	56,584	55,622	59,010	61,219
Real estate and rental and leasing	29,821	30,606	32,063	33,576	36,264	37,415	39,330
Professional, scientific, and technical services	43,405	44,955	47,551	49,175	50,327	51,550	53,774
Management of companies and enterprises	60,685	62,921	71,094	71,217	69,756	70,069	71,396
Administrative and waste services	22,054	23,299	24,251	25,038	25,716	26,379	26,248
Educational services	20,427	21,019	22,421	23,429	23,553	24,048	24,540
Health care and social assistance	32,049	32,831	33,972	35,418	35,900	36,388	37,364
Arts, entertainment, and recreation	18,447	20,194	21,342	20,534	20,120	20,702	20,698
Accommodation and food services	11,878	12,174	13,141	13,533	13,444	13,875	14,426
Other services, except public administration	21,566	22,462	23,804	24,852	25,407	26,192	26,827
Government and government enterprises	32,912	34,003	35,616	37,418	38,409	38,553	39,141

Table IA-10. Employment Characteristics by Family Type

(Number, percent.)

Family type and labor force status	2009		2010		2011	
	Total	Families with own children under 18 years	Total	Families with own children under 18 years	Total	Families with own children under 18 years
All families	798,262	354,635	793,768	346,995	784,895	344,983
Family type and labor force status						
Married-couple families	636,341	248,530	633,602	245,452	625,231	241,863
Both husband and wife in labor force	62.5	78.6	60.8	78.1	60.5	77.9
Husband in labor force, wife not in labor force	14.6	17.0	15.6	17.4	15.8	17.6
Wife in labor force, husband not in labor force	7.1	3.5	7.5	3.3	7.4	3.1
Both husband and wife not in labor force	15.8	1.0	16.1	1.3	16.3	1.4
Other families	161,921	106,105	160,166	101,543	159,664	103,120
Female householder, no husband present	70.4	72.9	70.8	73.4	70.4	73.6
In labor force	54.4	61.1	55.2	63.6	52.6	62.9
Not in labor force	15.9	11.8	15.5	9.8	17.8	10.7
Male householder, no wife present	29.6	27.1	29.2	26.6	29.6	26.4
In labor force	25.7	25.7	25.2	24.6	25.5	25.1
Not in labor force	3.9	1.4	4.0	1.9	4.1	1.3

Table IA-11. School Enrollment and Educational Attainment, 2011

(Number, percent.)

Item	State	U.S.
Enrollment		
Total population 3 years and over, enrolled in school	809,863	83,131,910
Enrolled in nursery school or preschool (percent)	6.9	6.0
Enrolled in kindergarten (percent)	5.1	5.1
Enrolled in elementary school, grades 1-8 (percent)	38.9	39.5
Enrolled in high school, grades 9-12 (percent)	20.4	20.7
Enrolled in college or graduate school (percent)	28.7	28.7
Attainment		
Total population 25 years and over	2,027,201	206,471,670
Less than ninth grade (percent)	3.7	6.0
9th to 12th grade, no diploma (percent)	5.7	8.1
High school graduate, including equivalency (percent)	33.1	28.4
Some college, no degree (percent)	21.3	21.2
Associate's degree (percent)	10.5	7.8
Bachelor's degree (percent)	17.7	17.9
Graduate or professional degree (percent)	8.1	10.6
High school graduate or higher (percent)	90.6	85.9
Bachelor's degree or higher (percent)	25.8	28.5

Table IA-12. Educational Indicators

(Number, percent; data derived from National Center of Education Statistics.)

Item	State	U.S.
Public Schools, 2009–2010 (except where noted)		
Number of school districts	361	13,629
Number of schools	1,468	99,834
Number of students (in thousands)	492	49,373
Student-teacher ratio	13.7	15.4
Expenditures per student (dollars)	11,647	10,591
Averaged freshman graduation rate, 2008–2009	85.7	75.5[1]
Dropout rate, 2008–2009	3.1	4.1
Students eligible for free or reduced-price lunch (percent)	38.7	48.0
English language learners, 2010–2011 (percent)	4.4	9.8[1]
Students with IEP (percent)	13.5	13.1
Private Schools, 2009–2010 (except where noted)		
Number of schools	230	33,366
Number of students (in thousands)	40	4,700
High school graduates, 2008–2009	2,249	308,813
Student-teacher ratio	12.3	10.7

[1] U.S. total includes estimates for nonreporting states.

Table IA-13. Reported Voting and Registration of the Voting-Age Population, November 2012

(Numbers in thousands, percent.)

Item	Total population	Total citizen population	Registered			Voted		
			Total registered	Percent registered (total population)	Percent registered (total citizen population)	Total voted	Percent voted (total population)	Percent voted (total citizen population)
U.S. Total	235,248	215,081	153,157	65.1	71.2	132,948	56.5	61.8
State Total	2,320	2,232	1,745	75.2	78.2	1,548	66.7	69.4
Sex								
Male	1,135	1,084	838	73.9	77.3	733	64.6	67.6
Female	1,186	1,148	906	76.4	79.0	816	68.8	71.1
Race								
White alone	2,173	2,123	1,673	77.0	78.8	1,482	68.2	69.8
White, non-Hispanic alone	2,067	2,057	1,644	79.5	79.9	1,455	70.4	70.7
Black alone	54	51	35	B	B	33	B	B
Asian alone	61	35	21	B	B	17	B	B
Hispanic (of any race)	120	71	32	26.8	B	30	25.1	B
Age								
18 to 24 years	260	243	150	57.7	61.8	121	46.6	49.9
25 to 44 years	787	737	551	70.0	74.8	476	60.5	64.6
45 to 64 years	828	812	652	78.7	80.3	586	70.8	72.2
65 to 74 years	239	237	214	89.7	90.2	201	84.0	84.6
75 years and over	206	203	177	86.3	87.4	164	79.8	80.8

B = Base is less than 75,000 and therefore too small to show the derived measure.

Table IA-14. Crime

(Number, rate per 100,000. Data are derived from the FBI Uniform Crime Reports.)

Item	State			U.S.		
	2010	2011	Percent change	2010	2011	Percent change
TOTAL POPULATION	3,050,202	3,062,309	0.4	309,330,219	311,591,917	0.7
VIOLENT CRIME						
Number	8,191	7,826	-4.5	1,251,248	1,203,564	-3.8
Rate	268.5	255.6	-4.8	404.5	386.3	-4.5
Murder and Nonnegligent Manslaughter						
Number	38	46	21.1	14,722	14,612	-0.7
Rate	1.2	1.5	25.0	4.8	4.7	-2.1
Forcible Rape						
Number	883	834	-5.5	85,593	83,425	-2.5
Rate	28.9	27.2	-5.9	27.7	26.8	-3.2
Robbery						
Number	1,012	825	-18.5	369,089	354,396	-4.0
Rate	33.2	26.9	-19.0	119.3	113.7	-4.7
Aggravated Assault						
Number	6,258	6,121	-2.2	781,844	751,131	-3.9
Rate	205.2	199.9	-2.6	252.8	241.1	-4.6
PROPERTY CRIME						
Number	68,740	71,361	3.8	9,112,625	9,063,173	-0.5
Rate	2,253.6	2,330.3	3.4	2,945.9	2,908.7	-1.3
Burglary						
Number	16,746	17,400	3.9	2,168,459	2,188,005	0.9
Rate	549.0	568.2	3.5	701.0	702.2	0.2
Larceny-Theft						
Number	48,194	50,025	3.8	6,204,601	6,159,795	-0.7
Rate	1,580.0	1,633.6	3.4	2,005.8	1,976.9	-1.4
Motor Vehicle Theft						
Number	3,800	3,936	3.6	739,565	715,373	-3.3
Rate	124.6	128.5	3.1	239.1	229.6	-4.0

Table IA-15. State Government Finances, 2011

(Dollar amounts in thousands, percent distribution.)

Item	Dollars	Percent distribution
Total Revenue	24,088,747	100.0
General revenue	18,097,362	75.1
Intergovernmental revenue	7,043,992	29.2
Taxes	7,236,476	30.0
General sales	2,232,028	9.3
Selective sales	1,094,387	4.5
License taxes	731,560	3.0
Individual income tax	2,851,449	11.8
Corporate income tax	250,272	1.0
Other taxes	76,780	0.3
Current charges	2,629,644	10.9
Miscellaneous general revenue	1,187,250	4.9
Utility revenue	0	0.0
Liquor stores revenue	213,972	0.9
Insurance trust revenue [1]	5,777,413	24.0
Total Expenditure	19,937,080	100.0
Intergovernmental expenditure	5,151,627	25.8
Direct expenditure	14,785,453	74.2
Current operation	9,984,903	50.1
Capital outlay	1,449,045	7.3
Insurance benefits and repayments	2,571,457	12.9
Assistance and subsidies	536,240	2.7
Interest on debt	243,808	1.2
Exhibit: Salaries and wages	2,402,356	12.0
Total Expenditure	19,937,080	100.0
General expenditure	17,218,913	86.4
Intergovernmental expenditure	5,151,627	25.8
Direct expenditure	12,067,286	60.5
General expenditure, by function:		
Education	6,269,650	31.4
Public welfare	4,900,757	24.6
Hospitals	1,090,080	5.5
Health	252,373	1.3
Highways	1,590,730	8.0
Police protection	96,692	0.5
Correction	332,291	1.7
Natural resources	314,102	1.6
Parks and recreation	24,953	0.1
Governmental administration	551,375	2.8
Interest on general debt	243,808	1.2
Other and unallocable	1,552,102	7.8
Utility expenditure	0	0.0
Liquor stores expenditure	146,710	0.7
Insurance trust expenditure	2,571,457	12.9
Debt at End of Fiscal Year	7,573,811	X
Cash and Security Holdings	35,356,891	X

X = Not applicable.
[1] Within insurance trust revenue, net earnings of state retirement systems is a calculated statistic (the item code in the data file is X08), and thus can be positive or negative. Net earnings is the sum of earnings on investments plus gains on investments minus losses on investments. The change made in 2002 for asset valuation from book to market value in accordance with Statement 34 of the Governmental Accounting Standards Board is reflected in the calculated statistics.

Table IA-16. State Government Tax Collections, 2012

(Dollars in thousands, percent.)

Item	Dollars	Percent distribution
Total Taxes	7,832,388	100.0
Property taxes	0	0.0
Sales and gross receipts	3,532,811	45.1
General sales and gross receipts	2,423,160	30.9
Selective sales and gross receipts	1,109,651	14.2
Alcoholic beverages	14,727	0.2
Amusements	294,886	3.8
Insurance premiums	101,406	1.3
Motor fuels	440,161	5.6
Pari-mutuels	4,054	0.1
Public utilities	0	0.0
Tobacco products	225,499	2.9
Other selective sales	28,918	0.4
Licenses	751,627	9.6
Alcoholic beverages	14,210	0.2
Amusements	19,239	0.2
Corporations in general	34,710	0.4
Hunting and fishing	29,286	0.4
Motor vehicle	520,946	6.7
Motor vehicle operators	8,062	0.1
Public utilities	11,711	0.1
Occupation and business, NEC	111,672	1.4
Other licenses	1,791	-
Income taxes	3,455,485	44.1
Individual income	3,029,709	38.7
Corporation net income	425,776	5.4
Other taxes	92,465	1.2
Death and gift	79,670	1.0
Documentary and stock transfer	12,795	0.2
Severance	0	0.0
Taxes, NEC	0	0.0

- = Rounds to zero.

Leading Exports, 2012

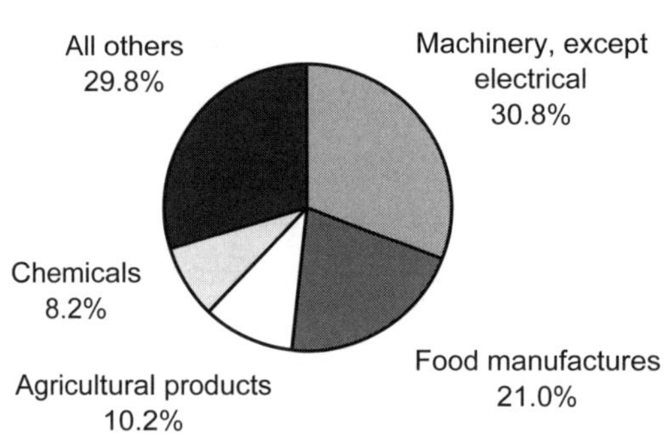

KANSAS

Facts and Figures

Location: Central United States; bordered on the N by Nebraska, on the E by Missouri, on the S by Oklahoma, and on the W by Colorado

Area: 82,277 sq. mi. (213,096 sq. km.); rank—15th

Population: 2,885,905 (2012 est.); rank—33rd

Principal Cities: capital—Topeka; largest—Wichita

Statehood: January 29, 1861; 34th state

U.S. Congress: 2 senators, 4 representatives

State Motto: *Ad astra per aspera* ("To the stars through difficulties")

State Song: "Home on the Range"

State Nicknames: The Sunflower State; The Jayhawk State

Abbreviations: KS; Kan.; Kans.

State Symbols: flower—wild native sunflower; tree—cottonwood; bird—Western meadowlark

At a Glance

- With an increase in population of 4.8 percent, Kansas ranked 32nd among the states in growth from 2000 to 2009.
- An estimated 18,500 marriages took place in Kansas in 2009, compared to 10,300 divorces.
- In 2011, 12.6 percent of Kansans did not have health insurance, compared to 15.1 percent of the total U.S. population.
- In the 2012 election, 63.3 percent of Kansas's eligible voters voted, compared to 61.8 percent of eligible voters nationwide.
- In 2007, Kansas exported $3.8 billion worth of agricultural products, about 4.7 percent of the U.S. total.

Table KS-1. Population by Age, Sex, Race, and Hispanic Origin

(Number, percent, except where noted.)

Sex, age, race, and Hispanic origin	2000	2010	2012[1]	Average annual percent change, 2010–2012
Total Population	2,688,418	2,853,118	2,885,905	0.4
Percent of total U.S. population	1.0	0.9	0.9	X
Sex				
Male	1,328,474	1,415,408	1,435,281	0.5
Female	1,359,944	1,437,710	1,450,624	0.3
Age				
Under 5 years	188,708	205,492	203,267	-0.4
5 to 19 years	609,710	605,152	604,278	-
20 to 64 years	1,533,771	1,666,358	1,684,091	0.4
65 years and over	356,229	376,116	394,269	1.5
Median age (years)	35.2	36.0	36.0	0.0
Race and Hispanic Origin				
One race				
White	2,313,944	2,501,057	2,517,663	0.2
Black	154,198	173,298	178,820	1.0
American Indian and Alaska Native	24,936	33,044	33,909	0.9
Asian	46,806	69,628	74,598	2.2
Native Hawaiian or Other Pacific Islander	1,313	2,864	2,953	1.0
Two or more races	56,496	73,227	77,962	2.0
Hispanic (of any race)	188,252	311,460	329,397	1.8

X = Not applicable.
- = Zero or rounds to zero.
[1] Population figures for 2012 are July 1 estimates. The 2010 estimates are taken from the 2010 Census.

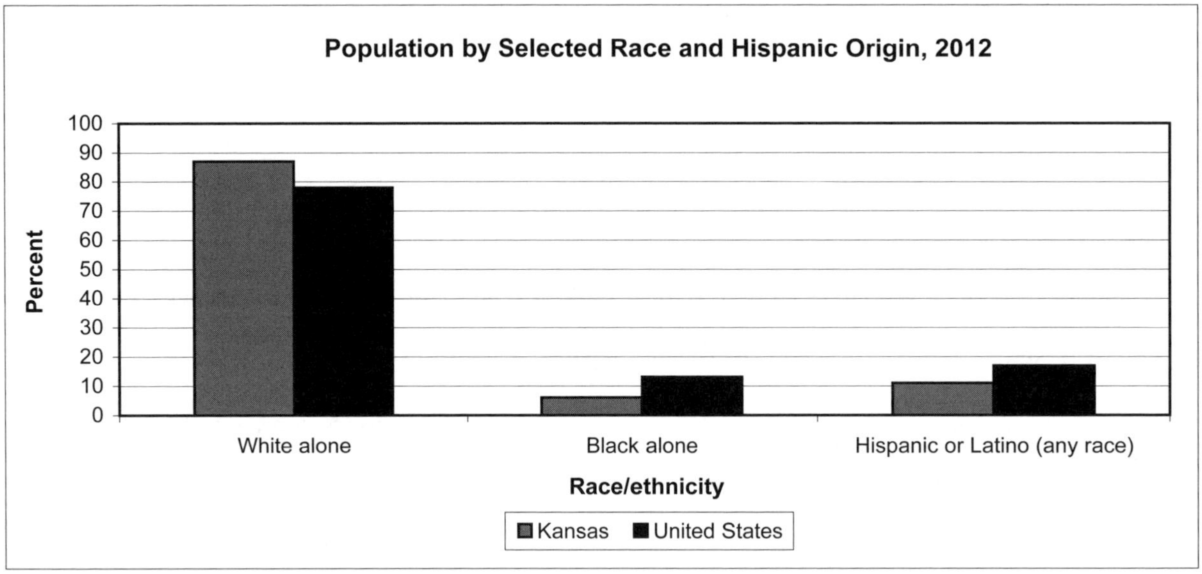

Table KS-2. Marital Status

(Number, percent distribution.)

Sex, age, race, and Hispanic origin	2000	2010	2011
Males, 15 Years and Over	1,025,114	1,106,102	1,114,875
Never married	27.4	31.6	32.7
Now married, except separated	59.9	53.9	53.6
Separated	1.1	1.4	1.2
Widowed	2.3	2.6	2.3
Divorced	9.2	10.5	10.2
Females, 15 Years and Over	1,075,542	1,145,453	1,152,191
Never married	20.8	25.1	25.1
Now married, except separated	56.4	51.4	50.8
Separated	1.3	1.7	1.8
Widowed	10.6	9.2	9.3
Divorced	10.9	12.6	13.1

Table KS-3. Households and Housing Characteristics

(Number, percent, dollars.)

Item	2000	2010	2011	Average annual percent change, 2000–2011
Total Households	1,037,891	1,101,658	1,101,701	0.5
Family households	701,547	721,592	722,016	0.2
Married-couple family	567,924	559,199	557,419	-0.2
Other family	133,623	162,393	164,597	1.9
Male householder, no wife present	36,962	46,692	46,960	2.3
Female householder, no husband present	96,661	115,701	117,637	1.8
Nonfamily households	336,344	380,066	379,685	1.1
Householder living alone	280,387	313,390	313,147	1.0
Householder not living alone	55,957	66,676	66,538	1.6
Housing Characteristics				
Total housing units	1,131,200	1,234,037	1,237,738	0.8
Occupied housing units	1,037,891	1,101,658	1,101,701	0.5
Owner occupied	718,703	749,907	747,079	0.3
Renter occupied	319,188	351,751	354,622	0.9
Average size	2.51	2.52	2.53	0.1
Financial Characteristics				
Median gross rent of renter-occupied housing	498	682	709	3.5
Median monthly owner costs for housing units with a mortgage	888	1,239	1,252	3.4
Median value of owner-occupied housing units	83,500	127,300	128,300	4.5

Table KS-4. Migration, Origin, and Language

(Number, percent.)

Characteristic	State			U.S.		
	2010	2011	Percent change	2010	2011	Percent change
Residence 1 Year Ago						
Population 1 year and over	2,820,894	2,833,584	0.4	305,628,607	307,900,319	0.7
Same house	83.0	83.7	0.8	84.6	84.8	0.2
Different house in the U.S.	16.6	15.8	-4.8	14.8	14.6	-1.4
Same county	9.7	9.5	-2.1	9.4	9.2	-2.1
Different county	6.9	6.3	-8.7	5.4	5.4	-
Same state	3.5	3.3	-5.7	3.2	3.1	-3.1
Different state	3.4	3.0	-11.8	2.2	2.3	4.5
Abroad	0.4	0.5	25.0	0.6	0.6	-
Place of Birth						
Native born	2,672,227	2,672,471	-	269,393,835	271,214,059	0.7
Male	49.4	49.4	-	49.2	49.2	-
Female	50.6	50.6	-	50.8	50.8	-
Foreign born	186,942	198,767	6.3	39,955,854	40,377,860	1.1
Male	51.7	51.8	0.2	49.1	48.9	-0.4
Female	48.3	48.2	-0.2	50.9	51.1	0.4
Foreign born; naturalized U.S. citizen	60,779	67,411	10.9	17,476,082	18,140,192	3.8
Male	46.1	49.8	8.0	45.8	45.8	-
Female	53.9	50.2	-6.9	54.2	54.2	-
Foreign born; not a U.S. citizen	126,163	131,356	4.1	22,479,772	22,237,668	-1.1
Male	54.3	52.8	-2.8	51.6	51.5	-0.2
Female	45.7	47.2	3.3	48.4	48.5	0.2
Entered 2000 or later	40.2	44.9	11.7	34.7	35.7	2.9
Entered 1990 to 1999	30.9	30.0	-2.9	27.2	26.7	-1.8
Entered before 1990	28.9	25.0	-13.5	38.1	37.6	-1.3
World Region of Birth, Foreign						
Foreign-born population, excluding population born at sea	186,942	198,767	6.3	39,955,673	40,377,757	1.1
Europe	8.9	7.5	-15.7	12.1	12.1	-
Asia	27.1	30.0	10.7	28.2	28.6	1.4
Africa	5.1	6.2	21.6	4	4.1	2.5
Oceania	0.4	0.4	-	0.5	0.5	-
Latin America	56.8	54.9	-3.3	53.1	52.6	-0.9
North America	1.7	1.1	-35.3	2	2.0	-
Language Spoken at Home and Ability to Speak English						
Population 5 years and over	2,654,069	2,669,198	0.6	289,215,746	291,524,091	0.8
English only	89.0	88.6	-0.4	79.4	79.2	-0.3
Language other than English	11.0	11.4	3.6	20.6	20.8	1.0
Speaks English less than "very well"	4.6	4.6	-	8.7	8.7	-

- = Zero or rounds to zero.

Table KS-5. Median Income and Poverty Status, 2011

(Number, percent, except as noted.)

Characteristic	State		U.S.	
	Number	Percent	Number	Percent
Median Income				
Households (dollars)	48,964	X	50,502	X
Families (dollars)	61,947	X	61,455	X
Below Poverty Level (All People)	383,467	13.8	48,452,035	15.9
Sex				
Male	170,564	12.4	21,825,281	14.7
Female	212,903	15.1	26,626,754	17.2
Age				
Under 18 years	133,556	18.8	16,386,500	22.5
Related children under 18 years	130,047	18.4	16,087,074	22.2
18 to 64 years	223,762	13.1	28,335,079	14.8
65 years and over	26,149	7.2	3,730,456	9.3

X = Not applicable.

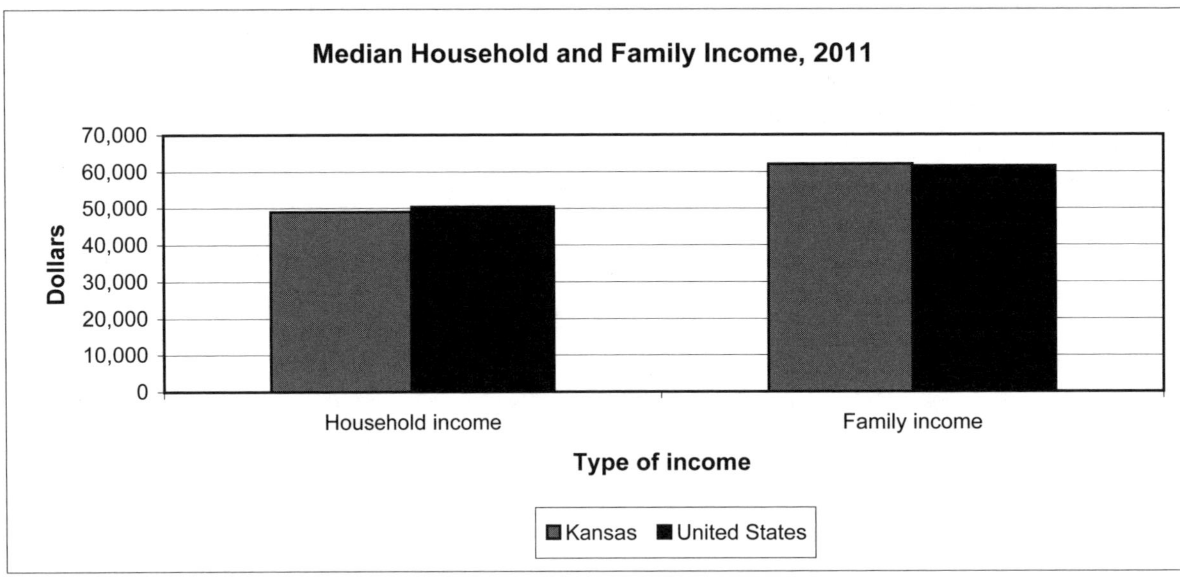

Table KS-6. Health Insurance Coverage Status for the Civilian Noninstitutionalized Population and Children Under 18 Years of Age

(Numbers in thousands, percent.)

Item	2004	2005	2006	2007	2008	2009	2010	2011
Civilian Noninstitutionalized Population	2,674	2,695	2,723	2,722	2,739	2,757	2,804	2,814
Covered by Private or Public Insurance								
Number	2,388	2,417	2,387	2,376	2,405	2,394	2,415	2,459
Percent	89.3	89.7	87.7	87.3	87.8	86.8	86.1	87.4
Not Covered								
Number	286	278	335	345	334	363	389	355
Percent	10.7	10.3	12.3	12.7	12.2	13.2	13.9	12.6
Percent in the U.S. not covered	14.9	15.3	15.8	15.3	15.1	15.1	15.5	15.1
Children Under 18 Years of Age	687	692	697	710	698	701	725	721
Covered by Private or Public Insurance								
Number	644	648	646	655	640	643	665	675
Percent	93.7	93.8	92.7	92.3	91.7	91.8	91.8	93.6
Not Covered								
Number	44	43	51	54	58	58	60	46
Percent	6.3	6.2	7.3	7.7	8.3	8.2	8.2	6.4
Percent in the U.S. not covered	10.5	10.9	11.7	11.0	9.7	8.6	8.0	7.5

Table KS-7. Employment Status by Demographic Group, Preliminary 2012

(Numbers in thousands, percent.)

Characteristic	Civilian noninstitutional population	Civilian labor force		Employed		Unemployed	
		Number	Percent of population	Number	Percent of population	Number	Percent of population
Total	2,182	1,482	67.9	1,400	64.1	82	5.6
Sex							
Male	1,062	781	73.6	736	69.3	45	5.8
Female	1,120	701	62.5	663	59.2	37	5.3
Race, Sex, and Hispanic Origin							
White	1,928	1,316	68.2	1,250	64.8	66	5.0
Male	943	700	74.2	665	70.5	34	4.9
Female	984	616	62.6	584	59.3	32	5.1
Black or African American	113	73	64.7	63	55.6	10	14.0
Male	52	37	70.0	30	58.0	6	17.3
Female	60	36	60.0	32	53.6	4	10.7
Hispanic	172	119	68.9	110	64.1	8	6.9
Male	86	65	75.6	62	71.8	3	5.1
Female	86	53	62.1	49	56.5	5	9.1
Age							
16 to 19 years	144	67	46.8	53	36.8	14	21.3
20 to 24 years	204	153	75.1	138	67.8	15	9.7
25 to 34 years	415	355	85.4	337	81.1	18	5.1
35 to 44 years	304	261	86.0	251	82.5	11	4.1
45 to 54 years	362	303	83.5	291	80.4	11	3.7
55 to 64 years	360	253	70.4	242	67.3	11	4.4
65 years and over	394	89	22.7	87	22.2	2	2.3

NOTE: Data in Table 7 are from the Current Population Survey (CPS) and do not match the estimates in Table 8. See notes and definitions for further information.

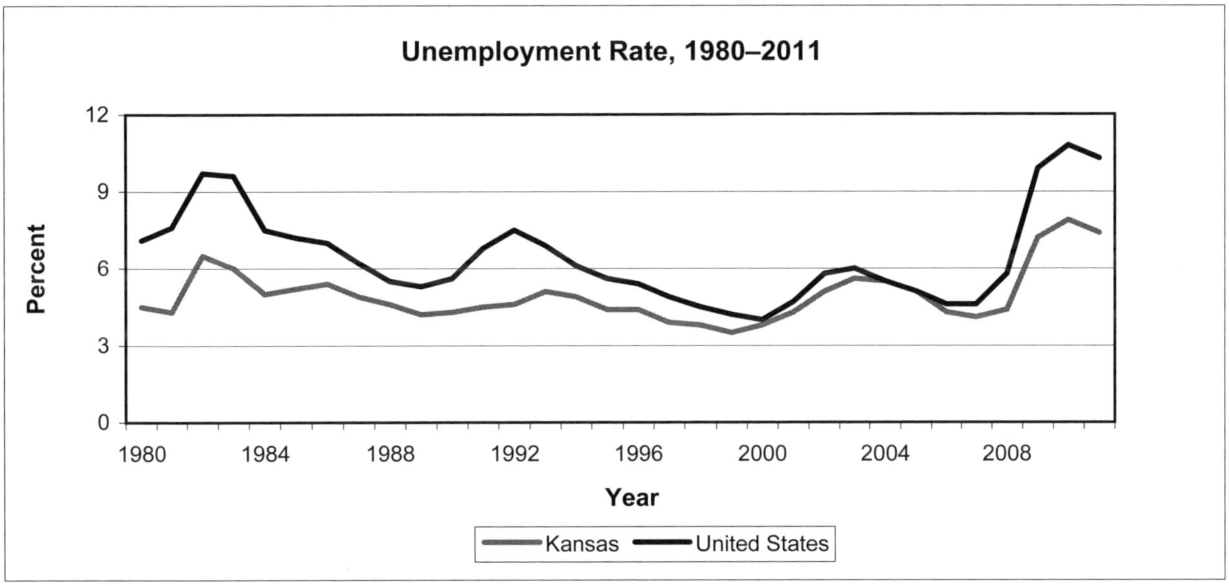

Table KS-8. Employment Status of the Civilian Noninstitutional Population Age 16 Years and Over

(Number, percent.)

Year	Civilian labor force	Civilian participation rate	Employed	Unemployed	Unemployment rate
2005	1,468,018	70.9	1,393,319	74,699	5.1
2006	1,474,044	70.8	1,410,048	63,996	4.3
2007	1,485,237	70.7	1,425,049	60,188	4.1
2008	1,496,943	70.7	1,431,340	65,603	4.4
2009	1,488,409	67.8	1,380,536	107,873	7.2
2010	1,491,225	67.4	1,373,030	118,195	7.9
2011	1,500,639	67.4	1,389,038	111,601	7.4

Table KS-9. Employment and Average Wages by Industry

(Estimates before 2007 are based on the 2002 *North American Industry Classification System* [NAICS]. Estimates from 2007 onward are based on the 2007 NAICS.)

Industry	2005	2006	2007	2008	2009	2010	2011
	Number of jobs						
Wage and Salary Employment by Industry	1,410,840	1,434,849	1,468,721	1,478,020	1,428,586	1,414,533	1,425,056
Farm Wage and Salary Employment	11,222	10,796	10,680	9,499	8,833	10,270	11,830
Nonfarm Wage and Salary Employment	1,399,618	1,424,053	1,458,041	1,468,521	1,419,753	1,404,263	1,413,226
Private wage and salary employment	1,116,926	1,135,851	1,163,765	1,170,143	1,119,434	1,100,661	1,113,281
Forestry, fishing, and related activities	3,759	3,608	3,557	3,621	3,489	3,646	3,799
Mining	7,584	8,836	9,347	10,010	8,353	8,521	9,047
Utilities	7,272	7,288	7,339	7,565	7,726	7,808	8,049
Construction	65,241	67,194	68,283	67,786	60,872	56,968	55,810
Manufacturing	180,529	183,005	187,260	187,572	167,633	160,506	161,350
Durable goods manufacturing	112,109	115,010	118,999	121,515	104,021	97,481	98,111
Nondurable goods manufacturing	68,420	67,995	68,261	66,057	63,612	63,025	63,239
Wholesale trade	59,723	59,838	61,246	63,280	61,439	59,981	59,911
Retail trade	149,343	148,797	150,366	148,774	144,390	143,075	143,980
Transportation and warehousing	46,174	47,147	48,358	48,206	45,379	44,651	46,482
Information	39,670	39,856	41,009	38,908	34,741	29,403	27,945
Finance and insurance	56,426	58,437	59,851	59,734	58,356	58,366	60,274
Real estate and rental and leasing	15,837	15,855	15,829	15,576	15,078	15,029	15,142
Professional, scientific, and technical services	55,841	58,001	60,855	63,482	61,957	61,452	61,464
Management of companies and enterprises	10,996	12,124	12,507	13,739	13,452	15,182	13,984
Administrative and waste services	70,209	72,780	76,859	75,664	69,727	71,027	75,368
Educational services	16,729	16,545	17,982	18,904	18,879	19,343	19,929
Health care and social assistance	151,589	153,870	157,722	161,946	165,136	164,929	168,169
Arts, entertainment, and recreation	13,758	13,934	14,010	13,572	13,403	13,336	14,033
Accommodation and food services	100,371	102,764	103,670	103,860	102,165	101,445	102,518
Other services, except public administration	65,875	65,972	67,715	67,944	67,259	65,993	66,027
Government and government enterprises	282,692	288,202	294,276	298,378	300,319	303,602	299,945
	Dollars						
Average Wages and Salaries by Industry	34,429	36,339	37,851	39,091	39,046	39,824	40,958
Average Farm Wages and Salaries	28,966	32,861	44,878	50,280	44,140	35,828	39,315
Average Nonfarm Wages and Salaries	34,473	36,365	37,800	39,018	39,014	39,853	40,972
Average private wages and salaries	35,022	36,985	38,418	39,594	39,330	40,320	41,464
Forestry, fishing, and related activities	19,477	20,777	21,731	22,236	23,230	24,442	24,710
Mining	44,891	48,018	49,567	52,426	49,114	50,987	54,896
Utilities	66,652	68,678	73,143	75,535	78,281	79,209	87,794
Construction	37,793	39,743	41,731	44,119	43,977	45,580	45,925
Manufacturing	44,926	48,237	49,289	49,673	50,051	52,052	53,411
Durable goods manufacturing	47,914	52,354	53,161	52,920	53,844	56,405	58,084
Nondurable goods manufacturing	40,029	41,273	42,538	43,701	43,849	45,319	46,163
Wholesale trade	49,635	52,422	54,548	56,712	56,822	59,143	59,887
Retail trade	22,100	22,877	23,358	23,895	23,839	24,134	24,788
Transportation and warehousing	40,036	40,857	42,076	43,448	42,853	43,871	45,997
Information	57,675	60,618	64,511	65,252	62,395	64,040	64,533
Finance and insurance	50,369	52,244	54,442	56,062	55,670	57,718	61,059
Real estate and rental and leasing	29,858	31,286	31,718	33,176	32,981	33,767	35,296
Professional, scientific, and technical services	48,768	51,255	53,896	55,782	56,122	57,269	59,584
Management of companies and enterprises	67,901	80,077	83,516	85,476	79,859	81,323	87,707
Administrative and waste services	27,554	29,859	31,085	32,468	32,645	33,615	35,543
Educational services	23,147	24,866	25,360	26,876	27,528	27,481	28,249
Health care and social assistance	33,315	34,475	35,849	37,175	38,033	38,688	39,262
Arts, entertainment, and recreation	15,661	16,649	17,557	17,247	17,222	17,872	18,328
Accommodation and food services	13,407	13,842	14,210	14,175	14,277	14,779	15,186
Other services, except public administration	23,119	24,128	25,344	26,447	26,097	26,898	27,605
Government and government enterprises	32,302	33,923	35,354	36,759	37,836	38,162	39,147

Table KS-10. Employment Characteristics by Family Type

(Number, percent.)

Family type and labor force status	2009 Total	2009 Families with own children under 18 years	2010 Total	2010 Families with own children under 18 years	2011 Total	2011 Families with own children under 18 years
All families	722,181	336,473	721,592	324,111	722,016	334,965
Family type and labor force status						
Married-couple families	557,648	233,695	559,199	221,090	557,419	233,734
Both husband and wife in labor force	59.7	71.3	58.7	72.0	59.3	71.3
Husband in labor force, wife not in labor force	19.7	24.3	19.3	24.4	20.1	24.8
Wife in labor force, husband not in labor force	6.7	2.9	7.4	2.7	6.8	3.0
Both husband and wife not in labor force	13.8	1.4	14.5	0.9	13.9	0.9
Other families	164,533	102,778	162,393	103,021	164,597	101,231
Female householder, no husband present	70.4	72.0	71.2	74.5	71.5	74.8
In labor force	54.9	63.7	56.4	64.6	55.8	63.7
Not in labor force	15.5	8.4	14.9	9.8	15.7	11.0
Male householder, no wife present	29.6	28.0	28.8	25.5	28.5	25.2
In labor force	25.3	26.4	24.2	23.5	23.8	23.6
Not in labor force	4.3	1.6	4.5	2.0	4.7	1.6

Table KS-11. School Enrollment and Educational Attainment, 2011

(Number, percent.)

Item	State	U.S.
Enrollment		
Total population 3 years and over, enrolled in school	801,598	83,131,910
Enrolled in nursery school or preschool (percent)	6.4	6.0
Enrolled in kindergarten (percent)	5.1	5.1
Enrolled in elementary school, grades 1-8 (percent)	39.9	39.5
Enrolled in high school, grades 9-12 (percent)	19.8	20.7
Enrolled in college or graduate school (percent)	28.8	28.7
Attainment		
Total population 25 years and over	1,852,094	206,471,670
Less than ninth grade (percent)	4.1	6.0
9th to 12th grade, no diploma (percent)	5.8	8.1
High school graduate, including equivalency (percent)	27.9	28.4
Some college, no degree (percent)	24.6	21.2
Associate's degree (percent)	7.4	7.8
Bachelor's degree (percent)	19.7	17.9
Graduate or professional degree (percent)	10.4	10.6
High school graduate or higher (percent)	90.0	85.9
Bachelor's degree or higher (percent)	30.1	28.5

Table KS-12. Educational Indicators

(Number, percent; data derived from National Center of Education Statistics.)

Item	State	U.S.
Public Schools, 2009–2010 (except where noted)		
Number of school districts	316	13,629
Number of schools	1,419	99,834
Number of students (in thousands)	474	49,373
Student-teacher ratio	13.7	15.4
Expenditures per student (dollars)	11,228	10,591
Averaged freshman graduation rate, 2008–2009	80.2	75.5[1]
Dropout rate, 2008–2009	2.1	4.1
Students eligible for free or reduced-price lunch (percent)	47.6	48.0
English language learners, 2010–2011 (percent)	8.1	9.8[1]
Students with IEP (percent)	14.0	13.1
Private Schools, 2009–2010 (except where noted)		
Number of schools	263	33,366
Number of students (in thousands)	40	4,700
High school graduates, 2008–2009	2,166	308,813
Student-teacher ratio	12.0	10.7

[1] U.S. total includes estimates for nonreporting states.

Table KS-13. Reported Voting and Registration of the Voting-Age Population, November 2012

(Numbers in thousands, percent.)

Item	Total population	Total citizen population	Registered			Voted		
			Total registered	Percent registered (total population)	Percent registered (total citizen population)	Total voted	Percent voted (total population)	Percent voted (total citizen population)
U.S. Total	235,248	215,081	153,157	65.1	71.2	132,948	56.5	61.8
State Total	2,120	1,973	1,467	69.2	74.4	1,249	58.9	63.3
Sex								
Male	1,029	953	671	65.2	70.4	567	55.1	59.5
Female	1,091	1,020	796	73.0	78.0	682	62.5	66.8
Race								
White alone	1,851	1,759	1,342	72.5	76.3	1,148	62.0	65.3
White, non-Hispanic alone	1,675	1,664	1,294	77.2	77.8	1,115	66.6	67.0
Black alone	105	103	64	61.3	62.5	54	51.4	52.4
Asian alone	66	27	9	B	B	6	B	B
Hispanic (of any race)	197	108	54	27.5	50.0	33	16.6	30.2
Age								
18 to 24 years	294	262	127	43.2	48.4	88	30.1	33.7
25 to 44 years	706	627	439	62.2	70.0	341	48.3	54.4
45 to 64 years	757	721	583	77.0	80.9	535	70.7	74.2
65 to 74 years	188	188	162	86.4	86.4	147	78.5	78.5
75 years and over	176	176	156	88.9	88.9	137	78.2	78.2

B = Base is less than 75,000 and therefore too small to show the derived measure.

Table KS-14. Crime

(Number, rate per 100,000. Data are derived from the FBI Uniform Crime Reports.)

Item	State			U.S.		
	2010	2011	Percent change	2010	2011	Percent change
TOTAL POPULATION	2,859,143	2,871,238	0.4	309,330,219	311,591,917	0.7
VIOLENT CRIME						
Number	10,602	10,162	-4.2	1,251,248	1,203,564	-3.8
Rate	370.8	353.9	-4.6	404.5	386.3	-4.5
Murder and Nonnegligent Manslaughter						
Number	97	110	13.4	14,722	14,612	-0.7
Rate	3.4	3.8	11.8	4.8	4.7	-2.1
Forcible Rape						
Number	1,146	1,085	-5.3	85,593	83,425	-2.5
Rate	40.1	37.8	-5.7	27.7	26.8	-3.2
Robbery						
Number	1,538	1,459	-5.1	369,089	354,396	-4.0
Rate	53.8	50.8	-5.6	119.3	113.7	-4.7
Aggravated Assault						
Number	7,821	7,508	-4.0	781,844	751,131	-3.9
Rate	273.5	261.5	-4.4	252.8	241.1	-4.6
PROPERTY CRIME						
Number	89,109	88,438	-0.8	9,112,625	9,063,173	-0.5
Rate	3,116.6	3,080.1	-1.2	2,945.9	2,908.7	-1.3
Burglary						
Number	19,315	18,789	-2.7	2,168,459	2,188,005	0.9
Rate	675.6	654.4	-3.1	701.0	702.2	0.2
Larceny-Theft						
Number	63,774	62,972	-1.3	6,204,601	6,159,795	-0.7
Rate	2,230.5	2,193.2	-1.7	2,005.8	1,976.9	-1.4
Motor Vehicle Theft						
Number	6,020	6,677	10.9	739,565	715,373	-3.3
Rate	210.6	232.5	10.4	239.1	229.6	-4.0

Table KS-15. State Government Finances, 2011

(Dollar amounts in thousands, percent distribution.)

Item	Dollars	Percent distribution
Total Revenue	18,613,184	100.0
General revenue	15,019,196	80.7
Intergovernmental revenue	4,940,903	26.5
Taxes	6,828,477	36.7
General sales	2,487,499	13.4
Selective sales	845,468	4.5
License taxes	333,916	1.8
Individual income tax	2,720,819	14.6
Corporate income tax	246,518	1.3
Other taxes	194,257	1.0
Current charges	2,369,426	12.7
Miscellaneous general revenue	880,390	4.7
Utility revenue	0	0.0
Liquor stores revenue	0	0.0
Insurance trust revenue [1]	3,593,988	19.3
Total Expenditure	16,686,643	100.0
Intergovernmental expenditure	4,208,664	25.2
Direct expenditure	12,477,979	74.8
Current operation	8,756,128	52.5
Capital outlay	1,088,586	6.5
Insurance benefits and repayments	2,159,915	12.9
Assistance and subsidies	201,483	1.2
Interest on debt	271,867	1.6
Exhibit: Salaries and wages	3,477,748	20.8
Total Expenditure	16,686,643	100.0
General expenditure	14,526,728	87.1
Intergovernmental expenditure	4,208,664	25.2
Direct expenditure	10,318,064	61.8
General expenditure, by function:		
Education	5,966,159	35.8
Public welfare	3,530,709	21.2
Hospitals	1,227,935	7.4
Health	322,888	1.9
Highways	1,238,789	7.4
Police protection	99,073	0.6
Correction	341,552	2.0
Natural resources	216,091	1.3
Parks and recreation	34,783	0.2
Governmental administration	456,464	2.7
Interest on general debt	271,867	1.6
Other and unallocable	820,418	4.9
Utility expenditure	0	0.0
Liquor stores expenditure	0	0.0
Insurance trust expenditure	2,159,915	12.9
Debt at End of Fiscal Year	6,893,030	X
Cash and Security Holdings	18,543,512	X

X = Not applicable.
[1] Within insurance trust revenue, net earnings of state retirement systems is a calculated statistic (the item code in the data file is X08), and thus can be positive or negative. Net earnings is the sum of earnings on investments plus gains on investments minus losses on investments. The change made in 2002 for asset valuation from book to market value in accordance with Statement 34 of the Governmental Accounting Standards Board is reflected in the calculated statistics.

Table KS-16. State Government Tax Collections, 2012

(Dollars in thousands, percent.)

Item	Dollars	Percent distribution
Total Taxes	7,418,341	100.0
Property taxes	74,413	1.0
Sales and gross receipts	3,685,595	49.7
General sales and gross receipts	2,825,880	38.1
Selective sales and gross receipts	859,715	11.6
Alcoholic beverages	118,202	1.6
Amusements	389	-
Insurance premiums	166,405	2.2
Motor fuels	435,049	5.9
Pari-mutuels	0	0.0
Public utilities	317	0.0
Tobacco products	103,639	1.4
Other selective sales	35,714	0.5
Licenses	315,411	4.3
Alcoholic beverages	4,530	0.1
Amusements	16	-
Corporations in general	21,180	0.3
Hunting and fishing	24,258	0.3
Motor vehicle	184,515	2.5
Motor vehicle operators	21,500	0.3
Public utilities	4,581	0.1
Occupation and business, NEC	52,267	0.7
Other licenses	2,564	-
Income taxes	3,209,321	43.3
Individual income	2,891,743	39.0
Corporation net income	317,578	4.3
Other taxes	133,601	1.8
Death and gift	694	-
Documentary and stock transfer	0	0.0
Severance	132,907	1.8
Taxes, NEC	0	0.0

- = Rounds to zero.

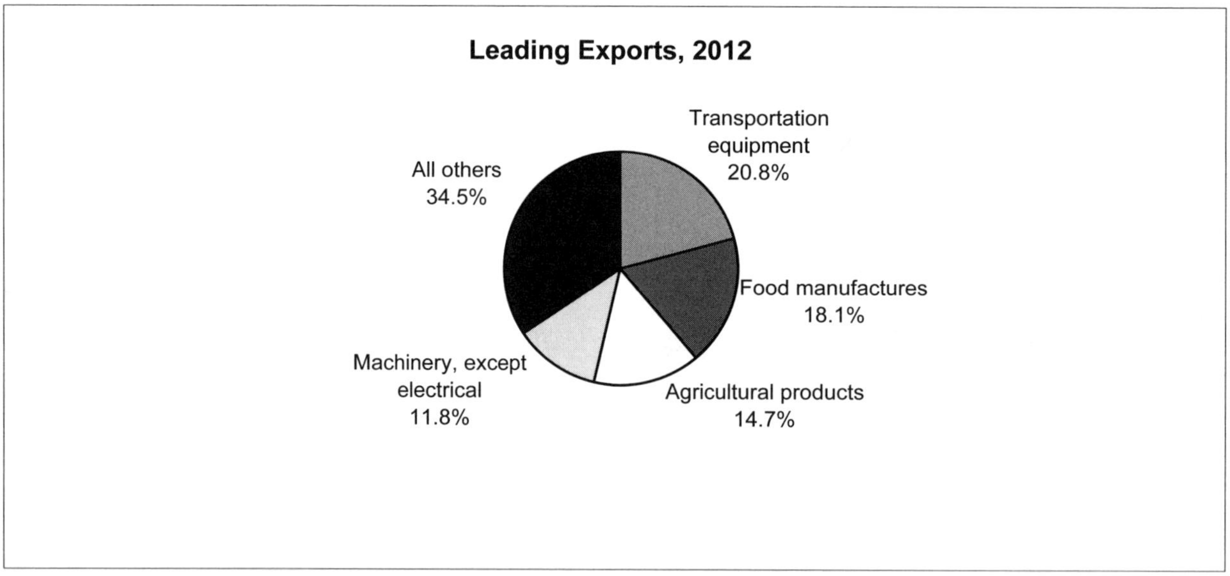

KENTUCKY

Facts and Figures

Location: East central United States; bordered on the N by Illinois, Indiana, and Ohio, on the E by West Virginia and Virginia, on the S by Tennessee, and on the W by Missouri and Illinois

Area: 40,409 sq. mi. (104,659 sq. km.); rank—37th

Population: 4,380,415 (2012 est.); rank—26th

Principal Cities: capital—Frankfort; largest—Lexington

Statehood: June 1, 1792; 15th state

U.S. Congress: 2 senators, 6 representatives

State Motto: United We Stand, Divided We Fall

State Song: "My Old Kentucky Home"

State Nickname: The Bluegrass State

Abbreviations: KY; Ky.

State Symbols: flower—goldenrod; tree—tulip poplar; bird—cardinal

At a Glance

- With an increase in population of 6.7 percent, Kentucky ranked 24th among the states in growth from 2000 to 2009.
- An estimated 33,400 marriages took place in Kentucky in 2009, compared to 19,900 divorces.
- Kentucky's median household income in 2011 was $41,141, and 19.1 percent of the population lived below the poverty level.
- In the 2012 election, 59.3 percent of Kentucky's eligible voters voted, compared to 61.8 percent of eligible voters nationwide.
- In 2007, Kentucky exported $1.2 billion worth of agricultural products, about 1.5 percent of the U.S. total.

Table KY-1. Population by Age, Sex, Race, and Hispanic Origin

(Number, percent, except where noted.)

Sex, age, race, and Hispanic origin	2000	2010	2012[1]	Average annual percent change, 2010–2012
Total Population	4,041,769	4,339,367	4,380,415	0.3
Percent of total U.S. population	1.4	1.4	1.4	X
Sex				
Male	1,975,368	2,134,952	2,157,711	0.4
Female	2,066,401	2,204,425	2,222,704	0.3
Age				
Under 5 years	265,901	282,367	279,535	-0.3
5 to 19 years	847,743	863,837	852,571	-0.4
20 to 64 years	2,423,332	2,614,936	2,633,656	0.2
65 years and over	504,793	578,227	614,653	2.0
Median age (years)	35.9	38.1	38.3	0.2
Race and Hispanic Origin				
One race				
White	3,640,889	3,864,193	3,882,987	0.2
Black	295,994	342,804	354,119	1.1
American Indian and Alaska Native	8,616	12,105	12,429	0.9
Asian	29,744	50,177	55,336	3.1
Native Hawaiian or Other Pacific Islander	1,460	3,199	3,441	2.3
Two or more races	42,443	66,889	72,103	2.4
Hispanic (of any race)	59,939	138,618	148,394	2.2

X = Not applicable.
[1] Population figures for 2012 are July 1 estimates. The 2010 estimates are taken from the 2010 Census.

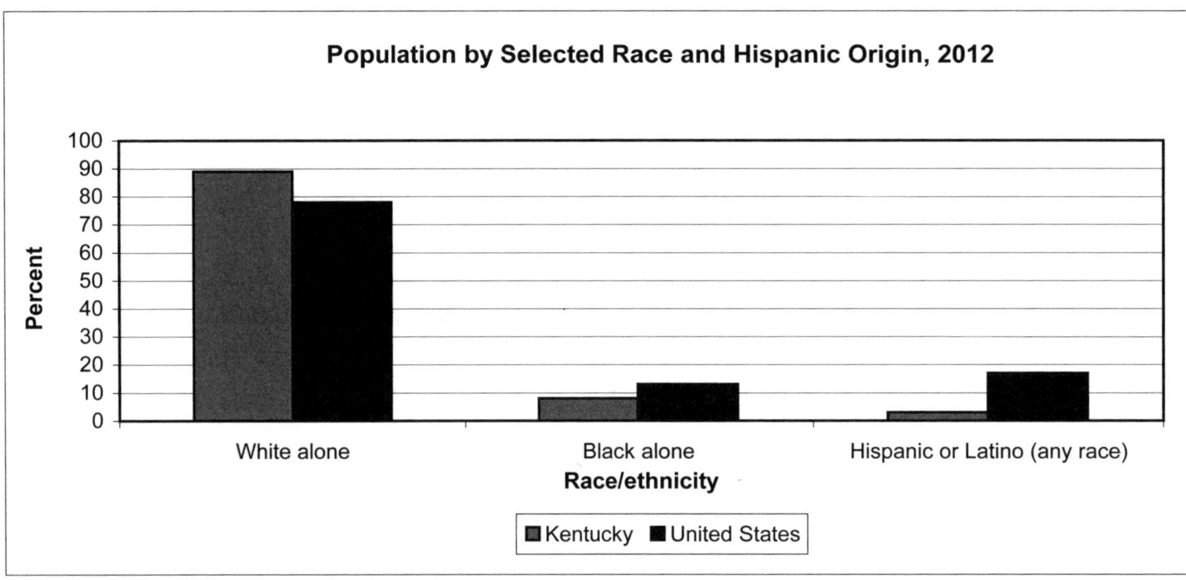

Table KY-2. Marital Status

(Number, percent distribution.)

Sex, age, race, and Hispanic origin	2000	2010	2011
Males, 15 Years and Over	1,551,174	1,702,020	1,710,913
Never married	25.9	30.8	31.2
Now married, except separated	59.9	52.0	51.5
Separated	1.5	2.1	2.2
Widowed	2.6	2.8	2.9
Divorced	10.2	12.3	12.2
Females, 15 Years and Over	1,665,993	1,794,164	1,807,329
Never married	19.7	24.2	24.6
Now married, except separated	55.0	48.9	48.5
Separated	2.1	2.6	2.5
Widowed	11.5	10.6	10.3
Divorced	11.8	13.7	14.1

Table KY-3. Households and Housing Characteristics

(Number, percent, dollars.)

Item	2000	2010	2011	Average annual percent change, 2000–2011
Total Households	1,590,647	1,684,348	1,672,134	0.4
Family households	1,104,398	1,126,685	1,119,880	0.1
Married-couple family	857,944	833,872	827,519	-0.3
Other family	246,454	292,813	292,361	1.6
Male householder, no wife present	58,497	76,832	75,067	2.4
Female householder, no husband present	187,957	215,981	217,294	1.3
Nonfamily households	486,249	557,663	552,254	1.1
Householder living alone	414,095	470,103	471,518	1.2
Householder not living alone	72,154	87,560	80,736	1.0
Housing Characteristics				
Total housing units	1,750,927	1,928,617	1,932,731	0.9
Occupied housing units	1,590,647	1,684,348	1,672,134	0.4
Owner occupied	1,125,397	1,156,292	1,151,479	0.2
Renter occupied	465,250	528,056	520,655	1.0
Average size	2.47	2.51	2.54	0.2
Financial Characteristics				
Median gross rent of renter-occupied housing	445	613	626	3.4
Median monthly owner costs for housing units with a mortgage	816	1,072	1,092	2.8
Median value of owner-occupied housing units	86,700	121,600	120,600	3.3

Table KY-4. Migration, Origin, and Language

(Number, percent.)

Characteristic	State			U.S.		
	2010	2011	Percent change	2010	2011	Percent change
Residence 1 Year Ago						
Population 1 year and over	4,296,639	4,316,297	0.5	305,628,607	307,900,319	0.7
Same house	84.7	85.4	0.8	84.6	84.8	0.2
Different house in the U.S.	14.9	14.3	-4.0	14.8	14.6	-1.4
Same county	8.7	8.4	-3.4	9.4	9.2	-2.1
Different county	6.2	5.9	-4.8	5.4	5.4	-
Same state	3.4	3.3	-2.9	3.2	3.1	-3.1
Different state	2.8	2.5	-10.7	2.2	2.3	4.5
Abroad	0.5	0.3	-40.0	0.6	0.6	-
Place of Birth						
Native born	4,205,683	4,228,923	0.6	269,393,835	271,214,059	0.7
Male	49.1	49.0	-0.2	49.2	49.2	-
Female	50.9	51.0	0.2	50.8	50.8	-
Foreign born	140,583	140,433	-0.1	39,955,854	40,377,860	1.1
Male	52.6	51.6	-1.9	49.1	48.9	-0.4
Female	47.4	48.4	2.1	50.9	51.1	0.4
Foreign born; naturalized U.S. citizen	48,069	49,981	4.0	17,476,082	18,140,192	3.8
Male	45.7	48.3	5.7	45.8	45.8	-
Female	54.3	51.7	-4.8	54.2	54.2	-
Foreign born; not a U.S. citizen	92,514	90,452	-2.2	22,479,772	22,237,668	-1.1
Male	56.3	53.5	-5.0	51.6	51.5	-0.2
Female	43.7	46.5	6.4	48.4	48.5	0.2
Entered 2000 or later	51.1	54.6	6.8	34.7	35.7	2.9
Entered 1990 to 1999	25.8	23.0	-10.9	27.2	26.7	-1.8
Entered before 1990	23.1	22.4	-3.0	38.1	37.6	-1.3
World Region of Birth, Foreign						
Foreign-born population, excluding population born at sea	140,583	140,433	-0.1	39,955,673	40,377,757	1.1
Europe	18.0	15.4	-14.4	12.1	12.1	-
Asia	30.9	32.9	6.5	28.2	28.6	1.4
Africa	5.6	9.2	64.3	4	4.1	2.5
Oceania	0.7	0.5	-28.6	0.5	0.5	-
Latin America	42.7	38.4	-10.1	53.1	52.6	-0.9
North America	2.1	3.6	71.4	2	2.0	-
Language Spoken at Home and Ability to Speak English						
Population 5 years and over	4,066,511	4,090,258	0.6	289,215,746	291,524,091	0.8
English only	95.2	95.2	-	79.4	79.2	-0.3
Language other than English	4.8	4.8	-	20.6	20.8	1.0
Speaks English less than "very well"	2.1	2.0	-4.8	8.7	8.7	-

- = Zero or rounds to zero.

Table KY-5. Median Income and Poverty Status, 2011

(Number, percent, except as noted.)

Characteristic	State		U.S.	
	Number	Percent	Number	Percent
Median Income				
Households (dollars)	41,141	X	50,502	X
Families (dollars)	51,917	X	61,455	X
Below Poverty Level (All People)	811,277	19.1	48,452,035	15.9
Sex				
Male	362,007	17.5	21,825,281	14.7
Female	449,270	20.7	26,626,754	17.2
Age				
Under 18 years	275,394	27.4	16,386,500	22.5
Related children under 18 years	269,406	27.0	16,087,074	22.2
18 to 64 years	468,189	17.6	28,335,079	14.8
65 years and over	67,694	11.8	3,730,456	9.3

X = Not applicable.

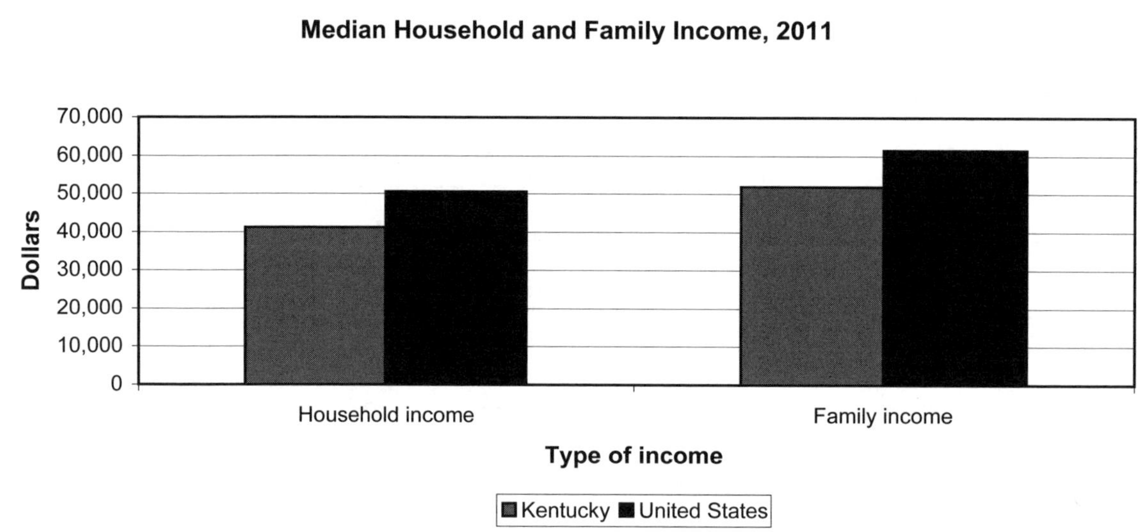

Table KY-6. Health Insurance Coverage Status for the Civilian Noninstitutionalized Population and Children Under 18 Years of Age

(Numbers in thousands, percent.)

Item	2004	2005	2006	2007	2008	2009	2010	2011
Civilian Noninstitutionalized Population	4,074	4,052	4,106	4,207	4,188	4,225	4,243	4,284
Covered by Private or Public Insurance								
Number	3,518	3,554	3,467	3,637	3,598	3,612	3,596	3,666
Percent	86.4	87.7	84.4	86.4	85.9	85.5	84.7	85.6
Not Covered								
Number	556	498	639	570	590	613	647	618
Percent	13.6	12.3	15.6	13.6	14.1	14.5	15.3	14.4
Percent in the U.S. not covered	14.9	15.3	15.8	15.3	15.1	15.1	15.5	15.1
Children Under 18 Years of Age	981	991	1,006	1,026	1,004	1,015	1,018	1,023
Covered by Private or Public Insurance								
Number	901	924	908	944	934	951	957	961
Percent	91.8	93.3	90.3	92.0	93.0	93.7	94.0	93.9
Not Covered								
Number	81	67	98	82	70	64	61	62
Percent	8.2	6.7	9.7	8.0	7.0	6.3	6.0	6.1
Percent in the U.S. not covered	10.5	10.9	11.7	11.0	9.7	8.6	8.0	7.5

Table KY-7. Employment Status by Demographic Group, Preliminary 2012

(Numbers in thousands, percent.)

Characteristic	Civilian noninstitutional population	Civilian labor force		Employed		Unemployed	
		Number	Percent of population	Number	Percent of population	Number	Percent of population
Total	3,394	2,074	61.1	1,908	56.2	166	8.0
Sex							
Male	1,633	1,090	66.8	995	61.0	95	8.7
Female	1,761	984	55.8	913	51.8	71	7.2
Race, Sex, and Hispanic Origin							
White	3,066	1,845	60.2	1,705	55.6	140	7.6
Male	1,476	980	66.4	898	60.9	81	8.3
Female	1,590	865	54.4	807	50.7	58	6.8
Black or African American	236	159	67.3	137	58.2	21	13.5
Male	108	74	68.0	63	58.3	11	14.3
Female	127	85	66.7	74	58.2	11	12.8
Hispanic	99	72	72.0	66	66.5	5	7.6
Male	64	51	80.7	47	73.6	5	8.9
Female	36	20	56.5	19	54.0	1	4.3
Age							
16 to 19 years	226	90	39.8	68	30.2	22	24.2
20 to 24 years	332	251	75.7	215	64.9	36	14.2
25 to 34 years	541	438	81.0	397	73.4	41	9.4
35 to 44 years	629	468	74.3	445	70.8	22	4.8
45 to 54 years	563	314	55.9	303	53.8	12	3.8
55 to 64 years	584	87	14.9	81	13.9	6	7.1
65 years and over	216	35	16.1	34	15.6	1	3.4

NOTE: Data in Table 7 are from the Current Population Survey (CPS) and do not match the estimates in Table 8. See notes and definitions for further information.

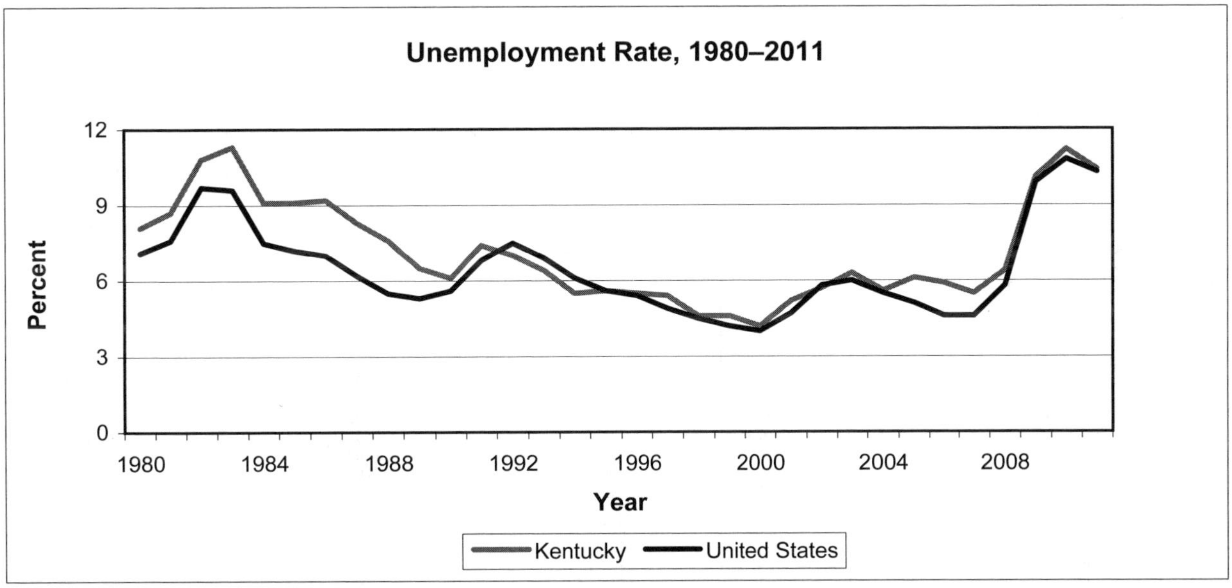

Table KY-8. Employment Status of the Civilian Noninstitutional Population Age 16 Years and Over

(Number, percent.)

Year	Civilian labor force	Civilian participation rate	Employed	Unemployed	Unemployment rate
2005	1,992,625	62.2	1,871,981	120,644	6.1
2006	2,027,794	62.6	1,908,784	119,010	5.9
2007	2,036,459	62.3	1,923,471	112,988	5.5
2008	2,042,915	61.9	1,911,240	131,675	6.4
2009	2,059,592	60.3	1,851,458	208,134	10.1
2010	2,044,016	59.5	1,815,971	228,045	11.2
2011	2,052,108	59.4	1,838,401	213,707	10.4

Table KY-9. Employment and Average Wages by Industry

(Estimates before 2007 are based on the 2002 *North American Industry Classification System* [NAICS]. Estimates from 2007 onward are based on the 2007 NAICS.)

Industry	2005	2006	2007	2008	2009	2010	2011
				Number of jobs			
Wage and Salary Employment by Industry	1,908,096	1,934,749	1,956,992	1,950,323	1,871,120	1,876,202	1,900,942
Farm Wage and Salary Employment	15,510	15,282	14,655	14,146	12,629	12,847	13,783
Nonfarm Wage and Salary Employment	1,892,586	1,919,467	1,942,337	1,936,177	1,858,491	1,863,355	1,887,159
Private wage and salary employment	1,537,808	1,558,010	1,575,798	1,565,902	1,483,765	1,478,322	1,501,396
Forestry, fishing, and related activities	7,348	7,433	7,400	7,594	7,351	7,362	7,437
Mining	20,888	22,551	21,735	23,671	23,299	21,807	22,654
Utilities	6,455	6,487	6,590	6,453	6,501	6,424	6,522
Construction	87,678	86,513	88,493	88,033	77,487	71,126	71,270
Manufacturing	262,372	261,284	255,994	245,322	213,078	209,208	213,009
Durable goods manufacturing	166,987	166,824	162,385	153,729	127,339	124,800	128,920
Nondurable goods manufacturing	95,385	94,460	93,609	91,593	85,739	84,408	84,089
Wholesale trade	75,452	76,663	78,230	77,519	73,268	72,395	72,816
Retail trade	214,713	214,691	217,042	213,372	204,735	203,527	204,083
Transportation and warehousing	85,576	86,996	89,801	88,992	83,173	83,287	86,108
Information	28,489	28,907	29,477	29,192	27,206	26,277	26,849
Finance and insurance	70,054	73,240	72,467	73,261	71,045	69,826	70,243
Real estate and rental and leasing	20,408	20,557	19,957	20,166	19,164	18,978	18,465
Professional, scientific, and technical services	61,252	63,453	67,085	70,664	71,154	70,580	70,323
Management of companies and enterprises	16,026	16,282	19,487	19,582	19,700	19,454	19,563
Administrative and waste services	97,087	101,736	101,489	95,691	83,516	92,469	99,465
Educational services	28,237	28,415	29,011	29,125	29,794	30,613	31,673
Health care and social assistance	205,430	208,899	212,476	216,916	219,644	222,834	226,556
Arts, entertainment, and recreation	18,864	19,134	20,004	19,967	19,779	18,950	18,845
Accommodation and food services	147,970	151,576	155,009	154,499	150,416	150,872	152,893
Other services, except public administration	83,509	83,193	84,051	85,883	83,455	82,333	82,622
Government and government enterprises	354,778	361,457	366,539	370,275	374,726	385,033	385,763
				Dollars			
Average Wages and Salaries by Industry	33,633	34,854	36,182	37,207	37,783	38,532	39,538
Average Farm Wages and Salaries	15,808	18,329	21,534	21,403	22,775	20,748	17,634
Average Nonfarm Wages and Salaries	33,779	34,985	36,293	37,323	37,885	38,655	39,698
Average private wages and salaries	33,437	34,597	35,918	36,732	37,264	38,090	39,080
Forestry, fishing, and related activities	22,590	24,469	24,876	25,728	26,215	26,453	26,682
Mining	52,250	55,499	56,778	61,405	63,143	67,281	69,509
Utilities	60,277	63,302	64,176	67,238	70,540	70,655	72,214
Construction	35,749	37,311	39,560	42,062	43,479	43,597	44,021
Manufacturing	43,961	45,357	46,894	47,555	47,944	49,665	51,294
Durable goods manufacturing	45,478	46,848	48,362	48,853	49,507	51,125	53,250
Nondurable goods manufacturing	41,304	42,725	44,347	45,376	45,622	47,506	48,295
Wholesale trade	46,513	48,197	50,733	51,269	51,022	51,741	53,665
Retail trade	21,293	21,982	22,410	22,719	23,356	23,743	24,117
Transportation and warehousing	43,406	43,618	46,336	45,791	46,490	47,938	47,876
Information	38,567	40,349	40,380	41,598	42,749	43,463	44,510
Finance and insurance	47,878	50,505	52,479	53,410	53,825	56,627	58,941
Real estate and rental and leasing	27,834	28,715	31,906	32,268	32,233	33,474	35,370
Professional, scientific, and technical services	46,366	48,241	49,603	49,993	49,913	50,984	52,753
Management of companies and enterprises	81,660	86,073	83,863	82,602	81,553	86,292	92,016
Administrative and waste services	21,037	21,906	22,679	24,093	25,148	25,445	25,779
Educational services	20,997	21,046	21,596	22,346	23,467	24,318	24,649
Health care and social assistance	35,056	36,224	37,742	38,881	40,139	40,801	41,958
Arts, entertainment, and recreation	20,151	21,192	22,346	21,450	20,804	21,594	21,953
Accommodation and food services	13,538	13,813	14,389	14,358	14,775	15,294	15,635
Other services, except public administration	22,986	23,548	24,303	25,670	26,183	26,923	27,379
Government and government enterprises	35,262	36,658	37,905	39,821	40,344	40,825	42,105

Table KY-10. Employment Characteristics by Family Type

(Number, percent.)

Family type and labor force status	2009		2010		2011	
	Total	Families with own children under 18 years	Total	Families with own children under 18 years	Total	Families with own children under 18 years
All families	1,146,621	507,942	1,126,685	484,616	1,119,880	475,828
Family type and labor force status						
Married-couple families	855,676	339,098	833,872	316,214	827,519	312,461
Both husband and wife in labor force	50.8	66.0	49.4	65.1	49.7	66.6
Husband in labor force, wife not in labor force	21.2	25.0	20.8	26.0	20.9	25.7
Wife in labor force, husband not in labor force	9.0	5.0	9.3	5.4	8.9	4.7
Both husband and wife not in labor force	18.9	3.9	20.5	3.5	20.4	3.1
Other families	290,945	168,844	292,813	168,402	292,361	163,367
Female householder, no husband present	76.2	80.1	73.8	76.2	74.3	76.1
In labor force	48.4	58.9	47.4	57.8	47.3	59.1
Not in labor force	27.8	21.2	26.4	18.4	27.0	17.0
Male householder, no wife present	23.8	19.9	26.2	23.8	25.7	23.9
In labor force	16.8	16.8	18.4	20.4	18.1	19.8
Not in labor force	7.0	3.0	7.8	3.4	7.6	4.0

Table KY-11. School Enrollment and Educational Attainment, 2011

(Number, percent.)

Item	State	U.S.
Enrollment		
Total population 3 years and over, enrolled in school	1,127,708	83,131,910
Enrolled in nursery school or preschool (percent)	5.6	6.0
Enrolled in kindergarten (percent)	5.5	5.1
Enrolled in elementary school, grades 1-8 (percent)	40.5	39.5
Enrolled in high school, grades 9-12 (percent)	21.0	20.7
Enrolled in college or graduate school (percent)	27.4	28.7
Attainment		
Total population 25 years and over	2,922,350	206,471,670
Less than ninth grade (percent)	7.0	6.0
9th to 12th grade, no diploma (percent)	10.0	8.1
High school graduate, including equivalency (percent)	34.1	28.4
Some college, no degree (percent)	20.9	21.2
Associate's degree (percent)	7.0	7.8
Bachelor's degree (percent)	12.3	17.9
Graduate or professional degree (percent)	8.8	10.6
High school graduate or higher (percent)	83.1	85.9
Bachelor's degree or higher (percent)	21.1	28.5

Table KY-12. Educational Indicators

(Number, percent; data derived from National Center of Education Statistics.)

Item	State	U.S.
Public Schools, 2009–2010 (except where noted)		
Number of school districts	174	13,629
Number of schools	1,542	99,834
Number of students (in thousands)	680	49,373
Student-teacher ratio	15.3	15.4
Expenditures per student (dollars)	10,436	10,591
Averaged freshman graduation rate, 2008–2009	77.6	75.5[1]
Dropout rate, 2008–2009	2.9	4.1
Students eligible for free or reduced-price lunch (percent)	56.5	48.0
English language learners, 2010–2011 (percent)	2.4	9.8[1]
Students with IEP (percent)	15.6	13.1
Private Schools, 2009–2010 (except where noted)		
Number of schools	358	33,366
Number of students (in thousands)	61	4,700
High school graduates, 2008–2009	3,937	308,813
Student-teacher ratio	11.6	10.7

[1] U.S. total includes estimates for nonreporting states.

Table KY-13. Reported Voting and Registration of the Voting-Age Population, November 2012

(Numbers in thousands, percent.)

Item	Total population	Total citizen population	Registered			Voted		
			Total registered	Percent registered (total population)	Percent registered (total citizen population)	Total voted	Percent voted (total population)	Percent voted (total citizen population)
U.S. Total	235,248	215,081	153,157	65.1	71.2	132,948	56.5	61.8
State Total	3,291	3,194	2,303	70.0	72.1	1,895	57.6	59.3
Sex								
Male	1,581	1,531	1,041	65.8	68.0	843	53.3	55.1
Female	1,710	1,663	1,262	73.8	75.9	1,052	61.5	63.3
Race								
White alone	2,966	2,899	2,091	70.5	72.1	1,733	58.4	59.8
White, non-Hispanic alone	2,908	2,886	2,082	71.6	72.1	1,723	59.3	59.7
Black alone	223	220	162	72.8	73.8	125	56.1	56.9
Asian alone	61	33	14	B	B	5	B	B
Hispanic (of any race)	82	34	20	24.0	B	13	15.5	B
Age								
18 to 24 years	446	437	225	50.5	51.6	165	37.1	37.9
25 to 44 years	1,060	996	731	69.0	73.4	565	53.3	56.7
45 to 64 years	1,173	1,152	879	74.9	76.3	757	64.6	65.7
65 to 74 years	357	352	258	72.5	73.4	223	62.4	63.3
75 years and over	256	256	210	81.8	81.8	185	72.3	72.3

B = Base is less than 75,000 and therefore too small to show the derived measure.

Table KY-14. Crime

(Number, rate per 100,000. Data are derived from the FBI Uniform Crime Reports.)

Item	State			U.S.		
	2010	2011	Percent change	2010	2011	Percent change
TOTAL POPULATION	4,347,223	4,369,356	0.5	309,330,219	311,591,917	0.7
VIOLENT CRIME						
Number	10,604	10,406	-1.9	1,251,248	1,203,564	-3.8
Rate	243.9	238.2	-2.3	404.5	386.3	-4.5
Murder and Nonnegligent Manslaughter						
Number	188	153	-18.6	14,722	14,612	-0.7
Rate	4.3	3.5	-18.6	4.8	4.7	-2.1
Forcible Rape						
Number	1,438	1,463	1.7	85,593	83,425	-2.5
Rate	33.1	33.5	1.2	27.7	26.8	-3.2
Robbery						
Number	3,748	3,693	-1.5	369,089	354,396	-4.0
Rate	86.2	84.5	-2.0	119.3	113.7	-4.7
Aggravated Assault						
Number	5,230	5,097	-2.5	781,844	751,131	-3.9
Rate	120.3	116.7	-3.0	252.8	241.1	-4.6
PROPERTY CRIME						
Number	111,170	118,358	6.5	9,112,625	9,063,173	-0.5
Rate	2,557.3	2,708.8	5.9	2,945.9	2,908.7	-1.3
Burglary						
Number	30,443	32,553	6.9	2,168,459	2,188,005	0.9
Rate	700.3	745.0	6.4	701.0	702.2	0.2
Larceny-Theft						
Number	74,488	79,132	6.2	6,204,601	6,159,795	-0.7
Rate	1,713.5	1,811.1	5.7	2,005.8	1,976.9	-1.4
Motor Vehicle Theft						
Number	6,239	6,673	7.0	739,565	715,373	-3.3
Rate	143.5	152.7	6.4	239.1	229.6	-4.0

Table KY-15. State Government Finances, 2011

(Dollar amounts in thousands, percent distribution.)

Item	Dollars	Percent distribution
Total Revenue	31,056,300	100.0
General revenue	23,572,816	100.0
Intergovernmental revenue	9,025,194	38.3
Taxes	10,203,241	43.3
General sales	2,896,252	12.3
Selective sales	1,998,095	8.5
License taxes	472,828	2.0
Individual income tax	3,417,779	14.5
Corporate income tax	516,523	2.2
Other taxes	901,764	3.8
Current charges	3,087,125	13.1
Miscellaneous general revenue	1,257,256	5.3
Utility revenue	0	0.0
Liquor stores revenue	0	0.0
Insurance trust revenue [1]	7,483,484	31.7
Total Expenditure	29,369,940	100.0
Intergovernmental expenditure	5,069,137	17.3
Direct expenditure	24,300,803	82.7
Current operation	16,042,722	54.6
Capital outlay	2,041,224	7.0
Insurance benefits and repayments	4,693,757	16.0
Assistance and subsidies	831,120	2.8
Interest on debt	691,980	2.4
Exhibit: Salaries and wages	3,873,887	13.2
Total Expenditure	29,369,940	100.0
General expenditure	24,676,183	84.0
Intergovernmental expenditure	5,069,137	17.3
Direct expenditure	19,607,046	66.8
General expenditure, by function:		
Education	9,415,111	32.1
Public welfare	7,334,231	25.0
Hospitals	1,135,081	3.9
Health	770,728	2.6
Highways	1,935,661	6.6
Police protection	195,356	0.7
Correction	518,890	1.8
Natural resources	357,155	1.2
Parks and recreation	110,142	0.4
Governmental administration	879,616	3.0
Interest on general debt	691,980	2.4
Other and unallocable	1,332,232	4.5
Utility expenditure	0	0.0
Liquor stores expenditure	0	0.0
Insurance trust expenditure	4,693,757	16.0
Debt at End of Fiscal Year	14,522,026	X
Cash and Security Holdings	39,925,843	X

X = Not applicable.

[1] Within insurance trust revenue, net earnings of state retirement systems is a calculated statistic (the item code in the data file is X08), and thus can be positive or negative. Net earnings is the sum of earnings on investments plus gains on investments minus losses on investments. The change made in 2002 for asset valuation from book to market value in accordance with Statement 34 of the Governmental Accounting Standards Board is reflected in the calculated statistics.

Table KY-16. State Government Tax Collections, 2012

(Dollars in thousands, percent.)

Item	Dollars	Percent distribution
Total Taxes	10,472,861	100.0
Property taxes	529,567	5.1
Sales and gross receipts	5,034,577	48.1
General sales and gross receipts	3,052,236	29.1
Selective sales and gross receipts	1,982,341	18.9
Alcoholic beverages	118,253	1.1
Amusements	164	-
Insurance premiums	133,070	1.3
Motor fuels	790,229	7.5
Pari-mutuels	3,601	-
Public utilities	64,919	0.6
Tobacco products	276,544	2.6
Other selective sales	595,561	5.7
Licenses	430,937	4.1
Alcoholic beverages	6,610	0.1
Amusements	272	-
Corporations in general	99,585	1.0
Hunting and fishing	27,344	0.3
Motor vehicle	188,714	1.8
Motor vehicle operators	15,738	0.2
Public utilities	0	0.0
Occupation and business, NEC	87,855	0.8
Other licenses	4,819	-
Income taxes	4,087,239	39.0
Individual income	3,512,075	33.5
Corporation net income	575,164	5.5
Other taxes	390,541	3.7
Death and gift	41,313	0.4
Documentary and stock transfer	3,178	-
Severance	346,050	3.3
Taxes, NEC	0	0.0

- = Rounds to zero.

Leading Exports, 2012

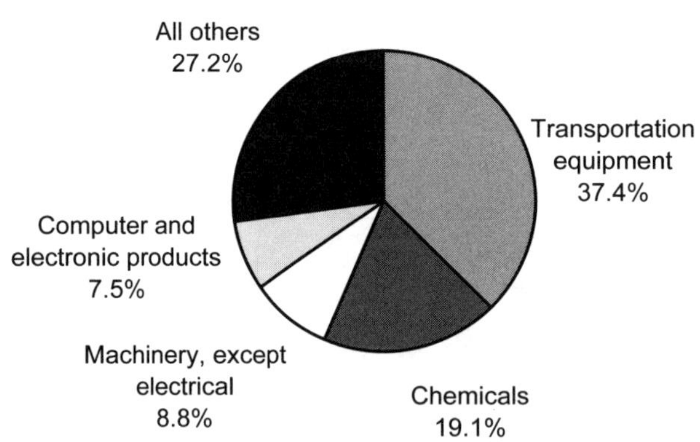

LOUISIANA

Facts and Figures

Location: South central United States; bordered on the N by Arkansas, on the E by Mississippi, on the S by the Gulf of Mexico, and on the W by Texas

Area: 51,840 sq. mi. (134,264 sq. km.); rank—31st

Population: 4,601,893 (2012 est.); rank—25th

Principal Cities: capital—Baton Rouge; largest—New Orleans

Statehood: April 30, 1812; 18th state

U.S. Congress: 2 senators, 6 representatives

State Motto: Union, Justice, Confidence

State Song: "Give Me Louisiana"

State Nicknames: The Pelican State; The Bayou State

Abbreviations: LA; La.

State Symbols: flower—magnolia; tree—bald cypress; bird—Eastern brown pelican

At a Glance

- With an increase in population of 0.5 percent, Louisiana ranked 46th in population growth from 2000 to 2009.
- An estimated 28,700 marriages took place in Louisiana in 2009; Louisiana does not report its number of divorces.
- Louisiana's median household income in 2007 was $41,374, and 20.4 percent of the population lived below the poverty level.
- Louisiana's violent crime rate in 2007 was 555.3 per 100,000 population, compared to 386.3 for the entire nation.
- In the 2012 election, 66.3 percent of Louisiana's eligible voters voted, compared to 61.8 percent of eligible voters nationwide.
- In 2007, Louisiana exported $695 million worth of agricultural products, less than 1 percent of the U.S. total.

Table LA-1. Population by Age, Sex, Race, and Hispanic Origin

(Number, percent, except where noted.)

Sex, age, race, and Hispanic origin	2000	2010	2012[1]	Average annual percent change, 2010–2012
Total Population	4,468,976	4,533,372	4,601,893	0.5
Percent of total U.S. population	1.6	1.5	1.5	X
Sex				
Male	2,162,903	2,219,292	2,252,050	0.5
Female	2,306,073	2,314,080	2,349,843	0.5
Age				
Under 5 years	317,392	314,260	314,766	0.1
5 to 19 years	1,050,637	939,977	926,421	-0.5
20 to 64 years	2,584,018	2,721,278	2,765,501	0.5
65 years and over	516,929	557,857	595,205	2.1
Median age (years)	34.0	35.8	35.9	0.1
Race and Hispanic Origin				
One race				
White	2,856,161	2,902,875	2,930,137	0.3
Black	1,451,944	1,462,969	1,491,433	0.6
American Indian and Alaska Native	25,477	33,037	34,249	1.2
Asian	54,758	71,829	77,252	2.3
Native Hawaiian or Other Pacific Islander	1,240	2,588	2,781	2.3
Two or more races	48,265	60,074	66,041	3.0
Hispanic (of any race)	107,738	200,653	217,417	2.6

X = Not applicable.
[1] Population figures for 2012 are July 1 estimates. The 2010 estimates are taken from the 2010 Census.

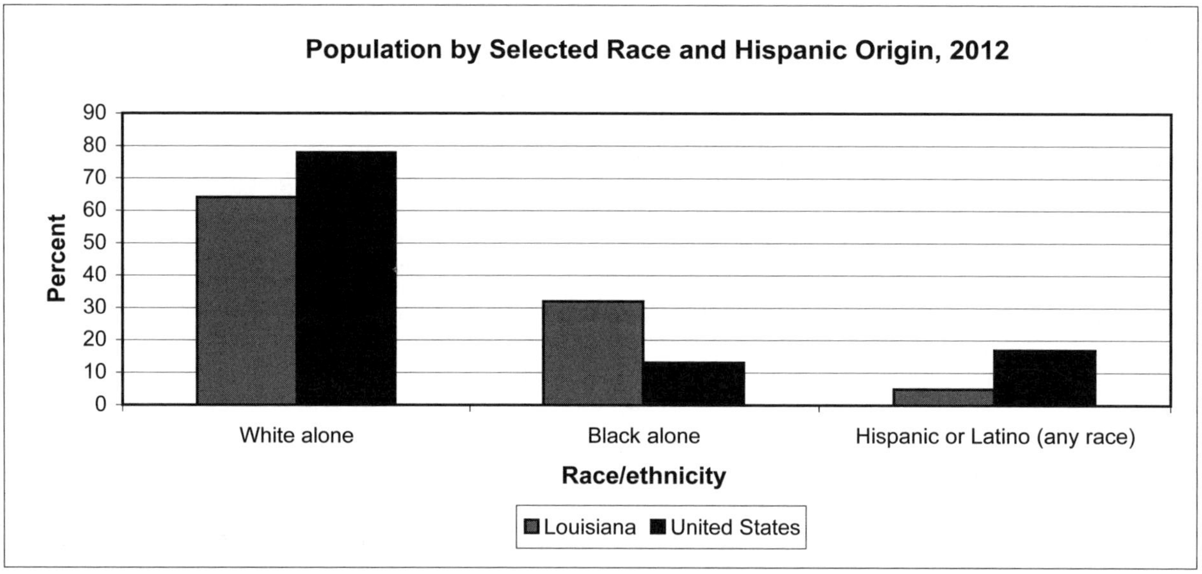

Table LA-2. Marital Status

(Number, percent distribution.)

Sex, age, race, and Hispanic origin	2000	2010	2011
Males, 15 Years and Over	1,648,133	1,751,556	1,758,929
Never married	31.2	37.0	37.7
Now married, except separated	54.5	47.2	46.6
Separated	2.2	2.2	2.2
Widowed	2.8	2.8	2.8
Divorced	9.2	10.8	10.8
Females, 15 Years and Over	1,828,247	1,861,490	1,882,493
Never married	26.3	30.8	31.6
Now married, except separated	48.2	42.6	41.7
Separated	2.9	3.2	3.3
Widowed	11.5	10.1	10.4
Divorced	11.1	13.3	13.1

Table LA-3. Households and Housing Characteristics

(Number, percent, dollars.)

Item	2000	2010	2011	Average annual percent change, 2000–2011
Total Households	1,656,053	1,689,822	1,702,030	0.2
Family households	1,156,438	1,129,117	1,118,217	-0.3
Married-couple family	809,498	753,423	743,138	-0.7
Other family	346,940	375,694	375,079	0.7
Male householder, no wife present	71,865	79,560	84,592	1.5
Female householder, no husband present	275,075	296,134	290,487	0.5
Nonfamily households	499,615	560,705	583,813	1.4
Householder living alone	419,200	468,853	492,531	1.5
Householder not living alone	80,415	91,852	91,282	1.1
Housing Characteristics				
Total housing units	1,847,181	1,967,947	1,978,974	0.6
Occupied housing units	1,656,053	1,689,822	1,702,030	0.2
Owner occupied	1,125,135	1,141,504	1,130,694	-
Renter occupied	530,918	548,318	571,336	0.6
Average size	2.62	2.61	2.61	-
Financial Characteristics				
Median gross rent of renter-occupied housing	466	736	747	5.0
Median monthly owner costs for housing units with a mortgage	816	1,163	1,176	3.7
Median value of owner-occupied housing units	85,000	137,500	139,400	5.3

- = Zero or rounds to zero.

Table LA-4. Migration, Origin, and Language

(Number, percent.)

Characteristic	State 2010	State 2011	State Percent change	U.S. 2010	U.S. 2011	U.S. Percent change
Residence 1 Year Ago						
Population 1 year and over	4,483,529	4,518,629	0.8	305,628,607	307,900,319	0.7
Same house	85.3	85.5	0.2	84.6	84.8	0.2
Different house in the U.S.	14.4	14.1	-2.1	14.8	14.6	-1.4
Same county	8.9	8.5	-4.5	9.4	9.2	-2.1
Different county	5.5	5.7	3.6	5.4	5.4	-
Same state	3.3	3.5	6.1	3.2	3.1	-3.1
Different state	2.2	2.2	-	2.2	2.3	4.5
Abroad	0.3	0.3	-	0.6	0.6	-
Place of Birth						
Native born	4,371,362	4,401,058	0.7	269,393,835	271,214,059	0.7
Male	48.7	48.7	-	49.2	49.2	-
Female	51.3	51.3	-	50.8	50.8	-
Foreign born	172,866	173,778	0.5	39,955,854	40,377,860	1.1
Male	55.9	53.4	-4.5	49.1	48.9	-0.4
Female	44.1	46.6	5.7	50.9	51.1	0.4
Foreign born; naturalized U.S. citizen	66,954	69,745	4.2	17,476,082	18,140,192	3.8
Male	51.5	47.6	-7.6	45.8	45.8	-
Female	48.5	52.4	8.0	54.2	54.2	-
Foreign born; not a U.S. citizen	105,912	104,033	-1.8	22,479,772	22,237,668	-1.1
Male	58.6	57.3	-2.2	51.6	51.5	-0.2
Female	41.4	42.7	3.1	48.4	48.5	0.2
Entered 2000 or later	45.2	46.8	3.5	34.7	35.7	2.9
Entered 1990 to 1999	20.3	20.1	-1.0	27.2	26.7	-1.8
Entered before 1990	34.5	33.1	-4.1	38.1	37.6	-1.3
World Region of Birth, Foreign						
Foreign-born population, excluding population born at sea	172,866	173,778	0.5	39,955,673	40,377,757	1.1
Europe	9.1	10.1	11.0	12.1	12.1	-
Asia	31.5	32.1	1.9	28.2	28.6	1.4
Africa	3.4	3.5	2.9	4	4.1	2.5
Oceania	0.6	0.4	-33.3	0.5	0.5	-
Latin America	53.7	52.5	-2.2	53.1	52.6	-0.9
North America	1.7	1.5	-11.8	2	2.0	-
Language Spoken at Home and Ability to Speak English						
Population 5 years and over	4,230,220	4,261,861	0.7	289,215,746	291,524,091	0.8
English only	91.1	91.3	0.2	79.4	79.2	-0.3
Language other than English	8.9	8.7	-2.2	20.6	20.8	1.0
Speaks English less than "very well"	2.8	2.9	3.6	8.7	8.7	-

- = Zero or rounds to zero.

Table LA-5. Median Income and Poverty Status, 2011

(Number, percent, except as noted.)

Characteristic	State		U.S.	
	Number	Percent	Number	Percent
Median Income				
Households (dollars)	41,734	X	50,502	X
Families (dollars)	53,601	X	61,455	X
Below Poverty Level (All People)	908,375	20.4	48,452,035	15.9
Sex				
Male	386,251	18.0	21,825,281	14.7
Female	522,124	22.7	26,626,754	17.2
Age				
Under 18 years	317,468	28.8	16,386,500	22.5
Related children under 18 years	314,203	28.6	16,087,074	22.2
18 to 64 years	520,986	18.7	28,335,079	14.8
65 years and over	69,921	12.7	3,730,456	9.3

X = Not applicable.

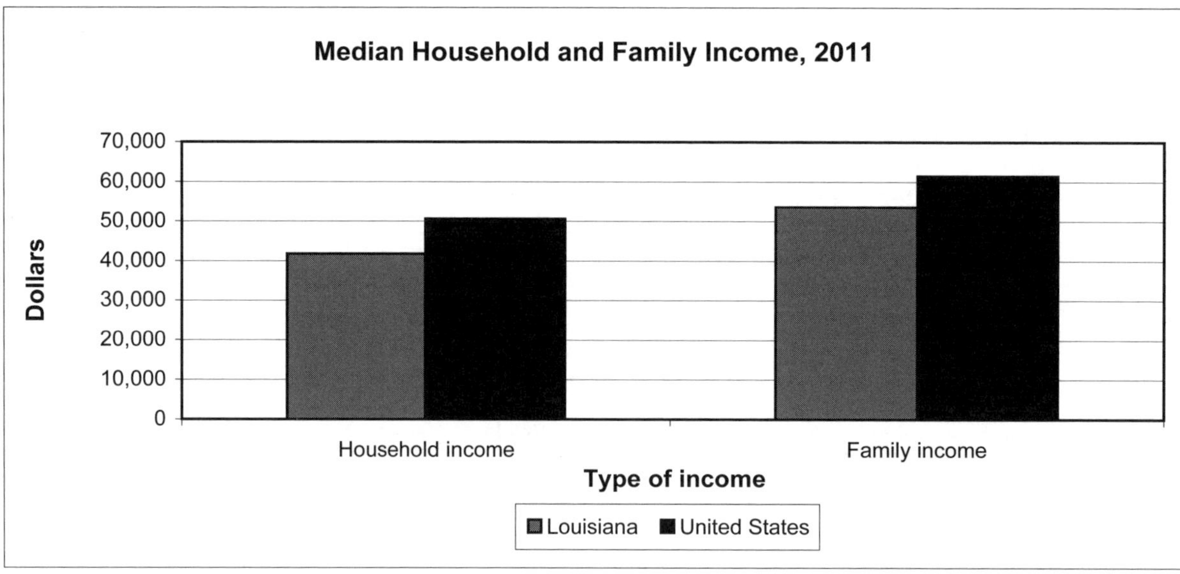

Table LA-6. Health Insurance Coverage Status for the Civilian Noninstitutionalized Population and Children Under 18 Years of Age

(Numbers in thousands, percent.)

Item	2004	2005	2006	2007	2008	2009	2010	2011
Civilian Noninstitutionalized Population	4,421	4,088	4,212	4,197	4,313	4,392	4,440	4,473
Covered by Private or Public Insurance								
Number	3,715	3,363	3,291	3,421	3,546	3,629	3,649	3,689
Percent	84.0	82.3	78.1	81.5	82.2	82.6	82.2	82.5
Not Covered								
Number	707	725	921	776	767	762	791	784
Percent	16.0	17.7	21.9	18.5	17.8	17.4	17.8	17.5
Percent in the U.S. not covered	14.9	15.3	15.8	15.3	15.1	15.1	15.5	15.1
Children Under 18 Years of Age	1,149	1,064	1,067	1,097	1,106	1,120	1,113	1,117
Covered by Private or Public Insurance								
Number	1,067	974	897	960	1,020	1,047	1,051	1,052
Percent	92.9	91.6	84.1	87.5	92.2	93.5	94.5	94.2
Not Covered								
Number	81	89	170	137	86	73	62	65
Percent	7.1	8.4	15.9	12.5	7.8	6.5	5.5	5.8
Percent in the U.S. not covered	10.5	10.9	11.7	11.0	9.7	8.6	8.0	7.5

Table LA-7. Employment Status by Demographic Group, Preliminary 2012

(Numbers in thousands, percent.)

Characteristic	Civilian noninstitutional population	Civilian labor force		Employed		Unemployed	
		Number	Percent of population	Number	Percent of population	Number	Percent of population
Total	3,500	2,078	59.4	1,932	55.2	147	7.1
Sex							
Male	1,661	1,106	66.6	1,027	61.8	79	7.1
Female	1,839	972	52.9	904	49.2	68	7.0
Race, Sex, and Hispanic Origin							
White	2,324	1,411	60.7	1,343	57.8	68	4.8
Male	1,133	790	69.8	758	66.9	32	4.1
Female	1,191	620	52.1	585	49.1	35	5.7
Black or African American	1,065	602	56.6	529	49.7	73	12.2
Male	477	279	58.5	237	49.7	42	15.0
Female	589	324	55.0	292	49.6	31	9.7
Hispanic	153	99	64.6	91	59.1	8	8.5
Male	81	63	77.7	59	73.0	4	6.1
Female	72	36	49.9	31	43.6	5	12.7
Age							
16 to 19 years	255	69	26.9	50	19.5	19	27.8
20 to 24 years	336	231	68.8	200	59.6	31	13.4
25 to 34 years	582	467	80.2	433	74.4	34	7.2
35 to 44 years	571	448	78.4	423	74.1	25	5.5
45 to 54 years	607	450	74.2	431	71.0	19	4.3
55 to 64 years	564	306	54.2	290	51.3	16	5.3
65 years and over	585	108	18.4	105	17.9	3	2.5

NOTE: Data in Table 7 are from the Current Population Survey (CPS) and do not match the estimates in Table 8. See notes and definitions for further information.

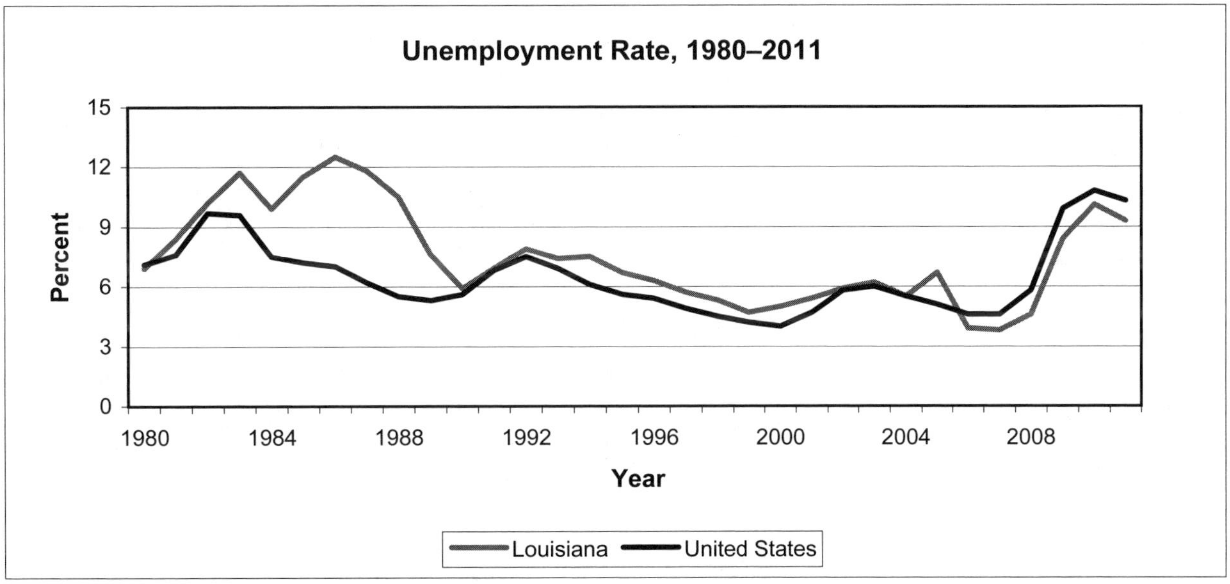

Table LA-8. Employment Status of the Civilian Noninstitutional Population Age 16 Years and Over

(Number, percent.)

Year	Civilian labor force	Civilian participation rate	Employed	Unemployed	Unemployment rate
2005	2,076,458	63.0	1,937,009	139,489	6.7
2006	1,985,462	61.8	1,907,465	78,007	3.9
2007	2,025,777	61.5	1,949,401	76,376	3.8
2008	2,078,935	62.3	1,983,220	95,715	4.6
2009	2,176,635	62.2	1,994,133	182,502	8.4
2010	2,187,678	61.6	1,967,523	220,155	10.1
2011	2,175,279	60.7	1,973,939	201,340	9.3

Table LA-9. Employment and Average Wages by Industry

(Estimates before 2007 are based on the 2002 *North American Industry Classification System* [NAICS]. Estimates from 2007 onward are based on the 2007 NAICS.)

Industry	2005	2006	2007	2008	2009	2010	2011
	Number of jobs						
Wage and Salary Employment by Industry	1,982,867	1,949,562	2,014,645	2,040,323	2,003,169	1,990,201	2,005,804
Farm Wage and Salary Employment	7,262	8,867	7,904	7,734	8,817	8,969	8,089
Nonfarm Wage and Salary Employment	1,975,605	1,940,695	2,006,741	2,032,589	1,994,352	1,981,232	1,997,715
Private wage and salary employment	1,568,746	1,558,008	1,617,588	1,631,605	1,587,934	1,572,459	1,600,373
Forestry, fishing, and related activities	7,421	7,287	7,387	7,311	7,062	7,230	7,227
Mining	41,805	45,321	47,789	51,888	48,039	48,652	49,902
Utilities	9,658	9,500	9,314	9,328	9,523	9,482	9,348
Construction	123,935	135,967	141,411	140,889	136,972	126,709	127,925
Manufacturing	152,059	152,502	157,536	152,927	142,703	137,621	139,983
Durable goods manufacturing	78,640	82,517	86,731	82,805	74,529	69,661	71,156
Nondurable goods manufacturing	73,419	69,985	70,805	70,122	68,174	67,960	68,827
Wholesale trade	74,239	73,415	76,624	76,499	72,598	71,035	72,873
Retail trade	222,376	223,120	228,862	228,562	224,211	221,236	224,125
Transportation and warehousing	71,865	72,023	74,394	75,311	70,438	69,810	72,335
Information	29,285	27,105	27,829	28,606	24,778	24,628	23,709
Finance and insurance	62,827	61,258	60,891	60,294	58,857	60,615	62,178
Real estate and rental and leasing	34,242	33,400	34,753	33,580	31,397	31,349	32,022
Professional, scientific, and technical services	75,182	79,066	82,942	83,757	80,848	80,830	82,403
Management of companies and enterprises	21,699	21,086	22,098	23,512	24,189	23,860	24,368
Administrative and waste services	93,295	96,552	99,418	99,858	91,546	91,510	92,439
Educational services	34,703	33,386	34,499	36,063	36,795	37,716	39,051
Health care and social assistance	213,186	205,999	216,247	224,622	232,150	236,656	240,782
Arts, entertainment, and recreation	35,779	30,987	33,230	33,506	28,899	28,522	28,412
Accommodation and food services	164,650	155,526	162,934	165,158	168,102	168,568	174,942
Other services, except public administration	100,540	94,508	99,430	99,934	98,827	96,430	96,349
Government and government enterprises	406,859	382,687	389,153	400,984	406,418	408,773	397,342
	Dollars						
Average Wages and Salaries by Industry	34,301	37,256	39,029	41,097	41,216	42,181	43,154
Average Farm Wages and Salaries	21,570	18,711	23,039	21,339	18,758	18,557	18,447
Average Nonfarm Wages and Salaries	34,348	37,340	39,092	41,172	41,315	42,288	43,254
Average private wages and salaries	34,172	37,602	39,231	41,181	41,190	42,276	43,353
Forestry, fishing, and related activities	27,311	28,595	29,924	31,593	30,515	32,382	33,109
Mining	65,334	72,641	75,708	82,414	79,934	82,129	85,218
Utilities	65,655	62,481	66,426	73,578	73,572	72,406	76,596
Construction	36,747	42,816	45,957	50,192	51,721	51,220	51,894
Manufacturing	50,635	53,650	55,474	58,606	58,888	61,563	64,047
Durable goods manufacturing	43,710	47,116	49,074	51,827	51,561	54,313	56,764
Nondurable goods manufacturing	58,051	61,354	63,315	66,611	66,898	68,994	71,578
Wholesale trade	46,150	50,915	52,302	54,488	54,591	55,825	57,293
Retail trade	22,386	24,631	24,764	25,043	25,087	25,536	25,983
Transportation and warehousing	43,746	48,189	52,239	54,998	54,755	57,247	57,858
Information	41,714	44,044	44,885	45,494	48,121	49,770	51,482
Finance and insurance	47,161	49,945	52,328	53,342	52,520	55,110	58,855
Real estate and rental and leasing	34,245	40,060	42,174	43,294	42,759	45,710	48,216
Professional, scientific, and technical services	46,803	51,206	54,501	58,536	59,248	61,153	63,001
Management of companies and enterprises	60,542	60,115	64,741	67,830	65,151	67,592	71,194
Administrative and waste services	26,424	31,073	31,564	33,186	33,480	34,920	34,460
Educational services	25,865	27,029	29,038	30,973	32,485	33,256	33,857
Health care and social assistance	32,146	34,323	35,358	36,633	37,597	38,116	38,808
Arts, entertainment, and recreation	30,667	31,798	33,959	34,339	33,016	35,217	35,272
Accommodation and food services	14,999	16,392	17,556	17,572	18,089	18,898	19,152
Other services, except public administration	22,522	25,047	25,906	27,492	27,758	28,751	29,368
Government and government enterprises	35,029	36,275	38,512	41,139	41,803	42,333	42,855

Table LA-10. Employment Characteristics by Family Type

(Number, percent.)

Family type and labor force status	2009 Total	2009 Families with own children under 18 years	2010 Total	2010 Families with own children under 18 years	2011 Total	2011 Families with own children under 18 years
All families	1,128,899	509,334	1,129,117	492,766	1,118,217	489,469
Family type and labor force status						
Married-couple families	774,011	315,510	753,423	290,484	743,138	286,474
Both husband and wife in labor force	51.8	67.3	50.7	66.1	48.9	65.2
Husband in labor force, wife not in labor force	23.3	26.6	23.9	27.8	24.1	28.8
Wife in labor force, husband not in labor force	8.1	4.2	8.0	4.0	8.6	4.0
Both husband and wife not in labor force	16.8	1.9	17.4	2.1	18.5	1.9
Other families	354,888	193,824	375,694	202,282	375,079	202,995
Female householder, no husband present	78.1	80.4	78.8	81.6	77.4	80.6
In labor force	52.5	64.4	53.6	64.9	52.6	64.5
Not in labor force	25.6	16.0	25.3	16.7	24.8	16.2
Male householder, no wife present	21.9	19.6	21.2	18.4	22.6	19.4
In labor force	17.0	17.8	15.5	16.2	15.9	16.6
Not in labor force	4.9	1.9	5.7	2.2	6.6	2.7

Table LA-11. School Enrollment and Educational Attainment, 2011

(Number, percent.)

Item	State	U.S.
Enrollment		
Total population 3 years and over, enrolled in school	1,213,228	83,131,910
Enrolled in nursery school or preschool (percent)	7.0	6.0
Enrolled in kindergarten (percent)	5.3	5.1
Enrolled in elementary school, grades 1-8 (percent)	41.9	39.5
Enrolled in high school, grades 9-12 (percent)	20.1	20.7
Enrolled in college or graduate school (percent)	25.6	28.7
Attainment		
Total population 25 years and over	2,972,737	206,471,670
Less than ninth grade (percent)	6.1	6.0
9th to 12th grade, no diploma (percent)	11.4	8.1
High school graduate, including equivalency (percent)	34.5	28.4
Some college, no degree (percent)	21.7	21.2
Associate's degree (percent)	5.2	7.8
Bachelor's degree (percent)	14	17.9
Graduate or professional degree (percent)	7.1	10.6
High school graduate or higher (percent)	82.5	85.9
Bachelor's degree or higher (percent)	21.1	28.5

Table LA-12. Educational Indicators

(Number, percent; data derived from National Center of Education Statistics.)

Item	State	U.S.
Public Schools, 2009–2010 (except where noted)		
Number of school districts	69	13,629
Number of schools	1,488	99,834
Number of students (in thousands)	691	49,373
Student-teacher ratio	13.9	15.4
Expenditures per student (dollars)	12,098	10,591
Averaged freshman graduation rate, 2008–2009	67.3	75.5[1]
Dropout rate, 2008–2009	6.8	4.1
Students eligible for free or reduced-price lunch (percent)	65.5	48.0
English language learners, 2010–2011 (percent)	1.7	9.8[1]
Students with IEP (percent)	12.3	13.1
Private Schools, 2009–2010 (except where noted)		
Number of schools	458	33,366
Number of students (in thousands)	132	4,700
High school graduates, 2008–2009	8,136	308,813
Student-teacher ratio	13.1	10.7

[1] U.S. total includes estimates for nonreporting states.

Table LA-13. Reported Voting and Registration of the Voting-Age Population, November 2012

(Numbers in thousands, percent.)

Item	Total population	Total citizen population	Registered			Voted		
			Total registered	Percent registered (total population)	Percent registered (total citizen population)	Total voted	Percent voted (total population)	Percent voted (total citizen population)
U.S. Total	235,248	215,081	153,157	65.1	71.2	132,948	56.5	61.8
State Total	3,321	3,239	2,498	75.2	77.1	2,148	64.7	66.3
Sex								
Male	1,554	1,494	1,102	70.9	73.7	931	59.9	62.4
Female	1,766	1,745	1,396	79.0	80.0	1,217	68.9	69.7
Race								
White alone	2,242	2,174	1,681	75.0	77.3	1,421	63.4	65.4
White, non-Hispanic alone	2,141	2,128	1,644	76.8	77.3	1,389	64.9	65.2
Black alone	996	996	768	77.1	77.1	692	69.5	69.5
Asian alone	37	23	6	B	B	6	B	B
Hispanic (of any race)	125	70	57	45.3	B	48	38.1	B
Age								
18 to 24 years	431	415	226	52.5	54.6	174	40.4	42.0
25 to 44 years	1,122	1,078	821	73.1	76.1	709	63.2	65.8
45 to 64 years	1,199	1,184	968	80.7	81.7	846	70.5	71.4
65 to 74 years	335	332	294	87.7	88.4	258	77.1	77.8
75 years and over	233	230	189	80.9	82.2	161	69.1	70.2

B = Base is less than 75,000 and therefore too small to show the derived measure.

Table LA-14. Crime

(Number, rate per 100,000. Data are derived from the FBI Uniform Crime Reports.)

Item	State			U.S.		
	2010	2011	Percent change	2010	2011	Percent change
TOTAL POPULATION	4,545,343	4,574,836	0.6	309,330,219	311,591,917	0.7
VIOLENT CRIME						
Number	25,241	25,406	0.7	1,251,248	1,203,564	-3.8
Rate	555.3	555.3	0.0	404.5	386.3	-4.5
Murder and Nonnegligent Manslaughter						
Number	500	513	2.6	14,722	14,612	-0.7
Rate	11.0	11.2	1.8	4.8	4.7	-2.1
Forcible Rape						
Number	1,230	1,268	3.1	85,593	83,425	-2.5
Rate	27.1	27.7	2.2	27.7	26.8	-3.2
Robbery						
Number	5,297	5,239	-1.1	369,089	354,396	-4.0
Rate	116.5	114.5	-1.7	119.3	113.7	-4.7
Aggravated Assault						
Number	18,214	18,386	0.9	781,844	751,131	-3.9
Rate	400.7	401.9	0.3	252.8	241.1	-4.6
PROPERTY CRIME						
Number	165,667	168,744	1.9	9,112,625	9,063,173	-0.5
Rate	3,644.8	3,688.5	1.2	2,945.9	2,908.7	-1.3
Burglary						
Number	45,437	46,320	1.9	2,168,459	2,188,005	0.9
Rate	999.6	1,012.5	1.3	701.0	702.2	0.2
Larceny-Theft						
Number	110,260	113,301	2.8	6,204,601	6,159,795	-0.7
Rate	2,425.8	2,476.6	2.1	2,005.8	1,976.9	-1.4
Motor Vehicle Theft						
Number	9,970	9,123	-8.5	739,565	715,373	-3.3
Rate	219.3	199.4	-9.1	239.1	229.6	-4.0

Table LA-15. State Government Finances, 2011

(Dollar amounts in thousands, percent distribution.)

Item	Dollars	Percent distribution
Total Revenue	33,974,652	100.0
General revenue	26,939,024	79.3
Intergovernmental revenue	12,532,918	36.9
Taxes	8,865,421	26.1
General sales	2,812,804	8.3
Selective sales	2,318,406	6.8
License taxes	351,398	1.0
Individual income tax	2,403,956	7.1
Corporate income tax	196,732	0.6
Other taxes	782,125	2.3
Current charges	3,299,702	9.7
Miscellaneous general revenue	2,240,983	6.6
Utility revenue	6,442	0.0
Liquor stores revenue	0	0.0
Insurance trust revenue [1]	7,029,186	20.7
Total Expenditure	33,396,449	100.0
Intergovernmental expenditure	6,580,164	19.7
Direct expenditure	26,816,285	80.3
Current operation	18,352,257	55.0
Capital outlay	2,631,116	7.9
Insurance benefits and repayments	4,254,973	12.7
Assistance and subsidies	535,045	1.6
Interest on debt	1,042,894	3.1
Exhibit: Salaries and wages	4,341,385	13.0
Total Expenditure	33,396,449	100.0
General expenditure	29,134,952	87.2
Intergovernmental expenditure	6,580,164	19.7
Direct expenditure	22,554,788	67.5
General expenditure, by function:		
Education	8,904,101	26.7
Public welfare	6,425,818	19.2
Hospitals	2,205,036	6.6
Health	597,955	1.8
Highways	2,184,629	6.5
Police protection	402,723	1.2
Correction	757,363	2.3
Natural resources	876,502	2.6
Parks and recreation	343,450	1.0
Governmental administration	981,958	2.9
Interest on general debt	1,042,894	3.1
Other and unallocable	4,412,523	13.2
Utility expenditure	6,524	0.0
Liquor stores expenditure	0	0.0
Insurance trust expenditure	4,254,973	12.7
Debt at End of Fiscal Year	18,447,200	X
Cash and Security Holdings	57,034,702	X

X = Not applicable.

[1] Within insurance trust revenue, net earnings of state retirement systems is a calculated statistic (the item code in the data file is X08), and thus can be positive or negative. Net earnings is the sum of earnings on investments plus gains on investments minus losses on investments. The change made in 2002 for asset valuation from book to market value in accordance with Statement 34 of the Governmental Accounting Standards Board is reflected in the calculated statistics.

Table LA-16. State Government Tax Collections, 2012

(Dollars in thousands, percent.)

Item	Dollars	Percent distribution
Total Taxes	8,994,053	100.0
Property taxes	50,937	0.6
Sales and gross receipts	4,888,854	54.4
General sales and gross receipts	2,815,919	31.3
Selective sales and gross receipts	2,072,935	23.0
Alcoholic beverages	56,869	0.6
Amusements	671,080	7.5
Insurance premiums	357,043	4.0
Motor fuels	575,063	6.4
Pari-mutuels	5,037	0.1
Public utilities	12,796	0.1
Tobacco products	133,194	1.5
Other selective sales	261,853	2.9
Licenses	402,212	4.5
Alcoholic beverages	0	0.0
Amusements	0	0.0
Corporations in general	105,495	1.2
Hunting and fishing	28,948	0.3
Motor vehicle	132,032	1.5
Motor vehicle operators	12,160	0.1
Public utilities	8,989	0.1
Occupation and business, NEC	110,325	1.2
Other licenses	4,263	-
Income taxes	2,764,995	30.7
Individual income	2,474,606	27.5
Corporation net income	290,389	3.2
Other taxes	887,055	9.9
Death and gift	1,073	-
Documentary and stock transfer	0	0.0
Severance	885,982	9.9
Taxes, NEC	0	0.0

- = Rounds to zero.

Leading Exports, 2012

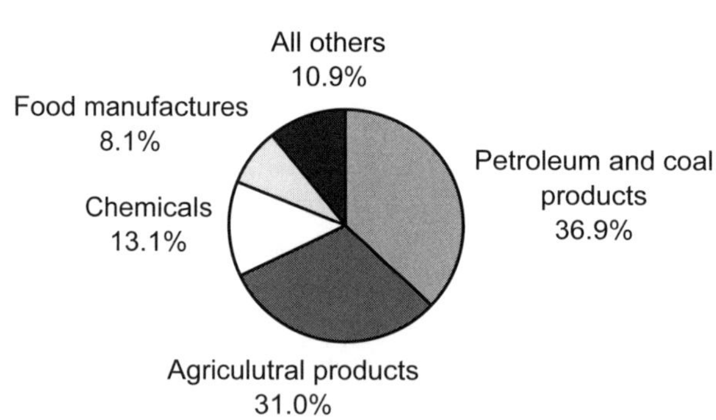

MAINE

Facts and Figures

Location: Northeast corner of the United States; bordered on the N and E by New Brunswick, Canada; on the S by the Atlantic Ocean; on the W by New Hampshire; and on the NW by Quebec, Canada

Area: 35,385 sq. mi. (91,646 sq. km.); rank—39th

Population: 1,329,192 (2012 est.); rank—41st

Principal Cities: capital—Augusta; largest—Portland

Statehood: March 15, 1820; 23rd state

U.S. Congress: 2 senators, 2 representatives

State Motto: *Dirigo* ("I lead")

State Song: "State of Maine Song"

State Nickname: The Pine Tree State

Abbreviations: ME; Me.

State Symbols: flower—white pinecone and tassel; tree—Eastern white pine; bird—chickadee

At a Glance

- With an increase in population of 3.4 percent, Maine ranked 44th among the states in growth from 2000 to 2009.
- An estimated 9,400 marriages took place in Maine in 2009, compared to 5,300 divorces.
- In 2011, 10.7 percent of Mainers did not have health insurance, compared to 15.1 percent of the total U.S. population.
- In the 2012 election, 68.6 percent of Maine's eligible voters voted, compared to 61.8 percent of eligible voters nationwide.
- In 2007, Maine exported $97 million worth of agricultural products, less than 1 percent of the U.S. total.

Table ME-1. Population by Age, Sex, Race, and Hispanic Origin

(Number, percent, except where noted.)

Sex, age, race, and Hispanic origin	2000	2010	2012[1]	Average annual percent change, 2010–2012
Total Population	1,274,923	1,328,361	1,329,192	-
Percent of total U.S. population	0.5	0.4	0.4	X
Sex				
Male	620,309	650,056	650,278	-
Female	654,614	678,305	678,914	-
Age				
Under 5 years	70,726	69,520	66,904	-1.3
5 to 19 years	264,729	241,439	234,910	-0.9
20 to 64 years	756,036	806,322	801,002	-0.2
65 years and over	183,402	211,080	226,376	2.3
Median age (years)	38.6	42.7	43.5	0.6
Race and Hispanic Origin				
One race				
White	1,236,014	1,269,764	1,266,849	-0.1
Black	6,760	16,269	17,603	2.5
American Indian and Alaska Native	7,098	8,771	8,859	0.3
Asian	9,111	13,783	14,810	2.3
Native Hawaiian or Other Pacific Islander	382	377	513	8.8
Two or more races	12,647	19,397	20,558	1.9
Hispanic (of any race)	9,360	18,261	20,023	2.9

X = Not applicable.
- = Zero or rounds to zero.
[1] Population figures for 2012 are July 1 estimates. The 2010 estimates are taken from the 2010 Census.

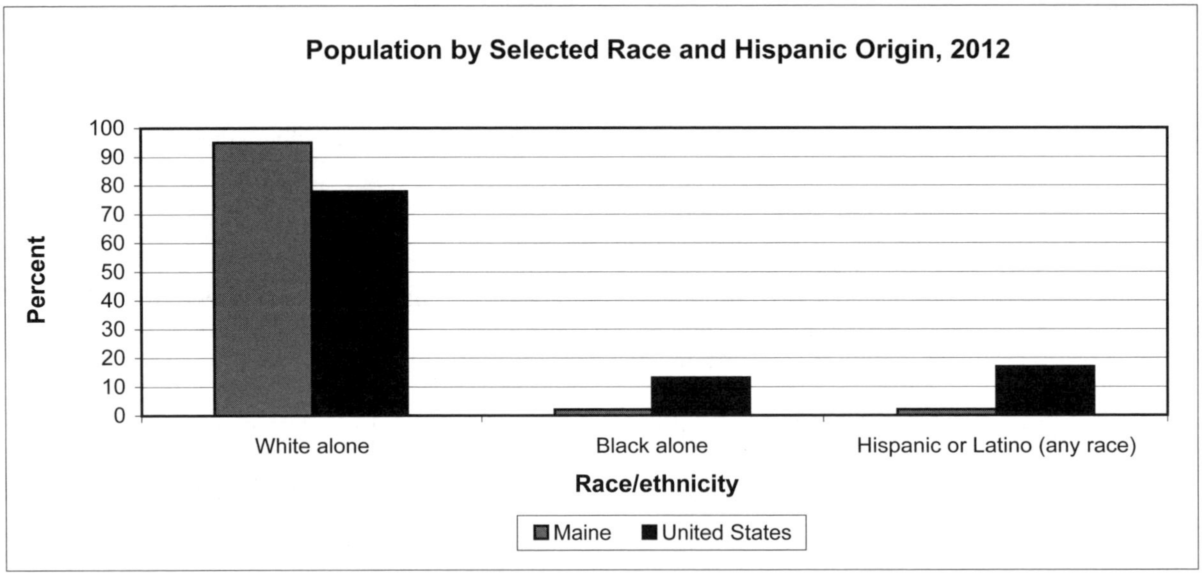

Table ME-2. Marital Status

(Number, percent distribution.)

Sex, age, race, and Hispanic origin	2000	2010	2011
Males, 15 Years and Over	494,217	534,474	536,592
Never married	26.8	31.0	30.9
Now married, except separated	58.8	52.5	52.8
Separated	1.1	1.2	0.9
Widowed	2.8	2.9	2.8
Divorced	10.5	12.5	12.5
Females, 15 Years and Over	534,606	570,281	571,004
Never married	21.2	24.2	24.3
Now married, except separated	54.1	49.3	49.7
Separated	1.3	1.6	1.4
Widowed	11.0	9.9	9.8
Divorced	12.4	15.0	14.8

Table ME-3. Households and Housing Characteristics

(Number, percent, dollars.)

Item	2000	2010	2011	Average annual percent change, 2000–2011
Total Households	518,200	545,417	552,051	0.5
Family households	340,685	345,328	347,960	0.2
Married-couple family	272,152	266,670	270,959	-
Other family	68,533	78,658	77,001	1.0
Male householder, no wife present	19,511	23,620	23,073	1.5
Female householder, no husband present	49,022	55,038	53,928	0.8
Nonfamily households	177,515	200,089	204,091	1.2
Householder living alone	139,969	155,623	156,958	1.0
Householder not living alone	37,546	44,466	47,133	2.1
Housing Characteristics				
Total housing units	651,901	722,217	725,650	0.9
Occupied housing units	518,200	545,417	552,051	0.5
Owner occupied	370,905	396,395	391,697	0.5
Renter occupied	147,295	149,022	160,354	0.7
Average size	2.39	2.37	2.34	-0.2
Financial Characteristics				
Median gross rent of renter-occupied housing	497	707	747	4.2
Median monthly owner costs for housing units with a mortgage	923	1,289	1,304	3.4
Median value of owner-occupied housing units	98,700	179,100	171,600	6.2

- = Zero or rounds to zero.

Table ME-4. Migration, Origin, and Language

(Number, percent.)

Characteristic	State			U.S.		
	2010	2011	Percent change	2010	2011	Percent change
Residence 1 Year Ago						
Population 1 year and over	1,313,902	1,315,833	0.1	305,628,607	307,900,319	0.7
Same house	86.5	85.1	-1.6	84.6	84.8	0.2
Different house in the U.S.	13.3	14.5	9.0	14.8	14.6	-1.4
Same county	8.3	8.6	3.6	9.4	9.2	-2.1
Different county	5.0	6.0	20.0	5.4	5.4	-
Same state	2.9	3.4	17.2	3.2	3.1	-3.1
Different state	2.1	2.6	23.8	2.2	2.3	4.5
Abroad	0.2	0.3	50.0	0.6	0.6	-
Place of Birth						
Native born	1,281,901	1,285,441	0.3	269,393,835	271,214,059	0.7
Male	49.1	49.2	0.2	49.2	49.2	-
Female	50.9	50.8	-0.2	50.8	50.8	-
Foreign born	45,666	42,747	-6.4	39,955,854	40,377,860	1.1
Male	41.9	42.8	2.1	49.1	48.9	-0.4
Female	58.1	57.2	-1.5	50.9	51.1	0.4
Foreign born; naturalized U.S. citizen	25,847	23,813	-7.9	17,476,082	18,140,192	3.8
Male	42.4	39.7	-6.4	45.8	45.8	-
Female	57.6	60.3	4.7	54.2	54.2	-
Foreign born; not a U.S. citizen	19,819	18,934	-4.5	22,479,772	22,237,668	-1.1
Male	41.2	46.6	13.1	51.6	51.5	-0.2
Female	58.8	53.4	-9.2	48.4	48.5	0.2
Entered 2000 or later	31.7	31.4	-0.9	34.7	35.7	2.9
Entered 1990 to 1999	19.0	19.4	2.1	27.2	26.7	-1.8
Entered before 1990	49.3	49.3	-	38.1	37.6	-1.3
World Region of Birth, Foreign						
Foreign-born population, excluding population born at sea	45,666	42,747	-6.4	39,955,673	40,377,757	1.1
Europe	23.9	24.0	0.4	12.1	12.1	-
Asia	26.8	26.1	-2.6	28.2	28.6	1.4
Africa	14.3	11.5	-19.6	4	4.1	2.5
Oceania	0.5	0.5	-	0.5	0.5	-
Latin America	9.2	9.3	1.1	53.1	52.6	-0.9
North America	25.4	28.7	13.0	2	2.0	-
Language Spoken at Home and Ability to Speak English						
Population 5 years and over	1,258,997	1,261,967	0.2	289,215,746	291,524,091	0.8
English only	93.3	93.4	0.1	79.4	79.2	-0.3
Language other than English	6.7	6.6	-1.5	20.6	20.8	1.0
Speaks English less than "very well"	1.7	1.5	-11.8	8.7	8.7	-

- = Zero or rounds to zero.

Table ME-5. Median Income and Poverty Status, 2011

(Number, percent, except as noted.)

Characteristic	State Number	State Percent	U.S. Number	U.S. Percent
Median Income				
Households (dollars)	46,033	X	50,502	X
Families (dollars)	58,375	X	61,455	X
Below Poverty Level (All People)	182,448	14.1	48,452,035	15.9
Sex				
Male	84,216	13.3	21,825,281	14.7
Female	98,232	14.9	26,626,754	17.2
Age				
Under 18 years	49,561	18.8	16,386,500	22.5
Related children under 18 years	47,593	18.2	16,087,074	22.2
18 to 64 years	115,981	14.2	28,335,079	14.8
65 years and over	16,906	8.0	3,730,456	9.3

X = Not applicable.

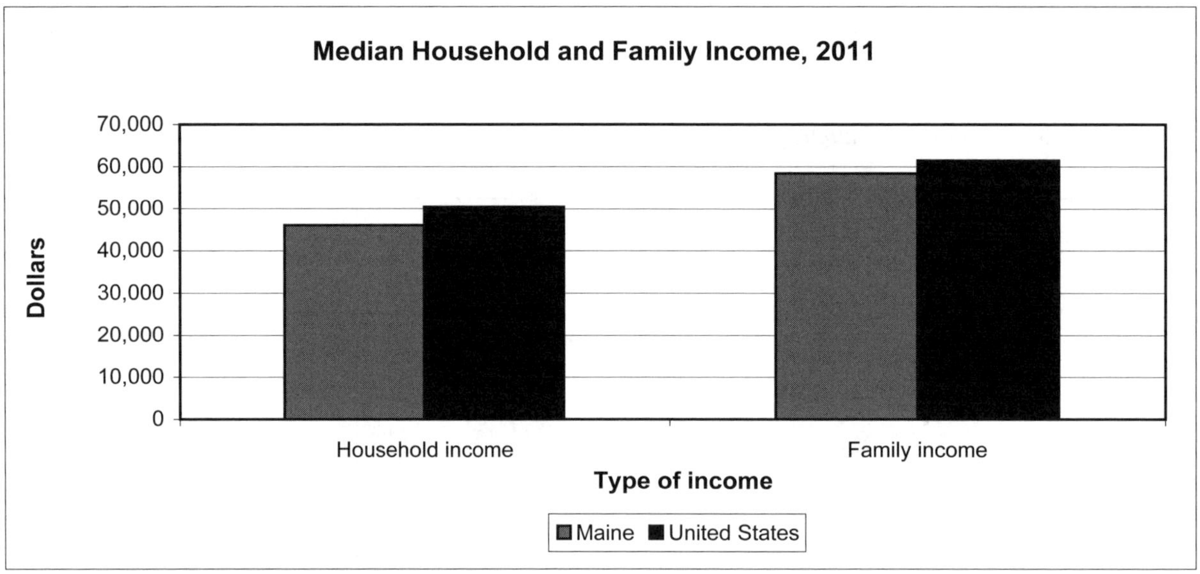

Table ME-6. Health Insurance Coverage Status for the Civilian Noninstitutionalized Population and Children Under 18 Years of Age

(Numbers in thousands, percent.)

Item	2004	2005	2006	2007	2008	2009	2010	2011
Civilian Noninstitutionalized Population	1,294	1,320	1,315	1,313	1,299	1,301	1,313	1,314
Covered by Private or Public Insurance								
Number	1,179	1,185	1,192	1,197	1,157	1,164	1,180	1,174
Percent	91.1	89.7	90.7	91.2	89.1	89.5	89.8	89.3
Not Covered								
Number	115	136	122	115	142	137	133	140
Percent	8.9	10.3	9.3	8.8	10.9	10.5	10.1	10.7
Percent in the U.S. not covered	14.9	15.3	15.8	15.3	15.1	15.1	15.5	15.1
Children Under 18 Years of Age	286	279	286	281	275	270	273	270
Covered by Private or Public Insurance								
Number	270	272	258	268	255	255	262	256
Percent	95.3	92.3	93.6	94.9	92.7	94.4	96.0	94.8
Not Covered								
Number	13	21	18	14	20	15	11	14
Percent	4.7	7.7	6.4	5.1	7.3	5.6	4.0	5.2
Percent in the U.S. not covered	10.5	10.9	11.7	11.0	9.7	8.6	8.0	7.5

Table ME-7. Employment Status by Demographic Group, Preliminary 2012

(Numbers in thousands, percent.)

Characteristic	Civilian noninstitutional population	Civilian labor force		Employed		Unemployed	
		Number	Percent of population	Number	Percent of population	Number	Percent of population
Total	1,084	704	64.9	650	59.9	54	7.7
Sex							
Male	525	366	69.7	336	64.0	30	8.2
Female	559	338	60.5	314	56.1	24	7.1
Race, Sex, and Hispanic Origin							
White	1,038	674	65.0	624	60.1	50	7.4
Male	501	350	69.7	322	64.3	27	7.8
Female	537	324	60.5	302	56.3	22	6.9
Black or African American	11	8	67.3	6	53.1	2	20.7
Male	NA	NA	NA	NA	NA	NA	NA
Female	NA	NA	NA	NA	NA	NA	NA
Hispanic	10	8	78.4	7	67.7	1	13.6
Male	NA	NA	NA	NA	NA	NA	NA
Female	NA	NA	NA	NA	NA	NA	NA
Age							
16 to 19 years	73	34	47.2	26	35.6	8	24.6
20 to 24 years	83	63	76.6	55	67.2	8	12.3
25 to 34 years	137	111	80.6	100	72.9	11	9.5
35 to 44 years	162	137	84.6	130	80.2	7	5.2
45 to 54 years							
55 to 64 years	204	140	68.6	133	65.2	7	4.9
65 years and over	210	43	20.3	40	18.8	3	7.1

NOTE: Data in Table 7 are from the Current Population Survey (CPS) and do not match the estimates in Table 8. See notes and definitions for further information.

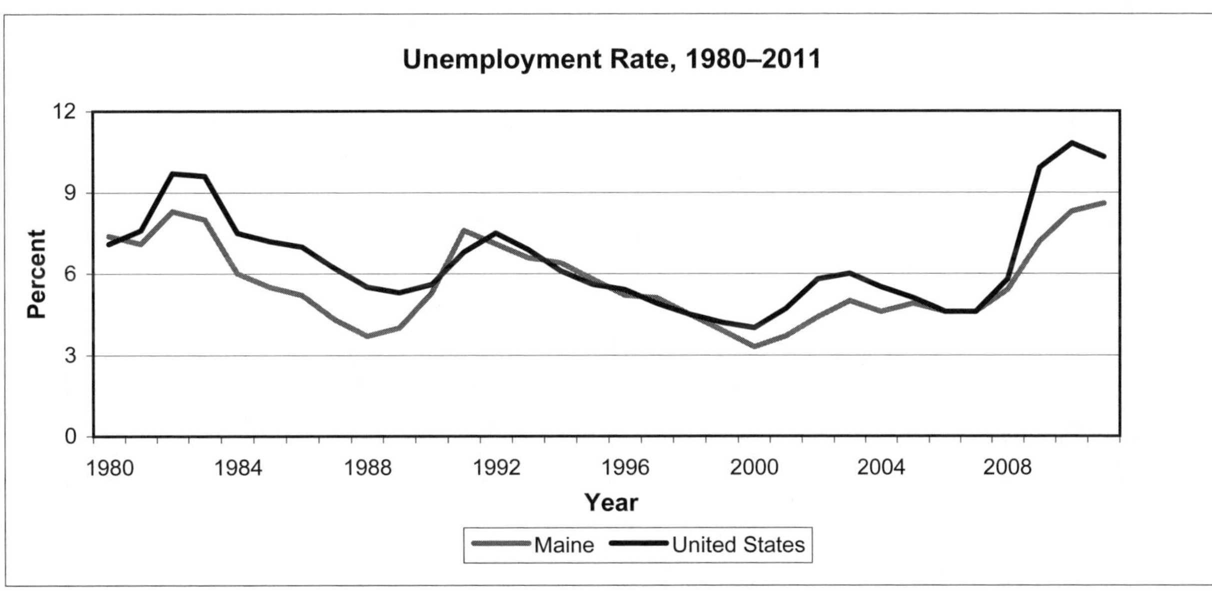

Table ME-8. Employment Status of the Civilian Noninstitutional Population Age 16 Years and Over

(Number, percent.)

Year	Civilian labor force	Civilian participation rate	Employed	Unemployed	Unemployment rate
2005	694,285	66.5	660,557	33,728	4.9
2006	701,505	66.8	669,067	32,438	4.6
2007	702,549	66.5	669,948	32,601	4.6
2008	706,829	66.6	668,724	38,105	5.4
2009	701,646	64.8	651,259	50,387	7.2
2010	699,627	64.3	641,665	58,162	8.3
2011	703,536	64.6	643,104	60,432	8.6

Table ME-9. Employment and Average Wages by Industry

(Estimates before 2007 are based on the 2002 *North American Industry Classification System* [NAICS]. Estimates from 2007 onward are based on the 2007 NAICS.)

Industry	2005	2006	2007	2008	2009	2010	2011
				Number of jobs			
Wage and Salary Employment by Industry	629,147	634,156	637,508	637,589	616,379	611,786	613,325
Farm Wage and Salary Employment	3,092	2,812	2,701	2,946	2,843	2,849	3,023
Nonfarm Wage and Salary Employment	626,055	631,344	634,807	634,643	613,536	608,937	610,302
Private wage and salary employment	514,193	518,766	521,979	521,727	501,937	498,170	501,526
Forestry, fishing, and related activities	4,061	4,124	4,104	D	D	4,071	4,094
Mining	114	126	109	D	D	179	203
Utilities	1,903	1,849	1,936	1,895	1,862	1,817	1,609
Construction	31,862	32,495	32,000	30,502	26,371	25,484	26,588
Manufacturing	60,913	59,937	59,449	58,801	52,436	50,716	50,855
Durable goods manufacturing	32,304	31,696	31,548	31,337	27,643	26,974	27,219
Nondurable goods manufacturing	28,609	28,241	27,901	27,464	24,793	23,742	23,636
Wholesale trade	21,557	21,491	21,498	20,968	19,746	19,170	19,190
Retail trade	88,416	86,702	87,064	86,720	83,496	82,742	82,565
Transportation and warehousing	14,938	17,063	17,567	16,929	15,944	15,696	15,875
Information	11,299	11,288	10,666	10,146	9,239	9,159	8,289
Finance and insurance	26,573	26,222	25,682	25,369	24,841	24,775	25,288
Real estate and rental and leasing	7,376	7,306	7,330	7,260	6,931	6,749	6,510
Professional, scientific, and technical services	23,243	23,836	24,032	24,812	24,128	23,830	23,854
Management of companies and enterprises	5,593	6,196	6,470	7,025	6,899	6,990	7,113
Administrative and waste services	21,978	23,005	24,743	26,028	25,314	25,808	27,120
Educational services	12,253	12,634	13,242	13,613	13,536	14,228	14,480
Health care and social assistance	95,832	97,843	98,826	100,355	101,479	101,138	101,362
Arts, entertainment, and recreation	8,154	8,027	8,355	8,399	8,170	8,182	8,251
Accommodation and food services	51,670	52,339	52,600	52,345	51,679	52,319	52,713
Other services, except public administration	26,458	26,283	26,306	26,365	25,743	25,117	25,567
Government and government enterprises	111,862	112,578	112,828	112,916	111,599	110,767	108,776
				Dollars			
Average Wages and Salaries by Industry	33,433	34,848	36,258	37,374	37,539	38,329	39,055
Average Farm Wages and Salaries	21,837	27,673	32,756	28,813	28,365	26,735	22,542
Average Nonfarm Wages and Salaries	33,491	34,880	36,273	37,413	37,582	38,384	39,137
Average private wages and salaries	32,962	34,416	35,808	36,904	36,846	37,766	38,691
Forestry, fishing, and related activities	32,698	34,816	36,625	D	D	38,248	40,511
Mining	32,535	33,825	40,046	D	D	53,469	53,493
Utilities	61,224	61,665	63,514	67,348	66,236	71,138	75,606
Construction	36,161	37,670	39,441	41,160	41,016	41,257	42,576
Manufacturing	42,904	44,685	46,273	48,074	48,119	51,576	52,263
Durable goods manufacturing	42,772	44,262	46,485	48,695	48,590	51,619	52,725
Nondurable goods manufacturing	43,052	45,160	46,033	47,365	47,594	51,526	51,730
Wholesale trade	46,670	49,227	51,325	51,944	52,209	52,979	54,738
Retail trade	23,049	23,687	24,201	24,459	24,763	25,083	25,349
Transportation and warehousing	35,092	35,027	36,040	37,684	38,349	38,928	38,772
Information	41,831	43,061	43,355	44,094	44,847	46,823	45,622
Finance and insurance	50,650	53,147	55,814	56,826	56,432	58,670	61,847
Real estate and rental and leasing	29,743	32,160	32,010	32,873	33,077	33,825	35,659
Professional, scientific, and technical services	48,048	50,315	53,044	55,986	55,621	56,290	58,089
Management of companies and enterprises	61,928	65,479	70,032	75,339	65,920	68,478	71,534
Administrative and waste services	27,145	28,309	30,840	31,891	31,622	32,479	32,886
Educational services	28,779	30,150	32,133	32,078	33,148	32,939	34,510
Health care and social assistance	34,735	36,444	37,988	39,522	40,296	40,756	41,901
Arts, entertainment, and recreation	20,940	23,989	25,406	24,421	24,304	24,738	25,049
Accommodation and food services	16,073	16,693	17,657	17,457	17,310	18,038	18,486
Other services, except public administration	21,996	22,699	23,358	24,330	24,498	25,657	26,155
Government and government enterprises	35,290	37,014	38,427	39,766	40,891	41,162	41,194

D = Not shown to avoid disclosure of confidential information, but the estimates for this item are included in the total.

Table ME-10. Employment Characteristics by Family Type

(Number, percent.)

Family type and labor force status	2009		2010		2011	
	Total	Families with own children under 18 years	Total	Families with own children under 18 years	Total	Families with own children under 18 years
All families	347,561	141,768	345,328	138,030	347,960	138,279
Family type and labor force status						
Married-couple families	271,143	93,871	266,670	90,004	270,959	88,876
Both husband and wife in labor force	55.7	72.7	56.2	75.6	55.4	73.8
Husband in labor force, wife not in labor force	17.7	21.4	15.7	18.3	16.8	19.9
Wife in labor force, husband not in labor force	8.0	3.7	8.7	4.0	8.9	4.1
Both husband and wife not in labor force	18.5	2.2	19.4	2.1	19.0	2.2
Other families	76,418	47,897	78,658	48,026	77,001	49,403
Female householder, no husband present	72.4	74.6	70.0	71.7	70.0	70.4
In labor force	52.9	60.4	49.7	56.6	50.1	56.2
Not in labor force	19.6	14.2	20.3	15.1	19.9	14.2
Male householder, no wife present	27.6	25.4	30.0	28.3	30.0	29.6
In labor force	22.4	22.5	22.6	24.9	24.0	26.1
Not in labor force	5.2	2.9	7.4	3.4	6.0	3.5

Table ME-11. School Enrollment and Educational Attainment, 2011

(Number, percent.)

Item	State	U.S.
Enrollment		
Total population 3 years and over, enrolled in school	304,531	83,131,910
Enrolled in nursery school or preschool (percent)	5.0	6.0
Enrolled in kindergarten (percent)	5.0	5.1
Enrolled in elementary school, grades 1-8 (percent)	40.8	39.5
Enrolled in high school, grades 9-12 (percent)	21.8	20.7
Enrolled in college or graduate school (percent)	27.4	28.7
Attainment		
Total population 25 years and over	942,537	206,471,670
Less than ninth grade (percent)	3.4	6.0
9th to 12th grade, no diploma (percent)	5.7	8.1
High school graduate, including equivalency (percent)	33.4	28.4
Some college, no degree (percent)	20.3	21.2
Associate's degree (percent)	8.9	7.8
Bachelor's degree (percent)	17.9	17.9
Graduate or professional degree (percent)	10.5	10.6
High school graduate or higher (percent)	90.9	85.9
Bachelor's degree or higher (percent)	28.4	28.5

Table ME-12. Educational Indicators

(Number, percent; data derived from National Center of Education Statistics.)

Item	State	U.S.
Public Schools, 2009–2010 (except where noted)		
Number of school districts	246	13,629
Number of schools	649	99,834
Number of students (in thousands)	189	49,373
Student-teacher ratio	11.6	15.4
Expenditures per student (dollars)	13,840	10,591
Averaged freshman graduation rate, 2008–2009	79.9[1]	75.5[2]
Dropout rate, 2008–2009	3.6	4.1
Students eligible for free or reduced-price lunch (percent)	43.0	48.0
English language learners, 2010–2011 (percent)	2.5	9.8[2]
Students with IEP (percent)	17.3	13.1
Private Schools, 2009–2010 (except where noted)		
Number of schools	163	33,366
Number of students (in thousands)	17	4,700
High school graduates, 2008–2009	2,362	308,813
Student-teacher ratio	9.0	10.7

[1] Includes 1,161 graduates in 2007-08 and 1,169 graduates in 2008-09 from private high schools that received a majority of their funding from public sources.
[2] U.S. total includes estimates for nonreporting states.

Table ME-13. Reported Voting and Registration of the Voting-Age Population, November 2012

(Numbers in thousands, percent.)

Item	Total population	Total citizen population	Registered: Total registered	Registered: Percent registered (total population)	Registered: Percent registered (total citizen population)	Voted: Total voted	Voted: Percent voted (total population)	Voted: Percent voted (total citizen population)
U.S. Total	235,248	215,081	153,157	65.1	71.2	132,948	56.5	61.8
State Total	1,042	1,020	787	75.5	77.1	700	67.2	68.6
Sex								
Male	509	501	383	75.2	76.4	333	65.5	66.5
Female	533	519	404	75.8	77.9	367	68.8	70.7
Race								
White alone	1,001	986	766	76.5	77.7	682	68.1	69.1
White, non-Hispanic alone	993	981	762	76.8	77.7	678	68.3	69.1
Black alone	8	7	4	B	B	4	B	B
Asian alone	14	8	3	B	B	2	B	B
Hispanic (of any race)	10	7	4	B	B	4	B	B
Age								
18 to 24 years	118	118	61	51.7	51.7	50	42.8	42.8
25 to 44 years	292	281	210	72.0	74.9	179	61.4	63.9
45 to 64 years	413	407	329	79.7	80.9	300	72.7	73.7
65 to 74 years	129	127	109	84.9	86.4	104	80.5	81.8
75 years and over	90	88	77	85.7	87.7	66	73.7	75.4

B = Base is less than 75,000 and therefore too small to show the derived measure.

Table ME-14. Crime

(Number, rate per 100,000. Data are derived from the FBI Uniform Crime Reports.)

Item	State: 2010	State: 2011	State: Percent change	U.S.: 2010	U.S.: 2011	U.S.: Percent change
TOTAL POPULATION	1,327,379	1,328,188	0.1	309,330,219	311,591,917	0.7
VIOLENT CRIME						
Number	1,621	1,636	0.9	1,251,248	1,203,564	-3.8
Rate	122.1	123.2	0.9	404.5	386.3	-4.5
Murder and Nonnegligent Manslaughter						
Number	24	26	8.3	14,722	14,612	-0.7
Rate	1.8	2.0	11.1	4.8	4.7	-2.1
Forcible Rape						
Number	389	393	1.0	85,593	83,425	-2.5
Rate	29.3	29.6	1.0	27.7	26.8	-3.2
Robbery						
Number	412	369	-10.4	369,089	354,396	-4.0
Rate	31.0	27.8	-10.3	119.3	113.7	-4.7
Aggravated Assault						
Number	796	848	6.5	781,844	751,131	-3.9
Rate	60.0	63.8	6.3	252.8	241.1	-4.6
PROPERTY CRIME						
Number	32,900	33,809	2.8	9,112,625	9,063,173	-0.5
Rate	2,478.6	2,545.5	2.7	2,945.9	2,908.7	-1.3
Burglary						
Number	7,364	7,854	6.7	2,168,459	2,188,005	0.9
Rate	554.8	591.3	6.6	701.0	702.2	0.2
Larceny-Theft						
Number	24,587	24,877	1.2	6,204,601	6,159,795	-0.7
Rate	1,849.3	1,873.0	1.3	2,005.8	1,976.9	-1.4
Motor Vehicle Theft						
Number	989	1,078	9.0	739,565	715,373	-3.3
Rate	74.5	81.2	9.0	239.1	229.6	-4.0

Table ME-15. State Government Finances, 2011

(Dollar amounts in thousands, percent distribution.)

Item	Dollars	Percent distribution
Total Revenue	10,611,116	100.0
General revenue	8,249,133	77.7
Intergovernmental revenue	3,241,435	30.5
Taxes	3,675,810	34.6
General sales	1,010,241	9.5
Selective sales	672,404	6.3
License taxes	248,730	2.3
Individual income tax	1,420,982	13.4
Corporate income tax	208,997	2.0
Other taxes	114,456	1.1
Current charges	791,648	7.5
Miscellaneous general revenue	540,240	5.1
Utility revenue	0	0.0
Liquor stores revenue	33	0.0
Insurance trust revenue [1]	2,361,950	22.3
Total Expenditure	9,099,085	100.0
Intergovernmental expenditure	1,301,692	14.3
Direct expenditure	7,797,393	85.7
Current operation	5,730,549	63.0
Capital outlay	492,329	5.4
Insurance benefits and repayments	1,089,136	12.0
Assistance and subsidies	236,004	2.6
Interest on debt	249,375	2.7
Exhibit: Salaries and wages	772,883	8.5
Total Expenditure	9,099,085	100.0
General expenditure	8,005,148	88.0
Intergovernmental expenditure	1,301,692	14.3
Direct expenditure	6,703,456	73.7
General expenditure, by function:		
Education	2,121,288	23.3
Public welfare	2,905,192	31.9
Hospitals	54,358	0.6
Health	445,881	4.9
Highways	647,106	7.1
Police protection	71,468	0.8
Correction	142,410	1.6
Natural resources	168,925	1.9
Parks and recreation	25,230	0.3
Governmental administration	286,203	3.1
Interest on general debt	249,375	2.7
Other and unallocable	887,712	9.8
Utility expenditure	4,801	0.1
Liquor stores expenditure	0	0.0
Insurance trust expenditure	1,089,136	12.0
Debt at End of Fiscal Year	5,904,221	X
Cash and Security Holdings	17,780,804	X

X = Not applicable.

[1] Within insurance trust revenue, net earnings of state retirement systems is a calculated statistic (the item code in the data file is X08), and thus can be positive or negative. Net earnings is the sum of earnings on investments plus gains on investments minus losses on investments. The change made in 2002 for asset valuation from book to market value in accordance with Statement 34 of the Governmental Accounting Standards Board is reflected in the calculated statistics.

Table ME-16. State Government Tax Collections, 2012

(Dollars in thousands, percent.)

Item	Dollars	Percent distribution
Total Taxes	3,777,130	100.0
Property taxes	38,360	1.0
Sales and gross receipts	1,748,815	46.3
General sales and gross receipts	1,064,342	28.2
Selective sales and gross receipts	684,473	18.1
Alcoholic beverages	17,352	0.5
Amusements	28,640	0.8
Insurance premiums	108,605	2.9
Motor fuels	242,124	6.4
Pari-mutuels	2,379	0.1
Public utilities	28,548	0.8
Tobacco products	139,729	3.7
Other selective sales	117,096	3.1
Licenses	252,404	6.7
Alcoholic beverages	4,827	0.1
Amusements	701	
Corporations in general	8,541	0.2
Hunting and fishing	15,904	0.4
Motor vehicle	99,135	2.6
Motor vehicle operators	10,660	0.3
Public utilities	0	0.0
Occupation and business, NEC	104,561	2.8
Other licenses	8,075	0.2
Income taxes	1,674,044	44.3
Individual income	1,441,926	38.2
Corporation net income	232,118	6.1
Other taxes	63,507	1.7
Death and gift	44,865	1.2
Documentary and stock transfer	18,642	0.5
Severance	0	0.0
Taxes, NEC	0	0.0

- = Rounds to zero.

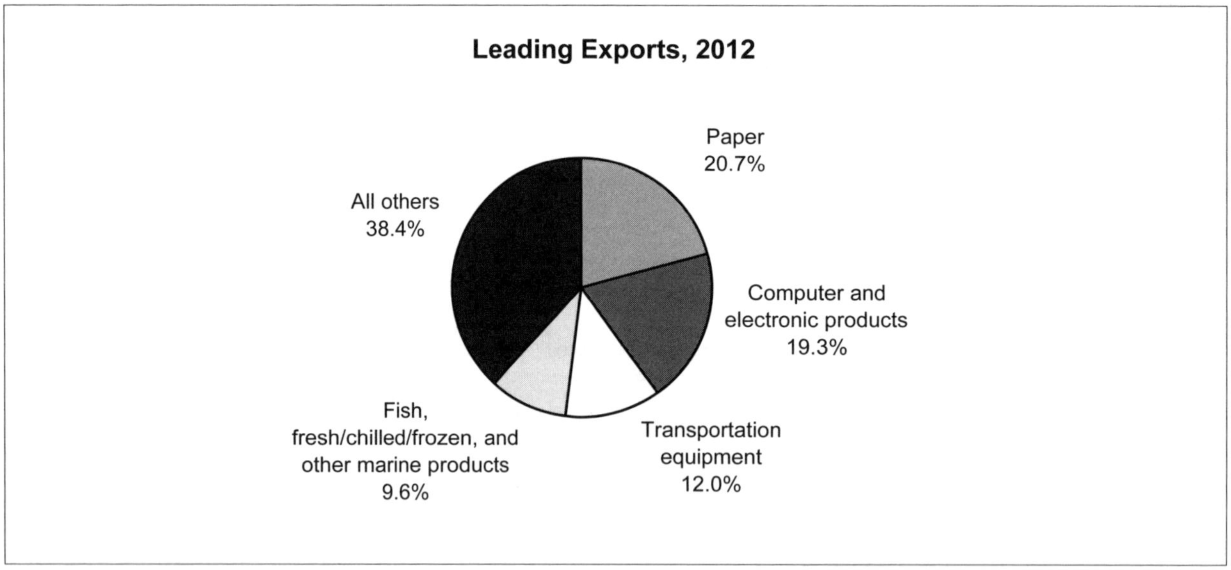

MARYLAND

Facts and Figures

Location: Eastern United States; bordered on the N by Pennsylvania, on the E by Delaware and the Atlantic Ocean, and on the S and W by Virginia and West Virginia

Area: 12,407 sq. mi. (32,133 sq. km.); rank—42nd

Population: 5,884,563 (2012 est.); rank—19th

Principal Cities: capital—Annapolis; largest—Baltimore

Statehood: April 28, 1788; 7th state

U.S. Congress: 2 senators, 8 representatives

State Motto: *Fatti maschii parole femine* ("Manly deeds, womanly words")

State Song: "Maryland, My Maryland"

State Nicknames: The Old Line State; The Free State

Abbreviations: MD; Md.

State Symbols: flower—black-eyed susan; tree—white oak; bird—Baltimore oriole

At a Glance

- With an increase in population of 7.6 percent, Maryland ranked 17th among the states in growth from 2000 to 2009.
- An estimated 32,400 marriages took place in Maryland in 2009, compared to 15,200 divorces.
- Maryland's median household income in 2007 was $70,004, and 10.1 percent of the population lived below the poverty level.
- Maryland's violent crime rate in 2007 was 494.1 per 100,000 population, compared to 386.3 for the entire nation.
- In 2007, Maryland exported $358 million worth of agricultural products, less than 1 percent of the U.S. total.

Table MD-1. Population by Age, Sex, Race, and Hispanic Origin

(Number, percent, except where noted.)

Sex, age, race, and Hispanic origin	2000	2010	2012[1]	Average annual percent change, 2010–2012
Total Population	5,296,486	5,773,552	5,884,563	0.6
Percent of total U.S. population	1.9	1.9	1.9	X
Sex				
Male	2,557,794	2,791,762	2,850,483	0.7
Female	2,738,692	2,981,790	3,034,160	0.6
Age				
Under 5 years	353,393	364,488	365,224	0.1
5 to 19 years	1,139,572	1,152,138	1,142,725	-0.3
20 to 64 years	3,204,214	3,549,284	3,613,595	0.6
65 years and over	599,307	707,642	763,019	2.4
Median age (years)	36.0	38.0	38.1	0.1
Race and Hispanic Origin				
One race				
White	3,391,308	3,542,379	3,579,276	0.3
Black	1,477,411	1,731,513	1,766,990	0.7
American Indian and Alaska Native	15,423	30,885	32,375	1.5
Asian	210,929	326,655	352,247	2.4
Native Hawaiian or Other Pacific Islander	2,303	5,391	5,674	1.7
Two or more races	103,587	137,729	148,001	2.3
Hispanic (of any race)	227,916	493,811	537,497	2.7

X = Not applicable.
[1] Population figures for 2012 are July 1 estimates. The 2010 estimates are taken from the 2010 Census.

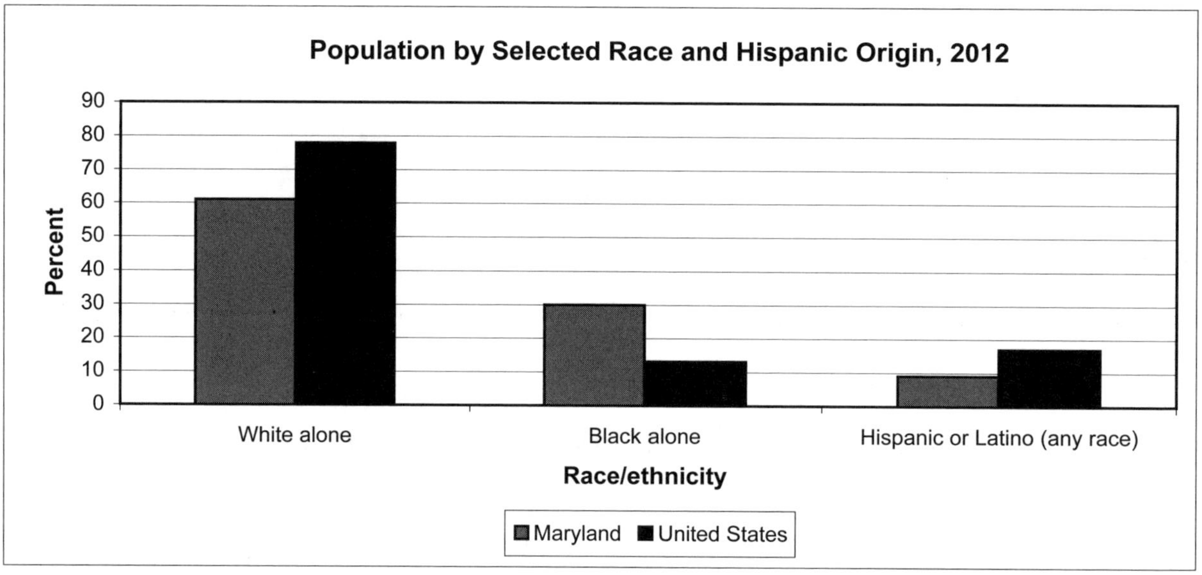

Table MD-2. Marital Status

(Number, percent distribution.)

Sex, age, race, and Hispanic origin	2000	2010	2011
Males, 15 Years and Over	1,972,921	2,232,162	2,256,241
Never married	31.0	36.8	37.5
Now married, except separated	56.3	50.2	49.0
Separated	2.8	2.3	2.3
Widowed	2.5	2.7	2.4
Divorced	7.4	8.0	8.8
Females, 15 Years and Over	2,186,715	2,442,021	2,461,615
Never married	26.8	32.2	33.0
Now married, except separated	49.7	45.3	43.7
Separated	3.4	2.9	3.0
Widowed	10.1	9.0	8.7
Divorced	10.1	10.7	11.6

Table MD-3. Households and Housing Characteristics

(Number, percent, dollars.)

Item	2000	2010	2011	Average annual percent change, 2000–2011
Total Households	1,980,859	2,127,439	2,134,517	0.6
Family households	1,359,318	1,431,958	1,415,576	0.3
Married-couple family	994,549	1,022,613	995,216	-
Other family	364,789	409,345	420,360	1.3
Male householder, no wife present	84,893	104,112	101,534	1.6
Female householder, no husband present	279,876	305,233	318,826	1.2
Nonfamily households	621,541	695,481	718,941	1.3
Householder living alone	495,459	570,388	592,823	1.6
Householder not living alone	126,082	125,093	126,118	-
Housing Characteristics				
Total housing units	2,145,283	2,380,605	2,391,508	1.0
Occupied housing units	1,980,859	2,127,439	2,134,517	0.6
Owner occupied	1,341,751	1,426,267	1,437,447	0.6
Renter occupied	639,108	701,172	697,070	0.8
Average size	2.61	2.65	2.67	0.2
Financial Characteristics				
Median gross rent of renter-occupied housing	689	1,131	1,153	5.6
Median monthly owner costs for housing units with a mortgage	1,296	2,016	1,961	4.3
Median value of owner-occupied housing units	146,000	301,400	287,100	8.1

- = Zero or rounds to zero.

Table MD-4. Migration, Origin, and Language

(Number, percent.)

Characteristic	State			U.S.		
	2010	2011	Percent change	2010	2011	Percent change
Residence 1 Year Ago						
Population 1 year and over	5,716,785	5,759,087	0.7	305,628,607	307,900,319	0.7
Same house	86.0	87.0	1.2	84.6	84.8	0.2
Different house in the U.S.	13.2	12.3	-6.8	14.8	14.6	-1.4
Same county	7.6	7.0	-7.9	9.4	9.2	-2.1
Different county	5.5	5.2	-5.5	5.4	5.4	-
Same state	2.7	2.6	-3.7	3.2	3.1	-3.1
Different state	2.9	2.7	-6.9	2.2	2.3	4.5
Abroad	0.8	0.7	-12.5	0.6	0.6	-
Place of Birth						
Native born	4,982,287	5,016,588	0.7	269,393,835	271,214,059	0.7
Male	48.2	48.3	0.2	49.2	49.2	-
Female	51.8	51.7	-0.2	50.8	50.8	-
Foreign born	803,695	811,701	1.0	39,955,854	40,377,860	1.1
Male	49.8	49.0	-1.6	49.1	48.9	-0.4
Female	50.2	51.0	1.6	50.9	51.1	0.4
Foreign born; naturalized U.S. citizen	360,932	372,873	3.3	17,476,082	18,140,192	3.8
Male	47.0	46.1	-1.9	45.8	45.8	-
Female	53.0	53.9	1.7	54.2	54.2	-
Foreign born; not a U.S. citizen	442,763	438,828	-0.9	22,479,772	22,237,668	-1.1
Male	52.0	51.5	-1.0	51.6	51.5	-0.2
Female	48.0	48.5	1.0	48.4	48.5	0.2
Entered 2000 or later	41.7	42.8	2.6	34.7	35.7	2.9
Entered 1990 to 1999	25.5	25.5	-	27.2	26.7	-1.8
Entered before 1990	32.8	31.7	-3.4	38.1	37.6	-1.3
World Region of Birth, Foreign						
Foreign-born population, excluding population born at sea	803,695	811,701	1.0	39,955,673	40,377,757	1.1
Europe	10.8	10.4	-3.7	12.1	12.1	-
Asia	33.1	32.4	-2.1	28.2	28.6	1.4
Africa	15.6	15.6	-	4	4.1	2.5
Oceania	0.3	0.2	-33.3	0.5	0.5	-
Latin America	38.8	40.2	3.6	53.1	52.6	-0.9
North America	1.3	1.1	-15.4	2	2.0	-
Language Spoken at Home and Ability to Speak English						
Population 5 years and over	5,421,054	5,465,168	0.8	289,215,746	291,524,091	0.8
English only	83.5	83.3	-0.2	79.4	79.2	-0.3
Language other than English	16.5	16.7	1.2	20.6	20.8	1.0
Speaks English less than "very well"	6.3	6.2	-1.6	8.7	8.7	-

- = Zero or rounds to zero.

Table MD-5. Median Income and Poverty Status, 2011

(Number, percent, except as noted.)

Characteristic	State		U.S.	
	Number	Percent	Number	Percent
Median Income				
Households (dollars)	70,004	X	50,502	X
Families (dollars)	83,823	X	61,455	X
Below Poverty Level (All People)	571,887	10.1	48,452,035	15.9
Sex				
Male	247,081	9.0	21,825,281	14.7
Female	324,806	11.0	26,626,754	17.2
Age				
Under 18 years	178,725	13.5	16,386,500	22.5
Related children under 18 years	174,219	13.2	16,087,074	22.2
18 to 64 years	340,370	9.3	28,335,079	14.8
65 years and over	52,792	7.5	3,730,456	9.3

X = Not applicable.

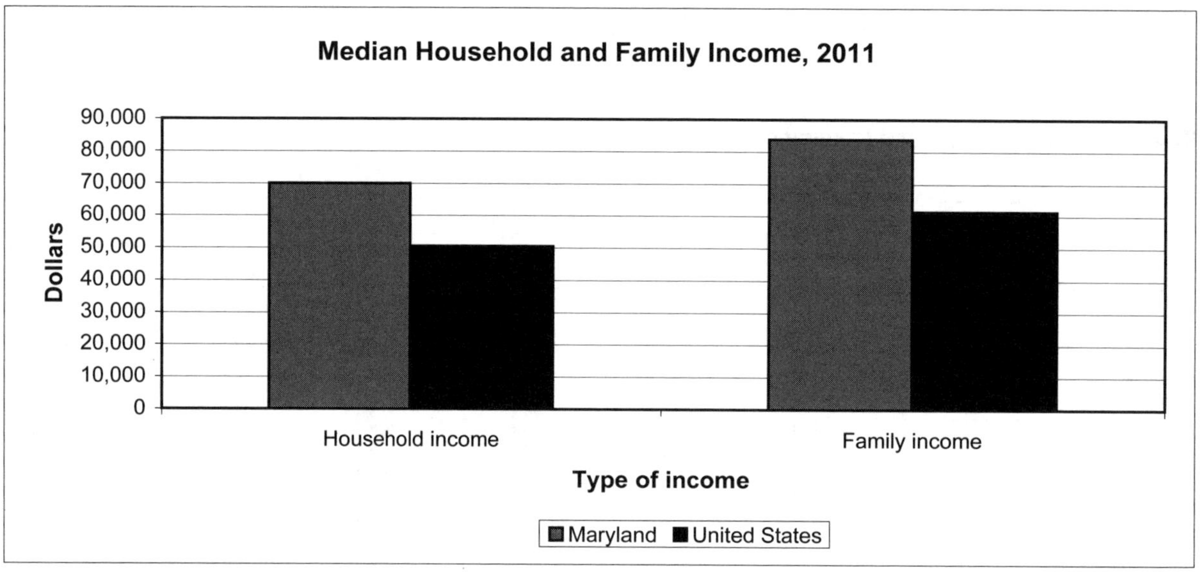

Table MD-6. Health Insurance Coverage Status for the Civilian Noninstitutionalized Population and Children Under 18 Years of Age

(Numbers in thousands, percent.)

Item	2004	2005	2006	2007	2008	2009	2010	2011
Civilian Noninstitutionalized Population	5,550	5,569	5,613	5,565	5,530	5,590	5,688	5,737
Covered by Private or Public Insurance								
Number	4,809	4,823	4,836	4,804	4,919	4,969	5,047	5,138
Percent	86.6	86.6	86.2	86.3	89.0	88.9	88.7	89.6
Not Covered								
Number	742	746	776	762	611	621	641	598
Percent	13.4	13.4	13.8	13.7	11.0	11.1	11.3	10.4
Percent in the U.S. not covered	14.9	15.3	15.8	15.3	15.1	15.1	15.5	15.1
Children Under 18 Years of Age	1,389	1,383	1,384	1,382	1,339	1,348	1,350	1,344
Covered by Private or Public Insurance								
Number	1,259	1,268	1,247	1,237	1,269	1,283	1,286	1,283
Percent	90.6	91.7	90.1	89.5	94.8	95.2	95.2	95.4
Not Covered								
Number	130	115	137	146	70	65	64	61
Percent	9.4	8.3	9.9	10.5	5.2	4.8	4.8	4.6
Percent in the U.S. not covered	10.5	10.9	11.7	11.0	9.7	8.6	8.0	7.5

Table MD-7. Employment Status by Demographic Group, Preliminary 2012

(Numbers in thousands, percent.)

Characteristic	Civilian noninstitutional population	Civilian labor force		Employed		Unemployed	
		Number	Percent of population	Number	Percent of population	Number	Percent of population
Total	4,585	3,110	67.8	2,893	63.1	217	7.0
Sex							
Male	2,168	1,569	72.4	1,455	67.1	114	7.3
Female	2,417	1,541	63.7	1,438	59.5	103	6.7
Race, Sex, and Hispanic Origin							
White	2,867	1,931	67.4	1,823	63.6	108	5.6
Male	1,405	1,026	73.1	965	68.7	61	5.9
Female	1,462	905	61.9	858	58.7	47	5.2
Black or African American	1,331	920	69.2	826	62.1	94	10.2
Male	590	414	70.2	367	62.2	47	11.3
Female	741	506	68.3	459	61.9	47	9.3
Hispanic	380	290	76.3	270	71.1	20	6.7
Male	188	164	87.0	154	81.8	10	6.0
Female	192	126	65.8	117	60.7	10	7.7
Age							
16 to 19 years	297	104	35.0	81	27.3	23	21.8
20 to 24 years	403	297	73.9	266	66.1	31	10.5
25 to 34 years	791	666	84.2	616	77.8	51	7.6
35 to 44 years	741	629	84.9	591	79.7	38	6.0
45 to 54 years	871	738	84.8	702	80.6	36	4.9
55 to 64 years	719	501	69.7	475	66.0	27	5.3
65 years and over	763	174	22.8	162	21.3	11	6.5

NOTE: Data in Table 7 are from the Current Population Survey (CPS) and do not match the estimates in Table 8. See notes and definitions for further information.

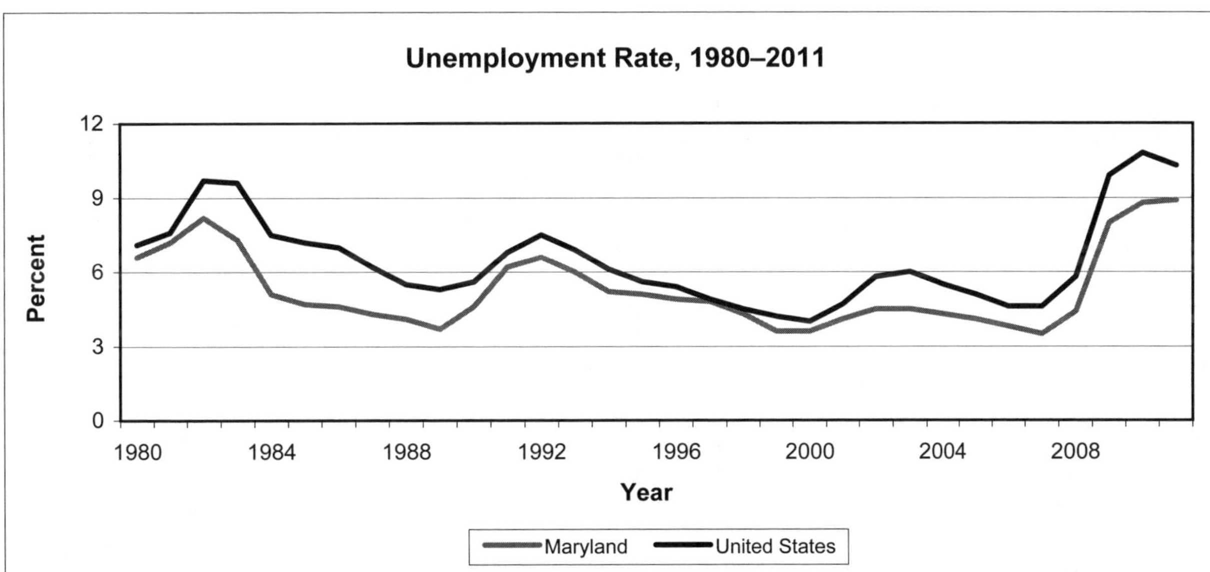

Table MD-8. Employment Status of the Civilian Noninstitutional Population Age 16 Years and Over

(Number, percent.)

Year	Civilian labor force	Civilian participation rate	Employed	Unemployed	Unemployment rate
2005	2,931,946	68.8	2,810,748	121,198	4.1
2006	2,983,937	69.4	2,871,176	112,761	3.8
2007	2,987,698	69.0	2,882,447	105,251	3.5
2008	2,997,709	68.8	2,857,178	130,531	4.4
2009	3,117,747	69.1	2,867,600	250,147	8.0
2010	3,164,140	68.8	2,886,015	278,125	8.8
2011	3,177,062	68.4	2,894,566	282,496	8.9

Table MD-9. Employment and Average Wages by Industry

(Estimates before 2007 are based on the 2002 *North American Industry Classification System* [NAICS]. Estimates from 2007 onward are based on the 2007 NAICS.)

Industry	2005	2006	2007	2008	2009	2010	2011
	Number of jobs						
Wage and Salary Employment by Industry	2,676,773	2,712,874	2,731,261	2,721,297	2,643,648	2,636,857	2,664,514
Farm Wage and Salary Employment	5,122	5,296	4,975	4,436	4,298	4,816	4,670
Nonfarm Wage and Salary Employment	2,671,651	2,707,578	2,726,286	2,716,861	2,639,350	2,632,041	2,659,844
Private wage and salary employment	2,141,822	2,170,389	2,184,135	2,165,616	2,081,971	2,066,491	2,089,409
Forestry, fishing, and related activities	2,480	2,392	2,146	2,166	2,109	2,186	2,094
Mining	1,711	1,795	1,650	1,616	1,492	1,468	1,431
Utilities	9,705	9,722	9,928	10,274	10,104	9,719	10,071
Construction	190,193	195,516	195,062	185,201	160,300	149,522	150,948
Manufacturing	139,750	135,518	131,846	128,368	118,788	115,083	112,946
Durable goods manufacturing	74,000	71,599	70,986	69,424	63,902	61,503	60,185
Nondurable goods manufacturing	65,750	63,919	60,860	58,944	54,886	53,580	52,761
Wholesale trade	95,039	95,941	95,991	93,753	88,238	86,123	86,777
Retail trade	302,104	303,808	305,675	296,824	281,097	281,817	284,893
Transportation and warehousing	67,814	69,757	69,799	68,277	65,511	66,017	66,581
Information	50,521	51,191	51,107	49,955	46,319	43,949	41,019
Finance and insurance	112,573	112,783	109,978	105,486	101,598	99,412	98,965
Real estate and rental and leasing	49,987	49,633	48,974	48,013	44,864	44,307	43,659
Professional, scientific, and technical services	216,736	221,936	224,145	229,406	227,426	227,311	232,290
Management of companies and enterprises	18,101	19,753	20,469	20,997	19,877	19,532	22,148
Administrative and waste services	156,165	157,766	157,442	153,452	141,599	145,057	147,597
Educational services	63,564	64,051	66,768	68,717	69,358	70,351	73,095
Health care and social assistance	292,435	300,436	307,718	315,336	324,909	329,891	335,766
Arts, entertainment, and recreation	36,425	36,865	37,125	37,072	35,893	36,289	37,094
Accommodation and food services	193,195	196,492	199,704	201,902	197,244	196,821	199,636
Other services, except public administration	143,324	145,034	148,608	148,801	145,245	141,636	142,399
Government and government enterprises	529,829	537,189	542,151	551,245	557,379	565,550	570,435
	Dollars						
Average Wages and Salaries by Industry	45,400	47,360	49,323	50,629	51,705	52,945	54,281
Average Farm Wages and Salaries	21,825	24,463	29,777	32,039	31,414	26,481	24,431
Average Nonfarm Wages and Salaries	45,445	47,404	49,359	50,660	51,738	52,993	54,333
Average private wages and salaries	43,624	45,564	47,350	48,463	49,201	50,463	51,659
Forestry, fishing, and related activities	24,155	24,908	25,080	25,850	25,811	26,607	27,450
Mining	51,747	51,075	52,562	54,404	53,982	55,858	61,188
Utilities	91,879	91,765	101,234	101,535	96,608	107,058	109,583
Construction	46,648	48,952	51,310	53,314	54,431	54,972	55,910
Manufacturing	55,587	57,699	61,807	63,443	64,848	67,792	68,579
Durable goods manufacturing	62,449	64,369	67,273	69,976	72,442	75,905	75,857
Nondurable goods manufacturing	47,864	50,227	55,433	55,748	56,006	58,479	60,276
Wholesale trade	60,662	63,426	66,000	67,812	68,505	70,546	72,673
Retail trade	27,552	28,314	28,459	28,262	28,394	28,841	28,948
Transportation and warehousing	42,053	43,224	44,585	45,986	46,262	47,989	50,118
Information	63,575	65,077	66,250	68,618	70,584	74,037	78,331
Finance and insurance	74,104	76,811	80,216	79,960	78,522	82,242	85,075
Real estate and rental and leasing	47,157	50,249	52,056	52,211	51,876	55,258	56,471
Professional, scientific, and technical services	70,041	74,135	77,415	80,094	82,925	85,262	88,177
Management of companies and enterprises	88,981	92,304	97,366	94,427	97,673	107,580	106,464
Administrative and waste services	31,704	33,401	35,426	36,580	37,256	38,149	38,668
Educational services	37,956	39,757	40,361	41,290	42,967	43,527	45,390
Health care and social assistance	41,392	43,036	44,576	46,612	47,362	47,646	48,623
Arts, entertainment, and recreation	27,914	29,962	31,591	29,359	29,861	31,151	31,522
Accommodation and food services	17,474	18,496	19,707	19,610	19,498	20,084	20,594
Other services, except public administration	29,656	31,075	32,083	33,191	33,741	34,951	35,414
Government and government enterprises	52,806	54,839	57,454	59,290	61,217	62,239	64,128

Table MD-10. Employment Characteristics by Family Type

(Number, percent.)

Family type and labor force status	2009 Total	2009 Families with own children under 18 years	2010 Total	2010 Families with own children under 18 years	2011 Total	2011 Families with own children under 18 years
All families	1,391,688	641,075	1,431,958	643,815	1,415,576	629,280
Family type and labor force status						
Married-couple families	1,012,157	433,179	1,022,613	430,441	995,216	411,914
Both husband and wife in labor force	61.6	74.0	61.4	73.5	59.2	72.6
Husband in labor force, wife not in labor force	19.2	22.6	19.1	22.7	19.4	22.4
Wife in labor force, husband not in labor force	6.6	2.5	6.9	3.1	7.8	3.9
Both husband and wife not in labor force	12.6	0.9	12.5	0.7	13.7	1.1
Other families	379,531	207,896	409,345	213,374	420,360	217,366
Female householder, no husband present	76.3	79.5	74.6	78.0	75.8	78.6
In labor force	59.5	69.3	57.7	67.5	59.1	70.0
Not in labor force	16.9	10.2	16.8	10.5	16.8	8.7
Male householder, no wife present	23.7	20.5	25.4	22.0	24.2	21.4
In labor force	19.5	19.0	21.0	20.6	19.8	20.2
Not in labor force	4.2	1.5	4.4	1.3	4.4	1.2

Table MD-11. School Enrollment and Educational Attainment, 2011

(Number, percent.)

Item	State	U.S.
Enrollment		
Total population 3 years and over, enrolled in school	1,577,839	83,131,910
Enrolled in nursery school or preschool (percent)	6.2	6.0
Enrolled in kindergarten (percent)	4.7	5.1
Enrolled in elementary school, grades 1-8 (percent)	36.9	39.5
Enrolled in high school, grades 9-12 (percent)	20.1	20.7
Enrolled in college or graduate school (percent)	32.1	28.7
Attainment		
Total population 25 years and over	3,915,657	206,471,670
Less than ninth grade (percent)	4.3	6.0
9th to 12th grade, no diploma (percent)	6.9	8.1
High school graduate, including equivalency (percent)	25.8	28.4
Some college, no degree (percent)	19.9	21.2
Associate's degree (percent)	6.3	7.8
Bachelor's degree (percent)	20.4	17.9
Graduate or professional degree (percent)	16.5	10.6
High school graduate or higher (percent)	88.9	85.9
Bachelor's degree or higher (percent)	36.9	28.5

Table MD-12. Educational Indicators

(Number, percent; data derived from National Center of Education Statistics.)

Item	State	U.S.
Public Schools, 2009–2010 (except where noted)		
Number of school districts	24	13,629
Number of schools	1,447	99,834
Number of students (in thousands)	848	49,373
Student-teacher ratio	14.6	15.4
Expenditures per student (dollars)	15,566	10,591
Averaged freshman graduation rate, 2008–2009	80.1	75.5[1]
Dropout rate, 2008–2009	3.0	4.1
Students eligible for free or reduced-price lunch (percent)	39.8	48.0
English language learners, 2010–2011 (percent)	5.3	9.8[1]
Students with IEP (percent)	12.1	13.1
Private Schools, 2009–2010 (except where noted)		
Number of schools	795	33,366
Number of students (in thousands)	126	4,700
High school graduates, 2008–2009	9,228	308,813
Student-teacher ratio	9.6	10.7

[1] U.S. total includes estimates for nonreporting states.

Table MD-13. Reported Voting and Registration of the Voting-Age Population, November 2012

(Numbers in thousands, percent.)

Item	Total population	Total citizen population	Registered			Voted		
			Total registered	Percent registered (total population)	Percent registered (total citizen population)	Total voted	Percent voted (total population)	Percent voted (total citizen population)
U.S. Total	235,248	215,081	153,157	65.1	71.2	132,948	56.5	61.8
State Total	4,449	4,007	2,888	64.9	72.1	2,609	58.7	65.1
Sex								
Male	2,101	1,914	1,336	63.6	69.8	1,189	56.6	62.1
Female	2,348	2,093	1,552	66.1	74.2	1,421	60.5	67.9
Race								
White alone	2,837	2,635	1,913	67.4	72.6	1,711	60.3	65.0
White, non-Hispanic alone	2,567	2,511	1,840	71.7	73.3	1,648	64.2	65.6
Black alone	1,276	1,167	850	66.6	72.8	788	61.8	67.5
Asian alone	260	131	78	29.9	59.4	66	25.4	50.4
Hispanic (of any race)	342	176	115	33.7	65.6	103	30.2	58.7
Age								
18 to 24 years	585	558	301	51.5	54.0	246	42.1	44.1
25 to 44 years	1,498	1,211	873	58.3	72.1	789	52.7	65.1
45 to 64 years	1,557	1,450	1,107	71.1	76.3	1,025	65.8	70.7
65 to 74 years	478	465	383	80.1	82.3	356	74.6	76.7
75 years and over	331	322	224	67.8	69.6	193	58.4	60.0

Table MD-14. Crime

(Number, rate per 100,000. Data are derived from the FBI Uniform Crime Reports.)

Item	State			U.S.		
	2010	2011	Percent change	2010	2011	Percent change
TOTAL POPULATION	5,785,681	5,828,289	0.7	309,330,219	311,591,917	0.7
VIOLENT CRIME						
Number	31,607	28,797	-8.9	1,251,248	1,203,564	-3.8
Rate	546.3	494.1	-9.6	404.5	386.3	-4.5
Murder and Nonnegligent Manslaughter						
Number	426	398	-6.6	14,722	14,612	-0.7
Rate	7.4	6.8	-8.1	4.8	4.7	-2.1
Forcible Rape						
Number	1,228	1,194	-2.8	85,593	83,425	-2.5
Rate	21.2	20.5	-3.3	27.7	26.8	-3.2
Robbery						
Number	11,054	10,343	-6.4	369,089	354,396	-4.0
Rate	191.1	177.5	-7.1	119.3	113.7	-4.7
Aggravated Assault						
Number	18,899	16,862	-10.8	781,844	751,131	-3.9
Rate	326.7	289.3	-11.4	252.8	241.1	-4.6
PROPERTY CRIME						
Number	173,309	166,699	-3.8	9,112,625	9,063,173	-0.5
Rate	2,995.5	2,860.2	-4.5	2,945.9	2,908.7	-1.3
Burglary						
Number	36,704	35,784	-2.5	2,168,459	2,188,005	0.9
Rate	634.4	614.0	-3.2	701.0	702.2	0.2
Larceny-Theft						
Number	118,578	114,847	-3.1	6,204,601	6,159,795	-0.7
Rate	2,049.5	1,970.5	-3.9	2,005.8	1,976.9	-1.4
Motor Vehicle Theft						
Number	18,027	16,068	-10.9	739,565	715,373	-3.3
Rate	311.6	275.7	-11.5	239.1	229.6	-4.0

Table MD-15. State Government Finances, 2011

(Dollar amounts in thousands, percent distribution.)

Item	Dollars	Percent distribution
Total Revenue	41,716,504	100.0
General revenue	32,998,746	79.1
Intergovernmental revenue	11,335,533	27.2
Taxes	16,002,529	38.4
General sales	3,896,700	9.3
Selective sales	2,757,314	6.6
License taxes	739,482	1.8
Individual income tax	6,644,962	15.9
Corporate income tax	775,845	1.9
Other taxes	1,188,226	2.8
Current charges	3,248,535	7.8
Miscellaneous general revenue	2,412,149	5.8
Utility revenue	152,836	0.4
Liquor stores revenue	0	0.0
Insurance trust revenue [1]	8,564,922	20.5
Total Expenditure	37,672,576	100.0
Intergovernmental expenditure	8,124,451	21.6
Direct expenditure	29,548,125	78.4
Current operation	19,699,511	52.3
Capital outlay	2,605,932	6.9
Insurance benefits and repayments	4,474,946	11.9
Assistance and subsidies	1,702,594	4.5
Interest on debt	1,065,142	2.8
Exhibit: Salaries and wages	4,711,684	12.5
Total Expenditure	37,672,576	100.0
General expenditure	32,305,854	85.8
Intergovernmental expenditure	8,124,451	21.6
Direct expenditure	24,181,403	64.2
General expenditure, by function:		
Education	11,212,610	29.8
Public welfare	9,274,305	24.6
Hospitals	495,596	1.3
Health	1,848,976	4.9
Highways	2,195,643	5.8
Police protection	521,332	1.4
Correction	1,383,744	3.7
Natural resources	467,720	1.2
Parks and recreation	128,763	0.3
Governmental administration	1,308,637	3.5
Interest on general debt	1,065,142	2.8
Other and unallocable	2,403,386	6.4
Utility expenditure	891,776	2.4
Liquor stores expenditure	0	0.0
Insurance trust expenditure	4,474,946	11.9
Debt at End of Fiscal Year	25,250,138	X
Cash and Security Holdings	58,515,287	X

X = Not applicable.
[1] Within insurance trust revenue, net earnings of state retirement systems is a calculated statistic (the item code in the data file is X08), and thus can be positive or negative. Net earnings is the sum of earnings on investments plus gains on investments minus losses on investments. The change made in 2002 for asset valuation from book to market value in accordance with Statement 34 of the Governmental Accounting Standards Board is reflected in the calculated statistics.

Table MD-16. State Government Tax Collections, 2012

(Dollars in thousands, percent.)

Item	Dollars	Percent distribution
Total Taxes	17,064,468	100.0
Property taxes	755,937	4.4
Sales and gross receipts	7,173,515	42.0
General sales and gross receipts	4,076,578	23.9
Selective sales and gross receipts	3,096,937	18.1
Alcoholic beverages	31,010	0.2
Amusements	27,504	0.2
Insurance premiums	428,024	2.5
Motor fuels	733,410	4.3
Pari-mutuels	1,267	-
Public utilities	127,106	0.7
Tobacco products	411,427	2.4
Other selective sales	1,337,189	7.8
Licenses	756,852	4.4
Alcoholic beverages	1,201	0.0
Amusements	26,000	0.2
Corporations in general	96,412	0.6
Hunting and fishing	15,858	0.1
Motor vehicle	443,956	2.6
Motor vehicle operators	26,244	0.2
Public utilities	0	0.0
Occupation and business, NEC	145,252	0.9
Other licenses	1,929	-
Income taxes	7,996,961	46.9
Individual income	7,116,605	41.7
Corporation net income	880,356	5.2
Other taxes	381,203	2.2
Death and gift	196,875	1.2
Documentary and stock transfer	127,575	0.7
Severance	0	0.0
Taxes, NEC	56,753	0.3

- = Rounds to zero.

Leading Exports, 2012

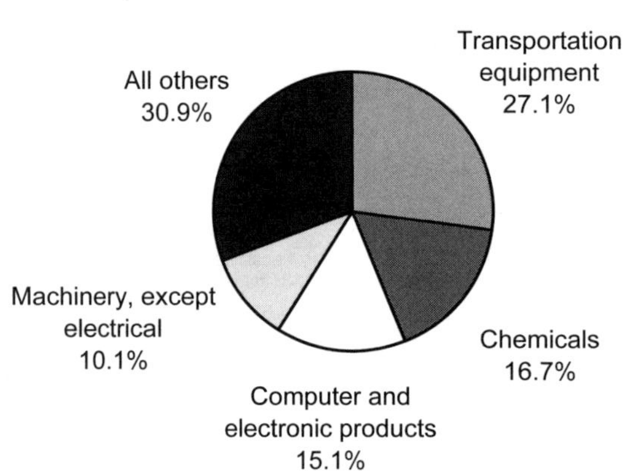

MASSACHUSETTS

Facts and Figures

Location: Northeastern United States; bordered on the N by Vermont and New Hampshire, on the E by the Atlantic Ocean, on the S by Connecticut and Rhode Island, and on the W by New York

Area: 10,555 sq. mi. (27,336 sq. km.); rank—44th

Population: 6,646,144 (2012 est.); rank—14th

Principal Cities: capital—Boston; largest—Boston

Statehood: February 6, 1788; 6th state

U.S. Congress: 2 senators, 9 representatives

State Motto: *Ense petit placidam sub libertate quietem* ("By the sword we seek peace, but peace only under liberty")

State Song: "All Hail to Massachusetts"

State Nickname: The Bay State

Abbreviations: MA; Mass.

State Symbols: flower—mayflower; tree—American elm; bird—chickadee

At a Glance

- With an increase in population of 3.9 percent, Massachusetts ranked 27th among the states in growth from 2000 to 2009.
- An estimated 36,700 marriages took place in Massachusetts in 2009, compared to 12,700 divorces.
- Massachusetts's median household income in 2011 was $62,859, and 11.6 percent of the population lived below the poverty level.
- Massachusetts's violent crime rate in 2011 was 428.4 per 100,000 population, compared to 386.3 for the entire nation.
- In 2007, Massachusetts exported $201 million worth of agricultural products, less than 1 percent of the U.S. total.

Table MA-1. Population by Age, Sex, Race, and Hispanic Origin

(Number, percent, except where noted.)

Sex, age, race, and Hispanic origin	2000	2010	2012[1]	Average annual percent change, 2010–2012
Total Population	6,349,097	6,547,629	6,646,144	0.5
Percent of total U.S. population	2.3	2.1	2.1	X
Sex				
Male	3,058,816	3,166,628	3,220,373	0.6
Female	3,290,281	3,381,001	3,425,771	0.4
Age				
Under 5 years	397,268	367,087	365,557	-0.1
5 to 19 years	1,277,845	1,254,056	1,245,485	-0.2
20 to 64 years	3,813,822	4,023,762	4,076,608	0.4
65 years and over	860,162	902,724	958,494	1.9
Median age (years)	36.5	39.1	39.3	0.2
Race and Hispanic Origin				
One race				
White	5,367,286	5,524,937	5,560,222	0.2
Black	343,454	504,365	525,799	1.4
American Indian and Alaska Native	15,015	29,944	31,172	1.3
Asian	238,124	359,673	387,770	2.4
Native Hawaiian or Other Pacific Islander	2,489	5,971	6,304	1.8
Two or more races	146,005	122,739	134,877	3.0
Hispanic (of any race)	428,729	656,888	708,296	2.4

X = Not applicable.
[1] Population figures for 2012 are July 1 estimates. The 2010 estimates are taken from the 2010 Census.

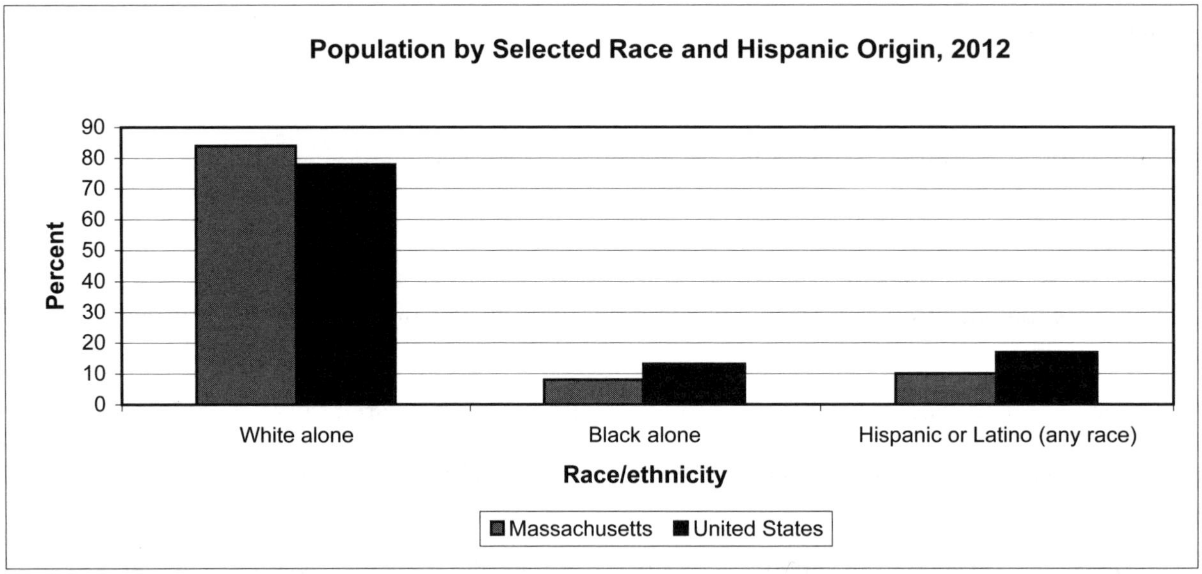

Table MA-2. Marital Status

(Number, percent distribution.)

Sex, age, race, and Hispanic origin	2000	2010	2011
Males, 15 Years and Over	2,412,349	2,579,221	2,601,690
Never married	33.9	38.7	38.2
Now married, except separated	54.7	49.1	49.6
Separated	1.6	1.6	1.6
Widowed	2.7	2.7	2.7
Divorced	7.0	8.0	7.9
Females, 15 Years and Over	2,679,020	2,819,768	2,838,556
Never married	28.5	33.2	33.2
Now married, except separated	48.9	44.1	44.4
Separated	2.3	2.4	2.3
Widowed	10.8	9.1	9.2
Divorced	9.5	11.1	10.9

Table MA-3. Households and Housing Characteristics

(Number, percent, dollars.)

Item	2000	2010	2011	Average annual percent change, 2000–2011
Total Households	2,443,580	2,520,419	2,532,067	0.3
Family households	1,576,696	1,590,257	1,597,920	0.1
Married-couple family	1,197,917	1,166,204	1,174,019	-0.2
Other family	378,779	424,053	423,901	1.0
Male householder, no wife present	88,835	100,400	99,872	1.0
Female householder, no husband present	289,944	323,653	324,029	1.0
Nonfamily households	866,884	930,162	934,147	0.6
Householder living alone	684,345	736,320	742,371	0.7
Householder not living alone	182,539	193,842	191,776	0.4
Housing Characteristics				
Total housing units	2,621,989	2,808,727	2,819,028	0.6
Occupied housing units	2,443,580	2,520,419	2,532,067	0.3
Owner occupied	1,508,052	1,568,382	1,573,279	0.4
Renter occupied	935,528	952,037	958,788	0.2
Average size	2.51	2.51	2.51	-
Financial Characteristics				
Median gross rent of renter-occupied housing	684	1,009	1,034	4.3
Median monthly owner costs for housing units with a mortgage	1,353	2,036	2,042	4.2
Median value of owner-occupied housing units	185,700	334,100	326,300	6.3

- = Zero or rounds to zero.

Table MA-4. Migration, Origin, and Language

(Number, percent.)

Characteristic	State			U.S.		
	2010	2011	Percent change	2010	2011	Percent change
Residence 1 Year Ago						
Population 1 year and over	6,489,250	6,515,057	0.4	305,628,607	307,900,319	0.7
Same house	86.0	86.9	1.0	84.6	84.8	0.2
Different house in the U.S.	13.0	12.2	-6.2	14.8	14.6	-1.4
Same county	8.2	7.4	-9.8	9.4	9.2	-2.1
Different county	4.8	4.8	-	5.4	5.4	-
Same state	2.7	2.7	-	3.2	3.1	-3.1
Different state	2.2	2.1	-4.5	2.2	2.3	4.5
Abroad	0.9	0.9	-	0.6	0.6	-
Place of Birth						
Native born	5,573,690	5,604,147	0.5	269,393,835	271,214,059	0.7
Male	48.4	48.4	-	49.2	49.2	-
Female	51.6	51.6	-	50.8	50.8	-
Foreign born	983,564	983,389	-	39,955,854	40,377,860	1.1
Male	47.9	48.2	0.6	49.1	48.9	-0.4
Female	52.1	51.8	-0.6	50.9	51.1	0.4
Foreign born; naturalized U.S. citizen	472,990	501,139	6.0	17,476,082	18,140,192	3.8
Male	44.2	45.8	3.6	45.8	45.8	-
Female	55.8	54.2	-2.9	54.2	54.2	-
Foreign born; not a U.S. citizen	510,574	482,250	-5.5	22,479,772	22,237,668	-1.1
Male	51.3	50.7	-1.2	51.6	51.5	-0.2
Female	48.7	49.3	1.2	48.4	48.5	0.2
Entered 2000 or later	38.1	39.3	3.1	34.7	35.7	2.9
Entered 1990 to 1999	24.6	24.4	-0.8	27.2	26.7	-1.8
Entered before 1990	37.3	36.3	-2.7	38.1	37.6	-1.3
World Region of Birth, Foreign						
Foreign-born population, excluding population born at sea	983,516	983,389	0.0	39,955,673	40,377,757	1.1
Europe	23.5	23.3	-0.9	12.1	12.1	-
Asia	29.1	29.3	0.7	28.2	28.6	1.4
Africa	7.9	8.4	6.3	4	4.1	2.5
Oceania	0.3	0.3	-	0.5	0.5	-
Latin America	36.2	35.7	-1.4	53.1	52.6	-0.9
North America	3.1	3.0	-3.2	2	2.0	-
Language Spoken at Home and Ability to Speak English						
Population 5 years and over	6,190,919	6,224,979	0.6	289,215,746	291,524,091	0.8
English only	78.3	78.0	-0.4	79.4	79.2	-0.3
Language other than English	21.7	22.0	1.4	20.6	20.8	1.0
Speaks English less than "very well"	8.8	8.9	1.1	8.7	8.7	-

- = Zero or rounds to zero.

Table MA-5. Median Income and Poverty Status, 2011

(Number, percent, except as noted.)

Characteristic	State		U.S.	
	Number	Percent	Number	Percent
Median Income				
Households (dollars)	62,859	X	50,502	X
Families (dollars)	80,425	X	61,455	X
Below Poverty Level (All People)	738,514	11.6	48,452,035	15.9
Sex				
Male	311,147	10.1	21,825,281	14.7
Female	427,367	13.0	26,626,754	17.2
Age				
Under 18 years	211,789	15.2	16,386,500	22.5
Related children under 18 years	206,694	14.9	16,087,074	22.2
18 to 64 years	444,249	10.9	28,335,079	14.8
65 years and over	82,476	9.3	3,730,456	9.3

X = Not applicable.

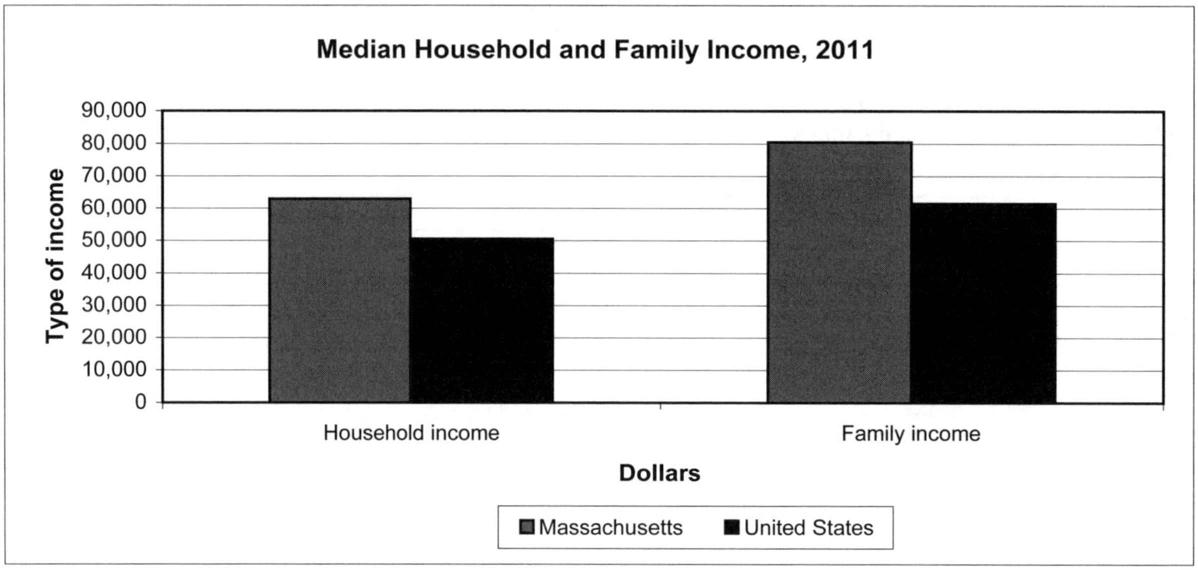

Table MA-6. Health Insurance Coverage Status for the Civilian Noninstitutionalized Population and Children Under 18 Years of Age

(Numbers in thousands, percent.)

Item	2004	2005	2006	2007	2008	2009	2010	2011
Civilian Noninstitutionalized Population	6,370	6,328	6,335	6,340	6,399	6,496	6,478	6,508
Covered by Private or Public Insurance								
Number	5,650	5,745	5,678	6,000	6,135	6,225	6,192	6,231
Percent	88.7	90.8	89.6	94.6	95.9	95.8	95.6	95.7
Not Covered								
Number	720	583	657	340	264	271	286	277
Percent	11.3	9.2	10.4	5.4	4.1	4.2	4.4	4.3
Percent in the U.S. not covered	14.9	15.3	15.8	15.3	15.1	15.1	15.5	15.1
Children Under 18 Years of Age	1,488	1,499	1,470	1,435	1,427	1,431	1,415	1,402
Covered by Private or Public Insurance								
Number	1,401	1,436	1,367	1,392	1,397	1,411	1,393	1,378
Percent	94.2	95.8	93.0	97.0	97.9	98.6	98.5	98.3
Not Covered								
Number	87	63	103	43	30	20	22	24
Percent	5.8	4.2	7.0	3.0	2.1	1.4	1.5	1.7
Percent in the U.S. not covered	10.5	10.9	11.7	11.0	9.7	8.6	8.0	7.5

Table MA-7. Employment Status by Demographic Group, Preliminary 2012

(Numbers in thousands, percent.)

Characteristic	Civilian noninstitutional population	Civilian labor force		Employed		Unemployed	
		Number	Percent of population	Number	Percent of population	Number	Percent of population
Total	5,320	3,476	65.3	3,245	61.0	231	6.7
Sex							
Male	2,540	1,762	69.3	1,629	64.1	133	7.5
Female	2,780	1,715	61.7	1,616	58.1	99	5.8
Race, Sex, and Hispanic Origin							
White	4,522	2,962	65.5	2,772	61.3	190	6.4
Male	2,172	1,520	70.0	1,412	65.0	108	7.1
Female	2,350	1,442	61.4	1,360	57.9	82	5.7
Black or African American	385	229	59.5	202	52.4	28	12.1
Male	180	107	59.7	92	51.1	16	14.5
Female	205	122	59.4	110	53.5	12	9.9
Hispanic	459	280	61.0	252	55.0	27	9.8
Male	225	152	67.6	133	59.4	19	12.2
Female	234	128	54.7	119	50.8	9	7.0
Age							
16 to 19 years	385	127	32.9	101	26.3	26	20.2
20 to 24 years	486	341	70.1	309	63.6	32	9.2
25 to 34 years	789	674	85.3	628	79.6	46	6.8
35 to 44 years	900	763	84.7	725	80.5	38	5.0
45 to 54 years	978	804	82.3	760	77.7	45	5.5
55 to 64 years	806	574	71.2	539	66.9	34	6.0
65 years and over	976	195	19.9	183	18.7	12	6.1

NOTE: Data in Table 7 are from the Current Population Survey (CPS) and do not match the estimates in Table 8. See notes and definitions for further information.

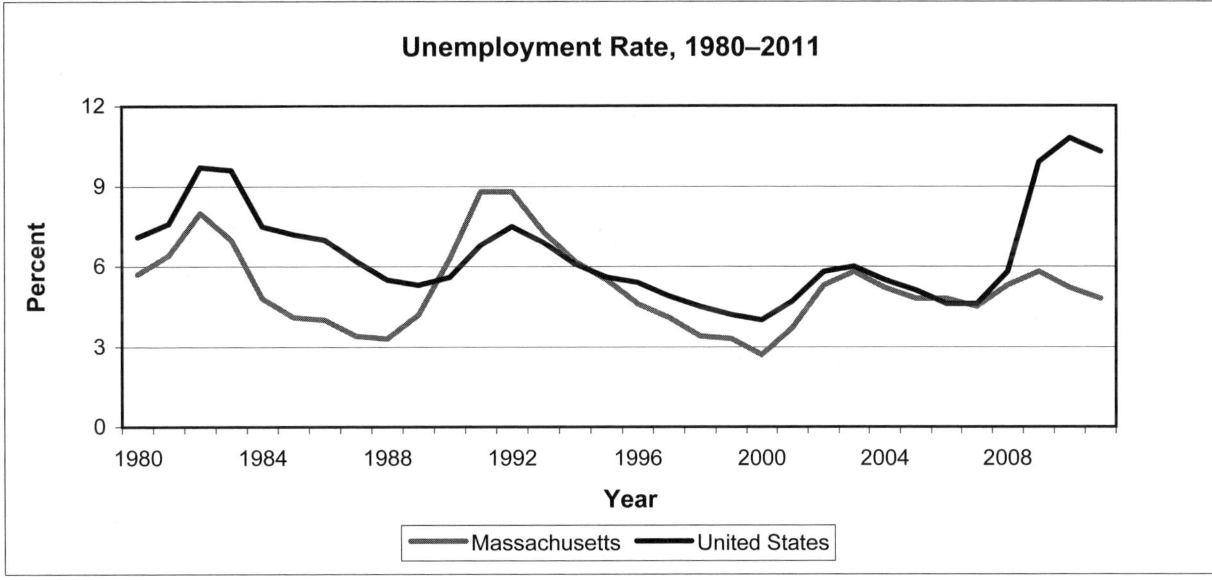

Table MA-8. Employment Status of the Civilian Noninstitutional Population Age 16 Years and Over

(Number, percent.)

Year	Civilian labor force	Civilian participation rate	Employed	Unemployed	Unemployment rate
2005	3,376,590	66.8	3,213,051	163,539	4.8
2006	3,407,957	67.1	3,245,374	162,583	4.8
2007	3,415,613	66.8	3,262,646	152,967	4.5
2008	3,424,018	66.5	3,243,779	180,239	5.3
2009	3,634,120	68.2	3,304,921	329,199	9.1
2010	3,590,908	67.6	3,225,103	365,805	10.2
2011	3,619,653	67.5	3,284,720	334,933	9.3

Table MA-9. Employment and Average Wages by Industry

(Estimates before 2007 are based on the 2002 *North American Industry Classification System* [NAICS]. Estimates from 2007 onward are based on the 2007 NAICS.)

Industry	2005	2006	2007	2008	2009	2010	2011
	Number of jobs						
Wage and Salary Employment by Industry	3,330,098	3,360,521	3,404,202	3,410,858	3,300,521	3,311,859	3,350,292
Farm Wage and Salary Employment	3,992	3,655	3,535	3,858	3,721	3,730	3,956
Nonfarm Wage and Salary Employment	3,326,106	3,356,866	3,400,667	3,407,000	3,296,800	3,308,129	3,346,336
Private wage and salary employment	2,888,537	2,914,370	2,952,145	2,953,629	2,844,590	2,853,964	2,896,415
Forestry, fishing, and related activities	4,660	4,660	4,591	4,578	4,879	4,971	4,058
Mining	1,834	1,727	1,485	1,273	1,220	1,048	1,002
Utilities	9,609	9,650	9,867	10,026	10,209	10,432	10,453
Construction	144,808	146,172	142,803	137,785	116,521	112,186	116,555
Manufacturing	305,864	299,786	295,949	287,097	259,629	254,857	254,195
Durable goods manufacturing	200,411	196,936	195,806	190,450	170,461	166,166	167,191
Nondurable goods manufacturing	105,453	102,850	100,143	96,647	89,168	88,691	87,004
Wholesale trade	134,865	137,589	139,063	137,445	128,466	123,891	124,165
Retail trade	360,064	355,680	354,301	352,469	339,954	345,194	348,742
Transportation and warehousing	73,957	74,478	76,131	76,041	72,101	73,879	74,670
Information	87,437	87,416	88,070	89,450	84,864	85,363	84,355
Finance and insurance	179,955	183,781	185,195	182,975	176,477	173,524	173,682
Real estate and rental and leasing	46,457	46,039	44,916	43,947	42,062	41,765	41,714
Professional, scientific, and technical services	234,734	244,604	250,762	261,255	254,688	251,989	259,996
Management of companies and enterprises	64,400	62,220	61,356	61,351	59,060	57,436	58,604
Administrative and waste services	165,114	170,379	174,984	169,591	151,742	158,625	163,472
Educational services	173,676	174,122	181,131	180,664	183,512	182,461	186,329
Health care and social assistance	446,874	458,939	476,832	488,580	498,869	510,601	518,706
Arts, entertainment, and recreation	47,158	47,323	48,943	49,935	48,383	49,611	50,570
Accommodation and food services	248,704	252,229	257,160	259,566	255,091	261,794	268,399
Other services, except public administration	158,367	157,576	158,606	159,601	156,863	154,337	156,748
Government and government enterprises	437,569	442,496	448,522	453,371	452,210	454,165	449,921
	Dollars						
Average Wages and Salaries by Industry	49,090	51,444	54,234	55,737	55,235	56,808	58,620
Average Farm Wages and Salaries	21,838	27,676	32,760	28,799	28,366	26,728	22,546
Average Nonfarm Wages and Salaries	49,122	51,470	54,256	55,767	55,265	56,842	58,662
Average private wages and salaries	49,614	52,082	55,062	56,563	55,879	57,689	59,541
Forestry, fishing, and related activities	51,904	48,587	51,269	51,525	51,403	54,008	57,093
Mining	50,436	53,456	54,881	51,901	53,072	56,133	57,184
Utilities	87,305	89,051	94,037	99,517	102,825	104,102	109,970
Construction	53,466	55,636	59,050	62,174	61,845	62,162	63,266
Manufacturing	62,460	65,048	69,540	68,978	69,237	75,206	77,553
Durable goods manufacturing	68,667	71,460	75,789	75,487	75,716	83,905	86,712
Nondurable goods manufacturing	50,662	52,771	57,323	56,151	56,850	58,908	59,953
Wholesale trade	67,184	72,794	74,693	76,919	76,456	79,192	82,166
Retail trade	27,509	27,353	27,620	27,741	27,777	27,823	27,919
Transportation and warehousing	40,242	41,521	43,184	43,716	43,730	44,150	45,425
Information	76,381	81,089	83,415	86,277	84,680	91,985	95,875
Finance and insurance	98,070	103,605	115,345	118,230	110,406	114,391	119,299
Real estate and rental and leasing	50,400	54,852	56,657	56,632	55,582	60,295	63,205
Professional, scientific, and technical services	83,418	87,853	92,900	96,720	95,743	100,957	103,816
Management of companies and enterprises	81,305	88,641	99,816	100,424	101,498	104,263	123,065
Administrative and waste services	34,259	35,697	37,767	38,683	38,397	38,535	39,779
Educational services	35,777	37,294	39,078	41,583	42,058	44,404	45,969
Health care and social assistance	42,929	45,066	46,771	49,150	50,269	51,327	52,111
Arts, entertainment, and recreation	32,894	34,447	38,465	37,412	36,356	37,237	37,556
Accommodation and food services	19,542	20,106	21,495	21,316	21,000	21,409	21,976
Other services, except public administration	27,774	28,684	30,023	31,103	30,998	31,666	32,245
Government and government enterprises	45,879	47,440	48,950	50,586	51,400	51,519	53,008

Table MA-10. Employment Characteristics by Family Type

(Number, percent.)

Family type and labor force status	2009		2010		2011	
	Total	Families with own children under 18 years	Total	Families with own children under 18 years	Total	Families with own children under 18 years
All families	1,557,057	702,831	1,590,257	725,898	1,597,920	718,136
Family type and labor force status						
Married-couple families	1,168,510	506,333	1,166,204	498,547	1,174,019	495,852
Both husband and wife in labor force	61.6	73.7	60.6	73.2	60.9	72.9
Husband in labor force, wife not in labor force	17.9	22.0	18.5	22.5	18.2	22.3
Wife in labor force, husband not in labor force	7.1	3.2	6.8	3.2	6.9	3.4
Both husband and wife not in labor force	13.5	1.1	14.0	1.1	14.0	1.3
Other families	388,547	196,498	424,053	227,351	423,901	222,284
Female householder, no husband present	74.6	79.1	76.3	80.0	76.4	81.5
In labor force	52.6	62.1	54.1	64.1	54.0	64.9
Not in labor force	22.0	17.0	22.3	16.0	22.5	16.6
Male householder, no wife present	25.4	20.9	23.7	20.0	23.6	18.5
In labor force	20.1	18.5	18.8	18.1	18.6	16.8
Not in labor force	5.3	2.5	4.9	1.9	5.0	1.7

Table MA-11. School Enrollment and Educational Attainment, 2011

(Number, percent.)

Item	State	U.S.
Enrollment		
Total population 3 years and over, enrolled in school	1,764,471	83,131,910
Enrolled in nursery school or preschool (percent)	6.5	6.0
Enrolled in kindergarten (percent)	4.6	5.1
Enrolled in elementary school, grades 1-8 (percent)	35.7	39.5
Enrolled in high school, grades 9-12 (percent)	19.6	20.7
Enrolled in college or graduate school (percent)	33.6	28.7
Attainment		
Total population 25 years and over	4,502,048	206,471,670
Less than ninth grade (percent)	5.0	6.0
9th to 12th grade, no diploma (percent)	5.8	8.1
High school graduate, including equivalency (percent)	25.9	28.4
Some college, no degree (percent)	16.4	21.2
Associate's degree (percent)	7.8	7.8
Bachelor's degree (percent)	22.3	17.9
Graduate or professional degree (percent)	16.8	10.6
High school graduate or higher (percent)	89.2	85.9
Bachelor's degree or higher (percent)	39.1	28.5

Table MA-12. Educational Indicators

(Number, percent; data derived from National Center of Education Statistics.)

Item	State	U.S.
Public Schools, 2009–2010 (except where noted)		
Number of school districts	244	13,629
Number of schools	1,836	99,834
Number of students (in thousands)	957	49,373
Student-teacher ratio	13.7	15.4
Expenditures per student (dollars)	15,790	10,591
Averaged freshman graduation rate, 2008–2009	83.3	75.5[1]
Dropout rate, 2008–2009	2.9	4.1
Students eligible for free or reduced-price lunch (percent)	33.5	48.0
English language learners, 2010–2011 (percent)	6.7	9.8[1]
Students with IEP (percent)	17.5	13.1
Private Schools, 2009–2010 (except where noted)		
Number of schools	830	33,366
Number of students (in thousands)	119	4,700
High school graduates, 2008–2009	20,630	308,813
Student-teacher ratio	8.0	10.7

[1] U.S. total includes estimates for nonreporting states.

Table MA-13. Reported Voting and Registration of the Voting-Age Population, November 2012

(Numbers in thousands, percent.)

Item	Total population	Total citizen population	Registered			Voted		
			Total registered	Percent registered (total population)	Percent registered (total citizen population)	Total voted	Percent voted (total population)	Percent voted (total citizen population)
U.S. Total	235,248	215,081	153,157	65.1	71.2	132,948	56.5	61.8
State Total	5,170	4,774	3,759	72.7	78.7	3,382	65.4	70.8
Sex								
Male	2,452	2,238	1,750	71.4	78.2	1,576	64.3	70.4
Female	2,718	2,537	2,009	73.9	79.2	1,807	66.5	71.2
Race								
White alone	4,358	4,128	3,331	76.4	80.7	3,009	69.0	72.9
White, non-Hispanic alone	3,991	3,877	3,161	79.2	81.5	2,839	71.1	73.2
Black alone	385	321	228	59.2	70.9	211	54.7	65.6
Asian alone	317	219	119	37.6	54.3	98	30.8	44.5
Hispanic (of any race)	453	322	216	47.6	66.9	202	44.6	62.7
Age								
18 to 24 years	694	633	395	56.9	62.4	316	45.6	49.9
25 to 44 years	1,697	1,489	1,107	65.2	74.3	980	57.7	65.8
45 to 64 years	1,784	1,677	1,424	79.8	84.9	1,327	74.4	79.2
65 to 74 years	584	573	494	84.6	86.1	465	79.7	81.2
75 years and over	411	402	339	82.5	84.3	294	71.5	73.1

Table MA-14. Crime

(Number, rate per 100,000. Data are derived from the FBI Uniform Crime Reports.)

Item	State			U.S.		
	2010	2011	Percent change	2010	2011	Percent change
TOTAL POPULATION	6,555,466	6,587,536	0.5	309,330,219	311,591,917	0.7
VIOLENT CRIME						
Number	30,737	28,219	-8.2	1,251,248	1,203,564	-3.8
Rate	468.9	428.4	-8.6	404.5	386.3	-4.5
Murder and Nonnegligent Manslaughter						
Number	214	185	-13.6	14,722	14,612	-0.7
Rate	3.3	2.8	-15.2	4.8	4.7	-2.1
Forcible Rape						
Number	1,784	1,628	-8.7	85,593	83,425	-2.5
Rate	27.2	24.7	-9.2	27.7	26.8	-3.2
Robbery						
Number	6,897	6,768	-1.9	369,089	354,396	-4.0
Rate	105.2	102.7	-2.4	119.3	113.7	-4.7
Aggravated Assault						
Number	21,842	19,638	-10.1	781,844	751,131	-3.9
Rate	333.2	298.1	-10.5	252.8	241.1	-4.6
PROPERTY CRIME						
Number	154,496	148,790	-3.7	9,112,625	9,063,173	-0.5
Rate	2,356.8	2,258.7	-4.2	2,945.9	2,908.7	-1.3
Burglary						
Number	37,903	36,533	-3.6	2,168,459	2,188,005	0.9
Rate	578.2	554.6	-4.1	701.0	702.2	0.2
Larceny-Theft						
Number	105,124	101,471	-3.5	6,204,601	6,159,795	-0.7
Rate	1,603.6	1,540.3	-3.9	2,005.8	1,976.9	-1.4
Motor Vehicle Theft						
Number	11,469	10,786	-6.0	739,565	715,373	-3.3
Rate	175.0	163.7	-6.5	239.1	229.6	-4.0

Table MA-15. State Government Finances, 2011

(Dollar amounts in thousands, percent distribution.)

Item	Dollars	Percent distribution
Total Revenue	56,636,798	100.0
General revenue	44,897,892	79.3
Intergovernmental revenue	14,136,989	25.0
Taxes	22,089,530	39.0
General sales	4,920,521	8.7
Selective sales	2,188,175	3.9
License taxes	854,458	1.5
Individual income tax	11,597,152	20.5
Corporate income tax	1,931,571	3.4
Other taxes	597,653	1.1
Current charges	4,576,524	8.1
Miscellaneous general revenue	4,094,849	7.2
Utility revenue	208,690	0.4
Liquor stores revenue	0	0.0
Insurance trust revenue [1]	11,530,216	20.4
Total Expenditure	52,550,586	100.0
Intergovernmental expenditure	8,826,190	16.8
Direct expenditure	43,724,396	83.2
Current operation	27,811,681	52.9
Capital outlay	2,758,230	5.2
Insurance benefits and repayments	9,141,544	17.4
Assistance and subsidies	795,029	1.5
Interest on debt	3,217,912	6.1
Exhibit: Salaries and wages	5,353,522	10.2
Total Expenditure	52,550,586	100.0
General expenditure	43,181,008	82.2
Intergovernmental expenditure	8,826,190	16.8
Direct expenditure	34,354,818	65.4
General expenditure, by function:		
Education	12,334,213	23.5
Public welfare	14,715,542	28.0
Hospitals	515,094	1.0
Health	1,112,022	2.1
Highways	1,907,814	3.6
Police protection	759,139	1.4
Correction	1,050,827	2.0
Natural resources	349,346	0.7
Parks and recreation	237,973	0.5
Governmental administration	1,648,292	3.1
Interest on general debt	3,131,246	6.0
Other and unallocable	5,419,500	10.3
Utility expenditure	228,034	0.4
Liquor stores expenditure	0	0.0
Insurance trust expenditure	9,141,544	17.4
Debt at End of Fiscal Year	74,315,823	X
Cash and Security Holdings	94,697,510	X

X = Not applicable.
[1] Within insurance trust revenue, net earnings of state retirement systems is a calculated statistic (the item code in the data file is X08), and thus can be positive or negative. Net earnings is the sum of earnings on investments plus gains on investments minus losses on investments. The change made in 2002 for asset valuation from book to market value in accordance with Statement 34 of the Governmental Accounting Standards Board is reflected in the calculated statistics.

Table MA-16. State Government Tax Collections, 2012

(Dollars in thousands, percent.)

Item	Dollars	Percent distribution
Total Taxes	22,805,644	100.0
Property taxes	4,441	-
Sales and gross receipts	7,319,030	32.1
General sales and gross receipts	5,079,105	22.3
Selective sales and gross receipts	2,239,925	9.8
Alcoholic beverages	77,861	0.3
Amusements	3,082	-
Insurance premiums	342,201	1.5
Motor fuels	668,112	2.9
Pari-mutuels	1,635	-
Public utilities	23,925	0.1
Tobacco products	573,759	2.5
Other selective sales	549,350	2.4
Licenses	899,682	3.9
Alcoholic beverages	3,003	-
Amusements	436	-
Corporations in general	25,968	0.1
Hunting and fishing	5,921	-
Motor vehicle	376,552	1.7
Motor vehicle operators	98,899	0.4
Public utilities	0	0.0
Occupation and business, NEC	258,897	1.1
Other licenses	130,006	0.6
Income taxes	13,935,232	61.1
Individual income	11,933,452	52.3
Corporation net income	2,001,780	8.8
Other taxes	647,259	2.8
Death and gift	293,269	1.3
Documentary and stock transfer	186,202	0.8
Severance	0	0.0
Taxes, NEC	167,788	0.7

- = Rounds to zero.

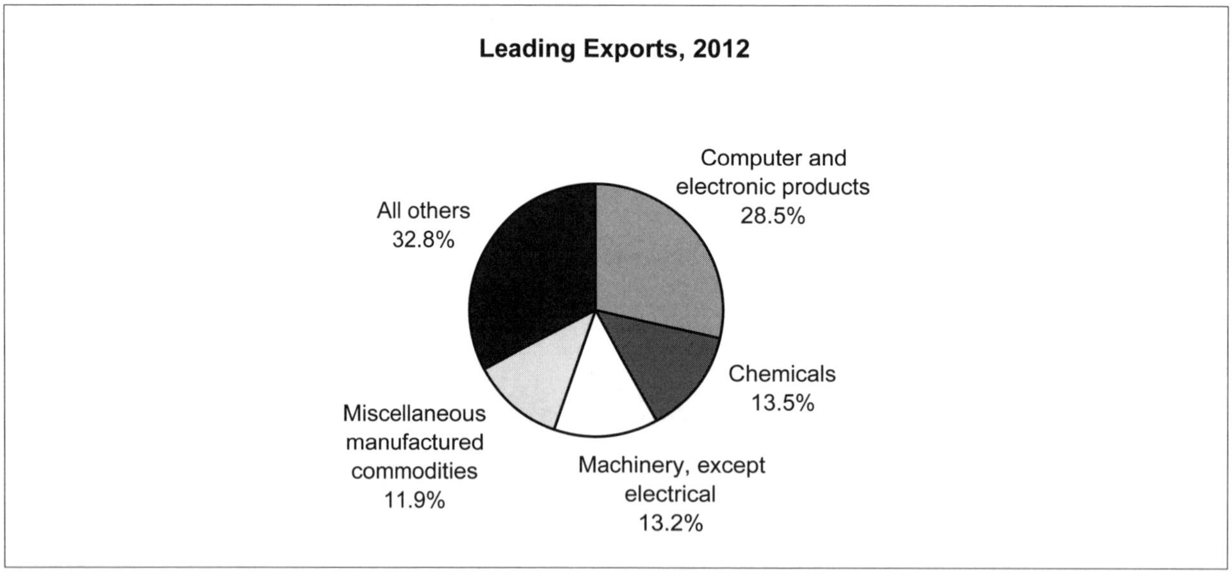

MICHIGAN

Facts and Figures

Location: East north central United States; bordered on the N by Lake Superior, on the E by Ontario, Canada, and Lakes Huron and Erie, on the S by Indiana and Ohio, and on the W by Wisconsin and Lake Michigan

Area: 96,716 sq. mi. (250,494 sq. km.); rank—11th

Population: 9,883,360 (2012 est.); rank—9th

Principal Cities: capital—Lansing; largest—Detroit

Statehood: January 26, 1837; 26th state

U.S. Congress: 2 senators, 14 representatives

State Motto: *Si quaeris peninsulam amoenam, circumspice* ("If you seek a pleasant peninsula, look about you")

State Song: "Michigan, My Michigan"

State Nicknames: The Wolverine State; The Great Lakes State

Abbreviations: MI; Mich.

State Symbols: flower—apple blossom; tree—Eastern white pine; bird—robin

At a Glance

- With an increase in population of 0.3 percent, Michigan ranked 45th among the states in growth from 2000 to 2009.
- An estimated 53,100 marriages took place in Michigan in 2009, compared to 32,500 divorces.
- In 2011, 11.8 percent of Michiganders did not have health insurance, compared to 15.1 percent of the total U.S. population.
- In the 2012 election, 66.8 percent of Michigan's eligible voters voted, compared to 61.8 percent of eligible voters nationwide.
- In 2007, Michigan exported $1.2 billion worth of agricultural products, about 1.5 percent of the U.S. total.

Table MI-1. Population by Age, Sex, Race, and Hispanic Origin

(Number, percent, except where noted.)

Sex, age, race, and Hispanic origin	2000	2010	2012[1]	Average annual percent change, 2010–2012
Total Population	9,938,444	9,883,640	9,883,360	-
Percent of total U.S. population	3.5	3.2	3.1	X
Sex				
Male	4,873,095	4,848,114	4,850,511	-
Female	5,065,349	5,035,526	5,032,849	-
Age				
Under 5 years	672,005	596,286	575,714	-1.2
5 to 19 years	2,212,060	2,052,599	1,975,839	-1.3
20 to 64 years	5,835,361	5,873,225	5,889,093	0.1
65 years and over	1,219,018	1,361,530	1,442,714	1.9
Median age (years)	35.5	38.9	39.4	0.4
Race and Hispanic Origin				
One race				
White	7,966,053	7,949,497	7,920,263	-0.1
Black	1,412,742	1,416,067	1,415,107	-
American Indian and Alaska Native	58,479	68,396	69,751	0.6
Asian	176,510	243,062	259,806	2.1
Native Hawaiian or Other Pacific Islander	2,692	3,442	3,720	2.5
Two or more races	192,416	203,176	214,713	1.8
Hispanic (of any race)	323,877	459,751	481,277	1.5

X = Not applicable.
- = Zero or rounds to zero.
[1] Population figures for 2012 are July 1 estimates. The 2010 estimates are taken from the 2010 Census.

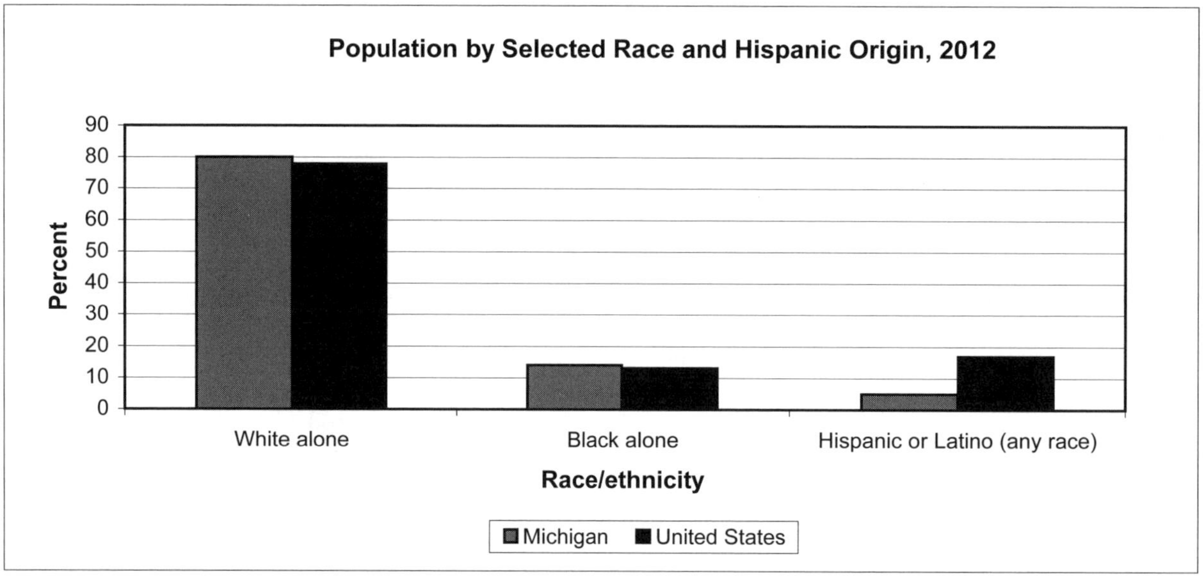

Table MI-2. Marital Status

(Number, percent distribution.)

Sex, age, race, and Hispanic origin	2000	2010	2011
Males, 15 Years and Over	3,761,881	3,875,107	3,890,962
Never married	30.8	34.9	35.9
Now married, except separated	56.1	50.5	49.6
Separated	1.3	1.3	1.3
Widowed	2.5	2.7	2.7
Divorced	9.3	10.6	10.6
Females, 15 Years and Over	4,013,722	4,099,384	4,114,716
Never married	25.0	29.0	29.2
Now married, except separated	51.8	47.2	46.8
Separated	1.6	1.6	1.7
Widowed	10.4	9.7	9.8
Divorced	11.2	12.5	12.4

Table MI-3. Households and Housing Characteristics

(Number, percent, dollars.)

Item	2000	2010	2011	Average annual percent change, 2000–2011
Total Households	3,785,661	3,806,621	3,772,433	-
Family households	2,575,699	2,508,780	2,472,884	-0.3
Married-couple family	1,947,610	1,845,094	1,817,454	-0.6
Other family	627,989	663,686	655,430	0.4
Male householder, no wife present	154,187	168,337	172,782	1.0
Female householder, no husband present	473,802	495,349	482,648	0.2
Nonfamily households	1,209,962	1,297,841	1,299,549	0.6
Householder living alone	993,607	1,090,126	1,092,559	0.8
Householder not living alone	216,335	207,715	206,990	-0.4
Housing Characteristics				
Total housing units	4,234,279	4,531,231	4,525,654	0.6
Occupied housing units	3,785,661	3,806,621	3,772,433	-
Owner occupied	2,793,124	2,769,474	2,706,280	-0.3
Renter occupied	992,537	1,037,147	1,066,153	0.6
Average size	2.56	2.53	2.56	-
Financial Characteristics				
Median gross rent of renter-occupied housing	546	730	739	2.9
Median monthly owner costs for housing units with a mortgage	972	1,288	1,275	2.6
Median value of owner-occupied housing units	115,600	123,300	118,100	0.2

Table MI-4. Migration, Origin, and Language

(Number, percent.)

Characteristic	State			U.S.		
	2010	2011	Percent change	2010	2011	Percent change
Residence 1 Year Ago						
Population 1 year and over	9,762,127	9,766,574	0.0	305,628,607	307,900,319	0.7
Same house	85.1	85.4	0.4	84.6	84.8	0.2
Different house in the U.S.	14.4	14.2	-1.4	14.8	14.6	-1.4
Same county	9.5	8.9	-6.3	9.4	9.2	-2.1
Different county	4.9	5.2	6.1	5.4	5.4	-
Same state	3.7	3.8	2.7	3.2	3.1	-3.1
Different state	1.2	1.4	16.7	2.2	2.3	4.5
Abroad	0.5	0.4	-20.0	0.6	0.6	-
Place of Birth						
Native born	9,289,827	9,272,173	-0.2	269,393,835	271,214,059	0.7
Male	49.0	49.1	0.2	49.2	49.2	-
Female	51.0	50.9	-0.2	50.8	50.8	-
Foreign born	587,747	604,014	2.8	39,955,854	40,377,860	1.1
Male	50.2	48.8	-2.8	49.1	48.9	-0.4
Female	49.8	51.2	2.8	50.9	51.1	0.4
Foreign born; naturalized U.S. citizen	288,460	307,726	6.7	17,476,082	18,140,192	3.8
Male	48.7	46.8	-3.9	45.8	45.8	-
Female	51.3	53.2	3.7	54.2	54.2	-
Foreign born; not a U.S. citizen	299,287	296,288	-1.0	22,479,772	22,237,668	-1.1
Male	51.6	50.9	-1.4	51.6	51.5	-0.2
Female	48.4	49.1	1.4	48.4	48.5	0.2
Entered 2000 or later	37.2	37.0	-0.5	34.7	35.7	2.9
Entered 1990 to 1999	28.0	28.3	1.1	27.2	26.7	-1.8
Entered before 1990	34.8	34.7	-0.3	38.1	37.6	-1.3
World Region of Birth, Foreign						
Foreign-born population, excluding population born at sea	587,747	603,954	2.8	39,955,673	40,377,757	1.1
Europe	22.6	24.1	6.6	12.1	12.1	-
Asia	46.0	46.1	0.2	28.2	28.6	1.4
Africa	4.2	4.4	4.8	4	4.1	2.5
Oceania	0.4	0.5	25.0	0.5	0.5	-
Latin America	20.1	18.5	-8.0	53.1	52.6	-0.9
North America	6.7	6.4	-4.5	2	2.0	-
Language Spoken at Home and Ability to Speak English						
Population 5 years and over	9,285,194	9,292,794	0.1	289,215,746	291,524,091	0.8
English only	91.4	90.9	-0.5	79.4	79.2	-0.3
Language other than English	8.6	9.1	5.8	20.6	20.8	1.0
Speaks English less than "very well"	3.1	3.2	3.2	8.7	8.7	-

- = Zero or rounds to zero.

Table MI-5. Median Income and Poverty Status, 2011

(Number, percent, except as noted.)

Characteristic	State		U.S.	
	Number	Percent	Number	Percent
Median Income				
Households (dollars)	45,981	X	50,502	X
Families (dollars)	58,068	X	61,455	X
Below Poverty Level (All People)	1,693,294	17.5	48,452,035	15.9
Sex				
Male	780,447	16.5	21,825,281	14.7
Female	912,847	18.5	26,626,754	17.2
Age				
Under 18 years	560,109	24.8	16,386,500	22.5
Related children under 18 years	548,145	24.4	16,087,074	22.2
18 to 64 years	1,022,144	16.9	28,335,079	14.8
65 years and over	111,041	8.2	3,730,456	9.3

X = Not applicable.

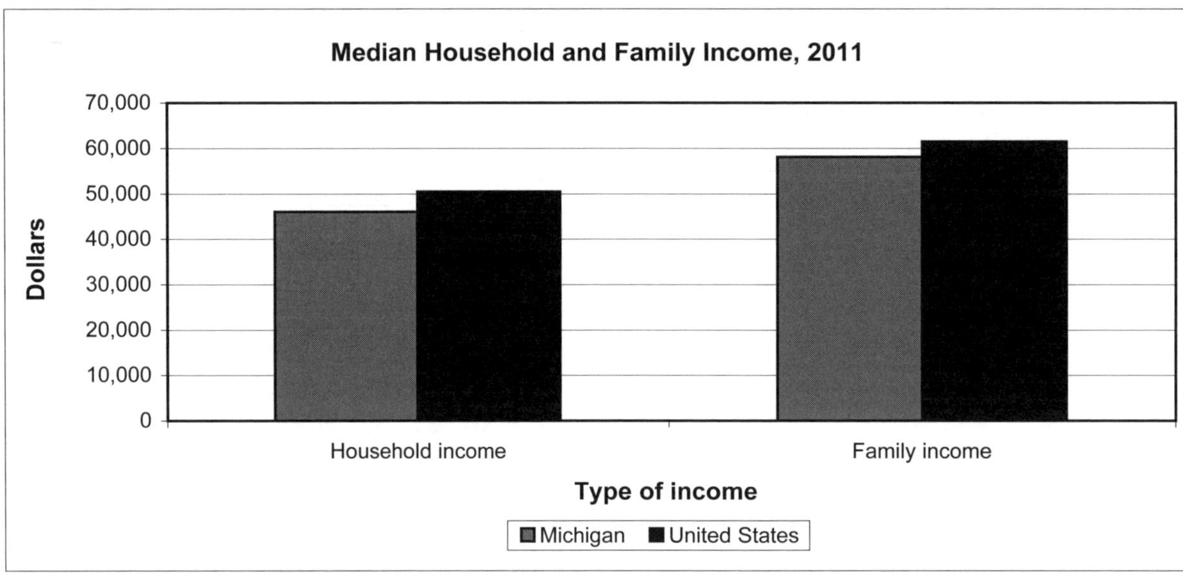

Table MI-6. Health Insurance Coverage Status for the Civilian Noninstitutionalized Population and Children Under 18 Years of Age

(Numbers in thousands, percent.)

Item	2004	2005	2006	2007	2008	2009	2010	2011
Civilian Noninstitutionalized Population	9,974	9,982	9,970	9,927	9,866	9,835	9,764	9,762
Covered by Private or Public Insurance								
Number	8,865	8,949	8,928	8,776	8,734	8,632	8,556	8,612
Percent	88.9	89.7	89.5	88.4	88.5	87.8	87.6	88.2
Not Covered								
Number	1,109	1,033	1,043	1,151	1,132	1,203	1,207	1,150
Percent	11.1	10.3	10.5	11.6	11.5	12.2	12.4	11.8
Percent in the U.S. not covered	14.9	15.3	15.8	15.3	15.1	15.1	15.5	15.1
Children Under 18 Years of Age	2,545	2,554	2,446	2,419	2,389	2,343	2,331	2,290
Covered by Private or Public Insurance								
Number	2,393	2,427	2,330	2,270	2,265	2,236	2,236	2,196
Percent	94.0	95.0	95.3	93.8	94.8	95.4	95.9	95.9
Not Covered								
Number	152	128	116	149	124	107	95	94
Percent	6.0	5.0	4.7	6.2	5.2	4.6	4.1	4.1
Percent in the U.S. not covered	10.5	10.9	11.7	11.0	9.7	8.6	8.0	7.5

Table MI-7. Employment Status by Demographic Group, Preliminary 2012

(Numbers in thousands, percent.)

Characteristic	Civilian noninstitutional population	Civilian labor force		Employed		Unemployed	
		Number	Percent of population	Number	Percent of population	Number	Percent of population
Total	7,787	4,673	60.0	4,247	54.5	426	9.1
Sex							
Male	3,752	2,474	65.9	2,239	59.7	235	9.5
Female	4,035	2,200	54.5	2,008	49.8	192	8.7
Race, Sex, and Hispanic Origin							
White	6,356	3,875	61.0	3,564	56.1	311	8.0
Male	3,095	2,083	67.3	1,904	61.5	179	8.6
Female	3,261	1,792	55.0	1,660	50.9	132	7.4
Black or African American	1,055	567	53.8	471	44.7	96	16.9
Male	475	262	55.3	215	45.3	47	18.0
Female	580	305	52.6	256	44.1	49	16.0
Hispanic	267	175	65.8	157	58.7	19	10.8
Male	150	106	71.0	93	62.0	13	12.6
Female	117	69	59.2	64	54.5	6	8.0
Age							
16 to 19 years	595	233	39.1	183	30.7	50	21.5
20 to 24 years	649	453	69.8	387	59.7	66	14.5
25 to 34 years	1,130	919	81.3	827	73.2	92	10.0
35 to 44 years	1,234	1,005	81.5	929	75.3	77	7.6
45 to 54 years	1,430	1,109	77.6	1,033	72.3	76	6.9
55 to 64 years	1,321	741	56.1	688	52.1	52	7.1
65 years and over	437	115	26.4	108	24.8	7	6.1

NOTE: Data in Table 7 are from the Current Population Survey (CPS) and do not match the estimates in Table 8. See notes and definitions for further information.

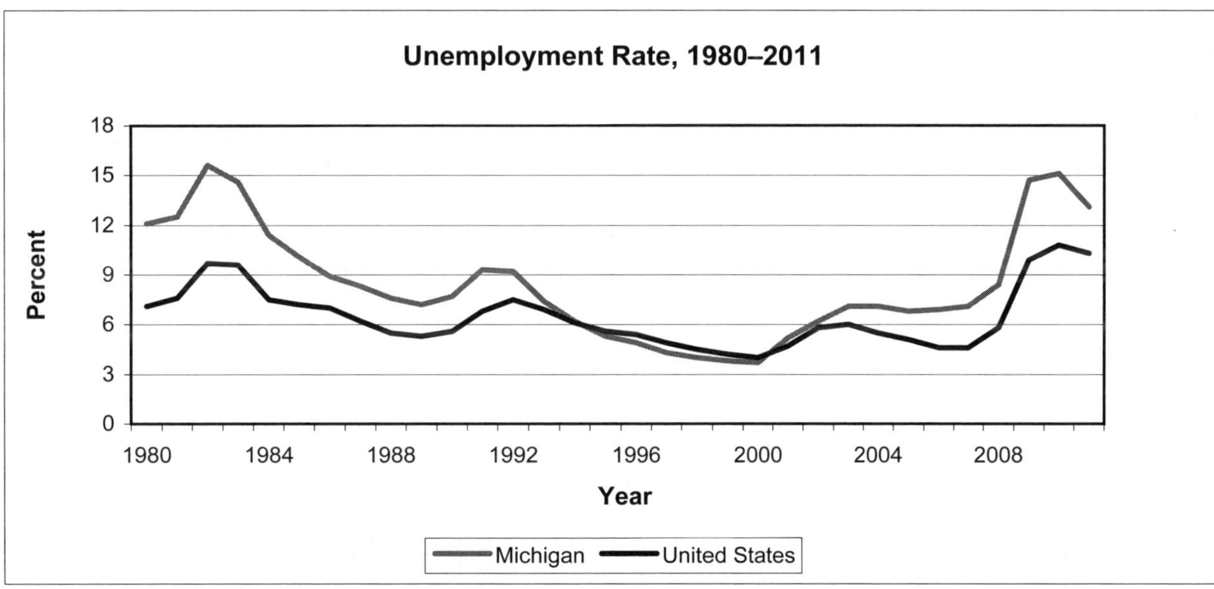

Table MI-8. Employment Status of the Civilian Noninstitutional Population Age 16 Years and Over

(Number, percent.)

Year	Civilian labor force	Civilian participation rate	Employed	Unemployed	Unemployment rate
2005	5,064,944	65.4	4,718,084	346,860	6.8
2006	5,068,179	65.2	4,718,676	349,503	6.9
2007	5,021,910	64.5	4,666,650	357,260	7.1
2008	4,935,584	63.4	4,519,476	416,108	8.4
2009	4,970,184	62.8	4,237,865	732,319	14.7
2010	4,870,674	62.2	4,137,510	733,164	15.1
2011	4,821,613	61.3	4,191,878	629,735	13.1

Table MI-9. Employment and Average Wages by Industry

(Estimates before 2007 are based on the 2002 *North American Industry Classification System* [NAICS]. Estimates from 2007 onward are based on the 2007 NAICS.)

Industry	2005	2006	2007	2008	2009	2010	2011
				Number of jobs			
Wage and Salary Employment by Industry	4,487,050	4,425,691	4,372,840	4,257,567	3,960,939	3,955,898	4,049,195
Farm Wage and Salary Employment	19,151	17,974	20,793	17,600	18,072	16,719	22,521
Nonfarm Wage and Salary Employment	4,467,899	4,407,717	4,352,047	4,239,967	3,942,867	3,939,179	4,026,674
Private wage and salary employment	3,778,635	3,728,382	3,677,963	3,576,307	3,283,032	3,288,111	3,394,605
Forestry, fishing, and related activities	6,766	6,334	6,362	6,518	6,529	6,914	7,197
Mining	6,705	6,513	6,170	6,372	5,561	5,616	5,913
Utilities	20,823	20,700	20,393	20,784	20,269	19,480	19,337
Construction	194,944	182,774	169,621	156,768	131,059	126,044	131,659
Manufacturing	679,719	652,607	625,517	580,835	469,570	478,601	513,416
Durable goods manufacturing	529,906	504,742	481,738	441,778	345,961	352,953	383,282
Nondurable goods manufacturing	149,813	147,865	143,779	139,057	123,609	125,648	130,134
Wholesale trade	170,817	170,721	169,360	167,482	153,228	151,528	156,142
Retail trade	511,559	501,669	496,113	484,299	458,394	452,882	454,646
Transportation and warehousing	108,565	109,234	109,829	105,892	94,526	95,225	100,170
Information	66,218	64,910	64,567	62,210	58,739	57,287	55,819
Finance and insurance	161,316	160,897	156,399	150,208	139,717	137,114	139,336
Real estate and rental and leasing	59,381	58,079	57,108	55,028	52,015	51,539	51,930
Professional, scientific, and technical services	250,792	248,754	247,713	243,722	223,044	226,352	238,825
Management of companies and enterprises	63,986	61,498	57,270	54,259	48,686	48,132	50,858
Administrative and waste services	284,108	281,185	279,248	267,688	233,079	247,251	270,635
Educational services	70,494	71,933	73,636	74,388	74,690	76,157	77,917
Health care and social assistance	504,988	515,069	528,109	537,862	538,699	540,771	548,958
Arts, entertainment, and recreation	62,776	61,477	57,231	56,812	53,730	51,868	49,049
Accommodation and food services	345,862	348,317	351,354	344,926	330,301	328,629	334,721
Other services, except public administration	208,816	205,711	201,963	200,254	191,196	186,721	188,077
Government and government enterprises	689,264	679,335	674,084	663,660	659,835	651,068	632,069
				Dollars			
Average Wages and Salaries by Industry	40,677	41,608	42,846	43,674	43,076	43,865	45,194
Average Farm Wages and Salaries	25,052	27,082	33,130	34,099	33,837	28,444	25,937
Average Nonfarm Wages and Salaries	40,744	41,668	42,893	43,713	43,118	43,930	45,302
Average private wages and salaries	40,961	41,795	43,043	43,665	42,693	43,557	45,219
Forestry, fishing, and related activities	21,886	22,521	23,056	23,844	24,077	25,024	25,591
Mining	53,040	56,853	62,554	64,932	62,502	73,681	74,926
Utilities	75,061	79,588	87,176	84,167	89,233	93,787	98,236
Construction	44,991	46,559	48,943	50,543	49,648	50,564	52,013
Manufacturing	56,771	57,995	59,555	59,557	58,613	59,744	62,235
Durable goods manufacturing	58,974	60,591	62,640	62,368	61,167	62,268	65,352
Nondurable goods manufacturing	48,979	49,135	49,219	50,628	51,464	52,655	53,054
Wholesale trade	57,548	59,100	61,421	63,504	61,587	64,279	67,009
Retail trade	23,808	24,205	24,634	25,035	25,250	25,648	26,037
Transportation and warehousing	45,295	44,552	46,316	46,459	45,789	47,516	49,077
Information	52,102	54,124	55,990	57,452	57,371	58,548	62,044
Finance and insurance	54,206	56,172	58,668	60,081	60,305	62,076	63,967
Real estate and rental and leasing	30,576	31,286	31,994	32,892	33,255	34,119	36,048
Professional, scientific, and technical services	67,028	68,750	71,822	74,099	70,491	70,668	73,096
Management of companies and enterprises	94,211	92,434	100,070	104,241	99,959	103,246	113,268
Administrative and waste services	30,906	31,272	30,759	30,908	30,661	30,907	31,068
Educational services	25,469	26,102	27,582	28,132	28,107	28,602	28,637
Health care and social assistance	38,104	39,373	40,419	42,059	42,996	43,341	44,373
Arts, entertainment, and recreation	27,529	30,048	30,238	30,364	30,594	30,778	30,484
Accommodation and food services	13,637	13,941	15,342	15,136	15,186	15,790	16,551
Other services, except public administration	25,436	26,263	27,272	27,906	27,711	28,533	29,016
Government and government enterprises	39,559	40,967	42,073	43,972	45,232	45,813	45,748

Table MI-10. Employment Characteristics by Family Type

(Number, percent.)

Family type and labor force status	2009		2010		2011	
	Total	Families with own children under 18 years	Total	Families with own children under 18 years	Total	Families with own children under 18 years
All families	2,523,758	1,126,790	2,508,780	1,085,689	2,472,884	1,051,743
Family type and labor force status						
Married-couple families	1,878,384	758,922	1,845,094	718,440	1,817,454	693,616
Both husband and wife in labor force	52.7	68.6	51.7	69.2	50.8	68.2
Husband in labor force, wife not in labor force	19.5	25.5	19.0	24.1	19.5	25.2
Wife in labor force, husband not in labor force	8.2	3.9	9.1	4.7	8.9	4.4
Both husband and wife not in labor force	19.6	2.0	20.2	2.0	20.8	2.2
Other families	645,374	367,868	663,686	367,249	655,430	358,127
Female householder, no husband present	74.2	77.1	74.6	77.3	73.6	75.5
In labor force	52.5	63.6	52.3	63.9	50.0	61.1
Not in labor force	21.7	13.5	22.3	13.4	23.6	14.4
Male householder, no wife present	25.8	22.9	25.4	22.7	26.4	24.5
In labor force	20.4	20.6	19.1	20.2	19.2	21.3
Not in labor force	5.4	2.3	6.2	2.5	7.2	3.2

Table MI-11. School Enrollment and Educational Attainment, 2011

(Number, percent.)

Item	State	U.S.
Enrollment		
Total population 3 years and over, enrolled in school	2,695,641	83,131,910
Enrolled in nursery school or preschool (percent)	5.4	6.0
Enrolled in kindergarten (percent)	4.8	5.1
Enrolled in elementary school, grades 1-8 (percent)	38.2	39.5
Enrolled in high school, grades 9-12 (percent)	21.0	20.7
Enrolled in college or graduate school (percent)	30.6	28.7
Attainment		
Total population 25 years and over	6,588,324	206,471,670
Less than ninth grade (percent)	3.5	6.0
9th to 12th grade, no diploma (percent)	7.7	8.1
High school graduate, including equivalency (percent)	30.8	28.4
Some college, no degree (percent)	23.9	21.2
Associate's degree (percent)	8.4	7.8
Bachelor's degree (percent)	15.7	17.9
Graduate or professional degree (percent)	9.9	10.6
High school graduate or higher (percent)	88.8	85.9
Bachelor's degree or higher (percent)	25.6	28.5

Table MI-12. Educational Indicators

(Number, percent; data derived from National Center of Education Statistics.)

Item	State	U.S.
Public Schools, 2009–2010 (except where noted)		
Number of school districts	551	13,629
Number of schools	3,879	99,834
Number of students (in thousands)	1,649	49,373
Student-teacher ratio	17.8	15.4
Expenditures per student (dollars)	12,002	10,591
Averaged freshman graduation rate, 2008–2009	75.3	75.5[1]
Dropout rate, 2008–2009	3.8	4.1
Students eligible for free or reduced-price lunch (percent)	46.0	48.0
English language learners, 2010–2011 (percent)	3.5	9.8[1]
Students with IEP (percent)	13.8	13.1
Private Schools, 2009–2010 (except where noted)		
Number of schools	1,069	33,366
Number of students (in thousands)	134	4,700
High school graduates, 2008–2009	8,519	308,813
Student-teacher ratio	12.3	10.7

[1] U.S. total includes estimates for nonreporting states.

Table MI-13. Reported Voting and Registration of the Voting-Age Population, November 2012

(Numbers in thousands, percent.)

Item	Total population	Total citizen population	Registered			Voted		
			Total registered	Percent registered (total population)	Percent registered (total citizen population)	Total voted	Percent voted (total population)	Percent voted (total citizen population)
U.S. Total	235,248	215,081	153,157	65.1	71.2	132,948	56.5	61.8
State Total	7,496	7,228	5,620	75.0	77.8	4,832	64.5	66.8
Sex								
Male	3,601	3,458	2,663	73.9	77.0	2,273	63.1	65.7
Female	3,895	3,769	2,957	75.9	78.4	2,559	65.7	67.9
Race								
White alone	6,103	5,971	4,758	78.0	79.7	4,065	66.6	68.1
White, non-Hispanic alone	5,918	5,816	4,629	78.2	79.6	3,951	66.8	67.9
Black alone	1,028	991	687	66.8	69.3	627	61.0	63.3
Asian alone	240	141	84	34.9	59.3	73	30.4	51.6
Hispanic (of any race)	285	225	193	67.9	86.0	158	55.4	70.3
Age								
18 to 24 years	905	894	536	59.2	59.9	394	43.5	44.0
25 to 44 years	2,403	2,242	1,729	72.0	77.1	1,397	58.1	62.3
45 to 64 years	2,676	2,611	2,141	80.0	82.0	1,906	71.2	73.0
65 to 74 years	871	855	703	80.6	82.1	670	77.0	78.4
75 years and over	641	624	512	79.8	82.0	464	72.4	74.3

Table MI-14. Crime

(Number, rate per 100,000. Data are derived from the FBI Uniform Crime Reports.)

Item	State			U.S.		
	2010	2011	Percent change	2010	2011	Percent change
TOTAL POPULATION	9,877,143	9,876,187	-	309,330,219	311,591,917	0.7
VIOLENT CRIME						
Number	48,693	43,983	-9.7	1,251,248	1,203,564	-3.8
Rate	493.0	445.3	-9.7	404.5	386.3	-4.5
Murder and Nonnegligent Manslaughter						
Number	580	613	5.7	14,722	14,612	-0.7
Rate	5.9	6.2	5.1	4.8	4.7	-2.1
Forcible Rape						
Number	4,733	4,347	-8.2	85,593	83,425	-2.5
Rate	47.9	44.0	-8.1	27.7	26.8	-3.2
Robbery						
Number	11,522	10,393	-9.8	369,089	354,396	-4.0
Rate	116.7	105.2	-9.9	119.3	113.7	-4.7
Aggravated Assault						
Number	31,858	28,630	-10.1	781,844	751,131	-3.9
Rate	322.5	289.9	-10.1	252.8	241.1	-4.6
PROPERTY CRIME						
Number	271,501	257,979	-5.0	9,112,625	9,063,173	-0.5
Rate	2,748.8	2,612.1	-5.0	2,945.9	2,908.7	-1.3
Burglary						
Number	74,345	71,596	-3.7	2,168,459	2,188,005	0.9
Rate	752.7	724.9	-3.7	701.0	702.2	0.2
Larceny-Theft						
Number	169,748	160,887	-5.2	6,204,601	6,159,795	-0.7
Rate	1,718.6	1,629.0	-5.2	2,005.8	1,976.9	-1.4
Motor Vehicle Theft						
Number	27,408	25,496	-7.0	739,565	715,373	-3.3
Rate	277.5	258.2	-7.0	239.1	229.6	-4.0

Table MI-15. State Government Finances, 2011

(Dollar amounts in thousands, percent distribution.)

Item	Dollars	Percent distribution
Total Revenue	64,440,454	100.0
General revenue	54,727,497	84.9
Intergovernmental revenue	19,914,367	30.9
Taxes	23,540,253	36.5
General sales	9,477,156	14.7
Selective sales	3,442,475	5.3
License taxes	1,403,872	2.2
Individual income tax	6,391,544	9.9
Corporate income tax	719,890	1.1
Other taxes	2,105,316	3.3
Current charges	7,395,302	11.5
Miscellaneous general revenue	3,877,575	6.0
Utility revenue	0	0.0
Liquor stores revenue	812,140	1.3
Insurance trust revenue [1]	8,900,817	13.8
Total Expenditure	63,108,508	100.0
Intergovernmental expenditure	19,878,322	31.5
Direct expenditure	43,230,186	68.5
Current operation	28,235,945	44.7
Capital outlay	2,246,088	3.6
Insurance benefits and repayments	10,245,923	16.2
Assistance and subsidies	1,364,321	2.2
Interest on debt	1,137,909	1.8
Exhibit: Salaries and wages	7,369,975	11.7
Total Expenditure	63,108,508	100.0
General expenditure	52,201,724	82.7
Intergovernmental expenditure	19,878,322	31.5
Direct expenditure	32,323,402	51.2
General expenditure, by function:		
Education	23,146,215	36.7
Public welfare	14,926,663	23.7
Hospitals	2,522,008	4.0
Health	1,156,070	1.8
Highways	2,464,441	3.9
Police protection	299,994	0.5
Correction	1,663,416	2.6
Natural resources	282,791	0.4
Parks and recreation	86,884	0.1
Governmental administration	823,221	1.3
Interest on general debt	1,137,909	1.8
Other and unallocable	3,692,112	5.9
Utility expenditure	0	0.0
Liquor stores expenditure	660,861	1.0
Insurance trust expenditure	10,245,923	16.2
Debt at End of Fiscal Year	30,975,273	X
Cash and Security Holdings	72,279,169	X

X = Not applicable.

[1] Within insurance trust revenue, net earnings of state retirement systems is a calculated statistic (the item code in the data file is X08), and thus can be positive or negative. Net earnings is the sum of earnings on investments plus gains on investments minus losses on investments. The change made in 2002 for asset valuation from book to market value in accordance with Statement 34 of the Governmental Accounting Standards Board is reflected in the calculated statistics.

Table MI-16. State Government Tax Collections, 2012

(Dollars in thousands, percent.)

Item	Dollars	Percent distribution
Total Taxes	23,968,760	100.0
Property taxes	1,797,508	7.5
Sales and gross receipts	13,118,854	54.7
General sales and gross receipts	9,565,702	39.9
Selective sales and gross receipts	3,553,152	14.8
Alcoholic beverages	149,159	0.6
Amusements	117,770	0.5
Insurance premiums	298,235	1.2
Motor fuels	973,502	4.1
Pari-mutuels	4,982	-
Public utilities	25,841	0.1
Tobacco products	951,319	4.0
Other selective sales	1,032,344	4.3
Licenses	1,416,186	5.9
Alcoholic beverages	16,572	0.1
Amusements	0	0.0
Corporations in general	21,959	0.1
Hunting and fishing	48,193	0.2
Motor vehicle	916,418	3.8
Motor vehicle operators	56,396	0.2
Public utilities	27,260	0.1
Occupation and business, NEC	149,604	0.6
Other licenses	179,784	0.8
Income taxes	7,436,742	31.0
Individual income	6,827,913	28.5
Corporation net income	608,829	2.5
Other taxes	199,470	0.8
Death and gift	198	-
Documentary and stock transfer	134,987	0.6
Severance	64,285	0.3
Taxes, NEC	0	0.0

- = Rounds to zero.

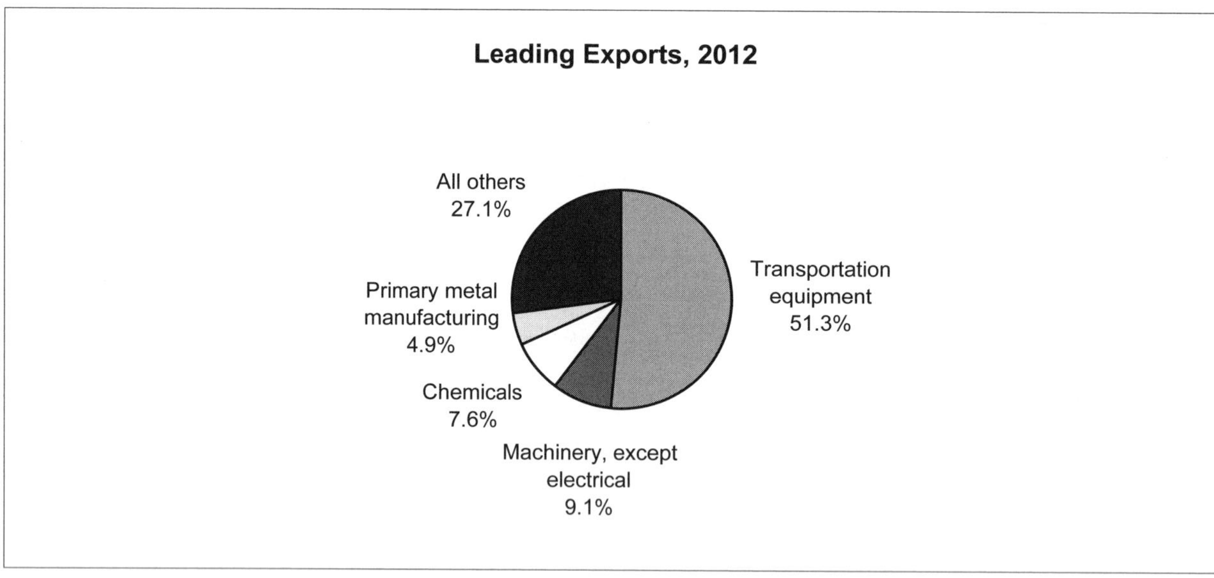

MINNESOTA

Facts and Figures

Location: North central United States; bordered on the N by Canada (Manitoba and Ontario), on the E by Lake Superior and Wisconsin, on the S by Iowa, and on the W by North Dakota and South Dakota

Area: 86,939 sq. mi. (225,171 sq. km.); rank—12th

Population: 5,379,139 (2012 est.); rank—21st

Principal Cities: capital—St. Paul; largest—Minneapolis

Statehood: May 11, 1858; 32nd state

U.S. Congress: 2 senators, 8 representatives

State Motto: *L'Etoile du Nord* ("The Star of the North")

State Song: "Hail! Minnesota"

State Nicknames: The North Star State; The Land of 10,000 Lakes; The Gopher State

Abbreviations: MN; Minn.

State Symbols: flower—showy (pink and white) lady's slipper; tree—red (Norway) pine; bird—loon

At a Glance

- With an increase in population of 7.0 percent, Minnesota ranked 19th among the states in growth from 2000 to 2009.
- An estimated 28,400 marriages took place in Minnesota in 2009; Minnesota does not report its number of divorces.
- Minnesota's violent crime rate in 2011 was 221.2 per 100,000 population, compared to 386.3 for the entire nation.
- In the 2012 election, 73.2 percent of Minnesota's eligible voters voted, compared to 61.8 percent of eligible voters nationwide.
- In 2007, Minnesota exported $3.6 billion worth of agricultural products, about 4.4 percent of the U.S. total.

Table MN-1. Population by Age, Sex, Race, and Hispanic Origin

(Number, percent, except where noted.)

Sex, age, race, and Hispanic origin	2000	2010	2012[1]	Average annual percent change, 2010–2012
Total Population	4,919,479	5,303,925	5,379,139	0.5
Percent of total U.S. population	1.7	1.7	1.7	X
Sex				
Male	2,435,631	2,632,132	2,672,169	0.5
Female	2,483,848	2,671,793	2,706,970	0.4
Age				
Under 5 years	329,594	355,504	348,338	-0.7
5 to 19 years	1,105,251	1,075,707	1,076,433	-
20 to 64 years	2,890,368	3,189,593	3,224,601	0.4
65 years and over	594,266	683,121	729,767	2.1
Median age (years)	35.4	37.4	37.6	0.2
Race and Hispanic Origin				
One race				
White	4,400,282	4,623,461	4,654,134	0.2
Black	171,731	280,949	297,962	1.9
American Indian and Alaska Native	54,967	67,325	68,961	0.8
Asian	141,968	217,792	235,120	2.5
Native Hawaiian or Other Pacific Islander	1,979	2,958	3,206	2.6
Two or more races	82,742	111,440	119,756	2.3
Hispanic (of any race)	143,382	264,432	279,594	5.4

X = Not applicable.
- = Zero or rounds to zero.
[1] Population figures for 2012 are July 1 estimates. The 2010 estimates are taken from the 2010 Census.

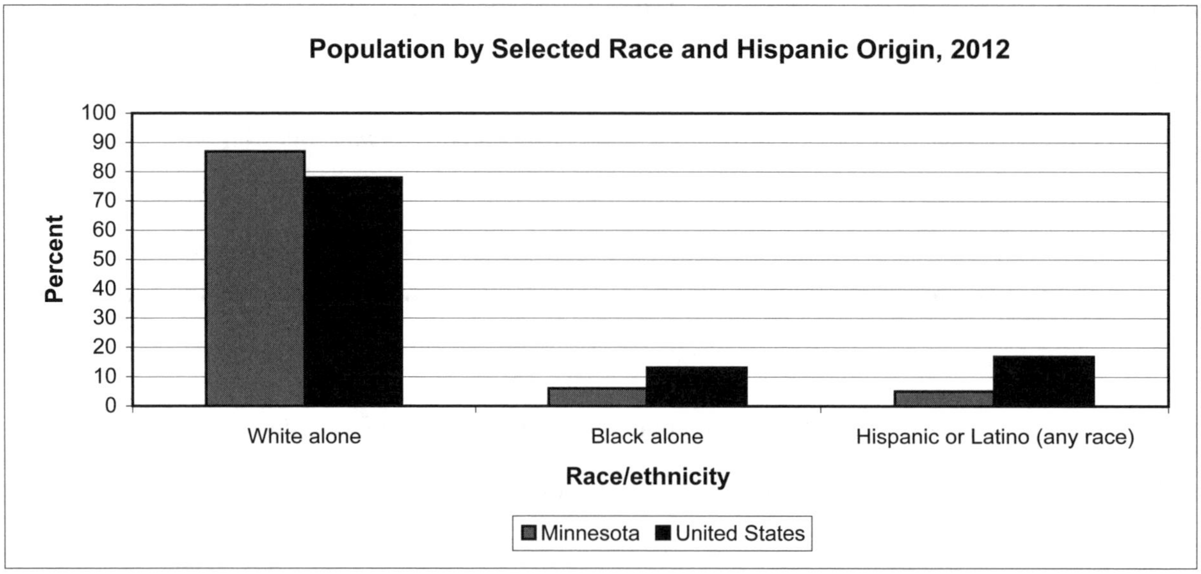

Table MN-2. Marital Status

(Number, percent distribution.)

Sex, age, race, and Hispanic origin	2000	2010	2011
Males, 15 Years and Over	1,889,936	2,090,940	2,113,814
Never married	31.3	34.6	35.1
Now married, except separated	57.7	53.5	52.9
Separated	0.9	0.9	1.1
Widowed	2.1	2.2	2.2
Divorced	8.0	8.7	8.7
Females, 15 Years and Over	1,967,819	2,155,042	2,169,757
Never married	25.0	28.2	28.1
Now married, except separated	55.0	51.5	51.4
Separated	1.2	1.2	1.3
Widowed	9.4	8.4	8.3
Divorced	9.5	10.7	10.9

Table MN-3. Households and Housing Characteristics

(Number, percent, dollars.)

Item	2000	2010	2011	Average annual percent change, 2000–2011
Total Households	1,895,127	2,091,548	2,096,477	0.9
Family households	1,255,141	1,353,758	1,356,466	0.7
Married-couple family	1,018,245	1,069,000	1,066,483	0.4
Other family	236,986	284,758	289,983	1.9
Male householder, no wife present	68,114	87,757	90,234	2.7
Female householder, no husband present	168,782	197,001	199,749	1.5
Nonfamily households	639,986	737,790	740,011	1.3
Householder living alone	509,468	591,124	600,179	1.5
Householder not living alone	130,518	146,666	139,832	0.6
Housing Characteristics				
Total housing units	2,065,946	2,348,242	2,354,075	1.2
Occupied housing units	1,895,127	2,091,548	2,096,477	0.9
Owner occupied	1,412,865	1,527,328	1,525,449	0.7
Renter occupied	482,262	564,220	571,028	1.5
Average size	2.52	2.47	2.48	-0.1
Financial Characteristics				
Median gross rent of renter-occupied housing	566	764	787	3.3
Median monthly owner costs for housing units with a mortgage	1,044	1,503	1,481	3.5
Median value of owner-occupied housing units	122,400	194,300	183,500	4.2

Table MN-4. Migration, Origin, and Language

(Number, percent.)

Characteristic	State			U.S.		
	2010	2011	Percent change	2010	2011	Percent change
Residence 1 Year Ago						
Population 1 year and over	5,244,256	5,277,329	0.6	305,628,607	307,900,319	0.7
Same house	85.4	85.4	-	84.6	84.8	0.2
Different house in the U.S.	14.1	14.2	0.7	14.8	14.6	-1.4
Same county	8.1	7.5	-7.4	9.4	9.2	-2.1
Different county	6.0	6.6	10.0	5.4	5.4	-
Same state	4.3	4.7	9.3	3.2	3.1	-3.1
Different state	1.7	1.9	11.8	2.2	2.3	4.5
Abroad	0.5	0.5	-	0.6	0.6	-
Place of Birth						
Native born	4,932,101	4,956,022	0.5	269,393,835	271,214,059	0.7
Male	49.6	49.8	0.4	49.2	49.2	-
Female	50.4	50.2	-0.4	50.8	50.8	-
Foreign born	378,483	388,839	2.7	39,955,854	40,377,860	1.1
Male	50.1	49.1	-2.0	49.1	48.9	-0.4
Female	49.9	50.9	2.0	50.9	51.1	0.4
Foreign born; naturalized U.S. citizen	169,246	178,569	5.5	17,476,082	18,140,192	3.8
Male	46.2	46.5	0.6	45.8	45.8	-
Female	53.8	53.5	-0.6	54.2	54.2	-
Foreign born; not a U.S. citizen	209,237	210,270	0.5	22,479,772	22,237,668	-1.1
Male	53.2	51.2	-3.8	51.6	51.5	-0.2
Female	46.8	48.8	4.3	48.4	48.5	0.2
Entered 2000 or later	43.8	46.4	5.9	34.7	35.7	2.9
Entered 1990 to 1999	28.9	28.6	-1.0	27.2	26.7	-1.8
Entered before 1990	27.3	25.0	-8.4	38.1	37.6	-1.3
World Region of Birth, Foreign						
Foreign-born population, excluding population born at sea	378,483	388,839	2.7	39,955,673	40,377,757	1.1
Europe	11.1	11.8	6.3	12.1	12.1	-
Asia	37.2	35.8	-3.8	28.2	28.6	1.4
Africa	20.2	20.6	2.0	4	4.1	2.5
Oceania	0.5	0.5	-	0.5	0.5	-
Latin America	27.4	28.1	2.6	53.1	52.6	-0.9
North America	3.6	3.2	-11.1	2	2.0	-
Language Spoken at Home and Ability to Speak English						
Population 5 years and over	4,954,466	4,992,262	0.8	289,215,746	291,524,091	0.8
English only	89.5	89.2	-0.3	79.4	79.2	-0.3
Language other than English	10.5	10.8	2.9	20.6	20.8	1.0
Speaks English less than "very well"	4.2	4.3	2.4	8.7	8.7	-

- = Zero or rounds to zero.

Table MN-5. Median Income and Poverty Status, 2011

(Number, percent, except as noted.)

Characteristic	State Number	State Percent	U.S. Number	U.S. Percent
Median Income				
Households (dollars)	56,954	X	50,502	X
Families (dollars)	71,321	X	61,455	X
Below Poverty Level (All People)	621,970	11.9	48,452,035	15.9
Sex				
Male	288,879	11.1	21,825,281	14.7
Female	333,091	12.7	26,626,754	17.2
Age				
Under 18 years	194,260	15.4	16,386,500	22.5
Related children under 18 years	188,495	15.0	16,087,074	22.2
18 to 64 years	374,105	11.4	28,335,079	14.8
65 years and over	53,605	8.0	3,730,456	9.3

X = Not applicable.

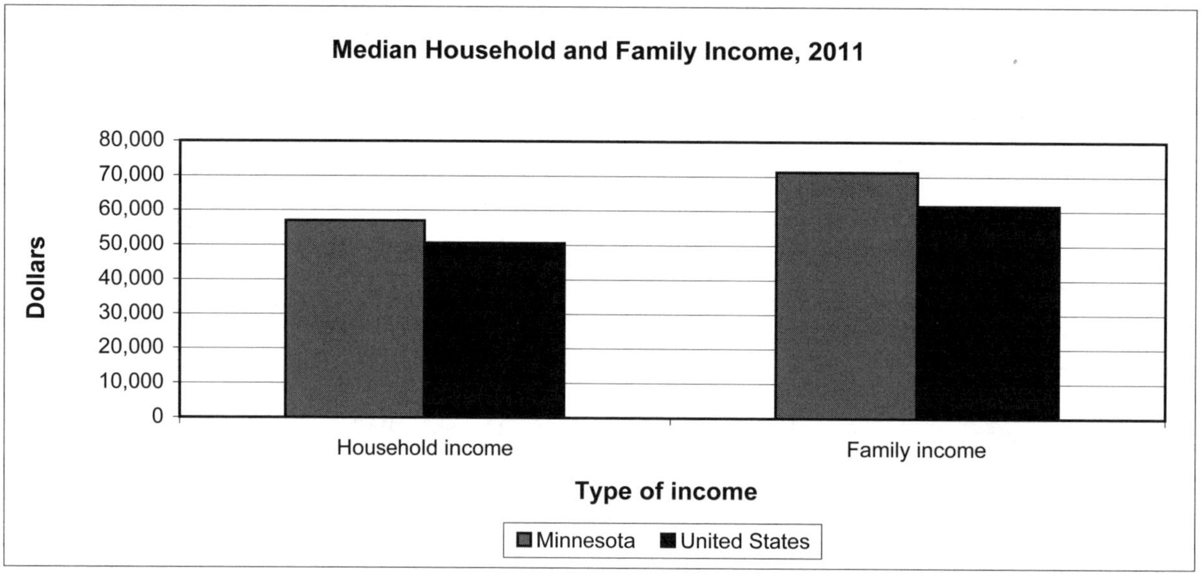

Table MN-6. Health Insurance Coverage Status for the Civilian Noninstitutionalized Population and Children Under 18 Years of Age

(Numbers in thousands, percent.)

Item	2004	2005	2006	2007	2008	2009	2010	2011
Civilian Noninstitutionalized Population	5,127	5,129	5,149	5,190	5,151	5,197	5,252	5,287
Covered by Private or Public Insurance								
Number	4,692	4,722	4,675	4,758	4,704	4,724	4,776	4,819
Percent	91.5	92.1	90.8	91.7	91.3	90.9	90.9	91.2
Not Covered								
Number	434	408	475	433	447	473	476	467
Percent	8.5	7.9	9.2	8.3	8.7	9.1	9.1	8.8
Percent in the U.S. not covered	14.9	15.3	15.8	15.3	15.1	15.1	15.5	15.1
Children Under 18 Years of Age	1,251	1,230	1,256	1,246	1,248	1,256	1,281	1,276
Covered by Private or Public Insurance								
Number	1,174	1,157	1,153	1,167	1,169	1,173	1,197	1,196
Percent	93.8	94.1	91.7	93.6	93.7	93.4	93.4	93.7
Not Covered								
Number	77	73	104	80	79	83	84	80
Percent	6.2	5.9	8.3	6.4	6.3	6.6	6.6	6.3
Percent in the U.S. not covered	10.5	10.9	11.7	11.0	9.7	8.6	8.0	7.5

Table MN-7. Employment Status by Demographic Group, Preliminary 2012

(Numbers in thousands, percent.)

Characteristic	Civilian noninstitutional population	Civilian labor force		Employed		Unemployed	
		Number	Percent of population	Number	Percent of population	Number	Percent of population
Total	4,188	2,946	70.3	2,776	66.3	169	5.8
Sex							
Male	2,061	1,562	75.8	1,466	71.1	97	6.2
Female	2,128	1,383	65.0	1,311	61.6	73	5.3
Race, Sex, and Hispanic Origin							
White	3,709	2,615	70.5	2,480	66.9	135	5.2
Male	1,826	1,383	75.7	1,306	71.5	77	5.5
Female	1,883	1,233	65.5	1,174	62.4	59	4.8
Black or African American	192	126	65.7	109	56.7	17	13.8
Male	94	66	70.0	56	59.3	10	15.3
Female	99	61	61.6	53	54.1	7	12.2
Hispanic	146	111	76.1	102	69.6	9	8.5
Male	77	63	82.3	58	75.6	5	8.1
Female	69	48	69.1	43	62.8	4	9.0
Age							
16 to 19 years	286	129	45.1	105	36.7	24	18.6
20 to 24 years	361	290	80.2	267	74.0	22	7.7
25 to 34 years	720	636	88.3	603	83.7	33	5.3
35 to 44 years	660	578	87.5	553	83.7	25	4.3
45 to 54 years	797	700	87.9	665	83.5	35	5.0
55 to 64 years	655	481	73.4	458	70.0	23	4.7
65 years and over	710	132	18.6	125	17.6	7	5.4

NOTE: Data in Table 7 are from the Current Population Survey (CPS) and do not match the estimates in Table 8. See notes and definitions for further information.

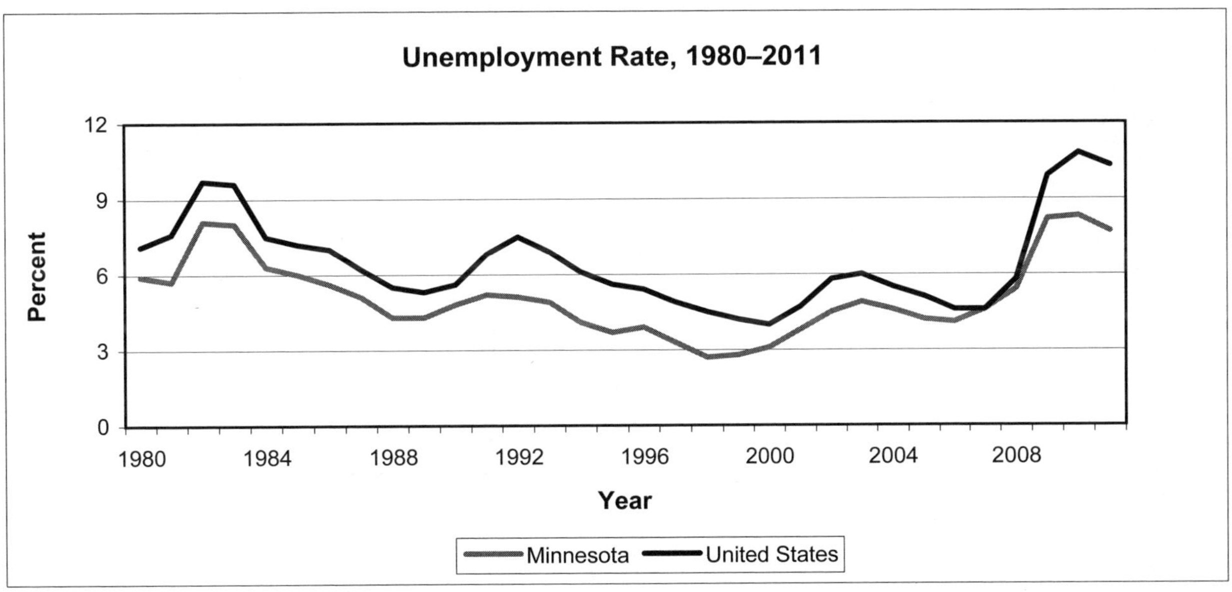

Table MN-8. Employment Status of the Civilian Noninstitutional Population Age 16 Years and Over

(Number, percent.)

Year	Civilian labor force	Civilian participation rate	Employed	Unemployed	Unemployment rate
2005	2,879,707	73.3	2,759,488	120,219	4.2
2006	2,893,112	72.9	2,774,941	118,171	4.1
2007	2,910,811	72.6	2,776,290	134,521	4.6
2008	2,932,961	72.5	2,773,136	159,825	5.4
2009	2,946,834	71.0	2,706,630	240,204	8.2
2010	2,938,277	70.4	2,693,645	244,632	8.3
2011	2,955,217	70.2	2,728,881	226,336	7.7

Table MN-9. Employment and Average Wages by Industry

(Estimates before 2007 are based on the 2002 *North American Industry Classification System* [NAICS]. Estimates from 2007 onward are based on the 2007 NAICS.)

Industry	2005	2006	2007	2008	2009	2010	2011
	Number of jobs						
Wage and Salary Employment by Industry	2,793,891	2,825,483	2,841,732	2,828,921	2,725,314	2,718,113	2,759,615
Farm Wage and Salary Employment	17,614	15,624	15,530	13,424	18,409	19,372	16,349
Nonfarm Wage and Salary Employment	2,776,277	2,809,859	2,826,202	2,815,497	2,706,905	2,698,741	2,743,266
Private wage and salary employment	2,361,014	2,390,148	2,406,818	2,395,555	2,288,567	2,278,070	2,329,716
Forestry, fishing, and related activities	5,129	5,200	5,177	5,343	5,305	5,560	5,857
Mining	5,120	5,183	5,236	5,549	4,423	5,220	5,812
Utilities	11,876	11,916	12,065	12,515	12,726	12,691	12,807
Construction	134,459	131,223	124,792	114,760	97,786	91,776	96,726
Manufacturing	346,903	346,505	341,507	335,168	300,075	292,717	301,429
Durable goods manufacturing	223,997	224,648	220,192	215,463	188,537	183,413	190,285
Nondurable goods manufacturing	122,906	121,857	121,315	119,705	111,538	109,304	111,144
Wholesale trade	131,886	133,725	133,871	133,858	126,920	124,523	126,851
Retail trade	306,049	305,107	305,062	298,169	284,478	282,103	284,601
Transportation and warehousing	84,525	82,439	83,312	83,086	78,347	77,968	80,081
Information	59,118	57,802	58,892	58,384	55,751	54,322	53,743
Finance and insurance	142,393	143,771	141,720	140,441	137,888	138,560	141,436
Real estate and rental and leasing	39,613	39,724	40,332	39,018	37,533	37,602	37,220
Professional, scientific, and technical services	123,345	128,007	132,715	134,271	127,256	125,404	130,053
Management of companies and enterprises	63,317	65,932	67,191	71,126	69,812	70,657	72,693
Administrative and waste services	124,062	130,572	132,816	127,456	114,424	122,830	130,706
Educational services	56,684	59,972	61,538	64,442	66,222	68,249	70,521
Health care and social assistance	341,272	355,994	370,641	382,788	392,413	395,097	400,501
Arts, entertainment, and recreation	37,492	38,522	39,170	39,253	38,709	37,762	38,719
Accommodation and food services	207,695	208,541	211,561	209,464	202,402	200,927	204,507
Other services, except public administration	140,076	140,013	139,220	140,464	136,097	134,102	135,453
Government and government enterprises	415,263	419,711	419,384	419,942	418,338	420,671	413,550
	Dollars						
Average Wages and Salaries by Industry	40,077	41,439	43,656	45,091	44,585	45,910	46,990
Average Farm Wages and Salaries	24,887	28,010	34,381	36,202	35,677	29,421	27,805
Average Nonfarm Wages and Salaries	40,173	41,513	43,707	45,133	44,646	46,029	47,105
Average private wages and salaries	40,607	41,949	44,262	45,592	44,814	46,510	47,659
Forestry, fishing, and related activities	21,277	22,239	23,517	24,652	25,112	25,894	27,025
Mining	60,885	64,721	65,454	71,798	63,524	73,484	81,167
Utilities	75,695	77,998	79,812	82,755	81,799	86,375	90,413
Construction	45,958	47,977	50,577	52,759	52,270	51,887	53,447
Manufacturing	48,848	50,277	52,182	53,154	53,552	56,320	57,531
Durable goods manufacturing	51,734	53,079	55,503	56,620	57,398	60,764	61,822
Nondurable goods manufacturing	43,587	45,112	46,156	46,914	47,052	48,863	50,184
Wholesale trade	59,653	62,240	64,770	68,081	66,800	69,494	71,753
Retail trade	22,808	23,145	23,585	23,973	24,118	24,477	24,886
Transportation and warehousing	43,529	41,608	45,645	47,436	44,281	44,607	46,035
Information	54,778	56,922	59,578	60,148	60,124	62,098	66,119
Finance and insurance	68,405	71,281	78,509	76,451	74,681	77,746	82,075
Real estate and rental and leasing	37,724	41,401	41,945	44,610	43,831	44,962	46,859
Professional, scientific, and technical services	62,678	65,571	69,675	72,001	72,030	74,432	76,038
Management of companies and enterprises	91,706	91,023	103,565	114,802	94,856	110,451	109,296
Administrative and waste services	27,599	27,710	29,282	30,678	31,042	31,377	31,635
Educational services	24,915	25,570	27,393	28,353	29,225	29,137	29,660
Health care and social assistance	37,330	38,951	40,578	41,160	42,135	43,231	43,429
Arts, entertainment, and recreation	25,158	29,051	29,573	29,938	28,869	31,935	31,887
Accommodation and food services	13,954	14,610	15,586	15,545	15,533	16,044	16,682
Other services, except public administration	24,799	25,638	26,578	27,296	27,546	27,716	28,474
Government and government enterprises	37,708	39,034	40,521	42,513	43,726	43,424	43,980

Table MN-10. Employment Characteristics by Family Type

(Number, percent.)

Family type and labor force status	2009 Total	2009 Families with own children under 18 years	2010 Total	2010 Families with own children under 18 years	2011 Total	2011 Families with own children under 18 years
All families	1,349,167	623,808	1,353,758	623,567	1,356,466	616,059
Family type and labor force status						
Married-couple families	1,076,694	454,188	1,069,000	447,290	1,066,483	437,819
Both husband and wife in labor force	62.9	76.6	62.3	76.4	62.1	77.3
Husband in labor force, wife not in labor force	15.7	19.4	15.6	19.0	15.7	18.8
Wife in labor force, husband not in labor force	6.6	3.1	7.0	3.5	7.2	2.9
Both husband and wife not in labor force	14.8	0.9	15.1	1.1	15.0	0.9
Other families	272,473	169,620	284,758	176,277	289,983	178,240
Female householder, no husband present	70.5	73.6	69.2	73.5	68.9	71.4
In labor force	55.4	61.9	54.2	62.7	53.8	60.9
Not in labor force	15.1	11.7	15.0	10.8	15.1	10.5
Male householder, no wife present	29.5	26.4	30.8	26.5	31.1	28.6
In labor force	25.6	24.4	25.6	23.9	26.3	26.5
Not in labor force	3.9	2.0	5.3	2.5	4.8	2.1

Table MN-11. School Enrollment and Educational Attainment, 2011

(Number, percent.)

Item	State	U.S.
Enrollment		
Total population 3 years and over, enrolled in school	1,423,499	83,131,910
Enrolled in nursery school or preschool (percent)	6.6	6.0
Enrolled in kindergarten (percent)	5.1	5.1
Enrolled in elementary school, grades 1-8 (percent)	39.5	39.5
Enrolled in high school, grades 9-12 (percent)	20.7	20.7
Enrolled in college or graduate school (percent)	28.1	28.7
Attainment		
Total population 25 years and over	3,560,801	206,471,670
Less than ninth grade (percent)	3.3	6.0
9th to 12th grade, no diploma (percent)	4.7	8.1
High school graduate, including equivalency (percent)	26.9	28.4
Some college, no degree (percent)	22.4	21.2
Associate's degree (percent)	10.3	7.8
Bachelor's degree (percent)	21.8	17.9
Graduate or professional degree (percent)	10.5	10.6
High school graduate or higher (percent)	92.0	85.9
Bachelor's degree or higher (percent)	32.4	28.5

Table MN-12. Educational Indicators

(Number, percent; data derived from National Center of Education Statistics.)

Item	State	U.S.
Public Schools, 2009–2010 (except where noted)		
Number of school districts	337	13,629
Number of schools	2,433	99,834
Number of students (in thousands)	837	49,373
Student-teacher ratio	15.8	15.4
Expenditures per student (dollars)	12,828	10,591
Averaged freshman graduation rate, 2008–2009	87.4	75.5[1]
Dropout rate, 2008–2009	1.9	4.1
Students eligible for free or reduced-price lunch (percent)	36.2	48.0
English language learners, 2010–2011 (percent)	5.1	9.8[1]
Students with IEP (percent)	14.5	13.1
Private Schools, 2009–2010 (except where noted)		
Number of schools	524	33,366
Number of students (in thousands)	78	4,700
High school graduates, 2008–2009	4,241	308,813
Student-teacher ratio	12.2	10.7

[1] U.S. total includes estimates for nonreporting states.

Table MN-13. Reported Voting and Registration of the Voting-Age Population, November 2012

(Numbers in thousands, percent.)

Item	Total population	Total citizen population	Registered			Voted		
			Total registered	Percent registered (total population)	Percent registered (total citizen population)	Total voted	Percent voted (total population)	Percent voted (total citizen population)
U.S. Total	235,248	215,081	153,157	65.1	71.2	132,948	56.5	61.8
State Total	4,055	3,903	3,085	76.1	79.0	2,859	70.5	73.2
Sex								
Male	1,993	1,921	1,496	75.1	77.9	1,374	68.9	71.5
Female	2,062	1,981	1,589	77.0	80.2	1,485	72.0	75.0
Race								
White alone	3,639	3,576	2,846	78.2	79.6	2,646	72.7	74.0
White, non-Hispanic alone	3,532	3,508	2,808	79.5	80.1	2,615	74.0	74.5
Black alone	179	142	95	52.9	66.9	88	49.2	62.1
Asian alone	174	125	110	63.1	87.6	98	56.2	78.1
Hispanic (of any race)	136	96	54	39.9	56.1	44	32.5	45.7
Age								
18 to 24 years	531	510	329	61.8	64.5	303	57.0	59.4
25 to 44 years	1,352	1,255	953	70.5	75.9	862	63.8	68.7
45 to 64 years	1,410	1,387	1,151	81.6	83.0	1,081	76.6	77.9
65 to 74 years	424	418	363	85.7	86.9	346	81.5	82.6
75 years and over	338	332	288	85.4	86.7	267	79.2	80.4

Table MN-14. Crime

(Number, rate per 100,000. Data are derived from the FBI Uniform Crime Reports.)

Item	State			U.S.		
	2010	2011	Percent change	2010	2011	Percent change
TOTAL POPULATION	5,310,658	5,344,861	0.6	309,330,219	311,591,917	0.7
VIOLENT CRIME						
Number	12,515	11,825	-5.5	1,251,248	1,203,564	-3.8
Rate	235.7	221.2	-6.2	404.5	386.3	-4.5
Murder and Nonnegligent Manslaughter						
Number	96	74	-22.9	14,722	14,612	-0.7
Rate	1.8	1.4	-22.2	4.8	4.7	-2.1
Forcible Rape						
Number	1,798	1,664	-7.5	85,593	83,425	-2.5
Rate	33.9	31.1	-8.3	27.7	26.8	-3.2
Robbery						
Number	3,388	3,386	-0.1	369,089	354,396	-4.0
Rate	63.8	63.4	-0.6	119.3	113.7	-4.7
Aggravated Assault						
Number	7,233	6,701	-7.4	781,844	751,131	-3.9
Rate	136.2	125.4	-7.9	252.8	241.1	-4.6
PROPERTY CRIME						
Number	136,431	136,264	-0.1	9,112,625	9,063,173	-0.5
Rate	2,569.0	2,549.4	-0.8	2,945.9	2,908.7	-1.3
Burglary						
Number	24,415	25,724	5.4	2,168,459	2,188,005	0.9
Rate	459.7	481.3	4.7	701.0	702.2	0.2
Larceny-Theft						
Number	103,429	102,358	-1.0	6,204,601	6,159,795	-0.7
Rate	1,947.6	1,915.1	-1.7	2,005.8	1,976.9	-1.4
Motor Vehicle Theft						
Number	8,587	8,182	-4.7	739,565	715,373	-3.3
Rate	161.1	153.1	-5.0	239.1	229.6	-4.0

Table MN-15. State Government Finances, 2011

(Dollar amounts in thousands, percent distribution.)

Item	Dollars	Percent distribution
Total Revenue	45,684,189	100.0
General revenue	33,451,689	73.2
Intergovernmental revenue	9,819,493	21.5
Taxes	18,952,919	41.5
General sales	4,657,395	10.2
Selective sales	3,578,288	7.8
License taxes	1,113,909	2.4
Individual income tax	7,482,396	16.4
Corporate income tax	1,003,657	2.2
Other taxes	1,117,274	2.4
Current charges	2,782,199	6.1
Miscellaneous general revenue	1,897,078	4.2
Utility revenue	0	0.0
Liquor stores revenue	0	0.0
Insurance trust revenue [1]	12,232,500	26.8
Total Expenditure	38,488,350	100.0
Intergovernmental expenditure	11,102,449	28.8
Direct expenditure	27,385,901	71.2
Current operation	18,649,448	48.5
Capital outlay	1,617,046	4.2
Insurance benefits and repayments	5,701,467	14.8
Assistance and subsidies	825,431	2.1
Interest on debt	592,509	1.5
Exhibit: Salaries and wages	5,221,569	13.6
Total Expenditure	38,488,350	100.0
General expenditure	32,670,505	84.9
Intergovernmental expenditure	11,102,449	28.8
Direct expenditure	21,568,056	56.0
General expenditure, by function:		
Education	12,406,335	32.2
Public welfare	10,872,302	28.2
Hospitals	288,254	0.7
Health	633,406	1.6
Highways	2,565,152	6.7
Police protection	396,442	1.0
Correction	508,237	1.3
Natural resources	690,585	1.8
Parks and recreation	280,770	0.7
Governmental administration	905,382	2.4
Interest on general debt	592,509	1.5
Other and unallocable	2,531,131	6.6
Utility expenditure	116,378	0.3
Liquor stores expenditure	0	0.0
Insurance trust expenditure	5,701,467	14.8
Debt at End of Fiscal Year	12,896,921	X
Cash and Security Holdings	60,605,879	X

X = Not applicable.

[1] Within insurance trust revenue, net earnings of state retirement systems is a calculated statistic (the item code in the data file is X08), and thus can be positive or negative. Net earnings is the sum of earnings on investments plus gains on investments minus losses on investments. The change made in 2002 for asset valuation from book to market value in accordance with Statement 34 of the Governmental Accounting Standards Board is reflected in the calculated statistics.

Table MN-16. State Government Tax Collections, 2012

(Dollars in thousands, percent.)

Item	Dollars	Percent distribution
Total Taxes	20,560,540	100.0
Property taxes	807,700	3.9
Sales and gross receipts	9,139,154	44.4
General sales and gross receipts	4,942,140	24.0
Selective sales and gross receipts	4,197,014	20.4
Alcoholic beverages	79,389	0.4
Amusements	42,182	0.2
Insurance premiums	360,794	1.8
Motor fuels	849,218	4.1
Pari-mutuels	577	-
Public utilities	49	-
Tobacco products	421,545	2.1
Other selective sales	2,443,260	11.9
Licenses	1,186,734	5.8
Alcoholic beverages	2,030	-
Amusements	1,130	-
Corporations in general	7,076	-
Hunting and fishing	55,638	0.3
Motor vehicle	631,436	3.1
Motor vehicle operators	45,095	0.2
Public utilities	137	-
Occupation and business, NEC	373,790	1.8
Other licenses	70,402	0.3
Income taxes	9,054,106	44.0
Individual income	7,988,084	38.9
Corporation net income	1,066,022	5.2
Other taxes	372,846	1.8
Death and gift	165,983	0.8
Documentary and stock transfer	160,493	0.8
Severance	46,370	0.2
Taxes, NEC	0	0.0

- = Rounds to zero.

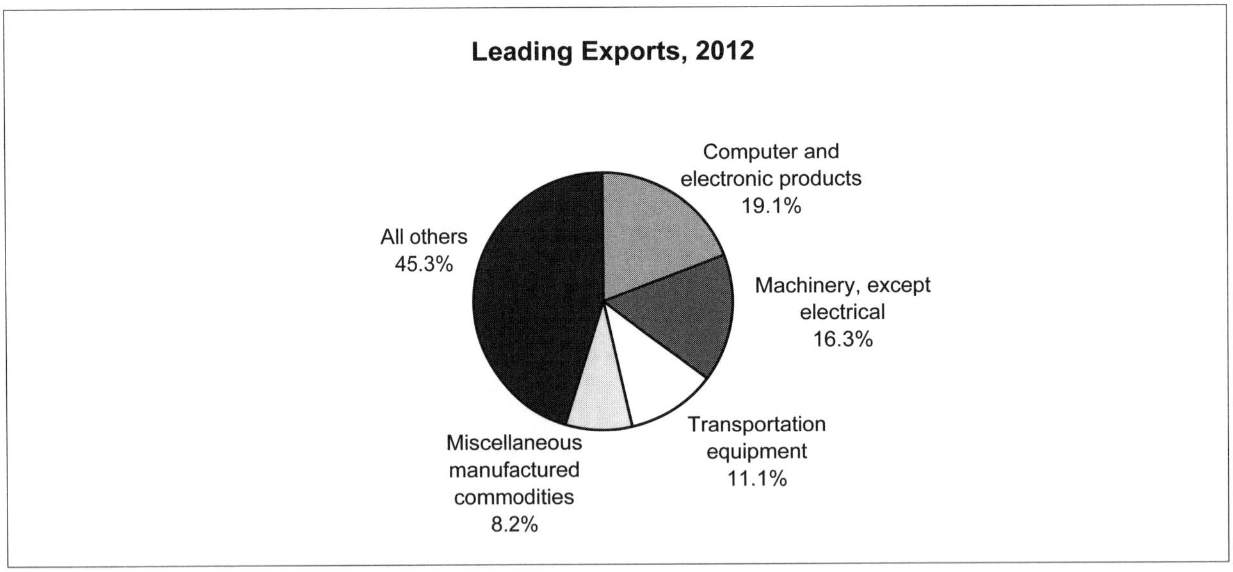

MISSISSIPPI

Facts and Figures

Location: South central United States; bordered on the N by Tennessee, on the E by Alabama, on the S by Louisiana and the Gulf of Mexico, and on the W by Arkansas and Louisiana

Area: 48,430 sq. mi. (125,434 sq. km.); rank—32nd

Population: 2,984,926 (2012 est.); rank—31st

Principal Cities: capital—Jackson; largest—Jackson

Statehood: December 10, 1817; 20th state

U.S. Congress: 2 senators, 4 representatives

State Motto: *Virtute et armis* ("By valor and arms")

State Song: "Go, Mississippi"

State Nicknames: The Magnolia State; The Hospitality State

Abbreviations: MS; Miss.

State Symbols: flower—magnolia blossom; tree—Southern magnolia; bird—mockingbird

At a Glance

- With an increase in population of 3.8 percent, Mississippi ranked 34th among the states in growth from 2000 to 2009.
- An estimated 14,500 marriages took place in Mississippi in 2009, compared to 12,200 divorces.
- Mississippi's median household income in 2011 was $36,919, and 22.6 percent of the population lived below the poverty level.
- In 2011, 17.7 percent of Mississippians did not have health insurance, compared to 15.1 percent of the total U.S. population.
- In 2007, Mississippi exported $1.1 billion worth of agricultural products, about 1.4 percent of the U.S. total.

Table MS-1. Population by Age, Sex, Race, and Hispanic Origin

(Number, percent, except where noted.)

Sex, age, race, and Hispanic origin	2000	2010	2012[1]	Average annual percent change, 2010–2012
Total Population	2,844,658	2,967,297	2,984,926	0.2
Percent of total U.S. population	1.0	1.0	1.0	X
Sex				
Male	1,373,554	1,441,240	1,449,291	0.2
Female	1,471,104	1,526,057	1,535,635	0.2
Age				
Under 5 years	204,364	210,956	203,828	-1.2
5 to 19 years	668,850	638,539	629,169	-0.5
20 to 64 years	1,627,921	1,737,395	1,747,854	0.2
65 years and over	343,523	380,407	404,075	2.0
Median age (years)	33.8	36.0	36.3	0.3
Race and Hispanic Origin				
One race				
White	1,746,099	1,789,391	1,788,664	-
Black	1,033,809	1,103,101	1,116,367	0.4
American Indian and Alaska Native	11,652	16,837	17,501	1.3
Asian	18,626	26,477	28,255	2.1
Native Hawaiian or Other Pacific Islander	667	1,700	1,715	0.3
Two or more races	20,021	29,791	32,424	2.7
Hispanic (of any race)	39,569	85,107	89,105	1.5

X = Not applicable.
- = Zero or rounds to zero.
[1] Population figures for 2012 are July 1 estimates. The 2010 estimates are taken from the 2010 Census.

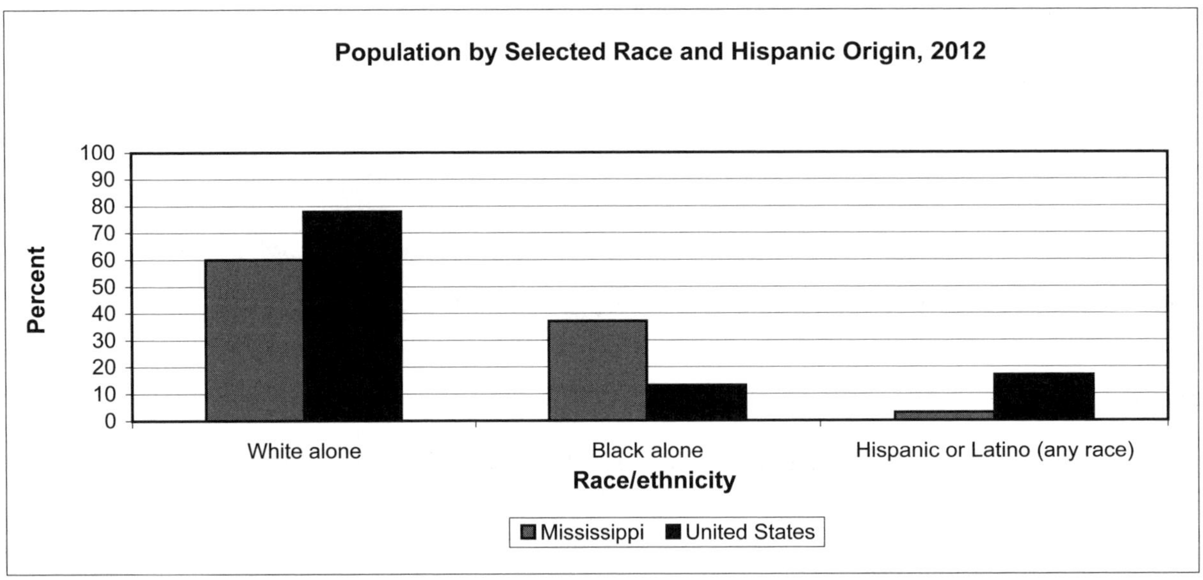

Table MS-2. Marital Status

(Number, percent distribution.)

Sex, age, race, and Hispanic origin	2000	2010	2011
Males, 15 Years and Over	1,046,252	1,121,265	1,122,460
Never married	30.6	34.9	35.9
Now married, except separated	54.6	48.3	48.2
Separated	2.4	2.5	2.9
Widowed	2.9	2.7	2.7
Divorced	9.5	11.7	10.4
Females, 15 Years and Over	1,157,363	1,224,423	1,227,559
Never married	25.1	29.8	31.2
Now married, except separated	48.6	43.8	41.6
Separated	3.2	3.4	3.5
Widowed	12.5	10.8	11.0
Divorced	10.6	12.3	12.6

Table MS-3. Households and Housing Characteristics

(Number, percent, dollars.)

Item	2000	2010	2011	Average annual percent change, 2000–2011
Total Households	1,046,434	1,079,999	1,080,991	0.3
Family households	747,159	746,115	740,958	-0.1
Married-couple family	520,884	501,571	487,509	-0.5
Other family	226,315	244,544	253,449	1.0
Male householder, no wife present	45,610	51,400	50,001	0.8
Female householder, no husband present	180,705	193,144	203,448	1.0
Nonfamily households	299,275	333,884	340,033	1.1
Householder living alone	257,708	293,185	297,896	1.3
Householder not living alone	41,567	40,699	42,137	0.1
Housing Characteristics				
Total housing units	1,161,953	1,276,441	1,281,760	0.9
Occupied housing units	1,046,434	1,079,999	1,080,991	0.3
Owner occupied	756,967	753,374	754,663	-
Renter occupied	289,467	326,625	326,328	1.1
Average size	2.63	2.66	2.67	0.1
Financial Characteristics				
Median gross rent of renter-occupied housing	439	672	689	4.7
Median monthly owner costs for housing units with a mortgage	762	1,043	1,048	3.1
Median value of owner-occupied housing units	71,400	100,100	99,900	3.3

- = Zero or rounds to zero.

Table MS-4. Migration, Origin, and Language

(Number, percent.)

Characteristic	State			U.S.		
	2010	2011	Percent change	2010	2011	Percent change
Residence 1 Year Ago						
Population 1 year and over	2,931,228	2,943,021	0.4	305,628,607	307,900,319	0.7
Same house	85.7	86.1	0.5	84.6	84.8	0.2
Different house in the U.S.	14.1	13.6	-3.5	14.8	14.6	-1.4
Same county	8.0	7.6	-5.0	9.4	9.2	-2.1
Different county	6.1	6.0	-1.6	5.4	5.4	-
Same state	3.6	3.7	2.8	3.2	3.1	-3.1
Different state	2.5	2.3	-8.0	2.2	2.3	4.5
Abroad	0.3	0.3	-	0.6	0.6	-
Place of Birth						
Native born	2,908,608	2,913,456	0.2	269,393,835	271,214,059	0.7
Male	48.4	48.4	-	49.2	49.2	-
Female	51.6	51.6	-	50.8	50.8	-
Foreign born	61,428	65,056	5.9	39,955,854	40,377,860	1.1
Male	53.5	56.5	5.6	49.1	48.9	-0.4
Female	46.5	43.5	-6.5	50.9	51.1	0.4
Foreign born; naturalized U.S. citizen	18,839	20,890	10.9	17,476,082	18,140,192	3.8
Male	41.7	45.3	8.6	45.8	45.8	-
Female	58.3	54.7	-6.2	54.2	54.2	-
Foreign born; not a U.S. citizen	42,589	44,166	3.7	22,479,772	22,237,668	-1.1
Male	58.7	61.8	5.3	51.6	51.5	-0.2
Female	41.3	38.2	-7.5	48.4	48.5	0.2
Entered 2000 or later	49.0	49.1	0.2	34.7	35.7	2.9
Entered 1990 to 1999	24.6	21.5	-12.6	27.2	26.7	-1.8
Entered before 1990	26.4	29.4	11.4	38.1	37.6	-1.3
World Region of Birth, Foreign						
Foreign-born population, excluding population born at sea	61,428	65,056	5.9	39,955,673	40,377,757	1.1
Europe	10.8	9.6	-11.1	12.1	12.1	-
Asia	33.6	31.0	-7.7	28.2	28.6	1.4
Africa	2.2	2.7	22.7	4	4.1	2.5
Oceania	0.3	0.4	-	0.5	0.5	-
Latin America	51.9	53.3	2.7	53.1	52.6	-0.9
North America	1.2	2.9	141.7	2	2.0	-
Language Spoken at Home and Ability to Speak English						
Population 5 years and over	2,760,957	2,773,115	0.4	289,215,746	291,524,091	0.8
English only	96.4	96.2	-0.2	79.4	79.2	-0.3
Language other than English	3.6	3.8	5.6	20.6	20.8	1.0
Speaks English less than "very well"	1.5	1.7	13.3	8.7	8.7	-

- = Zero or rounds to zero.

Table MS-5. Median Income and Poverty Status, 2011

(Number, percent, except as noted.)

Characteristic	State		U.S.	
	Number	Percent	Number	Percent
Median Income				
Households (dollars)	36,919	X	50,502	X
Families (dollars)	46,304	X	61,455	X
Below Poverty Level (All People)	650,524	22.6	48,452,035	15.9
Sex				
Male	282,033	20.3	21,825,281	14.7
Female	368,491	24.6	26,626,754	17.2
Age				
Under 18 years	235,727	31.8	16,386,500	22.5
Related children under 18 years	232,239	31.5	16,087,074	22.2
18 to 64 years	364,416	20.6	28,335,079	14.8
65 years and over	50,381	13.5	3,730,456	9.3

X = Not applicable.

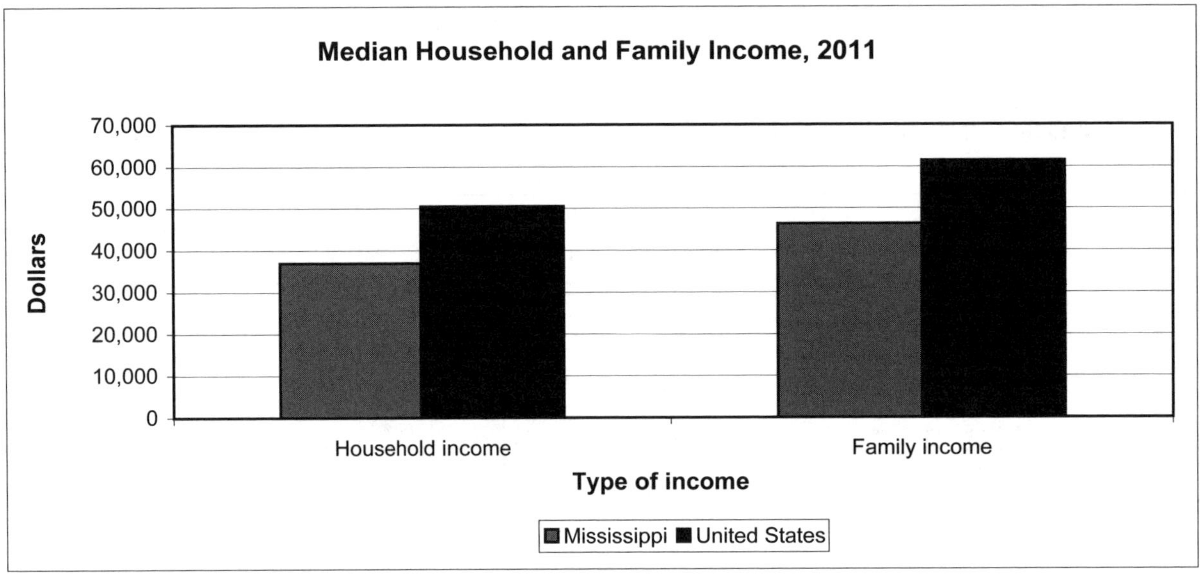

Table MS-6. Health Insurance Coverage Status for the Civilian Noninstitutionalized Population and Children Under 18 Years of Age

(Numbers in thousands, percent.)

Item	2004	2005	2006	2007	2008	2009	2010	2011
Civilian Noninstitutionalized Population	2,868	2,854	2,892	2,903	2,868	2,880	2,903	2,912
Covered by Private or Public Insurance								
Number	2,391	2,370	2,292	2,358	2,355	2,366	2,375	2,395
Percent	83.3	83.1	79.2	81.2	82.1	82.1	81.8	82.3
Not Covered								
Number	478	483	600	545	513	514	528	516
Percent	16.7	16.9	20.8	18.8	17.9	17.9	18.2	17.7
Percent in the U.S. not covered	14.9	15.3	15.8	15.3	15.1	15.1	15.5	15.1
Children Under 18 Years of Age	768	754	774	778	763	764	752	750
Covered by Private or Public Insurance								
Number	665	669	628	684	666	685	688	689
Percent	86.6	88.7	81.1	87.9	87.3	89.7	91.6	91.9
Not Covered								
Number	103	85	146	94	97	79	64	61
Percent	13.4	11.3	18.9	12.1	12.7	10.3	8.4	8.1
Percent in the U.S. not covered	10.5	10.9	11.7	11.0	9.7	8.6	8.0	7.5

Table MS-7. Employment Status by Demographic Group, Preliminary 2012

(Numbers in thousands, percent.)

Characteristic	Civilian noninstitutional population	Civilian labor force		Employed		Unemployed	
		Number	Percent of population	Number	Percent of population	Number	Percent of population
Total	2,256	1,329	58.9	1,211	53.7	118	8.9
Sex							
Male	1,061	691	65.2	632	59.6	59	8.5
Female	1,195	637	53.3	578	48.4	59	9.2
Race, Sex, and Hispanic Origin							
White	1,403	864	61.6	810	57.7	54	6.3
Male	681	472	69.2	447	65.6	25	5.3
Female	722	393	54.3	363	50.3	30	7.5
Black or African American	793	428	53.9	369	46.5	59	13.8
Male	355	201	56.7	170	48.0	31	15.4
Female	438	226	51.6	198	45.3	28	12.3
Hispanic	48	34	71.2	31	63.2	4	11.2
Male	27	21	77.8	20	73.8	1	5.3
Female	22	14	63.0	11	50.3	3	20.2
Age							
16 to 19 years	181	49	27.2	37	20.6	12	24.0
20 to 24 years	201	130	64.5	101	49.9	29	22.6
25 to 34 years	388	311	80.2	282	72.7	29	9.3
35 to 44 years	342	276	80.9	261	76.4	16	5.6
45 to 54 years	361	270	74.7	254	70.3	16	5.8
55 to 64 years	392	231	58.9	219	55.8	12	5.3
65 years and over	390	61	15.8	57	14.7	4	6.7

NOTE: Data in Table 7 are from the Current Population Survey (CPS) and do not match the estimates in Table 8. See notes and definitions for further information.

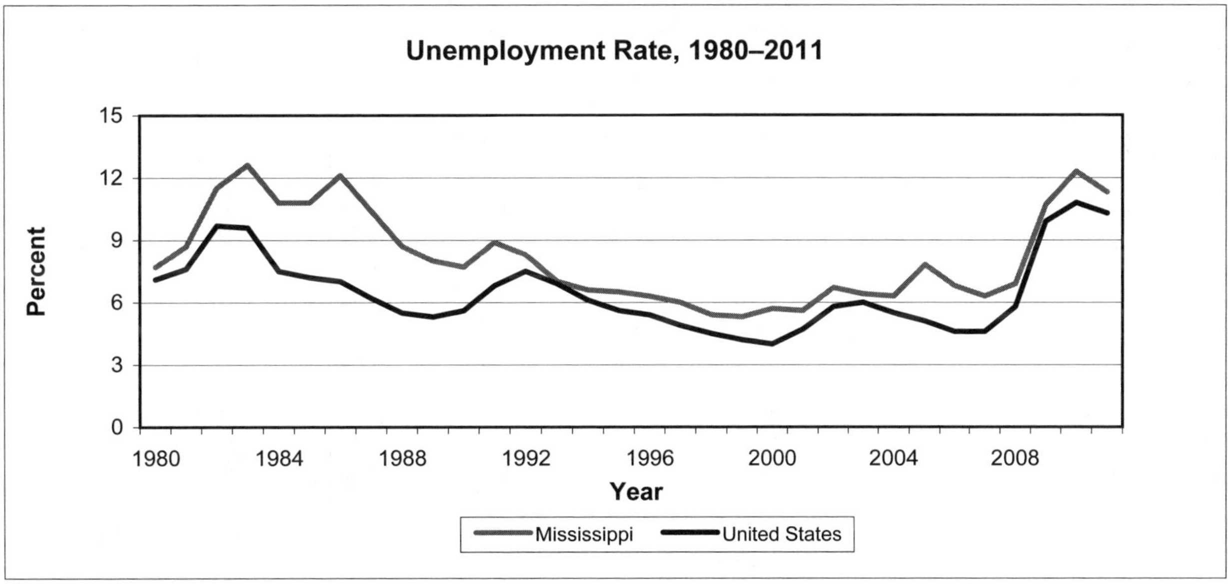

Table MS-8. Employment Status of the Civilian Noninstitutional Population Age 16 Years and Over

(Number, percent.)

Year	Civilian labor force	Civilian participation rate	Employed	Unemployed	Unemployment rate
2005	1,325,646	61.8	1,222,682	102,964	7.8
2006	1,297,954	60.3	1,210,245	97,709	6.8
2007	1,306,633	60.1	1,224,774	81,859	6.3
2008	1,314,444	60.0	1,223,858	90,586	6.9
2009	1,339,779	59.0	1,196,480	143,299	10.7
2010	1,340,288	58.2	1,175,203	165,085	12.3
2011	1,332,465	57.7	1,181,295	151,170	11.3

Table MS-9. Employment and Average Wages by Industry

(Estimates before 2007 are based on the 2002 *North American Industry Classification System* [NAICS]. Estimates from 2007 onward are based on the 2007 NAICS.)

Industry	2005	2006	2007	2008	2009	2010	2011
				Number of jobs			
Wage and Salary Employment by Industry	1,204,335	1,219,764	1,232,917	1,230,068	1,179,833	1,172,459	1,173,633
Farm Wage and Salary Employment	7,790	9,693	8,806	8,617	9,824	9,993	9,012
Nonfarm Wage and Salary Employment	1,196,545	1,210,071	1,224,111	1,221,451	1,170,009	1,162,466	1,164,621
Private wage and salary employment	919,882	934,709	944,704	937,690	885,322	880,596	885,304
Forestry, fishing, and related activities	9,324	9,000	8,591	8,183	7,591	7,994	8,230
Mining	4,813	5,778	6,140	6,513	5,667	5,700	6,126
Utilities	7,847	7,822	7,567	7,626	7,714	7,733	7,733
Construction	54,257	59,750	61,310	63,234	53,950	52,070	51,468
Manufacturing	178,729	176,108	169,416	159,641	141,508	136,188	135,493
Durable goods manufacturing	117,104	116,933	112,710	105,221	90,678	87,373	88,112
Nondurable goods manufacturing	61,625	59,175	56,706	54,420	50,830	48,815	47,381
Wholesale trade	35,404	36,655	37,243	36,773	35,103	34,521	34,561
Retail trade	140,496	144,249	143,575	141,108	135,253	134,361	134,996
Transportation and warehousing	39,295	39,936	41,381	41,408	39,490	39,545	40,037
Information	14,336	13,721	13,397	13,482	12,815	12,315	11,886
Finance and insurance	34,426	34,769	35,172	34,983	34,143	33,974	34,093
Real estate and rental and leasing	12,369	12,404	12,656	12,733	12,382	11,911	11,801
Professional, scientific, and technical services	32,640	33,260	33,192	33,876	32,219	32,138	32,161
Management of companies and enterprises	9,653	9,390	9,789	9,890	9,816	9,749	10,139
Administrative and waste services	46,238	50,764	51,972	52,431	46,671	51,490	52,749
Educational services	16,352	17,459	17,981	18,841	18,642	19,134	19,720
Health care and social assistance	106,334	110,164	114,565	116,457	118,460	120,870	122,437
Arts, entertainment, and recreation	12,523	11,232	13,319	12,895	12,260	12,074	11,021
Accommodation and food services	111,520	109,052	113,499	113,635	108,839	107,503	109,490
Other services, except public administration	53,326	53,196	53,939	53,981	52,799	51,326	51,163
Government and government enterprises	276,663	275,362	279,407	283,761	284,687	281,870	279,317
				Dollars			
Average Wages and Salaries by Industry	30,357	31,758	33,012	34,240	34,559	35,274	35,951
Average Farm Wages and Salaries	21,567	18,711	23,039	21,338	18,757	18,556	18,447
Average Nonfarm Wages and Salaries	30,414	31,863	33,083	34,331	34,692	35,418	36,086
Average private wages and salaries	29,910	31,493	32,686	33,839	34,004	34,699	35,486
Forestry, fishing, and related activities	25,056	26,585	27,601	28,441	28,466	29,121	29,948
Mining	50,983	56,340	61,486	67,919	64,256	65,743	70,024
Utilities	60,887	60,165	63,963	66,823	66,225	67,384	68,006
Construction	33,067	36,574	38,028	42,339	41,392	41,424	42,437
Manufacturing	35,559	37,040	38,624	40,150	41,196	42,220	43,610
Durable goods manufacturing	36,233	37,897	39,549	41,460	42,837	43,813	45,175
Nondurable goods manufacturing	34,279	35,346	36,785	37,618	38,267	39,368	40,699
Wholesale trade	43,184	46,258	47,793	48,838	48,284	48,893	50,327
Retail trade	21,141	22,448	22,500	22,854	23,062	23,691	24,012
Transportation and warehousing	36,820	38,052	38,991	40,173	39,800	40,843	41,834
Information	38,830	39,622	39,810	40,676	40,359	42,190	44,033
Finance and insurance	42,162	44,513	46,179	47,229	47,250	48,978	50,007
Real estate and rental and leasing	24,978	27,198	28,571	29,801	29,536	30,689	31,823
Professional, scientific, and technical services	41,970	45,334	48,220	50,764	52,024	52,203	53,074
Management of companies and enterprises	57,576	64,633	69,779	70,716	70,928	73,586	77,992
Administrative and waste services	21,402	22,730	23,771	24,452	25,108	25,816	25,596
Educational services	20,670	21,974	22,510	23,653	24,664	25,469	26,816
Health care and social assistance	33,803	35,170	36,283	37,562	38,602	38,853	39,568
Arts, entertainment, and recreation	24,186	25,038	26,569	24,819	24,332	24,800	24,240
Accommodation and food services	16,831	16,617	18,193	17,785	17,340	18,057	18,495
Other services, except public administration	20,946	22,396	23,402	24,684	24,744	26,043	26,362
Government and government enterprises	32,088	33,116	34,428	35,957	36,831	37,662	37,988

Table MS-10. Employment Characteristics by Family Type

(Number, percent.)

Family type and labor force status	2009 Total	2009 Families with own children under 18 years	2010 Total	2010 Families with own children under 18 years	2011 Total	2011 Families with own children under 18 years
All families	754,131	337,556	746,115	322,796	740,958	321,953
Family type and labor force status						
Married-couple families	506,527	197,137	501,571	193,319	487,509	186,686
Both husband and wife in labor force	50.5	67.3	50.1	66.8	49.5	67.3
Husband in labor force, wife not in labor force	21.6	25.8	22.3	26.3	22.5	26.1
Wife in labor force, husband not in labor force	8.9	4.9	8.8	4.7	9.0	4.6
Both husband and wife not in labor force	18.9	2.0	18.8	2.3	18.9	2.0
Other families	247,604	140,419	244,544	129,477	253,449	135,267
Female householder, no husband present	78.0	79.6	79.0	81.7	80.3	83.8
In labor force	51.9	64.1	49.9	64.2	52.0	67.0
Not in labor force	26.1	15.5	29.1	17.5	28.3	16.8
Male householder, no wife present	22.0	20.4	21.0	18.3	19.7	16.2
In labor force	16.7	17.7	14.5	15.2	13.6	14.4
Not in labor force	5.2	2.8	6.5	3.0	6.1	1.8

Table MS-11. School Enrollment and Educational Attainment, 2011

(Number, percent.)

Item	State	U.S.
Enrollment		
Total population 3 years and over, enrolled in school	830,815	83,131,910
Enrolled in nursery school or preschool (percent)	6.7	6.0
Enrolled in kindergarten (percent)	5.3	5.1
Enrolled in elementary school, grades 1-8 (percent)	40.7	39.5
Enrolled in high school, grades 9-12 (percent)	21.0	20.7
Enrolled in college or graduate school (percent)	26.3	28.7
Attainment		
Total population 25 years and over	1,912,708	206,471,670
Less than ninth grade (percent)	6.6	6.0
9th to 12th grade, no diploma (percent)	12.3	8.1
High school graduate, including equivalency (percent)	30.2	28.4
Some college, no degree (percent)	22.7	21.2
Associate's degree (percent)	8.3	7.8
Bachelor's degree (percent)	12.6	17.9
Graduate or professional degree (percent)	7.3	10.6
High school graduate or higher (percent)	81.1	85.9
Bachelor's degree or higher (percent)	19.8	28.5

Table MS-12. Educational Indicators

(Number, percent; data derived from National Center of Education Statistics.)

Item	State	U.S.
Public Schools, 2009–2010 (except where noted)		
Number of school districts	152	13,629
Number of schools	1,085	99,834
Number of students (in thousands)	492	49,373
Student-teacher ratio	14.9	15.4
Expenditures per student (dollars)	8,902	10,591
Averaged freshman graduation rate, 2008–2009	62.0	75.5[1]
Dropout rate, 2008–2009	4.2	4.1
Students eligible for free or reduced-price lunch (percent)	70.6	48.0
English language learners, 2010–2011 (percent)	1.1	9.8[1]
Students with IEP (percent)	13.0	13.1
Private Schools, 2009–2010 (except where noted)		
Number of schools	316	33,366
Number of students (in thousands)	47	4,700
High school graduates, 2008–2009	3,358	308,813
Student-teacher ratio	10.5	10.7

[1] U.S. total includes estimates for nonreporting states.

Table MS-13. Reported Voting and Registration of the Voting-Age Population, November 2012

(Numbers in thousands, percent.)

Item	Total population	Total citizen population	Registered			Voted		
			Total registered	Percent registered (total population)	Percent registered (total citizen population)	Total voted	Percent voted (total population)	Percent voted (total citizen population)
U.S. Total	235,248	215,081	153,157	65.1	71.2	132,948	56.5	61.8
State Total	2,166	2,130	1,794	82.8	84.2	1,588	73.3	74.5
Sex								
Male	1,019	995	824	80.9	82.8	710	69.7	71.4
Female	1,147	1,135	971	84.6	85.5	877	76.4	77.3
Race								
White alone	1,355	1,338	1,094	80.7	81.8	951	70.2	71.1
White, non-Hispanic alone	1,321	1,321	1,089	82.4	82.4	949	71.8	71.8
Black alone	748	744	674	90.2	90.6	613	82.0	82.4
Asian alone	26	10	5	B	B	2	B	B
Hispanic (of any race)	35	17	5	B	B	2	B	B
Age								
18 to 24 years	300	294	222	73.9	75.5	187	62.4	63.8
25 to 44 years	716	700	587	81.9	83.9	500	69.8	71.5
45 to 64 years	734	727	614	83.7	84.5	563	76.7	77.4
65 to 74 years	258	252	227	87.9	90.1	204	79.1	81.1
75 years and over	158	158	145	91.3	91.3	133	83.8	83.8

B = Base is less than 75,000 and therefore too small to show the derived measure.

Table MS-14. Crime

(Number, rate per 100,000. Data are derived from the FBI Uniform Crime Reports.)

Item	State			U.S.		
	2010	2011	Percent change	2010	2011	Percent change
TOTAL POPULATION	2,970,072	2,978,512	0.3	309,330,219	311,591,917	0.7
VIOLENT CRIME						
Number	7,999	8,036	0.5	1,251,248	1,203,564	-3.8
Rate	269.3	269.8	0.2	404.5	386.3	-4.5
Murder and Nonnegligent Manslaughter						
Number	204	239	17.2	14,722	14,612	-0.7
Rate	6.9	8.0	15.9	4.8	4.7	-2.1
Forcible Rape						
Number	931	865	-7.1	85,593	83,425	-2.5
Rate	31.3	29.0	-7.3	27.7	26.8	-3.2
Robbery						
Number	2,777	2,492	-10.3	369,089	354,396	-4.0
Rate	93.5	83.7	-10.5	119.3	113.7	-4.7
Aggravated Assault						
Number	4,087	4,440	8.6	781,844	751,131	-3.9
Rate	137.6	149.1	8.4	252.8	241.1	-4.6
PROPERTY CRIME						
Number	88,596	90,115	1.7	9,112,625	9,063,173	-0.5
Rate	2,983.0	3,025.5	1.4	2,945.9	2,908.7	-1.3
Burglary						
Number	30,453	30,907	1.5	2,168,459	2,188,005	0.9
Rate	1,025.3	1,037.7	1.2	701.0	702.2	0.2
Larceny-Theft						
Number	52,784	54,283	2.8	6,204,601	6,159,795	-0.7
Rate	1,777.2	1,822.5	2.5	2,005.8	1,976.9	-1.4
Motor Vehicle Theft						
Number	5,359	4,925	-8.1	739,565	715,373	-3.3
Rate	180.4	165.4	-8.3	239.1	229.6	-4.0

Table MS-15. State Government Finances, 2011

(Dollar amounts in thousands, percent distribution.)

Item	Dollars	Percent distribution
Total Revenue	23,606,197	100.0
General revenue	17,807,309	75.4
Intergovernmental revenue	8,726,548	37.0
Taxes	6,714,180	28.4
General sales	2,932,859	12.4
Selective sales	1,386,826	5.9
License taxes	455,473	1.9
Individual income tax	1,447,751	6.1
Corporate income tax	353,057	1.5
Other taxes	138,214	0.6
Current charges	1,764,127	7.5
Miscellaneous general revenue	602,454	2.6
Utility revenue	0	0.0
Liquor stores revenue	263,321	1.1
Insurance trust revenue [1]	5,535,567	23.4
Total Expenditure	20,157,417	100.0
Intergovernmental expenditure	5,253,307	26.1
Direct expenditure	14,904,110	73.9
Current operation	10,740,372	53.3
Capital outlay	1,255,919	6.2
Insurance benefits and repayments	2,397,687	11.9
Assistance and subsidies	242,417	1.2
Interest on debt	267,715	1.3
Exhibit: Salaries and wages	2,402,174	11.9
Total Expenditure	20,157,417	100.0
General expenditure	17,546,382	87.0
Intergovernmental expenditure	5,253,307	26.1
Direct expenditure	12,293,075	61.0
General expenditure, by function:		
Education	5,518,603	27.4
Public welfare	5,436,907	27.0
Hospitals	1,073,347	5.3
Health	434,010	2.2
Highways	1,377,654	6.8
Police protection	103,889	0.5
Correction	354,626	1.8
Natural resources	307,107	1.5
Parks and recreation	82,824	0.4
Governmental administration	395,498	2.0
Interest on general debt	267,715	1.3
Other and unallocable	2,194,202	10.9
Utility expenditure	0	0.0
Liquor stores expenditure	213,348	1.1
Insurance trust expenditure	2,397,687	11.9
Debt at End of Fiscal Year	6,768,371	X
Cash and Security Holdings	31,204,875	X

X = Not applicable.
[1] Within insurance trust revenue, net earnings of state retirement systems is a calculated statistic (the item code in the data file is X08), and thus can be positive or negative. Net earnings is the sum of earnings on investments plus gains on investments minus losses on investments. The change made in 2002 for asset valuation from book to market value in accordance with Statement 34 of the Governmental Accounting Standards Board is reflected in the calculated statistics.

Table MS-16. State Government Tax Collections, 2012

(Dollars in thousands, percent.)

Item	Dollars	Percent distribution
Total Taxes	6,953,362	100.0
Property taxes	23,982	0.3
Sales and gross receipts	4,396,669	63.2
General sales and gross receipts	3,072,243	44.2
Selective sales and gross receipts	1,324,426	19.0
Alcoholic beverages	42,183	0.6
Amusements	152,077	2.2
Insurance premiums	189,373	2.7
Motor fuels	417,048	6.0
Pari-mutuels	0	0.0
Public utilities	1,894	-
Tobacco products	157,433	2.3
Other selective sales	364,418	5.2
Licenses	517,982	7.4
Alcoholic beverages	2,918	-
Amusements	11,753	0.2
Corporations in general	146,254	2.1
Hunting and fishing	15,462	0.2
Motor vehicle	134,477	1.9
Motor vehicle operators	40,409	0.6
Public utilities	8,826	0.1
Occupation and business, NEC	91,660	1.3
Other licenses	66,223	1.0
Income taxes	1,896,945	27.3
Individual income	1,501,267	21.6
Corporation net income	395,678	5.7
Other taxes	117,784	1.7
Death and gift	12	-
Documentary and stock transfer	0	0.0
Severance	116,378	1.7
Taxes, NEC	1,394	-

- = Rounds to zero.

Leading Exports, 2012

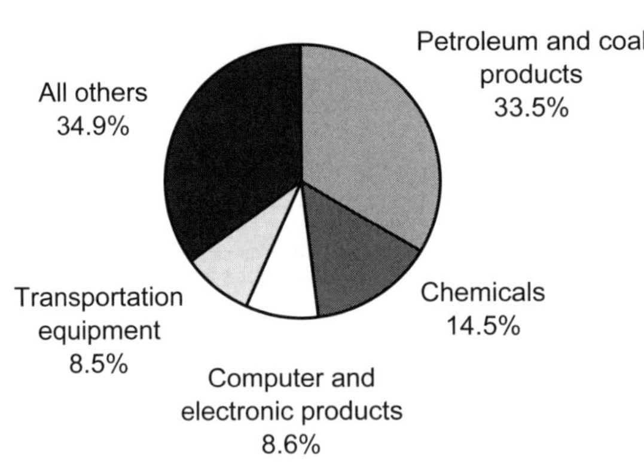

MISSOURI

Facts and Figures

Location: Central United States; bordered on the N by Iowa, on the E by Illinois, Kentucky, and Tennessee, on the S by Arkansas, and on the W by Oklahoma, Kansas, and Nebraska

Area: 69,704 sq. mi. (180,533 sq. km.); rank—21st

Population: 6,021,988 (2012 est.); rank—18th

Principal Cities: capital—Jefferson City; largest—Kansas City

Statehood: August 10, 1821; 24th state

U.S. Congress: 2 senators, 8 representatives

State Motto: *Salus populi suprema lex esto* ("The welfare of the people shall be the supreme law")

State Song: "Missouri Waltz"

State Nickname: The Show Me State

Abbreviations: MO; Mo

State Symbols: flower—hawthorn; tree—flowering dogwood; bird—Eastern bluebird

At a Glance

- With an increase in population of 7.0 percent, Missouri ranked 18th among the states in growth from 2000 to 2009.
- An estimated 39,800 marriages took place in Missouri in 2009, compared to 23,300 divorces.
- In 2011, 13.7 percent of Missourians did not have health insurance, compared to 15.1 percent of the total U.S. population.
- In the 2012 election, 63.9 percent of Missouri's eligible voters voted, compared to 61.8 percent of eligible voters nationwide.
- In 2007, Missouri exported $2.1 billion worth of agricultural products, about 2.5 percent of the U.S. total.

Table MO-1. Population by Age, Sex, Race, and Hispanic Origin

(Number, percent, except where noted.)

Sex, age, race, and Hispanic origin	2000	2010	2012[1]	Average annual percent change, 2010–2012
Total Population	5,595,211	5,988,927	6,021,988	0.2
Percent of total U.S. population	2.0	1.9	1.9	X
Sex				
Male	2,720,177	2,933,477	2,951,036	0.2
Female	2,875,034	3,055,450	3,070,952	0.2
Age				
Under 5 years	269,898	390,237	379,246	-1.0
5 to 19 years	1,224,274	1,211,174	1,189,179	-0.6
20 to 64 years	3,245,660	3,549,222	3,570,382	0.2
65 years and over	755,379	838,294	883,181	1.7
Median age (years)	36.1	37.9	38.1	0.2
Race and Hispanic Origin				
One race				
White	4,748,083	5,038,407	5,049,604	0.1
Black	629,391	700,178	708,079	0.4
American Indian and Alaska Native	25,076	30,595	31,631	1.1
Asian	61,595	100,213	107,092	2.1
Native Hawaiian or Other Pacific Islander	3,178	7,178	7,821	2.7
Two or more races	82,061	112,356	119,761	2.1
Hispanic (of any race)	118,592	223,421	237,319	2.0

X = Not applicable.
[1] Population figures for 2012 are July 1 estimates. The 2010 estimates are taken from the 2010 Census.

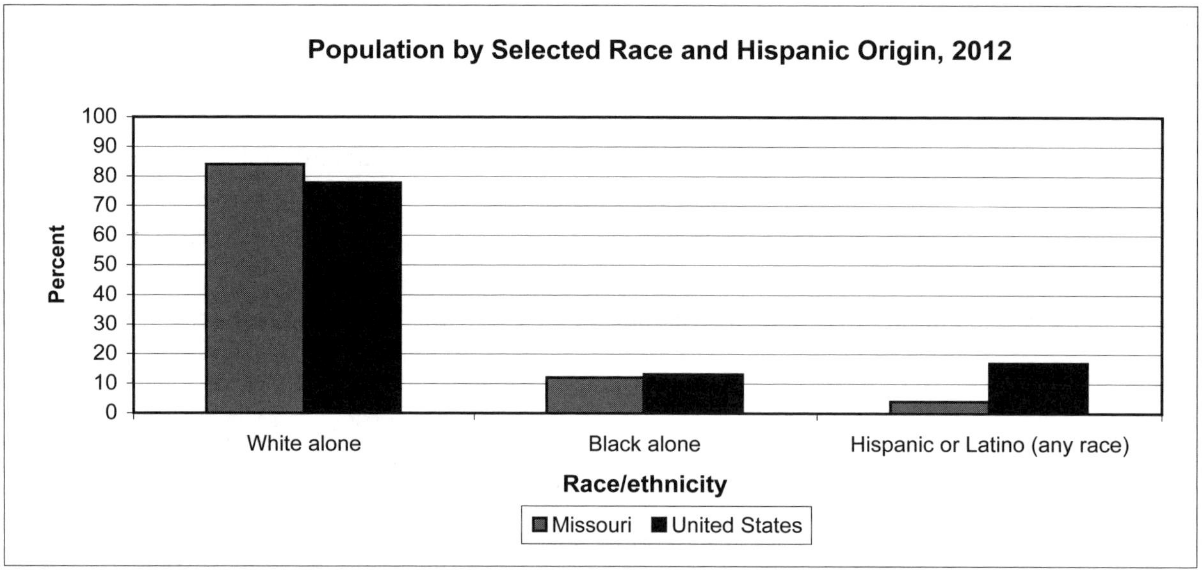

Table MO-2. Marital Status

(Number, percent distribution.)

Sex, age, race, and Hispanic origin	2000	2010	2011
Males, 15 Years and Over	2,114,280	2,332,888	2,348,195
Never married	27.8	32.1	32.7
Now married, except separated	58.0	52.5	51.9
Separated	1.6	1.7	1.7
Widowed	2.6	2.6	2.6
Divorced	10.0	11.0	11.1
Females, 15 Years and Over	2,300,111	2,492,198	2,493,306
Never married	22.1	26.8	26.4
Now married, except separated	53.1	48.2	48.6
Separated	2.0	2.2	2.1
Widowed	11.3	10.0	10.0
Divorced	11.5	12.8	13.0

Table MO-3. Households and Housing Characteristics

(Number, percent, dollars.)

Item	2000	2010	2011	Average annual percent change, 2000–2011
Total Households	2,194,594	2,350,628	2,341,074	0.6
Family households	1,476,516	1,524,078	1,534,831	0.3
Married-couple family	1,140,866	1,146,501	1,144,804	-
Other family	335,650	377,577	390,027	1.4
Male householder, no wife present	81,890	99,807	99,280	1.8
Female householder, no husband present	253,760	277,770	290,747	1.2
Nonfamily households	718,078	826,550	806,243	1.0
Householder living alone	599,808	689,361	668,566	1.0
Householder not living alone	118,270	137,189	137,677	1.4
Housing Characteristics				
Total housing units	2,442,017	2,714,017	2,723,449	1.0
Occupied housing units	2,194,594	2,350,628	2,341,074	0.6
Owner occupied	1,542,149	1,621,371	1,593,031	0.3
Renter occupied	652,445	729,257	748,043	1.2
Average size	2.48	2.48	2.49	-
Financial Characteristics				
Median gross rent of renter-occupied housing	484	682	708	3.9
Median monthly owner costs for housing units with a mortgage	861	1,182	1,199	3.3
Median value of owner-occupied housing units	89,900	139,000	136,900	4.4

- = Zero or rounds to zero.

Table MO-4. Migration, Origin, and Language

(Number, percent.)

Characteristic	State			U.S.		
	2010	2011	Percent change	2010	2011	Percent change
Residence 1 Year Ago						
Population 1 year and over	5,920,858	5,937,896	0.3	305,628,607	307,900,319	0.7
Same house	83.9	83.6	-0.4	84.6	84.8	0.2
Different house in the U.S.	15.7	16.0	1.9	14.8	14.6	-1.4
Same county	9.1	9.0	-1.1	9.4	9.2	-2.1
Different county	6.6	7.0	6.1	5.4	5.4	-
Same state	4.1	4.5	9.8	3.2	3.1	-3.1
Different state	2.5	2.5	-	2.2	2.3	4.5
Abroad	0.3	0.4	33.3	0.6	0.6	-
Place of Birth						
Native born	5,763,694	5,767,425	0.1	269,393,835	271,214,059	0.7
Male	48.8	49.0	0.4	49.2	49.2	-
Female	51.2	51.0	-0.4	50.8	50.8	-
Foreign born	232,537	243,263	4.6	39,955,854	40,377,860	1.1
Male	50.5	49.5	-2.0	49.1	48.9	-0.4
Female	49.5	50.5	2.0	50.9	51.1	0.4
Foreign born; naturalized U.S. citizen	100,144	101,137	1.0	17,476,082	18,140,192	3.8
Male	48.1	45.8	-4.8	45.8	45.8	-
Female	51.9	54.2	4.4	54.2	54.2	-
Foreign born; not a U.S. citizen	132,393	142,126	7.4	22,479,772	22,237,668	-1.1
Male	52.3	52.2	-0.2	51.6	51.5	-0.2
Female	47.7	47.8	0.2	48.4	48.5	0.2
Entered 2000 or later	44.9	48.0	6.9	34.7	35.7	2.9
Entered 1990 to 1999	28.1	26.3	-6.4	27.2	26.7	-1.8
Entered before 1990	27.0	25.8	-4.4	38.1	37.6	-1.3
World Region of Birth, Foreign						
Foreign-born population, excluding population born at sea	232,537	243,263	4.6	39,955,673	40,377,757	1.1
Europe	22.0	22.1	0.5	12.1	12.1	-
Asia	35.4	36.0	1.7	28.2	28.6	1.4
Africa	7.0	8.3	18.6	4	4.1	2.5
Oceania	1.9	0.9	-52.6	0.5	0.5	-
Latin America	30.8	30.8	-	53.1	52.6	-0.9
North America	3.0	1.9	-36.7	2	2.0	-
Language Spoken at Home and Ability to Speak English						
Population 5 years and over	5,608,805	5,629,071	0.4	289,215,746	291,524,091	0.8
English only	93.9	93.6	-0.3	79.4	79.2	-0.3
Language other than English	6.1	6.4	4.9	20.6	20.8	1.0
Speaks English less than "very well"	2.3	2.4	4.3	8.7	8.7	-

- = Zero or rounds to zero.

Table MO-5. Median Income and Poverty Status, 2011

(Number, percent, except as noted.)

Characteristic	State		U.S.	
	Number	Percent	Number	Percent
Median Income				
Households (dollars)	45,247	X	50,502	X
Families (dollars)	56,616	X	61,455	X
Below Poverty Level (All People)	920,118	15.8	48,452,035	15.9
Sex				
Male	410,068	14.4	21,825,281	14.7
Female	510,050	17.1	26,626,754	17.2
Age				
Under 18 years	306,038	22.1	16,386,500	22.5
Related children under 18 years	298,109	21.7	16,087,074	22.2
18 to 64 years	546,814	15.1	28,335,079	14.8
65 years and over	67,266	8.2	3,730,456	9.3

X = Not applicable.

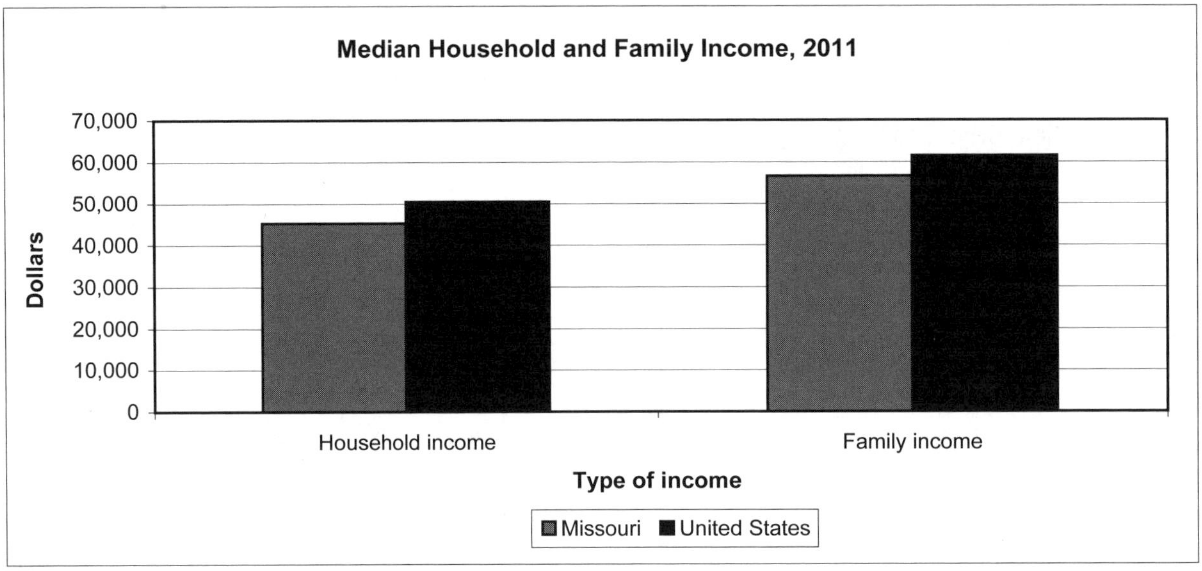

Table MO-6. Health Insurance Coverage Status for the Civilian Noninstitutionalized Population and Children Under 18 Years of Age

(Numbers in thousands, percent.)

Item	2004	2005	2006	2007	2008	2009	2010	2011
Civilian Noninstitutionalized Population	5,614	5,710	5,800	5,791	5,795	5,871	5,880	5,899
Covered by Private or Public Insurance								
Number	4,944	5,041	5,028	5,062	5,040	5,098	5,106	5,092
Percent	88.1	88.3	86.7	87.4	87.0	86.8	86.8	86.3
Not Covered								
Number	670	668	772	729	755	773	774	807
Percent	11.9	11.7	13.3	12.6	13.0	13.2	13.2	13.7
Percent in the U.S. not covered	14.9	15.3	15.8	15.3	15.1	15.1	15.5	15.1
Children Under 18 Years of Age	1,411	1,384	1,398	1,442	1,418	1,427	1,414	1,409
Covered by Private or Public Insurance								
Number	1,308	1,281	1,271	1,291	1,317	1,329	1,326	1,314
Percent	92.7	92.5	90.9	89.6	92.9	93.1	93.8	93.3
Not Covered								
Number	103	104	127	150	101	98	88	95
Percent	7.3	7.5	9.1	10.4	7.1	6.9	6.2	6.7
Percent in the U.S. not covered	10.5	10.9	11.7	11.0	9.7	8.6	8.0	7.5

Table MO-7. Employment Status by Demographic Group, Preliminary 2012

(Numbers in thousands, percent.)

Characteristic	Civilian noninstitutional population	Civilian labor force		Employed		Unemployed	
		Number	Percent of population	Number	Percent of population	Number	Percent of population
Total	4,679	3,018	64.5	2,810	60.1	208	6.9
Sex							
Male	2,249	1,578	70.2	1,466	65.2	112	7.1
Female	2,430	1,441	59.3	1,344	55.3	96	6.7
Race, Sex, and Hispanic Origin							
White	3,967	2,575	64.9	2,419	61.0	156	6.0
Male	1,919	1,356	70.6	1,271	66.2	85	6.2
Female	2,047	1,219	59.5	1,148	56.1	71	5.8
Black or African American	507	314	62.0	274	54.0	41	12.9
Male	227	151	66.7	129	57.0	22	14.5
Female	280	163	58.1	144	51.5	19	11.4
Hispanic	140	93	66.6	88	62.5	6	6.1
Male	67	48	71.6	46	67.7	3	5.4
Female	73	45	61.9	42	57.7	3	6.8
Age							
16 to 19 years	309	120	38.8	91	29.5	29	23.9
20 to 24 years	380	283	74.5	247	65.0	36	12.8
25 to 34 years	812	672	82.8	632	77.8	40	5.9
35 to 44 years	721	610	84.5	578	80.2	32	5.2
45 to 54 years	878	697	79.3	657	74.8	39	5.7
55 to 64 years	755	472	62.6	450	59.7	22	4.7
65 years and over	825	165	20.0	155	18.8	10	6.0

NOTE: Data in Table 7 are from the Current Population Survey (CPS) and do not match the estimates in Table 8. See notes and definitions for further information.

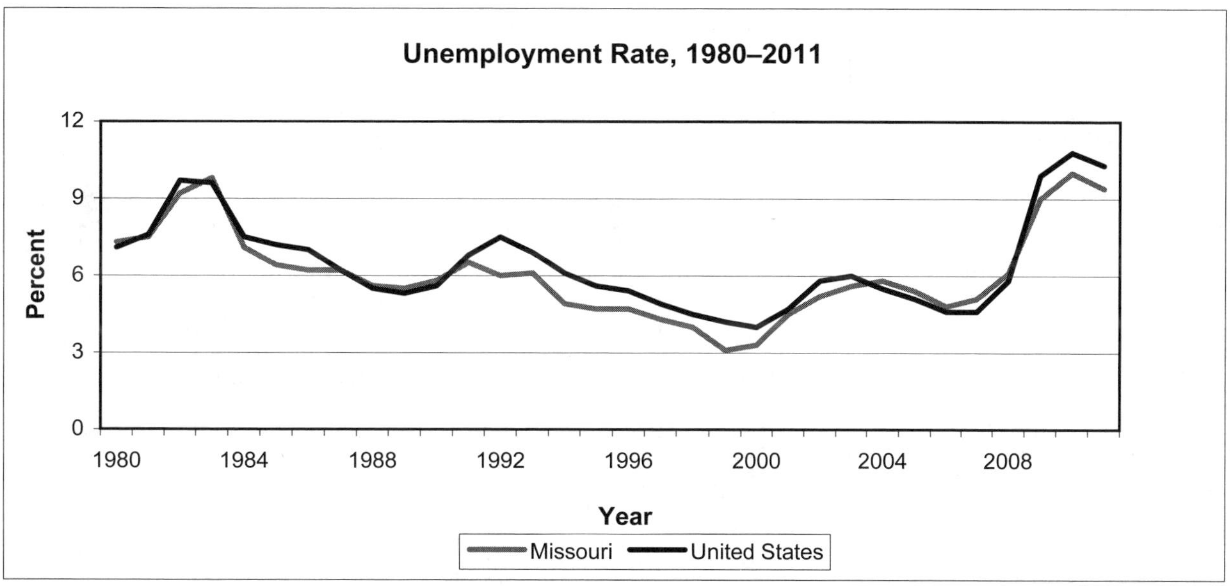

Table MO-8. Employment Status of the Civilian Noninstitutional Population Age 16 Years and Over

(Number, percent.)

Year	Civilian labor force	Civilian participation rate	Employed	Unemployed	Unemployment rate
2005	2,997,744	67.8	2,836,963	160,781	5.4
2006	3,014,920	67.4	2,868,857	145,263	4.8
2007	3,023,106	67.0	2,870,262	152,844	5.1
2008	3,012,126	66.3	2,829,289	182,837	6.1
2009	3,063,776	64.9	2,787,197	276,579	9.0
2010	3,036,146	64.0	2,733,876	302,270	10.0
2011	3,026,952	63.6	2,742,057	284,895	9.4

Table MO-9. Employment and Average Wages by Industry

(Estimates before 2007 are based on the 2002 *North American Industry Classification System* [NAICS]. Estimates from 2007 onward are based on the 2007 NAICS.)

Industry	2005	2006	2007	2008	2009	2010	2011
				Number of jobs			
Wage and Salary Employment by Industry	2,841,962	2,880,449	2,908,875	2,896,954	2,788,974	2,750,304	2,760,024
Farm Wage and Salary Employment	9,407	9,011	7,836	8,863	8,116	8,921	8,557
Nonfarm Wage and Salary Employment	2,832,555	2,871,438	2,901,039	2,888,091	2,780,858	2,741,383	2,751,467
Private wage and salary employment	2,356,995	2,391,727	2,415,088	2,394,176	2,281,338	2,250,632	2,268,829
Forestry, fishing, and related activities	4,884	4,693	4,262	4,264	4,226	4,495	4,814
Mining	5,067	4,852	5,033	4,941	4,134	4,092	4,018
Utilities	11,882	11,981	12,273	12,331	12,658	12,601	12,345
Construction	149,394	153,303	152,906	145,995	124,519	111,287	108,890
Manufacturing	309,249	308,019	301,245	289,656	255,609	243,699	246,939
Durable goods manufacturing	193,609	191,686	184,559	173,322	146,730	140,234	143,541
Nondurable goods manufacturing	115,640	116,333	116,686	116,334	108,879	103,465	103,398
Wholesale trade	122,225	123,461	125,564	126,199	119,174	117,277	117,049
Retail trade	320,558	320,562	321,041	315,917	305,987	303,854	306,198
Transportation and warehousing	95,733	97,908	99,348	97,805	91,795	87,770	88,187
Information	63,725	63,174	63,613	64,172	62,346	58,375	55,695
Finance and insurance	119,950	122,922	123,031	122,837	122,059	124,107	124,873
Real estate and rental and leasing	41,590	40,976	41,147	40,926	38,664	37,860	36,335
Professional, scientific, and technical services	121,668	126,699	129,326	132,081	126,273	123,375	125,928
Management of companies and enterprises	68,239	69,123	67,405	66,282	59,953	59,560	61,213
Administrative and waste services	133,226	139,408	144,762	147,292	134,528	141,668	147,755
Educational services	66,413	67,790	68,668	59,990	61,553	61,765	63,569
Health care and social assistance	306,932	314,157	330,508	337,906	344,115	348,782	355,202
Arts, entertainment, and recreation	45,079	43,449	44,068	45,422	43,689	43,236	42,394
Accommodation and food services	230,972	237,994	240,134	238,855	233,016	232,403	232,098
Other services, except public administration	140,209	141,256	140,754	141,305	137,040	134,426	135,327
Government and government enterprises	475,560	479,711	485,951	493,915	499,520	490,751	482,638
				Dollars			
Average Wages and Salaries by Industry	36,606	37,851	39,500	41,191	40,925	41,677	42,579
Average Farm Wages and Salaries	25,094	22,431	40,054	29,405	33,948	29,826	32,897
Average Nonfarm Wages and Salaries	36,644	37,899	39,498	41,227	40,945	41,716	42,609
Average private wages and salaries	37,094	38,368	40,000	41,772	41,259	42,051	43,052
Forestry, fishing, and related activities	23,586	24,458	26,482	29,364	29,782	27,610	25,881
Mining	73,741	53,096	64,035	70,036	61,185	59,665	70,043
Utilities	65,803	69,520	72,327	77,624	77,419	79,424	82,797
Construction	42,300	43,736	46,154	48,995	50,078	49,247	49,676
Manufacturing	45,216	46,968	48,111	51,072	50,285	50,976	52,163
Durable goods manufacturing	46,684	48,744	50,087	50,902	52,483	52,524	54,397
Nondurable goods manufacturing	42,757	44,042	44,987	51,325	47,324	48,878	49,060
Wholesale trade	51,417	53,646	55,996	57,906	57,634	58,917	60,403
Retail trade	22,935	23,580	24,114	24,823	25,070	25,389	25,698
Transportation and warehousing	40,488	41,542	42,674	44,092	43,071	44,087	44,978
Information	52,155	55,829	57,543	59,461	62,345	66,726	70,135
Finance and insurance	53,072	55,242	57,484	58,612	59,036	61,974	65,176
Real estate and rental and leasing	31,118	32,642	33,863	34,335	34,683	35,407	36,681
Professional, scientific, and technical services	57,861	60,727	64,239	66,875	67,871	67,950	68,890
Management of companies and enterprises	78,706	80,506	84,369	101,489	79,290	88,952	90,430
Administrative and waste services	26,524	26,617	28,476	29,889	30,634	31,365	32,092
Educational services	30,856	32,371	34,256	30,857	31,757	32,327	32,851
Health care and social assistance	35,862	36,783	38,856	40,261	41,288	41,649	42,546
Arts, entertainment, and recreation	31,521	34,914	36,247	34,415	35,426	35,997	38,107
Accommodation and food services	14,656	14,923	16,128	15,996	16,069	16,686	17,049
Other services, except public administration	25,359	26,169	27,073	27,957	28,106	28,755	29,192
Government and government enterprises	34,412	35,560	37,005	38,583	39,510	40,181	40,528

Table MO-10. Employment Characteristics by Family Type

(Number, percent.)

Family type and labor force status	2009		2010		2011	
	Total	Families with own children under 18 years	Total	Families with own children under 18 years	Total	Families with own children under 18 years
All families	1,543,375	687,666	1,524,078	656,551	1,534,831	665,667
Family type and labor force status						
Married-couple families	1,152,896	453,160	1,146,501	436,837	1,144,804	436,692
Both husband and wife in labor force	55.5	70.5	54.5	70.3	54.0	71.2
Husband in labor force, wife not in labor force	19.4	24.6	19.0	23.5	19.0	23.5
Wife in labor force, husband not in labor force	7.6	3.3	8.4	4.6	8.4	3.6
Both husband and wife not in labor force	17.5	1.6	18.1	1.6	18.7	1.7
Other families	390,479	234,506	377,577	219,714	390,027	228,975
Female householder, no husband present	74.9	77.4	73.6	74.7	74.5	76.4
In labor force	55.3	64.3	54.3	62.8	53.7	63.4
Not in labor force	19.6	13.2	19.2	11.9	20.8	13.0
Male householder, no wife present	25.1	22.6	26.4	25.3	25.5	23.6
In labor force	19.5	20.0	21.6	23.1	20.5	21.5
Not in labor force	5.5	2.6	4.9	2.3	4.9	2.1

Table MO-11. School Enrollment and Educational Attainment, 2011

(Number, percent.)

Item	State	U.S.
Enrollment		
Total population 3 years and over, enrolled in school	1,569,557	83,131,910
Enrolled in nursery school or preschool (percent)	6.7	6.0
Enrolled in kindergarten (percent)	5.2	5.1
Enrolled in elementary school, grades 1-8 (percent)	39.2	39.5
Enrolled in high school, grades 9-12 (percent)	20.6	20.7
Enrolled in college or graduate school (percent)	28.3	28.7
Attainment		
Total population 25 years and over	4,008,554	206,471,670
Less than ninth grade (percent)	3.9	6.0
9th to 12th grade, no diploma (percent)	8.5	8.1
High school graduate, including equivalency (percent)	31.4	28.4
Some college, no degree (percent)	22.9	21.2
Associate's degree (percent)	7.1	7.8
Bachelor's degree (percent)	16.4	17.9
Graduate or professional degree (percent)	9.7	10.6
High school graduate or higher (percent)	87.6	85.9
Bachelor's degree or higher (percent)	26.1	28.5

Table MO-12. Educational Indicators

(Number, percent; data derived from National Center of Education Statistics.)

Item	State	U.S.
Public Schools, 2009–2010 (except where noted)		
Number of school districts	523	13,629
Number of schools	2,427	99,834
Number of students (in thousands)	918	49,373
Student-teacher ratio	13.5	15.4
Expenditures per student (dollars)	11,332	10,591
Averaged freshman graduation rate, 2008–2009	83.1	75.5[1]
Dropout rate, 2008–2009	4.3	4.1
Students eligible for free or reduced-price lunch (percent)	45.0	48.0
English language learners, 2010–2011 (percent)	2.3	9.8[1]
Students with IEP (percent)	14.1	13.1
Private Schools, 2009–2010 (except where noted)		
Number of schools	693	33,366
Number of students (in thousands)	106	4,700
High school graduates, 2008–2009	7,043	308,813
Student-teacher ratio	11.7	10.7

[1] U.S. total includes estimates for nonreporting states.

Table MO-13. Reported Voting and Registration of the Voting-Age Population, November 2012

(Numbers in thousands, percent.)

Item	Total population	Total citizen population	Registered			Voted		
			Total registered	Percent registered (total population)	Percent registered (total citizen population)	Total voted	Percent voted (total population)	Percent voted (total citizen population)
U.S. Total	235,248	215,081	153,157	65.1	71.2	132,948	56.5	61.8
State Total	4,521	4,409	3,384	74.8	76.7	2,818	62.3	63.9
Sex								
Male	2,169	2,114	1,608	74.1	76.1	1,321	60.9	62.5
Female	2,352	2,295	1,776	75.5	77.4	1,497	63.7	65.2
Race								
White alone	3,887	3,830	2,923	75.2	76.3	2,452	63.1	64.0
White, non-Hispanic alone	3,765	3,732	2,857	75.9	76.6	2,395	63.6	64.2
Black alone	484	465	374	77.2	80.3	313	64.7	67.3
Asian alone	67	30	23	B	B	20	B	B
Hispanic (of any race)	140	104	71	50.9	68.6	63	45.0	60.7
Age								
18 to 24 years	525	520	332	63.3	64.0	223	42.5	42.9
25 to 44 years	1,526	1,460	1,083	71.0	74.2	875	57.4	60.0
45 to 64 years	1,714	1,684	1,344	78.4	79.8	1,175	68.5	69.8
65 to 74 years	425	425	358	84.2	84.2	308	72.4	72.4
75 years and over	330	320	266	80.7	83.2	237	71.9	74.0

B = Base is less than 75,000 and therefore too small to show the derived measure.

Table MO-14. Crime

(Number, rate per 100,000. Data are derived from the FBI Uniform Crime Reports.)

Item	State			U.S.		
	2010	2011	Percent change	2010	2011	Percent change
TOTAL POPULATION	5,995,715	6,101,688	1.8	309,330,219	311,591,917	0.7
VIOLENT CRIME						
Number	27,440	26,889	-2.0	1,251,248	1,203,564	-3.8
Rate	457.7	447.4	-2.3	404.5	386.3	-4.5
Murder and Nonnegligent Manslaughter						
Number	420	366	-12.9	14,722	14,612	-0.7
Rate	7.0	6.1	-12.9	4.8	4.7	-2.1
Forcible Rape						
Number	1,445	1,458	0.9	85,593	83,425	-2.5
Rate	24.1	24.3	0.8	27.7	26.8	-3.2
Robbery						
Number	6,185	6,269	1.4	369,089	354,396	-4.0
Rate	103.2	104.3	1.1	119.3	113.7	-4.7
Aggravated Assault						
Number	19,390	18,796	-3.1	781,844	751,131	-3.9
Rate	323.4	312.6	-3.3	252.8	241.1	-4.6
PROPERTY CRIME						
Number	200,858	198,882	-1.0	9,112,625	9,063,173	-0.5
Rate	3,350.0	3,308.8	-1.2	2,945.9	2,908.7	-1.3
Burglary						
Number	44,197	44,822	1.4	2,168,459	2,188,005	0.9
Rate	737.1	745.7	1.2	701.0	702.2	0.2
Larceny-Theft						
Number	140,526	138,743	-1.3	6,204,601	6,159,795	-0.7
Rate	2,343.8	2,308.3	-1.5	2,005.8	1,976.9	-1.4
Motor Vehicle Theft						
Number	16,135	15,317	-5.1	739,565	715,373	-3.3
Rate	269.1	254.8	-5.3	239.1	229.6	-4.0

Table MO-15. State Government Finances, 2011

(Dollar amounts in thousands, percent distribution.)

Item	Dollars	Percent distribution
Total Revenue	38,606,945	100.0
General revenue	27,082,904	70.2
Intergovernmental revenue	12,015,114	31.1
Taxes	10,109,918	26.2
General sales	2,972,654	7.7
Selective sales	1,654,538	4.3
License taxes	573,309	1.5
Individual income tax	4,534,346	11.7
Corporate income tax	323,593	0.8
Other taxes	51,478	0.1
Current charges	2,778,187	7.2
Miscellaneous general revenue	2,179,685	5.6
Utility revenue	0	0.0
Liquor stores revenue	0	0.0
Insurance trust revenue [1]	11,524,041	29.8
Total Expenditure	30,646,880	100.0
Intergovernmental expenditure	5,948,493	19.4
Direct expenditure	24,698,387	80.6
Current operation	16,709,191	54.5
Capital outlay	1,767,540	5.8
Insurance benefits and repayments	4,874,147	15.9
Assistance and subsidies	525,418	1.7
Interest on debt	822,091	2.7
Exhibit: Salaries and wages	3,764,288	12.3
Total Expenditure	30,646,880	100.0
General expenditure	25,772,733	84.1
Intergovernmental expenditure	5,948,493	19.4
Direct expenditure	19,824,240	64.7
General expenditure, by function:		
Education	8,854,989	28.9
Public welfare	7,586,724	24.8
Hospitals	1,492,957	4.9
Health	1,402,255	4.6
Highways	2,032,506	6.6
Police protection	218,447	0.7
Correction	720,834	2.4
Natural resources	307,101	1.0
Parks and recreation	37,915	0.1
Governmental administration	532,697	1.7
Interest on general debt	822,091	2.7
Other and unallocable	1,764,217	5.8
Utility expenditure	0	0.0
Liquor stores expenditure	0	0.0
Insurance trust expenditure	4,874,147	15.9
Debt at End of Fiscal Year	20,682,303	X
Cash and Security Holdings	70,741,709	X

X = Not applicable.

[1] Within insurance trust revenue, net earnings of state retirement systems is a calculated statistic (the item code in the data file is X08), and thus can be positive or negative. Net earnings is the sum of earnings on investments plus gains on investments minus losses on investments. The change made in 2002 for asset valuation from book to market value in accordance with Statement 34 of the Governmental Accounting Standards Board is reflected in the calculated statistics.

Table MO-16. State Government Tax Collections, 2012

(Dollars in thousands, percent.)

Item	Dollars	Percent distribution
Total Taxes	10,800,741	100.0
Property taxes	29,217	0.3
Sales and gross receipts	4,764,007	44.1
General sales and gross receipts	3,103,410	28.7
Selective sales and gross receipts	1,660,597	15.4
Alcoholic beverages	34,341	0.3
Amusements	390,779	3.6
Insurance premiums	270,169	2.5
Motor fuels	708,064	6.6
Pari-mutuels	0	0.0
Public utilities	0	0.0
Tobacco products	104,918	1.0
Other selective sales	152,326	1.4
Licenses	563,384	5.2
Alcoholic beverages	4,965	-
Amusements	1,617	-
Corporations in general	63,338	0.6
Hunting and fishing	32,489	0.3
Motor vehicle	267,641	2.5
Motor vehicle operators	17,686	0.2
Public utilities	19,495	0.2
Occupation and business, NEC	134,353	1.2
Other licenses	21,800	0.2
Income taxes	5,433,367	50.3
Individual income	5,131,686	47.5
Corporation net income	301,681	2.8
Other taxes	10,766	0.1
Death and gift	162	-
Documentary and stock transfer	4,611	-
Severance	2	-
Taxes, NEC	5,991	0.1

- = Rounds to zero.

Leading Exports, 2012

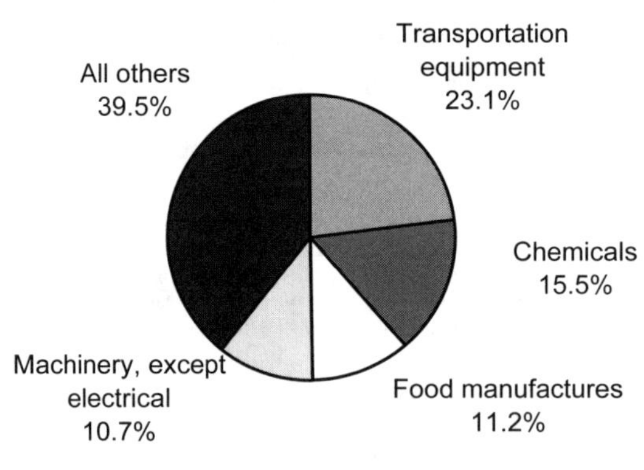

MONTANA

Facts and Figures

Location: Northwestern United States; bordered on the N by Canada (British Columbia, Alberta, and Saskatchewan), on the E by North Dakota and South Dakota, on the S by Idaho and Wyoming, and on the W by Idaho

Area: 147,042 sq. mi. (380,838 sq. km.); rank—4th

Population: 1,005,141 (2012 est.); rank—44th

Principal Cities: capital—Helena; largest—Billings

Statehood: November 8, 1889; 41st state

U.S. Congress: 2 senators, 1 representative

State Motto: *Oro y plata* ("Gold and silver")

State Song: "Montana"

State Nicknames: The Treasure State; Big Sky Country

Abbreviations: MT; Mont.

State Symbols: flower—bitterroot; tree—ponderosa pine; bird—Western meadowlark

At a Glance

- With an increase in population of 8.1 percent, Montana ranked 40th among the states in growth from 2000 to 2009.
- An estimated 7,100 marriages took place in Montana in 2009, compared to 3,900 divorces.
- Montana's violent crime rate in 2011 was 267.5 per 100,000 population, compared to 386.3 for the entire nation.
- In the 2012 election, 65.7 percent of Montana's eligible voters voted, compared to 61.8 percent of eligible voters nationwide.
- In 2007, Montana exported $723 million worth of agricultural products, less than 1 percent of the U.S. total.

Table MT-1. Population by Age, Sex, Race, and Hispanic Origin

(Number, percent, except where noted.)

Sex, age, race, and Hispanic origin	2000	2010	2012[1]	Average annual percent change, 2010–2012
Total Population	902,195	989,415	1,005,041	0.5
Percent of total U.S. population	0.3	0.3	0.3	X
Sex				
Male	449,480	496,667	504,949	0.5
Female	452,715	492,748	500,192	0.5
Age				
Under 5 years	54,869	62,423	60,964	-0.8
5 to 19 years	202,571	188,613	188,257	-0.1
20 to 64 years	523,806	591,637	597,531	0.3
65 years and over	120,949	146,742	158,289	2.4
Median age (years)	37.5	39.8	40.1	0.2
Race and Hispanic Origin				
One race				
White	817,229	891,529	901,340	0.4
Black	2,692	4,215	5,679	8.6
American Indian and Alaska Native	56,068	63,495	65,164	0.9
Asian	4,691	6,379	7,315	4.3
Native Hawaiian or Other Pacific Islander	470	734	774	1.7
Two or more races	15,730	23,063	24,869	2.4
Hispanic (of any race)	18,081	31,018	34,247	3.1

X = Not applicable.
[1] Population figures for 2012 are July 1 estimates. The 2010 estimates are taken from the 2010 Census.

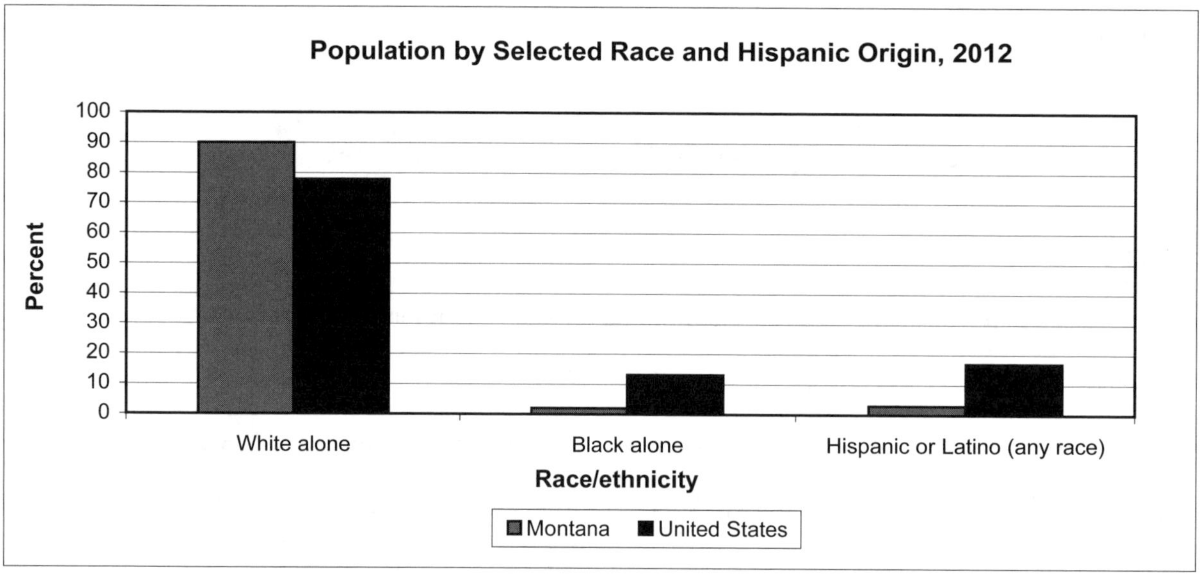

Table MT-2. Marital Status

(Number, percent distribution.)

Sex, age, race, and Hispanic origin	2000	2010	2011
Males, 15 Years and Over	353,801	404,179	405,999
Never married	27.7	30.5	32.6
Now married, except separated	58.3	53.4	51.9
Separated	1.2	1.5	1.0
Widowed	2.6	2.3	2.5
Divorced	10.2	12.4	12.1
Females, 15 Years and Over	362,114	403,766	408,822
Never married	20.4	23.5	24.0
Now married, except separated	56.3	52.9	51.3
Separated	1.3	1.6	1.4
Widowed	10.4	9.7	10.0
Divorced	11.6	12.3	13.3

Table MT-3. Households and Housing Characteristics

(Number, percent, dollars.)

Item	2000	2010	2011	Average annual percent change, 2000–2011
Total Households	358,667	402,747	404,250	1.1
Family households	237,407	255,199	253,131	0.6
Married-couple family	192,067	203,500	199,556	0.3
Other family	45,340	51,699	53,575	1.5
Male householder, no wife present	13,324	16,926	16,121	1.7
Female householder, no husband present	32,016	34,773	37,454	1.4
Nonfamily households	121,260	147,548	151,119	2.1
Householder living alone	98,422	119,762	123,553	2.1
Householder not living alone	22,838	27,786	27,566	1.7
Housing Characteristics				
Total housing units	412,633	483,006	489,183	1.5
Occupied housing units	358,667	402,747	404,250	1.1
Owner occupied	247,723	280,633	274,570	0.9
Renter occupied	110,944	122,114	129,680	1.4
Average size	2.45	2.39	2.40	-0.2
Financial Characteristics				
Median gross rent of renter-occupied housing	447	642	650	3.8
Median monthly owner costs for housing units with a mortgage	863	1,217	1,256	3.8
Median value of owner-occupied housing units	99,500	181,200	184,100	7.1

Table MT-4. Migration, Origin, and Language

(Number, percent.)

Characteristic	State			U.S.		
	2010	2011	Percent change	2010	2011	Percent change
Residence 1 Year Ago						
Population 1 year and over	978,507	987,076	0.9	305,628,607	307,900,319	0.7
Same house	84.0	83.9	-0.1	84.6	84.8	0.2
Different house in the U.S.	15.7	15.8	0.6	14.8	14.6	-1.4
Same county	8.7	9.1	4.6	9.4	9.2	-2.1
Different county	7.0	6.7	-4.3	5.4	5.4	-
Same state	3.3	3.3	-	3.2	3.1	-3.1
Different state	3.6	3.4	-5.6	2.2	2.3	4.5
Abroad	0.3	0.3	-	0.6	0.6	-
Place of Birth						
Native born	970,867	978,139	0.7	269,393,835	271,214,059	0.7
Male	50.7	50.4	-0.6	49.2	49.2	-
Female	49.3	49.6	0.6	50.8	50.8	-
Foreign born	20,031	20,060	0.1	39,955,854	40,377,860	1.1
Male	36.3	38.4	5.8	49.1	48.9	-0.4
Female	63.7	61.6	-3.3	50.9	51.1	0.4
Foreign born; naturalized U.S. citizen	11,506	9,662	-16.0	17,476,082	18,140,192	3.8
Male	30.6	34.5	12.7	45.8	45.8	-
Female	69.4	65.5	-5.6	54.2	54.2	-
Foreign born; not a U.S. citizen	8,525	10,398	22.0	22,479,772	22,237,668	-1.1
Male	44.1	42.1	-4.5	51.6	51.5	-0.2
Female	55.9	57.9	3.6	48.4	48.5	0.2
Entered 2000 or later	32.0	38.8	21.3	34.7	35.7	2.9
Entered 1990 to 1999	18.5	13.5	-27.0	27.2	26.7	-1.8
Entered before 1990	49.4	47.7	-3.4	38.1	37.6	-1.3
World Region of Birth, Foreign						
Foreign-born population, excluding population born at sea	20,031	20,060	0.1	39,955,673	40,377,757	1.1
Europe	37.1	31.5	-15.1	12.1	12.1	-
Asia	23.8	24.3	2.1	28.2	28.6	1.4
Africa	4.2	4.7	11.9	4	4.1	2.5
Oceania	2.4	2.4	-	0.5	0.5	-
Latin America	11.2	10.5	-6.2	53.1	52.6	-0.9
North America	21.3	26.7	25.4	2	2.0	-
Language Spoken at Home and Ability to Speak English						
Population 5 years and over	929,026	937,750	0.9	289,215,746	291,524,091	0.8
English only	95.4	95.3	-0.1	79.4	79.2	-0.3
Language other than English	4.6	4.7	2.2	20.6	20.8	1.0
Speaks English less than "very well"	0.9	0.8	-11.1	8.7	8.7	-

- = Zero or rounds to zero.

Table MT-5. Median Income and Poverty Status, 2011

(Number, percent, except as noted.)

Characteristic	State		U.S.	
	Number	Percent	Number	Percent
Median Income				
Households (dollars)	44,222	X	50,502	X
Families (dollars)	56,217	X	61,455	X
Below Poverty Level (All People)	144,054	14.8	48,452,035	15.9
Sex				
Male	69,483	14.3	21,825,281	14.7
Female	74,571	15.3	26,626,754	17.2
Age				
Under 18 years	43,110	19.7	16,386,500	22.5
Related children under 18 years	41,546	19.1	16,087,074	22.2
18 to 64 years	89,110	14.6	28,335,079	14.8
65 years and over	11,834	8.1	3,730,456	9.3

X = Not applicable.

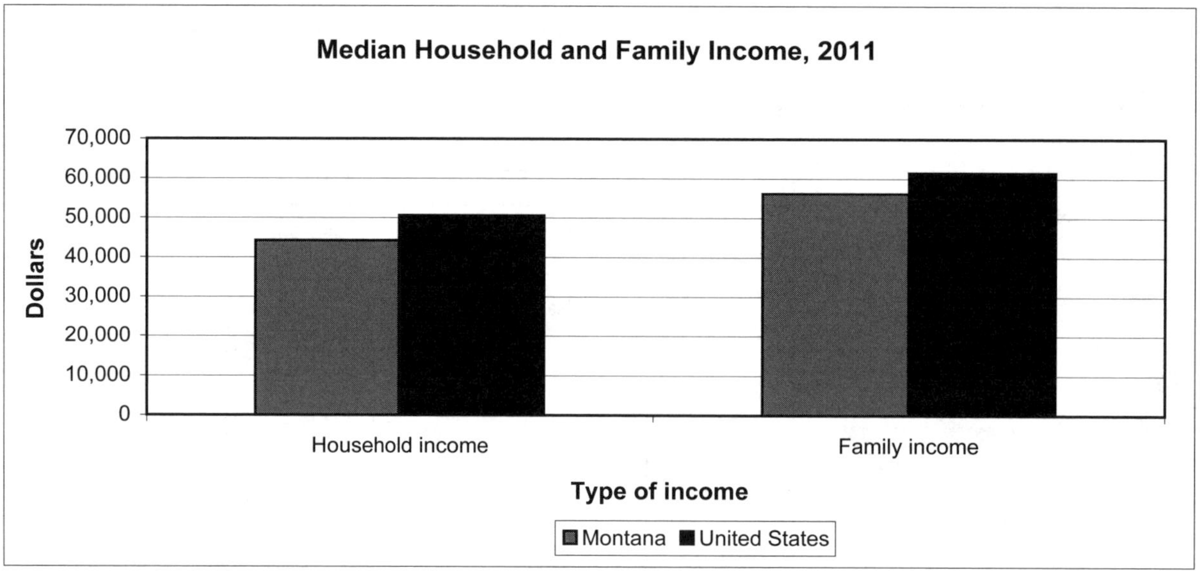

Table MT-6. Health Insurance Coverage Status for the Civilian Noninstitutionalized Population and Children Under 18 Years of Age

(Numbers in thousands, percent.)

Item	2004	2005	2006	2007	2008	2009	2010	2011
Civilian Noninstitutionalized Population	912	928	931	939	950	958	976	983
Covered by Private or Public Insurance								
Number	743	746	783	772	775	783	807	804
Percent	81.8	84.4	82.9	84.4	81.6	81.8	82.7	81.7
Not Covered								
Number	166	145	160	146	175	174	169	180
Percent	18.2	15.6	17.1	15.6	18.4	18.2	17.3	18.3
Percent in the U.S. not covered	14.9	15.3	15.8	15.3	15.1	15.1	15.5	15.1
Children Under 18 Years of Age	215	215	212	219	222	220	221	222
Covered by Private or Public Insurance								
Number	185	184	181	191	190	192	193	196
Percent	82.3	86.1	85.8	85.5	85.6	87.1	87.6	88.5
Not Covered								
Number	30	30	31	28	32	28	28	26
Percent	13.9	14.2	14.5	12.6	14.4	12.9	12.4	11.5
Percent in the U.S. not covered	10.5	10.9	11.7	11.0	9.7	8.6	8.0	7.5

Table MT-7. Employment Status by Demographic Group, Preliminary 2012

(Numbers in thousands, percent.)

Characteristic	Civilian noninstitutional population	Civilian labor force		Employed		Unemployed	
		Number	Percent of population	Number	Percent of population	Number	Percent of population
Total	793	506	63.8	476	59.9	31	6.1
Sex							
Male	394	265	67.4	246	62.5	19	7.2
Female	399	241	60.3	229	57.4	12	4.8
Race, Sex, and Hispanic Origin							
White	726	470	64.7	445	61.3	25	5.3
Male	362	246	68.1	231	63.8	16	6.3
Female	364	223	61.3	214	58.7	9	4.1
Black or African American	NA	NA	NA	NA	NA	NA	NA
Male	NA	NA	NA	NA	NA	NA	NA
Female	NA	NA	NA	NA	NA	NA	NA
Hispanic	18	9	52.3	8	46.8	1	10.7
Male	NA	NA	NA	NA	NA	NA	NA
Female	NA	NA	NA	NA	NA	NA	NA
Age							
16 to 19 years	47	20	43.2	18	38.6	2	10.8
20 to 24 years	66	47	71.5	42	63.5	5	11.3
25 to 34 years	133	110	82.9	102	76.3	9	8.0
35 to 44 years	108	91	84.3	85	78.8	6	6.5
45 to 54 years	122	100	82.3	98	80.0	3	2.8
55 to 64 years	142	94	65.9	90	62.9	4	4.5
65 years and over	174	43	24.4	41	23.6	1	3.3

NOTE: Data in Table 7 are from the Current Population Survey (CPS) and do not match the estimates in Table 8. See notes and definitions for further information.

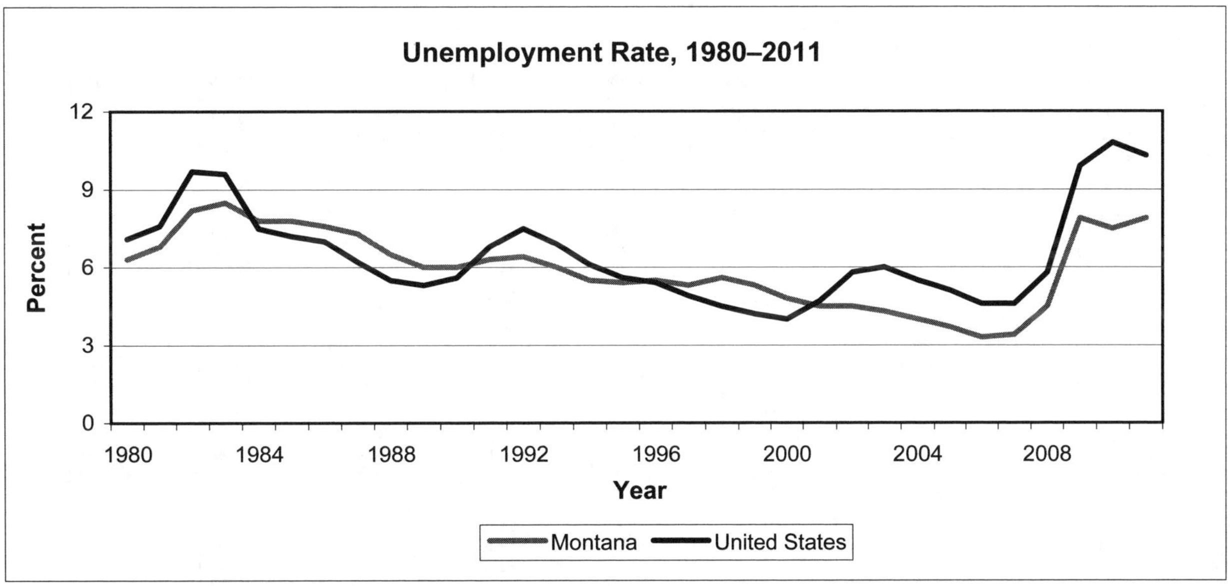

Table MT-8. Employment Status of the Civilian Noninstitutional Population Age 16 Years and Over

(Number, percent.)

Year	Civilian labor force	Civilian participation rate	Employed	Unemployed	Unemployment rate
2005	482,255	66.3	464,625	17,630	3.7
2006	493,469	66.9	477,256	16,213	3.3
2007	502,031	67.1	484,737	17,294	3.4
2008	506,159	66.8	483,455	22,704	4.5
2009	503,837	64.6	463,880	39,957	7.9
2010	505,674	63.6	467,674	38,000	7.5
2011	521,313	65.1	479,988	41,325	7.9

Table MT-9. Employment and Average Wages by Industry

(Estimates before 2007 are based on the 2002 *North American Industry Classification System* [NAICS]. Estimates from 2007 onward are based on the 2007 NAICS.)

Industry	2005	2006	2007	2008	2009	2010	2011
	Number of jobs						
Wage and Salary Employment by Industry	443,668	456,588	467,731	468,540	452,213	449,797	454,484
Farm Wage and Salary Employment	5,246	5,155	4,761	5,023	4,705	4,830	5,402
Nonfarm Wage and Salary Employment	438,422	451,433	462,970	463,517	447,508	444,967	449,082
Private wage and salary employment	345,627	358,715	369,433	369,354	351,490	347,936	352,843
Forestry, fishing, and related activities	2,864	2,846	2,864	2,771	2,444	2,616	2,742
Mining	6,700	7,297	7,466	7,541	6,489	6,835	7,561
Utilities	2,914	2,973	3,027	3,084	3,067	3,047	3,117
Construction	28,710	31,371	33,573	30,887	25,114	23,796	23,960
Manufacturing	19,478	20,167	20,430	19,939	17,331	16,352	16,864
Durable goods manufacturing	12,276	12,694	12,930	12,309	10,018	9,405	9,758
Nondurable goods manufacturing	7,202	7,473	7,500	7,630	7,313	6,947	7,106
Wholesale trade	16,404	16,636	17,052	16,887	16,118	15,788	15,770
Retail trade	56,102	56,992	59,395	59,660	56,579	55,568	55,609
Transportation and warehousing	13,537	14,008	14,115	13,803	13,334	13,371	13,848
Information	7,808	7,756	7,665	7,667	7,475	7,413	7,214
Finance and insurance	15,976	16,543	16,688	16,930	16,571	16,244	16,257
Real estate and rental and leasing	5,928	6,237	6,189	6,046	5,619	5,414	5,301
Professional, scientific, and technical services	17,836	18,895	19,289	19,607	18,842	18,945	19,341
Management of companies and enterprises	1,002	1,031	1,283	1,439	1,570	1,695	2,006
Administrative and waste services	16,672	18,396	19,844	19,210	18,019	18,458	19,283
Educational services	4,610	5,155	5,118	5,246	5,310	5,459	5,732
Health care and social assistance	53,007	54,259	55,475	57,541	59,202	59,969	60,186
Arts, entertainment, and recreation	10,210	10,897	11,619	11,759	11,415	10,894	10,965
Accommodation and food services	45,577	46,451	47,223	47,908	45,962	45,361	46,157
Other services, except public administration	20,292	20,805	21,118	21,429	21,029	20,711	20,930
Government and government enterprises	92,795	92,718	93,537	94,163	96,018	97,031	96,239
	Dollars						
Average Wages and Salaries by Industry	29,262	30,711	32,363	33,379	33,880	34,679	35,814
Average Farm Wages and Salaries	31,904	32,169	39,020	35,694	42,310	35,807	33,217
Average Nonfarm Wages and Salaries	29,230	30,695	32,294	33,354	33,791	34,667	35,846
Average private wages and salaries	28,284	29,766	31,404	32,316	32,605	33,637	34,986
Forestry, fishing, and related activities	24,404	26,575	27,734	28,327	28,029	27,305	28,833
Mining	58,117	64,575	67,500	72,383	70,377	74,599	80,502
Utilities	61,577	64,197	66,512	69,686	73,969	74,994	78,167
Construction	33,959	35,361	38,091	38,937	39,870	40,854	42,713
Manufacturing	36,884	37,695	39,781	40,594	41,224	42,588	42,588
Durable goods manufacturing	35,502	36,346	38,075	38,533	38,163	39,393	39,934
Nondurable goods manufacturing	39,240	39,986	42,722	43,920	45,417	46,914	46,232
Wholesale trade	38,091	40,476	43,246	45,040	44,642	45,187	47,891
Retail trade	21,176	22,187	23,099	23,475	23,613	24,217	24,685
Transportation and warehousing	38,238	39,765	40,537	42,222	42,125	44,085	47,294
Information	35,429	37,417	38,506	39,673	40,048	41,624	41,931
Finance and insurance	41,472	43,695	45,997	46,655	47,123	48,886	49,884
Real estate and rental and leasing	24,692	26,303	27,869	27,336	25,656	26,554	28,413
Professional, scientific, and technical services	40,383	41,947	45,330	47,435	48,237	49,575	51,672
Management of companies and enterprises	47,697	53,291	58,102	63,205	59,889	58,055	59,589
Administrative and waste services	20,851	22,249	23,601	24,981	25,690	27,130	27,858
Educational services	17,902	18,409	19,473	20,014	20,566	20,476	21,467
Health care and social assistance	31,357	33,026	34,184	35,745	36,876	37,713	39,103
Arts, entertainment, and recreation	16,373	18,371	19,857	18,767	19,194	19,567	20,341
Accommodation and food services	12,541	13,128	14,577	14,475	14,654	15,381	16,149
Other services, except public administration	21,120	21,379	22,555	23,544	23,789	24,511	25,008
Government and government enterprises	32,753	34,287	35,809	37,427	38,130	38,360	38,999

Table MT-10. Employment Characteristics by Family Type

(Number, percent.)

Family type and labor force status	2009 Total	2009 Families with own children under 18 years	2010 Total	2010 Families with own children under 18 years	2011 Total	2011 Families with own children under 18 years
All families	235,940	94,365	255,199	103,251	253,131	98,821
Family type and labor force status						
Married-couple families	187,966	65,006	203,500	72,739	199,556	68,083
Both husband and wife in labor force	54.4	68.2	54.3	69.2	54.1	70.2
Husband in labor force, wife not in labor force	18.1	24.7	18.7	23.7	18.4	24.6
Wife in labor force, husband not in labor force	9.1	4.3	8.4	4.3	8.2	3.2
Both husband and wife not in labor force	18.5	2.8	18.6	2.8	19.2	1.9
Other families	47,974	29,359	51,699	30,512	53,575	30,738
Female householder, no husband present	69.6	71.4	67.3	69.2	69.9	69.5
In labor force	52.3	59.8	49.4	58.2	54.1	60.4
Not in labor force	17.3	11.7	17.8	11.0	15.8	9.1
Male householder, no wife present	30.4	28.6	32.7	30.8	30.1	30.5
In labor force	23.4	23.1	24.1	25.1	25.2	27.4
Not in labor force	7.0	5.5	8.7	5.7	4.9	3.1

Table MT-11. School Enrollment and Educational Attainment, 2011

(Number, percent.)

Item	State	U.S.
Enrollment		
Total population 3 years and over, enrolled in school	242,981	83,131,910
Enrolled in nursery school or preschool (percent)	7.2	6.0
Enrolled in kindergarten (percent)	5.7	5.1
Enrolled in elementary school, grades 1-8 (percent)	38.9	39.5
Enrolled in high school, grades 9-12 (percent)	20.6	20.7
Enrolled in college or graduate school (percent)	27.6	28.7
Attainment		
Total population 25 years and over	676,793	206,471,670
Less than ninth grade (percent)	2.0	6.0
9th to 12th grade, no diploma (percent)	5.7	8.1
High school graduate, including equivalency (percent)	30.5	28.4
Some college, no degree (percent)	25.1	21.2
Associate's degree (percent)	8.4	7.8
Bachelor's degree (percent)	19.6	17.9
Graduate or professional degree (percent)	8.6	10.6
High school graduate or higher (percent)	92.3	85.9
Bachelor's degree or higher (percent)	28.2	28.5

Table MT-12. Educational Indicators

(Number, percent; data derived from National Center of Education Statistics.)

Item	State	U.S.
Public Schools, 2009–2010 (except where noted)		
Number of school districts	417	13,629
Number of schools	828	99,834
Number of students (in thousands)	142	49,373
Student-teacher ratio	13.5	15.4
Expenditures per student (dollars)	11,565	10,591
Averaged freshman graduation rate, 2008–2009	82.0	75.5[1]
Dropout rate, 2008–2009	5.0	4.1
Students eligible for free or reduced-price lunch (percent)	41.2	48.0
English language learners, 2010–2011 (percent)	2.3	9.8[1]
Students with IEP (percent)	12.1	13.1
Private Schools, 2009–2010 (except where noted)		
Number of schools	153[2]	33,366
Number of students (in thousands)	8	4,700
High school graduates, 2008–2009	372	308,813
Student-teacher ratio	9.1	10.7

[1] U.S. total includes estimates for nonreporting states.
[2] Interpret data with caution. The coefficient of variation for this estimate is larger than 25 percent.

Table MT-13. Reported Voting and Registration of the Voting-Age Population, November 2012

(Numbers in thousands, percent.)

Item	Total population	Total citizen population	Registered: Total registered	Registered: Percent registered (total population)	Registered: Percent registered (total citizen population)	Voted: Total voted	Voted: Percent voted (total population)	Voted: Percent voted (total citizen population)
U.S. Total	235,248	215,081	153,157	65.1	71.2	132,948	56.5	61.8
State Total	768	754	553	72.0	73.3	495	64.5	65.7
Sex								
Male	379	375	263	69.3	70.1	238	62.7	63.4
Female	389	380	290	74.5	76.3	258	66.2	67.9
Race								
White alone	698	689	506	72.5	73.5	461	66.1	67.0
White, non-Hispanic alone	688	680	500	72.7	73.6	457	66.4	67.2
Black alone	2	-	-	B	B	-	B	B
Asian alone	2	-	-	B	B	-	B	B
Hispanic (of any race)	15	13	8	B	B	7	B	B
Age								
18 to 24 years	82	79	53	65.0	66.9	33	40.7	41.9
25 to 44 years	247	242	146	59.2	60.3	127	51.7	52.7
45 to 64 years	254	249	201	79.1	80.5	189	74.3	75.6
65 to 74 years	115	114	95	82.3	83.2	90	78.1	79.0
75 years and over	71	70	58	B	B	56	B	B

- = Zero or rounds to zero.
B = Base is less than 75,000 and therefore too small to show the derived measure.

Table MT-14. Crime

(Number, rate per 100,000. Data are derived from the FBI Uniform Crime Reports.)

Item	State: 2010	State: 2011	State: Percent change	U.S.: 2010	U.S.: 2011	U.S.: Percent change
TOTAL POPULATION	990,958	998,199	0.7	309,330,219	311,591,917	0.7
VIOLENT CRIME						
Number	2,733	2,670	-2.3	1,251,248	1,203,564	-3.8
Rate	275.8	267.5	-3.0	404.5	386.3	-4.5
Murder and Nonnegligent Manslaughter						
Number	25	28	12.0	14,722	14,612	-0.7
Rate	2.5	2.8	12.0	4.8	4.7	-2.1
Forcible Rape						
Number	332	357	7.5	85,593	83,425	-2.5
Rate	33.5	35.8	6.9	27.7	26.8	-3.2
Robbery						
Number	154	169	9.7	369,089	354,396	-4.0
Rate	15.5	16.9	9.0	119.3	113.7	-4.7
Aggravated Assault						
Number	2,222	2,116	-4.8	781,844	751,131	-3.9
Rate	224.2	212.0	-5.4	252.8	241.1	-4.6
PROPERTY CRIME						
Number	25,409	23,155	-8.9	9,112,625	9,063,173	-0.5
Rate	2,564.1	2,319.7	-9.5	2,945.9	2,908.7	-1.3
Burglary						
Number	3,692	3,390	-8.2	2,168,459	2,188,005	0.9
Rate	372.6	339.6	-8.9	701.0	702.2	0.2
Larceny-Theft						
Number	20,166	18,307	-9.2	6,204,601	6,159,795	-0.7
Rate	2,035.0	1,834.0	-9.9	2,005.8	1,976.9	-1.4
Motor Vehicle Theft						
Number	1,551	1,458	-6.0	739,565	715,373	-3.3
Rate	156.5	146.1	-6.6	239.1	229.6	-4.0

Table MT-15. State Government Finances, 2011

(Dollar amounts in thousands, percent distribution.)

Item	Dollars	Percent distribution
Total Revenue	7,950,510	100.0
General revenue	5,768,585	72.6
Intergovernmental revenue	2,414,552	30.4
Taxes	2,303,516	29.0
General sales	0	0.0
Selective sales	533,372	6.7
License taxes	307,838	3.9
Individual income tax	812,629	10.2
Corporate income tax	123,985	1.6
Other taxes	525,692	6.6
Current charges	605,674	7.6
Miscellaneous general revenue	444,843	5.6
Utility revenue	0	0.0
Liquor stores revenue	73,456	0.9
Insurance trust revenue [1]	2,108,469	26.5
Total Expenditure	7,105,366	100.0
Intergovernmental expenditure	1,352,917	19.0
Direct expenditure	5,752,449	81.0
Current operation	3,811,860	53.6
Capital outlay	730,434	10.3
Insurance benefits and repayments	946,281	13.3
Assistance and subsidies	108,377	1.5
Interest on debt	155,497	2.2
Exhibit: Salaries and wages	980,364	13.8
Total Expenditure	7,105,366	100.0
General expenditure	6,082,012	85.6
Intergovernmental expenditure	1,352,917	19.0
Direct expenditure	4,729,095	66.6
General expenditure, by function:		
Education	1,840,578	25.9
Public welfare	1,390,134	19.6
Hospitals	47,762	0.7
Health	170,135	2.4
Highways	709,293	10.0
Police protection	48,159	0.7
Correction	188,537	2.7
Natural resources	259,715	3.7
Parks and recreation	31,274	0.4
Governmental administration	420,478	5.9
Interest on general debt	155,497	2.2
Other and unallocable	820,450	11.5
Utility expenditure	13,609	0.2
Liquor stores expenditure	63,464	0.9
Insurance trust expenditure	946,281	13.3
Debt at End of Fiscal Year	4,266,731	X
Cash and Security Holdings	16,596,265	X

X = Not applicable.
[1] Within insurance trust revenue, net earnings of state retirement systems is a calculated statistic (the item code in the data file is X08), and thus can be positive or negative. Net earnings is the sum of earnings on investments plus gains on investments minus losses on investments. The change made in 2002 for asset valuation from book to market value in accordance with Statement 34 of the Governmental Accounting Standards Board is reflected in the calculated statistics.

Table MT-16. State Government Tax Collections, 2012

(Dollars in thousands, percent.)

Item	Dollars	Percent distribution
Total Taxes	2,459,324	100.0
Property taxes	257,189	10.5
Sales and gross receipts	544,733	22.1
General sales and gross receipts	0	0.0
Selective sales and gross receipts	544,733	22.1
Alcoholic beverages	34,019	1.4
Amusements	53,596	2.2
Insurance premiums	70,779	2.9
Motor fuels	211,992	8.6
Pari-mutuels	15	-
Public utilities	49,740	2.0
Tobacco products	87,148	3.5
Other selective sales	37,444	1.5
Licenses	315,571	12.8
Alcoholic beverages	2,030	0.1
Amusements	4,409	0.2
Corporations in general	3,222	0.1
Hunting and fishing	44,661	1.8
Motor vehicle	142,901	5.8
Motor vehicle operators	8,950	0.4
Public utilities	10	-
Occupation and business, NEC	99,751	4.1
Other licenses	9,637	0.4
Income taxes	1,032,541	42.0
Individual income	900,180	36.6
Corporation net income	132,361	5.4
Other taxes	309,290	12.6
Death and gift	1	-
Documentary and stock transfer	0	0.0
Severance	305,617	12.4
Taxes, NEC	3,672	0.1

- = Rounds to zero.

Leading Exports, 2012

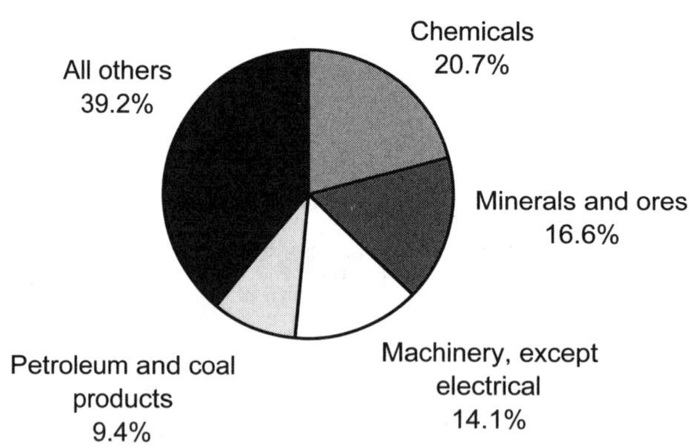

NEBRASKA

Facts and Figures

Location: Central United States; bordered on the N by South Dakota, on the E by Iowa and Missouri, on the S by Kansas and Colorado, and on the W by Wyoming

Area: 77,354 sq. mi. (200,345 sq. km.); rank—16th

Population: 1,855,525 (2012 est.); rank—37th

Principal Cities: capital—Lincoln; largest—Omaha

Statehood: March 1, 1867; 37th state

U.S. Congress: 2 senators, 3 representatives

State Motto: Equality Before the Law

State Song: "Beautiful Nebraska"

State Nickname: The Cornhusker State

Abbreviations: NE; Nebr.; Neb.

State Symbols: flower—goldenrod; tree—cottonwood; bird—Western meadowlark

At a Glance

- With an increase in population of 5.0 percent, Nebraska ranked 37th among the states in growth from 2000 to 2009.
- An estimated 12,500 marriages took place in Nebraska in 2009, compared to 5,400 divorces.
- In 2011, 11.4 percent of Nebraskans did not have health insurance, compared to 15.1 percent of the total U.S. population.
- In the 2012 election, 61.6 percent of Nebraska's eligible voters voted, compared to 61.8 percent of eligible voters nationwide.
- In 2007, Nebraska exported $4 billion worth of agricultural products, about 4.9 percent of the U.S. total.

Table NE-1. Population by Age, Sex, Race, and Hispanic Origin

(Number, percent, except where noted.)

Sex, age, race, and Hispanic origin	2000	2010	2012[1]	Average annual percent change, 2010–2012
Total Population	1,711,263	1,826,341	1,855,525	0.5
Percent of total U.S. population	0.6	0.6	0.6	X
Sex				
Male	843,351	906,296	922,302	0.6
Female	867,912	920,045	933,223	0.5
Age				
Under 5 years	117,048	131,908	132,268	0.1
5 to 19 years	387,288	380,564	385,109	0.4
20 to 64 years	974,732	1,067,192	1,080,794	0.4
65 years and over	232,195	246,677	257,354	1.4
Median age (years)	35.3	36.2	36.2	-
Race and Hispanic Origin				
One race				
White	1,533,261	1,649,264	1,668,779	0.4
Black	68,541	85,971	88,758	1.0
American Indian and Alaska Native	14,896	23,418	24,281	1.2
Asian	21,931	33,322	36,467	2.9
Native Hawaiian or Other Pacific Islander	836	2,061	2,163	1.6
Two or more races	23,953	32,305	35,077	2.6
Hispanic (of any race)	94,425	173,058	186,155	2.3

X = Not applicable.
- = Zero or rounds to zero.
[1] Population figures for 2012 are July 1 estimates. The 2010 estimates are taken from the 2010 Census.

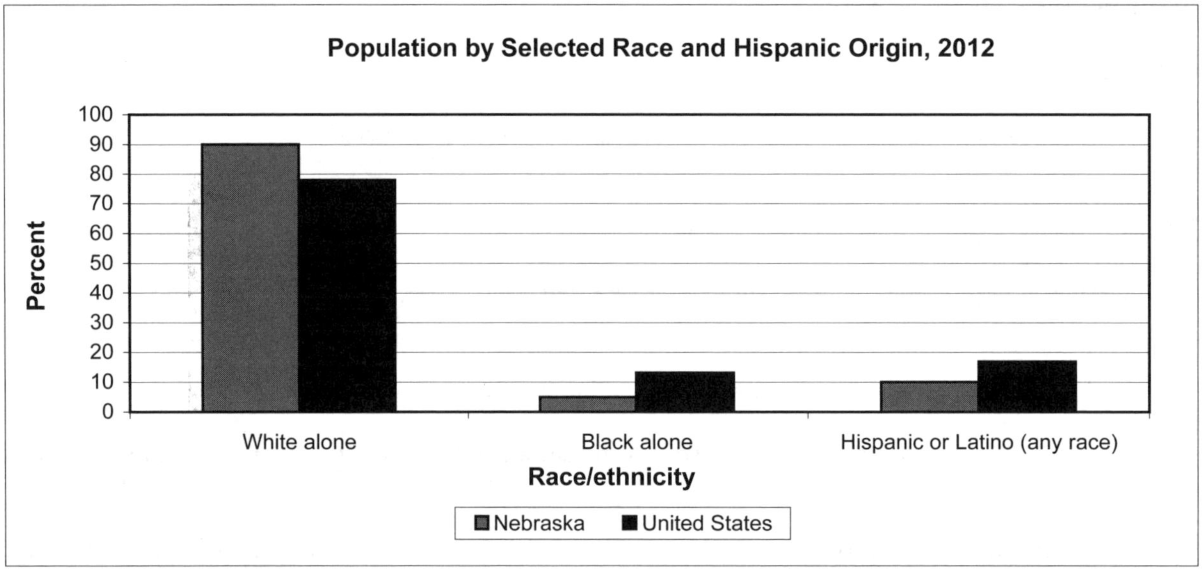

Table NE-2. Marital Status

(Number, percent distribution.)

Sex, age, race, and Hispanic origin	2000	2010	2011
Males, 15 Years and Over	654,559	708,783	715,219
Never married	29.2	32.4	32.2
Now married, except separated	59.1	54.0	54.4
Separated	1.0	1.4	1.2
Widowed	2.4	2.3	2.5
Divorced	8.3	9.9	9.7
Females, 15 Years and Over	687,863	735,744	741,573
Never married	22.5	25.3	26.0
Now married, except separated	55.7	52.7	52.1
Separated	1.3	1.5	1.3
Widowed	10.8	9.5	8.9
Divorced	9.7	10.9	11.7

Table NE-3. Households and Housing Characteristics

(Number, percent, dollars.)

Item	2000	2010	2011	Average annual percent change, 2000–2011
Total Households	666,184	719,304	723,800	0.7
Family households	443,411	468,407	470,445	0.5
Married-couple family	360,996	368,023	369,983	0.2
Other family	82,415	100,384	100,462	1.8
Male householder, no wife present	22,072	31,177	30,287	3.1
Female householder, no husband present	60,343	69,207	70,175	1.4
Nonfamily households	222,773	250,897	253,355	1.1
Householder living alone	183,550	205,263	208,428	1.1
Householder not living alone	39,223	45,634	44,927	1.2
Housing Characteristics				
Total housing units	722,668	797,677	801,182	0.9
Occupied housing units	666,184	719,304	723,800	0.7
Owner occupied	449,317	484,649	484,308	0.6
Renter occupied	216,867	234,655	239,492	0.9
Average size	2.49	2.47	2.48	-
Financial Characteristics				
Median gross rent of renter-occupied housing	491	669	673	3.1
Median monthly owner costs for housing units with a mortgage	895	1,218	1,237	3.2
Median value of owner-occupied housing units	88,000	127,600	127,400	3.7

- = Zero or rounds to zero.

Table NE-4. Migration, Origin, and Language

(Number, percent.)

Characteristic	State			U.S.		
	2010	2011	Percent change	2010	2011	Percent change
Residence 1 Year Ago						
Population 1 year and over	1,802,697	1,817,126	0.8	305,628,607	307,900,319	0.7
Same house	83.0	82.8	-0.2	84.6	84.8	0.2
Different house in the U.S.	16.5	16.8	1.8	14.8	14.6	-1.4
Same county	10.1	10.3	2.0	9.4	9.2	-2.1
Different county	6.4	6.5	1.6	5.4	5.4	-
Same state	3.6	3.6	-	3.2	3.1	-3.1
Different state	2.8	2.9	3.6	2.2	2.3	4.5
Abroad	0.4	0.4	-	0.6	0.6	-
Place of Birth						
Native born	1,718,251	1,726,517	0.5	269,393,835	271,214,059	0.7
Male	49.6	49.4	-0.4	49.2	49.2	-
Female	50.4	50.6	0.4	50.8	50.8	-
Foreign born	112,178	116,124	3.5	39,955,854	40,377,860	1.1
Male	49.0	52.0	6.1	49.1	48.9	-0.4
Female	51.0	48.0	-5.9	50.9	51.1	0.4
Foreign born; naturalized U.S. citizen	45,513	41,259	-9.3	17,476,082	18,140,192	3.8
Male	43.8	51.2	16.9	45.8	45.8	-
Female	56.2	48.8	-13.2	54.2	54.2	-
Foreign born; not a U.S. citizen	66,665	74,865	12.3	22,479,772	22,237,668	-1.1
Male	52.5	52.3	-0.4	51.6	51.5	-0.2
Female	47.5	47.7	0.4	48.4	48.5	0.2
Entered 2000 or later	38.5	49.3	28.1	34.7	35.7	2.9
Entered 1990 to 1999	34.7	29.2	-15.9	27.2	26.7	-1.8
Entered before 1990	26.7	21.5	-19.5	38.1	37.6	-1.3
World Region of Birth, Foreign						
Foreign-born population, excluding population born at sea	112,178	116,124	3.5	39,955,673	40,377,757	1.1
Europe	9.9	7.6	-23.2	12.1	12.1	-
Asia	24.6	27.0	9.8	28.2	28.6	1.4
Africa	8.7	6.9	-20.7	4	4.1	2.5
Oceania	0.7	0.1	-85.7	0.5	0.5	-
Latin America	54.7	57.0	4.2	53.1	52.6	-0.9
North America	1.4	1.3	-7.1	2	2.0	-
Language Spoken at Home and Ability to Speak English						
Population 5 years and over	1,698,792	1,711,659	0.8	289,215,746	291,524,091	0.8
English only	89.6	89.7	0.1	79.4	79.2	-0.3
Language other than English	10.4	10.3	-1.0	20.6	20.8	1.0
Speaks English less than "very well"	4.5	4.7	4.4	8.7	8.7	-

- = Zero or rounds to zero.

Table NE-5. Median Income and Poverty Status, 2011

(Number, percent, except as noted.)

Characteristic	State Number	State Percent	U.S. Number	U.S. Percent
Median Income				
Households (dollars)	50,296	X	50,502	X
Families (dollars)	63,491	X	61,455	X
Below Poverty Level (All People)	234,710	13.1	48,452,035	15.9
Sex				
Male	99,669	11.2	21,825,281	14.7
Female	135,041	15.0	26,626,754	17.2
Age				
Under 18 years	81,943	18.1	16,386,500	22.5
Related children under 18 years	78,831	17.6	16,087,074	22.2
18 to 64 years	134,137	12.2	28,335,079	14.8
65 years and over	18,630	7.8	3,730,456	9.3

X = Not applicable.

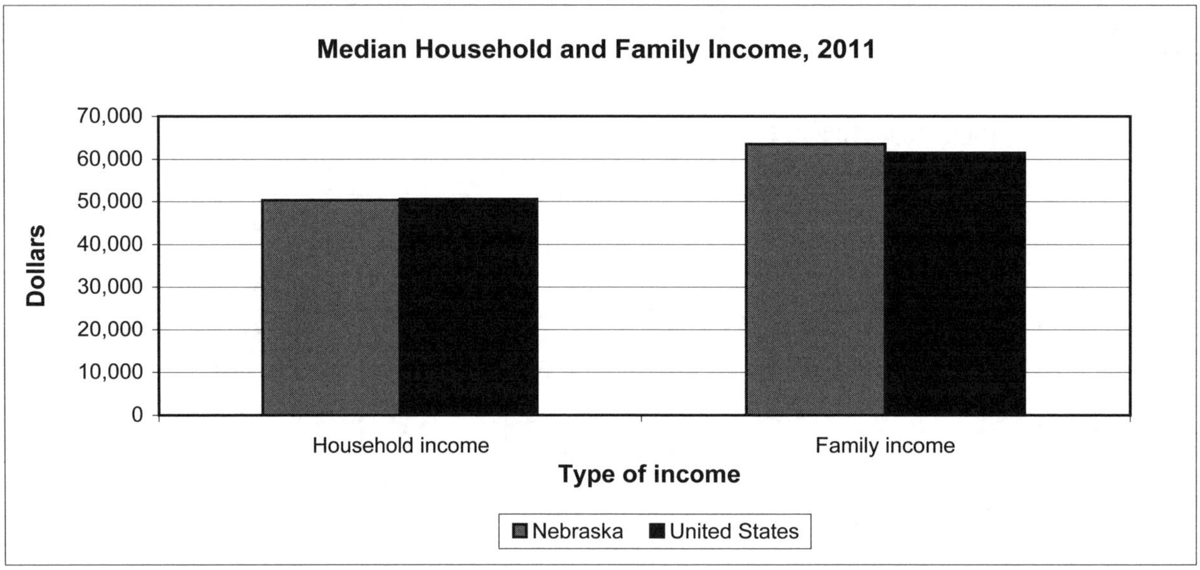

Table NE-6. Health Insurance Coverage Status for the Civilian Noninstitutionalized Population and Children Under 18 Years of Age

(Numbers in thousands, percent.)

Item	2004	2005	2006	2007	2008	2009	2010	2011
Civilian Noninstitutionalized Population	1,729	1,766	1,767	1,753	1,750	1,763	1,802	1,814
Covered by Private or Public Insurance								
Number	1,549	1,581	1,549	1,522	1,555	1,553	1,594	1,607
Percent	89.5	89.6	87.7	86.8	88.9	88.1	88.5	88.6
Not Covered								
Number	180	185	217	232	195	210	208	207
Percent	10.4	10.5	12.3	13.2	11.1	11.9	11.5	11.4
Percent in the U.S. not covered	14.9	15.3	15.8	15.3	15.1	15.1	15.5	15.1
Children Under 18 Years of Age	439	439	444	452	445	445	459	459
Covered by Private or Public Insurance								
Number	413	416	399	407	414	417	433	432
Percent	94.1	94.7	89.9	90.0	93.0	93.7	94.4	94.1
Not Covered								
Number	26	23	45	45	31	28	26	27
Percent	5.9	5.3	10.1	10.0	7.0	6.3	5.6	5.9
Percent in the U.S. not covered	10.5	10.9	11.7	11.0	9.7	8.6	8.0	7.5

Table NE-7. Employment Status by Demographic Group, Preliminary 2012

(Numbers in thousands, percent.)

Characteristic	Civilian noninstitutional population	Civilian labor force		Employed		Unemployed	
		Number	Percent of population	Number	Percent of population	Number	Percent of population
Total	1,417	1,027	72.5	986	69.6	41	4.0
Sex							
Male	695	538	77.4	517	74.5	20	3.8
Female	722	489	67.7	468	64.9	21	4.2
Race, Sex, and Hispanic Origin							
White	1,299	940	72.4	907	69.8	33	3.5
Male	637	494	77.5	477	74.9	16	3.3
Female	662	447	67.5	430	64.9	17	3.7
Black or African American	53	38	71.4	33	62.3	5	12.7
Male	26	19	74.0	17	65.0	2	12.3
Female	27	19	68.8	16	59.8	2	13.1
Hispanic	138	102	74.1	95	68.6	8	7.4
Male	76	63	83.4	59	77.9	4	6.5
Female	62	39	62.9	35	57.2	4	9.1
Age							
16 to 19 years	92	44	47.4	38	41.0	6	13.5
20 to 24 years	132	107	81.3	100	75.6	8	7.0
25 to 34 years	249	216	86.9	206	82.7	10	4.8
35 to 44 years	221	200	90.4	193	87.3	7	3.4
45 to 54 years	250	222	88.8	217	86.7	5	2.4
55 to 64 years	218	168	76.9	164	75.2	4	2.2
65 years and over	254	70	27.5	68	26.8	2	2.4

NOTE: Data in Table 7 are from the Current Population Survey (CPS) and do not match the estimates in Table 8. See notes and definitions for further information.

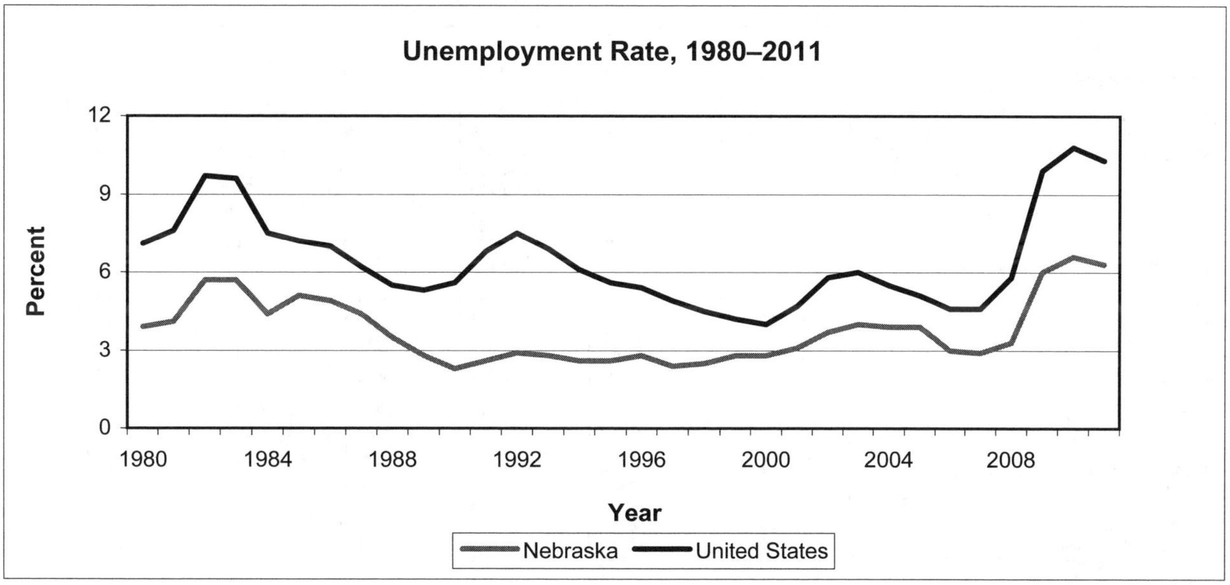

Table NE-8. Employment Status of the Civilian Noninstitutional Population Age 16 Years and Over

(Number, percent.)

Year	Civilian labor force	Civilian participation rate	Employed	Unemployed	Unemployment rate
2005	975,693	73.6	937,964	37,729	3.9
2006	974,888	73.0	945,288	29,600	3.0
2007	984,665	73.3	955,678	28,987	2.9
2008	995,635	73.5	962,418	33,217	3.3
2009	990,901	70.9	931,004	59,897	6.0
2010	1,000,833	70.5	935,104	65,779	6.6
2011	1,006,874	70.3	943,643	63,321	6.3

Table NE-9. Employment and Average Wages by Industry

(Estimates before 2007 are based on the 2002 *North American Industry Classification System* [NAICS]. Estimates from 2007 onward are based on the 2007 NAICS.)

Industry	2005	2006	2007	2008	2009	2010	2011
	Number of jobs						
Wage and Salary Employment by Industry	964,589	975,386	989,419	994,614	974,841	972,094	977,551
Farm Wage and Salary Employment	11,769	11,150	11,026	10,149	11,549	13,017	13,457
Nonfarm Wage and Salary Employment	952,820	964,236	978,393	984,465	963,292	959,077	964,094
Private wage and salary employment	782,032	791,881	806,706	811,170	787,107	782,045	789,051
Forestry, fishing, and related activities	3,768	3,763	4,268	4,156	4,398	4,634	4,958
Mining	1,360	1,316	961	982	938	940	1,022
Utilities	1,694	1,630	1,660	1,850	1,918	1,656	1,627
Construction	48,224	48,997	51,252	51,148	48,453	43,653	42,634
Manufacturing	101,329	101,950	101,695	101,599	93,466	91,740	93,723
Durable goods manufacturing	48,326	49,563	50,036	49,371	42,697	41,435	42,786
Nondurable goods manufacturing	53,003	52,387	51,659	52,228	50,769	50,305	50,937
Wholesale trade	40,920	41,193	41,296	42,354	41,593	40,945	41,178
Retail trade	108,634	108,082	109,277	109,204	106,159	106,114	106,433
Transportation and warehousing	52,911	53,501	55,302	54,573	51,764	51,086	51,873
Information	20,421	19,593	19,686	18,847	17,520	16,984	17,190
Finance and insurance	53,308	54,776	55,662	56,076	55,107	55,283	55,227
Real estate and rental and leasing	9,938	9,897	9,856	9,648	9,434	9,398	9,309
Professional, scientific, and technical services	37,621	40,608	41,595	43,687	43,063	43,570	43,950
Management of companies and enterprises	14,733	15,520	17,380	16,948	17,164	17,150	16,678
Administrative and waste services	45,329	45,881	46,325	46,263	41,816	41,965	43,251
Educational services	16,744	16,932	17,481	17,625	18,087	18,292	18,621
Health care and social assistance	101,230	103,074	105,713	108,710	109,967	111,811	113,518
Arts, entertainment, and recreation	11,525	11,596	12,371	12,822	12,906	12,413	12,583
Accommodation and food services	68,898	69,873	70,953	70,762	69,637	69,497	70,316
Other services, except public administration	43,445	43,699	43,973	43,916	43,717	44,914	44,960
Government and government enterprises	170,788	172,355	171,687	173,295	176,185	177,032	175,043
	Dollars						
Average Wages and Salaries by Industry	33,686	35,226	36,789	37,942	38,153	38,782	39,869
Average Farm Wages and Salaries	30,651	36,197	44,482	50,981	44,552	35,511	39,151
Average Nonfarm Wages and Salaries	33,724	35,214	36,703	37,808	38,076	38,826	39,879
Average private wages and salaries	33,400	34,960	36,495	37,546	37,643	38,325	39,359
Forestry, fishing, and related activities	17,336	17,973	18,648	21,497	20,949	20,996	23,706
Mining	41,945	42,432	42,287	44,410	43,762	45,790	48,119
Utilities	84,164	92,001	116,528	125,026	96,752	88,457	90,972
Construction	35,904	37,141	40,122	41,048	41,802	41,735	42,097
Manufacturing	37,860	39,736	40,765	42,117	41,983	43,695	44,641
Durable goods manufacturing	39,777	41,940	42,538	44,108	44,151	46,140	48,043
Nondurable goods manufacturing	36,112	37,651	39,048	40,235	40,160	41,681	41,783
Wholesale trade	43,757	45,635	47,905	50,131	49,940	51,243	52,832
Retail trade	21,255	22,010	22,557	23,069	23,133	23,859	24,064
Transportation and warehousing	44,651	46,563	47,507	48,770	47,360	48,605	51,136
Information	47,374	47,980	57,936	51,032	50,677	51,205	54,084
Finance and insurance	48,993	50,059	51,061	52,598	52,848	54,850	57,359
Real estate and rental and leasing	28,492	29,805	31,744	32,267	32,310	32,817	34,225
Professional, scientific, and technical services	49,040	51,052	53,350	56,601	57,806	58,533	59,706
Management of companies and enterprises	66,844	73,478	77,178	79,706	78,977	78,708	80,953
Administrative and waste services	25,442	27,936	27,635	28,341	29,233	29,039	30,080
Educational services	25,983	27,924	28,611	29,585	29,820	30,312	30,479
Health care and social assistance	35,176	36,506	37,808	39,140	39,857	40,084	41,068
Arts, entertainment, and recreation	15,661	17,054	17,552	16,663	16,825	17,683	18,106
Accommodation and food services	12,341	12,685	13,378	13,516	13,628	14,152	14,607
Other services, except public administration	21,930	22,846	24,001	25,181	25,518	26,120	26,637
Government and government enterprises	35,208	36,381	37,677	39,033	40,012	41,041	42,225

Table NE-10. Employment Characteristics by Family Type

(Number, percent.)

Family type and labor force status	2009 Total	2009 Families with own children under 18 years	2010 Total	2010 Families with own children under 18 years	2011 Total	2011 Families with own children under 18 years
All families	457,966	212,136	468,407	209,697	470,445	215,933
Family type and labor force status						
Married-couple families	362,370	152,871	368,023	148,405	369,983	152,305
Both husband and wife in labor force	63.0	75.9	63.9	77.0	63.1	76.3
Husband in labor force, wife not in labor force	16.9	20.6	15.8	19.4	17.3	20.1
Wife in labor force, husband not in labor force	6.3	2.6	6.7	2.3	6.1	2.6
Both husband and wife not in labor force	13.8	0.9	13.7	1.4	13.5	1.0
Other families	95,596	59,265	100,384	61,292	100,462	63,628
Female householder, no husband present	73.2	77.6	68.9	72.2	69.9	71.7
In labor force	58.9	69.2	55.3	64.7	56.7	64.0
Not in labor force	14.3	8.3	13.6	7.5	13.1	7.7
Male householder, no wife present	26.8	22.4	31.1	27.8	30.1	28.3
In labor force	22.6	21.1	27.2	26.1	24.9	26.0
Not in labor force	4.2	1.3	3.9	1.8	5.3	2.3

Table NE-11. School Enrollment and Educational Attainment, 2011

(Number, percent.)

Item	State	U.S.
Enrollment		
Total population 3 years and over, enrolled in school	515,647	83,131,910
Enrolled in nursery school or preschool (percent)	6.5	6.0
Enrolled in kindergarten (percent)	5.2	5.1
Enrolled in elementary school, grades 1-8 (percent)	39.2	39.5
Enrolled in high school, grades 9-12 (percent)	20.0	20.7
Enrolled in college or graduate school (percent)	29.2	28.7
Attainment		
Total population 25 years and over	1,196,112	206,471,670
Less than ninth grade (percent)	3.9	6.0
9th to 12th grade, no diploma (percent)	5.1	8.1
High school graduate, including equivalency (percent)	29.0	28.4
Some college, no degree (percent)	24.4	21.2
Associate's degree (percent)	9.6	7.8
Bachelor's degree (percent)	18.9	17.9
Graduate or professional degree (percent)	9.1	10.6
High school graduate or higher (percent)	91.0	85.9
Bachelor's degree or higher (percent)	27.9	28.5

Table NE-12. Educational Indicators

(Number, percent; data derived from National Center of Education Statistics.)

Item	State	U.S.
Public Schools, 2009–2010 (except where noted)		
Number of school districts	253	13,629
Number of schools	1,120	99,834
Number of students (in thousands)	295	49,373
Student-teacher ratio	13.3	15.4
Expenditures per student (dollars)	12,966	10,591
Averaged freshman graduation rate, 2008–2009	82.9	75.5[1]
Dropout rate, 2008–2009	2.4	4.1
Students eligible for free or reduced-price lunch (percent)	42.6	48.0
English language learners, 2010–2011 (percent)	6.7	9.8[1]
Students with IEP (percent)	14.7	13.1
Private Schools, 2009–2010 (except where noted)		
Number of schools	221	33,366
Number of students (in thousands)	35	4,700
High school graduates, 2008–2009	2,004	308,813
Student-teacher ratio	13.1	10.7

[1] U.S. total includes estimates for nonreporting states.

Table NE-13. Reported Voting and Registration of the Voting-Age Population, November 2012

(Numbers in thousands, percent.)

Item	Total population	Total citizen population	Registered			Voted		
			Total registered	Percent registered (total population)	Percent registered (total citizen population)	Total voted	Percent voted (total population)	Percent voted (total citizen population)
U.S. Total	235,248	215,081	153,157	65.1	71.2	132,948	56.5	61.8
State Total	1,371	1,296	901	65.7	69.5	798	58.2	61.6
Sex								
Male	677	639	441	65.1	69.0	386	57.1	60.4
Female	694	657	460	66.3	70.0	412	59.4	62.7
Race								
White alone	1,265	1,210	846	66.8	69.9	750	59.3	62.0
White, non-Hispanic alone	1,161	1,150	824	70.9	71.6	731	63.0	63.6
Black alone	51	45	32	B	B	29	B	B
Asian alone	31	18	7	B	B	5	B	B
Hispanic (of any race)	110	64	27	25.0	B	21	19.4	B
Age								
18 to 24 years	168	151	71	42.2	47.0	61	36.2	40.3
25 to 44 years	477	442	282	59.1	63.8	238	49.8	53.8
45 to 64 years	462	445	331	71.7	74.5	300	64.9	67.4
65 to 74 years	143	139	119	83.4	85.8	112	78.2	80.5
75 years and over	121	120	98	80.7	81.4	88	72.8	73.5

B = Base is less than 75,000 and therefore too small to show the derived measure.

Table NE-14. Crime

(Number, rate per 100,000. Data are derived from the FBI Uniform Crime Reports.)

Item	State			U.S.		
	2010	2011	Percent change	2010	2011	Percent change
TOTAL POPULATION	1,830,141	1,842,641	0.7	309,330,219	311,591,917	0.7
VIOLENT CRIME						
Number	5,093	4,665	-8.4	1,251,248	1,203,564	-3.8
Rate	278.3	253.2	-9.0	404.5	386.3	-4.5
Murder and Nonnegligent Manslaughter						
Number	54	67	24.1	14,722	14,612	-0.7
Rate	3.0	3.6	20.0	4.8	4.7	-2.1
Forcible Rape						
Number	674	695	3.1	85,593	83,425	-2.5
Rate	36.8	37.7	2.4	27.7	26.8	-3.2
Robbery						
Number	1,020	997	-2.3	369,089	354,396	-4.0
Rate	55.7	54.1	-2.9	119.3	113.7	-4.7
Aggravated Assault						
Number	3,345	2,906	-13.1	781,844	751,131	-3.9
Rate	182.8	157.7	-13.7	252.8	241.1	-4.6
PROPERTY CRIME						
Number	48,827	50,726	3.9	9,112,625	9,063,173	-0.5
Rate	2,667.9	2,752.9	3.2	2,945.9	2,908.7	-1.3
Burglary						
Number	8,318	8,714	4.8	2,168,459	2,188,005	0.9
Rate	454.5	472.9	4.0	701.0	702.2	0.2
Larceny-Theft						
Number	36,896	37,909	2.7	6,204,601	6,159,795	-0.7
Rate	2,016.0	2,057.3	2.0	2,005.8	1,976.9	-1.4
Motor Vehicle Theft						
Number	3,613	4,103	13.6	739,565	715,373	-3.3
Rate	197.4	222.7	12.8	239.1	229.6	-4.0

Table NE-15. State Government Finances, 2011

(Dollar amounts in thousands, percent distribution.)

Item	Dollars	Percent distribution
Total Revenue	11,523,401	100.0
General revenue	9,389,153	81.5
Intergovernmental revenue	3,401,587	29.5
Taxes	4,153,113	36.0
General sales	1,385,363	12.0
Selective sales	647,430	5.6
License taxes	227,377	2.0
Individual income tax	1,721,548	14.9
Corporate income tax	154,945	1.3
Other taxes	16,450	0.1
Current charges	1,037,362	9.0
Miscellaneous general revenue	797,091	6.9
Utility revenue	0	0.0
Liquor stores revenue	0	0.0
Insurance trust revenue [1]	2,134,248	18.5
Total Expenditure	9,356,473	100.0
Intergovernmental expenditure	2,306,692	24.7
Direct expenditure	7,049,781	75.3
Current operation	5,382,647	57.5
Capital outlay	670,217	7.2
Insurance benefits and repayments	739,408	7.9
Assistance and subsidies	165,892	1.8
Interest on debt	91,617	1.0
Exhibit: Salaries and wages	2,304,897	24.6
Total Expenditure	9,356,473	100.0
General expenditure	8,617,065	92.1
Intergovernmental expenditure	2,306,692	24.7
Direct expenditure	6,310,373	67.4
General expenditure, by function:		
Education	3,330,145	35.6
Public welfare	2,090,850	22.3
Hospitals	260,622	2.8
Health	455,621	4.9
Highways	602,273	6.4
Police protection	96,200	1.0
Correction	241,829	2.6
Natural resources	250,575	2.7
Parks and recreation	38,605	0.4
Governmental administration	210,568	2.3
Interest on general debt	91,617	1.0
Other and unallocable	948,160	10.1
Utility expenditure	0	0.0
Liquor stores expenditure	0	0.0
Insurance trust expenditure	739,408	7.9
Debt at End of Fiscal Year	2,345,750	X
Cash and Security Holdings	14,327,368	X

X = Not applicable.
[1] Within insurance trust revenue, net earnings of state retirement systems is a calculated statistic (the item code in the data file is X08), and thus can be positive or negative. Net earnings is the sum of earnings on investments plus gains on investments minus losses on investments. The change made in 2002 for asset valuation from book to market value in accordance with Statement 34 of the Governmental Accounting Standards Board is reflected in the calculated statistics.

Table NE-16. State Government Tax Collections, 2012

(Dollars in thousands, percent.)

Item	Dollars	Percent distribution
Total Taxes	4,358,328	100.0
Property taxes	78	-
Sales and gross receipts	2,085,484	47.9
General sales and gross receipts	1,456,625	33.4
Selective sales and gross receipts	628,859	14.4
Alcoholic beverages	28,472	0.7
Amusements	3,082	0.1
Insurance premiums	46,482	1.1
Motor fuels	299,764	6.9
Pari-mutuels	267	-
Public utilities	55,658	1.3
Tobacco products	33,725	0.8
Other selective sales	161,409	3.7
Licenses	183,035	4.2
Alcoholic beverages	1,405	-
Amusements	777	-
Corporations in general	26,330	0.6
Hunting and fishing	14,459	0.3
Motor vehicle	123,190	2.8
Motor vehicle operators	5,216	0.1
Public utilities	0	0.0
Occupation and business, NEC	11,658	0.3
Other licenses	0	0.0
Income taxes	2,072,640	47.6
Individual income	1,838,344	42.2
Corporation net income	234,296	5.4
Other taxes	17,091	0.4
Death and gift	1,017	-
Documentary and stock transfer	10,719	0.2
Severance	5,355	0.1
Taxes, NEC	0	0.0

- = Rounds to zero.

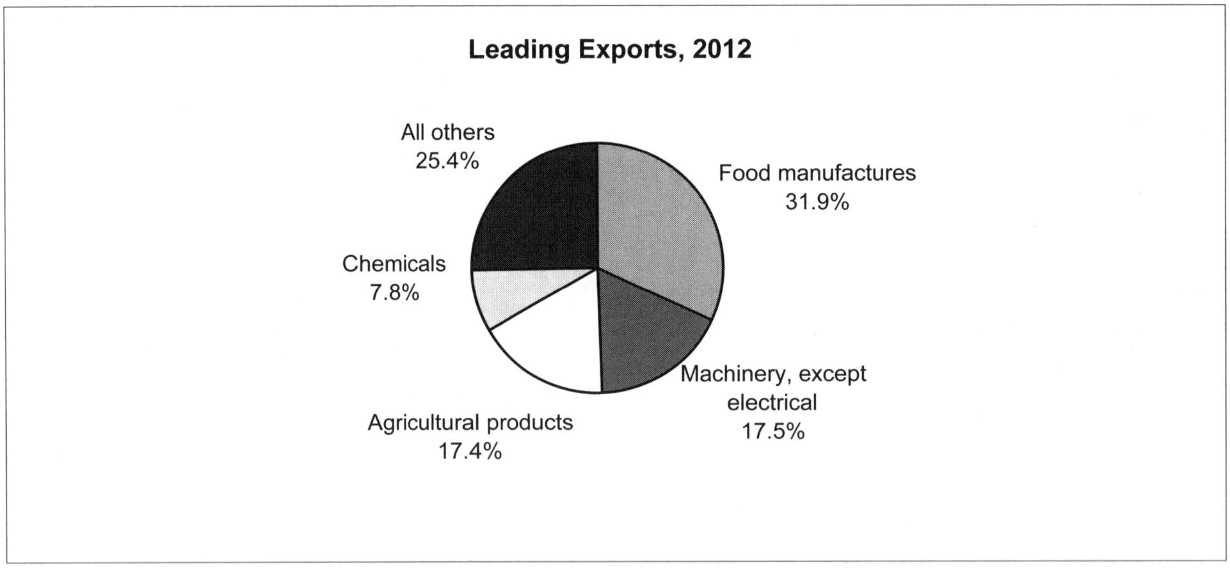

NEVADA

Facts and Figures

Location: Western United States; bordered on the N by Oregon and Idaho, on the E by Utah and Arizona, on the S by Arizona and California, and on the W by California

Area: 110,561 sq. mi. (286,351 sq. km.); rank—7th

Population: 2,758,931 (2012 est.); rank—35th

Principal Cities: capital—Carson City; largest—Las Vegas

Statehood: October 31, 1864; 36th state

U.S. Congress: 2 senators, 4 representatives

State Motto: All for Our Country

State Song: "Home Means Nevada"

State Nicknames: The Silver State; The Sagebrush State

Abbreviations: NV; Nev.

State Symbols: flower—sagebrush; tree—single-leaf piñon and bristlecone pine; bird—mountain bluebird

At a Glance

- With an increase in population of 32.3 percent, Nevada ranked 10th among the states in growth from 2000 to 2009.
- An estimated 108,200 marriages took place in Nevada in 2009, compared to 17,700 divorces.
- In 2011, 12.7 percent of Nevadans were unemployed, compared to 10.3 nationwide.
- Nevada's violent crime rate in 2011 was 562.1 per 100,000 population, compared to 386.3 for the entire nation.
- In 2007, Nevada exported $43 million worth of agricultural products, less than 1 percent of the U.S. total.

Table NV-1. Population by Age, Sex, Race, and Hispanic Origin

(Number, percent, except where noted.)

Sex, age, race, and Hispanic origin	2000	2010	2012[1]	Average annual percent change, 2010–2012
Total Population	1,998,257	2,700,551	2,758,931	0.7
Percent of total U.S. population	0.7	0.9	0.9	X
Sex				
Male	1,018,051	1,363,616	1,391,207	0.7
Female	980,206	1,336,935	1,367,724	0.8
Age				
Under 5 years	145,817	187,478	183,301	-0.8
5 to 19 years	415,684	548,850	545,929	-0.2
20 to 64 years	1,217,827	1,639,864	1,668,787	0.6
65 years and over	218,929	324,359	360,914	3.4
Median age (years)	35.0	36.3	36.9	0.5
Race and Hispanic Origin				
One race				
White	1,501,886	2,106,494	2,128,047	0.3
Black	135,477	231,224	244,462	1.8
American Indian and Alaska Native	26,420	42,965	44,571	1.2
Asian	90,266	203,478	217,264	2.1
Native Hawaiian or Other Pacific Islander	8,426	19,307	20,121	1.3
Two or more races	76,428	97,083	104,466	2.4
Hispanic (of any race)	393,970	741,200	779,222	1.6

X = Not applicable.
[1] Population figures for 2012 are July 1 estimates. The 2010 estimates are taken from the 2010 Census.

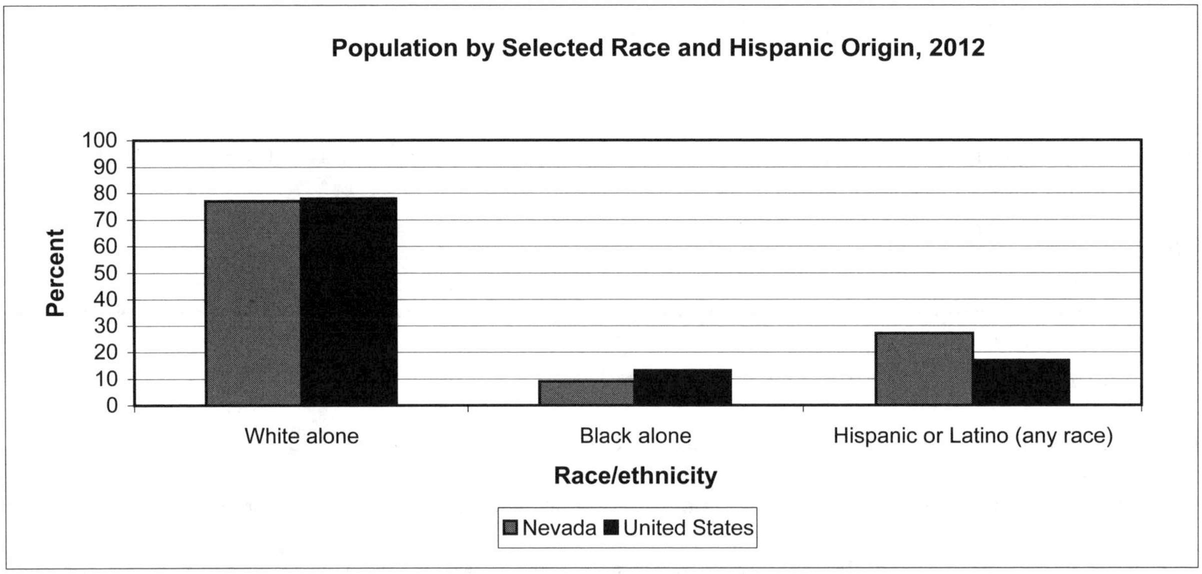

Table NV-2. Marital Status

(Number, percent distribution.)

Sex, age, race, and Hispanic origin	2000	2010	2011
Males, 15 Years and Over	792,317	1,081,514	1,090,897
Never married	28.8	35.0	35.2
Now married, except separated	53.8	47.6	46.7
Separated	2.0	2.0	2.5
Widowed	2.5	2.9	2.2
Divorced	12.9	12.5	13.4
Females, 15 Years and Over	771,263	1,069,123	1,081,640
Never married	20.9	27.2	28.5
Now married, except separated	53.1	47.2	46.3
Separated	2.7	2.8	3.0
Widowed	8.6	8.0	7.8
Divorced	14.7	14.8	14.5

Table NV-3. Households and Housing Characteristics

(Number, percent, dollars.)

Item	2000	2010	2011	Average annual percent change, 2000–2011
Total Households	751,165	989,811	982,352	2.6
Family households	298,333	639,686	636,981	9.5
Married-couple family	373,201	452,361	450,072	1.7
Other family	125,132	187,325	186,909	4.1
Male householder, no wife present	41,650	63,327	61,507	4.0
Female householder, no husband present	83,482	123,998	125,402	4.2
Nonfamily households	252,832	350,125	345,371	3.1
Householder living alone	186,745	266,232	271,647	3.8
Householder not living alone	66,087	83,893	73,724	1.0
Housing Characteristics				
Total housing units	827,457	1,175,070	1,183,917	3.6
Occupied housing units	751,165	989,811	982,352	2.6
Owner occupied	457,247	565,869	552,991	1.7
Renter occupied	293,918	423,942	429,361	3.8
Average size	2.62	2.70	2.74	0.4
Financial Characteristics				
Median gross rent of renter-occupied housing	699	952	936	2.8
Median monthly owner costs for housing units with a mortgage	1,190	1,638	1,529	2.4
Median value of owner-occupied housing units	142,000	174,800	158,000	0.9

Table NV-4. Migration, Origin, and Language

(Number, percent.)

Characteristic	State			U.S.		
	2010	2011	Percent change	2010	2011	Percent change
Residence 1 Year Ago						
Population 1 year and over	2,667,364	2,688,336	0.8	305,628,607	307,900,319	0.7
Same house	76.1	77.5	1.8	84.6	84.8	0.2
Different house in the U.S.	23.2	22.0	-5.2	14.8	14.6	-1.4
Same county	18.4	17.0	-7.6	9.4	9.2	-2.1
Different county	4.9	5.0	2.0	5.4	5.4	-
Same state	1.0	0.9	-	3.2	3.1	-3.1
Different state	3.8	4.1	7.9	2.2	2.3	4.5
Abroad	0.6	0.5	-	0.6	0.6	-
Place of Birth						
Native born	2,196,184	2,200,859	0.2	269,393,835	271,214,059	0.7
Male	50.8	50.8	-	49.2	49.2	-
Female	49.2	49.2	-	50.8	50.8	-
Foreign born	508,458	522,463	2.8	39,955,854	40,377,860	1.1
Male	49.3	48.9	-0.8	49.1	48.9	-0.4
Female	50.7	51.1	0.8	50.9	51.1	0.4
Foreign born; naturalized U.S. citizen	212,409	213,675	0.6	17,476,082	18,140,192	3.8
Male	48.3	45.6	-5.6	45.8	45.8	-
Female	51.7	54.4	5.2	54.2	54.2	-
Foreign born; not a U.S. citizen	296,049	308,788	4.3	22,479,772	22,237,668	-1.1
Male	49.9	51.2	2.6	51.6	51.5	-0.2
Female	50.1	48.8	-2.6	48.4	48.5	0.2
Entered 2000 or later	31.9	33.3	4.4	34.7	35.7	2.9
Entered 1990 to 1999	27.5	26.5	-3.6	27.2	26.7	-1.8
Entered before 1990	40.6	40.2	-1.0	38.1	37.6	-1.3
World Region of Birth, Foreign						
Foreign-born population, excluding population born at sea	508,458	522,463	2.8	39,955,673	40,377,757	1.1
Europe	8.5	8.3	-2.4	12.1	12.1	-
Asia	29.8	28.1	-5.7	28.2	28.6	1.4
Africa	2.3	2.2	-4.3	4	4.1	2.5
Oceania	0.5	0.8	60.0	0.5	0.5	-
Latin America	57.2	58.9	3.0	53.1	52.6	-0.9
North America	1.7	1.7	-	2	2.0	-
Language Spoken at Home and Ability to Speak English						
Population 5 years and over	2,517,937	2,538,136	0.8	289,215,746	291,524,091	0.8
English only	71.4	70.3	-1.5	79.4	79.2	-0.3
Language other than English	28.6	29.7	3.8	20.6	20.8	1.0
Speaks English less than "very well"	12.3	12.6	2.4	8.7	8.7	-

- = Zero or rounds to zero.

Table NV-5. Median Income and Poverty Status, 2011

(Number, percent, except as noted.)

Characteristic	State		U.S.	
	Number	Percent	Number	Percent
Median Income				
Households (dollars)	48,927	X	50,502	X
Families (dollars)	56,544	X	61,455	X
Below Poverty Level (All People)	426,741	15.9	48,452,035	15.9
Sex				
Male	200,293	14.9	21,825,281	14.7
Female	226,448	16.9	26,626,754	17.2
Age				
Under 18 years	144,440	22.1	16,386,500	22.5
Related children under 18 years	140,087	21.6	16,087,074	22.2
18 to 64 years	250,685	14.8	28,335,079	14.8
65 years and over	31,616	9.4	3,730,456	9.3

X = Not applicable.

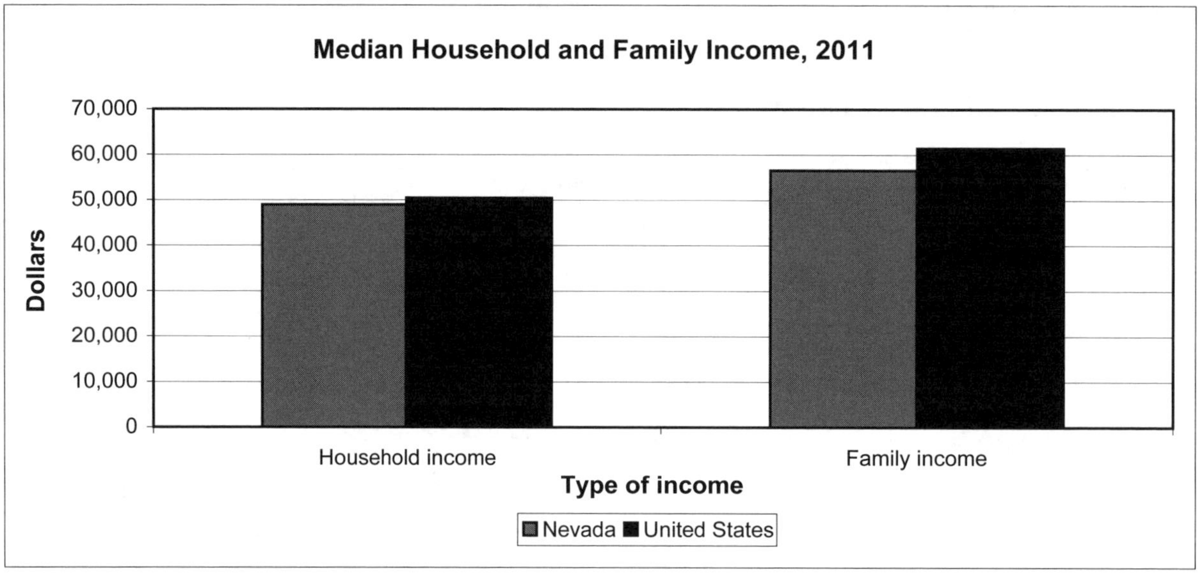

Table NV-6. Health Insurance Coverage Status for the Civilian Noninstitutionalized Population and Children Under 18 Years of Age

(Numbers in thousands, percent.)

Item	2004	2005	2006	2007	2008	2009	2010	2011
Civilian Noninstitutionalized Population	2,392	2,448	2,535	2,568	2,568	2,610	2,669	2,687
Covered by Private or Public Insurance								
Number	1,952	2,030	2,039	2,126	2,020	2,038	2,065	2,098
Percent	81.6	82.9	80.4	82.8	78.7	78.1	77.4	78.1
Not Covered								
Number	440	418	496	441	548	572	604	589
Percent	18.4	17.1	19.6	17.2	21.3	21.9	22.6	21.9
Percent in the U.S. not covered	14.9	15.3	15.8	15.3	15.1	15.1	15.5	15.1
Children Under 18 Years of Age	620	648	649	660	667	682	664	662
Covered by Private or Public Insurance								
Number	521	555	527	566	532	561	549	155
Percent	84.1	85.7	81.2	85.7	79.8	82.2	82.6	83.8
Not Covered								
Number	99	93	122	94	135	121	115	107
Percent	15.9	14.3	18.8	14.3	20.2	17.8	17.4	16.2
Percent in the U.S. not covered	10.5	10.9	11.7	11.0	9.7	8.6	8.0	7.5

Table NV-7. Employment Status by Demographic Group, Preliminary 2012

(Numbers in thousands, percent.)

Characteristic	Civilian noninstitutional population	Civilian labor force		Employed		Unemployed	
		Number	Percent of population	Number	Percent of population	Number	Percent of population
Total	2,108	1,363	64.7	1,214	57.6	150	11.0
Sex							
Male	1,047	744	71.0	654	62.5	90	12.0
Female	1,061	619	58.4	559	52.7	60	9.7
Race, Sex, and Hispanic Origin							
White	1,637	1,055	64.4	941	57.5	113	10.7
Male	825	584	70.8	516	62.5	69	11.7
Female	812	470	57.9	426	52.4	45	9.5
Black or African American	168	106	62.7	88	52.4	17	16.4
Male	81	56	68.1	45	55.6	10	18.4
Female	87	50	57.7	43	49.5	7	14.3
Hispanic	491	343	69.8	296	60.4	47	13.6
Male	244	196	80.3	167	68.4	29	14.9
Female	247	147	59.5	130	52.5	17	11.8
Age							
16 to 19 years	136	50	36.8	37	27.4	13	25.6
20 to 24 years	218	165	75.6	140	64.2	25	15.2
25 to 34 years	374	307	82.0	272	72.7	35	11.3
35 to 44 years	336	279	82.8	253	75.3	25	9.0
45 to 54 years	374	300	80.1	274	73.2	26	8.6
55 to 64 years	323	201	62.3	183	56.5	19	9.2
65 years and over	347	62	18.0	55	15.9	7	11.9

NOTE: Data in Table 7 are from the Current Population Survey (CPS) and do not match the estimates in Table 8. See notes and definitions for further information.

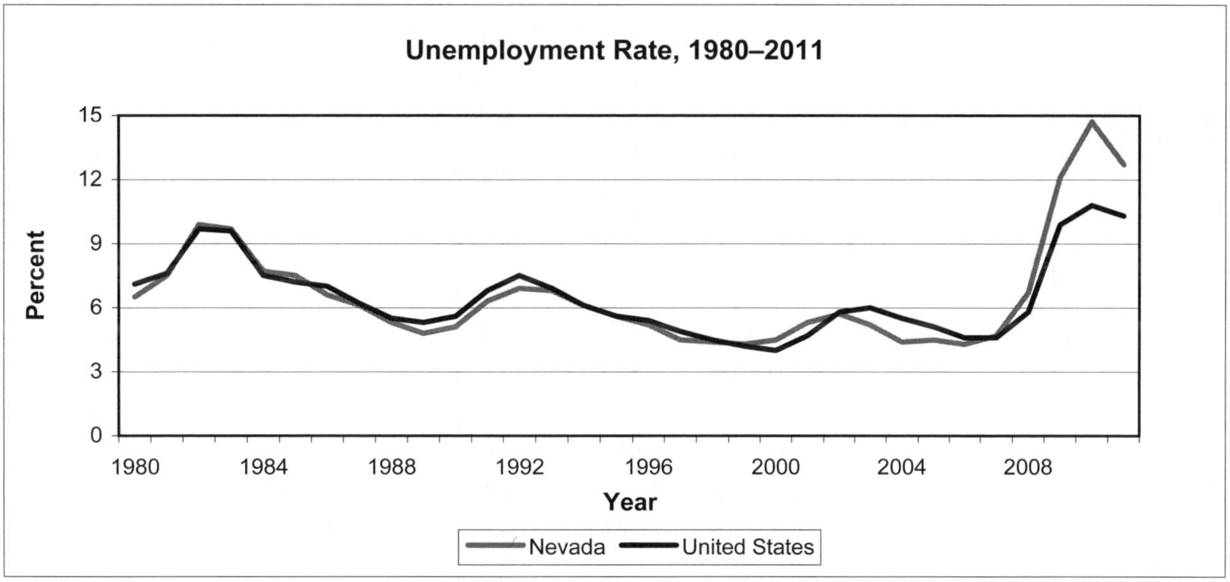

Table NV-8. Employment Status of the Civilian Noninstitutional Population Age 16 Years and Over

(Number, percent.)

Year	Civilian labor force	Civilian participation rate	Employed	Unemployed	Unemployment rate
2005	1,225,144	67.5	1,170,367	54,777	4.5
2006	1,277,197	68.0	1,222,183	55,014	4.3
2007	1,322,643	68.5	1,260,276	62,367	4.7
2008	1,373,462	69.7	1,282,012	91,450	6.7
2009	1,383,813	68.0	1,216,702	167,111	12.1
2010	1,393,170	65.8	1,196,894	196,276	14.1
2011	1,379,559	64.6	1,204,882	174,677	12.7

Table NV-9. Employment and Average Wages by Industry

(Estimates before 2007 are based on the 2002 *North American Industry Classification System* [NAICS]. Estimates from 2007 onward are based on the 2007 NAICS.)

Industry	2005	2006	2007	2008	2009	2010	2011
	Number of jobs						
Wage and Salary Employment by Industry	1,261,216	1,318,683	1,332,830	1,305,162	1,188,773	1,158,863	1,166,183
Farm Wage and Salary Employment	2,232	2,266	1,985	2,085	2,009	2,130	1,949
Nonfarm Wage and Salary Employment	1,258,984	1,316,417	1,330,845	1,303,077	1,186,764	1,156,733	1,164,234
Private wage and salary employment	1,103,077	1,154,514	1,161,947	1,128,518	1,015,497	987,759	998,170
Forestry, fishing, and related activities	479	475	482	532	524	566	591
Mining	10,696	11,475	12,025	12,292	11,630	12,200	13,884
Utilities	4,642	4,627	4,520	4,585	4,571	4,325	4,188
Construction	139,941	148,258	138,923	121,218	84,657	62,103	54,921
Manufacturing	48,465	50,760	50,487	48,260	40,303	38,004	38,259
Durable goods manufacturing	33,546	34,974	34,505	33,001	26,805	24,810	24,693
Nondurable goods manufacturing	14,919	15,786	15,982	15,259	13,498	13,194	13,566
Wholesale trade	37,675	39,293	39,878	39,389	35,343	33,281	33,009
Retail trade	132,834	138,925	141,945	140,500	130,421	129,415	131,017
Transportation and warehousing	42,985	46,331	50,027	50,686	47,125	46,689	47,965
Information	14,728	15,204	15,904	15,097	13,208	12,549	12,560
Finance and insurance	39,110	40,187	38,418	36,495	33,728	32,258	31,754
Real estate and rental and leasing	25,876	27,479	28,233	27,062	23,748	22,627	22,547
Professional, scientific, and technical services	51,011	54,810	55,797	54,667	49,649	48,141	47,896
Management of companies and enterprises	12,466	14,466	16,677	18,246	17,895	18,267	18,086
Administrative and waste services	86,264	91,276	88,554	81,042	69,953	71,705	75,552
Educational services	6,345	6,992	7,952	8,560	8,950	9,652	9,928
Health care and social assistance	79,944	82,792	86,919	90,841	92,172	94,135	96,043
Arts, entertainment, and recreation	29,772	30,286	31,175	29,294	26,540	25,786	27,388
Accommodation and food services	300,317	309,083	310,726	306,354	283,937	285,722	291,193
Other services, except public administration	39,527	41,795	43,305	43,398	41,143	40,334	41,389
Government and government enterprises	155,907	161,903	168,898	174,559	171,267	168,974	166,064
	Dollars						
Average Wages and Salaries by Industry	39,847	41,146	43,760	44,019	43,596	43,637	44,375
Average Farm Wages and Salaries	29,431	28,881	37,142	34,128	39,325	32,224	36,539
Average Nonfarm Wages and Salaries	39,865	41,167	43,769	44,035	43,603	43,658	44,388
Average private wages and salaries	39,165	40,371	43,089	43,119	42,265	42,328	43,227
Forestry, fishing, and related activities	25,681	26,634	28,602	32,778	34,977	34,133	36,203
Mining	62,900	69,048	74,839	77,126	78,537	82,914	84,536
Utilities	78,655	81,620	84,671	87,670	87,856	89,942	94,683
Construction	44,863	47,475	52,390	57,676	58,683	55,475	53,130
Manufacturing	43,580	45,124	47,794	49,764	49,928	50,384	51,753
Durable goods manufacturing	46,003	47,716	51,344	53,895	54,173	54,952	56,747
Nondurable goods manufacturing	38,134	39,380	40,128	40,829	41,499	41,795	42,663
Wholesale trade	53,383	55,738	58,034	59,277	59,428	60,609	62,925
Retail trade	28,061	28,462	28,415	28,015	27,488	27,711	28,220
Transportation and warehousing	38,489	40,368	41,504	44,431	46,410	48,525	50,346
Information	55,891	51,228	51,987	53,834	55,084	55,526	56,871
Finance and insurance	55,854	55,029	55,983	56,266	55,461	57,152	59,342
Real estate and rental and leasing	37,853	40,546	41,014	39,693	38,795	39,244	40,159
Professional, scientific, and technical services	61,121	63,411	65,005	66,208	65,794	66,306	68,210
Management of companies and enterprises	147,898	127,386	148,699	116,522	99,353	102,450	110,820
Administrative and waste services	25,643	26,801	27,886	29,497	29,904	29,739	30,023
Educational services	31,699	31,799	33,308	34,912	35,875	36,122	35,797
Health care and social assistance	43,391	45,133	46,889	47,976	48,944	48,533	49,399
Arts, entertainment, and recreation	29,878	32,872	34,074	33,225	32,949	32,806	34,671
Accommodation and food services	31,844	32,545	36,245	33,805	32,123	33,345	34,616
Other services, except public administration	27,458	28,724	29,537	30,282	30,384	30,909	31,324
Government and government enterprises	44,818	46,841	48,449	49,959	51,540	51,433	51,365

Table NV-10. Employment Characteristics by Family Type

(Number, percent.)

Family type and labor force status	2009 Total	2009 Families with own children under 18 years	2010 Total	2010 Families with own children under 18 years	2011 Total	2011 Families with own children under 18 years
All families	632,236	297,289	639,686	297,828	636,981	296,472
Family type and labor force status						
Married-couple families	451,914	197,306	452,361	193,732	450,072	191,500
Both husband and wife in labor force	54.4	64.8	52.0	64.3	50.9	62.3
Husband in labor force, wife not in labor force	23.2	30.7	22.5	28.7	23.7	32.2
Wife in labor force, husband not in labor force	7.2	3.4	8.7	5.3	7.9	3.8
Both husband and wife not in labor force	15.2	1.1	16.7	1.6	17.6	1.6
Other families	180,322	99,983	187,325	104,096	186,909	104,972
Female householder, no husband present	66.5	70.8	66.2	67.8	67.1	71.6
In labor force	50.1	58.9	49.1	57.7	50.8	62.0
Not in labor force	16.4	11.9	17.0	10.1	16.3	9.6
Male householder, no wife present	33.5	29.2	33.8	32.2	32.9	28.4
In labor force	29.2	27.4	28.9	30.0	27.0	26.6
Not in labor force	4.2	1.9	4.9	2.2	5.9	1.7

Table NV-11. School Enrollment and Educational Attainment, 2011

(Number, percent.)

Item	State	U.S.
Enrollment		
Total population 3 years and over, enrolled in school	684,009	83,131,910
Enrolled in nursery school or preschool (percent)	4.7	6.0
Enrolled in kindergarten (percent)	5.4	5.1
Enrolled in elementary school, grades 1-8 (percent)	42.1	39.5
Enrolled in high school, grades 9-12 (percent)	22.6	20.7
Enrolled in college or graduate school (percent)	25.2	28.7
Attainment		
Total population 25 years and over	1,810,960	206,471,670
Less than ninth grade (percent)	6.4	6.0
9th to 12th grade, no diploma (percent)	9.6	8.1
High school graduate, including equivalency (percent)	29.2	28.4
Some college, no degree (percent)	25.2	21.2
Associate's degree (percent)	7.2	7.8
Bachelor's degree (percent)	14.9	17.9
Graduate or professional degree (percent)	7.6	10.6
High school graduate or higher (percent)	84.0	85.9
Bachelor's degree or higher (percent)	22.5	28.5

Table NV-12. Educational Indicators

(Number, percent; data derived from National Center of Education Statistics.)

Item	State	U.S.
Public Schools, 2009–2010 (except where noted)		
Number of school districts	17	13,629
Number of schools	626	99,834
Number of students (in thousands)	429	49,373
Student-teacher ratio	19.4	15.4
Expenditures per student (dollars)	9,925	10,591
Averaged freshman graduation rate, 2008–2009	56.3	75.5[1]
Dropout rate, 2008–2009	5.1	4.1
Students eligible for free or reduced-price lunch (percent)	50.5	48.0
English language learners, 2010–2011 (percent)	19.4	9.8[1]
Students with IEP (percent)	11.2	13.1
Private Schools, 2009–2010 (except where noted)		
Number of schools	157	33,366
Number of students (in thousands)	20	4,700
High school graduates, 2008–2009	824	308,813
Student-teacher ratio	12.6	10.7

[1] U.S. total includes estimates for nonreporting states.

Table NV-13. Reported Voting and Registration of the Voting-Age Population, November 2012

(Numbers in thousands, percent.)

Item	Total population	Total citizen population	Registered			Voted		
			Total registered	Percent registered (total population)	Percent registered (total citizen population)	Total voted	Percent voted (total population)	Percent voted (total citizen population)
U.S. Total	235,248	215,081	153,157	65.1	71.2	132,948	56.5	61.8
State Total	2,039	1,808	1,176	57.7	65.0	1,048	51.4	57.9
Sex								
Male	1,015	910	574	56.5	63.1	511	50.3	56.2
Female	1,024	898	602	58.8	67.0	536	52.4	59.7
Race								
White alone	1,627	1,439	947	58.2	65.8	845	51.9	58.7
White, non-Hispanic alone	1,194	1,167	785	65.7	67.2	704	58.9	60.3
Black alone	169	164	107	63.3	65.1	101	60.2	61.8
Asian alone	152	115	82	54.4	71.9	67	44.5	58.8
Hispanic (of any race)	464	302	181	38.9	59.9	157	33.7	52.0
Age								
18 to 24 years	320	295	145	45.4	49.1	122	38.2	41.4
25 to 44 years	671	557	348	51.9	62.5	304	45.3	54.5
45 to 64 years	680	606	413	60.7	68.1	376	55.2	61.9
65 to 74 years	220	206	159	72.2	77.0	147	67.1	71.5
75 years and over	149	144	112	75.0	77.9	99	66.4	68.9

Table NV-14. Crime

(Number, rate per 100,000. Data are derived from the FBI Uniform Crime Reports.)

Item	State			U.S.		
	2010	2011	Percent change	2010	2011	Percent change
TOTAL POPULATION	2,704,283	2,723,322	0.7	309,330,219	311,591,917	0.7
VIOLENT CRIME						
Number	17,929	15,309	-14.6	1,251,248	1,203,564	-3.8
Rate	663.0	562.1	-15.2	404.5	386.3	-4.5
Murder and Nonnegligent Manslaughter						
Number	158	141	-10.8	14,722	14,612	-0.7
Rate	5.8	5.2	-10.3	4.8	4.7	-2.1
Forcible Rape						
Number	965	912	-5.5	85,593	83,425	-2.5
Rate	35.7	33.5	-6.2	27.7	26.8	-3.2
Robbery						
Number	5,298	4,299	-18.9	369,089	354,396	-4.0
Rate	195.9	157.9	-19.4	119.3	113.7	-4.7
Aggravated Assault						
Number	11,508	9,957	-13.5	781,844	751,131	-3.9
Rate	425.5	365.6	-14.1	252.8	241.1	-4.6
PROPERTY CRIME						
Number	75,004	69,731	-7.0	9,112,625	9,063,173	-0.5
Rate	2,773.5	2,560.5	-7.7	2,945.9	2,908.7	-1.3
Burglary						
Number	22,286	20,214	-9.3	2,168,459	2,188,005	0.9
Rate	824.1	742.3	-9.9	701.0	702.2	0.2
Larceny-Theft						
Number	42,533	40,032	-5.9	6,204,601	6,159,795	-0.7
Rate	1,572.8	1,470.0	-6.5	2,005.8	1,976.9	-1.4
Motor Vehicle Theft						
Number	10,185	9,485	-6.9	739,565	715,373	-3.3
Rate	376.6	348.3	-7.5	239.1	229.6	-4.0

Table NV-15. State Government Finances, 2011

(Dollar amounts in thousands, percent distribution.)

Item	Dollars	Percent distribution
Total Revenue	17,597,124	100.0
General revenue	10,443,848	59.3
Intergovernmental revenue	2,826,846	16.1
Taxes	6,332,128	36.0
General sales	2,931,547	16.7
Selective sales	1,757,619	10.0
License taxes	613,036	3.5
Individual income tax	0	0.0
Corporate income tax	0	0.0
Other taxes	1,029,926	5.9
Current charges	734,554	4.2
Miscellaneous general revenue	550,320	3.1
Utility revenue	89,488	0.5
Liquor stores revenue	0	0.0
Insurance trust revenue [1]	7,063,788	40.1
Total Expenditure	13,203,265	100.0
Intergovernmental expenditure	3,905,016	29.6
Direct expenditure	9,298,249	70.4
Current operation	5,006,214	37.9
Capital outlay	710,194	5.4
Insurance benefits and repayments	3,122,342	23.6
Assistance and subsidies	263,399	2.0
Interest on debt	196,100	1.5
Exhibit: Salaries and wages	1,540,187	11.7
Total Expenditure	13,203,265	100.0
General expenditure	9,990,585	75.7
Intergovernmental expenditure	3,905,016	29.6
Direct expenditure	6,085,569	46.1
General expenditure, by function:		
Education	4,148,254	31.4
Public welfare	2,127,591	16.1
Hospitals	236,250	1.8
Health	232,793	1.8
Highways	772,512	5.9
Police protection	101,648	0.8
Correction	275,865	2.1
Natural resources	129,928	1.0
Parks and recreation	19,759	0.1
Governmental administration	283,047	2.1
Interest on general debt	193,172	1.5
Other and unallocable	1,469,766	11.1
Utility expenditure	90,338	0.7
Liquor stores expenditure	0	0.0
Insurance trust expenditure	3,122,342	23.6
Debt at End of Fiscal Year	4,201,115	X
Cash and Security Holdings	27,490,790	X

X = Not applicable.
[1] Within insurance trust revenue, net earnings of state retirement systems is a calculated statistic (the item code in the data file is X08), and thus can be positive or negative. Net earnings is the sum of earnings on investments plus gains on investments minus losses on investments. The change made in 2002 for asset valuation from book to market value in accordance with Statement 34 of the Governmental Accounting Standards Board is reflected in the calculated statistics.

Table NV-16. State Government Tax Collections, 2012

(Dollars in thousands, percent.)

Item	Dollars	Percent distribution
Total Taxes	6,775,112	100.0
Property taxes	234,522	3.5
Sales and gross receipts	5,231,962	77.2
General sales and gross receipts	3,433,958	50.7
Selective sales and gross receipts	1,798,004	26.5
Alcoholic beverages	41,695	0.6
Amusements	910,839	13.4
Insurance premiums	237,861	3.5
Motor fuels	291,400	4.3
Pari-mutuels	0	0.0
Public utilities	22,717	0.3
Tobacco products	102,644	1.5
Other selective sales	190,848	2.8
Licenses	583,829	8.6
Alcoholic beverages	0	0.0
Amusements	95,410	1.4
Corporations in general	66,708	1.0
Hunting and fishing	9,810	0.1
Motor vehicle	160,840	2.4
Motor vehicle operators	22,036	0.3
Public utilities	0	0.0
Occupation and business, NEC	225,292	3.3
Other licenses	3,733	0.1
Income taxes	0	0.0
Individual income	0	0.0
Corporation net income	0	0.0
Other taxes	724,799	10.7
Death and gift	0	0.0
Documentary and stock transfer	52,131	0.8
Severance	303,038	4.5
Taxes, NEC	369,630	5.5

Leading Exports, 2012

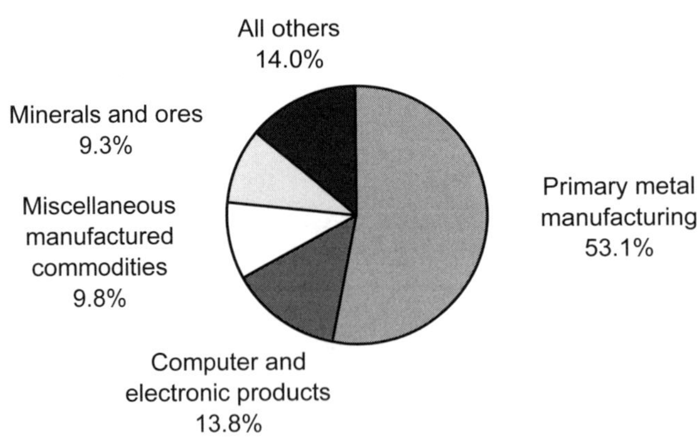

NEW HAMPSHIRE

Facts and Figures

Location: Northeastern United States; bordered on the N by Canada (Quebec), on the E by Maine, on the SE by the Atlantic Ocean, on the S by Massachusetts, and on the W by Vermont

Area: 9,350 sq. mi. (24,216 sq. km.); rank—46th

Population: 1,320,718 (2012 est.); rank—42nd

Principal Cities: capital—Concord; largest—Manchester

Statehood: June 21, 1788; 9th state

U.S. Congress: 2 senators, 2 representatives

State Motto: Live Free or Die

State Song: "Old New Hampshire"

State Nickname: The Granite State

Abbreviations: NH; N.H.

State Symbols: flower—purple lilac; tree—white birch; bird—purple finch

At a Glance

- With an increase in population of 7.2 percent, New Hampshire ranked 36th among the states in growth from 2000 to 2009.
- An estimated 8,500 marriages took place in New Hampshire in 2009, compared to 4,900 divorces.
- New Hampshire's violent crime rate in 2011 was 188.0 per 100,000 population, compared to 386.3 for the entire nation.
- In the 2012 election, 69.4 percent of New Hampshire's eligible voters voted, compared to 61.8 percent of eligible voters nationwide.
- In 2007, New Hampshire exported $19 million worth of agricultural products, less than 1 percent of the U.S. total.

Table NH-1. Population by Age, Sex, Race, and Hispanic Origin

(Number, percent, except where noted.)

Sex, age, race, and Hispanic origin	2000	2010	2012[1]	Average annual percent change, 2010–2012
Total Population	1,235,786	1,316,470	1,320,718	0.1
Percent of total U.S. population	0.4	0.4	0.4	X
Sex				
Male	607,687	649,394	652,237	0.1
Female	628,099	667,076	668,481	0.1
Age				
Under 5 years	75,685	69,806	65,953	-1.9
5 to 19 years	268,480	255,996	248,637	-1.0
20 to 64 years	743,651	812,400	812,325	-
65 years and over	147,970	178,268	193,803	2.7
Median age (years)	37.1	41.1	42.0	0.7
Race and Hispanic Origin				
One race				
White	1,186,851	1,248,321	1,247,076	-
Black	9,035	16,365	18,374	3.6
American Indian and Alaska Native	2,964	3,530	3,633	0.9
Asian	15,931	28,933	31,126	2.3
Native Hawaiian or Other Pacific Islander	371	532	596	3.6
Two or more races	13,214	18,789	19,913	1.9
Hispanic (of any race)	20,489	38,688	42,195	2.8

X = Not applicable.
- = Zero or rounds to zero.
[1] Population figures for 2012 are July 1 estimates. The 2010 estimates are taken from the 2010 Census.

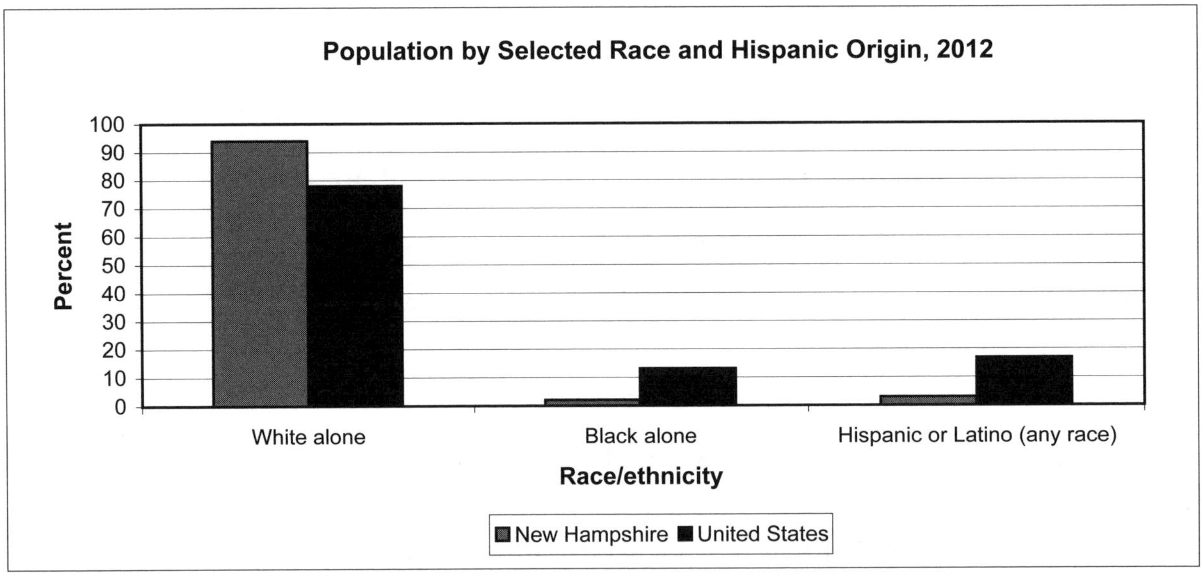

Table NH-2. Marital Status

(Number, percent distribution.)

Sex, age, race, and Hispanic origin	2000	2010	2011
Males, 15 Years and Over	476,409	529,439	534,297
Never married	27.7	30.5	30.9
Now married, except separated	59.1	54.7	55.6
Separated	1.2	1.3	1.1
Widowed	2.4	2.6	2.2
Divorced	9.6	10.9	10.3
Females, 15 Years and Over	502,232	555,698	556,645
Never married	22.3	25.4	25.3
Now married, except separated	55.7	51.4	51.6
Separated	1.5	1.3	1.5
Widowed	9.2	8.6	8.4
Divorced	11.3	13.4	13.2

Table NH-3. Households and Housing Characteristics

(Number, percent, dollars.)

Item	2000	2010	2011	Average annual percent change, 2000–2011
Total Households	474,606	515,431	516,454	0.7
Family households	323,651	344,057	349,501	0.7
Married-couple family	262,438	274,195	276,775	0.5
Other family	61,213	69,862	72,726	1.6
Male householder, no wife present	18,261	22,205	21,489	1.5
Female householder, no husband present	42,952	47,657	51,237	1.6
Nonfamily households	150,955	171,374	166,953	0.9
Householder living alone	116,014	130,327	130,657	1.1
Householder not living alone	34,941	41,047	36,296	0.3
Housing Characteristics				
Total housing units	547,024	614,996	617,702	1.1
Occupied housing units	474,606	515,431	516,454	0.7
Owner occupied	330,700	369,448	369,070	1.0
Renter occupied	143,906	145,983	147,384	0.2
Average size	2.53	2.48	2.47	-0.2
Financial Characteristics				
Median gross rent of renter-occupied housing	646	951	939	3.8
Median monthly owner costs for housing units with a mortgage	1,226	1,853	1,884	4.5
Median value of owner-occupied housing units	133,300	243,000	237,500	6.5

Table NH-4. Migration, Origin, and Language

(Number, percent.)

Characteristic	State			U.S.		
	2010	2011	Percent change	2010	2011	Percent change
Residence 1 Year Ago						
Population 1 year and over	1,303,865	1,305,678	0.1	305,628,607	307,900,319	0.7
Same house	85.8	87.4	1.9	84.6	84.8	0.2
Different house in the U.S.	13.8	12.2	-11.6	14.8	14.6	-1.4
Same county	8.4	7.1	-15.5	9.4	9.2	-2.1
Different county	5.4	5.1	-5.6	5.4	5.4	-
Same state	2.4	2.3	-4.2	3.2	3.1	-3.1
Different state	3.0	2.8	-6.7	2.2	2.3	4.5
Abroad	0.4	0.4	-	0.6	0.6	-
Place of Birth						
Native born	1,247,017	1,244,351	-0.2	269,393,835	271,214,059	0.7
Male	49.4	49.6	0.4	49.2	49.2	-
Female	50.6	50.4	-0.4	50.8	50.8	-
Foreign born	69,742	73,843	5.9	39,955,854	40,377,860	1.1
Male	45.8	46.1	0.7	49.1	48.9	-0.4
Female	54.2	53.9	-0.6	50.9	51.1	0.4
Foreign born; naturalized U.S. citizen	37,647	38,286	1.7	17,476,082	18,140,192	3.8
Male	43.4	46.8	7.8	45.8	45.8	-
Female	56.6	53.2	-6.0	54.2	54.2	-
Foreign born; not a U.S. citizen	32,095	35,557	10.8	22,479,772	22,237,668	-1.1
Male	48.7	45.4	-6.8	51.6	51.5	-0.2
Female	51.3	54.6	6.4	48.4	48.5	0.2
Entered 2000 or later	33.2	36.4	9.6	34.7	35.7	2.9
Entered 1990 to 1999	22.8	24.1	5.7	27.2	26.7	-1.8
Entered before 1990	44.0	39.5	-10.2	38.1	37.6	-1.3
World Region of Birth, Foreign						
Foreign-born population, excluding population born at sea	69,742	73,843	5.9	39,955,673	40,377,757	1.1
Europe	23.9	25.8	7.9	12.1	12.1	-
Asia	33.0	34.8	5.5	28.2	28.6	1.4
Africa	7.0	6.7	-4.3	4	4.1	2.5
Oceania	0.8	0.6	-25.0	0.5	0.5	-
Latin America	20.3	20.3	-	53.1	52.6	-0.9
North America	14.9	11.8	-20.8	2	2.0	-
Language Spoken at Home and Ability to Speak English						
Population 5 years and over	1,247,886	1,250,588	0.2	289,215,746	291,524,091	0.8
English only	92.2	92.2	-	79.4	79.2	-0.3
Language other than English	7.8	7.8	-	20.6	20.8	1.0
Speaks English less than "very well"	2.4	2.3	-4.2	8.7	8.7	-

- = Zero or rounds to zero.

Table NH-5. Median Income and Poverty Status, 2011

(Number, percent, except as noted.)

Characteristic	State		U.S.	
	Number	Percent	Number	Percent
Median Income				
Households (dollars)	62,647	X	50,502	X
Families (dollars)	76,609	X	61,455	X
Below Poverty Level (All People)	112,715	8.8	48,452,035	15.9
Sex				
Male	50,927	8.0	21,825,281	14.7
Female	61,788	9.6	26,626,754	17.2
Age				
Under 18 years	33,031	12.0	16,386,500	22.5
Related children under 18 years	32,092	11.7	16,087,074	22.2
18 to 64 years	68,785	8.3	28,335,079	14.8
65 years and over	10,899	6.2	3,730,456	9.3

X = Not applicable.

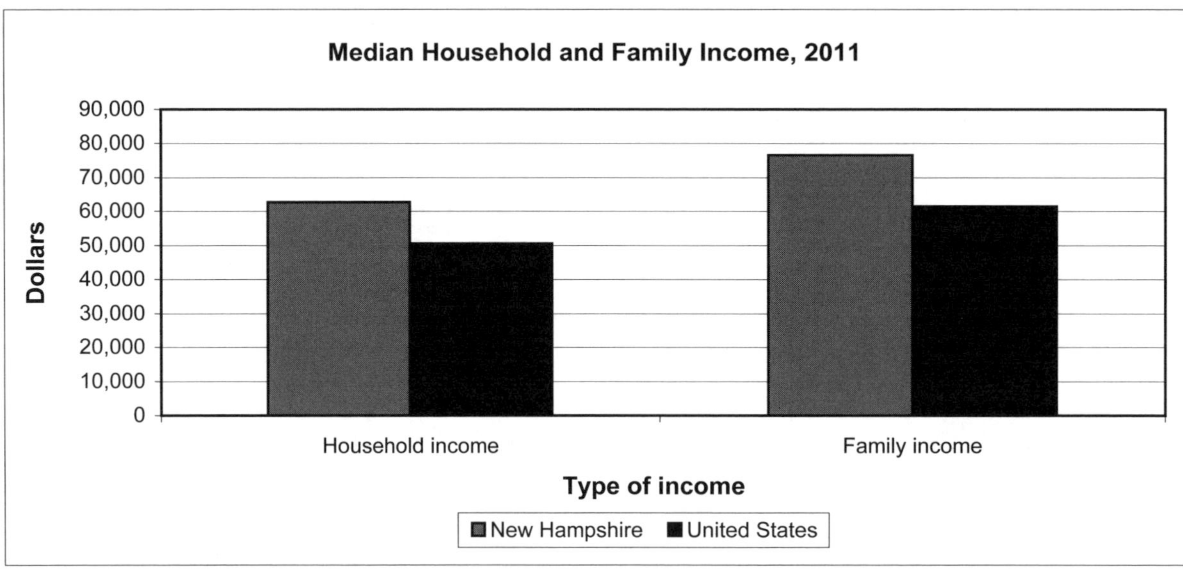

Table NH-6. Health Insurance Coverage Status for the Civilian Noninstitutionalized Population and Children Under 18 Years of Age

(Numbers in thousands, percent.)

Item	2004	2005	2006	2007	2008	2009	2010	2011
Civilian Noninstitutionalized Population	1,293	1,301	1,309	1,314	1,299	1,309	1,303	1,304
Covered by Private or Public Insurance								
Number	1,163	1,175	119	1,177	1,159	1,175	1,157	1,167
Percent	89.9	90.3	88.5	89.5	89.2	89.8	88.9	89.5
Not Covered								
Number	131	126	150	137	140	134	145	137
Percent	10.1	9.7	11.5	10.5	10.8	10.2	11.1	10.5
Percent in the U.S. not covered	14.9	15.3	15.8	15.3	15.1	15.1	15.5	15.1
Children Under 18 Years of Age	305	298	301	296	293	289	286	279
Covered by Private or Public Insurance								
Number	286	282	278	277	278	276	272	269
Percent	93.8	94.7	92.5	93.5	94.9	95.3	95.2	96.3
Not Covered								
Number	19	16	22	19	15	13	14	10
Percent	6.2	5.3	7.5	6.5	5.1	4.7	4.8	3.7
Percent in the U.S. not covered	10.5	10.9	11.7	11.0	9.7	8.6	8.0	7.5

Table NH-7. Employment Status by Demographic Group, Preliminary 2012

(Numbers in thousands, percent.)

Characteristic	Civilian noninstitutional population	Civilian labor force		Employed		Unemployed	
		Number	Percent of population	Number	Percent of population	Number	Percent of population
Total	1,065	739	69.4	697	65.5	42	5.6
Sex							
Male	521	387	74.2	363	69.6	24	6.2
Female	544	352	64.7	335	61.5	17	4.9
Race, Sex, and Hispanic Origin							
White	1,015	702	69.2	663	65.3	39	5.6
Male	498	368	74.0	345	69.4	23	6.2
Female	517	334	64.6	318	61.5	16	4.9
Black or African American	12	9	75.7	8	69.3	1	8.4
Male	NA	NA	NA	NA	NA	NA	NA
Female	NA	NA	NA	NA	NA	NA	NA
Hispanic	27	22	82.2	20	73.6	2	10.5
Male	14	12	86.9	11	77.0	1	11.4
Female	13	10	77.0	9	69.6	1	9.4
Age							
16 to 19 years	73	33	45.4	27	37.6	6	17.1
20 to 24 years	84	67	79.6	59	70.4	8	11.6
25 to 34 years	152	129	85.3	123	81.0	7	5.1
35 to 44 years	164	143	87.1	136	83.0	7	4.7
45 to 54 years	219	189	86.6	182	83.3	7	3.7
55 to 64 years	187	136	73.1	131	70.0	6	4.2
65 years and over	188	42	22.1	39	21.0	2	5.1

NOTE: Data in Table 7 are from the Current Population Survey (CPS) and do not match the estimates in Table 8. See notes and definitions for further information.
NA = Not available.

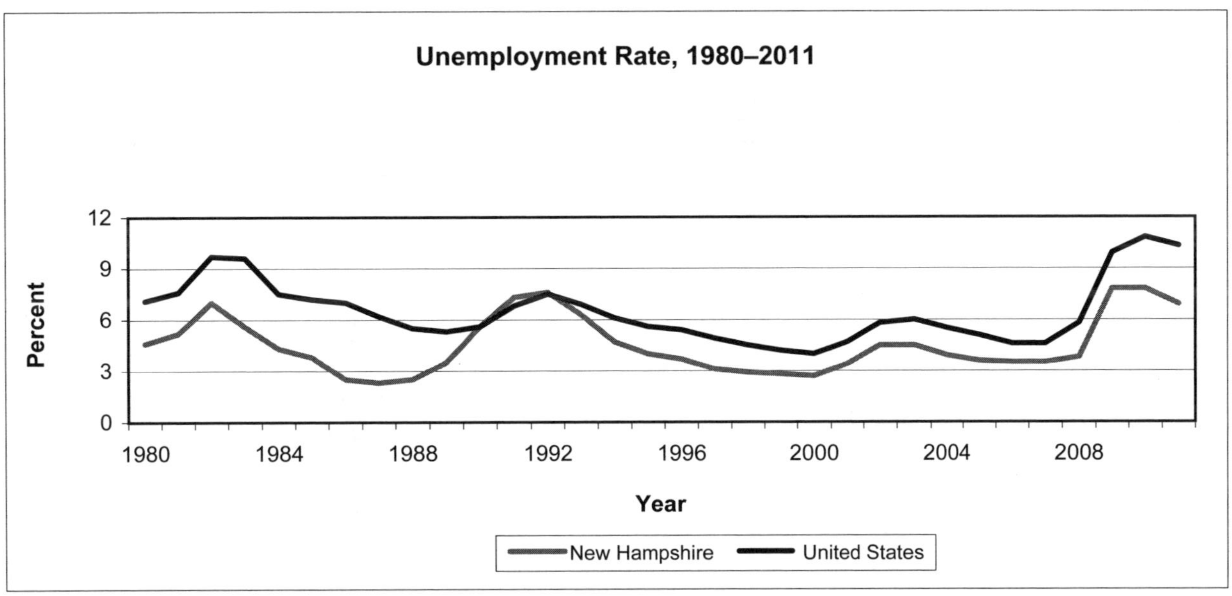

Table NH-8. Employment Status of the Civilian Noninstitutional Population Age 16 Years and Over

(Number, percent.)

Year	Civilian labor force	Civilian participation rate	Employed	Unemployed	Unemployment rate
2005	723,402	71.1	697,120	26,282	3.6
2006	732,808	71.2	707,129	25,709	3.5
2007	738,212	71.1	712,231	25,981	3.5
2008	738,858	70.7	710,623	28,235	3.8
2009	754,213	70.2	695,175	59,038	7.8
2010	742,209	69.6	684,575	57,634	7.8
2011	735,366	68.5	684,806	50,560	6.9

Table NH-9. Employment and Average Wages by Industry

(Estimates before 2007 are based on the 2002 *North American Industry Classification System* [NAICS]. Estimates from 2007 onward are based on the 2007 NAICS.)

Industry	2005	2006	2007	2008	2009	2010	2011
	Number of jobs						
Wage and Salary Employment by Industry	650,099	657,187	660,712	659,277	636,169	633,655	638,856
Farm Wage and Salary Employment	1,248	1,131	1,081	1,180	1,139	1,141	1,210
Nonfarm Wage and Salary Employment	648,851	656,056	659,631	658,097	635,030	632,514	637,646
Private wage and salary employment	556,958	562,461	564,948	562,461	538,792	534,869	541,705
Forestry, fishing, and related activities	923	852	805	810	785	775	778
Mining	562	587	682	607	510	490	493
Utilities	2,762	2,519	2,521	2,454	2,532	2,513	2,474
Construction	30,605	30,585	28,568	27,161	23,700	22,437	23,338
Manufacturing	80,126	78,529	77,974	76,095	68,115	65,821	66,667
Durable goods manufacturing	61,085	59,657	59,763	58,096	51,982	50,313	51,168
Nondurable goods manufacturing	19,041	18,872	18,211	17,999	16,133	15,508	15,499
Wholesale trade	27,671	28,183	28,574	28,289	26,649	26,093	26,383
Retail trade	98,949	99,826	99,293	98,298	94,565	94,033	94,604
Transportation and warehousing	13,229	13,225	13,139	12,930	12,383	12,346	12,524
Information	12,738	12,577	12,377	12,547	12,181	11,220	11,151
Finance and insurance	28,886	29,330	29,610	29,201	27,870	27,525	28,173
Real estate and rental and leasing	8,517	8,347	8,111	7,850	7,354	7,044	7,051
Professional, scientific, and technical services	28,326	29,583	30,525	31,433	29,948	29,686	30,345
Management of companies and enterprises	7,391	7,655	7,889	8,170	7,968	8,013	8,098
Administrative and waste services	25,254	26,389	27,815	27,753	25,864	27,661	28,856
Educational services	22,144	21,887	22,034	22,160	22,229	22,043	22,280
Health care and social assistance	75,920	78,529	80,862	82,900	84,749	85,391	85,739
Arts, entertainment, and recreation	11,073	11,181	10,969	11,099	11,081	11,199	11,479
Accommodation and food services	53,018	53,554	53,712	53,355	51,513	52,061	52,651
Other services, except public administration	28,864	29,123	29,488	29,349	28,796	28,518	28,621
Government and government enterprises	91,893	93,595	94,683	95,636	96,238	97,645	95,941
	Dollars						
Average Wages and Salaries by Industry	39,979	41,816	43,278	44,249	44,197	45,150	46,380
Average Farm Wages and Salaries	21,842	27,668	32,781	28,812	28,356	26,736	22,556
Average Nonfarm Wages and Salaries	40,014	41,840	43,295	44,277	44,225	45,183	46,425
Average private wages and salaries	40,644	42,644	44,066	44,918	44,684	45,896	47,183
Forestry, fishing, and related activities	31,061	33,964	37,652	34,717	34,851	36,034	37,478
Mining	49,548	49,617	50,419	50,936	52,245	55,849	55,507
Utilities	75,073	74,877	77,457	91,296	87,771	87,860	96,418
Construction	45,262	46,923	48,389	49,942	49,068	49,392	50,144
Manufacturing	51,931	55,506	57,843	58,738	58,299	61,926	63,219
Durable goods manufacturing	54,522	58,768	61,193	62,066	61,533	65,486	66,697
Nondurable goods manufacturing	43,617	45,193	46,849	47,995	47,876	50,376	51,735
Wholesale trade	66,368	68,607	71,292	72,268	70,957	74,646	77,793
Retail trade	26,071	26,288	26,490	26,502	26,350	26,760	27,406
Transportation and warehousing	33,919	35,339	36,016	36,684	36,602	37,434	38,705
Information	61,682	62,827	67,251	71,344	69,375	75,172	74,503
Finance and insurance	65,394	68,454	71,078	73,916	74,362	78,080	81,346
Real estate and rental and leasing	40,817	39,767	37,958	43,846	43,993	40,820	47,017
Professional, scientific, and technical services	63,918	68,947	69,018	73,296	72,500	74,270	76,812
Management of companies and enterprises	93,353	116,294	105,067	77,627	76,944	80,829	82,361
Administrative and waste services	32,977	34,778	38,534	38,712	40,207	40,031	40,296
Educational services	33,136	35,125	37,046	38,585	39,360	40,020	40,638
Health care and social assistance	39,225	40,599	42,406	44,568	45,709	46,500	47,829
Arts, entertainment, and recreation	21,287	23,106	25,338	21,981	21,073	21,263	21,597
Accommodation and food services	16,988	17,448	18,597	18,151	18,462	18,880	19,339
Other services, except public administration	26,274	27,227	28,060	29,282	28,856	29,739	30,126
Government and government enterprises	36,191	37,007	38,696	40,505	41,653	41,277	42,148

Table NH-10. Employment Characteristics by Family Type

(Number, percent.)

Family type and labor force status	2009		2010		2011	
	Total	Families with own children under 18 years	Total	Families with own children under 18 years	Total	Families with own children under 18 years
All families	336,491	148,230	344,057	143,634	349,501	145,570
Family type and labor force status						
Married-couple families	270,926	108,192	274,195	103,546	276,775	103,769
Both husband and wife in labor force	62.2	75.5	60.9	75.5	60.1	72.8
Husband in labor force, wife not in labor force	17.3	20.6	16.8	21.1	17.1	22.6
Wife in labor force, husband not in labor force	7.0	2.8	7.5	2.5	8.0	3.3
Both husband and wife not in labor force	13.5	1.0	14.8	1.0	14.8	1.3
Other families	65,565	40,038	69,862	40,088	72,726	41,801
Female householder, no husband present	69.9	72.9	68.2	68.7	70.5	72.5
In labor force	52.5	60.6	51.4	55.9	50.4	59.0
Not in labor force	17.4	12.3	16.9	12.8	20.0	13.5
Male householder, no wife present	30.1	27.1	31.8	31.3	29.5	27.5
In labor force	25.8	25.7	28.1	29.8	23.9	24.9
Not in labor force	4.3	1.4	3.7	1.5	5.7	2.6

Table NH-11. School Enrollment and Educational Attainment, 2011

(Number, percent.)

Item	State	U.S.
Enrollment		
Total population 3 years and over, enrolled in school	324,586	83,131,910
Enrolled in nursery school or preschool (percent)	5.5	6.0
Enrolled in kindergarten (percent)	4.6	5.1
Enrolled in elementary school, grades 1-8 (percent)	39.2	39.5
Enrolled in high school, grades 9-12 (percent)	21.8	20.7
Enrolled in college or graduate school (percent)	28.8	28.7
Attainment		
Total population 25 years and over	914,207	206,471,670
Less than ninth grade (percent)	2.8	6.0
9th to 12th grade, no diploma (percent)	5.8	8.1
High school graduate, including equivalency (percent)	29.3	28.4
Some college, no degree (percent)	19.2	21.2
Associate's degree (percent)	9.5	7.8
Bachelor's degree (percent)	21.0	17.9
Graduate or professional degree (percent)	12.4	10.6
High school graduate or higher (percent)	91.4	85.9
Bachelor's degree or higher (percent)	33.4	28.5

Table NH-12. Educational Indicators

(Number, percent; data derived from National Center of Education Statistics.)

Item	State	U.S.
Public Schools, 2009–2010 (except where noted)		
Number of school districts	180	13,629
Number of schools	484	99,834
Number of students (in thousands)	197	49,373
Student-teacher ratio	12.7	15.4
Expenditures per student (dollars)	14,004	10,591
Averaged freshman graduation rate, 2008–2009	84.3	75.5[1]
Dropout rate, 2008–2009	1.7	4.1
Students eligible for free or reduced-price lunch (percent)	25.2	48.0
English language learners, 2010–2011 (percent)	2.0	9.8[1]
Students with IEP (percent)	15.3	13.1
Private Schools, 2009–2010 (except where noted)		
Number of schools	285	33,366
Number of students (in thousands)	21	4,700
High school graduates, 2008–2009	2,463	308,813
Student-teacher ratio	8.0	10.7

[1] U.S. total includes estimates for nonreporting states.

Table NH-13. Reported Voting and Registration of the Voting-Age Population, November 2012

(Numbers in thousands, percent.)

Item	Total population	Total citizen population	Registered			Voted		
			Total registered	Percent registered (total population)	Percent registered (total citizen population)	Total voted	Percent voted (total population)	Percent voted (total citizen population)
U.S. Total	235,248	215,081	153,157	65.1	71.2	132,948	56.5	61.8
State Total	1,028	991	752	73.1	75.9	688	66.9	69.4
Sex								
Male	503	482	353	70.3	73.4	322	64.0	66.8
Female	525	509	398	75.8	78.2	366	69.7	71.9
Race								
White alone	980	958	730	74.5	76.1	670	68.4	69.9
White, non-Hispanic alone	952	935	715	75.1	76.4	655	68.8	70.0
Black alone	12	10	7	B	B	6	B	B
Asian alone	20	9	5	B	B	4	B	B
Hispanic (of any race)	29	23	15	B	B	15	B	B
Age								
18 to 24 years	123	119	71	57.5	59.6	61	50.0	51.9
25 to 44 years	309	290	199	64.3	68.6	180	58.3	62.2
45 to 64 years	425	414	337	79.4	81.5	312	73.4	75.4
65 to 74 years	97	96	84	87.0	87.4	79	81.6	82.0
75 years and over	74	72	61	B	B	55	B	B

B = Base is less than 75,000 and therefore too small to show the derived measure.

Table NH-14. Crime

(Number, rate per 100,000. Data are derived from the FBI Uniform Crime Reports.)

Item	State			U.S.		
	2010	2011	Percent change	2010	2011	Percent change
TOTAL POPULATION	1,316,807	1,318,194	0.1	309,330,219	311,591,917	0.7
VIOLENT CRIME						
Number	2,204	2,478	12.4	1,251,248	1,203,564	-3.8
Rate	167.4	188.0	12.3	404.5	386.3	-4.5
Murder and Nonnegligent Manslaughter						
Number	13	17	30.8	14,722	14,612	-0.7
Rate	1.0	1.3	30.0	4.8	4.7	-2.1
Forcible Rape						
Number	411	429	4.4	85,593	83,425	-2.5
Rate	31.2	32.5	4.2	27.7	26.8	-3.2
Robbery						
Number	450	474	5.3	369,089	354,396	-4.0
Rate	34.2	36.0	5.3	119.3	113.7	-4.7
Aggravated Assault						
Number	1,330	1,558	17.1	781,844	751,131	-3.9
Rate	101.0	118.2	17.0	252.8	241.1	-4.6
PROPERTY CRIME						
Number	29,230	30,106	3.0	9,112,625	9,063,173	-0.5
Rate	2,219.8	2,283.9	2.9	2,945.9	2,908.7	-1.3
Burglary						
Number	5,444	5,479	0.6	2,168,459	2,188,005	0.9
Rate	413.4	436.1	5.5	701.0	702.2	0.2
Larceny-Theft						
Number	22,789	23,383	2.6	6,204,601	6,159,795	-0.7
Rate	1,730.6	1,773.9	2.5	2,005.8	1,976.9	-1.4
Motor Vehicle Theft						
Number	997	974	-2.3	739,565	715,373	-3.3
Rate	75.7	73.9	-2.4	239.1	229.6	-4.0

Table NH-15. State Government Finances, 2011

(Dollar amounts in thousands, percent distribution.)

Item	Dollars	Percent distribution
Total Revenue	8,521,161	100.0
General revenue	6,252,239	73.4
Intergovernmental revenue	2,158,531	25.3
Taxes	2,320,014	27.2
General sales	0	
Selective sales	904,162	10.6
License taxes	271,223	3.2
Individual income tax	83,475	1.0
Corporate income tax	583,063	6.8
Other taxes	478,091	5.6
Current charges	985,980	11.6
Miscellaneous general revenue	787,714	9.2
Utility revenue	0.0	0.0
Liquor stores revenue	539,915	6.3
Insurance trust revenue [1]	1,729,007	20.3
Total Expenditure	7,638,166	100.0
Intergovernmental expenditure	1,191,097	15.6
Direct expenditure	6,447,069	84.4
Current operation	4,664,747	61.1
Capital outlay	425,324	5.6
Insurance benefits and repayments	799,660	10.5
Assistance and subsidies	164,490	2.2
Interest on debt	392,848	5.1
Exhibit: Salaries and wages	946,790	12.4
Total Expenditure	7,638,166	100.0
General expenditure	6,375,565	83.5
Intergovernmental expenditure	1,191,097	15.6
Direct expenditure	5,184,468	67.9
General expenditure, by function:		
Education	2,015,841	26.4
Public welfare	1,944,977	25.5
Hospitals	50,201	0.7
Health	88,265	1.2
Highways	552,523	7.2
Police protection	55,997	0.7
Correction	112,666	1.5
Natural resources	67,689	0.9
Parks and recreation	34,529	0.5
Governmental administration	256,033	3.4
Interest on general debt	392,848	5.1
Other and unallocable	803,996	10.5
Utility expenditure	8,549	0.1
Liquor stores expenditure	454,392	5.9
Insurance trust expenditure	799,660	10.5
Debt at End of Fiscal Year	8,450,218	X
Cash and Security Holdings	12,686,507	X

X = Not applicable.
[1] Within insurance trust revenue, net earnings of state retirement systems is a calculated statistic (the item code in the data file is X08), and thus can be positive or negative. Net earnings is the sum of earnings on investments plus gains on investments minus losses on investments. The change made in 2002 for asset valuation from book to market value in accordance with Statement 34 of the Governmental Accounting Standards Board is reflected in the calculated statistics.

Table NH-16. State Government Tax Collections, 2012

(Dollars in thousands, percent.)

Item	Dollars	Percent distribution
Total Taxes	2,206,329	100.0
Property taxes	380,682	17.3
Sales and gross receipts	875,037	39.7
General sales and gross receipts	0	0.0
Selective sales and gross receipts	875,037	39.7
Alcoholic beverages	9,723	0.4
Amusements	431	-
Insurance premiums	73,808	3.3
Motor fuels	143,794	6.5
Pari-mutuels	483	-
Public utilities	83,884	3.8
Tobacco products	215,161	9.8
Other selective sales	347,753	15.8
Licenses	263,683	12.0
Alcoholic beverages	4,011	0.2
Amusements	222	-
Corporations in general	47,308	2.1
Hunting and fishing	10,031	0.5
Motor vehicle	94,063	4.3
Motor vehicle operators	12,803	0.6
Public utilities	6,980	0.3
Occupation and business, NEC	87,606	4.0
Other licenses	659	-
Income taxes	602,866	27.3
Individual income	81,557	3.7
Corporation net income	521,309	23.6
Other taxes	84,061	3.8
Death and gift	0	0.0
Documentary and stock transfer	84,061	3.8
Severance	0	0.0
Taxes, NEC	0	0.0

- = Rounds to zero.

Leading Exports, 2012

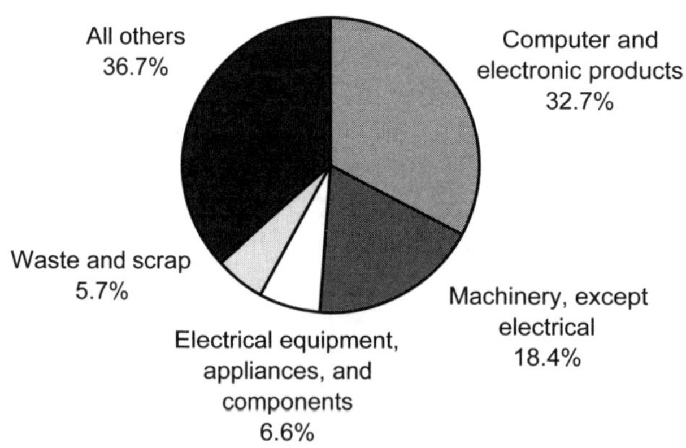

NEW JERSEY

Facts and Figures

Location: Middle Atlantic region of the United States; bordered on the N and NE by New York, on the E by the Atlantic Ocean, on the S by Delaware Bay, and on the W by Delaware and Pennsylvania

Area: 8,721 sq. mi. (22,588 sq. km.); rank—47th

Population: 8,864,590 (2012 est.); rank—11th

Principal Cities: capital—Trenton; largest—Newark

Statehood: December 18, 1787; 3rd state

U.S. Congress: 2 senators, 12 representatives

State Motto: Liberty and Prosperity

State Song: None

State Nickname: The Garden State

Abbreviations: NJ; N.J.

State Symbols: flower—common meadow violet; tree—red oak; bird—Eastern goldfinch

At a Glance

- With an increase in population of 3.5 percent, New Jersey ranked 22nd among the states in growth from 2000 to 2009.
- An estimated 46,300 marriages took place in New Jersey in 2009, compared to 24,000 divorces.
- New Jersey's median household income in 2007 was $67,458, and 10.4 percent of the population lived below the poverty level.
- In the 2012 election, 61.9 percent of New Jersey's eligible voters voted, compared to 61.8 percent of eligible voters nationwide.
- In 2007, New Jersey exported $245 million worth of agricultural products, less than 1 percent of the U.S. total.

Table NJ-1. Population by Age, Sex, Race, and Hispanic Origin

(Number, percent, except where noted.)

Sex, age, race, and Hispanic origin	2000	2010	2012[1]	Average annual percent change, 2010–2012
Total Population	8,414,350	8,791,894	8,864,590	0.3
Percent of total U.S. population	3.0	2.8	2.8	X
Sex				
Male	4,082,813	4,279,600	4,323,685	0.3
Female	4,331,357	4,512,294	4,540,905	0.2
Age				
Under 5 years	563,785	541,020	527,649	-0.8
5 to 19 years	1,720,332	1,750,184	1,728,623	-0.4
20 to 64 years	5,017,107	5,314,697	5,357,763	0.3
65 years and over	1,113,136	1,185,993	1,250,555	1.7
Median age (years)	36.7	39.0	39.3	0.3
Race and Hispanic Origin				
One race				
White	6,104,705	6,546,498	6,538,430	-
Black	1,141,821	1,282,005	1,298,879	0.4
American Indian and Alaska Native	19,492	49,907	52,255	1.5
Asian	480,276	746,212	794,923	2.0
Native Hawaiian or Other Pacific Islander	3,329	7,731	8,228	2.0
Two or more races	13,755	159,541	171,875	2.4
Hispanic (of any race)	1,117,191	1,606,006	1,637,921	0.6

X = Not applicable.
- = Zero or rounds to zero.
[1] Population figures for 2012 are July 1 estimates. The 2010 estimates are taken from the 2010 Census.

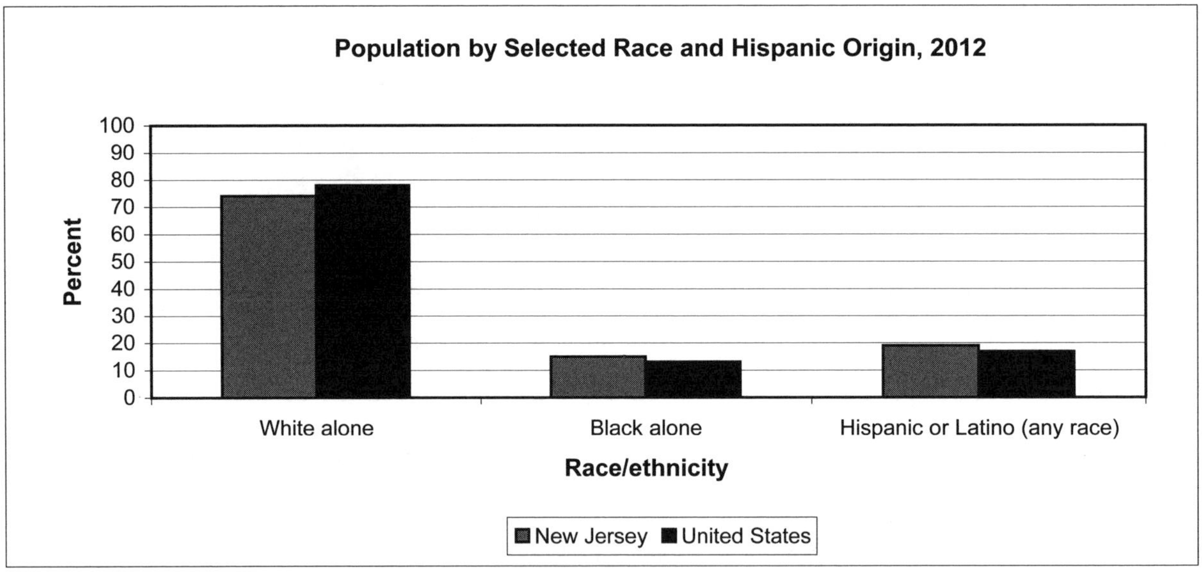

Table NJ-2. Marital Status

(Number, percent distribution.)

Sex, age, race, and Hispanic origin	2000	2010	2011
Males, 15 Years and Over	3,176,413	3,419,050	3,440,823
Never married	31.1	36.4	36.7
Now married, except separated	57.7	52.1	51.8
Separated	2.0	1.8	1.6
Widowed	2.9	2.6	2.7
Divorced	6.2	7.1	7.1
Females, 15 Years and Over	3,478,920	3,690,673	3,701,591
Never married	25.3	30.2	31.0
Now married, except separated	51.8	47.6	46.6
Separated	2.7	2.2	2.5
Widowed	11.5	10.2	9.9
Divorced	8.7	9.8	10.0

Table NJ-3. Households and Housing Characteristics

(Number, percent, dollars.)

Item	2000	2010	2011	Average annual percent change, 2000–2011
Total Households	3,064,645	3,172,421	3,167,629	0.3
Family households	2,154,539	2,185,732	2,191,404	0.1
Married-couple family	1,638,322	1,614,230	1,607,317	-0.2
Other family	516,217	571,502	584,087	1.1
Male householder, no wife present	129,205	154,036	152,932	1.5
Female householder, no husband present	387,012	417,466	431,155	1.0
Nonfamily households	910,106	986,689	976,225	0.6
Householder living alone	751,287	827,294	829,045	0.9
Householder not living alone	158,819	159,395	147,180	-0.6
Housing Characteristics				
Total housing units	3,310,275	3,554,909	3,562,720	0.6
Occupied housing units	3,064,645	3,172,421	3,167,629	0.3
Owner occupied	2,011,473	2,106,728	2,060,480	0.2
Renter occupied	1,053,172	1,065,693	1,107,149	0.4
Average size	2.68	2.72	2.73	0.2
Financial Characteristics				
Median gross rent of renter-occupied housing	751	1,114	1,135	4.3
Median monthly owner costs for housing units with a mortgage	1,560	2,370	2,397	4.5
Median value of owner-occupied housing units	170,800	339,200	324,900	7.5

Table NJ-4. Migration, Origin, and Language

(Number, percent.)

Characteristic	State			U.S.		
	2010	2011	Percent change	2010	2011	Percent change
Residence 1 Year Ago						
Population 1 year and over	8,709,933	8,719,952	0.1	305,628,607	307,900,319	0.7
Same house	90.0	89.7	-0.3	84.6	84.8	0.2
Different house in the U.S.	9.3	9.6	3.2	14.8	14.6	-1.4
Same county	5.7	5.9	3.5	9.4	9.2	-2.1
Different county	3.6	3.7	2.8	5.4	5.4	-
Same state	2.2	2.1	-4.5	3.2	3.1	-3.1
Different state	1.5	1.6	6.7	2.2	2.3	4.5
Abroad	0.6	0.7	16.7	0.6	0.6	-
Place of Birth						
Native born	6,957,043	6,927,969	-0.4	269,393,835	271,214,059	0.7
Male	48.6	48.7	0.2	49.2	49.2	-
Female	51.4	51.3	-0.2	50.8	50.8	-
Foreign born	1,844,581	1,893,186	2.6	39,955,854	40,377,860	1.1
Male	48.8	48.9	0.2	49.1	48.9	-0.4
Female	51.2	51.1	-0.2	50.9	51.1	0.4
Foreign born; naturalized U.S. citizen	919,882	959,342	4.3	17,476,082	18,140,192	3.8
Male	46.6	46.3	-0.6	45.8	45.8	-
Female	53.4	53.7	0.6	54.2	54.2	-
Foreign born; not a U.S. citizen	924,699	933,844	1.0	22,479,772	22,237,668	-1.1
Male	51.0	51.6	1.2	51.6	51.5	-0.2
Female	49.0	48.4	-1.2	48.4	48.5	0.2
Entered 2000 or later	34.1	36.4	6.7	34.7	35.7	2.9
Entered 1990 to 1999	27.7	26.6	-4.0	27.2	26.7	-1.8
Entered before 1990	38.1	37.1	-2.6	38.1	37.6	-1.3
World Region of Birth, Foreign						
Foreign-born population, excluding population born at sea	1,844,581	1,893,186	2.6	39,955,673	40,377,757	1.1
Europe	17.2	17.1	-0.6	12.1	12.1	-
Asia	30.8	31.3	1.6	28.2	28.6	1.4
Africa	4.5	4.5	-	4	4.1	2.5
Oceania	0.2	0.2	-	0.5	0.5	-
Latin America	46.2	46.1	-0.2	53.1	52.6	-0.9
North America	1.0	0.8	-20.0	2	2.0	-
Language Spoken at Home and Ability to Speak English						
Population 5 years and over	8,263,053	8,285,611	0.3	289,215,746	291,524,091	0.8
English only	70.3	69.6	-1.0	79.4	79.2	-0.3
Language other than English	29.7	30.4	2.4	20.6	20.8	1.0
Speaks English less than "very well"	12.5	13.0	4.0	8.7	8.7	-

- = Zero or rounds to zero.

Table NJ-5. Median Income and Poverty Status, 2011

(Number, percent, except as noted.)

Characteristic	State		U.S.	
	Number	Percent	Number	Percent
Median Income				
Households (dollars)	67,458	X	50,502	X
Families (dollars)	82,255	X	61,455	X
Below Poverty Level (All People)	897,376	10.4	48,452,035	15.9
Sex				
Male	396,753	9.5	21,825,281	14.7
Female	500,623	11.3	26,626,754	17.2
Age				
Under 18 years	296,198	14.7	16,386,500	22.5
Related children under 18 years	292,593	14.5	16,087,074	22.2
18 to 64 years	510,584	9.4	28,335,079	14.8
65 years and over	90,594	7.8	3,730,456	9.3

X = Not applicable.

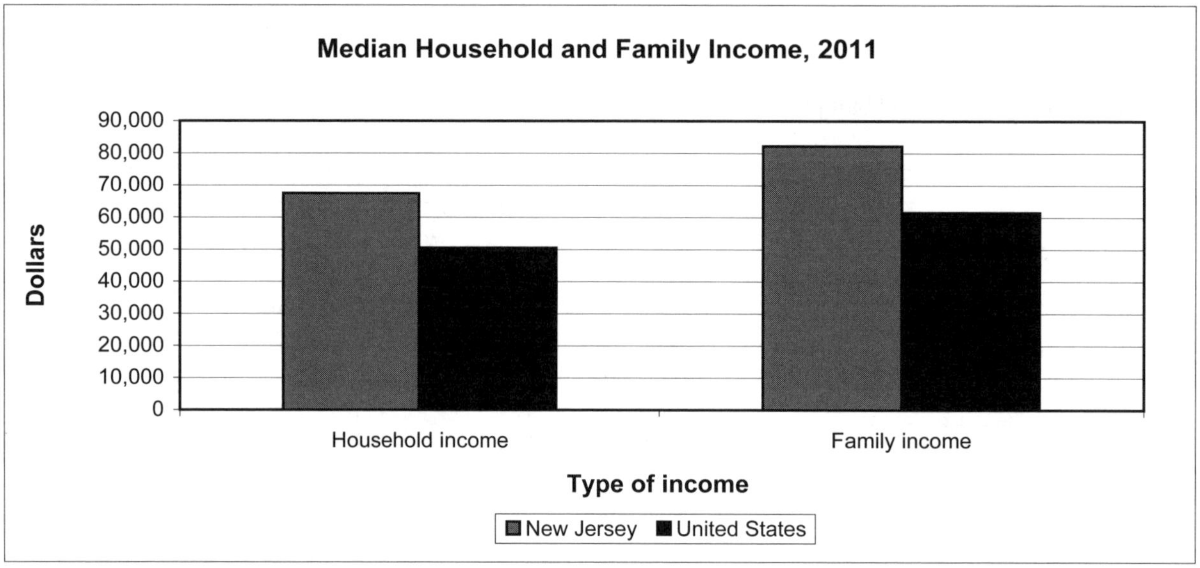

Table NJ-6. Health Insurance Coverage Status for the Civilian Noninstitutionalized Population and Children Under 18 Years of Age

(Numbers in thousands, percent.)

Item	2004	2005	2006	2007	2008	2009	2010	2011
Civilian Noninstitutionalized Population	8,662	8,725	8,660	8,556	8,557	8,583	8,694	8,713
Covered by Private or Public Insurance								
Number	7,430	7,461	7,319	7,208	7,499	7,499	7,542	7,574
Percent	86.1	85.5	84.5	84.2	87.6	87.4	86.8	86.9
Not Covered								
Number	1,201	1,265	1,341	1,348	1,058	1,084	1,151	1,139
Percent	13.9	14.5	15.5	15.8	12.4	12.6	13.2	13.1
Percent in the U.S. not covered	14.9	15.3	15.8	15.3	15.1	15.1	15.5	15.1
Children Under 18 Years of Age	2,208	2,172	2,088	2,091	2,045	2,044	2,057	2,038
Covered by Private or Public Insurance								
Number	1,986	1,944	1,810	1,821	1,897	1,914	1,934	1,933
Percent	90.0	89.5	86.7	87.1	92.8	93.6	94.0	94.8
Not Covered								
Number	222	228	277	270	148	130	123	105
Percent	10.0	10.5	13.3	12.9	7.2	6.4	6.0	5.2
Percent in the U.S. not covered	10.5	10.9	11.7	11.0	9.7	8.6	8.0	7.5

Table NJ-7. Employment Status by Demographic Group, Preliminary 2012

(Numbers in thousands, percent.)

Characteristic	Civilian noninstitutional population	Civilian labor force		Employed		Unemployed	
		Number	Percent of population	Number	Percent of population	Number	Percent of population
Total	6,958	4,584	65.9	4,150	59.6	434	9.5
Sex							
Male	3,338	2,425	72.6	2,194	65.7	231	9.5
Female	3,620	2,160	59.7	1,956	54.0	204	9.4
Race, Sex, and Hispanic Origin							
White	5,304	3,486	65.7	3,177	59.9	310	8.9
Male	2,552	1,866	73.1	1,698	66.5	169	9.0
Female	2,752	1,620	58.9	1,479	53.8	141	8.7
Black or African American	958	616	64.3	524	54.7	92	15.0
Male	430	288	66.9	241	56.1	47	16.2
Female	528	329	62.2	283	53.5	46	13.9
Hispanic	1,208	884	73.2	793	65.6	91	10.3
Male	618	487	78.9	438	71.0	49	10.0
Female	591	397	67.2	354	60.0	43	10.8
Age							
16 to 19 years	519	168	32.4	127	24.4	42	24.7
20 to 24 years	595	423	71.1	356	59.9	66	15.7
25 to 34 years	1,050	875	83.4	791	75.3	84	9.6
35 to 44 years	1,135	936	82.4	867	76.3	69	7.4
45 to 54 years	1,375	1,137	82.7	1,044	75.9	93	8.1
55 to 64 years	1,042	752	72.2	698	67.0	54	7.2
65 years and over	1,242	294	23.7	267	21.5	26	9.0

NOTE: Data in Table 7 are from the Current Population Survey (CPS) and do not match the estimates in Table 8. See notes and definitions for further information.

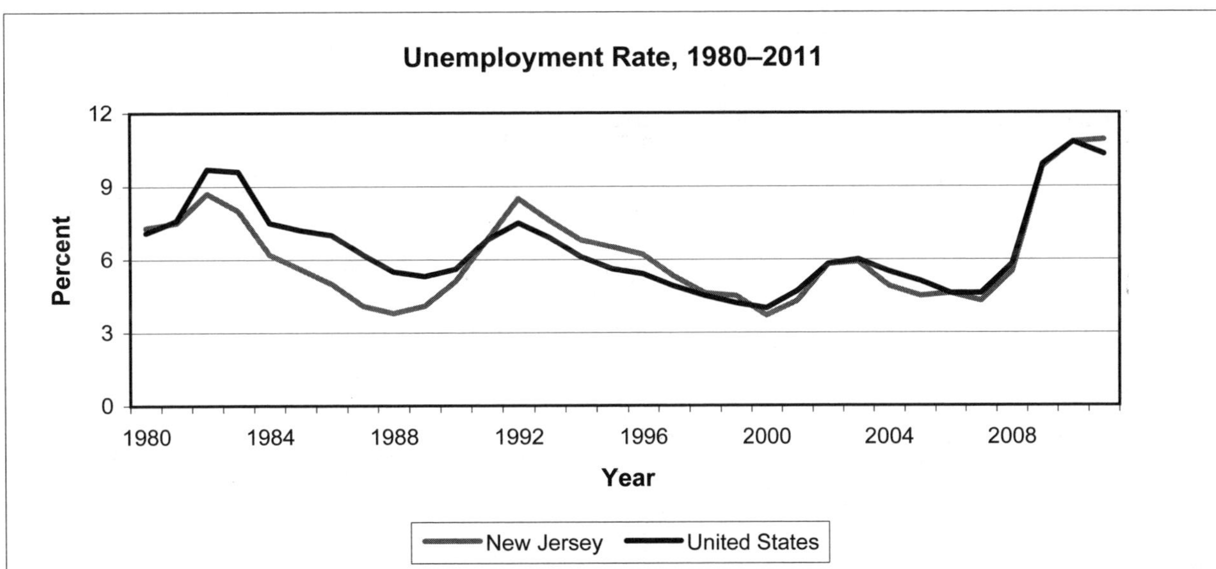

Table NJ-8. Employment Status of the Civilian Noninstitutional Population Age 16 Years and Over

(Number, percent.)

Year	Civilian labor force	Civilian participation rate	Employed	Unemployed	Unemployment rate
2005	4,416,087	66.3	4,218,485	197,602	4.5
2006	4,477,496	66.9	4,269,645	207,851	4.6
2007	4,462,253	66.4	4,271,652	190,601	4.3
2008	4,496,727	66.6	4,251,195	245,532	5.5
2009	4,638,181	67.2	4,184,978	453,203	9.8
2010	4,647,005	66.5	4,143,877	503,128	10.8
2011	4,662,195	66.4	4,152,513	509,682	10.9

Table NJ-9. Employment and Average Wages by Industry

(Estimates before 2007 are based on the 2002 *North American Industry Classification System* [NAICS]. Estimates from 2007 onward are based on the 2007 NAICS.)

Industry	2005	2006	2007	2008	2009	2010	2011
				Number of jobs			
Wage and Salary Employment by Industry	4,101,753	4,135,950	4,146,632	4,118,820	3,960,283	3,922,946	3,923,939
Farm Wage and Salary Employment	7,822	8,204	7,819	6,971	6,755	7,570	7,339
Nonfarm Wage and Salary Employment	4,093,931	4,127,746	4,138,813	4,111,849	3,953,528	3,915,376	3,916,600
Private wage and salary employment	3,438,244	3,471,355	3,481,911	3,452,565	3,293,683	3,267,478	3,290,968
Forestry, fishing, and related activities	2,786	2,726	2,842	2,945	3,078	3,677	3,811
Mining	1,687	1,688	1,604	1,605	1,492	1,371	1,305
Utilities	14,092	13,924	13,367	11,939	11,776	14,345	13,596
Construction	175,150	181,126	178,554	170,499	145,200	136,019	136,803
Manufacturing	331,492	323,792	308,113	298,064	266,926	257,696	253,333
Durable goods manufacturing	147,012	145,262	139,218	135,115	118,946	114,308	114,628
Nondurable goods manufacturing	184,480	178,530	168,895	162,949	147,980	143,388	138,705
Wholesale trade	234,805	233,615	236,155	234,458	218,250	212,135	211,455
Retail trade	475,042	473,437	473,982	464,036	443,251	444,675	448,211
Transportation and warehousing	159,646	162,603	164,622	163,582	153,789	151,198	152,332
Information	97,927	98,112	97,722	92,278	84,171	79,458	75,774
Finance and insurance	211,963	214,306	210,260	205,875	195,473	193,181	192,542
Real estate and rental and leasing	60,960	62,006	61,371	61,663	57,963	56,975	55,182
Professional, scientific, and technical services	272,409	280,438	290,167	293,729	281,110	276,511	281,203
Management of companies and enterprises	65,270	70,621	71,800	74,702	75,743	72,785	77,400
Administrative and waste services	260,282	258,008	260,041	252,539	235,034	241,793	250,969
Educational services	85,174	86,935	89,714	91,383	92,550	93,419	96,108
Health care and social assistance	461,063	472,091	481,320	490,545	497,698	505,292	509,745
Arts, entertainment, and recreation	50,529	50,312	52,621	54,877	53,763	53,664	54,897
Accommodation and food services	284,954	291,264	290,780	290,812	283,892	285,282	285,593
Other services, except public administration	193,013	194,351	196,876	197,034	192,524	188,002	190,709
Government and government enterprises	655,687	656,391	656,902	659,284	659,845	647,898	625,632
				Dollars			
Average Wages and Salaries by Industry	48,773	50,930	53,170	54,523	54,370	55,587	56,722
Average Farm Wages and Salaries	21,825	24,465	29,776	32,043	31,414	26,478	24,434
Average Nonfarm Wages and Salaries	48,825	50,983	53,215	54,561	54,409	55,643	56,783
Average private wages and salaries	48,650	50,904	53,160	54,412	53,986	55,228	56,377
Forestry, fishing, and related activities	20,985	21,466	22,755	23,952	24,754	23,878	24,140
Mining	57,992	57,159	60,415	62,782	64,157	67,177	66,959
Utilities	84,636	86,808	88,880	96,909	95,359	99,507	106,182
Construction	52,288	54,821	57,403	60,266	60,519	60,678	61,676
Manufacturing	61,249	64,869	68,313	70,564	71,230	74,016	74,981
Durable goods manufacturing	54,937	58,347	61,490	63,105	63,700	65,867	68,023
Nondurable goods manufacturing	66,280	70,175	73,937	76,748	77,283	80,512	80,732
Wholesale trade	65,928	68,987	72,320	73,633	74,077	76,696	79,469
Retail trade	28,405	29,215	29,880	29,742	29,686	30,003	30,390
Transportation and warehousing	44,120	44,877	46,696	47,455	47,215	48,360	49,321
Information	71,506	76,469	80,403	82,775	83,274	86,114	89,636
Finance and insurance	87,050	92,510	98,635	101,375	97,256	104,128	106,852
Real estate and rental and leasing	47,957	51,850	54,182	52,884	51,637	54,032	54,103
Professional, scientific, and technical services	75,546	78,134	82,957	85,411	85,976	88,091	90,889
Management of companies and enterprises	110,023	116,712	124,099	124,500	124,666	132,582	136,761
Administrative and waste services	33,899	34,903	35,630	37,284	36,723	37,264	38,182
Educational services	31,684	32,901	34,386	35,196	36,281	37,226	37,976
Health care and social assistance	42,224	43,568	44,691	46,364	46,792	46,802	47,448
Arts, entertainment, and recreation	29,244	34,349	34,648	35,863	35,868	36,633	35,269
Accommodation and food services	21,506	22,105	23,697	22,987	22,057	22,536	22,779
Other services, except public administration	29,576	30,187	30,699	31,519	31,359	32,027	32,429
Government and government enterprises	49,741	51,398	53,506	55,343	56,525	57,740	58,919

Table NJ-10. Employment Characteristics by Family Type

(Number, percent.)

Family type and labor force status	2009 Total	2009 Families with own children under 18 years	2010 Total	2010 Families with own children under 18 years	2011 Total	2011 Families with own children under 18 years
All families	2,172,031	1,011,680	2,185,732	1,007,512	2,191,404	1,003,032
Family type and labor force status						
Married-couple families	1,611,504	728,386	1,614,230	730,620	1,607,317	708,322
Both husband and wife in labor force	57.5	67.5	57.2	66.8	56.8	67.6
Husband in labor force, wife not in labor force	22.6	28.4	22.6	28.7	22.3	27.7
Wife in labor force, husband not in labor force	6.7	3.3	6.8	3.3	7.1	3.6
Both husband and wife not in labor force	13.3	0.8	13.4	1.1	13.8	1.2
Other families	560,527	283,294	571,502	276,892	584,087	294,710
Female householder, no husband present	73.7	77.6	73.0	76.1	73.8	77.6
In labor force	54.1	64.8	52.0	62.6	54.8	65.6
Not in labor force	19.6	12.7	21.0	13.4	19.1	12.0
Male householder, no wife present	26.3	22.4	27.0	23.9	26.2	22.4
In labor force	21.8	20.9	22.0	22.1	21.7	21.2
Not in labor force	4.5	1.5	5.0	1.8	4.5	1.2

Table NJ-11. School Enrollment and Educational Attainment, 2011

(Number, percent.)

Item	State	U.S.
Enrollment		
Total population 3 years and over, enrolled in school	2,289,399	83,131,910
Enrolled in nursery school or preschool (percent)	7.6	6.0
Enrolled in kindergarten (percent)	5.1	5.1
Enrolled in elementary school, grades 1-8 (percent)	39.4	39.5
Enrolled in high school, grades 9-12 (percent)	21.4	20.7
Enrolled in college or graduate school (percent)	26.4	28.7
Attainment		
Total population 25 years and over	6,004,613	206,471,670
Less than ninth grade (percent)	5.6	6.0
9th to 12th grade, no diploma (percent)	6.3	8.1
High school graduate, including equivalency (percent)	29.4	28.4
Some college, no degree (percent)	17.3	21.2
Associate's degree (percent)	6.1	7.8
Bachelor's degree (percent)	22.0	17.9
Graduate or professional degree (percent)	13.3	10.6
High school graduate or higher (percent)	88.1	85.9
Bachelor's degree or higher (percent)	35.3	28.5

Table NJ-12. Educational Indicators

(Number, percent; data derived from National Center of Education Statistics.)

Item	State	U.S.
Public Schools, 2009–2010 (except where noted)		
Number of school districts	603	13,629
Number of schools	2,590	99,834
Number of students (in thousands)	1,396	49,373
Student-teacher ratio	12.1	15.4
Expenditures per student (dollars)	18,737	10,591
Averaged freshman graduation rate, 2008–2009	85.3	75.5[1]
Dropout rate, 2008–2009	1.6	4.1
Students eligible for free or reduced-price lunch (percent)	32.7	48.0
English language learners, 2010–2011 (percent)	3.8	9.8[1]
Students with IEP (percent)	16.4	13.1
Private Schools, 2009–2010 (except where noted)		
Number of schools	1,385	33,366
Number of students (in thousands)	188	4,700
High school graduates, 2008–2009	14,348	308,813
Student-teacher ratio	9.9	10.7

[1] U.S. total includes estimates for nonreporting states.

Table NJ-13. Reported Voting and Registration of the Voting-Age Population, November 2012

(Numbers in thousands, percent.)

Item	Total population	Total citizen population	Registered: Total registered	Registered: Percent registered (total population)	Registered: Percent registered (total citizen population)	Voted: Total voted	Voted: Percent voted (total population)	Voted: Percent voted (total citizen population)
U.S. Total	235,248	215,081	153,157	65.1	71.2	132,948	56.5	61.8
State Total	6,730	5,929	4,326	64.3	73.0	3,670	54.5	61.9
Sex								
Male	3,215	2,795	1,982	61.6	70.9	1,676	52.1	60.0
Female	3,514	3,134	2,344	66.7	74.8	1,994	56.7	63.6
Race								
White alone	5,173	4,695	3,448	66.6	73.4	2,907	56.2	61.9
White, non-Hispanic alone	4,145	4,030	3,037	73.3	75.3	2,556	61.7	63.4
Black alone	907	789	586	64.7	74.3	540	59.6	68.5
Asian alone	566	373	243	43.0	65.2	179	31.7	48.1
Hispanic (of any race)	1,170	773	468	40.0	60.6	395	33.8	51.1
Age								
18 to 24 years	792	707	379	47.8	53.6	276	34.9	39.1
25 to 44 years	2,255	1,781	1,211	53.7	68.0	1,011	44.8	56.8
45 to 64 years	2,424	2,217	1,732	71.4	78.1	1,545	63.7	69.7
65 to 74 years	644	631	504	78.3	80.0	434	67.4	68.8
75 years and over	615	593	499	81.2	84.2	404	65.7	68.1

Table NJ-14. Crime

(Number, rate per 100,000. Data are derived from the FBI Uniform Crime Reports.)

Item	State: 2010	State: 2011	State: Percent change	U.S.: 2010	U.S.: 2011	U.S.: Percent change
TOTAL POPULATION	8,799,593	8,821,155	0.2	309,330,219	311,591,917	0.7
VIOLENT CRIME						
Number	27,055	27,203	0.5	1,251,248	1,203,564	-3.8
Rate	307.5	308.4	0.3	404.5	386.3	-4.5
Murder and Nonnegligent Manslaughter						
Number	371	380	2.4	14,722	14,612	-0.7
Rate	4.2	4.3	2.4	4.8	4.7	-2.1
Forcible Rape						
Number	981	1,006	2.5	85,593	83,425	-2.5
Rate	11.1	11.4	2.7	27.7	26.8	-3.2
Robbery						
Number	11,818	12,209	3.3	369,089	354,396	-4.0
Rate	134.3	138.4	3.1	119.3	113.7	-4.7
Aggravated Assault						
Number	13,885	13,608	-2.0	781,844	751,131	-3.9
Rate	157.8	154.3	-2.2	252.8	241.1	-4.6
PROPERTY CRIME						
Number	183,042	189,719	3.6	9,112,625	9,063,173	-0.5
Rate	2,080.1	2,150.7	3.4	2,945.9	2,908.7	-1.3
Burglary						
Number	38,732	43,238	11.6	2,168,459	2,188,005	0.9
Rate	440.2	490.2	11.4	701.0	702.2	0.2
Larceny-Theft						
Number	128,754	129,066	0.2	6,204,601	6,159,795	-0.7
Rate	1,463.2	1,463.1	-	2,005.8	1,976.9	-1.4
Motor Vehicle Theft						
Number	15,556	17,415	12.0	739,565	715,373	-3.3
Rate	176.8	197.4	11.7	239.1	229.6	-4.0

Table NJ-15. State Government Finances, 2011

(Dollar amounts in thousands, percent distribution.)

Item	Dollars	Percent distribution
Total Revenue	70,798,018	100.0
General revenue	51,676,400	73.0
Intergovernmental revenue	14,792,596	20.9
Taxes	27,182,753	38.4
General sales	8,144,397	11.5
Selective sales	3,777,428	5.3
License taxes	1,497,837	2.1
Individual income tax	10,617,034	15.0
Corporate income tax	2,216,438	3.1
Other taxes	929,619	1.3
Current charges	5,813,656	8.2
Miscellaneous general revenue	3,887,395	5.5
Utility revenue	986,028	1.4
Liquor stores revenue	0	0.0
Insurance trust revenue [1]	18,135,590	25.6
Total Expenditure	67,114,331	100.0
Intergovernmental expenditure	11,167,301	16.6
Direct expenditure	55,947,030	83.4
Current operation	32,945,972	49.1
Capital outlay	3,552,580	5.3
Insurance benefits and repayments	16,209,263	24.2
Assistance and subsidies	1,169,119	1.7
Interest on debt	2,070,096	3.1
Exhibit: Salaries and wages	10,246,367	15.3
Total Expenditure	67,114,331	100.0
General expenditure	48,732,533	72.6
Intergovernmental expenditure	11,167,301	16.6
Direct expenditure	37,565,232	56.0
General expenditure, by function:		
Education	15,710,434	23.4
Public welfare	14,213,978	21.2
Hospitals	2,119,042	3.2
Health	1,239,114	1.8
Highways	3,178,924	4.7
Police protection	620,379	0.9
Correction	1,453,667	2.2
Natural resources	615,808	0.9
Parks and recreation	293,283	0.4
Governmental administration	1,689,596	2.5
Interest on general debt	2,066,802	3.1
Other and unallocable	5,531,506	8.2
Utility expenditure	2,172,535	3.2
Liquor stores expenditure	0	0.0
Insurance trust expenditure	16,209,263	24.2
Debt at End of Fiscal Year	64,004,651	X
Cash and Security Holdings	114,090,081	X

X = Not applicable.
[1] Within insurance trust revenue, net earnings of state retirement systems is a calculated statistic (the item code in the data file is X08), and thus can be positive or negative. Net earnings is the sum of earnings on investments plus gains on investments minus losses on investments. The change made in 2002 for asset valuation from book to market value in accordance with Statement 34 of the Governmental Accounting Standards Board is reflected in the calculated statistics.

Table NJ-16. State Government Tax Collections, 2012

(Dollars in thousands, percent.)

Item	Dollars	Percent distribution
Total Taxes	27,456,175	100.0
Property taxes	5,650	-
Sales and gross receipts	12,009,552	43.7
General sales and gross receipts	8,099,549	29.5
Selective sales and gross receipts	3,910,003	14.2
Alcoholic beverages	135,304	0.5
Amusements	239,324	0.9
Insurance premiums	532,307	1.9
Motor fuels	539,714	2.0
Pari-mutuels	0	0.0
Public utilities	958,425	3.5
Tobacco products	792,066	2.9
Other selective sales	712,863	2.6
Licenses	1,425,441	5.2
Alcoholic beverages	3,960	-
Amusements	54,319	0.2
Corporations in general	214,348	0.8
Hunting and fishing	13,238	-
Motor vehicle	605,628	2.2
Motor vehicle operators	52,663	0.2
Public utilities	7,094	-
Occupation and business, NEC	472,006	1.7
Other licenses	2,185	-
Income taxes	13,057,551	47.6
Individual income	11,128,418	40.5
Corporation net income	1,929,133	7.0
Other taxes	957,981	3.5
Death and gift	641,868	2.3
Documentary and stock transfer	316,113	1.2
Severance	0	0.0
Taxes, NEC	0	0.0

- = Rounds to zero.

Leading Exports, 2012

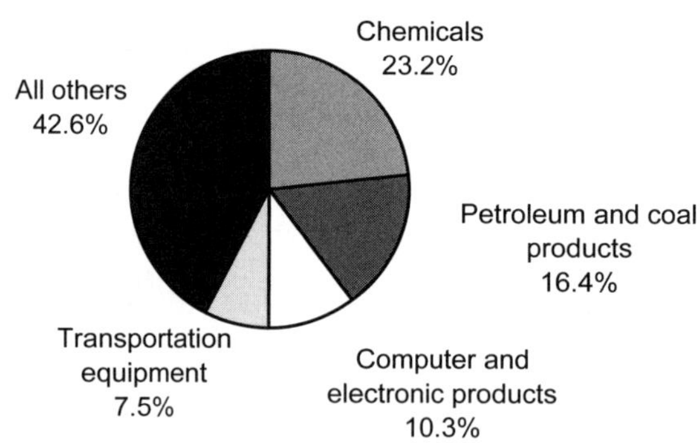

NEW MEXICO

Facts and Figures

Location: Southwestern United States; bordered on the N by Colorado, on the E by Oklahoma and Texas, on the S by Texas and Mexico, and on the W by Arizona; New Mexico is one of the Four Corner states—at its NW corner it touches Arizona, Colorado, and Utah

Area: 121,590 sq. mi. (314,915 sq. km.); rank—5th

Population: 2,085,538 (2012 est.); rank—36th

Principal Cities: capital—Santa Fe; largest—Albuquerque

Statehood: January 6, 1912; 47th state

U.S. Congress: 2 senators, 3 representatives

State Motto: *Crescit eundo* ("It grows as it goes")

State Song: "O, Fair New Mexico"

State Nickname: The Land of Enchantment

Abbreviations: NM; N. Mex.

State Symbols: flower—yucca; tree—piñon; bird—roadrunner

At a Glance

- With an increase in population of 10.5 percent, New Mexico ranked 30th among the states in growth from 2000 to 2009.
- An estimated 10,200 marriages took place in New Mexico in 2009, compared to 8,000 divorces.
- In 2011, 19.8 percent of New Mexicans did not have health insurance, compared to 15.1 percent of the total U.S. population.
- New Mexico's violent crime rate in 2011 was 567.5 per 100,000 population, compared to 386.3 for the entire nation.
- In 2007, New Mexico exported $269 million worth of agricultural products, less than 1 percent of the U.S. total.

Table NM-1. Population by Age, Sex, Race, and Hispanic Origin

(Number, percent, except where noted.)

Sex, age, race, and Hispanic origin	2000	2010	2012[1]	Average annual percent change, 2010–2012
Total Population	1,819,046	2,059,179	2,085,538	0.4
Percent of total U.S. population	0.6	0.7	0.7	X
Sex				
Male	894,317	1,017,421	1,032,707	0.5
Female	924,729	1,041,758	1,052,831	0.4
Age				
Under 5 years	130,628	144,981	143,536	-0.3
5 to 19 years	434,231	434,860	428,469	-0.5
20 to 64 years	1,041,962	1,207,083	1,218,700	0.3
65 years and over	212,225	272,255	294,833	2.6
Median age (years)	34.6	36.7	36.8	0.1
Race and Hispanic Origin				
One race				
White	1,214,253	1,720,992	1,735,255	0.3
Black	34,343	49,006	51,087	1.4
American Indian and Alaska Native	173,483	208,890	213,081	0.7
Asian	19,255	31,253	33,665	2.4
Native Hawaiian or Other Pacific Islander	1,503	3,132	3,327	2.0
Two or more races	66,327	45,906	49,123	2.2
Hispanic (of any race)	765,386	973,088	1,000,780	0.9

X = Not applicable.
[1] Population figures for 2012 are July 1 estimates. The 2010 estimates are taken from the 2010 Census.

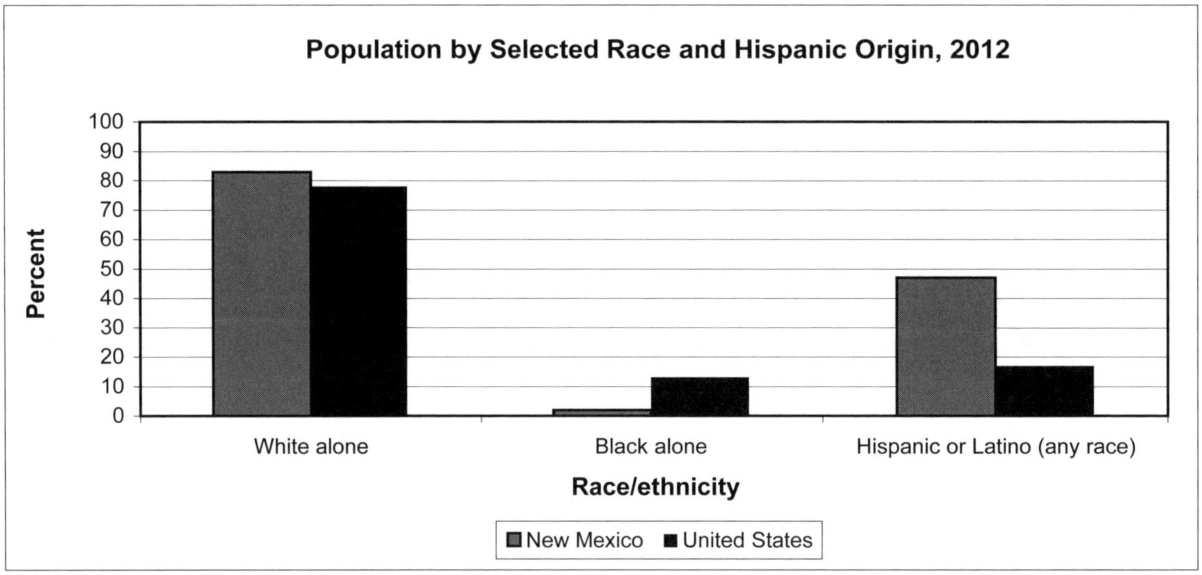

Table NM-2. Marital Status

(Number, percent distribution.)

Sex, age, race, and Hispanic origin	2000	2010	2011
Males, 15 Years and Over	677,967	801,901	812,152
Never married	30.5	35.4	35.6
Now married, except separated	55.0	48.4	48.2
Separated	1.6	1.6	1.3
Widowed	2.6	2.6	2.6
Divorced	10.4	11.9	12.2
Females, 15 Years and Over	720,529	833,357	835,962
Never married	24.7	29.9	29.7
Now married, except separated	51.2	45.0	44.6
Separated	2.0	2.6	2.4
Widowed	9.4	8.5	8.8
Divorced	12.8	14.1	14.5

Table NM-3. Households and Housing Characteristics

(Number, percent, dollars.)

Item	2000	2010	2011	Average annual percent change, 2000–2011
Total Households	677,971	765,183	767,285	1.1
Family households	466,515	501,092	502,498	0.6
Married-couple family	341,818	349,344	349,608	0.2
Other family	124,697	151,748	152,890	1.9
Male householder, no wife present	35,075	49,041	44,051	2.1
Female householder, no husband present	89,622	102,707	108,839	1.8
Nonfamily households	211,456	264,091	264,787	2.1
Householder living alone	172,181	216,704	220,008	2.3
Householder not living alone	39,275	47,387	44,779	1.2
Housing Characteristics				
Total housing units	780,579	902,242	908,168	1.4
Occupied housing units	677,971	765,183	767,285	1.1
Owner occupied	474,445	519,864	523,004	0.9
Renter occupied	203,526	245,319	244,281	1.7
Average size	2.63	2.64	2.66	0.1
Financial Characteristics				
Median gross rent of renter-occupied housing	503	699	729	3.7
Median monthly owner costs for housing units with a mortgage	929	1,202	1,216	2.6
Median value of owner-occupied housing units	108,100	161,200	159,000	3.9

Table NM-4. Migration, Origin, and Language

(Number, percent.)

Characteristic	State			U.S.		
	2010	2011	Percent change	2010	2011	Percent change
Residence 1 Year Ago						
Population 1 year and over	2,039,549	2,055,293	0.8	305,628,607	307,900,319	0.7
Same house	85.1	85.3	0.2	84.6	84.8	0.2
Different house in the U.S.	14.4	14.1	-2.1	14.8	14.6	-1.4
Same county	8.5	8.8	3.5	9.4	9.2	-2.1
Different county	6.0	5.4	-10.0	5.4	5.4	-
Same state	2.3	2.3	-	3.2	3.1	-3.1
Different state	3.6	3.0	-16.7	2.2	2.3	4.5
Abroad	0.5	0.6	20.0	0.6	0.6	-
Place of Birth						
Native born	1,860,791	1,871,117	0.6	269,393,835	271,214,059	0.7
Male	49.6	49.7	0.2	49.2	49.2	-
Female	50.4	50.3	-0.2	50.8	50.8	-
Foreign born	205,141	211,107	2.9	39,955,854	40,377,860	1.1
Male	47.6	50.1	5.3	49.1	48.9	-0.4
Female	52.4	49.9	-4.8	50.9	51.1	0.4
Foreign born; naturalized U.S. citizen	69,511	68,406	-1.6	17,476,082	18,140,192	3.8
Male	43.0	46.2	7.4	45.8	45.8	-
Female	57.0	53.8	-5.6	54.2	54.2	-
Foreign born; not a U.S. citizen	135,630	142,701	5.2	22,479,772	22,237,668	-1.1
Male	49.9	52.0	4.2	51.6	51.5	-0.2
Female	50.1	48.0	-4.2	48.4	48.5	0.2
Entered 2000 or later	35.0	35.1	0.3	34.7	35.7	2.9
Entered 1990 to 1999	23.8	27.1	13.9	27.2	26.7	-1.8
Entered before 1990	41.2	37.8	-8.3	38.1	37.6	-1.3
World Region of Birth, Foreign						
Foreign-born population, excluding population born at sea	205,141	211,107	2.9	39,955,673	40,377,757	1.1
Europe	7.8	7.7	-1.3	12.1	12.1	-
Asia	10.1	10.1	-	28.2	28.6	1.4
Africa	0.5	0.9	80.0	4	4.1	2.5
Oceania	0.3	0.2	-33.3	0.5	0.5	-
Latin America	79.7	79.5	-0.3	53.1	52.6	-0.9
North America	1.6	1.6	-	2	2.0	-
Language Spoken at Home and Ability to Speak English						
Population 5 years and over	1,921,916	1,937,824	0.8	289,215,746	291,524,091	0.8
English only	63.5	63.5	-	79.4	79.2	-0.3
Language other than English	36.5	36.5	-	20.6	20.8	1.0
Speaks English less than "very well"	9.2	10.1	9.8	8.7	8.7	-

- = Zero or rounds to zero.

Table NM-5. Median Income and Poverty Status, 2011

(Number, percent, except as noted.)

Characteristic	State		U.S.	
	Number	Percent	Number	Percent
Median Income				
Households (dollars)	41,963	X	50,502	X
Families (dollars)	51,744	X	61,455	X
Below Poverty Level (All People)	439,914	21.5	48,452,035	15.9
Sex				
Male	209,825	20.8	21,825,281	14.7
Female	230,089	22.2	26,626,754	17.2
Age				
Under 18 years	157,383	30.7	16,386,500	22.5
Related children under 18 years	156,369	30.6	16,087,074	22.2
18 to 64 years	249,661	19.9	28,335,079	14.8
65 years and over	32,870	11.8	3,730,456	9.3

X = Not applicable.

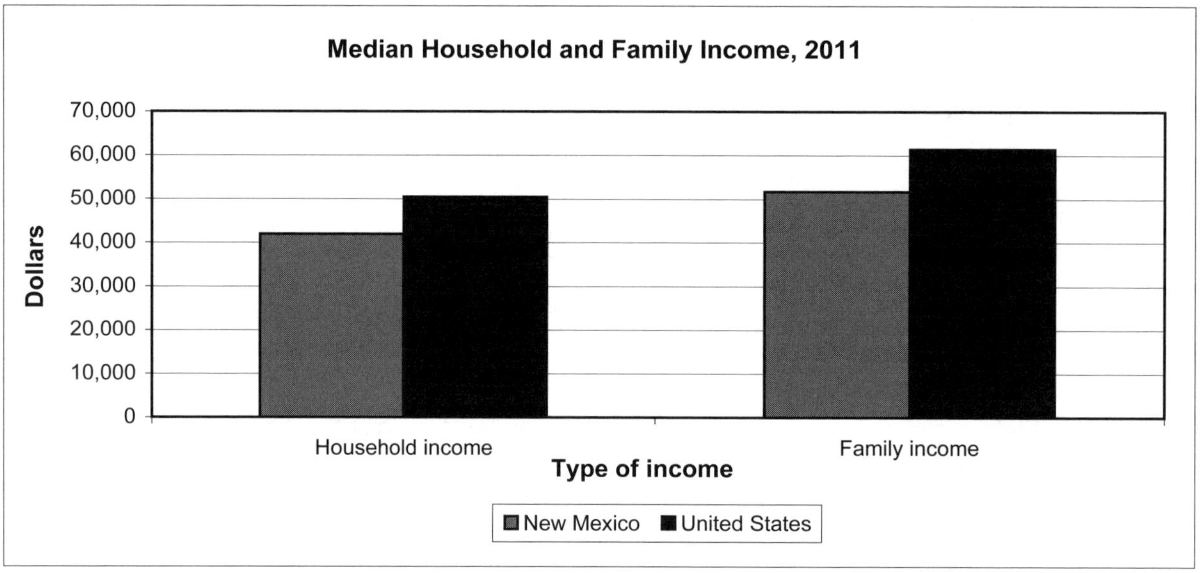

Table NM-6. Health Insurance Coverage Status for the Civilian Noninstitutionalized Population and Children Under 18 Years of Age

(Numbers in thousands, percent.)

Item	2004	2005	2006	2007	2008	2009	2010	2011
Civilian Noninstitutionalized Population	1,902	1,938	1,943	1,946	1,952	1,976	2,033	2,047
Covered by Private or Public Insurance								
Number	1,525	1,545	1,498	1,509	1,533	1,586	1,634	1,641
Percent	80.2	79.7	77.1	77.5	78.5	80.3	80.4	80.2
Not Covered								
Number	377	393	445	437	419	390	399	406
Percent	19.8	20.3	22.9	22.5	21.5	19.7	19.6	19.8
Percent in the U.S. not covered	14.9	15.3	15.8	15.3	15.1	15.1	15.5	15.1
Children Under 18 Years of Age	495	493	520	495	501	514	518	517
Covered by Private or Public Insurance								
Number	423	394	428	419	432	455	465	470
Percent	85.4	80.0	82.1	84.5	86.2	88.6	89.8	90.8
Not Covered								
Number	72	99	93	77	69	59	53	47
Percent	14.6	20.0	17.9	15.5	13.8	11.4	10.2	9.2
Percent in the U.S. not covered	10.5	10.9	11.7	11.0	9.7	8.6	8.0	7.5

Table NM-7. Employment Status by Demographic Group, Preliminary 2012

(Numbers in thousands, percent.)

Characteristic	Civilian noninstitutional population	Civilian labor force		Employed		Unemployed	
		Number	Percent of population	Number	Percent of population	Number	Percent of population
Total	1,594	952	59.7	884	55.4	68	7.1
Sex							
Male	773	500	64.8	462	59.7	39	7.7
Female	822	452	55.0	422	51.4	29	6.5
Race, Sex, and Hispanic Origin							
White	1,352	805	59.6	750	55.4	56	6.9
Male	657	430	65.4	398	60.5	32	7.5
Female	695	375	54.0	352	50.6	23	6.2
Black or African American	33	22	66.0	20	61.6	1	6.6
Male	NA	NA	NA	NA	NA	NA	NA
Female	NA	NA	NA	NA	NA	NA	NA
Hispanic	686	407	59.3	371	54.1	36	8.9
Male	339	227	66.9	204	60.3	22	9.8
Female	347	180	52.0	166	47.9	14	7.8
Age							
16 to 19 years	111	39	34.9	32	28.3	7	18.9
20 to 24 years	130	90	69.0	81	62.2	9	9.8
25 to 34 years	266	201	75.4	185	69.7	15	7.6
35 to 44 years	255	201	78.8	187	73.5	14	6.7
45 to 54 years	286	220	76.9	208	72.6	12	5.6
55 to 64 years	259	156	60.2	147	56.5	10	6.2
65 years and over	286	45	15.8	44	15.5	1	2.0

NOTE: Data in Table 7 are from the Current Population Survey (CPS) and do not match the estimates in Table 8. See notes and definitions for further information.
NA = Not available.

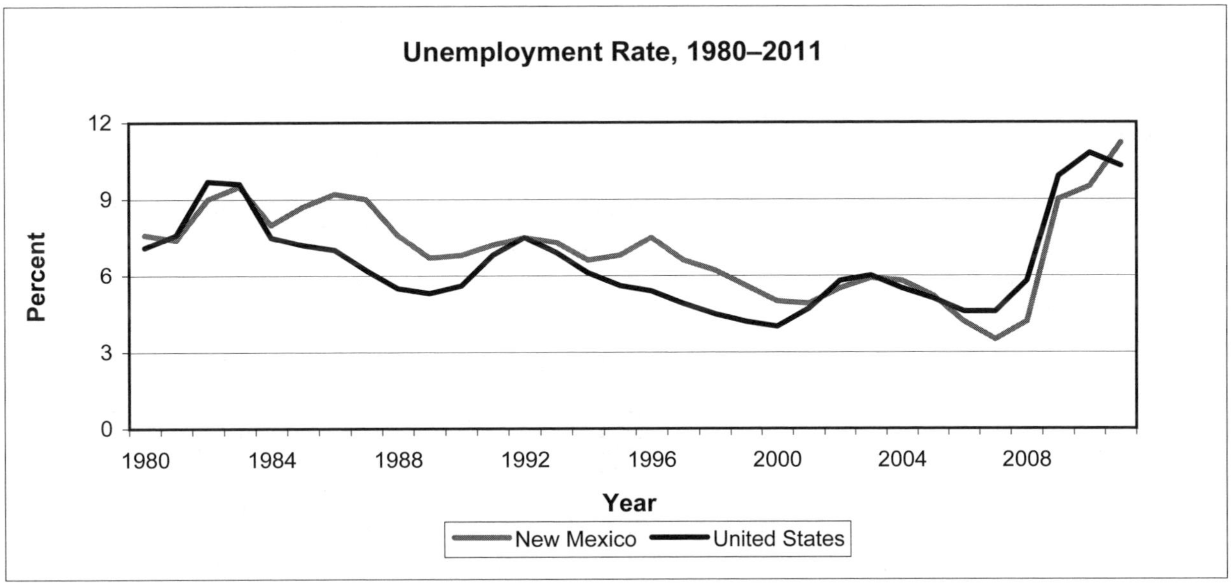

Table NM-8. Employment Status of the Civilian Noninstitutional Population Age 16 Years and Over

(Number, percent.)

Year	Civilian labor force	Civilian participation rate	Employed	Unemployed	Unemployment rate
2005	917,569	63.8	870,288	47,281	5.2
2006	935,396	63.9	896,359	39,037	4.2
2007	945,700	63.6	912,167	33,533	3.5
2008	949,458	63.7	919,466	39,992	4.2
2009	957,678	61.7	871,208	86,470	9.0
2010	959,218	59.7	868,276	90,942	9.5
2011	979,399	60.5	869,773	109,626	11.2

Table NM-9. Employment and Average Wages by Industry

(Estimates before 2007 are based on the 2002 *North American Industry Classification System* [NAICS]. Estimates from 2007 onward are based on the 2007 NAICS.)

Industry	2005	2006	2007	2008	2009	2010	2011
	Number of jobs						
Wage and Salary Employment by Industry	845,127	868,119	878,205	881,357	848,403	840,219	840,690
Farm Wage and Salary Employment	7,674	7,574	7,611	6,671	6,958	6,643	6,503
Nonfarm Wage and Salary Employment	837,453	860,545	870,594	874,686	841,445	833,576	834,187
Private wage and salary employment	618,801	646,269	660,727	661,461	625,304	616,320	620,357
Forestry, fishing, and related activities	3,035	2,976	2,792	2,858	2,753	2,923	3,034
Mining	16,893	18,840	19,616	21,111	17,511	18,284	21,096
Utilities	3,950	3,996	4,259	4,327	4,614	4,374	4,367
Construction	56,517	61,471	61,380	59,690	50,030	45,973	44,534
Manufacturing	35,994	37,407	36,818	35,080	30,075	29,064	29,602
Durable goods manufacturing	24,826	25,981	25,548	24,052	19,761	19,040	19,346
Nondurable goods manufacturing	11,168	11,426	11,270	11,028	10,314	10,024	10,256
Wholesale trade	22,747	23,560	23,714	23,777	21,870	22,074	21,162
Retail trade	94,886	95,555	97,317	97,673	93,059	91,272	91,545
Transportation and warehousing	19,728	20,138	20,942	20,632	18,301	17,812	18,475
Information	14,695	15,899	16,025	16,000	14,737	14,329	13,470
Finance and insurance	23,525	23,579	23,291	23,069	22,736	22,323	22,167
Real estate and rental and leasing	10,999	11,365	11,568	11,376	10,361	10,167	10,012
Professional, scientific, and technical services	44,235	51,338	56,698	56,951	55,923	54,422	54,174
Management of companies and enterprises	6,085	6,110	5,779	5,372	5,079	4,954	5,071
Administrative and waste services	43,884	46,238	47,395	47,419	42,544	41,722	42,179
Educational services	10,179	10,117	10,120	10,069	10,042	10,319	10,652
Health care and social assistance	88,935	91,612	95,131	98,316	101,908	103,733	105,592
Arts, entertainment, and recreation	8,337	8,357	8,692	8,763	8,779	8,648	8,668
Accommodation and food services	76,365	79,259	79,949	78,725	76,361	76,134	76,763
Other services, except public administration	37,812	38,452	39,241	40,253	38,621	37,793	37,794
Government and government enterprises	218,652	214,276	209,867	213,225	216,141	217,256	213,830
	Dollars						
Average Wages and Salaries by Industry	34,002	35,503	37,147	38,686	39,301	40,069	40,905
Average Farm Wages and Salaries	28,813	29,016	32,450	35,732	38,036	34,612	36,685
Average Nonfarm Wages and Salaries	34,050	35,560	37,188	38,709	39,312	40,112	40,938
Average private wages and salaries	32,274	34,215	36,158	37,663	37,998	38,919	39,741
Forestry, fishing, and related activities	18,460	19,733	20,447	21,006	21,433	21,521	22,348
Mining	55,387	60,884	62,802	68,956	66,837	75,764	72,876
Utilities	61,783	63,163	67,684	73,015	72,143	72,919	73,908
Construction	33,635	35,422	37,348	41,149	41,603	41,389	41,880
Manufacturing	42,959	45,150	48,557	48,893	50,838	53,528	55,293
Durable goods manufacturing	47,713	50,021	53,406	53,800	55,871	59,412	61,778
Nondurable goods manufacturing	32,391	34,075	37,564	38,189	41,197	42,351	43,062
Wholesale trade	42,473	45,206	47,766	49,257	49,111	50,051	50,329
Retail trade	23,771	24,692	25,406	25,684	25,631	26,042	26,471
Transportation and warehousing	40,257	42,145	43,791	45,026	44,328	45,490	48,050
Information	37,816	38,976	39,928	42,896	43,859	43,071	45,768
Finance and insurance	43,721	46,340	49,384	49,503	50,511	52,482	54,856
Real estate and rental and leasing	29,085	31,195	32,631	32,602	32,264	33,893	36,108
Professional, scientific, and technical services	57,247	61,080	65,149	67,105	68,167	70,507	71,223
Management of companies and enterprises	50,502	50,214	55,519	56,736	60,495	62,340	63,530
Administrative and waste services	27,759	28,679	30,033	31,433	32,809	32,980	34,530
Educational services	26,060	26,898	27,959	30,616	31,175	31,699	32,179
Health care and social assistance	33,143	34,551	35,613	37,295	38,311	38,503	39,074
Arts, entertainment, and recreation	19,590	20,637	22,341	22,225	21,554	21,532	21,844
Accommodation and food services	14,445	14,911	16,077	16,397	16,746	17,224	17,548
Other services, except public administration	21,989	23,080	24,326	25,444	25,567	26,325	26,768
Government and government enterprises	39,075	39,614	40,434	41,952	43,114	43,497	44,412

Table NM-10. Employment Characteristics by Family Type

(Number, percent.)

Family type and labor force status	2009		2010		2011	
	Total	Families with own children under 18 years	Total	Families with own children under 18 years	Total	Families with own children under 18 years
All families	489,296	218,304	501,092	223,212	502,498	214,387
Family type and labor force status						
Married-couple families	347,080	134,400	349,344	137,279	349,608	129,102
Both husband and wife in labor force	49.1	61.6	45.6	59.2	46.0	58.9
Husband in labor force, wife not in labor force	23.2	31.0	24.6	32.5	24.7	34.0
Wife in labor force, husband not in labor force	8.0	4.8	9.2	4.9	8.6	4.6
Both husband and wife not in labor force	19.8	2.6	20.6	3.3	20.7	2.5
Other families	142,216	83,904	151,748	85,933	152,890	85,285
Female householder, no husband present	70.5	71.2	67.7	71.7	71.2	75.3
In labor force	51.1	60.3	47.0	57.5	51.3	61.9
Not in labor force	19.4	10.9	20.7	14.2	19.9	13.4
Male householder, no wife present	29.5	28.8	32.3	28.3	28.8	24.7
In labor force	22.8	24.7	23.1	24.5	22.2	21.8
Not in labor force	6.8	4.1	9.3	3.8	6.6	3.0

Table NM-11. School Enrollment and Educational Attainment, 2011

(Number, percent.)

Item	State	U.S.
Enrollment		
Total population 3 years and over, enrolled in school	571,157	83,131,910
Enrolled in nursery school or preschool (percent)	5.2	6.0
Enrolled in kindergarten (percent)	5.1	5.1
Enrolled in elementary school, grades 1-8 (percent)	40.8	39.5
Enrolled in high school, grades 9-12 (percent)	19.8	20.7
Enrolled in college or graduate school (percent)	29.2	28.7
Attainment		
Total population 25 years and over	1,354,186	206,471,670
Less than ninth grade (percent)	7.3	6.0
9th to 12th grade, no diploma (percent)	9.6	8.1
High school graduate, including equivalency (percent)	26.6	28.4
Some college, no degree (percent)	23.6	21.2
Associate's degree (percent)	7.5	7.8
Bachelor's degree (percent)	14.4	17.9
Graduate or professional degree (percent)	11.1	10.6
High school graduate or higher (percent)	83.2	85.9
Bachelor's degree or higher (percent)	25.6	28.5

Table NM-12. Educational Indicators

(Number, percent; data derived from National Center of Education Statistics.)

Item	State	U.S.
Public Schools, 2009–2010 (except where noted)		
Number of school districts	89	13,629
Number of schools	855	99,834
Number of students (in thousands)	334	49,373
Student-teacher ratio	14.7	15.4
Expenditures per student (dollars)	11,342	10,591
Averaged freshman graduation rate, 2008–2009	64.8	75.5[1]
Dropout rate, 2008–2009	4.9	4.1
Students eligible for free or reduced-price lunch (percent)	67.7	48.0
English language learners, 2010–2011 (percent)	15.7	9.8[1]
Students with IEP (percent)	13.7	13.1
Private Schools, 2009–2010 (except where noted)		
Number of schools	187	33,366
Number of students (in thousands)	21	4,700
High school graduates, 2008–2009	2,463	308,813
Student-teacher ratio	10.1	10.7

[1] U.S. total includes estimates for nonreporting states.

Table NM-13. Reported Voting and Registration of the Voting-Age Population, November 2012

(Numbers in thousands, percent.)

Item	Total population	Total citizen population	Registered			Voted		
			Total registered	Percent registered (total population)	Percent registered (total citizen population)	Total voted	Percent voted (total population)	Percent voted (total citizen population)
U.S. Total	235,248	215,081	153,157	65.1	71.2	132,948	56.5	61.8
State Total	1,553	1,426	978	63.0	68.6	878	56.5	61.6
Sex								
Male	754	684	450	59.7	65.8	404	53.6	59.1
Female	799	742	528	66.1	71.2	474	59.3	63.9
Race								
White alone	1,310	1,215	875	66.8	72.0	789	60.2	64.9
White, non-Hispanic alone	729	713	545	74.8	76.4	503	69.0	70.5
Black alone	43	39	24	B	B	24	B	B
Asian alone	39	12	3	B	B	3	B	B
Hispanic (of any race)	624	544	349	55.9	64.1	306	49.0	56.2
Age								
18 to 24 years	177	163	84	47.4	51.3	66	37.1	40.2
25 to 44 years	542	471	296	54.5	62.7	253	46.7	53.7
45 to 64 years	588	551	414	70.4	75.1	390	66.3	70.8
65 to 74 years	129	124	87	67.3	70.0	82	63.7	66.3
75 years and over	118	116	99	83.9	85.0	87	74.3	75.2

B = Base is less than 75,000 and therefore too small to show the derived measure.

Table NM-14. Crime

(Number, rate per 100,000. Data are derived from the FBI Uniform Crime Reports.)

Item	State			U.S.		
	2010	2011	Percent change	2010	2011	Percent change
TOTAL POPULATION	2,065,913	2,082,224	0.8	309,330,219	311,591,917	0.7
VIOLENT CRIME						
Number	12,147	11,817	-2.7	1,251,248	1,203,564	-3.8
Rate	588.0	567.5	-3.5	404.5	386.3	-4.5
Murder and Nonnegligent Manslaughter						
Number	140	156	11.4	14,722	14,612	-0.7
Rate	6.8	7.5	10.3	4.8	4.7	-2.1
Forcible Rape						
Number	959	857	-10.6	85,593	83,425	-2.5
Rate	46.4	41.2	-11.2	27.7	26.8	-3.2
Robbery						
Number	1,616	1,722	6.6	369,089	354,396	-4.0
Rate	78.2	82.7	5.8	119.3	113.7	-4.7
Aggravated Assault						
Number	9,432	9,082	-3.7	781,844	751,131	-3.9
Rate	456.6	436.2	-4.5	252.8	241.1	-4.6
PROPERTY CRIME						
Number	70,776	73,534	3.9	9,112,625	9,063,173	-0.5
Rate	3,425.9	3,531.5	3.1	2,945.9	2,908.7	-1.3
Burglary						
Number	21,023	21,423	1.9	2,168,459	2,188,005	0.9
Rate	1,017.6	1,028.9	1.1	701.0	702.2	0.2
Larceny-Theft						
Number	44,503	46,703	4.9	6,204,601	6,159,795	-0.7
Rate	2,154.2	2,242.9	4.1	2,005.8	1,976.9	-1.4
Motor Vehicle Theft						
Number	5,250	5,408	3.0	739,565	715,373	-3.3
Rate	254.1	259.7	2.2	239.1	229.6	-4.0

Table NM-15. State Government Finances, 2011

(Dollar amounts in thousands, percent distribution.)

Item	Dollars	Percent distribution
Total Revenue	19,866,682	100.0
General revenue	14,949,450	75.2
Intergovernmental revenue	6,364,080	32.0
Taxes	4,980,115	25.1
General sales	1,880,400	9.5
Selective sales	693,335	3.5
License taxes	239,590	1.2
Individual income tax	1,066,200	5.4
Corporate income tax	229,800	1.2
Other taxes	870,790	4.4
Current charges	1,486,327	7.5
Miscellaneous general revenue	2,118,928	10.7
Utility revenue	0	0.0
Liquor stores revenue	0	0.0
Insurance trust revenue [1]	4,917,232	
Total Expenditure	17,865,171	100.0
Intergovernmental expenditure	4,325,766	24.2
Direct expenditure	13,539,405	75.8
Current operation	9,669,613	54.1
Capital outlay	1,020,848	5.7
Insurance benefits and repayments	2,253,681	12.6
Assistance and subsidies	255,451	1.4
Interest on debt	339,812	1.9
Exhibit: Salaries and wages	2,622,775	14.7
Total Expenditure	17,865,171	100.0
General expenditure	15,594,493	87.3
Intergovernmental expenditure	4,325,766	24.2
Direct expenditure	11,268,727	63.1
General expenditure, by function:		
Education	5,391,916	30.2
Public welfare	4,329,057	24.2
Hospitals	920,506	5.2
Health	494,774	2.8
Highways	805,745	4.5
Police protection	143,016	0.8
Correction	406,630	2.3
Natural resources	223,837	1.3
Parks and recreation	65,360	0.4
Governmental administration	637,398	3.6
Interest on general debt	339,812	1.9
Other and unallocable	1,836,442	10.3
Utility expenditure	16,997	0.1
Liquor stores expenditure	0	0.0
Insurance trust expenditure	2,253,681	12.6
Debt at End of Fiscal Year	8,118,832	X
Cash and Security Holdings	44,809,201	X

X = Not applicable.

[1] Within insurance trust revenue, net earnings of state retirement systems is a calculated statistic (the item code in the data file is X08), and thus can be positive or negative. Net earnings is the sum of earnings on investments plus gains on investments minus losses on investments. The change made in 2002 for asset valuation from book to market value in accordance with Statement 34 of the Governmental Accounting Standards Board is reflected in the calculated statistics.

Table NM-16. State Government Tax Collections, 2012

(Dollars in thousands, percent.)

Item	Dollars	Percent distribution
Total Taxes	5,088,335	100.0
Property taxes	60,195	1.2
Sales and gross receipts	2,651,121	52.1
General sales and gross receipts	1,990,535	39.1
Selective sales and gross receipts	660,586	13.0
Alcoholic beverages	40,574	0.8
Amusements	59,437	1.2
Insurance premiums	118,296	2.3
Motor fuels	234,796	4.6
Pari-mutuels	852	-
Public utilities	26,503	0.5
Tobacco products	74,800	1.5
Other selective sales	105,328	2.1
Licenses	177,398	3.5
Alcoholic beverages	1,597	-
Amusements	392	-
Corporations in general	21,754	0.4
Hunting and fishing	25,591	0.5
Motor vehicle	92,685	1.8
Motor vehicle operators	3,708	0.1
Public utilities	814	-
Occupation and business, NEC	26,435	0.5
Other licenses	4,422	0.1
Income taxes	1,431,515	28.1
Individual income	1,150,468	22.6
Corporation net income	281,047	5.5
Other taxes	768,106	15.1
Death and gift	0	0.0
Documentary and stock transfer	0	0.0
Severance	768,106	15.1
Taxes, NEC	0	0.0

- = Rounds to zero.

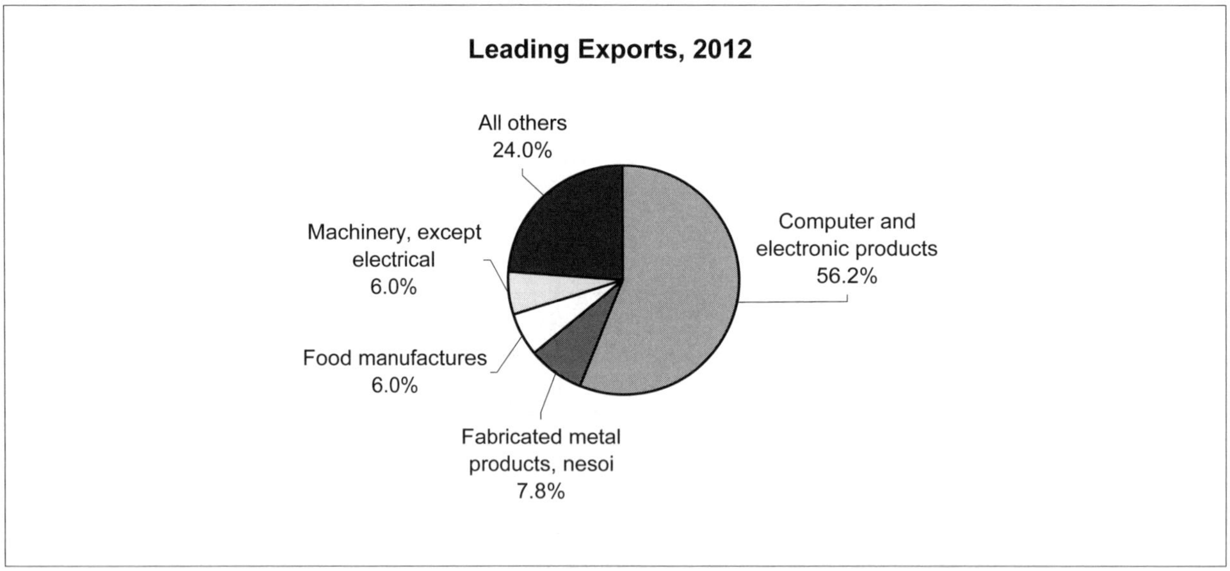

NEW YORK

Facts and Figures

Location: Northeastern United States; bordered on the N by Canada (Ontario and Quebec) and Lake Ontario; on the E by Vermont, Massachusetts, and Connecticut; on the S by New Jersey and Pennsylvania; and on the W by Pennsylvania, Lake Erie, Canada (Ontario), and Lake Ontario

Area: 54,556 sq. mi. (141,299 sq. km.); rank—27th

Population: 19,570,261 (2012 est.); rank—3rd

Principal Cities: capital—Albany; largest—New York City

Statehood: July 26, 1788; 11th state

U.S. Congress: 2 senators, 27 representatives

State Motto: *Excelsior* ("Ever upward")

State Song: "I Love New York"

State Nickname: The Empire State

Abbreviations: NY; N.Y.

State Symbols: flower—rose; tree—sugar maple; bird—bluebird

At a Glance

- With an increase in population of 3.0 percent, New York ranked 12th among the states in growth from 2000 to 2009.
- An estimated 120,100 marriages took place in New York in 2009, compared to 46,100 divorces.
- In 2011, 11.4 percent of New Yorkers did not have health insurance, compared to 15.1 percent of the total U.S. population.
- In the 2012 election, 58.7 percent of New York's eligible voters voted, compared to 61.8 percent of eligible voters nationwide.
- In 2007, New York exported $2.1 billion worth of agricultural products, about 2.6 percent of the U.S. total.

Table NY-1. Population by Age, Sex, Race, and Hispanic Origin

(Number, percent, except where noted.)

Sex, age, race, and Hispanic origin	2000	2010	2012[1]	Average annual percent change, 2010–2012
Total Population	18,976,457	19,378,102	19,570,261	0.3
Percent of total U.S. population	6.7	6.3	6.2	X
Sex				
Male	9,146,748	9,377,147	9,489,217	0.4
Female	9,829,709	10,000,955	10,081,044	0.3
Age				
Under 5 years	1,239,417	1,155,822	1,167,185	0.3
5 to 19 years	3,971,834	3,741,689	3,649,405	-0.8
20 to 64 years	11,316,854	11,862,648	11,996,099	0.4
65 years and over	2,448,352	2,617,943	2,757,572	1.7
Median age (years)	35.9	38.0	38.1	0.1
Race and Hispanic Origin				
One race				
White	12,893,689	13,901,661	13,930,819	0.1
Black	3,014,385	3,378,047	3,422,914	0.4
American Indian and Alaska Native	82,461	183,046	186,613	0.6
Asian	1,044,976	1,481,555	1,566,191	1.8
Native Hawaiian or Other Pacific Islander	8,818	24,000	25,101	1.5
Two or more races	590,182	409,793	438,623	2.2
Hispanic (of any race)	2,867,583	3,564,228	3,710,754	1.3

X = Not applicable.
[1] Population figures for 2012 are July 1 estimates. The 2010 estimates are taken from the 2010 Census.

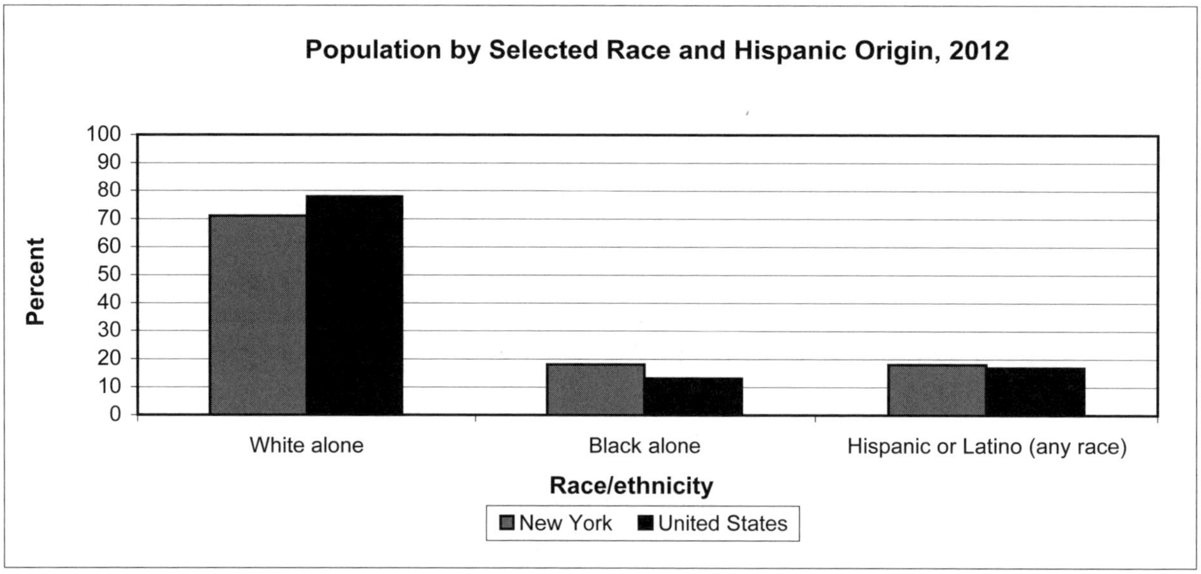

Table NY-2. Marital Status

(Number, percent distribution.)

Sex, age, race, and Hispanic origin	2000	2010	2011
Males, 15 Years and Over	7,125,715	7,586,733	7,642,666
Never married	34.7	40.5	40.6
Now married, except separated	53.3	47.6	47.1
Separated	2.7	2.2	2.3
Widowed	2.8	2.6	2.7
Divorced	6.5	7.2	7.3
Females, 15 Years and Over	7,932,161	8,283,542	8,314,855
Never married	29.0	34.8	34.9
Now married, except separated	47.1	42.8	42.3
Separated	3.7	3.1	3.3
Widowed	11.2	9.6	9.5
Divorced	8.9	9.7	10.0

Table NY-3. Households and Housing Characteristics

(Number, percent, dollars.)

Item	2000	2010	2011	Average annual percent change, 2000–2011
Total Households	7,056,860	7,196,427	7,187,938	0.2
Family households	4,639,387	4,632,676	4,607,636	-0.1
Married-couple family	3,289,514	3,210,895	3,166,722	-0.3
Other family	1,349,873	1,421,781	1,440,914	0.6
Male householder, no wife present	311,697	355,236	355,039	1.2
Female householder, no husband present	1,038,176	1,066,545	1,085,875	0.4
Nonfamily households	2,417,473	2,563,751	2,580,302	0.6
Householder living alone	1,982,742	2,089,816	2,119,464	0.6
Householder not living alone	434,731	473,935	460,838	0.5
Housing Characteristics				
Total housing units	7,679,301	8,108,211	8,119,804	0.5
Occupied housing units	7,056,860	7,196,427	7,187,938	0.2
Owner occupied	3,739,166	3,904,123	3,851,687	0.3
Renter occupied	3,317,694	3,292,304	3,336,251	-
Average size	2.61	2.61	2.63	0.1
Financial Characteristics				
Median gross rent of renter-occupied housing	627	1,020	1,058	5.7
Median monthly owner costs for housing units with a mortgage	1,357	1,963	1,977	3.8
Median value of owner-occupied housing units	148,700	296,500	285,300	7.7

- = Zero or rounds to zero.

Table NY-4. Migration, Origin, and Language

(Number, percent.)

Characteristic	State			U.S.		
	2010	2011	Percent change	2010	2011	Percent change
Residence 1 Year Ago						
Population 1 year and over	19,171,916	19,248,685	0.4	305,628,607	307,900,319	0.7
Same house	88.5	88.6	0.1	84.6	84.8	0.2
Different house in the U.S.	10.7	10.6	-0.9	14.8	14.6	-1.4
Same county	6.8	6.7	-1.5	9.4	9.2	-2.1
Different county	3.8	3.9	2.6	5.4	5.4	-
Same state	2.4	2.4	-	3.2	3.1	-3.1
Different state	1.4	1.5	7.1	2.2	2.3	4.5
Abroad	0.8	0.8	-	0.6	0.6	-
Place of Birth						
Native born	15,094,671	15,147,482	0.3	269,393,835	271,214,059	0.7
Male	48.8	48.8	-	49.2	49.2	-
Female	51.2	51.2	-	50.8	50.8	-
Foreign born	4,297,612	4,317,715	0.5	39,955,854	40,377,860	1.1
Male	47.2	47.4	0.4	49.1	48.9	-0.4
Female	52.8	52.6	-0.4	50.9	51.1	0.4
Foreign born; naturalized U.S. citizen	2,223,576	2,236,307	0.6	17,476,082	18,140,192	3.8
Male	44.6	44.7	0.2	45.8	45.8	-
Female	55.4	55.3	-0.2	54.2	54.2	-
Foreign born; not a U.S. citizen	2,074,036	2,081,408	0.4	22,479,772	22,237,668	-1.1
Male	49.9	50.3	0.8	51.6	51.5	-0.2
Female	50.1	49.7	-0.8	48.4	48.5	0.2
Entered 2000 or later	31.2	33.4	7.1	34.7	35.7	2.9
Entered 1990 to 1999	27.9	26.9	-3.6	27.2	26.7	-1.8
Entered before 1990	40.9	39.8	-2.7	38.1	37.6	-1.3
World Region of Birth, Foreign						
Foreign-born population, excluding population born at sea	4,297,612	4,317,715	0.5	39,955,673	40,377,757	1.1
Europe	17.8	18.0	1.1	12.1	12.1	-
Asia	26.8	27.2	1.5	28.2	28.6	1.4
Africa	3.7	4.0	8.1	4	4.1	2.5
Oceania	0.2	0.2	-	0.5	0.5	-
Latin America	50.1	49.2	-1.8	53.1	52.6	-0.9
North America	1.4	1.3	-7.1	2	2.0	-
Language Spoken at Home and Ability to Speak English						
Population 5 years and over	18,241,464	18,307,740	0.4	289,215,746	291,524,091	0.8
English only	70.0	69.9	-0.1	79.4	79.2	-0.3
Language other than English	30.0	30.1	0.3	20.6	20.8	1.0
Speaks English less than "very well"	13.5	13.5	-	8.7	8.7	-

- = Zero or rounds to zero.

Table NY-5. Median Income and Poverty Status, 2011

(Number, percent, except as noted.)

Characteristic	State		U.S.	
	Number	Percent	Number	Percent
Median Income				
Households (dollars)	55,246	X	50,502	X
Families (dollars)	66,852	X	61,455	X
Below Poverty Level (All People)	3,027,342	16.0	48,452,035	15.9
Sex				
Male	1,326,063	14.5	21,825,281	14.7
Female	1,701,279	17.4	26,626,754	17.2
Age				
Under 18 years	950,921	22.6	16,386,500	22.5
Related children under 18 years	934,807	22.3	16,087,074	22.2
18 to 64 years	1,775,899	14.6	28,335,079	14.8
65 years and over	300,522	11.7	3,730,456	9.3

X = Not applicable.

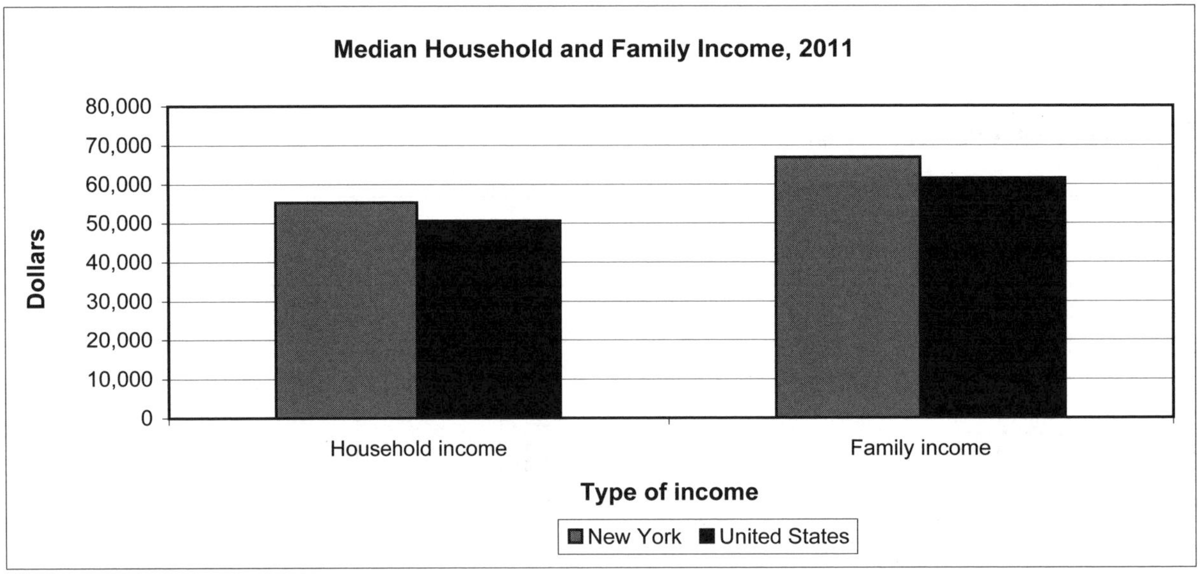

Table NY-6. Health Insurance Coverage Status for the Civilian Noninstitutionalized Population and Children Under 18 Years of Age

(Numbers in thousands, percent.)

Item	2004	2005	2006	2007	2008	2009	2010	2011
Civilian Noninstitutionalized Population	19,054	19,022	19,040	19,062	19,207	19,264	19,134	19,208
Covered by Private or Public Insurance								
Number	16,652	16,548	16,378	16,543	16,949	17,070	16,857	17,013
Percent	87.4	87.0	86.0	86.8	88.2	88.6	88.1	88.6
Not Covered								
Number	2,402	2,474	2,662	2,519	2,258	2,195	2,277	2,195
Percent	12.6	13.0	14.0	13.2	11.8	11.4	11.9	11.4
Percent in the U.S. not covered	14.9	15.3	15.8	15.3	15.1	15.1	15.5	15.1
Children Under 18 Years of Age	4,599	4,534	4,547	4,437	4,402	4,414	4,302	4,270
Covered by Private or Public Insurance								
Number	4,289	4,187	4,167	4,042	4,147	4,209	4,094	4,089
Percent	93.3	92.3	91.6	91.1	94.2	95.4	95.2	95.8
Not Covered								
Number	310	347	380	395	255	205	208	181
Percent	6.7	7.7	8.4	8.9	5.8	4.6	4.8	4.2
Percent in the U.S. not covered	10.5	10.9	11.7	11.0	9.7	8.6	8.0	7.5

Table NY-7. Employment Status by Demographic Group, Preliminary 2012

(Numbers in thousands, percent.)

Characteristic	Civilian noninstitutional population	Civilian labor force		Employed		Unemployed	
		Number	Percent of population	Number	Percent of population	Number	Percent of population
Total	15,554	9,556	61.4	8,726	56.1	830	8.7
Sex							
Male	7,408	5,019	67.8	4,545	61.4	474	9.4
Female	8,146	4,536	55.7	4,181	51.3	356	7.8
Race, Sex, and Hispanic Origin							
White	11,308	7,061	62.4	6,501	57.5	560	7.9
Male	5,484	3,778	68.9	3,453	63.0	325	8.6
Female	5,824	3,282	56.4	3,048	52.3	234	7.1
Black or African American	2,578	1,512	58.7	1,304	50.6	209	13.8
Male	1,144	704	61.6	586	51.2	118	16.8
Female	1,434	808	56.3	718	50.0	90	11.2
Hispanic	2,599	1,568	60.3	1,387	53.4	181	11.5
Male	1,205	837	69.5	746	61.9	92	11.0
Female	1,394	730	52.4	641	46.0	89	12.2
Age							
16 to 19 years	1,075	288	26.8	206	19.2	82	28.4
20 to 24 years	1,472	902	61.2	769	52.2	133	14.7
25 to 34 years	2,732	2,187	80.1	1,993	72.9	195	8.9
35 to 44 years	2,395	1,917	80.1	1,777	74.2	141	7.3
45 to 54 years	2,744	2,188	79.8	2,048	74.6	141	6.4
55 to 64 years	2,500	1,607	64.3	1,503	60.1	104	6.5
65 years and over	2,637	466	17.7	431	16.3	35	7.5

NOTE: Data in Table 7 are from the Current Population Survey (CPS) and do not match the estimates in Table 8. See notes and definitions for further information.

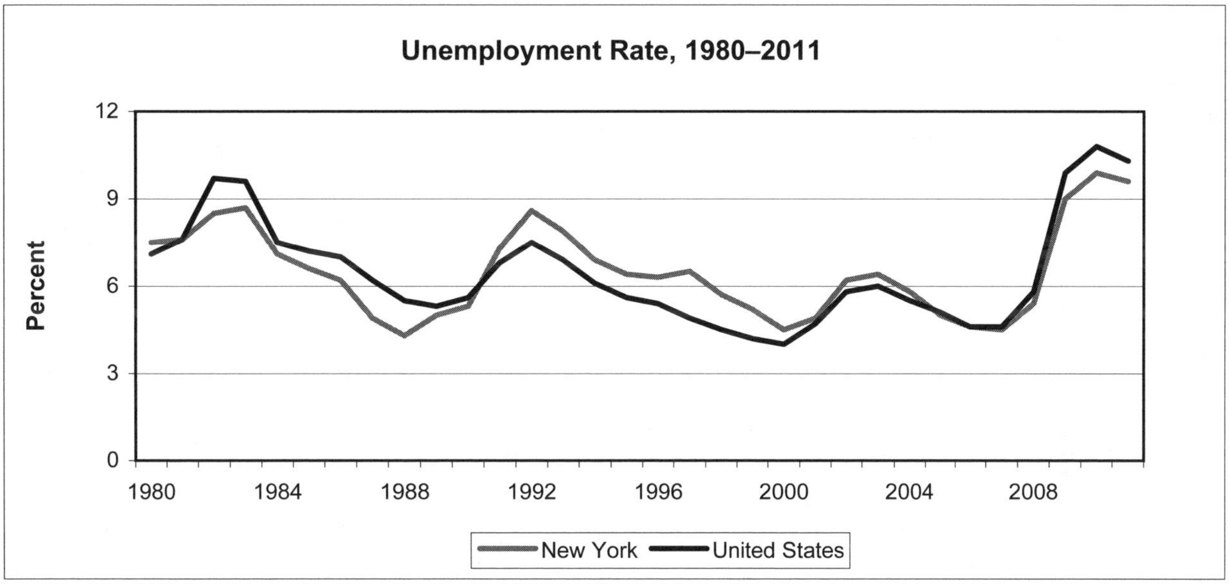

Table NY-8. Employment Status of the Civilian Noninstitutional Population Age 16 Years and Over

(Number, percent.)

Year	Civilian labor force	Civilian participation rate	Employed	Unemployed	Unemployment rate
2005	9,442,870	62.7	8,967,712	475,079	5.0
2006	9,530,103	62.9	9,091,712	438,391	4.6
2007	9,574,776	62.7	9,140,869	433,907	4.5
2008	9,679,617	63.1	9,152,934	526,683	5.4
2009	10,013,915	64.0	9,116,374	897,541	9.0
2010	9,888,442	63.3	8,913,640	974,802	9.9
2011	9,907,450	63.1	8,959,015	948,435	9.6

Table NY-9. Employment and Average Wages by Industry

(Estimates before 2007 are based on the 2002 *North American Industry Classification System* [NAICS]. Estimates from 2007 onward are based on the 2007 NAICS.)

Industry	2005	2006	2007	2008	2009	2010	2011
	Number of jobs						
Wage and Salary Employment by Industry	8,724,537	8,810,584	8,939,191	9,003,322	8,735,423	8,732,197	8,837,168
Farm Wage and Salary Employment	19,019	17,716	17,437	19,023	18,351	18,392	19,509
Nonfarm Wage and Salary Employment	8,705,518	8,792,868	8,921,754	8,984,299	8,717,072	8,713,805	8,817,659
Private wage and salary employment	7,205,578	7,293,560	7,410,505	7,455,737	7,191,241	7,195,895	7,339,851
Forestry, fishing, and related activities	4,728	4,842	4,814	5,029	5,045	5,158	5,446
Mining	4,935	5,289	5,493	5,635	4,777	4,634	4,681
Utilities	39,417	39,102	38,719	38,886	39,359	38,327	37,278
Construction	337,439	350,173	366,885	375,382	340,039	321,327	324,855
Manufacturing	583,280	568,773	554,240	534,317	477,631	458,109	459,252
Durable goods manufacturing	335,795	331,415	326,557	317,602	281,194	268,367	271,254
Nondurable goods manufacturing	247,485	237,358	227,683	216,715	196,437	189,742	187,998
Wholesale trade	356,082	356,984	360,553	354,528	332,696	328,545	334,142
Retail trade	891,317	895,754	909,619	910,003	878,238	891,411	907,655
Transportation and warehousing	233,257	237,432	240,727	242,217	230,532	226,846	230,202
Information	270,754	269,279	267,120	265,147	253,295	253,220	256,473
Finance and insurance	538,720	553,494	556,515	547,195	509,996	503,703	517,938
Real estate and rental and leasing	191,172	191,674	192,092	194,552	188,380	187,147	185,901
Professional, scientific, and technical services	540,756	562,546	584,206	597,315	571,505	564,281	584,824
Management of companies and enterprises	123,323	127,854	128,824	131,576	130,725	132,092	133,230
Administrative and waste services	432,365	431,538	441,932	443,118	410,762	420,108	432,763
Educational services	329,739	336,087	344,028	353,266	353,666	359,334	366,831
Health care and social assistance	1,203,106	1,227,826	1,249,795	1,271,880	1,293,921	1,318,983	1,331,403
Arts, entertainment, and recreation	134,374	136,169	140,971	146,531	143,117	143,118	145,968
Accommodation and food services	544,966	552,089	570,411	580,974	579,229	603,010	632,911
Other services, except public administration	445,848	446,655	453,561	458,186	448,328	436,542	448,098
Government and government enterprises	1,499,940	1,499,308	1,511,249	1,528,562	1,525,831	1,517,910	1,477,808
	Dollars						
Average Wages and Salaries by Industry	51,226	54,701	58,616	59,418	57,004	59,511	61,042
Average Farm Wages and Salaries	21,838	26,999	32,541	28,804	27,627	26,371	22,547
Average Nonfarm Wages and Salaries	51,290	54,757	58,667	59,483	57,066	59,581	61,127
Average private wages and salaries	52,323	56,193	60,602	61,252	58,106	60,831	62,437
Forestry, fishing, and related activities	24,473	25,296	26,542	27,844	28,753	28,865	29,137
Mining	48,793	50,271	54,095	60,086	55,486	58,210	67,444
Utilities	83,145	87,454	92,446	93,933	92,583	97,932	103,008
Construction	50,338	52,812	55,778	58,868	59,674	60,281	61,489
Manufacturing	51,840	53,600	55,679	57,040	57,052	59,391	59,979
Durable goods manufacturing	54,356	56,860	58,850	60,327	60,591	62,768	64,386
Nondurable goods manufacturing	48,426	49,047	51,132	52,223	51,987	54,614	53,620
Wholesale trade	62,301	65,453	69,067	68,900	68,769	71,633	73,738
Retail trade	27,251	28,174	29,169	29,469	29,215	29,626	30,299
Transportation and warehousing	40,099	41,584	43,664	44,356	44,025	45,460	46,132
Information	76,007	81,108	87,294	89,110	89,193	90,840	95,814
Finance and insurance	151,487	175,572	205,524	204,962	171,837	191,436	198,094
Real estate and rental and leasing	47,935	51,002	55,542	54,783	52,242	54,584	56,582
Professional, scientific, and technical services	76,945	80,222	84,184	87,363	86,296	90,752	93,826
Management of companies and enterprises	120,306	125,893	141,151	133,419	119,634	140,138	142,451
Administrative and waste services	35,474	36,703	39,383	40,668	40,503	42,540	41,922
Educational services	34,345	35,905	37,480	39,096	40,537	41,077	42,297
Health care and social assistance	38,222	39,611	41,038	42,536	43,733	44,359	45,135
Arts, entertainment, and recreation	41,821	46,927	47,769	47,315	46,484	47,111	48,224
Accommodation and food services	21,197	22,336	24,097	24,269	23,693	24,573	25,483
Other services, except public administration	28,529	29,779	30,919	32,397	32,576	33,582	33,971
Government and government enterprises	46,327	47,773	49,175	50,850	52,168	53,654	54,618

Table NY-10. Employment Characteristics by Family Type

(Number, percent.)

Family type and labor force status	2009 Total	2009 Families with own children under 18 years	2010 Total	2010 Families with own children under 18 years	2011 Total	2011 Families with own children under 18 years
All families	4,606,840	2,090,067	4,632,676	2,081,726	4,607,636	2,042,822
Family type and labor force status						
Married-couple families	3,214,598	1,387,954	3,210,895	1,373,666	3,166,722	1,330,561
Both husband and wife in labor force	54.3	65.2	53.9	65.3	53.4	64.9
Husband in labor force, wife not in labor force	22.0	28.7	21.7	28.5	21.9	28.7
Wife in labor force, husband not in labor force	7.9	4.5	8.2	4.3	8.2	4.5
Both husband and wife not in labor force	15.8	1.6	16.1	1.9	16.5	1.9
Other families	1,392,242	702,113	1,421,781	708,060	1,440,914	712,261
Female householder, no husband present	75.4	79.4	75.0	79.1	75.4	79.7
In labor force	52.6	63.5	51.8	63.2	51.5	63.4
Not in labor force	22.8	15.9	23.2	15.9	23.9	16.3
Male householder, no wife present	24.6	20.6	25.0	20.9	24.6	20.3
In labor force	19.2	18.3	19.6	18.8	18.9	18.1
Not in labor force	5.4	2.3	5.3	2.1	5.8	2.2

Table NY-11. School Enrollment and Educational Attainment, 2011

(Number, percent.)

Item	State	U.S.
Enrollment		
Total population 3 years and over, enrolled in school	5,020,940	83,131,910
Enrolled in nursery school or preschool (percent)	5.8	6.0
Enrolled in kindergarten (percent)	4.9	5.1
Enrolled in elementary school, grades 1-8 (percent)	37.4	39.5
Enrolled in high school, grades 9-12 (percent)	21.0	20.7
Enrolled in college or graduate school (percent)	30.9	28.7
Attainment		
Total population 25 years and over	13,197,704	206,471,670
Less than ninth grade (percent)	6.8	6.0
9th to 12th grade, no diploma (percent)	8.1	8.1
High school graduate, including equivalency (percent)	27.5	28.4
Some college, no degree (percent)	16.3	21.2
Associate's degree (percent)	8.3	7.8
Bachelor's degree (percent)	18.7	17.9
Graduate or professional degree (percent)	14.2	10.6
High school graduate or higher (percent)	85.0	85.9
Bachelor's degree or higher (percent)	32.9	28.5

Table NY-12. Educational Indicators

(Number, percent; data derived from National Center of Education Statistics.)

Item	State	U.S.
Public Schools, 2009–2010 (except where noted)		
Number of school districts	696	13,629
Number of schools	4,730	99,834
Number of students (in thousands)	2,766	49,373
Student-teacher ratio	12.9	15.4
Expenditures per student (dollars)	20,495	10,591
Averaged freshman graduation rate, 2008–2009	73.5	75.5[1]
Dropout rate, 2008–2009	4.2	4.1
Students eligible for free or reduced-price lunch (percent)	47.7	48.0
English language learners, 2010–2011 (percent)	7.8	9.8[1]
Students with IEP (percent)	16.7	13.1
Private Schools, 2009–2010 (except where noted)		
Number of schools	2,016	33,366
Number of students (in thousands)	431	4,700
High school graduates, 2008–2009	31,245	308,813
Student-teacher ratio	10.3	10.7

[1] U.S. total includes estimates for nonreporting states.

Table NY-13. Reported Voting and Registration of the Voting-Age Population, November 2012

(Numbers in thousands, percent.)

Item	Total population	Total citizen population	Registered			Voted		
			Total registered	Percent registered (total population)	Percent registered (total citizen population)	Total voted	Percent voted (total population)	Percent voted (total citizen population)
U.S. Total	235,248	215,081	153,157	65.1	71.2	132,948	56.5	61.8
State Total	15,066	13,082	8,887	59.0	67.9	7,675	50.9	58.7
Sex								
Male	7,151	6,194	4,084	57.1	65.9	3,503	49.0	56.5
Female	7,916	6,887	4,803	60.7	69.7	4,172	52.7	60.6
Race								
White alone	10,925	9,929	6,837	62.6	68.9	5,781	52.9	58.2
White, non-Hispanic alone	8,992	8,672	6,075	67.6	70.1	5,152	57.3	59.4
Black alone	2,482	2,103	1,542	62.1	73.3	1,456	58.7	69.2
Asian alone	1,442	848	384	26.6	45.3	333	23.1	39.2
Hispanic (of any race)	2,363	1,548	983	41.6	63.5	835	35.3	53.9
Age								
18 to 24 years	2,028	1,790	926	45.7	51.8	710	35.0	39.6
25 to 44 years	5,109	4,042	2,676	52.4	66.2	2,278	44.6	56.3
45 to 64 years	5,217	4,706	3,381	64.8	71.8	3,046	58.4	64.7
65 to 74 years	1,558	1,467	1,094	70.2	74.6	976	62.7	66.6
75 years and over	1,154	1,077	810	70.2	75.3	665	57.7	61.8

Table NY-14. Crime

(Number, rate per 100,000. Data are derived from the FBI Uniform Crime Reports.)

Item	State			U.S.		
	2010	2011	Percent change	2010	2011	Percent change
TOTAL POPULATION	19,395,206	19,465,197	0.4	309,330,219	311,591,917	0.7
VIOLENT CRIME						
Number	76,462	77,490	1.3	1,251,248	1,203,564	-3.8
Rate	394.4	398.1	0.9	404.5	386.3	-4.5
Murder and Nonnegligent Manslaughter						
Number	868	774	-10.8	14,722	14,612	-0.7
Rate	4.5	4.0	-11.1	4.8	4.7	-2.1
Forcible Rape						
Number	2,797	2,752	-1.6	85,593	83,425	-2.5
Rate	14.4	14.1	-2.1	27.7	26.8	-3.2
Robbery						
Number	28,630	28,396	-0.8	369,089	354,396	-4.0
Rate	147.6	145.9	-1.2	119.3	113.7	-4.7
Aggravated Assault						
Number	44,197	45,568	3.1	781,844	751,131	-3.9
Rate	227.9	234.1	2.7	252.8	241.1	-4.6
PROPERTY CRIME						
Number	379,710	372,255	-2.0	9,112,625	9,063,173	-0.5
Rate	1,957.8	1,912.4	-2.3	2,945.9	2,908.7	-1.3
Burglary						
Number	65,839	65,397	-0.7	2,168,459	2,188,005	0.9
Rate	339.5	336.0	-1.0	701.0	702.2	0.2
Larceny-Theft						
Number	293,232	287,547	-1.9	6,204,601	6,159,795	-0.7
Rate	1,511.9	1,477.2	-2.3	2,005.8	1,976.9	-1.4
Motor Vehicle Theft						
Number	20,639	19,311	-6.4	739,565	715,373	-3.3
Rate	106.4	99.2	-6.8	239.1	229.6	-4.0

Table NY-15. State Government Finances, 2011

(Dollar amounts in thousands, percent distribution.)

Item	Dollars	Percent distribution
Total Revenue	205,546,377	100.0
General revenue	148,840,822	72.4
Intergovernmental revenue	60,200,009	29.3
Taxes	67,945,152	33.1
General sales	11,581,018	5.6
Selective sales	10,786,944	5.2
License taxes	1,833,694	0.9
Individual income tax	36,209,216	17.6
Corporate income tax	4,015,628	2.0
Other taxes	3,518,652	1.7
Current charges	9,205,740	4.5
Miscellaneous general revenue	11,489,921	5.6
Utility revenue	7,990,745	3.9
Liquor stores revenue	0	0.0
Insurance trust revenue [1]	48,714,810	23.7
Total Expenditure	184,009,243	100.0
Intergovernmental expenditure	59,697,916	32.4
Direct expenditure	124,311,327	67.6
Current operation	80,841,845	43.9
Capital outlay	11,705,347	6.4
Insurance benefits and repayments	24,802,958	13.5
Assistance and subsidies	1,536,459	0.8
Interest on debt	5,424,718	2.9
Exhibit: Salaries and wages	17,791,144	9.7
Total Expenditure	184,009,243	100.0
General expenditure	146,077,903	79.4
Intergovernmental expenditure	59,697,916	32.4
Direct expenditure	86,379,987	46.9
General expenditure, by function:		
Education	45,218,649	24.6
Public welfare	51,131,664	27.8
Hospitals	6,113,751	3.3
Health	8,828,254	4.8
Highways	4,880,309	2.7
Police protection	953,450	0.5
Correction	2,995,539	1.6
Natural resources	506,181	0.3
Parks and recreation	523,176	0.3
Governmental administration	5,699,455	3.1
Interest on general debt	4,115,852	2.2
Other and unallocable	15,111,623	8.2
Utility expenditure	13,128,382	7.1
Liquor stores expenditure	0	0.0
Insurance trust expenditure	24,802,958	13.5
Debt at End of Fiscal Year	134,928,505	X
Cash and Security Holdings	317,212,468	X

X = Not applicable.
[1] Within insurance trust revenue, net earnings of state retirement systems is a calculated statistic (the item code in the data file is X08), and thus can be positive or negative. Net earnings is the sum of earnings on investments plus gains on investments minus losses on investments. The change made in 2002 for asset valuation from book to market value in accordance with Statement 34 of the Governmental Accounting Standards Board is reflected in the calculated statistics.

Table NY-16. State Government Tax Collections, 2012

(Dollars in thousands, percent.)

Item	Dollars	Percent distribution
Total Taxes	71,545,745	100.0
Property taxes	0	0.0
Sales and gross receipts	22,869,327	32.0
General sales and gross receipts	11,904,357	16.6
Selective sales and gross receipts	10,964,970	15.3
Alcoholic beverages	238,932	0.3
Amusements	769	-
Insurance premiums	1,339,033	1.9
Motor fuels	1,604,727	2.2
Pari-mutuels	22,361	-
Public utilities	942,585	1.3
Tobacco products	1,631,995	2.3
Other selective sales	5,184,568	7.2
Licenses	1,926,804	2.7
Alcoholic beverages	59,079	0.1
Amusements	40	-
Corporations in general	52,469	0.1
Hunting and fishing	56,286	0.1
Motor vehicle	1,418,700	2.0
Motor vehicle operators	132,129	0.2
Public utilities	20,347	-
Occupation and business, NEC	186,278	0.3
Other licenses	1,476	-
Income taxes	43,339,857	60.6
Individual income	38,771,968	54.2
Corporation net income	4,567,889	6.4
Other taxes	3,409,757	4.8
Death and gift	1,078,516	1.5
Documentary and stock transfer	710,877	1.0
Severance	0	0.0
Taxes, NEC	1,620,364	2.3

- = Rounds to zero.

Leading Exports, 2012

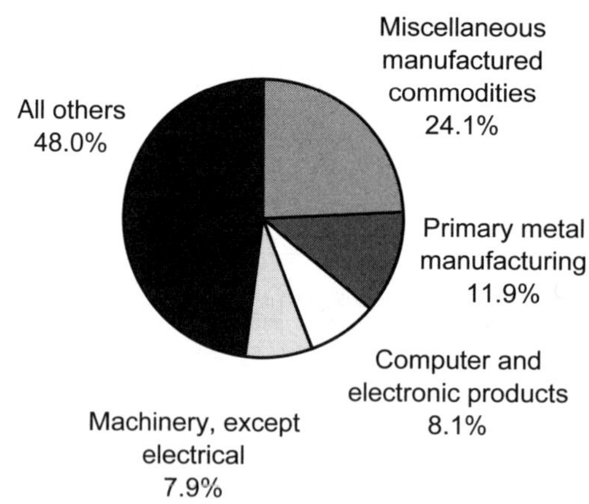

NORTH CAROLINA

Facts and Figures

Location: Southeastern United States; bordered on the N by Virginia, on the E by the Atlantic Ocean, on the S by South Carolina and Georgia, and on the W by Tennessee

Area: 53,819 sq. mi. (139,389 sq. km.); rank—28th

Population: 9,752,073 (2012 est.); rank—10th

Principal Cities: capital—Raleigh; largest—Charlotte

Statehood: November 21, 1789; 12th state

U.S. Congress: 2 senators, 13 representatives

State Motto: *Esse quam videri* ("To be rather than to seem")

State Song: "The Old North State"

State Nicknames: The Tar Heel State; The Old North State

Abbreviations: NC; N.C.

State Symbols: flower—flowering dogwood; tree—pine; bird—cardinal

At a Glance

- With an increase in population of 16.6 percent, North Carolina ranked 6th among the states in growth from 2000 to 2009.
- An estimated 65,800 marriages took place in North Carolina in 2009, compared to 36,700 divorces.
- North Carolina's median household income in 2011 was $43,916, and 17.9 percent of the population lived below the poverty level in 2011.
- North Carolina's violent crime rate in 2011 was 349.8 per 100,000 population, compared to 386.3 for the entire nation.
- In 2007, North Carolina exported $2.1 billion worth of agricultural products, about 2.6 percent of the U.S. total.

Table NC-1. Population by Age, Sex, Race, and Hispanic Origin

(Number, percent, except where noted.)

Sex, age, race, and Hispanic origin	2000	2010	2012[1]	Average annual percent change, 2010–2012
Total Population	8,049,313	9,535,483	9,752,073	0.7
Percent of total U.S. population	2.9	3.1	3.1	X
Sex				
Male	3,942,695	4,645,492	4,752,898	0.8
Female	4,106,618	4,889,991	4,999,175	0.7
Age				
Under 5 years	539,509	632,040	619,940	-0.7
5 to 19 years	1,653,851	1,926,640	1,941,523	0.3
20 to 64 years	4,886,905	5,742,724	5,842,741	0.6
65 years and over	969,048	1,234,079	1,347,869	2.8
Median age (years)	35.3	37.4	37.8	0.4
Race and Hispanic Origin				
One race				
White	5,804,656	6,898,296	7,013,116	0.5
Black	1,737,545	2,088,362	2,147,599	0.9
American Indian and Alaska Native	99,551	147,566	150,965	0.8
Asian	113,689	215,952	238,933	3.2
Native Hawaiian or Other Pacific Islander	3,983	10,309	10,834	1.6
Two or more races	103,260	174,998	190,626	2.7
Hispanic (of any race)	378,963	830,172	883,859	2.0

X = Not applicable.
[1] Population figures for 2012 are July 1 estimates. The 2010 estimates are taken from the 2010 Census.

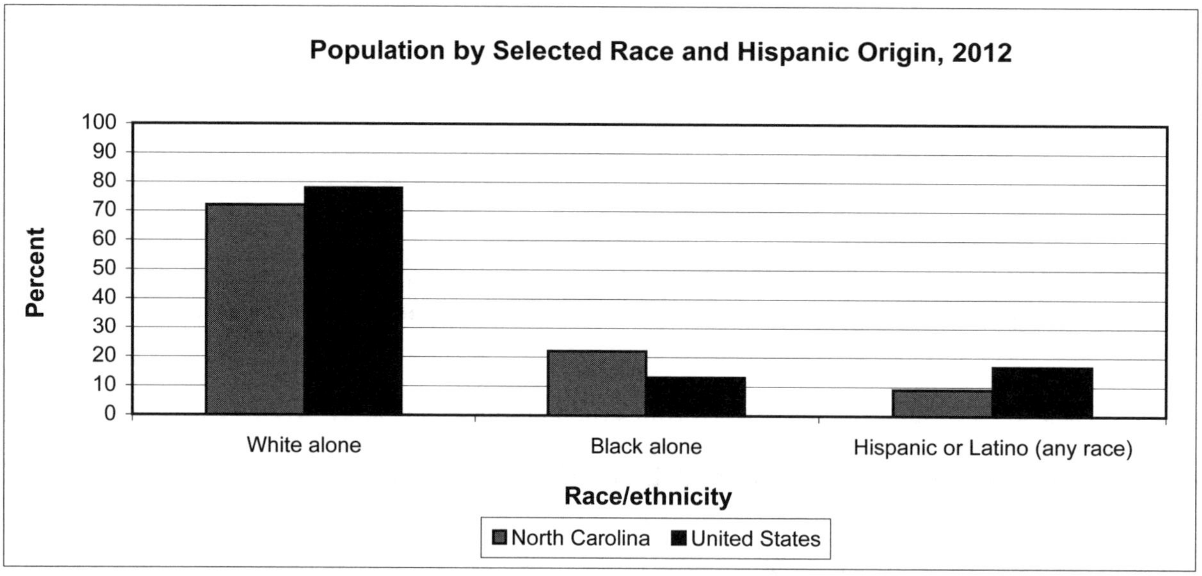

Table NC-2. Marital Status

(Number, percent distribution.)

Sex, age, race, and Hispanic origin	2000	2010	2011
Males, 15 Years and Over	3,092,380	3,678,950	3,718,727
Never married	28.2	33.3	33.5
Now married, except separated	58.7	51.8	51.8
Separated	2.7	2.9	2.8
Widowed	2.4	2.5	2.5
Divorced	8.1	9.6	9.3
Females, 15 Years and Over	3,301,327	3,975,748	4,021,355
Never married	22.0	27.3	27.8
Now married, except separated	53.9	47.3	47.1
Separated	3.3	3.5	3.7
Widowed	10.9	9.8	9.6
Divorced	9.9	12.1	11.9

Table NC-3. Households and Housing Characteristics

(Number, percent, dollars.)

Item	2000	2010	2011	Average annual percent change, 2000–2011
Total Households	3,132,013	3,670,859	3,683,364	1.5
Family households	2,158,869	2,441,916	2,455,564	1.1
Married-couple family	1,645,346	1,770,863	1,788,142	0.7
Other family	513,523	671,053	667,422	2.5
Male householder, no wife present	123,526	159,752	155,308	2.1
Female householder, no husband present	389,997	511,301	512,114	2.6
Nonfamily households	973,144	1,228,943	1,227,800	2.2
Householder living alone	795,271	1,022,017	1,031,543	2.5
Householder not living alone	177,873	206,926	196,257	0.9
Housing Characteristics				
Total housing units	3,523,944	4,333,479	4,362,956	2.0
Occupied housing units	3,132,013	3,670,859	3,683,364	1.5
Owner occupied	2,172,355	2,465,551	2,449,902	1.1
Renter occupied	959,658	1,205,308	1,233,462	2.4
Average size	2.49	2.53	2.55	0.2
Financial Characteristics				
Median gross rent of renter-occupied housing	548	731	745	3.0
Median monthly owner costs for housing units with a mortgage	985	1,250	1,246	2.2
Median value of owner-occupied housing units	108,300	154,200	153,700	3.5

Table NC-4. Migration, Origin, and Language

(Number, percent.)

Characteristic	State			U.S.		
	2010	2011	Percent change	2010	2011	Percent change
Residence 1 Year Ago						
Population 1 year and over	9,443,000	9,539,412	1.0	305,628,607	307,900,319	0.7
Same house	84.5	84.6	0.1	84.6	84.8	0.2
Different house in the U.S.	14.9	14.9	-	14.8	14.6	-1.4
Same county	8.7	8.7	-	9.4	9.2	-2.1
Different county	6.2	6.2	-	5.4	5.4	-
Same state	3.4	3.5	2.9	3.2	3.1	-3.1
Different state	2.8	2.8	-	2.2	2.3	4.5
Abroad	0.6	0.5	-16.7	0.6	0.6	-
Place of Birth						
Native born	8,842,421	8,948,051	1.2	269,393,835	271,214,059	0.7
Male	48.4	48.3	-0.2	49.2	49.2	-
Female	51.6	51.7	0.2	50.8	50.8	-
Foreign born	719,137	708,350	-1.5	39,955,854	40,377,860	1.1
Male	52.1	51.9	-0.4	49.1	48.9	-0.4
Female	47.9	48.1	0.4	50.9	51.1	0.4
Foreign born; naturalized U.S. citizen	217,183	234,546	8.0	17,476,082	18,140,192	3.8
Male	48.9	47.2	-3.5	45.8	45.8	-
Female	51.1	52.8	3.3	54.2	54.2	-
Foreign born; not a U.S. citizen	501,954	473,804	-5.6	22,479,772	22,237,668	-1.1
Male	53.4	54.3	1.7	51.6	51.5	-0.2
Female	46.6	45.7	-1.9	48.4	48.5	0.2
Entered 2000 or later	45.7	44.9	-1.8	34.7	35.7	2.9
Entered 1990 to 1999	31.1	31.6	1.6	27.2	26.7	-1.8
Entered before 1990	23.2	23.5	1.3	38.1	37.6	-1.3
World Region of Birth, Foreign						
Foreign-born population, excluding population born at sea	719,137	708,350	-1.5	39,955,673	40,377,757	1.1
Europe	10.5	11.1	5.7	12.1	12.1	-
Asia	22.7	22.6	-0.4	28.2	28.6	1.4
Africa	6.7	5.8	-13.4	4	4.1	2.5
Oceania	0.4	0.1	-75.0	0.5	0.5	-
Latin America	57.6	58.1	0.9	53.1	52.6	-0.9
North America	2.2	2.2	-	2	2.0	-
Language Spoken at Home and Ability to Speak English						
Population 5 years and over	8,929,538	9,029,678	1.1	289,215,746	291,524,091	0.8
English only	89.1	89.3	0.2	79.4	79.2	-0.3
Language other than English	10.9	10.7	-1.8	20.6	20.8	1.0
Speaks English less than "very well"	4.8	4.7	-2.1	8.7	8.7	-

- = Zero or rounds to zero.

Table NC-5. Median Income and Poverty Status, 2011

(Number, percent, except as noted.)

Characteristic	State		U.S.	
	Number	Percent	Number	Percent
Median Income				
Households (dollars)	43,916	X	50,502	X
Families (dollars)	54,082	X	61,455	X
Below Poverty Level (All People)	1,680,963	17.9	48,452,035	15.9
Sex				
Male	745,766	16.4	21,825,281	14.7
Female	935,197	19.2	26,626,754	17.2
Age				
Under 18 years	579,725	25.6	16,386,500	22.5
Related children under 18 years	572,095	25.3	16,087,074	22.2
18 to 64 years	982,046	16.6	28,335,079	14.8
65 years and over	119,192	9.7	3,730,456	9.3

X = Not applicable.

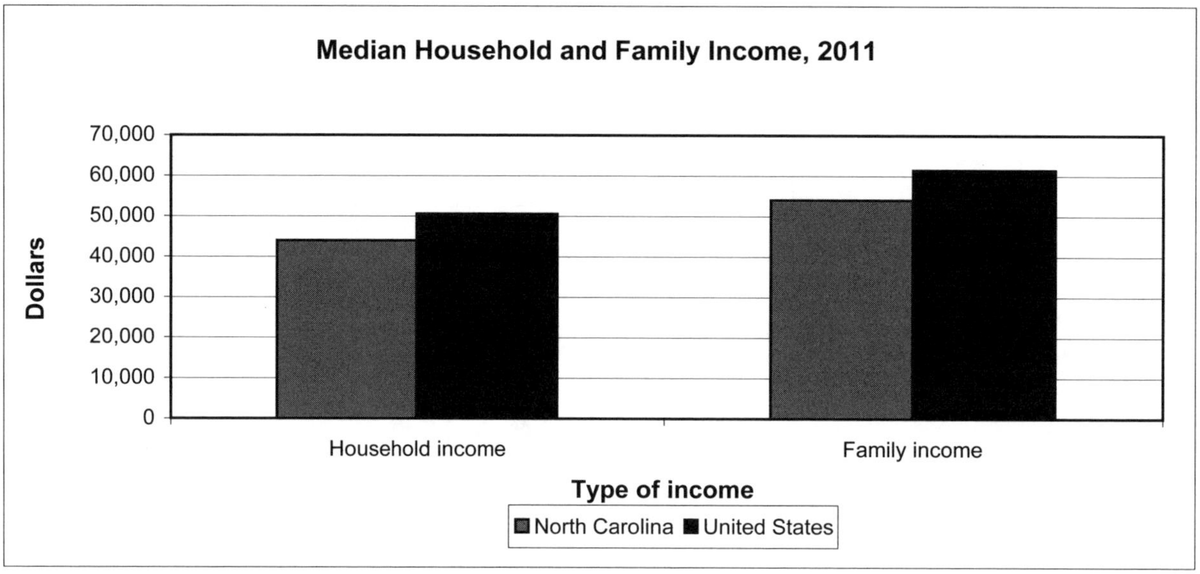

Table NC-6. Health Insurance Coverage Status for the Civilian Noninstitutionalized Population and Children Under 18 Years of Age

(Numbers in thousands, percent.)

Item	2004	2005	2006	2007	2008	2009	2010	2011
Civilian Noninstitutionalized Population	8,435	8,561	8,851	9,183	9,004	9,149	9,361	9,461
Covered by Private or Public Insurance								
Number	7,182	7,249	7,266	7,673	7,570	7,679	7,791	7,916
Percent	85.2	84.7	82.1	83.6	84.1	83.9	83.2	83.7
Not Covered								
Number	1,252	1,312	1,585	1,510	1,434	1,471	1,570	1,545
Percent	14.8	15.3	17.9	16.4	15.9	16.1	16.8	16.3
Percent in the U.S. not covered	14.9	15.3	15.8	15.3	15.1	15.1	15.5	15.1
Children Under 18 Years of Age	2,145	2,205	2,198	2,247	2,237	2,271	2,281	2,287
Covered by Private or Public Insurance								
Number	1,931	1,946	1,891	1,975	2,018	2,085	2,104	2,112
Percent	90.0	88.3	86.0	87.9	90.2	91.8	92.3	92.4
Not Covered								
Number	214	259	307	272	219	186	177	175
Percent	10.0	11.7	14.0	12.1	9.8	8.2	7.7	7.6
Percent in the U.S. not covered	10.5	10.9	11.7	11.0	9.7	8.6	8.0	7.5

Table NC-7. Employment Status by Demographic Group, Preliminary 2012

(Numbers in thousands, percent.)

Characteristic	Civilian noninstitutional population	Civilian labor force		Employed		Unemployed	
		Number	Percent of population	Number	Percent of population	Number	Percent of population
Total	7,485	4,693	62.7	4,262	56.9	431	9.2
Sex							
Male	3,530	2,475	70.1	2,257	63.9	218	8.8
Female	3,955	2,218	56.1	2,005	50.7	213	9.6
Race, Sex, and Hispanic Origin							
White	5,465	3,402	62.2	3,157	57.8	245	7.2
Male	2,643	1,885	71.3	1,764	66.7	121	6.4
Female	2,822	1,517	53.8	1,393	49.4	124	8.2
Black or African American	1,585	1,037	65.4	876	55.3	161	15.6
Male	700	471	67.3	387	55.4	84	17.7
Female	885	566	64.0	488	55.2	78	13.8
Hispanic	503	344	68.4	314	62.4	30	8.8
Male	258	217	84.2	201	78.1	16	7.3
Female	245	127	51.8	112	45.9	14	11.4
Age							
16 to 19 years	516	189	36.7	141	27.4	48	25.4
20 to 24 years	649	456	70.3	383	59.0	73	16.0
25 to 34 years	1,164	953	81.9	878	75.5	75	7.9
35 to 44 years	1,310	1,091	83.3	1,006	76.8	86	7.8
45 to 54 years	1,361	1,085	79.7	1,009	74.1	77	7.1
55 to 64 years	1,125	692	61.5	633	56.2	59	8.5
65 years and over	1,360	227	16.7	213	15.7	14	6.1

NOTE: Data in Table 7 are from the Current Population Survey (CPS) and do not match the estimates in Table 8. See notes and definitions for further information.

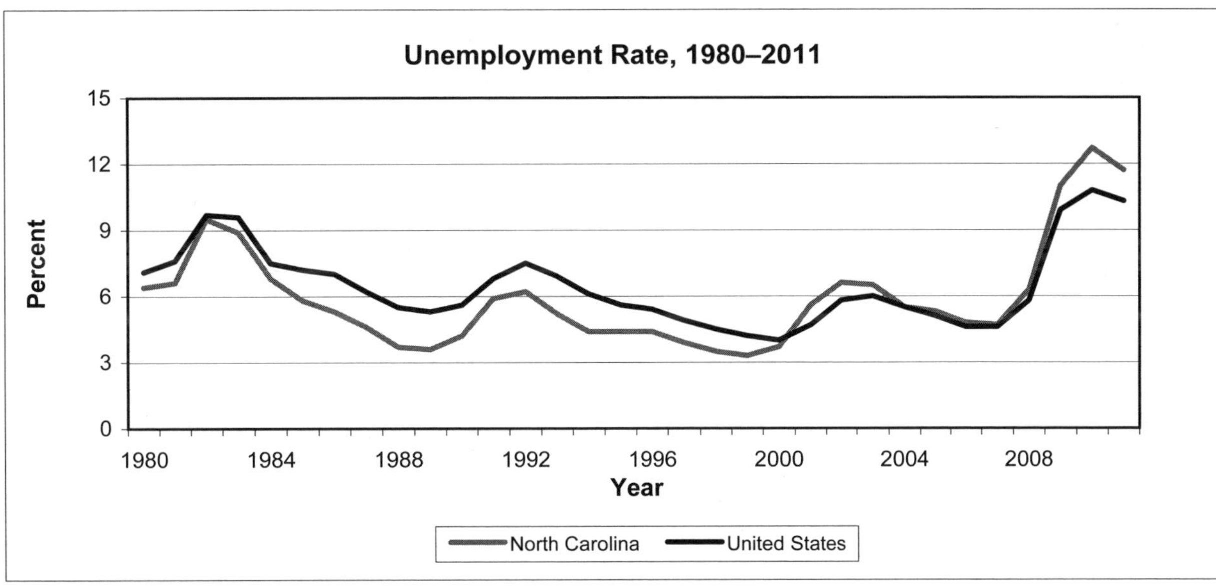

Table NC-8. Employment Status of the Civilian Noninstitutional Population Age 16 Years and Over

(Number, percent.)

Year	Civilian labor force	Civilian participation rate	Employed	Unemployed	Unemployment rate
2005	4,337,060	65.9	4,108,306	228,754	5.3
2006	4,449,262	66.2	1,237,729	211,533	4.8
2007	4,506,144	65.5	4,292,816	213,328	4.7
2008	4,543,754	64.8	4,256,815	286,939	6.3
2009	4,658,142	63.3	4,145,233	512,909	11.0
2010	4,727,122	62.8	4,128,576	598,546	12.7
2011	4,751,695	62.4	4,195,808	555,887	11.7

Table NC-9. Employment and Average Wages by Industry

(Estimates before 2007 are based on the 2002 *North American Industry Classification System* [NAICS]. Estimates from 2007 onward are based on the 2007 NAICS.)

Industry	2005	2006	2007	2008	2009	2010	2011
				Number of jobs			
Wage and Salary Employment by Industry	4,165,974	4,281,925	4,389,750	4,380,014	4,170,430	4,142,475	4,194,673
Farm Wage and Salary Employment	22,009	23,137	22,318	21,240	19,787	20,537	22,498
Nonfarm Wage and Salary Employment	4,143,965	4,258,788	4,367,432	4,358,774	4,150,643	4,121,938	4,172,175
Private wage and salary employment	3,344,708	3,453,688	3,543,270	3,509,755	3,291,218	3,255,024	3,311,094
Forestry, fishing, and related activities	12,785	13,200	13,434	13,276	13,184	13,756	14,185
Mining	3,512	3,739	3,977	3,857	3,421	3,017	3,041
Utilities	13,274	13,266	12,598	12,696	12,655	12,151	12,142
Construction	242,253	255,792	265,582	246,443	201,912	185,010	183,076
Manufacturing	572,362	556,899	544,235	520,425	450,378	432,671	435,641
Durable goods manufacturing	299,510	297,826	291,893	278,378	233,187	222,044	226,553
Nondurable goods manufacturing	272,852	259,073	252,342	242,047	217,191	210,627	209,088
Wholesale trade	170,770	177,646	182,479	180,249	168,500	166,187	169,313
Retail trade	453,750	461,707	475,162	470,147	445,199	441,978	447,766
Transportation and warehousing	118,136	120,258	119,826	116,205	106,853	104,879	108,408
Information	72,445	73,229	73,291	72,418	69,904	68,391	68,765
Finance and insurance	148,096	155,618	157,187	158,175	151,690	152,281	154,409
Real estate and rental and leasing	51,937	54,268	55,814	54,845	51,271	49,619	49,191
Professional, scientific, and technical services	163,246	175,947	186,384	190,501	182,479	183,673	191,014
Management of companies and enterprises	66,617	69,312	71,447	76,037	73,366	73,211	77,301
Administrative and waste services	226,929	240,083	249,721	243,984	217,521	234,201	251,092
Educational services	71,122	74,953	78,817	82,677	86,226	87,362	89,348
Health care and social assistance	406,541	432,926	455,994	464,786	470,835	465,393	465,269
Arts, entertainment, and recreation	46,804	49,694	52,701	53,965	57,441	56,560	58,051
Accommodation and food services	317,017	333,368	347,628	351,085	340,522	340,644	346,828
Other services, except public administration	187,112	191,783	196,993	197,984	187,861	184,040	186,254
Government and government enterprises	799,257	805,100	824,162	849,019	859,425	866,914	861,081
				Dollars			
Average Wages and Salaries by Industry	36,627	38,200	39,748	40,708	40,802	42,039	43,107
Average Farm Wages and Salaries	23,148	24,567	30,476	29,361	25,702	18,438	21,834
Average Nonfarm Wages and Salaries	36,699	38,274	39,795	40,763	40,874	42,157	43,221
Average private wages and salaries	36,542	38,083	39,480	40,274	40,185	41,689	42,827
Forestry, fishing, and related activities	24,135	24,568	25,360	25,890	26,470	27,046	27,915
Mining	59,766	62,948	64,642	53,137	51,558	43,772	46,996
Utilities	68,671	69,273	76,378	78,538	76,185	80,911	82,200
Construction	35,786	38,141	39,567	40,517	40,246	41,015	42,240
Manufacturing	43,948	46,093	48,429	49,177	50,468	52,809	54,176
Durable goods manufacturing	45,851	48,604	51,202	51,999	53,639	56,441	58,112
Nondurable goods manufacturing	41,859	43,206	45,222	45,931	47,064	48,980	49,910
Wholesale trade	52,646	54,826	57,069	58,029	57,951	60,561	62,665
Retail trade	24,006	24,603	25,204	25,175	24,984	25,594	25,625
Transportation and warehousing	38,247	38,874	40,164	42,174	42,055	42,980	43,845
Information	54,402	55,639	57,582	60,284	60,354	63,009	65,922
Finance and insurance	66,221	72,414	74,459	72,619	68,467	73,822	76,784
Real estate and rental and leasing	34,309	36,988	37,957	37,566	36,701	37,924	39,752
Professional, scientific, and technical services	54,707	57,370	60,420	62,622	63,425	66,463	68,258
Management of companies and enterprises	81,141	82,087	84,902	86,643	81,911	88,227	91,823
Administrative and waste services	25,430	26,377	27,784	29,370	30,103	30,982	31,550
Educational services	29,639	30,966	32,349	33,695	33,923	34,997	36,130
Health care and social assistance	35,477	36,514	37,458	38,926	39,811	40,599	41,688
Arts, entertainment, and recreation	27,899	31,648	32,885	32,648	30,330	30,474	31,388
Accommodation and food services	14,601	14,909	15,870	15,791	15,875	16,630	16,965
Other services, except public administration	23,872	24,564	26,752	26,632	27,128	28,223	28,798
Government and government enterprises	37,352	39,094	41,150	42,784	43,513	43,914	44,736

Table NC-10. Employment Characteristics by Family Type

(Number, percent.)

Family type and labor force status	2009 Total	2009 Families with own children under 18 years	2010 Total	2010 Families with own children under 18 years	2011 Total	2011 Families with own children under 18 years
All families	2,430,277	1,083,501	2,441,916	1,075,410	2,455,564	1,060,465
Family type and labor force status						
Married-couple families	1,791,515	712,126	1,770,863	702,528	1,788,142	675,851
Both husband and wife in labor force	53.8	68.1	53.0	67.6	52.2	66.8
Husband in labor force, wife not in labor force	21.4	27.0	21.6	27.0	21.7	27.7
Wife in labor force, husband not in labor force	7.8	3.4	8.2	3.8	8.2	4.1
Both husband and wife not in labor force	17.0	1.5	17.1	1.6	17.9	1.4
Other families	638,762	371,375	671,053	372,882	667,422	384,614
Female householder, no husband present	75.2	77.9	76.2	78.6	76.7	78.7
In labor force	53.8	64.0	53.4	64.0	54.9	64.8
Not in labor force	21.4	13.9	22.8	14.6	21.9	13.9
Male householder, no wife present	24.8	22.1	23.8	21.4	23.3	21.3
In labor force	20.5	20.5	18.8	19.7	18.3	19.4
Not in labor force	4.2	1.7	5.0	1.7	4.9	1.9

Table NC-11. School Enrollment and Educational Attainment, 2011

(Number, percent.)

Item	State	U.S.
Enrollment		
Total population 3 years and over, enrolled in school	2,557,304	83,131,910
Enrolled in nursery school or preschool (percent)	5.7	6.0
Enrolled in kindergarten (percent)	5.2	5.1
Enrolled in elementary school, grades 1-8 (percent)	40.2	39.5
Enrolled in high school, grades 9-12 (percent)	20.0	20.7
Enrolled in college or graduate school (percent)	29.0	28.7
Attainment		
Total population 25 years and over	6,399,357	206,471,670
Less than ninth grade (percent)	5.7	6.0
9th to 12th grade, no diploma (percent)	9.5	8.1
High school graduate, including equivalency (percent)	27.3	28.4
Some college, no degree (percent)	21.8	21.2
Associate's degree (percent)	8.7	7.8
Bachelor's degree (percent)	17.8	17.9
Graduate or professional degree (percent)	9.2	10.6
High school graduate or higher (percent)	84.7	85.9
Bachelor's degree or higher (percent)	26.9	28.5

Table NC-12. Educational Indicators

(Number, percent; data derived from National Center of Education Statistics.)

Item	State	U.S.
Public Schools, 2009–2010 (except where noted)		
Number of school districts	115	13,629
Number of schools	2,550	99,834
Number of students (in thousands)	1,483	49,373
Student-teacher ratio	14.1	15.4
Expenditures per student (dollars)	8,965	10,591
Averaged freshman graduation rate, 2008–2009	75.1	75.5[1]
Dropout rate, 2008–2009	5.3	4.1
Students eligible for free or reduced-price lunch (percent)	50.2	48.0
English language learners, 2010–2011 (percent)	7.1	9.8[1]
Students with IEP (percent)	12.5	13.1
Private Schools, 2009–2010 (except where noted)		
Number of schools	667	33,366
Number of students (in thousands)	99	4,700
High school graduates, 2008–2009	5,727	308,813
Student-teacher ratio	9.9	10.7

[1] U.S. total includes estimates for nonreporting states.

Table NC-13. Reported Voting and Registration of the Voting-Age Population, November 2012

(Numbers in thousands, percent.)

Item	Total population	Total citizen population	Registered			Voted		
			Total registered	Percent registered (total population)	Percent registered (total citizen population)	Total voted	Percent voted (total population)	Percent voted (total citizen population)
U.S. Total	235,248	215,081	153,157	65.1	71.2	132,948	56.5	61.8
State Total	7,265	6,712	5,295	72.9	78.9	4,624	63.7	68.9
Sex								
Male	3,439	3,125	2,401	69.8	76.8	2,103	61.2	67.3
Female	3,826	3,587	2,894	75.7	80.7	2,521	65.9	70.3
Race								
White alone	5,453	4,966	3,848	70.6	77.5	3,276	60.1	66.0
White, non-Hispanic alone	4,898	4,820	3,755	76.7	77.9	3,194	65.2	66.3
Black alone	1,529	1,501	1,279	83.7	85.3	1,203	78.7	80.2
Asian alone	95	57	34	35.4	B	34	35.4	B
Hispanic (of any race)	603	169	115	19.1	68.0	95	15.7	56.0
Age								
18 to 24 years	863	779	496	57.5	63.7	389	45.1	50.0
25 to 44 years	2,541	2,194	1,735	68.3	79.1	1,468	57.8	66.9
45 to 64 years	2,470	2,373	1,925	77.9	81.1	1,710	69.2	72.1
65 to 74 years	741	727	620	83.7	85.4	577	77.9	79.4
75 years and over	649	640	518	79.8	81.0	480	73.9	75.0

B = Base is less than 75,000 and therefore too small to show the derived measure.

Table NC-14. Crime

(Number, rate per 100,000. Data are derived from the FBI Uniform Crime Reports.)

Item	State			U.S.		
	2010	2011	Percent change	2010	2011	Percent change
TOTAL POPULATION	9,560,234	9,656,401	1.0	309,330,219	311,591,917	0.7
VIOLENT CRIME						
Number	34,679	33,774	-2.6	1,251,248	1,203,564	-3.8
Rate	362.7	349.8	-3.6	404.5	386.3	-4.5
Murder and Nonnegligent Manslaughter						
Number	474	508	7.2	14,722	14,612	-0.7
Rate	5.0	5.3	6.0	4.8	4.7	-2.1
Forcible Rape						
Number	2,002	1,995	-0.3	85,593	83,425	-2.5
Rate	20.9	20.7	-1.0	27.7	26.8	-3.2
Robbery						
Number	9,620	9,550	-0.7	369,089	354,396	-4.0
Rate	100.6	98.9	-1.7	119.3	113.7	-4.7
Aggravated Assault						
Number	22,583	21,721	-3.8	781,844	751,131	-3.9
Rate	236.2	224.9	-4.8	252.8	241.1	-4.6
PROPERTY CRIME						
Number	329,202	340,652	3.5	9,112,625	9,063,173	-0.5
Rate	3,443.5	3,526.8	2.4	2,945.9	2,908.7	-1.3
Burglary						
Number	102,826	106,144	3.2	2,168,459	2,188,005	0.9
Rate	1,075.6	1,099.2	2.2	701.0	702.2	0.2
Larceny-Theft						
Number	208,057	217,386	4.5	6,204,601	6,159,795	-0.7
Rate	2,176.3	2,251.2	3.4	2,005.8	1,976.9	-1.4
Motor Vehicle Theft						
Number	18,319	17,032	-7.0	739,565	715,373	-3.3
Rate	191.6	176.4	-7.9	239.1	229.6	-4.0

Table NC-15. State Government Finances, 2011

(Dollar amounts in thousands, percent distribution.)

Item	Dollars	Percent distribution
Total Revenue	63,199,284	100.0
General revenue	45,857,925	72.6
Intergovernmental revenue	16,048,794	25.4
Taxes	22,405,841	35.5
General sales	6,185,008	9.8
Selective sales	3,750,081	5.9
License taxes	1,449,051	2.3
Individual income tax	9,869,492	15.6
Corporate income tax	1,092,078	1.7
Other taxes	60,131	0.1
Current charges	4,688,504	7.4
Miscellaneous general revenue	2,714,786	4.3
Utility revenue	27	0.0
Liquor stores revenue	0	0.0
Insurance trust revenue [1]	17,341,332	27.4
Total Expenditure	53,088,745	100.0
Intergovernmental expenditure	13,633,379	25.7
Direct expenditure	39,455,366	74.3
Current operation	26,211,316	49.4
Capital outlay	3,364,839	6.3
Insurance benefits and repayments	8,705,210	16.4
Assistance and subsidies	603,558	1.1
Interest on debt	570,443	1.1
Exhibit: Salaries and wages	9,133,307	17.2
Total Expenditure	53,088,745	100.0
General expenditure	44,335,109	83.5
Intergovernmental expenditure	13,633,379	25.7
Direct expenditure	30,701,730	57.8
General expenditure, by function:		
Education	19,310,897	36.4
Public welfare	11,619,455	21.9
Hospitals	1,621,610	3.1
Health	1,567,085	3.0
Highways	3,432,887	6.5
Police protection	534,773	1.0
Correction	1,422,868	2.7
Natural resources	623,070	1.2
Parks and recreation	211,317	0.4
Governmental administration	1,145,911	2.2
Interest on general debt	570,443	1.1
Other and unallocable	2,274,793	4.3
Utility expenditure	48,426	0.1
Liquor stores expenditure	0	0.0
Insurance trust expenditure	8,705,210	16.4
Debt at End of Fiscal Year	18,556,175	X
Cash and Security Holdings	92,829,878	X

X = Not applicable.

[1] Within insurance trust revenue, net earnings of state retirement systems is a calculated statistic (the item code in the data file is X08), and thus can be positive or negative. Net earnings is the sum of earnings on investments plus gains on investments minus losses on investments. The change made in 2002 for asset valuation from book to market value in accordance with Statement 34 of the Governmental Accounting Standards Board is reflected in the calculated statistics.

Table NC-16. State Government Tax Collections, 2012

(Dollars in thousands, percent.)

Item	Dollars	Percent distribution
Total Taxes	22,713,357	100.0
Property taxes	0	0.0
Sales and gross receipts	9,539,299	42.0
General sales and gross receipts	5,573,658	24.5
Selective sales and gross receipts	3,965,641	17.5
Alcoholic beverages	322,970	1.4
Amusements	13,855	0.1
Insurance premiums	479,756	2.1
Motor fuels	1,861,838	8.2
Pari-mutuels	0	0.0
Public utilities	381,937	1.7
Tobacco products	294,754	1.3
Other selective sales	610,531	2.7
Licenses	1,475,960	6.5
Alcoholic beverages	16,026	0.1
Amusements	0	0.0
Corporations in general	523,262	2.3
Hunting and fishing	17,065	0.1
Motor vehicle	569,253	2.5
Motor vehicle operators	123,344	0.5
Public utilities	0	0.0
Occupation and business, NEC	219,080	1.0
Other licenses	7,930	-
Income taxes	11,603,868	51.1
Individual income	10,383,796	45.7
Corporation net income	1,220,072	5.4
Other taxes	94,230	0.4
Death and gift	58,323	0.3
Documentary and stock transfer	34,345	0.2
Severance	1,562	-
Taxes, NEC	0	0.0

- = Rounds to zero.

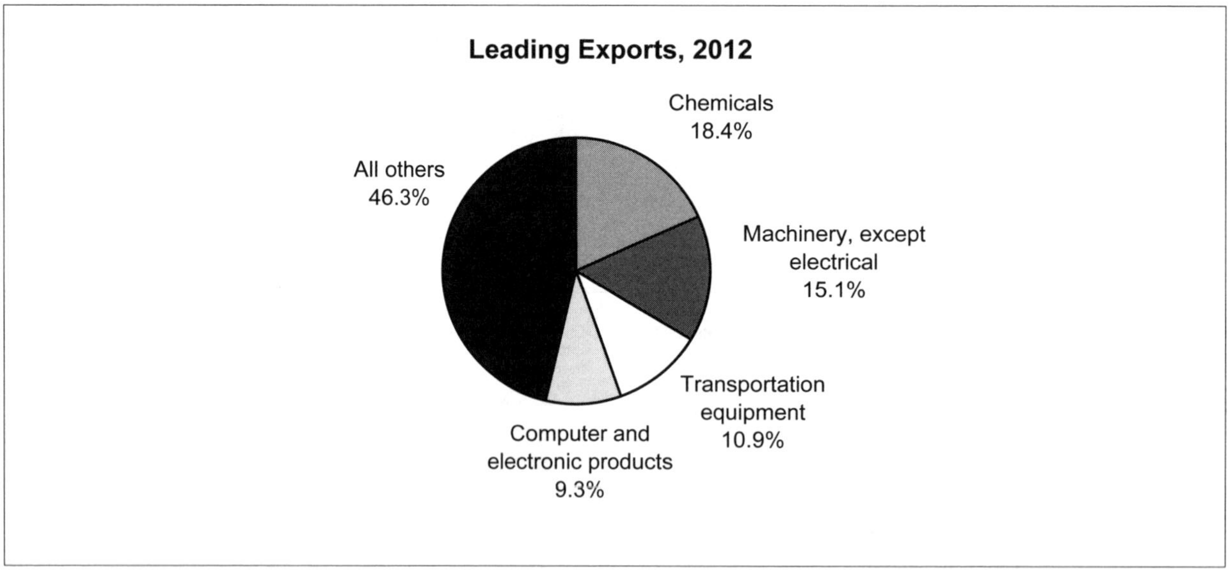

NORTH DAKOTA

Facts and Figures

Location: North central United States; bordered on the N by Canada (Manitoba and Saskatchewan), on the E by Minnesota, on the S by South Dakota, and on the W by Montana

Area: 70,700 sq. mi. (183,112 sq. km.); rank—19th

Population: 699,628 (2012 est.); rank—48th

Principal Cities: capital—Bismarck; largest—Fargo

Statehood: November 2, 1889; 39th state

U.S. Congress: 2 senators, 1 representative

State Motto: Liberty and Union, Now and Forever, One and Inseparable

State Song: "North Dakota Hymn"

State Nicknames: The Peace Garden State; The Flickertail State; The Rough Rider State

Abbreviations: ND; N.D.; N. Dak.

State Symbols: flower—wild prairie rose; tree—American elm; bird—Western meadowlark

At a Glance

- With an increase in population of 0.7 percent, North Dakota ranked 50th for population growth between 2000 and 2009.
- An estimated 4,300 marriages took place in North Dakota in 2009, compared to 1,600 divorces.
- In 2011, 9.8 percent of North Dakotans did not have health insurance, compared to 15.1 percent of the total U.S. population.
- In the 2012 election, 63.9 percent of North Dakota's eligible voters voted, compared to 61.8 percent of eligible voters nationwide.
- In 2007, North Dakota exported $2.6 billion worth of agricultural products, about 3.1 percent of the U.S. total.

Table ND-1. Population by Age, Sex, Race, and Hispanic Origin

(Number, percent, except where noted.)

Sex, age, race, and Hispanic origin	2000	2010	2012[1]	Average annual percent change, 2010–2012
Total Population	642,200	672,591	699,628	1.3
Percent of total U.S. population	0.2	0.2	0.2	X
Sex				
Male	320,524	339,864	355,742	1.5
Female	321,676	332,727	343,886	1.1
Age				
Under 5 years	39,400	44,595	46,109	1.1
5 to 19 years	144,064	127,340	131,115	1.0
20 to 64 years	364,258	403,179	421,738	1.5
65 years and over	94,478	97,477	100,666	1.1
Median age (years)	36.2	37.0	36.1	-0.8
Race and Hispanic Origin				
One race				
White	593,181	609,136	630,215	1.1
Black	3,916	8,248	10,547	7.3
American Indian and Alaska Native	31,329	36,948	38,283	1.2
Asian	3,606	7,032	7,840	3.4
Native Hawaiian or Other Pacific Islander	230	334	475	9.9
Two or more races	7,398	10,893	12,268	3.7
Hispanic (of any race)	7,786	14,407	18,301	7.1

X = Not applicable.
[1] Population figures for 2012 are July 1 estimates. The 2010 estimates are taken from the 2010 Census.

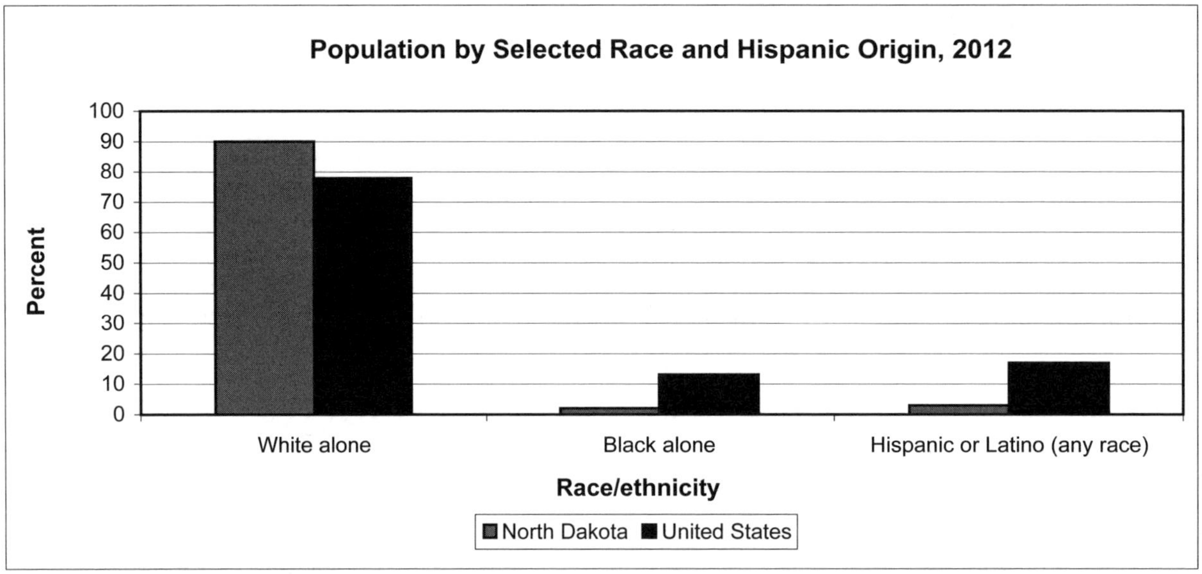

Table ND-2. Marital Status

(Number, percent distribution.)

Sex, age, race, and Hispanic origin	2000	2010	2011
Males, 15 Years and Over	253,900	278,276	280,190
Never married	32.0	35.8	96,741
Now married, except separated	57.5	53.1	149,275
Separated	0.6	0.6	2,023
Widowed	2.5	2.1	6,423
Divorced	7.3	8.4	25,728
Females, 15 Years and Over	258,381	271,462	276,998
Never married	23.2	26.6	72,880
Now married, except separated	56.0	52.5	146,237
Separated	0.8	0.7	2,508
Widowed	11.7	10.1	27,678
Divorced	8.2	10.2	27,695

Table ND-3. Households and Housing Characteristics

(Number, percent, dollars.)

Item	2000	2010	2011	Average annual percent change, 2000–2011
Total Households	257,252	280,412	283,440	0.8
Family households	166,150	171,945	175,219	0.5
Married-couple family	137,433	140,277	142,172	0.3
Other family	28,717	31,668	33,047	1.3
Male householder, no wife present	8,569	8,846	10,656	2.0
Female householder, no husband present	20,148	22,822	22,391	0.9
Nonfamily households	91,002	108,467	108,221	1.6
Householder living alone	75,420	87,883	88,099	1.4
Householder not living alone	15,582	20,584	20,122	2.4
Housing Characteristics				
Total housing units	289,677	318,099	320,888	0.9
Occupied housing units	257,252	280,412	283,440	0.8
Owner occupied	171,299	187,673	186,254	0.7
Renter occupied	85,853	92,739	97,186	1.1
Average size	2.41	2.32	2.32	-0.3
Financial Characteristics				
Median gross rent of renter-occupied housing	412	583	626	4.3
Median monthly owner costs for housing units with a mortgage	818	1,133	1,155	3.4
Median value of owner-occupied housing units	74,400	123,000	128,600	6.1

Table ND-4. Migration, Origin, and Language

(Number, percent.)

Characteristic	State			U.S.		
	2010	2011	Percent change	2010	2011	Percent change
Residence 1 Year Ago						
Population 1 year and over	665,654	675,161	1.4	305,628,607	307,900,319	0.7
Same house	83.6	82.9	-0.8	84.6	84.8	0.2
Different house in the U.S.	15.9	16.6	4.4	14.8	14.6	-1.4
Same county	8.5	8.6	1.2	9.4	9.2	-2.1
Different county	7.4	8.0	8.1	5.4	5.4	-
Same state	2.9	3.2	10.3	3.2	3.1	-3.1
Different state	4.5	4.8	6.7	2.2	2.3	4.5
Abroad	0.5	0.4	-20.0	0.6	0.6	-
Place of Birth						
Native born	657,860	667,306	1.4	269,393,835	271,214,059	0.7
Male	50.9	50.4	-1.0	49.2	49.2	-
Female	49.1	49.6	1.0	50.8	50.8	-
Foreign born	16,639	16,626	-0.1	39,955,854	40,377,860	1.1
Male	52.1	47.8	-8.3	49.1	48.9	-0.4
Female	47.9	52.2	9.0	50.9	51.1	0.4
Foreign born; naturalized U.S. citizen	6,190	5,837	-5.7	17,476,082	18,140,192	3.8
Male	42.3	42.8	1.2	45.8	45.8	-
Female	57.7	57.2	-0.9	54.2	54.2	-
Foreign born; not a U.S. citizen	10,449	10,789	3.3	22,479,772	22,237,668	-1.1
Male	57.9	50.5	-12.8	51.6	51.5	-0.2
Female	42.1	49.5	17.6	48.4	48.5	0.2
Entered 2000 or later	48.8	62.1	27.3	34.7	35.7	2.9
Entered 1990 to 1999	24.9	17.3	-30.5	27.2	26.7	-1.8
Entered before 1990	26.3	20.6	-21.7	38.1	37.6	-1.3
World Region of Birth, Foreign						
Foreign-born population, excluding population born at sea	16,639	16,626	-0.1	39,955,673	40,377,757	1.1
Europe	21.2	16.0	-24.5	12.1	12.1	-
Asia	37.7	43.7	15.9	28.2	28.6	1.4
Africa	19.3	17.8	-7.8	4	4.1	2.5
Oceania	0.0	0.5	-	0.5	0.5	-
Latin America	7.2	8.3	15.3	53.1	52.6	-0.9
North America	14.6	13.6	-6.8	2	2.0	-
Language Spoken at Home and Ability to Speak English						
Population 5 years and over	630,058	637,666	1.2	289,215,746	291,524,091	0.8
English only	94.9	94.9	-	79.4	79.2	-0.3
Language other than English	5.1	5.1	-	20.6	20.8	1.0
Speaks English less than "very well"	1.3	1.4	7.7	8.7	8.7	-

- = Zero or rounds to zero.

Table ND-5. Median Income and Poverty Status, 2011

(Number, percent, except as noted.)

Characteristic	State		U.S.	
	Number	Percent	Number	Percent
Median Income				
Households (dollars)	51,704	X	50,502	X
Families (dollars)	66,924	X	61,455	X
Below Poverty Level (All People)	80,882	12.2	48,452,035	15.9
Sex				
Male	35,734	10.8	21,825,281	14.7
Female	45,148	13.7	26,626,754	17.2
Age				
Under 18 years	21,827	14.6	16,386,500	22.5
Related children under 18 years	20,816	14.1	16,087,074	22.2
18 to 64 years	49,345	11.8	28,335,079	14.8
65 years and over	9,710	10.5	3,730,456	9.3

X = Not applicable.

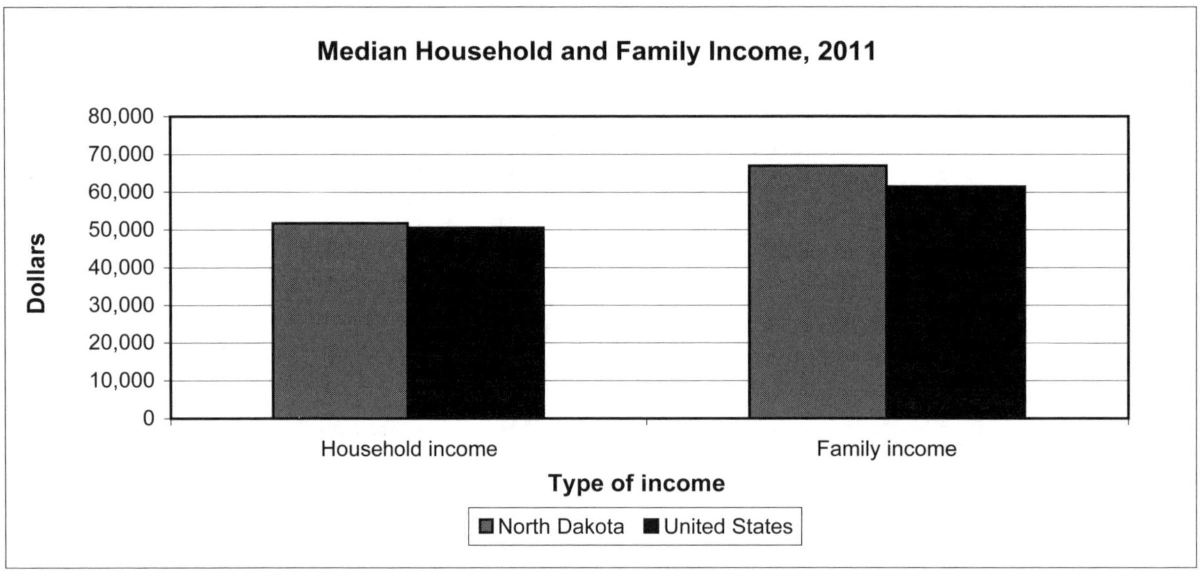

Table ND-6. Health Insurance Coverage Status for the Civilian Noninstitutionalized Population and Children Under 18 Years of Age

(Numbers in thousands, percent.)

Item	2004	2005	2006	2007	2008	2009	2010	2011
Civilian Noninstitutionalized Population	627	626	617	615	624	630	661	669
Covered by Private or Public Insurance								
Number	564	558	541	553	558	569	596	604
Percent	89.9	89.0	87.8	90.0	89.4	90.3	90.2	90.2
Not Covered								
Number	63	69	75	61	66	61	65	65
Percent	10.1	11.0	12.2	10.0	10.6	9.7	9.8	9.8
Percent in the U.S. not covered	14.9	15.3	15.8	15.3	15.1	15.1	15.5	15.1
Children Under 18 Years of Age	144	142	144	146	141	141	150	151
Covered by Private or Public Insurance								
Number	131	129	130	135	130	133	140	141
Percent	90.9	91.1	89.7	92.1	92.2	94.4	93.5	93.6
Not Covered								
Number	13	13	15	11	11	8	10	10
Percent	9.1	8.9	10.3	7.9	7.8	5.6	6.5	6.4
Percent in the U.S. not covered	10.5	10.9	11.7	11.0	9.7	8.6	8.0	7.5

Table ND-7. Employment Status by Demographic Group, Preliminary 2012

(Numbers in thousands, percent.)

Characteristic	Civilian noninstitutional population	Civilian labor force		Employed		Unemployed	
		Number	Percent of population	Number	Percent of population	Number	Percent of population
Total	542	394	72.6	381	70.3	13	3.2
Sex							
Male	272	211	77.6	203	74.8	8	3.6
Female	270	183	67.6	178	65.7	5	2.8
Race, Sex, and Hispanic Origin							
White	474	350	73.8	342	72.1	8	2.3
Male	237	187	78.9	182	76.8	5	2.6
Female	236	162	68.7	159	67.3	3	2.0
Black or African American	NA	NA	NA	NA	NA	NA	NA
Male	NA	NA	NA	NA	NA	NA	NA
Female	NA	NA	NA	NA	NA	NA	NA
Hispanic	13	10	71.7	9	68.9	...	4.1
Male	NA	NA	NA	NA	NA	NA	NA
Female	NA	NA	NA	NA	NA	NA	NA
Age							
16 to 19 years	35	18	49.7	15	43.5	2	12.4
20 to 24 years	55	44	79.5	42	75.5	2	5.0
25 to 34 years	100	86	86.7	84	84.0	3	3.2
35 to 44 years	75	69	91.5	67	89.0	2	2.8
45 to 54 years	98	87	89.2	85	87.5	2	2.0
55 to 64 years	90	68	76.5	67	74.6	2	2.4
65 years and over	90	21	23.9	21	23.6	...	1.4

NOTE: Data in Table 7 are from the Current Population Survey (CPS) and do not match the estimates in Table 8. See notes and definitions for further information.
NA = Not available.
... = Fewer than 500 persons.

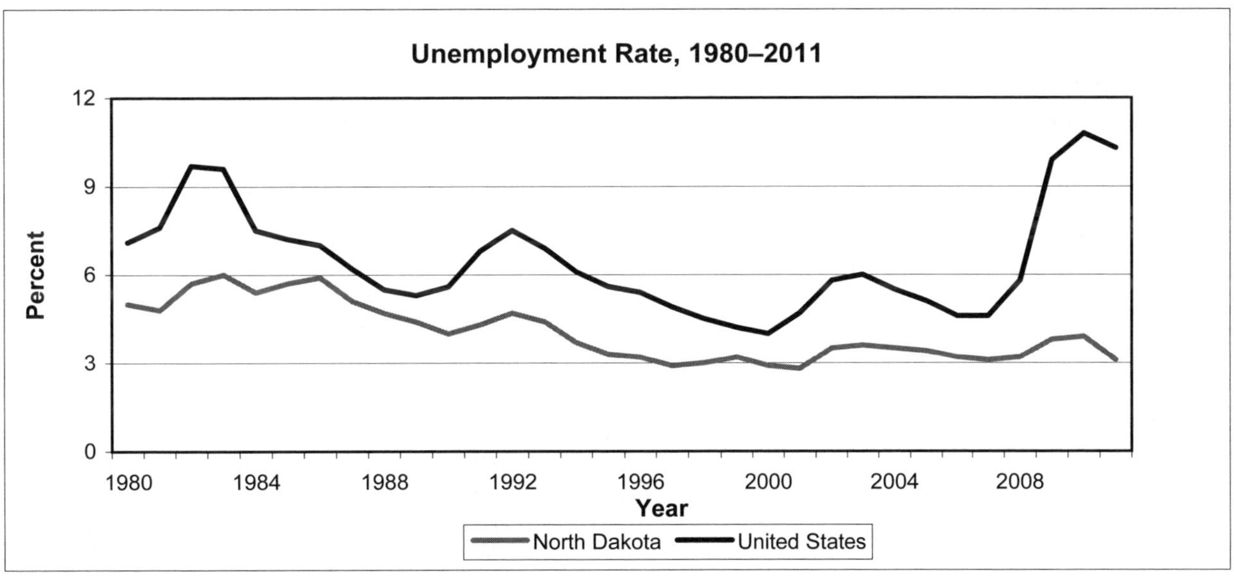

Table ND-8. Employment Status of the Civilian Noninstitutional Population Age 16 Years and Over

(Number, percent.)

Year	Civilian labor force	Civilian participation rate	Employed	Unemployed	Unemployment rate
2005	356,039	72.5	343,784	12,255	3.4
2006	361,210	73.2	349,662	11,548	3.2
2007	366,042	73.9	354,659	11,383	3.1
2008	369,671	74.2	358,001	11,670	3.2
2009	359,601	68.8	345,938	13,663	3.8
2010	377,605	69.7	362,895	14,710	3.9
2011	382,351	69.6	370,830	12,011	3.1

Table ND-9. Employment and Average Wages by Industry

(Estimates before 2007 are based on the 2002 *North American Industry Classification System* [NAICS]. Estimates from 2007 onward are based on the 2007 NAICS.)

Industry	2005	2006	2007	2008	2009	2010	2011
				Number of jobs			
Wage and Salary Employment by Industry	362,298	369,870	375,856	384,084	383,488	393,623	415,288
Farm Wage and Salary Employment	5,220	4,611	4,998	5,210	4,395	4,829	5,282
Nonfarm Wage and Salary Employment	357,078	365,259	370,858	378,874	379,093	388,794	410,006
Private wage and salary employment	276,358	283,652	289,663	298,381	296,084	304,071	325,678
Forestry, fishing, and related activities	1,559	1,531	1,538	1,630	1,639	1,713	1,790
Mining	4,069	4,645	5,075	6,791	6,906	10,523	16,580
Utilities	3,206	3,224	3,288	3,415	3,384	3,418	3,419
Construction	17,940	19,010	19,809	21,428	21,560	22,271	25,607
Manufacturing	25,898	26,003	26,099	26,362	23,607	22,591	23,792
Durable goods manufacturing	17,473	17,699	17,695	18,002	15,494	14,626	15,850
Nondurable goods manufacturing	8,425	8,304	8,404	8,360	8,113	7,965	7,942
Wholesale trade	18,955	19,200	19,498	20,045	20,377	21,252	22,885
Retail trade	42,622	43,772	43,691	43,692	43,438	44,221	45,418
Transportation and warehousing	10,274	10,807	11,048	11,854	12,038	12,965	16,287
Information	7,366	7,507	7,615	7,453	7,510	7,325	7,122
Finance and insurance	15,469	15,841	16,337	16,821	16,750	17,061	17,397
Real estate and rental and leasing	3,365	3,455	3,485	3,580	3,563	3,735	4,161
Professional, scientific, and technical services	11,201	11,959	12,332	13,115	12,661	12,657	12,869
Management of companies and enterprises	3,426	3,764	4,169	4,288	4,298	4,329	4,470
Administrative and waste services	12,395	12,866	13,264	13,216	12,420	11,752	12,852
Educational services	3,389	3,484	3,551	3,734	3,744	3,808	3,862
Health care and social assistance	46,362	47,356	48,103	49,289	50,325	52,031	53,345
Arts, entertainment, and recreation	3,503	3,513	3,619	3,765	3,760	3,863	3,829
Accommodation and food services	27,976	28,405	29,624	30,177	30,572	30,865	32,043
Other services, except public administration	17,383	17,310	17,518	17,726	17,532	17,691	17,950
Government and government enterprises	80,720	81,607	81,195	80,493	83,009	84,723	84,328
				Dollars			
Average Wages and Salaries by Industry	29,829	31,190	32,981	35,002	35,695	37,653	41,122
Average Farm Wages and Salaries	29,231	33,583	43,384	48,556	43,162	36,388	39,453
Average Nonfarm Wages and Salaries	29,838	31,160	32,841	34,815	35,609	37,668	41,143
Average private wages and salaries	29,573	31,044	32,845	34,861	35,599	37,915	41,952
Forestry, fishing, and related activities	20,509	21,214	22,540	23,642	25,836	26,684	27,991
Mining	56,926	64,268	69,506	74,767	72,801	79,246	89,204
Utilities	66,045	68,106	71,868	73,221	76,940	78,508	81,965
Construction	35,657	37,879	40,481	44,039	45,341	46,471	51,110
Manufacturing	36,370	38,274	40,149	41,725	41,559	43,376	44,736
Durable goods manufacturing	37,922	39,660	41,734	43,347	42,539	44,151	45,410
Nondurable goods manufacturing	33,152	35,320	36,812	38,233	39,687	41,953	43,390
Wholesale trade	40,092	41,914	44,389	48,136	48,743	51,324	57,530
Retail trade	20,224	20,696	21,718	22,883	23,268	24,198	25,689
Transportation and warehousing	39,154	40,968	42,654	46,134	46,621	50,095	56,400
Information	40,951	44,501	47,359	46,629	47,571	49,015	50,884
Finance and insurance	38,740	40,470	42,339	44,360	45,374	46,704	49,865
Real estate and rental and leasing	22,113	23,382	25,679	29,290	30,980	34,482	44,079
Professional, scientific, and technical services	38,731	40,627	42,993	44,349	46,514	51,424	55,841
Management of companies and enterprises	53,736	54,173	59,622	58,812	59,976	63,720	65,945
Administrative and waste services	19,881	20,992	21,630	22,135	23,060	25,166	27,901
Educational services	19,205	19,941	20,364	20,605	21,310	21,678	22,096
Health care and social assistance	32,140	33,196	34,839	36,783	37,922	39,366	41,243
Arts, entertainment, and recreation	13,522	14,576	15,145	14,667	15,121	15,562	16,327
Accommodation and food services	11,179	11,617	12,616	12,907	13,232	14,119	15,422
Other services, except public administration	19,370	20,099	21,166	22,051	22,856	23,847	25,122
Government and government enterprises	30,744	31,565	32,826	34,644	35,642	36,785	38,021

Table ND-10. Employment Characteristics by Family Type

(Number, percent.)

Family type and labor force status	2009 Total	2009 Families with own children under 18 years	2010 Total	2010 Families with own children under 18 years	2011 Total	2011 Families with own children under 18 years
All families	172,152	73,051	171,945	73,133	175,219	77,838
Family type and labor force status						
Married-couple families	140,848	53,878	140,277	53,463	142,172	56,394
Both husband and wife in labor force	63.9	81.9	63.5	78.0	62.5	77.8
Husband in labor force, wife not in labor force	13.8	14.0	15.0	18.1	16.8	19.3
Wife in labor force, husband not in labor force	7.4	2.9	7.4	2.9	6.6	2.2
Both husband and wife not in labor force	14.9	1.3	14.2	1.0	14.1	0.7
Other families	31,304	19,173	31,668	19,670	33,047	21,444
Female householder, no husband present	68.8	72.9	72.1	76.1	67.8	72.6
In labor force	52.1	63.8	56.2	66.2	51.7	61.2
Not in labor force	16.7	9.1	15.9	9.9	16.1	11.4
Male householder, no wife present	31.2	27.1	27.9	23.9	32.2	27.4
In labor force	26.7	24.8	24.2	21.6	28.7	26.5
Not in labor force	4.5	2.3	3.7	2.3	3.5	1.0

Table ND-11. School Enrollment and Educational Attainment, 2011

(Number, percent.)

Item	State	U.S.
Enrollment		
Total population 3 years and over, enrolled in school	172,936	83,131,910
Enrolled in nursery school or preschool (percent)	5.4	6.0
Enrolled in kindergarten (percent)	5.2	5.1
Enrolled in elementary school, grades 1-8 (percent)	35.4	39.5
Enrolled in high school, grades 9-12 (percent)	18.9	20.7
Enrolled in college or graduate school (percent)	35.2	28.7
Attainment		
Total population 25 years and over	448,145	206,471,670
Less than ninth grade (percent)	4.5	6.0
9th to 12th grade, no diploma (percent)	4.8	8.1
High school graduate, including equivalency (percent)	26.9	28.4
Some college, no degree (percent)	24.4	21.2
Associate's degree (percent)	13.1	7.8
Bachelor's degree (percent)	19.3	17.9
Graduate or professional degree (percent)	7.0	10.6
High school graduate or higher (percent)	90.7	85.9
Bachelor's degree or higher (percent)	26.3	28.5

Table ND-12. Educational Indicators

(Number, percent; data derived from National Center of Education Statistics.)

Item	State	U.S.
Public Schools, 2009–2010 (except where noted)		
Number of school districts	185	13,629
Number of schools	517	99,834
Number of students (in thousands)	95	49,373
Student-teacher ratio	11.4	15.4
Expenditures per student (dollars)	12,193	10,591
Averaged freshman graduation rate, 2008–2009	87.4	75.5[1]
Dropout rate, 2008–2009	2.5	4.1
Students eligible for free or reduced-price lunch (percent)	31.8	48.0
English language learners, 2010–2011 (percent)	3.0	9.8[1]
Students with IEP (percent)	13.9	13.1
Private Schools, 2009–2010 (except where noted)		
Number of schools	47	33,366
Number of students (in thousands)	7	4,700
High school graduates, 2008–2009	A	308,813
Student-teacher ratio	11.5	10.7

A = Reporting standards for NCES not met.
[1] U.S. total includes estimates for nonreporting states.

Table ND-13. Reported Voting and Registration of the Voting-Age Population, November 2012

(Numbers in thousands, percent.)

Item	Total population	Total citizen population	Registered			Voted		
			Total registered	Percent registered (total population)	Percent registered (total citizen population)	Total voted	Percent voted (total population)	Percent voted (total citizen population)
U.S. Total	235,248	215,081	153,157	65.1	71.2	132,948	56.5	61.8
State Total	528	514	383	72.5	74.5	328	62.2	63.9
Sex								
Male	263	256	192	73.0	74.9	165	62.8	64.5
Female	265	258	191	72.1	74.1	163	61.6	63.3
Race								
White alone	471	466	354	75.1	75.9	305	64.8	65.5
White, non-Hispanic alone	457	454	347	75.8	76.4	299	65.4	66.0
Black alone	6	4	2	B	B	2	B	B
Asian alone	7	1	-	B	B	-	B	B
Hispanic (of any race)	16	14	7	B	B	6	B	B
Age								
18 to 24 years	67	66	43	B	B	32	B	B
25 to 44 years	183	175	128	70.4	73.6	106	58.1	60.7
45 to 64 years	194	190	148	76.3	77.8	129	66.9	68.2
65 to 74 years	43	42	33	B	B	33	B	B
75 years and over	42	42	31	B	B	28	B	B

- = Zero or rounds to zero.
B = Base is less than 75,000 and therefore too small to show the derived measure.

Table ND-14. Crime

(Number, rate per 100,000. Data are derived from the FBI Uniform Crime Reports.)

Item	State			U.S.		
	2010	2011	Percent change	2010	2011	Percent change
TOTAL POPULATION	674,629	683,932	1.4	309,330,219	311,591,917	0.7
VIOLENT CRIME						
Number	1,548	1,689	9.1	1,251,248	1,203,564	-3.8
Rate	229.5	247.0	7.6	404.5	386.3	-4.5
Murder and Nonnegligent Manslaughter						
Number	10	24	140.0	14,722	14,612	-0.7
Rate	1.5	3.5	133.3	4.8	4.7	-2.1
Forcible Rape						
Number	245	259	5.7	85,593	83,425	-2.5
Rate	36.3	37.9	4.4	27.7	26.8	-3.2
Robbery						
Number	90	91	1.1	369,089	354,396	-4.0
Rate	13.3	13.3	-0.3	119.3	113.7	-4.7
Aggravated Assault						
Number	1,203	1,315	9.3	781,844	751,131	-3.9
Rate	178.3	192.3	7.9	252.8	241.1	-4.6
PROPERTY CRIME						
Number	12,010	13,246	10.3	9,112,625	9,063,173	0.5
Rate	1,780.2	1,936.7	8.8	2,945.9	2,908.7	-1.3
Burglary						
Number	2,000	2,433	21.7	2,168,459	2,188,005	0.9
Rate	296.5	355.7	20.0	701.0	702.2	0.2
Larceny-Theft						
Number	9,137	9,833	7.6	6,204,601	6,159,795	-0.7
Rate	1,354.4	1,437.7	6.2	2,005.8	1,976.9	-1.4
Motor Vehicle Theft						
Number	873	980	12.3	739,565	715,373	-3.3
Rate	129.4	143.3	10.7	239.1	229.6	-4.0

Table ND-15. State Government Finances, 2011

(Dollar amounts in thousands, percent distribution.)

Item	Dollars	Percent distribution
Total Revenue	7,805,674	100.0
General revenue	6,683,088	85.6
Intergovernmental revenue	1,737,078	22.3
Taxes	3,822,347	49.0
General sales	776,378	9.9
Selective sales	392,807	5.0
License taxes	173,298	2.2
Individual income tax	433,116	5.5
Corporate income tax	160,640	2.1
Other taxes	1,886,108	24.2
Current charges	742,377	9.5
Miscellaneous general revenue	381,286	4.9
Utility revenue	0	0.0
Liquor stores revenue	0	0.0
Insurance trust revenue [1]	1,122,586	14.4
Total Expenditure	5,515,725	100.0
Intergovernmental expenditure	1,300,989	23.6
Direct expenditure	4,214,736	76.4
Current operation	2,858,305	51.8
Capital outlay	607,335	11.0
Insurance benefits and repayments	483,268	8.8
Assistance and subsidies	164,512	3.0
Interest on debt	101,316	1.8
Exhibit: Salaries and wages	1,027,011	18.6
Total Expenditure	5,515,725	100.0
General expenditure	5,032,457	91.2
Intergovernmental expenditure	1,300,989	23.6
Direct expenditure	3,731,468	67.7
General expenditure, by function:		
Education	1,780,864	32.3
Public welfare	913,375	16.6
Hospitals	66,515	1.2
Health	109,839	2.0
Highways	716,704	13.0
Police protection	30,815	0.6
Correction	88,475	1.6
Natural resources	261,833	4.7
Parks and recreation	22,899	0.4
Governmental administration	159,562	2.9
Interest on general debt	101,316	1.8
Other and unallocable	780,260	14.1
Utility expenditure	0	0.0
Liquor stores expenditure	0	0.0
Insurance trust expenditure	483,268	8.8
Debt at End of Fiscal Year	2,060,516	X
Cash and Security Holdings	15,671,779	X

X = Not applicable.
[1] Within insurance trust revenue, net earnings of state retirement systems is a calculated statistic (the item code in the data file is X08), and thus can be positive or negative. Net earnings is the sum of earnings on investments plus gains on investments minus losses on investments. The change made in 2002 for asset valuation from book to market value in accordance with Statement 34 of the Governmental Accounting Standards Board is reflected in the calculated statistics.

Table ND-16. State Government Tax Collections, 2012

(Dollars in thousands, percent.)

Item	Dollars	Percent distribution
Total Taxes	5,620,036	100.0
Property taxes	2,398	-
Sales and gross receipts	1,594,529	28.4
General sales and gross receipts	1,122,783	20.0
Selective sales and gross receipts	471,746	8.4
Alcoholic beverages	8,463	0.2
Amusements	6,027	0.1
Insurance premiums	42,819	0.8
Motor fuels	204,573	3.6
Pari-mutuels	581	-
Public utilities	40,289	0.7
Tobacco products	28,240	0.5
Other selective sales	140,754	2.5
Licenses	187,847	3.3
Alcoholic beverages	325	-
Amusements	814	-
Corporations in general	0	0.0
Hunting and fishing	13,301	0.2
Motor vehicle	105,450	1.9
Motor vehicle operators	5,071	0.1
Public utilities	6	-
Occupation and business, NEC	62,880	1.1
Other licenses	0	0.0
Income taxes	648,149	11.5
Individual income	432,527	7.7
Corporation net income	215,622	3.8
Other taxes	3,187,113	56.7
Death and gift	1	-
Documentary and stock transfer	0	0.0
Severance	3,187,112	56.7
Taxes, NEC	0	0.0

- = Rounds to zero.

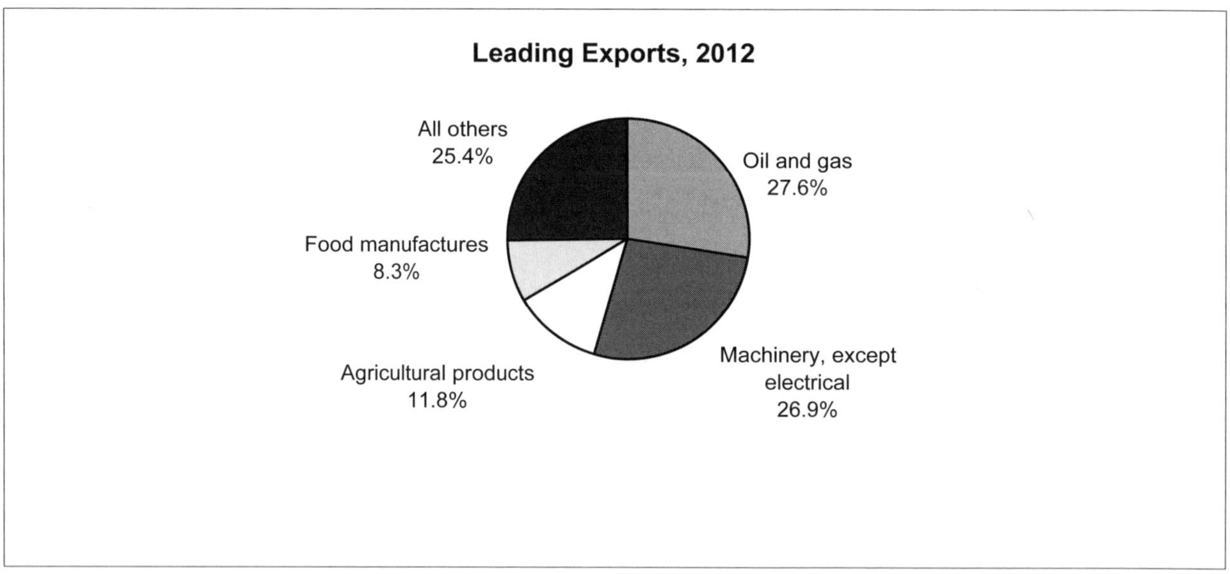

OHIO

Facts and Figures

Location: East north central United States; bordered on the N by Michigan and Lake Erie, on the E by Pennsylvania and West Virginia, on the S by West Virginia and Kentucky, and on the W by Indiana

Area: 44,825 sq. mi. (116,096 sq. km.); rank—34th

Population: 11,544,225 (2012 est.); rank—7th

Principal Cities: capital—Columbus; largest—Columbus

Statehood: March 1, 1803; 17th state

U.S. Congress: 2 senators, 16 representatives

State Motto: With God, All Things Are Possible

State Song: "Beautiful Ohio"

State Nickname: The Buckeye State

Abbreviations: OH

State Symbols: flower—scarlet carnation; tree—Ohio buckeye; bird—cardinal

At a Glance

- With an increase in population of 1.7 percent, Ohio ranked 31st among the states in growth from 2000 to 2009.
- An estimated 64,800 marriages took place in Ohio in 2009, compared to 36,900 divorces.
- Ohio's violent crime rate in 2011 was 307.4 per 100,000 population, compared to 386.3 for the entire nation.
- In the 2012 election, 63.1 percent of Ohio's eligible voters voted, compared to 61.8 percent of eligible voters nationwide.
- In 2007, Ohio exported $2.2 billion worth of agricultural products, about 2.7 percent of the U.S. total.

Table OH-1. Population by Age, Sex, Race, and Hispanic Origin

(Number, percent, except where noted.)

Sex, age, race, and Hispanic origin	2000	2010	2012[1]	Average annual percent change, 2010–2012
Total Population	11,353,140	11,536,504	11,544,225	-
Percent of total U.S. population	4.0	3.7	3.7	X
Sex				
Male	5,512,262	5,632,156	5,642,620	0.1
Female	5,840,878	5,904,348	5,901,605	-
Age				
Under 5 years	754,930	720,856	694,870	-1.2
5 to 19 years	2,461,025	2,346,270	2,288,803	-0.8
20 to 64 years	6,629,428	6,847,363	6,855,430	-
65 years and over	1,507,757	1,622,015	1,705,122	1.6
Median age (years)	36.2	38.8	39.2	0.3
Race and Hispanic Origin				
One race				
White	9,645,453	9,664,524	9,630,901	-0.1
Black	1,301,307	1,426,861	1,439,598	0.3
American Indian and Alaska Native	24,486	29,674	30,606	1.0
Asian	132,633	196,693	210,865	2.2
Native Hawaiian or Other Pacific Islander	2,749	5,336	5,597	1.6
Two or more races	157,885	213,416	228,658	2.2
Hispanic (of any race)	217,123	375,004	399,212	2.0

X = Not applicable.
- = Zero or rounds to zero.
[1] Population figures for 2012 are July 1 estimates. The 2010 estimates are taken from the 2010 Census.

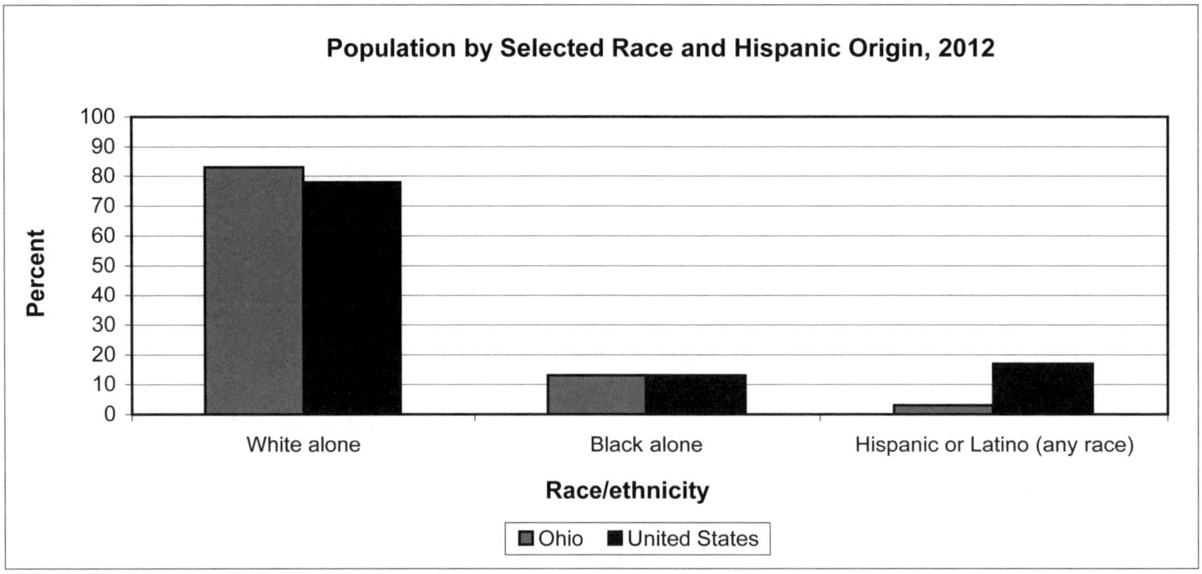

Table OH-2. Marital Status

(Number, percent distribution.)

Sex, age, race, and Hispanic origin	2000	2010	2011
Males, 15 Years and Over	4,281,736	4,487,900	4,505,750
Never married	29.2	33.5	34.1
Now married, except separated	57.0	51.2	50.2
Separated	1.4	1.7	1.6
Widowed	2.7	2.9	3.0
Divorced	9.7	10.8	11.1
Females, 15 Years and Over	4,670,985	4,809,613	4,820,580
Never married	23.5	27.9	28.2
Now married, except separated	52.1	46.9	46.4
Separated	1.7	2.1	2.1
Widowed	11.1	10.1	10.0
Divorced	11.5	12.9	13.3

Table OH-3. Households and Housing Characteristics

(Number, percent, dollars.)

Item	2000	2010	2011	Average annual percent change, 2000–2011
Total Households	4,445,773	4,525,066	4,538,555	0.2
Family households	2,993,023	2,960,107	2,915,927	-0.2
Married-couple family	2,285,798	2,169,003	2,137,964	-0.5
Other family	707,225	791,104	777,963	0.8
Male householder, no wife present	170,347	196,130	191,178	1.0
Female householder, no husband present	536,878	594,974	586,785	0.8
Nonfamily households	1,452,750	1,564,959	1,622,628	1.0
Householder living alone	1,215,614	1,315,321	1,364,722	1.0
Householder not living alone	237,136	249,638	257,906	0.7
Housing Characteristics				
Total housing units	4,783,051	5,128,113	5,133,528	0.6
Occupied housing units	4,445,773	4,525,066	4,538,555	0.2
Owner occupied	3,072,522	3,095,197	3,039,713	-0.1
Renter occupied	1,373,251	1,429,869	1,498,842	0.8
Average size	2.49	2.48	2.48	-
Financial Characteristics				
Median gross rent of renter-occupied housing	515	685	692	2.9
Median monthly owner costs for housing units with a mortgage	983	1,246	1,243	2.2
Median value of owner-occupied housing units	103,700	134,400	129,600	2.1

- = Zero or rounds to zero.

Table OH-4. Migration, Origin, and Language

(Number, percent.)

Characteristic	State			U.S.		
	2010	2011	Percent change	2010	2011	Percent change
Residence 1 Year Ago						
Population 1 year and over	11,405,101	11,418,944	0.1	305,628,607	307,900,319	0.7
Same house	85.4	85.5	0.1	84.6	84.8	0.2
Different house in the U.S.	14.3	14.2	-0.7	14.8	14.6	-1.4
Same county	9.5	9.5	-	9.4	9.2	-2.1
Different county	4.7	4.7	-	5.4	5.4	-
Same state	3.2	3.0	-6.3	3.2	3.1	-3.1
Different state	1.5	1.7	13.3	2.2	2.3	4.5
Abroad	0.3	0.3	-	0.6	0.6	-
Place of Birth						
Native born	11,066,434	11,088,529	0.2	269,393,835	271,214,059	0.7
Male	48.8	48.8	-	49.2	49.2	-
Female	51.2	51.2	-	50.8	50.8	-
Foreign born	469,748	456,422	-2.8	39,955,854	40,377,860	1.1
Male	49.2	49.3	0.2	49.1	48.9	-0.4
Female	50.8	50.7	-0.2	50.9	51.1	0.4
Foreign born; naturalized U.S. citizen	229,049	225,770	-1.4	17,476,082	18,140,192	3.8
Male	45.5	46.2	1.5	45.8	45.8	-
Female	54.5	53.8	-1.3	54.2	54.2	-
Foreign born; not a U.S. citizen	240,699	230,652	-4.2	22,479,772	22,237,668	-1.1
Male	52.8	52.3	-0.9	51.6	51.5	-0.2
Female	47.2	47.7	1.1	48.4	48.5	0.2
Entered 2000 or later	41.8	43.8	4.8	34.7	35.7	2.9
Entered 1990 to 1999	22.8	23.0	0.9	27.2	26.7	-1.8
Entered before 1990	35.4	33.2	-6.2	38.1	37.6	-1.3
World Region of Birth, Foreign						
Foreign-born population, excluding population born at sea	469,748	456,422	-2.8	39,955,673	40,377,757	1.1
Europe	26.4	25.2	-4.5	12.1	12.1	-
Asia	37.7	38.3	1.6	28.2	28.6	1.4
Africa	11.0	11.8	7.3	4	4.1	2.5
Oceania	0.4	0.5	25.0	0.5	0.5	-
Latin America	21.4	20.6	-3.7	53.1	52.6	-0.9
North America	3.1	3.5	12.9	2	2.0	-
Language Spoken at Home and Ability to Speak English						
Population 5 years and over	10,820,130	10,836,508	0.2	289,215,746	291,524,091	0.8
English only	93.3	93.3	0.0	79.4	79.2	-0.3
Language other than English	6.7	6.7	-	20.6	20.8	1.0
Speaks English less than "very well"	2.3	2.3	-	8.7	8.7	-

- = Zero or rounds to zero.

Table OH-5. Median Income and Poverty Status, 2011

(Number, percent, except as noted.)

Characteristic	State		U.S.	
	Number	Percent	Number	Percent
Median Income				
Households (dollars)	45,749	X	50,502	X
Families (dollars)	58,565	X	61,455	X
Below Poverty Level (All People)	1,845,800	16.4	48,452,035	15.9
Sex				
Male	825,757	15.1	21,825,281	14.7
Female	1,020,043	17.7	26,626,754	17.2
Age				
Under 18 years	640,884	24.2	16,386,500	22.5
Related children under 18 years	627,908	23.8	16,087,074	22.2
18 to 64 years	1,082,781	15.5	28,335,079	14.8
65 years and over	122,135	7.7	3,730,456	9.3

X = Not applicable.

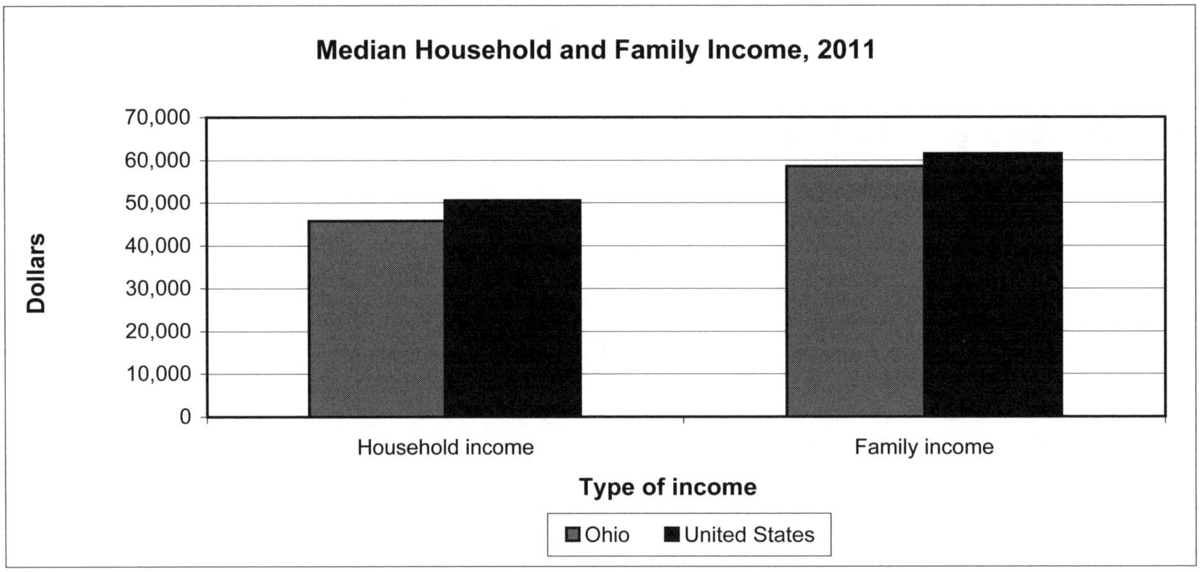

Table OH-6. Health Insurance Coverage Status for the Civilian Noninstitutionalized Population and Children Under 18 Years of Age

(Numbers in thousands, percent.)

Item	2004	2005	2006	2007	2008	2009	2010	2011
Civilian Noninstitutionalized Population	11,270	11,334	11,319	11,300	11,296	11,352	11,369	11,369
Covered by Private or Public Insurance								
Number	10,077	10,046	10,181	9,979	9,966	9,969	9,960	10,015
Percent	89.4	88.6	89.9	88.3	88.2	87.8	87.7	88.1
Not Covered								
Number	1,193	1,288	1,138	1,322	1,330	1,383	1,399	1,354
Percent	10.6	11.4	10.1	11.7	11.8	12.2	12.3	11.9
Percent in the U.S. not covered	14.9	15.3	15.8	15.3	15.1	15.1	15.5	15.1
Children Under 18 Years of Age	2,806	2,724	2,784	2,790	2,728	2,710	2,715	2,688
Covered by Private or Public Insurance								
Number	2,584	2,517	2,626	2,551	2,531	2,538	2,553	2,531
Percent	92.1	92.4	94.3	91.4	92.8	93.6	94.0	94.2
Not Covered								
Number	222	207	157	239	197	172	162	157
Percent	7.9	7.6	5.7	8.6	7.2	6.4	6.0	5.8
Percent in the U.S. not covered	10.5	10.9	11.7	11.0	9.7	8.6	8.0	7.5

Table OH-7. Employment Status by Demographic Group, Preliminary 2012

(Numbers in thousands, percent.)

Characteristic	Civilian noninstitutional population	Civilian labor force		Employed		Unemployed	
		Number	Percent of population	Number	Percent of population	Number	Percent of population
Total	9,042	5,729	63.4	5,317	58.8	412	7.2
Sex							
Male	4,342	3,013	69.4	2,792	64.3	221	7.3
Female	4,700	2,716	57.8	2,525	53.7	191	7.0
Race, Sex, and Hispanic Origin							
White	7,709	4,928	63.9	4,625	60.0	303	6.2
Male	3,736	2,619	70.1	2,455	65.7	163	6.2
Female	3,973	2,309	58.1	2,169	54.6	140	6.1
Black or African American	1,047	626	59.9	535	51.1	91	14.6
Male	473	300	63.4	249	52.7	50	16.8
Female	574	327	57.0	286	49.8	41	12.6
Hispanic	289	205	70.9	187	64.7	18	8.8
Male	169	133	78.8	123	72.8	10	7.7
Female	120	72	59.8	64	53.3	8	10.9
Age							
16 to 19 years	649	267	41.1	223	34.3	44	16.6
20 to 24 years	787	595	75.7	531	67.5	65	10.9
25 to 34 years	1,392	1,153	82.9	1,066	76.6	88	7.6
35 to 44 years	1,380	1,131	81.9	1,060	76.8	70	6.2
45 to 54 years	1,699	1,330	78.3	1,249	73.5	81	6.1
55 to 64 years	1,492	925	62.0	879	59.0	46	4.9
65 years and over	1,643	328	20.0	309	18.8	19	5.7

NOTE: Data in Table 7 are from the Current Population Survey (CPS) and do not match the estimates in Table 8. See notes and definitions for further information.

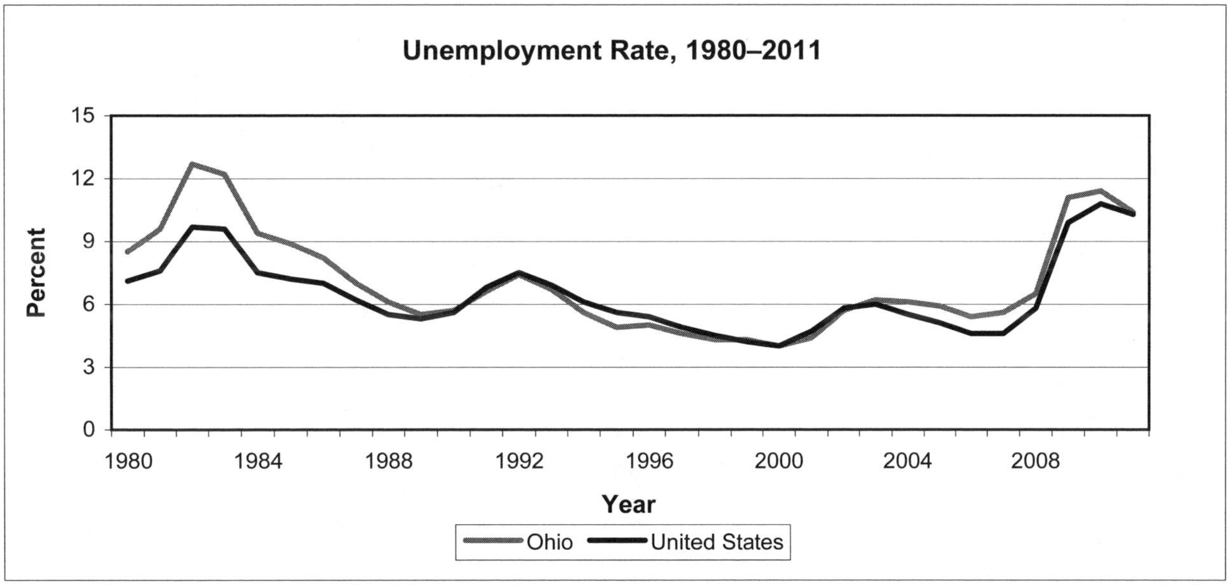

Table OH-8. Employment Status of the Civilian Noninstitutional Population Age 16 Years and Over

(Number, percent.)

Year	Civilian labor force	Civilian participation rate	Employed	Unemployed	Unemployment rate
2005	5,889,451	66.9	5,544,569	344,882	5.9
2006	5,942,053	67.2	5,619,810	322,243	5.4
2007	5,976,724	67.3	5,640,938	335,786	5.6
2008	5,971,874	67.1	5,582,127	389,747	6.5
2009	5,920,413	64.7	5,263,199	657,214	11.1
2010	5,844,911	64.0	5,176,890	668,021	11.4
2011	5,820,387	63.5	5,213,453	606,934	10.4

Table OH-9. Employment and Average Wages by Industry

(Estimates before 2007 are based on the 2002 *North American Industry Classification System* [NAICS]. Estimates from 2007 onward are based on the 2007 NAICS.)

Industry	2005	2006	2007	2008	2009	2010	2011
	Number of jobs						
Wage and Salary Employment by Industry	5,588,468	5,600,646	5,598,268	5,526,611	5,234,992	5,201,963	5,262,063
Farm Wage and Salary Employment	14,541	15,595	16,710	12,730	13,697	13,802	12,718
Nonfarm Wage and Salary Employment	5,573,927	5,585,051	5,581,558	5,513,881	5,221,295	5,188,161	5,249,345
Private wage and salary employment	4,731,078	4,743,067	4,737,170	4,670,242	4,382,490	4,352,940	4,431,887
Forestry, fishing, and related activities	4,106	4,099	4,176	4,247	4,166	4,392	4,529
Mining	10,815	10,997	11,304	11,681	11,450	10,914	11,393
Utilities	20,396	20,779	21,098	21,718	21,320	19,957	19,307
Construction	241,574	239,158	233,257	219,940	189,639	177,091	185,850
Manufacturing	812,869	798,489	773,857	740,114	630,843	621,438	638,984
Durable goods manufacturing	559,360	550,872	531,463	506,735	419,584	411,775	429,018
Nondurable goods manufacturing	253,509	247,617	242,394	233,379	211,259	209,663	209,966
Wholesale trade	239,080	240,825	241,645	239,183	223,515	218,849	220,413
Retail trade	617,690	610,403	610,473	597,304	569,535	561,431	564,106
Transportation and warehousing	180,510	188,920	193,984	191,370	169,014	164,862	168,885
Information	90,141	88,512	87,503	86,190	80,895	77,731	76,034
Finance and insurance	231,762	233,967	231,822	223,876	216,850	215,875	217,771
Real estate and rental and leasing	71,766	70,349	68,513	65,570	62,618	60,735	60,051
Professional, scientific, and technical services	236,380	243,246	250,537	254,371	243,084	242,733	249,760
Management of companies and enterprises	101,939	105,221	104,548	108,567	107,929	107,288	112,869
Administrative and waste services	315,530	316,033	317,496	310,400	271,613	282,344	295,856
Educational services	102,170	105,795	108,372	111,091	112,079	114,689	116,556
Health care and social assistance	677,351	691,752	703,795	721,396	731,134	741,362	750,158
Arts, entertainment, and recreation	69,521	66,876	67,086	65,933	64,222	63,308	64,865
Accommodation and food services	436,194	439,983	439,628	433,322	419,071	418,689	425,014
Other services, except public administration	271,284	267,663	268,076	263,969	253,513	249,252	249,486
Government and government enterprises	842,849	841,984	844,388	843,639	838,805	835,221	817,458
	Dollars						
Average Wages and Salaries by Industry	37,689	38,979	40,309	41,144	41,283	42,218	43,455
Average Farm Wages and Salaries	23,592	21,750	27,991	31,963	30,403	23,394	31,184
Average Nonfarm Wages and Salaries	37,726	39,028	40,346	41,165	41,312	42,268	43,485
Average private wages and salaries	37,569	38,959	40,284	41,039	40,988	41,986	43,270
Forestry, fishing, and related activities	20,976	21,562	22,930	23,940	24,931	25,591	26,626
Mining	56,026	58,902	59,670	61,679	62,894	66,664	71,352
Utilities	72,672	75,204	77,752	80,870	82,809	84,143	86,348
Construction	41,068	42,744	45,013	46,799	47,900	47,887	49,572
Manufacturing	49,318	51,294	52,684	53,103	52,790	54,852	56,921
Durable goods manufacturing	50,862	53,084	54,621	54,876	53,831	56,038	58,076
Nondurable goods manufacturing	45,912	47,314	48,435	49,254	50,723	52,523	54,562
Wholesale trade	52,563	54,689	56,959	58,427	57,871	60,005	62,244
Retail trade	23,560	23,832	24,203	24,445	24,501	25,095	25,698
Transportation and warehousing	40,794	42,164	43,034	44,342	45,055	45,019	46,216
Information	51,392	52,644	54,688	56,190	56,249	58,293	60,119
Finance and insurance	55,547	57,821	60,523	60,327	60,818	62,884	64,817
Real estate and rental and leasing	32,898	34,003	35,067	35,689	35,974	37,253	39,013
Professional, scientific, and technical services	54,632	57,084	60,094	61,854	62,153	63,559	65,853
Management of companies and enterprises	86,390	88,119	92,539	91,845	86,569	93,856	96,377
Administrative and waste services	25,529	26,563	28,176	29,099	29,782	29,943	30,547
Educational services	25,902	27,179	27,579	28,585	29,347	29,686	30,562
Health care and social assistance	36,420	37,641	38,353	39,538	40,411	40,701	41,351
Arts, entertainment, and recreation	25,753	28,722	30,355	30,293	29,997	31,335	30,675
Accommodation and food services	13,451	13,790	14,906	14,847	14,869	15,343	15,806
Other services, except public administration	23,797	24,624	25,369	26,024	26,134	26,991	27,575
Government and government enterprises	38,611	39,411	40,691	41,868	43,004	43,734	44,648

Table OH-10. Employment Characteristics by Family Type

(Number, percent.)

Family type and labor force status	2009		2010		2011	
	Total	Families with own children under 18 years	Total	Families with own children under 18 years	Total	Families with own children under 18 years
All families	2,947,214	1,306,350	2,960,107	1,284,364	2,915,927	1,244,537
Family type and labor force status						
Married-couple families	2,171,033	852,031	2,169,003	837,062	2,137,964	796,948
Both husband and wife in labor force	55.5	71.0	54.4	70.5	53.5	70.0
Husband in labor force, wife not in labor force	19.3	24.0	19.7	24.5	20.1	24.4
Wife in labor force, husband not in labor force	7.9	3.5	8.3	3.6	8.2	4.0
Both husband and wife not in labor force	17.3	1.5	17.6	1.5	18.2	1.6
Other families	776,181	454,319	791,104	447,302	777,963	447,589
Female householder, no husband present	75.5	77.8	75.2	77.7	75.4	78.6
In labor force	54.1	64.0	52.5	63.0	53.4	64.4
Not in labor force	21.4	13.8	22.7	14.7	22.0	14.2
Male householder, no wife present	24.5	22.2	24.8	22.3	24.6	21.4
In labor force	19.2	19.9	19.5	20.2	18.6	18.5
Not in labor force	5.3	2.3	5.3	2.2	5.9	2.9

Table OH-11. School Enrollment and Educational Attainment, 2011

(Number, percent.)

Item	State	U.S.
Enrollment		
Total population 3 years and over, enrolled in school	3,077,214	83,131,910
Enrolled in nursery school or preschool (percent)	6.2	6.0
Enrolled in kindergarten (percent)	4.9	5.1
Enrolled in elementary school, grades 1-8 (percent)	39.0	39.5
Enrolled in high school, grades 9-12 (percent)	20.7	20.7
Enrolled in college or graduate school (percent)	29.1	28.7
Attainment		
Total population 25 years and over	7,749,236	206,471,670
Less than ninth grade (percent)	3.3	6.0
9th to 12th grade, no diploma (percent)	8.4	8.1
High school graduate, including equivalency (percent)	34.8	28.4
Some college, no degree (percent)	21.1	21.2
Associate's degree (percent)	7.8	7.8
Bachelor's degree (percent)	15.4	17.9
Graduate or professional degree (percent)	9.2	10.6
High school graduate or higher (percent)	88.3	85.9
Bachelor's degree or higher (percent)	24.7	28.5

Table OH-12. Educational Indicators

(Number, percent; data derived from National Center of Education Statistics.)

Item	State	U.S.
Public Schools, 2009–2010 (except where noted)		
Number of school districts	615	13,629
Number of schools	3,796	99,834
Number of students (in thousands)	1,764	49,373
Student-teacher ratio	15.8	15.4
Expenditures per student (dollars)	13,185	10,591
Averaged freshman graduation rate, 2008–2009	79.6	75.5[1]
Dropout rate, 2008–2009	4.2	4.1
Students eligible for free or reduced-price lunch (percent)	42.6	48.0
English language learners, 2010–2011 (percent)	2.1	9.8[1]
Students with IEP (percent)	14.9	13.1
Private Schools, 2009–2010 (except where noted)		
Number of schools	1,759[2]	33,366
Number of students (in thousands)	222	4,700
High school graduates, 2008–2009	13,303	308,813
Student-teacher ratio	13.2	10.7

[1] U.S. total includes estimates for nonreporting states.
[2] Interpret data with caution. The coefficient of variation for this estimate is larger than 25 percent.

Table OH-13. Reported Voting and Registration of the Voting-Age Population, November 2012

(Numbers in thousands, percent.)

Item	Total population	Total citizen population	Registered			Voted		
			Total registered	Percent registered (total population)	Percent registered (total citizen population)	Total voted	Percent voted (total population)	Percent voted (total citizen population)
U.S. Total	235,248	215,081	153,157	65.1	71.2	132,948	56.5	61.8
State Total	8,750	8,550	6,076	69.4	71.1	5,395	61.7	63.1
Sex								
Male	4,175	4,074	2,798	67.0	68.7	2,463	59.0	60.4
Female	4,576	4,476	3,278	71.6	73.2	2,932	64.1	65.5
Race								
White alone	7,291	7,262	5,120	70.2	70.5	4,498	61.7	61.9
White, non-Hispanic alone	1,028	975	723	70.3	74.2	699	68.0	71.7
Black alone	104	60	41	40.0	B	38	36.4	B
Asian alone	252	173	116	45.9	67.0	98	39.0	56.9
Hispanic (of any race)								
Age								
18 to 24 years	1,145	1,105	629	55.0	57.0	511	44.7	46.3
25 to 44 years	2,753	2,626	1,820	66.1	69.3	1,544	56.1	58.8
45 to 64 years	3,213	3,179	2,325	72.4	73.1	2,159	67.2	67.9
65 to 74 years	859	859	667	77.7	77.7	605	70.4	70.4
75 years and over	781	781	635	81.3	81.3	576	73.7	73.7

B = Base is less than 75,000 and therefore too small to show the derived measure.

Table OH-14. Crime

(Number, rate per 100,000. Data are derived from the FBI Uniform Crime Reports.)

Item	State			U.S.		
	2010	2011	Percent change	2010	2011	Percent change
TOTAL POPULATION	11,537,968	11,544,951	0.1	309,330,219	311,591,917	0.7
VIOLENT CRIME						
Number	36,306	35,484	-2.3	1,251,248	1,203,564	-3.8
Rate	314.7	307.4	-2.3	404.5	386.3	-4.5
Murder and Nonnegligent Manslaughter						
Number	479	513	7.1	14,722	14,612	-0.7
Rate	4.2	4.4	4.8	4.8	4.7	-2.1
Forcible Rape						
Number	3,730	3,631	-2.7	85,593	83,425	-2.5
Rate	32.3	31.5	-2.5	27.7	26.8	-3.2
Robbery						
Number	16,486	16,057	-2.6	369,089	354,396	-4.0
Rate	142.9	139.1	-2.7	119.3	113.7	-4.7
Aggravated Assault						
Number	15,611	15,283	-2.1	781,844	751,131	-3.9
Rate	135.3	132.4	-2.1	252.8	241.1	-4.6
PROPERTY CRIME						
Number	376,836	387,297	2.8	9,112,625	9,063,173	-0.5
Rate	3,266.1	3,354.7	2.7	2,945.9	2,908.7	-1.3
Burglary						
Number	107,125	112,709	5.2	2,168,459	2,188,005	0.9
Rate	928.5	976.3	5.1	701.0	702.2	0.2
Larceny-Theft						
Number	248,581	253,520	2.0	6,204,601	6,159,795	-0.7
Rate	2,154.5	2,195.9	1.9	2,005.8	1,976.9	-1.4
Motor Vehicle Theft						
Number	21,130	21,068	-0.3	739,565	715,373	-3.3
Rate	183.1	182.5	-0.3	239.1	229.6	-4.0

Table OH-15. State Government Finances, 2011

(Dollar amounts in thousands, percent distribution.)

Item	Dollars	Percent distribution
Total Revenue	98,560,223	100.0
General revenue	61,983,770	62.9
Intergovernmental revenue	24,133,257	24.5
Taxes	25,176,562	25.5
General sales	7,767,709	7.9
Selective sales	4,823,542	4.9
License taxes	3,444,746	3.5
Individual income tax	8,820,082	8.9
Corporate income tax	237,205	0.2
Other taxes	83,278	0.1
Current charges	8,256,125	8.4
Miscellaneous general revenue	4,417,826	4.5
Utility revenue	0	0.0
Liquor stores revenue	808,533	0.8
Insurance trust revenue [1]	35,767,920	36.3
Total Expenditure	79,153,495	100.0
Intergovernmental expenditure	18,412,042	23.3
Direct expenditure	60,741,453	76.7
Current operation	33,666,658	42.5
Capital outlay	4,928,597	6.2
Insurance benefits and repayments	18,165,370	22.9
Assistance and subsidies	2,485,106	3.1
Interest on debt	1,495,722	1.9
Exhibit: Salaries and wages	8,896,903	11.2
Total Expenditure	79,153,495	100.0
General expenditure	60,490,876	76.4
Intergovernmental expenditure	18,412,042	23.3
Direct expenditure	42,078,834	53.2
General expenditure, by function:		
Education	22,408,315	28.3
Public welfare	18,421,960	23.3
Hospitals	2,660,362	3.4
Health	2,481,780	3.1
Highways	3,493,885	4.4
Police protection	292,834	0.4
Correction	1,625,282	2.1
Natural resources	423,554	0.5
Parks and recreation	91,288	0.1
Governmental administration	1,397,459	1.8
Interest on general debt	1,495,722	1.9
Other and unallocable	5,698,435	7.2
Utility expenditure	0	0.0
Liquor stores expenditure	497,249	0.6
Insurance trust expenditure	18,165,370	22.9
Debt at End of Fiscal Year	30,926,386	X
Cash and Security Holdings	195,145,374	X

X = Not applicable.

[1] Within insurance trust revenue, net earnings of state retirement systems is a calculated statistic (the item code in the data file is X08), and thus can be positive or negative. Net earnings is the sum of earnings on investments plus gains on investments minus losses on investments. The change made in 2002 for asset valuation from book to market value in accordance with Statement 34 of the Governmental Accounting Standards Board is reflected in the calculated statistics.

Table OH-16. State Government Tax Collections, 2012

(Dollars in thousands, percent.)

Item	Dollars	Percent distribution
Total Taxes	25,924,024	100.0
Property taxes	0	0.0
Sales and gross receipts	13,119,734	50.6
General sales and gross receipts	8,272,728	31.9
Selective sales and gross receipts	4,847,006	18.7
Alcoholic beverages	98,113	0.4
Amusements	19,760	0.1
Insurance premiums	477,982	1.8
Motor fuels	1,684,209	6.5
Pari-mutuels	7,122	0.0
Public utilities	1,051,730	4.1
Tobacco products	843,180	3.3
Other selective sales	664,910	2.6
Licenses	3,580,483	13.8
Alcoholic beverages	39,735	0.2
Amusements	120,505	0.5
Corporations in general	1,681,619	6.5
Hunting and fishing	39,096	0.2
Motor vehicle	714,980	2.8
Motor vehicle operators	81,026	0.3
Public utilities	25,436	0.1
Occupation and business, NEC	861,301	3.3
Other licenses	16,785	0.1
Income taxes	9,147,103	35.3
Individual income	9,029,657	34.8
Corporation net income	117,446	0.5
Other taxes	76,704	0.3
Death and gift	66,522	0.3
Documentary and stock transfer	0	0.0
Severance	10,182	-
Taxes, NEC	0	0.0

- = Rounds to zero.

Leading Exports, 2012

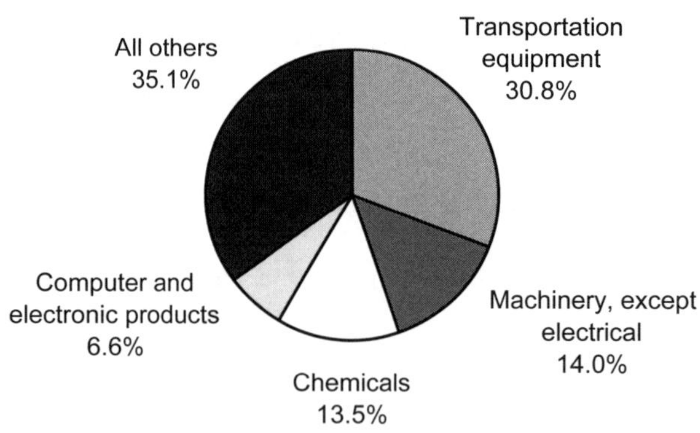

OKLAHOMA

Facts and Figures

Location: West south central United States; bordered on the N by Colorado and Kansas, on the E by Missouri and Arkansas, on the S by Texas, and on the W by Texas and New Mexico

Area: 69,898 sq. mi. (181,036 sq. km.); rank—20th

Population: 3,814,820 (2012 est.); rank—28th

Principal Cities: capital—Oklahoma City; largest—Oklahoma City

Statehood: November 16, 1907; 46th state

U.S. Congress: 2 senators, 5 representatives

State Motto: *Labor omnia vincit* ("Labor conquers all things")

State Song: "Oklahoma!"

State Nickname: The Sooner State

Abbreviations: OK; Okla.

State Symbols: flower—mistletoe; tree—redbud; bird—scissor-tailed flycatcher

At a Glance

- With an increase in population of 6.9 percent, Oklahoma ranked 28th among the states in growth from 2000 to 2009.
- An estimated 23,500 marriages took place in Oklahoma in 2009, compared to 16,900 divorces.
- Oklahoma's median household income in 2011 was $43,225, and 17.2 percent of the population lived below the poverty level.
- In 2011, 18.7 percent of Oklahomans did not have health insurance, compared to 15.1 percent of the total U.S. population.
- In 2007, Oklahoma exported $871 million worth of agricultural products, about 1 percent of the U.S. total.

Table OK-1. Population by Age, Sex, Race, and Hispanic Origin

(Number, percent, except where noted.)

Sex, age, race, and Hispanic origin	2000	2010	2012[1]	Average annual percent change, 2010–2012
Total Population	3,450,654	3,751,351	3,814,820	0.6
Percent of total U.S. population	1.2	1.2	1.2	X
Sex				
Male	1,695,895	1,856,977	1,889,825	0.6
Female	1,754,759	1,894,374	1,924,995	0.5
Age				
Under 5 years	236,353	264,126	261,958	-0.3
5 to 19 years	765,927	777,484	780,343	0.1
20 to 64 years	1,992,424	2,203,027	2,238,272	0.5
65 years and over	455,950	506,714	534,247	1.7
Median age (years)	35.5	36.2	36.2	-
Race and Hispanic Origin				
One race				
White	2,628,434	2,851,510	2,881,880	0.4
Black	260,968	284,332	291,551	0.8
American Indian and Alaska Native	273,230	335,664	341,844	0.6
Asian	46,767	67,126	72,539	2.5
Native Hawaiian or Other Pacific Islander	2,372	5,354	5,976	3.5
Two or more races	155,985	207,365	221,030	2.1
Hispanic (of any race)	179,304	351,542	377,578	2.3

X = Not applicable.
- = Zero or rounds to zero.
[1] Population figures for 2012 are July 1 estimates. The 2010 estimates are taken from the 2010 Census.

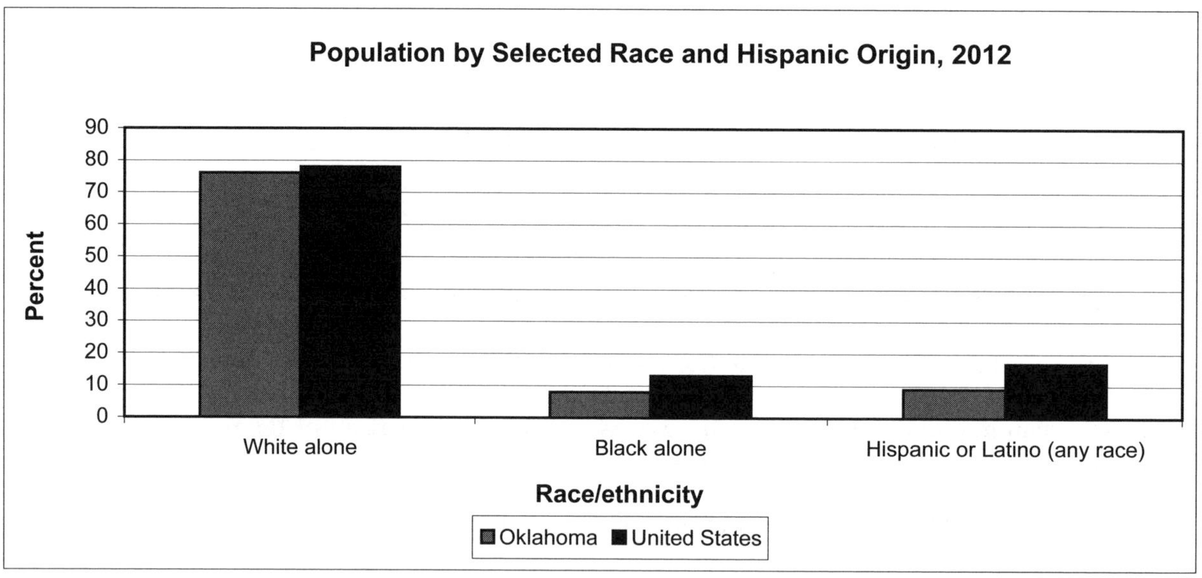

Table OK-2. Marital Status

(Number, percent distribution.)

Sex, age, race, and Hispanic origin	2000	2010	2011
Males, 15 Years and Over	1,318,729	1,457,860	1,476,110
Never married	25.8	30.7	30.2
Now married, except separated	59.5	52.2	52.7
Separated	1.6	1.8	1.9
Widowed	2.5	3.0	2.9
Divorced	10.6	12.3	12.4
Females, 15 Years and Over	1,398,823	1,521,546	1,531,015
Never married	19.1	23.8	23.4
Now married, except separated	55.3	49.7	50.3
Separated	1.9	2.7	2.4
Widowed	11.1	10.1	9.8
Divorced	12.5	13.7	14.2

Table OK-3. Households and Housing Characteristics

(Number, percent, dollars.)

Item	2000	2010	2011	Average annual percent change, 2000–2011
Total Households	1,342,293	1,432,959	1,442,731	0.6
Family households	921,750	954,622	957,855	0.3
Married-couple family	717,611	709,256	715,154	-
Other family	204,139	245,366	242,701	1.6
Male householder, no wife present	51,564	62,855	67,388	2.6
Female householder, no husband present	152,575	182,511	175,313	1.2
Nonfamily households	420,543	478,337	484,876	1.3
Householder living alone	358,560	400,840	408,924	1.2
Householder not living alone	61,983	77,497	75,952	1.9
Housing Characteristics				
Total housing units	1,514,400	1,666,205	1,674,724	0.9
Occupied housing units	1,342,293	1,432,959	1,442,731	0.6
Owner occupied	918,259	971,378	966,998	0.4
Renter occupied	424,034	461,581	475,733	1.0
Average size	2.49	2.55	2.55	0.2
Financial Characteristics				
Median gross rent of renter-occupied housing	456	659	675	4.0
Median monthly owner costs for housing units with a mortgage	764	1,089	1,108	3.8
Median value of owner-occupied housing units	70,700	111,400	112,600	4.9

- = Zero or rounds to zero.

Table OK-4. Migration, Origin, and Language

(Number, percent.)

Characteristic	State			U.S.		
	2010	2011	Percent change	2010	2011	Percent change
Residence 1 Year Ago						
Population 1 year and over	3,716,264	3,742,698	0.7	305,628,607	307,900,319	0.7
Same house	82.5	82.5	-	84.6	84.8	0.2
Different house in the U.S.	17.1	17.0	-0.6	14.8	14.6	-1.4
Same county	10.4	9.9	-4.8	9.4	9.2	-2.1
Different county	6.7	7.1	6.0	5.4	5.4	-
Same state	3.9	4.2	7.7	3.2	3.1	-3.1
Different state	2.9	2.9	-	2.2	2.3	4.5
Abroad	0.4	0.4	-	0.6	0.6	-
Place of Birth						
Native born	3,555,320	3,582,651	0.8	269,393,835	271,214,059	0.7
Male	49.2	49.3	0.2	49.2	49.2	-
Female	50.8	50.7	-0.2	50.8	50.8	-
Foreign born	206,382	208,857	1.2	39,955,854	40,377,860	1.1
Male	51.7	53.8	4.1	49.1	48.9	-0.4
Female	48.3	46.2	-4.3	50.9	51.1	0.4
Foreign born; naturalized U.S. citizen	65,938	70,407	6.8	17,476,082	18,140,192	3.8
Male	45.9	49.1	7.0	45.8	45.8	-
Female	54.1	50.9	-5.9	54.2	54.2	-
Foreign born; not a U.S. citizen	140,444	138,450	-1.4	22,479,772	22,237,668	-1.1
Male	54.4	56.1	3.1	51.6	51.5	-0.2
Female	45.6	43.9	-3.7	48.4	48.5	0.2
Entered 2000 or later	44.7	46.7	4.5	34.7	35.7	2.9
Entered 1990 to 1999	28.0	25.9	-7.5	27.2	26.7	-1.8
Entered before 1990	27.3	27.4	0.4	38.1	37.6	-1.3
World Region of Birth, Foreign						
Foreign-born population, excluding population born at sea	206,382	208,857	1.2	39,955,673	40,377,757	1.1
Europe	7.4	8.3	12.2	12.1	12.1	-
Asia	26.1	25.4	-2.7	28.2	28.6	1.4
Africa	4.4	4.7	6.8	4	4.1	2.5
Oceania	1.5	0.8	-46.7	0.5	0.5	-
Latin America	58.8	59.3	0.9	53.1	52.6	-0.9
North America	1.8	1.5	-16.7	2	2.0	-
Language Spoken at Home and Ability to Speak English						
Population 5 years and over	3,497,798	3,527,312	0.8	289,215,746	291,524,091	0.8
English only	90.9	90.7	-0.2	79.4	79.2	-0.3
Language other than English	9.1	9.3	2.2	20.6	20.8	1.0
Speaks English less than "very well"	3.9	3.8	-2.6	8.7	8.7	-

- = Zero or rounds to zero.

Table OK-5. Median Income and Poverty Status, 2011

(Number, percent, except as noted.)

Characteristic	State		U.S.	
	Number	Percent	Number	Percent
Median Income				
Households (dollars)	43,225	X	50,502	X
Families (dollars)	53,742	X	61,455	X
Below Poverty Level (All People)	633,298	17.2	48,452,035	15.9
Sex				
Male	291,220	16.1	21,825,281	14.7
Female	342,078	18.3	26,626,754	17.2
Age				
Under 18 years	215,804	23.4	16,386,500	22.5
Related children under 18 years	210,073	23.0	16,087,074	22.2
18 to 64 years	370,190	16.4	28,335,079	14.8
65 years and over	47,304	9.5	3,730,456	9.3

X = Not applicable.

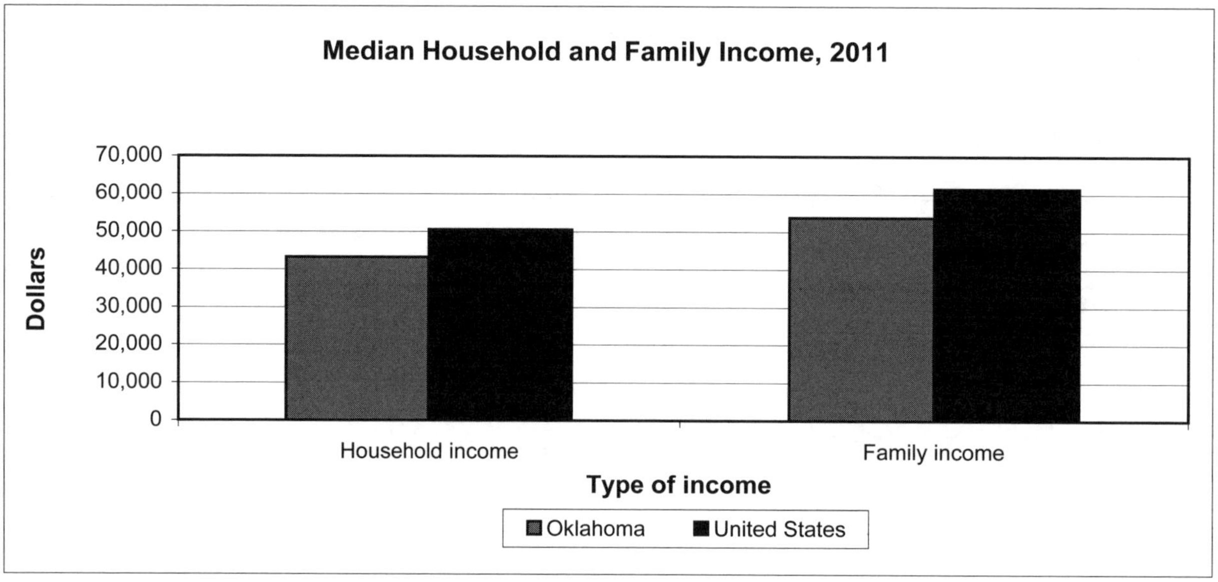

Table OK-6. Health Insurance Coverage Status for the Civilian Noninstitutionalized Population and Children Under 18 Years of Age

(Numbers in thousands, percent.)

Item	2004	2005	2006	2007	2008	2009	2010	2011
Civilian Noninstitutionalized Population	3,444	3,505	3,492	3,551	3,550	3,590	3,677	3,710
Covered by Private or Public Insurance								
Number	2,783	2,878	2,831	2,920	2,858	2,919	2,984	3,017
Percent	80.8	82.1	81.1	82.2	80.5	81.3	81.1	81.3
Not Covered								
Number	661	627	661	631	692	672	694	694
Percent	19.2	17.9	18.9	17.8	19.5	18.7	18.9	18.7
Percent in the U.S. not covered	14.9	15.3	15.8	15.3	15.1	15.1	15.5	15.1
Children Under 18 Years of Age	852	867	913	920	903	919	929	934
Covered by Private or Public Insurance								
Number	714	772	799	804	786	816	836	834
Percent	83.8	89.0	87.5	87.4	87.0	88.8	90.0	89.4
Not Covered								
Number	138	95	114	116	117	103	93	100
Percent	16.2	11.0	12.5	12.6	13.0	11.2	10.0	10.6
Percent in the U.S. not covered	10.5	10.9	11.7	11.0	9.7	8.6	8.0	7.5

Table OK-7. Employment Status by Demographic Group, Preliminary 2012

(Numbers in thousands, percent.)

Characteristic	Civilian noninstitutional population	Civilian labor force		Employed		Unemployed	
		Number	Percent of population	Number	Percent of population	Number	Percent of population
Total	2,897	1,818	62.8	1,726	59.6	93	5.1
Sex							
Male	1,400	994	71.0	945	67.5	48	4.9
Female	1,497	825	55.1	781	52.1	44	5.4
Race, Sex, and Hispanic Origin							
White	2,164	1,344	62.1	1,288	59.5	56	4.1
Male	1,048	741	70.7	713	68.0	28	3.8
Female	1,116	603	54.0	575	51.5	27	4.5
Black or African American	200	124	62.1	112	56.4	11	9.3
Male	91	59	64.6	54	59.5	5	7.8
Female	108	65	60.0	58	53.7	7	10.6
Hispanic	178	122	68.7	118	66.1	5	3.7
Male	97	80	82.8	77	80.1	3	3.2
Female	81	42	51.9	40	49.6	2	4.6
Age							
16 to 19 years	183	63	34.3	54	29.3	9	14.5
20 to 24 years	258	183	71.0	166	64.2	18	9.6
25 to 34 years	528	423	80.1	400	75.8	23	5.4
35 to 44 years	452	365	80.7	351	77.6	14	3.9
45 to 54 years	483	382	79.0	365	75.5	17	4.4
55 to 64 years	455	281	61.8	271	59.5	10	3.7
65 years and over	538	122	22.7	120	22.3	2	1.6

NOTE: Data in Table 7 are from the Current Population Survey (CPS) and do not match the estimates in Table 8. See notes and definitions for further information.

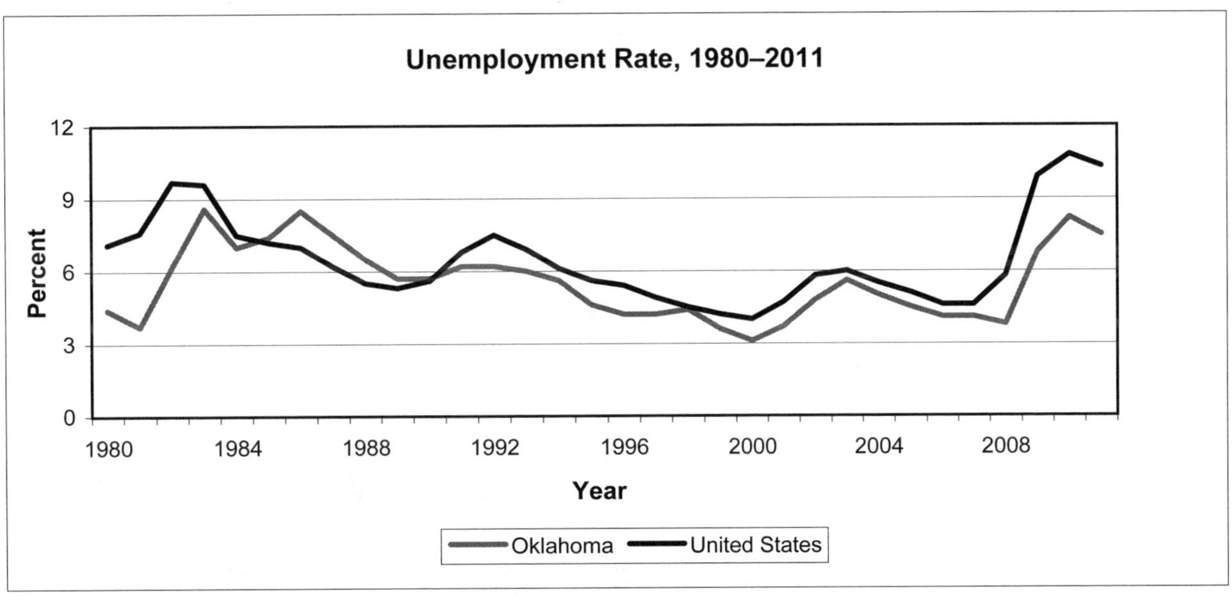

Table OK-8. Employment Status of the Civilian Noninstitutional Population Age 16 Years and Over

(Number, percent.)

Year	Civilian labor force	Civilian participation rate	Employed	Unemployed	Unemployment rate
2005	1,701,703	64.0	1,625,062	76,641	4.5
2006	1,719,613	63.9	1,648,828	70,785	4.1
2007	1,738,010	63.9	1,667,493	70,517	4.1
2008	1,748,416	63.6	1,681,854	66,562	3.8
2009	1,776,550	62.0	1,655,803	120,747	6.8
2010	1,815,022	61.9	1,666,604	148,418	8.2
2011	1,818,689	61.5	1,681,759	136,930	7.5

Table OK-9. Employment and Average Wages by Industry

(Estimates before 2007 are based on the 2002 *North American Industry Classification System* [NAICS]. Estimates from 2007 onward are based on the 2007 NAICS.)

Industry	2005	2006	2007	2008	2009	2010	2011
	Number of jobs						
Wage and Salary Employment by Industry	1,576,334	1,619,584	1,649,403	1,678,945	1,626,342	1,614,647	1,633,708
Farm Wage and Salary Employment	11,589	10,690	11,616	12,605	11,244	9,532	8,599
Nonfarm Wage and Salary Employment	1,564,745	1,608,894	1,637,787	1,666,340	1,615,098	1,605,115	1,625,109
Private wage and salary employment	1,217,036	1,251,958	1,275,458	1,298,032	1,236,244	1,225,337	1,253,214
Forestry, fishing, and related activities	4,088	4,157	4,131	4,189	3,949	4,128	4,111
Mining	35,630	41,617	46,344	50,710	42,591	43,229	50,925
Utilities	9,684	10,007	10,514	10,966	11,445	11,234	11,195
Construction	68,748	73,202	74,370	78,639	72,381	70,769	71,827
Manufacturing	145,192	149,455	150,496	150,338	132,008	125,385	132,255
Durable goods manufacturing	95,799	100,423	103,070	103,772	87,553	81,836	87,858
Nondurable goods manufacturing	49,393	49,032	47,426	46,566	44,455	43,549	44,397
Wholesale trade	57,075	59,307	60,256	60,227	56,970	56,037	58,651
Retail trade	171,534	172,570	173,596	175,088	172,028	171,161	172,829
Transportation and warehousing	44,097	45,996	47,737	46,540	44,482	42,453	43,280
Information	30,211	29,790	27,986	28,036	26,504	25,036	24,103
Finance and insurance	56,175	57,249	58,252	59,186	58,452	57,958	57,990
Real estate and rental and leasing	24,566	25,047	24,635	24,303	22,981	22,460	22,250
Professional, scientific, and technical services	60,635	62,447	65,267	66,899	64,137	63,806	65,688
Management of companies and enterprises	12,571	12,569	13,286	15,231	14,536	15,159	14,928
Administrative and waste services	99,278	102,663	106,144	107,178	92,240	93,926	94,967
Educational services	19,628	19,088	19,325	19,188	19,603	19,843	20,339
Health care and social assistance	165,416	169,239	173,659	178,613	181,094	183,915	185,043
Arts, entertainment, and recreation	14,537	15,615	14,637	14,905	14,561	14,477	14,976
Accommodation and food services	119,759	122,928	124,459	126,748	127,327	126,311	129,910
Other services, except public administration	78,212	79,012	80,364	81,048	78,955	78,050	77,947
Government and government enterprises	347,709	356,936	362,329	368,308	378,854	379,778	371,895
	Dollars						
Average Wages and Salaries by Industry	32,466	34,845	36,250	37,829	37,764	38,854	40,747
Average Farm Wages and Salaries	20,698	22,251	28,010	30,116	25,316	27,917	35,963
Average Nonfarm Wages and Salaries	32,553	34,929	36,308	37,887	37,851	38,919	40,772
Average private wages and salaries	32,179	34,897	36,174	37,860	37,596	38,745	40,918
Forestry, fishing, and related activities	20,811	21,309	22,183	22,223	22,178	22,920	23,605
Mining	65,985	87,531	79,401	86,657	81,300	84,802	95,092
Utilities	66,797	68,378	78,858	77,270	80,310	79,789	82,744
Construction	33,038	35,259	37,007	39,847	40,073	41,572	42,402
Manufacturing	40,655	42,824	43,969	45,600	45,737	47,704	49,460
Durable goods manufacturing	41,692	44,209	45,269	47,280	47,470	49,546	51,535
Nondurable goods manufacturing	38,644	39,988	41,144	41,857	42,325	44,244	45,353
Wholesale trade	44,186	47,248	49,257	52,032	50,717	50,318	52,424
Retail trade	21,973	23,015	23,679	24,304	24,436	25,234	25,957
Transportation and warehousing	42,156	44,030	45,944	47,540	47,528	50,334	53,017
Information	43,116	43,758	46,299	48,045	47,102	47,954	51,776
Finance and insurance	42,369	45,076	46,665	48,050	48,557	50,266	52,328
Real estate and rental and leasing	32,353	34,647	36,822	36,005	34,460	36,293	39,347
Professional, scientific, and technical services	44,937	47,265	49,713	51,206	52,315	54,200	55,811
Management of companies and enterprises	60,571	72,323	72,217	71,882	71,789	75,324	96,022
Administrative and waste services	24,424	26,344	27,667	29,639	30,517	30,975	31,846
Educational services	23,948	26,131	27,186	28,828	29,604	30,274	30,788
Health care and social assistance	32,481	34,212	35,710	37,031	37,965	38,640	39,954
Arts, entertainment, and recreation	18,671	25,043	25,313	23,067	27,201	28,064	28,805
Accommodation and food services	12,833	13,519	14,383	14,711	14,887	15,691	16,127
Other services, except public administration	21,948	23,218	24,238	25,653	25,637	26,721	27,496
Government and government enterprises	33,862	35,041	36,779	37,983	38,680	39,480	40,280

Table OK-10. Employment Characteristics by Family Type

(Number, percent.)

Family type and labor force status	2009		2010		2011	
	Total	Families with own children under 18 years	Total	Families with own children under 18 years	Total	Families with own children under 18 years
All families	949,299	433,422	954,622	418,419	957,855	424,367
Family type and labor force status						
Married-couple families	703,320	284,759	709,256	275,553	715,154	281,099
Both husband and wife in labor force	51.8	63.5	50.6	64.8	50.2	64.0
Husband in labor force, wife not in labor force	23.8	31.0	23.3	28.6	24.1	30.3
Wife in labor force, husband not in labor force	7.1	3.3	8.0	4.6	7.9	3.7
Both husband and wife not in labor force	17.3	2.2	18.1	1.9	17.8	2.0
Other families	245,979	148,663	245,366	142,866	242,701	143,268
Female householder, no husband present	71.5	72.6	74.4	77.2	72.2	74.0
In labor force	49.2	57.0	52.1	60.6	49.6	57.8
Not in labor force	22.2	15.7	22.2	16.6	22.6	16.2
Male householder, no wife present	28.5	27.4	25.6	22.8	27.8	26.0
In labor force	22.7	24.8	19.9	20.2	22.3	24.1
Not in labor force	5.8	2.6	5.7	2.6	5.5	1.9

Table OK-11. School Enrollment and Educational Attainment, 2011

(Number, percent.)

Item	State	U.S.
Enrollment		
Total population 3 years and over, enrolled in school	994,523	83,131,910
Enrolled in nursery school or preschool (percent)	6.5	6.0
Enrolled in kindergarten (percent)	5.8	5.1
Enrolled in elementary school, grades 1-8 (percent)	41.8	39.5
Enrolled in high school, grades 9-12 (percent)	20.3	20.7
Enrolled in college or graduate school (percent)	25.7	28.7
Attainment		
Total population 25 years and over	2,469,196	206,471,670
Less than ninth grade (percent)	4.8	6.0
9th to 12th grade, no diploma (percent)	8.9	8.1
High school graduate, including equivalency (percent)	31.4	28.4
Some college, no degree (percent)	24.1	21.2
Associate's degree (percent)	7.0	7.8
Bachelor's degree (percent)	16.0	17.9
Graduate or professional degree (percent)	7.8	10.6
High school graduate or higher (percent)	86.3	85.9
Bachelor's degree or higher (percent)	23.8	28.5

Table OK-12. Educational Indicators

(Number, percent; data derived from National Center of Education Statistics.)

Item	State	U.S.
Public Schools, 2009–2010 (except where noted)		
Number of school districts	532	13,629
Number of schools	1,795	99,834
Number of students (in thousands)	655	49,373
Student-teacher ratio	15.3	15.4
Expenditures per student (dollars)	8,651	10,591
Averaged freshman graduation rate, 2008–2009	77.3	75.5[1]
Dropout rate, 2008–2009	2.5	4.1
Students eligible for free or reduced-price lunch (percent)	60.5	48.0
English language learners, 2010–2011 (percent)	6.3	9.8[1]
Students with IEP (percent)	14.5	13.1
Private Schools, 2009–2010 (except where noted)		
Number of schools	252	33,366
Number of students (in thousands)	28	4,700
High school graduates, 2008–2009	1,531	308,813
Student-teacher ratio	9.6	10.7

[1] U.S. total includes estimates for nonreporting states.

Table OK-13. Reported Voting and Registration of the Voting-Age Population, November 2012

(Numbers in thousands, percent.)

Item	Total population	Total citizen population	Registered			Voted		
			Total registered	Percent registered (total population)	Percent registered (total citizen population)	Total voted	Percent voted (total population)	Percent voted (total citizen population)
U.S. Total	235,248	215,081	153,157	65.1	71.2	132,948	56.5	61.8
State Total	2,808	2,733	1,806	64.3	66.1	1,431	51.0	52.4
Sex								
Male	1,358	1,319	835	61.5	63.3	656	48.3	49.8
Female	1,449	1,414	970	66.9	68.6	775	53.5	54.8
Race								
White alone	2,072	2,018	1,364	65.8	67.6	1,101	53.1	54.6
White, non-Hispanic alone	1,931	1,925	1,331	68.9	69.2	1,076	55.7	55.9
Black alone	191	187	116	61.1	62.2	102	53.6	54.6
Asian alone	58	41	25	B	B	22	B	B
Hispanic (of any race)	174	127	53	30.4	41.8	36	20.9	28.7
Age								
18 to 24 years	325	323	130	40.1	40.3	88	27.2	27.3
25 to 44 years	1,000	958	577	57.7	60.2	396	39.6	41.4
45 to 64 years	1,001	980	720	72.0	73.5	602	60.1	61.4
65 to 74 years	275	269	240	87.4	89.2	217	79.1	80.7
75 years and over	208	204	138	66.5	67.9	128	61.4	62.8

B = Base is less than 75,000 and therefore too small to show the derived measure.

Table OK-14. Crime

(Number, rate per 100,000. Data are derived from the FBI Uniform Crime Reports.)

Item	State			U.S.		
	2010	2011	Percent change	2010	2011	Percent change
TOTAL POPULATION	3,760,184	3,791,508	0.8	309,330,219	311,591,917	0.7
VIOLENT CRIME						
Number	18,100	17,243	-4.7	1,251,248	1,203,564	-3.8
Rate	481.4	454.8	-5.5	404.5	386.3	-4.5
Murder and Nonnegligent Manslaughter						
Number	195	208	6.7	14,722	14,612	-0.7
Rate	5.2	5.5	5.8	4.8	4.7	-2.1
Forcible Rape						
Number	1,469	1,403	-4.5	85,593	83,425	-2.5
Rate	39.1	37.0	-5.4	27.7	26.8	-3.2
Robbery						
Number	3,345	3,282	-1.9	369,089	354,396	-4.0
Rate	89.0	86.6	-2.7	119.3	113.7	-4.7
Aggravated Assault						
Number	13,091	12,350	-5.7	781,844	751,131	-3.9
Rate	348.1	325.7	-6.4	252.8	241.1	-4.6
PROPERTY CRIME						
Number	129,464	127,252	-1.7	9,112,625	9,063,173	-0.5
Rate	3,443.0	3,356.2	-2.5	2,945.9	2,908.7	-1.3
Burglary						
Number	37,848	36,341	-4.0	2,168,459	2,188,005	0.9
Rate	1,006.5	958.6	-4.8	701.0	702.2	0.2
Larceny-Theft						
Number	81,303	79,880	-1.8	6,204,601	6,159,795	-0.7
Rate	2,162.2	2,106.8	-2.6	2,005.8	1,976.9	-1.4
Motor Vehicle Theft						
Number	10,313	11,031	7.0	739,565	715,373	-3.3
Rate	274.3	290.9	6.1	239.1	229.6	-4.0

Table OK-15. State Government Finances, 2011

(Dollar amounts in thousands, percent distribution.)

Item	Dollars	Percent distribution
Total Revenue	26,224,924	100.0
General revenue	20,189,621	77.0
Intergovernmental revenue	7,873,706	30.0
Taxes	7,766,332	29.6
General sales	2,177,458	8.3
Selective sales	1,058,677	4.0
License taxes	942,442	3.6
Individual income tax	2,385,413	9.1
Corporate income tax	353,972	1.3
Other taxes	848,370	3.2
Current charges	2,560,148	9.8
Miscellaneous general revenue	1,989,435	7.6
Utility revenue	572,875	2.2
Liquor stores revenue	0	0.0
Insurance trust revenue [1]	5,462,428	20.8
Total Expenditure	22,377,598	100.0
Intergovernmental expenditure	4,477,819	20.0
Direct expenditure	17,899,779	80.0
Current operation	12,076,949	54.0
Capital outlay	2,096,766	9.4
Insurance benefits and repayments	2,796,785	12.5
Assistance and subsidies	421,159	1.9
Interest on debt	508,120	2.3
Exhibit: Salaries and wages	3,030,813	13.5
Total Expenditure	22,377,598	100.0
General expenditure	19,011,589	85.0
Intergovernmental expenditure	4,477,819	20.0
Direct expenditure	14,533,770	64.9
General expenditure, by function:		
Education	7,491,074	33.5
Public welfare	5,456,745	24.4
Hospitals	283,449	1.3
Health	804,040	3.6
Highways	2,048,578	9.2
Police protection	217,134	1.0
Correction	530,853	2.4
Natural resources	221,443	1.0
Parks and recreation	96,949	0.4
Governmental administration	589,564	2.6
Interest on general debt	433,193	1.9
Other and unallocable	838,567	3.7
Utility expenditure	569,224	2.5
Liquor stores expenditure	0	0.0
Insurance trust expenditure	2,796,785	12.5
Debt at End of Fiscal Year	10,254,716	X
Cash and Security Holdings	37,423,346	X

X = Not applicable.
[1] Within insurance trust revenue, net earnings of state retirement systems is a calculated statistic (the item code in the data file is X08), and thus can be positive or negative. Net earnings is the sum of earnings on investments plus gains on investments minus losses on investments. The change made in 2002 for asset valuation from book to market value in accordance with Statement 34 of the Governmental Accounting Standards Board is reflected in the calculated statistics.

Table OK-16. State Government Tax Collections, 2012

(Dollars in thousands, percent.)

Item	Dollars	Percent distribution
Total Taxes	8,826,132	100.0
Property taxes	0	0.0
Sales and gross receipts	3,724,416	42.2
General sales and gross receipts	2,415,964	27.4
Selective sales and gross receipts	1,308,452	14.8
Alcoholic beverages	103,831	1.2
Amusements	18,946	0.2
Insurance premiums	228,915	2.6
Motor fuels	444,636	5.0
Pari-mutuels	1,388	-
Public utilities	39,353	0.4
Tobacco products	292,973	3.3
Other selective sales	178,410	2.0
Licenses	1,019,814	11.6
Alcoholic beverages	920	-
Amusements	148,684	1.7
Corporations in general	51,032	0.6
Hunting and fishing	22,082	0.3
Motor vehicle	665,123	7.5
Motor vehicle operators	15,066	0.2
Public utilities	4	-
Occupation and business, NEC	95,554	1.1
Other licenses	21,349	0.2
Income taxes	3,220,385	36.5
Individual income	2,774,376	31.4
Corporation net income	446,009	5.1
Other taxes	861,517	9.8
Death and gift	0	0.0
Documentary and stock transfer	12,570	0.1
Severance	848,947	9.6
Taxes, NEC	0	0.0

- = Rounds to zero.

Leading Exports, 2012

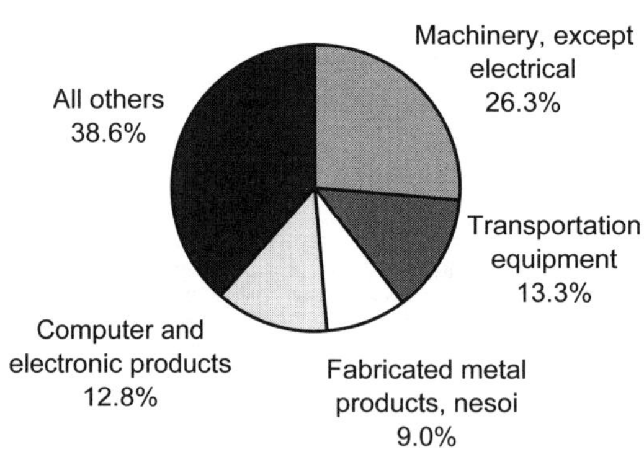

OREGON

Facts and Figures

Location: Northwestern United States; bordered on the N by Washington, on the E by Idaho, on the S by Nevada and California, and on the W by the Pacific Ocean

Area: 98,381 sq. mi. (254,805 sq. km.); rank—9th

Population: 3,889,353 (2012 est.); rank—27th

Principal Cities: capital—Salem; largest—Portland

Statehood: February 14, 1859; 33rd state

U.S. Congress: 2 senators, 5 representatives

State Motto: She Flies With Her Own Wings

State Song: "Oregon, My Oregon"

State Nickname: The Beaver State

Abbreviations: OR; Oreg.

State Symbols: flower—Oregon grape; tree—Douglas fir; bird—Western meadowlark

At a Glance

- With an increase in population of 11.8 percent, Oregon ranked 16th among the states in growth from 2000 to 2009.
- An estimated 23,500 marriages took place in Oregon in 2009, compared to 13,300 divorces.
- In 2011, 15.7 percent of Oregonians did not have health insurance, compared to 15.1 percent of the total U.S. population.
- Oregon's violent crime rate in 2011 was 247.6 per 100,000 population, compared to 386.3 for the entire nation.
- In 2007, Oregon exported $1.2 billion worth of agricultural products, about 1.5 percent of the U.S. total.

Table OR-1. Population by Age, Sex, Race, and Hispanic Origin

(Number, percent, except where noted.)

Sex, age, race, and Hispanic origin	2000	2010	2012[1]	Average annual percent change, 2010–2012
Total Population	3,421,399	3,831,074	3,889,353	0.5
Percent of total U.S. population	1.2	1.2	1.2	X
Sex				
Male	1,696,550	1,896,002	1,930,712	0.6
Female	1,724,849	1,935,072	1,968,641	0.6
Age				
Under 5 years	223,005	237,556	232,516	-0.7
5 to 19 years	720,999	734,627	726,775	-0.4
20 to 64 years	2,039,218	2,325,358	2,348,443	0.3
65 years and over	438,177	533,533	581,619	2.8
Median age (years)	36.3	38.4	38.8	0.3
Race and Hispanic Origin				
One race				
White	2,961,623	3,403,252	3,444,767	0.4
Black	55,662	74,414	77,564	1.4
American Indian and Alaska Native	45,211	66,784	69,955	1.5
Asian	101,350	145,009	156,077	2.4
Native Hawaiian or Other Pacific Islander	7,976	14,649	15,848	2.5
Two or more races	104,745	126,966	138,142	2.7
Hispanic (of any race)	275,314	467,030	499,067	2.1

X = Not applicable.
[1] Population figures for 2012 are July 1 estimates. The 2010 estimates are taken from the 2010 Census.

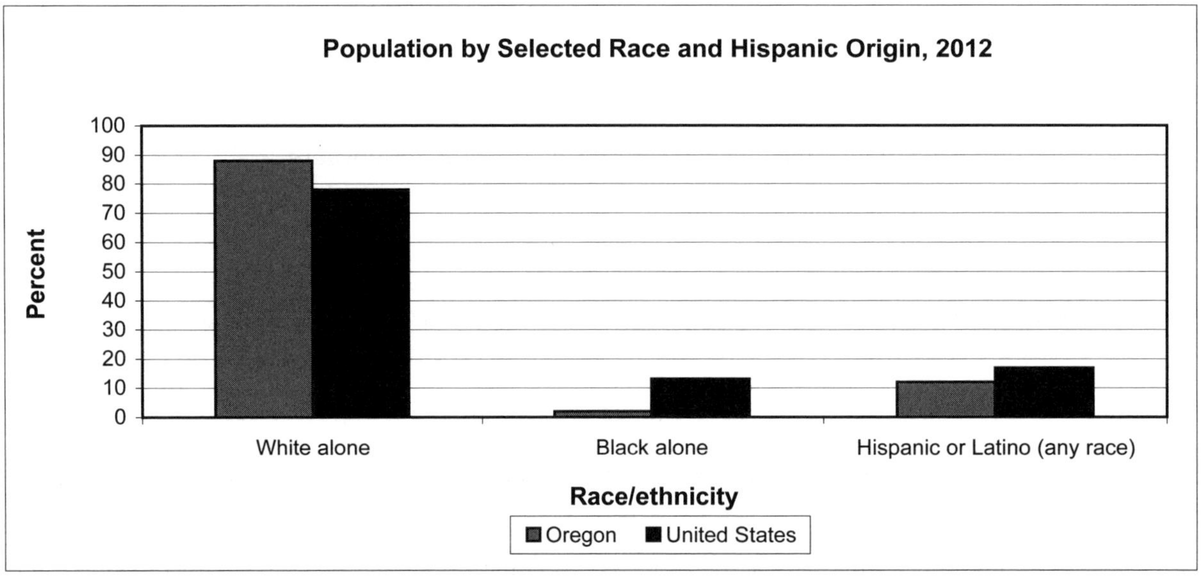

Table OR-2. Marital Status

(Number, percent distribution.)

Sex, age, race, and Hispanic origin	2000	2010	2011
Males, 15 Years and Over	1,336,805	1,533,177	1,546,819
Never married	28.5	32.6	33.2
Now married, except separated	57.1	51.4	51.2
Separated	1.5	1.6	1.5
Widowed	2.4	2.7	2.3
Divorced	10.6	11.8	11.8
Females, 15 Years and Over	1,385,329	1,588,428	1,608,158
Never married	21.9	25.8	26.5
Now married, except separated	53.9	48.9	49.1
Separated	1.9	1.9	2.0
Widowed	9.6	8.5	8.3
Divorced	12.7	14.9	14.0

Table OR-3. Households and Housing Characteristics

(Number, percent, dollars.)

Item	2000	2010	2011	Average annual percent change, 2000–2011
Total Households	1,333,723	1,507,137	1,516,979	1.1
Family households	877,671	963,362	956,746	0.8
Married-couple family	692,532	733,095	734,223	0.5
Other family	185,139	230,267	222,523	1.7
Male householder, no wife present	54,357	65,972	70,642	2.5
Female householder, no husband present	130,782	164,295	151,881	1.3
Nonfamily households	456,032	543,775	560,233	1.9
Householder living alone	347,624	416,500	431,258	2.0
Householder not living alone	108,428	127,275	128,975	1.6
Housing Characteristics				
Total housing units	1,452,709	1,676,476	1,684,244	1.3
Occupied housing units	1,333,723	1,507,137	1,516,979	1.1
Owner occupied	856,951	942,674	922,012	0.6
Renter occupied	476,772	564,463	594,967	2.1
Average size	2.51	2.49	2.50	-
Financial Characteristics				
Median gross rent of renter-occupied housing	620	816	840	3.0
Median monthly owner costs for housing units with a mortgage	1,125	1,577	1,546	3.1
Median value of owner-occupied housing units	152,100	244,500	232,900	4.4

- = Zero or rounds to zero.

Table OR-4. Migration, Origin, and Language

(Number, percent.)

Characteristic	State			U.S.		
	2010	2011	Percent change	2010	2011	Percent change
Residence 1 Year Ago						
Population 1 year and over	3,794,008	3,828,714	0.9	305,628,607	307,900,319	0.7
Same house	82.0	81.7	-0.4	84.6	84.8	0.2
Different house in the U.S.	17.5	17.7	1.1	14.8	14.6	-1.4
Same county	11.0	10.8	-1.8	9.4	9.2	-2.1
Different county	6.5	6.8	4.6	5.4	5.4	-
Same state	3.4	3.5	2.9	3.2	3.1	-3.1
Different state	3.1	3.3	6.5	2.2	2.3	4.5
Abroad	0.5	0.6	20.0	0.6	0.6	-
Place of Birth						
Native born	3,463,214	3,494,246	0.9	269,393,835	271,214,059	0.7
Male	49.5	49.4	-0.2	49.2	49.2	-
Female	50.5	50.6	0.2	50.8	50.8	-
Foreign born	375,743	377,613	0.5	39,955,854	40,377,860	1.1
Male	50.2	49.9	-0.6	49.1	48.9	-0.4
Female	49.8	50.1	0.6	50.9	51.1	0.4
Foreign born; naturalized U.S. citizen	140,491	143,433	2.1	17,476,082	18,140,192	3.8
Male	45.8	44.7	-2.4	45.8	45.8	-
Female	54.2	55.3	2.0	54.2	54.2	-
Foreign born; not a U.S. citizen	235,252	234,180	-0.5	22,479,772	22,237,668	-1.1
Male	52.9	53.1	0.4	51.6	51.5	-0.2
Female	47.1	46.9	-0.4	48.4	48.5	0.2
Entered 2000 or later	34.1	37.5	10.0	34.7	35.7	2.9
Entered 1990 to 1999	31.8	29.5	-7.2	27.2	26.7	-1.8
Entered before 1990	34.0	33.0	-2.9	38.1	37.6	-1.3
World Region of Birth, Foreign						
Foreign-born population, excluding population born at sea	375,743	377,613	0.5	39,955,673	40,377,757	1.1
Europe	15.4	15.0	-2.6	12.1	12.1	-
Asia	29.1	29.4	1.0	28.2	28.6	1.4
Africa	2.6	3.3	26.9	4	4.1	2.5
Oceania	1.9	1.7	-10.5	0.5	0.5	-
Latin America	46.5	46.8	0.6	53.1	52.6	-0.9
North America	4.5	3.8	-15.6	2	2.0	-
Language Spoken at Home and Ability to Speak English						
Population 5 years and over	3,602,925	3,633,190	0.8	289,215,746	291,524,091	0.8
English only	85.6	85.1	-0.6	79.4	79.2	-0.3
Language other than English	14.4	14.9	3.5	20.6	20.8	1.0
Speaks English less than "very well"	6.1	6.3	3.3	8.7	8.7	-

- = Zero or rounds to zero.

Table OR-5. Median Income and Poverty Status, 2011

(Number, percent, except as noted.)

Characteristic	State		U.S.	
	Number	Percent	Number	Percent
Median Income				
Households (dollars)	46,816	X	50,502	X
Families (dollars)	58,356	X	61,455	X
Below Poverty Level (All People)	662,283	17.5	48,452,035	15.9
Sex				
Male	308,549	16.5	21,825,281	14.7
Female	353,734	18.4	26,626,754	17.2
Age				
Under 18 years	199,489	23.6	16,386,500	22.5
Related children under 18 years	194,311	23.2	16,087,074	22.2
18 to 64 years	422,693	17.6	28,335,079	14.8
65 years and over	40,101	7.4	3,730,456	9.3

X = Not applicable.

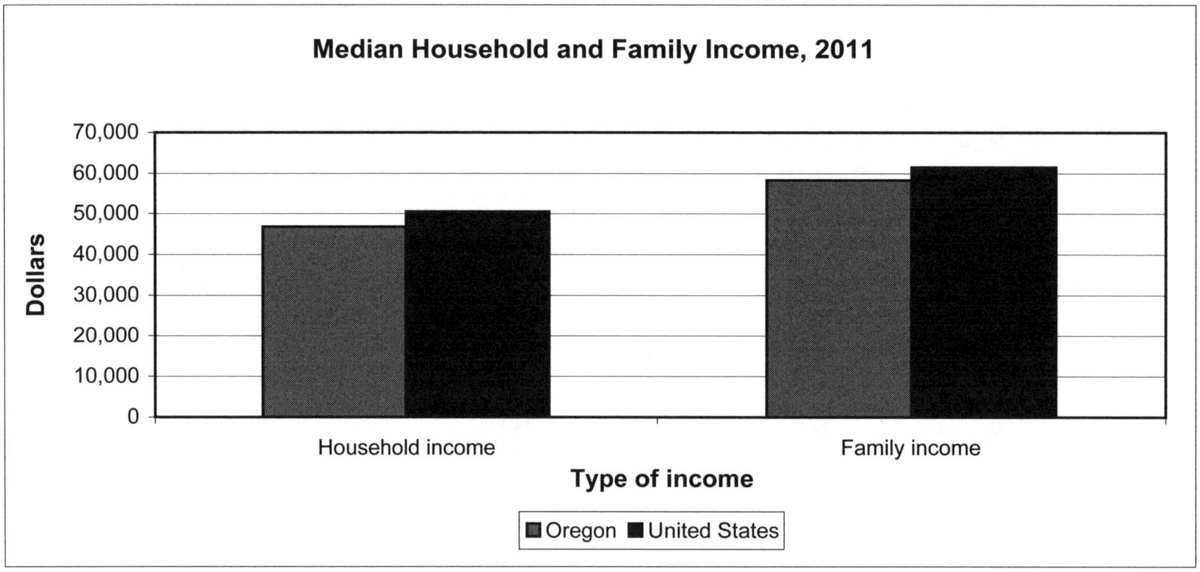

Table OR-6. Health Insurance Coverage Status for the Civilian Noninstitutionalized Population and Children Under 18 Years of Age

(Numbers in thousands, percent.)

Item	2004	2005	2006	2007	2008	2009	2010	2011
Civilian Noninstitutionalized Population	3,582	3,627	3,715	3,762	3,746	3,780	3,799	3,833
Covered by Private or Public Insurance								
Number	2,999	3,062	3,051	3,130	3,132	3,137	3,148	3,230
Percent	83.7	84.4	82.1	83.2	83.6	83.0	82.9	84.3
Not Covered								
Number	583	566	665	632	614	643	652	602
Percent	16.3	15.6	17.9	16.8	16.4	17.0	17.1	15.7
Percent in the U.S. not covered	14.9	15.3	15.8	15.3	15.1	15.1	15.5	15.1
Children Under 18 Years of Age	859	881	870	864	865	871	865	861
Covered by Private or Public Insurance								
Number	769	790	755	772	755	781	789	798
Percent	89.5	89.6	86.9	89.4	87.3	89.6	91.2	92.7
Not Covered								
Number	90	91	114	92	110	90	76	63
Percent	10.5	10.4	13.1	10.6	12.7	10.4	8.8	7.3
Percent in the U.S. not covered	10.5	10.9	11.7	11.0	9.7	8.6	8.0	7.5

Table OR-7. Employment Status by Demographic Group, Preliminary 2012

(Numbers in thousands, percent.)

Characteristic	Civilian noninstitutional population	Civilian labor force		Employed		Unemployed	
		Number	Percent of population	Number	Percent of population	Number	Percent of population
Total	3,097	1,958	63.2	1,785	57.6	173	8.9
Sex							
Male	1,513	1,032	68.2	936	61.9	96	9.3
Female	1,584	926	58.5	849	53.6	77	8.4
Race, Sex, and Hispanic Origin							
White	2,762	1,742	63.1	1,591	57.6	151	8.7
Male	1,346	923	68.5	839	62.3	83	9.0
Female	1,416	820	57.9	752	53.1	68	8.2
Black or African American	48	29	59.9	23	48.8	5	18.4
Male	24	16	67.3	12	52.2	4	22.6
Female	NA	NA	NA	NA	NA	NA	NA
Hispanic	252	185	73.6	164	65.2	21	11.4
Male	132	106	80.6	96	72.5	11	10.0
Female	120	79	65.9	68	57.1	11	13.4
Age							
16 to 19 years	194	71	36.5	54	28.0	16	23.3
20 to 24 years	270	198	73.3	166	61.7	32	15.9
25 to 34 years	513	411	80.1	379	73.8	32	7.9
35 to 44 years	509	420	82.5	383	75.3	37	8.7
45 to 54 years	523	350	67.0	326	62.4	24	6.9
55 to 64 years	579	99	17.0	94	16.3	4	4.3
65 years and over	216	35	16.1	34	15.6	1	3.4

NOTE: Data in Table 7 are from the Current Population Survey (CPS) and do not match the estimates in Table 8. See notes and definitions for further information.
NA = Not available.

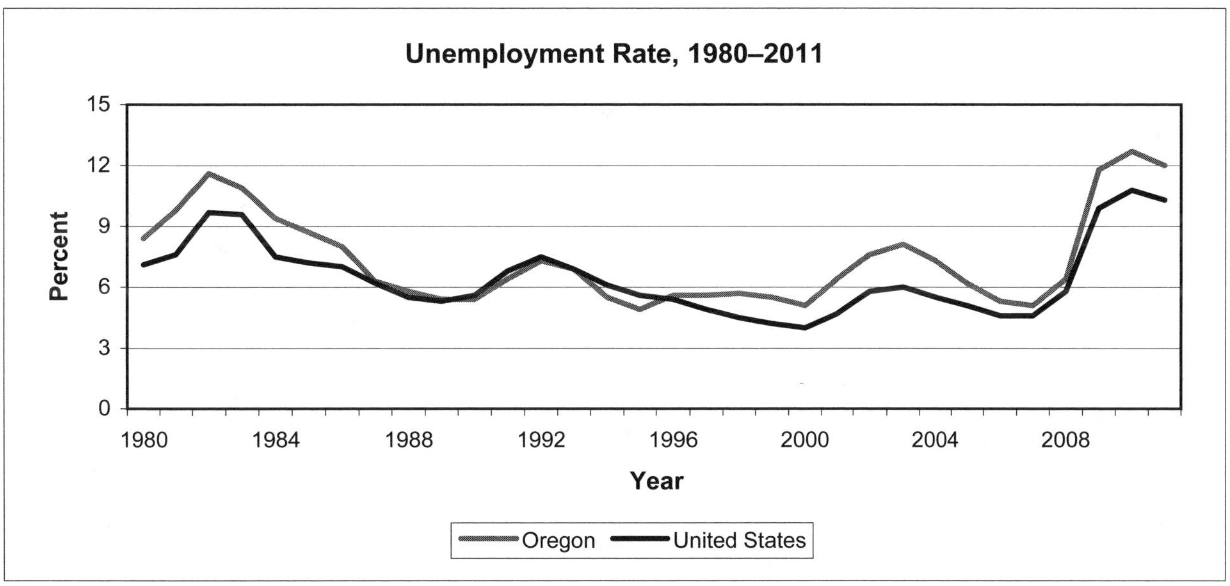

Table OR-8. Employment Status of the Civilian Noninstitutional Population Age 16 Years and Over

(Number, percent.)

Year	Civilian labor force	Civilian participation rate	Employed	Unemployed	Unemployment rate
2005	1,862,642	65.8	1,727,420	115,222	6.2
2006	1,898,090	65.8	1,796,832	101,258	5.3
2007	1,924,576	65.6	1,825,661	98,915	5.1
2008	1,957,953	65.7	1,833,374	124,579	6.4
2009	1,974,127	65.2	1,741,127	232,700	11.8
2010	1,948,885	63.4	1,701,473	247,412	12.7
2011	1,942,971	62.5	1,710,336	232,635	12.0

Table OR-9. Employment and Average Wages by Industry

(Estimates before 2007 are based on the 2002 *North American Industry Classification System* [NAICS]. Estimates from 2007 onward are based on the 2007 NAICS.)

Industry	2005	2006	2007	2008	2009	2010	2011
	Number of jobs						
Wage and Salary Employment by Industry	1,750,502	1,798,292	1,823,312	1,810,443	1,707,674	1,701,494	1,720,379
Farm Wage and Salary Employment	29,115	29,993	30,621	30,351	30,942	33,578	33,358
Nonfarm Wage and Salary Employment	1,721,387	1,768,299	1,792,691	1,780,092	1,676,732	1,667,916	1,687,021
Private wage and salary employment	1,436,278	1,481,713	1,503,391	1,484,093	1,378,007	1,367,286	1,392,299
Forestry, fishing, and related activities	20,265	20,316	20,614	20,701	18,818	19,157	19,894
Mining	2,079	2,151	2,153	1,989	1,676	1,575	1,600
Utilities	4,823	4,794	4,675	4,757	4,713	4,548	4,493
Construction	93,497	103,736	107,068	96,526	75,992	69,366	70,932
Manufacturing	203,472	207,055	203,829	195,054	166,964	163,545	167,984
Durable goods manufacturing	151,812	154,619	150,761	142,762	117,683	114,793	118,572
Nondurable goods manufacturing	51,660	52,436	53,068	52,292	49,281	48,752	49,412
Wholesale trade	78,364	80,630	81,469	80,878	75,856	73,576	74,573
Retail trade	195,187	199,899	203,498	199,067	185,856	185,643	187,109
Transportation and warehousing	53,560	54,764	55,093	54,585	49,670	48,640	49,738
Information	33,660	34,933	35,648	35,546	33,114	32,262	32,081
Finance and insurance	61,353	63,358	62,821	61,199	58,711	57,793	58,489
Real estate and rental and leasing	28,651	28,782	28,637	27,617	26,058	25,241	24,317
Professional, scientific, and technical services	66,144	69,318	71,838	73,537	70,752	71,233	74,713
Management of companies and enterprises	27,796	29,120	31,103	32,306	30,737	30,529	30,417
Administrative and waste services	94,435	97,875	97,028	92,256	80,225	81,936	84,103
Educational services	38,872	39,449	38,548	40,274	41,272	42,398	43,746
Health care and social assistance	187,585	191,710	196,930	203,894	207,421	212,172	215,966
Arts, entertainment, and recreation	21,040	22,007	23,352	23,489	22,212	21,827	22,402
Accommodation and food services	139,626	144,525	150,326	150,923	142,293	142,362	145,034
Other services, except public administration	85,869	87,291	88,761	89,495	85,667	83,483	84,708
Government and government enterprises	285,109	286,586	289,300	295,999	298,725	300,630	294,722
	Dollars						
Average Wages and Salaries by Industry	36,857	38,480	40,086	40,993	41,087	42,014	43,464
Average Farm Wages and Salaries	27,387	26,932	29,141	30,087	29,122	25,649	26,787
Average Nonfarm Wages and Salaries	37,018	38,675	40,272	41,179	41,308	42,343	43,794
Average private wages and salaries	36,849	38,568	40,154	40,930	40,842	41,985	43,486
Forestry, fishing, and related activities	29,825	30,647	31,782	32,026	30,616	30,165	32,435
Mining	43,661	46,556	49,182	47,813	45,646	45,480	48,768
Utilities	70,865	76,711	81,016	81,550	84,565	84,415	87,030
Construction	40,547	42,832	44,723	46,849	47,701	48,104	50,135
Manufacturing	49,435	51,170	53,180	54,743	55,243	59,172	62,062
Durable goods manufacturing	53,046	54,991	57,630	59,582	60,969	66,380	70,223
Nondurable goods manufacturing	38,823	39,902	40,540	41,532	41,567	42,200	42,479
Wholesale trade	57,282	59,790	62,791	63,628	63,188	66,367	69,594
Retail trade	25,292	26,182	26,671	26,521	26,556	26,970	27,377
Transportation and warehousing	39,264	41,108	41,791	42,335	42,123	43,417	44,345
Information	55,044	58,505	62,262	64,256	63,423	64,691	67,921
Finance and insurance	56,212	59,114	61,510	61,237	60,791	62,564	64,080
Real estate and rental and leasing	31,161	32,995	33,151	32,757	32,283	33,180	34,391
Professional, scientific, and technical services	52,665	54,827	57,738	59,581	59,170	61,348	63,638
Management of companies and enterprises	71,399	74,113	77,936	77,415	75,014	76,861	81,449
Administrative and waste services	25,341	26,577	28,136	29,578	30,308	30,294	30,931
Educational services	19,471	20,846	21,971	22,868	23,281	23,864	24,737
Health care and social assistance	36,387	38,437	40,227	41,870	42,419	42,924	44,224
Arts, entertainment, and recreation	23,409	24,326	25,723	24,917	24,686	26,357	25,509
Accommodation and food services	16,186	16,794	17,718	17,498	17,598	18,175	18,737
Other services, except public administration	24,684	25,886	26,883	27,148	27,009	27,986	28,489
Government and government enterprises	37,867	39,232	40,888	42,429	43,459	43,970	45,247

Table OR-10. Employment Characteristics by Family Type

(Number, percent.)

Family type and labor force status	2009 Total	2009 Families with own children under 18 years	2010 Total	2010 Families with own children under 18 years	2011 Total	2011 Families with own children under 18 years
All families	956,627	413,105	963,362	419,500	956,746	406,586
Family type and labor force status						
Married-couple families	739,731	285,258	733,095	287,606	734,223	278,537
Both husband and wife in labor force	52.8	66.7	51.9	65.4	50.7	64.2
Husband in labor force, wife not in labor force	20.3	27.2	20.7	28.6	21.0	29.8
Wife in labor force, husband not in labor force	7.9	4.2	8.5	3.8	8.3	4.2
Both husband and wife not in labor force	19.0	1.8	18.9	2.2	20.0	1.8
Other families	216,896	127,847	230,267	131,894	222,523	128,049
Female householder, no husband present	71.1	74.2	71.3	74.5	68.3	68.6
In labor force	50.7	59.5	49.2	57.8	45.8	52.5
Not in labor force	20.4	14.7	22.2	16.6	22.5	16.1
Male householder, no wife present	28.9	25.8	28.7	25.5	31.7	31.4
In labor force	22.8	22.8	23.1	22.9	24.8	27.6
Not in labor force	6.1	3.0	5.5	2.7	6.9	3.8

Table OR-11. School Enrollment and Educational Attainment, 2011

(Number, percent.)

Item	State	U.S.
Enrollment		
Total population 3 years and over, enrolled in school	973,213	83,131,910
Enrolled in nursery school or preschool (percent)	5.2	6.0
Enrolled in kindergarten (percent)	4.6	5.1
Enrolled in elementary school, grades 1-8 (percent)	39.6	39.5
Enrolled in high school, grades 9-12 (percent)	19.8	20.7
Enrolled in college or graduate school (percent)	30.8	28.7
Attainment		
Total population 25 years and over	2,644,754	206,471,670
Less than ninth grade (percent)	4.2	6.0
9th to 12th grade, no diploma (percent)	6.5	8.1
High school graduate, including equivalency (percent)	25.1	28.4
Some college, no degree (percent)	26.8	21.2
Associate's degree (percent)	8.2	7.8
Bachelor's degree (percent)	18.4	17.9
Graduate or professional degree (percent)	10.9	10.6
High school graduate or higher (percent)	89.4	85.9
Bachelor's degree or higher (percent)	29.3	28.5

Table OR-12. Educational Indicators

(Number, percent; data derived from National Center of Education Statistics.)

Item	State	U.S.
Public Schools, 2009–2010 (except where noted)		
Number of school districts	190	13,629
Number of schools	1,301	99,834
Number of students (in thousands)	583	49,373
Student-teacher ratio	20.3	15.4
Expenditures per student (dollars)	10,789	10,591
Averaged freshman graduation rate, 2008–2009	76.5	75.5[1]
Dropout rate, 2008–2009	3.4	4.1
Students eligible for free or reduced-price lunch (percent)	50.7	48.0
English language learners, 2010–2011 (percent)	10.5	9.8[1]
Students with IEP (percent)	13.7	13.1
Private Schools, 2009–2010 (except where noted)		
Number of schools	497	33,366
Number of students (in thousands)	47	4,700
High school graduates, 2008–2009	3,139	308,813
Student-teacher ratio	10.8	10.7

[1] U.S. total includes estimates for nonreporting states.

Table OR-13. Reported Voting and Registration of the Voting-Age Population, November 2012

(Numbers in thousands, percent.)

Item	Total population	Total citizen population	Registered			Voted		
			Total registered	Percent registered (total population)	Percent registered (total citizen population)	Total voted	Percent voted (total population)	Percent voted (total citizen population)
U.S. Total	235,248	215,081	153,157	65.1	71.2	132,948	56.5	61.8
State Total	2,998	2,806	2,086	69.6	74.3	1,897	63.3	67.6
Sex								
Male	1,480	1,377	990	66.9	71.9	893	60.3	64.8
Female	1,518	1,429	1,095	72.2	76.6	1,004	66.1	70.2
Race								
White alone	2,633	2,505	1,903	72.3	76.0	1,733	65.8	69.2
White, non-Hispanic alone	2,438	2,405	1,849	75.9	76.9	1,688	69.2	70.2
Black alone	57	40	32	B	B	26	B	B
Asian alone	101	71	23	22.5	B	23	22.5	B
Hispanic (of any race)	226	121	69	30.6	57.2	60	26.7	50.0
Age								
18 to 24 years	391	364	216	55.3	59.4	186	47.6	51.1
25 to 44 years	987	878	600	60.8	68.4	511	51.8	58.2
45 to 64 years	1,004	961	756	75.3	78.7	709	70.6	73.7
65 to 74 years	322	320	272	84.6	85.1	270	84.0	84.5
75 years and over	294	284	241	81.9	84.8	221	75.0	77.7

B = Base is less than 75,000 and therefore too small to show the derived measure.

Table OR-14. Crime

(Number, rate per 100,000. Data are derived from the FBI Uniform Crime Reports.)

Item	State			U.S.		
	2010	2011	Percent change	2010	2011	Percent change
TOTAL POPULATION	3,838,332	3,871,859	0.9	309,330,219	311,591,917	0.7
VIOLENT CRIME						
Number	9,648	9,586	-0.6	1,251,248	1,203,564	-3.8
Rate	251.4	247.6	-1.5	404.5	386.3	-4.5
Murder and Nonnegligent Manslaughter						
Number	96	82	-14.6	14,722	14,612	-0.7
Rate	2.5	2.1	-16.0	4.8	4.7	-2.1
Forcible Rape						
Number	1,239	1,217	-1.8	85,593	83,425	-2.5
Rate	32.3	31.4	-2.8	27.7	26.8	-3.2
Robbery						
Number	2,421	2,222	-8.2	369,089	354,396	-4.0
Rate	63.1	57.4	-9.0	119.3	113.7	-4.7
Aggravated Assault						
Number	5,892	6,065	2.9	781,844	751,131	-3.9
Rate	153.5	156.6	2.0	252.8	241.1	-4.6
PROPERTY CRIME						
Number	116,657	120,594	3.4	9,112,625	9,063,173	-0.5
Rate	3,039.3	3,114.6	2.5	2,945.9	2,908.7	-1.3
Burglary						
Number	20,035	20,448	2.1	2,168,459	2,188,005	0.9
Rate	522.0	528.1	1.2	701.0	702.2	0.2
Larceny-Theft						
Number	87,494	91,099	4.1	6,204,601	6,159,795	-0.7
Rate	2,279.5	2,352.8	3.2	2,005.8	1,976.9	-1.4
Motor Vehicle Theft						
Number	9,128	9,047	-0.9	739,565	715,373	-3.3
Rate	237.8	233.7	-1.7	239.1	229.6	-4.0

Table OR-15. State Government Finances, 2011

(Dollar amounts in thousands, percent distribution.)

Item	Dollars	Percent distribution
Total Revenue	34,991,146	100.0
General revenue	20,816,600	59.5
Intergovernmental revenue	7,608,740	21.7
Taxes	8,112,049	23.2
General sales	0	0.0
Selective sales	1,097,023	3.1
License taxes	939,978	2.7
Individual income tax	5,493,119	15.7
Corporate income tax	468,606	1.3
Other taxes	113,323	0.3
Current charges	3,356,236	9.6
Miscellaneous general revenue	1,739,575	5.0
Utility revenue	296	0.0
Liquor stores revenue	438,533	1.3
Insurance trust revenue [1]	13,735,717	39.3
Total Expenditure	27,334,818	100.0
Intergovernmental expenditure	5,774,682	21.1
Direct expenditure	21,560,136	78.9
Current operation	13,139,275	48.1
Capital outlay	1,466,251	5.4
Insurance benefits and repayments	5,992,007	21.9
Assistance and subsidies	508,046	1.9
Interest on debt	454,557	1.7
Exhibit: Salaries and wages	4,499,507	16.5
Total Expenditure	27,334,818	100.0
General expenditure	21,109,773	77.2
Intergovernmental expenditure	5,774,682	21.1
Direct expenditure	15,335,091	56.1
General expenditure, by function:		
Education	7,102,058	26.0
Public welfare	6,026,646	22.0
Hospitals	1,629,380	6.0
Health	495,366	1.8
Highways	1,671,863	6.1
Police protection	159,675	0.6
Correction	711,895	2.6
Natural resources	448,604	1.6
Parks and recreation	97,066	0.4
Governmental administration	785,777	2.9
Interest on general debt	454,557	1.7
Other and unallocable	1,526,886	5.6
Utility expenditure	18,397	0.1
Liquor stores expenditure	214,641	0.8
Insurance trust expenditure	5,992,007	21.9
Debt at End of Fiscal Year	14,069,253	X
Cash and Security Holdings	71,330,069	X

X = Not applicable.
[1] Within insurance trust revenue, net earnings of state retirement systems is a calculated statistic (the item code in the data file is X08), and thus can be positive or negative. Net earnings is the sum of earnings on investments plus gains on investments minus losses on investments. The change made in 2002 for asset valuation from book to market value in accordance with Statement 34 of the Governmental Accounting Standards Board is reflected in the calculated statistics.

Table OR-16. State Government Tax Collections, 2012

(Dollars in thousands, percent.)

Item	Dollars	Percent distribution
Total Taxes	8,699,626	100.0
Property taxes	15,710	0.2
Sales and gross receipts	1,398,998	16.1
General sales and gross receipts	0	0.0
Selective sales and gross receipts	1,398,998	16.1
Alcoholic beverages	17,322	0.2
Amusements	48	-
Insurance premiums	100,821	1.2
Motor fuels	533,420	6.1
Pari-mutuels	1,132	-
Public utilities	94,132	1.1
Tobacco products	255,652	2.9
Other selective sales	396,471	4.6
Licenses	903,132	10.4
Alcoholic beverages	3,577	-
Amusements	2,739	-
Corporations in general	19,425	0.2
Hunting and fishing	46,149	0.5
Motor vehicle	477,307	5.5
Motor vehicle operators	29,298	0.3
Public utilities	16,397	0.2
Occupation and business, NEC	301,940	3.5
Other licenses	6,300	0.1
Income taxes	6,258,923	71.9
Individual income	5,825,797	67.0
Corporation net income	433,126	5.0
Other taxes	122,863	1.4
Death and gift	101,816	1.2
Documentary and stock transfer	3,655	-
Severance	14,119	0.2
Taxes, NEC	3,273	-

- = Rounds to zero.

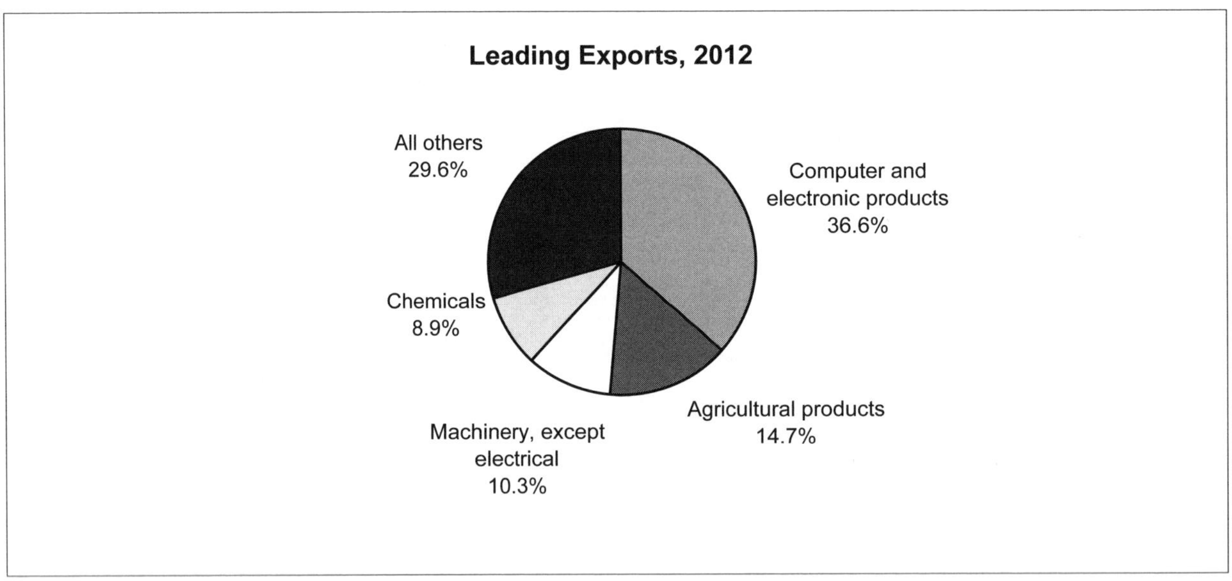

PENNSYLVANIA

Facts and Figures

Location: Northeastern United States; bordered on the N by Lake Erie and New York, on the E by New York and New Jersey, on the S by Delaware, Maryland, and West Virginia, and on the W by West Virginia and Ohio

Area: 46,055 sq. mi. (119,283 sq. km.); rank—33rd

Population: 12,763,536 (2012 est.); rank—6th

Principal Cities: capital—Harrisburg; largest—Philadelphia

Statehood: December 12, 1787; 2nd state

U.S. Congress: 2 senators, 18 representatives

State Motto: Virtue, Liberty, and Independence

State Song: "Pennsylvania"

State Nicknames: The Keystone State; The Quaker State

Abbreviations: PA; Penn.

State Symbols: flower—mountain laurel; tree—Eastern hemlock; bird—ruffed grouse

At a Glance

- With an increase in population of 2.6 percent, Pennsylvania ranked 21st among the states in growth from 2000 to 2009.
- An estimated 64,200 marriages took place in Pennsylvania in 2009, compared to 28,800 divorces.
- Pennsylvania's median household income in 2011 was $50,228, and 13.8 percent of the population lived below the poverty level in 2007.
- In the 2012 election, 61.6 percent of Pennsylvania's eligible voters voted, compared to 61.8 percent of eligible voters nationwide.
- In 2007, Pennsylvania exported $1.5 billion worth of agricultural products, about 1.8 percent of the U.S. total.

Table PA-1. Population by Age, Sex, Race, and Hispanic Origin

(Number, percent, except where noted.)

Sex, age, race, and Hispanic origin	2000	2010	2012[1]	Average annual percent change, 2010–2012
Total Population	12,281,054	12,702,379	12,763,536	0.2
Percent of total U.S. population	4.4	4.1	4.1	X
Sex				
Male	5,929,663	6,190,363	6,230,177	0.2
Female	6,351,391	6,512,016	6,533,359	0.1
Age				
Under 5 years	727,804	729,538	719,703	-0.5
5 to 19 years	2,542,780	2,449,852	2,393,925	-0.8
20 to 64 years	7,091,305	7,563,682	7,607,047	0.2
65 years and over	1,919,165	1,959,307	2,042,861	1.4
Median age (years)	38.0	40.1	40.5	0.3
Race and Hispanic Origin				
One race				
White	10,484,203	10,663,774	10,655,948	-
Black	1,224,612	1,431,826	1,456,977	0.6
American Indian and Alaska Native	18,348	39,735	41,680	1.6
Asian	219,813	358,195	383,917	2.2
Native Hawaiian or Other Pacific Islander	3,417	7,115	7,723	2.6
Two or more races	142,224	201,734	217,291	2.4
Hispanic (of any race)	394,088	758,058	823,684	2.7

X = Not applicable.
- = Zero or rounds to zero.
[1] Population figures for 2012 are July 1 estimates. The 2010 estimates are taken from the 2010 Census.

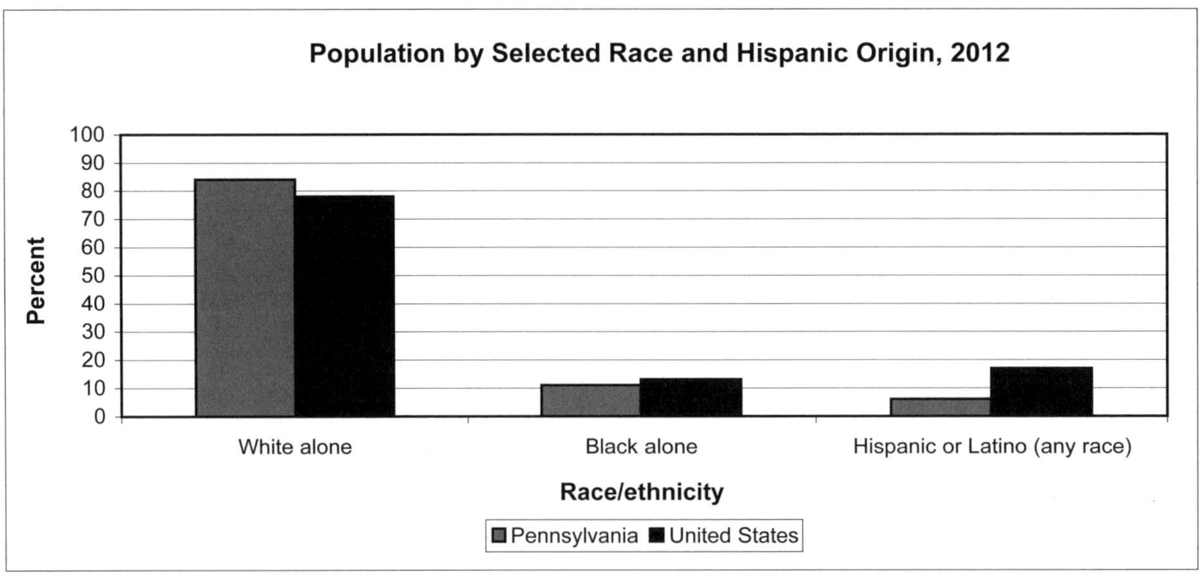

Table PA-2. Marital Status

(Number, percent distribution.)

Sex, age, race, and Hispanic origin	2000	2010	2011
Males, 15 Years and Over	4,686,277	5,031,761	5,063,080
Never married	30.1	35.9	36.4
Now married, except separated	57.4	50.6	50.1
Separated	1.9	2.0	2.0
Widowed	3.3	3.1	3.2
Divorced	7.3	8.5	8.4
Females, 15 Years and Over	5,175,436	5,406,494	5,425,119
Never married	24.6	29.8	30.4
Now married, except separated	51.5	46.2	45.9
Separated	2.4	2.7	2.5
Widowed	12.7	11.2	10.9
Divorced	8.8	10.2	10.4

Table PA-3. Households and Housing Characteristics

(Number, percent, dollars.)

Item	2000	2010	2011	Average annual percent change, 2000–2011
Total Households	4,777,003	4,936,030	4,937,333	0.3
Family households	3,208,388	3,197,710	3,193,701	-
Married-couple family	2,467,673	2,381,094	2,374,705	-0.3
Other family	740,715	816,616	818,996	0.9
Male householder, no wife present	186,022	215,082	221,386	1.6
Female householder, no husband present	554,693	601,534	597,610	0.6
Nonfamily households	1,568,615	1,738,320	1,743,632	0.9
Householder living alone	1,320,941	1,458,055	1,467,909	0.9
Householder not living alone	247,674	280,265	275,723	0.9
Housing Characteristics				
Total housing units	5,249,750	5,568,820	5,579,394	0.5
Occupied housing units	4,777,003	4,936,030	4,937,333	0.3
Owner occupied	3,406,337	3,461,678	3,431,023	0.1
Renter occupied	1,370,666	1,474,352	1,506,310	0.8
Average size	2.48	2.49	2.49	-
Financial Characteristics				
Median gross rent of renter-occupied housing	531	763	786	4.0
Median monthly owner costs for housing units with a mortgage	1,010	1,390	1,408	3.3
Median value of owner-occupied housing units	97,000	165,500	164,800	5.8

- = Zero or rounds to zero.

Table PA-4. Migration, Origin, and Language

(Number, percent.)

Characteristic	State			U.S.		
	2010	2011	Percent change	2010	2011	Percent change
Residence 1 Year Ago						
Population 1 year and over	12,577,555	12,610,486	0.3	305,628,607	307,900,319	0.7
Same house	87.9	88.0	0.1	84.6	84.8	0.2
Different house in the U.S.	11.7	11.6	-0.9	14.8	14.6	-1.4
Same county	7.3	7.3	-	9.4	9.2	-2.1
Different county	4.5	4.3	-4.4	5.4	5.4	-
Same state	2.6	2.4	-7.7	3.2	3.1	-3.1
Different state	1.9	1.9	-	2.2	2.3	4.5
Abroad	0.4	0.4	-	0.6	0.6	-
Place of Birth						
Native born	11,970,562	11,986,476	0.1	269,393,835	271,214,059	0.7
Male	48.7	48.8	0.2	49.2	49.2	-
Female	51.3	51.2	-0.2	50.8	50.8	-
Foreign born	739,068	756,410	2.3	39,955,854	40,377,860	1.1
Male	48.5	48.2	-0.6	49.1	48.9	-0.4
Female	51.5	51.8	0.6	50.9	51.1	0.4
Foreign born; naturalized U.S. citizen	366,119	395,879	8.1	17,476,082	18,140,192	3.8
Male	45.0	46.3	2.9	45.8	45.8	-
Female	55.0	53.7	-2.4	54.2	54.2	-
Foreign born; not a U.S. citizen	372,949	360,531	-3.3	22,479,772	22,237,668	-1.1
Male	52.0	50.3	-3.3	51.6	51.5	-0.2
Female	48.0	49.7	3.5	48.4	48.5	0.2
Entered 2000 or later	40.4	39.7	-1.7	34.7	35.7	2.9
Entered 1990 to 1999	25.6	26.3	2.7	27.2	26.7	-1.8
Entered before 1990	34.1	34.0	-0.3	38.1	37.6	-1.3
World Region of Birth, Foreign						
Foreign-born population, excluding population born at sea	739,068	756,410	2.3	39,955,673	40,377,757	1.1
Europe	22.3	24.1	8.1	12.1	12.1	-
Asia	37.7	37.5	-0.5	28.2	28.6	1.4
Africa	7.0	6.4	-8.6	4	4.1	2.5
Oceania	0.5	0.4	-20.0	0.5	0.5	-
Latin America	29.9	29.5	-1.3	53.1	52.6	-0.9
North America	2.6	2.2	-15.4	2	2.0	-
Language Spoken at Home and Ability to Speak English						
Population 5 years and over	11,983,239	12,021,912	0.3	289,215,746	291,524,091	0.8
English only	89.9	89.7	-0.2	79.4	79.2	-0.3
Language other than English	10.1	10.3	2.0	20.6	20.8	1.0
Speaks English less than "very well"	3.9	3.8	-2.6	8.7	8.7	-

- = Zero or rounds to zero.

Table PA-5. Median Income and Poverty Status, 2011

(Number, percent, except as noted.)

Characteristic	State		U.S.	
	Number	Percent	Number	Percent
Median Income				
Households (dollars)	50,228	X	50,502	X
Families (dollars)	63,283	X	61,455	X
Below Poverty Level (All People)	1,695,996	13.8	48,452,035	15.9
Sex				
Male	749,598	12.5	21,825,281	14.7
Female	946,398	14.9	26,626,754	17.2
Age				
Under 18 years	531,993	19.6	16,386,500	22.5
Related children under 18 years	521,160	19.2	16,087,074	22.2
18 to 64 years	1,012,696	13.1	28,335,079	14.8
65 years and over	151,307	8.0	3,730,456	9.3

X = Not applicable.

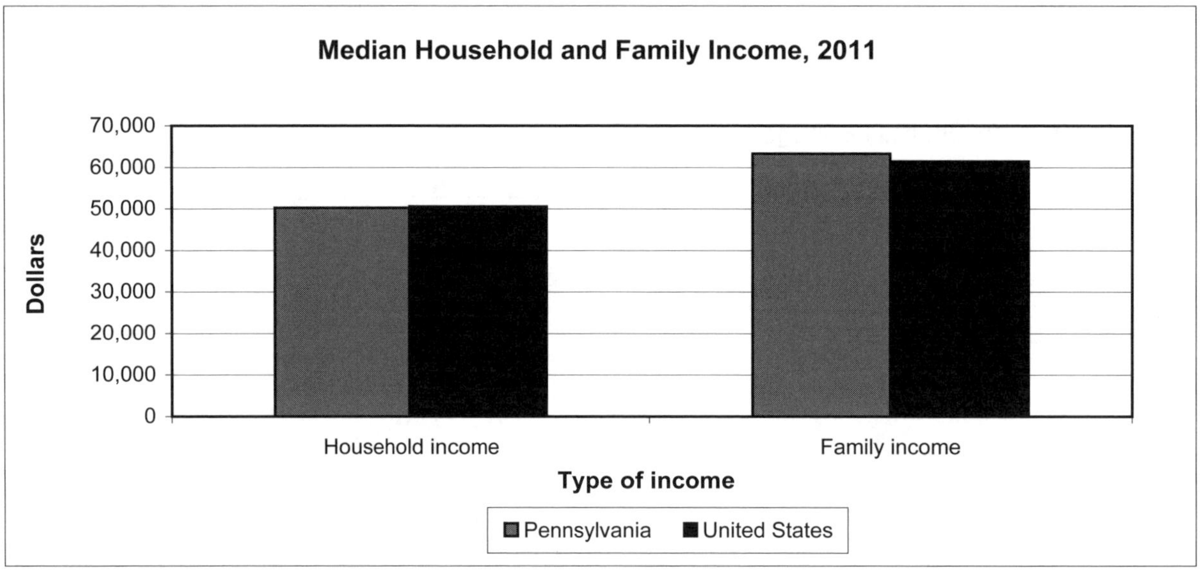

Table PA-6. Health Insurance Coverage Status for the Civilian Noninstitutionalized Population and Children Under 18 Years of Age

(Numbers in thousands, percent.)

Item	2004	2005	2006	2007	2008	2009	2010	2011
Civilian Noninstitutionalized Population	12,175	12,281	12,345	12,313	12,209	12,366	12,506	12,540
Covered by Private or Public Insurance								
Number	10,844	11,085	11,108	11,138	11,058	11,146	11,235	11,275
Percent	89.1	90.3	90.0	90.5	90.6	90.1	89.8	89.9
Not Covered								
Number	1,331	1,196	1,237	1,176	1,151	1,220	1,271	1,265
Percent	10.9	9.7	10.0	9.5	9.4	9.9	10.2	10.1
Percent in the U.S. not covered	14.9	15.3	15.8	15.3	15.1	15.1	15.5	15.1
Children Under 18 Years of Age	2,844	2,830	2,778	2,775	2,757	2,766	2,778	2,755
Covered by Private or Public Insurance								
Number	2,573	2,621	2,575	2,568	2,588	2,619	2,634	2,606
Percent	90.5	92.6	92.7	92.6	93.9	94.7	94.8	94.6
Not Covered								
Number	271	209	203	207	169	147	144	149
Percent	9.5	7.4	7.3	7.4	6.1	5.3	5.2	5.4
Percent in the U.S. not covered	10.5	10.9	11.7	11.0	9.7	8.6	8.0	7.5

Table PA-7. Employment Status by Demographic Group, Preliminary 2012

(Numbers in thousands, percent.)

Characteristic	Civilian noninstitutional population	Civilian labor force		Employed		Unemployed	
		Number	Percent of population	Number	Percent of population	Number	Percent of population
Total	10,193	6,521	64.0	6,012	59.0	509	7.8
Sex							
Male	4,886	3,451	70.6	3,177	65.0	273	7.9
Female	5,307	3,070	57.9	2,835	53.4	236	7.7
Race, Sex, and Hispanic Origin							
White	8,730	5,622	64.4	5,236	60.0	386	6.9
Male	4,214	3,010	71.4	2,792	66.3	218	7.2
Female	4,516	2,612	57.8	2,443	54.1	168	6.4
Black or African American	1,061	652	61.4	555	52.3	97	14.9
Male	477	302	63.3	259	54.3	43	14.1
Female	583	350	59.9	295	50.6	54	15.5
Hispanic	508	328	64.6	286	56.3	42	12.8
Male	273	199	72.9	175	64.1	24	12.0
Female	235	129	54.9	111	47.2	18	14.0
Age							
16 to 19 years	625	261	41.8	218	34.8	44	16.8
20 to 24 years	943	694	73.6	609	64.6	84	12.1
25 to 34 years	1,537	1,271	82.7	1,160	75.5	111	8.7
35 to 44 years	1,527	1,300	85.1	1,214	79.5	86	6.6
45 to 54 years	1,949	1,571	80.6	1,477	75.8	94	6.0
55 to 64 years	1,662	1,088	65.5	1,023	61.6	65	6.0
65 years and over	1,950	336	17.2	311	15.9	26	7.6

NOTE: Data in Table 7 are from the Current Population Survey (CPS) and do not match the estimates in Table 8. See notes and definitions for further information.

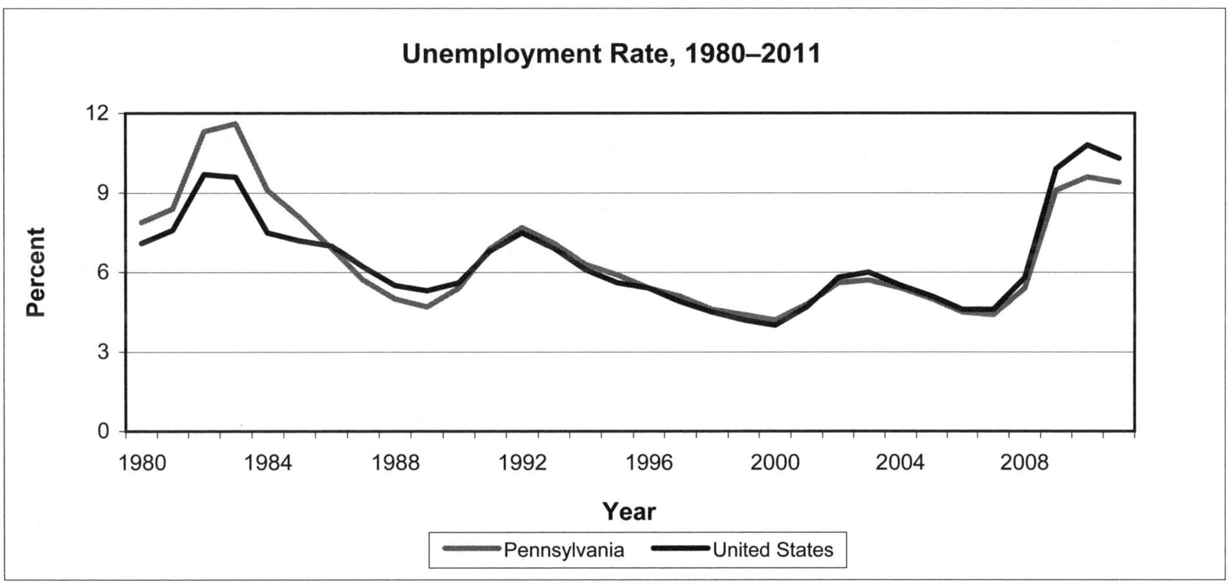

Table PA-8. Employment Status of the Civilian Noninstitutional Population Age 16 Years and Over

(Number, percent.)

Year	Civilian labor force	Civilian participation rate	Employed	Unemployed	Unemployment rate
2005	6,247,696	64.7	5,937,007	310,689	5.0
2006	6,281,121	64.7	5,996,036	285,085	4.5
2007	6,297,105	64.5	6,022,924	274,181	4.0
2008	6,394,884	65.2	6,050,623	344,261	5.4
2009	6,459,773	63.5	5,869,160	590,613	9.1
2010	6,463,490	62.9	5,842,790	620,700	9.6
2011	6,458,914	62.6	5,853,320	605,594	9.4

Table PA-9. Employment and Average Wages by Industry

(Estimates before 2007 are based on the 2002 *North American Industry Classification System* [NAICS]. Estimates from 2007 onward are based on the 2007 NAICS.)

Industry	2005	2006	2007	2008	2009	2010	2011
	Number of jobs						
Wage and Salary Employment by Industry	5,888,874	5,954,673	5,994,123	5,999,422	5,812,006	5,821,316	5,882,592
Farm Wage and Salary Employment	19,091	20,211	19,440	17,328	16,794	18,821	18,245
Nonfarm Wage and Salary Employment	5,869,783	5,934,462	5,974,683	5,982,094	5,795,212	5,802,495	5,864,347
Private wage and salary employment	5,055,585	5,119,581	5,163,874	5,165,218	4,972,955	4,978,951	5,061,393
Forestry, fishing, and related activities	7,199	7,356	7,391	7,711	7,699	8,047	8,442
Mining	18,676	19,840	20,546	21,573	21,563	25,871	32,359
Utilities	22,466	20,970	21,051	21,711	21,757	21,789	22,307
Construction	264,818	271,514	272,623	264,504	235,072	226,635	234,753
Manufacturing	674,760	670,971	656,542	643,396	576,265	561,421	565,523
Durable goods manufacturing	411,879	414,261	405,324	398,373	346,316	334,818	342,113
Nondurable goods manufacturing	262,881	256,710	251,218	245,023	229,949	226,603	223,410
Wholesale trade	235,118	240,081	242,427	241,597	227,853	225,618	229,466
Retail trade	668,619	665,110	665,740	657,690	635,555	636,332	639,415
Transportation and warehousing	211,458	216,613	221,211	220,879	212,539	212,878	219,226
Information	110,101	109,367	108,495	106,479	99,971	93,374	91,157
Finance and insurance	274,340	274,968	271,150	269,922	263,622	261,039	261,035
Real estate and rental and leasing	69,511	69,286	68,235	67,550	63,329	61,569	60,481
Professional, scientific, and technical services	299,616	308,654	315,371	321,572	310,690	307,556	312,866
Management of companies and enterprises	93,174	98,233	111,332	113,669	113,124	117,387	123,164
Administrative and waste services	278,425	279,643	288,872	282,632	256,985	272,269	286,829
Educational services	219,148	225,687	226,098	231,463	236,232	238,936	242,115
Health care and social assistance	816,098	844,042	860,627	882,144	895,324	907,540	919,745
Arts, entertainment, and recreation	81,345	82,538	85,615	88,252	88,277	90,597	94,463
Accommodation and food services	407,706	414,217	420,845	421,383	411,940	416,964	422,777
Other services, except public administration	303,007	300,491	299,703	301,091	295,158	293,129	295,270
Government and government enterprises	814,198	814,881	810,809	816,876	822,257	823,544	802,954
	Dollars						
Average Wages and Salaries by Industry	38,862	40,469	42,413	43,502	43,920	44,805	46,100
Average Farm Wages and Salaries	21,825	23,860	29,579	32,047	30,538	26,133	24,434
Average Nonfarm Wages and Salaries	38,918	40,526	42,455	43,535	43,959	44,865	46,168
Average private wages and salaries	38,833	40,538	42,497	43,592	43,851	44,795	46,160
Forestry, fishing, and related activities	22,486	22,954	23,265	23,902	24,674	25,283	25,795
Mining	53,461	54,519	56,497	59,901	61,585	67,930	72,635
Utilities	85,697	88,434	95,939	96,558	92,745	94,549	100,402
Construction	45,191	47,760	49,834	51,852	52,439	53,080	54,636
Manufacturing	46,785	48,661	49,904	51,203	51,527	53,646	55,211
Durable goods manufacturing	47,421	48,837	50,055	51,584	51,590	54,131	56,158
Nondurable goods manufacturing	45,789	48,378	49,662	50,583	51,432	52,928	53,761
Wholesale trade	55,578	58,713	61,775	63,407	63,607	65,473	68,682
Retail trade	23,042	23,622	24,125	24,438	24,676	25,028	25,347
Transportation and warehousing	37,319	37,986	39,128	39,813	39,795	40,556	41,626
Information	52,832	55,196	57,805	59,566	60,666	63,432	65,779
Finance and insurance	62,171	66,704	70,667	71,680	69,934	71,965	74,930
Real estate and rental and leasing	39,319	42,448	43,702	44,949	44,338	46,437	48,655
Professional, scientific, and technical services	65,000	67,638	71,653	73,643	75,651	77,352	78,901
Management of companies and enterprises	84,079	87,929	98,030	98,287	98,095	101,145	106,922
Administrative and waste services	27,339	28,410	29,881	30,914	31,024	31,168	31,316
Educational services	32,920	33,936	35,730	37,330	38,527	39,373	40,340
Health care and social assistance	36,783	38,006	39,518	40,937	41,838	42,260	43,178
Arts, entertainment, and recreation	25,434	27,673	28,639	28,790	29,414	30,550	32,233
Accommodation and food services	14,844	15,241	16,682	16,388	16,260	16,773	17,292
Other services, except public administration	24,599	25,509	26,472	27,319	27,588	28,299	28,828
Government and government enterprises	39,447	40,452	42,190	43,178	44,610	45,288	46,218

Table PA-10. Employment Characteristics by Family Type

(Number, percent.)

Family type and labor force status	2009		2010		2011	
	Total	Families with own children under 18 years	Total	Families with own children under 18 years	Total	Families with own children under 18 years
All families	3,195,832	1,349,177	3,197,710	1,325,520	3,193,701	1,319,563
Family type and labor force status						
Married-couple families	2,414,432	930,323	2,381,094	894,756	2,374,705	887,711
Both husband and wife in labor force	55.4	70.2	54.9	69.8	54.6	70.2
Husband in labor force, wife not in labor force	19.9	24.8	20.0	24.7	19.4	24.1
Wife in labor force, husband not in labor force	7.5	3.6	7.8	3.9	7.8	4.0
Both husband and wife not in labor force	17.2	1.4	17.3	1.6	18.2	1.6
Other families	781,400	418,854	816,616	430,764	818,996	431,852
Female householder, no husband present	73.7	76.3	73.7	76.9	73.0	75.2
In labor force	50.8	61.0	49.4	60.2	49.1	58.9
Not in labor force	22.9	15.3	24.3	16.7	23.9	16.3
Male householder, no wife present	26.3	23.7	26.3	23.1	27.0	24.8
In labor force	20.5	21.6	19.9	20.5	20.6	22.1
Not in labor force	5.9	2.2	6.5	2.6	6.4	2.7

Table PA-11. School Enrollment and Educational Attainment, 2011

(Number, percent.)

Item	State	U.S.
Enrollment		
Total population 3 years and over, enrolled in school	3,177,813	83,131,910
Enrolled in nursery school or preschool (percent)	6.2	6.0
Enrolled in kindergarten (percent)	4.6	5.1
Enrolled in elementary school, grades 1-8 (percent)	38.4	39.5
Enrolled in high school, grades 9-12 (percent)	21.2	20.7
Enrolled in college or graduate school (percent)	29.6	28.7
Attainment		
Total population 25 years and over	8,714,235	206,471,670
Less than ninth grade (percent)	3.6	6.0
9th to 12th grade, no diploma (percent)	7.7	8.1
High school graduate, including equivalency (percent)	37.5	28.4
Some college, no degree (percent)	16.6	21.2
Associate's degree (percent)	7.6	7.8
Bachelor's degree (percent)	16.6	17.9
Graduate or professional degree (percent)	10.4	10.6
High school graduate or higher (percent)	88.6	85.9
Bachelor's degree or higher (percent)	27.0	28.5

Table PA-12. Educational Indicators

(Number, percent; data derived from National Center of Education Statistics.)

Item	State	U.S.
Public Schools, 2009–2010 (except where noted)		
Number of school districts	500	13,629
Number of schools	3,244	99,834
Number of students (in thousands)	1,786	49,373
Student-teacher ratio	13.6	15.4
Expenditures per student (dollars)	14,849	10,591
Averaged freshman graduation rate, 2008–2009	80.5	75.5[1]
Dropout rate, 2008–2009	2.3	4.1
Students eligible for free or reduced-price lunch (percent)	39.1	48.0
English language learners, 2010–2011 (percent)	2.7	9.8[1]
Students with IEP (percent)	16.5	13.1
Private Schools, 2009–2010 (except where noted)		
Number of schools	2,276	33,366
Number of students (in thousands)	265	4,700
High school graduates, 2008–2009	18,663	308,813
Student-teacher ratio	11.2	10.7

[1] U.S. total includes estimates for nonreporting states.

Table PA-13. Reported Voting and Registration of the Voting-Age Population, November 2012

(Numbers in thousands, percent.)

Item	Total population	Total citizen population	Registered			Voted		
			Total registered	Percent registered (total population)	Percent registered (total citizen population)	Total voted	Percent voted (total population)	Percent voted (total citizen population)
U.S. Total	235,248	215,081	153,157	65.1	71.2	132,948	56.5	61.8
State Total	9,847	9,452	6,795	69.0	71.9	5,824	59.1	61.6
Sex								
Male	4,727	4,532	3,217	68.0	71.0	2,740	58.0	60.4
Female	5,120	4,919	3,578	69.9	72.7	3,084	60.2	62.7
Race								
White alone	8,382	8,228	5,951	71.0	72.3	5,074	60.5	61.7
White, non-Hispanic alone	7,994	7,901	5,779	72.3	73.1	4,937	61.8	62.5
Black alone	1,006	940	675	67.0	71.8	614	61.0	65.2
Asian alone	272	110	68	25.0	61.7	53	19.3	47.6
Hispanic (of any race)	501	407	225	45.0	55.3	184	36.7	45.1
Age								
18 to 24 years	1,198	1,137	645	53.8	56.7	478	39.9	42.1
25 to 44 years	3,063	2,884	2,038	66.5	70.7	1,718	56.1	59.6
45 to 64 years	3,674	3,547	2,648	72.1	74.6	2,331	63.4	65.7
65 to 74 years	998	978	740	74.2	75.7	673	67.5	68.8
75 years and over	915	905	723	79.0	79.9	624	68.1	68.9

Table PA-14. Crime

(Number, rate per 100,000. Data are derived from the FBI Uniform Crime Reports.)

Item	State			U.S.		
	2010	2011	Percent change	2010	2011	Percent change
TOTAL POPULATION	12,717,722	12,742,886	0.2	309,330,219	311,591,917	0.7
VIOLENT CRIME						
Number	46,612	45,240	-2.9	1,251,248	1,203,564	-3.8
Rate	366.5	355.0	-3.1	404.5	386.3	-4.5
Murder and Nonnegligent Manslaughter						
Number	653	637	-2.5	14,722	14,612	-0.7
Rate	5.1	5.0	-2.0	4.8	4.7	-2.1
Forcible Rape						
Number	3,472	3,324	-4.3	85,593	83,425	-2.5
Rate	27.3	26.1	-4.4	27.7	26.8	-3.2
Robbery						
Number	16,375	16,131	-1.5	369,089	354,396	-4.0
Rate	128.8	126.6	-1.7	119.3	113.7	-4.7
Aggravated Assault						
Number	26,112	25,148	-3.7	781,844	751,131	-3.9
Rate	205.3	197.3	-3.9	252.8	241.1	-4.6
PROPERTY CRIME						
Number	276,336	283,179	2.5	9,112,625	9,063,173	-0.5
Rate	2,173.1	2,222.3	2.3	2,945.9	2,908.7	-1.3
Burglary						
Number	55,206	57,850	4.8	2,168,459	2,188,005	0.9
Rate	434.1	454.0	4.6	701.0	702.2	0.2
Larceny-Theft						
Number	204,440	208,485	2.0	6,204,601	6,159,795	-0.7
Rate	1,607.5	1,636.1	1.8	2,005.8	1,976.9	-1.4
Motor Vehicle Theft						
Number	16,720	16,844	0.7	739,565	715,373	-3.3
Rate	131.5	132.2	0.5	239.1	229.6	-4.0

Table PA-15. State Government Finances, 2011

(Dollar amounts in thousands, percent distribution.)

Item	Dollars	Percent distribution
Total Revenue	91,705,305	100.0
General revenue	69,499,280	75.8
Intergovernmental revenue	23,842,639	26.0
Taxes	32,352,286	35.3
General sales	8,951,757	9.8
Selective sales	7,832,017	8.5
License taxes	2,578,020	2.8
Individual income tax	9,831,427	10.7
Corporate income tax	1,978,061	2.2
Other taxes	1,181,004	1.3
Current charges	8,622,614	9.4
Miscellaneous general revenue	4,681,741	5.1
Utility revenue	0	0.0
Liquor stores revenue	1,571,223	1.7
Insurance trust revenue [1]	20,634,802	22.5
Total Expenditure	90,791,525	100.0
Intergovernmental expenditure	19,944,576	22.0
Direct expenditure	70,846,949	78.0
Current operation	43,762,250	48.2
Capital outlay	7,291,907	8.0
Insurance benefits and repayments	15,844,146	17.5
Assistance and subsidies	2,146,870	2.4
Interest on debt	1,801,776	2.0
Exhibit: Salaries and wages	8,197,573	9.0
Total Expenditure	90,791,525	100.0
General expenditure	73,457,932	80.9
Intergovernmental expenditure	19,944,576	22.0
Direct expenditure	53,513,356	58.9
General expenditure, by function:		
Education	22,849,414	25.2
Public welfare	23,707,455	26.1
Hospitals	3,530,943	3.9
Health	2,759,144	3.0
Highways	7,790,203	8.6
Police protection	884,062	1.0
Correction	1,910,065	2.1
Natural resources	663,182	0.7
Parks and recreation	306,043	0.3
Governmental administration	2,956,520	3.3
Interest on general debt	1,801,776	2.0
Other and unallocable	4,299,125	4.7
Utility expenditure	0	0.0
Liquor stores expenditure	1,489,447	1.6
Insurance trust expenditure	15,844,146	17.5
Debt at End of Fiscal Year	45,267,281	X
Cash and Security Holdings	119,387,250	X

X = Not applicable.
[1] Within insurance trust revenue, net earnings of state retirement systems is a calculated statistic (the item code in the data file is X08), and thus can be positive or negative. Net earnings is the sum of earnings on investments plus gains on investments minus losses on investments. The change made in 2002 for asset valuation from book to market value in accordance with Statement 34 of the Governmental Accounting Standards Board is reflected in the calculated statistics.

Table PA-16. State Government Tax Collections, 2012

(Dollars in thousands, percent.)

Item	Dollars	Percent distribution
Total Taxes	32,949,917	100.0
Property taxes	38,452	0.1
Sales and gross receipts	17,151,633	52.1
General sales and gross receipts	9,166,842	27.8
Selective sales and gross receipts	7,984,791	24.2
Alcoholic beverages	324,024	1.0
Amusements	1,499,664	4.6
Insurance premiums	790,781	2.4
Motor fuels	2,073,677	6.3
Pari-mutuels	14,820	-
Public utilities	1,336,501	4.1
Tobacco products	1,118,961	3.4
Other selective sales	826,363	2.5
Licenses	2,646,493	8.0
Alcoholic beverages	16,304	0.0
Amusements	24,206	0.1
Corporations in general	656,221	2.0
Hunting and fishing	73,710	0.2
Motor vehicle	837,990	2.5
Motor vehicle operators	62,348	0.2
Public utilities	66,778	0.2
Occupation and business, NEC	890,117	2.7
Other licenses	18,819	0.1
Income taxes	11,939,487	36.2
Individual income	10,102,113	30.7
Corporation net income	1,837,374	5.6
Other taxes	1,173,852	3.6
Death and gift	804,731	2.4
Documentary and stock transfer	342,506	1.0
Severance	0	0.0
Taxes, NEC	26,615	0.1

- = Rounds to zero.

Leading Exports, 2012

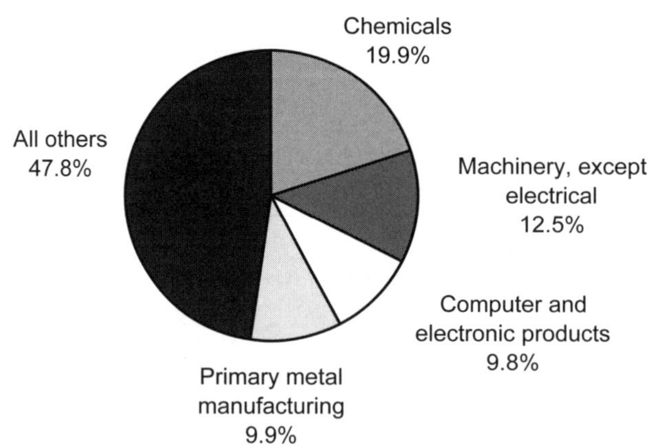

RHODE ISLAND

Facts and Figures

Location: Eastern United States; bordered on the N by Massachusetts, on the E by Massachusetts and the Atlantic Ocean, on the S by Block Island Sound and the Atlantic Ocean, and on the W by Connecticut

Area: 1,545 sq. mi. (4,002 sq. km.); rank—50th

Population: 1,050,292 (2012 est.); rank—43rd

Principal Cities: capital—Providence; largest—Providence

Statehood: May 29, 1790; 13th state

U.S. Congress: 2 senators, 2 representatives

State Motto: Hope

State Song: "Rhode Island"

State Nickname: The Ocean State

Abbreviations: RI; R.I.

State Symbols: flower—violet; tree—red maple; bird—Rhode Island red

At a Glance

- With an increase in population of 0.5 percent, Rhode Island ranked 49th among the states in growth from 2000 to 2009.
- An estimated 6,500 marriages took place in Rhode Island in 2009, compared to 3,300 divorces.
- In 2011, 10.8 percent of Rhode Islanders did not have health insurance, compared to 15.1 percent of the total U.S. population.
- Rhode Island's violent crime rate in 2011 was 247.5 per 100,000 population, compared to 386.3 for the entire nation.
- In 2007, Rhode Island exported $11 million worth of agricultural products, less than 1 percent of the U.S. total.

Table RI-1. Population by Age, Sex, Race, and Hispanic Origin

(Number, percent, except where noted.)

Sex, age, race, and Hispanic origin	2000	2010	2012[1]	Average annual percent change, 2010–2012
Total Population	1,048,319	1,052,567	1,050,292	-0.1
Percent of total U.S. population	0.4	0.3	0.3	X
Sex				
Male	503,635	508,400	508,276	-
Female	544,684	544,167	542,016	-0.1
Age				
Under 5 years	63,896	57,448	55,068	-1.4
5 to 19 years	218,720	204,310	198,191	-1.0
20 to 64 years	613,301	638,928	638,404	-
65 years and over	152,402	151,881	158,629	1.4
Median age (years)	36.7	39.4	39.8	0.3
Race and Hispanic Origin				
One race				
White	891,191	910,253	902,439	-0.3
Black	46,908	75,073	77,123	0.9
American Indian and Alaska Native	5,121	9,173	9,358	0.7
Asian	23,665	31,768	33,852	2.1
Native Hawaiian or Other Pacific Islander	567	1,602	1,648	0.9
Two or more races	28,251	24,698	25,872	1.5
Hispanic (of any race)	90,820	137,169	145,522	1.9

X = Not applicable.
- = Zero or rounds to zero.
[1] Population figures for 2012 are July 1 estimates. The 2010 estimates are taken from the 2010 Census.

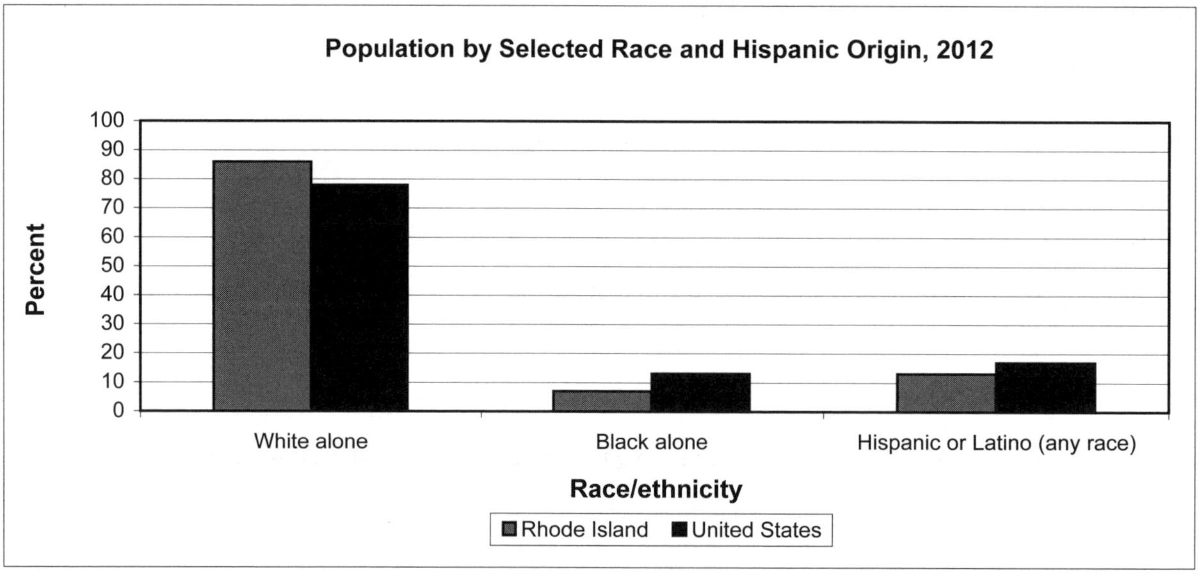

Table RI-2. Marital Status

(Number, percent distribution.)

Sex, age, race, and Hispanic origin	2000	2010	2011
Males, 15 Years and Over	396,396	414,628	416,897
Never married	32.5	39.8	38.9
Now married, except separated	54.9	45.2	47.3
Separated	1.5	1.6	1.6
Widowed	3.0	3.1	2.7
Divorced	8.0	10.3	9.5
Females, 15 Years and Over	445,107	456,425	455,766
Never married	27.1	32.4	32.0
Now married, except separated	48.5	41.8	42.7
Separated	2.3	2.4	2.3
Widowed	11.5	10.4	10.0
Divorced	10.7	13.0	13.0

Table RI-3. Households and Housing Characteristics

(Number, percent, dollars.)

Item	2000	2010	2011	Average annual percent change, 2000–2011
Total Households	408,424	402,295	412,259	0.1
Family households	265,398	246,028	256,181	-0.3
Married-couple family	196,757	173,848	181,495	-0.6
Other family	68,641	72,180	74,686	0.7
Male householder, no wife present	16,032	17,525	19,412	1.8
Female householder, no husband present	52,609	54,655	55,274	0.4
Nonfamily households	143,026	156,267	156,078	0.8
Householder living alone	116,678	125,371	126,149	0.7
Householder not living alone	26,348	30,896	29,929	1.1
Housing Characteristics				
Total housing units	439,837	463,416	464,741	0.5
Occupied housing units	408,424	402,295	412,259	0.1
Owner occupied	245,156	244,516	249,754	0.2
Renter occupied	163,268	157,779	162,505	-
Average size	2.47	2.51	2.45	-0.1
Financial Characteristics				
Median gross rent of renter-occupied housing	553	868	875	4.9
Median monthly owner costs for housing units with a mortgage	1,205	1,837	1,842	4.4
Median value of owner-occupied housing units	133,000	254,500	245,500	7.0

- = Zero or rounds to zero.

Table RI-4. Migration, Origin, and Language

(Number, percent.)

Characteristic	State			U.S.		
	2010	2011	Percent change	2010	2011	Percent change
Residence 1 Year Ago						
Population 1 year and over	1,042,240	1,040,022	-0.2	305,628,607	307,900,319	0.7
Same house	86.4	86.9	0.6	84.6	84.8	0.2
Different house in the U.S.	12.6	12.4	-1.6	14.8	14.6	-1.4
Same county	8.1	8.2	1.2	9.4	9.2	-2.1
Different county	4.5	4.2	-6.7	5.4	5.4	-
Same state	1.4	1.6	14.3	3.2	3.1	-3.1
Different state	3.1	2.6	-16.1	2.2	2.3	4.5
Abroad	1.0	0.7	-30.0	0.6	0.6	-
Place of Birth						
Native born	918,551	909,732	-1.0	269,393,835	271,214,059	0.7
Male	48.4	48.3	-0.2	49.2	49.2	-
Female	51.6	51.7	0.2	50.8	50.8	-
Foreign born	134,335	141,570	5.4	39,955,854	40,377,860	1.1
Male	47.4	48.9	3.2	49.1	48.9	-0.4
Female	52.6	51.1	-2.9	50.9	51.1	0.4
Foreign born; naturalized U.S. citizen	63,883	70,930	11.0	17,476,082	18,140,192	3.8
Male	43.0	45.4	5.6	45.8	45.8	-
Female	57.0	54.6	-4.2	54.2	54.2	-
Foreign born; not a U.S. citizen	70,452	70,640	0.3	22,479,772	22,237,668	-1.1
Male	51.4	52.4	1.9	51.6	51.5	-0.2
Female	48.6	47.6	-2.1	48.4	48.5	0.2
Entered 2000 or later	35.8	33.2	-7.3	34.7	35.7	2.9
Entered 1990 to 1999	21.8	23.9	9.6	27.2	26.7	-1.8
Entered before 1990	42.4	42.9	1.2	38.1	37.6	-1.3
World Region of Birth, Foreign						
Foreign-born population, excluding population born at sea	134,335	141,570	5.4	39,955,673	40,377,757	1.1
Europe	22.3	23.2	4.0	12.1	12.1	-
Asia	18.6	17.4	-6.5	28.2	28.6	1.4
Africa	12.5	10.6	-15.2	4	4.1	2.5
Oceania	0.2	0.2	0.0	0.5	0.5	-
Latin America	44.3	46.0	3.8	53.1	52.6	-0.9
North America	2.0	2.6	30.0	2	2.0	-
Language Spoken at Home and Ability to Speak English						
Population 5 years and over	995,774	995,856	-	289,215,746	291,524,091	0.8
English only	79.1	78.8	-0.4	79.4	79.2	-0.3
Language other than English	20.9	21.2	1.4	20.6	20.8	1.0
Speaks English less than "very well"	9.2	8.7	-5.4	8.7	8.7	-

- = Zero or rounds to zero.

Table RI-5. Median Income and Poverty Status, 2011

(Number, percent, except as noted.)

Characteristic	State		U.S.	
	Number	Percent	Number	Percent
Median Income				
Households (dollars)	53,636	X	50,502	X
Families (dollars)	69,604	X	61,455	X
Below Poverty Level (All People)	148,819	14.7	48,452,035	15.9
Sex				
Male	62,278	12.8	21,825,281	14.7
Female	86,541	16.6	26,626,754	17.2
Age				
Under 18 years	47,127	21.9	16,386,500	22.5
Related children under 18 years	46,391	21.6	16,087,074	22.2
18 to 64 years	86,800	13.4	28,335,079	14.8
65 years and over	14,892	10.2	3,730,456	9.3

X = Not applicable.

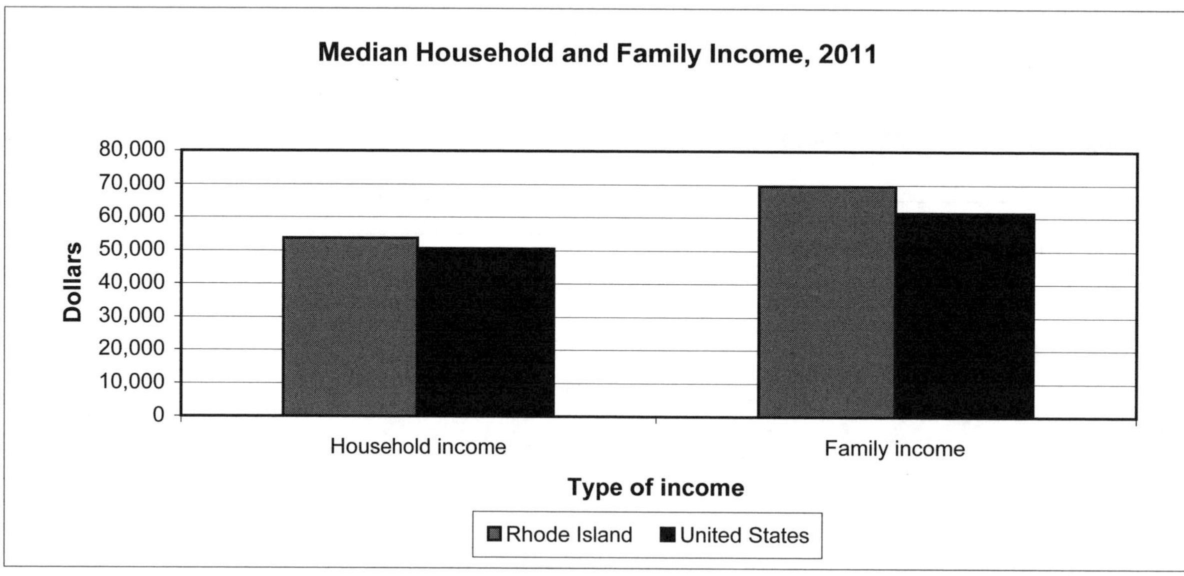

Table RI-6. Health Insurance Coverage Status for the Civilian Noninstitutionalized Population and Children Under 18 Years of Age

(Numbers in thousands, percent.)

Item	2004	2005	2006	2007	2008	2009	2010	2011
Civilian Noninstitutionalized Population	1,056	1,054	1,054	1,044	1,030	1,035	1,037	1,035
Covered by Private or Public Insurance								
Number	947	932	963	931	922	919	911	92,389
Percent	89.7	88.5	91.4	89.2	89.5	88.7	87.8	89.2
Not Covered								
Number	109	122	91	113	108	117	126	112
Percent	10.3	11.5	8.6	10.8	10.5	11.3	12.2	10.8
Percent in the U.S. not covered	14.9	15.3	15.8	15.3	15.1	15.1	15.5	15.1
Children Under 18 Years of Age	252	251	237	238	228	227	224	219
Covered by Private or Public Insurance								
Number	234	232	227	217	215	215	212	132
Percent	92.9	92.4	95.8	91.2	94.3	94.6	94.4	96.0
Not Covered								
Number	18	19	10	21	13	12	12	87
Percent	7.1	7.6	4.1	8.8	5.7	5.4	5.6	4.0
Percent in the U.S. not covered	10.5	10.9	11.7	11.0	9.7	8.6	8.0	7.5

Table RI-7. Employment Status by Demographic Group, Preliminary 2012

(Numbers in thousands, percent.)

Characteristic	Civilian noninstitutional population	Civilian labor force		Employed		Unemployed	
		Number	Percent of population	Number	Percent of population	Number	Percent of population
Total	846	558	66.0	499	59.0	59	10.5
Sex							
Male	402	285	70.8	253	62.9	32	11.1
Female	443	273	61.6	246	55.5	27	9.9
Race, Sex, and Hispanic Origin							
White	745	488	65.6	440	59.1	48	9.9
Male	355	250	70.3	223	62.8	27	10.7
Female	390	239	61.2	217	55.7	22	9.0
Black or African American	55	39	70.6	32	58.4	7	17.2
Male	27	20	75.2	17	61.9	4	17.7
Female	28	19	66.2	15	55.1	3	16.8
Hispanic	95	61	65.0	49	52.4	12	19.3
Male	42	31	73.8	25	59.9	6	18.9
Female	53	31	57.9	24	46.5	6	19.9
Age							
16 to 19 years	56	27	48.8	20	36.2	7	25.9
20 to 24 years	79	61	76.6	53	66.4	8	13.4
25 to 34 years	125	103	82.8	90	71.9	14	13.2
35 to 44 years	140	120	85.4	108	76.8	12	10.0
45 to 54 years	151	126	83.3	117	77.5	9	7.0
55 to 64 years	135	91	67.2	84	62.0	7	7.7
65 years and over	160	30	18.9	28	17.7	2	6.7

NOTE: Data in Table 7 are from the Current Population Survey (CPS) and do not match the estimates in Table 8. See notes and definitions for further information.

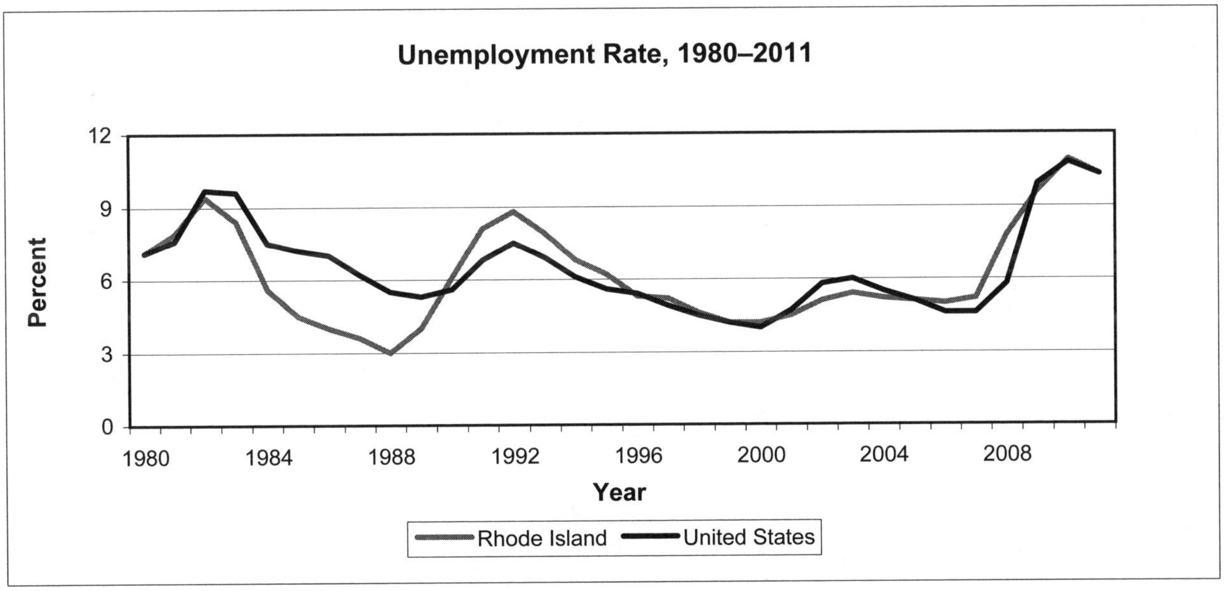

Table RI-8. Employment Status of the Civilian Noninstitutional Population Age 16 Years and Over

(Number, percent.)

Year	Civilian labor force	Civilian participation rate	Employed	Unemployed	Unemployment rate
2005	562,382	67.3	533,924	28,458	5.1
2006	571,454	68.4	542,632	28,822	5.0
2007	572,482	68.6	542,571	29,912	5.2
2008	567,597	68.1	523,226	44,371	7.8
2009	568,511	66.7	513,849	54,662	9.6
2010	551,014	64.2	490,964	60,050	10.9
2011	569,816	66.4	511,235	58,581	10.3

Table RI-9. Employment and Average Wages by Industry

(Estimates before 2007 are based on the 2002 *North American Industry Classification System* [NAICS]. Estimates from 2007 onward are based on the 2007 NAICS.)

Industry	2005	2006	2007	2008	2009	2010	2011
	Number of jobs						
Wage and Salary Employment by Industry	506,636	509,071	509,447	499,308	477,886	476,805	478,046
Farm Wage and Salary Employment	545	499	483	527	509	510	541
Nonfarm Wage and Salary Employment	506,091	508,572	508,964	498,781	477,377	476,295	477,505
Private wage and salary employment	430,389	433,402	433,561	424,126	403,989	403,247	405,394
Forestry, fishing, and related activities	559	548	530	514	558	D	D
Mining	252	260	279	246	194	D	D
Utilities	1,145	1,145	1,113	1,111	1,119	1,130	1,077
Construction	22,572	23,663	22,957	21,182	17,990	16,719	16,523
Manufacturing	55,113	52,854	50,920	48,034	41,841	40,431	40,416
Durable goods manufacturing	36,176	34,233	33,009	31,219	26,904	25,828	25,863
Nondurable goods manufacturing	18,937	18,621	17,911	16,815	14,937	14,603	14,553
Wholesale trade	16,769	17,071	17,325	16,957	16,226	15,935	16,278
Retail trade	53,222	52,468	52,221	50,320	47,840	47,701	47,640
Transportation and warehousing	9,800	9,880	10,017	9,883	9,186	9,247	9,693
Information	10,804	11,021	10,495	10,757	10,158	10,033	10,172
Finance and insurance	26,266	27,084	27,020	25,603	24,136	24,148	23,919
Real estate and rental and leasing	6,949	7,102	6,943	6,699	6,229	5,931	5,887
Professional, scientific, and technical services	21,201	21,805	22,141	21,967	21,470	21,248	21,287
Management of companies and enterprises	9,174	9,517	9,447	9,302	9,207	9,326	9,856
Administrative and waste services	25,559	25,623	25,203	24,211	22,483	23,554	23,702
Educational services	21,998	22,821	23,556	24,403	24,847	25,068	25,340
Health care and social assistance	74,004	75,732	77,501	78,004	78,388	79,691	79,534
Arts, entertainment, and recreation	7,582	7,780	8,286	8,166	7,768	7,679	7,703
Accommodation and food services	43,159	43,068	43,636	43,387	41,803	42,533	43,064
Other services, except public administration	24,261	23,960	23,971	23,380	22,546	22,127	22,554
Government and government enterprises	75,702	75,170	75,403	74,655	73,388	73,048	72,111
	Dollars						
Average Wages and Salaries by Industry	39,154	40,926	42,180	43,525	43,930	45,275	46,375
Average Farm Wages and Salaries	21,824	27,689	32,783	28,825	28,354	26,727	22,543
Average Nonfarm Wages and Salaries	39,172	40,939	42,189	43,541	43,947	45,295	46,402
Average private wages and salaries	37,893	39,633	40,847	42,069	42,271	43,650	44,760
Forestry, fishing, and related activities	36,234	39,688	38,649	39,484	37,618	D	D
Mining	44,357	48,027	48,229	48,297	48,582	D	D
Utilities	68,586	73,238	75,501	81,681	85,218	86,633	93,909
Construction	45,453	47,263	49,313	51,431	53,037	52,520	53,841
Manufacturing	43,002	44,946	47,457	47,975	48,872	50,989	52,722
Durable goods manufacturing	43,411	45,619	48,055	48,842	49,863	52,470	54,322
Nondurable goods manufacturing	42,221	43,708	46,355	46,365	47,087	48,371	49,877
Wholesale trade	55,643	56,863	60,364	61,469	61,378	64,751	65,451
Retail trade	25,782	26,185	27,572	27,456	27,294	28,154	27,821
Transportation and warehousing	34,449	36,303	36,491	37,934	38,992	39,861	40,949
Information	62,856	59,891	59,034	59,222	61,392	62,900	65,816
Finance and insurance	58,520	60,423	62,878	69,842	69,956	75,543	80,261
Real estate and rental and leasing	36,108	36,692	38,033	37,713	37,323	38,914	40,170
Professional, scientific, and technical services	55,756	65,091	60,714	63,007	63,211	65,446	66,555
Management of companies and enterprises	84,653	91,703	99,392	107,131	95,224	104,620	106,642
Administrative and waste services	26,476	27,522	29,526	30,903	31,200	31,606	32,403
Educational services	34,756	35,848	37,178	38,160	38,554	39,520	40,155
Health care and social assistance	37,511	38,570	39,227	40,384	41,708	42,311	43,169
Arts, entertainment, and recreation	24,249	26,284	28,031	26,444	26,487	27,149	28,115
Accommodation and food services	16,711	17,183	18,006	17,756	17,832	18,360	18,946
Other services, except public administration	25,212	26,031	27,025	27,915	28,124	28,941	29,190
Government and government enterprises	46,449	48,472	49,906	51,902	53,171	54,370	55,634

D = Not shown to avoid disclosure of confidential information, but the estimates for this item are included in the total.

Table RI-10. Employment Characteristics by Family Type

(Number, percent.)

Family type and labor force status	2009		2010		2011	
	Total	Families with own children under 18 years	Total	Families with own children under 18 years	Total	Families with own children under 18 years
All families	257,514	114,526	246,028	109,638	256,181	111,314
Family type and labor force status						
Married-couple families	187,192	74,633	173,848	71,052	181,495	70,306
Both husband and wife in labor force	59.1	73.2	58.1	71.9	58.5	74.3
Husband in labor force, wife not in labor force	18.3	20.9	17.8	21.0	17.8	21.0
Wife in labor force, husband not in labor force	8.3	5.0	9.6	6.2	8.3	3.6
Both husband and wife not in labor force	14.3	1.0	14.5	0.9	15.4	1.1
Other families	70,322	39,893	72,180	38,586	74,686	41,008
Female householder, no husband present	75.9	77.7	75.7	82.0	74.0	79.2
In labor force	53.4	59.9	54.0	67.6	54.0	65.1
Not in labor force	22.6	17.8	21.8	14.4	20.0	14.1
Male householder, no wife present	24.1	22.3	24.3	18.0	26.0	20.8
In labor force	19.6	19.6	18.1	15.4	19.7	18.4
Not in labor force	4.4	2.8	6.2	2.5	6.3	2.4

Table RI-11. School Enrollment and Educational Attainment, 2011

(Number, percent.)

Item	State	U.S.
Enrollment		
Total population 3 years and over, enrolled in school	277,923	83,131,910
Enrolled in nursery school or preschool (percent)	6.1	6.0
Enrolled in kindergarten (percent)	3.5	5.1
Enrolled in elementary school, grades 1-8 (percent)	34.6	39.5
Enrolled in high school, grades 9-12 (percent)	19.8	20.7
Enrolled in college or graduate school (percent)	35.9	28.7
Attainment		
Total population 25 years and over	712,266	206,471,670
Less than ninth grade (percent)	6.4	6.0
9th to 12th grade, no diploma (percent)	8.8	8.1
High school graduate, including equivalency (percent)	26.4	28.4
Some college, no degree (percent)	18.9	21.2
Associate's degree (percent)	8.4	7.8
Bachelor's degree (percent)	18.8	17.9
Graduate or professional degree (percent)	12.3	10.6
High school graduate or higher (percent)	84.8	85.9
Bachelor's degree or higher (percent)	31.1	28.5

Table RI-12. Educational Indicators

(Number, percent; data derived from National Center of Education Statistics.)

Item	State	U.S.
Public Schools, 2009–2010 (except where noted)		
Number of school districts	32	13,629
Number of schools	321	99,834
Number of students (in thousands)	145	49,373
Student-teacher ratio	12.8	15.4
Expenditures per student (dollars)	15,753	10,591
Averaged freshman graduation rate, 2008–2009	75.3	75.5[1]
Dropout rate, 2008–2009	4.4	4.1
Students eligible for free or reduced-price lunch (percent)	42.3	48.0
English language learners, 2010–2011 (percent)	5.5	9.8[1]
Students with IEP (percent)	18.1	13.1
Private Schools, 2009–2010 (except where noted)		
Number of schools	163	33,366
Number of students (in thousands)	22	4,700
High school graduates, 2008–2009	1,818	308,813
Student-teacher ratio	9.5	10.7

[1] U.S. total includes estimates for nonreporting states.

Table RI-13. Reported Voting and Registration of the Voting-Age Population, November 2012

(Numbers in thousands, percent.)

Item	Total population	Total citizen population	Registered			Voted		
			Total registered	Percent registered (total population)	Percent registered (total citizen population)	Total voted	Percent voted (total population)	Percent voted (total citizen population)
U.S. Total	235,248	215,081	153,157	65.1	71.2	132,948	56.5	61.8
State Total	9,847	9,452	6,795	69.0	71.9	5,824	59.1	61.6
Sex								
Male	384	352	254	66.1	72.0	212	55.3	60.2
Female	434	399	298	68.8	74.8	257	59.3	64.5
Race								
White alone	713	673	497	69.7	74.0	420	58.9	62.5
White, non-Hispanic alone	646	632	472	73.0	74.7	400	61.9	63.3
Black alone	50	43	33	B	B	30	B	B
Asian alone	25	16	6	B	B	5	B	B
Hispanic (of any race)	95	57	37	39.1	B	32	33.6	B
Age								
18 to 24 years	99	89	61	61.8	68.9	45	45.2	50.3
25 to 44 years	271	235	159	58.7	67.6	134	49.4	56.9
45 to 64 years	290	272	213	73.4	78.3	185	64.0	68.3
65 to 74 years	84	82	64	76.3	78.1	59	70.5	72.2
75 years and over	74	74	55	B	B	46	B	B

B = Base is less than 75,000 and therefore too small to show the derived measure.

Table RI-14. Crime

(Number, rate per 100,000. Data are derived from the FBI Uniform Crime Reports.)

Item	State			U.S.		
	2010	2011	Percent change	2010	2011	Percent change
TOTAL POPULATION	1,052,528	1,052,302	-.02	309,330,219	311,591,917	0.7
VIOLENT CRIME						
Number	2,709	2,602	-3.9	1,251,248	1,203,564	-3.8
Rate	257.4	247.5	-3.8	404.5	386.3	-4.5
Murder and Nonnegligent Manslaughter						
Number	29	14	-51.7	14,722	14,612	-0.7
Rate	2.8	1.3	-53.6	4.8	4.7	-2.1
Forcible Rape						
Number	298	304	2.0	85,593	83,425	-2.5
Rate	28.3	28.9	2.1	27.7	26.8	-3.2
Robbery						
Number	782	746	-4.6	369,089	354,396	-4.0
Rate	74.3	71.0	-4.4	119.3	113.7	-4.7
Aggravated Assault						
Number	1,600	1,538	-3.9	781,844	751,131	-3.9
Rate	152.0	146.3	-3.7	252.8	241.1	-4.6
PROPERTY CRIME						
Number	26,959	28,141	4.4	9,112,625	9,063,173	-0.5
Rate	2,561.4	2,676.8	4.5	2,945.9	2,908.7	-1.3
Burglary						
Number	6,124	6,964	13.7	2,168,459	2,188,005	0.9
Rate	581.8	662.4	13.9	701.0	702.2	0.2
Larceny-Theft						
Number	18,432	18,890	2.5	6,204,601	6,159,795	-0.7
Rate	1,751.2	1,796.8	2.6	2,005.8	1,976.9	-1.4
Motor Vehicle Theft						
Number	2,403	2,287	-4.8	739,565	715,373	-3.3
Rate	228.3	217.5	-4.7	239.1	229.6	-4.0

Table RI-15. State Government Finances, 2011

(Dollar amounts in thousands, percent distribution.)

Item	Dollars	Percent distribution
Total Revenue	9,371,534	100.0
General revenue	7,140,710	76.2
Intergovernmental revenue	2,731,772	29.1
Taxes	2,737,952	29.2
General sales	824,507	8.8
Selective sales	623,535	6.7
License taxes	95,804	1.0
Individual income tax	1,016,217	10.8
Corporate income tax	147,989	1.6
Other taxes	29,900	0.3
Current charges	793,659	8.5
Miscellaneous general revenue	877,327	9.4
Utility revenue	31,090	0.3
Liquor stores revenue	0	0.0
Insurance trust revenue [1]	2,199,734	23.5
Total Expenditure	8,270,898	100.0
Intergovernmental expenditure	1,074,302	13.0
Direct expenditure	7,196,596	87.0
Current operation	4,487,469	54.3
Capital outlay	522,157	6.3
Insurance benefits and repayments	1,623,507	19.6
Assistance and subsidies	135,696	1.6
Interest on debt	427,767	5.2
Exhibit: Salaries and wages	1,143,288	13.8
Total Expenditure	8,270,898	100.0
General expenditure	6,408,222	77.5
Intergovernmental expenditure	1,074,302	13.0
Direct expenditure	5,333,920	64.5
General expenditure, by function:		
Education	1,815,172	21.9
Public welfare	2,403,320	29.1
Hospitals	58,830	0.7
Health	170,829	2.1
Highways	254,778	3.1
Police protection	71,702	0.9
Correction	181,796	2.2
Natural resources	43,690	0.5
Parks and recreation	5,545	0.1
Governmental administration	320,660	3.9
Interest on general debt	427,767	5.2
Other and unallocable	654,133	7.9
Utility expenditure	239,169	2.9
Liquor stores expenditure	0	0.0
Insurance trust expenditure	1,623,507	19.6
Debt at End of Fiscal Year	9,173,572	X
Cash and Security Holdings	15,754,977	X

X = Not applicable.

[1] Within insurance trust revenue, net earnings of state retirement systems is a calculated statistic (the item code in the data file is X08), and thus can be positive or negative. Net earnings is the sum of earnings on investments plus gains on investments minus losses on investments. The change made in 2002 for asset valuation from book to market value in accordance with Statement 34 of the Governmental Accounting Standards Board is reflected in the calculated statistics.

Table RI-16. State Government Tax Collections, 2012

(Dollars in thousands, percent.)

Item	Dollars	Percent distribution
Total Taxes	2,805,287	100.0
Property taxes	2,093	0.1
Sales and gross receipts	1,474,739	52.6
General sales and gross receipts	839,414	29.9
Selective sales and gross receipts	635,325	22.6
Alcoholic beverages	12,785	0.5
Amusements	0	0.0
Insurance premiums	86,005	3.1
Motor fuels	117,663	4.2
Pari-mutuels	1,023	-
Public utilities	101,686	3.6
Tobacco products	130,811	4.7
Other selective sales	185,352	6.6
Licenses	105,911	3.8
Alcoholic beverages	69	-
Amusements	261	-
Corporations in general	4,611	0.2
Hunting and fishing	1,743	0.1
Motor vehicle	55,822	2.0
Motor vehicle operators	1,696	0.1
Public utilities	0	0.0
Occupation and business, NEC	40,383	1.4
Other licenses	1,326	-
Income taxes	1,186,644	42.3
Individual income	1,064,447	37.9
Corporation net income	122,197	4.4
Other taxes	35,900	1.3
Death and gift	27,913	1.0
Documentary and stock transfer	7,987	0.3
Severance	0	0.0
Taxes, NEC	0	0.0

- = Rounds to zero.

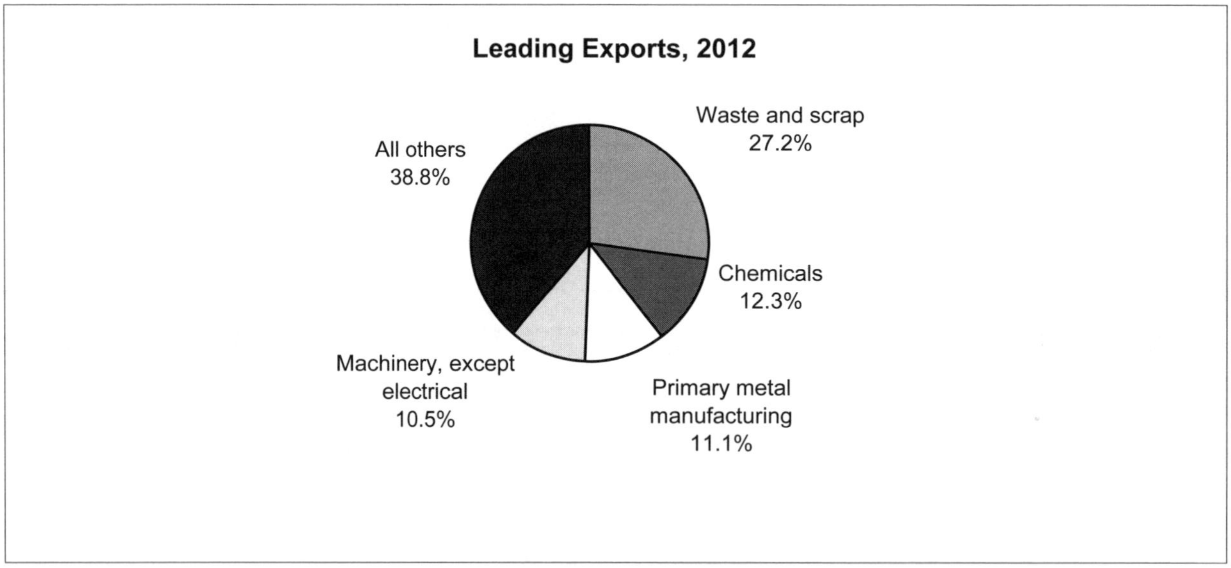

SOUTH CAROLINA

Facts and Figures

Location: Southeastern United States; bordered on the N by North Carolina, on the E by the Atlantic Ocean, on the S by the Atlantic Ocean and Georgia, and on the W by Georgia

Area: 32,020 sq. mi. (82,932 sq. km.); rank—40th

Population: 4,723,723 (2012 est.); rank—24th

Principal Cities: capital—Columbia; largest—Columbia

Statehood: May 23, 1788; 8th state

U.S. Congress: 2 senators, 7 representatives

State Mottoes: *Animis opibusque parati* ("Prepared in mind and resources"); *Dum spiro, spero* ("While I breathe, I hope")

State Songs: "Carolina"; "South Carolina on My Mind"

State Nickname: The Palmetto State

Abbreviations: SC; S.C.

State Symbols: flower—yellow jessamine; tree—cabbage palmetto; bird—Carolina wren

At a Glance

- With an increase in population of 13.7 percent, South Carolina ranked 14th among the states in growth from 2000 to 2009.
- An estimated 29,200 marriages took place in South Carolina in 2009, compared to 12,200 divorces.
- South Carolina's median household income in 2011 was $42,637, and 18.9 percent of the population lived below the poverty level.
- South Carolina's violent crime rate in 2011 was 571.9 per 100,000 population, compared to 386.3 for the entire nation.
- In 2007, South Carolina exported $436 million worth of agricultural products, less than 1 percent of the U.S. total.

Table SC-1. Population by Age, Sex, Race, and Hispanic Origin

(Number, percent, except where noted.)

Sex, age, race, and Hispanic origin	2000	2010	2012[1]	Average annual percent change, 2010–2012
Total Population	4,012,012	4,625,364	4,723,723	0.7
Percent of total U.S. population	1.4	1.5	1.5	X
Sex				
Male	1,948,929	2,250,101	2,297,213	0.7
Female	2,063,083	2,375,263	2,426,510	0.7
Age				
Under 5 years	264,679	302,297	296,401	-0.7
5 to 19 years	871,099	922,128	918,552	-0.1
20 to 64 years	2,390,901	2,769,065	2,813,311	0.5
65 years and over	485,333	631,874	695,459	3.0
Median age (years)	35.4	37.9	38.4	0.4
Race and Hispanic Origin				
One race				
White	2,695,560	3,164,143	3,229,346	0.7
Black	1,185,216	1,302,865	1,322,528	0.5
American Indian and Alaska Native	13,718	24,665	25,254	0.8
Asian	36,014	61,247	67,529	3.1
Native Hawaiian or Other Pacific Islander	1,628	3,957	4,104	1.2
Two or more races	39,950	68,487	74,962	2.9
Hispanic (of any race)	95,076	243,923	258,907	1.9

X = Not applicable.
[1] Population figures for 2012 are July 1 estimates. The 2010 estimates are taken from the 2010 Census.

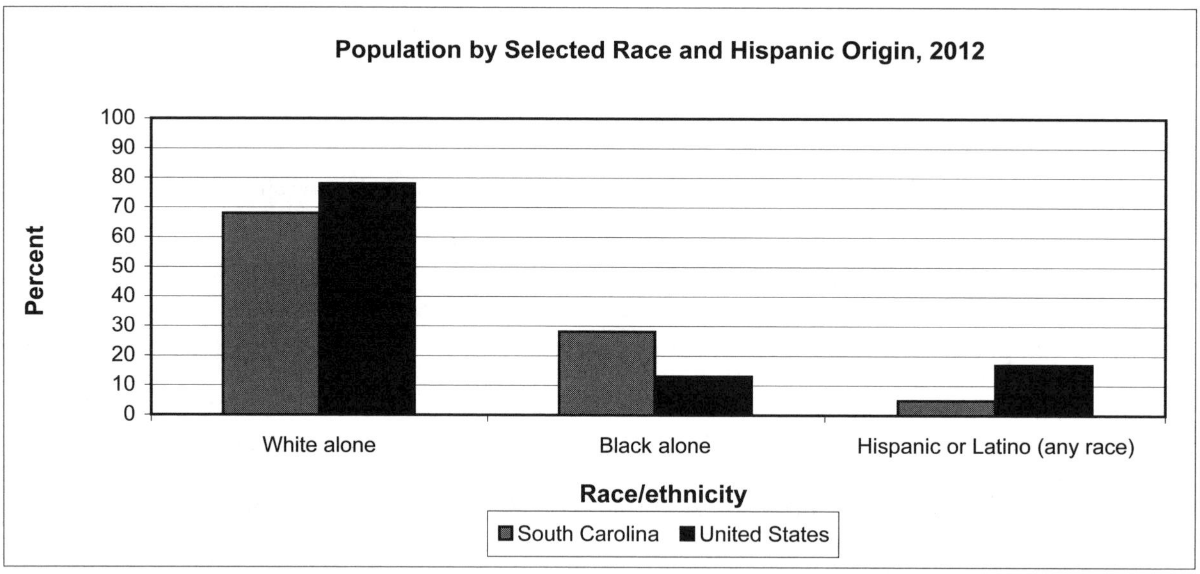

Table SC-2. Marital Status

(Number, percent distribution.)

Sex, age, race, and Hispanic origin	2000	2010	2011
Males, 15 Years and Over	1,516,125	1,797,441	1,818,218
Never married	28.8	35.2	34.4
Now married, except separated	57.3	49.4	50.3
Separated	2.8	3.0	3.1
Widowed	2.7	2.8	2.8
Divorced	8.3	9.5	9.4
Females, 15 Years and Over	1,652,793	1,939,054	1,957,930
Never married	23.4	29.1	28.3
Now married, except separated	51.4	45.2	46.1
Separated	3.8	3.9	4.1
Widowed	11.5	10.6	10.7
Divorced	9.9	11.2	10.8

Table SC-3. Households and Housing Characteristics

(Number, percent, dollars.)

Item	2000	2010	2011	Average annual percent change, 2000–2011
Total Households	1,533,854	1,761,393	1,768,834	1.3
Family households	1,072,822	1,180,687	1,201,688	1.0
Married-couple family	783,142	827,387	855,034	0.8
Other family	289,680	353,300	346,654	1.6
Male householder, no wife present	62,722	77,062	79,832	2.3
Female householder, no husband present	226,958	276,238	266,822	1.5
Nonfamily households	461,032	580,706	567,146	1.9
Householder living alone	383,142	489,995	483,491	2.2
Householder not living alone	77,890	90,711	83,655	0.6
Housing Characteristics				
Total housing units	1,753,670	2,140,337	2,157,063	1.9
Occupied housing units	1,533,854	1,761,393	1,768,834	1.3
Owner occupied	1,107,617	1,210,160	1,223,474	0.9
Renter occupied	426,237	551,233	545,360	2.3
Average size	2.53	2.55	2.57	0.1
Financial Characteristics				
Median gross rent of renter-occupied housing	510	728	741	3.8
Median monthly owner costs for housing units with a mortgage	894	1,177	1,175	2.6
Median value of owner-occupied housing units	94,900	138,100	136,000	3.6

Table SC-4. Migration, Origin, and Language

(Number, percent.)

Characteristic	State			U.S.		
	2010	2011	Percent change	2010	2011	Percent change
Residence 1 Year Ago						
Population 1 year and over	4,577,399	4,624,180	1.0	305,628,607	307,900,319	0.7
Same house	84.6	84.3	-0.4	84.6	84.8	0.2
Different house in the U.S.	15.1	15.2	0.7	14.8	14.6	-1.4
Same county	8.4	8.8	4.8	9.4	9.2	-2.1
Different county	6.6	6.4	-3.0	5.4	5.4	-
Same state	3.3	3.0	-9.1	3.2	3.1	-3.1
Different state	3.3	3.4	3.0	2.2	2.3	4.5
Abroad	0.4	0.4	-	0.6	0.6	-
Place of Birth						
Native born	4,417,818	4,457,297	0.9	269,393,835	271,214,059	0.7
Male	48.3	48.4	0.2	49.2	49.2	-
Female	51.7	51.6	-0.2	50.8	50.8	-
Foreign born	218,494	221,933	1.6	39,955,854	40,377,860	1.1
Male	53.7	52.0	-3.2	49.1	48.9	-0.4
Female	46.3	48.0	3.7	50.9	51.1	0.4
Foreign born; naturalized U.S. citizen	66,076	74,818	13.2	17,476,082	18,140,192	3.8
Male	47.4	46.5	-1.9	45.8	45.8	-
Female	52.6	53.5	1.7	54.2	54.2	-
Foreign born; not a U.S. citizen	152,418	147,115	-3.5	22,479,772	22,237,668	-1.1
Male	56.4	54.8	-2.8	51.6	51.5	-0.2
Female	43.6	45.2	3.7	48.4	48.5	0.2
Entered 2000 or later	50.7	45.6	-10.1	34.7	35.7	2.9
Entered 1990 to 1999	23.3	24.6	5.6	27.2	26.7	-1.8
Entered before 1990	25.9	29.8	15.1	38.1	37.6	-1.3
World Region of Birth, Foreign						
Foreign-born population, excluding population born at sea	218,494	221,933	1.6	39,955,673	40,377,757	1.1
Europe	16.9	18.3	8.3	12.1	12.1	-
Asia	20.4	22.2	8.8	28.2	28.6	1.4
Africa	3.8	1.8	-52.6	4	4.1	2.5
Oceania	0.3	0.2	-33.3	0.5	0.5	-
Latin America	54.8	53.7	-2.0	53.1	52.6	-0.9
North America	3.8	3.8	-	2	2.0	-
Language Spoken at Home and Ability to Speak English						
Population 5 years and over	4,334,519	4,376,509	1.0	289,215,746	291,524,091	0.8
English only	93.2	93.4	0.2	79.4	79.2	-0.3
Language other than English	6.8	6.6	-2.9	20.6	20.8	1.0
Speaks English less than "very well"	2.9	2.7	-6.9	8.7	8.7	-

- = Zero or rounds to zero.

Table SC-5. Median Income and Poverty Status, 2011

(Number, percent, except as noted.)

Characteristic	State		U.S.	
	Number	Percent	Number	Percent
Median Income				
Households (dollars)	42,367	X	50,502	X
Families (dollars)	52,240	X	61,455	X
Below Poverty Level (All People)	856,938	18.9	48,452,035	15.9
Sex				
Male	376,667	17.2	21,825,281	14.7
Female	480,271	20.4	26,626,754	17.2
Age				
Under 18 years	296,759	27.8	16,386,500	22.5
Related children under 18 years	293,522	27.6	16,087,074	22.2
18 to 64 years	495,522	17.5	28,335,079	14.8
65 years and over	64,657	10.1	3,730,456	9.3

X = Not applicable.

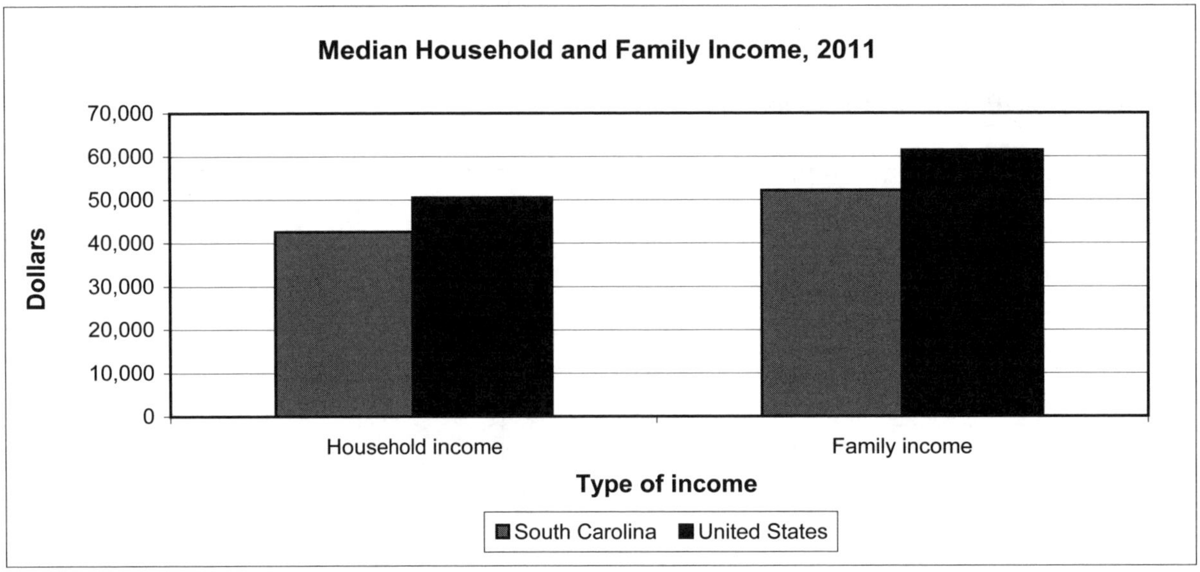

Table SC-6. Health Insurance Coverage Status for the Civilian Noninstitutionalized Population and Children Under 18 Years of Age

(Numbers in thousands, percent.)

Item	2004	2005	2006	2007	2008	2009	2010	2011
Civilian Noninstitutionalized Population	4,124	4,181	4,226	4,384	4,373	4,454	4,537	4,579
Covered by Private or Public Insurance								
Number	3,515	3,459	3,553	3,664	3,612	3,705	3,742	3,813
Percent	85.2	82.7	84.1	83.6	82.6	83.2	82.5	83.3
Not Covered								
Number	608	721	672	721	761	750	795	766
Percent	14.8	17.3	15.9	16.4	17.4	16.8	17.5	16.7
Percent in the U.S. not covered	14.9	15.3	15.8	15.3	15.1	15.1	15.5	15.1
Children Under 18 Years of Age	1,031	1,016	1,042	1,070	1,064	1,078	1,078	1,079
Covered by Private or Public Insurance								
Number	951	912	930	918	930	971	976	988
Percent	92.3	89.8	89.3	85.8	87.4	90.0	90.6	91.6
Not Covered								
Number	80	104	112	152	134	107	102	91
Percent	7.7	10.2	10.7	14.2	12.6	10.0	9.4	8.4
Percent in the U.S. not covered	10.5	10.9	11.7	11.0	9.7	8.6	8.0	7.5

Table SC-7. Employment Status by Demographic Group, Preliminary 2012

(Numbers in thousands, percent.)

Characteristic	Civilian noninstitutional population	Civilian labor force		Employed		Unemployed	
		Number	Percent of population	Number	Percent of population	Number	Percent of population
Total	3,646	2,161	59.3	1,958	53.7	203	9.4
Sex							
Male	1,720	1,104	64.2	1,007	58.6	97	8.8
Female	1,926	1,057	54.9	951	49.4	106	10.0
Race, Sex, and Hispanic Origin							
White	2,593	1,531	59.1	1,426	55.0	105	6.9
Male	1,251	821	65.6	768	61.4	53	6.4
Female	1,342	710	52.9	658	49.0	52	7.4
Black or African American	971	579	59.6	486	50.0	93	16.1
Male	431	256	59.5	215	49.9	41	16.1
Female	541	323	59.7	271	50.1	52	16.1
Hispanic	113	75	66.0	69	60.8	6	7.9
Male	60	51	84.0	48	79.7	3	5.2
Female	53	24	45.4	21	39.1	3	13.7
Age							
16 to 19 years	241	77	32.1	53	21.9	25	31.7
20 to 24 years	328	224	68.1	179	54.6	44	19.8
25 to 34 years	557	452	81.0	406	72.9	46	10.1
35 to 44 years	596	480	80.5	458	76.8	22	4.6
45 to 54 years	613	461	75.3	425	69.4	36	7.8
55 to 64 years	645	363	56.2	339	52.5	24	6.6
65 years and over	666	104	15.6	98	14.7	6	6.1

NOTE: Data in Table 7 are from the Current Population Survey (CPS) and do not match the estimates in Table 8. See notes and definitions for further information.

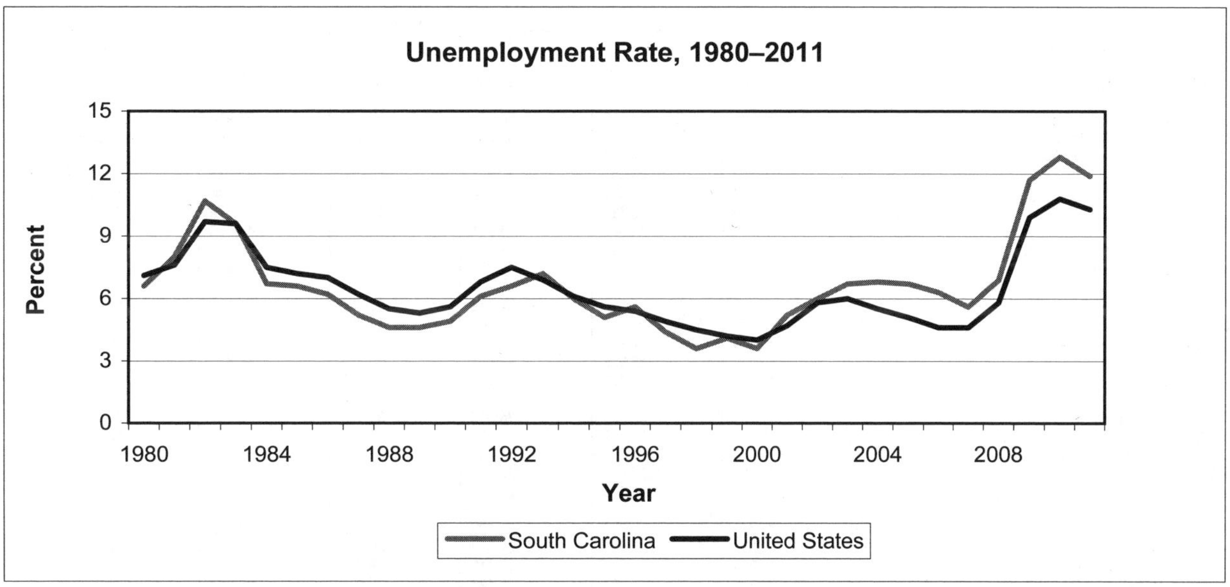

Table SC-8. Employment Status of the Civilian Noninstitutional Population Age 16 Years and Over

(Number, percent.)

Year	Civilian labor force	Civilian participation rate	Employed	Unemployed	Unemployment rate
2005	2,067,160	63.9	1,927,671	139,489	6.7
2006	2,109,916	63.9	1,976,648	133,268	6.3
2007	2,125,073	63.1	2,006,178	118,895	5.6
2008	2,152,965	62.7	2,004,241	148,724	6.9
2009	2,224,745	61.8	1,963,661	261,084	11.7
2010	2,241,088	61.0	1,955,035	286,053	12.8
2011	2,235,219	60.2	1,968,925	266,294	11.9

Table SC-9. Employment and Average Wages by Industry

(Estimates before 2007 are based on the 2002 *North American Industry Classification System* [NAICS]. Estimates from 2007 onward are based on the 2007 NAICS.)

Industry	2005	2006	2007	2008	2009	2010	2011
	Number of jobs						
Wage and Salary Employment by Industry	1,957,037	2,000,019	2,033,893	2,020,732	1,912,435	1,903,467	1,926,026
Farm Wage and Salary Employment	7,083	7,595	6,367	6,453	7,894	6,624	6,722
Nonfarm Wage and Salary Employment	1,949,954	1,992,424	2,027,526	2,014,279	1,904,541	1,896,843	1,919,304
Private wage and salary employment	1,568,584	1,605,346	1,636,554	1,613,489	1,502,296	1,498,976	1,526,368
Forestry, fishing, and related activities	7,169	7,322	6,740	6,635	6,468	6,697	6,905
Mining	1,523	1,509	1,453	1,482	1,340	1,244	1,232
Utilities	11,626	12,157	12,063	12,363	12,435	12,048	11,922
Construction	122,600	131,407	129,711	115,006	92,463	83,731	80,892
Manufacturing	260,561	255,410	250,677	243,301	214,821	208,203	216,381
Durable goods manufacturing	137,094	137,231	139,041	136,638	118,293	114,174	121,111
Nondurable goods manufacturing	123,467	118,179	111,636	106,663	96,528	94,029	95,270
Wholesale trade	67,776	70,101	71,870	71,671	65,668	64,222	65,039
Retail trade	235,060	237,900	243,762	239,826	227,174	226,866	228,832
Transportation and warehousing	51,912	53,549	54,730	52,830	47,673	47,205	48,312
Information	27,130	28,105	28,378	28,573	27,229	25,893	25,858
Finance and insurance	67,963	71,146	72,056	72,084	70,386	68,999	68,948
Real estate and rental and leasing	29,355	30,531	31,399	30,955	28,586	27,141	26,660
Professional, scientific, and technical services	67,584	70,377	74,048	77,270	74,138	75,713	80,155
Management of companies and enterprises	14,393	15,308	15,621	15,659	14,516	14,290	15,053
Administrative and waste services	129,143	132,362	138,265	131,288	115,370	129,873	136,527
Educational services	24,834	25,362	26,939	28,069	28,271	29,289	29,922
Health care and social assistance	149,682	155,573	161,332	166,737	168,480	172,707	175,238
Arts, entertainment, and recreation	25,583	26,107	27,249	28,779	27,029	26,044	26,805
Accommodation and food services	180,477	185,547	192,398	191,371	183,894	183,777	186,392
Other services, except public administration	94,213	95,573	97,863	99,590	96,355	95,034	95,295
Government and government enterprises	381,370	387,078	390,972	400,790	402,245	397,867	392,936
	Dollars						
Average Wages and Salaries by Industry	33,735	35,133	36,428	37,330	37,832	38,715	39,627
Average Farm Wages and Salaries	19,720	19,604	25,833	23,101	18,925	22,695	20,051
Average Nonfarm Wages and Salaries	33,786	35,192	36,461	37,375	37,910	38,771	39,696
Average private wages and salaries	33,215	34,689	35,764	36,469	36,798	37,836	38,842
Forestry, fishing, and related activities	26,910	27,627	29,978	29,913	29,906	31,148	31,518
Mining	45,385	46,541	47,912	46,090	43,035	48,012	50,545
Utilities	66,220	70,087	68,704	72,803	73,936	78,446	80,316
Construction	35,750	38,137	39,740	41,013	40,979	41,924	42,903
Manufacturing	43,131	45,040	46,341	47,851	48,779	51,196	52,793
Durable goods manufacturing	44,114	46,166	47,189	48,930	50,369	53,280	55,232
Nondurable goods manufacturing	42,041	43,733	45,284	46,468	46,832	48,666	49,693
Wholesale trade	48,454	51,244	54,112	55,336	54,676	55,975	58,095
Retail trade	23,625	24,393	24,668	24,850	24,928	25,432	25,518
Transportation and warehousing	36,868	37,730	38,521	38,908	39,240	40,449	41,243
Information	45,579	48,610	49,041	50,236	50,835	52,112	52,169
Finance and insurance	48,256	51,402	54,599	52,945	53,973	55,028	57,235
Real estate and rental and leasing	31,101	33,605	34,327	33,909	33,906	34,536	36,297
Professional, scientific, and technical services	51,325	53,387	56,492	57,089	57,937	59,901	61,272
Management of companies and enterprises	59,670	61,271	63,281	64,102	65,759	67,177	70,185
Administrative and waste services	27,197	27,997	29,084	30,739	32,200	32,930	33,796
Educational services	23,727	25,303	25,658	26,651	27,675	27,824	28,457
Health care and social assistance	36,272	37,297	38,125	39,183	40,059	41,319	42,089
Arts, entertainment, and recreation	20,072	21,002	21,769	20,390	20,026	20,396	21,023
Accommodation and food services	14,984	15,561	16,412	16,294	16,312	17,036	17,494
Other services, except public administration	23,259	24,094	25,120	26,071	26,257	27,246	27,792
Government and government enterprises	36,133	37,277	39,380	41,025	42,062	42,296	43,015

Table SC-10. Employment Characteristics by Family Type

(Number, percent.)

Family type and labor force status	2009 Total	2009 Families with own children under 18 years	2010 Total	2010 Families with own children under 18 years	2011 Total	2011 Families with own children under 18 years
All families	1,163,764	490,985	1,180,687	488,895	1,201,688	499,036
Family type and labor force status						
Married-couple families	833,306	306,512	827,387	303,324	855,034	313,733
Both husband and wife in labor force	52.0	68.7	50.4	68.6	48.6	65.0
Husband in labor force, wife not in labor force	20.4	25.0	21.2	25.1	22.6	28.7
Wife in labor force, husband not in labor force	8.4	4.1	8.8	4.3	8.7	3.9
Both husband and wife not in labor force	19.2	2.2	19.6	2.1	20.1	2.4
Other families	330,458	184,473	353,300	185,571	346,654	185,303
Female householder, no husband present	77.2	79.0	78.2	82.4	77.0	78.7
In labor force	54.6	67.1	54.6	68.6	52.2	64.6
Not in labor force	22.6	12.0	23.6	13.8	24.8	14.1
Male householder, no wife present	22.8	21.0	21.8	17.6	23.0	21.3
In labor force	17.7	18.7	16.2	15.7	17.5	18.7
Not in labor force	5.0	2.3	5.6	1.9	5.5	2.6

Table SC-11. School Enrollment and Educational Attainment, 2011

(Number, percent.)

Item	State	U.S.
Enrollment		
Total population 3 years and over, enrolled in school	1,199,462	83,131,910
Enrolled in nursery school or preschool (percent)	5.4	6.0
Enrolled in kindergarten (percent)	6.3	5.1
Enrolled in elementary school, grades 1-8 (percent)	39.9	39.5
Enrolled in high school, grades 9-12 (percent)	20.9	20.7
Enrolled in college or graduate school (percent)	27.5	28.7
Attainment		
Total population 25 years and over	3,110,532	206,471,670
Less than ninth grade (percent)	5.6	6.0
9th to 12th grade, no diploma (percent)	10.3	8.1
High school graduate, including equivalency (percent)	30.7	28.4
Some college, no degree (percent)	20.8	21.2
Associate's degree (percent)	8.6	7.8
Bachelor's degree (percent)	15.6	17.9
Graduate or professional degree (percent)	8.4	10.6
High school graduate or higher (percent)	84.2	85.9
Bachelor's degree or higher (percent)	24.1	28.5

Table SC-12. Educational Indicators

(Number, percent; data derived from National Center of Education Statistics.)

Item	State	U.S.
Public Schools, 2009–2010 (except where noted)		
Number of school districts	85	13,629
Number of schools	1,206	99,834
Number of students (in thousands)	723	49,373
Student-teacher ratio	15.4	15.4
Expenditures per student (dollars)	11,360	10,591
Averaged freshman graduation rate, 2008–2009	66.0	75.5[1]
Dropout rate, 2008–2009	3.4	4.1
Students eligible for free or reduced-price lunch (percent)	54.8	48.0
English language learners, 2010–2011 (percent)	5.1	9.8[1]
Students with IEP (percent)	14.0	13.1
Private Schools, 2009–2010 (except where noted)		
Number of schools	398	33,366
Number of students (in thousands)	49	4,700
High school graduates, 2008–2009	3,073	308,813
Student-teacher ratio	9.7	10.7

[1] U.S. total includes estimates for nonreporting states.

Table SC-13. Reported Voting and Registration of the Voting-Age Population, November 2012

(Numbers in thousands, percent.)

Item	Total population	Total citizen population	Registered			Voted		
			Total registered	Percent registered (total population)	Percent registered (total citizen population)	Total voted	Percent voted (total population)	Percent voted (total citizen population)
U.S. Total	235,248	215,081	153,157	65.1	71.2	132,948	56.5	61.8
State Total	3,516	3,380	2,479	70.5	73.3	2,187	62.2	64.7
Sex								
Male	1,660	1,580	1,096	66.1	69.4	940	56.6	59.5
Female	1,856	1,801	1,382	74.5	76.8	1,247	67.2	69.3
Race								
White alone	2,508	2,400	1,745	69.6	72.7	1,515	60.4	63.1
White, non-Hispanic alone	2,403	2,363	1,724	71.7	73.0	1,500	62.4	63.5
Black alone	919	911	691	75.1	75.8	631	68.7	69.3
Asian alone	48	30	17	B	B	17	B	B
Hispanic (of any race)	114	37	21	18.7	B	16	13.6	B
Age								
18 to 24 years	474	451	265	55.9	58.8	243	51.3	54.0
25 to 44 years	1,111	1,037	769	69.2	74.1	636	57.2	61.3
45 to 64 years	1,319	1,289	956	72.4	74.2	866	65.7	67.2
65 to 74 years	366	366	301	82.3	82.3	277	75.7	75.7
75 years and over	245	238	188	76.6	79.0	165	67.2	69.2

B = Base is less than 75,000 and therefore too small to show the derived measure.

Table SC-14. Crime

(Number, rate per 100,000. Data are derived from the FBI Uniform Crime Reports.)

Item	State			U.S.		
	2010	2011	Percent change	2010	2011	Percent change
TOTAL POPULATION	4,637,106	4,679,230	0.9	309,330,219	311,591,917	0.7
VIOLENT CRIME						
Number	27,923	26,760	-4.2	1,251,248	1,203,564	-3.8
Rate	602.2	571.9	-5.0	404.5	386.3	-4.5
Murder and Nonnegligent Manslaughter						
Number	265	320	20.8	14,722	14,612	-0.7
Rate	5.7	6.8	19.3	4.8	4.7	-2.1
Forcible Rape						
Number	1,551	1,612	3.9	85,593	83,425	-2.5
Rate	33.4	34.5	3.3	27.7	26.8	-3.2
Robbery						
Number	5,017	4,313	-14.0	369,089	354,396	-4.0
Rate	108.2	92.2	-14.8	119.3	113.7	-4.7
Aggravated Assault						
Number	21,090	20,515	-2.7	781,844	751,131	-3.9
Rate	454.8	438.4	-3.6	252.8	241.1	-4.6
PROPERTY CRIME						
Number	181,098	182,685	0.9	9,112,625	9,063,173	-0.5
Rate	3,905.4	3,905.2	-	2,945.9	2,908.7	-1.3
Burglary						
Number	46,261	46,921	1.4	2,168,459	2,188,005	0.9
Rate	997.6	1,002.8	0.5	701.0	702.2	0.2
Larceny-Theft						
Number	121,544	122,100	0.5	6,204,601	6,159,795	-0.7
Rate	2,621.1	2,609.4	-0.4	2,005.8	1,976.9	-1.4
Motor Vehicle Theft						
Number	13,293	13,664	2.8	739,565	715,373	-3.3
Rate	286.7	292.0	1.8	239.1	229.6	-4.0

Table SC-15. State Government Finances, 2011

(Dollar amounts in thousands, percent distribution.)

Item	Dollars	Percent distribution
Total Revenue	31,733,200	100.0
General revenue	22,791,506	71.8
Intergovernmental revenue	8,689,743	27.4
Taxes	7,687,496	24.2
General sales	2,793,683	8.8
Selective sales	1,271,982	4.0
License taxes	461,109	1.5
Individual income tax	2,907,731	9.2
Corporate income tax	216,082	0.7
Other taxes	36,909	0.1
Current charges	4,469,875	14.1
Miscellaneous general revenue	1,944,392	6.1
Utility revenue	1,881,095	5.9
Liquor stores revenue	0	0.0
Insurance trust revenue [1]	7,060,599	22.2
Total Expenditure	29,352,302	100.0
Intergovernmental expenditure	5,585,665	19.0
Direct expenditure	23,766,637	81.0
Current operation	16,510,702	56.3
Capital outlay	1,456,549	5.0
Insurance benefits and repayments	3,970,691	13.5
Assistance and subsidies	1,113,358	3.8
Interest on debt	715,337	2.4
Exhibit: Salaries and wages	3,493,175	11.9
Total Expenditure	29,352,302	100.0
General expenditure	23,659,459	80.6
Intergovernmental expenditure	5,585,665	19.0
Direct expenditure	18,073,794	61.6
General expenditure, by function:		
Education	8,080,658	27.5
Public welfare	6,831,297	23.3
Hospitals	1,478,463	5.0
Health	952,284	3.2
Highways	1,170,564	4.0
Police protection	192,294	0.7
Correction	445,612	1.5
Natural resources	200,164	0.7
Parks and recreation	80,878	0.3
Governmental administration	764,084	2.6
Interest on general debt	470,629	1.6
Other and unallocable	2,992,532	10.2
Utility expenditure	1,722,152	5.9
Liquor stores expenditure	0	0.0
Insurance trust expenditure	3,970,691	13.5
Debt at End of Fiscal Year	15,341,040	X
Cash and Security Holdings	38,698,667	X

X = Not applicable.

[1] Within insurance trust revenue, net earnings of state retirement systems is a calculated statistic (the item code in the data file is X08), and thus can be positive or negative. Net earnings is the sum of earnings on investments plus gains on investments minus losses on investments. The change made in 2002 for asset valuation from book to market value in accordance with Statement 34 of the Governmental Accounting Standards Board is reflected in the calculated statistics.

Table SC-16. State Government Tax Collections, 2012

(Dollars in thousands, percent.)

Item	Dollars	Percent distribution
Total Taxes	8,036,482	100.0
Property taxes	8,811	0.1
Sales and gross receipts	4,198,261	52.2
General sales and gross receipts	2,926,177	36.4
Selective sales and gross receipts	1,272,084	15.8
Alcoholic beverages	153,951	1.9
Amusements	38,848	0.5
Insurance premiums	144,072	1.8
Motor fuels	531,615	6.6
Pari-mutuels	0	0.0
Public utilities	45,680	0.6
Tobacco products	26,247	0.3
Other selective sales	331,671	4.1
Licenses	449,727	5.6
Alcoholic beverages	9,086	0.1
Amusements	1,953	-
Corporations in general	100,686	1.3
Hunting and fishing	18,176	0.2
Motor vehicle	135,022	1.7
Motor vehicle operators	44,128	0.5
Public utilities	0	0.0
Occupation and business, NEC	128,758	1.6
Other licenses	11,918	0.1
Income taxes	3,349,738	41.7
Individual income	3,096,834	38.5
Corporation net income	252,904	3.1
Other taxes	29,945	0.4
Death and gift	3	-
Documentary and stock transfer	29,942	0.4
Severance	0	0.0
Taxes, NEC	0	0.0

- = Rounds to zero.

Leading Exports, 2012

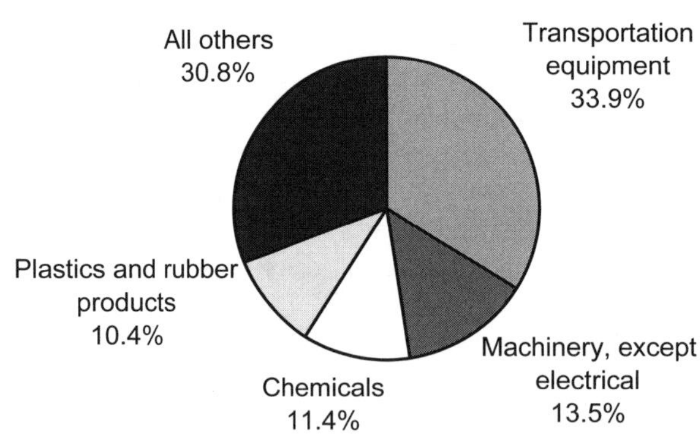

SOUTH DAKOTA

Facts and Figures

Location: North central United States; bordered on the N by North Dakota, on the E by Minnesota and Iowa, on the S by Nebraska, and on the W by Wyoming and Montana

Area: 77,117 sq. mi. (199,731 sq. km.); rank—17th

Population: 833,354 (2012 est.); rank—46th

Principal Cities: capital—Pierre; largest—Sioux Falls

Statehood: November 2, 1889; 40th state

U.S. Congress: 2 senators, 1 representative

State Motto: Under God the People Rule

State Song: "Hail, South Dakota"

State Nickname: The Mount Rushmore State

Abbreviations: SD; S.D.; S. Dak.

State Symbols: flower—pasqueflower; tree—Black Hills spruce; bird—ring-necked pheasant

At a Glance

- With an increase in population of 7.6 percent, South Dakota ranked 42nd among the states in growth from 2000 to 2009.
- An estimated 5,900 marriages took place in South Dakota in 2009, compared to 2,600 divorces.
- In 2011, 11.9 percent of South Dakotans did not have health insurance, compared to 15.1 percent of the total U.S. population.
- In the 2012 election, 61.0 percent of South Dakota's eligible voters voted, compared to 61.8 percent of eligible voters nationwide.
- In 2007, South Dakota exported $1.9 billion worth of agricultural products, about 2.3 percent of the U.S. total.

Table SD-1. Population by Age, Sex, Race, and Hispanic Origin

(Number, percent, except where noted.)

Sex, age, race, and Hispanic origin	2000	2010	2012[1]	Average annual percent change, 2010–2012
Total Population	754,844	814,180	833,354	0.8
Percent of total U.S. population	0.4	0.3	0.3	X
Sex				
Male	374,558	407,381	418,316	0.9
Female	380,286	406,799	415,038	0.7
Age				
Under 5 years	51,069	59,621	59,202	-0.2
5 to 19 years	176,412	167,119	169,405	0.4
20 to 64 years	419,232	470,859	482,564	0.8
65 years and over	108,131	116,581	122,183	1.5
Median age (years)	35.6	36.9	36.9	-
Race and Hispanic Origin				
One race				
White	669,404	706,690	718,352	0.5
Black	4,685	10,533	13,939	8.1
American Indian and Alaska Native	62,283	72,782	74,223	0.6
Asian	4,378	7,775	9,005	4.6
Native Hawaiian or Other Pacific Islander	261	517	608	5.0
Two or more races	10,156	15,883	17,227	2.6
Hispanic (of any race)	10,903	23,699	27,414	4.5

X = Not applicable.
- = Zero or rounds to zero.
[1] Population figures for 2012 are July 1 estimates. The 2010 estimates are taken from the 2010 Census.

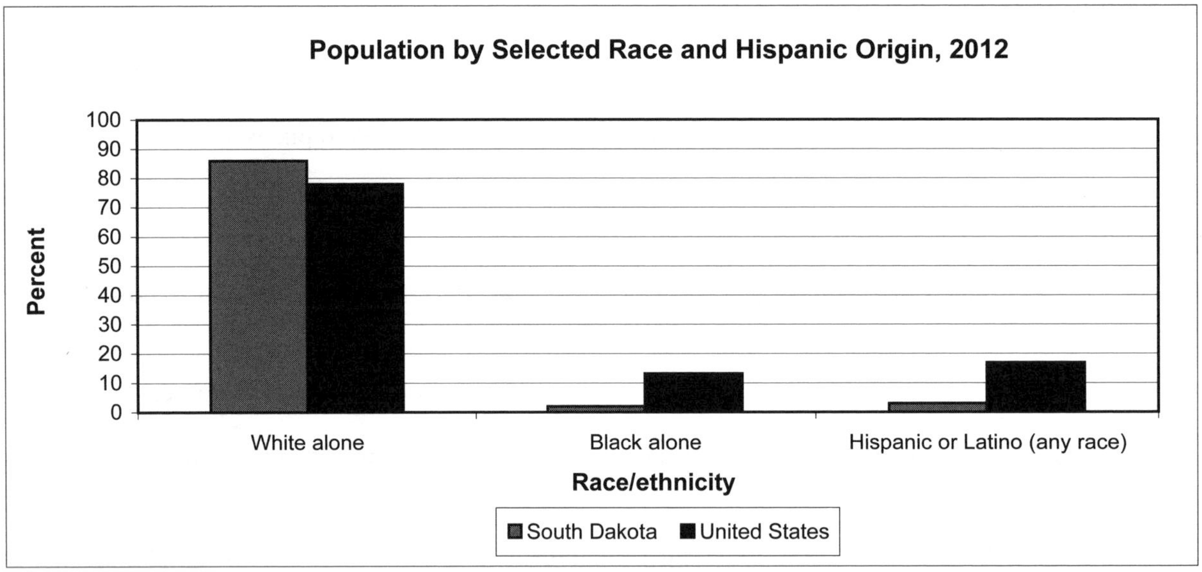

Table SD-2. Marital Status

(Number, percent distribution.)

Sex, age, race, and Hispanic origin	2000	2010	2011
Males, 15 Years and Over	289,858	322,689	324,608
Never married	29.8	33.5	33.0
Now married, except separated	58.2	52.5	52.9
Separated	1.0	0.9	1.0
Widowed	2.4	2.8	2.7
Divorced	8.5	10.3	10.4
Females, 15 Years and Over	299,754	325,640	330,772
Never married	22.5	26.0	27.3
Now married, except separated	55.9	52.1	51.5
Separated	1.1	1.0	1.3
Widowed	11.4	9.5	9.2
Divorced	9.0	11.4	10.7

Table SD-3. Households and Housing Characteristics

(Number, percent, dollars.)

Item	2000	2010	2011	Average annual percent change, 2000–2011
Total Households	290,245	318,955	323,215	0.9
Family households	194,330	204,029	210,679	0.7
Married-couple family	157,391	161,534	163,103	0.3
Other family	36,939	42,495	47,576	2.4
Male householder, no wife present	10,734	12,526	16,122	4.2
Female householder, no husband present	26,205	29,969	31,454	1.7
Nonfamily households	95,915	114,926	112,536	1.4
Householder living alone	80,040	95,610	93,067	1.4
Householder not living alone	15,875	19,316	19,469	1.9
Housing Characteristics				
Total housing units	323,208	364,031	366,521	1.1
Occupied housing units	290,245	318,955	323,215	0.9
Owner occupied	197,940	216,821	221,382	1.0
Renter occupied	92,305	102,134	101,833	0.9
Average size	2.50	2.45	2.44	-0.2
Financial Characteristics				
Median gross rent of renter-occupied housing	426	591	612	3.6
Median monthly owner costs for housing units with a mortgage	828	1,151	1,178	3.5
Median value of owner-occupied housing units	79,600	129,700	131,400	5.4

Table SD-4. Migration, Origin, and Language

(Number, percent.)

Characteristic	State			U.S.		
	2010	2011	Percent change	2010	2011	Percent change
Residence 1 Year Ago						
Population 1 year and over	805,616	814,175	1.1	305,628,607	307,900,319	0.7
Same house	84.5	84.6	0.1	84.6	84.8	0.2
Different house in the U.S.	15.2	15.0	-1.3	14.8	14.6	-1.4
Same county	7.9	7.8	-1.3	9.4	9.2	-2.1
Different county	7.3	7.2	-1.4	5.4	5.4	-
Same state	4.1	3.8	-7.3	3.2	3.1	-3.1
Different state	3.2	3.4	6.2	2.2	2.3	4.5
Abroad	0.3	0.4	33.3	0.6	0.6	-
Place of Birth						
Native born	794,225	802,067	1.0	269,393,835	271,214,059	0.7
Male	50.2	49.9	-0.6	49.2	49.2	-
Female	49.8	50.1	0.6	50.8	50.8	-
Foreign born	22,238	22,015	-1.0	39,955,854	40,377,860	1.1
Male	57.8	47.3	-18.2	49.1	48.9	-0.4
Female	42.2	52.7	24.9	50.9	51.1	0.4
Foreign born; naturalized U.S. citizen	9,083	6,686	-26.4	17,476,082	18,140,192	3.8
Male	59.8	42.7	-28.6	45.8	45.8	-
Female	40.2	57.3	42.5	54.2	54.2	-
Foreign born; not a U.S. citizen	13,155	15,329	16.5	22,479,772	22,237,668	-1.1
Male	56.4	49.3	-12.6	51.6	51.5	-0.2
Female	43.6	50.7	16.3	48.4	48.5	0.2
Entered 2000 or later	48.1	59.6	23.9	34.7	35.7	2.9
Entered 1990 to 1999	31.6	22.7	-28.2	27.2	26.7	-1.8
Entered before 1990	20.3	17.7	-12.8	38.1	37.6	-1.3
World Region of Birth, Foreign						
Foreign-born population, excluding population born at sea	22,238	22,015	-1.0	39,955,673	40,377,757	1.1
Europe	19.0	15.0	-21.1	12.1	12.1	-
Asia	29.4	29.1	-1.0	28.2	28.6	1.4
Africa	21.3	16.7	-21.6	4	4.1	2.5
Oceania	0.1	0.3	200.0	0.5	0.5	-
Latin America	25.8	33.8	31.0	53.1	52.6	-0.9
North America	4.4	5.0	13.6	2	2.0	-
Language Spoken at Home and Ability to Speak English						
Population 5 years and over	758,975	765,534	0.9	289,215,746	291,524,091	0.8
English only	92.5	93.4	1.0	79.4	79.2	-0.3
Language other than English	7.5	6.6	-12.0	20.6	20.8	1.0
Speaks English less than "very well"	2.1	2.2	4.8	8.7	8.7	-

- = Zero or rounds to zero.

Table SD-5. Median Income and Poverty Status, 2011

(Number, percent, except as noted.)

Characteristic	State Number	State Percent	U.S. Number	U.S. Percent
Median Income				
Households (dollars)	48,321	X	50,502	X
Families (dollars)	62,059	X	61,455	X
Below Poverty Level (All People)	110,681	13.9	48,452,035	15.9
Sex				
Male	50,155	12.7	21,825,281	14.7
Female	60,526	15.2	26,626,754	17.2
Age				
Under 18 years	35,793	18.2	16,386,500	22.5
Related children under 18 years	34,943	17.8	16,087,074	22.2
18 to 64 years	62,367	12.9	28,335,079	14.8
65 years and over	12,521	11.1	3,730,456	9.3

X = Not applicable.

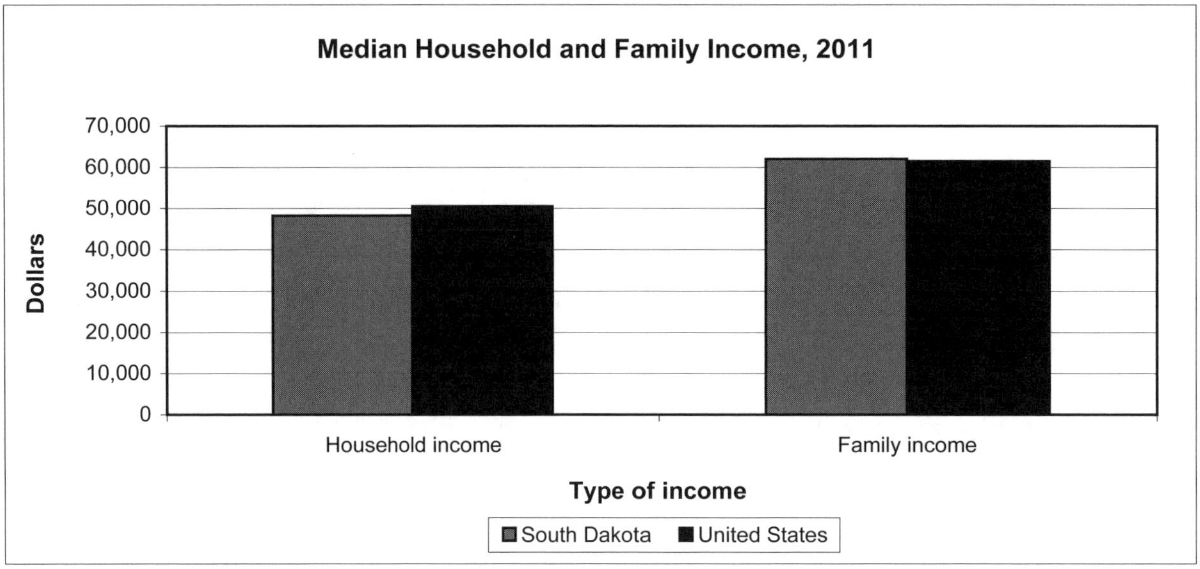

Table SD-6. Health Insurance Coverage Status for the Civilian Noninstitutionalized Population and Children Under 18 Years of Age

(Numbers in thousands, percent.)

Item	2004	2005	2006	2007	2008	2009	2010	2011
Civilian Noninstitutionalized Population	754	768	770	788	784	793	798	806
Covered by Private or Public Insurance								
Number	669	679	679	708	692	689	699	710
Percent	88.8	88.3	88.2	89.9	88.3	86.9	87.6	88.1
Not Covered								
Number	84	90	91	80	92	104	99	96
Percent	11.2	11.7	11.8	10.1	11.7	13.1	12.4	11.9
Percent in the U.S. not covered	14.9	15.3	15.8	15.3	15.1	15.1	15.5	15.1
Children Under 18 Years of Age	189	188	193	198	196	195	201	201
Covered by Private or Public Insurance								
Number	174	173	175	183	179	180	184	189
Percent	92.0	91.9	90.8	92.0	91.3	92.4	91.7	94.0
Not Covered								
Number	15	15	18	16	17	15	17	12
Percent	8.0	8.1	9.2	8.0	8.7	7.6	8.3	6.0
Percent in the U.S. not covered	10.5	10.9	11.7	11.0	9.7	8.6	8.0	7.5

Table SD-7. Employment Status by Demographic Group, Preliminary 2012

(Numbers in thousands, percent.)

Characteristic	Civilian noninstitutional population	Civilian labor force		Employed		Unemployed	
		Number	Percent of population	Number	Percent of population	Number	Percent of population
Total	633	440	69.6	420	66.4	20	4.6
Sex							
Male	313	235	75.1	223	71.5	11	4.8
Female	320	206	64.2	197	61.4	9	4.4
Race, Sex, and Hispanic Origin							
White	564	400	71.0	385	68.3	15	3.8
Male	278	213	76.7	205	73.6	9	4.0
Female	285	187	65.5	180	63.2	7	3.5
Black or African American	NA	NA	NA	NA	NA	NA	NA
Male	NA	NA	NA	NA	NA	NA	NA
Female	NA	NA	NA	NA	NA	NA	NA
Hispanic	17	11	66.6	10	60.6	1	8.9
Male	NA	NA	NA	NA	NA	NA	NA
Female	NA	NA	NA	NA	NA	NA	NA
Age							
16 to 19 years	40	21	51.1	18	45.2	2	11.4
20 to 24 years	63	49	77.7	45	70.4	5	9.4
25 to 34 years	106	92	86.8	88	82.8	4	4.6
35 to 44 years	89	78	87.5	74	83.8	3	4.3
45 to 54 years	104	92	88.0	89	85.5	3	2.8
55 to 64 years	104	79	75.3	76	72.8	3	3.2
65 years and over	126	31	24.4	30	23.8	1	2.5

NOTE: Data in Table 7 are from the Current Population Survey (CPS) and do not match the estimates in Table 8. See notes and definitions for further information.
NA = Not available.

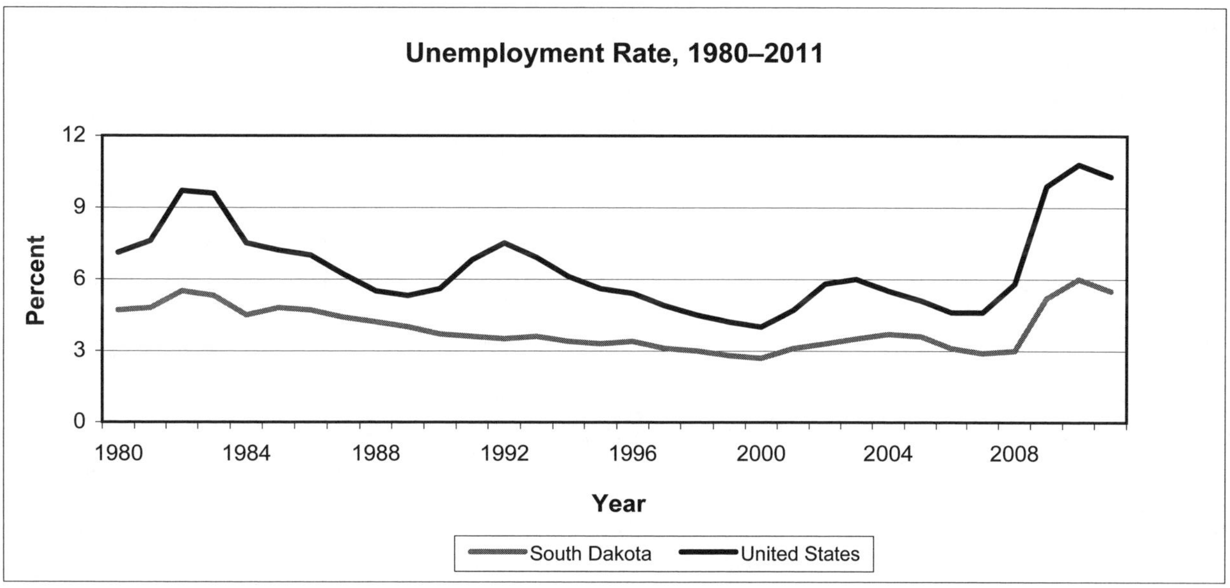

Table SD-8. Employment Status of the Civilian Noninstitutional Population Age 16 Years and Over

(Number, percent.)

Year	Civilian labor force	Civilian participation rate	Employed	Unemployed	Unemployment rate
2005	430,444	73.1	414,784	15,660	3.6
2006	435,733	73.1	422,355	13,378	3.1
2007	442,085	73.2	429,445	12,640	2.9
2008	444,890	72.8	431,379	13,511	3.0
2009	438,444	68.9	415,607	22,837	5.2
2010	435,452	68.3	409,194	26,258	6.0
2011	439,730	68.2	415,623	24,107	5.5

Table SD-9. Employment and Average Wages by Industry

(Estimates before 2007 are based on the 2002 *North American Industry Classification System* [NAICS]. Estimates from 2007 onward are based on the 2007 NAICS.)

Industry	2005	2006	2007	2008	2009	2010	2011
	Number of jobs						
Wage and Salary Employment by Industry	408,482	416,269	424,522	431,600	423,697	425,114	430,256
Farm Wage and Salary Employment	5,271	4,739	5,224	5,446	4,595	5,049	5,522
Nonfarm Wage and Salary Employment	403,211	411,530	419,298	426,154	419,102	420,065	424,734
Private wage and salary employment	322,930	331,130	338,828	344,190	334,741	334,353	339,612
Forestry, fishing, and related activities	1,459	1,572	1,653	1,685	1,659	1,750	1,887
Mining	788	790	849	932	836	818	832
Utilities	2,133	2,233	2,229	2,073	2,112	2,092	2,071
Construction	21,831	22,673	23,052	23,157	21,842	21,086	21,234
Manufacturing	39,898	41,443	42,105	42,789	37,806	37,044	39,291
Durable goods manufacturing	27,110	28,324	28,882	29,331	24,780	24,033	25,909
Nondurable goods manufacturing	12,788	13,119	13,223	13,458	13,026	13,011	13,382
Wholesale trade	17,841	18,254	18,502	18,854	18,474	18,741	19,138
Retail trade	49,673	49,807	50,641	50,829	50,351	50,354	50,958
Transportation and warehousing	10,323	10,710	10,923	11,012	10,617	10,484	10,576
Information	6,766	6,966	7,170	6,967	6,709	6,556	6,388
Finance and insurance	24,884	26,225	27,562	27,632	27,150	26,098	25,537
Real estate and rental and leasing	3,878	3,856	3,770	3,815	3,700	3,540	3,561
Professional, scientific, and technical services	9,760	10,143	10,630	11,167	11,210	11,363	11,353
Management of companies and enterprises	2,816	2,821	3,039	3,500	3,474	3,624	3,768
Administrative and waste services	12,470	13,115	14,155	13,925	12,568	12,965	13,850
Educational services	7,391	7,687	7,307	7,562	7,547	7,755	7,995
Health care and social assistance	50,794	51,617	53,089	55,047	56,043	57,046	57,726
Arts, entertainment, and recreation	6,617	6,491	6,828	6,694	6,564	6,492	6,494
Accommodation and food services	35,471	36,436	36,704	37,003	36,822	37,067	37,497
Other services, except public administration	18,137	18,291	18,620	19,547	19,257	19,478	19,456
Government and government enterprises	80,281	80,400	80,470	81,964	84,361	85,712	85,122
	Dollars						
Average Wages and Salaries by Industry	28,967	30,083	31,585	32,681	33,063	33,922	34,997
Average Farm Wages and Salaries	29,233	33,580	43,389	48,558	43,156	36,547	39,449
Average Nonfarm Wages and Salaries	28,964	30,043	31,438	32,478	32,952	33,890	34,939
Average private wages and salaries	28,577	29,733	31,205	32,238	32,635	33,664	34,871
Forestry, fishing, and related activities	20,217	20,520	22,878	23,228	23,896	25,166	26,424
Mining	42,279	44,472	46,789	51,013	46,606	49,559	55,826
Utilities	58,820	57,905	61,702	62,172	61,671	64,919	67,087
Construction	31,728	33,629	35,825	36,834	38,064	38,086	38,975
Manufacturing	34,387	35,508	37,078	37,766	38,331	39,905	41,470
Durable goods manufacturing	35,119	35,925	37,049	38,057	38,738	40,479	42,408
Nondurable goods manufacturing	32,836	34,607	37,140	37,130	37,556	38,844	39,653
Wholesale trade	40,004	41,138	43,183	45,108	45,552	46,634	48,900
Retail trade	20,162	20,823	21,489	21,951	22,174	23,106	23,737
Transportation and warehousing	34,594	36,599	37,116	38,531	38,151	39,442	41,362
Information	35,337	36,722	38,499	39,198	39,258	39,883	41,852
Finance and insurance	39,085	40,982	42,571	43,764	44,097	45,798	48,146
Real estate and rental and leasing	22,336	23,098	24,689	25,308	25,806	26,736	28,099
Professional, scientific, and technical services	38,380	41,212	43,329	45,148	44,612	46,400	49,024
Management of companies and enterprises	71,778	65,724	72,121	78,377	74,858	88,748	88,044
Administrative and waste services	22,074	22,441	24,236	23,904	24,478	25,336	25,528
Educational services	20,515	20,775	21,688	22,972	23,579	24,613	24,618
Health care and social assistance	33,773	35,192	36,510	38,257	39,496	40,093	41,580
Arts, entertainment, and recreation	15,625	17,387	17,867	17,459	17,863	17,795	18,001
Accommodation and food services	11,624	12,055	13,119	13,271	13,390	14,050	14,494
Other services, except public administration	20,409	21,276	22,182	22,661	23,171	23,623	24,220
Government and government enterprises	30,518	31,318	32,417	33,486	34,210	34,770	35,210

Table SD-10. Employment Characteristics by Family Type

(Number, percent.)

Family type and labor force status	2009		2010		2011	
	Total	Families with own children under 18 years	Total	Families with own children under 18 years	Total	Families with own children under 18 years
All families	204,649	92,593	204,029	89,204	210,679	91,614
Family type and labor force status						
Married-couple families	162,154	66,144	161,534	62,695	163,103	61,158
Both husband and wife in labor force	63.2	78.8	63.1	78.5	63.0	78.5
Husband in labor force, wife not in labor force	15.1	16.6	14.7	15.8	15.0	18.0
Wife in labor force, husband not in labor force	6.7	2.9	6.9	4.7	6.3	2.2
Both husband and wife not in labor force	15.0	1.7	15.2	0.9	15.8	1.2
Other families	42,495	26,449	42,495	26,509	47,576	30,456
Female householder, no husband present	74.9	78.7	70.5	73.1	66.1	70.3
In labor force	56.5	65.2	55.0	62.0	53.0	62.9
Not in labor force	18.4	13.5	15.5	11.0	13.1	7.4
Male householder, no wife present	25.1	21.3	29.5	26.9	33.9	29.7
In labor force	21.0	19.9	25.1	25.4	26.9	26.9
Not in labor force	4.1	1.4	4.4	1.5	6.9	2.8

Table SD-11. School Enrollment and Educational Attainment, 2011

(Number, percent.)

Item	State	U.S.
Enrollment		
Total population 3 years and over, enrolled in school	219,022	83,131,910
Enrolled in nursery school or preschool (percent)	6.6	6.0
Enrolled in kindergarten (percent)	5.2	5.1
Enrolled in elementary school, grades 1-8 (percent)	39.8	39.5
Enrolled in high school, grades 9-12 (percent)	20.6	20.7
Enrolled in college or graduate school (percent)	27.8	28.7
Attainment		
Total population 25 years and over	537,588	206,471,670
Less than ninth grade (percent)	4.1	6.0
9th to 12th grade, no diploma (percent)	5.3	8.1
High school graduate, including equivalency (percent)	31.4	28.4
Some college, no degree (percent)	23.1	21.2
Associate's degree (percent)	9.7	7.8
Bachelor's degree (percent)	18.2	17.9
Graduate or professional degree (percent)	8.1	10.6
High school graduate or higher (percent)	90.6	85.9
Bachelor's degree or higher (percent)	26.3	28.5

Table SD-12. Educational Indicators

(Number, percent; data derived from National Center of Education Statistics.)

Item	State	U.S.
Public Schools, 2009–2010 (except where noted)		
Number of school districts	156	13,629
Number of schools	714	99,834
Number of students (in thousands)	124	49,373
Student-teacher ratio	13.3	15.4
Expenditures per student (dollars)	10,422	10,591
Averaged freshman graduation rate, 2008–2009	81.7	75.5[1]
Dropout rate, 2008–2009	1.8	4.1
Students eligible for free or reduced-price lunch (percent)	37.1	48.0
English language learners, 2010–2011 (percent)	3.5	9.8[1]
Students with IEP (percent)	14.5	13.1
Private Schools, 2009–2010 (except where noted)		
Number of schools	75	33,366
Number of students (in thousands)	9	4,700
High school graduates, 2008–2009	518	308,813
Student-teacher ratio	11.1	10.7

[1] U.S. total includes estimates for nonreporting states.

Table SD-13. Reported Voting and Registration of the Voting-Age Population, November 2012

(Numbers in thousands, percent.)

Item	Total population	Total citizen population	Registered: Total registered	Registered: Percent registered (total population)	Registered: Percent registered (total citizen population)	Voted: Total voted	Voted: Percent voted (total population)	Voted: Percent voted (total citizen population)
U.S. Total	235,248	215,081	153,157	65.1	71.2	132,948	56.5	61.8
State Total	616	607	454	73.7	74.8	370	60.1	61.0
Sex								
Male	304	300	220	72.3	73.3	180	59.1	59.9
Female	312	307	235	75.1	76.3	191	61.1	62.0
Race								
White alone	541	536	405	74.9	75.6	341	63.0	63.5
White, non-Hispanic alone	527	526	400	75.9	76.1	338	64.2	64.3
Black alone	6	5	3	B	B	-	B	B
Asian alone	4	1	1	B	B	-	B	B
Hispanic (of any race)	16	13	6	B	B	3	B	B
Age								
18 to 24 years	95	94	52	54.4	54.7	31	32.7	32.9
25 to 44 years	186	180	130	69.8	71.9	99	53.2	54.7
45 to 64 years	204	202	167	82.0	82.7	145	70.9	71.5
65 to 74 years	77	76	61	79.7	80.9	56	73.4	74.4
75 years and over	55	55	45	B	B	40	B	B

- = Zero or rounds to zero.
B = Base is less than 75,000 and therefore too small to show the derived measure.

Table SD-14. Crime

(Number, rate per 100,000. Data are derived from the FBI Uniform Crime Reports.)

Item	State: 2010	State: 2011	State: Percent change	U.S.: 2010	U.S.: 2011	U.S.: Percent change
TOTAL POPULATION	816,598	824,082	0.9	309,330,219	311,591,917	0.7
VIOLENT CRIME						
Number	2,196	2,094	-4.6	1,251,248	1,203,564	-3.8
Rate	268.9	254.1	-5.5	404.5	386.3	-4.5
Murder and Nonnegligent Manslaughter						
Number	23	21	-8.7	14,722	14,612	-0.7
Rate	2.8	2.5	-10.7	4.8	4.7	-2.1
Forcible Rape						
Number	385	496	28.8	85,593	83,425	-2.5
Rate	47.1	60.2	27.8	27.7	26.8	-3.2
Robbery						
Number	154	167	8.4	369,089	354,396	-4.0
Rate	18.9	20.3	7.4	119.3	113.7	-4.7
Aggravated Assault						
Number	1,634	1,410	-13.7	781,844	751,131	-3.9
Rate	200.1	171.1	-14.5	252.8	241.1	-4.6
PROPERTY CRIME						
Number	15,188	14,979	-1.4	9,112,625	9,063,173	-0.5
Rate	1,859.9	1,817.7	-2.3	2,945.9	2,908.7	-1.3
Burglary						
Number	3,192	2,899	-9.2	2,168,459	2,188,005	0.9
Rate	390.9	351.8	-10.0	701.0	702.2	0.2
Larceny-Theft						
Number	11,196	11,134	-0.6	6,204,601	6,159,795	-0.7
Rate	1,371.1	1,351.1	-1.5	2,005.8	1,976.9	-1.4
Motor Vehicle Theft						
Number	800	946	18.3	739,565	715,373	-3.3
Rate	98.0	114.8	17.1	239.1	229.6	-4.0

Table SD-15. State Government Finances, 2011

(Dollar amounts in thousands, percent distribution.)

Item	Dollars	Percent distribution
Total Revenue	6,017,179	100.0
General revenue	4,124,318	68.5
Intergovernmental revenue	1,878,950	31.2
Taxes	1,379,607	22.9
General sales	808,091	13.4
Selective sales	345,406	5.7
License taxes	200,116	3.3
Individual income tax	0	0.0
Corporate income tax	15,208	0.3
Other taxes	10,786	0.2
Current charges	336,840	5.6
Miscellaneous general revenue	528,921	8.8
Utility revenue	0	0.0
Liquor stores revenue	0	0.0
Insurance trust revenue [1]	1,892,861	31.5
Total Expenditure	4,498,447	100.0
Intergovernmental expenditure	774,778	17.2
Direct expenditure	3,723,669	82.8
Current operation	2,441,343	54.3
Capital outlay	632,653	14.1
Insurance benefits and repayments	435,958	9.7
Assistance and subsidies	85,398	1.9
Interest on debt	128,317	2.9
Exhibit: Salaries and wages	909,103	20.2
Total Expenditure	4,498,447	100.0
General expenditure	4,062,489	90.3
Intergovernmental expenditure	774,778	17.2
Direct expenditure	3,287,711	73.1
General expenditure, by function:		
Education	1,300,189	28.9
Public welfare	965,643	21.5
Hospitals	61,421	1.4
Health	147,422	3.3
Highways	606,516	13.5
Police protection	32,484	0.7
Correction	112,316	2.5
Natural resources	164,535	3.7
Parks and recreation	43,484	1.0
Governmental administration	170,586	3.8
Interest on general debt	128,317	2.9
Other and unallocable	329,576	7.3
Utility expenditure	0	0.0
Liquor stores expenditure	0	0.0
Insurance trust expenditure	435,958	9.7
Debt at End of Fiscal Year	3,544,772	X
Cash and Security Holdings	12,917,402	X

X = Not applicable.
[1] Within insurance trust revenue, net earnings of state retirement systems is a calculated statistic (the item code in the data file is X08), and thus can be positive or negative. Net earnings is the sum of earnings on investments plus gains on investments minus losses on investments. The change made in 2002 for asset valuation from book to market value in accordance with Statement 34 of the Governmental Accounting Standards Board is reflected in the calculated statistics.

Table SD-16. State Government Tax Collections, 2012

(Dollars in thousands, percent.)

Item	Dollars	Percent distribution
Total Taxes	1,521,477	100.0
Property taxes	0	0.0
Sales and gross receipts	1,197,116	78.7
General sales and gross receipts	838,240	55.1
Selective sales and gross receipts	358,876	23.6
Alcoholic beverages	15,449	1.0
Amusements	9,200	0.6
Insurance premiums	67,000	4.4
Motor fuels	136,431	9.0
Pari-mutuels	183	-
Public utilities	3,676	0.2
Tobacco products	60,372	4.0
Other selective sales	66,565	4.4
Licenses	250,572	16.5
Alcoholic beverages	811	0.1
Amusements	7,568	0.5
Corporations in general	4,213	0.3
Hunting and fishing	29,352	1.9
Motor vehicle	64,710	4.3
Motor vehicle operators	3,792	0.2
Public utilities	0	0.0
Occupation and business, NEC	124,647	8.2
Other licenses	15,479	1.0
Income taxes	59,837	3.9
Individual income	0	0.0
Corporation net income	59,837	3.9
Other taxes	13,952	0.9
Death and gift	0	0.0
Documentary and stock transfer	193	-
Severance	13,759	0.9
Taxes, NEC	0	0.0

- = Rounds to zero.

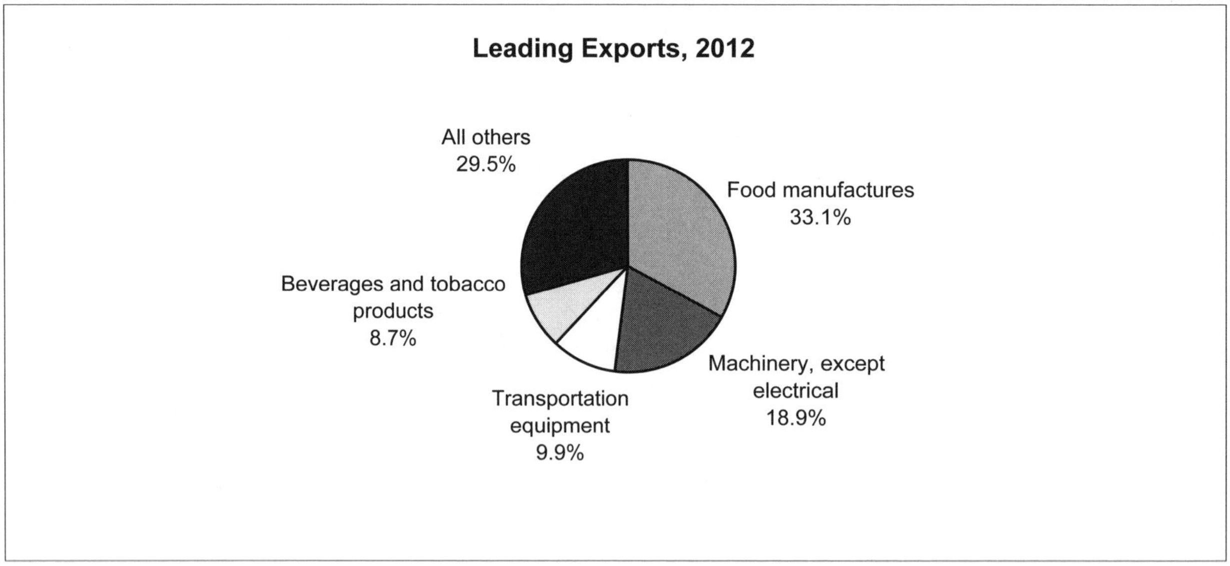

TENNESSEE

Facts and Figures

Location: South central United States; bordered on the N by Kentucky and Virginia, on the E by North Carolina, on the S by Georgia, Alabama, and Mississippi, and on the W by Arkansas and Missouri

Area: 42,143 sq. mi. (109,151 sq. km.); rank—36th

Population: 6,458,243 (2012 est.); rank—17th

Principal Cities: capital—Nashville; largest—Memphis

Statehood: June 1, 1796; 16th state

U.S. Congress: 2 senators, 9 representatives

State Motto: Agriculture and Commerce

State Song: "The Tennessee Waltz"

State Nickname: The Volunteer State

Abbreviations: TN; Tenn.

State Symbols: flower—iris; tree—yellow poplar (tulip poplar); bird—mockingbird

At a Glance

- With an increase in population of 10.7 percent, Tennessee ranked 11th among the states in growth from 2000 to 2009.
- An estimated 55,200 marriages took place in Tennessee in 2009, compared to 25,800 divorces.
- Tennessee's median household income in 2011 was $41,693, and 18.3 percent of the population lived below the poverty level.
- In 2011, 14.6 percent of Tennesseans did not have health insurance, compared to 15.1 percent of the total U.S. population.
- In 2007, Tennessee exported $770 million worth of agricultural products, almost 1 percent of the U.S. total.

Table TN-1. Population by Age, Sex, Race, and Hispanic Origin

(Number, percent, except where noted.)

Sex, age, race, and Hispanic origin	2000	2010	2012[1]	Average annual percent change, 2010–2012
Total Population	5,689,283	6,346,105	6,458,243	0.6
Percent of total U.S. population	2.0	2.1	2.0	X
Sex				
Male	2,770,275	3,093,504	3,148,763	0.6
Female	2,919,008	3,252,601	3,307,763	0.6
Age				
Under 5 years	374,880	407,813	403,976	-0.3
5 to 19 years	1,186,152	1,268,308	1,259,085	-0.2
20 to 64 years	3,424,940	3,816,522	3,876,675	0.5
65 years and over	703,311	853,462	918,507	2.4
Median age (years)	35.9	38.0	38.3	0.3
Race and Hispanic Origin				
One race				
White	4,563,310	5,056,311	5,117,456	0.4
Black	932,809	1,068,010	1,097,978	0.9
American Indian and Alaska Native	15,152	26,256	27,247	1.2
Asian	56,662	93,897	102,862	2.9
Native Hawaiian or Other Pacific Islander	2,205	5,426	5,788	2.1
Two or more races	63,109	96,205	104,912	2.8
Hispanic (of any race)	123,838	301,090	325,011	2.5

X = Not applicable.
[1] Population figures for 2012 are July 1 estimates. The 2010 estimates are taken from the 2010 Census.

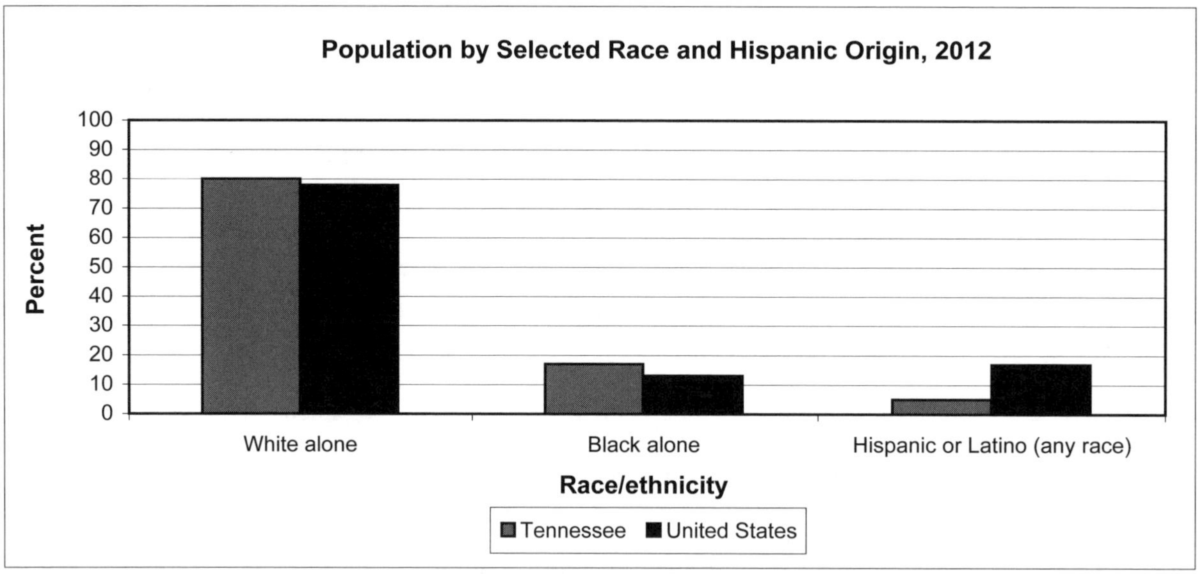

Table TN-2. Marital Status

(Number, percent distribution.)

Sex, age, race, and Hispanic origin	2000	2010	2011
Males, 15 Years and Over	2,169,327	2,461,573	2,490,152
Never married	26.6	31.4	32.0
Now married, except separated	58.9	52.2	51.2
Separated	1.7	2.1	1.9
Widowed	2.5	2.7	2.8
Divorced	10.4	11.7	12.0
Females, 15 Years and Over	2,353,303	2,652,823	2,678,163
Never married	20.7	25.3	25.7
Now married, except separated	53.6	47.9	47.3
Separated	2.3	2.7	2.7
Widowed	11.2	10.3	10.2
Divorced	12.2	13.7	14.1

Table TN-3. Households and Housing Characteristics

(Number, percent, dollars.)

Item	2000	2010	2011	Average annual percent change, 2000–2011
Total Households	2,232,905	2,440,663	2,467,428	0.9
Family households	1,547,835	1,644,896	1,625,686	0.4
Married-couple family	1,173,960	1,195,406	1,189,542	0.1
Other family	373,875	449,490	436,144	1.4
Male householder, no wife present	85,976	106,616	107,407	2.1
Female householder, no husband present	287,899	342,874	328,737	1.2
Nonfamily households	685,070	795,767	841,742	1.9
Householder living alone	576,401	675,565	715,609	2.0
Householder not living alone	108,669	120,202	126,133	1.3
Housing Characteristics				
Total housing units	2,439,443	2,815,087	2,829,125	1.3
Occupied housing units	2,232,905	2,440,663	2,467,428	0.9
Owner occupied	1,561,363	1,662,768	1,660,076	0.5
Renter occupied	671,542	777,895	807,352	1.7
Average size	2.48	2.54	2.53	0.2
Financial Characteristics				
Median gross rent of renter-occupied housing	505	697	715	3.5
Median monthly owner costs for housing units with a mortgage	882	1,161	1,172	2.7
Median value of owner-occupied housing units	93,000	139,000	138,300	4.1

Table TN-4. Migration, Origin, and Language

(Number, percent.)

Characteristic	State			U.S.		
	2010	2011	Percent change	2010	2011	Percent change
Residence 1 Year Ago						
Population 1 year and over	6,282,706	6,333,466	0.8	305,628,607	307,900,319	0.7
Same house	84.4	84.4	-	84.6	84.8	0.2
Different house in the U.S.	15.3	15.2	-0.7	14.8	14.6	-1.4
Same county	9.8	9.4	-4.1	9.4	9.2	-2.1
Different county	5.5	5.8	5.5	5.4	5.4	-
Same state	2.9	3.1	6.9	3.2	3.1	-3.1
Different state	2.5	2.7	8.0	2.2	2.3	4.5
Abroad	0.4	0.4	-	0.6	0.6	-
Place of Birth						
Native born	6,067,904	6,096,677	0.5	269,393,835	271,214,059	0.7
Male	48.5	48.6	0.2	49.2	49.2	-
Female	51.5	51.4	-0.2	50.8	50.8	-
Foreign born	288,993	306,676	6.1	39,955,854	40,377,860	1.1
Male	53.3	50.9	-4.5	49.1	48.9	-0.4
Female	46.7	49.1	5.1	50.9	51.1	0.4
Foreign born; naturalized U.S. citizen	96,905	106,035	9.4	17,476,082	18,140,192	3.8
Male	45.1	46.5	3.1	45.8	45.8	-
Female	54.9	53.5	-2.6	54.2	54.2	-
Foreign born; not a U.S. citizen	192,088	200,641	4.5	22,479,772	22,237,668	-1.1
Male	57.4	53.3	-7.1	51.6	51.5	-0.2
Female	42.6	46.7	9.6	48.4	48.5	0.2
Entered 2000 or later	51.6	48.8	-5.4	34.7	35.7	2.9
Entered 1990 to 1999	26.2	28.6	9.2	27.2	26.7	-1.8
Entered before 1990	22.3	22.6	1.3	38.1	37.6	-1.3
World Region of Birth, Foreign						
Foreign-born population, excluding population born at sea	288,993	306,676	6.1	39,955,673	40,377,757	1.1
Europe	11.3	12.7	12.4	12.1	12.1	-
Asia	26.8	27.0	0.7	28.2	28.6	1.4
Africa	9.5	8.9	-6.3	4	4.1	2.5
Oceania	0.6	0.8	33.3	0.5	0.5	-
Latin America	49.4	47.6	-3.6	53.1	52.6	-0.9
North America	2.3	3.0	30.4	2	2.0	-
Language Spoken at Home and Ability to Speak English						
Population 5 years and over	5,950,484	6,003,565	0.9	289,215,746	291,524,091	0.8
English only	93.6	93.1	-0.5	79.4	79.2	-0.3
Language other than English	6.4	6.9	7.8	20.6	20.8	1.0
Speaks English less than "very well"	2.9	2.9	-	8.7	8.7	-

- = Zero or rounds to zero.

Table TN-5. Median Income and Poverty Status, 2011

(Number, percent, except as noted.)

Characteristic	State		U.S.	
	Number	Percent	Number	Percent
Median Income				
Households (dollars)	41,693	X	50,502	X
Families (dollars)	52,273	X	61,455	X
Below Poverty Level (All People)	1,142,299	18.3	48,452,035	15.9
Sex				
Male	508,174	16.8	21,825,281	14.7
Female	634,125	19.7	26,626,754	17.2
Age				
Under 18 years	385,931	26.3	16,386,500	22.5
Related children under 18 years	380,055	26.0	16,087,074	22.2
18 to 64 years	664,983	16.9	28,335,079	14.8
65 years and over	91,385	10.7	3,730,456	9.3

X = Not applicable.

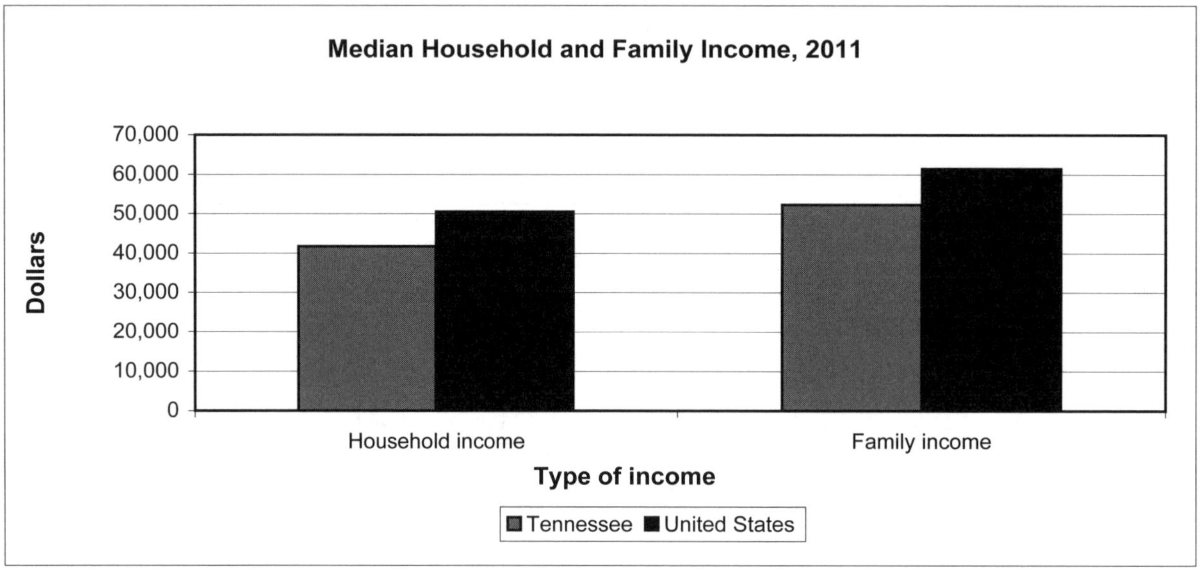

Table TN-6. Health Insurance Coverage Status for the Civilian Noninstitutionalized Population and Children Under 18 Years of Age

(Numbers in thousands, percent.)

Item	2004	2005	2006	2007	2008	2009	2010	2011
Civilian Noninstitutionalized Population	5,857	5,867	5,920	6,150	6,113	6,188	6,260	6,302
Covered by Private or Public Insurance								
Number	5,091	5,069	5,111	5,268	5,279	5,305	5,361	5,380
Percent	86.9	86.4	86.3	85.6	86.4	85.7	85.6	85.4
Not Covered								
Number	766	798	809	883	834	883	899	923
Percent	13.1	13.6	13.7	14.4	13.6	14.3	14.4	14.6
Percent in the U.S. not covered	14.9	15.3	15.8	15.3	15.1	15.1	15.5	15.1
Children Under 18 Years of Age	1,409	1,403	1,468	1,479	1,476	1,488	1,493	1,488
Covered by Private or Public Insurance								
Number	1,276	1,276	1,376	1,344	1,370	1,401	1,414	1,403
Percent	90.6	90.9	93.6	90.9	92.8	94.1	94.7	94.3
Not Covered								
Number	133	127	94	135	106	87	79	85
Percent	9.4	9.1	6.4	9.1	7.2	5.9	5.3	5.7
Percent in the U.S. not covered	10.5	10.9	11.7	11.0	9.7	8.6	8.0	7.5

Table TN-7. Employment Status by Demographic Group, Preliminary 2012

(Numbers in thousands, percent.)

Characteristic	Civilian noninstitutional population	Civilian labor force		Employed		Unemployed	
		Number	Percent of population	Number	Percent of population	Number	Percent of population
Total	5,021	3,094	61.6	2,853	56.8	242	7.8
Sex							
Male	2,395	1,658	69.2	1,523	63.6	135	8.1
Female	2,626	1,437	54.7	1,330	50.6	107	7.5
Race, Sex, and Hispanic Origin							
White	4,060	2,483	61.2	2,314	57.0	169	6.8
Male	1,960	1,357	69.2	1,263	64.4	95	7.0
Female	2,100	1,126	53.6	1,051	50.1	74	6.6
Black or African American	795	507	63.7	440	55.4	67	13.1
Male	355	244	68.8	207	58.3	37	15.2
Female	441	263	59.6	233	53.0	29	11.2
Hispanic	209	152	72.8	144	68.8	8	5.5
Male	122	107	87.3	103	84.5	3	3.2
Female	87	46	52.6	41	46.9	5	10.9
Age							
16 to 19 years	331	125	37.7	99	30.0	25	20.4
20 to 24 years	415	302	72.7	270	65.0	32	10.6
25 to 34 years	840	688	81.9	620	73.9	67	9.8
35 to 44 years	825	669	81.1	619	75.0	51	7.6
45 to 54 years	853	649	76.1	609	71.4	40	6.2
55 to 64 years	837	499	59.6	477	57.1	22	4.3
65 years and over	921	162	17.6	158	17.2	4	2.6

NOTE: Data in Table 7 are from the Current Population Survey (CPS) and do not match the estimates in Table 8. See notes and definitions for further information.

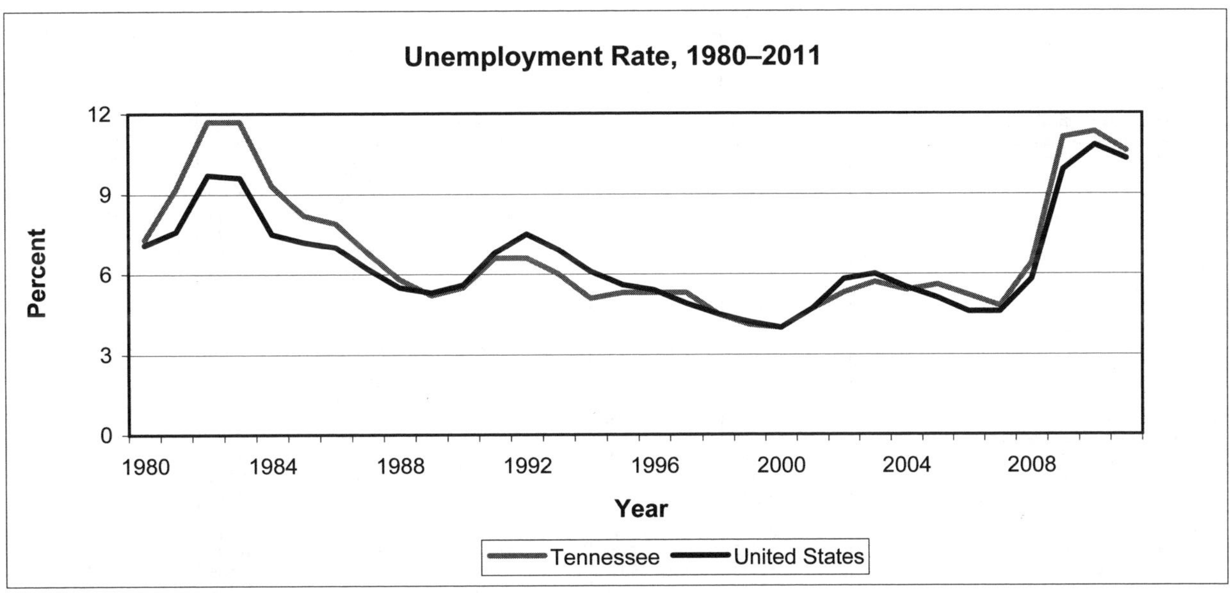

Table TN-8. Employment Status of the Civilian Noninstitutional Population Age 16 Years and Over

(Number, percent.)

Year	Civilian labor force	Civilian participation rate	Employed	Unemployed	Unemployment rate
2005	2,934,586	63.8	2,771,206	163,380	5.6
2006	2,998,586	64.1	2,843,716	155,089	5.2
2007	3,013,380	62.5	2,867,579	145,801	4.8
2008	3,041,276	63.2	2,846,096	195,180	6.4
2009	3,115,748	62.6	2,771,090	344,658	11.1
2010	3,081,522	61.3	2,734,829	346,693	11.3
2011	3,113,007	61.3	2,784,462	328,545	10.6

Table TN-9. Employment and Average Wages by Industry

(Estimates before 2007 are based on the 2002 *North American Industry Classification System* [NAICS]. Estimates from 2007 onward are based on the 2007 NAICS.)

Industry	2005	2006	2007	2008	2009	2010	2011
	Number of jobs						
Wage and Salary Employment by Industry	2,847,003	2,893,408	2,910,068	2,888,909	2,728,711	2,724,777	2,769,845
Farm Wage and Salary Employment	9,849	9,935	9,757	9,417	8,408	8,553	9,176
Nonfarm Wage and Salary Employment	2,837,154	2,883,473	2,900,311	2,879,492	2,720,303	2,716,224	2,760,669
Private wage and salary employment	2,400,254	2,441,228	2,453,858	2,425,718	2,267,069	2,258,202	2,306,093
Forestry, fishing, and related activities	4,493	4,533	4,500	4,435	4,364	4,640	4,946
Mining	3,217	3,321	3,878	3,921	3,228	3,549	3,595
Utilities	3,538	3,512	3,576	3,502	3,557	3,358	3,318
Construction	126,135	135,363	138,403	133,007	110,843	105,805	110,330
Manufacturing	410,903	401,661	383,093	361,391	310,581	300,054	304,462
Durable goods manufacturing	257,889	253,913	239,260	220,844	183,414	177,658	183,824
Nondurable goods manufacturing	153,014	147,748	143,833	140,547	127,167	122,396	120,638
Wholesale trade	130,990	133,147	133,539	133,097	121,872	117,878	118,463
Retail trade	328,321	332,266	335,739	330,882	311,720	312,020	314,622
Transportation and warehousing	144,862	147,307	147,527	142,618	132,539	131,704	135,709
Information	49,496	49,744	49,312	49,457	46,328	44,465	43,166
Finance and insurance	107,277	109,297	109,967	110,908	108,330	108,748	107,450
Real estate and rental and leasing	36,766	37,154	37,045	37,054	34,418	33,566	32,197
Professional, scientific, and technical services	105,259	108,899	110,464	113,057	109,270	108,798	111,188
Management of companies and enterprises	19,965	20,971	23,623	25,011	25,384	26,049	28,981
Administrative and waste services	186,649	189,846	191,668	186,666	162,171	172,034	186,512
Educational services	50,016	44,911	47,201	50,179	51,646	52,859	54,018
Health care and social assistance	287,422	303,689	312,185	319,706	324,095	329,625	337,410
Arts, entertainment, and recreation	30,029	30,678	31,102	31,678	30,643	30,098	30,688
Accommodation and food services	235,062	242,845	248,741	245,713	236,137	235,798	240,228
Other services, except public administration	139,854	142,084	142,295	143,436	139,943	137,154	138,810
Government and government enterprises	436,900	442,245	446,453	453,774	453,234	458,022	454,576
	Dollars						
Average Wages and Salaries by Industry	35,405	37,031	38,606	39,445	39,703	41,014	41,876
Average Farm Wages and Salaries	15,808	18,327	21,533	21,405	22,775	21,148	17,635
Average Nonfarm Wages and Salaries	35,473	37,095	38,664	39,504	39,755	41,076	41,957
Average private wages and salaries	35,625	37,334	38,933	39,735	39,966	41,469	42,371
Forestry, fishing, and related activities	20,556	21,110	21,635	21,564	21,791	22,823	23,723
Mining	51,223	56,695	54,177	58,717	56,977	63,525	61,540
Utilities	50,975	54,212	55,732	58,384	60,849	61,574	63,018
Construction	37,615	40,276	42,673	43,717	43,063	44,294	45,565
Manufacturing	42,766	44,671	46,235	48,142	48,676	51,869	52,883
Durable goods manufacturing	41,678	43,771	45,300	47,416	47,799	50,763	51,775
Nondurable goods manufacturing	44,598	46,218	47,791	49,282	49,942	53,474	54,572
Wholesale trade	49,767	52,869	55,362	55,927	55,571	57,503	59,658
Retail trade	24,279	25,027	26,105	26,000	26,140	27,034	27,726
Transportation and warehousing	42,979	44,584	46,120	46,866	46,212	48,116	49,590
Information	44,677	49,855	51,833	52,288	52,156	54,018	57,046
Finance and insurance	55,581	59,171	62,742	62,796	62,915	66,006	68,066
Real estate and rental and leasing	34,505	36,822	38,003	37,351	37,077	38,103	39,862
Professional, scientific, and technical services	52,528	55,244	58,272	60,904	61,699	64,532	65,860
Management of companies and enterprises	66,304	74,527	75,943	77,906	73,568	82,160	83,175
Administrative and waste services	25,776	26,904	28,624	29,674	30,985	31,425	31,174
Educational services	34,842	31,648	32,705	32,786	33,462	33,653	34,218
Health care and social assistance	38,650	40,305	41,624	42,791	44,015	44,835	45,500
Arts, entertainment, and recreation	33,256	38,344	39,156	38,710	37,798	40,385	41,880
Accommodation and food services	15,710	16,117	17,620	16,981	17,059	17,829	18,186
Other services, except public administration	24,232	25,312	26,217	27,052	27,517	28,455	29,204
Government and government enterprises	34,638	35,777	37,182	38,271	38,701	39,142	39,856

Table TN-10. Employment Characteristics by Family Type

(Number, percent.)

Family type and labor force status	2009		2010		2011	
	Total	Families with own children under 18 years	Total	Families with own children under 18 years	Total	Families with own children under 18 years
All families	1,638,789	712,529	1,644,896	684,351	1,625,686	674,287
Family type and labor force status						
Married-couple families	1,207,312	473,002	1,195,406	443,527	1,189,542	445,519
Both husband and wife in labor force	51.9	67.7	50.6	65.2	50.6	65.9
Husband in labor force, wife not in labor force	22.0	26.7	21.6	27.4	21.8	27.1
Wife in labor force, husband not in labor force	7.9	3.5	8.8	4.6	8.4	4.4
Both husband and wife not in labor force	18.3	2.1	19.0	2.8	19.2	2.6
Other families	431,477	239,527	449,490	240,824	436,144	228,768
Female householder, no husband present	75.3	76.5	76.3	79.2	75.4	79.1
In labor force	51.3	61.2	51.2	61.8	51.1	63.6
Not in labor force	24.0	15.2	25.1	17.4	24.3	15.5
Male householder, no wife present	24.7	23.5	23.7	20.8	24.6	20.9
In labor force	19.0	20.9	17.5	17.5	18.1	18.4
Not in labor force	5.8	2.7	6.2	3.3	6.6	2.5

Table TN-11. School Enrollment and Educational Attainment, 2011

(Number, percent.)

Item	State	U.S.
Enrollment		
Total population 3 years and over, enrolled in school	1,594,654	83,131,910
Enrolled in nursery school or preschool (percent)	5.6	6.0
Enrolled in kindergarten (percent)	4.7	5.1
Enrolled in elementary school, grades 1-8 (percent)	42.6	39.5
Enrolled in high school, grades 9-12 (percent)	20.9	20.7
Enrolled in college or graduate school (percent)	26.1	28.7
Attainment		
Total population 25 years and over	4,294,392	206,471,670
Less than ninth grade (percent)	6.1	6.0
9th to 12th grade, no diploma (percent)	9.7	8.1
High school graduate, including equivalency (percent)	33.4	28.4
Some college, no degree (percent)	21.2	21.2
Associate's degree (percent)	6.0	7.8
Bachelor's degree (percent)	15.3	17.9
Graduate or professional degree (percent)	8.3	10.6
High school graduate or higher (percent)	84.2	85.9
Bachelor's degree or higher (percent)	23.6	28.5

Table TN-12. Educational Indicators

(Number, percent; data derived from National Center of Education Statistics.)

Item	State	U.S.
Public Schools, 2009–2010 (except where noted)		
Number of school districts	140	13,629
Number of schools	1,772	99,834
Number of students (in thousands)	973	49,373
Student-teacher ratio	14.9	15.4
Expenditures per student (dollars)	9,007	10,591
Averaged freshman graduation rate, 2008–2009	77.4	75.5[1]
Dropout rate, 2008–2009	3.2	4.1
Students eligible for free or reduced-price lunch (percent)	55.1	48.0
English language learners, 2010–2011 (percent)	3.0	9.8[1]
Students with IEP (percent)	12.2	13.1
Private Schools, 2009–2010 (except where noted)		
Number of schools	525	33,366
Number of students (in thousands)	88	4,700
High school graduates, 2008–2009	6,219	308,813
Student-teacher ratio	10.2	10.7

[1] U.S. total includes estimates for nonreporting states.

Table TN-13. Reported Voting and Registration of the Voting-Age Population, November 2012

(Numbers in thousands, percent.)

Item	Total population	Total citizen population	Registered: Total registered	Registered: Percent registered (total population)	Registered: Percent registered (total citizen population)	Voted: Total voted	Voted: Percent voted (total population)	Voted: Percent voted (total citizen population)
U.S. Total	235,248	215,081	153,157	65.1	71.2	132,948	56.5	61.8
State Total	4,849	4,678	3,210	66.2	68.6	2,606	53.7	55.7
Sex								
Male	2,300	2,203	1,432	62.3	65.0	1,172	50.9	53.2
Female	2,548	2,475	1,778	69.8	71.8	1,434	56.3	57.9
Race								
White alone	3,925	3,836	2,621	66.8	68.3	2,098	53.4	54.7
White, non-Hispanic alone	3,768	3,746	2,559	67.9	68.3	2,052	54.5	54.8
Black alone	768	722	513	66.8	71.1	441	57.4	61.1
Asian alone	50	20	13	B	B	13	B	B
Hispanic (of any race)	241	134	107	44.4	79.7	84	34.7	62.3
Age								
18 to 24 years	610	590	306	50.2	51.9	207	34.0	35.2
25 to 44 years	1,615	1,513	1,030	63.8	68.1	796	49.3	52.6
45 to 64 years	1,607	1,563	1,081	67.2	69.1	904	56.3	57.9
65 to 74 years	631	628	503	79.7	80.1	457	72.3	72.7
75 years and over	385	385	290	75.4	75.4	241	62.7	62.7

B = Base is less than 75,000 and therefore too small to show the derived measure.

Table TN-14. Crime

(Number, rate per 100,000. Data are derived from the FBI Uniform Crime Reports.)

Item	State: 2010	State: 2011	State: Percent change	U.S.: 2010	U.S.: 2011	U.S.: Percent change
TOTAL POPULATION	6,357,436	6,403,353	0.7	309,330,219	311,591,917	0.7
VIOLENT CRIME						
Number	38,909	38,944	0.1	1,251,248	1,203,564	-3.8
Rate	612.0	608.2	-0.6	404.5	386.3	-4.5
Murder and Nonnegligent Manslaughter						
Number	359	373	3.9	14,722	14,612	-0.7
Rate	5.6	5.8	3.6	4.8	4.7	-2.1
Forcible Rape						
Number	2,173	2,024	-6.9	85,593	83,425	-2.5
Rate	34.2	31.6	-7.6	27.7	26.8	-3.2
Robbery						
Number	8,361	8,081	-3.3	369,089	354,396	-4.0
Rate	131.5	126.2	-4.0	119.3	113.7	-4.7
Aggravated Assault						
Number	28,016	28,466	1.6	781,844	751,131	-3.9
Rate	440.7	444.5	0.9	252.8	241.1	-4.6
PROPERTY CRIME						
Number	232,855	230,261	-1.1	9,112,625	9,063,173	-0.5
Rate	3,662.7	3,595.9	-1.8	2,945.9	2,908.7	-1.3
Burglary						
Number	64,293	62,749	-2.4	2,168,459	2,188,005	0.9
Rate	1,011.3	979.9	-3.1	701.0	702.2	0.2
Larceny-Theft						
Number	153,729	153,476	-0.2	6,204,601	6,159,795	-0.7
Rate	2,418.1	2,396.8	-0.9	2,005.8	1,976.9	-1.4
Motor Vehicle Theft						
Number	14,833	14,036	-5.4	739,565	715,373	-3.3
Rate	233.3	219.2	-6.0	239.1	229.6	-4.0

Table TN-15. State Government Finances, 2011

(Dollar amounts in thousands, percent distribution.)

Item	Dollars	Percent distribution
Total Revenue	34,680,853	100.0
General revenue	27,520,317	79.4
Intergovernmental revenue	12,116,843	34.9
Taxes	11,235,404	32.4
General sales	6,186,336	17.8
Selective sales	2,417,783	7.0
License taxes	1,099,020	3.2
Individual income tax	189,518	0.5
Corporate income tax	1,068,573	3.1
Other taxes	274,174	0.8
Current charges	2,287,931	6.6
Miscellaneous general revenue	1,880,139	5.4
Utility revenue	0	0.0
Liquor stores revenue	0	0.0
Insurance trust revenue [1]	7,160,536	20.6
Total Expenditure	30,841,226	100.0
Intergovernmental expenditure	7,104,790	23.0
Direct expenditure	23,736,436	77.0
Current operation	17,559,644	56.9
Capital outlay	1,532,498	5.0
Insurance benefits and repayments	3,275,456	10.6
Assistance and subsidies	1,112,983	3.6
Interest on debt	255,855	0.8
Exhibit: Salaries and wages	3,542,148	11.5
Total Expenditure	30,841,226	100.0
General expenditure	27,565,770	89.4
Intergovernmental expenditure	7,104,790	23.0
Direct expenditure	20,460,980	66.3
General expenditure, by function:		
Education	9,176,744	29.8
Public welfare	10,746,576	34.8
Hospitals	415,026	1.3
Health	1,118,539	3.6
Highways	1,704,659	5.5
Police protection	221,624	0.7
Correction	796,449	2.6
Natural resources	312,772	1.0
Parks and recreation	90,361	0.3
Governmental administration	763,799	2.5
Interest on general debt	255,855	0.8
Other and unallocable	1,963,366	6.4
Utility expenditure	0	0.0
Liquor stores expenditure	0	0.0
Insurance trust expenditure	3,275,456	10.6
Debt at End of Fiscal Year	5,899,369	X
Cash and Security Holdings	41,692,841	X

X = Not applicable.
[1] Within insurance trust revenue, net earnings of state retirement systems is a calculated statistic (the item code in the data file is X08), and thus can be positive or negative. Net earnings is the sum of earnings on investments plus gains on investments minus losses on investments. The change made in 2002 for asset valuation from book to market value in accordance with Statement 34 of the Governmental Accounting Standards Board is reflected in the calculated statistics.

Table TN-16. State Government Tax Collections, 2012

(Dollars in thousands, percent.)

Item	Dollars	Percent distribution
Total Taxes	11,982,345	100.0
Property taxes	0	0.0
Sales and gross receipts	8,962,195	74.8
General sales and gross receipts	6,512,362	54.3
Selective sales and gross receipts	2,449,833	20.4
Alcoholic beverages	133,055	1.1
Amusements	0	0.0
Insurance premiums	639,222	5.3
Motor fuels	837,787	7.0
Pari-mutuels	0	0.0
Public utilities	9,318	0.1
Tobacco products	279,017	2.3
Other selective sales	551,434	4.6
Licenses	1,282,015	10.7
Alcoholic beverages	1,320	-
Amusements	290	-
Corporations in general	626,236	5.2
Hunting and fishing	32,592	0.3
Motor vehicle	262,243	2.2
Motor vehicle operators	46,494	0.4
Public utilities	6,967	0.1
Occupation and business, NEC	297,235	2.5
Other licenses	8,638	0.1
Income taxes	1,408,141	11.8
Individual income	182,251	1.5
Corporation net income	1,225,890	10.2
Other taxes	329,994	2.8
Death and gift	149,344	1.2
Documentary and stock transfer	136,224	1.1
Severance	2,450	-
Taxes, NEC	41,976	0.4

- = Rounds to zero.

Leading Exports, 2012

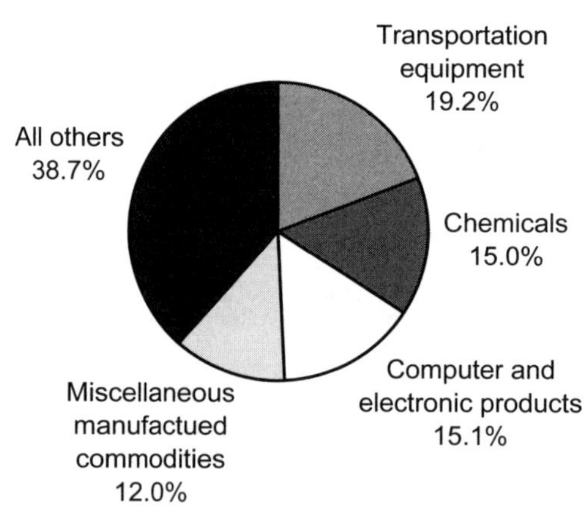

TEXAS

Facts and Figures

Location: West South Central United States; bordered on the N by Oklahoma, on the E by Arkansas and Louisiana, on the S by Mexico and the Gulf of Mexico, and on the W by Mexico and New Mexico

Area: 268,581 sq. mi. (695,621 sq. km.); rank—2nd

Population: 26,059,203 (2012 est.); rank—2nd

Principal Cities: capital—Austin; largest—Houston

Statehood: December 29, 1845; 28th state

U.S. Congress: 2 senators, 36 representatives

State Motto: Friendship

State Song: "Texas, Our Texas"

State Nickname: The Lone Star State

Abbreviations: TX; Tex.

State Symbols: flower—bluebonnet; tree—pecan; bird—mockingbird

At a Glance

- With an increase in population of 18.8 percent, Texas ranked 1st among the states in growth from 2000 to 2009.
- An estimated 179,800 marriages took place in Texas in 2009, compared to 76,900 divorces.
- Texas's median household income in 2011 was $49,392, and 18.5 percent of the population lived below the poverty level.
- In 2011, 23 percent of Texans did not have health insurance, compared to 15.1 percent of the total U.S. population.
- In 2007, Texas exported $5.2 billion worth of agricultural products, about 6.3 percent of the U.S. total.

Table TX-1. Population by Age, Sex, Race, and Hispanic Origin

(Number, percent, except where noted.)

Sex, age, race, and Hispanic origin	2000	2010	2012[1]	Average annual percent change, 2010–2012
Total Population	20,851,820	25,145,561	26,059,203	1.2
Percent of total U.S. population	7.4	8.1	8.3	X
Sex				
Male	10,352,910	12,472,280	12,947,734	1.2
Female	10,498,910	12,673,281	13,111,469	1.1
Age				
Under 5 years	1,625,628	1,928,473	1,941,845	0.2
5 to 19 years	4,291,608	5,693,241	5,793,060	0.6
20 to 64 years	12,233,052	14,921,961	15,485,003	1.2
65 years and over	2,072,532	2,601,886	2,839,295	2.8
Median age (years)	32.3	33.6	33.9	0.3
Race and Hispanic Origin				
One race				
White	14,799,505	20,389,793	21,001,450	1.0
Black	2,404,566	3,070,440	3,216,242	1.5
American Indian and Alaska Native	118,362	251,209	265,563	1.8
Asian	562,319	1,000,473	1,095,443	2.9
Native Hawaiian or Other Pacific Islander	14,434	31,242	33,980	2.7
Two or more races	514,633	402,404	446,525	3.3
Hispanic (of any race)	6,699,666	9,578,505	10,091,933	1.7

X = Not applicable.
[1] Population figures for 2012 are July 1 estimates. The 2010 estimates are taken from the 2010 Census.

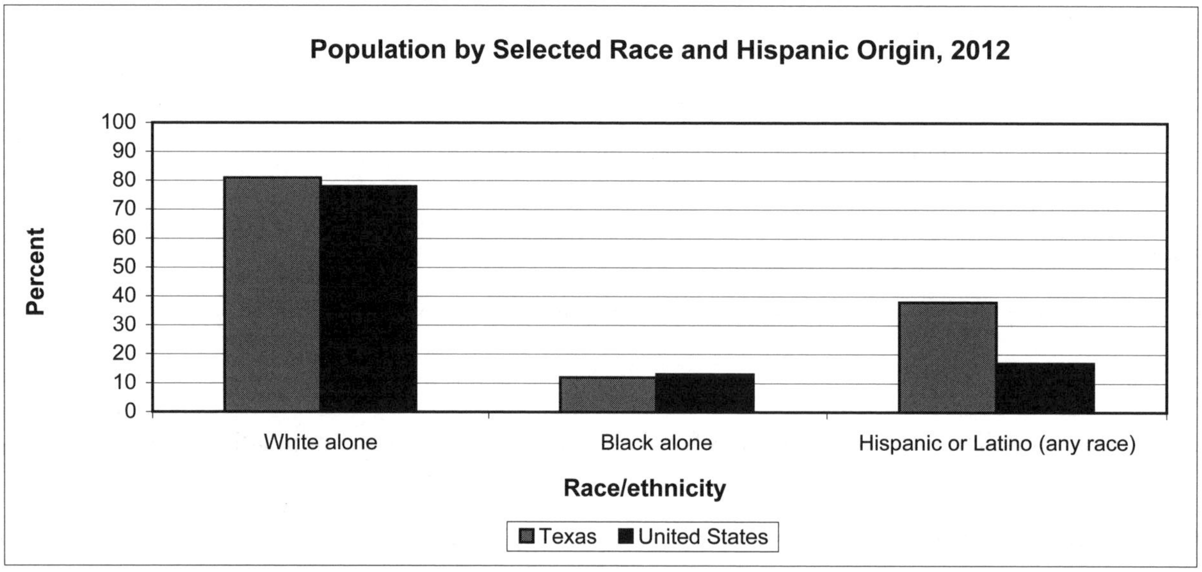

Table TX-2. Marital Status

(Number, percent distribution.)

Sex, age, race, and Hispanic origin	2000	2010	2011
Males, 15 Years and Over	7,820,248	9,587,343	9,761,236
Never married	28.6	34.6	34.7
Now married, except separated	58.8	51.6	51.2
Separated	2.0	2.3	2.2
Widowed	2.1	2.2	2.2
Divorced	8.5	9.4	9.6
Females, 15 Years and Over	8,117,395	9,903,147	10,077,282
Never married	22.6	27.6	28.2
Now married, except separated	54.3	48.5	48.0
Separated	2.9	3.3	3.2
Widowed	9.1	8.1	8.2
Divorced	11.0	12.5	12.4

Table TX-3. Households and Housing Characteristics

(Number, percent, dollars.)

Item	2000	2010	2011	Average annual percent change, 2000–2011
Total Households	7,393,354	8,738,664	8,850,370	1.6
Family households	5,247,794	6,091,590	6,171,317	1.5
Married-couple family	3,989,741	4,386,996	4,429,883	0.9
Other family	1,258,053	1,704,594	1,741,434	3.2
Male householder, no wife present	320,464	436,727	456,464	3.5
Female householder, no husband present	937,489	1,267,867	1,284,970	3.1
Nonfamily households	2,145,560	2,647,074	2,679,053	2.1
Householder living alone	1,752,141	2,166,469	2,210,249	2.2
Householder not living alone	393,419	480,605	468,804	1.6
Housing Characteristics				
Total housing units	8,157,575	9,996,209	10,099,242	2.0
Occupied housing units	7,393,354	8,738,664	8,850,370	1.6
Owner occupied	4,716,959	5,555,903	5,568,300	1.5
Renter occupied	2,676,395	3,182,761	3,282,070	1.9
Average size	2.74	2.82	2.84	0.3
Financial Characteristics				
Median gross rent of renter-occupied housing	574	801	813	3.5
Median monthly owner costs for housing units with a mortgage	986	1,402	1,398	3.5
Median value of owner-occupied housing units	82,500	128,100	127,700	4.6

Table TX-4. Migration, Origin, and Language

(Number, percent.)

Characteristic	State			U.S.		
	2010	2011	Percent change	2010	2011	Percent change
Residence 1 Year Ago						
Population 1 year and over	24,899,075	25,327,104	1.7	305,628,607	307,900,319	0.7
Same house	82.3	82.9	0.7	84.6	84.8	0.2
Different house in the U.S.	17.0	16.4	-3.5	14.8	14.6	-1.4
Same county	10.9	10.6	-2.8	9.4	9.2	-2.1
Different county	6.1	5.8	-4.9	5.4	5.4	-
Same state	4.2	3.8	-9.5	3.2	3.1	-3.1
Different state	2.0	2.0	-	2.2	2.3	4.5
Abroad	0.7	0.7	-	0.6	0.6	-
Place of Birth						
Native born	21,115,083	21,473,006	1.7	269,393,835	271,214,059	0.7
Male	49.4	49.4	-	49.2	49.2	-
Female	50.6	50.6	-	50.8	50.8	-
Foreign born	4,142,031	4,201,675	1.4	39,955,854	40,377,860	1.1
Male	50.8	50.7	-0.2	49.1	48.9	-0.4
Female	49.2	49.3	0.2	50.9	51.1	0.4
Foreign born; naturalized U.S. citizen	1,325,501	1,393,937	5.2	17,476,082	18,140,192	3.8
Male	47.3	47.3	-	45.8	45.8	-
Female	52.7	52.7	-	54.2	54.2	-
Foreign born; not a U.S. citizen	2,816,530	2,807,738	-0.3	22,479,772	22,237,668	-1.1
Male	52.4	52.4	-	51.6	51.5	-0.2
Female	47.6	47.6	-	48.4	48.5	0.2
Entered 2000 or later	36.4	37.2	2.2	34.7	35.7	2.9
Entered 1990 to 1999	28.8	28.4	-1.4	27.2	26.7	-1.8
Entered before 1990	34.8	34.4	-1.1	38.1	37.6	-1.3
World Region of Birth, Foreign						
Foreign-born population, excluding population born at sea	4,142,031	4,201,675	1.4	39,955,673	40,377,757	1.1
Europe	4.2	4.5	7.1	12.1	12.1	-
Asia	18.6	18.5	-0.5	28.2	28.6	1.4
Africa	3.3	3.4	3.0	4	4.1	2.5
Oceania	0.2	0.2	-	0.5	0.5	-
Latin America	72.8	72.2	-0.8	53.1	52.6	-0.9
North America	1.0	1.1	10.0	2	2.0	-
Language Spoken at Home and Ability to Speak English						
Population 5 years and over	23,327,776	23,721,334	1.7	289,215,746	291,524,091	0.8
English only	65.2	65.3	0.2	79.4	79.2	-0.3
Language other than English	34.8	34.7	-0.3	20.6	20.8	1.0
Speaks English less than "very well"	14.4	14.5	0.7	8.7	8.7	-

- = Zero or rounds to zero.

Table TX-5. Median Income and Poverty Status, 2011

(Number, percent, except as noted.)

Characteristic	State		U.S.	
	Number	Percent	Number	Percent
Median Income				
Households (dollars)	49,392	X	50,502	X
Families (dollars)	58,016	X	61,455	X
Below Poverty Level (All People)	4,628,758	18.5	48,452,035	15.9
Sex				
Male	2,089,526	16.9	21,825,281	14.7
Female	2,539,232	19.9	26,626,754	17.2
Age				
Under 18 years	1,829,214	26.6	16,386,500	22.5
Related children under 18 years	1,809,923	26.4	16,087,074	22.2
18 to 64 years	2,499,622	16.1	28,335,079	14.8
65 years and over	299,922	11.4	3,730,456	9.3

X = Not applicable.

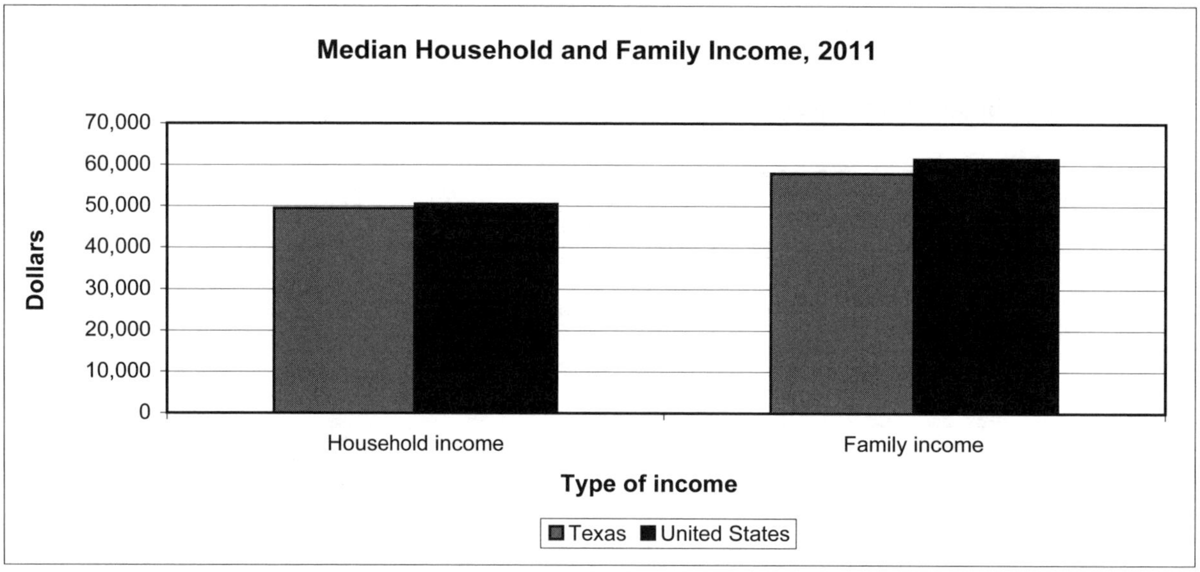

Table TX-6. Health Insurance Coverage Status for the Civilian Noninstitutionalized Population and Children Under 18 Years of Age

(Numbers in thousands, percent.)

Item	2004	2005	2006	2007	2008	2009	2010	2011
Civilian Noninstitutionalized Population	22,331	22,819	23,236	23,704	23,827	24,292	24,779	25,197
Covered by Private or Public Insurance								
Number	16,926	17,426	17,533	17,742	18,082	18,508	18,904	19,408
Percent	75.8	76.4	75.5	74.8	75.9	76.2	76.3	77.0
Not Covered								
Number	5,405	5,394	5,704	5,962	5,745	5,783	5,875	5,790
Percent	24.2	23.6	24.5	25.2	24.1	23.8	23.7	23.0
Percent in the U.S. not covered	14.9	15.3	15.8	15.3	15.1	15.1	15.5	15.1
Children Under 18 Years of Age	6,306	6,477	6,556	6,720	6,714	6,878	6,876	6,947
Covered by Private or Public Insurance								
Number	5,000	5,253	5,164	5,285	5,518	5,758	5,880	6,030
Percent	79.3	81.1	78.8	78.6	82.2	83.7	85.5	86.8
Not Covered								
Number	1,307	1,224	1,392	1,435	1,196	1,120	996	917
Percent	20.7	18.9	21.2	21.4	17.8	16.3	14.5	13.2
Percent in the U.S. not covered	10.5	10.9	11.7	11.0	9.7	8.6	8.0	7.5

Table TX-7. Employment Status by Demographic Group, Preliminary 2012

(Numbers in thousands, percent.)

Characteristic	Civilian noninstitutional population	Civilian labor force		Employed		Unemployed	
		Number	Percent of population	Number	Percent of population	Number	Percent of population
Total	19,287	12,640	65.5	11,797	61.2	843	6.7
Sex							
Male	9,360	6,915	73.9	6,475	69.2	440	6.4
Female	9,927	5,725	57.7	5,323	53.6	402	7.0
Race, Sex, and Hispanic Origin							
White	15,653	10,256	65.5	9,638	61.6	618	6.0
Male	7,662	5,713	74.6	5,382	70.2	332	5.8
Female	7,991	4,543	56.8	4,257	53.3	286	6.3
Black or African American	2,279	1,499	65.8	1,335	58.6	164	11.0
Male	1,039	702	67.6	625	60.1	78	11.0
Female	1,240	797	64.3	710	57.3	87	10.9
Hispanic	7,238	4,790	66.2	4,421	61.1	370	7.7
Male	3,564	2,723	76.4	2,515	70.6	208	7.6
Female	3,674	2,067	56.3	1,905	51.9	161	7.8
Age							
16 to 19 years	1,423	450	31.6	355	24.9	95	21.1
20 to 24 years	1,782	1,255	70.4	1,120	62.8	135	10.8
25 to 34 years	3,756	3,034	80.8	2,815	74.9	219	7.2
35 to 44 years	3,430	2,808	81.9	2,640	76.9	168	6.0
45 to 54 years	3,351	2,688	80.2	2,578	76.9	110	4.1
55 to 64 years	2,826	1,856	65.7	1,764	62.4	93	5.0
65 years and over	2,718	549	20.2	526	19.4	23	4.1

NOTE: Data in Table 7 are from the Current Population Survey (CPS) and do not match the estimates in Table 8. See notes and definitions for further information.

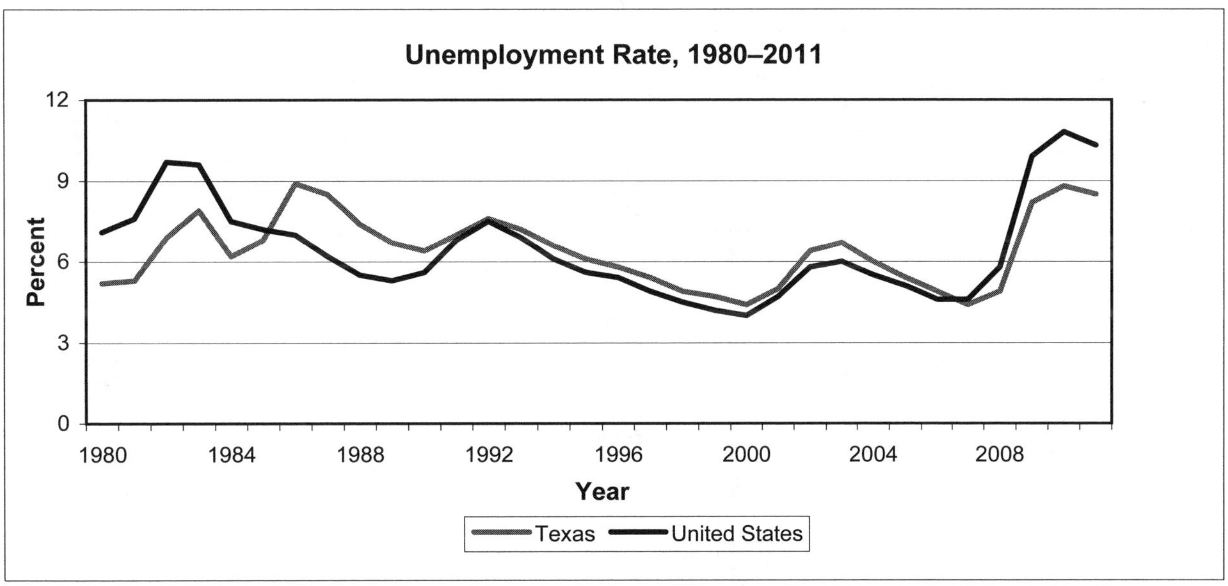

Table TX-8. Employment Status of the Civilian Noninstitutional Population Age 16 Years and Over

(Number, percent.)

Year	Civilian labor force	Civilian participation rate	Employed	Unemployed	Unemployment rate
2005	11,170,574	67.0	10,568,414	602,160	5.4
2006	11,348,147	66.5	10,787,397	560,750	4.9
2007	11,474,987	65.8	10,972,152	502,835	4.4
2008	11,701,585	65.7	11,126,436	575,149	4.9
2009	12,210,524	65.6	11,211,611	998,913	8.2
2010	12,363,612	64.7	11,271,851	1,091,761	8.8
2011	12,520,343	64.4	11,455,069	1,065,274	8.5

Table TX-9. Employment and Average Wages by Industry

(Estimates before 2007 are based on the 2002 *North American Industry Classification System* [NAICS]. Estimates from 2007 onward are based on the 2007 NAICS.)

Industry	2005	2006	2007	2008	2009	2010	2011
	Number of jobs						
Wage and Salary Employment by Industry	10,170,768	10,525,419	10,858,772	11,096,319	10,808,235	10,828,653	11,072,783
Farm Wage and Salary Employment	46,382	39,303	43,404	42,703	48,479	44,051	41,328
Nonfarm Wage and Salary Employment	10,124,386	10,486,116	10,815,368	11,053,616	10,759,756	10,784,602	11,031,455
Private wage and salary employment	8,297,798	8,624,328	8,929,873	9,116,924	8,776,668	8,771,530	9,046,768
Forestry, fishing, and related activities	29,786	28,725	28,504	28,127	27,127	28,302	28,775
Mining	162,851	183,999	204,434	230,088	203,229	203,461	234,092
Utilities	45,842	44,559	45,605	47,516	48,042	48,316	49,026
Construction	590,088	630,584	673,014	700,532	626,586	592,472	595,688
Manufacturing	902,404	929,803	934,915	924,271	838,653	811,550	837,471
Durable goods manufacturing	574,911	604,208	615,008	608,562	537,342	515,868	543,706
Nondurable goods manufacturing	327,493	325,595	319,907	315,709	301,311	295,682	293,765
Wholesale trade	479,965	502,819	523,444	533,936	502,987	501,522	519,424
Retail trade	1,125,959	1,150,056	1,179,228	1,190,978	1,159,288	1,155,041	1,178,723
Transportation and warehousing	365,542	381,071	393,727	398,766	376,704	377,833	391,232
Information	223,480	223,675	222,003	217,408	205,464	196,069	195,523
Finance and insurance	438,413	457,311	465,602	467,810	458,773	464,849	477,157
Real estate and rental and leasing	178,562	182,459	187,041	192,012	182,340	179,127	180,900
Professional, scientific, and technical services	500,700	533,483	566,421	595,415	570,446	577,632	596,946
Management of companies and enterprises	53,284	56,862	67,858	74,981	77,042	79,307	83,489
Administrative and waste services	615,405	656,842	679,395	683,145	622,713	637,018	676,759
Educational services	128,945	132,270	138,053	143,269	148,431	153,919	158,713
Health care and social assistance	1,004,597	1,037,872	1,073,888	1,108,291	1,155,375	1,196,470	1,228,565
Arts, entertainment, and recreation	103,167	105,035	108,673	110,219	111,675	111,881	112,998
Accommodation and food services	817,047	850,022	884,080	908,255	905,928	909,188	942,578
Other services, except public administration	531,761	536,881	553,988	561,905	555,865	547,573	558,709
Government and government enterprises	1,826,588	1,861,788	1,885,495	1,936,692	1,983,088	2,013,072	1,984,687
	Dollars						
Average Wages and Salaries by Industry	39,730	42,024	44,272	45,526	45,255	46,542	48,351
Average Farm Wages and Salaries	22,838	23,553	27,864	31,452	25,333	27,486	35,284
Average Nonfarm Wages and Salaries	39,807	42,093	44,338	45,580	45,345	46,619	48,400
Average private wages and salaries	40,412	42,807	45,065	46,247	45,703	47,146	49,079
Forestry, fishing, and related activities	21,636	22,385	23,092	24,408	24,805	25,451	25,907
Mining	98,087	102,168	107,182	113,073	111,559	117,244	122,085
Utilities	76,195	81,989	93,955	88,718	88,531	90,004	90,239
Construction	40,522	44,496	46,599	48,950	48,943	49,195	50,908
Manufacturing	54,322	57,400	59,903	60,462	60,239	63,181	65,897
Durable goods manufacturing	55,659	59,237	60,927	61,921	62,256	65,452	68,327
Nondurable goods manufacturing	51,976	53,991	57,934	57,648	56,641	59,220	61,401
Wholesale trade	58,490	61,363	64,610	65,786	65,020	67,874	71,415
Retail trade	25,561	26,205	26,633	26,668	26,511	27,165	27,902
Transportation and warehousing	45,515	48,009	50,457	51,143	50,639	53,376	55,373
Information	56,978	60,480	64,618	67,122	66,835	67,330	70,722
Finance and insurance	59,423	62,774	66,544	67,795	65,364	68,514	71,569
Real estate and rental and leasing	39,666	43,167	45,050	45,620	44,045	45,764	49,099
Professional, scientific, and technical services	65,026	69,140	71,659	73,749	73,877	76,448	79,425
Management of companies and enterprises	87,339	92,147	102,335	96,622	94,096	100,017	106,866
Administrative and waste services	29,061	30,778	33,788	34,895	35,198	36,084	36,965
Educational services	29,985	30,971	32,197	34,008	35,127	35,508	36,131
Health care and social assistance	35,318	36,598	38,106	39,377	40,482	40,945	41,719
Arts, entertainment, and recreation	27,489	30,868	32,072	31,476	31,916	31,827	32,702
Accommodation and food services	16,232	16,842	17,765	17,625	17,679	18,429	18,982
Other services, except public administration	23,287	24,729	25,839	27,049	27,341	28,346	29,197
Government and government enterprises	37,061	38,788	40,891	42,445	43,757	44,323	45,306

Table TX-10. Employment Characteristics by Family Type

(Number, percent.)

Family type and labor force status	2009 Total	2009 Families with own children under 18 years	2010 Total	2010 Families with own children under 18 years	2011 Total	2011 Families with own children under 18 years
All families	5,956,367	2,957,134	6,091,590	2,990,774	6,171,317	2,990,780
Family type and labor force status						
Married-couple families	4,313,750	2,019,949	4,386,996	2,021,898	4,429,883	2,017,757
Both husband and wife in labor force	53.4	61.8	52.6	61.2	51.6	59.9
Husband in labor force, wife not in labor force	27.0	33.4	27.0	34.2	27.8	35.2
Wife in labor force, husband not in labor force	6.2	3.2	6.5	3.1	6.7	3.3
Both husband and wife not in labor force	13.4	1.6	13.8	1.5	13.9	1.7
Other families	1,642,617	937,185	1,704,594	968,876	1,741,434	973,023
Female householder, no husband present	73.6	78.1	74.4	78.6	73.8	78.4
In labor force	52.9	63.8	54.6	65.1	53.3	64.1
Not in labor force	20.6	14.3	19.8	13.5	20.4	14.3
Male householder, no wife present	26.4	21.9	25.6	21.4	26.2	21.6
In labor force	21.9	20.3	20.9	19.8	21.3	19.8
Not in labor force	4.6	1.6	4.7	1.6	4.9	1.8

Table TX-11. School Enrollment and Educational Attainment, 2011

(Number, percent.)

Item	State	U.S.
Enrollment		
Total population 3 years and over, enrolled in school	7,320,055	83,131,910
Enrolled in nursery school or preschool (percent)	6.2	6.0
Enrolled in kindergarten (percent)	5.7	5.1
Enrolled in elementary school, grades 1-8 (percent)	42.6	39.5
Enrolled in high school, grades 9-12 (percent)	20.6	20.7
Enrolled in college or graduate school (percent)	25.0	28.7
Attainment		
Total population 25 years and over	16,074,391	206,471,670
Less than ninth grade (percent)	9.5	6.0
9th to 12th grade, no diploma (percent)	9.4	8.1
High school graduate, including equivalency (percent)	25.5	28.4
Some college, no degree (percent)	22.6	21.2
Associate's degree (percent)	6.5	7.8
Bachelor's degree (percent)	17.7	17.9
Graduate or professional degree (percent)	8.7	10.6
High school graduate or higher (percent)	81.1	85.9
Bachelor's degree or higher (percent)	26.4	28.5

Table TX-12. Educational Indicators

(Number, percent; data derived from National Center of Education Statistics.)

Item	State	U.S.
Public Schools, 2009–2010 (except where noted)		
Number of school districts	1,032	13,629
Number of schools	8,619	99,834
Number of students (in thousands)	4,850	49,373
Student-teacher ratio	14.6	15.4
Expenditures per student (dollars)	11,000	10,591
Averaged freshman graduation rate, 2008–2009	75.4	75.5[1]
Dropout rate, 2008–2009	3.2	4.1
Students eligible for free or reduced-price lunch (percent)	50.1	48.0
English language learners, 2010–2011 (percent)	15.0	9.8[1]
Students with IEP (percent)	9.2	13.1
Private Schools, 2009–2010 (except where noted)		
Number of schools	1,852	33,366
Number of students (in thousands)	246	4,700
High school graduates, 2008–2009	12,903	308,813
Student-teacher ratio	9.6	10.7

[1] U.S. total includes estimates for nonreporting states.

Table TX-13. Reported Voting and Registration of the Voting-Age Population, November 2012

(Numbers in thousands, percent.)

Item	Total population	Total citizen population	Registered			Voted		
			Total registered	Percent registered (total population)	Percent registered (total citizen population)	Total voted	Percent voted (total population)	Percent voted (total citizen population)
U.S. Total	235,248	215,081	153,157	65.1	71.2	132,948	56.5	61.8
State Total	18,642	16,062	10,749	57.7	66.9	8,643	46.4	53.8
Sex								
Male	9,046	7,719	4,977	55.0	64.5	3,925	43.4	50.8
Female	9,596	8,344	5,772	60.1	69.2	4,719	49.2	56.6
Race								
White alone	15,029	12,989	8,643	57.5	66.5	6,900	45.9	53.1
White, non-Hispanic alone	8,512	8,360	6,101	71.7	73.0	5,087	59.8	60.9
Black alone	2,213	2,144	1,569	70.9	73.2	1,352	61.1	63.1
Asian alone	900	506	299	33.2	59.1	214	23.8	42.4
Hispanic (of any race)	6,831	4,867	2,652	38.8	54.5	1,890	27.7	38.8
Age								
18 to 24 years	2,538	2,249	971	38.2	43.1	572	22.5	25.4
25 to 44 years	7,140	5,713	3,573	50.0	62.5	2,701	37.8	47.3
45 to 64 years	6,115	5,429	3,981	65.1	73.3	3,399	55.6	62.6
65 to 74 years	1,719	1,610	1,329	77.4	82.6	1,201	69.9	74.6
75 years and over	1,131	1,061	895	79.2	84.4	770	68.1	72.6

Table TX-14. Crime

(Number, rate per 100,000. Data are derived from the FBI Uniform Crime Reports.)

Item	State			U.S.		
	2010	2011	Percent change	2010	2011	Percent change
TOTAL POPULATION	25,253,466	25,674,681	1.7	309,330,219	311,591,917	0.7
VIOLENT CRIME						
Number	113,231	104,873	-7.4	1,251,248	1,203,564	-3.8
Rate	448.4	408.5	-8.9	404.5	386.3	-4.5
Murder and Nonnegligent Manslaughter						
Number	1,249	1,126	-9.8	14,722	14,612	-0.7
Rate	4.9	4.4	-10.2	4.8	4.7	-2.1
Forcible Rape						
Number	7,622	7,439	-2.4	85,593	83,425	-2.5
Rate	30.2	29.0	-4.0	27.7	26.8	-3.2
Robbery						
Number	32,843	28,395	-13.5	369,089	354,396	-4.0
Rate	130.1	110.6	-15.0	119.3	113.7	-4.7
Aggravated Assault						
Number	71,517	67,913	-5.0	781,844	751,131	-3.9
Rate	283.2	264.5	-6.6	252.8	241.1	-4.6
PROPERTY CRIME						
Number	951,246	891,499	-6.3	9,112,625	9,063,173	-0.5
Rate	3,766.8	3,472.3	-7.8	2,945.9	2,908.7	-1.3
Burglary						
Number	228,597	215,223	-5.9	2,168,459	2,188,005	0.9
Rate	905.2	838.3	-7.4	701.0	702.2	0.2
Larceny-Theft						
Number	654,626	612,938	-6.4	6,204,601	6,159,795	-0.7
Rate	2,592.2	2,387.3	-7.9	2,005.8	1,976.9	-1.4
Motor Vehicle Theft						
Number	68,023	63,338	-6.9	739,565	715,373	-3.3
Rate	269.4	246.7	-8.4	239.1	229.6	-4.0

Table TX-15. State Government Finances, 2011

(Dollar amounts in thousands, percent distribution.)

Item	Dollars	Percent distribution
Total Revenue	134,344,602	100.0
General revenue	107,189,851	79.8
Intergovernmental revenue	42,858,907	31.9
Taxes	43,188,251	32.1
General sales	21,793,858	16.2
Selective sales	12,004,561	8.9
License taxes	6,712,228	5.0
Individual income tax	0	0.0
Corporate income tax	0	0.0
Other taxes	2,677,604	2.0
Current charges	12,442,051	9.3
Miscellaneous general revenue	8,700,642	6.5
Utility revenue	0	0.0
Liquor stores revenue	0	0.0
Insurance trust revenue [1]	27,154,751	20.2
Total Expenditure	125,939,778	100.0
Intergovernmental expenditure	29,665,803	23.6
Direct expenditure	96,273,975	76.4
Current operation	68,088,408	54.1
Capital outlay	7,157,024	5.7
Insurance benefits and repayments	17,340,283	13.8
Assistance and subsidies	2,264,173	1.8
Interest on debt	1,424,087	1.1
Exhibit: Salaries and wages	16,179,202	12.8
Total Expenditure	125,939,778	100.0
General expenditure	108,599,495	86.2
Intergovernmental expenditure	29,665,803	23.6
Direct expenditure	78,933,692	62.7
General expenditure, by function:		
Education	48,809,392	38.8
Public welfare	31,269,267	24.8
Hospitals	4,196,479	3.3
Health	2,732,257	2.2
Highways	6,558,148	5.2
Police protection	882,787	0.7
Correction	3,764,642	3.0
Natural resources	924,825	0.7
Parks and recreation	199,538	0.2
Governmental administration	2,039,063	1.6
Interest on general debt	1,424,087	1.1
Other and unallocable	5,799,010	4.6
Utility expenditure	0	0.0
Liquor stores expenditure	0	0.0
Insurance trust expenditure	17,340,283	13.8
Debt at End of Fiscal Year	38,530,338	X
Cash and Security Holdings	268,468,004	X

X = Not applicable.

[1] Within insurance trust revenue, net earnings of state retirement systems is a calculated statistic (the item code in the data file is X08), and thus can be positive or negative. Net earnings is the sum of earnings on investments plus gains on investments minus losses on investments. The change made in 2002 for asset valuation from book to market value in accordance with Statement 34 of the Governmental Accounting Standards Board is reflected in the calculated statistics.

Table TX-16. State Government Tax Collections, 2012

(Dollars in thousands, percent.)

Item	Dollars	Percent distribution
Total Taxes	48,596,548	100.0
Property taxes	0	0.0
Sales and gross receipts	37,431,966	77.0
General sales and gross receipts	24,500,909	50.4
Selective sales and gross receipts	12,931,057	26.6
Alcoholic beverages	937,614	1.9
Amusements	39,375	0.1
Insurance premiums	1,508,157	3.1
Motor fuels	3,178,419	6.5
Pari-mutuels	7,142	-
Public utilities	619,670	1.3
Tobacco products	1,469,712	3.0
Other selective sales	5,170,968	10.6
Licenses	7,509,000	15.5
Alcoholic beverages	73,118	0.2
Amusements	9,854	-
Corporations in general	4,543,589	9.3
Hunting and fishing	102,661	0.2
Motor vehicle	1,832,791	3.8
Motor vehicle operators	130,838	0.3
Public utilities	18,509	-
Occupation and business, NEC	619,851	1.3
Other licenses	177,789	0.4
Income taxes	0	0.0
Individual income	0	0.0
Corporation net income	0	0.0
Other taxes	3,655,582	7.5
Death and gift	0	0.0
Documentary and stock transfer	0	0.0
Severance	3,655,582	7.5
Taxes, NEC	0	0.0

- = Rounds to zero.

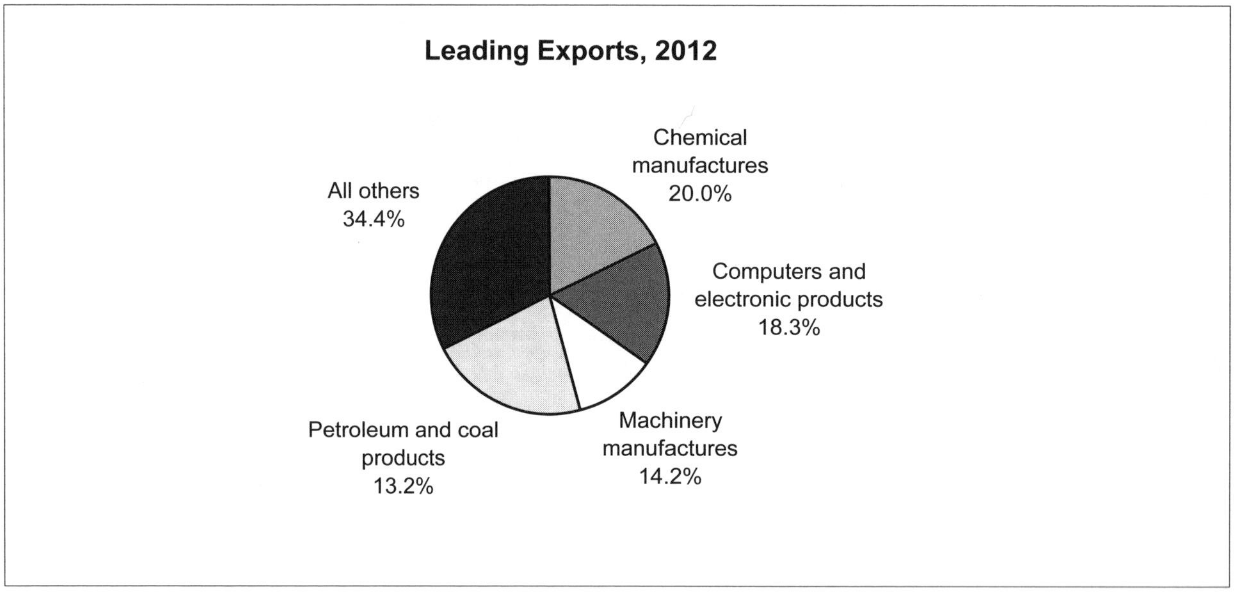

UTAH

Facts and Figures

Location: Western United States; bordered on the N by Idaho and Wyoming, on the E by Colorado, on the S by Arizona, and on the W by Nevada; Utah is one of the Four Corner states—at its SE corner it touches Arizona, Colorado, and New Mexico

Area: 84,899 sq. mi. (219,887 sq. km.); rank—13th

Population: 2,855,287 (2012 est.); rank—34th

Principal Cities: capital—Salt Lake City; largest—Salt Lake City

Statehood: January 4, 1896; 45th state

U.S. Congress: 2 senators, 4 representatives

State Motto: Industry

State Song: "Utah, We Love Thee"

State Nickname: The Beehive State

Abbreviations: UT

State Symbols: flower—sego lily; tree—blue spruce; bird—California seagull

At a Glance

- With an increase in population of 24.7 percent, Utah ranked 13th among the states in growth from 2000 to 2009.
- An estimated 23,900 marriages took place in Utah in 2009, compared to 10,700 divorces.
- Utah's violent crime rate in 2011 was 195.0 per 100,000 population, compared to 386.3 for the entire nation.
- In the 2012 election, 57.0 percent of Utah's eligible voters voted, compared to 61.8 percent of eligible voters nationwide.
- In 2007, Utah exported $344 million worth of agricultural products, less than 1 percent of the U.S. total.

Table UT-1. Population by Age, Sex, Race, and Hispanic Origin

(Number, percent, except where noted.)

Sex, age, race, and Hispanic origin	2000	2010	2012[1]	Average annual percent change, 2010–2012
Total Population	2,233,169	2,763,885	2,855,287	1.1
Percent of total U.S. population	0.8	0.9	0.9	X
Sex				
Male	1,119,031	1,388,317	1,435,860	1.1
Female	1,114,138	1,375,568	1,419,427	1.0
Age				
Under 5 years	209,378	263,924	257,848	-0.8
5 to 19 years	601,599	698,613	715,491	0.8
20 to 64 years	1,231,970	1,551,886	1,610,529	1.2
65 years and over	190,222	249,462	271,419	2.7
Median age (years)	27.1	29.2	29.9	0.8
Race and Hispanic Origin				
One race				
White	1,992,975	2,547,328	2,620,788	0.9
Black	17,657	33,864	38,717	4.2
American Indian and Alaska Native	29,684	40,729	42,049	1.0
Asian	37,108	57,800	63,857	3.2
Native Hawaiian or Other Pacific Islander	15,145	26,049	27,563	1.8
Two or more races	47,185	58,114	64,313	3.2
Hispanic (of any race)	201,559	370,870	393,267	1.9

X = Not applicable.
[1] Population figures for 2012 are July 1 estimates. The 2010 estimates are taken from the 2010 Census.

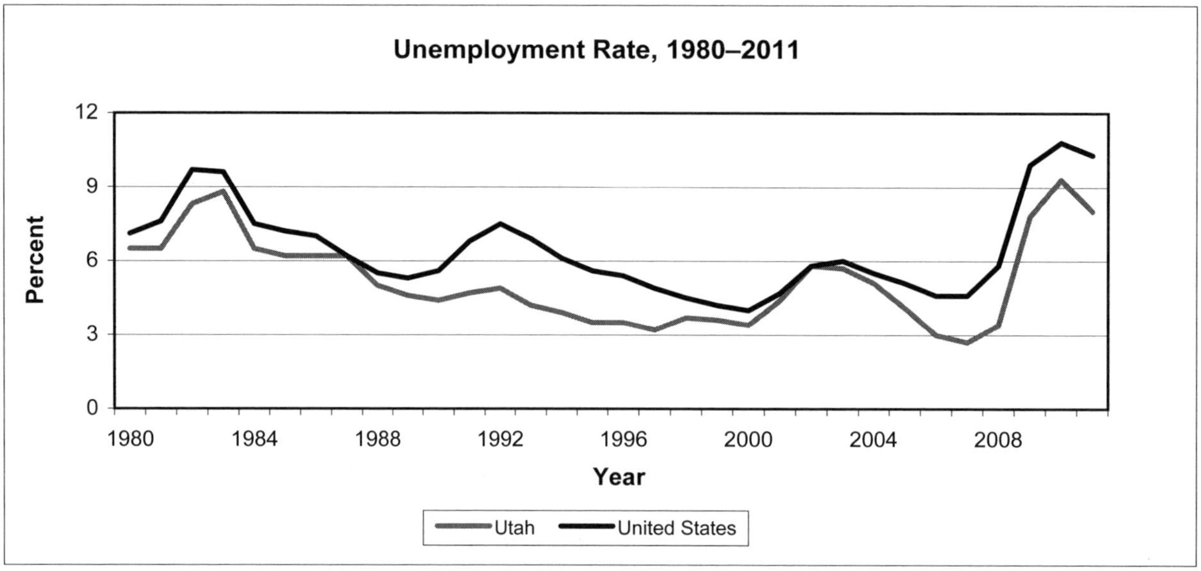

Table UT-2. Marital Status

(Number, percent distribution.)

Sex, age, race, and Hispanic origin	2000	2010	2011
Males, 15 Years and Over	813,693	1,014,706	1,031,388
Never married	30.6	31.3	32.5
Now married, except separated	59.5	58.0	56.3
Separated	1.1	1.3	1.3
Widowed	1.6	1.8	1.6
Divorced	7.3	7.6	8.3
Females, 15 Years and Over	852,995	1,019,010	1,033,823
Never married	25.2	25.8	25.9
Now married, except separated	58.0	56.6	56.1
Separated	1.4	1.6	1.9
Widowed	6.6	5.8	5.6
Divorced	8.8	10.1	10.5

Table UT-3. Households and Housing Characteristics

(Number, percent, dollars.)

Item	2000	2010	2011	Average annual percent change, 2000–2011
Total Households	701,281	880,025	884,253	2.2
Family households	535,294	665,964	662,478	2.0
Married-couple family	442,931	543,212	534,006	1.7
Other family	92,363	122,752	128,472	3.3
Male householder, no wife present	26,422	37,258	38,126	3.7
Female householder, no husband present	65,941	85,494	90,346	3.1
Nonfamily households	165,987	214,061	221,775	2.8
Householder living alone	124,756	164,863	175,353	3.4
Householder not living alone	41,231	49,198	46,422	1.0
Housing Characteristics				
Total housing units	768,594	981,821	993,125	2.4
Occupied housing units	701,281	880,025	884,253	2.2
Owner occupied	501,547	615,142	613,499	1.9
Renter occupied	188,734	264,883	270,754	3.6
Average size	3.13	3.10	3.13	-
Financial Characteristics				
Median gross rent of renter-occupied housing	597	796	822	3.1
Median monthly owner costs for housing units with a mortgage	1,102	1,433	1,418	2.4
Median value of owner-occupied housing units	146,100	217,200	207,500	3.5

- = Zero or rounds to zero.

Table UT-4. Migration, Origin, and Language

(Number, percent.)

Characteristic	State			U.S.		
	2010	2011	Percent change	2010	2011	Percent change
Residence 1 Year Ago						
Population 1 year and over	2,724,064	2,769,627	1.7	305,628,607	307,900,319	0.7
Same house	82.3	82.9	0.7	84.6	84.8	0.2
Different house in the U.S.	17.1	16.6	-2.9	14.8	14.6	-1.4
Same county	11.3	10.5	-7.1	9.4	9.2	-2.1
Different county	5.8	6.1	5.2	5.4	5.4	-
Same state	2.9	3.0	3.4	3.2	3.1	-3.1
Different state	2.9	3.1	6.9	2.2	2.3	4.5
Abroad	0.6	0.5	-16.7	0.6	0.6	-
Place of Birth						
Native born	2,553,831	2,579,179	1.0	269,393,835	271,214,059	0.7
Male	50.3	50.4	0.2	49.2	49.2	-
Female	49.7	49.6	-0.2	50.8	50.8	-
Foreign born	222,638	238,043	6.9	39,955,854	40,377,860	1.1
Male	50.4	49.6	-1.6	49.1	48.9	-0.4
Female	49.6	50.4	1.6	50.9	51.1	0.4
Foreign born; naturalized U.S. citizen	74,756	86,081	15.1	17,476,082	18,140,192	3.8
Male	45.1	47.0	4.2	45.8	45.8	-
Female	54.9	53.0	-3.5	54.2	54.2	-
Foreign born; not a U.S. citizen	147,882	151,962	2.8	22,479,772	22,237,668	-1.1
Male	53.2	51.0	-4.1	51.6	51.5	-0.2
Female	46.8	49.0	4.7	48.4	48.5	0.2
Entered 2000 or later	37.7	40.0	6.1	34.7	35.7	2.9
Entered 1990 to 1999	31.4	32.8	4.5	27.2	26.7	-1.8
Entered before 1990	30.9	27.3	-11.7	38.1	37.6	-1.3
World Region of Birth, Foreign						
Foreign-born population, excluding population born at sea	222,638	238,043	6.9	39,955,673	40,377,757	1.1
Europe	11.1	11.5	3.6	12.1	12.1	-
Asia	16.8	16.7	-0.6	28.2	28.6	1.4
Africa	2.9	2.7	-6.9	4	4.1	2.5
Oceania	3.7	3.6	-2.7	0.5	0.5	-
Latin America	62.3	61.5	-1.3	53.1	52.6	-0.9
North America	3.2	4.0	25.0	2	2.0	-
Language Spoken at Home and Ability to Speak English						
Population 5 years and over	2,512,866	2,554,924	1.7	289,215,746	291,524,091	0.8
English only	85.8	85.1	-0.8	79.4	79.2	-0.3
Language other than English	14.2	14.9	4.9	20.6	20.8	1.0
Speaks English less than "very well"	5.4	5.3	-1.9	8.7	8.7	-

- = Zero or rounds to zero.

Table UT-5. Median Income and Poverty Status, 2011

(Number, percent, except as noted.)

Characteristic	State Number	State Percent	U.S. Number	U.S. Percent
Median Income				
Households (dollars)	55,869	X	50,502	X
Families (dollars)	62,809	X	61,455	X
Below Poverty Level (All People)	374,859	13.5	48,452,035	15.9
Sex				
Male	177,414	12.8	21,825,281	14.7
Female	197,445	14.3	26,626,754	17.2
Age				
Under 18 years	138,024	15.9	16,386,500	22.5
Related children under 18 years	135,200	15.6	16,087,074	22.2
18 to 64 years	223,484	13.6	28,335,079	14.8
65 years and over	13,351	5.3	3,730,456	9.3

X = Not applicable.

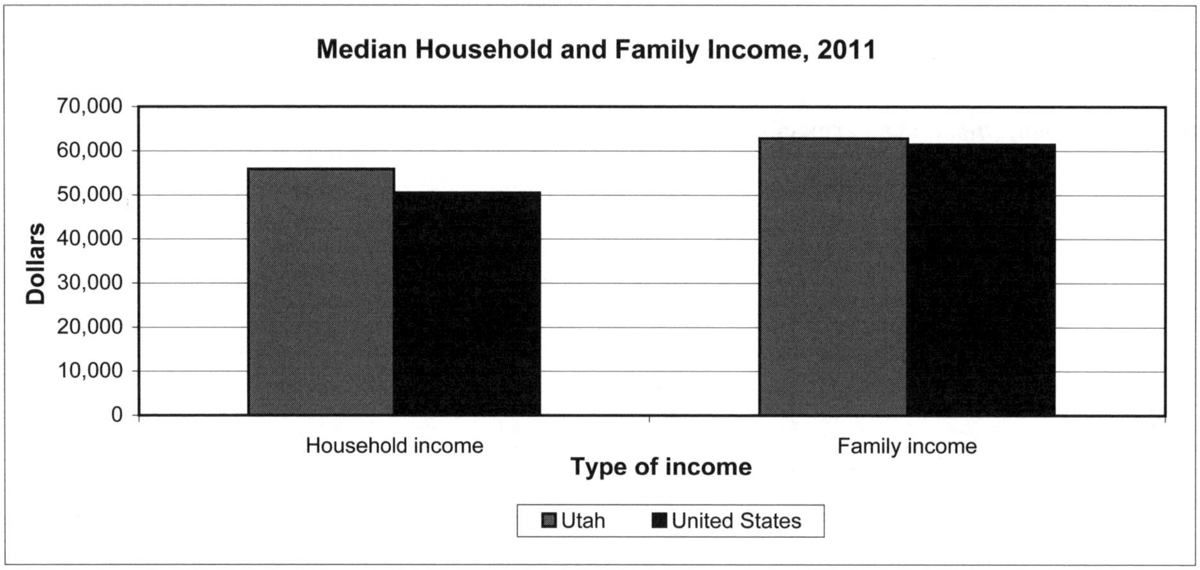

Table UT-6. Health Insurance Coverage Status for the Civilian Noninstitutionalized Population and Children Under 18 Years of Age

(Numbers in thousands, percent.)

Item	2004	2005	2006	2007	2008	2009	2010	2011
Civilian Noninstitutionalized Population	2,393	2,524	2,537	2,657	2,705	2,755	2,750	2,790
Covered by Private or Public Insurance								
Number	2,075	2,110	2,094	2,317	2,286	2,354	2,328	2,364
Percent	86.7	83.6	82.6	87.2	84.5	85.4	84.7	84.7
Not Covered								
Number	318	414	442	340	419	401	422	426
Percent	13.3	16.4	17.4	12.8	15.5	14.6	15.3	15.3
Percent in the U.S. not covered	14.9	15.3	15.8	15.3	15.1	15.1	15.5	15.1
Children Under 18 Years of Age	773	762	801	832	849	869	870	878
Covered by Private or Public Insurance								
Number	693	668	681	746	738	780	775	781
Percent	89.7	87.7	85.0	89.6	86.9	89.7	89.1	88.9
Not Covered								
Number	79	94	120	87	111	89	95	97
Percent	10.3	12.3	15.0	10.4	13.1	10.3	10.9	11.1
Percent in the U.S. not covered	10.5	10.9	11.7	11.0	9.7	8.6	8.0	7.5

Table UT-7. Employment Status by Demographic Group, Preliminary 2012

(Numbers in thousands, percent.)

Characteristic	Civilian noninstitutional population	Civilian labor force		Employed		Unemployed	
		Number	Percent of population	Number	Percent of population	Number	Percent of population
Total	2,028	1,365	67.3	1,285	63.4	80	5.8
Sex							
Male	1,005	768	76.5	721	71.8	47	6.1
Female	1,023	597	58.3	564	55.1	33	5.5
Race, Sex, and Hispanic Origin							
White	1,886	1,275	67.6	1,205	63.9	71	5.5
Male	935	721	77.2	680	72.7	42	5.8
Female	951	554	58.2	525	55.2	29	5.2
Black or African American	NA	NA	NA	NA	NA	NA	NA
Male	NA	NA	NA	NA	NA	NA	NA
Female	NA	NA	NA	NA	NA	NA	NA
Hispanic	245	174	71.1	160	65.4	14	7.9
Male	129	102	79.2	93	72.2	9	8.8
Female	116	72	62.1	67	57.9	5	6.7
Age							
16 to 19 years	179	84	46.6	66	37.0	17	20.7
20 to 24 years	215	173	80.5	160	74.3	13	7.7
25 to 34 years	432	344	79.5	329	76.2	14	4.1
35 to 44 years	373	301	80.7	290	77.7	11	3.6
45 to 54 years	283	227	80.4	214	75.7	13	5.8
55 to 64 years	266	185	69.5	176	66.0	9	5.0
65 years and over	279	52	18.6	50	17.9	2	3.5

NOTE: Data in Table 7 are from the Current Population Survey (CPS) and do not match the estimates in Table 8. See notes and definitions for further information.
NA = Not available.

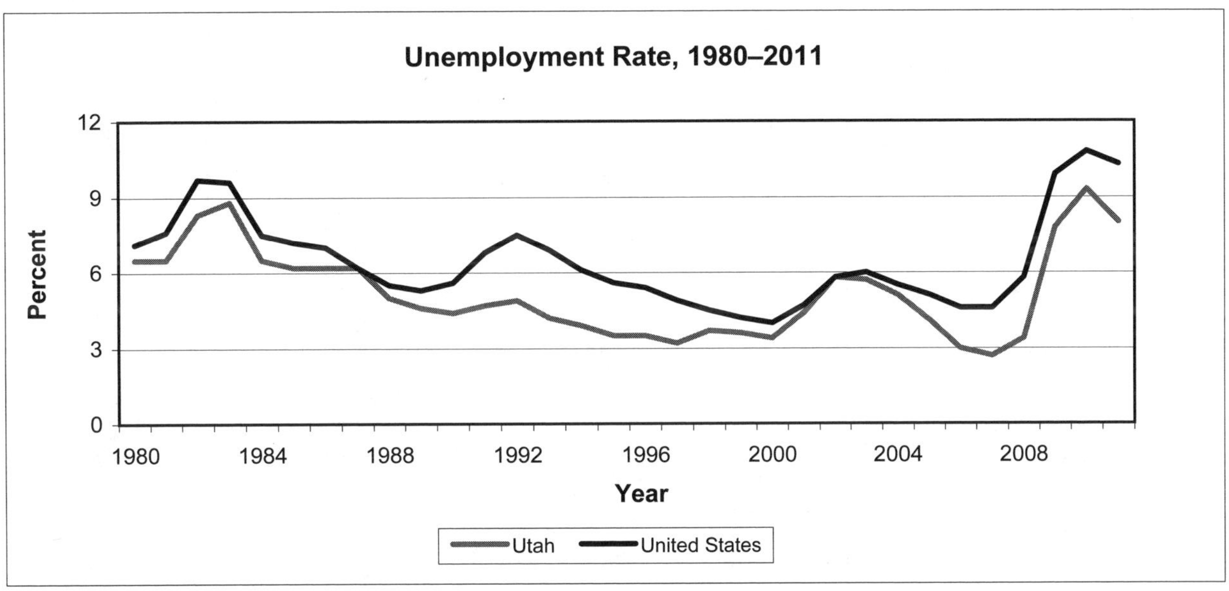

Table UT-8. Employment Status of the Civilian Noninstitutional Population Age 16 Years and Over

(Number, percent.)

Year	Civilian labor force	Civilian participation rate	Employed	Unemployed	Unemployment rate
2005	1,280,038	71.8	1,226,922	53,116	4.1
2006	1,320,504	71.8	1,281,029	39,475	3.0
2007	1,356,550	71.5	1,319,784	36,766	2.7
2008	1,383,743	71.1	1,336,156	47,587	3.4
2009	1,380,269	69.1	1,271,981	108,188	7.8
2010	1,355,406	68.2	1,229,064	126,342	9.3
2011	1,370,085	67.8	1,260,806	109,279	8.0

Table UT-9. Employment and Average Wages by Industry

(Estimates before 2007 are based on the 2002 *North American Industry Classification System* [NAICS]. Estimates from 2007 onward are based on the 2007 NAICS.)

Industry	2005	2006	2007	2008	2009	2010	2011
	Number of jobs						
Wage and Salary Employment by Industry	1,201,884	1,260,325	1,310,226	1,311,608	1,247,606	1,241,818	1,268,399
Farm Wage and Salary Employment	4,929	5,063	4,486	4,713	4,542	4,814	4,406
Nonfarm Wage and Salary Employment	1,196,955	1,255,262	1,305,740	1,306,895	1,243,064	1,237,004	1,263,993
Private wage and salary employment	976,794	1,032,507	1,080,328	1,078,399	1,011,524	1,002,726	1,026,412
Forestry, fishing, and related activities	1,180	1,220	1,330	1,382	1,345	1,416	1,520
Mining	8,454	10,129	11,147	12,538	10,661	10,377	11,594
Utilities	3,941	4,042	4,116	4,152	4,138	4,063	4,020
Construction	84,881	98,779	107,457	94,065	73,808	68,344	68,728
Manufacturing	118,555	122,351	127,071	125,310	112,322	110,493	113,063
Durable goods manufacturing	80,397	83,097	87,208	84,643	73,484	71,763	74,057
Nondurable goods manufacturing	38,158	39,254	39,863	40,667	38,838	38,730	39,006
Wholesale trade	43,908	45,362	47,549	48,489	45,518	44,329	46,413
Retail trade	137,034	142,721	149,607	150,693	143,176	140,395	140,822
Transportation and warehousing	43,619	45,536	47,108	47,263	44,387	43,566	45,111
Information	30,999	31,029	29,143	29,633	28,441	28,184	28,366
Finance and insurance	52,213	55,232	57,591	57,218	55,562	53,534	54,128
Real estate and rental and leasing	17,054	18,211	19,004	18,706	17,314	17,051	17,247
Professional, scientific, and technical services	55,897	61,823	65,664	69,048	66,306	66,276	69,200
Management of companies and enterprises	17,248	17,509	18,459	18,575	17,631	16,747	16,759
Administrative and waste services	70,789	74,994	78,741	74,471	65,477	69,473	73,645
Educational services	30,607	32,526	34,865	36,706	37,869	39,440	40,781
Health care and social assistance	99,149	103,487	108,005	113,600	116,693	119,358	121,951
Arts, entertainment, and recreation	16,618	17,512	18,333	17,880	17,726	17,724	18,363
Accommodation and food services	88,576	92,073	95,730	98,236	94,413	94,375	96,696
Other services, except public administration	56,072	57,971	59,408	60,434	58,737	57,581	58,005
Government and government enterprises	220,161	222,755	225,412	228,496	231,540	234,278	237,581
	Dollars						
Average Wages and Salaries by Industry	34,058	35,828	37,697	38,692	39,319	40,174	41,105
Average Farm Wages and Salaries	29,433	28,881	37,146	34,123	39,314	32,225	36,531
Average Nonfarm Wages and Salaries	34,077	35,856	37,699	38,708	39,319	40,205	41,121
Average private wages and salaries	33,992	35,882	37,748	38,652	39,162	40,273	41,292
Forestry, fishing, and related activities	20,613	22,975	25,381	25,229	25,462	26,348	26,901
Mining	57,997	63,270	68,266	70,405	66,927	70,788	74,076
Utilities	72,699	80,680	80,223	81,494	83,143	87,092	87,564
Construction	32,982	36,112	38,204	39,977	41,563	42,876	43,528
Manufacturing	40,892	43,108	45,274	47,864	49,081	50,872	51,558
Durable goods manufacturing	42,784	45,250	47,679	50,955	52,739	54,604	55,385
Nondurable goods manufacturing	36,905	38,572	40,012	41,429	42,159	43,958	44,293
Wholesale trade	47,887	51,201	54,101	54,896	54,677	55,743	58,575
Retail trade	23,855	25,289	26,710	26,213	26,129	26,850	27,280
Transportation and warehousing	40,325	40,368	45,031	42,733	42,455	43,839	44,729
Information	47,234	46,434	48,899	49,037	50,251	53,670	57,933
Finance and insurance	48,469	50,496	52,386	52,538	53,399	55,963	58,425
Real estate and rental and leasing	31,700	34,334	36,183	35,780	35,628	36,662	38,749
Professional, scientific, and technical services	51,587	53,842	57,318	59,646	60,220	60,855	62,758
Management of companies and enterprises	59,868	64,545	66,759	68,704	70,365	80,746	78,792
Administrative and waste services	23,355	25,060	26,586	27,890	28,582	28,863	29,656
Educational services	24,482	25,494	25,777	26,326	26,558	27,559	28,441
Health care and social assistance	33,487	35,419	36,222	37,112	38,548	38,536	39,100
Arts, entertainment, and recreation	21,424	23,770	25,158	24,260	24,477	25,277	25,180
Accommodation and food services	14,187	15,081	16,266	16,298	15,971	16,567	17,056
Other services, except public administration	32,756	33,619	34,661	36,713	38,518	40,508	40,876
Government and government enterprises	34,457	35,738	37,464	38,977	40,005	39,914	40,384

Table UT-10. Employment Characteristics by Family Type

(Number, percent.)

Family type and labor force status	2009		2010		2011	
	Total	Families with own children under 18 years	Total	Families with own children under 18 years	Total	Families with own children under 18 years
All families	648,732	341,128	665,964	348,660	662,478	339,646
Family type and labor force status						
Married-couple families	532,818	276,256	543,212	280,917	534,006	267,353
Both husband and wife in labor force	53.6	57.9	52.3	57.0	51.3	55.0
Husband in labor force, wife not in labor force	29.2	39.0	29.7	39.8	29.7	41.4
Wife in labor force, husband not in labor force	4.7	2.2	5.3	2.3	5.5	2.6
Both husband and wife not in labor force	12.5	0.9	12.7	0.9	13.4	1.1
Other families	115,914	64,872	122,752	67,743	128,472	72,293
Female householder, no husband present	70.0	72.1	69.6	72.1	70.3	74.7
In labor force	53.2	62.1	53.0	61.1	52.4	63.5
Not in labor force	16.8	10.0	16.6	11.0	17.9	11.2
Male householder, no wife present	30.0	27.9	30.4	27.9	29.7	25.3
In labor force	25.5	26.4	26.0	26.4	24.8	24.0
Not in labor force	4.5	1.5	4.3	1.6	4.9	1.3

Table UT-11. School Enrollment and Educational Attainment, 2011

(Number, percent.)

Item	State	U.S.
Enrollment		
Total population 3 years and over, enrolled in school	926,365	83,131,910
Enrolled in nursery school or preschool (percent)	6.4	6.0
Enrolled in kindergarten (percent)	5.5	5.1
Enrolled in elementary school, grades 1-8 (percent)	41.3	39.5
Enrolled in high school, grades 9-12 (percent)	18.8	20.7
Enrolled in college or graduate school (percent)	28.0	28.7
Attainment		
Total population 25 years and over	1,608,668	206,471,670
Less than ninth grade (percent)	3.2	6.0
9th to 12th grade, no diploma (percent)	6.5	8.1
High school graduate, including equivalency (percent)	23.7	28.4
Some college, no degree (percent)	27.7	21.2
Associate's degree (percent)	9.2	7.8
Bachelor's degree (percent)	20.1	17.9
Graduate or professional degree (percent)	9.7	10.6
High school graduate or higher (percent)	90.3	85.9
Bachelor's degree or higher (percent)	29.7	28.5

Table UT-12. Educational Indicators

(Number, percent; data derived from National Center of Education Statistics.)

Item	State	U.S.
Public Schools, 2009–2010 (except where noted)		
Number of school districts	41	13,629
Number of schools	1,046	99,834
Number of students (in thousands)	583	49,373
Student-teacher ratio	22.9	15.4
Expenditures per student (dollars)	8,102	10,591
Averaged freshman graduation rate, 2008–2009	79.4	75.5[1]
Dropout rate, 2008–2009	3.3	4.1
Students eligible for free or reduced-price lunch (percent)	38.3	48.0
English language learners, 2010–2011 (percent)	7.7	9.8[1]
Students with IEP (percent)	11.6	13.1
Private Schools, 2009–2010 (except where noted)		
Number of schools	185	33,366
Number of students (in thousands)	18	4,700
High school graduates, 2008–2009	1,270	308,813
Student-teacher ratio	9.8	10.7

[1] U.S. total includes estimates for nonreporting states.

Table UT-13. Reported Voting and Registration of the Voting-Age Population, November 2012

(Numbers in thousands, percent.)

Item	Total population	Total citizen population	Registered			Voted		
			Total registered	Percent registered (total population)	Percent registered (total citizen population)	Total voted	Percent voted (total population)	Percent voted (total citizen population)
U.S. Total	235,248	215,081	153,157	65.1	71.2	132,948	56.5	61.8
State Total	1,917	1,793	1,138	59.4	63.5	1,022	53.3	57.0
Sex								
Male	940	869	543	57.8	62.4	494	52.6	56.9
Female	977	924	595	60.9	64.4	528	54.0	57.1
Race								
White alone	1,780	1,683	1,089	61.2	64.7	989	55.6	58.8
White, non-Hispanic alone	1,561	1,546	1,030	66.0	66.6	943	60.4	61.0
Black alone	23	18	9	B	B	9	B	B
Asian alone	57	37	20	B	B	12	B	B
Hispanic (of any race)	233	151	61	26.1	40.1	49	20.9	32.1
Age								
18 to 24 years	279	263	115	41.2	43.7	97	34.8	36.9
25 to 44 years	803	714	418	52.1	58.5	355	44.2	49.7
45 to 64 years	592	576	396	67.0	68.8	375	63.4	65.1
65 to 74 years	141	138	118	83.8	85.5	111	78.9	80.5
75 years and over	101	101	90	88.9	88.9	84	82.5	82.5

B = Base is less than 75,000 and therefore too small to show the derived measure.

Table UT-14. Crime

(Number, rate per 100,000. Data are derived from the FBI Uniform Crime Reports.)

Item	State			U.S.		
	2010	2011	Percent change	2010	2011	Percent change
TOTAL POPULATION	2,775,479	2,817,222	1.5	309,330,219	311,591,917	0.7
VIOLENT CRIME						
Number	5,925	5,494	-7.3	1,251,248	1,203,564	-3.8
Rate	213.5	195.0	-8.7	404.5	386.3	-4.5
Murder and Nonnegligent Manslaughter						
Number	53	54	1.9	14,722	14,612	-0.7
Rate	1.9	1.9	0.0	4.8	4.7	-2.1
Forcible Rape						
Number	983	854	-13.1	85,593	83,425	-2.5
Rate	35.4	30.3	-14.4	27.7	26.8	-3.2
Robbery						
Number	1,269	1,081	-14.8	369,089	354,396	-4.0
Rate	45.7	38.4	-16.0	119.3	113.7	-4.7
Aggravated Assault						
Number	3,620	3,505	-3.2	781,844	751,131	-3.9
Rate	130.4	124.4	-4.6	252.8	241.1	-4.6
PROPERTY CRIME						
Number	88,316	83,758	-5.2	9,112,625	9,063,173	-0.5
Rate	3,182.0	2,973.1	-6.6	2,945.9	2,908.7	-1.3
Burglary						
Number	15,095	13,122	-13.1	2,168,459	2,188,005	0.9
Rate	543.9	465.8	-14.4	701.0	702.2	0.2
Larceny-Theft						
Number	67,242	64,453	-4.1	6,204,601	6,159,795	-0.7
Rate	2,422.7	2,287.8	-5.6	2,005.8	1,976.9	-1.4
Motor Vehicle Theft						
Number	5,979	6,183	3.4	739,565	715,373	-3.3
Rate	215.4	219.5	1.9	239.1	229.6	-4.0

Table UT-15. State Government Finances, 2011

(Dollar amounts in thousands, percent distribution.)

Item	Dollars	Percent distribution
Total Revenue	16,984,797	100.0
General revenue	13,834,601	81.5
Intergovernmental revenue	4,364,882	25.7
Taxes	5,475,904	32.2
General sales	1,843,856	10.9
Selective sales	699,376	4.1
License taxes	284,996	1.7
Individual income tax	2,298,220	13.5
Corporate income tax	247,661	1.5
Other taxes	101,795	0.6
Current charges	2,955,511	17.4
Miscellaneous general revenue	1,038,304	6.1
Utility revenue	0	0.0
Liquor stores revenue	250,241	1.5
Insurance trust revenue [1]	2,899,955	17.1
Total Expenditure	16,682,581	100.0
Intergovernmental expenditure	3,106,230	18.6
Direct expenditure	13,576,351	81.4
Current operation	8,841,878	53.0
Capital outlay	1,913,474	11.5
Insurance benefits and repayments	1,790,077	10.7
Assistance and subsidies	755,983	4.5
Interest on debt	274,939	1.6
Exhibit: Salaries and wages	2,715,369	16.3
Total Expenditure	16,682,581	100.0
General expenditure	14,708,284	88.2
Intergovernmental expenditure	3,106,230	18.6
Direct expenditure	11,602,054	69.5
General expenditure, by function:		
Education	6,516,379	39.1
Public welfare	2,812,493	16.9
Hospitals	955,956	5.7
Health	349,500	2.1
Highways	1,514,147	9.1
Police protection	143,677	0.9
Correction	297,609	1.8
Natural resources	177,299	1.1
Parks and recreation	44,743	0.3
Governmental administration	800,404	4.8
Interest on general debt	274,939	1.6
Other and unallocable	821,138	4.9
Utility expenditure	0	0.0
Liquor stores expenditure	184,220	1.1
Insurance trust expenditure	1,790,077	10.7
Debt at End of Fiscal Year	7,205,779	X
Cash and Security Holdings	27,064,212	X

X = Not applicable.
[1] Within insurance trust revenue, net earnings of state retirement systems is a calculated statistic (the item code in the data file is X08), and thus can be positive or negative. Net earnings is the sum of earnings on investments plus gains on investments minus losses on investments. The change made in 2002 for asset valuation from book to market value in accordance with Statement 34 of the Governmental Accounting Standards Board is reflected in the calculated statistics.

Table UT-16. State Government Tax Collections, 2012

(Dollars in thousands, percent.)

Item	Dollars	Percent distribution
Total Taxes	5,809,953	100.0
Property taxes	0	0.0
Sales and gross receipts	2,722,128	46.9
General sales and gross receipts	1,857,035	32.0
Selective sales and gross receipts	865,093	14.9
Alcoholic beverages	45,823	0.8
Amusements	0	0.0
Insurance premiums	104,443	1.8
Motor fuels	372,212	6.4
Pari-mutuels	0	0.0
Public utilities	25,824	0.4
Tobacco products	123,988	2.1
Other selective sales	192,803	3.3
Licenses	255,677	4.4
Alcoholic beverages	1,936	-
Amusements	0	0.0
Corporations in general	547	-
Hunting and fishing	28,720	0.5
Motor vehicle	158,169	2.7
Motor vehicle operators	14,987	0.3
Public utilities	0	0.0
Occupation and business, NEC	47,698	0.8
Other licenses	3,620	0.1
Income taxes	2,725,073	46.9
Individual income	2,466,495	42.5
Corporation net income	258,578	4.5
Other taxes	107,075	1.8
Death and gift	0	0.0
Documentary and stock transfer	0	0.0
Severance	107,075	1.8
Taxes, NEC	0	0.0

- = Rounds to zero.

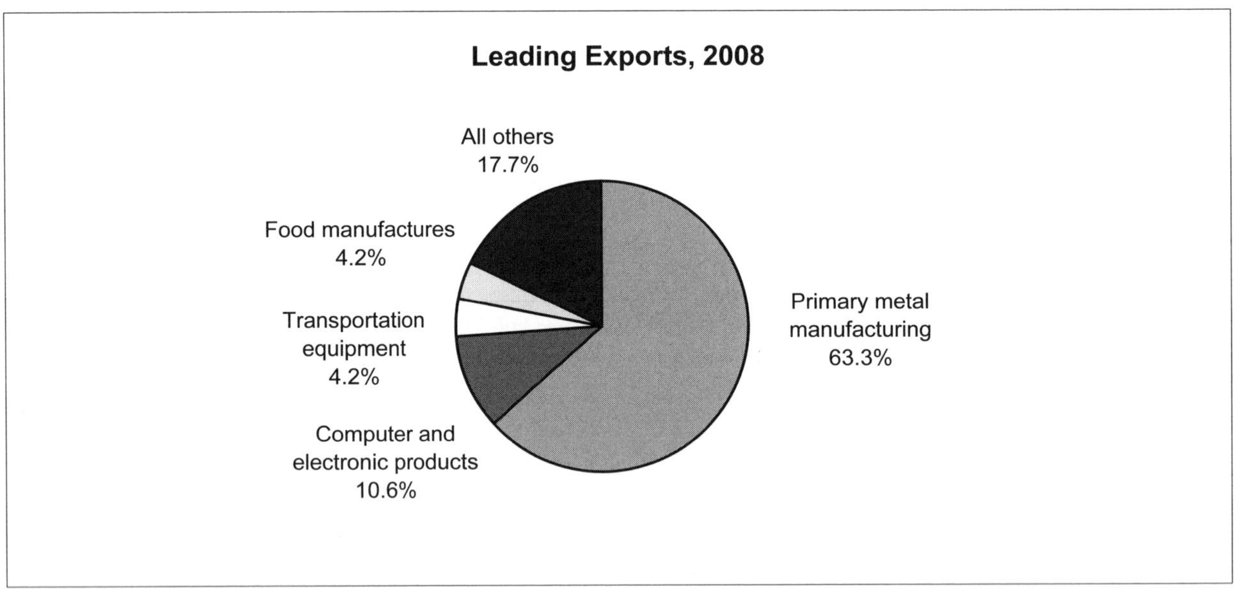

VERMONT

Facts and Figures

Location: Northeastern United States; bordered on the N by Canada (Quebec), on the E by New Hampshire, on the S by Massachusetts, and on the W by New York

Area: 9,614 sq. mi. (24,901 sq. km.); rank—45th

Population: 626,011 (2012 est.); rank—50th

Principal Cities: capital—Montpelier; largest—Burlington

Statehood: March 4, 1791; the 14th state

U.S. Congress: 2 senators, 1 representative

State Motto: Freedom and Unity

State Song: "These Green Mountains"

State Nickname: The Green Mountain State

Abbreviations: VT; Vt.

State Symbols: flower—red clover; tree—sugar maple; bird—hermit thrush

At a Glance

- With an increase in population of 2.1 percent, Vermont ranked 47th among the states in growth from 2000 to 2009.
- An estimated 4,700 marriages took place in Vermont in 200, compared to 2,100 divorces.
- Vermont's median household income in 2011 was $52,776, and 11.5 percent of the population lived below the poverty level in 2007.
- In the 2012 election, 63.3 percent of Vermont's eligible voters voted, compared to 61.8 percent of eligible voters nationwide.
- In 2007, Vermont exported $47 million worth of agricultural products, less than 1 percent of the U.S. total.

Table VT-1. Population by Age, Sex, Race, and Hispanic Origin

(Number, percent, except where noted.)

Sex, age, race, and Hispanic origin	2000	2010	2012[1]	Average annual percent change, 2010–2012
Total Population	608,827	625,741	626,011	-
Percent of total U.S. population	0.2	0.2	0.2	X
Sex				
Male	298,337	308,206	308,778	0.1
Female	310,490	317,535	317,233	-
Age				
Under 5 years	33,989	31,952	30,521	-1.6
5 to 19 years	132,268	118,323	115,486	-0.8
20 to 64 years	365,060	384,388	381,560	-0.2
65 years and over	77,510	91,078	98,444	2.5
Median age (years)	37.7	41.5	42.3	0.6
Race and Hispanic Origin				
One race				
White	589,208	598,592	597,050	-0.1
Black	3,063	6,456	6,879	2.0
American Indian and Alaska Native	2,420	2,308	2,280	-0.4
Asian	5,217	8,069	8,912	3.2
Native Hawaiian or Other Pacific Islander	141	175	203	4.6
Two or more races	7,335	10,141	10,687	1.7
Hispanic (of any race)	5,504	9,962	10,894	2.9

X = Not applicable.
- = Zero or rounds to zero.
[1] Population figures for 2012 are July 1 estimates. The 2010 estimates are taken from the 2010 Census.

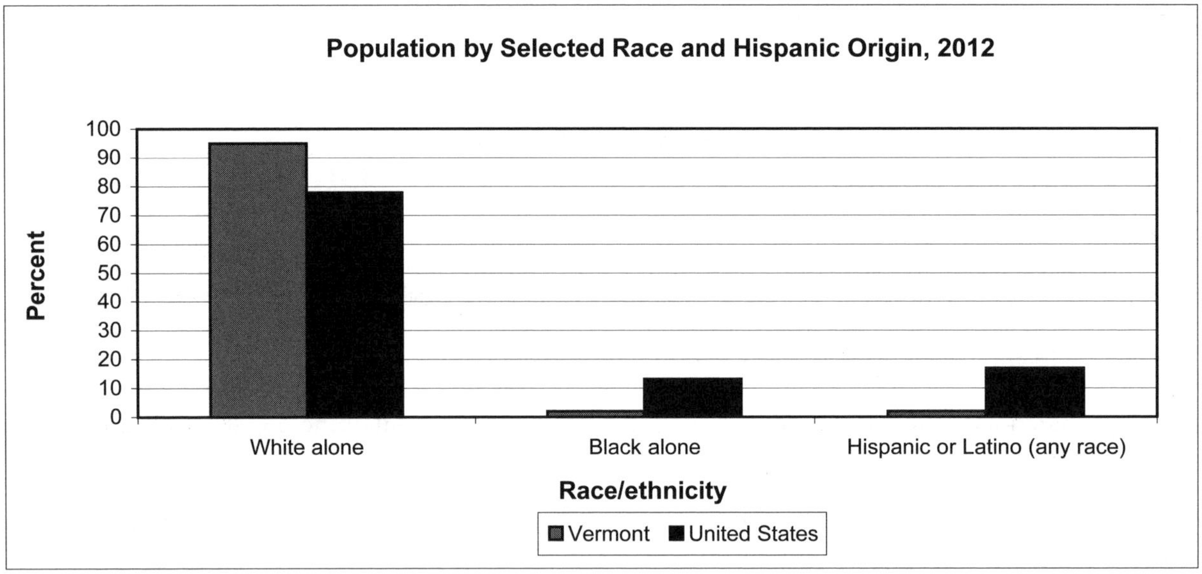

Table VT-2. Marital Status

(Number, percent distribution.)

Sex, age, race, and Hispanic origin	2000	2010	2011
Males, 15 Years and Over	236,517	254,288	256,055
Never married	29.7	34.2	33.8
Now married, except separated	57.1	51.3	52.0
Separated	1.2	1.3	0.9
Widowed	2.4	2.5	2.0
Divorced	9.6	10.7	11.3
Females, 15 Years and Over	251,764	266,860	268,534
Never married	23.9	27.7	27.8
Now married, except separated	53.3	49.7	49.9
Separated	1.4	1.4	1.3
Widowed	10.0	8.2	8.2
Divorced	11.5	13.0	12.8

Table VT-3. Households and Housing Characteristics

(Number, percent, dollars.)

Item	2000	2010	2011	Average annual percent change, 2000–2011
Total Households	240,634	256,922	257,358	0.6
Family households	157,763	159,846	161,619	0.2
Married-couple family	126,413	125,678	128,267	0.1
Other family	31,350	34,168	33,352	0.5
Male householder, no wife present	9,078	10,887	11,331	2.1
Female householder, no husband present	22,272	23,281	22,021	-0.1
Nonfamily households	82,871	97,076	95,739	1.3
Householder living alone	63,112	75,243	71,136	1.1
Householder not living alone	19,759	21,833	24,603	2.0
Housing Characteristics				
Total housing units	294,382	322,698	324,385	0.8
Occupied housing units	240,634	256,922	257,358	0.6
Owner occupied	169,784	180,847	183,452	0.7
Renter occupied	70,850	76,075	73,906	0.4
Average size	2.44	2.34	2.34	-0.3
Financial Characteristics				
Median gross rent of renter-occupied housing	553	823	849	4.5
Median monthly owner costs for housing units with a mortgage	1,021	1,445	1,487	3.8
Median value of owner-occupied housing units	111,500	216,800	213,700	7.6

Table VT-4. Migration, Origin, and Language

(Number, percent.)

Characteristic	State			U.S.		
	2010	2011	Percent change	2010	2011	Percent change
Residence 1 Year Ago						
Population 1 year and over	619,363	621,354	0.3	305,628,607	307,900,319	0.7
Same house	86.4	86.5	0.1	84.6	84.8	0.2
Different house in the U.S.	13.2	13.1	-0.8	14.8	14.6	-1.4
Same county	7.6	7.6	-	9.4	9.2	-2.1
Different county	5.6	5.4	-3.6	5.4	5.4	-
Same state	1.9	2.1	10.5	3.2	3.1	-3.1
Different state	3.6	3.3	-8.3	2.2	2.3	4.5
Abroad	0.5	0.5	-	0.6	0.6	-
Place of Birth						
Native born	598,400	602,188	0.6	269,393,835	271,214,059	0.7
Male	49.4	49.5	0.2	49.2	49.2	-
Female	50.6	50.5	-0.2	50.8	50.8	-
Foreign born	27,560	24,243	-12.0	39,955,854	40,377,860	1.1
Male	45.1	41.8	-7.3	49.1	48.9	-0.4
Female	54.9	58.2	6.0	50.9	51.1	0.4
Foreign born; naturalized U.S. citizen	16,594	14,836	-10.6	17,476,082	18,140,192	3.8
Male	42.8	40.7	-4.9	45.8	45.8	-
Female	57.2	59.3	3.7	54.2	54.2	-
Foreign born; not a U.S. citizen	10,966	9,407	-14.2	22,479,772	22,237,668	-1.1
Male	48.5	43.7	-9.9	51.6	51.5	-0.2
Female	51.5	56.3	9.3	48.4	48.5	0.2
Entered 2000 or later	36.1	28.7	-20.5	34.7	35.7	2.9
Entered 1990 to 1999	25.7	22.5	-12.5	27.2	26.7	-1.8
Entered before 1990	38.2	48.8	27.7	38.1	37.6	-1.3
World Region of Birth, Foreign						
Foreign-born population, excluding population born at sea	27,560	24,243	-12.0	39,955,673	40,377,757	1.1
Europe	30.5	30.3	-0.7	12.1	12.1	-
Asia	28.1	25.6	-8.9	28.2	28.6	1.4
Africa	7.6	6.2	-18.4	4	4.1	2.5
Oceania	0.4	0.9	125.0	0.5	0.5	-
Latin America	10.1	12.3	21.8	53.1	52.6	-0.9
North America	23.4	24.7	5.6	2	2.0	-
Language Spoken at Home and Ability to Speak English						
Population 5 years and over	593,692	595,658	0.3	289,215,746	291,524,091	0.8
English only	94.4	95.1	0.7	79.4	79.2	-0.3
Language other than English	5.6	4.9	-12.5	20.6	20.8	1.0
Speaks English less than "very well"	1.8	1.4	-22.2	8.7	8.7	-

- = Zero or rounds to zero.

Table VT-5. Median Income and Poverty Status, 2011

(Number, percent, except as noted.)

Characteristic	State		U.S.	
	Number	Percent	Number	Percent
Median Income				
Households (dollars)	52,776	X	50,502	X
Families (dollars)	66,190	X	61,455	X
Below Poverty Level (All People)	69,075	11.5	48,452,035	15.9
Sex				
Male	30,978	10.5	21,825,281	14.7
Female	38,097	12.5	26,626,754	17.2
Age				
Under 18 years	18,263	14.9	16,386,500	22.5
Related children under 18 years	17,299	14.2	16,087,074	22.2
18 to 64 years	44,485	11.5	28,335,079	14.8
65 years and over	6,327	7.0	3,730,456	9.3

X = Not applicable.

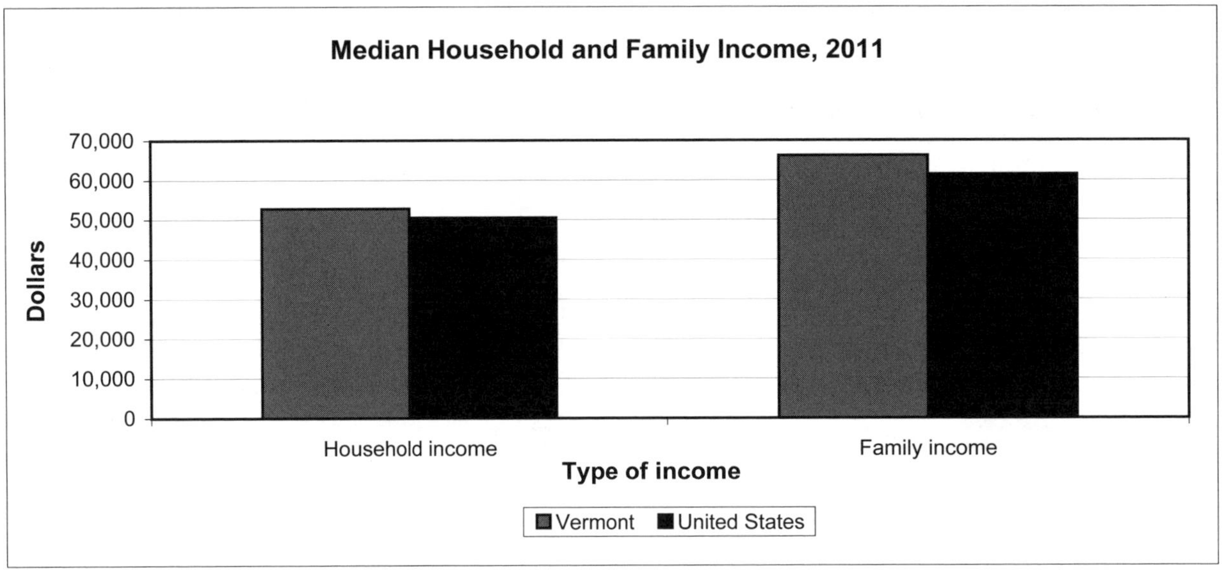

Table VT-6. Health Insurance Coverage Status for the Civilian Noninstitutionalized Population and Children Under 18 Years of Age

(Numbers in thousands, percent.)

Item	2004	2005	2006	2007	2008	2009	2010	2011
Civilian Noninstitutionalized Population	617	622	620	614	615	615	620	620
Covered by Private or Public Insurance								
Number	552	550	557	545	559	562	570	579
Percent	89.5	88.5	89.8	88.8	90.9	91.4	92.0	93.4
Not Covered								
Number	65	72	63	69	56	53	50	41
Percent	10.5	11.5	10.2	11.2	9.1	8.6	8.0	6.6
Percent in the U.S. not covered	14.9	15.3	15.8	15.3	15.1	15.1	15.5	15.1
Children Under 18 Years of Age	134	133	133	129	129	126	130	126
Covered by Private or Public Insurance								
Number	128	126	122	117	124	122	127	123
Percent	95.3	94.7	92.0	90.6	96.1	96.8	98.0	97.6
Not Covered								
Number	6	7	11	12	5	4	3	3
Percent	4.7	5.3	8.0	9.4	3.9	3.2	2.0	2.4
Percent in the U.S. not covered	10.5	10.9	11.7	11.0	9.7	8.6	8.0	7.5

Table VT-7. Employment Status by Demographic Group, Preliminary 2012

(Numbers in thousands, percent.)

Characteristic	Civilian noninstitutional population	Civilian labor force		Employed		Unemployed	
		Number	Percent of population	Number	Percent of population	Number	Percent of population
Total	513	356	69.5	338	65.9	18	5.1
Sex							
Male	250	183	73.0	173	69.1	10	5.4
Female	262	173	66.1	165	62.9	8	4.9
Race, Sex, and Hispanic Origin							
White	488	338	69.2	321	65.8	16	4.9
Male	239	174	72.7	165	68.9	9	5.1
Female	250	164	65.9	157	62.9	8	4.6
Black or African American	NA	NA	NA	NA	NA	NA	NA
Male	NA	NA	NA	NA	NA	NA	NA
Female	NA	NA	NA	NA	NA	NA	NA
Hispanic	NA	NA	NA	NA	NA	NA	NA
Male	NA	NA	NA	NA	NA	NA	NA
Female	NA	NA	NA	NA	NA	NA	NA
Age							
16 to 19 years	35	16	45.8	13	37.8	3	17.7
20 to 24 years	39	28	72.7	25	65.1	3	10.5
25 to 34 years	76	65	85.3	61	80.6	4	5.5
35 to 44 years	77	68	88.1	66	85.4	2	3.1
45 to 54 years	103	88	86.2	85	82.9	3	3.8
55 to 64 years	91	70	76.2	67	73.6	2	3.4
65 years and over	93	22	23.6	21	22.3	1	5.6

NOTE: Data in Table 7 are from the Current Population Survey (CPS) and do not match the estimates in Table 8. See notes and definitions for further information.
NA = Not available.

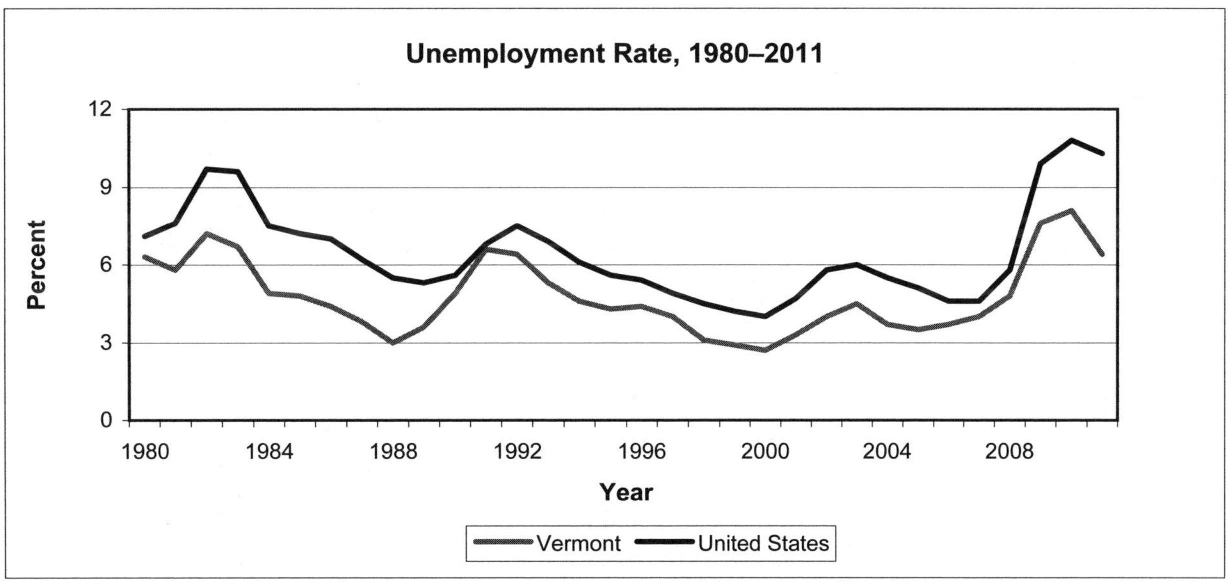

Table VT-8. Employment Status of the Civilian Noninstitutional Population Age 16 Years and Over

(Number, percent.)

Year	Civilian labor force	Civilian participation rate	Employed	Unemployed	Unemployment rate
2005	349,093	70.5	336,849	12,244	3.5
2006	355,463	71.3	342,204	13,259	3.7
2007	353,992	70.6	339,945	14,047	4.0
2008	355,432	70.6	338,517	16,915	4.8
2009	351,341	68.6	324,467	26,874	7.6
2010	350,829	68.3	322,432	28,397	8.1
2011	349,718	67.8	327,302	22,416	6.4

Table VT-9. Employment and Average Wages by Industry

(Estimates before 2007 are based on the 2002 *North American Industry Classification System* [NAICS]. Estimates from 2007 onward are based on the 2007 NAICS.)

Industry	2005	2006	2007	2008	2009	2010	2011
	Number of jobs						
Wage and Salary Employment by Industry	320,101	322,438	322,306	321,435	311,317	312,230	314,778
Farm Wage and Salary Employment	2,475	2,251	2,163	2,359	2,276	2,282	2,420
Nonfarm Wage and Salary Employment	317,626	320,187	320,143	319,076	309,041	309,948	312,358
Private wage and salary employment	262,126	264,187	263,884	262,280	251,913	252,545	255,425
Forestry, fishing, and related activities	779	803	796	801	886	903	950
Mining	695	835	834	740	650	594	611
Utilities	1,703	1,725	1,738	1,699	1,756	1,801	1,801
Construction	17,516	18,050	17,494	16,221	14,400	14,201	14,835
Manufacturing	36,819	36,163	35,949	34,790	31,153	30,853	30,948
Durable goods manufacturing	26,455	26,217	26,165	25,179	22,088	21,787	21,628
Nondurable goods manufacturing	10,364	9,946	9,784	9,611	9,065	9,066	9,320
Wholesale trade	10,213	10,594	10,602	10,347	9,675	9,634	9,687
Retail trade	41,052	40,992	40,646	40,675	38,854	38,709	38,661
Transportation and warehousing	7,318	7,211	7,173	7,101	6,763	6,896	7,191
Information	6,241	6,069	5,949	5,777	5,510	5,369	4,945
Finance and insurance	9,943	10,024	9,897	9,618	9,373	9,348	9,370
Real estate and rental and leasing	3,360	3,375	3,403	3,388	3,157	3,093	3,066
Professional, scientific, and technical services	13,025	13,488	13,616	13,728	13,450	13,795	13,881
Management of companies and enterprises	308	198	201	735	778	893	1,417
Administrative and waste services	8,814	8,755	8,811	8,995	8,424	8,867	9,705
Educational services	13,807	14,058	13,886	13,785	13,641	13,683	13,916
Health care and social assistance	42,700	43,753	45,353	46,670	47,664	47,699	47,799
Arts, entertainment, and recreation	3,929	3,952	3,996	3,994	3,866	3,880	3,981
Accommodation and food services	29,423	29,703	29,172	29,080	28,145	28,853	29,023
Other services, except public administration	14,481	14,439	14,368	14,136	13,768	13,474	13,638
Government and government enterprises	55,500	56,000	56,259	56,796	57,128	57,403	56,933
	Dollars						
Average Wages and Salaries by Industry	33,572	34,906	36,405	37,682	38,085	38,735	39,541
Average Farm Wages and Salaries	21,832	27,671	32,749	28,809	28,367	26,723	22,544
Average Nonfarm Wages and Salaries	33,664	34,957	36,429	37,748	38,157	38,823	39,672
Average private wages and salaries	33,181	34,478	35,951	37,110	37,411	38,141	39,048
Forestry, fishing, and related activities	24,827	25,417	26,275	28,313	27,828	28,373	29,278
Mining	41,655	50,600	52,637	53,784	55,386	55,665	54,286
Utilities	80,917	80,493	87,365	88,943	87,929	92,295	92,736
Construction	36,299	37,979	39,984	41,293	41,697	42,705	43,287
Manufacturing	46,369	47,796	49,241	50,530	51,677	53,103	53,784
Durable goods manufacturing	49,857	51,315	53,076	54,343	56,034	57,401	58,356
Nondurable goods manufacturing	37,464	38,519	38,986	40,541	41,061	42,774	43,174
Wholesale trade	45,839	46,975	47,874	50,397	51,531	52,483	54,634
Retail trade	23,773	24,301	24,815	25,291	25,572	25,990	26,772
Transportation and warehousing	33,610	34,971	36,152	36,821	36,804	37,304	37,830
Information	39,583	41,039	42,995	44,230	45,173	45,091	49,309
Finance and insurance	54,711	55,944	61,802	64,673	61,497	62,219	64,123
Real estate and rental and leasing	29,611	29,855	31,269	32,135	32,853	33,356	34,472
Professional, scientific, and technical services	52,055	57,160	57,171	59,530	60,257	63,808	64,562
Management of companies and enterprises	63,068	56,949	53,114	79,751	77,545	78,471	78,258
Administrative and waste services	25,363	26,469	28,559	29,521	30,555	28,779	29,257
Educational services	26,104	27,148	28,677	30,689	31,420	30,674	31,054
Health care and social assistance	32,280	33,930	35,150	36,793	37,601	38,420	39,255
Arts, entertainment, and recreation	20,089	22,119	23,119	22,383	22,841	23,529	23,643
Accommodation and food services	17,965	18,206	20,070	19,587	19,387	19,802	20,710
Other services, except public administration	22,145	22,737	23,678	24,985	25,123	25,701	26,235
Government and government enterprises	35,941	37,216	38,674	40,695	41,444	41,826	42,474

Table VT-10. Employment Characteristics by Family Type

(Number, percent.)

Family type and labor force status	2009		2010		2011	
	Total	Families with own children under 18 years	Total	Families with own children under 18 years	Total	Families with own children under 18 years
All families	159,445	69,687	159,846	65,676	161,619	66,084
Family type and labor force status						
Married-couple families	125,522	47,258	125,678	45,063	128,267	44,516
Both husband and wife in labor force	62.2	77.4	60.7	77.1	61.4	78.1
Husband in labor force, wife not in labor force	14.4	16.0	15.7	17.0	13.7	16.9
Wife in labor force, husband not in labor force	8.7	4.2	7.9	3.1	8.2	4.1
Both husband and wife not in labor force	14.8	2.4	15.8	2.8	16.7	0.9
Other families	33,923	22,429	34,168	20,613	33,352	21,568
Female householder, no husband present	70.9	73.4	68.1	71.2	66.0	69.1
In labor force	52.0	58.8	50.3	57.2	48.3	54.3
Not in labor force	19.0	14.6	17.8	14.0	17.8	14.9
Male householder, no wife present	29.1	26.6	31.9	28.8	34.0	30.9
In labor force	24.7	25.2	26.6	26.3	27.0	27.5
Not in labor force	4.4	1.4	5.3	2.5	7.0	3.4

Table VT-11. School Enrollment and Educational Attainment, 2011

(Number, percent.)

Item	State	U.S.
Enrollment		
Total population 3 years and over, enrolled in school	155,911	83,131,910
Enrolled in nursery school or preschool (percent)	5.3	6.0
Enrolled in kindergarten (percent)	3.9	5.1
Enrolled in elementary school, grades 1-8 (percent)	36.3	39.5
Enrolled in high school, grades 9-12 (percent)	20.3	20.7
Enrolled in college or graduate school (percent)	34.2	28.7
Attainment		
Total population 25 years and over	434,652	206,471,670
Less than ninth grade (percent)	2.8	6.0
9th to 12th grade, no diploma (percent)	5.5	8.1
High school graduate, including equivalency (percent)	30.2	28.4
Some college, no degree (percent)	17.8	21.2
Associate's degree (percent)	8.4	7.8
Bachelor's degree (percent)	21.4	17.9
Graduate or professional degree (percent)	14	10.6
High school graduate or higher (percent)	91.8	85.9
Bachelor's degree or higher (percent)	35.4	28.5

Table VT-12. Educational Indicators

(Number, percent; data derived from National Center of Education Statistics.)

Item	State	U.S.
Public Schools, 2009–2010 (except where noted)		
Number of school districts	291	13,629
Number of schools	323	99,834
Number of students (in thousands)	92	49,373
Student-teacher ratio	10.6	15.4
Expenditures per student (dollars)	17,007	10,591
Averaged freshman graduation rate, 2008–2009	89.6	75.5[1]
Dropout rate, 2008–2009	2.6	4.1
Students eligible for free or reduced-price lunch (percent)	36.8	48.0
English language learners, 2010–2011 (percent)	1.9[2]	9.8[1]
Students with IEP (percent)	15.3	13.1
Private Schools, 2009–2010 (except where noted)		
Number of schools	119	33,366
Number of students (in thousands)	10	4,700
High school graduates, 2008–2009	1,167	308,813
Student-teacher ratio	7.2	10.7

[1] U.S. total includes estimates for nonreporting states.
[2] Imputation for survey nonresponse. State-level imputations were based on the percentages reported by the state for other years applied to the enrollment for the given year.

Table VT-13. Reported Voting and Registration of the Voting-Age Population, November 2012

(Numbers in thousands, percent.)

Item	Total population	Total citizen population	Registered			Voted		
			Total registered	Percent registered (total population)	Percent registered (total citizen population)	Total voted	Percent voted (total population)	Percent voted (total citizen population)
U.S. Total	235,248	215,081	153,157	65.1	71.2	132,948	56.5	61.8
State Total	496	487	357	72.0	73.4	308	62.1	63.3
Sex								
Male	241	237	168	69.8	70.7	146	60.6	61.4
Female	255	249	189	74.2	75.9	162	63.5	65.0
Race								
White alone	470	464	341	72.6	73.5	293	62.4	63.2
White, non-Hispanic alone	466	461	339	72.8	73.6	291	62.5	63.2
Black alone	5	5	3	B	B	3	B	B
Asian alone	7	4	4	B	B	3	B	B
Hispanic (of any race)	6	5	3	B	B	3	B	B
Age								
18 to 24 years	61	59	30	B	B	23	B	B
25 to 44 years	147	144	94	64.1	65.7	77	52.0	53.3
45 to 64 years	195	193	153	78.8	79.6	133	68.5	69.2
65 to 74 years	49	47	40	B	B	39	B	B
75 years and over	44	44	39	B	B	36	B	B

B = Base is less than 75,000 and therefore too small to show the derived measure.

Table VT-14. Crime

(Number, rate per 100,000. Data are derived from the FBI Uniform Crime Reports.)

Item	State			U.S.		
	2010	2011	Percent change	2010	2011	Percent change
TOTAL POPULATION	625,909	626,431	0.1	309,330,219	311,591,917	0.7
VIOLENT CRIME						
Number	820	847	3.3	1,251,248	1,203,564	-3.8
Rate	131.0	135.2	3.2	404.5	386.3	-4.5
Murder and Nonnegligent Manslaughter						
Number	7	8	14.3	14,722	14,612	-0.7
Rate	1.1	1.3	18.2	4.8	4.7	-2.1
Forcible Rape						
Number	141	119	-15.6	85,593	83,425	-2.5
Rate	22.5	19.0	-15.6	27.7	26.8	-3.2
Robbery						
Number	76	85	11.8	369,089	354,396	-4.0
Rate	12.1	13.6	12.4	119.3	113.7	-4.7
Aggravated Assault						
Number	596	635	6.5	781,844	751,131	-3.9
Rate	95.2	101.4	6.5	252.8	241.1	-4.6
PROPERTY CRIME						
Number	14,160	14,464	2.1	9,112,625	9,063,173	-0.5
Rate	2,262.3	2,309.0	2.1	2,945.9	2,908.7	-1.3
Burglary						
Number	3,348	3,643	8.8	2,168,459	2,188,005	0.9
Rate	534.9	581.5	8.7	701.0	702.2	0.2
Larceny-Theft						
Number	10,373	10,322	-0.5	6,204,601	6,159,795	-0.7
Rate	1,657.3	1,647.7	-0.6	2,005.8	1,976.9	-1.4
Motor Vehicle Theft						
Number	439	499	13.7	739,565	715,373	-3.3
Rate	70.1	79.7	13.7	239.1	229.6	-4.0

Table VT-15. State Government Finances, 2011

(Dollar amounts in thousands, percent distribution.)

Item	Dollars	Percent distribution
Total Revenue	6,506,203	100.0
General revenue	5,627,897	86.5
Intergovernmental revenue	2,035,378	31.3
Taxes	2,687,926	41.3
General sales	325,622	5.0
Selective sales	578,446	8.9
License taxes	99,870	1.5
Individual income tax	556,013	8.5
Corporate income tax	105,077	1.6
Other taxes	1,022,898	15.7
Current charges	606,611	9.3
Miscellaneous general revenue	297,982	4.6
Utility revenue	0	0.0
Liquor stores revenue	46,973	0.7
Insurance trust revenue [1]	831,333	12.8
Total Expenditure	5,853,842	100.0
Intergovernmental expenditure	1,552,853	26.5
Direct expenditure	4,300,989	73.5
Current operation	3,294,655	56.3
Capital outlay	319,259	5.5
Insurance benefits and repayments	417,185	7.1
Assistance and subsidies	144,081	2.5
Interest on debt	125,809	2.1
Exhibit: Salaries and wages	762,976	13.0
Total Expenditure	5,853,842	100.0
General expenditure	5,390,621	92.1
Intergovernmental expenditure	1,552,853	26.5
Direct expenditure	3,837,768	65.6
General expenditure, by function:		
Education	2,322,901	39.7
Public welfare	1,462,903	25.0
Hospitals	20,260	0.3
Health	190,986	3.3
Highways	419,173	7.2
Police protection	90,175	1.5
Correction	128,356	2.2
Natural resources	78,892	1.3
Parks and recreation	18,367	0.3
Governmental administration	137,715	2.4
Interest on general debt	125,809	2.1
Other and unallocable	395,084	6.7
Utility expenditure	0	0.0
Liquor stores expenditure	46,036	0.8
Insurance trust expenditure	417,185	7.1
Debt at End of Fiscal Year	3,485,346	X
Cash and Security Holdings	7,198,185	X

X = Not applicable.

[1] Within insurance trust revenue, net earnings of state retirement systems is a calculated statistic (the item code in the data file is X08), and thus can be positive or negative. Net earnings is the sum of earnings on investments plus gains on investments minus losses on investments. The change made in 2002 for asset valuation from book to market value in accordance with Statement 34 of the Governmental Accounting Standards Board is reflected in the calculated statistics.

Table VT-16. State Government Tax Collections, 2012

(Dollars in thousands, percent.)

Item	Dollars	Percent distribution
Total Taxes	2,757,370	100.0
Property taxes	948,749	34.4
Sales and gross receipts	968,303	35.1
General sales and gross receipts	342,085	12.4
Selective sales and gross receipts	626,218	22.7
Alcoholic beverages	22,403	0.8
Amusements	0	0.0
Insurance premiums	59,000	2.1
Motor fuels	108,177	3.9
Pari-mutuels	0	0.0
Public utilities	13,267	0.5
Tobacco products	80,230	2.9
Other selective sales	343,141	12.4
Licenses	101,161	3.7
Alcoholic beverages	391	-
Amusements	35	-
Corporations in general	2,023	0.1
Hunting and fishing	6,502	0.2
Motor vehicle	64,294	2.3
Motor vehicle operators	7,963	0.3
Public utilities	0	0.0
Occupation and business, NEC	18,103	0.7
Other licenses	1,850	0.1
Income taxes	695,029	25.2
Individual income	598,450	21.7
Corporation net income	96,579	3.5
Other taxes	44,128	1.6
Death and gift	13,335	0.5
Documentary and stock transfer	26,334	1.0
Severance	0	0.0
Taxes, NEC	4,459	0.2

- = Rounds to zero.

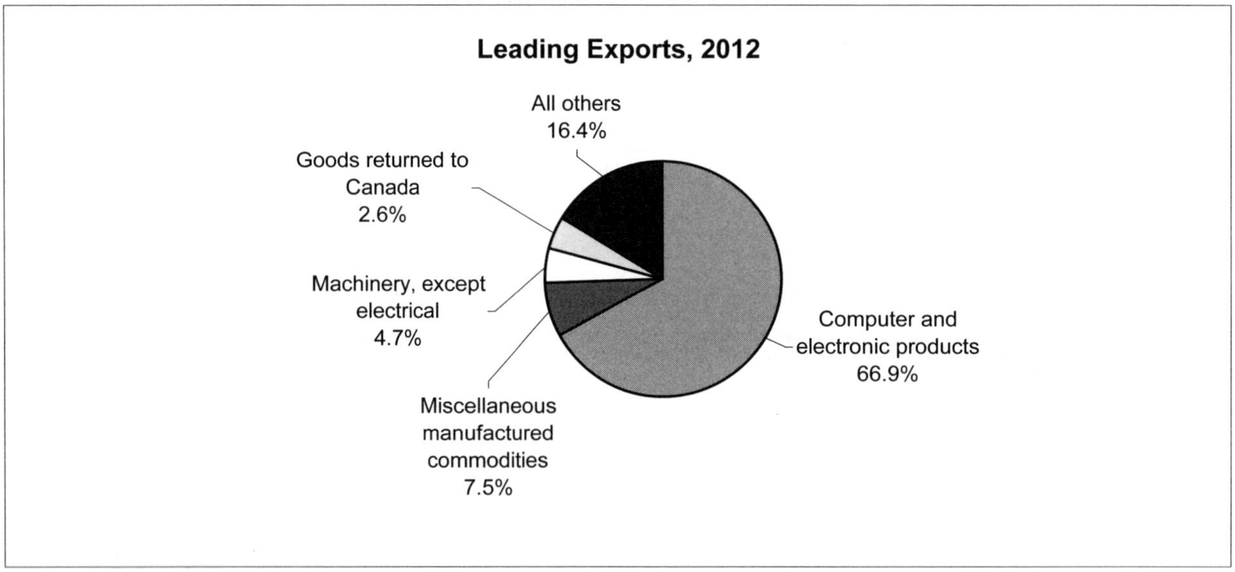

VIRGINIA

Facts and Figures

Location: Eastern United States; bordered on the N and NE by Maryland and the District of Columbia, on the E by the Atlantic Ocean, on the S by North Carolina and Tennessee, and on the W by Kentucky and West Virginia

Area: 42,774 sq. mi. (110,785 sq. km.); rank—35th

Population: 8,185,867 (2012 est.); rank—12th

Principal Cities: capital—Richmond; largest—Virginia Beach

Statehood: June 25, 1788; 10th state

U.S. Congress: 2 senators, 11 representatives

State Motto: *Sic semper tyrannis* ("Thus always to tyrants")

State Song: "Carry Me Back to Old Virginia"; the Virginia General Assembly (legislature) is in the process of selecting a new state song

State Nickname: The Old Dominion State

Abbreviations: VA; Va.

State Symbols: flower—flowering dogwood; tree—flowering dogwood; bird—cardinal

At a Glance

- With an increase in population of 11.4 percent, Virginia ranked 7th among the states in growth from 2000 to 2009.
- An estimated 54,100 marriages took place in Virginia in 2009, compared to 28,500 divorces.
- Virginia's violent crime rate in 2011 was 196.7 per 100,000 population, compared to 386.6 for the entire nation.
- In the 2012 election, 66.9 percent of Virginia's eligible voters voted, compared to 61.8 percent of eligible voters nationwide.
- In 2007, Virginia exported $622 million worth of agricultural products, less than 1 percent of the U.S. total.

Table VA-1. Population by Age, Sex, Race, and Hispanic Origin

(Number, percent, except where noted.)

Sex, age, race, and Hispanic origin	2000	2010	2012[1]	Average annual percent change, 2010–2012
Total Population	7,078,515	8,001,024	8,185,867	0.8
Percent of total U.S. population	2.5	2.6	2.6	X
Sex				
Male	3,471,895	3,925,983	4,021,525	0.8
Female	3,606,620	4,075,041	4,164,342	0.7
Age				
Under 5 years	461,982	509,625	509,602	-
5 to 19 years	1,475,104	1,574,060	1,577,474	0.1
20 to 64 years	4,349,096	4,940,402	5,036,286	0.6
65 years and over	79,233	976,937	1,062,505	2.7
Median age (years)	35.7	37.5	37.6	0.1
Race and Hispanic Origin				
One race				
White	5,120,110	5,725,432	5,818,810	0.5
Black	1,390,293	1,579,414	1,612,713	0.7
American Indian and Alaska Native	21,172	41,525	43,768	1.7
Asian	261,025	449,149	487,505	2.6
Native Hawaiian or Other Pacific Islander	3,946	8,201	8,830	2.4
Two or more races	143,069	197,303	214,241	2.6
Hispanic (of any race)	329,540	660,501	685,712	1.2

X = Not applicable.
- = Zero or rounds to zero.
[1] Population figures for 2012 are July 1 estimates. The 2010 estimates are taken from the 2010 Census.

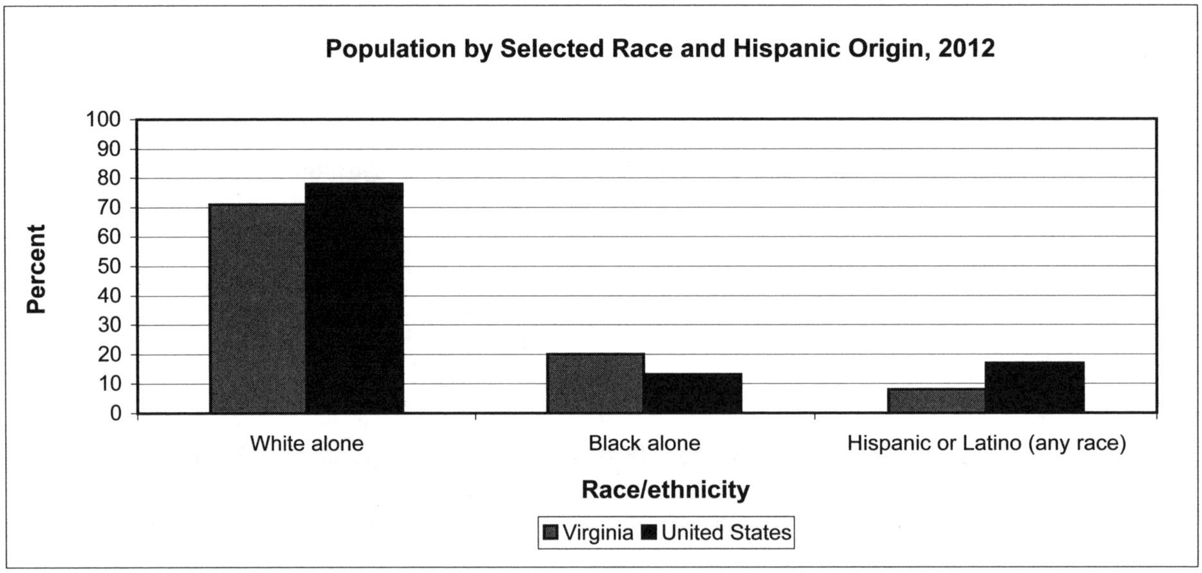

Table VA-2. Marital Status

(Number, percent distribution.)

Sex, age, race, and Hispanic origin	2000	2010	2011
Males, 15 Years and Over	2,724,334	3,156,115	3,191,036
Never married	29.1	34.2	34.7
Now married, except separated	58.2	52.6	52.1
Separated	2.6	2.3	2.3
Widowed	2.3	2.3	2.3
Divorced	7.9	8.5	8.6
Females, 15 Years and Over	2,899,294	3,331,264	3,365,742
Never married	23.5	28.0	28.2
Now married, except separated	53.4	49.0	48.5
Separated	3.2	2.9	2.9
Widowed	9.9	8.7	8.8
Divorced	10.0	11.4	11.6

Table VA-3. Households and Housing Characteristics

(Number, percent, dollars.)

Item	2000	2010	2011	Average annual percent change, 2000–2011
Total Households	2,699,173	2,992,732	2,990,650	0.9
Family households	1,847,796	2,013,520	2,010,914	0.7
Married-couple family	1,426,044	1,517,627	1,518,944	0.5
Other family	421,752	495,893	491,970	1.4
Male householder, no wife present	101,462	124,273	126,534	2.1
Female householder, no husband present	320,290	371,620	365,436	1.2
Nonfamily households	851,377	979,212	979,736	1.3
Householder living alone	676,907	794,535	787,081	1.4
Householder not living alone	174,470	184,677	192,655	0.9
Housing Characteristics				
Total housing units	2,904,192	3,368,674	3,387,801	1.4
Occupied housing units	2,699,173	2,992,732	2,990,650	0.9
Owner occupied	1,837,939	2,025,240	2,013,595	0.8
Renter occupied	861,234	967,492	977,055	1.1
Average size	2.54	2.60	2.63	0.3
Financial Characteristics				
Median gross rent of renter-occupied housing	650	1,019	1,062	5.3
Median monthly owner costs for housing units with a mortgage	1,144	1,728	1,707	4.1
Median value of owner-occupied housing units	125,400	249,100	243,100	7.8

Table VA-4. Migration, Origin, and Language

(Number, percent.)

Characteristic	State			U.S.		
	2010	2011	Percent change	2010	2011	Percent change
Residence 1 Year Ago						
Population 1 year and over	7,930,773	7,996,552	0.8	305,628,607	307,900,319	0.7
Same house	85.1	84.9	-0.2	84.6	84.8	0.2
Different house in the U.S.	14.2	14.3	0.7	14.8	14.6	-1.4
Same county	6.2	6.5	4.8	9.4	9.2	-2.1
Different county	8.0	7.8	-2.5	5.4	5.4	-
Same state	4.7	4.6	-2.1	3.2	3.1	-3.1
Different state	3.3	3.2	-3.0	2.2	2.3	4.5
Abroad	0.6	0.8	33.3	0.6	0.6	-
Place of Birth						
Native born	7,113,498	7,196,361	1.2	269,393,835	271,214,059	0.7
Male	49.2	49.3	0.2	49.2	49.2	-
Female	50.8	50.7	-0.2	50.8	50.8	-
Foreign born	911,119	900,243	-1.2	39,955,854	40,377,860	1.1
Male	48.2	47.9	-0.6	49.1	48.9	-0.4
Female	51.8	52.1	0.6	50.9	51.1	0.4
Foreign born; naturalized U.S. citizen	414,714	423,345	2.1	17,476,082	18,140,192	3.8
Male	46.4	45.8	-1.3	45.8	45.8	-
Female	53.6	54.2	1.1	54.2	54.2	-
Foreign born; not a U.S. citizen	496,405	476,898	-3.9	22,479,772	22,237,668	-1.1
Male	49.7	49.8	0.2	51.6	51.5	-0.2
Female	50.3	50.2	-0.2	48.4	48.5	0.2
Entered 2000 or later	41.6	43.0	3.4	34.7	35.7	2.9
Entered 1990 to 1999	27.3	26.5	-2.9	27.2	26.7	-1.8
Entered before 1990	31.2	30.5	-2.2	38.1	37.6	-1.3
World Region of Birth, Foreign						
Foreign-born population, excluding population born at sea	911,058	900,243	-1.2	39,955,673	40,377,757	1.1
Europe	11.3	11.4	0.9	12.1	12.1	-
Asia	39.7	40.7	2.5	28.2	28.6	1.4
Africa	9.8	9.5	-3.1	4	4.1	2.5
Oceania	0.4	0.4	-	0.5	0.5	-
Latin America	37.1	36.4	-1.9	53.1	52.6	-0.9
North America	1.7	1.6	-5.9	2	2.0	-
Language Spoken at Home and Ability to Speak English						
Population 5 years and over	7,517,185	7,588,188	0.9	289,215,746	291,524,091	0.8
English only	85.2	85.1	-0.1	79.4	79.2	-0.3
Language other than English	14.8	14.9	0.7	20.6	20.8	1.0
Speaks English less than "very well"	5.7	5.5	-3.5	8.7	8.7	-

- = Zero or rounds to zero.

Table VA-5. Median Income and Poverty Status, 2011

(Number, percent, except as noted.)

Characteristic	State		U.S.	
	Number	Percent	Number	Percent
Median Income				
Households (dollars)	61,882	X	50,502	X
Families (dollars)	74,500	X	61,455	X
Below Poverty Level (All People)	905,914	11.5	48,452,035	15.9
Sex				
Male	391,420	10.2	21,825,281	14.7
Female	514,494	12.8	26,626,754	17.2
Age				
Under 18 years	280,115	15.3	16,386,500	22.5
Related children under 18 years	273,819	15.0	16,087,074	22.2
18 to 64 years	552,097	10.9	28,335,079	14.8
65 years and over	73,702	7.5	3,730,456	9.3

X = Not applicable.

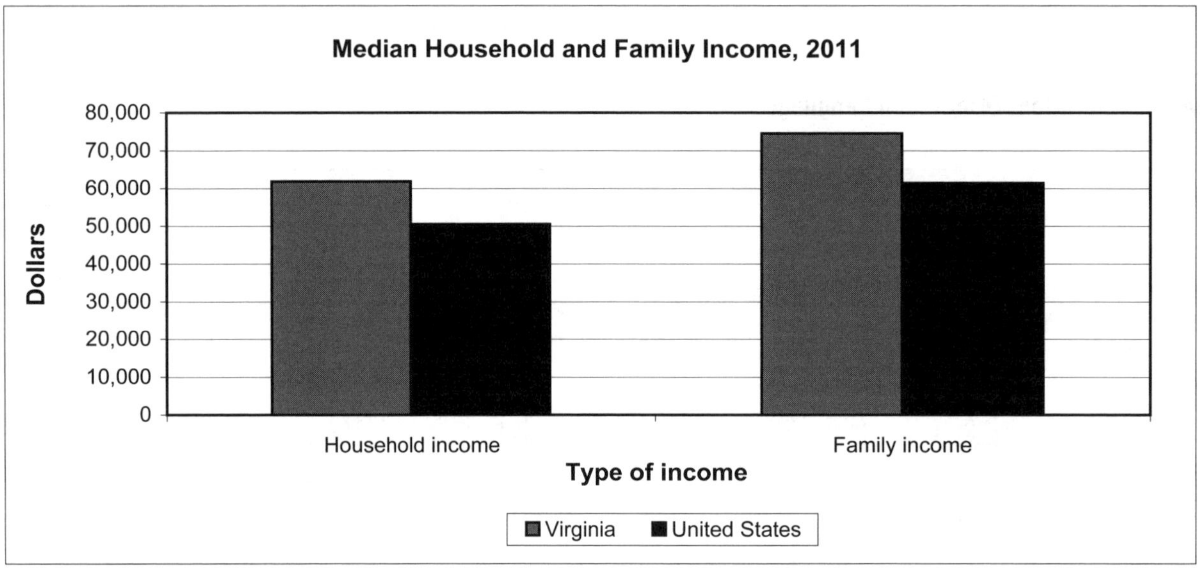

Table VA-6. Health Insurance Coverage Status for the Civilian Noninstitutionalized Population and Children Under 18 Years of Age

(Numbers in thousands, percent.)

Item	2004	2005	2006	2007	2008	2009	2010	2011
Civilian Noninstitutionalized Population	7,386	7,454	7,538	7,684	7,520	7,644	7,807	7,887
Covered by Private or Public Insurance								
Number	6,465	6,503	6,532	6,548	6,621	6,736	6,787	6,904
Percent	87.5	87.2	86.7	85.2	88.0	88.1	86.9	87.5
Not Covered								
Number	922	951	1,006	1,135	899	908	1,020	983
Percent	12.5	12.8	13.3	14.8	12.0	11.9	13.1	12.5
Percent in the U.S. not covered	14.9	15.3	15.8	15.3	15.1	15.1	15.5	15.1
Children Under 18 Years of Age	1,837	1,828	1,827	1,833	1,815	1,843	1,850	1,849
Covered by Private or Public Insurance								
Number	1,705	1,672	1,643	1,646	1,677	1,721	1,729	1,741
Percent	92.8	91.5	89.9	89.8	92.4	93.4	93.4	94.1
Not Covered								
Number	132	156	185	187	138	122	121	108
Percent	7.2	8.5	10.1	10.2	7.6	6.6	6.6	5.9
Percent in the U.S. not covered	10.5	10.9	11.7	11.0	9.7	8.6	8.0	7.5

Table VA-7. Employment Status by Demographic Group, Preliminary 2012

(Numbers in thousands, percent.)

Characteristic	Civilian noninstitutional population	Civilian labor force		Employed		Unemployed	
		Number	Percent of population	Number	Percent of population	Number	Percent of population
Total	6,298	4,184	66.4	3,934	62.5	251	6.0
Sex							
Male	3,008	2,202	73.2	2,078	69.1	124	5.6
Female	3,290	1,982	60.2	1,856	56.4	126	6.4
Race, Sex, and Hispanic Origin							
White	4,626	3,106	67.1	2,950	63.8	156	5.0
Male	2,248	1,675	74.5	1,597	71.0	77	4.6
Female	2,378	1,431	60.2	1,352	56.9	79	5.5
Black or African American	1,179	759	64.3	684	58.0	75	9.9
Male	531	359	67.6	323	60.7	37	10.2
Female	648	400	61.7	361	55.8	38	9.6
Hispanic	385	283	73.5	274	71.0	9	3.3
Male	200	171	85.4	166	83.0	5	2.9
Female	185	112	60.5	108	58.1	4	3.9
Age							
16 to 19 years	448	159	35.6	118	26.4	41	25.9
20 to 24 years	531	390	73.4	339	63.7	51	13.1
25 to 34 years	1,074	896	83.4	840	78.1	56	6.3
35 to 44 years	1,048	903	86.2	872	83.3	31	3.4
45 to 54 years	1,151	953	82.8	913	79.3	40	4.2
55 to 64 years	975	667	68.4	643	66.0	23	3.5
65 years and over	1,071	216	20.2	208	19.5	8	3.6

NOTE: Data in Table 7 are from the Current Population Survey (CPS) and do not match the estimates in Table 8. See notes and definitions for further information.

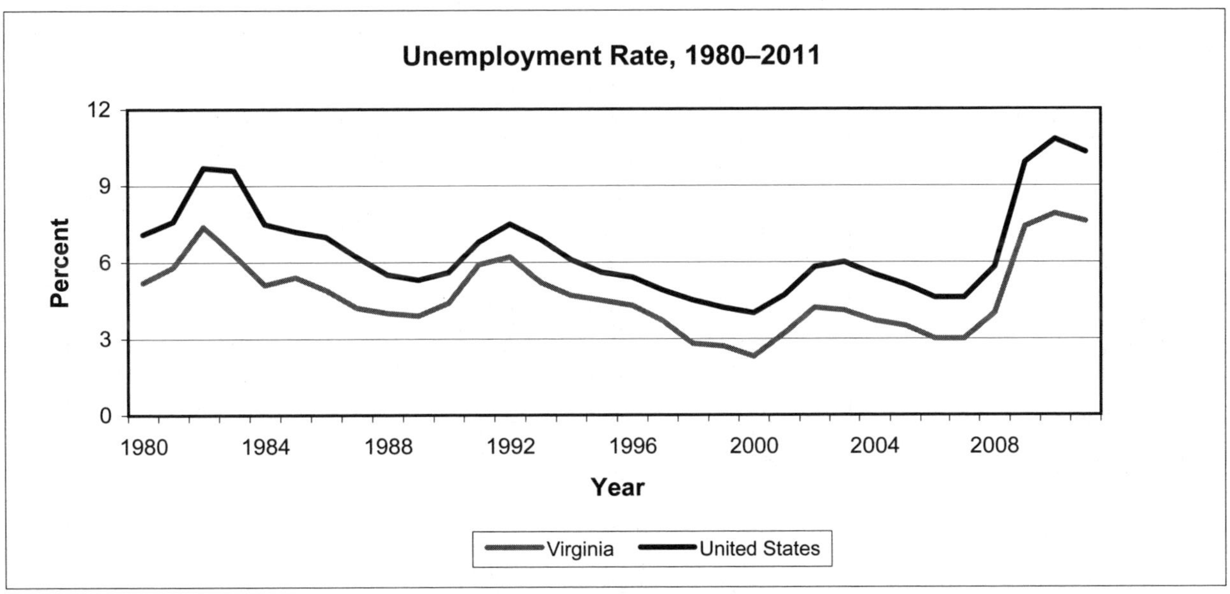

Table VA-8. Employment Status of the Civilian Noninstitutional Population Age 16 Years and Over

(Number, percent.)

Year	Civilian labor force	Civilian participation rate	Employed	Unemployed	Unemployment rate
2005	3,935,250	68.9	3,797,488	137,762	3.5
2006	4,010,565	69.3	3,890,060	120,505	3.0
2007	4,067,520	69.4	3,945,479	122,041	3.0
2008	4,124,766	69.6	3,960,011	164,755	4.0
2009	4,081,593	65.4	3,778,949	302,644	7.4
2010	4,141,905	64.9	3,814,199	327,706	7.9
2011	4,175,698	64.7	3,860,131	315,567	7.6

Table VA-9. Employment and Average Wages by Industry

(Estimates before 2007 are based on the 2002 *North American Industry Classification System* [NAICS]. Estimates from 2007 onward are based on the 2007 NAICS.)

Industry	2005	2006	2007	2008	2009	2010	2011
	Number of jobs						
Wage and Salary Employment by Industry	3,922,024	3,973,298	4,009,016	4,006,870	3,882,095	3,874,473	3,909,375
Farm Wage and Salary Employment	9,775	9,859	9,308	9,264	9,879	13,127	10,085
Nonfarm Wage and Salary Employment	3,912,249	3,963,439	3,999,708	3,997,606	3,872,216	3,861,346	3,899,290
Private wage and salary employment	3,064,114	3,112,309	3,141,107	3,125,203	2,998,974	2,987,308	3,027,512
Forestry, fishing, and related activities	5,467	5,426	5,495	5,452	5,348	5,498	5,694
Mining	8,742	9,459	9,086	9,288	8,489	8,593	9,040
Utilities	10,999	10,939	11,173	11,479	11,448	10,917	10,892
Construction	253,882	259,144	249,949	232,599	199,691	192,176	188,046
Manufacturing	295,662	286,636	276,625	264,666	239,445	230,767	230,872
Durable goods manufacturing	169,291	167,702	161,966	153,764	137,113	132,380	134,413
Nondurable goods manufacturing	126,371	118,934	114,659	110,902	102,332	98,387	96,459
Wholesale trade	118,952	120,794	123,359	121,211	114,278	111,017	113,126
Retail trade	424,662	430,209	433,918	425,957	404,814	404,937	408,642
Transportation and warehousing	112,185	110,352	110,424	109,508	103,624	103,663	104,960
Information	93,675	91,891	91,019	87,883	81,318	76,442	74,404
Finance and insurance	135,231	137,784	135,099	130,268	124,833	124,539	128,440
Real estate and rental and leasing	60,871	60,377	59,896	58,634	56,098	54,237	52,920
Professional, scientific, and technical services	335,054	352,790	365,058	378,425	381,689	387,686	396,367
Management of companies and enterprises	73,392	75,701	78,096	77,465	74,741	73,963	73,355
Administrative and waste services	206,786	210,115	215,152	211,823	193,815	197,862	204,193
Educational services	60,747	63,289	66,153	68,208	68,662	70,827	73,178
Health care and social assistance	327,375	337,902	350,104	364,700	374,283	381,407	389,687
Arts, entertainment, and recreation	45,221	45,969	47,355	48,248	47,108	47,434	48,582
Accommodation and food services	288,647	296,871	302,569	305,294	298,526	298,471	305,160
Other services, except public administration	206,564	206,661	210,577	214,095	210,764	206,872	209,954
Government and government enterprises	848,135	851,130	858,601	872,403	873,242	874,038	871,778
	Dollars						
Average Wages and Salaries by Industry	43,166	45,092	47,221	48,470	49,461	50,948	52,072
Average Farm Wages and Salaries	22,002	25,413	30,939	29,824	25,703	18,648	21,993
Average Nonfarm Wages and Salaries	43,219	45,141	47,259	48,513	49,521	51,057	52,150
Average private wages and salaries	42,593	44,471	46,497	47,667	48,533	50,122	51,372
Forestry, fishing, and related activities	23,928	25,175	26,265	26,746	26,474	27,556	28,453
Mining	53,097	54,798	56,147	60,398	61,570	67,349	70,807
Utilities	77,259	87,002	89,122	91,812	93,856	100,019	100,599
Construction	40,803	42,830	44,536	45,565	46,052	47,559	48,597
Manufacturing	44,889	46,594	48,904	50,193	51,111	53,412	54,527
Durable goods manufacturing	46,040	47,382	50,394	51,970	52,904	55,166	57,091
Nondurable goods manufacturing	43,348	45,483	46,799	47,729	48,710	51,051	50,954
Wholesale trade	59,003	62,393	65,077	66,487	67,121	69,087	72,211
Retail trade	24,759	25,419	25,673	25,823	25,992	26,482	26,853
Transportation and warehousing	40,736	42,744	43,696	45,326	45,935	47,102	48,214
Information	76,313	76,833	76,435	77,818	78,360	80,670	81,724
Finance and insurance	71,363	70,660	73,134	72,672	72,433	75,333	78,514
Real estate and rental and leasing	41,209	43,481	43,703	44,021	43,876	45,192	46,823
Professional, scientific, and technical services	75,155	79,332	84,389	87,808	90,030	93,372	96,059
Management of companies and enterprises	88,650	93,245	100,704	98,278	98,693	103,532	107,867
Administrative and waste services	28,743	30,118	32,391	33,861	35,412	36,980	37,923
Educational services	31,319	33,181	35,833	37,631	39,014	39,727	40,256
Health care and social assistance	38,547	40,194	41,881	43,340	44,110	44,676	45,691
Arts, entertainment, and recreation	22,541	25,815	26,997	26,107	26,084	27,443	26,558
Accommodation and food services	16,568	17,148	18,316	18,100	17,906	18,614	19,030
Other services, except public administration	29,385	30,980	32,301	33,828	34,073	35,211	35,625
Government and government enterprises	45,479	47,592	50,044	51,547	52,916	54,253	54,851

Table VA-10. Employment Characteristics by Family Type

(Number, percent.)

Family type and labor force status	2009		2010		2011	
	Total	Families with own children under 18 years	Total	Families with own children under 18 years	Total	Families with own children under 18 years
All families	1,987,501	900,927	2,013,520	884,969	2,010,914	893,805
Family type and labor force status						
Married-couple families	1,509,508	637,159	1,517,627	617,975	1,518,944	630,339
Both husband and wife in labor force	56.6	66.8	56.3	69.2	55.3	67.2
Husband in labor force, wife not in labor force	22.1	28.8	21.3	26.3	22.3	28.0
Wife in labor force, husband not in labor force	7.1	3.1	7.3	3.3	7.0	3.1
Both husband and wife not in labor force	14.2	1.3	15.0	1.2	15.3	1.7
Other families	477,993	263,768	495,893	266,994	491,970	263,466
Female householder, no husband present	74.1	76.3	74.9	78.0	74.3	76.9
In labor force	55.1	64.8	54.0	65.5	54.6	65.2
Not in labor force	19.0	11.5	20.9	12.5	19.7	11.8
Male householder, no wife present	25.9	23.7	25.1	22.0	25.7	23.1
In labor force	20.9	22.1	20.0	20.0	20.5	21.2
Not in labor force	4.9	1.6	5.1	1.9	5.2	1.9

Table VA-11. School Enrollment and Educational Attainment, 2011

(Number, percent.)

Item	State	U.S.
Enrollment		
Total population 3 years and over, enrolled in school	2,156,250	83,131,910
Enrolled in nursery school or preschool (percent)	5.9	6.0
Enrolled in kindergarten (percent)	5.0	5.1
Enrolled in elementary school, grades 1-8 (percent)	38.1	39.5
Enrolled in high school, grades 9-12 (percent)	19.7	20.7
Enrolled in college or graduate school (percent)	31.2	28.7
Attainment		
Total population 25 years and over	5,418,844	206,471,670
Less than ninth grade (percent)	4.8	6.0
9th to 12th grade, no diploma (percent)	7.3	8.1
High school graduate, including equivalency (percent)	25.6	28.4
Some college, no degree (percent)	20.1	21.2
Associate's degree (percent)	7.0	7.8
Bachelor's degree (percent)	20.5	17.9
Graduate or professional degree (percent)	14.6	10.6
High school graduate or higher (percent)	87.8	85.9
Bachelor's degree or higher (percent)	35.1	28.5

Table VA-12. Educational Indicators

(Number, percent; data derived from National Center of Education Statistics.)

Item	State	U.S.
Public Schools, 2009–2010 (except where noted)		
Number of school districts	134	13,629
Number of schools	2,164	99,834
Number of students (in thousands)	1,245	49,373
Student-teacher ratio	17.6	15.4
Expenditures per student (dollars)	11,683	10,591
Averaged freshman graduation rate, 2008–2009	78.4	75.5[1]
Dropout rate, 2008–2009	2.5	4.1
Students eligible for free or reduced-price lunch (percent)	36.7	48.0
English language learners, 2010–2011 (percent)	7.1	9.8[1]
Students with IEP (percent)	13.2	13.1
Private Schools, 2009–2010 (except where noted)		
Number of schools	915	33,366
Number of students (in thousands)	103	4,700
High school graduates, 2008–2009	6,511	308,813
Student-teacher ratio	9.1	10.7

[1] U.S. total includes estimates for nonreporting states.

Table VA-13. Reported Voting and Registration of the Voting-Age Population, November 2012

(Numbers in thousands, percent.)

Item	Total population	Total citizen population	Registered			Voted		
			Total registered	Percent registered (total population)	Percent registered (total citizen population)	Total voted	Percent voted (total population)	Percent voted (total citizen population)
U.S. Total	235,248	215,081	153,157	65.1	71.2	132,948	56.5	61.8
State Total	6,094	5,645	4,210	69.1	74.6	3,778	62.0	66.9
Sex								
Male	2,890	2,648	1,931	66.8	72.9	1,709	59.1	64.5
Female	3,204	2,998	2,279	71.1	76.0	2,069	64.6	69.0
Race								
White alone	4,496	4,245	3,222	71.7	75.9	2,872	63.9	67.6
White, non-Hispanic alone	4,169	4,114	3,118	74.8	75.8	2,778	66.6	67.5
Black alone	1,133	1,063	772	68.1	72.6	715	63.1	67.2
Asian alone	316	223	136	43.1	61.1	118	37.3	53.0
Hispanic (of any race)	375	154	114	30.3	73.6	103	27.5	66.8
Age								
18 to 24 years	695	612	351	50.5	57.4	292	42.0	47.7
25 to 44 years	2,181	1,914	1,415	64.9	73.9	1,239	56.8	64.7
45 to 64 years	2,140	2,050	1,591	74.3	77.6	1,473	68.9	71.9
65 to 74 years	627	625	506	80.7	81.1	468	74.6	74.9
75 years and over	452	444	347	76.8	78.0	306	67.7	68.8

Table VA-14. Crime

(Number, rate per 100,000. Data are derived from the FBI Uniform Crime Reports.)

Item	State			U.S.		
	2010	2011	Percent change	2010	2011	Percent change
TOTAL POPULATION	8,023,953	8,096,604	0.9	309,330,219	311,591,917	0.7
VIOLENT CRIME						
Number	17,184	15,923	-7.3	1,251,248	1,203,564	-3.8
Rate	214.2	196.7	-8.2	404.5	386.3	-4.5
Murder and Nonnegligent Manslaughter						
Number	376	303	-19.4	14,722	14,612	-0.7
Rate	4.7	3.7	-21.3	4.8	4.7	-2.1
Forcible Rape						
Number	1,580	1,536	-2.8	85,593	83,425	-2.5
Rate	19.7	19.0	-3.6	27.7	26.8	-3.2
Robbery						
Number	5,678	5,430	-4.4	369,089	354,396	-4.0
Rate	70.8	67.1	-5.2	119.3	113.7	-4.7
Aggravated Assault						
Number	9,550	8,654	-9.4	781,844	751,131	-3.9
Rate	119.0	106.9	-10.2	252.8	241.1	-4.6
PROPERTY CRIME						
Number	187,403	182,141	-2.8	9,112,625	9,063,173	-0.5
Rate	2,335.5	2,249.6	-3.7	2,945.9	2,908.7	-1.3
Burglary						
Number	30,804	30,597	-0.7	2,168,459	2,188,005	0.9
Rate	383.9	377.9	-1.6	701.0	702.2	0.2
Larceny-Theft						
Number	145,990	141,820	-2.9	6,204,601	6,159,795	-0.7
Rate	1,819.4	1,751.6	-3.7	2,005.8	1,976.9	-1.4
Motor Vehicle Theft						
Number	10,609	9,724	-8.3	739,565	715,373	-3.3
Rate	132.2	120.1	-9.2	239.1	229.6	-4.0

Table VA-15. State Government Finances, 2011

(Dollar amounts in thousands, percent distribution.)

Item	Dollars	Percent distribution
Total Revenue	50,781,571	100.0
General revenue	39,194,046	77.2
Intergovernmental revenue	10,512,522	20.7
Taxes	17,409,072	34.3
General sales	3,460,741	6.8
Selective sales	2,389,808	4.7
License taxes	774,505	1.5
Individual income tax	9,530,628	18.8
Corporate income tax	798,404	1.6
Other taxes	454,986	0.9
Current charges	7,696,778	15.2
Miscellaneous general revenue	3,575,674	7.0
Utility revenue	0	0.0
Liquor stores revenue	575,722	1.1
Insurance trust revenue [1]	11,011,803	21.7
Total Expenditure	45,549,347	100.0
Intergovernmental expenditure	11,489,163	25.2
Direct expenditure	34,060,184	74.8
Current operation	23,523,940	51.6
Capital outlay	3,238,159	7.1
Insurance benefits and repayments	4,732,113	10.4
Assistance and subsidies	1,460,216	3.2
Interest on debt	1,105,756	2.4
Exhibit: Salaries and wages	6,326,449	13.9
Total Expenditure	45,549,347	100.0
General expenditure	40,350,197	88.6
Intergovernmental expenditure	11,489,163	25.2
Direct expenditure	28,861,034	63.4
General expenditure, by function:		
Education	14,372,117	31.6
Public welfare	9,347,936	20.5
Hospitals	3,253,555	7.1
Health	1,019,470	2.2
Highways	3,327,572	7.3
Police protection	531,978	1.2
Correction	1,679,294	3.7
Natural resources	687,664	1.5
Parks and recreation	114,237	0.3
Governmental administration	1,341,453	2.9
Interest on general debt	1,105,756	2.4
Other and unallocable	3,569,165	7.8
Utility expenditure	0	0.0
Liquor stores expenditure	467,037	1.0
Insurance trust expenditure	4,732,113	10.4
Debt at End of Fiscal Year	26,479,450	X
Cash and Security Holdings	78,914,816	X

X = Not applicable.

[1] Within insurance trust revenue, net earnings of state retirement systems is a calculated statistic (the item code in the data file is X08), and thus can be positive or negative. Net earnings is the sum of earnings on investments plus gains on investments minus losses on investments. The change made in 2002 for asset valuation from book to market value in accordance with Statement 34 of the Governmental Accounting Standards Board is reflected in the calculated statistics.

Table VA-16. State Government Tax Collections, 2012

(Dollars in thousands, percent.)

Item	Dollars	Percent distribution
Total Taxes	18,137,586	100.0
Property taxes	34,297	0.2
Sales and gross receipts	5,853,266	32.3
General sales and gross receipts	3,487,343	19.2
Selective sales and gross receipts	2,365,923	13.0
Alcoholic beverages	190,796	1.1
Amusements	81	-
Insurance premiums	390,950	2.2
Motor fuels	866,243	4.8
Pari-mutuels	0	0.0
Public utilities	150,759	0.8
Tobacco products	192,441	1.1
Other selective sales	574,653	3.2
Licenses	777,187	4.3
Alcoholic beverages	12,038	0.1
Amusements	93	0.0
Corporations in general	57,209	0.3
Hunting and fishing	27,491	0.2
Motor vehicle	431,651	2.4
Motor vehicle operators	60,282	0.3
Public utilities	0	0.0
Occupation and business, NEC	183,905	1.0
Other licenses	4,518	-
Income taxes	11,054,938	61.0
Individual income	10,216,148	56.3
Corporation net income	838,790	4.6
Other taxes	417,898	2.3
Death and gift	298	-
Documentary and stock transfer	313,052	1.7
Severance	1,986	-
Taxes, NEC	102,562	0.6

- = Rounds to zero.

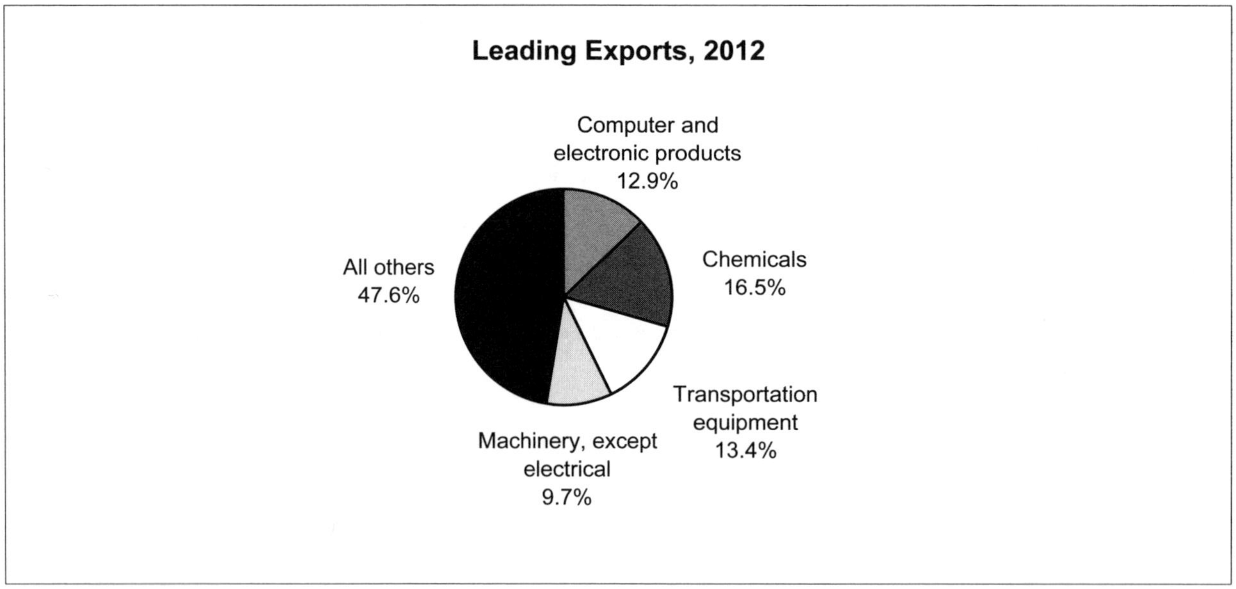

WASHINGTON

Facts and Figures

Location: Northwestern United States; bordered on the N by Canada (British Columbia), on the E by Idaho, on the S by Oregon, and on the W by the Pacific Ocean

Area: 71,300 sq. mi. (184,665 sq. km.); rank—18th

Population: 6,897,012 (2012 est.); rank—13th

Principal Cities: capital—Olympia; largest—Seattle

Statehood: November 11, 1889; 42nd state

U.S. Congress: 2 senators, 10 representatives

State Motto: *Alki* ("By and by")

State Song: "Washington, My Home"

State Nickname: The Evergreen State

Abbreviations: WA; Wash.

State Symbols: flower—coast rhododendron; tree—Western hemlock; bird—willow goldfinch

At a Glance

- With an increase in population of 13.1 percent, Washington ranked 8th among the states in growth from 2000 to 2009.
- An estimated 40,400 marriages took place in Washington in 2009, compared to 26,300 divorces.
- Washington's median household income in 2007 was $56,835, and 13.9 percent of the population lived below the poverty level.
- In 2011, 14.2 percent of Washingtonians did not have health insurance, compared to 15.1 percent of the total U.S. population.
- In 2007, Washington exported $2.6 billion worth of agricultural products, about 3.2 percent of the U.S. total.

Table WA-1. Population by Age, Sex, Race, and Hispanic Origin

(Number, percent, except where noted.)

Sex, age, race, and Hispanic origin	2000	2010	2012[1]	Average annual percent change, 2010–2012
Total Population	5,894,121	6,724,540	6,897,012	0.8
Percent of total U.S. population	2.1	2.2	2.2	X
Sex				
Male	2,934,300	3,349,707	3,441,550	0.9
Female	2,959,821	3,374,833	3,455,462	0.8
Age				
Under 5 years	394,306	439,657	443,157	0.3
5 to 19 years	1,288,713	1,330,238	1,317,947	-0.3
20 to 64 years	3,548,954	4,126,968	4,227,491	0.8
65 years and over	662,148	827,677	908,417	3.0
Median age (years)	35.9	37.3	37.5	0.2
Race and Hispanic Origin				
One race				
White	4,821,823	5,535,262	5,625,335	0.5
Black	190,267	252,333	268,660	2.0
American Indian and Alaska Native	93,301	122,649	126,526	1.0
Asian	322,335	491,685	531,395	2.5
Native Hawaiian or Other Pacific Islander	23,953	43,505	46,143	1.9
Two or more races	213,519	279,106	298,953	2.2
Hispanic (of any race)	441,509	776,539	856,880	3.1

X = Not applicable.
[1] Population figures for 2012 are July 1 estimates. The 2010 estimates are taken from the 2010 Census.

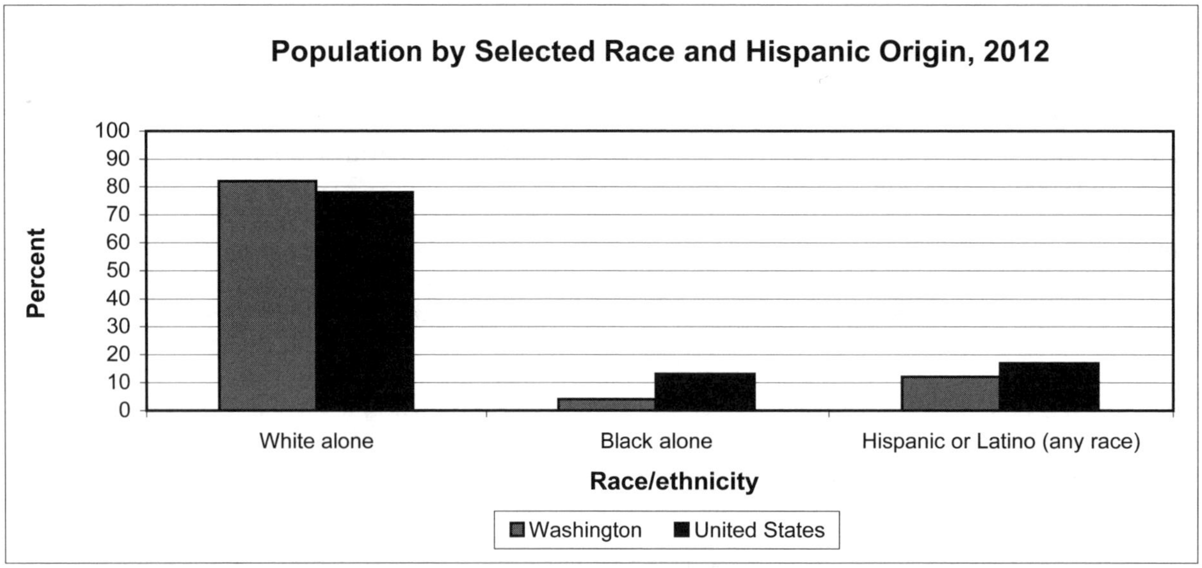

Table WA-2. Marital Status

(Number, percent distribution.)

Sex, age, race, and Hispanic origin	2000	2010	2011
Males, 15 Years and Over	2,287,431	2,686,801	2,735,194
Never married	29.8	33.8	34.0
Now married, except separated	56.6	52.0	51.4
Separated	1.4	1.6	1.4
Widowed	2.1	2.1	2.1
Divorced	10.1	10.5	11.0
Females, 15 Years and Over	2,352,091	2,746,158	2,781,549
Never married	22.8	26.4	26.5
Now married, except separated	54.1	50.6	49.8
Separated	1.8	2.1	2.0
Widowed	8.6	7.8	7.9
Divorced	12.7	13.2	13.9

Table WA-3. Households and Housing Characteristics

(Number, percent, dollars.)

Item	2000	2010	2011	Average annual percent change, 2000–2011
Total Households	2,271,398	2,606,863	2,632,621	1.3
Family households	1,499,127	1,681,386	1,699,851	1.1
Married-couple family	1,181,995	1,297,240	1,303,418	0.9
Other family	317,132	384,146	396,433	2.1
Male householder, no wife present	92,514	114,187	116,352	2.1
Female householder, no husband present	224,618	269,959	280,081	2.1
Nonfamily households	772,271	925,477	932,770	1.7
Householder living alone	594,325	731,452	724,391	1.8
Householder not living alone	117,946	194,025	208,379	6.4
Housing Characteristics				
Total housing units	2,451,075	2,888,594	2,907,605	1.6
Occupied housing units	2,271,398	2,606,863	2,632,621	1.3
Owner occupied	1,467,009	1,644,939	1,653,712	1.1
Renter occupied	804,389	961,924	978,909	1.8
Average size	2.53	2.53	2.54	-
Financial Characteristics				
Median gross rent of renter-occupied housing	663	908	930	3.4
Median monthly owner costs for housing units with a mortgage	1,268	1,736	1,733	3.1
Median value of owner-occupied housing units	168,300	271,800	256,300	4.4

- = Zero or rounds to zero.

Table WA-4. Migration, Origin, and Language

(Number, percent.)

Characteristic	State			U.S.		
	2010	2011	Percent change	2010	2011	Percent change
Residence 1 Year Ago						
Population 1 year and over	6,661,321	6,748,474	1.3	305,628,607	307,900,319	0.7
Same house	82.0	82.5	0.6	84.6	84.8	0.2
Different house in the U.S.	17.1	16.7	-2.3	14.8	14.6	-1.4
Same county	11.2	10.8	-3.6	9.4	9.2	-2.1
Different county	5.9	5.9	0.0	5.4	5.4	-
Same state	3.1	2.9	-6.5	3.2	3.1	-3.1
Different state	2.9	3.1	6.9	2.2	2.3	4.5
Abroad	0.9	0.8	-11.1	0.6	0.6	-
Place of Birth						
Native born	5,858,234	5,920,726	1.1	269,393,835	271,214,059	0.7
Male	50.1	50.3	0.4	49.2	49.2	-
Female	49.9	49.7	-0.4	50.8	50.8	-
Foreign born	886,262	909,312	2.6	39,955,854	40,377,860	1.1
Male	47.6	47.4	-0.4	49.1	48.9	-0.4
Female	52.4	52.6	0.4	50.9	51.1	0.4
Foreign born; naturalized U.S. citizen	403,280	417,019	3.4	17,476,082	18,140,192	3.8
Male	44.4	45.4	2.3	45.8	45.8	-
Female	55.6	54.6	-1.8	54.2	54.2	-
Foreign born; not a U.S. citizen	482,982	492,293	1.9	22,479,772	22,237,668	-1.1
Male	50.3	49.1	-2.4	51.6	51.5	-0.2
Female	49.7	50.9	2.4	48.4	48.5	0.2
Entered 2000 or later	37.5	38.4	2.4	34.7	35.7	2.9
Entered 1990 to 1999	28.9	28.4	-1.7	27.2	26.7	-1.8
Entered before 1990	33.6	33.2	-1.2	38.1	37.6	-1.3
World Region of Birth, Foreign						
Foreign-born population, excluding population born at sea	886,262	909,269	2.6	39,955,673	40,377,757	1.1
Europe	16.8	17.2	2.4	12.1	12.1	-
Asia	40.2	39.8	-1.0	28.2	28.6	1.4
Africa	4.8	5.4	12.5	4	4.1	2.5
Oceania	1.3	1.5	15.4	0.5	0.5	-
Latin America	31.3	30.7	-1.9	53.1	52.6	-0.9
North America	5.7	5.4	-5.3	2	2.0	-
Language Spoken at Home and Ability to Speak English						
Population 5 years and over	6,306,287	6,390,691	1.3	289,215,746	291,524,091	0.8
English only	81.7	81.4	-0.4	79.4	79.2	-0.3
Language other than English	18.3	18.6	1.6	20.6	20.8	1.0
Speaks English less than "very well"	8.1	8.0	-1.2	8.7	8.7	-

- = Zero or rounds to zero.

Table WA-5. Median Income and Poverty Status, 2011

(Number, percent, except as noted.)

Characteristic	State Number	State Percent	U.S. Number	U.S. Percent
Median Income				
Households (dollars)	56,835	X	50,502	X
Families (dollars)	68,628	X	61,455	X
Below Poverty Level (All People)	929,258	13.9	48,452,035	15.9
Sex				
Male	428,418	12.9	21,825,281	14.7
Female	500,840	14.9	26,626,754	17.2
Age				
Under 18 years	283,176	18.3	16,386,500	22.5
Related children under 18 years	273,660	17.8	16,087,074	22.2
18 to 64 years	574,933	13.4	28,335,079	14.8
65 years and over	71,149	8.5	3,730,456	9.3

X = Not applicable.

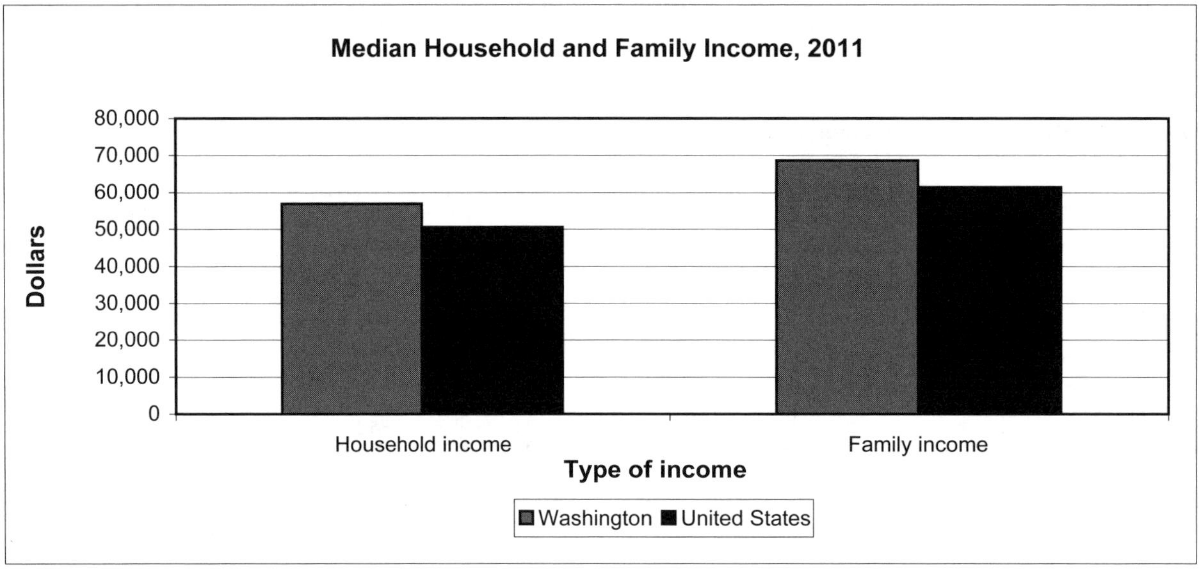

Table WA-6. Health Insurance Coverage Status for the Civilian Noninstitutionalized Population and Children Under 18 Years of Age

(Numbers in thousands, percent.)

Item	2004	2005	2006	2007	2008	2009	2010	2011
Civilian Noninstitutionalized Population	6,118	6,250	6,318	6,509	6,428	6,546	6,638	6,717
Covered by Private or Public Insurance								
Number	5,359	5,422	5,572	5,773	5,586	5,669	5,692	5,764
Percent	87.6	86.7	88.2	88.7	86.9	86.6	85.8	85.8
Not Covered								
Number	759	828	746	737	842	878	946	952
Percent	12.4	13.3	11.8	11.3	13.1	13.4	14.2	14.2
Percent in the U.S. not covered	14.9	15.3	15.8	15.3	15.1	15.1	15.5	15.1
Children Under 18 Years of Age	1,512	1,525	1,518	1,558	1,541	1,570	1,583	1,578
Covered by Private or Public Insurance								
Number	1,412	1,391	1,413	1,452	1,411	1,462	1,481	1,481
Percent	93.4	91.3	93.1	93.2	91.6	93.1	93.6	93.8
Not Covered								
Number	100	133	105	106	130	108	102	97
Percent	6.6	8.7	6.9	6.8	8.4	6.9	6.4	6.2
Percent in the U.S. not covered	10.5	10.9	11.7	11.0	9.7	8.6	8.0	7.5

Table WA-7. Employment Status by Demographic Group, Preliminary 2012

(Numbers in thousands, percent.)

Characteristic	Civilian noninstitutional population	Civilian labor force		Employed		Unemployed	
		Number	Percent of population	Number	Percent of population	Number	Percent of population
Total	5,377	3,469	64.5	3,181	59.2	288	8.3
Sex							
Male	2,639	1,851	70.2	1,696	64.3	155	8.4
Female	2,739	1,618	59.1	1,485	54.2	133	8.2
Race, Sex, and Hispanic Origin							
White	4,410	2,833	64.2	2,598	58.9	234	8.3
Male	2,157	1,504	69.7	1,380	64.0	124	8.2
Female	2,252	1,328	59.0	1,218	54.1	110	8.3
Black or African American	173	124	71.6	106	61.1	18	14.7
Male	88	72	81.7	61	70.0	10	14.3
Female	85	52	61.2	44	51.9	8	15.2
Hispanic	470	324	68.9	288	61.2	36	11.2
Male	248	192	77.4	175	70.5	17	9.0
Female	222	131	59.3	113	50.8	19	14.3
Age							
16 to 19 years	359	127	35.4	90	25.2	36	28.6
20 to 24 years	455	323	70.8	284	62.4	39	12.0
25 to 34 years	898	740	82.4	684	76.2	55	7.5
35 to 44 years	948	775	81.8	727	76.7	48	6.3
45 to 54 years	932	763	81.9	704	75.5	59	7.8
55 to 64 years	871	579	66.4	542	62.2	37	6.4
65 years and over	915	163	17.8	150	16.4	13	8.1

NOTE: Data in Table 7 are from the Current Population Survey (CPS) and do not match the estimates in Table 8. See notes and definitions for further information.

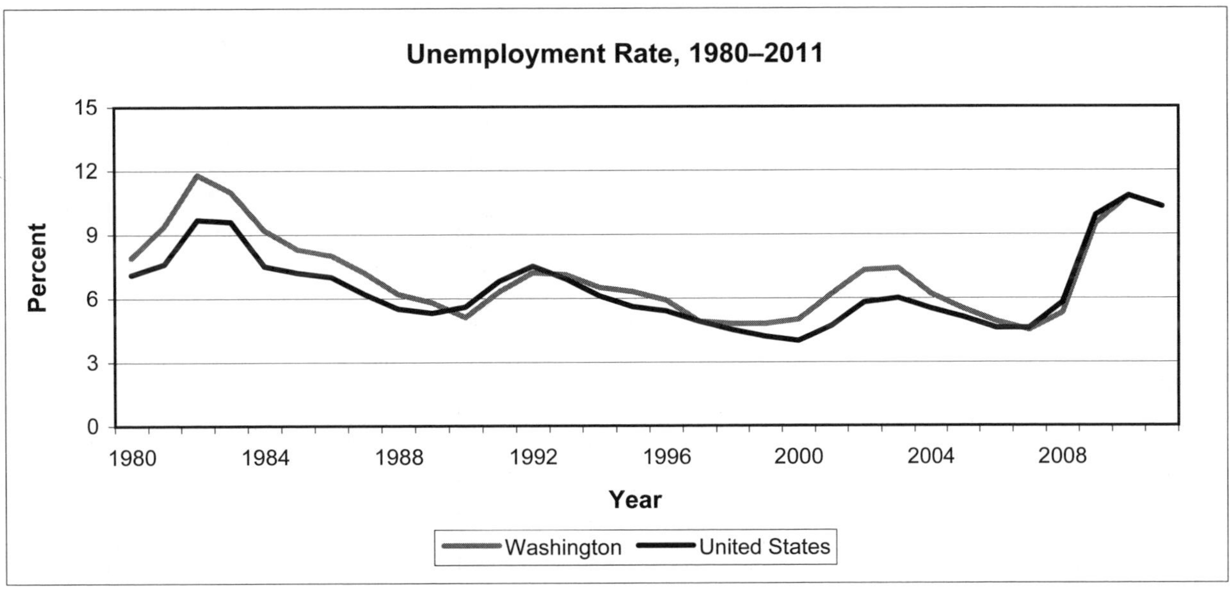

Table WA-8. Employment Status of the Civilian Noninstitutional Population Age 16 Years and Over

(Number, percent.)

Year	Civilian labor force	Civilian participation rate	Employed	Unemployed	Unemployment rate
2005	3,258,844	67.6	3,079,482	179,362	5.5
2006	3,319,593	67.6	3,156,995	162,598	4.9
2007	3,391,248	67.8	3,237,358	153,890	4.5
2008	3,476,766	68.4	3,290,993	185,773	5.3
2009	3,438,309	65.2	3,110,366	327,954	9.5
2010	3,440,495	64.4	3,070,269	370,226	10.8
2011	3,477,743	64.0	3,117,998	358,745	10.3

Table WA-9. Employment and Average Wages by Industry

(Estimates before 2007 are based on the 2002 *North American Industry Classification System* [NAICS]. Estimates from 2007 onward are based on the 2007 NAICS.)

Industry	2005	2006	2007	2008	2009	2010	2011
				Number of jobs			
Wage and Salary Employment by Industry	2,988,867	3,080,441	3,154,787	3,190,328	3,055,064	3,017,067	3,050,198
Farm Wage and Salary Employment	42,649	43,496	40,162	47,160	49,636	48,890	46,644
Nonfarm Wage and Salary Employment	2,946,218	3,036,945	3,114,625	3,143,168	3,005,428	2,968,177	3,003,554
Private wage and salary employment	2,345,212	2,432,206	2,504,769	2,516,679	2,374,663	2,336,116	2,378,200
Forestry, fishing, and related activities	26,278	26,658	26,441	26,002	27,210	26,656	28,470
Mining	3,373	3,465	3,135	2,955	2,367	2,202	2,205
Utilities	4,461	4,583	4,460	4,703	4,767	4,863	4,870
Construction	184,876	203,601	217,517	208,581	166,336	146,762	143,279
Manufacturing	271,774	285,726	293,283	291,067	265,520	257,913	268,681
Durable goods manufacturing	191,073	203,802	211,983	211,250	190,284	183,718	193,063
Nondurable goods manufacturing	80,701	81,924	81,300	79,817	75,236	74,195	75,618
Wholesale trade	122,143	125,871	130,037	130,798	123,355	121,554	123,051
Retail trade	319,687	326,647	330,505	330,081	314,067	313,189	317,476
Transportation and warehousing	88,712	90,717	92,556	92,072	87,026	85,243	87,156
Information	94,378	98,605	102,859	105,724	103,817	102,884	104,202
Finance and insurance	106,766	108,572	106,589	104,081	97,037	93,785	93,779
Real estate and rental and leasing	51,320	53,069	53,185	52,951	49,519	47,356	46,216
Professional, scientific, and technical services	145,202	151,194	161,895	169,754	163,556	164,645	170,210
Management of companies and enterprises	33,436	33,619	34,678	34,783	32,178	31,796	33,282
Administrative and waste services	142,734	149,584	153,566	149,209	132,706	134,751	140,112
Educational services	45,093	46,091	47,336	49,357	49,032	49,908	51,700
Health care and social assistance	291,020	299,996	308,949	321,880	331,044	333,660	337,636
Arts, entertainment, and recreation	45,542	45,413	46,785	48,459	46,577	45,883	46,782
Accommodation and food services	221,263	229,708	237,226	238,717	225,921	224,183	227,794
Other services, except public administration	147,154	149,087	153,767	155,505	152,628	148,883	151,299
Government and government enterprises	601,006	604,739	609,856	626,489	630,765	632,061	625,354
				Dollars			
Average Wages and Salaries by Industry	41,723	43,863	46,223	47,231	48,087	49,282	51,036
Average Farm Wages and Salaries	27,680	26,045	28,025	29,672	27,635	25,520	26,156
Average Nonfarm Wages and Salaries	41,926	44,118	46,458	47,495	48,425	49,673	51,423
Average private wages and salaries	42,002	44,317	46,706	47,552	48,240	49,598	51,602
Forestry, fishing, and related activities	30,446	32,088	33,265	34,826	32,324	33,267	34,648
Mining	53,194	55,657	58,502	55,819	53,328	56,188	59,809
Utilities	64,771	69,484	73,380	76,188	83,464	77,235	81,878
Construction	42,929	45,287	48,308	50,782	52,150	51,817	52,859
Manufacturing	55,534	58,776	60,114	61,573	63,039	65,280	68,479
Durable goods manufacturing	60,221	64,039	64,959	66,644	69,068	72,104	75,748
Nondurable goods manufacturing	44,436	45,681	47,482	48,153	47,792	48,381	49,920
Wholesale trade	54,655	57,937	60,646	62,211	62,367	64,253	66,665
Retail trade	28,714	29,487	30,759	30,791	31,024	31,586	32,647
Transportation and warehousing	44,874	46,174	47,172	47,439	48,340	49,589	51,898
Information	89,283	95,619	106,526	104,789	106,908	111,436	121,621
Finance and insurance	63,007	67,413	70,358	72,858	71,286	70,283	73,173
Real estate and rental and leasing	34,564	36,596	37,537	37,586	37,330	38,878	40,332
Professional, scientific, and technical services	62,871	65,473	72,263	71,567	73,019	76,181	77,882
Management of companies and enterprises	75,625	86,522	90,161	88,966	89,733	100,110	103,999
Administrative and waste services	33,810	34,952	36,604	38,106	39,972	41,923	43,211
Educational services	23,486	24,221	25,625	26,698	27,684	28,562	29,142
Health care and social assistance	37,918	39,367	41,033	42,812	44,377	45,386	46,582
Arts, entertainment, and recreation	28,503	31,025	31,822	29,727	28,123	27,871	27,657
Accommodation and food services	17,183	18,535	18,813	18,723	19,121	20,277	21,311
Other services, except public administration	25,582	26,661	27,969	28,756	28,931	29,844	30,305
Government and government enterprises	41,631	43,320	45,437	47,268	49,121	49,953	50,741

Table WA-10. Employment Characteristics by Family Type

(Number, percent.)

Family type and labor force status	2009		2010		2011	
	Total	Families with own children under 18 years	Total	Families with own children under 18 years	Total	Families with own children under 18 years
All families	1,650,579	753,552	1,681,586	759,227	1,699,851	767,324
Family type and labor force status						
	1,284,279	533,861	1,297,240	535,314	1,303,418	538,771
Married-couple families	53.8	64.0	53.8	64.1	52.5	61.9
Both husband and wife in labor force	23.1	31.2	22.5	30.3	23.5	32.4
Husband in labor force, wife not in labor force	7.3	3.7	7.4	3.7	7.3	3.8
Wife in labor force, husband not in labor force	15.8	1.2	16.3	1.9	16.7	1.8
Both husband and wife not in labor force						
	366,240	219,691	384,146	223,913	396,433	228,553
Other families	69.4	72.5	70.3	74.2	70.7	72.9
Female householder, no husband present	51.0	58.9	51.8	60.2	51.0	58.9
In labor force	18.3	13.5	18.5	14.1	19.7	14.0
Not in labor force						
	30.6	27.5	29.7	25.8	29.3	27.1
Male householder, no wife present	25.3	25.1	24.6	23.3	24.1	24.2
In labor force	5.3	2.5	5.2	2.4	5.2	2.9
Not in labor force	4.9	1.6	7.1	3.1	6.5	3.0

Table WA-11. School Enrollment and Educational Attainment, 2011

(Number, percent.)

Item	State	U.S.
Enrollment		
Total population 3 years and over, enrolled in school	1,710,462	83,131,910
Enrolled in nursery school or preschool (percent)	6.0	6.0
Enrolled in kindergarten (percent)	5.0	5.1
Enrolled in elementary school, grades 1-8 (percent)	40.4	39.5
Enrolled in high school, grades 9-12 (percent)	20.8	20.7
Enrolled in college or graduate school (percent)	27.7	28.7
Attainment		
Total population 25 years and over	4,583,426	206,471,670
Less than ninth grade (percent)	4.2	6.0
9th to 12th grade, no diploma (percent)	5.6	8.1
High school graduate, including equivalency (percent)	23.8	28.4
Some college, no degree (percent)	24.7	21.2
Associate's degree (percent)	9.7	7.8
Bachelor's degree (percent)	20.2	17.9
Graduate or professional degree (percent)	11.7	10.6
High school graduate or higher (percent)	90.1	85.9
Bachelor's degree or higher (percent)	31.9	28.5

Table WA-12. Educational Indicators

(Number, percent; data derived from National Center of Education Statistics.)

Item	State	U.S.
Public Schools, 2009–2010 (except where noted)		
Number of school districts	295	13,629
Number of schools	2,318	99,834
Number of students (in thousands)	1,035	49,373
Student-teacher ratio	19.4	15.4
Expenditures per student (dollars)	11,395	10,591
Averaged freshman graduation rate, 2008–2009	73.7	75.5[1]
Dropout rate, 2008–2009	4.7	4.1
Students eligible for free or reduced-price lunch (percent)	40.9	48.0
English language learners, 2010–2011 (percent)	8.7	9.8[1]
Students with IEP (percent)	12.2	13.1
Private Schools, 2009–2010 (except where noted)		
Number of schools	656	33,366
Number of students (in thousands)	77	4,700
High school graduates, 2008–2009	4,448	308,813
Student-teacher ratio	11.1	10.7

[1] U.S. total includes estimates for nonreporting states.

Table WA-13. Reported Voting and Registration of the Voting-Age Population, November 2012

(Numbers in thousands, percent.)

Item	Total population	Total citizen population	Registered			Voted		
			Total registered	Percent registered (total population)	Percent registered (total citizen population)	Total voted	Percent voted (total population)	Percent voted (total citizen population)
U.S. Total	235,248	215,081	153,157	65.1	71.2	132,948	56.5	61.8
State Total	5,230	4,832	3,533	67.6	73.1	3,172	60.7	65.6
Sex								
Male	2,546	2,338	1,658	65.1	70.9	1,491	58.5	63.8
Female	2,684	2,495	1,875	69.9	75.2	1,682	62.7	67.4
Race								
White alone	4,301	4,039	2,987	69.4	74.0	2,696	62.7	66.8
White, non-Hispanic alone	3,936	3,829	2,875	73.0	75.1	2,603	66.1	68.0
Black alone	162	149	103	63.8	69.5	72	44.3	48.3
Asian alone	377	255	178	47.2	69.7	169	44.7	66.0
Hispanic (of any race)	460	298	172	37.5	58.0	139	30.2	46.6
Age								
18 to 24 years	563	511	275	48.8	53.8	215	38.2	42.1
25 to 44 years	1,933	1,719	1,244	64.4	72.4	1,064	55.1	61.9
45 to 64 years	1,660	1,570	1,183	71.3	75.3	1,101	66.4	70.1
65 to 74 years	625	605	487	77.9	80.4	471	75.5	77.9
75 years and over	449	427	344	76.5	80.5	320	71.3	75.0

Table WA-14. Crime

(Number, rate per 100,000. Data are derived from the FBI Uniform Crime Reports.)

Item	State			U.S.		
	2010	2011	Percent change	2010	2011	Percent change
TOTAL POPULATION	6,742,950	6,830,038	1.3	309,330,219	311,591,917	0.7
VIOLENT CRIME						
Number	21,138	20,121	-4.8	1,251,248	1,203,564	-3.8
Rate	313.5	294.6	-6.0	404.5	386.3	-4.5
Murder and Nonnegligent Manslaughter						
Number	154	162	5.2	14,722	14,612	-0.7
Rate	2.3	2.4	4.3	4.8	4.7	-2.1
Forcible Rape						
Number	2,579	2,290	-11.2	85,593	83,425	-2.5
Rate	38.3	33.5	-12.5	27.7	26.8	-3.2
Robbery						
Number	5,929	5,638	-4.9	369,089	354,396	-4.0
Rate	87.9	82.5	-6.1	119.3	113.7	-4.7
Aggravated Assault						
Number	12,476	12,031	-3.6	781,844	751,131	-3.9
Rate	185.0	176.1	-4.8	252.8	241.1	-4.6
PROPERTY CRIME						
Number	249,426	244,146	-2.1	9,112,625	9,063,173	-0.5
Rate	3,669.1	3,574.6	-2.6	2,945.9	2,908.7	-1.3
Burglary						
Number	55,192	56,532	2.4	2,168,459	2,188,005	0.9
Rate	818.5	827.7	1.1	701.0	702.2	0.2
Larceny-Theft						
Number	168,490	162,779	-3.4	6,204,601	6,159,795	-0.7
Rate	2,498.8	2,383.3	-4.6	2,005.8	1,976.9	-1.4
Motor Vehicle Theft						
Number	25,744	24,835	-3.5	739,565	715,373	-3.3
Rate	381.8	363.6	-4.8	239.1	229.6	-4.0

Table WA-15. State Government Finances, 2011

(Dollar amounts in thousands, percent distribution.)

Item	Dollars	Percent distribution
Total Revenue	50,420,289	100.0
General revenue	34,993,013	69.4
Intergovernmental revenue	10,944,017	21.7
Taxes	17,411,033	34.5
General sales	10,580,395	21.0
Selective sales	3,523,309	7.0
License taxes	931,427	1.8
Individual income tax	0	0.0
Corporate income tax	0	0.0
Other taxes	2,375,902	4.7
Current charges	4,500,974	8.9
Miscellaneous general revenue	2,136,989	4.2
Utility revenue	0	0.0
Liquor stores revenue	587,475	1.2
Insurance trust revenue [1]	14,839,801	29.4
Total Expenditure	45,999,749	100.0
Intergovernmental expenditure	9,346,712	20.3
Direct expenditure	36,653,037	79.7
Current operation	21,817,601	47.4
Capital outlay	3,456,637	7.5
Insurance benefits and repayments	8,575,604	18.6
Assistance and subsidies	1,533,462	3.3
Interest on debt	1,269,733	2.8
Exhibit: Salaries and wages	9,987,655	21.7
Total Expenditure	45,999,749	100.0
General expenditure	36,888,688	80.2
Intergovernmental expenditure	9,346,712	20.3
Direct expenditure	27,541,976	59.9
General expenditure, by function:		
Education	14,886,147	32.4
Public welfare	8,668,902	18.8
Hospitals	2,051,272	4.5
Health	1,797,324	3.9
Highways	3,029,932	6.6
Police protection	322,098	0.7
Correction	1,002,442	2.2
Natural resources	885,585	1.9
Parks and recreation	134,623	0.3
Governmental administration	714,305	1.6
Interest on general debt	1,269,733	2.8
Other and unallocable	2,126,325	4.6
Utility expenditure	47,600	0.1
Liquor stores expenditure	487,857	1.1
Insurance trust expenditure	8,575,604	18.6
Debt at End of Fiscal Year	28,153,562	X
Cash and Security Holdings	81,974,098	X

X = Not applicable.

[1] Within insurance trust revenue, net earnings of state retirement systems is a calculated statistic (the item code in the data file is X08), and thus can be positive or negative. Net earnings is the sum of earnings on investments plus gains on investments minus losses on investments. The change made in 2002 for asset valuation from book to market value in accordance with Statement 34 of the Governmental Accounting Standards Board is reflected in the calculated statistics.

Table WA-16. State Government Tax Collections, 2012

(Dollars in thousands, percent.)

Item	Dollars	Percent distribution
Total Taxes	17,624,715	100.0
Property taxes	1,897,095	10.8
Sales and gross receipts	14,171,443	80.4
General sales and gross receipts	10,614,137	60.2
Selective sales and gross receipts	3,557,306	20.2
Alcoholic beverages	349,164	2.0
Amusements	0	0.0
Insurance premiums	430,052	2.4
Motor fuels	1,177,987	6.7
Pari-mutuels	1,734	-
Public utilities	460,025	2.6
Tobacco products	470,765	2.7
Other selective sales	667,579	3.8
Licenses	994,819	5.6
Alcoholic beverages	33,912	0.2
Amusements	6,116	-
Corporations in general	30,083	0.2
Hunting and fishing	41,826	0.2
Motor vehicle	471,016	2.7
Motor vehicle operators	69,745	0.4
Public utilities	18,862	0.1
Occupation and business, NEC	253,245	1.4
Other licenses	70,014	0.4
Income taxes	0	0.0
Individual income	0	0.0
Corporation net income	0	0.0
Other taxes	561,358	3.2
Death and gift	104,592	0.6
Documentary and stock transfer	420,464	2.4
Severance	36,302	0.2
Taxes, NEC	0	0.0

- = Rounds to zero.

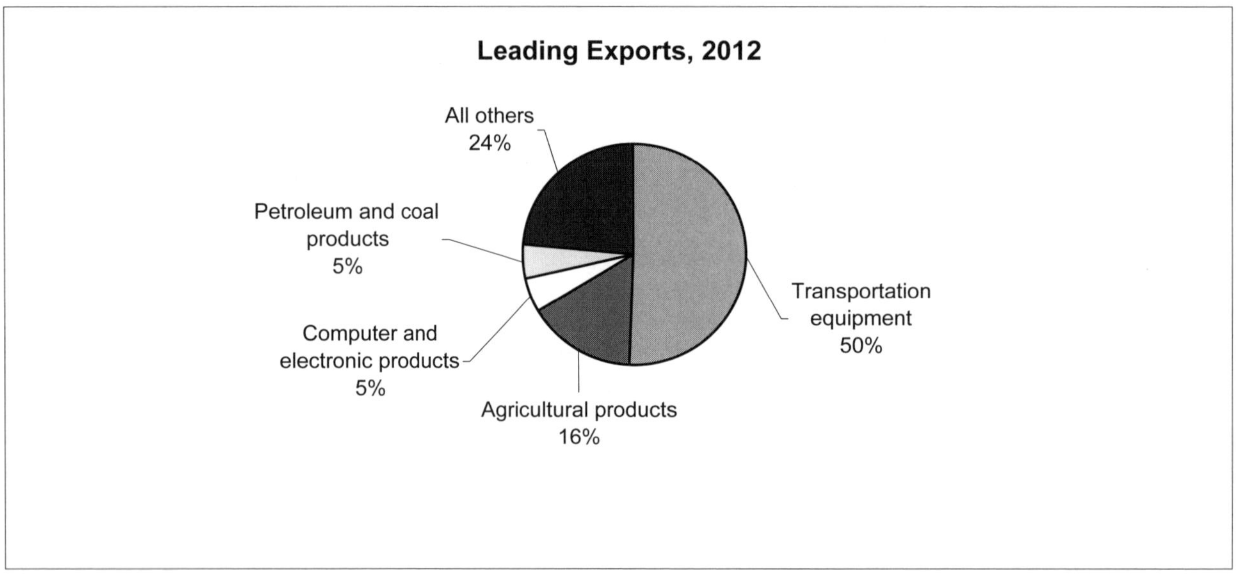

WEST VIRGINIA

Facts and Figures

Location: East central United States; bordered on the N by Ohio and Pennsylvania, on the E by Pennsylvania, Maryland, and Virginia, on the S by Virginia and Kentucky, and on the W by Kentucky and Ohio

Area: 24,230 sq. mi. (62,755 sq. km.); rank—41st

Population: 1,855,413 (2012 est.); rank—38th

Principal Cities: capital—Charleston; largest—Charleston

Statehood: June 20, 1863; 35th state

U.S. Congress: 2 senators, 3 representatives

State Motto: *Montani semper liberi* (Mountaineers are always free)

State Songs: "West Virginia Hills"; "This Is My West Virginia"; "West Virginia, My Home Sweet Home"

State Nickname: The Mountain State

Abbreviations: WV; W. Va.

State Symbols: flower—rhododendron (great laurel); tree—sugar maple; bird—cardinal

At a Glance

- With an increase in population of 0.6 percent, West Virginia ranked 48th among the states in growth from 2000 to 2009.
- An estimated 12,400 marriages took place in West Virginia in 2009, compared to 9,200 divorces.
- West Virginia's median household income in 2007 was $38,482, and 18.6 percent of the population lived below the poverty level.
- In 2011, 14.9 percent of West Virginians did not have health insurance, compared to 15.1 percent of the total U.S. population.
- In 2007, West Virginia exported $46 million worth of agricultural products, less than 1 percent of the U.S. total.

Table WV-1. Population by Age, Sex, Race, and Hispanic Origin

(Number, percent, except where noted.)

Sex, age, race, and Hispanic origin	2000	2010	2012[1]	Average annual percent change, 2010–2012
Total Population	1,808,344	1,852,994	1,855,413	-
Percent of total U.S. population	0.6	0.6	0.6	X
Sex				
Male	879,170	913,586	915,405	0.1
Female	929,174	939,408	940,008	-
Age				
Under 5 years	101,805	104,060	103,071	-0.3
5 to 19 years	352,910	335,153	327,782	-0.7
20 to 64 years	1,076,734	1,116,377	1,112,611	-0.1
65 years and over	276,895	297,404	311,949	1.6
Median age (years)	38.9	41.3	41.7	0.3
Race and Hispanic Origin				
One race				
White	1,718,777	1,746,513	1,743,721	-0.1
Black	57,232	63,885	65,787	1.0
American Indian and Alaska Native	3,606	3,975	4,104	1.0
Asian	9,434	12,637	13,796	2.8
Native Hawaiian or Other Pacific Islander	400	485	563	4.6
Two or more races	15,788	25,499	27,442	2.4
Hispanic (of any race)	12,279	23,679	26,035	3.0

X = Not applicable.
- = Zero or rounds to zero.
[1] Population figures for 2012 are July 1 estimates. The 2010 estimates are taken from the 2010 Census.

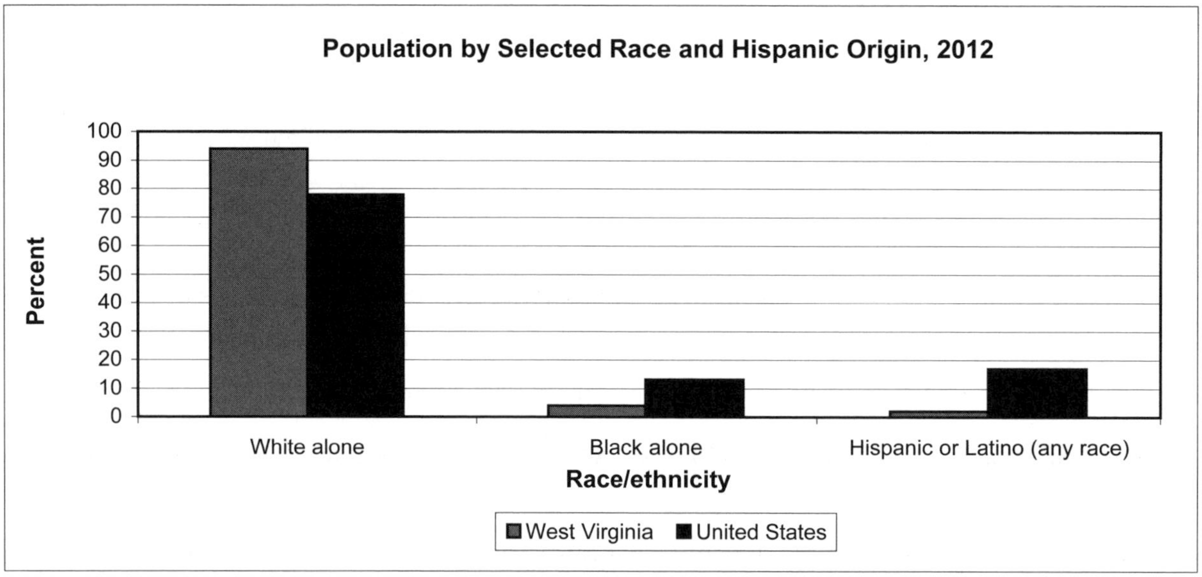

Table WV-2. Marital Status

(Number, percent distribution.)

Sex, age, race, and Hispanic origin	2000	2010	2011
Males, 15 Years and Over	710,443	750,542	749,911
Never married	25.4	30.3	31.7
Now married, except separated	59.9	52.1	50.8
Separated	1.3	1.6	1.5
Widowed	3.2	3.4	3.5
Divorced	10.1	12.6	12.5
Females, 15 Years and Over	768,858	785,182	786,147
Never married	19.1	22.6	23.7
Now married, except separated	54.7	49.7	48.1
Separated	1.6	1.7	2.4
Widowed	13.9	12.8	12.5
Divorced	10.8	13.2	13.4

Table WV-3. Households and Housing Characteristics

(Number, percent, dollars.)

Item	2000	2010	2011	Average annual percent change, 2000–2011
Total Households	736,481	741,940	735,408	-
Family households	504,055	485,652	477,809	-0.4
Married-couple family	397,499	372,301	356,697	-0.9
Other family	106,556	113,351	121,112	1.1
Male householder, no wife present	27,436	28,515	35,308	2.4
Female householder, no husband present	79,120	84,836	85,804	0.7
Nonfamily households	232,426	256,288	257,599	0.9
Householder living alone	199,587	219,848	221,498	0.9
Householder not living alone	32,839	36,440	36,101	0.8
Housing Characteristics				
Total housing units	844,623	882,213	881,821	0.4
Occupied housing units	736,481	741,940	735,408	-
Owner occupied	553,699	553,429	531,392	-0.3
Renter occupied	182,782	188,511	204,016	1.0
Average size	2.40	2.43	2.46	0.2
Financial Characteristics				
Median gross rent of renter-occupied housing	401	571	599	4.1
Median monthly owner costs for housing units with a mortgage	713	918	937	2.6
Median value of owner-occupied housing units	72,800	95,100	99,300	3.0

- = Zero or rounds to zero.

Table WV-4. Migration, Origin, and Language

(Number, percent.)

Characteristic	State			U.S.		
	2010	2011	Percent change	2010	2011	Percent change
Residence 1 Year Ago						
Population 1 year and over	1,833,535	1,836,614	0.2	305,628,607	307,900,319	0.7
Same house	88.6	87.6	-1.1	84.6	84.8	0.2
Different house in the U.S.	11.2	12.1	8.0	14.8	14.6	-1.4
Same county	6.6	6.9	4.5	9.4	9.2	-2.1
Different county	4.7	5.2	10.6	5.4	5.4	-
Same state	2.5	2.4	-4.0	3.2	3.1	-3.1
Different state	2.2	2.7	22.7	2.2	2.3	4.5
Abroad	0.1	0.3	200.0	0.6	0.6	-
Place of Birth						
Native born	1,831,462	1,831,535	-	269,393,835	271,214,059	0.7
Male	49.2	49.2	-	49.2	49.2	-
Female	50.8	50.8	-	50.8	50.8	-
Foreign born	22,511	23,829	5.9	39,955,854	40,377,860	1.1
Male	52.6	53.8	2.3	49.1	48.9	-0.4
Female	47.4	46.2	-2.5	50.9	51.1	0.4
Foreign born; naturalized U.S. citizen	10,281	10,599	3.1	17,476,082	18,140,192	3.8
Male	50.1	47.0	-6.2	45.8	45.8	-
Female	49.9	53.0	6.2	54.2	54.2	-
Foreign born; not a U.S. citizen	12,230	13,230	8.2	22,479,772	22,237,668	-1.1
Male	54.8	59.3	8.2	51.6	51.5	-0.2
Female	45.2	40.7	-10.0	48.4	48.5	0.2
Entered 2000 or later	41.3	43.6	5.6	34.7	35.7	2.9
Entered 1990 to 1999	18.3	20.7	13.1	27.2	26.7	-1.8
Entered before 1990	40.4	35.7	-11.6	38.1	37.6	-1.3
World Region of Birth, Foreign						
Foreign-born population, excluding population born at sea	22,511	23,829	5.9	39,955,673	40,377,757	1.1
Europe	19.0	24.4	28.4	12.1	12.1	-
Asia	43.8	41.7	-4.8	28.2	28.6	1.4
Africa	8.2	6.3	-23.2	4	4.1	2.5
Oceania	0.2	0.3	50.0	0.5	0.5	-
Latin America	23.6	22.6	-4.2	53.1	52.6	-0.9
North America	5.1	4.7	-7.8	2	2.0	-
Language Spoken at Home and Ability to Speak English						
Population 5 years and over	1,752,096	1,751,216	-0.1	289,215,746	291,524,091	0.8
English only	97.8	97.7	-0.1	79.4	79.2	-0.3
Language other than English	2.2	2.3	4.5	20.6	20.8	1.0
Speaks English less than "very well"	0.7	0.8	14.3	8.7	8.7	-

- = Zero or rounds to zero.

Table WV-5. Median Income and Poverty Status, 2011

(Number, percent, except as noted.)

Characteristic	State		U.S.	
	Number	Percent	Number	Percent
Median Income				
Households (dollars)	38,482	X	50,502	X
Families (dollars)	49,693	X	61,455	X
Below Poverty Level (All People)	334,885	18.6	48,452,035	15.9
Sex				
Male	150,778	17.1	21,825,281	14.7
Female	184,107	20.0	26,626,754	17.2
Age				
Under 18 years	97,677	25.8	16,386,500	22.5
Related children under 18 years	94,852	25.3	16,087,074	22.2
18 to 64 years	209,714	18.5	28,335,079	14.8
65 years and over	27,494	9.4	3,730,456	9.3

X = Not applicable.

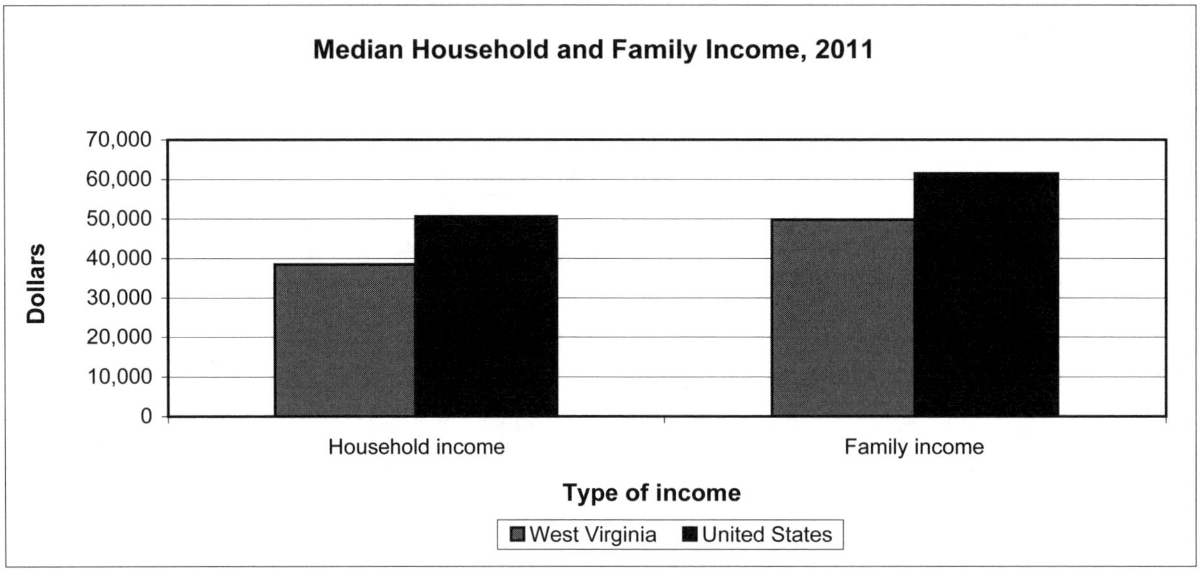

Table WV-6. Health Insurance Coverage Status for the Civilian Noninstitutionalized Population and Children Under 18 Years of Age

(Numbers in thousands, percent.)

Item	2004	2005	2006	2007	2008	2009	2010	2011
Civilian Noninstitutionalized Population	1,792	1,799	1,814	1,795	1,788	1,793	1,823	1,826
Covered by Private or Public Insurance								
Number	1,503	1,495	1,570	1,541	1,505	1,539	1,557	1,554
Percent	83.9	83.1	86.5	85.9	84.2	85.8	85.4	85.1
Not Covered								
Number	289	304	245	254	283	254	266	272
Percent	16.1	16.9	13.5	14.1	15.8	14.2	14.6	14.9
Percent in the U.S. not covered	14.9	15.3	15.8	15.3	15.1	15.1	15.5	15.1
Children Under 18 Years of Age	388	387	395	394	385	383	385	385
Covered by Private or Public Insurance								
Number	354	361	361	376	359	362	367	368
Percent	91.3	93.4	91.5	95.4	93.2	94.5	95.5	95.6
Not Covered								
Number	34	26	34	18	26	21	18	17
Percent	8.7	6.6	8.5	4.6	6.8	5.5	4.5	4.4
Percent in the U.S. not covered	10.5	10.9	11.7	11.0	9.7	8.6	8.0	7.5

Table WV-7. Employment Status by Demographic Group, Preliminary 2012

(Numbers in thousands, percent.)

Characteristic	Civilian noninstitutional population	Civilian labor force		Employed		Unemployed	
		Number	Percent of population	Number	Percent of population	Number	Percent of population
Total	1,492	811	54.3	751	50.3	60	7.4
Sex							
Male	725	436	60.1	398	54.9	38	8.7
Female	767	375	48.9	353	46.0	22	5.9
Race, Sex, and Hispanic Origin							
White	1,415	764	53.9	707	49.9	57	7.4
Male	688	410	59.6	375	54.5	35	8.6
Female	727	353	48.6	332	45.6	21	6.0
Black or African American	48	31	65.6	29	60.5	2	7.7
Male	25	18	72.7	16	65.9	2	9.4
Female	23	13	58.0	13	54.7	1	5.5
Hispanic	NA	NA	NA	NA	NA	NA	NA
Male	NA	NA	NA	NA	NA	NA	NA
Female	NA	NA	NA	NA	NA	NA	NA
Age							
16 to 19 years	81	24	29.9	20	24.3	5	18.8
20 to 24 years	118	77	65.5	66	55.9	11	14.7
25 to 34 years	237	177	74.7	159	66.9	18	10.4
35 to 44 years	222	167	75.5	158	71.3	9	5.6
45 to 54 years	252	172	68.2	162	64.4	10	5.6
55 to 64 years	283	151	53.5	147	51.9	4	2.9
65 years and over	300	43	14.3	40	13.4	3	5.8

NOTE: Data in Table 7 are from the Current Population Survey (CPS) and do not match the estimates in Table 8. See notes and definitions for further information.
NA = Not available.

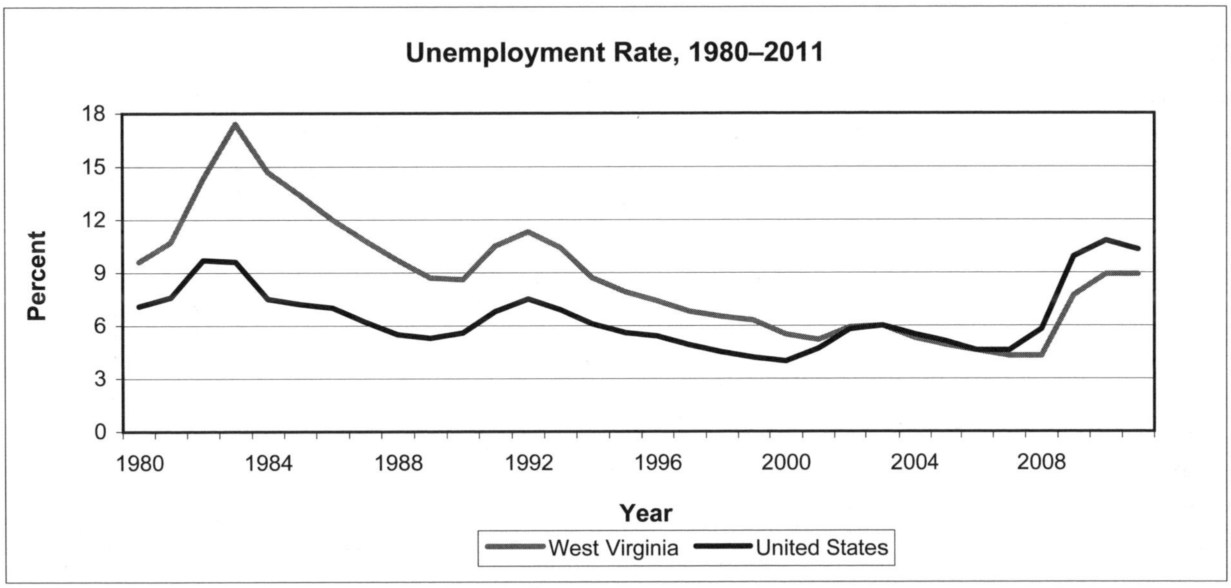

Table WV-8. Employment Status of the Civilian Noninstitutional Population Age 16 Years and Over

(Number, percent.)

Year	Civilian labor force	Civilian participation rate	Employed	Unemployed	Unemployment rate
2005	797,844	55.5	758,525	39,319	4.9
2006	810,437	56.2	773,118	37,319	4.6
2007	813,195	56.3	777,961	35,234	4.3
2008	806,152	55.6	771,805	34,347	4.3
2009	826,113	55.8	726,233	63,880	7.7
2010	820,067	54.2	746,844	73,223	8.9
2011	821,367	54.3	748,558	72,809	8.9

Table WV-9. Employment and Average Wages by Industry

(Estimates before 2007 are based on the 2002 *North American Industry Classification System* [NAICS]. Estimates from 2007 onward are based on the 2007 NAICS.)

Industry	2005	2006	2007	2008	2009	2010	2011
	Number of jobs						
Wage and Salary Employment by Industry	736,791	746,689	751,719	755,780	737,945	738,582	747,666
Farm Wage and Salary Employment	1,627	1,580	1,492	1,440	1,286	1,308	1,403
Nonfarm Wage and Salary Employment	735,164	745,109	750,227	754,340	736,659	737,274	746,263
Private wage and salary employment	583,875	593,588	595,452	597,771	577,417	575,076	584,884
Forestry, fishing, and related activities	1,721	1,718	1,664	1,549	1,367	1,320	1,254
Mining	24,719	26,886	27,631	30,483	28,947	29,251	32,910
Utilities	6,123	6,183	6,121	6,201	6,194	5,632	5,439
Construction	38,350	41,091	40,543	40,830	35,866	34,324	34,794
Manufacturing	62,005	60,858	58,899	56,586	50,767	49,180	49,560
Durable goods manufacturing	39,006	38,232	37,017	35,426	30,942	29,651	29,944
Nondurable goods manufacturing	22,999	22,626	21,882	21,160	19,825	19,529	19,616
Wholesale trade	24,115	24,922	24,954	24,702	23,555	23,130	23,454
Retail trade	90,704	91,868	92,707	91,213	88,334	88,004	88,367
Transportation and warehousing	20,411	20,732	20,771	20,763	19,485	19,376	19,847
Information	11,648	11,479	11,450	11,175	10,468	10,334	10,369
Finance and insurance	21,464	22,179	22,094	21,846	20,932	20,705	20,429
Real estate and rental and leasing	7,602	7,782	7,727	7,645	7,294	7,259	6,966
Professional, scientific, and technical services	24,491	24,937	24,801	25,182	24,467	24,843	25,421
Management of companies and enterprises	4,097	4,340	4,846	5,116	5,430	5,469	5,699
Administrative and waste services	31,091	31,445	32,024	31,565	30,410	31,060	32,341
Educational services	8,481	8,385	8,598	8,625	8,477	8,835	9,154
Health care and social assistance	100,105	100,604	101,963	104,748	107,358	109,010	110,883
Arts, entertainment, and recreation	9,347	9,186	9,455	9,147	9,305	9,536	7,366
Accommodation and food services	60,821	62,610	63,083	64,562	63,450	63,555	66,294
Other services, except public administration	36,580	36,383	36,121	35,833	35,311	34,253	34,337
Government and government enterprises	151,289	151,521	154,775	156,569	159,242	162,198	161,379
	Dollars						
Average Wages and Salaries by Industry	31,029	32,391	33,632	35,468	36,326	37,098	38,477
Average Farm Wages and Salaries	15,809	18,328	21,531	21,402	22,767	21,144	17,636
Average Nonfarm Wages and Salaries	31,063	32,420	33,656	35,495	36,350	37,126	38,516
Average private wages and salaries	30,400	31,870	33,232	35,073	35,863	36,857	38,463
Forestry, fishing, and related activities	20,918	22,726	23,964	24,680	24,825	26,023	27,258
Mining	57,139	59,700	63,147	69,067	72,252	73,284	78,917
Utilities	64,171	68,090	68,690	71,679	76,112	77,029	80,512
Construction	34,140	37,922	39,977	43,696	44,623	47,229	46,962
Manufacturing	43,097	44,207	45,717	47,564	47,934	49,963	51,693
Durable goods manufacturing	39,318	40,875	42,450	44,552	45,019	46,548	48,386
Nondurable goods manufacturing	49,505	49,836	51,243	52,607	52,484	55,147	56,741
Wholesale trade	42,106	44,478	46,039	48,153	49,287	49,810	51,245
Retail trade	19,854	20,421	21,080	21,891	22,608	23,173	23,729
Transportation and warehousing	39,853	41,082	42,769	45,693	46,467	46,947	49,182
Information	37,498	39,348	40,054	42,125	43,604	46,228	48,520
Finance and insurance	35,630	37,077	38,701	40,220	41,323	42,470	46,743
Real estate and rental and leasing	25,046	27,234	28,180	29,854	31,033	34,849	34,923
Professional, scientific, and technical services	39,380	41,621	43,960	46,393	48,247	50,439	50,623
Management of companies and enterprises	56,259	58,883	65,485	66,177	64,248	67,681	81,738
Administrative and waste services	20,788	21,711	22,619	24,682	25,383	26,618	28,502
Educational services	18,096	19,548	19,995	21,205	22,646	23,274	23,980
Health care and social assistance	31,688	32,899	34,258	35,567	36,934	37,129	37,800
Arts, entertainment, and recreation	17,111	18,862	20,137	19,448	20,694	22,315	19,473
Accommodation and food services	13,543	13,856	14,995	15,104	15,231	15,994	17,304
Other services, except public administration	20,642	21,742	22,518	23,503	24,025	25,163	25,599
Government and government enterprises	33,621	34,578	35,288	37,105	38,118	38,082	38,708

Table WV-10. Employment Characteristics by Family Type

(Number, percent.)

Family type and labor force status	2009		2010		2011	
	Total	Families with own children under 18 years	Total	Families with own children under 18 years	Total	Families with own children under 18 years
All families	492,279	192,889	485,652	176,631	477,809	176,454
Family type and labor force status						
Married-couple families	377,805	133,985	372,301	122,282	356,697	115,050
Both husband and wife in labor force	44.7	60.1	43.4	61.2	43.3	59.9
Husband in labor force, wife not in labor force	22.1	30.0	22.0	29.3	21.1	28.9
Wife in labor force, husband not in labor force	9.6	5.1	10.1	5.6	10.6	7.4
Both husband and wife not in labor force	23.6	4.8	24.5	3.9	25.0	3.8
Other families	114,474	58,904	113,351	54,349	121,112	61,404
Female householder, no husband present	72.1	74.3	74.8	75.1	70.8	73.2
In labor force	40.4	52.0	40.6	53.5	38.4	50.9
Not in labor force	31.7	22.3	34.3	21.7	32.5	22.3
Male householder, no wife present	27.9	25.7	25.2	24.9	29.2	26.8
In labor force	18.6	21.1	15.8	20.8	19.4	23.0
Not in labor force	9.3	4.6	9.3	4.1	9.8	3.8

Table WV-11. School Enrollment and Educational Attainment, 2011

(Number, percent.)

Item	State	U.S.
Enrollment		
Total population 3 years and over, enrolled in school	420,204	83,131,910
Enrolled in nursery school or preschool (percent)	5.5	6.0
Enrolled in kindergarten (percent)	4.8	5.1
Enrolled in elementary school, grades 1-8 (percent)	41.6	39.5
Enrolled in high school, grades 9-12 (percent)	20.6	20.7
Enrolled in college or graduate school (percent)	27.6	28.7
Attainment		
Total population 25 years and over	1,294,198	206,471,670
Less than ninth grade (percent)	5.8	6.0
9th to 12th grade, no diploma (percent)	10.0	8.1
High school graduate, including equivalency (percent)	41.6	28.4
Some college, no degree (percent)	17.7	21.2
Associate's degree (percent)	6.4	7.8
Bachelor's degree (percent)	11.7	17.9
Graduate or professional degree (percent)	6.8	10.6
High school graduate or higher (percent)	84.2	85.9
Bachelor's degree or higher (percent)	18.5	28.5

Table WV-12. Educational Indicators

(Number, percent; data derived from National Center of Education Statistics.)

Item	State	U.S.
Public Schools, 2009–2010 (except where noted)		
Number of school districts	55	13,629
Number of schools	759	99,834
Number of students (in thousands)	283	49,373
Student-teacher ratio	13.9	15.4
Expenditures per student (dollars)	12,153	10,591
Averaged freshman graduation rate, 2008–2009	77.0	75.5[1]
Dropout rate, 2008–2009	4.1	4.1
Students eligible for free or reduced-price lunch (percent)	51.4	48.0
English language learners, 2010–2011 (percent)	0.6	9.8[1]
Students with IEP (percent)	16.3	13.1
Private Schools, 2009–2010 (except where noted)		
Number of schools	137	33,366
Number of students (in thousands)	12	4,700
High school graduates, 2008–2009	739	308,813
Student-teacher ratio	9.6	10.7

[1] U.S. total includes estimates for nonreporting states.

Table WV-13. Reported Voting and Registration of the Voting-Age Population, November 2012

(Numbers in thousands, percent.)

Item	Total population	Total citizen population	Registered			Voted		
			Total registered	Percent registered (total population)	Percent registered (total citizen population)	Total voted	Percent voted (total population)	Percent voted (total citizen population)
U.S. Total	235,248	215,081	153,157	65.1	71.2	132,948	56.5	61.8
State Total	1,452	1,442	982	67.6	68.1	690	47.5	47.8
Sex								
Male	705	700	474	67.3	67.7	332	47.0	47.4
Female	747	742	508	67.9	68.4	358	47.9	48.2
Race								
White alone	1,391	1,386	948	68.2	68.4	665	47.8	48.0
White, non-Hispanic alone	1,381	1,378	944	68.4	68.6	662	48.0	48.1
Black alone	40	38	23	B	B	19	B	B
Asian alone	7	5	3	B	B	1	B	B
Hispanic (of any race)	14	13	8	B	B	4	B	B
Age								
18 to 24 years	163	162	78	47.8	48.1	37	22.6	22.7
25 to 44 years	450	447	293	65.1	65.6	178	39.5	39.8
45 to 64 years	479	475	326	68.0	68.6	253	52.9	53.3
65 to 74 years	205	204	168	81.7	82.2	134	65.3	65.7
75 years and over	155	155	118	75.8	75.8	88	56.5	56.5

B = Base is less than 75,000 and therefore too small to show the derived measure.

Table WV-14. Crime

(Number, rate per 100,000. Data are derived from the FBI Uniform Crime Reports.)

Item	State			U.S.		
	2010	2011	Percent change	2010	2011	Percent change
TOTAL POPULATION	1,854,368	1,855,364	0.1	309,330,219	311,591,917	0.7
VIOLENT CRIME						
Number	5,586	5,861	4.9	1,251,248	1,203,564	-3.8
Rate	301.2	315.9	4.9	404.5	386.3	-4.5
Murder and Nonnegligent Manslaughter						
Number	58	80	37.9	14,722	14,612	-0.7
Rate	3.1	4.3	38.7	4.8	4.7	-2.1
Forcible Rape						
Number	352	388	10.2	85,593	83,425	-2.5
Rate	19.5	20.9	7.2	27.7	26.8	-3.2
Robbery						
Number	776	910	17.3	369,089	354,396	-4.0
Rate	41.8	49.0	17.2	119.3	113.7	-4.7
Aggravated Assault						
Number	4,390	4,483	2.1	781,844	751,131	-3.9
Rate	236.7	241.6	2.1	252.8	241.1	-4.6
PROPERTY CRIME						
Number	41,301	42,189	2.2	9,112,625	9,063,173	-0.5
Rate	2,227.2	2,273.9	2.1	2,945.9	2,908.7	-1.3
Burglary						
Number	10,778	11,192	3.8	2,168,459	2,188,005	0.9
Rate	581.2	603.2	3.8	701.0	702.2	0.2
Larceny-Theft						
Number	28,104	28,743	2.3	6,204,601	6,159,795	-0.7
Rate	1,515.6	1,549.2	2.2	2,005.8	1,976.9	-1.4
Motor Vehicle Theft						
Number	2,419	2,254	-6.8	739,565	715,373	-3.3
Rate	130.4	121.5	-6.8	239.1	229.6	-4.0

Table WV-15. State Government Finances, 2011

(Dollar amounts in thousands, percent distribution.)

Item	Dollars	Percent distribution
Total Revenue	15,329,476	100.0
General revenue	12,646,080	82.5
Intergovernmental revenue	4,748,528	31.0
Taxes	5,142,771	33.5
General sales	1,210,255	7.9
Selective sales	1,209,208	7.9
License taxes	150,029	1.0
Individual income tax	1,665,885	10.9
Corporate income tax	307,278	2.0
Other taxes	600,116	3.9
Current charges	1,483,565	9.7
Miscellaneous general revenue	1,271,216	8.3
Utility revenue	2,108	0.0
Liquor stores revenue	84,268	0.5
Insurance trust revenue [1]	2,597,020	16.9
Total Expenditure	13,000,033	100.0
Intergovernmental expenditure	2,533,582	19.5
Direct expenditure	10,466,451	80.5
Current operation	7,372,142	56.7
Capital outlay	1,100,556	8.5
Insurance benefits and repayments	1,480,834	11.4
Assistance and subsidies	269,701	2.1
Interest on debt	243,218	1.9
Exhibit: Salaries and wages	1,771,738	13.6
Total Expenditure	13,000,033	100.0
General expenditure	11,445,676	88.0
Intergovernmental expenditure	2,533,582	19.5
Direct expenditure	8,912,094	68.6
General expenditure, by function:		
Education	4,161,900	32.0
Public welfare	3,287,709	25.3
Hospitals	120,540	0.9
Health	318,411	2.4
Highways	1,224,162	9.4
Police protection	76,036	0.6
Correction	275,564	2.1
Natural resources	227,838	1.8
Parks and recreation	60,557	0.5
Governmental administration	418,183	3.2
Interest on general debt	243,218	1.9
Other and unallocable	1,031,558	7.9
Utility expenditure	3,728	0.0
Liquor stores expenditure	69,795	0.5
Insurance trust expenditure	1,480,834	11.4
Debt at End of Fiscal Year	7,406,254	X
Cash and Security Holdings	20,305,005	X

X = Not applicable.

[1] Within insurance trust revenue, net earnings of state retirement systems is a calculated statistic (the item code in the data file is X08), and thus can be positive or negative. Net earnings is the sum of earnings on investments plus gains on investments minus losses on investments. The change made in 2002 for asset valuation from book to market value in accordance with Statement 34 of the Governmental Accounting Standards Board is reflected in the calculated statistics.

Table WV-16. State Government Tax Collections, 2012

(Dollars in thousands, percent.)

Item	Dollars	Percent distribution
Total Taxes	5,355,809	100.0
Property taxes	6,039	0.1
Sales and gross receipts	2,629,622	49.1
General sales and gross receipts	1,277,328	23.8
Selective sales and gross receipts	1,352,294	25.2
Alcoholic beverages	87,240	1.6
Amusements	78,121	1.5
Insurance premiums	144,786	2.7
Motor fuels	387,040	7.2
Pari-mutuels	2,337	-
Public utilities	155,560	2.9
Tobacco products	109,618	2.0
Other selective sales	387,592	7.2
Licenses	137,670	2.6
Alcoholic beverages	1,337	-
Amusements	3,745	0.1
Corporations in general	4,323	0.1
Hunting and fishing	104	-
Motor vehicle	3,261	0.1
Motor vehicle operators	104,388	1.9
Public utilities	395	-
Occupation and business, NEC	12,994	0.2
Other licenses	7,123	0.1
Income taxes	1,948,131	36.4
Individual income	1,755,746	32.8
Corporation net income	192,385	3.6
Other taxes	634,347	11.8
Death and gift	16	-
Documentary and stock transfer	8,128	0.2
Severance	626,203	11.7
Taxes, NEC	0	0.0

- = Rounds to zero.

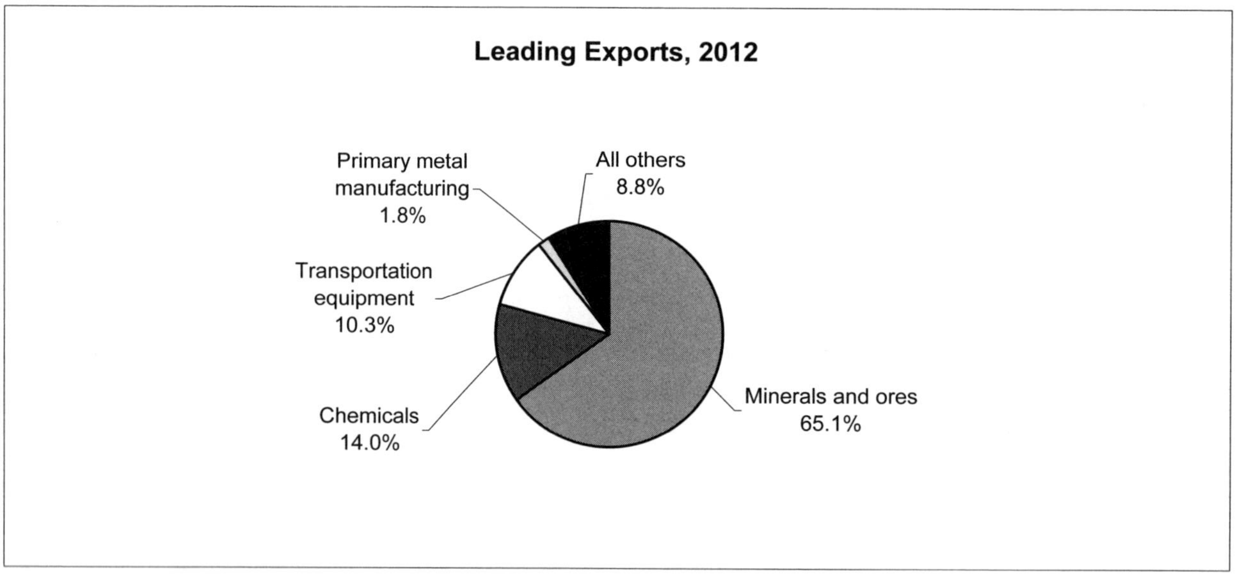

WISCONSIN

Facts and Figures

Location: North central United States; bordered on the N by Michigan and Lake Superior, on the E by Lake Michigan, on the S by Illinois, and on the W by Iowa and Minnesota

Area: 65,498 sq. mi. (169,639 sq. km.); rank—23rd

Population: 5,726,398 (2012 est.); rank—20th

Principal Cities: capital—Madison; largest—Milwaukee

Statehood: May 29, 1848; 30th state

U.S. Congress: 2 senators, 8 representatives

State Motto: Forward

State Song: "On, Wisconsin!"

State Nickname: The Badger State

Abbreviations: WI; Wis.; Wisc.

State Symbols: flower—wood violet; tree—sugar maple; bird—robin

At a Glance

- With an increase in population of 5.4 percent, Wisconsin ranked 23rd among the states in growth from 2000 to 2009.
- An estimated 30,300 marriages took place in Wisconsin in 2009, compared to 17,300 divorces.
- Wisconsin's violent crime rate in 2011 was 236.9 per 100,000 population, compared to 386.3 for the entire nation.
- In the 2012 election, 73.6 percent of Wisconsin's eligible voters voted, compared to 61.8 percent of eligible voters nationwide.
- In 2007, Wisconsin exported $2.1 billion worth of agricultural products, about 2.6 percent of the U.S. total.

Table WI-1. Population by Age, Sex, Race, and Hispanic Origin

(Number, percent, except where noted.)

Sex, age, race, and Hispanic origin	2000	2010	2012[1]	Average annual percent change, 2010–2012
Total Population	5,363,675	5,686,986	5,726,398	0.2
Percent of total U.S. population	1.9	1.8	1.8	X
Sex				
Male	2,649,041	2,822,400	2,843,072	0.2
Female	2,714,634	2,864,586	2,883,326	0.2
Age				
Under 5 years	342,340	358,443	350,581	-0.7
5 to 19 years	1,189,753	1,143,753	1,129,893	-0.4
20 to 64 years	3,129,029	3,407,476	3,421,424	0.1
65 years and over	702,553	777,314	824,500	1.9
Median age (years)	36.0	38.5	38.9	0.3
Race and Hispanic Origin				
One race				
White	4,769,857	5,036,923	5,052,112	0.1
Black	304,460	367,021	373,275	0.6
American Indian and Alaska Native	47,228	60,100	62,021	1.0
Asian	88,763	131,828	140,885	2.1
Native Hawaiian or Other Pacific Islander	1,630	2,505	2,640	1.7
Two or more races	66,895	88,609	95,465	2.4
Hispanic (of any race)	192,291	349,366	370,044	1.9

X = Not applicable.
[1] Population figures for 2012 are July 1 estimates. The 2010 estimates are taken from the 2010 Census.

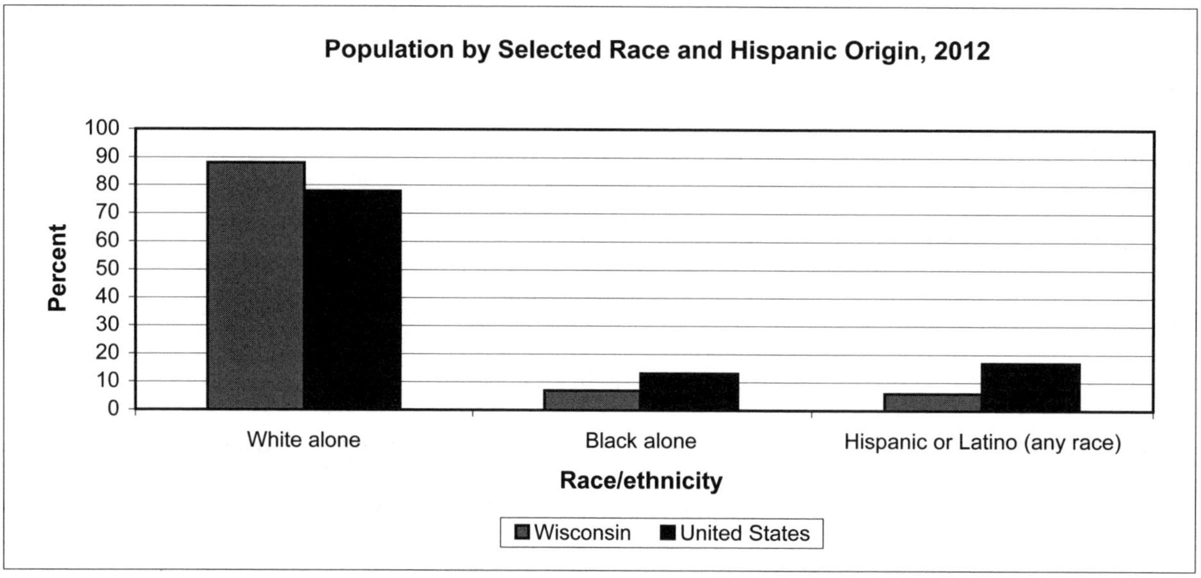

Table WI-2. Marital Status

(Number, percent distribution.)

Sex, age, race, and Hispanic origin	2000	2010	2011
Males, 15 Years and Over	2,072,397	2,261,022	2,276,263
Never married	30.2	34.1	34.5
Now married, except separated	57.9	52.1	52.5
Separated	1.1	1.0	1.1
Widowed	2.4	2.6	2.4
Divorced	8.4	10.2	9.6
Females, 15 Years and Over	2,167,164	2,328,733	2,342,294
Never married	24.3	28.1	28.1
Now married, except separated	54.6	50.1	50.2
Separated	1.3	1.2	1.3
Widowed	10.2	9.2	9.1
Divorced	9.7	11.4	11.3

Table WI-3. Households and Housing Characteristics

(Number, percent, dollars.)

Item	2000	2010	2011	Average annual percent change, 2000–2011
Total Households	2,084,544	2,279,532	2,275,352	0.8
Family households	1,386,815	1,453,332	1,462,927	0.5
Married-couple family	1,108,597	1,125,314	1,134,124	0.2
Other family	278,218	328,018	328,803	1.5
Male householder, no wife present	77,918	96,237	99,723	2.3
Female householder, no husband present	200,300	231,781	229,080	1.2
Nonfamily households	697,729	826,200	812,425	1.4
Householder living alone	557,875	669,106	655,662	1.5
Householder not living alone	139,854	157,094	156,763	1.0
Housing Characteristics				
Total housing units	2,321,144	2,625,477	2,634,806	1.1
Occupied housing units	2,084,544	2,279,532	2,275,352	0.8
Owner occupied	1,426,361	1,566,039	1,543,908	0.7
Renter occupied	658,183	713,493	731,444	0.9
Average size	2.50	2.43	2.44	-0.2
Financial Characteristics				
Median gross rent of renter-occupied housing	540	715	739	3.1
Median monthly owner costs for housing units with a mortgage	1,024	1,404	1,402	3.1
Median value of owner-occupied housing units	112,200	169,400	166,700	4.0

Table WI-4. Migration, Origin, and Language

(Number, percent.)

Characteristic	State			U.S.		
	2010	2011	Percent change	2010	2011	Percent change
Residence 1 Year Ago						
Population 1 year and over	5,623,196	5,647,213	0.4	305,628,607	307,900,319	0.7
Same house	85.8	85.8	-	84.6	84.8	0.2
Different house in the U.S.	14.0	13.9	-0.7	14.8	14.6	-1.4
Same county	9.2	8.7	-5.4	9.4	9.2	-2.1
Different county	4.7	5.2	10.6	5.4	5.4	-
Same state	3.1	3.2	3.2	3.2	3.1	-3.1
Different state	1.7	1.9	11.8	2.2	2.3	4.5
Abroad	0.3	0.3	-	0.6	0.6	-
Place of Birth						
Native born	5,436,127	5,442,033	0.1	269,393,835	271,214,059	0.7
Male	49.6	49.6	-	49.2	49.2	-
Female	50.4	50.4	-	50.8	50.8	-
Foreign born	254,920	269,734	5.8	39,955,854	40,377,860	1.1
Male	51.0	51.2	0.4	49.1	48.9	-0.4
Female	49.0	48.8	-0.4	50.9	51.1	0.4
Foreign born; naturalized U.S. citizen	103,035	119,363	15.8	17,476,082	18,140,192	3.8
Male	47.2	48.5	2.8	45.8	45.8	-
Female	52.8	51.5	-2.5	54.2	54.2	-
Foreign born; not a U.S. citizen	151,885	150,371	-1.0	22,479,772	22,237,668	-1.1
Male	53.6	53.4	-0.4	51.6	51.5	-0.2
Female	46.4	46.6	0.4	48.4	48.5	0.2
Entered 2000 or later	40.4	40.9	1.2	34.7	35.7	2.9
Entered 1990 to 1999	26.4	26.7	1.1	27.2	26.7	-1.8
Entered before 1990	33.3	32.5	-2.4	38.1	37.6	-1.3
World Region of Birth, Foreign						
Foreign-born population, excluding population born at sea	254,920	269,734	5.8	39,955,673	40,377,757	1.1
Europe	18.2	19.9	9.3	12.1	12.1	-
Asia	32.7	32.4	-0.9	28.2	28.6	1.4
Africa	3.0	5.4	80.0	4	4.1	2.5
Oceania	0.4	0.6	50.0	0.5	0.5	-
Latin America	43.3	39.4	-9.0	53.1	52.6	-0.9
North America	2.5	2.3	-8.0	2	2.0	-
Language Spoken at Home and Ability to Speak English						
Population 5 years and over	5,335,995	5,362,567	0.5	289,215,746	291,524,091	0.8
English only	91.7	91.3	-0.4	79.4	79.2	-0.3
Language other than English	8.3	8.7	4.8	20.6	20.8	1.0
Speaks English less than "very well"	3.2	3.3	3.1	8.7	8.7	-

- = Zero or rounds to zero.

Table WI-5. Median Income and Poverty Status, 2011

(Number, percent, except as noted.)

Characteristic	State		U.S.	
	Number	Percent	Number	Percent
Median Income				
Households (dollars)	50,395	X	50,502	X
Families (dollars)	63,732	X	61,455	X
Below Poverty Level (All People)	725,797	13.1	48,452,035	15.9
Sex				
Male	330,314	12.0	21,825,281	14.7
Female	395,483	14.1	26,626,754	17.2
Age				
Under 18 years	236,730	18.2	16,386,500	22.5
Related children under 18 years	230,521	17.9	16,087,074	22.2
18 to 64 years	431,861	12.4	28,335,079	14.8
65 years and over	57,206	7.5	3,730,456	9.3

X = Not applicable.

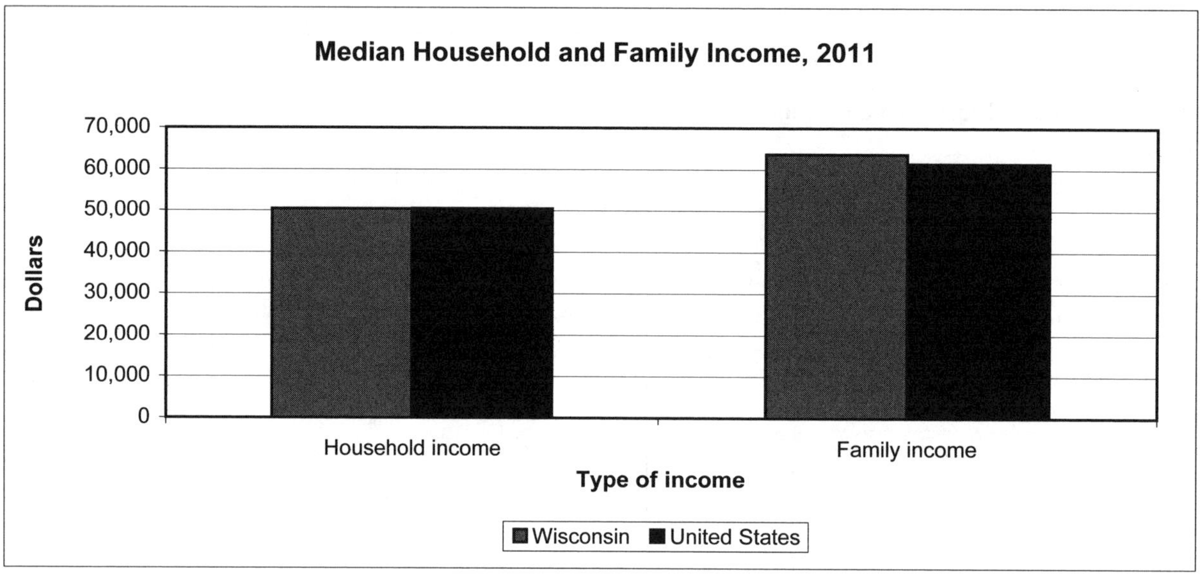

Table WI-6. Health Insurance Coverage Status for the Civilian Noninstitutionalized Population and Children Under 18 Years of Age

(Numbers in thousands, percent.)

Item	2004	2005	2006	2007	2008	2009	2010	2011
Civilian Noninstitutionalized Population	5,463	5,447	5,476	5,473	5,540	5,566	5,613	5,634
Covered by Private or Public Insurance								
Number	4,912	4,938	4,995	5,023	5,034	5,045	5,084	5,127
Percent	89.8	90.7	91.2	91.8	90.9	90.6	90.6	91.0
Not Covered								
Number	551	509	481	451	506	521	529	507
Percent	10.1	9.3	8.8	8.2	9.1	9.4	9.4	9.0
Percent in the U.S. not covered	14.9	15.3	15.8	15.3	15.1	15.1	15.5	15.1
Children Under 18 Years of Age	1,308	1,303	1,290	1,329	1,309	1,303	1,334	1,323
Covered by Private or Public Insurance								
Number	1,246	1,212	1,227	1,252	1,241	1,238	1,267	1,265
Percent	95.3	93.1	95.1	94.2	94.8	95.0	95.0	95.6
Not Covered								
Number	62	90	63	77	68	65	67	58
Percent	4.7	6.9	4.9	5.8	5.2	5.0	5.0	4.4
Percent in the U.S. not covered	10.5	10.9	11.7	11.0	9.7	8.6	8.0	7.5

Table WI-7. Employment Status by Demographic Group, Preliminary 2012

(Numbers in thousands, percent.)

Characteristic	Civilian noninstitutional population	Civilian labor force		Employed		Unemployed	
		Number	Percent of population	Number	Percent of population	Number	Percent of population
Total	4,495	3,084	68.6	2,866	63.7	219	7.1
Sex							
Male	2,206	1,602	72.6	1,482	67.2	120	7.5
Female	2,289	1,482	64.7	1,384	60.5	98	6.6
Race, Sex, and Hispanic Origin							
White	4,011	2,784	69.4	2,613	65.1	171	6.1
Male	1,971	1,465	74.3	1,369	69.4	97	6.6
Female	2,040	1,318	64.6	1,244	61.0	74	5.6
Black or African American	256	153	59.8	124	48.6	29	18.7
Male	121	64	52.7	49	40.3	15	23.5
Female	135	89	66.3	76	56.1	14	15.3
Hispanic	250	166	66.5	147	58.9	19	11.4
Male	134	99	74.1	88	65.8	11	11.1
Female	115	67	57.6	59	50.9	8	11.7
Age							
16 to 19 years	305	157	51.6	125	41.1	32	20.4
20 to 24 years	396	319	80.5	289	73.0	29	9.2
25 to 34 years	689	598	86.8	551	80.0	47	7.8
35 to 44 years	723	648	89.6	602	83.2	46	7.1
45 to 54 years	786	666	84.7	639	81.3	27	4.0
55 to 64 years	775	540	69.7	513	66.2	27	5.0
65 years and over	822	157	19.1	147	17.9	10	6.5

NOTE: Data in Table 7 are from the Current Population Survey (CPS) and do not match the estimates in Table 8. See notes and definitions for further information.

Unemployment Rate, 1980–2011

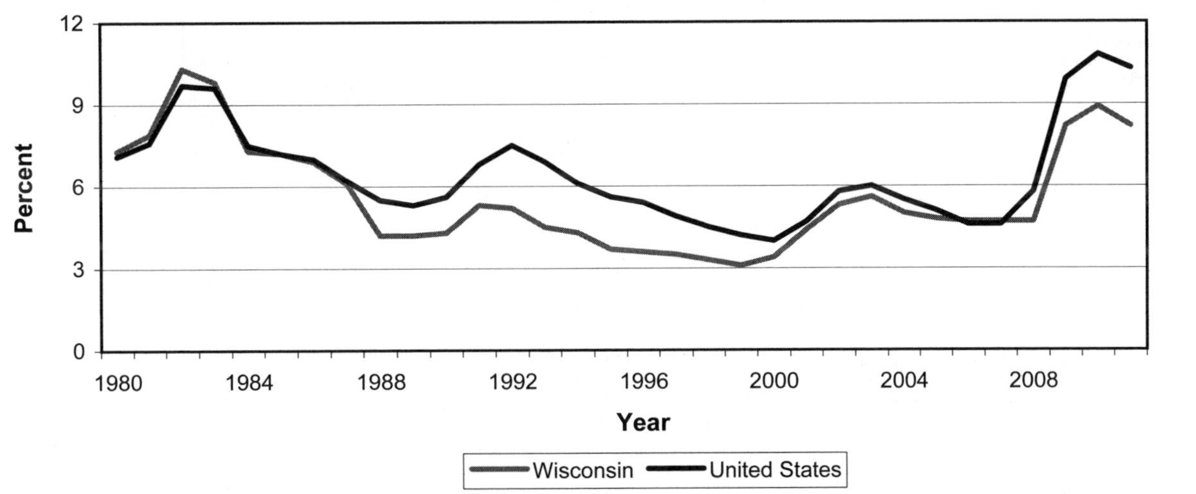

Table WI-8. Employment Status of the Civilian Noninstitutional Population Age 16 Years and Over

(Number, percent.)

Year	Civilian labor force	Civilian participation rate	Employed	Unemployed	Unemployment rate
2005	3,031,825	70.8	2,886,560	145,265	4.8
2006	3,070,465	71.0	2,927,307	143,158	4.7
2007	3,093,763	71.0	2,948,131	145,632	4.7
2008	3,084,130	70.3	2,937,871	146,259	4.7
2009	3,117,785	69.1	2,863,518	254,267	8.2
2010	3,080,461	68.3	2,805,102	275,359	8.9
2011	3,070,131	67.6	2,819,477	250,654	8.2

Table WI-9. Employment and Average Wages by Industry

(Estimates before 2007 are based on the 2002 *North American Industry Classification System* [NAICS]. Estimates from 2007 onward are based on the 2007 NAICS.)

Industry	2005	2006	2007	2008	2009	2010	2011
	Number of jobs						
Wage and Salary Employment by Industry	2,903,601	2,926,765	2,940,888	2,932,840	2,803,520	2,795,211	2,824,652
Farm Wage and Salary Employment	24,503	22,695	23,717	24,483	22,753	23,468	24,791
Nonfarm Wage and Salary Employment	2,879,098	2,904,070	2,917,171	2,908,357	2,780,767	2,771,743	2,799,861
Private wage and salary employment	2,454,283	2,477,653	2,489,895	2,476,599	2,344,911	2,334,467	2,368,305
Forestry, fishing, and related activities	4,821	4,919	4,991	5,115	5,250	5,412	5,700
Mining	2,968	3,052	2,849	2,631	2,308	2,227	2,293
Utilities	11,500	11,330	11,145	11,319	11,271	11,113	10,920
Construction	133,250	132,826	131,085	123,236	106,731	99,226	97,761
Manufacturing	507,926	508,889	503,084	494,458	437,035	431,729	445,665
Durable goods manufacturing	318,968	321,494	317,404	310,980	264,048	258,729	270,714
Nondurable goods manufacturing	188,958	187,395	185,680	183,478	172,987	173,000	174,951
Wholesale trade	119,158	122,523	123,475	123,652	116,786	113,855	115,475
Retail trade	322,036	320,110	320,447	314,818	302,760	299,011	299,853
Transportation and warehousing	98,623	100,191	100,979	97,099	91,549	90,637	91,926
Information	50,311	49,664	50,428	50,426	48,040	46,890	47,056
Finance and insurance	132,191	133,358	134,141	134,603	132,910	130,529	130,186
Real estate and rental and leasing	29,054	29,179	28,766	28,348	26,645	26,027	25,295
Professional, scientific, and technical services	94,952	98,251	100,288	102,257	97,654	95,303	97,667
Management of companies and enterprises	41,352	41,700	43,534	45,930	46,393	47,130	50,719
Administrative and waste services	131,619	134,959	138,756	138,480	119,381	131,733	139,142
Educational services	47,674	48,149	49,816	51,450	52,492	54,321	55,609
Health care and social assistance	331,980	339,423	345,264	353,683	358,739	361,818	364,486
Arts, entertainment, and recreation	35,293	35,796	36,886	36,279	35,227	35,238	35,954
Accommodation and food services	224,314	227,830	228,642	226,511	220,452	219,644	219,657
Other services, except public administration	135,261	135,504	135,319	136,304	133,288	132,624	132,941
Government and government enterprises	424,815	426,417	427,276	431,758	435,856	437,276	431,556
	Dollars						
Average Wages and Salaries by Industry	35,811	37,208	38,588	39,678	39,613	40,479	41,558
Average Farm Wages and Salaries	25,132	27,699	34,611	35,038	35,292	29,335	27,175
Average Nonfarm Wages and Salaries	35,902	37,283	38,621	39,717	39,649	40,573	41,686
Average private wages and salaries	35,930	37,374	38,755	39,814	39,642	40,697	41,876
Forestry, fishing, and related activities	25,905	26,774	27,827	29,241	28,691	29,757	30,923
Mining	47,182	48,091	50,027	52,482	53,359	56,996	60,382
Utilities	73,650	74,812	78,590	91,695	93,364	92,701	95,756
Construction	43,418	45,222	48,177	50,503	49,693	50,070	51,149
Manufacturing	45,558	47,265	48,470	49,672	49,355	51,943	53,093
Durable goods manufacturing	46,387	48,425	49,399	50,813	50,468	53,717	55,081
Nondurable goods manufacturing	44,160	45,274	46,882	47,739	47,657	49,291	50,016
Wholesale trade	49,470	51,296	52,558	54,176	53,362	55,180	57,311
Retail trade	21,846	22,451	22,823	23,275	23,343	23,834	24,204
Transportation and warehousing	37,447	38,247	39,440	39,976	39,272	39,724	40,815
Information	45,245	47,723	50,649	52,156	52,629	54,155	56,149
Finance and insurance	51,678	54,742	57,028	58,325	57,581	59,821	62,356
Real estate and rental and leasing	29,798	31,394	31,992	33,097	33,784	33,071	34,171
Professional, scientific, and technical services	52,606	54,471	57,396	58,692	58,569	59,652	61,676
Management of companies and enterprises	76,645	83,675	85,071	80,226	78,337	85,041	87,493
Administrative and waste services	22,673	23,541	25,250	26,110	26,445	26,507	27,239
Educational services	27,246	28,933	30,330	31,454	32,112	33,076	34,023
Health care and social assistance	37,490	38,598	40,029	41,594	42,487	42,855	43,680
Arts, entertainment, and recreation	23,088	25,594	26,878	27,523	27,283	28,299	29,215
Accommodation and food services	12,174	12,626	13,455	13,405	13,369	13,956	14,418
Other services, except public administration	22,990	23,751	24,869	25,680	25,765	26,596	27,231
Government and government enterprises	35,739	36,753	37,840	39,160	39,686	39,910	40,638

Table WI-10. Employment Characteristics by Family Type

(Number, percent.)

Family type and labor force status	2009 Total	2009 Families with own children under 18 years	2010 Total	2010 Families with own children under 18 years	2011 Total	2011 Families with own children under 18 years
All families	1,476,615	660,200	1,453,332	644,861	1,462,927	633,636
Family type and labor force status						
Married-couple families	1,148,612	455,520	1,125,314	437,433	1,134,124	429,500
Both husband and wife in labor force	61.0	75.5	60.4	75.8	59.4	75.7
Husband in labor force, wife not in labor force	15.6	20.0	15.3	19.8	15.9	19.4
Wife in labor force, husband not in labor force	7.7	3.5	7.7	3.2	8.2	3.6
Both husband and wife not in labor force	15.8	0.9	16.6	1.1	16.5	1.3
Other families	328,003	204,680	328,018	207,428	328,803	204,136
Female householder, no husband present	70.1	72.9	70.7	72.9	69.7	71.8
In labor force	53.9	62.8	54.3	61.6	53.1	60.6
Not in labor force	16.2	10.1	16.3	11.4	16.6	11.2
Male householder, no wife present	29.9	27.1	29.3	27.1	30.3	28.2
In labor force	24.9	25.0	24.3	24.2	24.7	25.9
Not in labor force	5.0	2.1	5.0	2.9	5.6	2.3

Table WI-11. School Enrollment and Educational Attainment, 2011

(Number, percent.)

Item	State	U.S.
Enrollment		
Total population 3 years and over, enrolled in school	1,506,580	83,131,910
Enrolled in nursery school or preschool (percent)	5.1	6.0
Enrolled in kindergarten (percent)	5.8	5.1
Enrolled in elementary school, grades 1-8 (percent)	39.3	39.5
Enrolled in high school, grades 9-12 (percent)	20.9	20.7
Enrolled in college or graduate school (percent)	28.9	28.7
Attainment		
Total population 25 years and over	3,831,373	206,471,670
Less than ninth grade (percent)	3.4	6.0
9th to 12th grade, no diploma (percent)	6.3	8.1
High school graduate, including equivalency (percent)	33.1	28.4
Some college, no degree (percent)	21.3	21.2
Associate's degree (percent)	9.6	7.8
Bachelor's degree (percent)	17.4	17.9
Graduate or professional degree (percent)	9.0	10.6
High school graduate or higher (percent)	90.4	85.9
Bachelor's degree or higher (percent)	26.5	28.5

Table WI-12. Educational Indicators

(Number, percent; data derived from National Center of Education Statistics.)

Item	State	U.S.
Public Schools, 2009–2010 (except where noted)		
Number of school districts	425	13,629
Number of schools	2,242	99,834
Number of students (in thousands)	872	49,373
Student-teacher ratio	14.9	15.4
Expenditures per student (dollars)	13,244	10,591
Averaged freshman graduation rate, 2008–2009	90.7	75.5[1]
Dropout rate, 2008–2009	2.3	4.1
Students eligible for free or reduced-price lunch (percent)	39.2	48.0
English language learners, 2010–2011 (percent)	5.0	9.8[1]
Students with IEP (percent)	14.4	13.1
Private Schools, 2009–2010 (except where noted)		
Number of schools	894	33,366
Number of students (in thousands)	116	4,700
High school graduates, 2008–2009	5,607	308,813
Student-teacher ratio	12.1	10.7

[1] U.S. total includes estimates for nonreporting states.

Table WI-13. Reported Voting and Registration of the Voting-Age Population, November 2012

(Numbers in thousands, percent.)

Item	Total population	Total citizen population	Registered			Voted		
			Total registered	Percent registered (total population)	Percent registered (total citizen population)	Total voted	Percent voted (total population)	Percent voted (total citizen population)
U.S. Total	235,248	215,081	153,157	65.1	71.2	132,948	56.5	61.8
State Total	4,352	4,247	3,318	76.3	78.1	3,127	71.9	73.6
Sex								
Male	2,115	2,058	1,554	73.5	75.5	1,460	69.0	70.9
Female	2,236	2,189	1,764	78.9	80.6	1,667	74.6	76.2
Race								
White alone	3,920	3,856	3,030	77.3	78.6	2,854	72.8	74.0
White, non-Hispanic alone	3,751	3,728	2,968	79.1	79.6	2,797	74.6	75.0
Black alone	242	227	184	76.1	81.0	178	73.7	78.5
Asian alone	35	20	15	B	B	15	B	B
Hispanic (of any race)	214	163	76	35.5	46.8	71	33.3	43.9
Age								
18 to 24 years	539	513	308	57.1	60.1	287	53.3	56.0
25 to 44 years	1,413	1,357	1,024	72.4	75.4	951	67.3	70.1
45 to 64 years	1,552	1,532	1,224	78.9	79.9	1,192	76.8	77.8
65 to 74 years	444	444	398	89.7	89.7	383	86.3	86.3
75 years and over	403	401	364	90.4	90.8	313	77.8	78.1

B = Base is less than 75,000 and therefore too small to show the derived measure.

Table WI-14. Crime

(Number, rate per 100,000. Data are derived from the FBI Uniform Crime Reports.)

Item	State			U.S.		
	2010	2011	Percent change	2010	2011	Percent change
TOTAL POPULATION	5,691,659	5,711,767	0.4	309,330,219	311,591,917	0.7
VIOLENT CRIME						
Number	14,167	13,532	-4.5	1,251,248	1,203,564	-3.8
Rate	248.9	236.9	-4.8	404.5	386.3	-4.5
Murder and Nonnegligent Manslaughter						
Number	155	136	-12.3	14,722	14,612	-0.7
Rate	2.7	2.4	-11.1	4.8	4.7	-2.1
Forcible Rape						
Number	1,191	1,163	-2.4	85,593	83,425	-2.5
Rate	20.9	20.4	-2.4	27.7	26.8	-3.2
Robbery						
Number	4,516	4,469	-1.0	369,089	354,396	-4.0
Rate	79.3	78.2	-1.4	119.3	113.7	-4.7
Aggravated Assault						
Number	8,305	7,764	-6.5	781,844	751,131	-3.9
Rate	145.9	135.9	-6.9	252.8	241.1	-4.6
PROPERTY CRIME						
Number	142,781	138,949	-2.7	9,112,625	9,063,173	-0.5
Rate	2,508.6	2,432.7	-3.0	2,945.9	2,908.7	-1.3
Burglary						
Number	26,636	26,654	0.1	2,168,459	2,188,005	0.9
Rate	468.0	466.7	-0.3	701.0	702.2	0.2
Larceny-Theft						
Number	107,993	104,063	-3.6	6,204,601	6,159,795	-0.7
Rate	1,897.4	1,821.9	-4.0	2,005.8	1,976.9	-1.4
Motor Vehicle Theft						
Number	8,152	8,232	1.0	739,565	715,373	-3.3
Rate	143.2	144.1	0.6	239.1	229.6	-4.0

Table WI-15. State Government Finances, 2011

(Dollar amounts in thousands, percent distribution.)

Item	Dollars	Percent distribution
Total Revenue	44,807,389	100.0
General revenue	32,132,862	71.7
Intergovernmental revenue	10,535,845	23.5
Taxes	15,347,327	34.3
General sales	4,109,019	9.2
Selective sales	2,700,050	6.0
License taxes	1,058,464	2.4
Individual income tax	6,429,115	14.3
Corporate income tax	850,647	1.9
Other taxes	200,032	0.4
Current charges	3,817,453	8.5
Miscellaneous general revenue	2,432,237	5.4
Utility revenue	0	0.0
Liquor stores revenue	0	0.0
Insurance trust revenue [1]	12,674,527	28.3
Total Expenditure	39,349,832	100.0
Intergovernmental expenditure	10,428,954	26.5
Direct expenditure	28,920,878	73.5
Current operation	18,220,639	46.3
Capital outlay	2,656,015	6.7
Insurance benefits and repayments	6,303,922	16.0
Assistance and subsidies	712,575	1.8
Interest on debt	1,027,727	2.6
Exhibit: Salaries and wages	4,218,700	10.7
Total Expenditure	39,349,832	100.0
General expenditure	33,040,658	84.0
Intergovernmental expenditure	10,428,954	26.5
Direct expenditure	22,611,704	57.5
General expenditure, by function:		
Education	11,345,332	28.8
Public welfare	8,969,198	22.8
Hospitals	1,187,957	3.0
Health	744,851	1.9
Highways	2,432,125	6.2
Police protection	133,915	0.3
Correction	1,160,898	3.0
Natural resources	694,882	1.8
Parks and recreation	50,974	0.1
Governmental administration	716,003	1.8
Interest on general debt	1,027,727	2.6
Other and unallocable	4,576,796	11.6
Utility expenditure	5,252	0.0
Liquor stores expenditure	0	0.0
Insurance trust expenditure	6,303,922	16.0
Debt at End of Fiscal Year	22,878,524	X
Cash and Security Holdings	97,615,538	X

X = Not applicable.
[1] Within insurance trust revenue, net earnings of state retirement systems is a calculated statistic (the item code in the data file is X08), and thus can be positive or negative. Net earnings is the sum of earnings on investments plus gains on investments minus losses on investments. The change made in 2002 for asset valuation from book to market value in accordance with Statement 34 of the Governmental Accounting Standards Board is reflected in the calculated statistics.

Table WI-16. State Government Tax Collections, 2012

(Dollars in thousands, percent.)

Item	Dollars	Percent distribution
Total Taxes	14,747,971	100.0
Property taxes	155,556	1.1
Sales and gross receipts	6,394,748	43.4
General sales and gross receipts	3,871,581	26.3
Selective sales and gross receipts	2,523,167	17.1
Alcoholic beverages	49,661	0.3
Amusements	248	-
Insurance premiums	152,188	1.0
Motor fuels	893,771	6.1
Pari-mutuels	0	0.0
Public utilities	384,780	2.6
Tobacco products	597,866	4.1
Other selective sales	444,653	3.0
Licenses	995,018	6.7
Alcoholic beverages	1,525	-
Amusements	585	-
Corporations in general	18,789	0.1
Hunting and fishing	68,583	0.5
Motor vehicle	455,446	3.1
Motor vehicle operators	41,146	0.3
Public utilities	80,942	0.5
Occupation and business, NEC	323,364	2.2
Other licenses	4,638	-
Income taxes	7,150,055	48.5
Individual income	6,260,550	42.5
Corporation net income	889,505	6.0
Other taxes	52,594	0.4
Death and gift	310	-
Documentary and stock transfer	35,728	0.2
Severance	5,013	-
Taxes, NEC	11,543	0.1

- = Rounds to zero.

Leading Exports, 2012

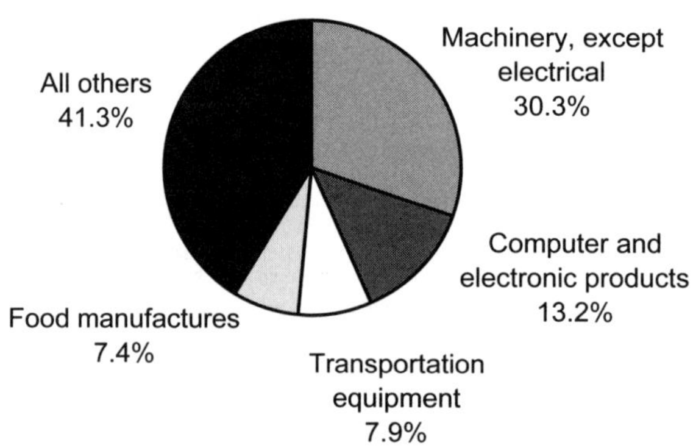

WYOMING

Facts and Figures

Location: Western United States; bordered on the N by Montana, on the E by South Dakota and Nebraska, on the S by Colorado and Utah, and on the W by Utah and Idaho

Area: 97,814 sq. mi. (253,336 sq. km.); rank—10th

Population: 576,412 (2012 est.); rank—51st

Principal Cities: capital—Cheyenne; largest—Cheyenne

Statehood: July 10, 1890; 44th state

U.S. Congress: 2 senators, 1 representative

State Motto: Equal Rights

State Song: "Wyoming"

State Nicknames: The Equality State; The Cowboy State

Abbreviations: WY; Wyo.

State Symbols: flower—Indian paintbrush; tree—cottonwood; bird—Western meadowlark

At a Glance

- With an increase in population of 10.2 percent, Wyoming ranked 43rd among the states in growth from 2000 to 2009.
- An estimated 4,700 marriages took place in Wyoming in 2009, compared to 2,800 divorces.
- Wyoming's violent crime rate in 2011 was 219.3 per 100,000 population, compared to 386.3 for the entire nation.
- In the 2012 election, 58.9 percent of Wyoming's eligible voters voted, compared to 61.8 percent of eligible voters nationwide.
- In 2007, Wyoming exported $61 million worth of agricultural products, less than 1 percent of the U.S. total.

Table WY-1. Population by Age, Sex, Race, and Hispanic Origin

(Number, percent, except where noted.)

Sex, age, race, and Hispanic origin	2000	2010	2012[1]	Average annual percent change, 2010–2012
Total Population	493,782	563,626	576,412	0.7
Percent of total U.S. population	0.2	0.2	0.2	X
Sex				
Male	248,374	287,437	294,281	0.8
Female	245,408	276,189	282,131	0.7
Age				
Under 5 years	30,940	40,203	38,592	-1.4
5 to 19 years	114,406	111,310	112,451	0.3
20 to 64 years	290,743	342,023	349,861	0.7
65 years and over	57,693	70,090	75,508	2.4
Median age (years)	36.2	36.8	36.9	0.1
Race and Hispanic Origin				
One race				
White	454,670	529,110	537,450	0.5
Black	3,722	5,135	8,555	13.3
American Indian and Alaska Native	11,133	14,457	15,003	1.2
Asian	2,771	4,649	5,183	3.4
Native Hawaiian or Other Pacific Islander	302	521	575	3.1
Two or more races	8,883	9,754	10,646	2.8
Hispanic (of any race)	31,669	52,112	56,779	2.7

X = Not applicable.
[1] Population figures for 2012 are July 1 estimates. The 2010 estimates are taken from the 2010 Census.

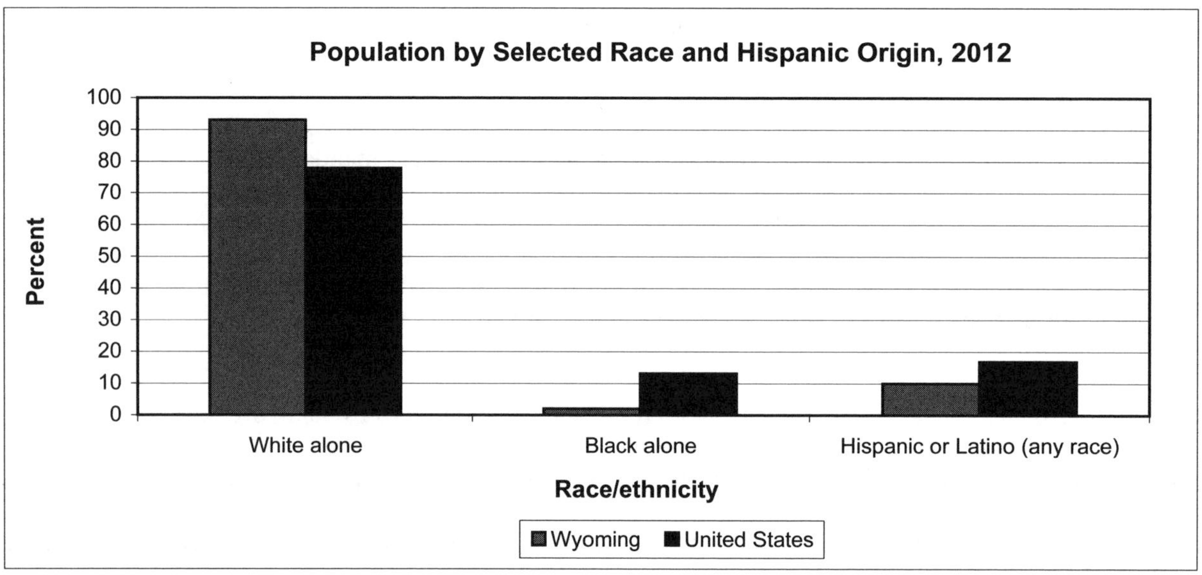

Table WY-2. Marital Status

(Number, percent distribution.)

Sex, age, race, and Hispanic origin	2000	2010	2011
Males, 15 Years and Over	195,412	228,725	230,621
Never married	26.6	29.0	32.4
Now married, except separated	58.8	56.2	52.1
Separated	1.0	1.3	1.4
Widowed	2.3	2.4	2.3
Divorced	11.3	11.2	11.8
Females, 15 Years and Over	195,433	220,169	223,960
Never married	20.0	20.7	23.6
Now married, except separated	57.5	55.1	52.8
Separated	1.3	2.0	1.3
Widowed	9.2	8.6	8.2
Divorced	12.0	13.6	14.1

Table WY-3. Households and Housing Characteristics

(Number, percent, dollars.)

Item	2000	2010	2011	Average annual percent change, 2000–2011
Total Households	193,608	222,803	222,539	1.2
Family households	130,497	147,394	142,618	0.8
Married-couple family	106,179	119,756	114,463	0.7
Other family	24,318	27,638	28,155	1.3
Male householder, no wife present	7,481	7,804	8,700	1.4
Female householder, no husband present	16,837	19,834	19,455	1.3
Nonfamily households	63,111	75,409	79,921	2.2
Householder living alone	50,980	61,775	60,037	1.5
Householder not living alone	12,131	13,634	19,884	5.3
Housing Characteristics				
Total housing units	223,854	262,286	265,554	1.6
Occupied housing units	193,608	222,803	222,539	1.2
Owner occupied	135,514	155,278	157,223	1.3
Renter occupied	58,094	67,525	65,316	1.0
Average size	2.48	2.47	2.49	-
Financial Characteristics				
Median gross rent of renter-occupied housing	437	693	759	6.1
Median monthly owner costs for housing units with a mortgage	825	1,300	1,269	4.5
Median value of owner-occupied housing units	96,600	180,100	179,900	7.2

- = Zero or rounds to zero.

Table WY-4. Migration, Origin, and Language

(Number, percent.)

Characteristic	State			U.S.		
	2010	2011	Percent change	2010	2011	Percent change
Residence 1 Year Ago						
Population 1 year and over	556,954	561,389	0.8	305,628,607	307,900,319	0.7
Same house	79.8	82.4	3.3	84.6	84.8	0.2
Different house in the U.S.	19.8	17.3	-12.6	14.8	14.6	-1.4
Same county	11.9	9.1	-23.5	9.4	9.2	-2.1
Different county	7.9	8.2	3.8	5.4	5.4	-
Same state	2.9	2.7	-6.9	3.2	3.1	-3.1
Different state	5.0	5.5	10.0	2.2	2.3	4.5
Abroad	0.4	0.2	-50.0	0.6	0.6	-
Place of Birth						
Native born	548,617	549,768	0.2	269,393,835	271,214,059	0.7
Male	50.9	51.0	0.2	49.2	49.2	-
Female	49.1	49.0	-0.2	50.8	50.8	-
Foreign born	15,843	18,390	16.1	39,955,854	40,377,860	1.1
Male	49.0	49.6	1.2	49.1	48.9	-0.4
Female	51.0	50.4	-1.2	50.9	51.1	0.4
Foreign born; naturalized U.S. citizen	6,447	5,973	-7.4	17,476,082	18,140,192	3.8
Male	47.6	47.2	-0.8	45.8	45.8	-
Female	52.4	52.8	0.8	54.2	54.2	-
Foreign born; not a U.S. citizen	9,396	12,417	32.2	22,479,772	22,237,668	-1.1
Male	50.0	50.7	1.4	51.6	51.5	-0.2
Female	50.0	49.3	-1.4	48.4	48.5	0.2
Entered 2000 or later	49.6	55.6	12.1	34.7	35.7	2.9
Entered 1990 to 1999	20.6	19.3	-6.3	27.2	26.7	-1.8
Entered before 1990	29.8	25.1	-15.8	38.1	37.6	-1.3
World Region of Birth, Foreign						
Foreign-born population, excluding population born at sea	15,843	18,390	16.1	39,955,673	40,377,757	1.1
Europe	16.0	11.9	-25.6	12.1	12.1	-
Asia	18.4	17.1	-7.1	28.2	28.6	1.4
Africa	1.9	2.3	21.1	4	4.1	2.5
Oceania	1.5	1.0	-33.3	0.5	0.5	-
Latin America	56.9	62.1	9.1	53.1	52.6	-0.9
North America	5.4	5.5	1.9	2	2.0	-
Language Spoken at Home and Ability to Speak English						
Population 5 years and over	523,440	529,136	1.1	289,215,746	291,524,091	0.8
English only	93.6	93.6	-	79.4	79.2	-0.3
Language other than English	6.4	6.4	-	20.6	20.8	1.0
Speaks English less than "very well"	1.8	1.7	-5.6	8.7	8.7	-

- = Zero or rounds to zero.

Table WY-5. Median Income and Poverty Status, 2011

(Number, percent, except as noted.)

Characteristic	State		U.S.	
	Number	Percent	Number	Percent
Median Income				
Households (dollars)	56,322	X	50,502	X
Families (dollars)	68,629	X	61,455	X
Below Poverty Level (All People)	62,629	11.3	48,452,035	15.9
Sex				
Male	27,950	9.9	21,825,281	14.7
Female	34,679	12.7	26,626,754	17.2
Age				
Under 18 years	20,689	15.6	16,386,500	22.5
Related children under 18 years	20,017	15.2	16,087,074	22.2
18 to 64 years	37,643	10.7	28,335,079	14.8
65 years and over	4,297	6.2	3,730,456	9.3

X = Not applicable.

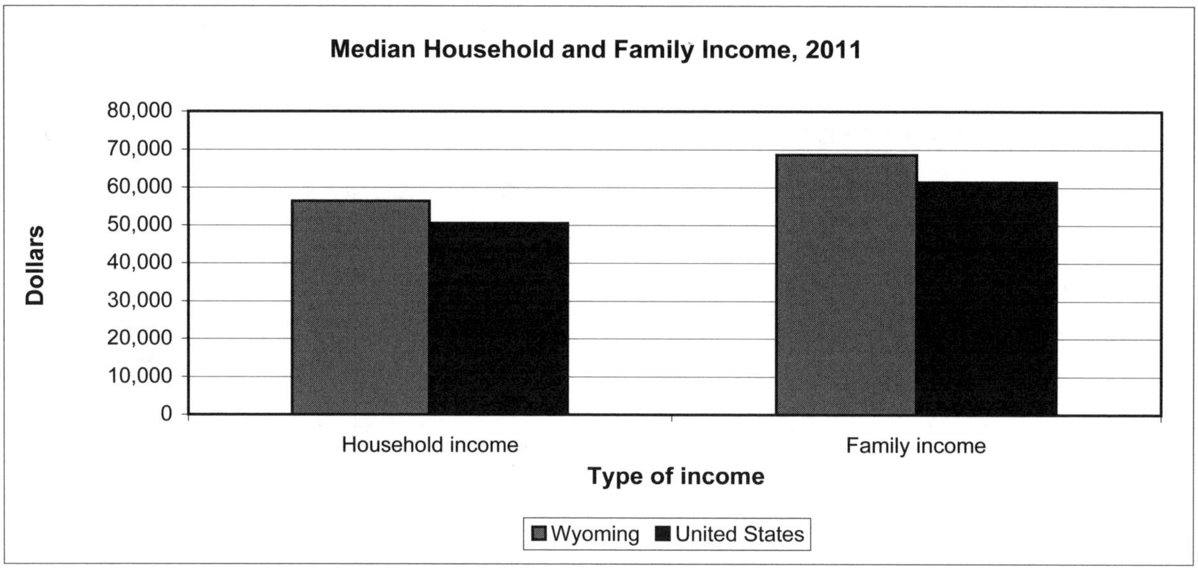

Table WY-6. Health Insurance Coverage Status for the Civilian Noninstitutionalized Population and Children Under 18 Years of Age

(Numbers in thousands, percent.)

Item	2004	2005	2006	2007	2008	2009	2010	2011
Civilian Noninstitutionalized Population	498	511	516	518	523	534	555	559
Covered by Private or Public Insurance								
Number	435	436	441	447	451	453	472	473
Percent	87.2	85.4	85.4	86.4	86.2	84.8	85.1	84.6
Not Covered								
Number	64	75	75	70	72	81	83	86
Percent	12.8	14.6	14.6	13.6	13.8	15.2	14.9	15.4
Percent in the U.S. not covered	14.9	15.3	15.8	15.3	15.1	15.1	15.5	15.1
Children Under 18 Years of Age	117	118	123	127	127	128	136	135
Covered by Private or Public Insurance								
Number	107	105	113	115	116	117	125	123
Percent	91.2	89.2	91.8	90.4	91.3	91.0	92.1	91.4
Not Covered								
Number	10	13	10	12	11	11	11	12
Percent	8.8	10.8	8.2	9.6	8.7	9.0	7.9	8.6
Percent in the U.S. not covered	10.5	10.9	11.7	11.0	9.7	8.6	8.0	7.5

Table WY-7. Employment Status by Demographic Group, Preliminary 2012

(Numbers in thousands, percent.)

Characteristic	Civilian noninstitutional population	Civilian labor force		Employed		Unemployed	
		Number	Percent of population	Number	Percent of population	Number	Percent of population
Total	441	305	69.2	288	65.4	17	5.5
Sex							
Male	222	169	75.9	160	71.8	9	5.4
Female	219	136	62.3	128	58.8	8	5.6
Race, Sex, and Hispanic Origin							
White	414	287	69.4	273	65.9	14	5.0
Male	207	158	76.4	150	72.7	8	4.9
Female	207	129	62.4	123	59.2	7	5.1
Black or African American	4	3	79.1	3	71.9	...	9.5
Male	NA	NA	NA	NA	NA	NA	NA
Female	NA	NA	NA	NA	NA	NA	NA
Hispanic	37	25	66.4	22	60.4	2	9.0
Male	21	15	71.4	13	65.1	1	8.8
Female	17	10	60.3	9	54.7	1	9.3
Age							
16 to 19 years	27	14	51.3	12	42.5	2	17.1
20 to 24 years	40	31	77.0	27	68.8	3	10.6
25 to 34 years	79	65	82.7	63	79.5	3	3.9
35 to 44 years	66	56	85.1	54	81.2	3	4.6
45 to 54 years	79	68	85.6	64	81.4	3	5.0
55 to 64 years	74	52	69.8	50	67.3	2	3.6
65 years and over	76	19	25.7	19	24.7	1	3.7

NOTE: Data in Table 7 are from the Current Population Survey (CPS) and do not match the estimates in Table 8. See notes and definitions for further information.
NA = Not available.
... = Fewer than 500 persons.

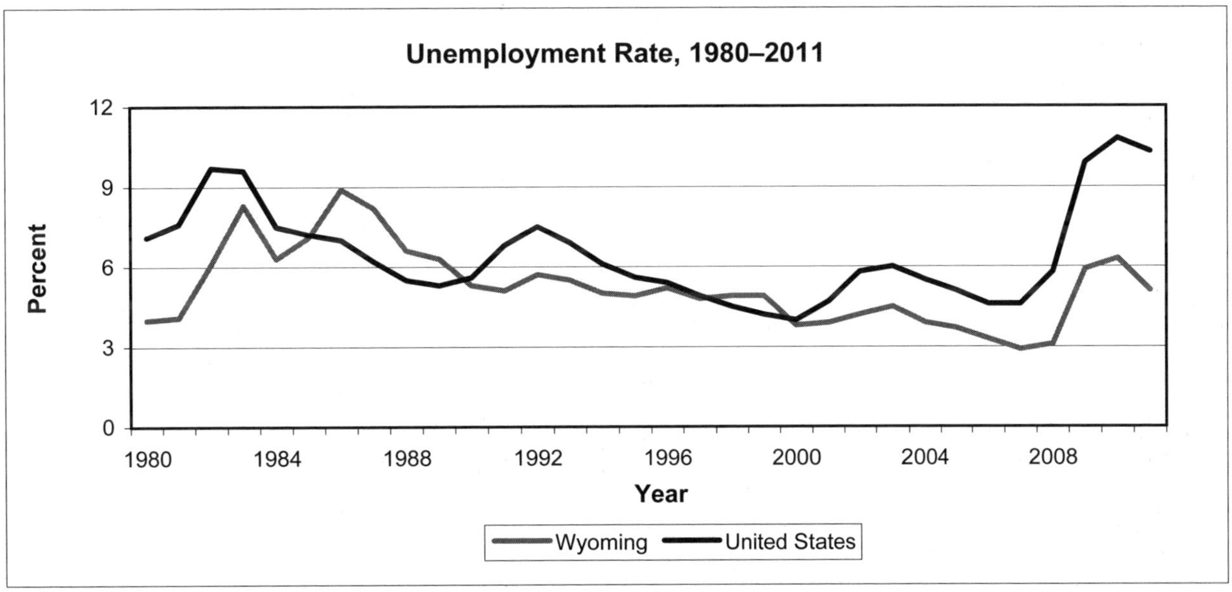

Table WY-8. Employment Status of the Civilian Noninstitutional Population Age 16 Years and Over

(Number, percent.)

Year	Civilian labor force	Civilian participation rate	Employed	Unemployed	Unemployment rate
2005	277,238	71.2	266,966	10,252	3.7
2006	283,410	71.6	274,198	9,212	3.3
2007	288,433	71.6	280,087	8,346	2.9
2008	292,606	71.4	283,598	9,008	3.1
2009	296,944	69.2	279,544	17,400	5.9
2010	299,393	67.7	280,614	18,779	6.3
2011	305,529	68.5	289,976	15,553	5.1

Table WY-9. Employment and Average Wages by Industry

(Estimates before 2007 are based on the 2002 *North American Industry Classification System* [NAICS]. Estimates from 2007 onward are based on the 2007 NAICS.)

Industry	2005	2006	2007	2008	2009	2010	2011
	Number of jobs						
Wage and Salary Employment by Industry	275,063	287,821	298,916	307,460	295,383	291,969	295,870
Farm Wage and Salary Employment	3,107	3,064	2,837	2,993	2,805	2,878	3,220
Nonfarm Wage and Salary Employment	271,956	284,757	296,079	304,467	292,578	289,091	292,650
Private wage and salary employment	203,462	216,255	225,873	232,960	218,671	214,098	217,690
Forestry, fishing, and related activities	946	901	887	888	868	902	956
Mining	22,442	26,385	27,238	29,320	25,344	24,933	27,215
Utilities	2,274	2,309	2,466	2,507	2,493	2,483	2,489
Construction	21,592	24,889	27,602	29,299	25,036	23,470	22,221
Manufacturing	9,713	10,160	10,192	9,964	9,125	8,727	9,185
Durable goods manufacturing	5,148	5,445	5,463	5,209	4,589	4,265	4,617
Nondurable goods manufacturing	4,565	4,715	4,729	4,755	4,536	4,462	4,568
Wholesale trade	7,799	8,250	8,818	9,174	8,809	8,529	8,901
Retail trade	30,737	31,300	32,451	32,605	31,156	29,989	29,639
Transportation and warehousing	10,591	11,475	12,255	12,364	11,668	11,516	12,077
Information	4,306	4,182	4,030	4,011	3,960	3,891	3,850
Finance and insurance	6,997	7,193	7,172	7,441	7,336	7,169	7,108
Real estate and rental and leasing	4,062	4,285	4,543	4,539	4,219	4,101	4,115
Professional, scientific, and technical services	8,506	9,174	9,665	10,064	9,432	9,300	9,236
Management of companies and enterprises	762	843	845	801	773	857	865
Administrative and waste services	6,896	7,296	8,143	8,070	7,380	7,332	7,920
Educational services	1,699	1,744	1,748	1,876	1,984	2,101	2,077
Health care and social assistance	20,323	20,736	21,527	22,663	23,587	23,903	24,147
Arts, entertainment, and recreation	2,746	2,804	2,914	2,896	2,798	2,786	2,835
Accommodation and food services	29,587	30,099	30,822	31,931	30,425	30,194	30,561
Other services, except public administration	11,484	12,230	12,555	12,547	12,278	11,915	12,293
Government and government enterprises	68,494	68,502	70,206	71,507	73,907	74,993	74,960
	Dollars						
Average Wages and Salaries by Industry	34,013	37,334	39,985	42,235	41,416	42,587	44,033
Average Farm Wages and Salaries	31,910	32,158	39,030	35,704	42,300	35,817	33,215
Average Nonfarm Wages and Salaries	34,037	37,390	39,995	42,300	41,407	42,655	44,152
Average private wages and salaries	33,717	37,456	40,089	42,439	40,933	42,410	44,204
Forestry, fishing, and related activities	19,826	20,169	21,202	21,499	21,665	22,879	24,353
Mining	62,416	68,164	72,663	76,850	74,342	77,821	80,948
Utilities	69,522	73,663	74,752	76,946	78,796	81,400	84,114
Construction	35,807	40,307	45,291	48,963	46,153	48,298	48,334
Manufacturing	41,500	43,508	46,838	50,023	51,068	52,997	56,101
Durable goods manufacturing	36,110	38,322	41,328	44,921	45,518	47,135	48,502
Nondurable goods manufacturing	47,579	49,498	53,203	55,613	56,682	58,601	63,781
Wholesale trade	44,458	49,264	51,537	55,730	53,876	55,449	57,451
Retail trade	22,177	23,688	24,869	25,637	25,446	25,975	26,736
Transportation and warehousing	46,133	49,860	51,049	53,998	51,566	53,696	56,461
Information	31,324	34,329	37,512	38,495	38,927	39,983	41,812
Finance and insurance	40,739	43,491	47,357	50,883	47,880	49,398	50,982
Real estate and rental and leasing	31,691	35,032	38,507	38,304	36,601	38,757	42,987
Professional, scientific, and technical services	41,439	44,547	48,754	51,820	52,648	53,936	55,925
Management of companies and enterprises	87,979	93,675	93,140	99,074	95,708	103,743	105,391
Administrative and waste services	23,244	25,325	28,132	30,079	29,254	29,052	32,177
Educational services	22,998	24,558	26,368	26,960	27,387	27,683	28,898
Health care and social assistance	32,821	34,332	36,250	38,401	38,435	39,328	40,364
Arts, entertainment, and recreation	18,161	20,433	21,272	20,696	21,594	21,526	21,483
Accommodation and food services	15,502	18,506	18,824	18,401	17,977	18,517	19,058
Other services, except public administration	21,440	24,538	27,452	28,269	28,212	30,297	30,209
Government and government enterprises	34,987	37,179	39,692	41,846	42,811	43,354	44,001

Table WY-10. Employment Characteristics by Family Type

(Number, percent.)

Family type and labor force status	2009		2010		2011	
	Total	Families with own children under 18 years	Total	Families with own children under 18 years	Total	Families with own children under 18 years
All families	143,459	62,775	147,394	63,001	142,618	60,196
Family type and labor force status						
Married-couple families	116,350	46,174	119,756	46,694	114,463	41,491
Both husband and wife in labor force	60.4	69.7	56.9	67.6	56.2	67.9
Husband in labor force, wife not in labor force	19.6	26.3	22.1	28.5	22.0	27.4
Wife in labor force, husband not in labor force	6.5	2.7	7.4	2.2	6.7	3.5
Both husband and wife not in labor force	13.5	1.3	13.6	1.7	15.2	1.2
Other families	27,109	16,601	27,638	16,307	28,155	18,705
Female householder, no husband present	64.5	63.8	71.8	73.3	69.1	69.3
In labor force	47.5	53.2	56.2	63.8	53.5	57.0
Not in labor force	16.9	10.5	15.6	9.5	15.6	12.2
Male householder, no wife present	35.5	36.2	28.2	26.7	30.9	30.7
In labor force	30.8	34.6	22.7	22.9	25.9	28.1
Not in labor force	4.8	1.6	5.6	3.8	5.0	2.6

Table WY-11. School Enrollment and Educational Attainment, 2011

(Number, percent.)

Item	State	U.S.
Enrollment		
Total population 3 years and over, enrolled in school	145,877	83,131,910
Enrolled in nursery school or preschool (percent)	6.3	6.0
Enrolled in kindergarten (percent)	5.3	5.1
Enrolled in elementary school, grades 1-8 (percent)	41.5	39.5
Enrolled in high school, grades 9-12 (percent)	20.2	20.7
Enrolled in college or graduate school (percent)	26.6	28.7
Attainment		
Total population 25 years and over	375,608	206,471,670
Less than ninth grade (percent)	1.8	6.0
9th to 12th grade, no diploma (percent)	6.2	8.1
High school graduate, including equivalency (percent)	30.8	28.4
Some college, no degree (percent)	26.6	21.2
Associate's degree (percent)	9.9	7.8
Bachelor's degree (percent)	16.5	17.9
Graduate or professional degree (percent)	8.3	10.6
High school graduate or higher (percent)	92.0	85.9
Bachelor's degree or higher (percent)	24.7	28.5

Table WY-12. Educational Indicators

(Number, percent; data derived from National Center of Education Statistics.)

Item	State	U.S.
Public Schools, 2009–2010 (except where noted)		
Number of school districts	48	13,629
Number of schools	363	99,834
Number of students (in thousands)	88	49,373
Student-teacher ratio	12.3	15.4
Expenditures per student (dollars)	19,238	10,591
Averaged freshman graduation rate, 2008–2009	75.2	75.5[1]
Dropout rate, 2008–2009	1.1	4.1
Students eligible for free or reduced-price lunch (percent)	36.9	48.0
English language learners, 2010–2011 (percent)	2.9	9.8[1]
Students with IEP (percent)	17.1	13.1
Private Schools, 2009–2010 (except where noted)		
Number of schools	39	33,366
Number of students (in thousands)	2	4,700
High school graduates, 2008–2009	A	308,813
Student-teacher ratio	7.4	10.7

A = Reporting standards for NCES not met.
[1] U.S. total includes estimates for nonreporting states.

Table WY-13. Reported Voting and Registration of the Voting-Age Population, November 2012

(Numbers in thousands, percent.)

Item	Total population	Total citizen population	Registered			Voted		
			Total registered	Percent registered (total population)	Percent registered (total citizen population)	Total voted	Percent voted (total population)	Percent voted (total citizen population)
U.S. Total	235,248	215,081	153,157	65.1	71.2	132,948	56.5	61.8
State Total	427	419	268	62.8	63.9	247	57.8	58.9
Sex								
Male	213	209	127	59.6	61.0	118	55.2	56.4
Female	213	211	141	65.9	66.7	129	60.4	61.2
Race								
White alone	403	396	259	64.2	65.3	240	59.4	60.4
White, non-Hispanic alone	373	372	249	66.8	67.0	232	62.1	62.3
Black alone	3	3	1	B	B	1	B	B
Asian alone	2	-	-	B	B	-	B	B
Hispanic (of any race)	32	27	10	B	B	8	B	B
Age								
18 to 24 years	56	55	21	B	B	18	B	B
25 to 44 years	142	137	84	59.4	61.3	75	52.7	54.4
45 to 64 years	155	154	101	65.1	65.8	95	61.1	61.8
65 to 74 years	45	45	38	B	B	36	B	B
75 years and over	29	29	24	B	B	23	B	B

- = Zero or rounds to zero.
B = Base is less than 75,000 and therefore too small to show the derived measure.

Table WY-14. Crime

(Number, rate per 100,000. Data are derived from the FBI Uniform Crime Reports.)

Item	State			U.S.		
	2010	2011	Percent change	2010	2011	Percent change
TOTAL POPULATION	564,554	568,158	0.6	309,330,219	311,591,917	0.7
VIOLENT CRIME						
Number	1,117	1,246	11.5	1,251,248	1,203,564	-3.8
Rate	197.9	219.3	10.8	404.5	386.3	-4.5
Murder and Nonnegligent Manslaughter						
Number	8	18	125.0	14,722	14,612	-0.7
Rate	1.4	3.2	128.6	4.8	4.7	-2.1
Forcible Rape						
Number	162	146	-9.9	85,593	83,425	-2.5
Rate	28.7	25.7	-10.5	27.7	26.8	-3.2
Robbery						
Number	77	71	-7.8	369,089	354,396	-4.0
Rate	13.6	12.5	-8.1	119.3	113.7	-4.7
Aggravated Assault						
Number	870	1,011	16.2	781,844	751,131	-3.9
Rate	154.1	177.9	15.4	252.8	241.1	-4.6
PROPERTY CRIME						
Number	13,869	12,877	-7.2	9,112,625	9,063,173	-0.5
Rate	2,456.6	2,266.4	-7.7	2,945.9	2,908.7	-1.3
Burglary						
Number	2,151	1,863	-13.4	2,168,459	2,188,005	0.9
Rate	381.0	327.9	-13.9	701.0	702.2	0.2
Larceny-Theft						
Number	11,126	10,493	-5.7	6,204,601	6,159,795	-0.7
Rate	1,970.8	1,846.8	-6.3	2,005.8	1,976.9	-1.4
Motor Vehicle Theft						
Number	592	521	-12.0	739,565	715,373	-3.3
Rate	104.9	91.7	-12.6	239.1	229.6	-4.0

Table WY-15. State Government Finances, 2011

(Dollar amounts in thousands, percent distribution.)

Item	Dollars	Percent distribution
Total Revenue	7,494,341	100.0
General revenue	6,056,459	80.8
Intergovernmental revenue	2,400,542	32.0
Taxes	2,461,977	32.9
General sales	862,805	11.5
Selective sales	124,412	1.7
License taxes	140,989	1.9
Individual income tax	0	0.0
Corporate income tax	0	0.0
Other taxes	1,333,771	17.8
Current charges	190,588	2.5
Miscellaneous general revenue	1,003,352	13.4
Utility revenue	0	0.0
Liquor stores revenue	84,752	1.1
Insurance trust revenue [1]	1,353,130	18.1
Total Expenditure	5,673,561	100.0
Intergovernmental expenditure	1,653,068	29.1
Direct expenditure	4,020,493	70.9
Current operation	2,707,379	47.7
Capital outlay	476,969	8.4
Insurance benefits and repayments	694,965	12.2
Assistance and subsidies	75,270	1.3
Interest on debt	65,910	1.2
Exhibit: Salaries and wages	723,619	12.8
Total Expenditure	5,673,561	100.0
General expenditure	4,904,854	86.5
Intergovernmental expenditure	1,653,068	29.1
Direct expenditure	3,251,786	57.3
General expenditure, by function:		
Education	1,679,054	29.6
Public welfare	739,851	13.0
Hospitals	4,468	0.1
Health	281,932	5.0
Highways	536,582	9.5
Police protection	49,415	0.9
Correction	137,518	2.4
Natural resources	354,083	6.2
Parks and recreation	29,364	0.5
Governmental administration	238,113	4.2
Interest on general debt	65,910	1.2
Other and unallocable	788,564	13.9
Utility expenditure	0	0.0
Liquor stores expenditure	73,742	1.3
Insurance trust expenditure	694,965	12.2
Debt at End of Fiscal Year	1,364,404	X
Cash and Security Holdings	22,233,323	X

X = Not applicable.

[1] Within insurance trust revenue, net earnings of state retirement systems is a calculated statistic (the item code in the data file is X08), and thus can be positive or negative. Net earnings is the sum of earnings on investments plus gains on investments minus losses on investments. The change made in 2002 for asset valuation from book to market value in accordance with Statement 34 of the Governmental Accounting Standards Board is reflected in the calculated statistics.

Table WY-16. State Government Tax Collections, 2012

(Dollars in thousands, percent.)

Item	Dollars	Percent distribution
Total Taxes	2,550,991	100.0
Property taxes	316,734	12.4
Sales and gross receipts	1,120,203	43.9
General sales and gross receipts	994,167	39.0
Selective sales and gross receipts	126,036	4.9
Alcoholic beverages	1,742	0.1
Amusements	0	0.0
Insurance premiums	26,056	1.0
Motor fuels	66,443	2.6
Pari-mutuels	68	-
Public utilities	4,443	0.2
Tobacco products	25,984	1.0
Other selective sales	1,300	0.1
Licenses	140,045	5.5
Alcoholic beverages	0	0.0
Amusements	0	0.0
Corporations in general	12,720	0.5
Hunting and fishing	35,612	1.4
Motor vehicle	65,733	2.6
Motor vehicle operators	2,158	0.1
Public utilities	0	0.0
Occupation and business, NEC	23,822	0.9
Other licenses	0	0.0
Income taxes	0	0.0
Individual income	0	0.0
Corporation net income	0	0.0
Other taxes	974,009	38.2
Death and gift	38	-
Documentary and stock transfer	0	0.0
Severance	968,525	38.0
Taxes, NEC	5,446	0.2

- = Rounds to zero.

Leading Exports, 2012

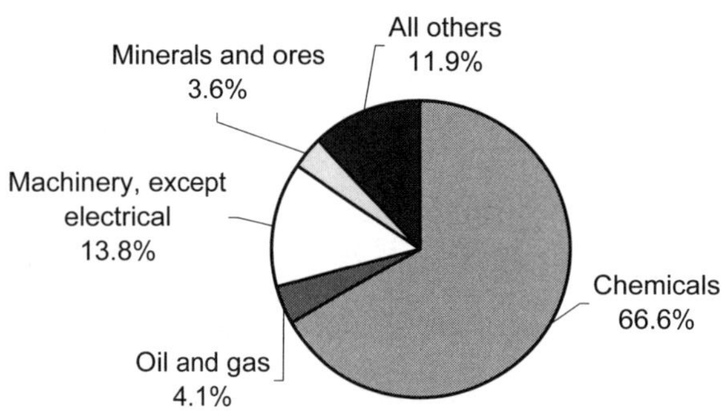

NOTES AND DEFINITIONS

The state chapters in this book follow a standard plan of organization, and the same data sources are used for the tables and figures found in each chapter. These notes describe the standard data sources, which are presented by topic in the order in which they appear in each chapter. Definitions, brief descriptions of methodology, and sources of additional information are also provided.

Symbols used are included in the footnotes of the tables.

Table 1.
Source: U.S. Department of Commerce. U.S Census Bureau. 2000 and 2010 Decennial Census. Census statistics, 2012.
<http://factfinder2.census.gov/>.

Population estimates data are accessed through American FactFinder. U.S. Census Bureau, as well as from the Census Bureau itself. The data for average annual percent change, 2010–2012, were calculated by the editor.

Population estimates and the decennial census. Population data are estimates produced by the Census Bureau. The Bureau's Population Estimates Program (PEP) produces estimates of the population as of July 1 for each year following the most recently published decennial census (the actual physical count of the population made every ten years, which is described below). Existing data on births, deaths, and domestic and international immigration are used to update the decennial census base. PEP estimates are used to set federal funding allocations, update national surveys, and monitor recent demographic changes.

Noncitizens residing in the United States are included, regardless of their immigration status.

Persons temporarily away from their usual residence on Census Day (April 1), for reasons such as vacation or business trips, were counted as being at their usual residence. People who live at more than one residence during the week, month, or year were counted as being at the place in which they lived most of the year. However, people without a usual residence were counted as being where they were staying on Census Day.

Age, sex, race, and ethnicity. While estimates of the age and sex of the population are straightforward, estimates of race and ethnicity are not. Decennial census data on race and ethnicity are based on self-identification by the respondent, and the same respondent may answer differently on separate occasions. On the 2000 decennial census, respondents could report more than one race; in previous censuses, respondents had to identify themselves as belonging to only one race.

The Census Bureau treats Hispanic or Latino origin as a separate and distinct concept from race. Beginning with the 2000 census, a separate self-identification question was asked regarding Hispanic or Latino origin. Persons of Hispanic or Latino origin are those who classified themselves as belonging to one of the specific categories listed on the questionnaire—Mexican, Puerto Rican, Cuban, or Other Spanish/Hispanic origin (including those whose origins are from Spain, the Spanish-speaking countries of Central and South America, or the Dominican Republic). People who are Hispanic may be of any race and people in each race group may be Hispanic. The overlap of race and Hispanic origin is a major comparability issue, because Hispanics may be of any race. For a further discussion of this issue, see: U.S. Census Bureau. *U.S. Census Bureau Guidance on the Presentation and Comparison of Race and Hispanic Origin Data.* (June 12, 2003.) <http://www.census.gov/population/www/socdemo/compraceho.html>.

Table 2.
Source: U.S. Department of Commerce. U.S Census Bureau. 2000 Decennial Census. American Community Survey, 2010 and 2011.
<http://factfinder2.census.gov/>.

Data on marital status was tabulated for persons 15 years and over. Marital status was reported for each person as either "now married," "widowed," "divorced," "separated," or "never married." Individuals who were living together (unmarried people, people in commonlaw marriages) reported the marital status which they considered most appropriate.

Now Married, Except Separated. Includes people whose current marriage has not ended through widowhood, divorce, or separation (regardless of previous marital history). The category may also include couples who live together or people in common-law marriages if they consider this category the most appropriate. In certain tabulations, currently married people are further classified as "spouse present" or "spouse absent."

Separated. Refers to people who were not living with their spouse due to marital discord.

Divorced. Indicates people who reported being divorced and had not remarried.

Widowed. Refers to people whose last marriage ended with the death of their spouse and they had not remarried.

Never married. The term applies to those who had never been legally married or people whose only marriage ended in an annulment.

Table 3.
Source: U.S. Department of Commerce. U.S Census Bureau. 2000 Decennial Census. American Community Survey, 2010 and 2011.
<http://factfinder2.census.gov/>.

The annual data were obtained from the Census Bureau. The data for average annual percent change, 2000–2011, were calculated by the editor.

Households. A household comprises one or more persons occupying a single housing unit, such as a house, apartment, or a room occupied as separate living quarters. A household may consist of a person living alone, a single family, two or more families living together, or any other group of unrelated individuals sharing a housing unit.

Householder. The person, or one of the people, in whose name the home is owned, being bought, or rented. If there is no such person present, any household member 15 years old and over can serve as the householder for the purposes of the census. Two types of householders are distinguished: a family householder and a nonfamily householder. A family householder is a householder living with one or more people related to him or her by birth, marriage, or adoption. The householder and all people in the household related to him are family members. A nonfamily householder is a householder living alone or with nonrelatives only.

Housing unit. A house, an apartment, a mobile home or trailer, a group of rooms, or a single room occupied as separate living quarters, or if vacant, intended for occupancy as separate living quarters.

Median gross rent. The monthly amount of contract rent plus the estimated average monthly cost of utilities (electricity, gas, water and sewer) and fuels (oil, coal, kerosene, wood, etc.).

Median monthly owner-costs for housing units with a mortgage. The sum of payments for mortgages, deeds of trust, contracts to purchase, or similar debts on the property (including payments for the first mortgage, second mortgages, home equity loans, and other junior mortgages); real estate taxes; fire, hazard, and flood insurance on the property; utilities (electricity, gas, and water and sewer); and fuels (oil, coal, kerosene, wood, etc.). It also includes, where appropriate, the monthly condominium fee for condominiums and mobile home costs (installment loan payments, personal property taxes, site rent, registration fees, and license fees). Selected monthly owner costs were tabulated for all owner-occupied units, and usually are shown separately for units "with a mortgage" and for units "not mortgaged.

Median value of owner-occupied housing units. Data for the median value of owner-occupied housing units are respondents' estimates of how much their property would sell for if it was currently on the market.

Table 4.
Source: U.S. Department of Commerce. U.S Census Bureau. American Community Survey, 2010 and 2011.
<http://factfinder2.census.gov/>.

The annual data derives from Census estimates. The data for percent change were calculated by the editor.

Residence 1 year ago. The data on residence 1 year ago were derived from answers to Question 15, which were asked of the population 1 year and older. For the American Community Survey, people who had moved from another residence in the United States or Puerto Rico 1 year earlier were asked to report the exact address (number and street name); the name of the city, town, or post office; the name of the U.S. county; and the ZIP Code where they lived 1 year ago. People living outside the United States and Puerto Rico were asked to report the name of the foreign country or U.S. Island Area where they were living 1 year ago.

Native born. The native population includes anyone who was a U.S. citizen or a U.S. national at birth. This includes respondents who indicated they were born in the United States, Puerto Rico, a U.S. Island Area (such as Guam), or abroad of American (U.S. citizen) parent or parents.

Foreign born. The foreign-born population includes anyone who was not a U.S. citizen or a U.S. national at birth. This includes respondents who indicated they were a U.S. citizen by naturalization or not a U.S. citizen.

Respondent's ability to speak English. Respondents who reported speaking a language other than English were asked to indicate their English-speaking ability based on one of the following categories: "Very well," "Well," "Not well," or "Not at all." Those who answered "Well," "Not well," or "Not at all" are sometimes referred as "Less than 'very well.'" Respondents were not instructed on how to interpret the response categories in this question. Households in which no one 14 and over speaks English only or speaks a language other than English at home and speaks English "very well" identifies households that may need English language assistance. This arises when no one 14 and over meets either of two conditions (1) they speak English at home or (2) even though they speak another language, they also report that they speak English "very well."

Table 5.
Source: U.S. Department of Commerce. U.S Census Bureau. American Community Survey.
<http://factfinder2.census.gov/>.

Median household income. Includes the income of the householder and all other individuals 15 years old and over in the household, whether they are related to the householder or not. Because many households consist of only one person, average household income is usually less than average family income. Total income is the sum of the amounts reported separately for wage or salary income; net self-employment income; interest, dividends, or net rental or royalty income or income from estates and trusts; Social Security or railroad retirement income; Supplemental Security Income (SSI); public assistance or welfare payments; retirement, survivor, or disability pensions; and all other income. Receipts from the following sources are not included as income: capital gains, money received from the sale of property (unless the recipient was engaged in the business of selling such property); the value of income "in kind" from food stamps, public housing subsidies, medical care, employer contributions for individuals, etc.; withdrawal of bank deposits; money borrowed; tax refunds; exchange of money between relatives living in the same household; gifts and lump-sum inheritances, insurance payments, and other types of lump-sum receipts.

Median family income. The incomes of all members 15 years old and over related to the householder are summed and treated as a single amount.

Poverty. Following OMB standards that have been in use since the late 1960s, the Census Bureau uses a set of money income thresholds that vary by family size and composition to determine the proportion of Americans in poverty. If a household's total income is less than the threshold for the applicable family size, age of householder, and number of children present in the family under 18 years of age, every individual in that household is considered to be living in poverty.

Table 6.
Source: U.S. Department of Commerce. U.S. Census Bureau. American Community Survey.
<http://factfinder2.census.gov/>.

The Census Bureau collects health insurance data from two surveys. The data in Table 5 are from The Annual Social and Economic Supplement (ASEC) to the Current Population Survey (CPS). The CPS ASEC is a survey of about 78,000 households and includes detailed health insurance questions asked of the household respondent for every household resident. Respondents are asked about health insurance coverage in the previous calendar year. This survey is useful as a source of estimates of the insured and uninsured populations at the state level and is the most widely used source of data on health insurance coverage in the United States. In addition, it is the official source of estimates used to allocate federal funding to states for the State Children's Health Insurance Program (SCHIP).

Private health insurance. Coverage by a health plan provided through an employer or union or purchased by an individual from a private health insurance company.

Government health insurance includes plans funded by governments as the federal, state, or local level. The major categories of government health insurance are Medicare, Medicaid, the State Children's Health Insurance Program (SCHIP), military health care, state plans, and the Indian Health Service.

Table 7.
Source: U.S. Department of Labor. Bureau of Labor Statistics. Current Population Survey.
<http://www.bls.gov/cps/>.

Annual data on the labor force, employment, and unemployment for state and local areas are available from two major sources: the Current Population Survey (CPS) and the Local Area Unemployment Statistics (LAUS) program. In Table 6, the data are obtained from the CPS. The CPS is a monthly survey of approximately 60,000 households conducted by the Census Bureau for the Bureau of Labor Statistics. It provides comprehensive data on topics such as the labor force, employment, unemployment, and persons not in the labor force.

Civilian noninstitutional population included are persons 16 years of age and older residing in the 50 States and the District of Columbia who are not inmates of institutions (for example, penal and mental facilities, homes for the aged), and who are not on active duty in the Armed Forces.

Civilian labor force includes all persons classified as employed or unemployed who are not inmates of institutions (for example, penal and mental facilities, homes for the aged), and who are not on active duty in the Armed Forces. Civilians 16 years of age and over in the noninstitutional population who are not classified as employed or unemployed are defined as not in the labor force.

Employment includes persons 16 years and over in the civilian noninstitutional population who, during the reference week, (a) did any work at all (at least 1 hour) as paid employees; worked in their own business, profession, or on their own farm, or worked 15 hours or more as unpaid workers in an enterprise operated by a member of the family; and (b) all those who were not working but who had jobs or businesses from which they were temporarily absent because of vacation, illness, bad weather, childcare problems, maternity or paternity leave, labor-management dispute, job training, or other family or personal reasons, whether or not they were paid for the time off or were seeking other jobs.

Unemployed persons. All civilians who were not employed (according to the above definition) during the reference week, but who were available for work—except for temporary illness—and who had made specific efforts to find employment sometime during the previous four weeks. Persons who did not look for work because they were on layoff are also counted as unemployed.

Unemployment rate. The number of unemployed as a percentage of the civilian labor force.

Table 8.
Source: U.S. Department of Labor. Bureau of Labor Statistics. Local Area Unemployment Statistics.
<http://www.bls.gov/lau/home.htm>.

The Local Area Unemployment Statistics (LAUS) program is a Federal-State cooperative effort in which monthly estimates of total employment and unemployment are prepared for approximately 7,300 areas.

The concepts and definitions underlying LAUS data come from the Current Population Survey (CPS), the household survey that is the official measure of the labor force for the nation. State monthly model estimates are controlled in "real time" to sum to national monthly labor force estimates from the CPS. These models combine current and historical data from the CPS, the Current Employment Statistics (CES) program, and State unemployment insurance (UI) systems. Estimates for seven large areas and their respective balances of State are also model-based. Estimates for the remainder of the substate labor market areas are produced through a building-block approach known as the "Handbook method." This procedure also uses data from several sources, including the CPS, the CES program, State UI systems, and the decennial census, to create estimates that are adjusted to the statewide measures of employment and unemployment. Below the labor market area level, estimates are prepared using disaggregation techniques based on inputs from the decennial census, annual population estimates, and current UI data.

Table 9.
Source: U.S. Department of Commerce. Bureau of Economic Analysis. <http://www.bea.gov/regional>.

In this table, the data by industry reflect the North American Industry Classification System (NAICS), a supply- or production-based system that replaced the Standard Industrial Classification (SIC) system in January 2003. Estimates of state employment and earnings by industry use NAICS from 2001 forward. NAICS was adopted to more fully reflect the current composition of U.S. businesses and to establish a standard measure of industry classification throughout the United States, Canada, and Mexico, in accordance with the North American Free Trade Agreement, to enhance cross-border comparisons among these trading partners.

Wage and salary employment, also referred to as wage and salary jobs, measures the average annual number of full-time and part-time jobs in each area by place-of-work. All jobs for which wages and salaries are paid are counted. Full-time and part-time jobs are counted with equal weight. Jury and witness service, as well as paid employment of prisoners, are not counted as wage and salary employment; the payments for these activities are classified as "other labor income" in the personal income measure. Corporate directorships are counted as self-employment. This concept of employment differs from that in the Current Population Survey (CPS), which is the source of the employment data in the table on population and labor force. The CPS is a household survey. It counts each individual only once, no matter how many jobs the person holds, and it includes only civilian employment.

Wages and salaries consist of the monetary remuneration of employees, including corporate officers salaries and bonuses, commissions, pay-in-kind, incentive payments, and tips. It reflects the amount of payments disbursed, but not necessarily earned during the year. Wage and salary disbursements are measured before deductions, such as social security contributions and union dues. In recent years, stock options have become a point of discussion. Wage and salary disbursements include stock options of nonqualified plans at the time that they have been exercised by the individual. Stock options are reported in wage and salary disbursements. The value that is included in wages is the difference between the exercise price and the price that the stock options were granted. Average annual wages and salaries were calculated by the editors by dividing total wages and salaries paid during the year in each sector by total wage and salary employment in that sector.

Table 10.
Source: U.S. Department of Commerce. U.S. Census Bureau. American Community Survey, 2009, 2010, 2011.
<http://factfinder2.census.gov/>.

Civilian labor force. (See definition under Table 7.)

Employment. (See definition under Table 7.)

Family. A family consists of a householder and one or more other people living in the same household who are related to the householder by birth, marriage, or adoption. All people in a household who are related to the householder are regarded as members of his or her family. A family household may contain people not related to the householder, but those people are not included as part of the householder's family in tabulations. Thus, the number of family households is equal to the number of families, but family households may include more members than do families. A household can contain only one family for purposes of tabulations. Not all households contain families since a household may be comprised of a group of unrelated people or of one person living alone – these are called nonfamily households. Families are classified by type as either a "married-couple family" or "other family" according to the sex of the householder and the presence of relatives. The data on family type are based on answers to questions on sex and relationship that were asked of all people.

Married-couple family. A family in which the householder and his or her spouse are listed as members of the same household.

Other family:

Male householder, no wife present. A family with a male householder and no spouse of householder present.

Female householder, no husband present. A family with a female householder and no spouse of householder present.

Table 11.
Source: U.S. Department of Commerce. U.S. Census Bureau. American Community Survey, 2011.
<http://www.census.gov/acs/www/index.html>.

Data on school enrollment and educational attainment were derived from a sample of the population. Persons were classified as enrolled in school if they reported attending a "regular" public or private school (or college) during the year. The instructions were to "include only nursery school, kindergarten, elementary school, and schooling which would lead to a high school diploma or a college degree" as regular school. The Census Bureau defines a public school as "any school or college controlled and supported by a local, county, state, or federal government." Schools primarily supported and controlled by religious organizations or other private groups are defined as private schools.

Data on educational attainment are tabulated for the population 25 years old and over. The data were derived from a question that asked respondents for the highest level of school completed or the highest degree received. Persons who had passed a high school equivalency examination were considered high school graduates. Schooling received in foreign schools was to be reported as the equivalent grade or years in the regular American school system.

Vocational and technical training, such as barber school training; business, trade, technical, and vocational schools; or other training for a specific trade are specifically excluded.

High school graduate or more. This category includes persons whose highest degree was a high school diploma or its equivalent, and those who reported any level higher than a high school diploma.

Bachelor's degree or more. This category includes persons who have received bachelor's degrees, master's degrees, professional school degrees (such as law school or medical school degrees), and doctoral degrees.

Graduate degree or more. This category includes persons who have a master's degree, including the traditional MA and MS degrees and field-specific degrees, such as MSW, MEd, MBA, MLS, and MEng., or a professional school degree: medicine, dentistry, chiropractic, optometry, osteopathic medicine, pharmacy, podiatry, veterinary medicine, law, and theology.

Table 12.
Source: U.S. Department of Education, National Center for Education Statistics. ***Common Core of Data.*** <http://nces.ed.gov/ccd/>.
Private School Universe Survey. <http://nces.ed.gov/surveys/pss/>.

Public Schools

The data are from the Common Core of Data (CCD) state universe and include approximately 17,000 regular school districts with students in membership. Not included are special districts that typically offer research, administrative, or other support services to client agencies. The CCD data now include charter schools. Since charter schools are managed independently from the local school district, each one is considered a single district. Most of the CCD state data were compiled through the CCD "Build a Table" feature, which can be found on the Internet at <http://nces.ed.gov/ccd/bat>.

A **school district** or Local Education Agency (LEA) is a local-level education agency that exists primarily to operate public schools or to contract for public school services. A public school is controlled and operated by publicly elected or appointed officials, and it derives its primary support from public funds.

Regular schools do not focus primarily on special, vocational, or alternative education, though they may offer these programs in addition to the regular curriculum.

The primary grades include pre-kindergarten through grade 4. Middle school grades included grades 5 through 8. High school grades include grades 9 through 12. Ungraded students are included in the total but are not separately listed. Some states have no ungraded students.

The student-teacher ratio is calculated by dividing the number of students in all schools by the number of full-time equivalent teachers employed by all schools and agencies.

Current expenditures per student are derived by dividing total current expenditures by the fall student membership count from the CCD. Student membership consists of the count of students enrolled on or about October 1 and is comparable across all states.

The averaged freshman graduation rate provides an estimate of the percentage of high school students who graduate on time. The rate uses aggregate student enrollment data (to estimate the size of an incoming freshman class) and aggregate counts of the number of diplomas awarded 4 years later. The incoming freshman class size is estimated by summing the enrollment in 8th grade in one year, 9th grade in the next year, and 10th grade in the year after that, and then dividing by three. The averaging is intended to account for prior-year retentions in the 9th grade.

A **dropout** is a student who was enrolled in school at some time during the previous school year who was not enrolled at the beginning of the current school year and who had not graduated from high school or completed a state or district-approved educational program and who did not meet any of the following exclusionary conditions: transferal to another public school district, private school, or state- or district-approved educational program; temporary absence due to suspension or school-approved illness; or death.

Most of the states that reported on dropouts used an October through September cycle; however, the following states reported on a July through June cycle: Alabama, Arizona, Florida, Illinois, Maryland, New Jersey, New York, Tennessee, and Vermont.

The **Free and Reduced-Price Lunch** Program is a program under the National School Lunch Act that provides cash subsidies for free or reduced-price meals to students based on family size and income criteria. Participation in the Free and Reduced-Price Lunch Program depends on income, and eligibility is often used to estimate student needs.

Students Who Are English-Language Learners. This category includes the number of students who are served in appropriate programs of language assistance (e.g., English as a Second Language, High Intensity Language Training, and bilingual education). This designation changed from Limited-English Proficient (LEP) to English-Language Learners (ELL) in the 2001–2002 school year.

An **Individualized Education Program (IEP)** is a written instructional plan for students with disabilities who are designated as special education students under IDEA (Individuals with Disabilities Education Act). An IEP includes a statement of present levels of educational performance of a child; a statement of annual goals, including short-term instructional objectives; a statement of specific educational services to be provided and the extent to which the child will be able to participate in regular educational programs; a projected date for initiation and the anticipated duration of services; appropriate objectives, criteria, and evaluation procedures; and schedules for determining, on at least an annual basis, whether instructional objectives are being achieved.

Private Schools

Since 1989, the Census Bureau has conducted the biennial Private School Universe Survey (PSS) for NCES. The PSS is designed to generate biennial data on the total number of private schools, students, and teachers and to build a universe of private schools in all of the states and the District of Columbia to serve as a sampling frame of private schools for NCES sample surveys. The target population for the PSS is every school in all of the states and the District of Columbia that are not primarily supported by public funds, provide instruction for one or more grades between kindergarten and grade 12 (or comparable ungraded levels), and have one or more teachers. Organizations or institutions that provide support for home schooling, but do not provide classroom instruction, are not included. Although the PSS has begun to collect limited data on the many private schools for which kindergarten is the highest grade, the data in this volume are for (traditional) schools that include at least one grade between grades 1 and 12.

A **private school** is controlled by an individual or agency other than a state, a subdivision of a state, or the federal government; is usually supported primarily by nonpublic funds; and the operation of its program does not rest with publicly elected or appointed officials. Private schools include both nonprofit and proprietary institutions.

The **student-teacher ratio** is calculated by dividing the number of students enrolled in all schools by the number of full-time equivalent teachers employed by all schools.

Table 13.
Source: U.S. Department of Commerce. U.S. Census Bureau. November Supplement to the Current Population Survey (CPS). *Voting and Registration in the Election of November 2012.*
<http://www.census.gov/hhes/www/socdemo/voting/publications/p20/2012/tables.html>

Voter participation data are obtained from additional questions regarding voting and voter registration, which are added to the Current Population Survey each November. Because these data are from a sample of the noninstitutional population, they differ from the "official" tally of voter participation reported by the Clerk of the U.S. House of Representatives.

Voting, people eligible to register. The population of voting age includes a considerable number of people who meet the age requirement but cannot register and vote. People who are not citizens are not eligible to vote. Among citizens of voting age, some people are not permitted to vote because they have been committed to penal institutions, mental hospitals, or other institutions, or because they fail to meet state and local resident requirements for various reasons. The eligibility to register is governed by state laws which differ in many respects.

Registration is the act of qualifying to vote by formally enrolling on a list of voters. People who have moved to another election district must take steps to have their names placed on the voting rolls in their new place of residence.

In a few states or parts of states, no formal registration is required. Voters merely present themselves at the polling place on election day with proof that they are of age and have met the appropriate residence requirements. Therefore, in these areas people who are citizens and of voting age, and who meet the residence requirement, would be considered as being registered.

Voter, reported participation. Voter participation data are derived from replies to the following question asked of people (excluding noncitizens) of voting age: "In any election some people are not able to vote because they are sick or busy, or have some other reason, and others do not want to vote. Did (this person) vote in the election held on November (date varies)?"

Those of voting age were classified as "voted" or "did not vote." In most tables, this "did not vote" class includes those reported as "did not vote," "do not know," noncitizens, and nonrespondents. Nonrespondents and people who reported that they did not know if they voted were included in the "did not vote" class because of the general over-reporting by respondents in the sample.

Voter, reported registration. The data on registration were obtained by tabulating replies to the following question for those people included in the category "did not vote." "Was (this person) registered to vote in the November (date varies) election?"

All people reported as having voted were assumed to have been registered. Therefore, the total registered population is obtained by combining the number of people who voted and people included in the category "did not vote," but who had registered.

Table 14.
Source: U.S. Department of Justice. Federal Bureau of Investigation. Uniform Crime Reports. *Crime in the United States, 2011.*
< http://www.fbi.gov/about-us/cjis/ucr/crime-in-the-u.s/2011/crime-in-the-u.s.-2011/about-cius>

The Uniform Crime Reports (UCR) Program, administered by the Federal Bureau of Investigation (FBI), was created in 1929 and collects information on the following crimes reported to law enforcement authorities: murder and nonnegligent manslaughter, forcible rape, robbery, aggravated assault, burglary, larceny-theft, motor vehicle theft, and arson. Law enforcement agencies also report arrest data for 21 additional crime categories.

The UCR Program compiles data from monthly law enforcement reports and from individual crime incident records transmitted directly to the FBI or to centralized state agencies that report to the FBI. The program thoroughly examines each report it receives for reasonableness, accuracy, and deviations that may indicate errors. Large variations in crime levels may indicate modified records procedures, incomplete reporting, or changes in a jurisdiction's boundaries. To identify any unusual fluctuations in an agency's crime counts, the program compares monthly reports to previous submissions of the agency and to those for similar agencies.

The FBI annually publishes its findings in a preliminary release in the spring of the following calendar year, followed by a detailed annual report, *Crime in the United States*, issued in the fall. (The printed copy of *Crime in the United States* is now published by Bernan Press.) In addition to crime counts and trends, this report includes data on crimes cleared, persons arrested (age, sex, and race), law enforcement personnel (including the number of sworn officers killed or assaulted), and the characteristics of homicides (including age, sex, and race of victims and offenders; victim-offender relationships; weapons used; and circumstances surrounding the homicides). Other periodic reports are also available from the UCR Program.

Note for Users

Since crime is a sociological phenomenon influenced by a variety of factors, the FBI discourages data users from ranking agencies and using the data as a measurement of the effectiveness of law enforcement. Until data users examine all the variables that affect crime in a town, city, county, state, region, or college or university, they can make no meaningful comparisons.

Violent crime is composed of four offenses: murder and nonnegligent manslaughter, forcible rape, robbery, and aggravated assault. According to the UCR Program's definition, violent crimes involve force or threat of force.

Criminal homicide. a.) Murder and nonnegligent manslaughter: the willful (nonnegligent) killing of one human being by another. Deaths caused by negligence, attempts to kill, assaults to kill, suicides, and accidental deaths are excluded. The program classifies justifiable homicides separately and limits the definition to (1) the killing of a felon by a law enforcement officer in the line of duty; or (2) the killing of a felon, during the commission of a felony, by a private citizen. b.) Manslaughter by negligence: the killing of another person through gross negligence. Traffic fatalities are excluded.

Forcible rape. The carnal knowledge of a female forcibly and against her will. Assaults and attempts to commit rape by force or threat of force are also included. Statutory rape (no force used—female victim is under the age of consent) and other sex offenses are excluded. Sexual attacks on males are counted as aggravated assaults or sex offenses, depending on the circumstances and the extent of any injuries.

Robbery. The taking or attempted taking of anything of value from the care, custody, or control of a person or persons by force or threat of force or violence and/or by putting the victim in fear.

Aggravated assault. An unlawful attack by one person upon another for the purpose of inflicting severe or aggravated bodily injury. This type of assault usually is accompanied by the use of a weapon or by means likely to produce death or great bodily harm. Attempted aggravated assaults that involve the display of—or threat to use—a gun, knife, or other weapon is included in this crime category because serious personal injury would likely result if the assault were completed. When aggravated assault and larceny-theft occur together, the offense falls under the category of robbery. Simple assaults are excluded.

Property crime includes the offenses of burglary, larceny-theft, motor vehicle theft, and arson. The object of the theft-type offenses is the taking of money or property, but there is no force or threat of force against the victims. The property crime category includes arson because the offense involves the destruction of property; however, arson victims may be subjected to force.

Burglary (breaking or entering). The unlawful entry of a structure to commit a felony or a theft. The use of force to gain entry need not have occurred. The Program has three subclassifications for burglary: forcible entry, unlawful entry where no force is used, and attempted forcible entry. The UCR definition of "structure" includes, for example, apartment, barn, house trailer or houseboat when used as a permanent dwelling, office, railroad car (but not automobile), stable, and vessel (i.e., ship).

Larceny-theft (except motor vehicle theft). The unlawful taking, carrying, leading, or riding away of property from the possession or constructive possession of another. Examples are thefts of bicycles or automobile accessories, shoplifting, pocket-picking, or the stealing of any property or article that is not taken by force and violence or by fraud. Attempted larcenies are included. Embezzlement, confidence games, forgery, worthless checks, and the like, are excluded.

Motor vehicle theft. The theft or attempted theft of a motor vehicle. It includes the stealing of automobiles, trucks, buses, motorcycles, snowmobiles, and the like. The taking of a motor vehicle for temporary use by persons having lawful access is excluded from this definition. A motor vehicle is self-propelled and runs on land surface and not on rails. Motorboats, construction equipment, airplanes, and farming equipment are specifically excluded from this category.

Table 15.
Source: U.S. Department of Commerce. U.S Census Bureau.
<http://www.census.gov/govs/index.html>.

The Census Bureau conducts an annual survey covering a range of government finance activities carried out by all state and local governments in the United States, including revenue, expenditures, debt, and assets. The data in this volume relate to state revenues and expenditures only, with the exception of the District of Columbia. Data generally reference state government fiscal year 2011. General revenue comprises all revenue except utilities, liquor store, and insurance trust revenue. Intergovernmental revenue is funds from other governments (mainly the federal government), including general support, grants, shared taxes, and loans or advances. Other data on government finance by state, not shown in this volume, include federal government expenditures, obligations, contract awards, and insurance programs.

Table 16.
Source: U.S. Department of Commerce. U.S Census Bureau.
<http://www.census.gov/govs/www/statetax.html>.

State tax data include all required taxes taken by government for public purposes, except for employer and employee assessments for Social Security and unemployment compensation. The data are shown in this volume are generally for each state's fiscal year 2011. For more information, see the text under Table 15.

INDEX